D1707939

LONGITUDINAL ANALYSIS

Longitudinal Analysis provides an accessible, application-oriented treatment of introductory and advanced linear models for within-person fluctuation and change. Organized by research design and data type, the text uses in-depth examples to provide a complete description of the model-building process. The core longitudinal models and their extensions are presented within a multilevel modeling framework, paying careful attention to the modeling concerns that are unique to longitudinal data. Written in a conversational style, the text provides verbal and visual interpretation of model equations to aid in their translation to empirical research results. Overviews and summaries, boldfaced key terms, and review questions will help readers synthesize the key concepts in each chapter.

Written for non-mathematically oriented readers, this text features:

- A description of the data manipulation steps required prior to model estimation so readers can more easily apply the steps to their own data.
- An emphasis on how the terminology, interpretation, and estimation of familiar general linear models relate to those of more complex models for longitudinal data.
- Integrated model comparisons, effect sizes, and statistical inference in each example to strengthen readers' understanding of the overall model-building process.
- Sample results sections for each example to provide useful templates for published reports.
- Examples using both real and simulated data in the text, along with syntax and output for SAS, SPSS, STATA, and M*plus* at www.PilesOfVariance.com to help readers apply the models to their own data.

Class-tested at the University of Nebraska–Lincoln and in intensive summer workshops, this is an ideal text for graduate-level courses on longitudinal analysis or general multilevel modeling taught in psychology, human development and family studies, education, business, and other behavioral, social, and health sciences. The book's accessible approach will also help those trying to learn on their own. Only familiarity with general linear models (regression, analysis of variance) is needed for this text.

Lesa Hoffman is the Scientific Director of the Research Design and Analysis Unit and Associate Professor of Quantitative Methods in the Schiefelbusch Institute for Life Span Studies at the University of Kansas.

MULTIVARIATE APPLICATIONS BOOK SERIES

The Multivariate Applications book series was developed to encourage the use of rigorous methodology in the study of meaningful scientific issues and to describe the applications in easy-to-understand language. The series is sponsored by the Society of Multivariate Experimental Psychology and welcomes methodological applications from a variety of disciplines, such as psychology, public health, sociology, education, and business. Books can be single authored, multiple authored, or edited volumes. The ideal book for this series would take on one of several approaches: (1) demonstrate the application of several multivariate methods to a single, major area of research; (2) describe a multivariate procedure or framework that could be applied to a number of research areas; or (3) present a discussion of a topic of interest to applied multivariate researchers. Previous books in the series:

What If There Were No Significance Tests? co-edited by Lisa L. Harlow, Stanley A. Mulaik and James H. Steiger (1997)

Structural Equation Modeling with LISREL, PRELIS, and SIMPLIS: Basic Concepts, Applications, and Programming by Barbara M. Byrne (1998)

Multivariate Applications in Substance Use Research co-edited by Jennifer S. Rose, Laurie Chassin, Clark C. Presson, and Steven J. Sherman (2000)

Item Response Theory for Psychologists co-authored by Susan E. Embretson and Steven P. Reise (2000)

Structural Equation Modeling with AMOS by Barbara M. Byrne (2001)

Conducting Meta-Analysis Using SAS co-authored by Winfred Arthur, Jr., Winston Bennett, Jr., and Allen I. Huffcutt (2001)

Modeling Intraindividual Variability with Repeated Measures Data: Methods and Applications co-edited by D.S. Moskowitz and Scott L. Hershberger (2002)

Multilevel Modeling: Methodological Advances, Issues, and Applications co-edited by Steven P. Reise and Naihua Duan (2003)

The Essence of Multivariate Thinking: Basic Themes and Methods by Lisa L. Harlow (2005)

Structural Equation Modeling with EQS: Basic Concepts, Applications, and Programming, Second Edition by Barbara M. Byrne (2006)

A Paul Meehl Reader: Essays on the Practice of Scientific Psychology co-edited by Niels G. Waller, Leslie J. Yonce, William M. Grove, David Faust, Mark F. Lenzenweger (2006)

Introduction to Statistical Mediation Analysis by David P. MacKinnon (2008)

Applied Data Analytic Techniques for Turning Points Research edited by Patricia Cohen (2008)

Cognitive Assessment: An Introduction to the Rule Space Method by
Kikumi K. Tatsuoka (2009)

*Structural Equation Modeling with AMOS: Basic Concepts, Applications, and
Programming, Second Edition* by Barbara M. Byrne (2009)

Handbook of Ethics in Quantitative Methodology co-edited by A. T. Panter,
Sonya K. Sterba (2011)

*Longitudinal Data Analysis: A Practical Guide for Researchers in Aging, Health, and
Social Sciences* co-edited by Jason Newsom, Richard N. Jones, Scott M. Hofer (2011)

Understanding the New Statistics: Effect Sizes, Confidence Intervals, and Meta-Analysis
by Geoff Cumming (2011)

*Structural Equation Modeling with Mplus: Basic Concepts, Applications, and
Programming* by Barbara M. Byrne (2011)

Frontiers of Test Validity Theory: Measurement, Causation, and Meaning co-authored by
Keith A. Markus, Denny Borsboom (2013)

The Essence of Multivariate Thinking: Basic Themes and Methods, Second Edition by
Lisa L. Harlow (2014)

More information can be obtained from the editor, Lisa L. Harlow, at: Department
of Psychology, University of Rhode Island, 10 Chafee Rd., Suite 8, Kingston, RI
02881–0808; Phone: 401–874–4242; FAX: 401–874–5562; or E-Mail: Lharlow@uri.edu.

LONGITUDINAL ANALYSIS

Modeling Within-Person Fluctuation
and Change

Lesa Hoffman

Routledge
Taylor & Francis Group

NEW YORK AND LONDON

First published 2015
by Routledge
711 Third Avenue, New York, NY 10017

and by Routledge
27 Church Road, Hove, East Sussex BN3 2FA

*Routledge is an imprint of the Taylor & Francis Group, an informa
business*

© 2015 Taylor & Francis

The right of Lesa Hoffman to be identified as the author of this work
has been asserted by her in accordance with sections 77 and 78 of
the Copyright, Designs and Patents Act 1988.

All rights reserved. No part of this book may be reprinted or
reproduced or utilised in any form or by any electronic, mechanical,
or other means, now known or hereafter invented, including
photocopying and recording, or in any information storage or
retrieval system, without permission in writing from the publishers.

Trademark notice: Product or corporate names may be trademarks
or registered trademarks, and are used only for identification and
explanation without intent to infringe.

Library of Congress Cataloging-in-Publication Data

Hoffman, Lesa.
    Longitudinal analysis : modeling within-person fluctuation and
change / Lesa Hoffman. — 1 Edition.
        pages cm. — (Multivariate applications series)
    Includes bibliographical references and index.
    1. Longitudinal method.   2. Psychology—Research.   I. Title.
    BF76.6.L65H64 2014
    001.4'33—dc23
    2014020352

ISBN: 978-0-415-87600-1 (hbk)
ISBN: 978-0-415-87602-5 (pbk)
ISBN: 978-1-315-74409-4 (ebk)

Typeset in StoneSerif
by Apex CoVantage, LLC

BRIEF CONTENTS

BRIEF CONTENTS

CONTENTS

SECTION II Modeling the Effects of Time   **111**

CHAPTER 4 Describing Within-Person Fluctuation
Over Time   113

▓ **CHAPTER 6** Describing Within-Person Change Over Time   207

CHAPTER 12 Analysis of Repeated Measures Designs Not Involving Time   551

PREFACE

The purpose of this text is to provide an application-oriented and technically accessible treatment of introductory and advanced linear models for within-person fluctuation and change. This text begins with general linear models (i.e., regression and analysis of variance), and then shows their extensions into general linear mixed models (*aka*, multilevel models or hierarchical linear models) and multivariate versions thereof. Based on my experiences in teaching these models, I have three aims for this text: (1) it presents the core models and their more complex extensions from a longitudinal perspective, (2) it gives sufficient attention to the substantive modeling decisions that are unique to longitudinal or repeated measures data within complex designs, and (3) it is sufficiently accessible for non-mathematically-oriented students and colleagues (like me). This text is designed for students, faculty, and other researchers from the social sciences who may have exposure to general linear models, but who may not have the technical background needed to understand longitudinal (or multilevel) models when introduced from a more statistical perspective. This text could be used in graduate-level classes for longitudinal or multilevel models, such as in psychology, education, human development and family studies, sociology, political science, business, speech-language-hearing, and survey research methodology. However, this text is also designed for those who are trying to teach themselves on their own; accordingly, the accompanying website (as described shortly) contains considerable electronic resources to do so. My overall goal is for you to learn how to thoughtfully use these models to analyze your existing data, and that these new models in turn may unlock new research questions for you as well. In striving to meet this goal, you may find that this text differs in several respects from other texts you have read—these deliberate differences and my rationale for them are as follows.

1. Why This Text?

To begin, many statistical texts are organized by model. Although a model-based type of organization makes sense to those who already understand the purposes for which models can be used, it is less ideal for beginners—in essence, readers must know what they should be looking for in order to find it! Instead, this text is organized by *research design and type of data,* and then proceeds through the series of model-building steps that would be relevant under particular scenarios. In addition, rather than placing more general concepts (e.g., model comparisons, effect size, statistical inference) in separate chapters, these topics are instead integrated into each example; that way they are ingrained as a natural part of every analysis. As a result, you should be less likely to inadvertently omit relevant material (before you know how to look for it) and to have a better handle on the model-building and model-evaluation process as a whole.

In addition, rather than using abstract language and generic notation, I will generally use specific data-driven examples to introduce each new type of model. I have chosen this strategy based on my own difficulty in following abstract material without a more concrete exemplar in place. You should feel free to mentally substitute your own examples to make the material more concrete to you as well. In fact, being able to translate from my examples into your own data will be helpful in assessing your comprehension as you read. On that note, I recognize that many researchers (me included) do not find formulas full of matrices particularly intuitive on their own. So, although the text will necessarily contain a lot of equations (some with matrices), I promise to supplement all equations with verbal and visual explanation as much as possible. By the way, I hate footnotes and the flipping-back-and-forth-to-the-end-of-the-chapter that they require, so in this text there are no footnotes—all I have to say will be right there on the page.

I know there is a big difference between following a textbook example and actually being able to apply it to your own data—no doubt the end goal for anyone voluntarily reading a stats book! To help maintain continuity while reading, each chapter has intermediate summaries as well as a final summary at the end, along with review questions you can use to test your own comprehension of the "bigger picture" ideas addressed by each chapter. In addition, in order to facilitate the process of applying these models to your own data, I have included three other key features. First, data, syntax, and output (as well as spreadsheets for other calculations) for all examples in the text are provided on this website: www.PilesOfVariance.com. Currently, the website includes analysis files for SPSS, SAS, STATA, and Mplus; more programs may be added in the future. I strongly encourage you to play along at home by estimating the example models in your software of choice (whose syntax can then serve as a template to be modified for your own data). Second, I recognize that before you can try a new model, you have to have your data set up correctly. To that end, any restructuring of data and creation of new variables needed in order to estimate these models is described in the text along with the model and its results. The example syntax online will also include these *a priori* data manipulations. Third, because even the most sophisticated model is inherently useless if no one understands it, this text will show you how to clearly convey model results by using equations, words, tables, and figures. Each example also includes a sample results section that provides a template to illustrate what a complete published report should contain, including model specification, decision making, and the substantive interpretation of model effects. As a result of this emphasis on accessibility, I hope you will have all the tools you need to make your results accessible to others as well.

2. Organization of Topics by Section and Chapter

The text is organized into four primary sections. In Section I, chapters 1, 2, and 3 will provide the building blocks of longitudinal analysis. Chapter 1 introduces some general ideas and key terminology. Chapter 2 begins by reviewing the general linear model for between-person analysis in order to build on a common foundation of linear models. Because readers are likely to vary in how much training they've had in interpreting interactions among continuous and/or categorical predictors, the rest of chapter 2 is dedicated to interpreting interaction effects. Chapter 3 begins by distinguishing between-person and within-person models for the variance, and then describes the options within repeated measures analysis of variance (and why they may be inadequate for real-world longitudinal data). Notably, chapter 3 also introduces the logic and rules for comparing relative model fit (which will also be used throughout the text).

In Section II, chapters 4, 5, and 6 will present *unconditional* longitudinal models (i.e., models with effects of time but no other predictors). Chapter 4 presents alternative covariance structure models for the variance used to describe within-person fluctuation over time. Although some may evaluate alternative models for the variance only *after* including predictors, I believe it is useful to obtain a plausible variance model *before* including predictors, given that the significance tests of the predictors depend on having the "right" (i.e., most plausible) model for the variance in the first place. Chapters 5 and 6 then focus on models for within-person change rather than fluctuation. Chapter 5 introduces fixed and random effects of time using a simple linear model for change, including the primary roles of fixed and random effects and how random effects of time create non-constant variance and covariance over time. Chapter 5 also uses a random linear time model to describe how maximum likelihood estimation actually happens, thus providing a more thorough rationale for the rules of model comparisons. Finally, chapter 6 presents a variety of functions for describing more complex patterns of within-person change, including polynomial models, nonlinear models, and discontinuous change models.

In Section III, chapters 7, 8, and 9 will present *conditional* longitudinal models (i.e., models with effects of additional predictors besides time). Chapter 7 describes the process of adding time-invariant predictors to models of within-person fluctuation and change, as well as an appendix that addresses how to examine the adequacy of assumptions about model residuals. Chapters 8 and 9 tackle the process of adding time-varying predictors to models of within-person fluctuation or change, respectively. Modeling time-varying predictors is really complicated, and so considerable space is devoted to issues of centering time-varying predictors and the resulting interpretation of model effects. Furthermore, because time-varying predictors that change over time are often better modeled using multivariate models, these are also presented in Chapter 9.

In Section IV, chapters 10 to 13 will present advanced applications for use with more complex designs. Chapter 10 evaluates alternative metrics of time (e.g., time since birth, time from/to an event) in accelerated longitudinal designs, describing how to describe effects of time when it differs both between persons (e.g., when people begin the study at different points in time) and within persons (e.g., when people are measured repeatedly). Chapter 10 also illustrates three-level models for multiple dimensions of within-person time, such as those found in ecological momentary assessment designs and measurement burst designs. Chapter 11 then focuses on the analysis of individuals in groups over time, both when group membership is constant over time (e.g., children attend the same school at each occasion) and when group membership varies over time (e.g., when children change classrooms at each occasion). Chapter 12 heads in a different direction—that of repeated measures designs not involving time—which occurs in experimental studies in which persons respond to the same items such that persons and items are crossed. Historically, such designs have been analyzed via analyses of variance that focus on one sampling dimension to the detriment of the other, but chapter 12 shows how models with crossed random effects can quantify and predict variation across both persons and items simultaneously. Finally, chapter 13 briefly discusses some additional considerations and future directions for learning about longitudinal analysis, such as the evaluation of statistical power in planning longitudinal studies, generalized longitudinal models for non-normal outcomes, and other useful extensions of the longitudinal models for event timing or intensive longitudinal data.

3. Advice for Reading the Text

Unlike many textbooks, this book is not meant to serve only as a reference—instead, I hope you will actually sit down and read it! The chapters build sequentially to tell an overall story, even though not every part of the story may be immediately relevant to you. Accordingly, I would recommend proceeding through the text as follows. For instructors, experience suggests that the material from chapters 1–7 and 12 can be covered in one semester of a graduate course on longitudinal analysis, and chapters 8–13 could be covered in a second, more advanced course.

First, everyone should begin with chapters 1–3. If you will be modeling within-person fluctuation, then chapters 4 and 5 should follow (but not necessarily chapter 6). If you will be modeling within-person change, then chapters 5 and 6 should follow (but not necessarily chapter 4). Please note that the rules of model comparisons introduced in chapter 3 (with more technical detail in chapter 5) may not make sense immediately without a familiar context in which to apply them. So it may be useful to revisit this material after completing the subsequent chapters, at which point the abstract rules of model comparisons should be more relatable. Everyone should read chapters 7, 8, and 9 because these are likely to be most important in answering research questions about longitudinal effects of predictors.

If you will be analyzing data from an accelerated longitudinal design (e.g., in which persons begin at different ages, grade levels, etc.) or multiple dimensions of time (e.g., occasions within days for multiple days), then chapter 10 is a must as well. Likewise, if your sample is organized within groups, chapter 11 is absolutely necessary. Furthermore, although it may appear that the remaining chapters could be read only as needed given your research design, I'd still recommend that you read them (and not just because I took the time to write them). This is because through the process of acquiring advanced material, the earlier material will be ingrained more deeply. Certainly, no single text can cover every relevant topic, but I do hope that after finishing this text you will have the necessary frame of reference with which to acquire new related models as needed (as overviewed in chapter 13).

However, there are two related limitations to this text that you should be aware of with respect to the treatment of the models and the description of their results. First, this book will have little to say about research design as a topic unto itself. This is because the inferences to be made about the effects estimated by a model (e.g., correlational or causal) depend on the research design, not the analysis, and so the fundamentals of research design (as presented in other texts for that purpose) translate readily to longitudinal models. We will instead focus primarily on the between-person and within-person levels of inference, issues that are unique to longitudinal models. Second, although a sample results section is provided at the end of every chapter that includes an extended example, it is important to recognize that this type of results section by itself would not be sufficient for the purposes of publication. That is, although the results sections will demonstrate how to present and interpret the model results, they do not place those empirical findings within the context of a substantively meaningful story, theoretical framework, or set of research hypotheses to be tested. Although critically important, such contextual information will be far too study-idiosyncratic to be sufficiently addressed in this text, and as such it will need to be incorporated by you once you become sufficiently well versed in each type of longitudinal models and in the general interpretation of their parameters.

Finally, the reader should be aware that references to published empirical work will be rare within the text, and this is a deliberate strategy so that this text will retain as much generality as possible. Once you better understand the terminology and concepts of longitudinal analysis, you will be able to more carefully consider the longitudinal research within your own field, and thus to find your own examples that will be more immediately useful. Furthermore, any generally accepted statistical or methodological concepts (i.e., concepts that can be readily found in many other texts) will usually not have explicit references given, but ideas taken from more specific or recent sources will be referenced accordingly (with full citations appearing in the reference section the end of each chapter). However, references for more in-depth treatments of particular topics that could provide useful elaboration are provided where appropriate.

4. Acknowledgments

A project of this size could never be completed alone, and this text would have never been imagined or completed without the invaluable assistance of my family, friends, and colleagues. First, I owe a huge debt of gratitude to my parents, who always told me I could do anything, and who have always done their absolute best to give me everything I needed to do so. Second, I offer a huge thank you to my previous instructors, mentors, and all of you who have patiently answered my questions over the years. You've taught me so much not only about statistics, but also about how to be an effective instructor, mentor, and scientist. This thank-you list includes (but is not limited to) Calvin Garbin, John Flowers, Dave Hansen, Dan Bernstein, Janet Marquis, Susan Embretson, Xiangdong Yang, Susan Kemper, Mabel Rice, Joan McDowd, Scott Hofer, Andrea Piccinin, Martin Sliwinski, Mike Rovine, Don Hedeker, and Walter Stroup.

A huge thank you also goes to the persons who generously provided their data for the examples in the text or to motivate the examples in the text. This list includes (but is not limited to) Boo Johansson, David Almeida, Nan Crouter, Susan McHale, Robert Stawski, Scott Hofer, Martin Sliwinski, Scott Gest, and Kelli Rulison. I am exceedingly grateful for all of the helpful comments I've received on the drafts of each chapter from my students at the University of Nebraska–Lincoln and from students in other workshops. I sincerely appreciate the careful feedback of chapter drafts by Ryan Walters, Lucas Wang, and Catharine Sparks and by the reviewers including Lisa L. Harlow, University of Rhode Island; Scott M. Hofer, University of Victoria; Andrea Piccinin, University of Victoria; Kristopher J. Preacher, Vanderbilt University; Michael J. Rovine, Penn State University; and three anonymous reviewers. Another huge thank you goes to Debra Riegert for her never-ending patience and flexibility as I missed deadline after deadline (and yet kept asking for more pages to complete this work).

Finally, my biggest thank you yet is reserved for my best friend, husband, and the smartest person I've ever known, Jonathan Templin. I cannot thank you enough for reading every word I wrote (multiple times) and for providing me with the careful feedback I always needed to hear (even when I didn't want to hear it). You have been beyond generous with your time and energy, and have taught me pretty much everything I know about estimation and about countless other topics as well. But most of all, I thank you for the indispensable amount of support you've given me throughout every day of this process. I could not have done this without you. (And I promise that now I'll be the one to cook you dinner for a change.)

ABOUT THE AUTHOR

Dr. Lesa Hoffman received her Ph.D. in psychology at the University of Kansas in 2003, and completed a post-doctoral fellowship at The Pennsylvania State University before joining the Department of Psychology at the University of Nebraska–Lincoln as an Assistant Professor in 2006 (and as Associate Professor in 2011). Dr. Hoffman became the scientific director of the Research Design and Analysis (RDA) Unit and Associate Professor of Quantitative Methods in the Schiefelbusch Institute for Life Span Studies in August 2014. Her program of research seeks to empirically examine and to thoughtfully disseminate how developments in quantitative psychology can best be utilized to advance empirical work in psychology, human development, and other social sciences. Recent projects have focused on the measurement of visual attention in older adults, the methodological barriers to examining longitudinal changes in cognition, and innovative applications of multilevel modeling for within-person experimental designs. She has received support for her research from NIH and NSF as a principal, co-investigator, and consultant. Her work has been featured in both methodological and area-specific journals, such as *Multivariate Behavioral Research, Behavioral Research Methods, Psychology and Aging,* and the *Journal of Speech-Language-Hearing Research*. Lesa was also elected to the Society of Multivariate Experimental Psychology in 2009. She received their Tanaka Award for Most Outstanding Article in 2007 in Multivariate Behavioral Research as well as their Cattell Early Career Research Award in 2011. She teaches graduate courses and intensive workshops in advanced quantitative methods, such as latent trait measurement models, multilevel modeling, and longitudinal data analysis. Visit Lesa's home page for more information about her research and teaching: www.lesahoffman.com.

SECTION I

BUILDING BLOCKS FOR LONGITUDINAL ANALYSIS

CHAPTER 1

INTRODUCTION TO THE ANALYSIS OF LONGITUDINAL DATA

Welcome to the wonderful world of longitudinal analysis! The overall purpose of this book is to take you, the reader, on a highly detailed and pedagogical tour of statistical models for analyzing longitudinal data. Entering a new world of statistical models can be like entering a foreign country—no matter how prepared you may try to be, challenges are bound to arise due to the unfamiliar language, routines, and customs used in that new land. Accordingly, the goal of this first chapter is to begin orienting you to some of the more prominent themes in analyzing longitudinal data, as well as to the varying terminology by which these ideas can be described. To that end, the overall purpose of this chapter is to identify the salient features of longitudinal data and longitudinal models, as well as to highlight the advantages that the models offered in this text have over more traditional ways of analyzing longitudinal data.

More specifically, this chapter begins with the idea of *levels of analysis*—that is, by distinguishing longitudinal research questions about between-person relationships from questions about within-person relationships (and how longitudinal data can be used to address each of these). And as you already may know, there are many different kinds of longitudinal data that can be collected over varying time scales (e.g., ranging from moment-to-moment fluctuation to long-term change observed over the span of several decades). As such, we will also examine a useful heuristic with which to organize longitudinal data—its location on a *data continuum* ranging from pure within-person fluctuation to pure within-person change (growth or decline).

But in addition to the new concepts and vocabulary in the land of longitudinal analysis, there are also unfamiliar statistical modeling frameworks to be learned. Because readers of this text will have different backgrounds in terms of their topics of interest and with which models they are already familiar, it is imperative for us to establish a common analytic viewpoint and set of terminology before we can move forward. Accordingly, this chapter will introduce the two-sided lens through which each of the to-be-presented statistical models can be viewed—the *model for the means* and the *model for the variance*. Although statistical models are logically separate from the software with which they are estimated, their method of presentation usually favors one modeling framework or another, and so this chapter also overviews the two modeling frameworks employed in this text, those of *multilevel models* (which are featured predominantly in the text) and *structural equation models* (which are discussed briefly in chapter 9). Furthermore, because the to-be-presented models were originally developed for use with certain kinds of outcome variables, this chapter will also introduce the necessary features any outcome variable must have in order to be analyzed using models presented in this text.

Learning a new set of concepts, vocabulary, and models is never a simple task, and the material presented in this text will be no exception. But I strongly believe that transitioning to this new land of longitudinal analysis does have many significant advantages, and I want to assure you that it will be worth your while to do so before diving into the model specifics. Thus, the end of this chapter also highlights the flexibility and power of the to-be-presented models for not only specifying many kinds of research questions, but also for answering them as accurately as possible. Finally, this chapter concludes by describing the datasets that will be used in the forthcoming examples.

1. Features of Longitudinal Data

We now turn to two prominent features of longitudinal data: (a) the levels of analysis they can address, and (b) a data continuum for kinds of longitudinal variability.

1.A. Levels of Analysis: Between-Person and Within-Person Relationships

Why conduct longitudinal research? It requires a lot of time, money, and energy to conduct a longitudinal study. If you are reading this book, chances are you already know this all too well! And chances are, your answer to this question would be something like, "Because I am interested in seeing how people change over time," or perhaps, "Because I want to see how daily fluctuations across variables are related." Both of these answers reflect an appreciation for the need to distinguish *between-person relationships* from *within-person relationships*.

The phrase **between-person** simply refers to the existence of **interindividual variation** (i.e., differences between people). The term **between-person relationship** is used to capture how individual differences on one outcome are related to individual differences on another outcome. People can differ from each other in stable attributes, such as ethnicity or biological sex. People can also differ from each other in attributes like intelligence, personality, or socioeconomic status that could potentially change over time. But if those attributes are assessed at only a single point in time, then those values obtained at that particular occasion are assumed to be stable and reflective of the person as a whole—in other words, the attributes are considered **time-invariant.** Thus, the phrase *between-person* refers to relationships among *interindividual differences* in variables that are *time-invariant.* Furthermore, in the longitudinal models to be presented, the between-person level of analysis is usually labeled as **level 2,** or the **macro** level of analysis.

But what if it is unreasonable to assume that attributes remain constant over time? In that case, it may be more useful to examine *within-person* relationships rather than *between-person* relationships. The phrase **within-person** refers to the existence of **intraindividual variation** within a person when measured repeatedly over time—in other words, how a person varies from his or her own baseline level (in which baseline can be an assessment at a particular point in time or a constructed average of assessments over time). Within-person variation is only directly observable when each person is measured more than once (i.e., in a longitudinal study). The term **within-person relationship** is used to capture how variation relative to a person's own baseline is related across variables, regardless of the baseline values *per se.* Some attributes are expected to vary over time, such as levels of stress, emotion, or physiological arousal—such variables when measured repeatedly are called **time-varying.** Yet people may also show variation over time in attributes that are supposedly stable, like personality. So long as a variable measured repeatedly actually shows within-person variation over time, that variable can be considered time-varying and has the potential to show a within-person relationship. Thus, the phrase *within-person* refers to relationships among *intraindividual differences* in variables that are *time-varying.* Furthermore, in the models to be presented, the within-person level of analysis is usually labeled as **level 1,** or the **micro** level of analysis. The *micro* level 1 of longitudinal observations is nested within the *macro* level 2 of persons (e.g., time-specific outcomes at level 1 are nested within persons at level 2).

Furthermore, although the language used so far assumes that person is the unit of analysis, it still applies to any other entity that is measured repeatedly over time. For instance, research with animal models might examine variation in drug response between and within *rats* over time; organizational research might examine variation in company performance outcomes between and within *companies* over time. For this reason, in the notation used in this text, level-2 units will be represented generically with an *i* subscript for *individuals* to recognize that the individual unit of study could be many things (and not just person, although person will be featured in this text).

The primary benefit of a longitudinal study is its capacity to inform about within-person relationships (and not just between-person relationships, as in cross-sectional studies). But another important benefit is that longitudinal studies provide the opportunity to test hypotheses at multiple levels of analysis simultaneously (see Hofer & Sliwinski, 2006). That is, the models in this text will allow us to examine both between-person and within-person relationships in the same variables at the same time. In fact, much of this text will emphasize the need to distinguish between-person from within-person relationships (as well as relationships at other levels when applicable), both in terms of specifying longitudinal research questions and in examining these relationships with longitudinal models. Although human development, psychology, and other fields are replete with theoretical explanations of human behavior, it can often be a challenge to identify theoretical implications at both the between-person and within-person levels of analysis.

For example, we might posit a link between stress and negative mood, such that greater amounts of stress will result in greater negative mood. But at what level of analysis is this relationship likely to hold: between persons, within persons, or both? People who are chronically stressed may have more generally elevated levels of negative mood than people with less chronic stress. Such a relationship, if found, would be *between persons* (i.e., *inter*individual differences in stress related to *inter*individual differences in negative mood). This stress–mood relationship would be considered *between persons* if stress and mood were assessed only once *or* if they were assessed repeatedly, but then only their average values across time were computed per person and then analyzed (i.e., a relationship among across-time averages in a longitudinal study is still *between persons*). But by collecting repeated measurements of stress and negative mood, we could also examine the extent to which negative mood may be greater *than usual* when someone is under more stress *than usual*. This is an example of a *within-person* relationship in which *intra*individual differences in stress are related to *intra*individual differences in negative mood (i.e., greater than baseline amounts of stress predict greater than baseline amounts of negative mood, in which each person's baseline serves as his or her own reference).

In this example, both the between-person and within-person relationships of stress with negative mood would be expected to be positive—higher stress relates to more negative mood, in which "higher stress" could be relative to other people (between persons) or relative to one's own baseline (within persons). But in other instances, different relationships may be expected between persons rather than within persons. For example, people who undergo regular physical activity are likely in better shape (e.g., have a lower resting heart rate) than people who do not. Thus, a between-person relationship between activity level and resting heart rate is likely to be negative. Yet, when someone is more active than usual (e.g., when actually exercising), his or her active heart rate is elevated relative to his or her resting heart rate. Similarly, during a period of intense training that is more than to what a person is accustomed, his or her resting heart rate is likely to be more elevated than usual while the body adapts to the training demands. Thus, in contrast to a negative between-person relationship, these within-person relationships between activity level and resting heart rate are likely to be positive instead, even over different time scales. In general, different relationships would be expected at each level of analysis (between persons and within persons) because these relationships reflect different phenomena at each level of analysis.

This brings us to a fundamental tenet of longitudinal research: *relationships observed at the within-person level of analysis need not (and often will not) mirror those observed at the between-person level of analysis.* Accordingly, it is critical to frame hypotheses about the phenomena of interest to address these differing expectations. And relevant to this text, it is equally important to conduct statistical analyses that also explicitly separate between-person relationships from within-person relationships among variables measured repeatedly over time. Longitudinal variables usually contain both between-person and within-person variation, and so each source of variation has the potential to show its own relationship with other variables—in other words, variables measured over time are usually really two variables instead of one.

In addition, there is potentially greater complexity to be found due to interactions across levels of analysis. For example, consider a hypothetical relationship between positive mood and amount of sleep. Is it that people who routinely get more sleep are routinely in better moods (i.e., a positive between-person relationship)? Or is it that after getting more sleep than usual, your mood is better than usual (i.e., a positive within-person relationship)? Does getting more sleep than usual *matter more* for people who don't get that much sleep in general? If so, we would find a *cross-level interaction*, such that the within-person relationship between sleep and positive mood would depend upon a person's usual (between-person) level of sleep. You can likely think of many similar examples where the effects of within-person variation matter more for certain kinds of people. The point of these examples is simply that differences between people aren't usually a good proxy for variation within a person, and that the simultaneous modeling of both between-person and within-person relationships in longitudinal data requires careful attention to these distinctions. These points will be reiterated throughout the text.

1.B. A Data Continuum: Within-Person Fluctuation to Within-Person Change

In addition to distinguishing interindividual (between-person) variation from intraindividual (within-person) variation, another distinction that is important to make when conducting longitudinal research relates to the *type* of intraindividual variation to be examined—do you expect within-person *change* or within-person *fluctuation?* These concepts will be introduced briefly below, and more extended discussion can be found in the work of Nesselroade and colleagues (e.g., Nesselroade, 1991; Nesselroade & Ram, 2004).

Within-person change is a more specific type of within-person variation, and it refers to any kind of systematic change that is expected as a result of the meaningful passage of time (i.e., the predictor of *time* serves as an index of a causal process thought to be responsible for the observed change). Children grow in mathematical ability as a function of years of schooling, the symptoms of persons with illness may improve as a function of time in treatment, and older adults may decline in cognition and health as they near the end of their lifespan. Although these changes may manifest themselves in different patterns or at different rates across people, the key idea is that some kind of systematic change is expected as a function of time—that is, time is meaningfully sampled with the goal of studying change. The aim of such studies is often to describe and predict individual differences in change over time (e.g., which persons benefit most from a treatment, which older adults are most likely to show the most pronounced decline).

In contrast, **within-person fluctuation** refers to undirected variation over repeated assessments and is seen in contexts in which one would not expect any systematic change, and in which time is simply a way to obtain multiple observations per person (rather than serving as a meaningful index of a causal process). People *fluctuate* in things like stress, mood, and energy level across days, weeks, months, or years, but *systematic increases or decreases* in the levels of these variables may not be expected as a function of time, specifically. The goal of this type of longitudinal study is often to describe and predict relationships in within-person fluctuation among *short-term* processes, rather than within-person relationships in *long-term* change.

Because this text will present models for examining both within-person fluctuation and within-person change over time, in the text notation, level-1 units will be represented generically with a *t* subscript for *time* to recognize that time could be measured in any metric (seconds, hours, days, months, years, etc.). However, the distinction of *fluctuation* versus *change* will be relevant in framing within-person hypotheses about variation around one's own baseline level in longitudinal studies. That is, given the study design and its resulting data, what should the *baseline* be? If the within-person variation is thought to reflect mostly fluctuation, then it may be useful for the baseline to be the variable's average over time (i.e., such that within-person variation would reflect having more of variable X than usual at a given occasion). In contrast, if the within-person variation is thought to reflect mostly change, then it may be more useful for the baseline to be a particular occasion instead, such as the beginning of the study (i.e., such that within-person variation would reflect having more of variable X now than at the first occasion, or more directly, change from baseline).

In thinking about your own research, you may discover that distinguishing within-person fluctuation from within-person change is not always as straightforward as it seems! In reality, there is a continuum ranging from "pure" fluctuation to "pure" change, with many possible intermediate points given differences in study designs and in the variables being assessed. For instance, systematic effects of time (i.e., within-person change) may be relevant in short-term longitudinal studies designed to examine within-person fluctuation (e.g., negative mood may change systematically across days of the week). The reverse may be true as well, in that within-person fluctuation may be present in addition to more systematic within-person change in longer-term studies. Furthermore, we might predict both fluctuation and change in studies that feature multiple time scales (e.g., *measurement burst designs,* in which the process of collecting multiple observations over a short period of time is repeated across several more widely spaced intervals).

In any event, the expected location for your data on the continuum of fluctuation to change will be important when deciding which longitudinal models will be most useful for describing any within-person patterns in your data and for testing your hypotheses. Fortunately, the extent to which your data show systematic within-person change (on average or at the individual level) can be assessed empirically, as we will see later on. An absence of systematic change over time suggests that the models designed for fluctuation may be more useful instead.

2. Features of Longitudinal Models

2.A. The Two Sides of Any Model: Means and Variances

The models in this book require knowledge of the general linear model (and so its most relevant concepts will be reviewed in chapters 2 and 3). But before diving in, this requirement first needs to be clarified, as the term *general linear model* can sometimes be intimidating in and of itself! People who are familiar with multiple regression and analysis of variance (ANOVA) are often unnecessarily hesitant in confirming that they are, in fact, familiar with the general linear model. Simply put—if you know regression and ANOVA, then you do know the general linear model! The term **general linear model** encompasses a number of models for continuous outcome variables whose names differ according to the type of predictor variables included. Throughout the text, I will use the phrase **continuous** for quantitative variables (even if they are not truly continuous in the sense of having all possible intermediate values between integers), and the phrase **categorical** for discrete, grouping variables (i.e., in which differences between specific levels are of interest, although those levels may or may not be ordered). General linear models with slopes for continuous predictors are called *regression,* models with mean differences across levels of categorical predictors are called *analyses of variance,* and models with both types of predictors are called *analysis of covariance* (or just *regression* in some texts).

More technically, the general linear model is used to predict continuous outcomes that are thought to be conditionally normally distributed (i.e., in contrast to general*ized* linear models, in which the outcomes take on other conditional distributions). But what general linear models and those in this text have in common is that they have *two sides,* or ways in which they can be distinguished—in their model for the means or in their model for the variance, as described next.

The term **model for the means** refers to the *structural* or the *fixed effects* side of the model and is what you are likely used to caring about for testing hypotheses. Does predictor X relate to outcome Y? Are there mean differences in outcome Y across the categories of X? In each of these statements, the effect of predictor X is part of the model for the means. In general, *the model for the means states how the expected (or predicted) outcome for each person varies as a function of his or her predictor values.* The phrase *model for the means* is based on the idea that if you know nothing else for a person, the best naïve guess for his or her Y outcome will be the grand mean of Y for the sample. A better guess for each person's Y outcome can then be made by taking into account his or her X predictor values. But because all persons with the same predictor values will have the same expected outcome, that predicted Y is still a *mean*—just now it's a **conditional mean,** so named because it depends on, or is *conditional* on, the values of the predictors. These X predictors can be continuous variables, categorical variables, or a mixture of both, and the predictors can each be measured just once or repeatedly over time. The X predictors are weighted and linearly combined to generate an expected Y outcome for each person. The predictor weights are called **fixed effects** because they are constant for everyone in the sample. The fixed effects in the model for the means are always specified as a function of known predictor variables, and they are estimated by fitting the chosen model to the data.

Three general labels for specific versions of the model for the means will be used in this text. First is an **empty model**, which is just as it sounds—a model for the means that contains a fixed intercept but no predictors. Although an empty model is usually not that informative, it will serve as a useful baseline against which to compare the utility of more complex models. Next will be **unconditional models**, which in this text will refer to models that contain fixed effects to describe within-person change or fluctuation over time, but that do not contain any other predictors besides those representing the effects of time. And finally, a **conditional model** in this text will be a model in which fixed effects for other predictors besides time are then included.

Formulating the model for the means and comparing alternative versions thereof requires making choices about which predictors to include as well as the form of their effects (e.g., linear or nonlinear, additive or interactive with other predictors). Such choices in the model for the means are often made on substantive grounds in order to answer research questions. This is usually not the case for the other side of any model—the model for the variance.

The term **model for the variance** refers to the *stochastic* or *error* part of the model and describes *how the residuals of the Y outcome (i.e., the differences between the Y values observed in the data and the Y values predicted by the model for the means) are distributed and related across observations*. That is, whereas the model for the means is specified to predict the Y outcome values themselves, the model for the variance is specified to predict the *pattern of variance and covariance* for the residuals of the Y outcomes instead. In contrast to the model for the means, the model for the variance is likely *not* something you are used to contemplating. That is, rather than making *choices* as in the model for the means, you are likely used to making *assumptions* about the model for the variance due to a lack of available options in general linear models. For instance, very simple assumptions are made about the residuals in regression or ANOVA: in addition to their conditionally normal distribution, we assume the residuals are unrelated across persons and that their variance is the same across persons (i.e., *homogeneity of variance*, or *constant variance*). Such simplifying assumptions are highly unlikely to hold when moving to the analysis of longitudinal and repeated measures data, however. The benefit of a modeling framework that allows more choices and greater flexibility in the variance side of the model (as well as in the means side of the model) is twofold.

First, such choices in modeling variance will allow you to test substantive hypotheses about variation between and within persons. For example, do people change over time at different rates? If so, then the effect of time shouldn't be included just as a *fixed effect* in the model for the means, or as constant effect across the sample. Instead, the effect of time should also be included as a *random effect*, which would allow each person to have his or her own slope for the effect of time. Rather than estimating these person-specific slopes directly as a different fixed slope for each person, the models in this text will estimate their random variance across persons instead. That is, random effects are included as part of the model for the variance instead of the model for the means. In general, when describing kinds of model effects, the term **fixed** means that everyone gets the same effect (i.e., a single slope estimated for the predictor's effect in the model for the means), whereas the term **random** means that everyone gets his or her own effect (i.e., achieved by estimating a *variance* across persons for the slope of the predictor).

As another example of a substantive hypothesis about variation, what if people differ in how much within-person fluctuation they show over time? For instance, what if some people are just "moodier" (i.e., show more fluctuation in reported mood over time) than other people? Within a longitudinal model, the residual variance characterizes within-person fluctuation. If people differ in the amount of within-person fluctuation they exhibit (e.g., moodiness) as a function of specific variables (e.g., personality characteristics), then the residual variance (representing outcome fluctuation) should be allowed to differ over persons as a function of those characteristics instead of assuming the residual variance is constant over persons.

Finally, even if research hypotheses about the model for the variance are not a part of your analysis goals, there is a second important reason why having choices available for the model for the variance can be helpful. Namely, the validity of the standard errors for the tests of the fixed effects (and thus their accompanying *p*-values) in the model for the means depends on having the "right" model for the variance. In reality, given that we never know what the "right" model is, we simply try to find the model that is "least wrong" among the plausible alternatives. Thus, having the power to *make choices* (instead of merely *making assumptions*) about what belongs in the model for the variance will permit greater confidence in the tests of fixed effects for predictors in the model for the means—tests that are more often the purpose of our analyses.

2.B. Longitudinal Modeling Frameworks

One of the most confusing parts of learning new quantitative methods is the process of sorting out hypotheses, models, modeling frameworks, and software packages. That is, it can be challenging to determine how research questions can be examined in statistical models, how those models can be implemented within different modeling frameworks, and which software packages can be used as a result. A key idea underlying this series of decisions, however, is that *statistical models are logically separate from the software used to estimate them*. Furthermore, the majority of the longitudinal models presented in this book can be estimated within two general modeling frameworks: multilevel modeling and structural equation modeling. Although this text will describe longitudinal models as multilevel models, structural equation models could also be used as well (as well as hybrids of both approaches). Both of these frameworks offer greater flexibility than can be found in the general linear model, as overviewed briefly below.

The term **multilevel model** (*aka,* **hierarchical linear model** or **general linear mixed model**) describes an analytic framework that includes both fixed effects (that are the same for everyone) and random effects (that vary across persons). Multilevel models are used for data collected through multiple dimensions of sampling, which likely results in multiple sources of variation in the outcomes and predictors. For instance, because longitudinal data include two dimensions of sampling (between persons and within persons over time), this creates between-person and within-person variation, respectively. The purpose of multilevel models is to quantify and then explain each source of variation with predictors that correspond to each sampling dimension. In multilevel models for longitudinal data, time-invariant predictors can account for between-person variance, and time-varying predictors can account for within-person variance.

The idea that multiple dimensions of sampling lead to distinct kinds of variance in the outcome is often described as the problem of **dependency.** That is, because observations from the same person will tend to be more alike than observations from different people, model residuals from the same person will tend to be correlated (i.e., to covary), and thus violate the general linear model assumption of independent residuals. This correlation or dependency results in distorted standard errors for the fixed effects of the predictors, whose significance tests may then be too conservative or too liberal, depending on the form of the dependency and the sampling dimension for each predictor (e.g., over time or persons). The purpose of multilevel models for longitudinal data is to add terms to the model for the variance that will represent those sources of dependency. After doing so, the model for the variance and covariance in the outcome over time will better match the actual patterns in the data, thereby ensuring that the tests of the fixed effects for predictors will take those sources of dependency into account where necessary. Multilevel models have numerous and flexible options for addressing sources of dependency.

More generally, because multilevel models can include many types of dependency due to multiple dimensions of sampling in an outcome, they can also be used in **clustered data**, or when persons from different groups are sampled (and in which independence of residuals may also be violated). For example, people from the same schools, families, or organizations may be more similar in their responses than people from different schools, families, or organizations, causing dependency of the residuals of persons from the same group. Thus, a significant advantage of working within the multilevel modeling framework is the capacity to simultaneously model dependency of all different kinds (e.g., across time, across persons, across groups), thus testing the fixed effects of the predictors within each dimension of sampling as accurately as possible.

Just as general linear models include special cases that go by specific names, so do multilevel models. Models for describing and predicting individual differences in change are known as **growth curve models** or **latent growth curve models** (the term *latent* will be addressed in the next section). Models for describing fluctuation rather than change are known as **within-person variation models.** Models for examining predictors across levels of sampling (e.g., in students sampled from multiple schools) are known as **clustered models.** Models for data in which the higher-level grouping dimensions are crossed instead of nested (e.g., when students who attend different schools live in different neighborhoods, or when students change classrooms at each occasion) are known as **cross-classified models** or **crossed random effects models.** Finally, any general linear model can be operationalized as some kind of multilevel model via certain restrictions in the model for the variance (as will be shown in chapter 3).

Although multilevel models offer many flexible strategies for quantifying and predicting dependency due to multiple dimensions of sampling, they are estimated on observed variables that are assumed to be perfectly reliable. This limitation is not found within **structural equation models,** a general framework for estimating relationships among observed variables *or* among unobserved **latent variables,** which are the underlying traits or abilities thought to produce the observed variables (which are known as *indicators* in latent variable models). By defining a latent variable from the common variance across indicators thought to measure the same construct (e.g., a latent factor of *intelligence* can be defined from scores from a set of items or tests measuring IQ), the latent variable should measure the underlying construct more reliably than would any single indicator. Thus, potentially stronger relationships may be observed among the latent variables than among any of their less reliable single-indicator counterparts.

Included within the structural equation modeling framework are **measurement models** for how latent variables relate to their observed indicators, such as *confirmatory factor models* (that relate continuous latent variables to their observed continuous indicators), *item response models* (that relate continuous latent variables to their observed categorical indicators), and *diagnostic classification models* (that relate categorical latent variables to their observed continuous or categorical indicators). Upon defining the latent variables through their measurement models, **structural models** then specify relationships among those latent variables. Structural equation models can be especially useful when a measurement procedure differs over time because rather than modeling within-person change in an *observed* variable (e.g., a sum score ignoring which items were given at each occasion), change in a *latent* variable (as defined by different but overlapping sets of items at each occasion) can be examined more meaningfully instead.

Although usually thought of as underlying abilities like *intelligence,* latent variables can also be used for within-person change. Structural equation models for longitudinal data are often called **latent growth curve models**, in which the latent variables of *intercept* and *time slope* can represent underlying individual differences in levels and rates of change over time, as formed from the sources of common variance of an outcome measured repeatedly. However, you will see that in this text I have chosen to present longitudinal models using multilevel model notation rather than structural equation model notation. This is because I believe multilevel models are an easier starting point given how readily they map onto familiar linear models (e.g., regression).

Software for structural equation models can also be used to conduct multivariate analysis of observed variables only. Such models are sometimes referred to as **path models,** and a special case is **mediation models,** in which variables can be both predictors and outcomes simultaneously (i.e., in which X predicts M, and in which M then predicts Y). Multilevel versions of path models have recently become more commonplace, in which random effects can account for sampling-related dependency and relations through intermediate outcomes can also be examined. Such models have been referred to (somewhat confusingly) as **multilevel structural equation models,** even when they do not include latent variable measurement models (although truly multilevel measurement models are possible as well). To avoid confusion, this text will reserve the term *structural equation models* for analyses including latent variable measurement structures, and instead use the term *multivariate model* for analyses involving observed variables only.

Before moving on, it is important to recognize that nearly all longitudinal modeling concepts presented in this text will apply to either observed variables or to latent variables. But because the construction of measurement models for latent variables is a complex separate topic unto itself, this text will present examples using observed variables only. This should not imply a preference for observed variables over latent variables, though. Instead, the focus of the text is how to analyze within-person change or fluctuation in variables of interest over time, which is logically separate from how those variables should be constructed *per se.*

2.C. Data Formats Across Modeling Frameworks

In order to use most multilevel modeling software programs, longitudinal datasets will need to be organized in one of two formats: stacked or multivariate. The **stacked format,** otherwise known as *univariate, long,* or *person-period,* is utilized primarily within multilevel modeling programs and requires *one row per occasion per person.* Thus, for a longitudinal study with five measurement occasions, each person would have five rows of data. In contrast, the **multivariate format,** otherwise known as *wide* or *person-level,* is utilized primarily within structural equation modeling programs and requires *one row per person,* such that the multiple observations per occasion are placed in multiple columns (one column for each occasion).

Table 1.1 shows an example of a two-occasion dataset under the *stacked format* on the left and the *multivariate format* on the right. In the stacked format, two index variables are used: *ID,* which keeps track of the person contributing each observation, and *Age,* which identifies the occasion at which the observation occurred. In the example data, there is a single time-invariant variable of *Treat,* which keeps track of whether each person was in a treatment group (0 = *no,* 1 = *yes*). There are two time-varying variables, labeled generically X and Y, and the observation of X and Y at each age is given in its corresponding row for each person. Thus, in a stacked format, time-varying variables (like X and Y here) will vary across the rows for the same person, whereas time-invariant variables (like *ID* and *Treat* here) will be constant across the rows for the same person instead. In contrast, in the multivariate format the observations for each person are constrained to one row, with time-varying variables transposed across columns instead of rows per person. The time identification in the multivariate format is contained in the names of the columns (e.g., *X10* is X at age 10), instead of as a separate variable as in the stacked format.

Table 1.1 Example of data in stacked (left) and multivariate (right) formats.

Stacked Format					Multivariate Format					
ID	Age	Treat	X	Y	ID	Treat	X10	X11	Y10	Y11
1	10	0	5	54.40	1	0	5	3	54.40	56.50
1	11	0	3	56.50	2	0	6	9	52.71	55.97
2	10	0	6	52.71	3	1	2	4	52.24	57.93
2	11	0	9	55.97	4	1	7	8	54.68	58.32
3	10	1	2	52.24						
3	11	1	4	57.93						
4	10	1	7	54.68						
4	11	1	8	58.32						

2.D. Features of Outcome Variables

Although this chapter has presented some of the major themes in modeling longitudinal data, it hasn't yet discussed the data themselves—the kinds of outcome variables that will be most appropriately analyzed with the models presented in this text. First is the most obvious requirement: The outcomes must be measured longitudinally, or at least twice per person. As discussed earlier, the term *longitudinal* does not imply that observations must occur far apart in time—studies whose occasions span only seconds or that span many years are considered equally longitudinal (although studies over such different time frames may logically be placed at different points along the data continuum of within-person fluctuation to within-person change). As will be discussed in chapter 3, however, the minimum of two occasions per person will not be sufficient to examine hypotheses about individual differences in change over time (or in other kinds of within-person relationships). Because a line will fit two points perfectly, error cannot be distinguished from real differences in change unless each person has three or more observations.

Second, the models presented in this text are for *continuous, conditionally normally distributed outcomes:* the outcomes must be measured on an interval scale in which a one-unit change has the same meaning across all points of the scale, and for which a normal distribution for all model residuals after including all model predictors is a tenable assumption. Although this is the same requirement for outcomes within almost *any* linear model, it is not a death knell for outcomes that do not have normally distributed residuals. Considerable research has shown that general models tend to be fairly robust to deviations of normality of the residuals. Furthermore, *generalized mixed linear models* for non-normal longitudinal outcomes are also becoming increasingly more available. It's just that the added complexity involved in estimating models for non-normal longitudinal outcomes makes them a difficult place to begin for the novice reader (for whom this text is intended). After becoming familiar with the models for normal longitudinal outcomes, however, the transition to other outcomes such as binary, categorical, or count data should be more straightforward; these models are described briefly in chapter 13.

Note that, as in the general linear model, no assumptions are made about the distributions of the predictor variables. The model assumptions explicitly pertain to the residuals of the *outcome* only (i.e., the model is Y given X, not X given Y), so it is not a problem to include the effects of categorical predictors via dummy codes. In estimating slopes for continuous variables, though, it is important to remember that meaningful slope estimates require that a one-unit change in the predictor has the same meaning across all values of the predictor. This may not be reasonable in ordinal variables for which the differences between the assigned numeric values are arbitrary, but this caution is relevant in any linear model, longitudinal or otherwise. Finally, although skewness or kurtosis of predictors may not be a problem *per se*, extreme predictor values could end up having stronger leverage (i.e., to be weighted more heavily in estimating the predictor's slope), and non-normality of predictors could be problematic for that reason instead.

A final requirement is that the outcome variable (and any time-varying predictor in this case) needs to have *invariant meaning and measurement over time*. First, variables should have the same conceptual meaning at each occasion, an assumption that may not be testable empirically. For instance, a test of single-digit multiplication that assesses mathematical ability in second-graders may assess memory instead in high school students, and so using it to measure growth in mathematical ability from childhood through adolescence may not be meaningful. Second, variables need to be measured in the same way at each occasion. This may entail using the same physical devices and procedures when measuring observed quantities, or using the same items when assessing latent constructs, in which case the items should also relate to the construct being measured in the same manner at each occasion. If this is not the case, then latent variable measurement models that can explicitly account for changes in the items administered or in the item properties over time should first be used to construct meaningful latent variables instead. Although often more theoretical than empirical, such considerations are nevertheless important precursors to any analysis, longitudinal or otherwise, because even the most sophisticated statistical models in the world cannot save poorly defined or measured variables.

Thus, in summary, the models used in this text will require outcome variables measured at least twice per person (preferably more) whose residuals should be (reasonably) normally distributed after including all model predictors. Furthermore, the outcome variable should be measured on an interval scale and have the same conceptual meaning over time. Any kind of predictor variable can be included, but you should be watchful of extreme predictor values having undue influence (leverage) on the model effects, just as you would in any linear model.

3. Advantages Over General Linear Models

This chapter so far has introduced us to some of the recurring themes in longitudinal analysis: (1) the idea of levels of analysis (*between person* and *within person*); (2) the continuum for kinds of within-person variation that can be found in longitudinal data (ranging from *undirected fluctuation* to *systematic change*); (3) the two sides of any statistical model (*the model for the means* and *the model for the variance*); (4) the frameworks in which longitudinal models can be estimated (*multilevel modeling* and *structural equation modeling*); (5) the data formats that are required within different analysis programs (*stacked* or *multivariate*); and, finally, (6) the kinds of outcome variables that will be needed to utilize the models in the text. Before diving into any modeling specifics, though, I think it will be useful to overview the advantages to be found in moving away from the general linear model for analyzing longitudinal data. Don't worry if all of the points introduced below don't make sense immediately, as they will be elaborated and demonstrated repeatedly throughout the text as they become relevant.

3.A. Modeling Dependency Across Observations

As introduced earlier, models for longitudinal data need to address **dependency**, or the fact that the model residuals from the same person will usually be correlated. This phrasing as *dependency* implies the existence of a single problem to be overcome, or that you must "deal with" or "control for" this dependency in order to analyze the data. In reality there are usually multiple plausible sources of dependency present in longitudinal data that need to be considered in building a reasonable model, as elaborated below. But rather than being seen as a nuisance to overcome, our perspective will be that these sources of dependency are interesting phenomena to be quantified and explored in their own right. Multilevel models in particular offer many useful strategies to do so by modifying the model for the variance to describe the patterns of correlation in the outcome over time as accurately as possible. Although later chapters will describe each of these strategies more specifically, the general ideas are introduced below.

Dependency in longitudinal data can be thought of as arising from three different sources. The first is *dependency due to constant mean differences across persons*, and it is this specific form of person dependency that is usually being referred to when the term *dependency* is used in the first place. For example, consider changes in scholastic achievement in elementary school children over time. Although ability will grow over time, some children may show higher ability than other children at every occasion. That is, the residuals across occasions from the same child may all deviate from the predicted mean in the same direction, such that a residual correlation occurs in that child's data just because he or she is higher than other children on average.

This residual correlation due to constant mean differences (or more precisely, *intercept differences*) between persons is the most anticipated kind of dependency in longitudinal models. It can be addressed by adding a **random intercept variance** to the model for the variance, which allows each person to have his or her own random intercept deviation across time. By adding the random intercept variance, the outcome variance is partitioned into variation due to *constant mean (intercept) differences between persons* and remaining variation due to *within-person deviations around each person's mean*. However, adding only a random intercept variance implies that the residuals from the same person would have a constant correlation over time, which is not usually the case in longitudinal data. Thus, two other sources of dependency may need to be considered in addition to intercept differences across persons.

The second source of dependency is due to *individual differences in the effects of predictors*. That is, continuing our example, some children may increase in achievement at a faster rate over time (in addition to showing higher achievement in general). These individual differences in the effect of time can create an additional form of person dependency in the outcome that is *specifically related to time*. As another example, parental involvement at each occasion may predict achievement at each occasion, but the effect of this time-varying predictor may differ across children. If so, these individual differences can create a separate form of person dependency in the outcome that is *specifically related to parental involvement*.

Dependency caused by individual differences in the effects of time or other time-varying predictors can be represented in longitudinal models via *fixed effects* and/or *random effects*. For instance, individual differences in change over time may result if girls and boys increase at different rates. Accordingly, adding a gender by time interaction as a *fixed effect* in the model for the means would allow girls and boys to have different time slopes, thus accounting for any of the time-specific dependency that had to do with gender. But individual differences in change over time may still be present even after considering gender. If so, this can be addressed by adding a **random slope variance** in the model for the variance, by which each child is allowed his or her own *time slope deviation*. Similarly, individual differences in the effect of parental involvement can be addressed by allowing its slope to be random over persons as well. More generally, the idea of a random slope in longitudinal models is that *each person needs his or her own version of a predictor's effect*, with the result that the correlation of the residuals from the same person is not constant, but instead varies as a function of that predictor. The outcome variance becomes heterogeneous (non-constant) as a function of those predictors as well. By adding random slope variances to represent differential effects across persons, any predictor-specific person dependency is then explicitly accounted for by the model for the variance.

Finally, the third kind of dependency that may be found in longitudinal data can be classified as *non-constant within-person correlation for unknown reasons*. That is, residuals from observations that are closer together in time may simply be more related than those further apart in time. These time-specific patterns of correlation are not due to differences between persons in the mean outcome over time (which could have been captured by a random intercept), in the rates of change over time (which could have been captured by a random slope for time), or in the effects of other time-varying predictors (which could have been captured by random slopes for those predictors). Instead, the model should just allow this additional time-specific pattern of correlation to exist (instead of or in addition to random intercepts and slopes). Fortunately, a large variety of alternative structures are available to model the patterns of correlation in longitudinal data as accurately as possible, even when that correlation is not due to known predictor variables. These potential patterns of correlation will be the focus of chapter 4.

It is important to note that, of these three kinds of dependency in longitudinal data, repeated measures analysis of variance models are really only designed to handle one of them—dependency due to constant mean differences (i.e., as a random intercept across persons). That is, the univariate approach to repeated measures analysis of variance assumes that everyone changes at the same rate and that the correlation of the outcome over time is constant as a result. In contrast, the models for the variance that follow in the rest of the text can include random intercepts as well as random slopes and/or additional patterns of correlation as needed. These flexible alternatives will allow us to better describe the variation and covariation over time and persons in the actual data, thus ensuring that tests of the fixed effects are as accurate as possible.

In addition, these same techniques can be used to include other kinds of dependency in the model as well, such as *dependency due to clustering of persons*. For instance, what if our longitudinal sample of children was obtained from different classrooms? Students may be assigned to a classroom based on their levels of ability, or the effectiveness of the teacher could create a similar advantage for all students in the classroom. In either case, students from the same classroom may perform better on average than students from different classrooms. This mean difference between classrooms is exactly the same type of dependency created by mean differences over time between persons. Accordingly, we can model classroom mean differences by including a *random classroom intercept,* which would allow each classroom to have its own deviation from the predicted sample mean, further partitioning the between-person outcome variance into variation that is between classrooms (differences among the classroom means) and variation within classrooms (variation of the children in a classroom around their classroom mean). Similarly, systematic differences between classrooms in the effects of predictors (e.g., rate of change over time, parental involvement) could be modeled by including a *random classroom slope* of the predictor (in addition to a *random person slope* of the predictor). Such extensions for longitudinal clustered data will be elaborated in chapter 11, but suffice to say for now that the multilevel models we will use for longitudinal data can be augmented as needed to describe almost any kind of dependency or correlation across time, persons, or groups.

3.B. Including Predictors at Multiple Levels of Analysis

Another advantage of the models in this text pertains to the evaluation of predictors—because the dependency that arises due to each level of sampling is explicitly represented in the model for the variance, effects of predictors pertaining to multiple levels of analysis can be examined simultaneously and accurately. For instance, as discussed earlier, longitudinal models have at least two levels of analysis: between persons and within persons. Continuing with the example of growth in achievement over time, time-invariant predictors (e.g., child gender, age at school entry), as well as the between-person, time-invariant part of any time-varying predictors (e.g., mean parental involvement over time), could be used to help explain between-person variation at level 2 (i.e., why each child needs his or her own random intercept). The within-person part of any time-varying predictors (e.g., deviation from mean parental involvement at each occasion) could then be used to explain within-person outcome variation at level 1 (i.e., the time-specific remaining deviations at each occasion). In addition, the between-person variance in the random slopes (i.e., individual-specific effects of time or parental involvement) at level 2 can be explained by *cross-level* interactions of time-invariant predictors with the time-varying predictor with a random slope. For instance, an interaction of sex by time could explain why some children grow faster than others, or an interaction of age at school entry by time-varying parental involvement could explain differential benefits of parental involvement across children.

All of this is possible because the model for the variance accounts for each dimension of sampling (or level of analysis), and thus ensures that any predictor is tested against the most relevant source(s) of outcome variation. In contrast, if general linear models were used instead, because only one source of error variance is assumed, predictors may be tested against too much or too little error, depending on their level of analysis. Furthermore, in repeated measures analysis of variance, although the model does distinguish between-person variation in the mean outcome over time from within-person variation, there is no direct way to test the effect of a continuous predictor that varies over time (i.e., covariates are only allowed as time-*invariant* predictors). Predictors at higher levels of analysis (e.g., classroom characteristics) would also not be tested appropriately without differences between classrooms (in the mean outcome or in the effects of predictors) explicitly represented in the model for the variance as another level of analysis. Thus, the models presented in this text offer significant advantages for testing complex hypotheses at and across multiple levels of analysis simultaneously and accurately.

3.C. Does Not Require the Same Time Observations per Person

The complications that can arise due to variation in the sampling of time are yet another reason to move beyond general linear models for longitudinal data. Consider the following data scenario as an example. Let's say you are interested in infant development, and you decide to measure the performance of infants at 3, 6, 9, and 12 months. The mean trajectory for your sample is shown in the middle of Figure 1.1, along with the data from two hypothetical infants. One of these infants, Bill, attended the 3-month assessment as planned, returned for his 6-month assessment, but then his parents stopped returning your phone calls, and he never came back. Because he missed his 9-month and 12-month assessments, Bill's data will be *incomplete*.

This example illustrates one of the most challenging aspects of longitudinal research—keeping it longitudinal! People may become disinterested in the study, people may relocate, and people may even die—missing or **incomplete data** can result from many different causes, and the havoc that it can wreak on an analysis depends to a large extent on how well those causes can be identified and measured.

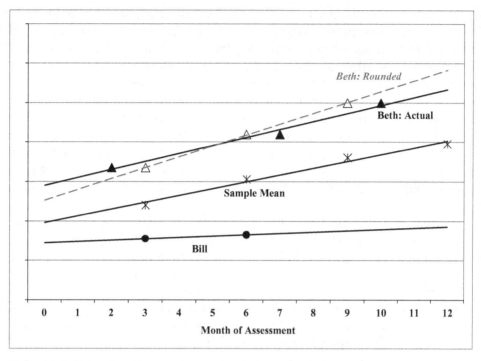

Figure 1.1 Example of incomplete and unbalanced time.

Unfortunately, in the usual approach to longitudinal analysis via repeated measures analysis of variance, missing data is handled via **listwise deletion,** such that if any of a person's responses over time was missing, this would result in not being able to use *any* of that person's data. In contrast, in the longitudinal models to be presented in this text, we will be able to use whatever data are available (e.g., Bill's 3-month and 6-month observations could still be used). This advantage is significant not only in terms of preserving statistical power but also in preserving the validity of the inferences we could make. That is, given that persons who drop out of a study may differ in important ways from persons who do complete the study, it is important to include all available data in order to generalize from the results as intended.

As elaborated in chapter 9, the multilevel modeling and structural equation modeling (i.e., "truly multivariate") frameworks for longitudinal data analysis differ in the extent to which persons with incomplete predictor data can still contribute to an analysis. Furthermore, although state-of-the art methods for addressing incomplete data (e.g., full-information maximum likelihood, multiple imputation, and Bayesian models; see Enders 2010) are continually being refined, they carry with them certain (untestable) assumptions that may not be tenable in some data.

But incomplete or missing data is only one potential complication. Another very likely problem is **unbalanced time,** which occurs when persons are not measured at the exact same occasions, either deliberately or accidentally. An example of unbalanced time can be seen by looking at the data from Beth, the other infant in our current example. Beth attended the 3-month assessment as requested, but due to a clerical error she was actually only 2 months old at the time. She was then unable to return at *exactly* 6 months, and by the time she was assessed again, she was actually 7 months old. The same problem happened at her 9-month assessment, in which Beth was actually 10 months old, and unfortunately, she did not complete her fourth assessment. So what should one do with Beth's incomplete and unbalanced data? One might be tempted to simply include all of her observations within the rest of the intended observations (i.e., treat her 2-month observation as if it were "time 1" at 3 months, her 7-month observation as if it were "time 2" at 6 months, and her 10-month observation as if it were "time 3" at 9 months). This would be required for use with repeated measures ANOVA, in which time must be balanced.

The top lines in Figure 1.1 illustrate the result of ignoring this unbalance in time. The solid line shows the best-fitting slope through Beth's actual data, and the dashed line shows the incorrect slope (i.e., in which Beth appears to be growing at a faster rate than she really is) that would result from "rounding" her data into balanced time. Thus, in situations like these it would be far better to use longitudinal models in which time can be a *continuous* variable, so that whatever occasions were actually observed for each person can be included instead. The time occasions can even be completely distinct for each person—the model operates on whatever outcome data are present, whenever they were measured. In general one should never introduce measurement error by rounding time, just as one would never deliberately introduce error into any other predictor variable. Thus, a significant advantage of the longitudinal models to be presented is that deletion or distortion of "messy" unbalanced time data will never be required.

The infant example above illustrates how unbalanced time may arise inadvertently. In other scenarios, however, unbalanced time may be the natural result of modeling change as a function of time metric not initially conceived in the study design. For instance, in the example of growth in scholastic achievement, children's current grade level would mostly likely be the metric of *time* by which change in achievement is assessed. But if you wished to examine change in other variables as a function of chronological age instead, then *time* as indexed by age would be unbalanced, given that children at the same grade level are not necessarily the same age.

In longitudinal studies in which the goal is to examine change over time, it is important to consider the theoretical mechanism that underlies the observed changes, and to try and select a time metric that best matches that process. A careful consideration of what *time* should be may lead to the conclusion that there are many plausible alternative ways of clocking time, such as time in study, time since birth, time until death, time since event, and so forth (as elaborated in chapter 10). As a result, persons may have incomplete and unbalanced data depending on exactly what *time* is. Furthermore, if persons vary in their initial locations along the temporal process under study (e.g., differ in their age at the beginning of a study), then the timing of their observations may still be unbalanced as a result of these initial differences. Determining an appropriate metric for *time* is a critical part of a longitudinal analysis whenever you are measuring a developmental process that has already commenced prior to beginning the study (and that will likely continue past the end of the study)—in other words, most of the time! Thus, statistical models that can incorporate unbalanced time in repeated measures data without listwise deletion and without unnecessary measurement error created by rounding the metric of time will be very valuable.

3.D. Utility for Other Repeated Measures Data

Although this text is focused predominantly on models for longitudinal data, these same models may also be useful for repeated measures data more broadly defined. Chapter 12 presents multilevel models for data in which persons and items (e.g., trials or stimuli) are *crossed,* and in which both sources of variance must be accounted for to properly test the effects of predictors for each. Chapter 12 also presents other advantages of these models over repeated measures analysis of variance, such as their flexibility in including continuous item predictors, use in testing exchangeability of the items within the same experimental condition, use in testing hypotheses about variability in response to item manipulations, and their use of incomplete data.

3.E. You Already Know How (Even if You Don't Know It Yet)

Perhaps the strongest argument I can make for why you should continue with the rest of the text is that you will already be familiar with many of the concepts based on the models you do know, and that great care has been taken to emphasize these parallels whenever possible. For instance, much of what follows focuses on interpreting intercepts, slopes, interactions, and variance components—these concepts are the same in longitudinal models as they are regression or analysis of variance. That is, an **intercept** is still the expected outcome when all predictors = 0. Second, a **slope** is still the expected difference in the outcome for a one-unit difference in the predictor. Although the slopes may pertain to different kinds of predictors (e.g., measured across time, across persons, or across groups), a slope is still a slope. Third, an **interaction** is still the *difference of the difference*—how the effect of a predictor depends on (or is *moderated* by) the value of its interacting predictor. Many of the fixed effects in longitudinal models will be interaction terms. Because they so often can be confusing, chapter 2 provides a detailed treatment of interactions within general linear models without additional longitudinal complexity. Fourth, a **variance component** is simply the idea of unaccounted for or leftover variance—the collection of residual deviations between each actual outcome and the outcome predicted by the model for the means. In longitudinal models there will be more than one kind of variance component to keep track of simultaneously (i.e., between-person variance and within-person variance), but the idea of leftover variance in an outcome variable is still the same.

In addition, you may not necessarily need to learn a new statistical package in order to estimate these models. General purpose programs like R, SPSS, SAS, and

STATA can be used, as well as multilevel modeling programs (HLM, MlwiN) and some structural equation modeling programs (M*plus*, LISREL). The online resources for the text will provide syntax and data for the example models in several different programs, thus hopefully reducing the reader's learning workload to just the new models, and not new programs as well. Finally, because even the most sophisticated model is inherently useless if no one understands it, the chapter examples are summarized with a sample results section so that you can see how the model results would be described in practice. Together the online syntax and text examples should provide a complete template that you can follow initially and then modify as needed for analysis of your own data.

4. Description of Example Datasets

Although many examples in the text will use simulated data, real data are also analyzed in order to illustrate some of the complexity and ambiguity that is unavoidable when using these models with actual data. Furthermore, all simulated data were created to mimic real data (and all their complexity). The datasets that will serve as the basis for chapter examples (either based on the actual data or as the basis for simulation) are described briefly below, although in every case the actual data have been selected or altered to demonstrate specific principles, and as such the example results presented should NOT be interpreted as meaningful empirical findings. I am exceedingly grateful to these original authors for allowing the use of these modified data.

The *Octogenarian Twin Study of Aging* (OCTO) consists of same-sex twins of initial age 80 years or older. They were measured every two years over an eight-year span, up to five observations per person. A variety of physical, cognitive, and psychosocial measures were collected (see Johansson et al., 1999, and Johansson et al., 2004, for information about the OCTO study). Known dates of birth and death are available for most of the sample, as well as approximate dates of onset of dementia for a third of the sample who was diagnosed with dementia. The OCTO data will be the basis of the example between-person general linear models in chapter 2 and the models for alternative metrics of time in accelerated longitudinal designs in section 2 of chapter 10.

The *Cognition, Health, and Aging Project* (CHAP) consists of a sample of both younger and older adults collected using a measurement burst design. A single measurement burst included six observations over a two-week period. Bursts were then separated by 6-month intervals. In this manner, both shorter-term (within-burst) and longer-term (between-burst) change was observed during the study. A variety of measures of physical, cognitive, and emotional well-being were collected (for more information about the CHAP data, see Sliwinski, Almeida, Smyth, & Stawski, 2009; Sliwinski, Smyth, Hofer, & Stawski, 2006; and Stawski, Sliwinski, Almeida, & Smyth, 2008). The CHAP data will be the basis of many examples in this text. These include the repeated measures analyses of variance in section 2 of chapter 3, models for nonlinear change in chapter 6, models for time-invariant and time-varying predictors of within-person fluctuation (section 2 of chapter 7 and chapter 8, respectively), and three-level models for multiple dimensions of within-person time in section 3 of chapter 10.

The *National Study of Daily Experiences* (NSDE) includes a subset of persons sampled as part of a larger study of *Midlife Development in the United States* (MIDUS; see Brim, Ryff, & Kessler, 2004) that included a national probability sample. NSDE participants were measured for eight days to examine the effects of daily stressors on daily outcomes related to health, life, work, and family (see Almeida, Wethington, & Kessler, 2002, for more about the NSDE study). The NSDE data were used to simulate seven days of data for the examples of alternative covariance structures for describing within-person fluctuation in chapter 4.

The *Pennsylvania State University Family Relationships Project* (FRP) includes a sample of families in which the perspectives of multiple family members—mothers, fathers, and two siblings— whose data were collected to learn about family dynamics, developmental trends, and work experiences. For more information about the original study, see www.hhdev.psu.edu/hdfs/frp/publications. The FRP data were used as the basis of the simulated data to illustrate time-invariant predictors of within-person change in section 3 of chapter 7 as well as time-varying predictors that show individual change over time in chapter 9.

Finally, the *Classroom Peer Ecologies Project* (CPE) includes a large sample of youth in first-, third-, and fifth-grade classrooms. The project focused on how aspects of classroom peer networks are related to the children's academic and social outcomes and how teachers can better manage social dynamics of their classroom. For more information about the project and other related research, see Gest, Madill, Zadzora, Miller, and Rodkin (2014); Gest, Rulison, Davidson, and Welsh (2008); and Madill, Gest, and Rodkin (2014). The CPE data were the basis of the examples in chapter 11 of persons nested in time-invariant or time-varying groups.

5. Chapter Summary

The purpose of this chapter was to introduce some of the recurring themes in longitudinal analysis. In terms of levels of analysis, longitudinal data provide information about *between-person* relationships (i.e., level-2, time-invariant relationships for attributes measured only once, or for their average values over time), as well as about *within-person* relationships (i.e., level-1, time-varying relationships for attributes measured repeatedly that vary over time). Longitudinal data can be organized along a continuum ranging from *within-person fluctuation,* which is often the goal of short-term studies (e.g., daily diary or ecological momentary assessment studies), to *within-person change,* which is often the goal of longer-term studies (e.g., data collected over multiple years in order to observe systematic change). In reality, however, these distinctions may not always be so obvious and will need to be examined empirically.

This chapter then turned to the statistical aspects of longitudinal data, beginning by describing the two-sided lens through which we can view any statistical model. On one side is its *model for the means* (i.e., fixed effects), which is how the predictors combine to create an expected outcome for each observation. On the other side is its *model for the variance* (i.e., random effects and residuals), which describes how the deviations between the observed and model-predicted outcomes vary and covary across observations. The longitudinal models to be presented differ from general linear models primarily in their model for the variance, for which we will now make choices, rather than assumptions. Longitudinal models can generally be estimated as *multilevel models* (used predominantly throughout the text, and which require a *stacked* or *long* data format) or as *structural equation models* (used for assessing mediation and changes in latent variables, and which generally require a *multivariate* or *wide* data format).

This chapter then highlighted five advantages the models to be presented can provide: (1) flexibility in modeling dependency across observations, (2) inclusion of predictors at multiple levels of analysis, (3) flexibility in including data that are incomplete or unbalanced with respect to time, (4) utility for other kinds of repeated measures data, and (5) similarity with general linear models in terms of general concepts and the software with which they can be estimated. Finally, this chapter described the example data to be featured in the rest of the text.

Review Questions

1. How does a *between-person* relationship differ from a *within-person* relationship? Provide an example of each type from your own area of research or experience.
2. What is the difference between a *fixed effect* and a *random effect?* To which side of the model (means or variance) does each type of effect belong?
3. What are some of the most common sources of *dependency* found in longitudinal data?

References

Almeida, D. M., Wethington, E., & Kessler, R. C. (2002). The daily inventory of stressful events: An interview-based approach for measuring daily stressors. *Assessment, 9,* 41–55.
Brim, O. G., Ryff, C. D., & Kessler, R. C. (2004). *How healthy are we?: A national study of well-being at midlife.* Chicago, IL: University of Chicago Press.
Enders, C. K. (2010). *Applied missing data analysis.* New York, NY: Guilford.
Gest, S. D., Madill, R. A., Zadzora, K. M., Miller, A. M., & Rodkin, P. C. (2014). Teacher management of elementary classroom social dynamics: Associations with changes in student adjustment. *Journal of Emotional and Behavioral Disorders,* 1063426613512677, first published on February 3, 2014.
Gest, S. D., Rulison, K. L., Davidson, A. J., & Welsh, J. A. (2008). A reputation for success (or failure): The association of peer academic reputations with academic self-concept, effort, and performance across the upper elementary grades. *Developmental Psychology, 44*(3), 625–636.

Hofer, S. M., & Sliwinski, M. J. (2006). Design and analysis of longitudinal studies of aging. In J. E. Birren & K. W. Schaie (Eds.), *Handbook of the psychology of aging* (6th ed., pp. 15–37). San Diego, CA: Academic Press.

Johansson, B., Hofer, S. M., Allaire, J. C., Maldonado-Molina, M., Piccinin, A. M., Berg, S., Pedersen, N., & McClearn, G. E. (2004). Change in memory and cognitive functioning in the oldest-old: The effects of proximity to death in genetically related individuals over a six-year period. *Psychology and Aging, 19,* 145–156.

Johansson, B., Whitfield, K., Pedersen, N. L., Hofer, S. M., Ahern, F., & McClearn, G. E. (1999). Origins of individual differences in episodic memory in the oldest-old: A population-based study of identical and same-sex fraternal twins aged 80 and older. *Journal of Gerontology: Psychological Sciences, 54B,* P173–P179.

Madill, R. A., Gest, S. D., & Rodkin, P. C. (2014). Students' perceptions of relatedness in the classroom: The roles of emotionally supportive teacher–child interactions, children's aggressive–disruptive behaviors, and peer social preference. *School Psychology Review, 43*(1), 86–105.

Nesselroade, J. R. (1991). The warp and woof of the developmental fabric. In R. Downs, L. Liben, & D. Palermo (Eds.), *Visions of development, the environment, and aesthetics: The legacy of Joachim F. Wohlwill* (pp. 213–240). Hillsdale, NJ: Lawrence Erlbaum Associates.

Nesselroade, J. R., & Ram, N. (2004). Studying intraindividual variability: What we have learned that will help us understand lives in context. *Research in Human Development, 1,* 9–29.

Sliwinski, M. J., Almeida, D. M., Smyth, J. M., & Stawski, R. S. (2009). Intraindividual change and variability in daily stress processes: Findings from two diary burst studies. *Psychology and Aging, 24,* 828–840.

Sliwinski, M. J., Smyth, J. M., Hofer, S. M., & Stawski, R. S. (2006). Intraindividual coupling of daily stress and cognition. *Psychology and Aging, 21,* 545–557.

Stawski, R. S., Sliwinski, M. J., Almeida, D. M., & Smyth, J. M. (2008). Reported exposure and emotional reactivity to daily stressors: The roles of adult-age and global perceived stress. *Psychology and Aging, 23,* 52–61.

CHAPTER 2

BETWEEN-PERSON ANALYSIS AND INTERPRETATION OF INTERACTIONS

Chapter 2 presents some of the necessary building blocks that we'll need to have in place before diving into longitudinal analysis. It uses a single continuous example to meet two goals. The first goal is to review general linear models for **between-person analysis**, in which each person has only one outcome (i.e., cross-sectional data) and thus only one model residual (i.e., the difference between the observed and model-predicted outcome). Second, this chapter will describe how to specify and interpret interactions among continuous or categorical predictors in general linear models. Although interactions are a default in some variants of general linear models (e.g., ANOVA), they are less common in others (e.g., regression), particularly among continuous predictors. Because interactions play a prominent role in the longitudinal models in the rest of this text, though, it is important to understand them thoroughly before proceeding any further. Thus, this chapter tackles interaction effects in familiar general linear models for cross-sectional data prior to presenting them within more complex longitudinal models.

1. Between-Person (Cross-Sectional; Between-Groups) Analysis

1.A. Decomposing General Linear Models

In the phrase **general linear model**, the term *general* means that we are assuming all model residuals have a normal distribution with a mean of 0 and some estimated variance that is constant over persons and across the values of any predictors. Critically, the model residuals are assumed to be independent of each other as well, which is why longitudinal data will require a different model. The term *linear* means that a linear combination of the predictors is used to create an expected outcome, in which the contribution of each predictor is weighted by an estimated slope parameter that describes the size of its unique relationship with the outcome.

Finally, the term *model* implies that we are not just trying to *describe* the outcome, but that we are trying to *predict* the outcome using other information (i.e., the model predictors). This chapter is intended to serve only as a refresher of general linear models, with the goal of reinforcing the concepts and vocabulary that will be necessary for us to move forward into more complex models. Before continuing, though, it is necessary to discuss the different names possessed by the different general linear model variants and how they relate to each other.

Traditionally, general linear models including continuous predictors are called **regression models,** in which the slope of the line relating each continuous predictor to a continuous outcome is estimated. Of interest in regression models is the size and direction of each of these slopes, how these slopes differ after including slopes for additional predictors, and how much variance in the outcome is explained by the predictors. In contrast, general linear models including categorical (grouping) predictors are called **analyses of variance models** (or **ANOVA models**). Of interest in ANOVA models is the size and direction of mean differences between groups as well as how much variation in the outcome can be attributed to those mean differences. General linear models with both continuous and categorical predictors are called **analysis of covariance models** (or **ANCOVA models**) if the continuous predictors are allowed only main effects, or *regression* models if the continuous predictors are allowed to interact with other predictors.

Ultimately, though, these naming conventions serve only to maintain the arbitrary distinctions among variants of what is essentially just one kind of model— a *between-person general linear model,* as defined above. Many of the distinctions among these models arise from the use of different statistical routines (e.g., SAS PROC REG vs. GLM, or SPSS Regression vs. GLM). These routines differ by default in how they represent the effects of categorical predictors and in how they summarize and evaluate model effects in their output.

In addition, regression and ANOVA models have historically been taught using different mathematical representations for the sake of convenience, and this may be another reason why their underlying communalities are not always readily apparent. For instance, because predictors in regression models are treated as continuous variables, they have many possible values that can create many different expected outcomes. As a result, regression models are usually summarized using equations that show how the combination of model predictors, each weighted by its slope, creates an expected outcome for each observation (i.e., a predicted outcome for each person). This can be a very general and useful way of expressing a model. In contrast, ANOVA models are not commonly expressed using equations that predict individual outcomes. This may be because the same expected outcome would be received by all individuals within the same group (or crossing of groups in designs with multiple grouping variables), and so simply describing the model via differences in group means is a more direct way to convey ANOVA results. Thus, although ANOVA models could be expressed using individual prediction equations like in regression, it can be less convenient to do so. However, because the models we will cover in the rest of this text will include continuous and categorical predictors, for continuity the models will be presented as equations that describe how a predicted outcome is created for each observation.

Furthermore, because ANOVA models rely on least squares estimation, their presentation usually emphasizes how evaluation of group mean differences operates through sums of squares, mean squares, F-ratios, and other statistics that are fundamental to least squares estimation. And because ANOVA models are special cases of regression models, these summary statistics also appear in evaluating the overall quality of a regression model (such as an F-test for whether the variance accounted for by a set of predictors is significantly different than 0). But because the models in the rest of this text will require other methods of estimation (such as *maximum likelihood,* as described in subsequent chapters), we will emphasize interpretation of the fixed effects for the predictors and residual variance components *per se,* rather than the least squares routes by which they are obtained. In cross-sectional analyses with complete data, least squares and maximum likelihood estimation will result in the same model estimates anyway.

Finally, there is another salient difference in how the effects of predictors are typically specified in regression versus ANOVA models. In regression models, predictors are included primarily as main effects, such that their slope is assumed to be linear and constant over all other predictors. Although interactions can be included among predictors, this is not the default model specification. In contrast, whenever two or more grouping variables are included in ANOVA, all possible interactions among them tend to be estimated by default. As a result, it has become standard practice in ANOVA to interpret both main effects and interaction effects, and much attention is given to decomposing interaction effects via contrasts of specific group means. This difference in typical procedure leads to a few important distinctions between ANOVA and regression in the way main effects and interactions effects are most often interpreted.

Specifically, in anticipation of including interaction effects in ANOVA, the main effects of grouping variables are usually coded with **contrasts,** or by coding the predictor variable such that the mean across all possible predictor groups is 0. (These concepts will be illustrated in more detail later in the chapter.) For instance, given equal group sizes, a two-group variable may be represented as −0.5 for one group and +0.5 for the other group, so that the mean across groups is 0. This way, if the main effects and interaction effects of multiple grouping variables are included in an ANOVA model, the main effects can be interpreted as the *overall mean difference* across the levels of each grouping variable (i.e., averaged across all other predictors), or what is known as a **marginal main effect.** For groups with more than two levels (and especially when different sizes of the groups are to be represented), this coding can be tedious, but software packages will take care of all such coding so as to retain marginal main effects in the presence of interactions.

In contrast, regression software requires the user to specify how the predictor effects are to be entered into the model. For instance, given two continuous predictors, we can multiply them together and include their product to represent an interaction between them in the model (as demonstrated later in the chapter). Unlike ANOVA models in which the grouping variables are coded such that the mean across groups is 0, the mean of the continuous predictors is usually not 0 by default. As a result, although interactions can be interpreted the same as in ANOVA, the main effects cannot. Rather than remaining marginal main effects (such that the main effect is interpreted as the average effect across all other predictors), the main effects become **simple main effects**, such that they are interpreted as *the main effect specifically when the interacting predictor is 0.* These distinctions can be confusing, and so the examples in this chapter are designed to help illustrate them more fully. Suffice to say for now that in general, when learning regression models, the interpretation of interactions (and the impact they have on the main effects of the predictors) is not as heavily emphasized as when learning ANOVA models, and as a result, the consequences of including interactions between continuous predictors in regression models may be less well understood. But because many of the fixed effects to be interpreted in longitudinal models will be interactions, the goal of this chapter is to remedy any misconceptions in interpreting main effects and interactions in between-person (cross-sectional) models first.

To summarize, this chapter will review underlying concepts and vocabulary across general linear model variants in order to build a common language with which to move forward. Persons wanting a more thorough discussion of general linear models *per se* should consult any of the excellent texts that address these models, such as Maxwell and Delaney (2004) for ANOVA, and Cohen, Cohen, West, and Aiken (2002) for regression. We now illustrate between-person general linear models that include main effects of continuous and categorical predictors.

1.B. A Between-Person Empty Model

As introduced in chapter 1, all statistical models have two sides: The model for the means and the model for the variance. The **model for the means** (i.e., fixed effects, structural model) describes how the predictors are weighted and combined to create an expected outcome for each observation. The **model for the variance** (i.e., random effects and residuals, stochastic model) describes how the model residuals (the difference between the actual outcome for each observation and the outcome predicted by the model for the means) are distributed and related to each other. All general models, no matter how complex they become, begin with one term for each side of the model, as in the **between-person empty model** shown in Equation (2.1):

$$y_i = \beta_0 + e_i \qquad\qquad (2.1)$$

in which y_i is the outcome for individual i. The model for the means contains just a single fixed effect: an intercept, β_0 (pronounced "beta zero"). An **intercept** is defined as the expected outcome when all predictors = 0. But because there are no predictors in Equation (2.1)—hence the name *empty model*—the intercept β_0 is just the grand mean of y_i. That is, if we know nothing else about a person, our best naïve guess for his or her y_i outcome is its grand mean. This is the clearest example of where the term *model for the means* comes from—in the empty model in Equation (2.1), the model for the means literally contains just the grand mean, β_0.

When we fit this model to an outcome variable, we receive an estimate of what β_0 is for that sample along with its **standard error** (to be described shortly) that indicates how precise the intercept estimate is. The model for the variance contains just a single **residual** (i.e., error term), e_i, which is the difference between the predicted and the actual outcome for individual i. Here we note a critical distinction between the model for the means and the model for the variance regarding their focus of interest. Unlike the fixed effects (in the model for the means) that each receive an estimate with a standard error, in the model for the variance, each term (just e_i here) is used to represent a *variance* that is estimated instead. That is, rather than estimating an e_i residual value for each person, the model focuses on providing an estimate of the *variance of the e_i values* across the sample of N persons given k fixed effects, given by Equation (2.2):

$$\sigma_e^2 = \frac{\sum_{i=1}^{N}(y_i - \hat{y}_i)^2}{N - k} \tag{2.2}$$

in which the variance of the e_i values, typically denoted as σ_e^2 and called **residual variance** or **error variance**, represents all the unknown reasons why the observed y_i outcome differs from the predicted y_i outcome (known as $\hat{y}_i$, pronounced "y hat") for each person. The $y_i - \hat{y}_i$ deviations are then squared, summed over N persons, and that quantity is divided by N persons minus the k number of fixed effects (including the fixed intercept). In a between-person general linear model, we assume that the e_i residuals are normally distributed with a mean = 0 and a variance = σ_e^2, and that the e_i residuals are also independent with constant variance across persons and predictors. The models for longitudinal data in the rest of the text will modify these assumptions of independence and constant variance, but not the assumption about normality of the e_i residuals (although chapter 13 will have more to say about this topic).

The empty model in Equation (2.1) represents the starting point of every statistical model that could possibly follow. From the perspective of predicting the outcome, it is absolutely the worst we can do—all the variance in the y_i outcome is yet to be accounted for because everyone is predicted to have its grand mean (that is, $\hat{y}_i$ is predicted from only β_0 so far, or k fixed effects = 1). Thus, the next logical step is to include predictors that might help create more accurate predicted outcomes and reduce or explain the σ_e^2 residual variance.

To illustrate the empty model and those that follow, consider the following example: A researcher is interested in describing individual differences in cognitive functioning. To suit the goals of the chapter, data were generated for a single occasion based loosely on patterns found in the *Octogenarian Twin Study of Aging* (OCTO, a longitudinal study described in chapter 1). Our example data include 550 older adults age 80 to 97 years ($M = 84.93$, $SD = 3.43$). Cognition was assessed by the *Information Test,* a measure of general world knowledge (i.e., crystallized intelligence; $M = 24.82$, $SD = 10.99$, range = 0 to 44). For simplicity, the Information Test outcome will be called *cognition* throughout this example. Although we could use software for general linear models (e.g., SAS or SPSS GLM, STATA REGRESS), we will instead use restricted maximum likelihood estimation within the more flexible software for general linear

Table 2.1 Results from between-person models including main effects only. Bold values are $p < .05$.

Model Parameters	Equation 2.3: Empty Model			Equation 2.4: Add Age			Equation 2.6: Add Grip Strength			Equation 2.7: Add Sex			Equation 2.8: Add Dementia		
	Est	SE	p <	Est	SE	p <	Est	SE	p <	Est	SE	p <	Est	SE	p <
Model for the Means															
β_0 Intercept	**24.82**	0.47	.001	**24.78**	0.46	.001	**24.70**	0.45	.001	**26.96**	0.74	.001	**29.26**	0.70	.001
β_1 Age (0 = 85 years)				**−0.55**	0.13	.001	**−0.42**	0.13	.002	**−0.43**	0.13	.001	**−0.41**	0.12	.001
β_2 Grip Strength (0 = 9 lbs)							**0.80**	0.15	.001	**0.55**	0.17	.001	**0.60**	0.15	.001
β_3 Sex (0 = Men, 1 = Women)										**−3.80**	0.99	.001	**−3.66**	0.89	.001
Dementia Group															
β_4 None vs. Future													**−5.72**	1.02	.001
β_5 None vs. Current													**−16.48**	1.52	.001
$\beta_5 - \beta_4$ Future vs. Current													**−10.76**	1.71	.001
Model for the Variance															
σ_e^2 Residual Variance	120.76			117.46			112.12			109.38			88.07		
R^2 relative to Empty Model				.03			.07			.10			.27		

mixed models to be featured in the rest of the text (e.g., SAS, SPSS, or STATA MIXED), of which the general linear models are a special case. Table 2.1 shows the results for each incremental model in this section.

Although atypical when conducting a regression analysis, we will begin by estimating the empty between-person model in Equation (2.1) for our example data, as shown in Equation (2.3):

$$\text{Cognition}_i = \beta_0 + e_i \qquad\qquad\qquad (2.3)$$

in which Cognition_i is the Information Test outcome for individual *i*. As shown in the first set of columns in Table 2.1, the estimate we obtain for the intercept $\beta_0 = 24.82$ (with a standard error, or SE = 0.47) exactly matches the grand mean of Cognition_i in this sample. We also obtain an estimate of the variability of the e_i residuals of $\sigma_e^2 = 120.76$ (typically labeled as *Mean Square Error* or MSE in GLM output). The square root of this variance exactly matches the standard deviation reported for the cognition outcome as well. Not surprisingly, the variance accounted for in cognition (given as R^2 in the output) is exactly 0, because σ_e^2 still contains all possible variance in cognition (i.e., $\hat{y}_i$ is based only on the grand mean β_0 so far). Although uninformative in a predictive sense, this empty model does provide a useful baseline for further models, in that by knowing how much outcome variance there is in the first place, we can more directly see how the predictors we subsequently include will reduce this variation. This will be especially helpful in later chapters.

1.C. Between-Persons Analysis Using Continuous Predictors

To continue our example, many characteristics can potentially relate to cognition, but perhaps a reasonable place to start in this sample of older adults is chronological age. Thus, we can expand the model shown in Equation (2.3) to include a predictor for age (*M* = 84.93 years, *SD* = 3.43, range = 80 to 97 years), as shown in Equation (2.4):

$$\text{Cognition}_i = \beta_0 + \beta_1 \left(\text{Age}_i - 85 \right) + e_i \qquad\qquad (2.4)$$

in which the model for the means now contains two fixed effects (β_0 and β_1). The model for the variance still contains just e_i, which still represents the difference between the observed outcome and the outcome predicted by the model for the means for each person. In this model, though, e_i is the discrepancy in the actual cognition outcome that remains after predicting cognition from age, now given by $\beta_0 + \beta_1(\text{Age}_i - 85)$ instead of just β_0. As seen in the second set of columns in Table 2.1, the variance of the e_i residuals was reduced to $\sigma_e^2 = 117.46$. The R^2 value for reduction in σ_e^2 that would be reported from GLM output is calculated as the model sum of squares divided by the total sums of squares from the model plus error. After adding a main effect of age, this is a reduction of approximately 3% relative to the empty model. Another way to arrive at approximately this same figure that will generalize to later models is by calculating the proportion reduction in σ_e^2 relative to that of the empty model, or $R^2 = (120.76 - 117.46)/120.76 = .03$ here.

The new fixed effect β_1 is a **slope,** defined as the difference in the expected outcome for a one-unit difference in the predictor. The reason that Age_i – 85 was included as a predictor rather than Age_i was to keep the intercept interpretable. That is, because the intercept is the expected outcome when all predictors are 0, the scale of each predictor should include a meaningful 0 point. In this case, because our example includes data from adults age 80 to 97 years, an intercept at $Age_i = 0$ would fall far outside the range of the data (i.e., it would be the expected cognition outcome at birth). Accordingly, we changed the scale of our age predictor so that it includes 0 by **centering:** We subtracted a constant from each person's age so that 0 would fall within the range of the new age predictor. Thus, 85 years is the new 0 for age in the model. Age 85 was chosen for the centering point because it is near the sample mean, but other ages observed in the sample (e.g., age 80 or 90) could have been chosen as well. Given the scaling of age in years, $\beta_1 = -0.55$ is the expected difference in cognition for a one-unit difference in age: for each year older, cognition is expected to be lower by 0.55. The age slope is assumed to be linear, such that a one-unit difference in age has the exact same effect on cognition at all ages. Although nonlinear effects of age could also be added (e.g., age^2 to represent a quadratic effect of age), the models in this example will include linear slopes for continuous predictors only.

Whether or not the age slope $\beta_1 = -0.55$ is significantly different from 0 depends on its **standard error,** which can be derived using the formula in Equation (2.5):

$$SE_{\beta_x} = \sqrt{\frac{Var(y_i) * (1 - R_Y^2)}{Var(x_i) * (1 - R_X^2) * (N - k)}} = \sqrt{\frac{120.76 * (1 - 0.03)}{11.75 * (1 - 0) * (550 - 2)}} = 0.13 \qquad (2.5)$$

in which the β_1 SE = 0.13, as calculated using the original variance in the cognition outcome (120.76), the proportion reduction in cognition variance from the model for the means (0.03), and the variance in the age predictor (11.75). More generally, Equation (2.5) shows how the standard error of any fixed effect (SE of β_x) depends on a few key pieces of information. First, in the numerator, the SE depends on how well the model for the means can predict the outcome, as indexed by the amount of outcome variance that remains. All things being equal, fixed effects in models for the means that account for more outcome variance will have smaller SE values. Second, the denominator serves to scale that remaining outcome variance based on the scale of the original x_i predictor for which we are deriving an SE. More specifically, the denominator starts with the original amount of variance in the x_i predictor, multiplied by how much of its variance can be accounted for by the other predictors in the model (i.e., the reciprocal of its VIF, variance inflation factor). So far, because age is the only predictor, its R^2 from other predictors is 0, and so its total variance is then multiplied by the N sample size minus k fixed effects ($k = 2$ for β_0 and β_1). Thus, given the same amount of remaining outcome variance, to the extent that a predictor has more variance in general, or has less shared variance with the other predictors in the model, the SE for its effect will be smaller. Finally, by taking the square root, the entire quantity is transformed from a variance metric to a standard deviation metric (i.e., SE is the *standard deviation* of the sampling distribution for the fixed effect, rather than its *variance*).

In general for any fixed effect, the ratio of its estimate divided by its SE is distributed as a *t*-statistic, or what is known as a **Wald test.** Here, $t = -0.55/0.13 = -4.23$ (within rounding error). That *t*-statistic can be compared to a *t*-distribution to determine the probability (the *p*-value) that the β_1 age slope estimate is different from 0. The degrees of freedom for the *t*-statistic here is $N - 2$ for the two fixed effects (β_0 and β_1). Thus, relative to a critical value of ±1.96 for $p < .05$, the age slope estimate β_1 is significantly different than 0. Said differently, the 3% of the variance in cognition that age accounted for was a statistically significant reduction.

In addition to evaluating whether a given fixed effect is significantly different than 0, we can also form a confidence interval around any fixed effect using its standard error. For instance, a *95% confidence interval* around the age slope β_1 can be found as ($\beta_1 \pm 1.96*$SE). That is, if the study was replicated numerous times, the confidence interval would include the true value of the age slope 95% of the time. Thus, smaller SE values lead to narrower intervals, or less expected variability in the size of the effect across samples. In this example, the confidence interval for the age slope would be: CI = $-0.55 \pm 1.96*0.13$, or -0.80 to -0.30, within rounding error. The fact that the interval does not overlap 0 also means the age slope is significantly different from 0.

The other fixed effect, the intercept, was estimated as $\beta_0 = 24.78$ (SE = 0.46), which can be interpreted as the expected cognition outcome for someone who is 85 years old (i.e., given that the intercept is the expected outcome when all predictors are 0, which is 85 for $Age_i - 85$). Had we not centered Age_i at 85, the intercept would have been estimated as $\beta_0 = 71.20$ (SE = 11.46), which would have been the expected cognition outcome at birth, an impossible (and thus highly imprecise) value of cognition given its range of 0 to 44. However, the age slope β_1 and the error variance σ_e^2 would still be the same, because *centering* (i.e., subtracting a constant from the predictor variable) does not change the predictor's main effect, so long as no interactions with the predictor are included in the model. We will elaborate on this point in the sections to come.

In studies with older adults, age is usually included as a control variable prior to examining the effects of other predictors. But another factor that may relate to cognition is physical condition—more frail individuals may have diminished cognition. We can examine this idea in our example data by including a predictor of *grip strength,* measured in pounds per square inch ($M = 9.11$ pounds, $SD = 2.99$, range = 0 to 19 pounds). After centering grip strength at 9 pounds, we can then add the centered predictor to the model, as shown in Equation (2.6):

$$\text{Cognition}_i = \beta_0 + \beta_1 (\text{Age}_i - 85) + \beta_2 (\text{Grip}_i - 9) + e_i \qquad (2.6)$$

the results for which are shown in the third set of columns in Table 2.1. The model for the means now contains three fixed effects: β_0, β_1, and β_2. The intercept $\beta_0 = 24.70$ (SE = 0.45) is the expected cognition for someone who is both age 85 and has a grip strength of 9 pounds (i.e., when $Age_i - 85$ and $Grip_i - 9$ are both 0). The age slope is still the expected difference in cognition for a one-unit difference in age, but is now $\beta_1 = -0.42$ (SE = 0.13): for each additional year of age, cognition is expected to be significantly lower by 0.42. The age slope is closer to 0 than in the previous age-only model in Equation (2.4) because it now reflects the *unique contribution of age* holding constant the grip strength of each person. Because age and grip strength are correlated in the sample ($r = -.18$), the contribution of age after controlling for grip strength is smaller (with a slightly larger SE due to a reduction in the amount of unique age variance unrelated to grip strength). The grip strength slope $\beta_2 = 0.80$ (SE = 0.15) indicates that for each additional pound of grip strength (holding age constant), cognition is expected to be significantly higher by 0.80. Finally, the variance in cognition that remains after controlling for age and grip strength is $\sigma_e^2 = 112.12$, which has now been reduced by 7% relative to the original variance in cognition as given by the empty model, $R^2 = (120.76 - 112.12) / 120.76 = .07$.

1.D. Between-Person Analysis Using Categorical Predictors

So far we have only considered continuous predictors of cognition (i.e., a *regression*). Now we consider categorical or grouping predictors as well (i.e., *analysis of covariance*). Continuing with our example, another factor that might relate to cognition is sex—there may be differences in cognition between men and women. Our example data is 41.27% men and 58.73% women. Because there are only two groups, we can represent the difference between them with a single variable. To make sure the intercept stays interpretable, we include a dummy-coded predictor for sex such that 0 = men and 1 = women, as shown in Equation (2.7):

$$\text{Cognition}_i = \beta_0 + \beta_1 (\text{Age}_i - 85) + \beta_2 (\text{Grip}_i - 9) + \beta_3 (\text{SexMW}_i) + e_i \qquad (2.7)$$

results for which are shown in the fourth set of columns in Table 2.1. The estimated fixed effect for the sex difference of $\beta_3 = -3.80$ (SE = 0.99) indicates that women ($\text{SexMW}_i = 1$) are predicted to have significantly lower cognition by 3.80 than men ($\text{SexMW}_i = 0$). As a result of including the sex difference β_3, the intercept $\beta_0 = 26.96$ (SE = 0.74), which is now the expected cognition specifically for a man who is age 85 and has 9 pounds of grip strength. The residual variance has been reduced to $\sigma_e^2 = 109.38$, or a total reduction of 9% relative to the empty model, $R^2 = (120.76 - 109.38)/120.76 = .09$. The age slope β_1 and the grip strength slope β_2 are still significant after controlling for differences between men and women in cognition. However, the unique effect of grip strength is reduced ($\beta_2 = 0.80$ vs. $\beta_2 = 0.55$) with a higher SE due to the correlation between grip strength and sex (i.e., there are sex differences in grip strength favoring men, $r = -.40$), whereas the unique effect of age and its SE are similar with or without sex in the model given the low correlation between age and sex ($r = .05$).

The choice to represent the sex predictor such that men were the reference (0) group was arbitrary; other versions of the sex predictor could also have been used. For instance, if we had dummy-coded the sex predictor such that women were the reference group instead (i.e., 0 = Women, 1 = Men), then the intercept would be $\beta_0 = 26.96 - 3.80 = 23.16$. Another alternative is *effects coding*, in which 0 becomes the mean of the grouping variable (i.e., as more commonly used in ANOVA). In our example, had we coded men as -0.4127 and women as 0.5873 to match the proportion of men and women in the sample, then the intercept would have been $\beta_0 = 25.39$ instead, which could then be interpreted as the intercept averaged across men and women (but also still conditional on age = 85 and grip strength = 9 pounds). If we wished to give each group equal weight instead of weighting based on sample size, group values of ± 0.5 could have been used instead. Regardless of the coding of the sex predictor, however, so long as there is a difference of exactly 1.0 between the two possible values of the sex predictor, the main effect of sex representing the difference between men and women and the rest of the model estimates will stay the same, because centering does not change the model-predicted outcome.

In addition to age, grip strength, and sex, the final predictor of cognition we will consider is a dementia diagnosis during the rest of the longitudinal study. Specifically, we will evaluate differences among three types of persons: those who will *not* be diagnosed with dementia (*none* group = 1; 72.55%), those who will *eventually* be diagnosed with dementia later in the study (*future* group = 2; 19.82%), and those who *already* have been diagnosed with dementia (*current* group = 3; 7.64%). Although there are three possible differences among the three groups, only two group differences need to be represented in the model, as the third is redundant (i.e., it could be determined by the other two group differences). Given that it is the largest in the sample, we will select the *none* group as our reference by creating two new variables to represent the difference between the *none* group and the other groups: $DemNF_i$ (none = 0, future = 1, current = 0) and $DemNC_i$ (none = 0, future = 0, current = 1). We then include both dementia group contrasts as predictor variables simultaneously in the model, as shown in Equation (2.8):

$$\text{Cognition}_i = \beta_0 + \beta_1 (\text{Age}_i - 85) + \beta_2 (\text{Grip}_i - 9) + \beta_3 (\text{SexMW}_i) \\ + \beta_4 (\text{DemNF}_i) + \beta_5 (\text{DemNC}_i) + e_i \tag{2.8}$$

in which Cognition$_i$ is still the outcome for individual *i*, as now predicted by age, grip strength, sex, and the two grouping variables for dementia diagnosis. Results from the model in Equation (2.8) are shown in the fifth set of columns in Table 2.1; each effect was significant.

The *none* group is the reference because it is the only group that has a 0 for both DemNF$_i$ and DemNC$_i$. Thus, the intercept $\beta_0 = 29.26$ is now the expected cognition outcome for a man who is age 85, who has 9 pounds of grip strength, and who will not be diagnosed with dementia. By including both group contrasts simultaneously as predictors, we can interpret them as the difference between the reference group and the alternative group coded 1 for each contrast. Thus, the slope for DemNF$_i$ $\beta_4 = -5.72$ indicates that relative to persons who will not be diagnosed with dementia (none), those who will be diagnosed with dementia (future) are expected to have significantly lower cognition by 5.72. Likewise, the slope for DemNC$_i$ $\beta_5 = -16.48$ indicates that relative to persons who will not be diagnosed with dementia (none), those who have already been diagnosed with dementia (current) are expected to have significantly lower cognition by 16.48. The slopes for the other predictors remained significant after controlling for dementia diagnosis. Although the other predictor variables are related to dementia group, the SE values for their slopes are still smaller because of the reduction in the residual variance after including effects of dementia group. Specifically, the residual variance has been reduced to $\sigma_e^2 = 88.07$, or a total reduction of 27% relative to the empty model, $R^2 = (120.76 - 88.07) / 120.76 = .27$.

The manual coding of group differences in dementia diagnosis using $DemNF_i$ and $DemNC_i$ is not typically how such categorical grouping variables are specified in a general linear model (i.e., as in ANOVA). When differences between groups are coded manually as we've done here, the model reports significance tests for each specific group contrast separately. But what may be of interest instead is whether there are significant differences across the groups in general—this omnibus effect is what a typical ANOVA would report instead of (or in addition to) the separate group contrasts. To obtain this omnibus information for the model in Equation (2.8), we would remove the two dementia group contrasts we created, and instead indicate that the original three-category dementia variable is a categorical predictor within the program syntax (i.e., on the CLASS statement in SAS, on the BY statement in SPSS, or using the i. option in STATA). After doing so, we obtain an omnibus overall test (i.e., a multivariate Wald test with two degrees of freedom) of whether there is a significant difference across the three groups, $F(2, 544) = 67.06$, $p < .001$.

This designation of a categorical grouping variable is also convenient in that any desired comparisons between groups can then be requested (not just those that are explicitly given by the manual contrast variables in the model). For instance, our model has only given us two of the three possible group differences—we do not know yet if the future and current dementia groups also differ significantly. One way to obtain this contrast is to make future dementia the reference group by replacing $DemNF_i$ and $DemNC_i$ with new contrasts of $DemFN_i$ (none = 1, future = 0, current = 0) and $DemFC_i$ (none = 0, future = 0, current = 1) and re-estimating the model. But this is not necessary if your software provides estimates and standard errors for any fixed effect that is *implied* by the model, even if not given directly by a model parameter. These statements (e.g., ESTIMATE in SAS, TEST in SPSS, LINCOM in STATA, or NEW in M*plus*, as included in the syntax online) are much more convenient than changing the reference group and re-estimating the model. Using this approach here, we can obtain the model-implied difference between the future and current groups as $\beta_5 - \beta_4 = -16.48 + 5.72 = -10.76$ (SE = 1.71, $p < .001$).

However, an unfortunate side effect is that the group differences provided directly within the model may not be what you had intended—in SAS and SPSS, they are relative to the group coded *highest* numerically or last alphabetically; in STATA, they are relative to the group coded *lowest* numerically (although this can be changed). As such, you should be extra cautious in assessing differences between groups when the program is in charge of creating the contrasts instead of you! These issues are further elaborated in the appendix at the end of this chapter.

2. Interpreting Interactions Among Continuous Predictors

So far we have assumed that the effects of age, grip strength, sex, and dementia group are additive. But what if age differences in cognition are greater in those with worse grip strength? Similarly, what if the sex difference in cognition favoring men that we found earlier depends on dementia group? The general idea that the effect of a model predictor "depends on" another model predictor is referred to more generally as **moderation**, which is tested by including an interaction term between the predictors whose effects are thought to depend on one another (see Aiken & West, 1991). Interaction variables may need to be created in advance depending on the particular software routine used. This is yet another reason why we are using general linear mixed modeling procedures in our statistical packages, which generally do not require that interaction terms be created ahead of time—instead, interaction effects can be estimated directly in the syntax by specifying a special character (such as an asterisk in SAS or SPSS or a hashtag in STATA) between the predictor variables that will interact in the model.

Interpretation of interactions and their constituent main effects has historically been fraught with difficulty, primarily resulting from confusion as to how those main effects should then be interpreted. Some authors have suggested that main effects should *not* be interpreted when they are included in an interaction, but I will take a decidedly different perspective—*main effects can and should be interpreted, especially when included in an interaction.* The trick is to interpret the main effects correctly! As described in the next sections, the correct way to interpret main effects is *conditionally on their interacting predictor,* not marginally, as when they are included only as main effects. Using our working example predicting cognition, we next illustrate how to interpret interactions among continuous predictors, followed by interactions among categorical predictors, and then interactions among continuous and categorical predictors. For clarity, new interaction effects are underlined in each of the model equations that follow.

To provide an example of moderation between continuous predictors, we add to our previous model an interaction effect between age and grip strength, as shown in Equation (2.9):

$$\text{Cognition}_i = \beta_0 + \beta_1 (\text{Age}_i - 85) + \beta_2 (\text{Grip}_i - 9) + \beta_3 (\text{SexMW}_i)$$
$$+ \beta_4 (\text{DemNF}_i) + \beta_5 (\text{DemNC}_i) + \underline{\beta_6 (\text{Age}_i - 85)(\text{Grip}_i - 9)} + e_i \quad (2.9)$$

in which an additional slope β_6 has been added to represent the interaction of age and grip strength. Fixed effects from the model in Equation (2.9) are shown in the first set of columns in Table 2.2. Some of the effects originally present in the main effects model in Equation (2.8) now take on different interpretations due to the age by grip strength interaction. We will discuss each of these effects in turn. Throughout this section, small differences (i.e., ≤ 0.01) between the values calculated in the text and those reported in the tables may occur due to rounding error.

To begin, some of the fixed effects in the model for the means are interpreted the same as in the previous main effects only model in Equation (2.8). These include

Table 2.2 Fixed effects from models with an age by grip strength interaction. Bold values are $p < .05$.

Model Parameters		Equation 2.9 when Age = 85, Grip = 9			Equation 2.9 when Age = 80, Grip = 12			Equation 2.9 when Age = 90, Grip = 6		
		Est	SE	p<	Est	SE	p<	Est	SE	p<
β_0	Intercept	**29.41**	0.69	.001	**31.09**	1.09	.001	**24.03**	1.15	.001
β_1	Age									
	Grip Strength (0 = 6 lbs)							**–0.70**	0.15	.001
	Grip Strength (0 = 9 lbs)	**–0.33**	0.12	.006						
	Grip Strength (0 = 12 lbs)				0.04	0.19	.851			
β_2	Grip Strength									
	Age (0 = 80 years)				0.00	0.25	.986			
	Age (0 = 85 years)	**0.62**	0.15	.001						
	Age (0 = 90 years)							**1.23**	0.26	.001
β_3	Sex (0 = Men, 1 = Women)	**–3.46**	0.89	.001	**–3.46**	0.89	.001	**–3.46**	0.89	.001
	Dementia Group									
β_4	None vs. Future	**–5.92**	1.01	.001	**–5.92**	1.01	.001	**–5.92**	1.01	.001
β_5	None vs. Current	**–16.30**	1.51	.001	**–16.30**	1.51	.001	**–16.30**	1.51	.001
$\beta_5 - \beta_4$	Future vs. Current	**–10.38**	1.70	.001	**–10.38**	1.70	.001	**–10.38**	1.70	.001
β_6	Age by Grip Interaction									
	Age (0 = 85) by Grip (0 = 9)	**0.12**	0.04	.003						
	Age (0 = 80) by Grip (0 = 12)				**0.12**	0.04	.003			
	Age (0 = 90) by Grip (0 = 6)							**0.12**	0.04	.003

the intercept β_0, the main effect of sex β_3, and the main effects of dementia diagnosis group β_4 and β_5. Although these fixed effects are now the unique effects after controlling for the age by grip strength interaction, their interpretations do not change because they are not part of the interaction. Because no new predictors have been added to the model, the intercept β_0 is still the expected cognition outcome for an 85-year-old man with 9 pounds of grip strength who will not be diagnosed with dementia. Likewise, because they are not part of an interaction, the main effects of sex β_3 and dementia group β_4 and β_5 continue to represent their group mean differences in cognition. We would use the terms **unconditional main effect** or **marginal main effect** to describe the main effects of sex and dementia group, in that their effects do not depend on the value of any other predictor because they are not part of an interaction with any other predictors—not yet, anyway!

What have changed in the model for the means after adding the age by grip strength interaction β_6, however, are the interpretations of the main effects for age β_1 and grip strength β_2. Previously, these slopes indicated the expected difference in cognition for a one-unit difference in age or grip strength, respectively, and these effects were expected to hold equally across the sample (i.e., they were *unconditional* when they were not included in an interaction). As seen by comparing the last set of columns in Table 2.1 to the first set of columns in Table 2.2, after adding an interaction between them, the main effect of age β_1 changed from –0.41 to –0.33 and the main effect of grip strength β_2 changed from 0.60 to 0.62. Although small in this instance, these changes are necessary and expected because main effects that are part of an interaction can no longer be considered main effects. Instead, they become **simple (conditional) main effects**, such they become the effect of the predictor *specifically when their interacting predictor = 0*. Here, because of the age by grip strength interaction, the simple main effect of age β_1 is now the *age slope when grip strength = 0*. Because centered grip strength = 0 is really 9 pounds, the age slope β_1 indicates that *specifically for someone with 9 pounds of grip strength,* for every year older, cognition is expected to be significantly lower by 0.33. Likewise, the simple main effect of grip strength β_2 is now the *grip strength slope when age = 0*. Because centered age = 0 is really 85 years, the grip strength slope β_2 indicates that *specifically for someone who is age 85,* for every additional pound of grip strength, cognition is expected to be significantly higher by 0.62.

2.A. Implications of Centering for Interpreting Simple Main Effects of Interactions

In general, the correct way to interpret main effects that are included in an interaction is to make a *conditional* (not marginal) interpretation—they become *simple* main effects that apply only when the interacting predictor is 0. For this reason, it is imperative that the predictors have a meaningful 0 value. Otherwise, the intercept and main effects can be nonsense. For instance, in this example, what if we had not centered our predictors—what if we had used the original values of age and grip strength and their interaction instead? The intercept β_0 and the simple main effects of age β_1 and grip strength β_2 would change radically, because they would then be conditional on the 0 values of the original predictors instead. Thus, the intercept β_0 would be the expected cognition outcome at birth (age = 0 years) for someone with absolutely no grip strength (grip strength = 0 pounds). Likewise, the simple age main effect β_1 would describe age differences in cognition specifically for persons with absolutely no grip strength (grip strength = 0 pounds), and the grip strength simple main effect β_2 would describe grip strength differences in cognition specifically at birth (age = 0 years). By centering age at 85 years and grip strength at 9 pounds, we ensure that the intercept (and the simple main effects of their interaction) are evaluated conditionally for persons who actually exist in our data, and therefore are useful to us. The most typical centering point for a predictor is its grand mean, so that the intercept and main effects are evaluated where there is the most data (i.e., the center of the predictor's distribution). In reality, however, any centering constant within the observed scale of the predictor can be used to facilitate interpretation of the intercept and the simple main effects of an interaction, and sometimes the grand mean may not be as useful as other constants with more inherent meaning.

Consider, for example, a predictor of years of education when measured in adults. In a sample of persons with high school degrees, college degrees, or graduate degrees, the grand mean for years of education could be something like 14.67 years. Although you could use 14.67 years of education as a reference point, it's an odd choice because no one in the sample is likely to have provided 14.67 years as a response. In this case, it may be more meaningful to pick 12 years of education as a centering point instead, such that the reference group would become persons who graduated high school, or perhaps 16 years of education, such that the reference group would become persons who graduated college. Such absolute centering points can also be helpful for emphasizing the absolute values of predictors within a given sample, as well as why potentially different findings may be reported for a predictor whose absolute values differ across samples. For instance, "mean education" could be 10 years in one sample but 18 years in another sample, and the simple main effect of an interacting predictor may look very different when evaluated as conditional on 10 years of education rather than conditional on 18 years of education. Interpreting interacting main effects as conditional simply on "mean education" can mask such important distinctions when the mean education differs across samples; centering at an absolutely meaningful value (like 12 years of education) can emphasize them instead.

There is nothing inherently wrong with using any centering point of your choosing. You can subtract from each predictor the grand mean, a meaningful constant, or perform no centering at all, and the model will still account for the same amount of outcome variance and predict the same expected outcomes. That is, your results will not become incorrect as a consequence of centering or not centering, but your coefficients will be strange if the 0 values of your predictors extend beyond the possible range of their scales. Simply put, the problem with not centering is that the intercept and simple main effects of an interaction may not provide useful information. For this reason, I strongly recommend centering each predictor so that the intercept is an interpretable and meaningful value as evaluated when the predictor is 0, but this is especially important when evaluating simple main effects that are conditional on their interacting predictor.

2.B. Interaction Coefficients Modify Their Simple Main Effects

Now that we have considered how the main effects become conditional on the interacting predictor, it's time to interpret the significant interaction coefficient itself. As shown in the first set of columns in Table 2.2, the interaction coefficient from the model in Equation (2.9) was $\beta_6 = 0.12$. Its inclusion reduced the residual variance from $\sigma_e^2 = 88.07$ to 86.76 (for a total reduction of approximately 28% of the original variation in cognition, $R^2 = (120.76 - 86.76)/120.76 = .28$.

The trick to correctly interpreting interaction coefficients is to remember their role in the model. More specifically, whereas the role of main effects is to adjust the *intercept* (i.e., a positive main effect makes the expected outcome or intercept go up, a negative main effect makes the intercept go down), the *role of two-way interactions is to adjust the slopes of the simple main effects.* That is, the interaction effect operates only indirectly on the intercept by adjusting the simple main effects (which then adjust the intercept more directly). Given two interacting simple main effects, there are two possible ways to interpret the interaction, which would describe how each simple main effect depends on the value of the other predictor. Both interpretations will always be correct, but one may be more convenient to present than the other. That is, there is no way to distinguish statistically which is "the moderator"—that is a distinction to be made in interpretation, because the interaction moderates both main effects at once.

Accordingly, one way to interpret the age by grip strength interaction β_6 is to describe how the *effect of age depends on grip strength.* To do so, we start with the simple main effect of age $\beta_1 = -0.33$ as evaluated specifically when grip strength = 9 pounds (because 9 is the new 0 in the centered grip strength predictor). For every additional pound of grip strength, *the age slope β_1 becomes less negative by the interaction of $\beta_6 = 0.12$.* Thus, the interaction *weakens* the effect of age, such that the β_1 slope for the expected change in cognition for each year of age is *less negative* in stronger people (smaller by 0.12 per pound of grip strength). To put it in more simply in plain English, we would say that age matters *less* for predicting cognition in stronger people.

The other way to interpret the age by grip strength interaction is to describe how the effect of grip strength depends on age. To do so, we start with the simple main effect of grip strength $\beta_2 = 0.62$ as evaluated specifically when age = 85 years (because age 85 is the new 0 in the centered age predictor). For every additional year of age, *the grip strength slope β_2 becomes more positive by the interaction of $\beta_6 = 0.12$.* Thus, the interaction also *strengthens* the effect of grip strength, such that the β_2 slope for the expected change in cognition for each pound of grip strength is *more positive* in older people (larger by 0.12 per year of age). Or, to put it in English, we would say that strength matters *more* for predicting cognition in older people.

This example also illustrates an important point about interaction coefficients—we cannot simply look at the direction of the interaction to determine its influence in the model. Here, the positive interaction coefficient $\beta_6 = 0.12$ served to make the age slope $\beta_1 = -0.33$ *less negative* (weaker by 0.12 per additional pound of grip strength), Furthermore, because *less negative* is in the same direction as *more positive,* the positive interaction effect implies that not only would the negative age slope become less negative as grip strength increases, but that the age slope would eventually become positive in very strong people. At the same time, however, the positive interaction $\beta_6 = 0.12$ made the grip strength slope $\beta_2 = 0.62$ *more positive* (stronger by 0.12 per additional year of age), but it also implies that the grip strength slope would become *less positive* as age decreases, eventually becoming negative in much younger people. In contrast, had the interaction been *negative,* it could have made the negative main effect of age more negative (stronger), or it could have made the positive main effect of grip strength less positive (weaker). Thus, interaction effects must be interpreted relative to their simple main effects in the model.

2.C. Re-Centering Main Effects to Decompose Interactions

We can see more directly how the model predicts what the simple main effects of age and grip strength will be for any value of the interacting predictor by using a little bit of calculus. More specifically, if we take the first derivative of the function given in Equation (2.9) with respect to age and then with respect to grip strength, the result is shown in Equation (2.10):

$$\text{Age Slope} = \beta_1 + \beta_6(\text{Grip}_i - 9)$$

$$\text{Age Slope at Grip Strength} = 6: \quad \beta_{1new} = -0.33 + (0.12 * -3) = -0.70$$

$$\text{Age Slope at Grip Strength} = 9: \quad \beta_{1new} = -0.33 + (0.12 * 0) = -0.33$$

$$\text{Age Slope at Grip Strength} = 12: \quad \beta_{1new} = -0.33 + (0.12 * 3) = -0.04$$

$$(2.10)$$

$$\text{Grip Strength Slope} = \beta_2 + \beta_6(\text{Age}_i - 85)$$

$$\text{Grip Strength Slope at Age} = 80: \quad \beta_{2new} = 0.62 + (0.12 * -5) = 0.00$$

$$\text{Grip Strength Slope at Age} = 85: \quad \beta_{2new} = 0.62 + (0.12 * 0) = 0.62$$

$$\text{Grip Strength Slope at Age} = 90: \quad \beta_{2new} = 0.62 + (0.12 * 5) = 1.23$$

in which the simple main effects of age under different centering points for grip strength (6, 9, or 12 pounds) as well as the simple main effects of grip strength under different centering points for age (80, 85, or 90 years) have been calculated. For each additional pound of grip strength, the age slope β_1 becomes less negative by the interaction $\beta_6 = 0.12$, and for each additional year of age, the grip strength slope β_2 becomes more positive by the interaction $\beta_6 = 0.12$.

Fortunately, we can also calculate any model-implied simple main effect without using calculus, and it involves three steps. First, we would examine the model equation and extract any terms that include the predictor whose simple slope we wish to find. For instance, to find the simple slope for age, we would examine Equation (2.9), and extract only the following terms that include the age predictor: $\beta_1(\text{Age}_i - 85) + \beta_6(\text{Age}_i - 85)(\text{Grip}_i - 9)$. Second, we would factor out the predictor variable—here, this would result in: $(\text{Age}_i - 85)[\beta_1 + \beta_6(\text{Grip}_i - 9)]$. Third, the term that then multiplies the predictor in [ ] then becomes its new slope—as shown in the first line of Equation (2.10). This logic and process generalizes to models with higher-order interactions (i.e., three-way and four-way interactions) as well.

Although we can use these slope equations to calculate what the simple main effects would be under any centering constant, we cannot easily obtain their SEs (and their significance tests) this way. But we can do so simply by re-estimating the model using different centering points for each interacting predictor. For instance, in the first set of columns in Table 2.2, age is centered at 85 years and grip strength is centered at 9 pounds. Given the negative correlation between age and grip strength, I opted to pair younger and stronger persons to create a second reference point, and to pair older and weaker persons to create a third reference point. Thus, in the second set of columns in Table 2.2, age is centered at 80 years and grip strength is centered at

12 pounds. In the third set of columns in Table 2.2, age is centered at 90 years and grip strength is centered at 6 pounds. The additional age values of 80 and 90 years were chosen as specific values of interest within the ages sampled, and the grip strength values of 6 and 12 pounds were chosen as ±1 standard deviation (SD) around the mean of 9 pounds. By re-estimating the same model using different centering points for the simple main effects and interaction, we can obtain estimates and SEs for the simple main effects *as evaluated at specific values of the interacting predictors.* Although it is common to use ±1 SD of the predictors as points with which to re-center, any meaningful value can be used to decompose an interaction in this fashion.

Let us examine the results in Table 2.2. The interaction of age and grip strength $\beta_6 = 0.12$ is the same across models with differing centering points because it is the highest order effect—it does not depend on any other predictor. Likewise, the main effects of sex β_3 and of dementia group β_4 and β_5 are the same as well because they are not part of the interaction. Although not shown, the amount of outcome variance accounted for is the same across models with different centering points, because centering will not change the predictions of a model.

But what have changed are the intercept β_0, simple main effect of age β_1, and simple main effect of grip strength β_2 because they are conditional on the 0 value of each predictor. The fixed intercept varied from 24.03 to 29.41 to 31.09 across models because it is the expected cognition outcome when age = 0 and grip strength = 0, and the location of 0 depends on which centering point was used (e.g., 80, 85, or 90 years of age; 6, 9, or 12 pounds for grip strength). In each case, however, the intercept is also still specifically for a man who will not be diagnosed with dementia given that the reference groups for sex and dementia are the same. Similarly, the age slope β_1 varied from –0.70 (for 6 pounds of grip strength, third set of columns) to –0.33 (for 9 pounds of grip strength, first set of columns) to 0.04 (for 12 pounds of grip strength, second set of columns). Likewise, the grip strength slope β_2 varied from 0.00 (for age 80, second set of columns) to 0.62 (for age 85, first set of columns) to 1.23 (for age 90, third set of columns).

Thus, when answering the general questions of "does age matter" and "does grip strength matter" in predicting cognition, we might come to very different conclusions across versions of the same model due to differences in centering. But to resolve this apparent discrepancy, we must realize that because these effects moderate one another, the correct answer is "it depends" to both questions. In weaker persons (grip strength = 6), age *does* matter (significant simple main effect of age). In stronger persons (grip strength = 12), age *does not* matter (nonsignificant simple main effect of age). In younger persons (age = 80), grip strength *does not* matter (nonsignificant simple main effect of grip strength). In older persons (age = 90), grip strength *does* matter (significant simple main effect of grip strength).

2.D. Plotting Interactions Using Hypothetical People

Perhaps the easiest way to convey the pattern of any interaction effect is to create a figure that illustrates how the slopes of the predictors are moderated by each other. To do so, we will use the method of plotting interactions via **hypothetical people.**

In this approach, we first create fictional cases with targeted values for their predictor variables. We can then illustrate the pattern of the interaction by plotting the predicted outcomes for these hypothetical people as calculated from the fixed effects in the model and their values of the model predictors. Typically the predictors that are not part of the interaction to be plotted are held constant (i.e., sex and dementia group here). Furthermore, although it is common to use ±1 SD of the predictors as the plotted values, any meaningful value of the predictor can be used to generate predicted outcomes for the hypothetical people. Here we will create model-predicted cognition outcomes using the same predictor values as when we re-centered the predictors to examine simple slopes. The manual calculations needed to obtain each predicted outcome are shown in Equation (2.11):

$$\text{Predicted Cognition}_i = \beta_0 + \beta_1(\text{Age}_i - 85) + \beta_2(\text{Grip}_i - 9) + \beta_6(\text{Age}_i - 85)(\text{Grip}_i - 9)$$

Grip Strength = 12, Age = 80: $29.41 - 0.33(-5) + 0.62(\ 3) + 0.12(-5)(\ 3) = 31.09$

Grip Strength = 12, Age = 85: $29.41 - 0.33(\ 0) + 0.62(\ 3) + 0.12(\ 0)(\ 3) = 31.27$

Grip Strength = 12, Age = 90: $29.41 - 0.33(\ 5) + 0.62(\ 3) + 0.12(\ 5)(\ 3) = 31.44$

Grip Strength = 9, Age = 80: $29.41 - 0.33(-5) + 0.62(\ 0) + 0.12(-5)(\ 0) = 31.08$

Grip Strength = 9, Age = 85: $29.41 - 0.33(\ 0) + 0.62(\ 0) + 0.12(\ 0)(\ 0) = 29.41$

Grip Strength = 9, Age = 90: $29.41 - 0.33(\ 5) + 0.62(\ 0) + 0.12(\ 5)(\ 0) = 27.74$

Grip Strength = 6, Age = 80: $29.41 - 0.33(-5) + 0.62(-3) + 0.12(-5)(-3) = 31.06$

Grip Strength = 6, Age = 85: $29.41 - 0.33(\ 0) + 0.62(-3) + 0.12(\ 0)(-3) = 27.55$

Grip Strength = 6, Age = 90: $29.41 - 0.33(\ 5) + 0.62(-3) + 0.12(\ 5)(-3) = 24.03$

(2.11)

in which nine possible values are calculated (using the original fixed effect estimates) for each pairing of age (80, 85, or 90) and grip strength (6, 9, or 12). Note that the centered values of the predictors are included in Equation (2.11) rather than the original values. Also note that because the terms unrelated to age or grip strength (main effects of sex β_3 and dementia group β_4 and β_5) are not included, the predicted cognition outcomes are implicitly for a man (SexMW$_i$ = 0) who will not be diagnosed with dementia (DemNF$_i$ = 0 and DemNC$_i$ = 0). Although using different values for these other predictors would adjust the intercept up or down, they would not adjust the simple main effects or interaction between age and grip strength, because sex and dementia group do not interact with age or grip strength in this model. Thus, we do not need to include the sex and dementia group variables to demonstrate the age by grip strength interaction, as now shown in Figure 2.1.

Figure 2.1 illustrates both interpretations of the two-way interaction between age and grip strength. First, using the top panel, consider the original version of the model in Equation (2.9), as shown in the first set of columns in Table 2.2, in which age was centered at 85 years and grip strength was centered at 9 pounds. The predicted intercept from that model of 29.41 is shown in the center point of the second line for age = 85 and grip strength = 9. The simple main effect of age is displayed via the slope of the second line (the difference in cognition across age for grip strength = 9 pounds). Similarly, the simple main effect of grip strength is displayed as the vertical distance between the lines at the middle points (the difference in cognition across grip strength for age 85). Still using the top panel of Figure 2.1, next consider

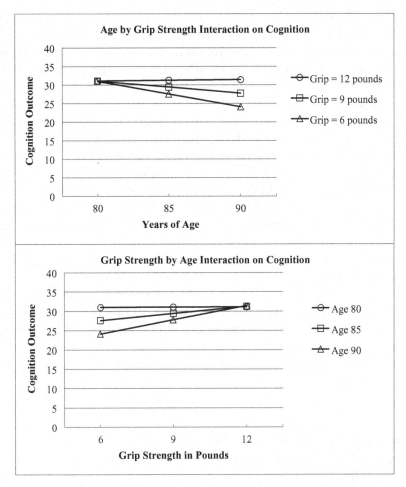

Figure 2.1 Decomposing an age by grip strength interaction via simple slopes for age (top) and simple slopes for grip strength (bottom).

the second reference point we created, as shown in the second set of columns in Table 2.2, in which age was centered at 80 years and grip strength was centered at 12 pounds. For that model, the intercept of 31.09 is shown as the left point on the top line, the simple main effect of age is shown by the slope of the top line, and the simple main effect of grip is shown by the vertical distance across the left points. Finally, still using the top panel of Figure 2.1, consider the third reference point we created, as shown in the third set of columns in Table 2.2, in which age was centered at 90 years and grip strength was centered at 6 pounds. For that model, the intercept of 24.03 is shown as the right point on the bottom line, the simple main effect of age is shown by the slope of the bottom line, and the simple main effect of grip is shown by the vertical distance across the right points.

To summarize, the top panel in Figure 2.1 shows how the main effect of age (as the slope of the lines) becomes less negative as grip strength is greater, as well as how the main effect of grip strength (as the distance between the lines) becomes more positive in older persons. The bottom panel of Figure 2.1 then shows these same ideas but with grip strength on the *x*-axis instead, such that the slopes of the lines show the simple main effects of grip strength for each age, whereas the vertical distances between the lines then show the simple effects of age.

Although calculating the nine predicted outcomes to be plotted in Figure 2.1 was straightforward, such manual calculations (even via spreadsheets) can quickly become tedious and error prone. To automate the calculation of predicted outcomes to be plotted, we can take the concept of hypothetical people even further— by adding them to our dataset! More specifically, we would add to the data cases that carry all necessary combinations of the predictor values to be plotted. In this example, nine fake persons would be added to show every possible pairing of age (80, 85, or 90) and grip strength (6, 9, or 12). We could then take advantage of the fact that most software routines will provide model-predicted outcomes for each observation. Given that the hypothetical people do not have values for the outcome variable, their data will not be used in estimating the model, so no harm will come from including these hypothetical cases in the analysis. The model for the means then creates an expected outcome for all observations with values for the predictor variables. Thus one can easily obtain predicted outcomes to create plots for any person, hypothetical or real. Syntax for the creation and addition of hypothetical people and generation of predicted outcomes is given in the files for this example online.

2.E. Assessing Regions of Significance of Main Effects Within Interactions

So far we have examined how the interaction moderates each main effect (which then become simple main effects). We have also re-centered the predictors to get a sense of whether these simple main effects remain significant when evaluated at different values of the interacting predictor. For instance, we have learned that the effect of age is significantly negative when evaluated at the mean grip strength or 1 SD below the mean (grip strength = 9 and 6 pounds, respectively), but is nonsignificant when evaluated at 1 SD above the mean (grip strength = 12 pounds). Likewise, we have learned that the effect of grip strength is significantly positive when evaluated at age 90 or age 85, but is nonsignificant at age 80. A natural follow-up question, then, is across what range of the interacting predictor will a given simple main effect be significant?

Methods for decomposing an interaction effect via **regions of significance** (e.g., Johnson & Fay, 1950) have been extended more recently for use with interactions among continuous predictors (e.g., Bauer & Curran, 2005; Preacher, Curran, & Bauer, 2006). The idea behind *regions of significance* is this: Rather than picking arbitrary values of the interacting predictor at which to evaluate the significance of each simple main effect, we can instead determine the threshold values of the interacting predictor after which the simple main effect of the interacting predictor becomes nonsignificant. For instance, rather than asking "is the effect of grip strength still significant at age 80?" we could instead ask "at what age does the grip strength effect become nonsignificant?" Alternatively, we could ask "at what level of grip strength does the age effect become nonsignificant?" In other words, assessing regions of significance allows us to obtain the points at which the simple slopes turn on, turn off, or even change direction (given that interaction effects imply nonparallel lines that will eventually cross).

As presented earlier in the chapter, the significance of a given fixed effect is determined by a Wald test: the t-statistic formed by the ratio of its estimated slope over its SE. If the t-statistic is smaller than -1.96 or greater than 1.96, the slope is deemed significant at the $\alpha = .05$ level. Thus, we can determine if a simple slope is significant for any value of the interacting predictor. To obtain the simple slopes that lie at the boundaries of significance, we need to turn this formula around—we must find the simple slopes that correspond to the desired t-statistics of ± 1.96 (for slope / SE), and the values of the interacting predictor at which they occur.

To illustrate regions of significance using our current example, let us first determine the boundary ages at which the grip strength effect is no longer significant. To do so, we consider grip strength as the effect of interest and age as the moderator effect. Recall from Table 2.2 that the simple main effect of grip strength was nonsignificant at age 80 but was significantly positive at age 85. At what age does the effect of grip strength become significantly positive (i.e., when does the grip strength slope turn on)? To determine this, we need to consider which model effects are responsible for modifying the grip strength slope. Recall from Equation (2.10) that the simple slope for grip strength is a function of its simple main effect β_2 and its interaction with age β_6, such that grip strength slope = $\beta_2 + \beta_6(\text{Age}_i - 85)$. Thus, the grip strength slope SE is also a function of its simple main effect and interaction with age. The formulas to derive the simple slope estimate and its SE to compute the t-statistic for significance are shown in Equation (2.12):

$$\pm t = \pm 1.96 = \frac{\text{Slope Estimate}}{\sqrt{\text{Variance of Slope Estimate}}}, \text{ where:}$$

$$\text{Grip Strength Slope Estimate} = \beta_2 + \beta_6(\text{Age} - 85) \tag{2.12}$$

$$\text{Variance of Slope Estimate} = \text{Var}(\beta_2) + 2\text{Cov}(\beta_2\beta_6)(\text{Age} - 85)$$

$$+ \text{Var}(\beta_6)(\text{Age} - 85)^2$$

in which Age $-$ 85 is the value at which the simple slope of grip strength is to be evaluated. As shown in Equation (2.12), the total sampling variance of the grip strength slope estimate (i.e., its SE squared) is a complex function of the sampling variance of its own slope β_2 and the sampling variance of the interaction slope β_6. This latter equation is derived from general mathematical rules about how to find the expected variance of a random variable. In this case, the random variable is the grip strength slope estimate, computed as: $\beta_2 + \beta_6(\text{Age} - 85)$. Contributing to the total sampling variance of the slope estimate is not only the sampling variance of each part, but also the covariance among the parts. Accordingly, in this case, the total sampling variance of the slope estimate includes the variance of the β_2 estimate, the variance of the β_6 estimate, and twice the covariance between them (given that a covariance matrix is symmetric and thus the covariance shows up twice). Because the interaction slope β_6 is a function of age, age is also included in the covariance with β_2. Finally, age is squared in the last term because it is treated as a constant, and constants can be removed from the expected variance if they are squared. Finally, through some tedious algebra we can solve for the slopes needed to obtain $t = \pm 1.96$ (see Bauer & Curran, 2005).

Although we can readily obtain the sampling variance of each estimated slope (i.e., as its SE squared), covariances among the estimates are generally not provided by default. However, one can request the **asymptotic covariance matrix**, which will contain the sampling variance of each estimated fixed effect as well as the covariances among the estimates of the fixed effects. The asymptotic covariance matrix is available only in some software procedures, which is another reason why we are using procedures for general linear mixed models to estimate these general linear models (as shown in the example syntax files online). Table 2.3 provides the asymptotic covariance matrix for the estimates of the fixed effects in the model in Equation (2.9) as well as the original fixed effect estimates when age is centered at 85 years and grip strength is centered at 9 pounds (bottom row). The values in bold are those needed to calculate regions of significance for the simple effect of grip strength as moderated by age, including the grip strength slope estimate β_2 and its sampling variance, the interaction slope estimate β_6 and its sampling variance, and the covariance between the β_2 and β_6 slope estimates.

Table 2.3 Covariance matrix for the Equation 2.9 parameter estimates. Bold values are used for assessing regions of significance.

Estimate Covariance	Intercept β_0	Age β_1	Grip Strength β_2	Sex β_3	DemNF β_4	DemNC β_5	Age by Grip Strength β_6
Intercept	0.4829						
Age	0.0005	0.0145					
Grip Strength	−0.0308	0.0033	**0.0221**				
Sex (0 = Men, 1 = Women)	−0.4507	0.0050	0.0537	0.7873			
DemNF (None vs. Future)	−0.1820	−0.0041	−0.0134	−0.0710	1.0274		
DemNC (None vs. Current)	−0.2263	−0.0012	−0.0003	0.0237	0.2129	2.2878	
Age by Grip Strength	0.0019	0.0010	**0.0002**	0.0027	−0.0027	0.0024	**0.0016**
Fixed Effect Estimate	29.4078	−0.3340	**0.6194**	−3.4556	−5.9225	−16.3004	**0.1230**

Calculators for computing regions of significance are available in the online resources; results may differ slightly depending on how many digits are carried forward into the calculations. When using all possible digits, the upper threshold for age is −2.29 (where $t = 1.96$) and the lower threshold for age is −14.82 (where $t = −1.96$). Given the centering of age as 0 = 85 years, these values translate (within rounding error) into −2.29 + 85 = 82.71 years and −14.82 + 85 = 70.18 years. Although the estimated values will differ if other centering points of age were used instead, the resulting thresholds will be the same, and can be interpreted as follows. Above age 82.71, there will be a significant *positive* effect of grip strength on cognition (i.e., as found when evaluating the effect of grip strength at age 85 or age 90 in Table 2.2). Between age 70.18 and 82.71, there will be a *nonsignificant* effect of grip strength on cognition (i.e., as found when evaluating the effect of grip strength at age 80 in Table 2.2). In addition, at age 70.18 or younger, there will be a significant *negative* effect of grip strength. Although this reversal of the effect of grip strength may seem strange, it is a natural consequence of any linear interaction effect—nonparallel lines eventually cross, so any positive effect must eventually become negative (and any negative effect must eventually become positive). In these data, the youngest person is 80 years old, and thus for most persons we would expect a positive effect of grip strength, which becomes even more positive in older persons via the age by grip strength interaction effect.

We can also assess the region of significance for the age slope as moderated by grip strength. In this case, we will need the age slope estimate β_1 and its sampling variance, the interaction slope estimate β_6 and its sampling variance, and the covariance between the β_1 and β_6 slope estimates. Using these values, the upper threshold for grip strength is 9.52 (where $t = 1.96$) and the lower threshold for grip strength is 0.67 (where $t = −1.96$). Given the centering of grip strength as 0 = 9 pounds, these values translate into 9.52 + 9 = 18.52 pounds and 0.67 + 9 = 9.67 pounds and can be interpreted as follows. Above 18.52 pounds of grip strength, there will be a significant *positive* effect of age on cognition. Between 9.67 and 18.52 pounds of grip strength, there will be a *nonsignificant* effect of age on cognition. Below 9.67 pounds of grip strength, there will be a significant *negative* effect of age on cognition (i.e., as found when evaluating the effect age at grip strength = 6 or 9 pounds in Table 2.2). Given that grip strength values in the current sample range from 0 to 19 with a mean of 9 pounds, for about half the sample we would expect to see a significant negative effect of age (which would become more negative as grip strength is weaker), while we would expect to see a minimal effect of age for the other upper half of the sample (and for almost no one would we expect to see a positive effect of age).

So far we have examined several tools to describe two-way interactions between continuous predictors. These include the process of translating marginal main effects into simple main effects when part of an interaction, re-centering predictors to obtain simple main effects at various points of interest, showing differences in simple slopes by plotting model-predicted outcomes for hypothetical people, and computing regions of significance to explore the point of the moderator at which the simple main effects turn on or turn off (and perhaps turn back on again in the opposite direction). Later in this chapter we will use some of these same tools to decompose three-way and higher-order interactions as well. For now, though, we focus on expanding our repertoire to include interpretation of interactions among categorical predictors.

3. Interpreting Interactions Involving Categorical Predictors

To continue with our example, we can examine whether the differences in cognition that were found as a function of dementia diagnosis differ by sex. In this section the sex by dementia group interaction will be examined using each dementia group as the reference in turn.

The interaction of sex by dementia group is first specified using the no dementia group as the reference, as shown in Equation (2.13):

$$
\begin{aligned}
\text{Cognition}_i = {} & \beta_0 + \beta_1 \left(\text{Age}_i - 85\right) + \beta_2 \left(\text{Grip}_i - 9\right) + \beta_3 \left(\text{SexMW}_i\right) \\
& + \beta_4 \left(\text{DemNF}_i\right) + \beta_5 \left(\text{DemNC}_i\right) + \beta_6 \left(\text{Age}_i - 85\right)\left(\text{Grip}_i - 9\right) \\
& + \beta_7 \left(\text{SexMW}_i\right)\left(\text{DemNF}_i\right) + \beta_8 \left(\text{SexMW}_i\right)\left(\text{DemNC}_i\right) + e_i
\end{aligned} \tag{2.13}
$$

in which two new effects, β_7 and β_8, represent the interaction of sex with the three dementia groups (none, future, and current). Just as we needed two contrasts for the main effects of how the three dementia groups differ in cognition (β_4 and β_5), we need two contrasts to indicate how the three dementia groups differ in their effect of sex on cognition (or equivalently, to represent how dementia group differences manifest differently in women than in men). The fixed effects from this model are shown in the first set of columns in Table 2.4. Adding the β_7 and β_8 interaction terms further reduced the error variance in cognition to $\sigma_e^2 = 85.97$, for a total reduction from the original variation in cognition of approximately 29%, or $R^2 =$ (120.76 − 85.97) / 120.76 = .29. Some of the effects from in the previous model with only main effects of sex and dementia group from Equation (2.9) now take on different interpretations due to the sex by dementia group interaction terms of β_7 and β_8. We will discuss each of these effects in turn. As in the previous section, small differences (i.e., ≤ 0.01) between the values calculated in the text and those reported in the tables may occur due to rounding error.

To begin, we note the terms in the model for the means that carry the same interpretation as in the previous model in Equation (2.9). Because no new predictors have been added to the model, the intercept β_0 is still the expected cognition outcome for an 85-year-old man with 9 pounds of grip strength who will not be diagnosed with dementia. Similarly, although the age slope β_1, the grip strength slope β_2, and the age by grip strength interaction β_6 are now the unique effects after also controlling for the sex by dementia group interaction, their interpretations do not change because they are not a part of the new interaction terms. Their obtained regions of significance are very similar to those found in the previous model. That is, the age slope will be significantly negative below a grip strength of 9.68 pounds, significantly positive above 18.65 pounds, and nonsignificant between 9.68 and 18.65 pounds. Likewise, the grip strength slope will be significantly negative below

Table 2.4 Fixed effects from models with sex by dementia interactions. Bold values are $p < .05$.

Model Parameters		Equation 2.13 Reference = Men without Dementia			Equation 2.13 Reference = Women without Dementia		
		Est	SE	p <	Est	SE	p <
β_0	Intercept	**29.07**	0.75	.001	**26.19**	0.64	.001
β_1	Age Slope (0 = 85 years)	**−0.33**	0.12	.005	**−0.33**	0.12	.005
β_2	Grip Strength Slope (0 = 9 lbs)	**0.62**	0.15	.001	**0.62**	0.15	.001
β_6	Age by Grip Interaction	**0.12**	0.04	.003	**0.12**	0.04	.003
β_3	Sex						
	Dementia: 0 = None	**−2.88**	1.01	.005	**2.88**	1.01	.005
	Dementia: 0 = Future						
	Dementia: 0 = Current						
	Dementia Group (None as Reference)						
β_4	DemNF: None vs. Future (0 = Men)	**−6.06**	1.64	.001			
β_4	DemNF: None vs. Future (0 = Women)				**−5.89**	1.28	.001
β_5	DemNC: None vs. Current (0 = Men)	**−11.97**	2.25	.001			
β_5	DemNC: None vs. Current (0 = Women)				**−19.85**	2.03	.001
	Dementia Group (Future as Reference)						
β_4	DemFN: Future vs. None (0 = Men)						
β_4	DemFN: Future vs. None (0 = Women)						
β_5	DemFC: Future vs. Current (0 = Men)						
β_5	DemFC: Future vs. Current (0 = Women)						
	Dementia Group (Current as Reference)						
β_4	DemCN: Current vs. None (0 = Men)						
β_4	DemCN: Current vs. None (0 = Women)						
β_5	DemCF: Current vs. Future (0 = Men)						
β_5	DemCF: Current vs. Future (0 = Women)						
	Sex by Dementia Group Interaction						
β_7	Sex by DemNF (None vs. Future)	0.16	2.07	.937	−0.16	2.07	.937
β_7	Sex by DemFN (Future vs. None)						
β_7	Sex by DemCN (Current vs. None)						
β_8	Sex by DemNC (None vs. Current)	**−7.88**	3.02	.010	**7.88**	3.02	.010
β_8	Sex by DemFC (Future vs. Current)						
β_8	Sex by DemCF (Current vs. Future)						

Table 2.4 (Continued)

Model Parameters		Equation 2.15 Reference = Men with Future Dementia			Equation 2.15 Reference = Women with Future Dementia		
		Est	SE	p <	Est	SE	p <
β_0	Intercept	**23.01**	1.49	.001	**20.30**	1.12	.001
β_1	Age Slope (0 = 85 years)	**−0.33**	0.12	.005	**−0.33**	0.12	.005
β_2	Grip Strength Slope (0 = 9 lbs)	**0.62**	0.15	.001	**0.62**	0.15	.001
β_6	Age by Grip Interaction	**0.12**	0.04	.003	**0.12**	0.04	.003
β_3	Sex						
	Dementia: 0 = None						
	Dementia: 0 = Future	−2.71	1.87	.149	2.71	1.87	.149
	Dementia: 0 = Current						
	Dementia Group (None as Reference)						
β_4	DemNF: None vs. Future (0 = Men)						
β_4	DemNF: None vs. Future (0 = Women)						
β_5	DemNC: None vs. Current (0 = Men)						
β_5	DemNC: None vs. Current (0 = Women)						
	Dementia Group (Future as Reference)						
β_4	DemFN: Future vs. None (0 = Men)	**6.06**	1.64	.001			
β_4	DemFN: Future vs. None (0 = Women)				**5.89**	1.28	.001
β_5	DemFC: Future vs. Current (0 = Men)	**−5.91**	2.59	.023			
β_5	DemFC: Future vs. Current (0 = Women)				**−13.95**	2.24	.001
	Dementia Group (Current as Reference)						
β_4	DemCN: Current vs. None (0 = Men)						
β_4	DemCN: Current vs. None (0 = Women)						
β_5	DemCF: Current vs. Future (0 = Men)						
β_5	DemCF: Current vs. Future (0 = Women)						
	Sex by Dementia Group Interaction						
β_7	Sex by DemNF (None vs. Future)						
β_7	Sex by DemFN (Future vs. None)	−0.16	2.07	.937	0.16	2.07	.937
β_7	Sex by DemCN (Current vs. None)						
β_8	Sex by DemNC (None vs. Current)						
β_8	Sex by DemFC (Future vs. Current)	**−8.04**	3.42	.019	**8.04**	3.42	.019
β_8	Sex by DemCF (Current vs. Future)						

Model Parameters	Equation 2.16 Reference = Men with Current Dementia			Equation 2.16 Reference = Women with Current Dementia		
	Est	SE	$p <$	Est	SE	$p <$
β_0 Intercept	**17.10**	2.14	.001	6.35	1.95	.001
β_1 Age Slope (0 = 85 years)	**−0.33**	0.12	.005	−0.33	0.12	.005
β_2 Grip Strength Slope (0 = 9 lbs)	**0.62**	0.15	.001	0.62	0.15	.001
β_6 Age by Grip Interaction	**0.12**	0.04	.003	0.12	0.04	.003
β_3 Sex						
Dementia: 0 = None						
Dementia: 0 = Future						
Dementia: 0 = Current	**−10.75**	2.90	.001	10.75	2.90	.001
Dementia Group (None as Reference)						
β_4 DemNF: None vs. Future (0 = Men)						
β_4 DemNF: None vs. Future (0 = Women)						
β_5 DemNC: None vs. Current (0 = Men)						
β_5 DemNC: None vs. Current (0 = Women)						
Dementia Group (Future as Reference)						
β_4 DemFN: Future vs. None (0 = Men)						
β_4 DemFN: Future vs. None (0 = Women)						
β_5 DemFC: Future vs. Current (0 = Men)						
β_5 DemFC: Future vs. Current (0 = Women)						
Dementia Group (Current as Reference)						
β_4 DemCN: Current vs. None (0 = Men)	**11.97**	2.25	.001			
β_4 DemCN: Current vs. None (0 = Women)				19.85	2.03	.001
β_5 DemCF: Current vs. Future (0 = Men)	**5.91**	2.59	.023			
β_5 DemCF: Current vs. Future (0 = Women)				13.95	2.24	.001
Sex by Dementia Group Interaction						
β_7 Sex by DemNF (None vs. Future)						
β_7 Sex by DemFN (Future vs. None)						
β_7 Sex by DemCN (Current vs. None)	**7.88**	3.02	.010	−7.88	3.02	.010
β_8 Sex by DemNC (None vs. Current)						
β_8 Sex by DemFC (Future vs. Current)						
β_8 Sex by DemCF (Current vs. Future)	**8.04**	3.42	.019	−8.04	3.42	.019

70.06 years, significantly positive above 82.70 years, and nonsignificant between 70.06 and 82.70 years.

What have changed after adding the sex by dementia group interaction slopes β_7 and β_8 are the interpretations of the main effects for sex β_3 and dementia group β_4 and β_5. Previously, β_3 was the difference in cognition between men and women (with men as the reference group), β_4 was the difference in cognition between the none and future dementia groups, and β_5 was the difference in cognition between the none and current dementia groups. Previously these effects were expected to hold equally across the sample (i.e., they were *unconditional* when they were not included in an interaction). But as seen by comparing the first set of columns in Table 2.2 to the first set of columns in Table 2.4, after adding their interactions, the main effect of sex β_3 changed from –3.46 to –2.88, the main effect of $DemNF_i$ β_4 changed from –5.92 to –6.06, and the main effect of $DemNC_i$ β_5 changed from –16.30 to –11.97.

These changes are again necessary and expected because, as we learned before, the main effects of an interaction become *conditional* on each other, such that they become the simple effects specifically when their interacting predictor is 0. To help us in interpreting these new simple main effects (as well as the interactions), we can use the model coefficients from the first set of columns in Table 2.4 to generate predicted values for all possible combinations of men and women in the three dementia groups, as shown in Equation (2.14):

$$\text{Predicted Cognition}_i = \beta_0 + \beta_3\left(\text{SexMW}_i\right) + \beta_4\left(\text{DemNF}_i\right) + \beta_5\left(\text{DemNC}_i\right)$$
$$+ \beta_7\left(\text{SexMW}_i\right)\left(\text{DemNF}_i\right) + \beta_8\left(\text{SexMW}_i\right)\left(\text{DemNC}_i\right)$$

Men, None:	$29.07 - 2.88(0) - 6.06(0) - 11.97(0) + 0.16(0)(0) - 7.88(0)(0) = 29.07$
Women, None:	$29.07 - 2.88(1) - 6.06(0) - 11.97(0) + 0.16(1)(0) - 7.88(1)(0) = 26.19$
Men, Future:	$29.07 - 2.88(0) - 6.06(1) - 11.97(0) + 0.16(0)(1) - 7.88(0)(0) = 23.01$
Women, Future:	$29.07 - 2.88(1) - 6.06(1) - 11.97(0) + 0.16(1)(1) - 7.88(1)(0) = 20.30$
Men, Current:	$29.07 - 2.88(0) - 6.06(0) - 11.97(1) + 0.16(0)(0) - 7.88(0)(1) = 17.10$
Women, Current:	$29.07 - 2.88(1) - 6.06(0) - 11.97(1) + 0.16(1)(0) - 7.88(1)(1) = 6.35$

$$(2.14)$$

in which the intercept, main effects of sex and dementia group, and their two interactions are used to generate six predicted group means (each of which is assuming age = 85 years and grip strength = 9 pounds). Figure 2.2 illustrates these six group means as well. Now let us examine which of these group differences are given to us directly by the model in Equation (2.13), and which are not. Estimated group means are provided in parentheses to facilitate interpretation of the group mean differences represented by the coefficients, as described below.

Our reference point is men who will not be diagnosed with dementia ($SexMW_i = 0$, $DemNF_i = 0$, and $DemNC_i = 0$; the top left point in Figure 2.2). Accordingly, the simple main effect of sex β_3 is now the difference between men and women *specifically in the no dementia group* (the vertical distance between the left points in Figure 2.2), in which women without dementia (26.19) are predicted to have significantly lower cognition by 2.88 than men without dementia (29.07). Similarly, the simple main effect of $DemNF_i$ β_4 is now conditional on men (the difference between the left and center points on the top line in Figure 2.2), such that men who will eventually be diagnosed with dementia (23.01) are expected to have significantly lower cognition by 6.06 than men who will not be diagnosed (29.07). Likewise, the simple main effect of $DemNC_i$ β_5 is now conditional on men (the difference from the left to right

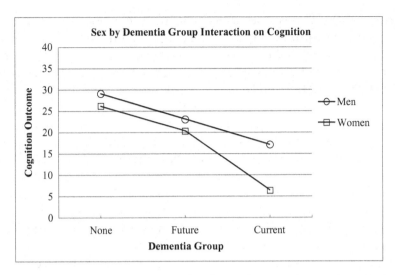

Figure 2.2 Decomposing a sex by dementia group interaction via simple slopes for dementia diagnosis group for each sex.

points on the top line in Figure 2.2), such that men who already have been diagnosed with dementia (17.10) are predicted to have significantly lower cognition by 11.97 than men who will not be diagnosed (29.07). These interpretations are based on the no dementia group as the reference (i.e., the group that has a value of 0 for both the $DemNF_i$ and $DemNC_i$ contrasts).

Turning to the two new interaction terms, we first consider the two possible (and equally correct) ways to interpret the nonsignificant interaction $\beta_7 = 0.16$ between $SexMW_i$ and $DemNF_i$. One way to interpret β_7 is as how the sex difference in cognition differs in the none versus future dementia groups. To do so, we start with the simple main effect of sex β_3: cognition in women and men without dementia differs by –2.88 (men = 29.07, women = 26.19 for no dementia). According to the interaction $\beta_7 = 0.16$, this sex difference of –2.88 becomes nonsignificantly less negative (smaller) by 0.16 in persons with future dementia ($DemNF_i = 1$), in which the sex difference is expected to be $\beta_3 + \beta_7 = -2.88 + 0.16 = -2.72$ (men = 23.01, women = 20.30 for future dementia). In other words, the nonsignificant interaction $\beta_7 = 0.16$ means that the sex difference (the vertical distance between the lines in Figure 2.2) is equivalent in the no dementia (–2.88; between left points) and future dementia groups (–2.72; between middle points).

The other way of interpreting the nonsignificant interaction $\beta_7 = 0.16$ is as how the difference in cognition between the none and future dementia groups differs by sex. To do so, we start with the simple main effect of $DemNF_i$ β_4: men with future dementia are expected to have lower cognition by 6.06 than men with no dementia (none = 29.07, future = 23.01 in men). The interaction $\beta_7 = 0.16$ tells us that the none versus future group difference of –6.06 in men becomes nonsignificantly less negative (smaller) by 0.16 in women, in which the none versus future group difference is expected to be $\beta_4 + \beta_7 = -6.06 + 0.16 = -5.91$ (none = 26.19, future = 20.30

in women). In other words, the nonsignificant interaction $\beta_7 = 0.16$ also means that the none versus future group difference (between the left and center points in Figure 2.2) is equivalent in men (–6.06; top line) and women (–5.91; bottom line).

Next, consider the two possible interpretations of the significant interaction $\beta_8 = -7.88$ between $SexMW_i$ and $DemNC_i$. Similar to the previous interaction β_7, one way to interpret the interaction β_8 is as how the sex difference in cognition differs in the none versus current dementia groups. To do so, we again start with the simple main effect of sex β_3: women and men without dementia differ by –2.88 (men = 29.07, women = 26.19 for no dementia). This sex difference of –2.88 becomes significantly more negative (larger) by 7.88 in persons currently with dementia ($DemNC_i = 1$), in which the sex difference is expected to be $\beta_3 + \beta_8 = -2.88 - 7.88 = -10.75$ (men = 17.10, women = 6.35 for current dementia). Thus, the significant interaction $\beta_8 = -7.88$ means that the sex difference favoring men (the vertical distance between the lines in Figure 2.2) is significantly larger in the current dementia group (–10.75; between right points) than in the no dementia group (–2.88; between left points).

The other way of interpreting the significant interaction β_8 is as how the difference in cognition between the none and current dementia groups differs by sex. To do so, we start with the simple main effect of $DemNC_i$ β_5: men with current dementia are expected to have lower cognition by 11.97 than men without dementia (none = 29.07, current = 17.10 in men). This none versus current group difference of –11.97 in men becomes significantly more negative (larger) by 7.88 in women, in which the none versus current group difference is expected to be $\beta_4 + \beta_8 = -11.97 - 7.88 = -19.85$ (none = 26.19, current = 6.35 in women). Thus, the significant interaction $\beta_8 = -7.88$ also means that the none versus current group difference (between the left and right points in Figure 2.2) is significantly larger in women (–19.85; bottom line) than in men (–11.97; top line).

Although the model in Equation (2.13) provides us with many possible contrasts among the six group means for sex by dementia group, it does not provide us with all of them. First, because men were used as the reference group, we now know whether two of the dementia group differences are significant for men (via the main effects of dementia group), and whether these dementia group differences are *different* for women (via their interactions with sex). But what is missing from our results is the explicit test of whether the implied dementia group differences for women are significant in and of themselves. To obtain the two simple main effects of dementia group specifically in women, we can change the reference group for sex to women by coding sex such that women = 0 and men = 1 instead. Results for this women-referenced model are shown in the second set of columns in Table 2.4, in which the intercept β_0 and the simple main effects of dementia group β_4 and β_5 are now specifically for women. Although the men-referenced model told us what these simple main effects for women should be (i.e., each is the simple main effect for men plus the interaction effect of how it differs for women), by using women as the reference group instead we can obtain the simple effect SEs and their corresponding *p*-values.

Accordingly, the none (26.19) versus future (20.30) dementia group difference $\beta_4 = -5.89$ in women (as could be calculated from the previous effect of $DemNF_i$ plus how it differs in women of $\beta_4 + \beta_7 = -6.06 + 0.16 = -5.89$) is indeed significant, as is the none (26.19) versus current (6.35) group difference of -19.85 for women (as could be calculated from the previous effect of DemNC_i plus how it differs for women of $\beta_5 + \beta_8 = -11.97 - 7.88 = -19.85$). Because centering does not change the predictions of a model, the predicted outcomes from this women-referenced model will match those of the men-referenced model. Also, we see that any fixed effects that are unconditional with respect to sex (the age slope β_1, the grip strength slope β_2, and the age by grip interaction slope β_6) are the same as in the men-referenced model. Finally, we note that relative to the men-referenced model, the simple main effect of sex is exactly backwards, as are the interaction terms of sex by dementia group, as expected given the 0–1 switch in the coding for sex. Thus, the point of re-centering sex to make women the reference group is *not* to obtain a new simple main effect of sex or new interaction terms with sex, but to obtain new simple main effects for dementia group that test dementia group differences *specifically in women*.

In addition, our models thus far have included specific contrasts for the none versus current dementia groups and for the none versus future dementia groups, but we have not yet obtained explicit tests of the differences between the current and future dementia groups. To do so, we can change the coding of the dementia group predictors to make the future dementia group the reference instead of the no dementia group, as shown in Equation (2.15):

$$
\begin{aligned}
\text{Cognition}_i = {} & \beta_0 + \beta_1 \left(\text{Age}_i - 85\right) + \beta_2 \left(\text{Grip}_i - 9\right) + \beta_3 \left(\text{SexMW}_i\right) \\
& + \beta_4 \left(\text{DemFN}_i\right) + \beta_5 \left(\text{DemFC}_i\right) + \beta_6 \left(\text{Age}_i - 85\right)\left(\text{Grip}_i - 9\right) \qquad (2.15) \\
& + \beta_7 \left(\text{SexMW}_i\right)\left(\text{DemFN}_i\right) + \beta_8 \left(\text{SexMW}_i\right)\left(\text{DemFC}_i\right) + e_i
\end{aligned}
$$

in which contrasts are now included for DemFN_i (none = 1, future = 0, current = 0) and DemFC_i (none = 0, future = 0, current = 1). Results from this model are shown in the third set of columns in Table 2.4. The results obtained for the simple main effect of future versus no dementia β_4 and its interaction with sex β_7 exactly mirror those found in the first set of columns in Table 2.4 from Equation (2.13), just in the opposite direction, as the reference group is now the future dementia group instead of the no dementia group. But new information is provided by the simple main effect of sex β_3, the simple main effect of future versus current dementia β_5, and their interaction β_8.

Specifically, the nonsignificant simple main effect of sex $\beta_3 = -2.71$ is now the difference between men and women *specifically in the future dementia group* (the vertical distance between the middle points in Figure 2.2). Although this effect could have been calculated from the model in Equation (2.13) (i.e., as the previous simple main effect of sex plus how it differs in the future dementia group of $\beta_3 + \beta_7 = -2.88 + 0.16 = -2.71$), these calculations would not provide an SE and p-value to assess its significance. This distinction turns out to be important, because although it is almost as large as was found in the no dementia group (-2.88, SE = 1.01), the estimated sex difference of -2.71 (SE = 1.87) in the future dementia group is nonsignificant. This is because there are fewer persons in future dementia group (20%)

than in the no dementia group (73%), and so the sex difference in the smaller future dementia group is estimated less precisely. Thus, although the interaction β_7 from the previous model in Equation (2.13) told us that the sex differences in cognition are equivalent in the none and future dementia groups, the sex difference is significant in the no dementia group only, likely due to differences in group sample size.

Additional new information is provided by the simple main effect of future versus current dementia (DemFC$_i$) $\beta_5 = -5.91$ (the difference between the middle and right points on the top line in Figure 2.2), indicating that men with current dementia (17.10) were predicted to have significantly lower cognition by 5.91 than men with future dementia (23.01). Finally, we also have the sex by future versus current dementia interaction $\beta_8 = -8.04$. This interaction indicates that the sex difference favoring men (the vertical difference between the lines in Figure 2.2) in the future dementia group (–2.71; between middle points) was significantly smaller than the sex difference in the current dementia group (–2.71 – 8.04 = –10.75; between right points). Or interpreted the other way, the difference between the future and current dementia groups (between the middle and right points in Figure 2.2) in men (–5.91; top line) was significantly smaller than in women (–5.91 – 8.04 = –13.95; bottom line).

As we did previously, we can re-estimate the model in Equation (2.15) using women as the reference group to obtain an SE and p-value for the future–current dementia group difference in women. As seen in the fourth set of columns in Table 2.4, the simple main effect of future versus current dementia $\beta_5 = -13.95$ in women (as could be calculated for the previous effect for men plus how it differs in women of $\beta_5 + \beta_8 = -5.91 – 8.04 = -13.95$) was also significant.

Let us now try to summarize our results, and see if we have missed any comparisons. First, consider the differences in cognition by dementia group within sex. We have learned that men and women with future or current dementia are predicted to have significantly lower cognition than men and women without dementia, as indicated by the simple main effects of DemNF$_i$/DemFN$_i$ and DemNC$_i$. Also, men and women with current dementia are predicted to have significantly lower cognition than men and women with future dementia, as indicated by the simple main effect of DemFC$_i$. The difference between the none and current dementia groups is the same for both sexes (as given by the nonsignificant sex by DemNF$_i$/DemFN$_i$ interaction), the difference between the none and future dementia groups is significantly greater for women (as given by the sex by DemNC$_i$ interaction), and the difference between the future and current dementia groups is also significantly greater for women (as given by the sex by DemFC$_i$ interaction).

Finally, let us consider the simple effects of sex within dementia group. In persons without dementia, men are expected to have significantly higher cognition than women (as given by the simple main effect of sex when none is the reference for dementia group). In persons with future dementia, men and women do not differ significantly (as given by the simple main effect of sex when future is the reference for dementia group). In persons with current dementia . . . this one is still missing! Working backwards from the previous model in Equation (2.15), we could calculate the sex difference for the current dementia group as the simple main effect of sex for future dementia plus the interaction for how it differs in for current dementia, or $\beta_3 + \beta_8 = -2.71 - 8.04 = -10.75$. But is this sex effect significant, given that only 7% of the sample currently had dementia?

To obtain the missing simple main effect of sex, we can estimate one last set of models in which the current dementia group is the reference, as shown in Equation (2.16):

$$\begin{aligned} \text{Cognition}_i = & \beta_0 + \beta_1 \left(\text{Age}_i - 85\right) + \beta_2 \left(\text{Grip}_i - 9\right) + \beta_3 \left(\text{SexMW}_i\right) \\ & + \beta_4 \left(\text{DemCN}_i\right) + \beta_5 \left(\text{DemCF}_i\right) + \beta_6 \left(\text{Age}_i - 85\right) \left(\text{Grip}_i - 9\right) \quad (2.16) \\ & + \beta_7 \left(\text{SexMW}_i\right) \left(\text{DemCN}_i\right) + \beta_8 \left(\text{SexMW}_i\right) \left(\text{DemCF}_i\right) + e_i \end{aligned}$$

in which contrasts are now included for DemCN_i (none = 1, future = 0, current = 0) and DemCF_i (none = 0, future = 1, current = 0). Results from the model in Equation (2.16) are shown in the fifth set of columns in Table 2.4. The missing simple effect of sex for the current dementia group is given by $\beta_3 = -10.75$, which is significant. And although it provides no new information, the same model with women as the reference group instead of men is also reported for completeness in the sixth set of columns in Table 2.4. Thus, we can now conclude our summary of results with respect to sex differences in cognition (as given by the simple main effect of sex from each set of models): Men are predicted to have significantly higher cognition than women in the none and current dementia groups, but not in the future dementia group. Furthermore, the advantage for men is significantly greater in the current group than in the none group (by the sex by DemNC_i interaction) or than in the future group (by the sex by DemFC_i interaction), but the sex difference is equivalent in the none and future dementia groups (by the sex by DemNF_i interaction). Phew!

3.A. Requesting Simple Main Effects via Syntax From a Single Model

At this point you may notice all the redundancy in Table 2.4 and question whether all these re-centered versions of the same model are really necessary. The answer is both yes and no. Re-centering and re-estimating the same model multiple times may be necessary if you wish to obtain all possible simple main effects *directly from the fixed effects*, as we've done here. But as discussed earlier, this is not necessary if your software can provide estimates and standard errors for any fixed effect that is *implied* by the model (i.e., that is a linear combination of estimated fixed effects). In addition, by specifying predictors as "categorical" in the program syntax you can request all possible group means and comparisons among them directly (i.e., via LSMEANS in SAS, EMMEANS in SPSS, or MARGINS in STATA). This categorical predictor approach also often provides omnibus tests of whether the overall set of interactions is significant. In these data, the omnibus F-test of the sex by dementia group interaction (i.e., a multivariate Wald test) was $F(2, 541) = 3.49$, $p = .03$. From there, you can decompose the omnibus interaction into any specific group contrasts of interest—as we have already done the hard way by re-estimating the same model six times!

One important caveat (as illustrated in the appendix at the end of this chapter) is that you need to pay close attention to how the differences between groups are coded when interacting predictors are both specified as categorical. The programs will report group contrasts in which the main effects become *marginalized* over the interacting predictor (i.e., so that the main effect of sex is averaged across the three dementia groups rather than evaluated for the reference group, and so that the main effect of dementia group is averaged across men and women). Thus, these marginal main effects reported by the program may not agree with the simple (conditional) main effects obtained listed in the fixed effects—they shouldn't, because they mean different things.

Although they are both equally viable alternative representations of a main effect, a simple main effect may be more straightforward to interpret because it pertains to someone in a specific reference group that actually exists in the data. In contrast, because a marginal main effect (averaged across values of the interacting predictor) does not apply to a specific group, it may not be descriptive at any value of the interacting predictor. For instance, if a sex difference favoring men was found for one dementia group but a sex difference favoring women was found for another group, the *marginal* main effect of sex averaged across groups may be 0, because these two sex effects in different directions could cancel each other out. But the 0 marginal main effect of sex would not have any practical meaning in that case because it would not accurately describe the sex differences for any group. For this reason, in this text categorical predictors will be coded so that when they are included in an interaction, their main effects become conditional, simple effects (that refer to specific groups that actually exist in the data) rather than marginal effects (that refer to aggregate estimates created from combining across groups instead).

As discussed earlier in this chapter, when interpreting interactions among categorical predictors (e.g., as is typically done in ANOVA), summarizing the model via group means and their specific comparisons can be more convenient than describing the same model via simple main effects and specific interaction contrasts, as we've done instead here. But the purpose of this extended presentation was to demonstrate how we can estimate and interpret any kind of interaction within a general linear model, and not just those that are conveniently summarized via group means! Accordingly, in order to complete our interaction repertoire for use with more complex longitudinal models in later chapters, we now continue with an example of how to examine interactions between categorical and continuous predictors as well.

3.B. Interpreting Interactions Among Continuous and Categorical Predictors

Thus far we have examined whether cognition in older adults is related to age, grip strength, sex, and dementia diagnosis (none, future, or current). We have also examined whether the effect of age depends on grip strength (and vice-versa), as well as whether the effect of sex depends on dementia group (and vice-versa). To illustrate how to interpret interactions among a mix of categorical and continuous predictors, we now examine whether the effect of sex depends on age or on grip strength (and vice-versa), as shown in Equation (2.17):

$$
\begin{aligned}
\text{Cognition}_i = {} & \beta_0 + \beta_1(\text{Age}_i - 85) + \beta_2(\text{Grip}_i - 9) + \beta_3(\text{SexMW}_i) \\
& + \beta_4(\text{DemNF}_i) + \beta_5(\text{DemNC}_i) + \beta_6(\text{Age}_i - 85)(\text{Grip}_i - 9) \\
& + \beta_7(\text{SexMW}_i)(\text{DemNF}_i) + \beta_8(\text{SexMW}_i)(\text{DemNC}_i) \\
& + \beta_9(\text{Age}_i - 85)(\text{SexMW}_i) + \beta_{10}(\text{Grip}_i - 9)(\text{SexMW}_i) + e_i
\end{aligned}
\tag{2.17}
$$

in which two new interactions of sex (using men as the reference) with age (centered at 85 years) and sex with grip strength (centered at 9 pounds) have now been included via β_9 and β_{10}, respectively. Results from the model in Equation (2.17) are shown in Table 2.5. Adding the β_9 and β_{10} interaction terms did not account for any additional variance in cognition ($R^2 = .30$, still); actually, the error variance from the model in Equation (2.17) was slightly larger than in the previous model ($\sigma_e^2 = 86.22$ vs. 85.97, previously). This strange result occurs because although the model sum of squares error term is indeed reduced slightly by the two new interactions, when divided by the residual degrees of freedom, the mean square error term is actually slightly higher than in the previous model. This kind of anomaly can happen for effects that are "really nonsignificant"—such as the two new interaction terms here. Nevertheless, we retain and interpret them for the sake of illustration and because they will be necessary to further augment the model to examine a three-way interaction in the next section.

Let us first consider how the simple effects change after adding interactions of age with sex (β_9) and grip strength with sex (β_{10}). Because of the age by sex interaction β_9, the significant simple main effect of age $\beta_1 = -0.39$ now applies specifically to men (as well as to grip strength of 9 pounds because of the previous age by grip strength interaction β_6). Because of the grip strength by sex interaction β_{10}, the main effect of grip strength $\beta_2 = 0.72$ is also now specific to men (as well as to an 85-year-old because of the previous age by grip strength interaction β_6). The significant simple main effect of sex $\beta_3 = -2.76$ is conditional on both new interactions—it now applies specifically to an 85-year-old with 9 pounds of grip strength (as well as to the no dementia group because of the previous sex by dementia group interactions β_7 and β_8).

There are two possible ways to interpret the nonsignificant age by sex interaction $\beta_9 = 0.08$, with each main effect serving as the moderator in turn. First, the significant age slope $\beta_1 = -0.39$ in men is nonsignificantly less negative by 0.08 in women (in which it would be $\beta_1 + \beta_9 = -0.39 + 0.08 = -0.31$, which was marginally significant, as shown in Table 2.5). Second, the significant advantage for men of $\beta_3 = -2.76$ found at age 85 narrows nonsignificantly by 0.08 per year of age (e.g., the advantage for men at age 86 would be $\beta_3 + \beta_9[\text{Age}_i - 85] = -2.76 + 0.08[1] = -2.68$). Although the simple effects of sex at other ages besides 85 are not shown in Table 2.5, in theory we could test the significance of any such alternative simple effects, or we could also examine regions of significance to determine at what ages the sex difference in cognition turns on or off. But these steps would be unnecessary here—the fact that the age by sex interaction β_9 is nonsignificant tells us that the

Table 2.5 Results from model including interactions of age by sex and grip strength by sex. Bold values are $p < .05$.

Model Parameters		Equation 2.17		
		Est	SE	$p <$
β_0	Intercept	**28.91**	0.80	.001
	Age Slope (0 = 85 years)			
β_1	Grip = 9, Men	−0.39	0.19	0.05
$\beta_1 + \beta_9$	Grip = 9, Women	−0.31	0.17	0.07
	Grip Strength Slope (0 = 9 lbs)			
β_2	Age = 85, Men	**0.72**	0.24	.002
$\beta_2 + \beta_{10}$	Age = 85, Women	**0.56**	0.19	.004
	Sex (0 = Men, 1 = Women)			
β_3	Grip = 9, Age = 85, No Dementia	**−2.76**	1.03	.008
$\beta_3 + \beta_7$	Grip = 9, Age = 85, Future Dementia	−2.53	1.90	.184
$\beta_3 + \beta_8$	Grip = 9, Age = 85, Current Dementia	**−10.64**	2.91	.001
	Dementia Group			
β_4	Men: None vs. Future	**−6.08**	1.64	.001
β_5	Men: None vs. Current	**−11.95**	2.25	.001
$\beta_5 - \beta_4$	Men: Future vs. Current	**−5.86**	2.59	.024
$\beta_4 + \beta_7$	Women: None vs. Future	**−5.86**	1.28	.001
$\beta_5 + \beta_8$	Women: None vs. Current	**−19.84**	2.03	.001
$\beta_5 + \beta_8 - \beta_4 - \beta_7$	Women: Future vs. Current	**−13.98**	2.24	.001
β_6	Age by Grip Interaction	**0.13**	0.05	.005
	Sex by Dementia Group Interaction			
β_7	Sex by None vs. Future	0.23	2.08	.913
β_8	Sex by None vs. Current	**−7.89**	3.03	.010
$\beta_8 - \beta_7$	Sex by Future vs. Current	**−8.12**	3.42	.018
β_9	Age by Sex Interaction	0.08	0.27	.774
β_{10}	Grip by Sex Interaction	−0.16	0.30	.590

effect of sex is the same across age. In addition, even if the age by sex interaction were significant, obtaining regions of significance for the age slope with respect to sex would not make any sense, because there are only two possible values of sex at which to evaluate of the age slope in predicting cognition anyway (as given in Table 2.5).

Let us now consider the two ways to interpret the other new (and also nonsignificant) interaction of grip strength by sex $\beta_{10} = -0.16$. First, the significant grip strength slope $\beta_2 = 0.72$ in men is nonsignificantly smaller (less positive) by 0.16 than in women (in which it would be $\beta_2 + \beta_{10} = 0.72 - 0.16 = 0.56$, which was still significant, as shown in Table 2.5). Second, the significant sex difference favoring men $\beta_3 = -2.76$ at a grip strength of 9 pounds becomes nonsignificantly larger (more negative) by 0.16 for each additional pound of grip strength (e.g., the sex difference at a grip strength of 10 pounds would be $\beta_3 + \beta_{10}[\text{Grip}_i - 9] = -2.76 - 0.16[1] = -2.92$). It again would not make sense to determine the regions of grip strength for which the sex difference would remain significant because the nonsignificant grip strength by sex interaction tells us that the effect of grip strength on cognition is equivalent in men and women (and thus that the sex difference in cognition is the same across levels of grip strength as well).

Keeping track of the conditionality of the fixed effects in our current model is a little tricky, but we can do so as follows. The intercept β_0 is conditional on the 0 value for all model predictors (so age 85, grip strength of 9 pounds, men, no dementia group). Each main effect is then conditional on where its interacting predictors = 0, but not on the predictors with which it does not have an interaction. Thus, the age slope β_1 is conditional on grip strength of 9 pounds and men (but not on dementia group because age does not interact with dementia group). The grip strength slope β_2 is conditional on age 85 and men (but not on dementia group because grip strength does not interact with dementia group). The sex difference β_3 is conditional on age 85, grip strength of 9 pounds, and no dementia diagnosis. The dementia group differences for none versus future β_4 and none versus current β_5 are both conditional on men (but not on age or grip strength because they do not interact with age or grip strength). Finally, because the two-way interactions are the highest-order terms, they are unconditional. That is, the age by grip strength interaction is assumed constant over both sexes and dementia groups, the age by sex interaction is assumed constant over all grip strength and dementia groups, and the grip strength by sex interaction is assumed constant over all ages and dementia groups. To test these assumptions about the two-way interactions, we would need to estimate three-way interactions, as illustrated next.

3.C. Interpreting Three-Way and Higher-Order Interactions

Let us now consider how to interpret three-way (and higher-order) interactions. Although examples will also follow in later chapters, we will illustrate the general rules of interpreting higher-order interactions using our current example predicting cognition. For instance, let us examine a three-way interaction of age by grip strength by sex, as shown in Equation (2.18):

$$
\begin{aligned}
\text{Cognition}_i = {} & \beta_0 + \beta_1 \left(\text{Age}_i - 85\right) + \beta_2 \left(\text{Grip}_i - 9\right) + \beta_3 \left(\text{SexMW}_i\right) \\
& + \beta_4 \left(\text{DemNF}_i\right) + \beta_5 \left(\text{DemNC}_i\right) + \beta_6 \left(\text{Age}_i - 85\right)\left(\text{Grip}_i - 9\right) \\
& + \beta_7 \left(\text{SexMW}_i\right)\left(\text{DemNF}_i\right) + \beta_8 \left(\text{SexMW}_i\right)\left(\text{DemNC}_i\right) \\
& + \beta_9 \left(\text{Age}_i - 85\right)\left(\text{SexMW}_i\right) + \beta_{10}\left(\text{Grip}_i - 9\right)\left(\text{SexMW}_i\right) \\
& + \beta_{11}\left(\text{Age}_i - 85\right)\left(\text{Grip}_i - 9\right)\left(\text{SexMW}_i\right) + e_i
\end{aligned}
\tag{2.18}
$$

the results for which are shown in Table 2.6. The three-way interaction $\beta_{11} = -0.16$ was not significant and did not account for any additional variance in cognition

68 Building Blocks for Longitudinal Analysis

$(\sigma_e^2 = 85.94; R^2 = .29)$. Nevertheless, we will retain and interpret it for the sake of illustration. But before we begin to decompose this model, note that in order for the three-way interaction to be interpreted correctly, all of its lower-order main effects and two-way interactions must be included in the model, regardless of their significance. In our case, this includes three main effects for age, grip strength, and

Table 2.6 Results from model including three-way interaction of age grip strength by sex. Bold values are p < .05.

Model Parameters		Equation 2.18		
		Est	*SE*	*p <*
β_0	Intercept	**28.96**	0.80	**.001**
	Age Slope (0 = 85 years)			
β_1	Grip = 9, Men	**−0.50**	0.21	**.016**
$\beta_1 + \beta_9$	Grip = 9, Women	**−0.40**	0.18	**.026**
	Grip Strength Slope (0 = 9 lbs)			
β_2	Age = 85, Men	**0.74**	0.24	**.002**
$\beta_2 + \beta_{10}$	Age = 85, Women	**0.54**	0.19	**.005**
	Sex (0 = Men, 1 = Women)			
β_3	Grip = 9, Age = 85, No Dementia	**−2.97**	1.04	**.004**
$\beta_3 + \beta_7$	Grip = 9, Age = 85, Future Dementia	−2.58	1.90	.175
$\beta_3 + \beta_8$	Grip = 9, Age = 85, Current Dementia	**−11.12**	2.92	**.001**
	Dementia Group			
β_4	Men: None vs. Future	**−6.17**	1.64	**.001**
β_5	Men: None vs. Current	**−11.78**	2.25	**.001**
$\beta_5 - \beta_4$	Men: Future vs. Current	**−5.62**	2.59	**.031**
$\beta_4 + \beta_7$	Women: None vs. Future	**−5.77**	1.28	**.001**
$\beta_5 + \beta_8$	Women: None vs. Current	**−19.93**	2.03	**.001**
$\beta_5 + \beta_8 - \beta_4 - \beta_7$	Women: Future vs. Current	**−14.16**	2.24	**.001**
	Age by Grip Interaction			
β_6	Men	**0.23**	0.08	**.003**
$\beta_6 + \beta_{11}$	Women	0.07	0.06	.214
	Sex by Dementia Group Interaction			
β_7	Sex by None vs. Future	0.40	2.08	.849
β_8	Sex by None vs. Current	**−8.15**	3.03	**.007**
$\beta_8 - \beta_7$	Sex by Future vs. Current	**−8.54**	3.43	**.013**
β_9	Age by Sex Interaction (for Grip = 9)	0.10	0.28	.729
β_{10}	Grip by Sex Interaction (for Age = 85)	−0.20	0.30	.512
β_{11}	Age by Grip by Sex Interaction	−0.16	0.10	.097

sex, as well as three two-way interactions of age by grip strength, age by sex, and grip strength by sex. Thus, even though the two latter two-way interactions were not significant, we must retain them to examine whether they depend on the third predictor (i.e., if the interaction of age by sex depends on grip strength, or if the interaction of sex by grip strength depends on age). Similarly, were we to estimate other three-way interactions (e.g., age by sex by dementia group), all of their lower-order main effects and two-way interactions would need to be included as well.

So what do we do with this three-way interaction? The rules are the same as when interpreting two-way interactions but are applied at a higher level of complexity. That is, just as two-way interactions modify their lower-order main effects (which then modify the intercept), three-way interactions modify their lower-order two-way interactions (which then modify their lower-order main effects, which modify the intercept). Furthermore, just as the main effects of an interaction become simple main effects specifically when the interacting predictor is 0, the two-way interactions within a three-way interaction become conditional on the third predictor = 0 as well. Thus, the simple two-way interaction of age by sex is specifically for grip strength = 0 (9 pounds), the simple two-way interaction of age by grip is specifically for sex = 0 (men), and the simple two-way interaction of sex by grip strength is specifically for age = 0 (85 years). Next we will examine all three possible interpretations of the three-way interaction. To do so, we will refer to Figure 2.3, which shows predicted cognition for a series of hypothetical people (men in the left panel, women in the right panel) who are age 80, 85, or 90 and who have grip strength of 6, 9, or 12 pounds (its mean and ± 1 SD).

First, we could describe how the two-way interaction of age by grip strength differs by sex. Previously we found that greater grip strength made the age slope less negative (and that older age made the grip strength slope more positive). Given the three-way interaction, the two-way interaction of age by grip strength $\beta_6 = 0.23$ is now specifically for men (the difference between the slope of the lines in the left

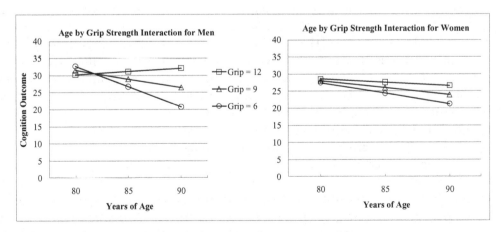

Figure 2.3 Decomposing an age by grip strength by sex interaction via simple slopes for age by grip strength for each sex.

panel of Figure 2.3). As reported in Table 2.6, the three-way interaction $\beta_{11} = -0.16$ indicates that the significant age by grip strength interaction $\beta_6 = 0.23$ in men is weaker (less positive) by 0.16 in women ($\beta_6 + \beta_{11} = 0.23 - 0.16 = 0.07$, which is not significant). This means age and grip strength depend on each other nonsignificantly more in men than women (i.e., the lines are more parallel in the right panel of Figure 2.3 for women).

Second, we could describe how the two-way interaction of age by sex differs for every additional pound of grip strength. Previously we found that the age slope was equivalent in men and women. Given the three-way interaction, the two-way interaction of age by sex $\beta_9 = 0.10$ is now specifically for someone with grip strength of 9 pounds (the non-difference in the slope of the middle line between men and women in Figure 2.3). The three-way interaction $\beta_{11} = -0.16$ indicates that the nonsignificant age by sex interaction $\beta_9 = 0.10$ at 9 pounds is nonsignificantly more negative by 0.16 for each additional pound of grip strength (so for someone with grip strength of 10 pounds, the age by sex interaction β_9 would be $\beta_9 + \beta_{11}[\text{Grip}_i - 9] = 0.10 - 0.16[1] = -0.06$). In other words, as grip strength is *lower*, the sex difference in the age slope becomes nonsignificantly *greater* (i.e., the difference between men and women in the slope of the bottom line in Figure 2.3 is greater than the difference between men and women in the slope of the other lines). If the three-way interaction were significant, we might also want to find the grip strength at which the sex difference in the age slope becomes significant (which would happen at some point below 9 pounds given the nonsignificant age by sex interaction $\beta_9 = 0.10$ at 9 pounds).

Third, we could describe how the two-way interaction of sex by grip strength differs for every additional year of age. Previously we found that the grip strength slope was equivalent in men and women. Given the three-way interaction, the two-way interaction of grip strength by sex $\beta_{10} = -0.20$ is now specifically for an 85-year-old (how the vertical difference between the middle points doesn't differ between men and women in Figure 2.3). The three-way interaction $\beta_{11} = -0.16$ indicates that the nonsignificant grip strength by sex interaction $\beta_{10} = -0.20$ for an 85-year-old is nonsignificantly more negative by 0.16 for each additional year of age (so for someone who is age 86, the grip strength by sex interaction β_{10} would be $\beta_{10} + \beta_{11}[\text{Age}_i - 85] = -0.20 - 0.16[1] = -0.36$). In other words, the nonsignificantly larger effect of grip strength in men than women is magnified nonsignificantly in older persons (the difference between men and women in the vertical difference between the lines in Figure 2.3 becomes larger in older ages). If the three-way interaction were significant, we might also want to find the age at which the sex difference in the grip strength slope becomes significant (somewhere past age 85, given the nonsignificant grip strength by sex interaction β_{10} at age 85).

Although the last model was quite complex, it could actually have been much worse, in that not all possible interactions were estimated! If we were feeling brave, we could try the two possible four-way interactions (age by grip by sex by none vs. future dementia; age by grip by sex by none vs. current dementia), which would each require two more two-way interactions (age by dementia, grip by dementia) and three more three-way interactions (age by grip by dementia; age by sex by dementia; grip by sex by dementia). We could decompose the four-way interactions using the same basic strategies: we would discuss how a four-way interaction modifies each of its simple three-way interactions, which then modify their simple two-way interactions, which then modify their simple main effects (which then modify the intercept). Finally, because three-way and higher-order interactions can be more challenging to interpret, in addition to describing differences in simple main effects and interaction terms, plotting predicted outcomes created for hypothetical people with example values of the interacting predictors can be of great assistance. Such figures will be indispensable for the presentation of interaction results as well.

4. Chapter Summary

This chapter focused on between-person analysis via general linear models for predicting continuous outcomes (whose residuals should be conditionally normally distributed with constant variance and independence across persons). When each person has only one outcome and thus only one model residual, general linear models including one source of variation for differences between persons are useful for examining the effects of continuous (quantitative) or categorical (grouping) predictors, as well as interactions thereof. Traditionally, general linear models with continuous predictors are called *regression,* models with categorical predictors are called *analysis of variance,* and models with both kinds of predictors are called *analysis of covariance* or *regression.* Additional superficial differences between these models are found in how they are presented (i.e., via equations predicting individual outcomes or via tables of group mean outcomes), in the output provided by statistical programs (i.e., regression coefficients or cell mean differences), and in how main effects and interactions are specified (i.e., conditionally or marginally). Yet underneath all of these seemingly disparate models is a single general model that can be augmented to include any kind of predictor effect that is needed.

This chapter then tackled in great detail the potentially confusing world of interpreting interactions, beginning with interactions among continuous predictors, followed by interactions among categorical predictors, and then interactions among continuous and categorical predictors. Along the way we examined a new set of tools for decomposing any kind of interaction. First, you can always describe how the simple main effects are modified by their interaction terms (e.g., a positive main effect can become less positive or more positive; a negative main effect can become less negative or more negative). Second, you can change the 0 or conditional value of a predictor to evaluate the main effect of its interacting predictors at specific points of interest (e.g., to test the age slope specifically for men or women, to test the sex difference specifically among 80-year-olds or 90-year-olds), or accomplish the same goal by requesting fixed effects that are linear combinations of existing fixed effects in the program syntax. Third, you can calculate model-predicted outcomes for hypothetical people with prototypical values of the predictors in the interaction. These predicted outcomes can be created manually from the model equation, which can be useful for pedagogical purposes. Predicted outcomes can also be calculated more quickly and with less error in three steps: (1) add the hypothetical people to your data set, (2) ask the program to create predicted values for each observation, and then (3) re-estimate the model. Predicted outcomes can then be plotted to more directly convey the pattern of the interaction. Finally, you can determine the regions along each moderator through which its interacting main effect is expected to be significant, or the values of the moderator at which the interacting main effect turns on or turns off. Calculating regions of significance can be especially useful when evaluating moderation by continuous predictors for which no particularly meaningful specific values exist. Furthermore, all four of these strategies can be used to decompose two-way, three-way, or even higher-order interactions.

In conclusion, let me say this: It is one thing to avoid retaining higher-order interaction terms because they are not statistically or practically significant; it is quite another to shy away from interactions because you don't know what they mean! Armed with a new (or revisited) set of tools for decomposing interactions, hopefully you will now approach any interaction effect with the confidence and clarity you've earned by making it all the way though this chapter!

5. Sample Results Section

The analyses in this chapter could be summarized into the beginning of a results section as follows (which would then need to be expanded to better capture the substantively meaningful story, theoretical framework, or set of research hypotheses to be tested). You'll note that instead of reporting by model parameter as we've done so far (i.e., all main effects, then all interactions), the text and table below are presented by predictor effect, which can be more intuitive to follow in models in which many of the main effects are conditional on higher-order interactions.

Between-person differences in cognition were examined in 550 older adults age 80 to 97 ($M = 84.93$ years, $SD = 3.43$). Cognition was measured by the Information Test, a measure of crystallized intelligence ($M = 24.82$, $SD = 10.99$, possible scores range from 0 to 44). The sample consisted of 41% men and 59% women. Other predictors included grip strength as measured in pounds per square inch ($M = 9.11$ pounds, $SD = 2.99$, range = 0 to 19 pounds) and dementia diagnosis group (none = 73%, future = 20%, or current = 7%). To facilitate interpretation of the intercept and main effects, each predictor was centered such that 0 was a meaningful value, including age (0 = 85 years), grip strength (0 = 9 pounds), and sex (0 = men, 1 = women). Finally, two contrasts were used represent differences among the three dementia diagnosis groups: DemNF (none = 0, future = 1, current = 0) and DemNC (none = 0, future = 0, current = 1). Main effects and interactions were added in sequential models. Significant effects were retained, as well as nonsignificant lower-order effects needed for significant interaction effects. Equation (2.13) provides the final model, the results of which are summarized in Table 2.7, Figure 2.1, and Figure 2.2. The significance of model parameters not directly given by Equation (2.13) was evaluated by requesting additional model-implied fixed effects.

Table 2.7 Example table of model results. Bold values are $p < .05$.

Model Effects		Est	SE	$p <$
Model for the Means				
β_0	Intercept	**29.07**	0.75	.001
β_1	Age Slope (0 = 85 years)	**−0.33**	0.12	.005
β_2	Grip Strength Slope (0 = 9 lbs)	**0.62**	0.15	.001
β_6	Age by Grip Interaction	**0.12**	0.04	.003
	Sex (0 = Men, 1 = Women) Differences			
β_3	No Dementia	**−2.88**	1.01	.005
$\beta_3 + \beta_7$	Future Dementia	−2.71	1.87	.149
$\beta_3 + \beta_8$	Current Dementia	**−10.75**	2.90	.001
	Dementia Group Differences			
	None vs. Future Dementia			
β_4	Men	**−6.06**	1.64	.001
$\beta_4 + \beta_7$	Women	**−5.89**	1.28	.001
β_7	Sex by None vs. Future	0.16	2.07	.937
	None vs. Current Dementia			
β_5	Men	**−11.97**	2.25	.001
$\beta_5 + \beta_8$	Women	**−19.85**	2.02	.001
β_8	Sex by None vs. Current	**−7.88**	3.02	.010
	Future vs. Current Dementia			
$\beta_5 - \beta_4$	Men	**−5.91**	2.59	.023
$\beta_5 + \beta_8 - \beta_4 - \beta_7$	Women	**−13.95**	2.24	.001
$\beta_8 - \beta_7$	Sex by Future vs. Current	**−8.04**	3.42	.019
Model for the Variance				
σ_e^2	Residual Variance	85.97		
	R^2 relative to Empty Model	.30		

The intercept $\beta_0 = 29.07$ is the expected cognition outcome for an 85-year-old man with 9 pounds of grip strength who will not be diagnosed with dementia later in the study. The main effect of age $\beta_1 = -0.33$ indicated that cognition is predicted to be significantly lower by 0.33 for every additional year of age (in persons with grip strength of 9 pounds). The main effect of grip strength $\beta_2 = 0.62$ indicated that cognition is predicted to be significantly greater by 0.62 for every additional pound of grip strength (in persons who are age 85). As shown in Figure 2.1, the age by grip strength interaction $\beta_6 = 0.12$ indicated the age slope predicting cognition became significantly less negative by 0.12 for each additional pound of grip strength (as shown by the differences in the slope of the lines). Equivalently, the grip strength slope predicting cognition became significantly more positive by 0.12 for each additional year of age (as shown by the differences in the vertical distance between the lines).

To further decompose the age by grip strength interaction, the regions along each moderator through which the other main effect is expected to be significant were then calculated using the fixed effect estimates and their associated covariance matrix, as described in Bauer and Curran (2005). For the effect of age, the obtained threshold values of grip strength were 9.68 and 18.65 pounds. Given the range of grip strength of 0 to 19 pounds in the current sample ($M = 9$), the effect of age is expected to be negative for about half of the sample (below 9.68 pounds), the effect of age is expected to be nonsignificant for the other half (between 9.68 and 18.65 pounds), and the effect of age expected to be positive for almost no one (above 18.65 pounds). Similarly, for the effect of grip strength, the obtained threshold values of age were 70.06 and 82.70 years. Given the range of age of 80 to 97 years in the sample ($M = 85$), the effect of grip strength is expected to be negative for no one (below 70.06 years), the effect of grip strength is expected to be nonsignificant for a small part of the sample (between 70.06 and 82.70 years), and the effect of grip strength is expected to be positive for the majority of the sample (above 82.70 years).

The main and interactive effects of sex by dementia diagnosis group are presented next, as illustrated in Figure 2.2, in which the sex differences are shown by the vertical distances between the lines, and the diagnosis group differences are shown by the differences within the lines. First, with respect to sex differences, there was a significant main effect of sex $\beta_3 = -2.88$ such that in the no dementia group, cognition was significantly lower by 2.88 in women than in men. The sex difference in cognition was equivalent in no dementia and future dementia groups, as shown by the nonsignificant sex by no dementia versus future dementia interaction $\beta_7 = 0.16$. However, the resulting sex difference in cognition favoring men in the future dementia group of $\beta_3 + \beta_7 = -2.88 + 0.16 = -2.71$ was not significant, likely a result of the small number of persons with future dementia (only 20% of the sample). In addition, the sex difference in cognition was significantly larger in the current dementia group than in the no dementia group, as shown by the significant sex by no dementia versus current dementia interaction $\beta_8 = -7.88$, and the resulting sex difference in the current dementia group of $\beta_3 + \beta_8 = 2.88 - 7.88 = -10.75$ was also significant. The sex difference in cognition was also significantly larger in the current dementia group than in the future dementia group, as found by $\beta_8 - \beta_7 = -7.88 - 0.16 = -8.04$.

Next, with respect to differences among the dementia groups, cognition was significantly lower in the future dementia than no dementia group both in men, $\beta_4 = -6.06$, and in women, $\beta_4 + \beta_7 = -6.06 + 0.16 = -5.89$. This group difference was equivalent across sexes, as indicated by the nonsignificant sex by no dementia versus future dementia interaction $\beta_4 = 0.16$. Cognition was also significantly lower in the current dementia than no dementia group both in men, $\beta_5 = -11.97$, and in women, $\beta_5 + \beta_8 = -11.97 - 7.88 = -19.85$. This group difference was significantly larger in women, as indicated by the sex by no dementia versus current dementia interaction $\beta_8 = -7.88$. Finally, cognition was also significantly lower in the current dementia group than future diagnosis group both in men, $\beta_5 - \beta_4 = -11.97 + 6.06 = -5.91$, and in women, $\beta_5 + \beta_8 - \beta_4 - \beta_7 = -11.97 - 7.88 + 6.06 + 0.16 = -13.95$. This group difference was significantly larger in women, as indicated by the additional interaction contrast of $\beta_8 - \beta_7 = -7.88 - 0.16 = -8.04$.

Review Questions

1. What makes a model *between-person*? Why might you predict that between-person models (i.e., general linear models) will not be suitable for longitudinal data?
2. Describe the process of centering continuous predictors. Which model effects should change as a result of choosing a different centering point, and which should not?
3. Describe the process of centering categorical predictors. What are the interpretational advantages and disadvantages of creating marginal vs. conditional (simple) contrasts?
4. Create your own examples to describe how a two-way interaction effect would be interpreted between all possible combinations of continuous with categorical predictors.

References

Aiken, L. S., & West, S. G. (1991). *Multiple regression: Testing and probing interactions.* Thousand Oaks, CA: Sage.

Bauer, D. J., & Curran, P. J. (2005). Probing interactions in fixed and multilevel regression: Inferential and graphical techniques. *Multivariate Behavioral Research, 40,* 373–400.

Cohen, J., Cohen, P., West, S. G., & Aiken, L. S. (2002). *Applied multiple regression/correlation analysis for the behavioral sciences* (3rd ed.). Hillsdale, NJ: Erlbaum.

Johnson, P. O., & Fay, L. C. (1950). The Johnson-Neyman technique, its theory and application. *Psychometrika, 15,* 349–367.

Maxwell, S. E., & Delaney, H. D. (2004). *Designing experiments and analyzing data.* Mahwah, NJ: Erlbaum.

Preacher, K. J., Curran, P. J., & Bauer, D. J. (2006). Computational tools for probing interaction effects in multiple linear regression, multilevel modeling, and latent curve analysis. *Journal of Educational and Behavioral Statistics, 31,* 437–448.

Appendix 2.A: Marginal Versus Simple Main Effects in General Linear Modeling Output

As introduced earlier in the chapter, there are two choices as to how to specify fixed effects of categorical predictors in a general linear model (as well as in the general linear mixed model or multilevel models we'll see later). One option is for the user to code the differences between groups manually as separate variables (e.g., by creating the DemNF$_i$ and DemNC$_i$ dummy codes for the contrasts among the three groups). The other option is to let the software program create group contrasts by denoting the predictor as "categorical" (e.g., via the CLASS statement in SAS, the BY statement in SPSS, or by using the i. indicator in STATA). Although neither approach is more correct than the other, you should be aware of how this choice will change the output that is then provided and what the resulting significance tests will then mean. Note that the following discussion does not apply to slopes for continuous variables, however.

Table 2.8 summarizes the output from Equation (2.13) when manually creating contrasts for dementia group in which the no dementia group is as the reference (i.e., $DemNF_i$ and $DemNC_i$, in which none = 0). Sex is represented by a single contrast between men (0) and women (1). The results under the heading "Parameter Estimates," provided by requesting the "solution for fixed effects" or "parameter estimates solution," for each fixed effect include an estimate, standard error, a t-statistic, and a p-value for the t-statistic (using denominator degrees of freedom = 541). For ease of comparison with the ANOVA solution, I have also computed the corresponding F-statistic (given as t^2 because each effect is tested using 1 degree of freedom in the numerator). The results under the heading "ANOVA" are provided by the Type III tests of the fixed effects in the ANOVA solution, which provides F-statistics instead of t-statistics. What Table 2.8 shows is the exact same information is provided by both output tables—the F-statistics match within rounding error, and the p-values match exactly. Furthermore, the interpretation of the estimates is based on the manual coding—in this case, men without dementia were the reference group for each of their simple main effects.

Table 2.9 provides the results from Equation (2.13) when sex and dementia group are specified as *categorical* predictors instead, such that the program then creates the contrasts instead of the user. First, notice that for each of the main effects of the categorical predictors (sex and dementia group), one row of output lists an estimate of 0.00 with dots where the standard errors and significance tests should be, which denotes the level of the grouping predictor that is serving as the reference category. Here, the highest coded group (or last alphabetically) is the reference, as

Table 2.8 Fixed effects significance tests given by the solution for fixed effects and analysis of variance (ANOVA) results when denoting sex and dementia group as continuous variables using manually coded contrasts. Bold values are $p < .05$.

Fixed Effects	Parameter Estimates					ANOVA	
	Est	SE	t-value	F-value	p <	F-value	p <
Intercept	**29.07**	0.75	38.84	1508.55	.001		
Age (0 = 85 years)	**−0.33**	0.12	−2.79	7.78	.005	7.80	.005
Grip Strength (0 = 9 lbs)	**0.62**	0.15	4.17	17.39	.001	17.41	.001
Age by Grip Strength	**0.12**	0.04	3.03	9.18	.003	9.16	.003
Sex (0 = Men, 1 = Women)	**−2.88**	1.01	−2.84	8.07	.005	8.09	.005
Dementia: None vs. Future	**−6.06**	1.64	−3.70	13.69	.000	13.72	.000
Dementia: None vs. Current	**−11.97**	2.25	−5.33	28.41	.001	28.43	.001
Sex by Dementia: None vs. Current	0.16	2.07	0.08	0.01	.937	0.01	.937
Sex by Dementia: None vs. Future	**−7.88**	3.02	−2.60	6.76	.010	6.78	.010

Table 2.9 Fixed effects significance tests given by the solution for fixed effects and analysis of variance (ANOVA) results when denoting sex and dementia group as categorical variables instead of using manually coded contrasts. Bold values are $p < .05$.

Fixed Effects	Categorical Variables		Parameter Estimates					ANOVA	
	Sex	Dementia	Est	SE	t-value	F-value	p <	F-value	p <
Intercept			**6.35**	1.95	3.26	10.63	.001		
Age (0 = 85 years)			**−0.33**	0.12	−2.79	7.78	.005	7.80	.005
Grip Strength (0 = 9 lbs)			**0.62**	0.15	4.17	17.39	.001	17.41	.001
Age by Grip Strength			**0.12**	0.04	3.03	9.18	.003	9.16	.003
Sex (0 = Men, 1 = Women)	Men		**10.75**	2.90	3.71	13.76	.000		
	Women		0.00	.	.		.	19.45	.001
Dementia Group (None, Future, or Current)		None	**19.85**	2.03	9.78	95.65	.001		
		Future	**13.95**	2.24	6.23	38.81	.001		
		Current	0.00	.	.		.	64.62	.001
Sex by Dementia Group	Men	None	**−7.88**	3.02	−2.6	6.76	.010		
	Men	Future	**−8.04**	3.42	−2.35	5.52	.019		
	Men	Current	0.00	.	.		.		
	Women	None	0.00	.	.		.		
	Women	Future	0.00	.	.		.		
	Women	Current	0.00	.	.		.	3.49	.031

in SAS or SPSS by default, although the lowest is the default in STATA (although this can be changed). Thus, for the effect of sex (a variable in which men = 0 and women = 1 in the dataset), the program essentially codes it backwards, such that women = 0 and men = 1. Similarly, for dementia group (a variable in which 1 = none, 2 = future, and 3 = current in the dataset), the highest-coded group, current dementia, becomes the reference instead.

This means that, in contrast to how the variables are actually coded in the dataset, the reference group in the parameter estimates solution for the intercept is a women with current dementia, the simple main effect of sex is the difference between women and men specifically in the current dementia group, and the simple main effects of dementia group are the differences specifically in women between current dementia and no dementia or between current dementia and future dementia. Likewise, the sex by dementia group interaction has four rows of 0.00 estimates and dots, but provides interaction effects for how the sex difference reported for the current dementia group differs in the no dementia or future dementia groups. Thus, the program has overridden the reference groups originally created by the user in estimating the categorical predictors. Further complicating our interpretation is the fact that the *F*-statistics and significance tests thereof for the effects of the categorical predictors do not match across the parameter estimates solution and the ANOVA results. This is due to two factors.

First, for the main effects, whereas the *F*-statistics calculated in the parameter estimates solution are assessing *simple main effects,* the *F*-statistics provided in the ANOVA solution are assessing *marginal main effects* instead. For instance, the *F*-statistic for the main effect of sex in the parameter estimates (13.76) is testing the sex difference in the current dementia group specifically, whereas the *F*-statistic in the ANOVA solution (19.45) is testing the sex difference on average across the dementia groups. Thus, these *F*-statistics for the main effect of sex have different values because they mean different things (simple versus marginal main effects).

Second, for categorical predictors with more than two groups, the *F*-statistics also do not have the same degrees of freedom. As a result, the *F*-statistics for the main effect of dementia group do not correspond at all. Whereas the *F*-statistics in the parameter estimates solution are testing simple main effects for each group contrast with one degree of freedom (current vs. none, current vs. future, both specifically in women), the *F*-statistic for the main effect of dementia group in the ANOVA solution is testing the overall (i.e., "omnibus") difference across the groups using two degrees of freedom, *and* is testing those omnibus dementia group differences averaged across sex. Thus, the *F*-statistics for the main effect of group (two values in the parameter estimates solution; one value in the ANOVA solution) are providing completely different information. The same is true for the sex by dementia group interaction: the two single degree of freedom *F*-statistics in the parameter estimates solution are testing how the sex effect found in the current dementia group differs in each of the other groups, whereas the single *F*-statistic with two degrees of freedom in the ANOVA solution instead is testing the overall or omnibus interaction between the two levels of sex and the three levels of dementia group.

But specifying categorical predictors with the program rather than creating manual contrasts can still be advantageous despite the interpretational challenges the resulting output can present. Letting the program do the coding can be much easier than determining the exact coding scheme needed to represent complex interaction effects. It also makes it easier for the user to follow-up on an omnibus effect to request any additional group comparisons of interest, as well as to determine if a set of contrasts representing an overall omnibus interaction (e.g., as in sex by dementia group) is significant (rather than each contrast individually).

Finally, given an interaction effect, which should be reported, simple or marginal main effects? I believe that you as the analyst should decide which effects correspond more closely to your research questions, and report the effects that answer those questions accordingly. I personally find little use in marginal main effects when an interaction is present, because marginal main effects do not apply to any specific person or group, and thus may not describe anyone in the sample. However, there may be situations in which the main effect averaged over other interacting predictors can be useful. The main thing to remember in either case, though, is to be absolutely clear about what a given effect represents, and not just whether it is significant!

INTRODUCTION TO WITHIN-PERSON ANALYSIS AND MODEL COMPARISONS

Although chapter 1 introduced some of the themes, concepts, and vocabulary recurring in longitudinal analysis, chapter 2 focused exclusively on *between-person models* instead. More specifically, chapter 2 reviewed the general linear models that would be used for cross-sectional data (i.e., in which each person has only one outcome and thus one model residual). We will build on these ideas to continue into chapter 3, whose purpose is to introduce **within-person models**, in which each person has more than one observation of the outcome variable because of repeated measurements (e.g., over time in longitudinal studies; across trials or conditions in other types of repeated measures studies), and thus more than one model residual. Furthermore, although the primary focus of chapter 2 was on the *model for the means* (i.e., interpreting fixed main effects and interactions among predictors), the primary focus of chapter 3 will be on the *model for the variance* (i.e., how the model residuals are distributed and related across observations).

Accordingly, this chapter begins using a two-occasion example to distinguish *between-person* from *within-person* models, and in doing so introduces the *intraclass correlation,* a useful way of quantifying the proportion of between-person variance in a longitudinal outcome. This chapter then describes how the general linear model can be extended for longitudinal analysis via different variants of repeated measures analysis of variance (ANOVA), including the univariate model, the univariate model with adjustments, and the multivariate model. It also discusses the limitations of these models in their suitability for real-world longitudinal data. Finally, this chapter introduces the rules for comparing alternative models, and illustrates these rules by comparing across the variants of ANOVA models seen so far. These rules of model comparisons will be applied throughout the text; a more technical treatment is also provided in chapter 5.

1. Extending Between-Person Models to Within-Person Models

As presented in chapter 1, longitudinal data are unique in their capacity to provide information about between-person (BP) relationships and within-person (WP) relationships simultaneously. This is accomplished by quantifying and predicting the variation in the outcome due to each source, as will be illustrated using simulated two-occasion data in this section.

Consider a hypothetical example: A researcher is interested in examining the effects of a new approach to instruction on an elementary student learning outcome ($M = 53.34$, $SD = 6.35$, range = 37.54 to 68.62). She randomly assigns 25 students to a control group (group = 1) and 25 students to a treatment group (group = 2), and collects student data at the beginning of the semester (pre-test is time = 1) and again at the end of the semester (post-test is time = 2), with no missing data. Individual trajectories are shown in Figure 3.1. She hypothesizes that students will score higher on the outcome at post-test than at pre-test (i.e., a positive main effect of time), and also that time and group will have a positive interaction, such that the change over time will be greater for students in the treatment group than in the control group, or equivalently, that the difference between the control and treatment groups will be greater at post-test than at pre-test (and there should be no group difference at pre-test). Let us now examine two different ways we might test these hypotheses in longitudinal data: by using a between-person model for the variance or a within-person model for the variance.

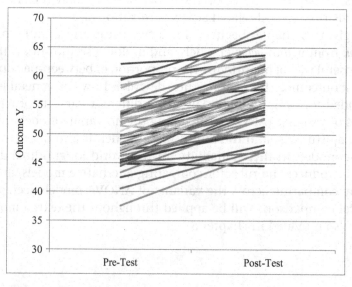

Figure 3.1 Individual trajectories for two-occasion example learning data.

1.A. A Between-Person Empty Model

We can begin by considering the simplest possible model for any outcome variable, a **between-person empty model**, as introduced in chapter 2 and as shown in Equation (3.1):

$$y_{ti} = \beta_0 + e_{ti} \qquad\qquad (3.1)$$

in which y_{ti} is the outcome at time t for individual i, β_0 is the intercept, and e_{ti} is the deviation from the intercept at time t for individual i. In estimating this model for our example data, as shown in the first set of columns of Table 3.1, the intercept $\beta_0 = 53.34$, which is just the grand mean of the outcome over all persons and occasions because we have no predictors included in the model for the means so far. The e_{ti} variance was estimated as $\sigma_e^2 = 40.34$, which so far includes all possible variation in the outcome across persons and occasions.

However, to what extent is this between-person model containing only a single residual appropriate for these longitudinal data? Recall the assumptions of the σ_e^2-only between-person models (e.g., between-groups analysis of variance, regression) as introduced in chapter 2: the e_{ti} residuals are supposed to be conditionally normally distributed (i.e., after including model predictors) with constant variance (across all observations and predictors) and to be independent across observations. Thus, the model in Equation (3.1) assumes that participants varied just as much from each other at pre-test as at post-test (i.e., constant variance across time), which may not be likely. More problematically, it also assumes that the residuals for the pre-test and post-test occasions from the same person have no relationship at all. This independence assumption is highly unlikely to hold in longitudinal data, even for just two occasions. Fortunately, this independence assumption is testable. To do so, we need to augment our between-person model for the variance to be able to represent and quantify the separate contributions of cross-sectional, between-person variation as well as longitudinal, within-person variation, as presented next.

1.B. A Within-Person Empty Model

A **within-person model** uses two parameters in the model for the variance to distinguish between-person (BP) from within-person (WP) variance in longitudinal data. Note that the within-person model does not remove between-person variation, but instead includes *both* sources of variation simultaneously. A **within-person empty model** is shown in Equation (3.2):

$$y_{ti} = \beta_0 + U_{0i} + e_{ti} \qquad\qquad (3.2)$$

in which the model for the means includes just the intercept β_0, which is now the mean of the person means given that the model for the variance now contains two residual terms to represent the variance in the outcome, U_{0i} and e_{ti}. The interpretation of these residual terms is illustrated in Figure 3.2, which contrasts how

Table 3.1 Results for the two-occasion example data from the between-person and within-person models. Bold values are $p < .05$.

Model Parameters		Equation 3.1: Between-Person Empty Model			Equation 3.2: Within-Person Empty Model			Equation 3.6: Between-Person Conditional Model			Equation 3.7: Within-Person Conditional Model		
		Est	SE	p <	Est	SE	p <	Est	SE	p <	Est	SE	p <
Model for the Means													
β_0	Intercept	**53.34**	0.64	.001	**53.34**	0.73	.001	**49.08**	1.04	.001	**49.08**	1.04	.001
	Time Effect												
β_1	Control Group							**5.82**	1.48	.001	**5.82**	0.60	.001
$\beta_1 + \beta_3$	Treatment Group							**7.86**	1.48	.001	**7.86**	0.60	.001
	Group Effect												
β_2	Pre-Test							1.68	1.48	.260	1.68	1.48	.260
$\beta_2 + \beta_3$	Post-Test							**3.72**	1.48	.015	**3.72**	1.48	.015
	Time by Group Interaction												
β_3	Difference of Difference							2.04	2.09	.333	**2.04**	0.84	.019
Predicted Cell Means													
β_0	= Control Group, Pre-Test							**49.08**	1.04	.001	**49.08**	1.04	.001
$\beta_0 + \beta_1$	= Control Group, Post-Test							**54.90**	1.04	.001	**54.90**	1.04	.001
$\beta_0 + \beta_2$	= Treatment Group, Pre-Test							**50.76**	1.04	.001	**50.76**	1.04	.001
$\beta_0 + \beta_1 + \beta_2 + \beta_3$	= Treatment Group, Post-Test							**58.62**	1.04	.001	**58.62**	1.04	.001
Model for the Variance													
σ_e^2	Residual Variance	**40.34**	5.73	.001	**28.21**	5.64	.001	**27.22**	3.93	.001	**4.45**	0.91	.001
$\tau_{U_0}^2$	Random Intercept Variance				**12.25**	6.03	.042				**22.78**	5.12	.001
	Intraclass Correlation	.00			.30			.00			.84		

the residuals are defined in a *between-person empty model* (top panel) versus a *within-person empty model* (bottom panel). In both panels, the dashed line through the squares represents prediction of the grand mean outcome from the intercept β_0. Outcomes for two hypothetical persons (A and B) are shown by the dots and triangles, respectively.

Let us first consider the outcomes for Person A in the top panel of Figure 3.2, in which the differences between the actual outcomes and the outcomes predicted from the model for the means (just β_0 so far) are represented by the e_{ti} deviations. Because Person A performs better than average at both pre-test and post-test, Person A's e_{ti} residuals are likely to be correlated (or *dependent*) as a result. The same is true for the outcomes for Person B, whose outcomes are both below average, and

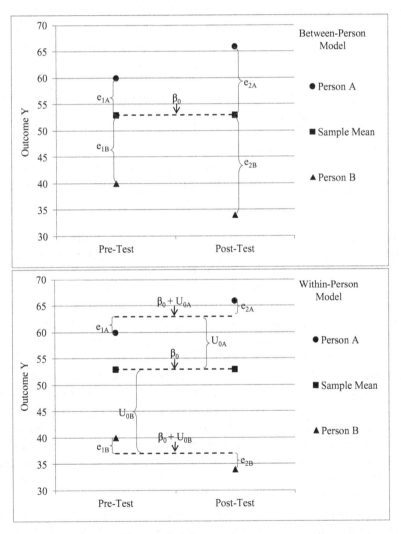

Figure 3.2 Illustration of empty between-person (top) and within-person (bottom) models for the variance. The data for the sample and for two hypothetical individuals are shown.

whose e_{ti} residuals will also be dependent. As you might remember from chapter 1, this illustrates one of several kinds of dependency possible in longitudinal data—correlation among the residuals from the same person due to constant mean differences over time. The trick to solving this problem is to add a residual term to the model for the variance that will accurately represent this type of dependency, rather than assuming no dependency at all.

Accordingly, this dependency due to constant mean differences can be included in the model for the variance as U_{0i} as shown in the bottom panel of Figure 3.2. This new term, U_{0i}, is called a **random intercept**, and is *the difference between the conditional mean predicted by the model for the means (here, just β_0) and the person's mean across time.* As a result, we must now explicitly differentiate two kinds of intercepts: not only do we have the *fixed* intercept β_0 that is shared by all observations in the sample, but now we also have a *random* intercept U_{0i}, by which each person gets his or her own *deviation* from the fixed intercept. The β_0 and U_{0i} terms share a *0* subscript because they are both intercepts, but only the random intercept U_{0i} gets an *i* subscript to indicate that each person has a different U_{0i}. In the bottom panel of Figure 3.2, $\beta_0 = 53$ (still the grand mean over time). For Person A, $U_{0i} = 10$, such that $\beta_0 + U_{0A} = 53 + 10 = 63$, Person A's mean across time. Similarly, for Person B, $U_{0i} = -16$, so $\beta_0 + U_{0B} = 53 - 16 = 37$, Person B's mean across time. Although the individual U_{0i} values could be calculated, longitudinal models instead estimate the variance of the U_{0i} values across persons as $\tau_{U_0}^2$. That is, because U_{0i} is considered a random variable (i.e., just like e_{ti} is a random variable), it doesn't really matter what the individual U_{0i} values are. As such, although the residual term U_{0i} is included in the model equations to represent the *idea* of between-person variance in the mean over time, its variance $\tau_{U_0}^2$ is the actual model parameter to be estimated. In keeping with the notation used in other books (e.g., Raudenbush & Bryk, 2002; Snijders & Bosker, 2012), τ_U^2 will be used for variances of random effects (i.e., just U_{0i} for now), and σ_e^2 will be used for the variance of the e_{ti} residuals.

After accounting for dependency due to between-person mean differences by including the random intercept U_{0i}, the remaining within-person deviation of the outcome at each occasion from the person's mean is then represented by e_{ti}. Thus, for Person A, e_{ti} at pre-test would be -3, such that the pre-test outcome is created by $\beta_0 + U_{0A} + e_{1A} = 53 + 10 - 3 = 60$, whereas e_{ti} at post-test would be 3, such that the post-test outcome is created by $\beta_0 + U_{0A} + e_{2A} = 53 + 10 + 3 = 66$. For Person B, the pre-test outcome is created by $\beta_0 + U_{0B} + e_{1B} = 53 - 16 + 3 = 40$, and the post-test outcome is created by $\beta_0 + U_{0B} + e_{2B} = 53 - 16 - 3 = 34$. Both the U_{0i} and e_{ti} residuals are assumed to be conditionally normally distributed with constant variance across persons and occasions—although we will see how the latter assumption about constant variance across occasions can be relaxed in the models presented in the next few chapters.

It is important to note that the total amount of variation around the grand mean at each occasion will be approximately the same when including only e_{ti} (as in the between-person empty model in the top panel of Figure 3.2) as when including U_{0i} and e_{ti} (as in the within-person empty model in the bottom panel of Figure 3.2). Because the within-person empty model in Equation (3.2) contains only the fixed intercept β_0 in the model for the means (thus the name "empty"), we have not yet *explained* any outcome variance. Instead, we have simply *partitioned* the total outcome variance into different sources for its two dimensions of sampling: variation between persons in $\tau^2_{U_0}$ and variation within persons in σ^2_e, rather than keeping all of the outcome variance in σ^2_e. In doing so we have allowed a correlation across occasions, as explained next.

1.C. Intraclass Correlation

As shown in the second set of columns of Table 3.1, estimating the within-person empty model in Equation (3.2) in our example yields a random intercept variance of the U_{0i} values of $\tau^2_{U_0}$ = 12.25 and a residual variance for the e_{ti} values of σ^2_e = 28.21. Their total variance of 40.46 is slightly higher than the total variance from the between-person empty model of σ^2_e = 40.34. This illustrates how the partitioning of variance in the within-person empty model (into $\tau^2_{U_0}$ and σ^2_e) will result in a total variance that is approximately (but not always exactly) the same as the total variance in the between-person empty model (from σ^2_e).

But why should we care what the variances of the U_{0i} and e_{ti} terms are? Although not helpful for the prediction of our outcome, the results of a within-person empty model will provide a baseline with which to judge the contribution of other effects to be added to the model. It also provides a means with which to calculate a useful descriptive statistic, the **intraclass correlation**, or **ICC**, as shown for our example data in Equation (3.3):

$$
\begin{aligned}
\text{ICC} &= \frac{\text{BP variation}}{\text{BP + WP variation}} = \frac{\text{Var}(U_{0i})}{\text{Var}(U_{0i}) + \text{Var}(e_{ti})} = \frac{\tau^2_{U_0}}{\tau^2_{U_0} + \sigma^2_e} \\
&= \frac{12.25}{12.25 + 28.21} = .30
\end{aligned}
\tag{3.3}
$$

in which the ICC can range between 0 and 1. One way to interpret the ICC is as *the proportion of outcome variation due to between-person differences in the intercept* (i.e., due to variance in the between-person U_{0i} random intercepts, relative to the total variation from the between-person U_{0i} random intercepts and the within-person e_{ti} residuals). Thus, 30% of the original outcome variation (i.e., before adding any predictors) is due to between-person mean differences over time. In other words, 30% of the outcome variance is cross-sectional and 70% is longitudinal.

To understand the implications of this ICC value for our data analysis, it may be helpful to consider the results from fitting the between-person (BP) and within-person (WP) empty models to our example data. As shown in Table 3.1, both models result in the exact same fixed intercept of β_0 = 53.34, which is the grand mean over time given that we do not yet have any predictors. This is because both models have specified the same *model for the means*—an empty model, which (so far) excludes any predictors for change over time or mean differences across groups. Instead, the BP and WP models differ in their *model for the variance*, such that the BP model includes σ^2_e only, whereas the WP model includes both $\tau^2_{U_0}$ and σ^2_e. The implications of this difference with respect to what these models predict are shown in Equation (3.4):

$$
\begin{aligned}
\text{BP model:} & \begin{pmatrix} \text{Var}(y_1) & \text{Cov}(y_1,y_2) \\ \text{Cov}(y_1,y_2) & \text{Var}(y_2) \end{pmatrix} = \begin{pmatrix} \sigma_e^2 & 0 \\ 0 & \sigma_e^2 \end{pmatrix} = \begin{pmatrix} 40.34 & 0 \\ 0 & 40.34 \end{pmatrix} \\
\text{WP model:} & \begin{pmatrix} \text{Var}(y_1) & \text{Cov}(y_1,y_2) \\ \text{Cov}(y_1,y_2) & \text{Var}(y_2) \end{pmatrix} = \begin{pmatrix} \sigma_e^2 + \tau_{U_0}^2 & \tau_{U_0}^2 \\ \tau_{U_0}^2 & \sigma_e^2 + \tau_{U_0}^2 \end{pmatrix} = \begin{pmatrix} 40.46 & 12.25 \\ 12.25 & 40.46 \end{pmatrix}
\end{aligned} \quad (3.4)
$$

in which the variance across persons at each occasion (in which y_1 = pre-test and y_2 = post-test) and the covariance between occasions are abbreviated as *Var* and *Cov*, respectively. As a brief refresher, Equation (3.5) provides the formulas for the variance of the outcome at each occasion (left equation) and for the covariance between two occasions (right equation):

$$
\text{Variance }(y_t) = \frac{\sum_{i=1}^{N}(y_{ti} - \hat{y}_{ti})^2}{N-k} \quad \text{Covariance }(y_1,y_2) = \frac{\sum_{i=1}^{N}(y_{1i} - \hat{y}_{1i})(y_{2i} - \hat{y}_{2i})}{N-k} \quad (3.5)
$$

in which the variance of the outcome at time t can be calculated as the sum over N persons of the squared deviations of each actual y_{ti} from the $\hat{y}_{ti}$ predicted from the model for the means divided by N persons minus k fixed effects ($k = 1$ for just β_0 so far), and the covariance between occasions can be calculated as the sum over N persons of the product of those $y_{ti} - \hat{y}_{ti}$ deviations at each occasion divided by N persons minus k fixed effects. Covariance tells us the direction and extent to which the residuals of the pre-test and post-test occasions are related in the unstandardized metric of the outcome. Although these formulas in Equation (3.5) are based on least squares estimation, they are also equivalent in this case to the restricted maximum likelihood results that we will utilize later (because in this example we have complete data that is balanced over time).

For the predicted variance and covariance using the BP model in the top of Equation (3.4), all the variance in the outcome at each occasion is represented by the single residual e_{ti} (which is the difference between y_{ti} and $\hat{y}_{ti}$ for each observation, as shown in the top panel of Figure 3.2). In our example, the BP model predicts the variance at each occasion to be 40.34. It assumes the e_{ti} residuals have a normal distribution and are independent with constant variance across observations. Thus, the BP model predicts no covariance whatsoever between the pre-test and post-test residuals for each person (indicated by 0 for the covariance in the off-diagonal).

In contrast, for the predicted variance and covariance using the WP model shown in the bottom of Equation (3.4), the total outcome variance at each occasion (estimated as 40.46) is predicted from the variance of the e_{ti} residuals (WP variance of $\sigma_e^2 = 28.21$) plus the variance of the U_{0i} random intercepts (BP variance of $\tau_{U_0}^2 = 12.25$). Like the BP model, the WP model predicts the same total outcome variation at pre-test and post-test. But unlike the BP model, the WP model also predicts a covariance between the pre-test and post-test outcomes, and this covariance is entirely due to the random intercept variance ($\tau_{U_0}^2 = 12.25$). Although it may seem odd that a variance could become a covariance, in this case, what the WP model is saying is that *the only reason why the pre-test and post-test outcomes are related is because of constant mean differences between persons over time.* After including the U_{0i} random intercept to represent those constant person mean differences (i.e., deviating each y_{ti} from $\hat{y}_{ti} + U_{0i}$ in the bottom panel of Figure 3.2 instead of just $\hat{y}_{ti}$ as in the top panel), the e_{ti} residuals from the same person are then independent. Both the BP and WP models assume the residuals from different people are independent as well—although in chapter 11 we'll see how the model for the variance can be further modified if persons are not actually independent, such as when nested in groups.

We can convert the *covariance* between occasions to a *correlation* using Equation (3.6):

$$\text{Correlation } (y_1, y_2) = \frac{\text{Cov}(y_1, y_2)}{\sqrt{\text{Var}(y_1)} * \sqrt{\text{Var}(y_2)}} = \frac{\tau^2_{U_0}}{\sqrt{\tau^2_{U_0} + \sigma^2_e} * \sqrt{\tau^2_{U_0} + \sigma^2_e}}$$

$$= \frac{12.25}{40.46} = .30$$

(3.6)

resulting in a correlation between occasions of $r = .30$, as reported in the second set of columns of Table 3.1. It is not a coincidence that .30 is what we found for the **intraclass correlation** (ICC) earlier—another way of interpreting the ICC is as *the correlation of the outcome residuals over time.* Although with only two occasions there is only one correlation to consider, once we have more than two occasions, the ICC will become the average correlation across time.

In summary, in our empty models so far, the within-person model with $\tau^2_{U_0}$ and σ^2_e predicts a constant correlation between occasions due to the random intercept U_{0i} (i.e., the only dependency is due to constant person mean differences over time), whereas the between-person model with σ^2_e only predicts no correlation between occasions at all. As a result, a between-person model is not likely to be plausible for longitudinal data, in which the residuals from the same person will usually be dependent because of constant person mean differences, as well as for other reasons, as introduced in chapter 1. But why should we care? That is, the hypotheses in this example concern the effects in the model for the means for time, group, and their interaction, and not how much between-person or within-person variance our outcome has. As we will see next, though, because the model for the variance can result in different inferences about the model's fixed effects, the model for the variance can be just as important to consider.

1.D. Comparing Between-Person and Within-Person Conditional Model Results

Let us now examine the hypothesized effects in the model for the means under between-person (BP) and within-person (WP) versions of the same *conditional* model with predictors of time, group, and their interaction, as shown in Equation (3.7):

$$\text{BP model: } y_{ti} = \beta_0 + \beta_1 (\text{Time}_{ti}) + \beta_2 (\text{Group}_i) + \beta_3 (\text{Time}_{ti})(\text{Group}_i) + e_{ti}$$

$$\text{WP model: } y_{ti} = \beta_0 + \beta_1 (\text{Time}_{ti}) + \beta_2 (\text{Group}_i) + \beta_3 (\text{Time}_{ti})(\text{Group}_i)$$
$$+ U_{0i} + e_{ti}$$

(3.7)

in which the BP and WP models differ only in their model for the variance (σ_e^2-only versus $\tau_{U_0}^2$ and σ_e^2, respectively). Their fixed effects in the model for the means are the same: β_0 is the fixed intercept, β_1 is the simple main effect of time, β_2 is the simple main effect of group, and β_3 is the two-way interaction of time by group. The subscript ti is used for any variable that varies over both time and individuals (here, the y_{ti} outcome, the predictor of Time$_{ti}$, and the e_{ti} residual). The subscript i is used for Group$_i$ because each person is only in one group across all occasions (so group membership varies across individuals, but does not vary over time), as well as for the random intercept U_{0i}, for which each person gets his or her own value (that is constant across time).

As we learned in chapter 2, the interpretation of these fixed effects of time and group and their tests of significance will depend on the reference value for each predictor. In the example dataset, the time variable has possible values of 1 = pre-test and 2 = post-test, and the group variable has values of 1 = control and 2 = treatment. One option is to make the reference point for the model the pre-test observation for the control group by coding the time variable as pre-test = 0 and post-test = 1, and by coding the group variable as control = 0 and treatment = 1. Alternatively, we could make the reference point the treatment group at post-test by coding the time variable as pre-test = 1 and post-test = 0, and by coding the group variable as control = 1 and treatment = 0. There is no wrong way to code the predictor variables, but the choices we make for how they are included will impact the intercept and main effect parameters in model solution we receive (although it will not change the amount of outcome variance the model accounts for, nor will it change the predicted outcome for any observation).

The model results for the BP and WP models in Equation (3.7) are shown in the third and fourth sets of columns of Table 3.1, respectively, along with the model-predicted means for each combination of time and group. The predictors of time and group have been coded so that the reference is the control group at pre-test; thus the fixed intercept $\beta_0 = 49.08$ is predicted outcome for the control group at pre-test. The *simple main effect of time* $\beta_1 = 5.82$ is the difference between the pre-test and the post-test occasions specifically for the control group, which was significant (in both models) as expected. The *simple main effect of group* $\beta_2 = 1.68$ is the difference between the control and treatment groups specifically at pre-test, which was not significant (in either model) as expected. Finally, the two-way time by group interaction $\beta_3 = 2.04$ is the *difference of the differences* and can be interpreted in two alternative but equally correct ways. First, $\beta_3 = 2.04$ is how the difference between the pre-test and post-test occasions differs between the control and treatment groups, such that the change over time is larger by 2.04 in the treatment group. Second, $\beta_3 = 2.04$ is also how the difference between the control and treatment groups differs between pre-test and post-test, such that the group difference is larger by 2.04 at post-test than at pre-test. Interestingly, while the time by group interaction β_3 was not significant in the BP model, it was significant in the WP model. We'll revisit this result shortly.

To examine the significance of the other simple effects not provided directly by the model, we could re-code the time and group predictor variables so that the reference is the treatment group at post-test, or we could use additional programming statements instead (as shown in the example syntax online). In doing so, also as provided in Table 3.1, we find that the simple main effect of time for the treatment group of $\beta_1 + \beta_3 = 5.82 + 2.04 = 7.86$ and the simple main effect of group at post-test of $\beta_2 + \beta_3 = 1.68 + 2.04 = 3.72$ were also significant (in both models) as expected. Thus, the researcher's hypotheses were partially supported—both the control and treatment groups did improve significantly from pre-test to post-test, and the group difference was not significant at pre-test (i.e., before the treatment) but was significant at post-test (i.e., after the treatment). But the other hypothesis for the time by group interaction β_3—that the treatment group would improve more over time than the control group—was supported in the WP model, but not in the BP model. Why did this happen, and which answer is the right one?

Before answering these questions, we must consider the kind of outcome variance each fixed effect could explain. First, the predictor for control versus treatment group varies between persons (but not within persons because each person is in the same group at both occasions). Thus, including the effect of group in the model should reduce the model's BP variance (the U_{0i} random intercept variance $\tau_{U_0}^2$). Second, the predictor for pre-test versus post-test time varies within persons but not between persons (because each person has the same two possible occasions). Thus, including the effect of time in the model should reduce the model's WP variance (the e_{ti} residual variance σ_e^2). Third, although the interaction of time by group varies both between persons and within persons, it serves to predict why some people change differently from pre-test to post-test. Thus, including the interaction of time by group should further reduce the model's WP variance—because the interaction allows each group to have their own slope for time, the remaining time- and individual-specific e_{ti} deviations around the time slope should be reduced.

With these differences as to whether the predictor is accounting for BP variance or WP variance in mind, let us now note some important similarities and differences in the results in Table 3.1. First, we note that the parameter estimates for the fixed effects (β_0, β_1, β_2, and β_3, and the model-implied additional simple main effects of $\beta_1 + \beta_3$ and $\beta_2 + \beta_3$) are exactly the same across the BP and WP models. This is not a coincidence—the BP and WP models in Equation (3.7) include the same model for the means, and so their estimates of these fixed effects are the same. However, the BP and WP models include different models for their variance. So, what does differ between models are the *standard errors* (and resulting *p*-values) of the effects that account for within-person variance: those for time and time by group. Standard errors (SE) for the main effects or interactions from our models can be calculated as shown in Equation (3.8):

$$\text{BP effect SE}_{\beta_x} = \sqrt{\frac{\sigma_e^2 + \tau_{U_0}^2}{\text{Var}(x_i) * (1 - R_X^2) * (T - 1)}}$$

$$\text{WP effect SE}_{\beta_x} = \sqrt{\frac{\sigma_e^2}{\text{Var}(x_i) * (1 - R_X^2) * (T - 1)}}$$

(3.8)

in which the square root is used to transform the sampling variance of the fixed effect into a SE metric (i.e., from a variance to a standard deviation metric). The denominator is based on the variance in the predictor x_i that is not accounted for by the other predictors and the product of *T* total observations minus 1; thus, to the extent that x_i has more variance in general (or less shared variance with other predictors), the SE for its effect will be smaller. Here, though, the numerator includes the remaining outcome variance that is relevant for assessing the strength of the predictor's effect, but which sources of variance are relevant will depend on the source of the effect. The SE for all effects will include at least σ_e^2, but the SE for any BP effect will also include $\tau_{U_0}^2$. This difference is the source of the differing SEs for the WP effects in Table 3.1.

Let us first examine the SE for the simple main effect of group (either at pre-test or post-test) in both models for $T = 100$ total observations (50 persons by two occasions). Because the binary group variable has a mean of 0.50 (i.e., half of the sample is in each group), its variance is $0.5*(1 - 0.5) = 0.25$. Given the coding of time (0 = pre-test, 1 = post-test) and group (0 = control, 1 = treatment), the variables for group and the time by group interaction are correlated, such that half of the variance in the group variable is predicted by the interaction ($1 - R_X^2 = .50$). Using these values, the denominator of the SE equation will be 12.50 in either model. Critically, because the simple effect of group accounts for BP variance, the numerator is calculated as $\tau_{U_0}^2 + \sigma_e^2 = 22.78 + 4.45 = 27.22$. The square root of $27.22 / 12.5 = 1.48$, which is the SE for the group effect at either occasion. Because the SE for the group effect is calculated using the total remaining outcome variance, the SE is the same in the WP model (in which the remaining outcome variance has been partitioned into two sources of $\tau_{U_0}^2$ and σ_e^2) as in the BP model (in which all remaining variance is contained within σ_e^2). The significance of the group effect can then be determined by a Wald test, in which the slope estimate is divided by its SE to form a t-statistic, which is then compared to a t-distribution with denominator degrees of freedom equal to N persons minus k fixed effects. In both models, the Wald test returns a t-statistic > 1.96 at the post-test occasion only, and thus the effect of group is significant at post-test but not at pre-test, as found in both models.

Next, let us consider the SE for the simple main effect of time (for either group). The binary time variable also has a variance of 0.25, of which 50% is predicted by the time by group interaction, resulting in a denominator of the SE equation of 12.50 in either model. In contrast, the numerator of the SE equation will differ across models. Because the effect of time operates within persons, its SE is calculated using only σ_e^2, which is defined differently across models, as illustrated in Figure 3.3. In the BP model (top panel), $\sigma_e^2 = 27.22$ and contains *all remaining outcome variation:* e_{ti} is the difference between the observed y_{ti} outcome and the $\hat{y}_{ti}$ outcome predicted by time, group, and their interaction (as shown by the dashed line for each group). In contrast, in the WP model (bottom panel), $\sigma_e^2 = 4.45$ and contains only the remaining y_{ti} variation relative to the dashed line for each person created from $\hat{y}_{ti} + U_{0i}$ (i.e., after taking into account constant person mean differences). Because of this difference in σ_e^2, the fixed effect of time is tested against less variance in the WP model, reducing its SE from 1.48 in the BP model to 0.60 in the WP model. Its resulting Wald test is significant for both groups in both models, however.

Finally, let us examine the interaction of time by group, whose SE also includes σ_e^2 only, and thus differs from 2.09 in the BP model to 0.84 in the WP model. As a

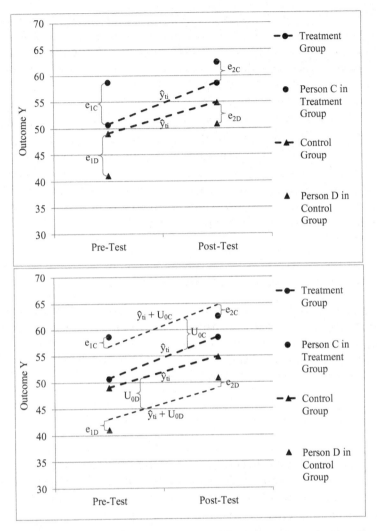

Figure 3.3 Illustration of conditional between-person (top) and
within-person (bottom) models for the variance.
The data for two hypothetical individuals from different groups are shown.

result, the interaction is not significant in the BP model but is significant in the WP
model. So, which set of results should we believe? Although later we will use more
formal methods of comparing models, for now we can take a simpler approach.
As shown in Equation (3.4), the BP model predicts a correlation of exactly 0 for
the model residuals between occasions. We can test this assumption by calculat-
ing the e_{ti} model residuals for each observation as: $e_{ti} = y_{ti} - \hat{y}_{ti}$, in which $\hat{y}_{ti} = 49.08 +$
$5.82(\text{Time}_{ti}) + 1.62(\text{Group}_i) + 2.04(\text{Time}_{ti})(\text{Group}_i)$. The Pearson correlation of
the e_{ti} residuals between pre-test and post-test was significantly different from 0 at
$r = .84$ ($p < .001$ for $N = 50$ total observations), which strongly suggests that the BP
model assumption of 0 residual correlation is incorrect.

In contrast, the WP model predicts a correlation of $r = .84$ for the model residuals between occasions, which can be calculated as the conditional ICC using Equation (3.3) and the estimated $\tau^2_{U_0}$ and σ^2_e variances in the fourth set of columns in Table 3.1 as ICC = 22.78 / (22.78 + 4.45) = 0.84. Because the example data were generated using the WP model in Equation (3.7), in this case the actual residual correlation exactly matches that predicted from the WP model, although this won't always happen. But for now, we can conclude that because the residual correlation is significantly different from 0, the WP model (in which $\tau^2_{U_0}$ predicts a constant correlation of the residuals across time) matches the data better than the BP model (that includes only the σ^2_e residual variance, and thus which predicts 0 correlation of the residuals over time). So, the results from the WP model in which the time by group interaction β_3 was significant are more trustworthy than the results from the BP model—good news for our example researcher!

1.E. Generalizing Results: Fixed and Random Effects

Another way to interpret the results from the WP model is to think of it as a three-way design (with factors of group, time, and person) rather than as a two-way design (with factors of just group and time). In doing so, we will try to identify all possible main effects and interactions and see which our WP model contains, as repeated below from Equation (3.7) in Equation (3.9):

$$\text{WP model: } y_{ti} = \beta_0 + \beta_1(\text{Time}_{ti}) + \beta_2(\text{Group}_i) + \beta_3(\text{Time}_{ti})(\text{Group}_i) \\ + U_{0i} + e_{ti} \tag{3.9}$$

in which the main effects of time, group, and person are given by β_1, β_2, and U_{0i}, respectively. Whereas β_1 and β_2 are *fixed* main effects (that belong to the model for the means), U_{0i} is a *random* main effect (that belongs to the model for the variance instead). The difference between fixed and random effects will be elaborated throughout the text, but for now it can be thought of as follows. The **fixed effects** for time and group are used to make inferences about differences in the outcome between *the specific and non-exchangeable variants observed in the study*—here, the pre-test versus post-test occasions and the control versus treatment groups, specifically. In contrast, the **random effect** is not *designed to make inferences between the specific variants examined in the study*—we do not care how participant 1 compares with participants 2, 3, or 50, as our sample instead represents a larger population of persons who are seen as exchangeable. We simply want to know if *persons matter*—if there is significant *variance* in the outcome due to systematic mean differences between persons. Because each person provides more than one outcome, we can observe the contribution due to each specific person. Although we could also model differences between persons as fixed effects instead, our current example would require 49 dummy codes to represent all possible differences among the 50 persons. So, rather than model differences between persons with fixed effects, we have modeled differences between persons using the variance of a single random effect U_{0i} that adjusts each

y_{ti} outcome by a constant intercept difference for each person (and we can test if persons matter as whether $\tau_{U_0}^2 > 0$). Critically, by treating persons as random we can explore *why* people differ (i.e., explain the $\tau_{U_0}^2$ variance with person characteristics such as group) rather than simply control for those person intercept differences via 49 uninformative fixed effects tied to their ID numbers.

In addition to the three main effects, there are also three possible two-way interactions in our three-way design, as well as one three-way interaction—which of these are included in our model? Although the interaction of time by group is included via the fixed effect β_3, the interaction of person by group cannot be determined, given that each person is in the same group on both occasions. For the same reason, the three-way interaction of time by group by person cannot be determined. That leaves us with the interaction of time by person, reflecting how persons change differently between pre-test and post-test. Although not obvious, the time by person interaction *is* the residual e_{ti}! The only systematic reason left why the observed y_{ti} values do not match those predicted from $\hat{y}_{ti} + U_{0i}$ is because *people change differently over time*. For instance, as shown in Figure 3.3, Person D improved more than was predicted from being in the control group, whereas Person C improved less than was predicted from being in the treatment group. These differences in the time slopes between persons must be considered "error" (as the e_{ti} residuals) given only two occasions, because if we were to give each person his or her own random time slope in addition to a random intercept, the prediction would be perfect! We cannot have a random time slope for each person that is separate from the e_{ti} values without at least three occasions, as we will see starting in chapter 5.

2. Within-Person Models via Repeated Measures Analysis of Variance

The previous example was presented to illustrate the primary difference between between-person and within-person models but was limited to two occasions. This next section addresses traditional models for longitudinal data more generally, in which *within-person models* are more commonly referred to as **repeated measures** (or **within-subjects**) **analysis of variance** (**ANOVA**). In practice, however, there is more than one approach to repeated measures ANOVA resulting from different variants of the basic within-person model, as described next.

To continue, we will use a new example taken from a subset of the *Cognition, Health, and Aging Project* data (as described in chapter 1) in which 101 older adults were measured on six occasions (once per day) over a span of two weeks (with no missing data). The outcome variable was a measure of processing speed—the average response time (RT) across trials (in milliseconds; $M = 1{,}770.70$, $SD = 494.09$, range $= 917.67$ to $4{,}159.14$) needed to accurately judge whether two series of three numbers were the same or different. The purpose of the study was to assess individual differences in short-term learning; individual trajectories for the

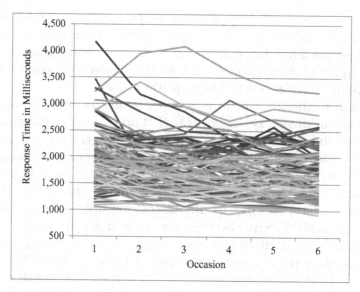

Figure 3.4 Individual trajectories for six-occasion example response time data.

change in RT across the six occasions are shown in Figure 3.4. Descriptive statistics for RT at each occasion are given in the bottom panel of Table 3.2, in which the variance of RT at each occasion is given on the diagonal, the covariance between occasions is given above the diagonal, the correlation between occasions is given below the diagonal, and the means and their SEs at each occasion are given in the bottom rows. Before explaining how three different approaches to repeated measures ANOVA would describe these data (for which the rest of Table 3.2 will be relevant), let us first examine what they have in common—their model for the means over time.

2.A. Saturated Model for the Means in Repeated Measures Analysis of Variance

The repeated measures analysis of variance (ANOVA) model for longitudinal data treats time as a categorical factor. That is, *time* is considered as a set of discrete, fixed conditions in which each person (or individual observational unit: organization, animal, etc.) contributes one outcome variable per time *condition*. The ANOVA model for describing mean change over time uses as many parameters as there are discrete occasions and is thus referred to as a **saturated means model** (i.e., the model for time is *saturated* by using all possible degrees of freedom for differences across conditions of the time variable). A saturated ANOVA model for the means for our six-occasion example response time (RT) data (without yet considering what

Table 3.2 Observed and model-predicted variances (on the diagonal), covariances (above the diagonal), correlations (below the diagonal), means (with SE = standard errors), and fit by model for the six-occasion example response time data.

Between-Person (Independent) ANOVA Model Fit and Predictions
Variance Parameters = 1, −2LL = 9155.4, AIC = 9157.4, BIC = 9160.0

Occasion	1	2	3	4	5	6
1	236,813	0	0	0	0	0
2	0	236,813	0	0	0	0
3	0	0	236,813	0	0	0
4	0	0	0	236,813	0	0
5	0	0	0	0	236,813	0
6	0	0	0	0	0	236,813
Mean	1961.89	1815.17	1750.03	1717.80	1707.18	1672.14
SE	48.42	48.42	48.42	48.42	48.42	48.42

Univariate Within-Person (Repeated Measures) ANOVA Model Fit and Predictions
Variance Parameters = 2, −2LL = 8353.4, AIC = 8357.4, BIC = 8362.6

Occasion	1	2	3	4	5	6
1	236,813	202,677	202,677	202,677	202,677	202,677
2	0.856	236,813	202,677	202,677	202,677	202,677
3	0.856	0.856	236,813	202,677	202,677	202,677
4	0.856	0.856	0.856	236,813	202,677	202,677
5	0.856	0.856	0.856	0.856	236,813	202,677
6	0.856	0.856	0.856	0.856	0.856	236,813
Mean	1961.89	1815.17	1750.03	1717.80	1707.18	1672.14
SE	48.42	48.42	48.42	48.42	48.42	48.42

Multivariate Within-Person (Repeated Measures) ANOVA Model Fit and Predictions
(are same as in original data)
Variance Parameters = 21, −2LL = 8229.8, AIC = 8271.8, BIC = 8326.7

Occasion	1	2	3	4	5	6
1	301,985	235,659	217,994	202,607	192,154	195,360
2	0.842	259,150	230,217	213,232	202,092	193,268
3	0.821	0.936	233,368	205,209	196,919	188,604
4	0.791	0.898	0.911	217,544	193,676	185,321
5	0.759	0.862	0.885	0.902	212,098	187,840
6	0.802	0.856	0.880	0.896	0.920	196,733
Mean	1961.89	1815.17	1750.03	1717.80	1707.18	1672.14
SE	54.68	50.65	48.07	46.41	45.83	44.13

kind of model for the variance we will need, thus predicting $\widehat{RT}_{ti}$ rather than RT) is shown in Equation (3.10):

$$\widehat{RT}_{ti} = \beta_0 + \beta_1\left(T1_{ti}\right) + \beta_2\left(T2_{ti}\right) + \beta_3\left(T3_{ti}\right) + \beta_4\left(T4_{ti}\right) + \beta_5\left(T5_{ti}\right) \qquad (3.10)$$

in which five dummy code predictors are used to distinguish the six occasions: T1 = 1 for time 1 and is 0 otherwise, T2 = 1 for time 2 and is 0 otherwise, and so forth. A dummy code for time 6 is not included because time 6 is the reference: β_0 is the mean for time 6, and β_1 through β_5 are the mean differences between time 6 and each other occasion (this coding in which the last category is the reference is the default in SPSS MIXED and SAS MIXED). Because this saturated model for the means contains six fixed effects, it will perfectly reproduce the mean RT at each of the six occasions. Although many other ways of creating contrasts across occasions are also possible, the point is that the default repeated measures ANOVA model for six occasions will include one intercept and five contrasts of some kind. The goal of the ANOVA model is *not to predict* or *summarize* the pattern of means via some parsimonious functional form; instead, it simply *reproduces* the observed mean per occasion using fixed effects equal to the number of occasions minus 1 (given that the fixed intercept is already included). This is the case for all repeated measures ANOVA variants that follow—their differences lie not in their (saturated) model for the means, but in their model for the variance.

2.B. Univariate Model for Repeated Measures Analysis of Variance

The univariate model for repeated measures ANOVA is exactly the within-person model for the variance that was described earlier. That is, the univariate model adds two residual terms to the saturated means model in Equation (3.10): the random intercept U_{0i} as the difference between the overall predicted mean (here, $\hat{y}_{ti}$ is just the mean at each occasion) and the mean for person i over time (as predicted from $\hat{y}_{ti} + U_{0i}$), and the residual e_{ti} as the time-specific and person-specific deviation of the actual y_{ti} values from those predicted by $\hat{y}_{ti} + U_{0i}$.

Estimating the univariate model for our example data yields a random intercept variance of $\tau^2_{U_0} = 202{,}677$ and a residual variance of $\sigma^2_e = 34{,}316$. Through Equation (3.4) we can find the predicted variances and covariances over the six occasions from the univariate model, as shown in the middle panel of Table 3.2. We can evaluate the accuracy of these predictions informally by comparing them with the actual data shown in the bottom panel of Table 3.2. Later in this chapter we will examine a more formal way to compare alternative models for the variance.

First, the univariate model in the middle panel of Table 3.2 predicts the total variance at each occasion to be $\tau^2_{U_0} + \sigma^2_e = 202{,}677 + 34{,}316 = 236{,}813$, which is exactly the average total variance across the six occasions. As seen in the bottom panel of Table 3.2, however, 236,813 is an underestimate of the total variance for occasions 1 to 2, but is an overestimate for occasions 3 to 6. Similarly, the univariate model predicts the covariance between occasions to be constant over time at $\tau^2_{U_0}$ = 202,677, which is exactly the average covariance across the 15 possible covariances between occasions 1 to 6. It is an underestimate for 5 of the 15 covariances and is an overestimate for the other 10 covariances. Finally, the **conditional intraclass correlation** (i.e., after including the mean differences between occasions) in the univariate model from Equation (3.3) is predicted to be ICC = $\tau^2_{U_0}$/ $(\tau^2_{U_0} + \sigma^2_e)$ = 202,677 / (202,677 + 34,316) = .86. The correlation between occasions is predicted to result only from the random intercept variance because the model says that the only reason the six outcomes from the same person are related is because of person mean differences (i.e., intercept differences) over time. Because person mean differences are constant over time, the predicted correlation should be constant over time as well. But of the 15 possible correlations between occasions, r = .86 is an underestimate for 9 of the correlations, but is an overestimate for the other 6, indicating that something else is likely causing the correlation over time in addition to constant person mean differences through U_{0i}. But what is the ultimate impact of these discrepancies between the actual data (the variances, covariances, and correlations over time) and the patterns predicted by the univariate repeated measures ANOVA model?

In ANOVA parlance, the pattern of equal variances over time (from $\tau^2_{U_0} + \sigma^2_e$) and equal covariance over time (from $\tau^2_{U_0}$) found in the univariate model is called **compound symmetry**. Considerable research has examined what can happen when compound symmetry does not hold (as in our data). The essential problem is that the SEs for testing mean differences between occasions become biased (and thus so do the p-values based on those SEs). Because the model assumes constant variance over time, it uses the same amount of σ^2_e in the numerator of each SE calculation (which may be an overestimate or an underestimate). The result is that for some comparisons the SEs (and thus their accompanying p-values) will be too big or too small.

However, as discussed in Maxwell and Delaney (2004, chapter 11), all that is technically needed to obtain unbiased tests of significance of the differences between occasions is for the data to show **sphericity**, otherwise known as the *homogeneity of treatment-difference variances assumption*. Whereas compound symmetry requires equal variances and equal covariances over time, the less restrictive form of sphericity instead requires *equal variance and equal covariance of the pairwise differences between occasions* (e.g., the difference between time 1 and 2, time 2 and 3, and so forth). If the more restrictive assumption of compound symmetry is satisfied, then so is the less restrictive assumption of sphericity. Sphericity is also always satisfied when there are only two occasions, as there is only one possible difference between time 1 and 2 to consider, resulting in a single difference variance and no difference covariances. But for more than two occasions, there are two other variants of repeated measures ANOVA models for addressing violations of sphericity. These approaches will be summarized below; readers who seek greater detail are referred to the excellent treatment by Maxwell and Delaney (2004, chapters 11–14).

2.C. Adjustments to the Univariate Model Tests Based on Degrees of Freedom

Although sphericity tests are available to determine whether the assumption of sphericity has been violated, empirical work has suggested their utility is questionable. Alternative approaches were developed to conduct adjusted significance tests based on a parameter called ε (pronounced "epsilon") that indexes how far off from sphericity the pattern of pairwise variance and covariance over time is determined to be. If sphericity holds perfectly then $\varepsilon = 1$; otherwise ε ranges from 0 to 1, with lower values indicating more deviation from sphericity. Because ε must be estimated from the data, many approaches have been developed to adjust the sample estimate of ε, including the Geisser-Greenhouse lower-bound ε correction, the Huynh-Feldt $\tilde{\varepsilon}$ adjustment, and the Geisser and Greenhouse $\hat{\varepsilon}$ adjustment, the latter of which is recommended by Maxwell and Delaney (2004, p. 545). The goal of each approach is to reduce the degrees of freedom used for the omnibus F-test of the overall difference across occasions, creating a more conservative omnibus test. However, the ε adjustment cannot be used to adjust post-hoc comparisons between particular occasions (i.e., at which a single σ_e^2 value may be too big or too small), and an alternative repeated measures ANOVA model is recommended instead, as presented next.

2.D. Multivariate Model for Repeated Measures Analysis of Variance

Although the univariate model (or sphericity-based adjustments thereof) is perhaps the most common repeated measures ANOVA model for longitudinal data, a **multivariate model** could also be used instead. Although both use the same saturated model for the means (i.e., use all possible fixed effects of time to perfectly reproduce the means at each occasion), they differ in what they assume the pattern of variance and covariance over time to be after accounting for all model predictors. The multivariate model cannot be described succinctly by an equation predicting the outcome at any occasion because, unlike the univariate model, it does not include the U_{0i} and e_{ti} terms that imply constant variance over time. Instead, the variance at each occasion and the covariances between occasions are all estimated separately. Another way to say this is that the form of the variance–covariance matrix over time is **unstructured,** meaning that every individual element (variance and covariance) gets to be whatever the data wants it to be. If there are n occasions per person, this will result in $(n*[n + 1]) / 2$ estimated parameters, or for our current 6-occasion example, $6*7 / 2 = 21$ estimated parameters (6 variances and 15 covariances).

Because the multivariate model describes the data as they are, the mean differences between occasions are tested more precisely (e.g., the difference between occasions 1 and 2 is tested using their specific variances and covariance, and not the average variance and covariance across all six occasions instead), resulting in SEs and p-values for the comparisons that are as accurate as possible. Thus, an important advantage of the multivariate model is that it can never be wrong—because no assumptions are made about the pattern of variance and covariance across time, concerns about violating sphericity do not apply. A disadvantage of the multivariate model is that the denominator degrees of freedom for these comparisons are based on N persons, and not $T = N * n$ total observations as in the univariate model. Another disadvantage is that the estimation of all possible variances and covariances over time (rather than just $\tau_{U_0}^2$ and σ_e^2) may require large sample sizes, a problem that is compounded as the number of occasions increases.

3. Comparing Alternative Models for Longitudinal Data

So far in this chapter we have seen three model variants for analysis of variance: *between persons, univariate within persons,* and *multivariate within persons.* Although each has the same saturated model for the means over time, they have different models for the variance. So far we have evaluated them informally by observing how well the variances and covariances over time predicted by the model match those observed in the actual data, but there are more formal, empirical ways by which alternative models can be compared. What follows next is intended to introduce the basic concepts and rules for longitudinal model comparison; more technical details will be presented in chapter 5. The indices we will use for model comparison throughout the text are described first, followed by the three primary decision points required to successfully follow the rules of the model comparison process. This section concludes by using these new tools to compare the three ANOVA models and discusses their likely suitability for longitudinal data.

3.A. Introduction to Relative Model Fit Statistics

Although more detail on their origin will be provided in chapter 5, for now we briefly introduce three indices by which **relative model fit** can be judged. The idea of *relative* model fit means that none of these indices can tell us whether a given model fits the data in an absolute sense, but these indices can tell us which of competing models fits relatively better. Indices of absolute fit (i.e., as often provided by structural equation modeling programs by default) are only possible for longitudinal data that have balanced occasions, such that there is a finite set of possible per-occasion means to be predicted by the model for the means, and a finite set of per-occasion variances and covariances to be predicted by the model for the variance.

The three indices of fit we will consider are based on the concept of **model likelihood,** which is an overall summary of the likelihood of observing the y_{ti} outcomes given the estimated model parameters. In likelihood estimation, the program tries out different possible values for the model parameters, and based on the model's assumptions (e.g., multivariate normality of all random effects and residuals), calculates the *likelihood* of observing each y_{ti} value given each set of possible values for the model parameters. Although similar to the idea of probability, the term *likelihood* is used instead for continuous outcomes. The estimation process terminates (or *converges*) when the next parameter values it tries no longer substantially increase the model likelihood (as indicating by meeting *convergence criteria,* whose values are set by default in the software). The parameter values that result in the highest likelihood are then provided by the program, along with standard errors (SEs) that describe the precision of each parameter estimate. This process of likelihood estimation will be explained in substantially more detail in chapter 5. What is important to remember for now is that through this process we obtain a single value for the likelihood of the model that we will use as the basis of assessing relative model fit.

However, because calculating the likelihood function involves multiplying together the likelihood values for all possible y_{ti} values, the result becomes numerically unstable (i.e., the consequences of rounding error are very large). So, instead of multiplying the likelihood values together to calculate a likelihood function, the natural logarithm of the likelihood function is calculated instead. The **natural log** (abbreviated as just *log* in this text) is the power to which the constant *e* (where $e = 2.718 \ldots$) must be raised to return a given number. One of its properties is that by calculating the log of the likelihood function, the likelihood values can then be added together rather than multiplied together, solving the numerical instability problem.

As an end-product of estimation, each model gets a **log-likelihood (LL)** value that reflects how well the estimated model parameters fit the data, which serves as the basis for comparing model fit. The LL value gets multiplied by –2 so that the difference between LL values for two competing models becomes approximately **chi-square (χ^2)** distributed with **degrees of freedom (*df*)** equal to the difference in the number of model parameters. A significance test can then be conducted to see which of two models (if nested; see below) fits better. Accordingly, for many programs (e.g., SAS, SPSS), the overall index of model fit is given not as *likelihood,* but as **–2 log likelihood (–2LL)**. Other programs (M*plus*, STATA) provide the LL values instead of the –2LL values (so that you must multiply those LL values by –2 in order to compare models).

The –2LL value, also referred to as **deviance** in multilevel modeling, will serve as our primary index of relative model fit, in which smaller deviance values (i.e., less positive or more negative) indicate better fit. (Please note that we will refer to the –2LL value *itself* as *deviance* here, even though in other contexts the term *deviance* is sometimes used to describe a *difference* in –2LL values between nested models instead.) However, we will also consider two related indices that take into account *model parsimony,* as shown in Equation (3.11):

$$\text{AIC} = -2\text{LL} + 2 * (\#\,\text{parameters})$$
$$\text{BIC} = -2\text{LL} + \log(N) * (\#\,\text{parameters})$$

$$(3.11)$$

in which the **AIC** is the **Akaike Information Criterion** and the **BIC** is the **Bayesian Information Criterion** (also known as the **Schwarz Criterion**). Smaller values indicate a better model for both indices. Often used in this context is the term **parsimony**, which reflects a balance between model complexity and model fit. Although the fit of any model (as indexed by its –2LL value) will be improved by adding more parameters, the improvement should be meaningful in order for the more complex model to be retained. Thus, if two models achieve the same degree of fit, the more parsimonious model with fewer parameters is preferred.

The AIC tries to balance fit (as indexed by the –2LL) with parsimony (via a correction factor of twice the number of model parameters). So, in considering two models with equivalent fit according to the –2LL, the AIC will prefer the more parsimonious model with fewer parameters. The BIC uses a different parsimony correction, the natural log of N persons times the number of model parameters. The BIC is more heavily weighted to favor parsimonious models in larger samples, in which the number of parameters will thus count more. Because of these differences in how they correct for parsimony, the AIC and BIC indices may not always agree on which model is relatively best. Nevertheless, these indices of –2LL (deviance), AIC, and BIC will be used throughout the text to compare relative model fit. However, the rules by which they can be used for model comparisons depend on three key decision points, as described next.

3.B. Three Decision Points in Conducting Model Comparisons

First, are the models to be compared **nested** or **non-nested**? That is, can one model be viewed as a subset of the other, such that we only need to add OR remove parameters to get from one model to the other? For instance, if we wished to compare model A whose parameters included main effects of time and group, to model B whose parameters included main effects of time, group, and gender, then model A is *nested* within model B: we can go from model A to model B by just adding gender (or equivalently, go from model B to model A just by removing gender). In contrast, if we wished to compare model A that included effects of time and group to model C that included effects of time and gender instead, then model A and model C would be non-nested: we can only go from model A to model C by adding gender *and* removing group (or equivalently, go from model C to model A by removing gender *and* adding group).

Whether the difference in fit of a nested model is significant can be assessed via the difference in the model –2LL deviance values, or **–2ΔLL** (in which the Greek letter Δ stands for the difference in the –2LL values, pronounced "delta"). This –2ΔLL **deviance difference test** (known more generally as a **likelihood ratio test**, as will be presented in chapter 5) involves three steps: (1) Calculate the deviance difference as: $-2\Delta LL = -2LL_{fewer}$ minus $-2LL_{more}$. The model with *fewer* parameters will have a higher –2LL than the model with *more* parameters, and so the –2ΔLL will be positive. (2) Calculate the difference in the number of model parameters as: $\Delta df = df_{more}$ minus df_{fewer}, so that the Δdf will also be positive. (3) Compare the –2ΔLL deviance difference to a χ^2-distribution with degrees of freedom = Δdf and your chosen alpha level (e.g., $\alpha < .05$). If the –2ΔLL value exceeds the critical χ^2 value for that df, then the difference in model fit *is* significant: the model with more parameters *fits better* than the model with fewer parameters (or equivalently, the model with fewer parameters *fits worse* than the model with more parameters). If the $-2\Delta LL$ value does *not* exceed the critical χ^2 value for that *df*, then the difference in fit is *not* significant: The model with more parameters *does not fit better* than the model with fewer parameters (or equivalently, the model with fewer parameters *does not fit worse* than the model with more parameters). In summary, when relative fit is indicated by the $-2\Delta LL$ deviance difference, if adding parameters, model fit can only get *better* or *not better*; if removing parameters, model fit can only get *worse* or *not worse*.

When the models to be compared are *non-nested*, however, no direct significance tests of the difference in their fit are available. Instead, we can compare their AIC and BIC values (given by most programs), such that smaller values indicate better fit. We cannot say the model with the smaller AIC and BIC values fits *significantly better*; instead, we can only say that the model with the smaller AIC and/or BIC *is preferred* given that differences in information criteria do not follow a known distribution and thus no cut-off values are available. Furthermore, unlike the $-2LL$ index of fit, the AIC and BIC indices can indicate worse fit even if model parameters are added, which would mean that the improvement in model fit was not enough to offset the cost from reduced parsimony. AIC and BIC can also be used with nested models as additional evidence that the improvement in fit due to adding parameters is *really* worth it (i.e., ideally, the AIC and BIC will also be smaller if the $-2\Delta LL$ test is significant). Thus, the $-2LL$, AIC, and BIC indices may not necessarily agree on whether a new parameter is helpful to the model.

In addition to whether the models to be compared are nested or non-nested, we must also know exactly *how* they differ from each other. As introduced in chapter 1, all statistical models have two sides: the model for the means and the model for the variance. The model for the means describes how fixed effects of predictors create expected outcome values; the model for the variance describes how model residuals are distributed and related across observations. Thus, a second decision point is, do the models to be compared differ with respect to their model for the means, their model for the variance, or on both sides at once? In the previous comparison example, the models differed only in which fixed effects (e.g., time, group, or gender) were included in the model for the means. As an alternative example, the difference between the univariate and multivariate within-person ANOVA models lies entirely in their model for the variance; both have the same saturated model for the means. As we will see in later chapters, the models to be compared could also differ in both their model for the means and for the variance.

Finally, after determining whether the models to be compared are nested or non-nested and exactly how they differ, we must consider which estimator has been used: **maximum likelihood (ML)** or **restricted (residual) maximum likelihood (REML)**. As explained in more detail in chapter 5, ML maximizes the likelihood of the *full data*, treating the fixed effects as *known*, whereas REML maximizes the likelihood of the *residuals* only, treating the fixed effects as *unknown*. These two differences in how the ML and REML likelihoods are computed lead to an important difference in which aspects of model fit will be indexed by their $-2LL$, AIC, and

BIC values. When using ML estimation, the –2LL, AIC, and BIC indices describe the fit of the *entire model*. As a result, models that differ on either side—in their model for the means and/or in their model for the variance—can be compared using the –2LL, AIC, and BIC indices from ML. In contrast, these indices in REML estimation only describe the fit of the *model for the variance,* and thus can only be used to compare models that differ in their random effects or residual variance parameters. This is because REML maximizes the likelihood of the model residuals specifically—and because the residuals from models with different fixed effects are defined differently, the REML likelihoods based on these different definitions of residuals will not be on the same comparable scale. Thus, the –2LL, AIC, and BIC indices from REML *cannot* be used to indicate if adding new fixed effects in the model for the means has improved model fit. This is not a serious limitation to the use of REML estimation, however, because the significance of each fixed effect can each be assessed more directly via its Wald test *p*-value (i.e., based on its estimate/SE, as we have been doing so far) and multiple fixed effects can be tested simultaneously using multivariate Wald tests (as discussed in chapter 5) within ML or REML.

Given that the REML fit indices can only be used to compare different models for the variance, you might be wondering why anyone would ever use REML estimation in the first place. The reason is that ML has a downside—as stated earlier, ML does not take into account the uncertainty from estimating the model fixed effects, whereas REML does. As a result, REML estimates of variances will be correct, but ML estimates of variances will be downwardly biased (too small) by a factor of $(N – k) / N$, where N is the number of persons and k is the number of fixed effects. This bias in the estimated variances will propagate to create SEs for the fixed effects that are too small under ML as well. However, the difference in the variances estimated in ML or REML will diminish as the number of people increases, and so it will be more important if you are analyzing smaller samples to use REML than if you are analyzing larger samples (in which the bias in ML estimates may be negligible). On that note, be careful to check which estimator is being invoked: REML is the default in some programs (SAS, SPSS, and STATA), but not in others (M*plus*). When using REML, the –2LL value will usually be provided as *–2 res log likelihood* (or something similar), rather than *–2 log likelihood* as provided when using ML.

3.C. Comparisons of Analysis of Variance Models for Longitudinal Data

Now that the rules of model comparisons have been introduced, let us formally compare the three potential ANOVA models (between-persons, univariate within-persons, multivariate within-persons) for our six-occasion example response time data. We will also consider the pattern of variance and covariance they predict over time and their resulting implied patterns of longitudinal change. Although the results reported previously were from REML estimation, because these models all contain the same saturated means model, we can compare the fit of their different variance models using their –2LL, AIC, and BIC values, as given for each model in Table 3.2. Furthermore, recall that the actual data (means and their SEs, variances, covariances, and correlations across occasions) provided in the bottom of Table 3.2 can be considered the correct answer for what these models are trying to predict.

Our first alternative, the between-persons (BP) ANOVA model (in the top panel of Table 3.2) includes only a single residual e_{ti} (with constant predicted variance across occasions of $\sigma_e^2 = 236{,}813$) that captures all the deviations between each actual y_{ti} and the $\hat{y}_{ti}$ values predicted by the model for the means. The BP model predicts zero covariance between occasions—that the residuals from the same person will be no more related than those from different persons. Although this independence assumption is unlikely to be met in longitudinal data, it is actually an empirical question that we'll answer shortly. Furthermore, in terms of the model for the means, while the means at each occasion are perfectly reproduced, their SEs are not—the BP model predicts them to be constant across occasions (because the variance over time is predicted to be constant), whereas in the original data the SEs decline steadily across occasions instead (because the variance in the original data declines over time as well). The omnibus F-test for the mean differences across occasions is reported as $F(5, 500) = 4.73$, $p < .001$. But given the misfit of the BP model to the variances and covariances over time, should we believe it?

Our second alternative, the univariate within-persons (WP) ANOVA model (in the middle panel of Table 3.2) includes two residual terms: (1) the random intercept U_{0i} (with a variance of $\tau_{U_0}^2$) to represent deviations from the predicted $\hat{y}_{ti}$ values to each person's mean (then given by $\hat{y}_{ti} + U_{0i}$), and (2) the residual e_{ti} (with a variance still denoted as σ_e^2) that now represents the remaining deviation from $\hat{y}_{ti} + U_{0i}$ to each actual y_{ti}. The total variance is still predicted to be constant across occasions at $\tau_{U_0}^2 + \sigma_e^2 = 202{,}677 + 34{,}316 = 236{,}813$. Furthermore, just as in the BP model, the means at each occasion are perfectly reproduced by the univariate WP model, with predicted SEs that are again constant across occasions (because the variance is still predicted to be constant). The omnibus F-test for the mean differences across occasions from the univariate WP model is $F(5, 500) = 32.85$, $p < .001$. This F-value is much larger than in the BP model because 86% of the original remaining variance was moved into $\tau_{U_0}^2$, resulting in much less within-person error (σ_e^2) with which to test the mean differences across occasions.

This partitioning of the outcome variance into $\tau_{U_0}^2$ and σ_e^2 also serves an important role in modifying the predicted covariance across occasions. Rather than assuming *no* covariance over time as in the BP model, the univariate (*compound symmetry*) WP model assumes a *constant* covariance over time that is due entirely to the random intercept variance $\tau_{U_0}^2 = 202{,}677$ (as seen in the upper off-diagonal in the middle panel of Table 3.2). What this says is that the only reason why the e_{ti} residuals from the same person were correlated originally is because that person was simply higher or lower than the rest of the sample at every occasion. After incorporating each person's mean difference into the model via the U_{0i} random intercept, the e_{ti} residuals are no longer correlated (i.e., independence holds for the e_{ti} residuals only after accounting for U_{0i}). What this implies less directly is that *everyone changes the same*—the only way that people are allowed to differ from each other is in their intercept. As will be discussed in chapter 5, though, if people change differently over time, then the variance over time cannot be constant, and the covariance or correlation over time cannot be constant, either. Thus, to the extent that individual differences in change are observed, the univariate WP model is not likely to describe the data sufficiently (and creating more conservative omnibus tests by adjusting the degrees of freedom based on deviations from sphericity does not solve this fundamental problem).

So which is the better model for these data: the BP model (with σ_e^2 only) or the univariate WP model (with $\tau_{U_0}^2$ and σ_e^2)? Because the BP model is nested within the univariate WP model (i.e., they differ by $\tau_{U_0}^2$), we can use the 3-step likelihood ratio test that was described earlier (i.e., calculate the deviance difference, calculate the df difference, and then compare against the χ^2-distribution). For step 1, the $-2\Delta LL =$ 9155.4 – 8353.4 = 802.0. For step 2, the $\Delta df = 2 - 1 = 1$. For step 3, the critical χ^2 value for df = 1 at $\alpha < .05$ is 3.84, which is much smaller than the obtained $-2\Delta LL =$ 802.0. We can obtain the exact p-value for the obtained $-2\Delta LL = 802.0$ for $df = 1$ by using the χ^2 function in Microsoft Excel (or other programs) as $p = 1.98E^{-176}$ (a number so small it has 176 zeros after the decimal, which we will summarize as $p <$ .001). The likelihood ratio test results would be written like this, with the number of parameters added between models as the df in parentheses: $-2\Delta LL(1) = 802.0$, $p < .001$. Equivalently, it could also be written as: $\Delta \chi_1^2 = 802.1$, $p < .001$, explicitly recognizing that $-2\Delta LL$ value is χ^2-distributed with one degree of freedom here.

One complication that you should be aware of when using $-2\Delta LL$ tests (as will be elaborated in chapter 5) is that the $-2\Delta LL$ is only χ^2-distributed with $df = \Delta df$ for the number of added parameters when those added parameters do not have a boundary. This means that the $-2\Delta LL$ is χ^2-distributed with df = Δdf when adding new fixed effects (i.e., that could be estimated as any positive or negative value), but not when adding a random intercept variance (which can only be 0 or greater and implies a positive average covariance across time). Instead, the $-2\Delta LL$ when adding a random intercept variance is distributed as a mixture of the χ^2-distributions for $df = 0$ (for the missing negative side of the sampling distribution for the random intercept variance) and for df = 1 (for the observed positive side of its sampling distribution).

Several remedies to this problem have been proposed; a simple solution that works when testing a new random intercept variance as we've done so far is to use a one-tailed test (or $\alpha < .10$) instead of a two-tailed test ($\alpha < .05$), which would result in a critical χ^2 value for $df = 1$ of 2.71 instead of 3.84. Unfortunately, this simple solution may not always apply when testing the differences between more complex variance models, as will be discussed in chapter 5. For now, though, we note that the traditional $-2\Delta LL$ test (in which the χ^2 $df = \Delta df$ for the number of added parameters) is overly conservative when used to test new random effects variances. As such, any significant result can be accepted without concern, whereas the influence of using the incorrect χ^2-distribution should be considered in evaluating any nonsignificant results. In our current example, the $-2\Delta LL = 802.0$ would be significant according to either χ^2 critical value (the more conservative but approximately correct critical value of 3.84 from assuming $df = 1$, or the more correct critical value of 2.71 assuming that $df = 1$ only 50% of the time), so the boundary issue is moot. But from this point forward we will explicitly acknowledge the conservative nature of the $-2\Delta LL$ test when relevant (i.e., for the addition of new random effects variances, in which the Δdf is used as the χ^2 *df* naively without regard to the boundary problem) by including a ~ with the *df*. So, for example, our comparison of the BP model (σ_e^2 only) to the univariate WP model ($\tau_{U_0}^2$ and σ_e^2) model would be written as: $-2\Delta LL(\sim 1) = 802.0, p < .001$.

The significant $-2\Delta LL$ value indicates that the univariate WP model (with $\tau_{U_0}^2$ and σ_e^2) fits significantly better than the BP model (with σ_e^2 only), or more directly, that $\tau_{U_0}^2$ is significantly larger than 0. The smaller AIC and BIC values from the univariate WP model also support it as the better model. The *conditional intraclass correlation* we calculated previously as ICC $= \tau_{U_0}^2 / (\tau_{U_0}^2 + \sigma_e^2) = 202{,}677 / (202{,}677 + 34{,}316) = .86$ (as seen in the lower off-diagonal in the middle of Table 3.2) provides an effect size for this comparison. So, we know that after controlling for occasion mean differences, the outcome contains 86% between-person (random intercept) variance, and that .86 is indeed significantly larger than 0. Thus, the univariate WP model results are more trustworthy than the BP model results. But is the univariate WP model (that predicts constant variance and constant covariance across occasions) good enough *per se*?

As a final point of comparison, we turn to the multivariate WP ANOVA model (reported in the bottom of Table 3.2). Unlike the univariate model that tries to predict the variances and covariances using just $\tau_{U_0}^2$ and σ_e^2, the *unstructured* multivariate model estimates each variance and covariance over time separately, and uses those separate estimates in testing fixed effects. This is why the SEs for the means across occasions are exactly right—because the variances and covariances predicted by the multivariate model are exactly right. The omnibus *F*-test for the mean differences across occasions from the multivariate model is $F(5, 100) = 16.72, p < .001$, a more conservative result than the *F*-test returned by the univariate model.

To see if the 21-parameter multivariate model that uses all possible degrees of freedom to reproduce the 21 variances and covariances over time is "better enough" than the two-parameter univariate model that uses just $\tau_{U_0}^2$ and σ_e^2 (which is thus nested within the multivariate model), we can compare their fit via a likelihood ratio test. To conduct our test, we calculate $-2\Delta LL = 8353.4 - 8229.8 = 123.6$ and $\Delta df = 21 - 2 = 19$. In this case, though, we don't need to worry about the validity of the $-2\Delta LL$ test because the extra variances and covariances can be thought of as time-specific deviations from the average variance and covariance over time that were given by the $\tau_{U_0}^2$ and σ_e^2 model, and those deviations are not bounded. The critical χ^2 value for $df = 19$ at $\alpha < .05$ is 30.14, which is smaller than the obtained $-2\Delta LL = 123.6$ (with an exact *p*-value of 2.35E^{-17}). So, the multivariate model fits significantly better than the univariate model, $-2\Delta LL(19) = 123.6, p < .001$, and the smaller AIC and BIC values for the multivariate model concur. Because it will always fit perfectly, the only real question is whether the improvement in fit of the multivariate model is enough to justify its extra parameters (i.e., all possible variances and covariances over time, rather than just $\tau_{U_0}^2$ and σ_e^2). On this basis you might conclude that the multivariate WP ANOVA model should always be used for longitudinal data. Unfortunately, though, it has two data requirements (which are common to the BP and univariate WP ANOVA models as well) that can severely limit its usefulness for longitudinal data in practice.

First, because ANOVA results are obtained via least squares estimation, complete data are required—persons who miss just one of the time conditions will have *all* their observations dropped from analysis (i.e., listwise deletion). Second, all ANOVA models require that time is balanced across persons—that *time* is composed of a set of common, discrete conditions. As discussed in chapter 1, this requirement will not be satisfied when persons are not measured at exactly the same occasions. For instance, in the current example, *occasion* was our index of time under the assumption that it only mattered how many times during the two weeks participants had practiced the test; accordingly, everyone had the same balanced occasions of 1 to 6. In contrast, if we thought the number of days that had passed between occasions was more relevant, then we could have used *day* as our index of time instead, in which each person would have had a distinct set of values corresponding to his or her time observations during the two-week period. But then the multivariate model with a separate mean and variance at each occasion would not have been estimable because no one would have had observations for each of the 14 days.

Although these are serious practical limitations to the use of WP ANOVA models for longitudinal data, the predictions that they make (e.g., *compound symmetry* or *unstructured* models for the variance) will re-appear as special cases of the models to be presented (but in which listwise deletion will no longer be required). So, ANOVA models are still useful to understand before moving forward to more complex longitudinal models in the next chapters.

4. Chapter Summary

This chapter covered three topics with respect to models for the variance in longitudinal data. First, this chapter introduced the need to distinguish variation in a longitudinal outcome that is *between persons* (BP) from variation that is *within persons* (WP) over time. So far, the only kind of BP variation we have examined is in the mean outcome over time, as represented by a random intercept U_{0i} (and whose variance across persons $\tau_{U_0}^2$ is the estimated model parameter rather than the individual random U_{0i} values). The remaining within-person deviations between the actual y_{ti} outcomes and the person's predicted outcomes (from $\hat{y}_{ti} + U_{0i}$) are then represented by the residual e_{ti}, whose variance across occasions and persons is estimated as σ_e^2. Although no additional outcome variance is explained through this process of partitioning the outcome variation into $\tau_{U_0}^2$ and σ_e^2, it does change the standard errors for the fixed effects in the model for the means, as was demonstrated using an example of treatment and control groups measured at pre-test and post-test. Specifically, we saw that effects targeting BP variation will be tested using both $\tau_{U_0}^2$ and σ_e^2, whereas effects targeting WP variation will be tested using only σ_e^2.

Second, this chapter presented analysis of variance (ANOVA) models for longitudinal data in terms of their implied model for the variance (using a working example of improvement in response time over six occasions). The BP (i.e., between-groups, σ_e^2 only) ANOVA model predicts constant variance but no covariance over time whatsoever. In contrast, the WP (repeated measures) ANOVA models do predict some covariance over time, but the univariate and multivariate versions do so differently. The univariate WP ANOVA model predicts constant variance over time as $\tau_{U_0}^2 + \sigma_e^2$ and constant covariance over time as $\tau_{U_0}^2$, a pattern known as *compound symmetry*. Technically, only the less restrictive form of *sphericity* (constant variance and covariance of the pairwise differences between occasions) is required for the univariate WP ANOVA results to be accurate. Although adjustments have been proposed (based on deviations from sphericity) to the degrees of freedom by which the overall mean differences across time are then tested more conservatively, they don't really solve the problem that compound symmetry often doesn't fit longitudinal data. This is because if people change differently over time, then the variances and covariances have to change over time, too. Even in data showing within-person fluctuation, occasions closer together in time may be more related than occasions further apart. In either case, a compound symmetry model may not be adequate for longitudinal data.

As an alternative, the multivariate or *unstructured* WP ANOVA model does not assume compound symmetry, sphericity, or anything else. In fact, it is not really a model at all—it simply estimates all possible variances and covariances over time as is, and so it can never be wrong. However, the multivariate WP model has some practical limitations. It requires a total of $(n*[n + 1]) / 2$ estimated parameters for n occasions. And like the other ANOVA models, it requires complete and balanced data (i.e., all persons are measured at exactly the same occasions), and models mean differences between occasions using $n - 1$ contrasts across the discrete time conditions, rather than trying to summarize the overall trajectory over time.

Finally, this chapter presented some new indices of model fit (–2LL, AIC, and BIC, in which smaller is better for each) and practiced the rules by which they can be used to assess relative model fit. These model fit comparisons will recur frequently in the text, and so it is important to understand three key decision points for their use: whether the models to be compared are nested or non-nested, exactly how they differ (in their model for the means, their model for the variance, or on both sides), and which estimator was used to obtain model parameters—either maximum likelihood (ML) or restricted maximum likelihood (REML). With these answers at hand, the rules for model comparisons can thus be summarized as follows.

First, the difference in fit of nested models can be compared via –2LL likelihood ratio tests, in which the $-2\Delta LL$ is compared to a χ^2-distribution with degrees of freedom equal to the difference in the number of model parameters. Second, the difference in fit of non-nested models cannot be formally tested, but models with smaller AIC and BIC values are "preferred" (and AIC and BIC can also be used to compare the fit of nested models as well). Third, the fit of *all* nested models can be compared using the –2LL, AIC, and BIC indices from ML estimation, but only different models for the variance can be compared with the –2LL, AIC, and BIC indices from REML estimation. This is because REML maximizes the likelihood of the model residuals rather than the likelihood of the full data as in ML, and so the REML indices from models with different fixed effects in the model for the means are not on the same scale (and will thus not be comparable). But given that Wald tests for fixed effects will provide p-values to assess their significance in both ML and REML, this is not really a problem. Lastly, because it assumes fixed effects are unknown, REML estimation provides more accurate estimates of variances than does ML estimation by a factor of $(N - k) / N$, where N is the number of persons and k is the number of fixed effects. Thus, it is especially important to use REML rather than ML in smaller samples, which is why we did so in this chapter.

5. Sample Results Sections

The analyses in this chapter could each be summarized into the beginning of a results section as follows (each of which would then need to be expanded to better capture the substantively meaningful story, theoretical framework, or research hypotheses to be tested).

5.A. Two-Occasion Example

The extent to which a new approach to instruction resulted in greater student learning outcomes ($M = 53.34$, $SD = 6.35$, range = 37.54 to 68.62) between pre-test and post-test was examined in 50 elementary school children, of which 25 were in a control group and 25 were in the treatment group. A univariate repeated measures analysis of variance model in which persons were treated as a random effect was used to distinguish between-person variation in the mean outcome over time from within-person, time-specific variation. Fixed effects for time (coded such that 0 = pre-test, 1 = post-test), for group (coded such that 0 = control, 1 = treatment), and for a time by group interaction were then examined as shown in the second line of Equation (3.7), and standard errors for the additional model simple effects were obtained via separate syntax statements. Results are shown in the fourth set of columns of Table 3.1; differences in the group means over time are shown in the bottom panel of Figure 3.3 (Note: just the mean trajectories for each group would be shown). The expected outcome for the control group at pre-test was $\beta_0 = 49.08$. The positive effect of time was significant in both the control group ($\beta_1 = 5.82$, SE = 0.60, $p < .001$) and in the treatment group (as given by $\beta_1 + \beta_3 = 5.82 + 2.04 = 7.86$, SE = 0.60, $p < .001$). The higher performance for the treatment group than the control group was not significant at pre-test as expected ($\beta_2 = 1.68$, SE = 1.48, $p = .26$), but was significant at post-test (as given by $\beta_2 + \beta_3 = 1.68 + 2.04 = 3.72$, SE = 1.48, $p = .02$). Finally, the larger improvement over time of the treatment group relative to the control group (the time by group interaction) was significant as expected ($\beta_3 = 2.04$, SE = 0.84, $p = .02$).

5.B. Six-Occasion Example

The extent to which response time (RT in milliseconds) to a measure of processing speed ($M = 1,770.70$, $SD = 494.09$, range = 917.67 to 4,159.14) improved over six occasions was examined in a sample of 101 older adults via a saturated means model (i.e., including five contrasts for mean differences in RT among the six occasions). The extent to which the residual variances and covariances of RT across occasions would be adequately described by three variants of ANOVA models was then examined. As expected, substantial covariance among the residuals from the same person was observed (conditional ICC = .86), as indicated by the significantly better fit of a compound symmetry model (with equal variance and equal covariance over time) than a model with no predicted covariance over time, $-2\Delta LL(\sim 1) = 802.0$, $p < .001$. However, the prediction of equal variance and equal covariance did not adequately describe the actual RT data, as indicated by the significantly better fit of a multivariate (unstructured) model in which each variance and covariance was estimated separately, $-2\Delta LL(19) = 123.6$, $p < .001$. Significant mean differences in RT were observed across occasions within the multivariate model, $F(5, 100) = 16.72$, $p < .001$.

Review Questions

1. Why is it necessary to consider what to include in the model for the variance in longitudinal data? Refer in your answer to the statistical and substantive reasons for doing so.
2. What predictions do the three types of analysis of variance (ANOVA) models (between-persons, univariate within-persons, and multivariate within-persons) make about the pattern of means, variances, and covariances over time for a longitudinal outcome? What are the limitations of these ANOVA models for longitudinal data?
3. How are the −2LL, AIC, and BIC indices used to compare relative fit? What kinds of model comparisons can be made using these indices when using ML versus REML?

References

Maxwell, S. E., & Delaney, H. D. (2004). *Designing experiments and analyzing data*. Mahwah, NJ: Erlbaum.

Raudenbush, S. W., & Bryk, A. S. (2002). *Hierarchical linear models: Applications and data analysis methods* (2nd ed.). Thousand Oaks, CA: Sage.

Snijders, T.A.B., & Bosker, R. (2012). *Multilevel analysis* (2nd ed). Thousand Oaks, CA: Sage.

SECTION II

MODELING THE EFFECTS OF TIME

CHAPTER 4

DESCRIBING WITHIN-PERSON FLUCTUATION OVER TIME

The first three chapters in this text were meant to provide the necessary building blocks for conducting longitudinal analysis. These initial building blocks included new concepts, new vocabulary, and an overview of how the longitudinal models to be presented will differ from traditional approaches (chapter 1), followed by a review of how to interpret main effects and interactions among predictors (chapter 2). Recall that while the purpose of the model for the means is to predict the outcome *values,* the model for the variance tries to predict the pattern of *variance and covariance* of the outcome residuals across observations instead. In chapter 3 we examined how and why the model for the variance needs to differ from those of traditional general linear models in order to be suitable for longitudinal data: to separate between-person from within-person variance and to allow residuals from the same person to covary over time, so that the effects of within-person predictors can be tested accurately. Chapter 3 also introduced how to compare the fit of alternative models, which we'll be doing frequently.

The next three chapters will use these building blocks in order to model the effects of time in longitudinal data. All models from this point forward will be estimated using likelihood-based approaches (maximum likelihood or restricted maximum likelihood, as introduced at the end of chapter 3) and thus can include persons with incomplete outcomes. Recall from chapter 1 that different types of within-person variation can be located on a data continuum ranging from *within-person fluctuation* over time (i.e., as is typical for short-term studies) to *within-person change* over time (i.e., as is typical for longer-term studies in which time is meaningfully sampled with the goal of observing systematic change). The models in chapter 4 focus on describing *within-person fluctuation* over time, whereas the models in chapters 5 and 6 will focus on describing *within-person change* instead.

Accordingly, this chapter introduces **alternative covariance structure (ACS) models** for describing the pattern (or *structure*) of the variance and covariance over time in a longitudinal outcome that shows within-person fluctuation over time. We will see that the compound symmetry and unstructured models (found in the repeated measures ANOVA models from chapter 3) will reappear as special cases of the ACS models, and other new variants will be introduced as well. Only the ACS models most commonly used for dependency related to time will be presented in this chapter, although there are similar models for other types of covariance as well (e.g., for spatial dependency in SAS MIXED; see Littell, Milliken, Stroup, Wolfinger, & Schabenberger, 2006, chapter 11). Furthermore, the ACS models presented here will be distinguished into models *without* a random intercept (which are relatively well known) and models *with* a random intercept (which are less well known). An excellent additional treatment of both types of ACS models can also be found in Hedeker and Gibbons (2006, chapters 6–7).

It is important to note before beginning that most of the ACS models to be presented in this chapter require **equal-interval** time observations that are **balanced** across persons—that is, although the data from persons with missing outcomes can still be included, everyone must have the same set of equidistant time observations (the few exceptions to this requirement will be noted). Furthermore, ACS models simply describe the pattern of outcome variance and covariance over time as observed in the data—ACS models say nothing about the potential *reasons* for any non-constant variance and covariance over time. In contrast, we will see in chapter 5 how models that include random slopes for time do not require equal-interval and balanced time observations and explicitly postulate *individual differences in change* as the source behind differing variance and covariance over time instead. But for outcomes in which people show within-person *fluctuation* over time rather than systematic *change* over time, random time slopes for individual differences in change won't be relevant for describing patterns of outcome variance and covariance over time—this is where ACS models are more useful.

1. Unconditional Models for Describing Within-Person Fluctuation Over Time

Before diving into the specifics of alternative covariance structure (ACS) models, it is useful to examine the bigger picture—which data characteristics will be important to consider, and how they can be used to construct an organizational schema by which specific variants of ACS models can then be distinguished. This section covers each of these topics in turn.

1.A. Concerns in Evaluating Alternative Models for the Variance

When systematic change over time is not expected, the ACS models to be presented for such outcomes showing only within-person fluctuation will generally not need any fixed effects of time in their model for the means. However, fixed effects of time could be added and tested as needed to account for any unexpected mean differences across occasions (i.e., as in the saturated means model in chapter 3). Everything that follows in this chapter will focus exclusively on the *model for the variance*—what parameters are needed to describe the pattern or structure of the outcome variance and covariance over time as parsimoniously but accurately as possible (i.e., using as few parameters as needed to achieve good fit to the data).

In selecting an ACS model for the variance for a longitudinal outcome, we will need to consider two main issues. First, is the variance across persons the same or different across occasions (i.e., **homogeneous variance** or **heterogeneous variance**, respectively)? Second, although we expect the model residuals from the same person to be related across occasions (i.e., to covary or show *covariance*), are these covariances the same or different over time? So far we have seen two limited choices through repeated measures ANOVA models—either the outcome variance and covariance is the same over time (*univariate* or *compound symmetry* model), or the outcome variances and covariances all differ over time (*multivariate* or *unstructured* model). Although the ACS models presented in this chapter only permit homogeneous or heterogeneous variance over time (i.e., all the same or all different), they do offer more flexibility in the patterns of covariance they predict over time. The random slopes models presented in chapters 5 and 6 will be even more flexible in the patterns of non-constant variance and covariance they can predict.

But why should we care? Even if the model for the variance is not of theoretical interest, it is nevertheless an important concern when modeling longitudinal data for two reasons. First, as was shown in chapter 3, if the variances and covariances predicted by the model over time do not adequately reflect those in the actual data, then the standard errors and p-values for the fixed effects of the model predictors may be incorrect—they can be too conservative or too liberal, depending on how the model for the variance is misspecified. This is why we will evaluate both the model for the means and the model for the variance with respect to time *before* testing the effects of other predictors—so that they will be tested as accurately as possible. However, the model for the variance should be re-evaluated after examining all predictors to ensure it is still adequate (and perhaps it can then be simplified without compromising the accuracy of the SEs and p-values for the fixed effects of predictors that were retained).

Second, understanding the structure of outcome variance and covariance over time can be informative for subsequent model building. For instance, consider an intraclass correlation (from the compound symmetry model in chapter 3) that reflects how much outcome variance is due to between-person mean (intercept) differences rather than due to within-person variation over time. If most of an outcome's variance is between persons, then stable person characteristics will be more useful for explaining its variance than will person characteristics that change over time. Furthermore, if a compound symmetry model (that predicts equal variance and covariance over time) does not adequately describe the outcome, this may indicate that people differ from each other in more ways than just in their intercept—they may also differ from each other in their rates of change or in their effects of other time-varying predictors. Thus, considering which parameters are necessary to build a suitable model for the variance and covariance over time may be informative for the more substantive model building process that follows.

Finally, it is important to note that the phrase *over time* will be used frequently with the implicit assumption that you have already chosen what *time* should be.

As also elaborated in chapters 5 and 10, there are sometimes multiple metrics by which to organize fluctuation or change over time. For instance, in this chapter's example study, data on positive mood were collected daily from persons who began the study on different days of the week. Thus, at least two different metrics of time could be used. First, the data from different persons could be organized by *day of study*—this would make sense if the number of times someone has been assessed is most likely to be most relevant for understanding the data. Alternatively, the data from different persons could be organized by *day of the week*—this would make sense if the outcome variation was more likely to be systematic to chronological time instead (e.g., if variability in positive mood differs between weekends and weekdays). These kinds of theoretical expectations may not provide a single right answer for what *time* should be. Fortunately, the utility of these alternative metrics of time (and of others as well) can be compared empirically, such that the model with the smaller AIC and BIC values (from ML estimation if the models differ on both sides, as introduced in chapter 3) would be preferred. In sum, because the ACS models for describing within-person fluctuation over time that follow are agnostic with respect to what *time* should be, the onus is on you to consider which metric of time for organizing data from different persons that will be most theoretically appropriate and empirically informed.

1.B. Two Families of Models for Describing Within-Person Fluctuation

The ACS models presented in this chapter form a continuum ranging from the most parsimonious (but likely worst-fitting) to the least parsimonious (but likely best-fitting). Figure 4.1 depicts the dimensions along which ACS models can be organized, and will be referred to throughout the chapter as we examine each specific model. As seen via the two halves of its horizontal axis, the variances in each model will be either homogeneous or heterogeneous across time. As seen within each half of Figure 4.1, there are two families of models, labeled as **R-only models** or as **G and R combined models** that differ by whether a random intercept is *not* included or *is* included, respectively. These new organizing names correspond to the output in software for mixed models (i.e., programs for estimating models that may include random effects).

As introduced in chapter 3, one way by which the residuals from the same person are allowed to covary is through distinguishing variance that is between persons (BP) from variance which is within persons (WP), such that the expected covariance between occasions is then due to the BP variance (i.e., due to the random intercept variance, as seen in chapter 3). Accordingly, the parameters from models that take this BP–WP variance partitioning approach will be shown using three different matrices in the output, and so you'll have to learn the names of these three matrices in order to link the ACS models to an actual data analysis. Each is a *square* matrix (i.e., it has the same number of rows as columns) and is *symmetric* as well (i.e., the terms above and below the diagonal are reflective; for example, the

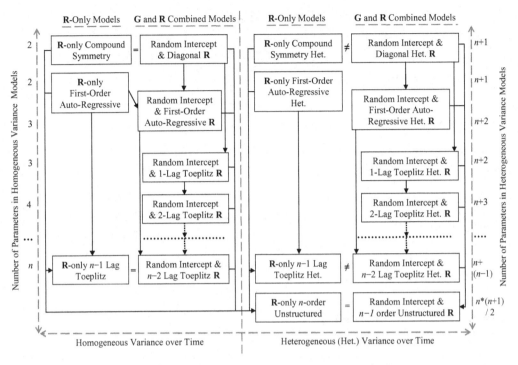

Figure 4.1 Organization of alternative covariance structure models. The arrows depict the direction of nesting, and *n* is the number of occasions per person.

matrix *element* or number in the second row, first column [2,1] will be the same as the element in the first row, second column [1,2]). To distinguish them as matrices, the names of matrices will always be bolded in this text. I promise you won't need to know matrix algebra to follow this chapter, as Figure 4.2 shows (for only four occasions to save space) exactly how the parameters of each ACS model combine to create the predicted outcome variances and covariances. These predictions will also be illustrated more concretely in the chapter's example (and these matrices will re-appear in chapter 5).

So for now, your goal is simply to learn the names of the three new matrices used within ACS models for constructing the predicted outcome variance and covariance over time. Please note that each of these matrices is specified per individual, and in this chapter will be the same across individuals because we are using balanced data for the example. But as we'll see in more detail in chapter 5, the matrices for everyone in a sample will eventually be combined into a more complex version of each. To begin, let's examine the kind of variance and covariance that each matrix contains and how they work together conceptually in the model for the variance.

First, the **G matrix** holds any BP variances and covariances. So far, the only kind of BP variance we have seen is variance across persons is the U_{0i} random intercepts $(\tau_{U_0}^2)$ and so the **G** matrix will have just 1 row and 1 column (i.e., it will be a 1x1

R-only Models

n-order Unstructured (UNn):

parameters = $n*(n + 1) / 2$
total variances and covariances

$$\begin{bmatrix} \sigma_{T1}^2 & \sigma_{T12} & \sigma_{T13} & \sigma_{T14} \\ \sigma_{T21} & \sigma_{T2}^2 & \sigma_{T23} & \sigma_{T24} \\ \sigma_{T31} & \sigma_{T32} & \sigma_{T3}^2 & \sigma_{T34} \\ \sigma_{T41} & \sigma_{T42} & \sigma_{T43} & \sigma_{T4}^2 \end{bmatrix}$$

Compound Symmetry (CS):

parameters = 1 covariance ($\tau_{U_0}^2$, also known as CS) and 1 residual variance (σ_e^2)

$$\begin{bmatrix} \tau_{U_0}^2 + \sigma_e^2 & \tau_{U_0}^2 & \tau_{U_0}^2 & \tau_{U_0}^2 \\ \tau_{U_0}^2 & \tau_{U_0}^2 + \sigma_e^2 & \tau_{U_0}^2 & \tau_{U_0}^2 \\ \tau_{U_0}^2 & \tau_{U_0}^2 & \tau_{U_0}^2 + \sigma_e^2 & \tau_{U_0}^2 \\ \tau_{U_0}^2 & \tau_{U_0}^2 & \tau_{U_0}^2 & \tau_{U_0}^2 + \sigma_e^2 \end{bmatrix}$$

Compound Symmetry Heterogeneous (CSH):

parameters = n total variances (σ_{Tn}^2), 1 total correlation (CSH)

$$\begin{bmatrix} \sigma_{T1}^2 & CSH\sigma_{T1}\sigma_{T2} & CSH\sigma_{T1}\sigma_{T3} & CSH\sigma_{T1}\sigma_{T4} \\ CSH\sigma_{T2}\sigma_{T1} & \sigma_{T2}^2 & CSH\sigma_{T2}\sigma_{T3} & CSH\sigma_{T2}\sigma_{T4} \\ CSH\sigma_{T3}\sigma_{T1} & CSH\sigma_{T3}\sigma_{T2} & \sigma_{T3}^2 & CSH\sigma_{T3}\sigma_{T4} \\ CSH\sigma_{T4}\sigma_{T1} & CSH\sigma_{T4}\sigma_{T2} & CSH\sigma_{T4}\sigma_{T3} & \sigma_{T4}^2 \end{bmatrix}$$

Auto-Regressive (AR1):

parameters = 1 total variance (σ_T^2), 1 total auto-correlation (r_T)

$$\begin{bmatrix} \sigma_T^2 & r_T^1\sigma_T^2 & r_T^2\sigma_T^2 & r_T^3\sigma_T^2 \\ r_T^1\sigma_T^2 & \sigma_T^2 & r_T^1\sigma_T^2 & r_T^2\sigma_T^2 \\ r_T^2\sigma_T^2 & r_T^1\sigma_T^2 & \sigma_T^2 & r_T^1\sigma_T^2 \\ r_T^3\sigma_T^2 & r_T^2\sigma_T^2 & r_T^1\sigma_T^2 & \sigma_T^2 \end{bmatrix}$$

Auto-Regressive Heterogeneous (ARH1):

parameters = n total variances (σ_{Tn}^2), 1 total auto-correlation (r_T)

$$\begin{bmatrix} \sigma_{T1}^2 & r_T^1\sigma_{T1}\sigma_{T2} & r_T^2\sigma_{T1}\sigma_{T3} & r_T^3\sigma_{T1}\sigma_{T4} \\ r_T^1\sigma_{T2}\sigma_{T1} & \sigma_{T2}^2 & r_T^1\sigma_{T2}\sigma_{T3} & r_T^2\sigma_{T2}\sigma_{T4} \\ r_T^2\sigma_{T3}\sigma_{T1} & r_T^1\sigma_{T3}\sigma_{T2} & \sigma_{T3}^2 & r_T^1\sigma_{T3}\sigma_{T4} \\ r_T^3\sigma_{T4}\sigma_{T1} & r_T^2\sigma_{T4}\sigma_{T2} & r_T^1\sigma_{T4}\sigma_{T3} & \sigma_{T4}^2 \end{bmatrix}$$

---

n-order Toeplitz (TOEPn):

parameters = 1 total variance (σ_T^2), $n - 1$ banded total covariances (c_{Tb})

$$\begin{bmatrix} \sigma_T^2 & & & \\ c_{T1} & \sigma_T^2 & & \\ c_{T2} & c_{T1} & \sigma_T^2 & \\ c_{T3} & c_{T2} & c_{T1} & \sigma_T^2 \end{bmatrix}$$

---

n-order Toeplitz Heterogeneous (TOEPHn):

parameters = n total variances (σ_{Tn}^2), $n - 1$ banded total correlations (r_{Tb})

$$\begin{bmatrix} \sigma_{T1}^2 & r_{T1}\sigma_{T1}\sigma_{T2} & r_{T2}\sigma_{T1}\sigma_{T3} & r_{T3}\sigma_{T1}\sigma_{T4} \\ r_{T1}\sigma_{T2}\sigma_{T1} & \sigma_{T2}^2 & r_{T1}\sigma_{T2}\sigma_{T3} & r_{T2}\sigma_{T2}\sigma_{T4} \\ r_{T2}\sigma_{T3}\sigma_{T1} & r_{T1}\sigma_{T3}\sigma_{T2} & \sigma_{T3}^2 & r_{T1}\sigma_{T3}\sigma_{T4} \\ r_{T3}\sigma_{T4}\sigma_{T1} & r_{T2}\sigma_{T4}\sigma_{T2} & r_{T1}\sigma_{T4}\sigma_{T3} & \sigma_{T4}^2 \end{bmatrix}$$

G and R Combined Models

Random Intercept Variance in G and $n - 1$ order Unstructured R (RI and UN$n - 1$):

parameters = $\tau_{U_0}^2$ in **G**; $[n*(n + 1) / 2] - 1$ residual variances and covariances in **R**

$$\mathbf{V} = \mathbf{Z} * \mathbf{G} * \mathbf{Z}^T + \mathbf{R} = \mathbf{V}$$

$$\mathbf{V} = \begin{bmatrix} 1 \\ 1 \\ 1 \\ 1 \end{bmatrix} \begin{bmatrix} \tau_{U_0}^2 \end{bmatrix} \begin{bmatrix} 1 & 1 & 1 & 1 \end{bmatrix} + \begin{bmatrix} \sigma_{e1}^2 & \sigma_{e12} & \sigma_{e13} & 0 \\ \sigma_{e21} & \sigma_{e2}^2 & \sigma_{e23} & \sigma_{e24} \\ \sigma_{e31} & \sigma_{e32} & \sigma_{e3}^2 & \sigma_{e34} \\ 0 & \sigma_{e42} & \sigma_{e43} & \sigma_{e4}^2 \end{bmatrix} = \begin{bmatrix} \tau_{U_0}^2 + \sigma_{e1}^2 & \tau_{U_0}^2 + \sigma_{e12} & \tau_{U_0}^2 + \sigma_{e13} & \tau_{U_0}^2 \\ \tau_{U_0}^2 + \sigma_{e21} & \tau_{U_0}^2 + \sigma_{e2}^2 & \tau_{U_0}^2 + \sigma_{e23} & \tau_{U_0}^2 + \sigma_{e24} \\ \tau_{U_0}^2 + \sigma_{e31} & \tau_{U_0}^2 + \sigma_{e32} & \tau_{U_0}^2 + \sigma_{e3}^2 & \tau_{U_0}^2 + \sigma_{e34} \\ \tau_{U_0}^2 & \tau_{U_0}^2 + \sigma_{e42} & \tau_{U_0}^2 + \sigma_{e43} & \tau_{U_0}^2 + \sigma_{e4}^2 \end{bmatrix}$$

Figure 4.2 Parameterization of the alternative covariance structure models, in which T refers to total variance, e refers to residual variance, and n is the number of occasions per person ($n = 4$ here).

Random Intercept Variance in G and Diagonal R (RI and DIAG):

parameters $= \tau_{U_0}^2$ in **G**; 1 residual variance σ_e^2, 0 residual covariances in **R**

$$\mathbf{V} = \mathbf{Z} * \mathbf{G} * \mathbf{Z}^T + \mathbf{R} = \mathbf{V}$$

$$\mathbf{V} = \begin{bmatrix} 1 \\ 1 \\ 1 \\ 1 \end{bmatrix} \begin{bmatrix} \tau_{U_0}^2 \end{bmatrix} \begin{bmatrix} 1 & 1 & 1 & 1 \end{bmatrix} + \begin{bmatrix} \sigma_e^2 & 0 & 0 & 0 \\ 0 & \sigma_e^2 & 0 & 0 \\ 0 & 0 & \sigma_e^2 & 0 \\ 0 & 0 & 0 & \sigma_e^2 \end{bmatrix} = \begin{bmatrix} \tau_{U_0}^2 + \sigma_e^2 & \tau_{U_0}^2 & \tau_{U_0}^2 & \tau_{U_0}^2 \\ \tau_{U_0}^2 & \tau_{U_0}^2 + \sigma_e^2 & \tau_{U_0}^2 & \tau_{U_0}^2 \\ \tau_{U_0}^2 & \tau_{U_0}^2 & \tau_{U_0}^2 + \sigma_e^2 & \tau_{U_0}^2 \\ \tau_{U_0}^2 & \tau_{U_0}^2 & \tau_{U_0}^2 & \tau_{U_0}^2 + \sigma_e^2 \end{bmatrix}$$

Random Intercept Variance in G and Diagonal Heterogeneous R (RI and DIAGH):

parameters $= \tau_{U_0}^2$ in **G**; n residual variances (σ_{en}^2), 0 residual covariances in **R**

$$\mathbf{V} = \mathbf{Z} * \mathbf{G} * \mathbf{Z}^T + \mathbf{R} = \mathbf{V}$$

$$\mathbf{V} = \begin{bmatrix} 1 \\ 1 \\ 1 \\ 1 \end{bmatrix} \begin{bmatrix} \tau_{U_0}^2 \end{bmatrix} \begin{bmatrix} 1 & 1 & 1 & 1 \end{bmatrix} + \begin{bmatrix} \sigma_{e1}^2 & 0 & 0 & 0 \\ 0 & \sigma_{e2}^2 & 0 & 0 \\ 0 & 0 & \sigma_{e3}^2 & 0 \\ 0 & 0 & 0 & \sigma_{e4}^2 \end{bmatrix} = \begin{bmatrix} \tau_{U_0}^2 + \sigma_{e1}^2 & \tau_{U_0}^2 & \tau_{U_0}^2 & \tau_{U_0}^2 \\ \tau_{U_0}^2 & \tau_{U_0}^2 + \sigma_{e2}^2 & \tau_{U_0}^2 & \tau_{U_0}^2 \\ \tau_{U_0}^2 & \tau_{U_0}^2 & \tau_{U_0}^2 + \sigma_{e3}^2 & \tau_{U_0}^2 \\ \tau_{U_0}^2 & \tau_{U_0}^2 & \tau_{U_0}^2 & \tau_{U_0}^2 + \sigma_{e4}^2 \end{bmatrix}$$

Random Intercept Variance in G and Auto-Regressive R (RI and AR1):

parameters $= \tau_{U_0}^2$ in **G**; 1 residual variance σ_e^2, 1 residual auto-correlation r_e in **R**

$$\mathbf{V} = \mathbf{Z} * \mathbf{G} * \mathbf{Z}^T + \mathbf{R} = \mathbf{V}$$

$$\mathbf{V} = \begin{bmatrix} 1 \\ 1 \\ 1 \\ 1 \end{bmatrix} \begin{bmatrix} \tau_{U_0}^2 \end{bmatrix} \begin{bmatrix} 1 & 1 & 1 & 1 \end{bmatrix} + \begin{bmatrix} \sigma_e^2 & r_e^1\sigma_e^2 & r_e^2\sigma_e^2 & r_e^3\sigma_e^2 \\ r_e^1\sigma_e^2 & \sigma_e^2 & r_e^1\sigma_e^2 & r_e^2\sigma_e^2 \\ r_e^2\sigma_e^2 & r_e^1\sigma_e^2 & \sigma_e^2 & r_e^1\sigma_e^2 \\ r_e^3\sigma_e^2 & r_e^2\sigma_e^2 & r_e^1\sigma_e^2 & \sigma_e^2 \end{bmatrix} = \begin{bmatrix} \tau_{U_0}^2 + \sigma_e^2 & \tau_{U_0}^2 + r_e^1\sigma_e^2 & \tau_{U_0}^2 + r_e^2\sigma_e^2 & \tau_{U_0}^2 + r_e^3\sigma_e^2 \\ \tau_{U_0}^2 + r_e^1\sigma_e^2 & \tau_{U_0}^2 + \sigma_e^2 & \tau_{U_0}^2 + r_e^1\sigma_e^2 & \tau_{U_0}^2 + r_e^2\sigma_e^2 \\ \tau_{U_0}^2 + r_e^2\sigma_e^2 & \tau_{U_0}^2 + r_e^1\sigma_e^2 & \tau_{U_0}^2 + \sigma_e^2 & \tau_{U_0}^2 + r_e^1\sigma_e^2 \\ \tau_{U_0}^2 + r_e^3\sigma_e^2 & \tau_{U_0}^2 + r_e^2\sigma_e^2 & \tau_{U_0}^2 + r_e^1\sigma_e^2 & \tau_{U_0}^2 + \sigma_e^2 \end{bmatrix}$$

Random Intercept Variance in G and Auto-Regressive Heterogeneous R (RI and ARH1):

parameters $= \tau_{U_0}^2$ in **G**; n residual variances (σ_{en}^2), 1 residual auto-correlation r_e in **R**

$$\mathbf{V} = \mathbf{Z} * \mathbf{G} * \mathbf{Z}^T + \mathbf{R} = \mathbf{V}$$

$$\mathbf{V} = \begin{bmatrix} 1 \\ 1 \\ 1 \\ 1 \end{bmatrix} \begin{bmatrix} \tau_{U_0}^2 \end{bmatrix} \begin{bmatrix} 1 & 1 & 1 & 1 \end{bmatrix} + \begin{bmatrix} \sigma_{e1}^2 & r_e^1\sigma_{e1}\sigma_{e2} & r_e^2\sigma_{e1}\sigma_{e3} & r_e^3\sigma_{e1}\sigma_{e4} \\ r_e^1\sigma_{e2}\sigma_{e1} & \sigma_{e2}^2 & r_e^1\sigma_{e2}\sigma_{e3} & r_e^2\sigma_{e2}\sigma_{e4} \\ r_e^2\sigma_{e3}\sigma_{e1} & r_e^1\sigma_{e3}\sigma_{e2} & \sigma_{e3}^2 & r_e^1\sigma_{e3}\sigma_{e4} \\ r_e^3\sigma_{e4}\sigma_{e1} & r_e^2\sigma_{e4}\sigma_{e2} & r_e^1\sigma_{e4}\sigma_{e3} & \sigma_{e4}^2 \end{bmatrix}$$

$$= \begin{bmatrix} \tau_{U_0}^2 + \sigma_{e1}^2 & \tau_{U_0}^2 + r_e^1\sigma_{e1}\sigma_{e2} & \tau_{U_0}^2 + r_e^2\sigma_{e1}\sigma_{e3} & \tau_{U_0}^2 + r_e^3\sigma_{e1}\sigma_{e4} \\ \tau_{U_0}^2 + r_e^1\sigma_{e2}\sigma_{e1} & \tau_{U_0}^2 + \sigma_{e2}^2 & \tau_{U_0}^2 + r_e^1\sigma_{e2}\sigma_{e3} & \tau_{U_0}^2 + r_e^2\sigma_{e2}\sigma_{e4} \\ \tau_{U_0}^2 + r_e^2\sigma_{e3}\sigma_{e1} & \tau_{U_0}^2 + r_e^1\sigma_{e3}\sigma_{e2} & \tau_{U_0}^2 + \sigma_{e3}^2 & \tau_{U_0}^2 + r_e^1\sigma_{e3}\sigma_{e4} \\ \tau_{U_0}^2 + r_e^3\sigma_{e4}\sigma_{e1} & \tau_{U_0}^2 + r_e^2\sigma_{e4}\sigma_{e2} & \tau_{U_0}^2 + r_e^1\sigma_{e4}\sigma_{e3} & \tau_{U_0}^2 + \sigma_{e4}^2 \end{bmatrix}$$

Random Intercept Variance in G and 1-Lag Toeplitz R (RI and TOEP2):

parameters $= \tau_{U_0}^2$ in **G**; 1 residual variance σ_e^2, 1 banded residual covariance c_{e1} in **R**

$$\mathbf{V} = \mathbf{Z} * \mathbf{G} * \mathbf{Z}^T + \mathbf{R} = \mathbf{V}$$

$$\mathbf{V} = \begin{bmatrix} 1 \\ 1 \\ 1 \\ 1 \end{bmatrix} \begin{bmatrix} \tau_{U_0}^2 \end{bmatrix} \begin{bmatrix} 1 & 1 & 1 & 1 \end{bmatrix} + \begin{bmatrix} \sigma_e^2 & c_{e1} & 0 & 0 \\ c_{e1} & \sigma_e^2 & c_{e1} & 0 \\ 0 & c_{e1} & \sigma_e^2 & c_{e1} \\ 0 & 0 & c_{e1} & \sigma_e^2 \end{bmatrix} = \begin{bmatrix} \tau_{U_0}^2 + \sigma_e^2 & \tau_{U_0}^2 + c_{e1} & \tau_{U_0}^2 & \tau_{U_0}^2 \\ \tau_{U_0}^2 + c_{e1} & \tau_{U_0}^2 + \sigma_e^2 & \tau_{U_0}^2 + c_{e1} & \tau_{U_0}^2 \\ \tau_{U_0}^2 & \tau_{U_0}^2 + c_{e1} & \tau_{U_0}^2 + \sigma_e^2 & \tau_{U_0}^2 + c_{e1} \\ \tau_{U_0}^2 & \tau_{U_0}^2 & \tau_{U_0}^2 + c_{e1} & \tau_{U_0}^2 + \sigma_e^2 \end{bmatrix}$$

Random Intercept Variance in G and 1-Lag Toeplitz Heterogeneous R (RI and TOEPH2):

parameters $= \tau_{U_0}^2$ in **G**; n residual variances (σ_{en}^2), 1 banded residual correlation r_{e1} in **R**

$$\mathbf{V} = \mathbf{Z} * \mathbf{G} * \mathbf{Z}^T + \mathbf{R} = \mathbf{V}$$

$$\mathbf{V} = \begin{bmatrix} 1 \\ 1 \\ 1 \\ 1 \end{bmatrix} \begin{bmatrix} \tau_{U_0}^2 \end{bmatrix} \begin{bmatrix} 1 & 1 & 1 & 1 \end{bmatrix} + \begin{bmatrix} \sigma_{e1}^2 & r_{e1}\sigma_{e1}\sigma_{e2} & 0 & 0 \\ r_{e1}\sigma_{e2}\sigma_{e1} & \sigma_{e2}^2 & r_{e1}\sigma_{e2}\sigma_{e3} & 0 \\ 0 & r_{e1}\sigma_{e3}\sigma_{e2} & \sigma_{e3}^2 & r_{e1}\sigma_{e3}\sigma_{e4} \\ 0 & 0 & r_{e1}\sigma_{e4}\sigma_{e3} & \sigma_{e4}^2 \end{bmatrix} = \begin{bmatrix} \tau_{U_0}^2 + \sigma_{e1}^2 & \tau_{U_0}^2 + r_{e1}\sigma_{e1}\sigma_{e2} & \tau_{U_0}^2 & \tau_{U_0}^2 \\ \tau_{U_0}^2 + r_{e1}\sigma_{e2}\sigma_{e1} & \tau_{U_0}^2 + \sigma_{e2}^2 & \tau_{U_0}^2 + r_{e1}\sigma_{e2}\sigma_{e3} & \tau_{U_0}^2 \\ \tau_{U_0}^2 & \tau_{U_0}^2 + r_{e1}\sigma_{e3}\sigma_{e2} & \tau_{U_0}^2 + \sigma_{e3}^2 & \tau_{U_0}^2 + r_{e1}\sigma_{e3}\sigma_{e4} \\ \tau_{U_0}^2 & \tau_{U_0}^2 & \tau_{U_0}^2 + r_{e1}\sigma_{e4}\sigma_{e3} & \tau_{U_0}^2 + \sigma_{e4}^2 \end{bmatrix}$$

Figure 4.2 (Continued)

Random Intercept Variance in **G** and $n-1$ order Toeplitz **R** (RI and TOEP$n-1$):
parameters = $\tau_{U_0}^2$ in **G**; 1 residual variance σ_e^2, $n-2$ banded residual covariances (c_{eb}) in **R**

$$\mathbf{V} = \mathbf{Z} * \mathbf{G} * \mathbf{Z}^T \; + \; \mathbf{R} \; = \; \mathbf{V}$$

$$
\mathbf{V} = \begin{bmatrix} 1 \\ 1 \\ 1 \\ 1 \end{bmatrix} \left[\tau_{U_0}^2 \right] \begin{bmatrix} 1 & 1 & 1 & 1 \end{bmatrix} +
\begin{bmatrix}
\sigma_e^2 & c_{e1} & c_{e2} & 0 \\
c_{e1} & \sigma_e^2 & c_{e1} & c_{e2} \\
c_{e2} & c_{e1} & \sigma_e^2 & c_{e1} \\
0 & c_{e2} & c_{e1} & \sigma_e^2
\end{bmatrix}
=
\begin{bmatrix}
\tau_{U_0}^2 + \sigma_e^2 & \tau_{U_0}^2 + c_{e1} & \tau_{U_0}^2 + c_{e2} & \tau_{U_0}^2 \\
\tau_{U_0}^2 + c_{e1} & \tau_{U_0}^2 + \sigma_e^2 & \tau_{U_0}^2 + c_{e1} & \tau_{U_0}^2 + c_{e2} \\
\tau_{U_0}^2 + c_{e2} & \tau_{U_0}^2 + c_{e1} & \tau_{U_0}^2 + \sigma_e^2 & \tau_{U_0}^2 + c_{e1} \\
\tau_{U_0}^2 & \tau_{U_0}^2 + c_{e2} & \tau_{U_0}^2 + c_{e1} & \tau_{U_0}^2 + \sigma_e^2
\end{bmatrix}
$$

Random Intercept Variance in **G** and $n-1$ order Toeplitz Heterogeneous **R** (RI and TOEPH $n-1$):
parameters = $\tau_{U_0}^2$ in **G**; n residual variances (σ_{en}^2), $n-2$ banded residual correlations (r_{eb}) in **R**

$$\mathbf{V} = \mathbf{Z} * \mathbf{G} * \mathbf{Z}^T \; + \; \mathbf{R} \; = \; \mathbf{V}$$

$$
\mathbf{V} = \begin{bmatrix} 1 \\ 1 \\ 1 \\ 1 \end{bmatrix} \left[\tau_{U_0}^2 \right] \begin{bmatrix} 1 & 1 & 1 & 1 \end{bmatrix} +
\begin{bmatrix}
\sigma_{e1}^2 & r_{e1}\sigma_{e1}\sigma_{e2} & r_{e2}\sigma_{e1}\sigma_{e3} & 0 \\
r_{e1}\sigma_{e2}\sigma_{e1} & \sigma_{e2}^2 & r_{e1}\sigma_{e2}\sigma_{e3} & r_{e2}\sigma_{e2}\sigma_{e4} \\
r_{e2}\sigma_{e3}\sigma_{e1} & r_{e1}\sigma_{e3}\sigma_{e2} & \sigma_{e3}^2 & r_{e1}\sigma_{e3}\sigma_{e4} \\
0 & r_{e2}\sigma_{e4}\sigma_{e2} & r_{e1}\sigma_{e4}\sigma_{e3} & \sigma_{e4}^2
\end{bmatrix}
=
\begin{bmatrix}
\tau_{U_0}^2 + \sigma_{e1}^2 & \tau_{U_0}^2 + r_{e1}\sigma_{e1}\sigma_{e2} & \tau_{U_0}^2 + r_{e2}\sigma_{e1}\sigma_{e3} & \tau_{U_0}^2 \\
\tau_{U_0}^2 + r_{e1}\sigma_{e2}\sigma_{e1} & \tau_{U_0}^2 + \sigma_{e2}^2 & \tau_{U_0}^2 + r_{e1}\sigma_{e2}\sigma_{e3} & \tau_{U_0}^2 + r_{e2}\sigma_{e2}\sigma_{e4} \\
\tau_{U_0}^2 + r_{e2}\sigma_{e3}\sigma_{e1} & \tau_{U_0}^2 + r_{e1}\sigma_{e3}\sigma_{e2} & \tau_{U_0}^2 + \sigma_{e3}^2 & \tau_{U_0}^2 + r_{e1}\sigma_{e3}\sigma_{e4} \\
\tau_{U_0}^2 & \tau_{U_0}^2 + r_{e2}\sigma_{e4}\sigma_{e2} & \tau_{U_0}^2 + r_{e1}\sigma_{e4}\sigma_{e3} & \tau_{U_0}^2 + \sigma_{e4}^2
\end{bmatrix}
$$

Figure 4.2 (Continued)

scalar value for $\tau_{U_0}^2$). Second, after estimating $\tau_{U_0}^2$ in the **G** matrix, the **R matrix** holds the remaining WP variances and covariances of the e_{ti} residuals over time. The **R** matrix will have n by n rows and columns (where n is the number of occasions per person). In mixed model programs like SAS or SPSS MIXED, the form of the **G** and **R** matrices are specified by the RANDOM and REPEATED commands, respectively. Third, the **V matrix** holds the total predicted variation and covariation over time resulting from the **G** and **R** matrices. The **V** matrix will have n by n rows and columns and can be requested on the RANDOM command in SAS MIXED. Given that they are of different dimensions, how the **G** and **R** matrices get combined to create the **V** matrix for the total predicted variance and covariance over time will be explained when we examine these models.

In estimating longitudinal models within mixed model programs, the **R** matrix is required (because all models have at least a residual variance), but the **G** matrix is not required because the random intercept variance is optional. When the **G** matrix is omitted, the **R** matrix *becomes* the **V** matrix for the total predicted variance and covariance over time directly. So, whether or not a random intercept variance is included in the **G** matrix is the basis for the two families of ACS models we will examine. First, R-only models will not distinguish BP from WP variance through the **G** and **R** matrices; instead they try to predict the *total* variance and covariance directly in the **R** matrix (so that **R = V**). Second, **G** and **R** combined models will control for BP random intercept variance in the **G** matrix, with the result that the **R** matrix then predicts just the *WP residual* (not *total*) variance and covariance over time. The **G** and **R** combined models are especially useful given that they can not only reproduce some of the **R**-only models, but they can also potentially offer more parsimony in modeling the covariance over time, as we'll see later.

1.C. Example Data

This chapter presents each ACS model in the context of a working example of simulated data based on the *National Study of Daily Experience* (NSDE, as described in chapter 1). Our current sample includes 200 adults responding once daily, for seven consecutive days, to six items inquiring how much of that day they experienced aspects of positive mood (i.e., *cheerful, in good spirits, extremely happy, calm and peaceful, satisfied,* and *full of life*). The daily outcome will be the mean across items, ranging from 1 to 5, where 1 = *none of the time,* 2 = *a little of the time,* 3 = *some of the time,* 4 = *most of the time,* and 5 = *all of the time,* with a grand mean across days of 3.7. As discussed earlier, although other metrics of time could also be useful (e.g., *day of the week*), *time* in this example will simply be *day in study* (ranging from 1 to 7). REML estimation will be used throughout this example given that our focus lies solely on the model for the variance. Accordingly, we can use the REML −2LL, AIC, and BIC indices from each ACS model to help guide us to the model that appears to best balance parsimony with good fit. We will also use −2ΔLL likelihood ratio tests to compare the fit of nested models when possible.

As introduced in chapter 1, there are (at least) three kinds of dependency (or correlation) among observations to consider when persons are measured repeatedly: (1) constant correlation due to individual differences in the mean outcome over time, (2) non-constant correlation due to individual differences in the effects of time or time-varying predictors, and (3) non-constant within-person correlation over time for unknown reasons. The ACS models presented next will be most useful in addressing the first and third kinds of dependency that result from within-person fluctuation primarily, rather than dependency resulting from systematic within-person change. In this example, because study participants simply reported their positive mood each day (i.e., no intervention to improve mood occurred), no systematic within-person change across the seven days of the study was expected. The data support this conjecture; the omnibus *F*-test of mean differences across days was not statistically significant. However, this won't always be the case for within-person fluctuation studies, and any unexpected mean differences across time would thus need to be modeled with fixed effects of time (as we'll do in chapters 5 and 6). But for this example we will proceed with only a single fixed intercept in the model for the means and focus solely on describing the pattern of variance and covariance in positive mood across seven days via the two families of ACS models, starting with **R**-only models in the next section.

It is important to note before diving in, though, that the more general purpose of this chapter is to describe and compare the ACS models that will be most useful for characterizing patterns of variance and covariance arising from within-person fluctuation over time. As such, we will examine many different ACS models with our example data. In other contexts, however, such exploratory data analysis may be frowned upon, in which the danger of inflated Type I error rates would discourage you from testing "too many" effects or making "too many" comparisons. But in this context we are not testing multitudes of predictor effects to try to find something significant—instead, we are trying to find a model that best matches the outcome variance and covariance over time so that subsequent predictor effects will be tested as *accurately* as possible. Thus, I do not believe that the data exploration needed to accurately describe the outcome variance and covariance over time is inherently problematic—in fact, I would rather err on the side of trying too many ACS models than too few. Fortunately, though, the characteristics of the data and the constructs being measured may help limit the models in practice to some that are more plausible than others, and these guiding considerations will be mentioned where relevant as we proceed through the two families of ACS model variants in the next sections.

2. Alternative Covariance Structure Models Using the **R** Matrix Only

2.A. Baseline Model: *n*-Order Unstructured (UN*n*)

The **R**-only family of ACS models tries to predict the pattern or structure of the *total* variance and covariance over time using just the **R** matrix. All ACS models can be located on a continuum ranging from parsimony to good fit, as represented by the vertical axis of Figure 4.1. The complexity continuum of **R**-only models (located in the left-hand side of each column) begins with the compound symmetry model and ends with the unstructured model, which will serve as the baselines against which to compare other **R**-only models of intermediate parsimony.

The predictions for our example 7-day positive mood data for each **R**-only model are shown in Table 4.1. The first column describes the model parameters used to create the structure of the total variance and covariance over time in the **R** matrix. Although all models will include parameters for the variance across time, the way that the relationships across days are expressed will differ across models— some models will include parameters for *covariance* across time while others will include parameters for *correlation* instead of covariance. But each can be calculated given the other, as shown for an example between days 1 and 2 in Equation (4.1):

$$\text{Correlation}_{y1,y2} = \frac{\text{Covariance}_{y1,y2}}{\sqrt{\text{Variance}_{y1}} * \sqrt{\text{Variance}_{y2}}}$$

$$\text{Covariance}_{y1,y2} = \text{Correlation}_{y1,y2} * \sqrt{\text{Variance}_{y1}} * \sqrt{\text{Variance}_{y2}}$$

(4.1)

The second column of Table 4.1 shows the model predictions across days, with variances on the diagonal, covariances above the diagonal, and correlations below the diagonal. In reality the **R** matrix of predicted variances and covariances is symmetric, with the same covariances above and below the diagonal, and the predicted correlations would be found in another symmetric matrix instead (i.e., referred to as **RCORR** in SAS MIXED). To save space, though, these separate **R** and **RCORR** matrices have been concatenated to show the model-predicted total variances, covariances, and correlations all at once in Table 4.1. To help separate the values from each matrix visually, three digits are

Table 4.1 R-only alternative covariance structure models for the $n = 7$ day example positive mood data (* indicates selected R-only model). R matrix predicted variances are shown in the diagonal, R matrix predicted covariances are shown above the diagonal, and RCORR matrix predicted correlations are shown below the diagonal.

Model Description	R/RCORR Matrices							
	Day	1	2	3	4	5	6	7
n-order Unstructured (UNn)								
$n*(n + 1) / 2 = 28$ parameters:	1	.595	.450	.411	.416	.397	.360	.353
7 separate total variances	2	.78	.563	.398	.427	.408	.353	.367
21 separate total covariances	3	.70	.70	.578	.414	.414	.354	.390
(these create the 21 separate total correlations)	4	.70	.74	.71	.589	.424	.415	.388
	5	.70	.74	.74	.75	.541	.364	.382
	6	.65	.66	.65	.76	.69	.512	.343
	7	.61	.66	.69	.68	.70	.64	.557
Compound Symmetry (CS)								
2 parameters: $\tau^2_{U_0} = CS = .390$ and $\sigma^2_e = .170$	1	.560	.390	.390	.390	.390	.390	.390
total variance $= \tau^2_{U_0} + \sigma^2_e = .560$	2	.70	.560	.390	.390	.390	.390	.390
total covariance $= \tau^2_{U_0} = .390$	3	.70	.70	.560	.390	.390	.390	.390
(these create the equal total correlations)	4	.70	.70	.70	.560	.390	.390	.390
	5	.70	.70	.70	.70	.560	.390	.390
	6	.70	.70	.70	.70	.70	.560	.390
	7	.70	.70	.70	.70	.70	.70	.560
Compound Symmetry Heterogeneous (CSH)								
$n + 1 = 8$ parameters:	1	.597	.399	.409	.406	.390	.391	.411
7 separate total variances (σ^2_{Tn})	2	.70	.550	.392	.390	.374	.375	.395
1 total correlation $= CSH = .70$	3	.70	.70	.577	.399	.383	.384	.404
(these create the unequal total covariances)	4	.70	.70	.70	.568	.380	.381	.401
	5	.70	.70	.70	.70	.523	.366	.385
	6	.70	.70	.70	.70	.70	.526	.386
	7	.70	.70	.70	.70	.70	.70	.584
Auto-Regressive (AR1)								
2 parameters:	1	.563	.401	.286	.204	.145	.104	.074
1 total variance $= \sigma^2_T = .563$	2	.71	.563	.401	.286	.204	.145	.104
1 total auto-correlation $= r = .71$	3	.51	.71	.563	.401	.286	.204	.145
lag-1 $= r^1_T = .71$, lag-2 $= r^2_T = .51$,	4	.36	.51	.71	.563	.401	.286	.204
lag-3 $= r^3_T = .36$, lag-4 $= r^4_T = .26$,	5	.26	.36	.51	.71	.563	.401	.286
lag-5 $= r^5_T = .18$, lag-6 $= r^6_T = .13$	6	.18	.26	.36	.51	.71	.563	.401
(these create the equal total covariances)	7	.13	.18	.26	.36	.51	.71	.563

(Continued)

Table 4.1 (Continued)

Auto-Regressive Heterogeneous (ARH1)

$n + 1 = 8$ parameters:
  7 separate total variances (σ_{Tn}^2)
  1 total auto-correlation = $r_T = .71$
   lag-1 = $r_T^1 = .71$, lag-2 = $r_T^2 = .51$,
   lag-3 = $r_T^3 = .36$, lag-4 = $r_T^4 = .26$,
   lag-5 = $r_T^5 = .18$, lag-6 = $r_T^6 = .13$
(these create the unequal total covariances)

1	.544	.383	.283	.200	.139	.101	.075
2	.71	.531	.393	.278	.193	.140	.104
3	.51	.71	.573	.406	.282	.204	.152
4	.36	.51	.71	.568	.394	.285	.212
5	.26	.36	.51	.71	.539	.390	.290
6	.18	.26	.36	.51	.71	.558	.415
7	.13	.18	.26	.36	.51	.71	.609

$n - 1$ Lag Toeplitz (TOEPn)*

$n = 7$ parameters:
  1 total variance = $\sigma_T^2 = .561$
  6 banded total covariances (c_{Tb})
   lag-1 = $c_{T1} = .399$, lag-2 = $c_{T2} = .406$,
   lag-3 = $c_{T3} = .385$, lag-4 = $c_{T4} = .382$,
   lag-5 = $c_{T5} = .371$, lag-6 = $c_{T6} = .348$
(these create the banded total correlations)

1	.561	.399	.406	.385	.382	.371	.348
2	.71	.561	.399	.406	.385	.382	.371
3	.72	.71	.561	.399	.406	.385	.382
4	.69	.72	.71	.561	.399	.406	.385
5	.68	.69	.72	.71	.561	.399	.406
6	.66	.68	.69	.72	.71	.561	.399
7	.62	.66	.68	.69	.72	.71	.561

$n - 1$ Lag Toeplitz Heterogeneous (TOEPHn)

$n + (n - 1) = 13$ parameters:
  7 separate total variances (σ_{Tn}^2)
  6 banded total correlations (r_{Tb})
   lag-1 = $r_{T1} = .71$, lag-2 = $r_{T2} = .72$,
   lag-3 = $r_{T3} = .69$, lag-4 = $r_{T4} = .68$,
   lag-5 = $r_{T5} = .66$, lag-6 = $r_{T6} = .62$
(these create the unequal total covariances)

1	.580	.399	.421	.396	.380	.365	.359
2	.71	.544	.399	.405	.371	.364	.371
3	.72	.71	.582	.410	.405	.380	.395
4	.69	.72	.71	.573	.393	.398	.395
5	.68	.69	.72	.71	.536	.377	.404
6	.66	.68	.69	.72	.71	.525	.391
7	.62	.66	.68	.69	.72	.71	.579

used after the decimal for variances and covariances, whereas two digits are used for the correlations.

First, in the top row of Table 4.1 is the least parsimonious **n-order unstructured** (UNn) model, which estimates all possible total variances and covariances across the n occasions (i.e., values for the 1 diagonal and for all 6 off-diagonals for $n = 7$ days), or $(n*[n + 1]) / 2 = 28$ total parameters. In our data, the total variances across days ranged from 0.512 to 0.595 and the total covariances ranged from 0.343 to 0.450 (resulting in correlations that ranged from .61 to .78), such that the days closer together were more strongly related (for the most part). But are these values different enough to warrant using all 28 possible parameters to describe these patterns? We will answer this empirical question by comparing the fit of the n-order unstructured (UNn) model to more parsimonious ACS models.

Because the UNn model simply estimates the actual total variances and covariances over time and does not try to summarize them using fewer model parameters, it will fit best relative to other models as indexed by the –2LL, but it may not be preferred by the AIC and BIC due to its lack of parsimony. When outcome data are balanced over time such that the UNn model is estimable, it provides the "answer key" for the pattern of variances and covariances over time we are trying to predict—this is why we consider it first. Because it will always have the lowest –2LL, the UNn model could be used by default in balanced data with few occasions (e.g., 3 or 4). It could be used for our example data, too, given that we have 200 persons with which to estimate the 7 variances and 21 covariances across the 7 days. However, in order for the chapter example to generalize more broadly, we will try to find a more parsimonious model that can still accurately predict the pattern of total variance and covariance over time. This is because as the number of occasions increases, the concomitant increase in the number of estimated parameters may prohibit use of the UNn model in longer studies—and the UNn model sometimes may not be estimable at all, depending on the number of persons and the amount of missing data. In sum, although finding a simpler but still-plausible model will be absolutely necessary for studies in which the UNn model may be impossible to estimate, achieving parsimony without compromising good fit (when possible) is a desirable objective more generally.

2.B. Compound Symmetry (CS) and Compound Symmetry Heterogeneous (CSH)

Rather than starting with the most complex model, it may be easier to start the model comparison process with the most parsimonious model instead (and it will be necessary to do so whenever the UNn model is not estimable). Accordingly, the second row in Table 4.1 shows the most parsimonious alternative for longitudinal data, the **compound symmetry** (CS) model, which uses only 2 parameters no matter how many occasions there are. That is, although the σ_e^2-only model (i.e., an R matrix with equal total variances on the diagonal but 0's on the off-diagonal) is even more parsimonious, it is not included given that its assumption of no covariance over time will likely never hold. The compound symmetry model predicts a constant total variance per day of $\tau_{U_0}^2 + \sigma_e^2 = 0.390 + 0.170 = 0.560$, a constant total covariance across days of $\tau_{U_0}^2 = 0.390$ (listed as the CS parameter in the output), and a constant total correlation across days, calculated as the **intraclass correlation**, or $ICC = \tau_{U_0}^2 / (\tau_{U_0}^2 + \sigma_e^2) = 0.390 / 0.560 = .700$. In other words, the constant total covariance across days predicted by the compound symmetry model is entirely due to constant mean differences across persons (through the variance of the U_{0i} random intercepts).

But do just 2 parameters for $\tau_{U_0}^2$ and σ_e^2 in the CS model do a good enough job predicting all 28 possible total variances and covariances? Among the R-only models, each is nested within the UNn model (as shown in Figure 4.1 by the arrows going into the UNn model), such that –2ΔLL likelihood ratio tests can be used to compare the fit of each lower-order alternative model to the fit of the highest-order UNn model (when it is estimable, as it is here). As reported in Table 4.2,

Table 4.2 Fit statistics and model comparisons for the R-only alternative covariance structure models for the $n = 7$ day example positive mood data (* indicates selected R-only model).

R-Only Models	Variance Parameters	−2LL	AIC	BIC
n-order Unstructured (UNn)	28	1983	2039	2131
Compound Symmetry (CS)	2	2029	2033	2040
Compound Symmetry Heterogeneous (CSH)	8	2026	2042	2068
Auto-Regressive (AR1)	2	2280	2284	2290
Auto-Regressive Heterogeneous (ARH1)	8	2278	2294	2320
$n − 1$ Lag Toeplitz (TOEPn)*	7	2010	2024	2047
$n − 1$ Lag Toeplitz Heterogeneous (TOEPHn)	13	2008	2034	2076

Deviance Difference Tests	Δdf	$-2\Delta LL$	$p <$
Tests for n-order unstructured vs. others			
UNn vs. CS	26	46.1	.009
UNn vs. CSH	20	43.0	.002
UNn vs. AR1	26	296.7	.001
UNn vs. ARH1	20	294.6	.001
UNn vs. TOEPn	21	26.8	.178
UNn vs. TOEPHn	15	24.5	.058
Tests for heterogeneity of variance			
CSH vs. CS	6	3.1	.796
ARH1 vs. AR1	6	2.1	.912
TOEPHn vs. TOEPn	6	2.3	.885
Tests for nested correlation structures			
TOEPn vs. CS	5	19.3	.002
TOEPHn vs. CSH	5	18.5	.002
TOEPn vs. AR1	5	269.9	.001
TOEPHn vs. ARH1	5	270.1	.001

the 2-parameter compound symmetry (CS) model fit significantly worse than the 28-parameter UNn model, $-2\Delta LL(26) = 46.1$, $p = .009$, indicating that just $\tau_{U_0}^2$ and σ_e^2 are not enough to describe the total pattern of variance and covariance over time. So, we must continue by considering other less parsimonious model alternatives. However, the CS model is still useful in serving as the lowest-order baseline against which the fit of more complex models can be compared (which is especially useful whenever the UNn model is not estimable).

The CS model can be extended to include heterogeneous variances across time as the **compound symmetry heterogeneous** (CSH) model, which uses $n + 1$ parameters for n separate total variances across time and a single constant correlation over time as the *CS* parameter in the output. As seen in the third row of Table 4.1, $n = 7$ separate total variances are now estimated on the diagonal of the **R** matrix, 1 for each day. As a result of these differing total variances, the predicted total covariances across days are no longer constant, but the predicted total correlations (based on the single CS parameter) are still constant at $r = .70$. The CSH model may be useful for outcomes in which the total variability differs across occasions, but in which person mean differences are still the primary cause of the total correlation over time.

Unfortunately, the 8-parameter CSH model fit significantly worse than 28-parameter UN*n* model, $-2\Delta LL(20) = 43.0$, $p = .002$, so adding separate variances across days was not enough to obtain predicted variances and covariances across days that would be comparable to the original data. But we can also compare the fit of the 8-parameter CSH model against the most parsimonious baseline, the CS model, to see if the separate variances helped at all. Although not explicitly depicted in Figure 4.1, the homogeneous variance version of each **R**-only model is nested within its heterogeneous variance version. Thus, the 2-parameter CS model is nested within the 8-parameter CSH model (i.e., the CSH model would become the CS model if the 7 different variances across days were constrained to be equal), and so a $-2\Delta LL$ test can also be used to compare their fit. As seen in Table 4.2, $-2\Delta LL(6) = 3.1$, $p = .796$, indicating a nonsignificant improvement to the model after allowing 7 different total variances across days rather than just 1 common total variance across days. The AIC and BIC are also smaller for the CS than CSH model, further indicating that the separate total variances across days in the CSH model are unnecessary. Putting these results together, the reason for the misfit does not appear to be due to the assumption of equal total variance across days—otherwise the CSH model would have been an improvement over the CS model. Instead, the misfit is likely due to the pattern of covariance or correlation over time, so we need to consider other potential patterns (besides the CS and CSH models that predict a constant covariance or correlation, which doesn't fit here).

2.C. First-Order Auto-Regressive (AR1) and First-Order Auto-Regressive Heterogeneous (ARH1)

The next **R**-only model in the fourth row of Table 4.1 also has 2 parameters but differs from compound symmetry in two respects. First, rather than partitioning the total variance into $\tau^2_{U_0}$ and σ^2_e, the **first-order auto-regressive** (AR1) model estimates a single constant total variance across days. Second, it predicts a specific pattern of correlation over time based on the idea of a *time lag* as the distance between subsequent occasions. Relationships between outcomes one day apart are called *lag-1* (e.g., day 1 to 2, day 2 to 3, day 3 to 4 . . .), those at two days apart are called *lag-2* (e.g., day 1 to 3, day 2 to 4 . . .), and so forth. The AR1 model predicts all lag-1 total correlations to be equal to the r_T auto-correlation parameter, as shown in the first lower off-diagonal in the fourth row of Table 4.1, in which $r_T^1 = .71$. The lag-2 total correlations are all predicted by squaring the r parameter (lag-2 = $.71^2 = .51$), the lag-3 total correlations are all predicted by cubing the r parameter (lag-3 $= .71^3 = .36$), and so forth. Thus, the 2 parameters in the AR1 model are for the total variance and the total auto-correlation (from which the predicted total covariance over time is calculated, as shown in Figure 4.2). In our data, the auto-correlation in the AR1 model results in a sharp decay of the predicted total correlations across days, ranging from $r_T^1 = .71$ at lag-1 to just $r_T^6 = .13$ by lag-6 (days 1 and 7).

So how did the AR1 model do relative to our other alternatives? The CS and AR1 models each have 2 parameters and are thus non-nested, but the AIC and BIC prefer the CS model over the AR1 model. However, the 2-parameter AR1 model fit significantly worse than the 28-parameter UNn model, $-2\Delta LL(26) = 296.7$, $p < .001$, most likely due to the mismatch between the predicted total correlations over time in the AR1 model (which decay sharply) and the observed total correlations over time in the UNn model (which are somewhat constant, but not completely constant, or else the CS model would have fit equivalently to the UNn model). In general, the AR1 model is not likely to be useful for data in which most of the total correlation over time is likely due to constant person mean differences (i.e., with a large ICC), and therefore, in which the total correlations should not decay substantially across time.

The AR1 model can also include heterogeneous variances. As seen in the fifth row of Table 4.1, the **first-order autoregressive heterogeneous** (ARH1) model has $n + 1$ parameters, in which 7 total variances have been estimated (1 for each day). As also shown in Figure 4.2, although the predicted total covariances now vary due to the separate total variances for each day, they are still based on the single total auto-correlation parameter. The 2-parameter AR1 model is nested within the 8-parameter ARH1 model, and a comparison of their fit (as seen in Table 4.2) yields $-2\Delta LL(6) = 2.1$, $p = .912$. Thus, there is no significant improvement from allowing 7 different total variances across days; the AIC and BIC concur. The 8-parameter ARH1 model also fit significantly worse than the 28-parameter UNn model, $-2\Delta LL(20) = 294.6$, $p < .001$, indicating that we still need to consider other alternatives.

Although not shown here, the AR1 model can be extended in two other ways. First, the AR1/ARH1 models can be extended to include higher-order auto-regressive relationships (e.g., AR2/ARH2), in which additional auto-correlation parameters for direct relationships at longer lags would then also contribute to the predicted correlations over time. Second, it is also possible to estimate an AR1 model on *unbalanced* or unequal interval data over time (e.g., by using SAS MIXED with TYPE = SP[POW] [time]), in which the correlation decays exponentially as a function of continuous time rather than discrete time.

2.D. *n*-1 Lag Toeplitz (TOEP*n*) and *n*-1 Lag Toeplitz Heterogeneous (TOEPH*n*)

The next **R**-only model in the sixth row of Table 4.1 also relies on the concept of a time lag but does so differently than the auto-regressive models. The **n-1 lag Toeplitz** (TOEP*n*; also known as a *banded* model) has n parameters, including

1 total variance across days and $n-1$ separate total covariances for each time lag (i.e., 6 separate total covariances for the 6 time lags in our data, from which 6 total correlations can be calculated). The name of the Toeplitz models can be confusing, because a TOEPn model (of n order) includes covariances for only $n-1$ lags. That is, the 1 extra for the n-order is for the total variance. So, a TOEP7 model has 1 band of variances on the diagonal and 6 off-diagonals of lagged covariances, a TOEP6 model has 1 band of variances on the diagonal and 5 off-diagonals of lagged covariances, and so on. Unlike the AR1 models, the lagged relationships in the TOEPn model are not exponential functions of a single auto-correlation parameter—instead, the total covariance at each time lag is estimated separately, allowing for much more flexibility in how the total covariance changes over time. For instance, in our example, the predicted total covariance between observations at lag-1 = 0.399, at lag-2 = 0.406, at lag-3 = 0.385, at lag-4 = 0.382, at lag-5 = 0.371, and at lag-6 = 0.348, which translates into predicted correlations at lags 1 to 6 of .71, .72, .69, .68, .66, and .62, respectively.

As shown in Figure 4.1, the 2-parameter CS model and 2-parameter AR1 model are each nested within the 7-parameter $n-1$ lag Toeplitz (TOEPn) model. As reported in Table 4.2, the TOEPn model fit significantly better than both the CS model, $-2\Delta LL(5) = 19.3$, $p = .002$, and the AR1 model, $-2\Delta LL(5) = 269.9$, $p < .001$. Whereas the AIC also prefers the TOEPn model over the CS and AR1 models, the BIC prefers the CS model instead (likely because the TOEPn model has 5 more parameters than the CS model). However, the 7-parameter $n-1$ lag (TOEPn) model did *not* fit significantly worse than the 28-parameter UNn model, $-2\Delta LL(21) = 26.8$, $p = .178$, such that the $n-1$ lag Toeplitz model was able to reproduce the total variances and covariances over time using 21 fewer parameters than the UNn model. So, we may have a winner!

Finally, as seen in the last row of Table 4.1, the $n-1$ Lag Toeplitz model can also include heterogeneous total variances across time as the **n-1 lag Toeplitz heterogeneous** (TOEPHn) model with a total of $n + (n-1)$ parameters (for n separate total variances on the diagonal and $n-1$ separate lags on the off-diagonals). As also shown in Figure 4.2, its $n-1$ lagged relationships are specified as total *correlations* that are still held equal within-lag, but which translate into unequal total *covariances* within-lag given the different total variances across days. The 7-parameter $n-1$ lag TOEPn model is nested within the 13-parameter $n-1$ lag TOEPHn model and a comparison of their fit (as seen in Table 4.2) yields $-2\Delta LL(6) = 2.4$, $p = .885$, or a nonsignificant improvement by adding heterogeneous total variance across days; the AIC and BIC concur. Finally, a comparison of the 13-parameter $n-1$ lag TOEPHn model and the 28-parameter UNn model yields $-2\Delta LL(15) = 24.5$, $p = .058$, indicating that the TOEPHn model is also not significantly worse than the UNn model. But because the $-2\Delta LL$ is evaluated per difference in degrees of freedom, the model comparison is closer to significance in this case given how many extra parameters for heterogeneous total variances across days were used by the TOEPHn model than the TOEPn model without a commensurate improvement in model fit.

2.E. Summary of R-Only Models and Model Comparisons

Let us now summarize our findings regarding prediction of the total variances and covariances across time from the **R**-only models so far. First, in asking whether the total variance of positive mood needs to be estimated separately across the 7 days, the answer is no—as seen in Table 4.2, the heterogeneous variance models did not fit better than their homogeneous variance versions. Second, we have seen that the total covariances and correlations across days appear mostly similar, but do appear to have some drop across time lags (given that the n–1 lag Toeplitz model that allows the covariances to differ by time lag fit better than the compound symmetry model in which the covariances are predicted to be the same across days instead). The total correlations over time definitely don't decay as sharply as predicted by the AR1 model, which had the worst fit. So far, our most parsimonious model that still exhibits good fit to the total variances and covariances over time in positive mood is the 6-lag Toeplitz model (TOEPn).

It is also useful at this point to review the general rules by which to consider whether any two **R**-only models are nested, as shown by the directed arrows in Figure 4.1 and summarized as follows. First, all models are nested within the n-order unstructured (UNn) model because they can each be created through restrictions on the separate parameters in the UNn model. Second, the compound symmetry (CS) and auto-regressive (AR1) models each have two parameters and thus cannot be nested, but the CS and AR1 models are each nested within the n-order, n–1 lag Toeplitz (TOEPn) model with n parameters (which can become CS or AR1 by restricting its parameters as well). Analogously, the heterogeneous variance CSH and ARH1 models with $n + 1$ parameters are non-nested relative to each other but are each nested within the heterogeneous variance n-order, n–1 lag TOEPHn model with $n + (n - 1)$ parameters. Third, the homogeneous variance version of each model is nested within its heterogeneous variance version, including CS within CSH, AR1 within ARH1, and TOEPn within TOEPHn. There is no homogeneous version of the UNn model (in which all total variances and covariances are always separate), however.

You may have noticed that these rules of nesting can create many other possible model comparisons that we have not considered here, as illustrated in Table 4.2. However, it is generally most helpful to compare models that differ either in their covariance pattern *or* in their variance pattern but not in both dimensions at once. For instance, the CS model (with homogeneous variance and constant covariance and correlation over days) is nested within the TOEPHn model (with heterogeneous variance and different lagged correlations over days), and so their fit could be compared via a -2ΔLL test. But if the TOEPHn model fit significantly better than the CS model, we wouldn't know whether the improvement in fit came from allowing heterogeneous rather than homogeneous variances over time, from allowing a non-constant pattern of correlation over time, or for both reasons. To prevent this ambiguity, the comparisons in this example have generally focused on models that differ in one dimension only—the exceptions to this rule are comparisons with the n-order unstructured model as the "answer key" for the original outcome variances and covariances. Furthermore, to limit the number of comparisons necessary, it may be useful to use the heterogeneous variance versions of each model (if possible) when initially evaluating which pattern of correlation fits best (e.g., constant correlation via CSH, auto-regressive correlation via ARH1, or banded correlation via TOEPH*n*) given that the worst the heterogeneous variances can be is overkill. After seeing which pattern of correlation fits best, you can then test whether heterogeneous variances are really necessary.

Now that we've examined a plethora of options within the **R**-only alternative covariance structure (ACS) models, it's time to introduce the other family of ACS models for describing the pattern of variance and covariance over time in outcomes showing within-person fluctuation: the **G** and **R** combined family of ACS models, which also include a random intercept variance.

3. Models Combining a Random Intercept Variance in the **G** Matrix With a Covariance Structure Model in the **R** Matrix

In the **R**-only ACS models for our example so far, it appeared that most of the covariance or correlation across days was relatively (but not completely) constant. When this is the case, it may be advantageous to specify our models to include a random intercept variance ($\tau_{U_0}^2$) in the **G** matrix to explicitly account for between-person (BP) intercept differences, and to then evaluate the pattern of within-person (WP) residual variance and covariance that remains in the **R** matrix. The logic behind such **G** and **R** combined models is this: it may be that the only reason why observations far apart in time (e.g., days 1 and 7) are still correlated is because of constant person mean differences ($\tau_{U_0}^2$). So, after moving the part of the total variance and covariance due to $\tau_{U_0}^2$ to the **G** matrix, the remaining residual WP e_{ti} variances and covariances in the **R** matrix can often be predicted using a simpler model (i.e., fewer lagged covariances may remain after controlling for the part of the lagged covariance created by the random intercept variance $\tau_{U_0}^2$).

As indicated by their name, the **G** and **R** combined models use both the **G** and **R** matrices to construct the **V** matrix for the total predicted variance and covariance over time. That is, in the previous **R**-only models, the **R** matrix held the *total* predicted variance and covariance over time such that the **R** matrix = **V** matrix directly (but it is still referred to as the **R** matrix rather than as the **V** matrix by convention). Accordingly, in the **G** and **R** combined models that follow, the **V** matrix (rather than the **R** matrix as in the previous **R**-only models) will hold the *total* predicted variance and covariance over time, and the **R** matrix will instead hold only the *WP e_{ti} residual* variance and covariance after controlling for the random intercept variance $\tau_{U_0}^2$ in the **G** matrix. As we will see next, the **G** and **R** combined models can not only reproduce some of the **R**-only models, but they also can potentially offer some more parsimonious alternatives as well.

How **G** and **R** combined models are specified more generally is shown in Figure 4.2, and the results for the **G** and **R** combined models we will examine for our example positive mood data are given in Table 4.3. The first column of Table 4.3 describes the

Table 4.3 G and R combined models (with a random intercept variance in the G matrix and a covariance structure in the R matrix) for the $n = 7$ day example positive mood data (* indicates selected G and R combined model). R matrix and V matrix predicted variances are shown in the diagonals, R matrix and V matrix predicted covariances are shown above the diagonals, and RCORR and VCORR matrix predicted correlations are shown below the diagonals.

Random Intercept Variance in G and n–1 order Unstructured R (RI and UNn–1)

Model Description:
1 G Matrix parameter = $\tau^2_{U_0}$ = .353
$[n*(n + 1) / 2] - 1 = 27$ R matrix parameters:
7 separate residual variances (σ^2_{en})
20 residual covariances (lag 6 is omitted)
(these create the residual correlations)

Day	R/RCORR 1	2	3	4	5	6	7	V/VCORR 1	2	3	4	5	6	7
1	.243	.097	.058	.063	.044	.007	0	.595	.450	.411	.416	.397	.360	.353
2	.43	.211	.045	.074	.056	.001	.015	.78	.563	.398	.427	.408	.353	.367
3	.25	.21	.225	.061	.062	.001	.037	.70	.70	.578	.414	.414	.354	.390
4	.26	.33	.27	.236	.071	.062	.035	.70	.74	.71	.589	.424	.415	.388
5	.21	.28	.30	.34	.188	.011	.029	.70	.74	.74	.75	.541	.364	.382
6	.04	.00	.01	.32	.06	.160	–.010	.65	.66	.65	.76	.69	.512	.343
7	0	.07	.17	.16	.15	–.05	.204	.61	.66	.69	.68	.70	.64	.557

Random Intercept Variance in G and Diagonal R (RI and DIAG)

Model Description:
1 G Matrix parameter = $\tau^2_{U_0}$ = .390
1 R matrix parameter:
1 residual variance = σ^2_e = .170
0 residual covariances
(these create the 0 residual correlations)

Day	R/RCORR 1	2	3	4	5	6	7	V/VCORR 1	2	3	4	5	6	7
1	.170	0	0	0	0	0	.0	.560	.390	.390	.390	.390	.390	.390
2	0	.170	0	0	0	0	0	.70	.560	.390	.390	.390	.390	.390
3	0	0	.170	0	0	0	0	.70	.70	.560	.390	.390	.390	.390
4	0	0	0	.170	0	0	0	.70	.70	.70	.560	.390	.390	.390
5	0	0	0	0	.170	0	0	.70	.70	.70	.70	.560	.390	.390
6	0	0	0	0	0	.170	0	.70	.70	.70	.70	.70	.560	.390
7	0	0	0	0	0	0	.170	.70	.70	.70	.70	.70	.70	.560

Model Description	R/RCORR Matrices							V/VCORR Matrices (from G and R)						
Day	1	2	3	4	5	6	7	1	2	3	4	5	6	7
Random Intercept Variance in G and Diagonal Heterogeneous R (RI and DIAGH)														
1 **G** Matrix parameter = $\tau^2_{U_0}$ = .394 1	.189	0	0	0	0	0	0	.582	.394	.394	.394	.394	.394	.394
<u>n = 7 **R** matrix parameters:</u> 2	0	.153	0	0	0	0	0	.70	.547	.394	.394	.394	.394	.394
7 separate residual variances (σ^2_{en}) 3	0	0	.176	0	0	0	0	.68	.71	.570	.394	.394	.394	.394
0 residual correlations 4	0	0	0	.148	0	0	0	.70	.72	.71	.541	.394	.394	.394
(these create the 0 residual covariances) 5	0	0	0	0	.135	0	0	.71	.73	.72	.74	.529	.394	.394
6	0	0	0	0	0	.179	0	.68	.70	.69	.71	.72	.572	.394
7	0	0	0	0	0	0	.212	.66	.68	.67	.69	.70	.67	.605
Random Intercept Variance in G and Auto-Regressive R (RI and AR1)														
1 **G** Matrix parameter = $\tau^2_{U_0}$ = .388 1	.173	.008	.000	.000	.000	.000	.000	.561	.396	.388	.388	.388	.388	.388
<u>2 **R** matrix parameters:</u> 2	.05	.173	.008	.000	.000	.000	.000	.71	.561	.396	.388	.388	.388	.388
1 residual variance = σ^2_e = .173 3	.00	.05	.173	.008	.000	.000	.000	.69	.71	.561	.396	.388	.388	.388
1 residual auto-correlation = r_e = .05 4	.00	.00	.05	.173	.008	.000	.000	.69	.69	.71	.561	.396	.388	.388
lag-1 = r^1_e = .05, lag-2 = r^2_e = .00… 5	.00	.00	.00	.05	.173	.008	.000	.69	.69	.69	.71	.561	.396	.388
(these create the residual covariances) 6	.00	.00	.00	.00	.05	.173	.008	.69	.69	.69	.69	.71	.561	.396
7	.00	.00	.00	.00	.00	.05	.173	.69	.69	.69	.69	.69	.71	.561
Random Intercept Variance in G and Auto-Regressive Heterogeneous R (RI and ARH1)														
1 **G** Matrix parameter = $\tau^2_{U_0}$ = .392 1	.187	.006	.000	.000	.000	.000	.000	.582	.394	.394	.394	.394	.394	.394
<u>$n+1$ = 8 **R** matrix parameters:</u> 2	.03	.153	.005	.000	.000	.000	.000	.70	.547	.394	.394	.394	.394	.394
7 separate residual variances (σ^2_{en}) 3	.00	.03	.180	.005	.000	.000	.000	.68	.71	.570	.394	.394	.394	.394
1 residual auto-correlation = r = .03 4	.00	.00	.03	.151	.005	.000	.000	.70	.72	.71	.541	.394	.394	.394
lag-1 = r^1_e = .03, lag-2 = r^2_e = .00… 5	.00	.00	.00	.03	.138	.005	.000	.71	.73	.72	.74	.529	.394	.394
(these create the residual covariances) 6	.00	.00	.00	.00	.03	.181	.006	.68	.70	.69	.71	.72	.572	.394
7	.00	.00	.00	.00	.00	.03	.212	.66	.68	.67	.69	.70	.67	.605

(Continued)

Table 4.3 (Continued)

Model Description		R/RCORR Matrices							V/VCORR Matrices (from G and R)						
	Day	1	2	3	4	5	6	7	1	2	3	4	5	6	7

Random Intercept Variance in G and 1-Lag Toeplitz R (RI and TOEP2)

1 G Matrix parameter = $\tau^2_{U_0}$ = .388
2 R matrix parameters:
  1 residual variance = σ^2_e = .172
  1 banded residual covariance (c_{e1})
    lag-1 = c_{e1} = .007
  (*these create the residual correlation*)

Day	1	2	3	4	5	6	7	1	2	3	4	5	6	7
1	.172	.007	0	0	0	0	0	.560	.395	.388	.388	.388	.388	.388
2	.04	.172	.007	0	0	0	0	.70	.560	.395	.388	.388	.388	.388
3	0	.04	.172	.007	0	0	0	.69	.70	.560	.395	.388	.388	.388
4	0	0	.04	.172	.007	0	0	.69	.69	.70	.560	.395	.388	.388
5	0	0	0	.04	.172	.007	0	.69	.69	.69	.70	.560	.395	.388
6	0	0	0	0	.04	.172	.007	.69	.69	.69	.69	.70	.560	.395
7	0	0	0	0	0	.04	.172	.69	.69	.69	.69	.69	.70	.560

Random Intercept Variance in G and 1-Lag Toeplitz Heterogeneous R (RI and TOEPH2)

1 G Matrix parameter = $\tau^2_{U_0}$ = .392
$n+1$ = 8 R matrix parameters:
  7 separate residual variances (σ^2_{en})
  1 banded residual correlation (r_{e1})
    lag-1 = r_{e1} = .03
  (*these create the residual covariance*)

Day	1	2	3	4	5	6	7	1	2	3	4	5	6	7
1	.188	.005	0	0	0	0	0	.572	.398	.407	.384	.384	.384	.384
2	.03	.153	.005	0	0	0	0	.71	.541	.398	.403	.384	.384	.384
3	0	.03	.179	.004	0	0	0	.71	.71	.578	.398	.404	.384	.384
4	0	0	.03	.150	.004	0	0	.69	.74	.71	.546	.398	.404	.384
5	0	0	0	.03	.137	.004	0	.69	.71	.73	.73	.533	.397	.405
6	0	0	0	0	.03	.181	.005	.67	.69	.67	.73	.72	.568	.400
7	0	0	0	0	0	.03	.212	.65	.67	.65	.67	.72	.68	.603

Random Intercept Variance in G and 2-Lag Toeplitz R (RI and TOEP3)*

1 G Matrix parameter = $\tau^2_{U_0}$ = .380
3 R matrix parameters:
  1 residual variance = σ^2_e = .181
  2 banded residual covariances (c_{eb})
    lag-1 = c_{e1} = .017, lag-2 = c_{e2} = .023
  (*these create the residual correlations*)

Day	1	2	3	4	5	6	7	1	2	3	4	5	6	7
1	.181	.017	.023	0	0	0	0	.560	.396	.403	.380	.380	.380	.380
2	.09	.181	.017	.023	0	0	0	.71	.560	.396	.403	.380	.380	.380
3	.13	.09	.181	.017	.023	0	0	.72	.71	.560	.396	.403	.380	.380
4	0	.13	.09	.181	.017	.023	0	.68	.72	.71	.560	.396	.403	.380
5	0	0	.13	.09	.181	.017	.023	.68	.68	.72	.71	.560	.396	.403
6	0	0	0	.13	.09	.181	.017	.68	.68	.68	.72	.71	.560	.396
7	0	0	0	0	.13	.09	.181	.68	.68	.68	.68	.72	.71	.560

Model Description		R/RCORR Matrices							V/VCORR Matrices (from G and R)						
	Day	1	2	3	4	5	6	7	1	2	3	4	5	6	7

Random Intercept Variance in G and 2-Lag Toeplitz Heterogeneous R (RI and TOEPH3)

Model Description	Day	1	2	3	4	5	6	7	1	2	3	4	5	6	7
1 G Matrix parameter = $\tau^2_{U_0}$ = .384	1	.188	.014	.023	0	0	0	0	.572	.398	.407	.384	.384	.384	.384
$n+2=9$ R matrix parameters:	2	.08	.157	.014	.019	0	0	0	.71	.541	.398	.403	.384	.384	.384
7 separate residual variances (σ^2_{en})	3	.12	.08	.195	.014	.020	0	0	.71	.71	.578	.398	.404	.384	.384
2 banded residual correlations (r_{eb})	4	0	.12	.08	.162	.013	.021	0	.69	.74	.71	.546	.396	.404	.384
lag-1 = r_{e1} = .08, lag-2 = r_{e2} = .12	5	0	0	.12	.08	.149	.013	.022	.69	.71	.73	.73	.533	.397	.405
(these create the residual covariances)	6	0	0	0	.12	.08	.184	.016	.67	.69	.67	.73	.72	.568	.400
	7	0	0	0	0	.12	.08	.219	.65	.67	.65	.67	.72	.68	.603

Random Intercept Variance in G and 3-Lag Toeplitz R (RI and TOEP4)

Model Description	Day	1	2	3	4	5	6	7	1	2	3	4	5	6	7
1 G Matrix parameter = $\tau^2_{U_0}$ = .376	1	.184	.021	.027	.008	0	0	0	.560	.397	.403	.384	.376	.376	.376
3 R matrix parameters:	2	.11	.184	.021	.027	.008	0	0	.71	.560	.397	.403	.384	.376	.376
1 residual variance = σ^2_e = .184	3	.15	.11	.184	.021	.027	.008	0	.72	.71	.560	.397	.403	.384	.376
3 banded residual covariances (c_{eb})	4	.05	.15	.11	.184	.021	.027	.008	.69	.72	.71	.560	.397	.403	.384
lag-1 = c_{e1} = .021, lag-2 = c_{e2} = .027,	5	0	.05	.15	.11	.184	.021	.027	.67	.69	.72	.71	.560	.397	.403
lag-3 = c_{e3} = .008	6	0	0	.05	.15	.11	.184	.021	.67	.67	.69	.72	.71	.560	.397
(these create the residual correlations)	7	0	0	0	.05	.15	.11	.184	.67	.67	.67	.69	.72	.71	.560

Random Intercept Variance in G and 3-Lag Toeplitz Heterogeneous R (RI and TOEPH4)

Model Description	Day	1	2	3	4	5	6	7	1	2	3	4	5	6	7
1 G Matrix parameter = $\tau^2_{U_0}$ = .380	1	.190	.017	.027	.007	0	0	0	.570	.398	.407	.387	.380	.380	.380
$n+3=10$ R matrix parameters:	2	.10	.159	.018	.023	.006	0	0	.72	.539	.398	.403	.386	.380	.380
7 separate residual variances (σ^2_{en})	3	.14	.10	.200	.018	.024	.007	0	.71	.71	.580	.399	.404	.387	.380
3 banded residual correlations (r_{eb})	4	.04	.14	.10	.168	.016	.024	.007	.69	.74	.71	.548	.396	.405	.387
lag-1 = r_{e1} = .10, lag-2 = r_{e2} = .14,	5	0	.04	.14	.10	.153	.017	.025	.69	.72	.73	.73	.533	.397	.406
lag-3 = r_{e3} = .04	6	0	0	.04	.14	.10	.187	.020	.67	.69	.68	.73	.72	.567	.401
(these create the residual covariances)	7	0	0	0	.04	.14	.10	.222	.65	.67	.64	.67	.72	.69	.602

(Continued)

Table 4.3 (Continued)

Random Intercept Variance in G and 4-Lag Toeplitz R (RI and TOEP5)

Model Description:

1 G Matrix parameter = $\tau^2_{U_0}$ = .365
4 R matrix parameters:
1 residual variance = σ^2_e = .196
4 banded residual covariances (c_{eb})
lag-1 = c_{e1} = .032, lag-2 = c_{e2} = .041, lag-3 = c_{e3} = .019, lag-4 = c_{e4} = .019
(these create the residual correlations)

Day	R/RCORR Matrices							V/VCORR Matrices (from G and R)						
	1	2	3	4	5	6	7	1	2	3	4	5	6	7
1	.196	.032	.041	.019	.019	0	0	.560	.397	.405	.384	.384	.365	.365
2	.17	.196	.032	.041	.019	.019	0	.71	.560	.397	.405	.384	.384	.365
3	.21	.17	.196	.032	.041	.019	.019	.72	.71	.560	.397	.405	.384	.384
4	.10	.21	.17	.196	.032	.041	.019	.69	.72	.71	.560	.397	.405	.384
5	.10	.10	.21	.17	.196	.032	.041	.68	.69	.72	.71	.560	.397	.405
6	0	.10	.10	.21	.17	.196	.032	.65	.68	.69	.72	.71	.560	.397
7	0	0	.10	.10	.21	.17	.196	.65	.65	.68	.69	.72	.71	.560

Random Intercept Variance in G and 4-Lag Toeplitz Heterogeneous R (RI and TOEPH5)

Model Description:

1 G Matrix parameter = $\tau^2_{U_0}$ = .371
$n + 4 = 11$ R matrix parameters:
7 separate residual variances (σ^2_e)
4 banded residual correlations (r_{eb})
lag-1 = r_{e1} = .15, lag-2 = r_{e2} = .19, lag-3 = r_{e3} = .08, lag-4 = r_{e4} = .08
(these create the residual covariances)

Day	R/RCORR Matrices							V/VCORR Matrices (from G and R)						
	1	2	3	4	5	6	7	1	2	3	4	5	6	7
1	.196	.027	.039	.016	.014	0	0	.566	.397	.410	.386	.385	.371	.371
2	.15	.167	.028	.033	.014	.014	0	.72	.538	.399	.404	.385	.385	.371
3	.19	.15	.213	.029	.036	.017	.017	.71	.71	.583	.400	.406	.388	.388
4	.08	.19	.15	.180	.026	.036	.017	.71	.74	.71	.550	.396	.406	.387
5	.08	.08	.19	.15	.166	.027	.037	.69	.72	.73	.73	.537	.397	.408
6	0	.08	.08	.19	.15	.196	.031	.70	.72	.67	.73	.72	.567	.402
7	0	0	.08	.08	.19	.15	.227	.65	.70	.66	.68	.72	.69	.597

Random Intercept Variance in G and 5-Lag Toeplitz R (RI and TOEP6)

Model Description:

1 G Matrix parameter = $\tau^2_{U_0}$ = .348
5 R matrix parameters:
1 residual variance = σ^2_e = .213
5 banded residual covariances (c_{eb})
lag-1 = c_{e1} = .051, lag-2 = c_{e2} = .059, lag-3 = c_{e3} = .037, lag-4 = c_{e4} = .035, lag-5 = c_{e5} = .023
(these create the residual correlations)

Day	R/RCORR Matrices							V/VCORR Matrices (from G and R)						
	1	2	3	4	5	6	7	1	2	3	4	5	6	7
1	.213	.051	.059	.037	.035	.023	0	.561	.399	.406	.385	.382	.371	.348
2	.24	.213	.051	.059	.037	.035	.023	.71	.561	.399	.406	.385	.382	.371
3	.27	.24	.213	.051	.059	.037	.035	.72	.71	.561	.399	.406	.385	.382
4	.18	.27	.24	.213	.051	.059	.037	.69	.72	.71	.561	.399	.406	.385
5	.16	.18	.27	.24	.213	.051	.059	.68	.69	.72	.71	.561	.399	.406
6	.11	.16	.18	.27	.24	.213	.051	.66	.68	.69	.72	.71	.561	.399
7	0	.11	.16	.18	.27	.24	.213	.62	.66	.68	.69	.72	.71	.561

(these create the residual correlations)

Model Description	R/RCORR Matrices							V/VCORR Matrices (from G and R)						
	Day	1	2	3	4	5	6	7	1	2	3	4	5	6	7

Model Description	Day	1	2	3	4	5	6	7	1	2	3	4	5	6	7
Random Intercept Variance in **G** and 5-Lag Toeplitz Heterogeneous **R** (RI and TOEPH6)															
1 **G** Matrix parameter = $\tau^2_{U_0}$ = .356	1	.208	.042	.055	.031	.027	.019	0	.564	.398	.411	.387	.383	.375	.356
$n + 5 = 12$ **R** matrix parameters:	2	.21	.181	.044	.048	.028	.027	.019	.72	.538	.400	.404	.384	.383	.375
7 separate residual variances (σ^2_{en})	3	.25	.21	.229	.045	.051	.034	.032	.72	.71	.586	.402	.408	.390	.389
5 banded residual correlations (r_{eb})	4	.15	.25	.21	.197	.040	.051	.033	.69	.74	.71	.553	.397	.408	.389
lag-1 = r_{e1} = .21, lag-2 = r_{e2} = .25,	5	.14	.15	.25	.21	.181	.042	.052	.70	.71	.73	.73	.537	.398	.409
lag-3 = r_{e3} = .15, lag-4 = r_{e4} = .04,	6	.09	.14	.15	.25	.21	.212	.048	.66	.69	.68	.73	.72	.568	.404
lag-5 = r_{e5} = .09	7	0	.09	.14	.15	.25	.21	.240	.61	.66	.66	.68	.72	.70	.596
(these create the residual covariances)															

model parameters and provides the estimated random intercept variance $\tau_{U_0}^2$ from the **G** matrix. In the second column the **R** and **RCORR** matrices have again been concatenated to save space, with the predicted WP e_{ti} variances on the diagonal, the WP e_{ti} covariances above the diagonal, and the WP e_{ti} correlations below the diagonal. The third column of Table 4.3 provides the *total* pattern of variance, covariance, and correlation over time based on the **G** and **R** matrices *combined,* as now found within the **V** matrix for *total* variance and covariance and the **VCORR** matrix for *total* correlation. As with the **R** and **RCORR** matrices, the **V** and **VCORR** matrices have also been concatenated to show both at once: the total variances are on the diagonal, the total covariances are above the diagonal, and the total correlations are below the diagonal. Finally, the fit of each model (and $-2\Delta LL$ tests for nested comparisons thereof) are given in Table 4.4.

To describe how the **G** and **R** matrices create the **V** matrix, the phrase **G** *and* **R** *combined* is used deliberately because, following the rules of matrix algebra, the **G** and **R** matrices cannot be added together directly because they have different dimensions (i.e., in which *dimensions* are the number of rows by the number of columns). Here, **G** is a 1x1 matrix (or *scalar*) that contains only $\tau_{U_0}^2$, whereas **R** is a 7x7 matrix for the e_{ti} variances and covariances across the $n = 7$ days. Accordingly, as shown in Figure 4.2, the **G** matrix must be pre-multiplied by a 7x1 column vector

Table 4.4 Fit statistics and model comparisons for the **G** and **R** combined alternative covariance structure models for the $n = 7$ day example positive mood data (* indicates selected **G** and **R** combined model).

Random Intercept Variance in G (RI) and Covariance Structure in R Combined Models	Variance Parameters	−2LL	AIC	BIC
RI and n-1 order Unstructured **R** (RI and UNn-1)	28	1983	2039	2131
RI and Diagonal **R** (RI and DIAG)	2	2029	2033	2040
RI and Diagonal Heterogeneous **R** (RI and DIAGH)	8	2019	2035	2061
RI and Auto-Regressive **R** (RI and AR1)	3	2027	2033	2043
RI and Auto-Regressive Heterogeneous **R** (RI and ARH1)	9	2018	2036	2066
RI and 1-Lag Toeplitz **R** (RI and TOEP2)	3	2028	2034	2044
RI and 1-Lag Toeplitz Heterogeneous **R** (RI and TOEPH2)	9	2018	2036	2066
RI and 2-Lag Toeplitz **R** (RI and TOEP3)*	4	2017	2025	2038
RI and 2-Lag Toeplitz Heterogeneous **R** (RI and TOEPH3)	10	2009	2029	2062
RI and 3-Lag Toeplitz **R** (RI and TOEP4)	5	2016	2026	2042
RI and 3-Lag Toeplitz Heterogeneous **R** (RI and TOEPH4)	11	2008	2030	2067
RI and 4-Lag Toeplitz **R** (RI and TOEP5)	6	2012	2024	2044
RI and 4-Lag Toeplitz Heterogeneous **R** (RI and TOEPH5)	12	2006	2030	2070
RI and 5-Lag Toeplitz **R** (RI and TOEP6)	7	2010	2024	2047
RI and 5-Lag Toeplitz Heterogeneous **R** (RI and TOEPH6)	13	2005	2031	2074

Deviance Difference Tests	Δdf	$-2\Delta LL$	$p <$
Tests for RI and *n*-1 order unstructured vs. others:			
RI and UN*n*-1 vs. RI and DIAG	26	46.1	.009
RI and UN*n*-1 vs. RI and DIAGH	20	35.6	.017
RI and UN*n*-1 vs. RI and AR1	25	44.3	.010
RI and UN*n*-1 vs. RI and ARH1	19	34.8	.015
RI and UN*n*-1 vs. RI and TOEP2	25	44.6	.009
RI and UN*n*-1 vs. RI and TOEPH2	19	34.9	.014
RI and UN*n*-1 vs. RI and TOEP3	24	33.7	.091
RI and UN*n*-1 vs. RI and TOEPH3	18	25.9	.103
RI and UN*n*-1 vs. RI and TOEP4	23	32.7	.086
RI and UN*n*-1 vs. RI and TOEPH4	17	25.3	.089
RI and UN*n*-1 vs. RI and TOEP5	22	29.1	.143
RI and UN*n*-1 vs. RI and TOEPH5	16	23.3	.107
RI and UN*n*-1 vs. RI and TOEP6	21	26.8	.178
RI and UN*n*-1 vs. RI and TOEPH6	15	22.0	.109
Tests for heterogeneity of variance:			
RI and DIAGH vs. RI and DIAG	6	10.5	.105
RI and AR1H vs. RI and AR1	6	9.5	.146
RI and TOEPH2 vs. RI and TOEP2	6	9.7	.137
RI and TOEPH3 vs. RI and TOEP3	6	7.8	.252
RI and TOEPH4 vs. RI and TOEP4	6	7.4	.282
RI and TOEPH5 vs. RI and TOEP5	6	5.8	.445
RI and TOEPH6 vs. RI and TOEP6	6	4.9	.563
Tests for number of lagged relationships:			
1 vs. 0 lags: RI and TOEP2 vs. RI and DIAG	1	1.5	.227
1 vs. 0 lags: RI and TOEPH2 vs. RI and DIAGH	1	0.7	.410
2 vs. 1 lags: RI and TOEP3 vs. RI and TOEP2	1	11.0	.001
2 vs. 1 lags: RI and TOEPH3 vs. RI and TOEPH2	1	9.1	.003
3 vs. 2 lags: RI and TOEP4 vs. RI and TOEP3	1	1.0	.327
3 vs. 2 lags: RI and TOEPH4 vs. RI and TOEPH3	1	0.6	.442
4 vs. 3 lags: RI and TOEP5 vs. RI and TOEP4	1	3.7	.056
4 vs. 3 lags: RI and TOEPH5 vs. RI and TOEPH4	1	2.0	.155
5 vs. 4 lags: RI and TOEP6 vs. RI and TOEP5	1	2.3	.133
5 vs. 4 lags: RI and TOEPH6 vs. RI and TOEPH5	1	1.3	.254
Tests for nested correlation structures:			
RI and AR1 vs. R-only AR1	~1	252.4	.001
RI and AR1 vs. RI and DIAG	1	1.8	.182

of 1's and post-multiplied by a 1x7 row vector of 1's (labeled as the **Z** and **Z** transpose matrices, respectively) in order to get to the right 7x7 size to then be added to the 7x7 **R** matrix. We'll examine these matrices in more detail in chapter 5, but for now this **G** and **R** combination process can be understood conceptually as adding the random intercept variance $\tau_{U_0}^2$ in **G** to each residual variance and covariance in the 7x7 **R** matrix (to the diagonal and upper off-diagonal elements in the second column of Table 4.3), resulting in the 7x7 **V** matrix (the diagonal and upper off-diagonal elements in the third column of Table 4.3). These total variances and covariances (in **V**) can then be used to calculate the total correlations (in **VCORR**).

As seen in Figure 4.1, just like the **R**-only models, the **G** and **R** combined models can also be viewed along a continuum of most to least parsimonious (and each has a homogeneous variance or heterogeneous variance version as well). Furthermore, the endpoints of this continuum are functionally equivalent across both families of models, as described next.

3.A. Baseline Model: Random Intercept Variance in G With an n–1 Order Unstructured R (RI and UNn–1)

Accordingly, our first **G** and **R** combined model, as seen in the first row of Table 4.3, combines a *random intercept variance in G with an $n - 1$ order unstructured R matrix* (RI and UNn–1). As shown by the equal sign in Figure 4.1, the RI and UNn–1 model has equivalent fit to the **R**-only n-order unstructured (UNn) model we saw before. The difference in order of n–1 versus n for the unstructured **R** matrix arises because the UNn model for the **R** matrix would use all possible degrees of freedom, so then we couldn't also estimate one more parameter for $\tau_{U_0}^2$ in the **G** matrix. If we tried to estimate 29 parameters for the 28 possible variances and covariances, at least one of the parameters will be unidentified (and no standard error for it would be given).

One of many potential ways of solving this problem is to constrain the covariance on the last off-diagonal (i.e., between days 1 and 7) of the **R** matrix to be 0 so as to remain at 28 total parameters. Thus, the term *UNn–1* for an n–1 order unstructured **R** matrix means that the last off-diagonal element in the **R** matrix has been eliminated in order to be able to estimate the random intercept variance $\tau_{U_0}^2$ in the **G** matrix. But this does NOT mean that we are assuming no covariance between days 1 and 7. Instead, it means that we are assuming no *extra* covariance between the e_{ti} residuals for days 1 and 7 *after controlling for the covariance implied by* $\tau_{U_0}^2$. That is, although there is no within-person covariance in the last off-diagonal for day 1 to 7 in the **R** matrix, there is still a covariance in the resulting total **V** matrix for days 1 and 7, as created by $\tau_{U_0}^2$ from the **G** matrix (as shown in Figure 4.2). Accordingly, the UNn–1 **R** matrix then describes the *within-person residual* variance and covariance that is left after subtracting $\tau_{U_0}^2$.

By comparing the **V** matrix for the RI and UNn–1 model (first row of Table 4.3) to the **R** matrix for the **R**-only UNn model (first row of Table 4.1), we can see that their predictions and model fit are the same. That is, the point of estimating the RI and UNn–1 model is not to improve fit by adding $\tau^2_{U_0}$; rather, it is to see the "answer key" for the pattern of within-person, residual e_{ti} variance and covariance *that is left* after controlling for $\tau^2_{U_0}$ in the G matrix. This is just a different view of the same data than that given by the **R**-only UNn model without a random intercept, whose role is to provide the "answer key" for the *total* variance and covariance over time instead (as still seen in the **V** matrix of the RI and UNn–1 model created by **G** and **R**).

More generally in these **G** and **R** combined models, $\tau^2_{U_0}$ will be estimated to reflect the expected covariance among any occasions that have 0 covariance specified in the **R** matrix. So, in the most complex RI and UNn–1 model, because the only **R** matrix covariance that is set to 0 is between the first and last occasions, $\tau^2_{U_0}$ will reflect this actual covariance specifically. Thus, in the RI and UNn–1 model, $\tau^2_{U_0} = 0.353$, as based only on the observed covariance between days 1 and 7; that is why it is smaller than the estimate of $\tau^2_{U_0} = 0.390$ from the **R**-only CS model (which was based on all possible covariances across days instead). Similarly, in the less complex models that follow, $\tau^2_{U_0}$ will essentially reflect the average covariance across any sets of occasions that have 0 covariance specified in the **R** matrix (as also shown more generally in Figure 4.2).

But despite this difference in which information is used to estimate $\tau^2_{U_0}$, the **R** matrix obtained in the RI and UNn–1 model can still provide the general pattern of how the WP residual variances and covariances differ over time. As seen in Table 4.3, although the leftover WP e_{ti} residual variance on the diagonal of the **R** matrix seems fairly constant across days, the residual correlations are fairly substantial from lag-1 to lag-4, but seem to drop off after that. As before, we can consider more parsimonious models for **R** matrix to try and describe these patterns.

3.B. Random Intercept Variance in G With a Diagonal R (RI and DIAG) or With a Diagonal Heterogeneous R (RI and DIAGH)

The most parsimonious **G** and **R** combined model has 2 parameters and combines a *random intercept variance in the **G** matrix with a diagonal structure in the **R** matrix* (RI and DIAG), as seen in the second row of Table 4.3. Also known as a *variance components* **R** matrix, a **diagonal R** matrix predicts equal residual variances and no covariances across days at all. A diagonal **R** matrix used by itself without $\tau^2_{U_0}$ in the **G** matrix would be the same as an σ^2_e-only model (because without the **G** matrix, the **R** matrix = the **V** matrix). But in our case, a diagonal **R** matrix combined with $\tau^2_{U_0}$ in the **G** matrix results in a **V** matrix that then predicts a constant total variance across days of $\tau^2_{U_0} + \sigma^2_e$, with a constant covariance across days of $\tau^2_{U_0}$. Sound familiar? It should—as noted by the equal sign between them in Figure 4.1, a model with a random intercept variance in **G** with a diagonal **R** matrix (RI and DIAG) is the same as the **R**-only compound symmetry (CS) model, with the same model fit. It assumes that the total covariance across days is due solely to $\tau^2_{U_0}$, such that the e_{ti} residuals should then be unrelated across days. Thus, there is a significant decrease in fit between the 28-parameter RI and UNn–1 model and the 2-parameter RI and DIAG model of $-2\Delta LL(26) = 46.1$, $p = .009$, exactly the same result we saw in comparing the R-only UNn and CS models in Table 4.2.

The RI and DIAG model can be extended to allow heterogeneity of residual variance across days as the *random intercept variance in G and diagonal heterogeneous R matrix* (RI and DIAGH) model with $n + 1$ parameters. As seen in the third row of Table 4.3, although the residual variance in the R matrix is allowed to differ across days, there is still no e_{ti} correlation in the R matrix at all. The 2-parameter RI and DIAG model is nested within the 8-parameter RI and DIAGH model, and a comparison of their fit as seen in Table 4.4 yields $-2\Delta LL(6) = 10.5$, $p = .105$, or a nonsignificant improvement by adding heterogeneous residual variances across days; the AIC and BIC concur. However, unlike their homogeneous variance counterparts (RI and DIAG = R-only CS), the RI and DIAGH and the R-only CSH models are *not* equivalent, as indicated in Figure 4.1. This is due to the difference in what type of variance is heterogeneous in each model—heterogeneous *residual* variances in the RI and DIAGH model rather than heterogeneous *total* variances in the CSH model. Although the AIC and BIC prefer the RI and DIAGH model over the CSH model, both fit significantly worse than their unstructured baseline models, as seen in Table 4.2 for the CSH versus UNn models, $-2\Delta LL(20) = 42.9$, $p = .002$, and in Table 4.4 for the RI and DIAGH versus RI and UNn–1 models, $-2\Delta LL(20) = 35.6$, $p = .017$. So, there is still room for improvement by considering some additional G and R combined models.

3.C. Random Intercept Variance in G With a First-Order Auto-Regressive R (RI and AR1) or With a First-Order Auto-Regressive Heterogeneous R (RI and ARH1)

The next G and R combined model has three parameters and combines *a random intercept variance in the G matrix with a first-order auto-regressive structure in the R matrix* (RI and AR1). Unlike the R-only AR1 model in which the *total* correlation over time is predicted to decay exponentially by the auto-correlation parameter (so lag-1 = r_T^1, lag-2 = r_T^2, etc.), in the RI and AR1 model, the *WP residual* correlation is predicted to decay by the auto-correlation parameter instead. As seen in the fourth row of Table 4.3, the correlation between the lag-1 e_{ti} residuals is predicted to be $r_e^1 = .05^1$, at lag-2 to be $r_e^2 = .05^2$, at lag-3 to be $r_e^3 = .05^3$, and so on.

As indicated in Figure 4.1, two other models are nested within the RI and AR1 model. First, the 2-parameter R-only AR1 model is nested within the 3-parameter RI and AR1 model, and a comparison of their fit as seen in Table 4.4 yields $-2\Delta LL(\sim1) = 252.4$, $p < .001$, indicating that the addition of the random intercept variance in the RI and AR1 model results in a significant improvement in fit over the R-only AR1 model (and the AIC and BIC concur). (Recall from chapter 3 that the $\sim$ is used to acknowledge that $-2\Delta LL$ is only approximately distributed as a χ^2 with $df = \Delta df$ between models when some of the added parameters have a boundary for their possible values, resulting in a conservative significance test for the difference in model fit.) This means that predicting a sharp decay in only the *residual* correlation across days fits the data better than predicting a sharp decay in the *total* correlation across days instead. Second, the 2-parameter RI and DIAG model is also nested within the 3-parameter RI and AR1 model, and a comparison of their fit yields $-2\Delta\text{LL}(1) = 1.8$, $p = .182$, indicating that the addition of the WP auto-correlation parameter in the RI and AR1 model does not significantly improve model fit. The AIC likes both of these equally, but the BIC prefers the more parsimonious RI and DIAG model over the RI and AR1 model. Finally, the 3-parameter RI and AR1 model also fit significantly worse than the 28-parameter RI and UN$n-1$ model, $-2\Delta\text{LL}(25) = 44.3$, $p = .010$.

The RI and AR1 model can be extended to include heterogeneous residual variances across days by combining a *random intercept variance in G with a first-order auto-regressive heterogeneous R matrix* (RI and ARH1), as seen in the fifth row of Table 4.3. The RI and ARH1 model has $n + 2$ parameters, including n residual variances, 1 random intercept variance, and 1 residual auto-correlation parameter (by which residual covariances are created in the **R** matrix). The 9-parameter RI and ARH1 model did not have significantly better fit than the 3-parameter RI and AR1 model, $-2\Delta\text{LL}(6) = 9.52$, $p = .146$; the AIC and BIC concur, indicating that adding heterogeneous residual variances did not help. The AIC and BIC also prefer the RI and ARH1 model over the **R**-only ARH1 model (which are not nested given their difference in whether the *residual* or *total* variance is heterogeneous). Finally, the 9-parameter RI and ARH1 model also fit significantly worse than the 28-parameter RI and UN$n-1$ model, $-2\Delta\text{LL}(19) = 34.8$, $p = .015$, indicating that further **G** and **R** combined models should be considered.

3.D. Random Intercept Variance in G With a Reduced-Lag Toeplitz R (RI and TOEP*x*) or Reduced-Lag Toeplitz Heterogeneous R (RI and TOEPH*x*)

Finally, the last of **G** and **R** combined models we will examine combines a *random intercept variance in the G matrix with a reduced-lag Toeplitz structure in the R matrix* (RI and TOEP*x*) or a *with a reduced-lag Toeplitz heterogeneous structure in the R matrix* (RI and TOEPH*x*), as seen in Table 4.3. Similar to the **R**-only $n-1$ lag Toeplitz model that predicts the *total* covariance (or *total* correlation in the heterogeneous version) to be the same within lags but to differ between lags, the RI and TOEP*x* (or RI and TOEPH*x*) models predict the *residual* covariance (or *residual* correlation in the heterogeneous versions) in the **R** matrix to be the same within lags, but to differ between lags. The order of the Toeplitz models is always one higher than the number of lags included because of the 1 band of variances on the diagonal.

But there is an important distinction to be made between the **R**-only Toeplitz models and their analogs also including the random intercept variance $\tau_{U_0}^2$ in the **G** matrix. In the **R**-only Toeplitz models, it would not be logical to reduce the number of lagged *total* covariances or correlations estimated, because outcomes from the same person are usually at least somewhat related, no matter how far apart in time they occur. Therefore, for our 7-occasion example data, we only considered the 6-lag TOEPn and 6-lag TOEPHn **R**-only models with all possible $n-1$ lags (i.e., up to an order of n occasions). But after controlling for the constant covariance due to person mean differences through $\tau_{U_0}^2$ in the **G** matrix, relationships may only remain among the residuals closest in time, such that fewer lagged *residual* covariances or correlations may be necessary (and thus the abbreviations TOEP*x* and TOEPH*x* that imply a variable number of *x* parameters independent of the *n* occasions). Thus, the benefit of adding $\tau_{U_0}^2$ to the **G** matrix is not to improve the fit of the Toeplitz models, but to be able to potentially fit fewer lagged relationships among the residuals in the **R** matrix after accounting for the covariance due to $\tau_{U_0}^2$ in the **G** matrix, thus potentially offering greater parsimony than the **R**-only Toeplitz models.

For our 7-occasion example data, Table 4.4 provides the fit of models combining $\tau_{U_0}^2$ in the **G** matrix with Toeplitz-structured **R** matrices (with either homogeneous or heterogeneous residual variance across days) that range from residual covariances or correlations only at lag-1 (RI and TOEP2 or TOEPH2) all the way through lag-5 (RI and TOEP6 or TOEPH6). Within each model, although the off-diagonals for the non-estimated lags are fixed to 0 in the **R** matrix, covariances and correlations for those lags are still predicted in the total **V** matrix due to $\tau_{U_0}^2$ in the **G** matrix, with Toeplitz-structured **R** matrices (with either homogeneous or heterogeneous residual variance across days) that range from residual covariances or correlations only at lag-1 (RI and TOEP2 or TOEPH2) all the way through lag-5 (RI and TOEP6 or TOEPH6). Within each model, although the off-diagonals for the non-estimated lags are fixed to 0 in the **R** matrix, covariances and correlations for those lags are still predicted in the total **V** matrix due to $\tau_{U_0}^2$ in the **G** matrix. You may notice a smaller estimate of $\tau_{U_0}^2$ in the **G** matrix as more lags are added—this is because its estimate is based on which **R** matrix lagged covariances are still set to 0, which are just for the occasions further apart in time (that are less related) as more lags are added.

The covariance at the last lag (at lag-6 here) is not separately estimable from $\tau_{U_0}^2$ in the **G** matrix, so the maximum number of lags in a Toeplitz **R** residual structure combined with $\tau_{U_0}^2$ in **G** is *n*–2, rather than *n*–1 as in an **R**-only Toeplitz model. In fact, the **R**-only *n*–1 lag Toeplitz model and the RI and *n*–2 lag Toeplitz model each have *n* parameters and will have the same fit and model predictions in their **R** and **V** matrices, respectively (but their heterogeneous variance versions will not be equivalent, given heterogeneous *total* variances in the **R**-only *n*–1 lag TOEPH model versus heterogeneous *residual* variances in the RI and *n*–2 lag TOEPH model).

So how do we know how many lagged relationships among the e_{ti} residuals should be included? Conveniently, models with fewer lags are nested within models with more lags, and so Table 4.4 provides comparisons of fit across lags for both the homogeneous and heterogeneous variance versions of the models. As shown, although there was no significant improvement when going from a 0-lag to a 1-lag model (RI and DIAG vs. RI and TOEP2; RI and DIAGH vs. RI and TOEPH2), there was a significant improvement in fit when going from a 1-lag to a 2-lag model (RI and TOEP2 vs. RI and TOEP3; RI and TOEPH2 vs. RI and TOEPH3), but nonsignificant improvements in fit when adding additional lags (3 to 5). In addition, none of the tests for heterogeneity of residual variance (e.g., RI and TOEP2 vs. RI and TOEPH2) was significant.

In summary, of the **G** and **R** combined models with Toeplitz **R** structures, the RI and 2-lag TOEP3 model fit relatively best as indicated by the series of –2ΔLL tests. Furthermore, although the AIC was slightly smaller for the RI and 4-lag TOEP5 model and for the RI and 5-lag TOEP6 model, the BIC is smallest for the RI and 2-lag TOEP3 model. All things considered, it seems the RI and 2-lag TOEP3 model provides the best balance of good fit and parsimony in describing the pattern of variance and covariance in positive mood across days. It does so using just 4 parameters: a random intercept variance $\tau^2_{U_0}$ that allows a constant covariance across all days, a single residual variance σ^2_e across days, and additional covariances between the WP e_{ti} residuals one day apart and two days apart (at lag-1 and lag-2). In analyzing these data further, we would proceed using the RI and 2-lag TOEP3 model to examine our predictors of interest. We would then have greater confidence in the accuracy of the standard errors for subsequent fixed effects than if we had not investigated how well the model for the variance actually predicted the variances and covariances over time. However, given that the RI and 2-lag TOEP3 model would also need to describe the pattern of remaining variance and covariance after including *all* model predictors, we may wish to re-examine its suitability after evaluating all of our predictors as well.

4. Chapter Summary

This chapter presented **alternative covariance structure** (ACS) models for describing patterns of variance and covariance over time in a longitudinal outcome. ACS models offer more flexibility than ANOVA models for accurate but parsimonious prediction of the observed pattern of variation and covariation over time and can be viewed along a continuum of least to most complex (i.e., from *compound symmetry* to *unstructured*). Although they do not require complete data, most ACS models do require balanced data with equal time intervals between occasions (given that most models employ the idea of a *lag*, which implies equidistant time observations). ACS models are best-suited for outcomes showing within-person fluctuation (that often show a dependency pattern of non-constant within-person correlation for unknown reasons), rather than outcomes showing within-person change (in which the primary source of dependency is likely to be individual differences in intercept and change over time instead). We then used a working example of self-reported positive mood over seven days to examine two families of ACS models: those without or with a random intercept variance that predicts constant covariance over time.

First, in ACS models employing an **R** matrix without a **G** matrix (i.e., the **R**-only models), the *total* variances and covariances over time are predicted in the **R** matrix. In addition to the *compound symmetry* and *unstructured* models, we also examined *first-order auto-regressive* models (by which the correlation over time is predicted to decay exponentially) and *Toeplitz* models (in which the correlation between occasions within the same time lag is assumed equal, but in which different correlations are estimated across time lags). Each of these models can have homogeneous or heterogeneous variance across occasions as well.

Second, in the **G** and **R** combined ACS models, a random intercept variance is estimated in the **G** matrix, such that the remaining within-person residual variances and covariances are then estimated in the **R** matrix (of which homogeneous or heterogeneous variance versions of the diagonal, first-order auto-regressive, or Toeplitz structures can be estimated). In these **G** and **R** combined models, the random intercept variance in the **G** matrix is added to every variance and covariance in the **R** matrix to construct a **V** matrix for the total predicted pattern of variance and covariance over time. The **G** and **R** combined models are best suited for outcomes with a large intraclass correlation (i.e., much of the variance is between persons and constant over time). In those cases, the **G** and **R** combined models can offer the opportunity for greater parsimony, in that relationships among the residuals at distant time lags in the **R** matrix may not be necessary after controlling for covariance due to constant mean differences between persons (i.e., by including the random intercept variance in the **G** matrix).

Numerous variants of the ACS models were presented so that you could be aware of a full catalog of options for predicting variance and covariance over time, and there are many others that are available (e.g., for spatial correlation) that were not presented. In practice, though, you may not need to consider all possible alternative models, and may instead wish to focus on those that seem most plausible given the variances and covariances estimated in the unstructured model (i.e., the "answer key" for what the other models are trying to predict) when it's possible to do so. Furthermore, if you have relatively few occasions of balanced data (e.g., 3 to 4), then there may not be much point in trying to evaluate alternative models for the variances and covariances. Instead, you may simply choose to use an unstructured model (given that it can never be wrong), and call it good. However, it can be advantageous to try and predict the total variance and covariance over time using a simpler model (with fewer parameters), especially when there are too few people or too many occasions to make estimation of an unstructured model feasible.

5. Sample Results Section

Because the process of finding an unconditional model that best describes the observed pattern of variation and covariation over time is usually not of substantive interest, in most written reports it can be summarized substantially, as shown for the positive mood data below.

A series of unconditional models (i.e., without predictors) were estimated to describe the variances and covariances of positive mood over 7 days using restricted maximum likelihood (REML). An unstructured model (i.e., in which 7 variances and 21 covariances were estimated separately) was first examined to provide a baseline for comparison. Although the variances appeared relatively homogeneous across days, the covariances did appear to decline slightly with increasing time lags. Because no systematic change in positive mood was expected or observed across days, alternative covariance structure models were evaluated to ensure appropriate tests of subsequent fixed effects. To predict the total pattern of variance and covariance over time, we examined the **R**-matrix-only models of compound symmetry (CS; equal variances, equal covariances), first-order auto-regressive (AR1; equal variances, a correlation of r^1 for lag-1, r^2 for lag-2, r^3 for lag-3, and so forth), and Toeplitz (TOEP or banded; all variances equal, equal covariance within a time lag, but separate covariances across time lags), as well as heterogeneous variance versions of each. A combination approach was also taken, in which a random intercept was estimated in the **G** matrix, and alternative covariances structures for the residual variances and covariances were then estimated in the **R** matrix (including a diagonal model with no additional residual covariation, an AR1 model, and reduced Toeplitz models with additional residual covariances up to lag-5, as well heterogeneous variance versions of each).

Table 4.2 and Table 4.4 provide the model –2LL value and information criteria (AIC and BIC) for the **R**-only models and for the **G** and **R** combined models, respectively. The model that provided the most parsimonious representation of the variances and covariances over time that still exhibited reasonable fit to the observed data, as indicated by the AIC and BIC, included 4 parameters: a random intercept variance that allows a constant covariance across all days, a single residual variance across days, and additional Toeplitz (banded) covariances between the residuals one day apart (lag-1) and two days apart (lag-2). Allowing the residual variances in this model to differ across days did not result in a better fit according to a likelihood ratio test, $-2\Delta LL(6) = 7.8$, $p = .252$, as well as higher AIC and BIC values indicating worse fit. Thus, the random intercept and 2-lag Toeplitz homogeneous variance model was used as the basis for all subsequent analyses. The model-predicted variances, covariances, and correlations over time given in the **V** matrix after combining the **G** and **R** matrices are given in Table 4.3.

Review Questions

1. What characteristics of longitudinal data should be considered in choosing an ACS model?
2. What is the difference between alternative covariance structure models that use only the **R** matrix versus those that use the **G** and **R** matrices? What advantage does the latter have?
3. Describe the rules for which ACS models can be considered nested or non-nested, as well as which **R**-only models or **G** and **R** combined models will be equivalent or nonequivalent.

References

Hedeker, D., & Gibbons, D. (2006). *Longitudinal data analysis* (Wiley series in probability and statistics). Hoboken, NJ: Wiley.

Littell, R. C., Milliken, G. A., Stroup, W. W., Wolfinger, R. D., & Schabenberger, O. (2006). *SAS for mixed models* (2nd ed.). Cary, NC: SAS Institute.

CHAPTER 5

INTRODUCTION TO RANDOM EFFECTS OF TIME AND MODEL ESTIMATION

The first section of this text (chapters 1–3) presented the necessary building blocks for conducting longitudinal analysis, and the current section of the text (chapters 4–6) has been using those building blocks to describe the effects of time in *unconditional* models (i.e., in which time is the only predictor variable). Whereas chapter 4 presented models for describing patterns of outcome variance and covariance arising primarily from within-person fluctuation over time, chapters 5 and 6 will focus instead on models for describing within-person change over time.

This chapter has two related goals. First, it will introduce the idea of fixed and random effects of time in modeling within-person change. We'll begin by considering some conceptual issues, including the potential metrics by which to index change and the overall purpose of fixed and random effects of time. The chapter will then use a simple linear model for change over time to introduce the multilevel specification of longitudinal models, to show how fixed and random effects of time generate predictions for the means, variances, and covariances of the outcome (even for unbalanced time), and to show how random effects models may be combined with alternative covariance structure (ACS) models for even more flexibility. That will bring us to the second goal—to describe the likelihood-based estimation processes by which we obtain our model results. Although the basics of likelihood estimation as they relate to conducting model comparisons were introduced in chapter 3, this chapter will provide more detail and explanation for this challenging but necessary topic. Although a somewhat disparate subject, likelihood estimation is presented within this chapter deliberately because we will use the random linear model for time that is introduced in the first half of the chapter as a specific working example in order to present the topic of likelihood estimation as concretely as possible in the second half.

Once this new general foundation of fixed and random effects of time is in place, chapter 6 will then follow with alternative families of models for describing patterns of change over time, including polynomial models, nonlinear models, and piecewise (discontinuous) models. At the end of chapter 6 we will then be poised to transition from unconditional longitudinal models to more informative and interesting *conditional* models in the third section of the text, including models with time-invariant predictors (chapter 7) and time-varying predictors (chapters 8 and 9).

1. Conceptualizing Models of Change Over Time

1.A. What Should "Time" Be? Where Should "Time 0" Be?

Before diving into the specifics of modeling change, it is important to understand the big picture of what each part of these models will be trying to do. Statistical models of change over time often begin with two initial goals. One goal is *description*—to describe the average pattern of change over time and individual differences therein. The other goal is *prediction*—to predict those *between-person* or *interindividual* differences in change over time, and to predict remaining *within-person* or *intraindividual* variation over time. In pursuing these and more complex aims regarding change over time, however, we are implicitly assuming that we know what *time* is. Yet in many contexts exactly what *time* should be is both a theoretical and empirical question in that different metrics for indexing time that reflect alternative causal models of change may yield different conclusions. For instance, in studying learning in elementary school children, does it matter what grade a child is in, does it matter how old the child is, or do both matter? In studying relationship satisfaction, does it matter how long a couple has been married, how long they've been together in total (i.e., including time spent dating), or is change in relationship satisfaction more closely tied to the timing of a critical event, such as the birth of their first child together?

Chapter 10 will address the topic of alternative metrics of time in greater detail, but a careful consideration of what *time* should be is always an important first step in any longitudinal analysis. This is especially the case when your goal is to model change over time—which is why this concern about time is mentioned here prior to examining any models of change. Although the examples in chapters 5 to 9 will utilize a naïve and generic metric of *time in study,* in your own data other metrics of time may be more relevant or salient, such as *chronological age, time in treatment,* and so forth. It is fine for now for you to think of *time* as whichever metric best indexes the causal process thought to be responsible for the observed change in your data, and to proceed through chapters 5 to 9 with that personal definition of *time* in mind.

However, a caution needs to be made in advance if your data result from an **accelerated longitudinal design** (i.e., a sequential overlapping cohort design; see chapter 10), in which people differ in that metric of time at their baseline observation (e.g., people who begin the study at different ages are followed as they age; separate cohorts of children who begin in different grades of school are followed as they progress through school). In these kinds of accelerated designs, it is likely that more complex unconditional models will be required to fully capture the multiple effects of *time* that result. But using *time in study* as *time* will allow us to ignore such complications for now so that we can focus on the basic features of models for change over time.

Finally, another important consideration prior to defining models of change is where time 0 should be. Recall from chapter 2 that after including predictors, the intercept becomes the expected outcome when all predictors = 0. The same is true for longitudinal models—in order for the intercept to be meaningful, the scale of your metric of time should include a meaningful 0 value. Although centering time or any other predictor (i.e., subtracting a constant so that 0 is within the scale of the new predictor) will not change the predicted outcomes or the fit of the model, choosing different constants at which to center time will change the interpretation of some of the model parameters, rendering them more or less useful to you as the data analyst.

For instance, consider a study of adult development in which age ranges from 25 to 50—if you believe age should be the metric by which to index change over time, you might include *age* as the *time* predictor variable. But if the age predictor were included as is, the intercept would be the expected outcome at birth (age = 0). Further, if an interaction of sex by age were included, the simple main effect of sex would be the difference in the outcome between boys and girls specifically at birth. While there is technically nothing wrong with this, the resulting model parameters may be very strange given how far outside the data they are located (i.e., no one in the study has age = 0). A more useful time 0 could be created by centering age at 25 (i.e., by subtracting 25 from the age variable and including that new age predictor variable instead), such that time 0 would then refer to a 25-year-old. Accordingly, the intercept would then be the expected outcome at age 25; the simple main effect of sex would become the difference between 25-year-old men and women. But time 0 doesn't always have to be at the beginning—centering at any age actually included in the study (e.g., an age between 25 and 50) may be just as useful, depending on the research questions to be addressed. However, it is important to note that the precision with which the intercept and subsequent effects conditional on it are estimated varies across the possible values of time 0, with the most precision generally found toward the mean of time (see Biesanz, Deeb-Sossa, Papadakis, Bollen, & Curran, 2004, for further discussion).

Similarly, in studies of childhood development, if *grade in school* was the *time* predictor variable, then including *grade* in the model as is would create an intercept (and simple main effects of any interacting predictors) that would refer specifically to grade 0 (at kindergarten). Centering at one of the grades observed in the study is likely to be more useful. No matter what your chosen metric of time is, for the sake of interpretability, the location of time 0 should exist in your observed data. If you are still uncertain, consider this question: At what point in time do you want a snapshot of individual differences? Centering your time predictor so that 0 refers to that specific point in time will result in model effects that are as useful to you as possible.

With these ideas of what *time* should be in mind, let us now overview the separate roles the effects of time can play in the model for the means and in the model for the variance.

1.B. Two Different Effects of Time: Fixed and Random

In thinking about the roles a predictor of *time* can play in a model of change, there are two relevant questions to be answered. First, *is there change over time on average?* That is, if you were to graph the means of your outcome over time, would the slope through those means be something other than flat? The model parameters that will describe any change over time on average are the *fixed effects of time* in the model for the means. Although the terms *fixed* and *random* have been introduced previously, they have a more direct interpretation in this context: the term **fixed effect** means *everybody gets the same effect.* Fixed effects of time are what analysis of variance models are designed specifically to test (i.e., mean differences over time), and thus, so far fixed effects are the only effects of time we have really considered.

But in addition to change on average, the second question to be answered is about individual change: *Does everybody change the same?* In other words, is the fixed effect for the slope across time that everybody would get sufficient, or does each person need his or her own *random effect* for the slope across time instead? The term **random effect** means *everybody gets his or her own effect.* In contrast to fixed effects of time that represent change on average in the model for the means, random effects of time represent *individual differences* in change as part of the model for the variance instead. That is, rather than estimating a different fixed time slope for each person, we will estimate the *variance* across persons of *individual deviations* from the fixed time slope. Random slopes for the effect of time are not a part of analysis of variance (ANOVA), and are thus a new addition to our toolbox so far. Although specific terminology differs across disciplines, the terms *random effect of time* and *random slope for time* are synonymous—the key idea is that *random* means each person gets his or her own *effect* or *slope* of a predictor.

Before diving into any model equations, it is important to recognize that any combination of fixed and/or random effects of time can be observed in a given longitudinal outcome. This is depicted by the four panels in Figure 5.1, in which the *x*-axis is time, the *y*-axis is the outcome variable, the heavy line is meant to convey the fixed slope for mean change over time for the sample, and the thin lines show the time slopes for hypothetical individuals in the sample. In each panel, a "yes" indicates a significant effect; a "no" indicates a nonsignificant effect.

First, the top left panel (a) in Figure 5.1 shows effects of time that are neither fixed nor random—no significant effects of time, period. There is no *fixed* effect of time because the slope of the heavy line for the means over time is flat—there is no change on average. But there is also no *random* effect of time because that flat fixed slope for time is sufficient for everybody. That is, although each person does still need his or her own random *intercept* (i.e., so that the vertical distance between the parallel lines differs between persons), each person does not need his or her own random *slope* for the effect of time beyond the fixed slope. Second, the top right panel (b) in Figure 5.1 shows a fixed effect of time, but no random effect of time. There is a *fixed* effect of time because the slope of the heavy line for the means over time is not flat (i.e., the outcome increases over time on average). But there is no *random* effect of time because that fixed slope for the mean increase over time is sufficient to describe each person's individual rate of change.

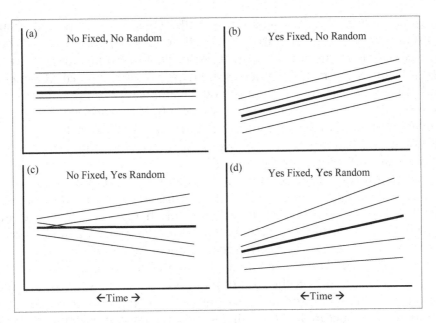

Figure 5.1 Illustration of fixed and random effects of time.

Third, the bottom left panel (c) in Figure 5.1 shows perhaps the most interesting scenario: when there is no fixed effect of time, but there is a random effect of time. There is no *fixed* effect of time because the slope of the heavy line for the means over time is flat—there is no change on average, as in the top left panel (a). But in the bottom left panel (c), however, because the flat fixed effect of time does *not* describe the individual slopes, there is a *random* effect of time, such that each person needs his or her own different slope for the effect of time beyond the fixed slope. In this case, the fact that some people increase over time while others decrease results in a pattern of no mean change overall (and thus no fixed effect of time), but that zero fixed effect of time may not describe anyone in the sample (and thus is not informative). Finally, the bottom right panel (d) in Figure 5.1 shows perhaps the most common pattern, in which there are both fixed and random effects of time. There is a *fixed* effect of time because the slope of the heavy line for the means over time is not flat (i.e., the outcome increases over time on average). But there is also a *random* effect of time because that fixed effect slope does not adequately describe the individual slopes. Instead, because some people increase at a *faster* rate than average while others increase at a *slower* rate than average, people still need their own different slopes for time beyond the fixed slope—there is a random effect of time.

One other feature of Figure 5.1 to mention is that the univariate ANOVA (compound symmetry) model for the variance will only be appropriate for data that resemble the top panels, in which people differ in their intercept (i.e., location on y-axis), but not in their rates of change (i.e., no random effects of time). This is because, as illustrated in the bottom panels, if people change differently over time, then the variance of the outcome over time has to change, too (and by extension, the covariance over time will change as well). Thus, the compound symmetry model that predicts constant variance over time (from $\tau_{U_0}^2$ and σ_e^2) and constant covariance over time (from just $\tau_{U_0}^2$) will not fit data like that shown in the lower panels of Figure 5.1 very well. Whereas in chapter 4 we evaluated ACS models to try and predict the pattern of variance and covariances over time directly, in this chapter we will instead focus on random effects of time that also allow the variances and covariances to change over time but that do so more indirectly.

Although the patterns of change over time shown in Figure 5.1 are very simplistic, they are still useful for conveying the idea that in the models that follow, any of the four combinations of fixed and random effects of time can be observed (neither, just fixed, just random, or both). To summarize, the purpose of any *fixed* effects of time is to describe the *mean* pattern of change over time. The purpose of *random* effects of time is to describe *individual differences* in those patterns of change while simultaneously allowing the variance and covariance to change over time as needed. Thus, models including random effects of time serve as another kind of "happy medium" on the spectrum of potential models for the variance for longitudinal data ranging from most parsimonious (compound symmetry) to least parsimonious (unstructured). As we will see, though, random effects of time do not require complete data or balanced time data across persons, and as such can offer great flexibility for describing within-person change over time.

2. A Random Linear Model for Change Over Time

This section will introduce the formal specification of models with fixed and random effects of time using the simplest type of change: linear change, or constant change over time. Our working example will be a simulated dataset of 25 persons assessed on a single test score outcome ($M = 12.85$, $SD = 3.14$, range = 6.96 to 22.41) at four annual occasions. Individual trajectories are shown in Figure 5.2. All

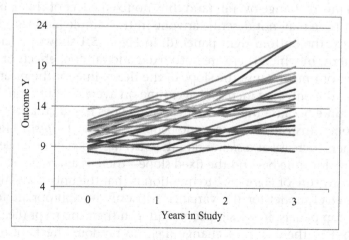

Figure 5.2 Individual trajectories for four-occasion example data.

models in this section will be estimated using *restricted maximum likelihood* (REML; as introduced in chapter 3 and elaborated later in this chapter). *Years in study* will be our metric of time, such that time 0 will represent the first occasion. For ease of exposition, these example data are complete and balanced across persons, such that each person has an outcome at year 0, 1, 2, and 3. Later in this section we will see how these models can also include unbalanced data in which the observed time observations differ across persons.

We begin by introducing a new way of writing longitudinal models: as **multilevel models**, in which the **level-1** model predicts outcome variation within persons (WP) over time and the **level-2** model predicts variation between persons (BP). A synonym for multilevel models is the term **mixed models**, which is used to describe models that have both fixed and random effects. We will also continue to use the terminology introduced in chapter 4 to describe the contents of the model for the variance. To review, any within-person variances and covariances at level 1 will be in the **R** matrix, a symmetric matrix with n by n rows and columns (in which n is the number of occasions per person, or $n = 4$ in our example here). Any between-person variances and covariances at level 2 will be in the symmetric **G** matrix. Previously, **G** was a 1x1 matrix (or scalar) that held only a random intercept variance $\tau_{U_0}^2$, but from now on the **G** matrix may hold other elements as well. Later in this section we will see exactly how in random effects models the **G** and **R** matrices combine to create the total predicted **V** matrix of variances and covariances over time (in which **V** is also a symmetric matrix with n by n rows and columns).

For now, though, we will proceed through a sequence of models for linear change over time so that the ideas of *fixed* and *random* effects of time can be demonstrated more concretely.

2.A. Specification of Fixed and Random Effects Through Multilevel Models

The starting point for any longitudinal analysis is to estimate the *within-person empty model* that was originally introduced in chapter 3, as shown in multilevel form in Equation (5.1):

Level 1: $y_{ti} = \beta_{0i} + e_{ti}$

Level 2: $\beta_{0i} = \gamma_{00} + U_{0i}$ (5.1)

Composite: $y_{ti} = (\gamma_{00} + U_{0i}) + e_{ti}$

in which the within-person (level-1) and between-person (level-2) models are written separately. First, in the within-person level-1 model, the outcome y_{ti} at time t for individual i is defined by an individual intercept, β_{0i}, as well as a time-specific and person-specific within-person residual e_{ti}. The β_{0i} intercept term in the level-1 model has an i subscript to indicate that β_{0i} varies over individuals. But β_{0i} is not an estimated parameter—β_{0i} is just a placeholder that gets defined at level 2 by two terms: the fixed intercept, which we now denote as γ_{00} (pronounced "gamma"), and the random intercept U_{0i}. Given that this is an empty model that contains no predictors, the fixed intercept γ_{00} is the grand mean of the person means, and the random intercept U_{0i} is the individual-specific deviation between the grand mean and each person's mean over time. This model has 3 estimated parameters: 1 parameter in the model for the means (the fixed intercept γ_{00}) and 2 parameters in the model for the variance ($\tau^2_{U_0}$, the between-person variance of the level-2 U_{0i} random intercepts in the **G** matrix, and σ^2_e, the remaining within-person variance across time of the level-1 e_{ti} residuals in the **R** matrix). That there are only 3 total parameters is shown directly in the composite single-level model in the last line of Equation (5.1), in which the β_{0i} intercept placeholder has been replaced by its contents ($\gamma_{00} + U_{0i}$).

With regard to the name of the model in Equation (5.1), we can drop the *within-person* part of the name because all longitudinal models will include both between-person and within-person variance. In the multilevel modeling literature, the model in Equation (5.1) is often called an *empty model* because it has only a fixed intercept in the model for the means. But it may also be called a *random intercept model* or a *variance components model* because the only variance term besides σ^2_e is $\tau^2_{U_0}$. We wouldn't have to call it a *fixed and random intercept model* because the random intercept U_{0i} is defined as a deviation from the fixed intercept γ_{00} such that the fixed intercept has to be there already. So, to avoid confusion and clearly define what it contains on *each* side of the model, we will refer to the model in Equation (5.1) as an **empty means, random intercept model.** In general, the way that each person gets his or her own model effect (such as an intercept here) is by combining a fixed effect with an individual-specific random effect that is the person's deviation from the fixed effect. So, when describing a model that has an effect with both a fixed and a random part, it is sufficient to name only the random part. When a model effect has *only* a fixed part without a random part, it will be named as such, as will be seen later.

Finally, the subscripts of fixed effects keep track of that term's order within each level of the model. For instance, in the fixed intercept γ_{00}, the first subscript is 0 because it contributes to β_{0i} in the level-1 model (just as the first subscript is 0 in U_{0i} because it also contributes to β_{0i}). The second subscript in γ_{00} is 0 because γ_{00} is the lowest-order fixed effect in its level-2 equation. These subscripts will make more sense once there are more fixed effects to keep track of, though.

The results from our example data of 25 persons across four annual occasions (year 0, 1, 2, and 3) for the empty means, random intercept only model from REML estimation are shown in the first column of Table 5.1. The three model parameters are the fixed intercept of $\gamma_{00} = 12.85$, a level-2 random intercept variance in the **G** matrix of $\tau^2_{U_0} = 2.88$, and a level-1 residual variance in the **R** matrix of $\sigma^2_e = 7.06$. According to this model, the total variance at each occasion in the **V** matrix is predicted to be constant at $\tau^2_{U_0} + \sigma^2_e = 2.88 + 7.06 = 9.94$, and the total covariance across occasions in the **V** matrix is predicted to be constant at $\tau^2_{U_0} = 2.88$. We can predict the total

Table 5.1 Model parameters for the four-occasion example data. Bold values are $p < .05$.

Model Parameters	Equation 5.1: Empty Means, Random Intercept Model			Equation 5.3: Fixed Linear Time, Random Intercept Model			Equation 5.5: Random Linear Time Model		
	Est	SE	p <	Est	SE	p <	Est	SE	p <
Model for the Means									
β_0 Intercept	**12.85**	**0.43**	**.001**	**10.27**	**0.47**	**.001**	**10.27**	**0.33**	**.001**
β_1 Linear Time				**1.72**	**0.13**	**.001**	**1.72**	**0.20**	**.001**
Model for the Variance									
$\tau^2_{U_0}$ Random Intercept Variance	**2.88**	**1.37**	**.018**	**4.10**	**1.34**	**.001**	**2.26**	**0.80**	**.002**
$\tau_{U_{01}}$ Intercept-Linear Covariance							0.05	0.35	.876
$\tau^2_{U_1}$ Random Linear Slope Variance							**0.91**	**0.30**	**.001**
σ^2_e Residual Variance	**7.06**	**1.15**	**.001**	**2.17**	**0.36**	**.001**	**0.70**	**0.14**	**.001**
REML Model Fit									
Number of Parameters	3			4			6		
–2LL	502.2			415.1			366.7		
AIC	506.2			419.1			374.7		
BIC	508.7			421.5			379.6		

constant correlation across occasions and assess the relative magnitude of each source of variation via an **intraclass correlation** (ICC), as seen in chapter 3 and shown in Equation (5.2):

$$\text{ICC} = \frac{\text{BP variation}}{\text{BP} + \text{WP variation}} = \frac{\text{Var}(U_{0i})}{\text{Var}(U_{0i}) + \text{Var}(e_{ti})} = \frac{\tau^2_{U_0}}{\tau^2_{U_0} + \sigma^2_e} \tag{5.2}$$

$$= \frac{2.88}{2.88 + 7.06} = .29$$

in which the ICC = .29. Thus, of the total variation in our outcome over time, 29% is due to constant mean differences between persons (the between-person variance of the U_{0i} random intercepts at level 2), and 71% is due to the remaining variation around those person means (the within-person variance of the e_{ti} residuals at level 1). To test whether the ICC = 0.29 is greater than 0, we can compare the fit of the empty means, random intercept model from Equation (5.1) to the fit of an empty means, σ^2_e-only model via a –2ΔLL likelihood ratio test (as introduced in chapter 3). In doing so we find –2ΔLL(~1) = 9.8, p = .002 (recall from chapter 3 that the ~ is used to acknowledge that –2ΔLL is only approximately distributed as a χ^2 with $df = \Delta df$ between models when some of the added parameters have a boundary for their possible values, resulting in a conservative significance test for the difference in model fit). This result indicates that the addition of $\tau^2_{U_0}$ did significantly improve model fit, or that the ICC = .29 is significantly greater than 0 (and the smaller AIC and BIC for the empty means, random intercept model concur).

Figure 5.3 illustrates how the model parameters create predicted trajectories on average and for specific individuals by showing the sample means at each occasion (in squares), as well as the outcomes for two hypothetical individuals in the sample (person A in dots; person B in triangles). First, the top panel of Figure 5.3a depicts the predicted trajectories over time from the empty means, random intercept model in Equation (5.1). Without any fixed effects of time, the sample means over time are predicted to be constant (as shown by the flat heavy dashed line predicted by the fixed intercept $\gamma_{00} = 12.85$), which doesn't fit the observed means at all. In

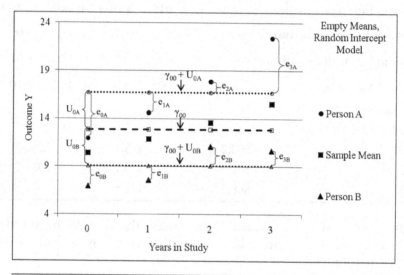

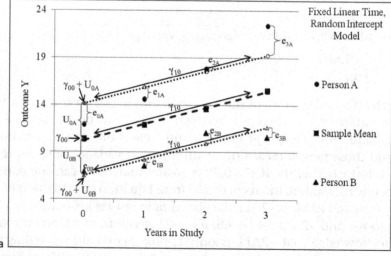

Figure 5.3 Partitioning of variance across models for the four-occasion example data.

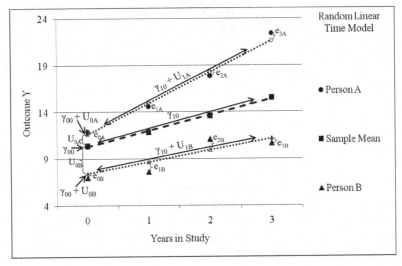

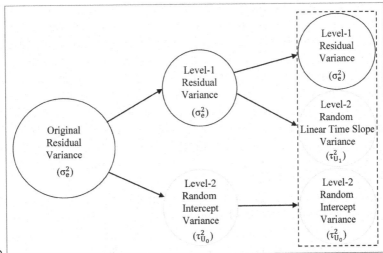

Figure 5.3 (Continued)

the model for the variance, each person gets his or her own U_{0i} that allows the person intercepts to differ, as formed by $\beta_{0i} = \gamma_{00} + U_{0i}$. That is, because person A's intercept is higher than $\gamma_{00} = 12.85$, U_{0A} will be positive, whereas because person B's intercept is lower than $\gamma_{00} = 12.85$, U_{0B} will be negative. The e_{ti} residuals are the remaining deviations between the actual outcome at each occasion and each person's intercept. Because these predicted trajectories don't really fit the individual data that well, this empty means, random intercept model is probably not going to be adequate. Nevertheless, it still provides a useful baseline with which to compare more complex models given that it can be estimated for balanced or unbalanced data across time.

The first section in this chapter discussed two different questions related to the roles that *time* can play in a longitudinal model for within-person change. We can now answer the first of these two questions—whether there is change over time on average—by adding a **fixed linear effect of time** to our model, as shown in Equation (5.3):

Level 1: $\quad y_{ti} = \beta_{0i} + \beta_{1i}(\text{Time}_{ti}) + e_{ti}$

Level 2: $\quad \beta_{0i} = \gamma_{00} + U_{0i}$ $\qquad\qquad\qquad\qquad\qquad\qquad$ (5.3)

$\qquad\qquad \beta_{1i} = \gamma_{10}$

Composite: $\quad y_{ti} = (\gamma_{00} + U_{0i}) + \gamma_{10}(\text{Time}_{ti}) + e_{ti}$

in which a new β_{1i} placeholder for the individual linear effect of time has been added to the level-1 model, which is then defined in the level-2 model solely by the fixed linear slope for time γ_{10}. The first subscript for γ_{10} is 1 because it predicts β_{1i} in the level-1 model, and the second subscript for γ_{10} is 0 because it is the lowest-order fixed effect in its level-2 equation. This 4-parameter model would be called a **fixed linear time, random intercept model** to indicate that the effect of time is *fixed*, not *random*—the time slope so far is assumed to be the same for everyone. In the results for our example data shown in the second column of Table 5.1, the fixed linear effect of time was estimated as $\gamma_{10} = 1.72$, indicating for every additional year in the study, the outcome is predicted to increase significantly by 1.72. We cannot test the addition of the fixed linear effect of time by comparing the fit of the fixed linear time, random intercept model to the fit of the empty means, random intercept model given that we are using REML estimation (whose –2LL, AIC, and BIC can only be used to compare different models for the variance instead, as elaborated later). But the *p*-value from the Wald test for the fixed linear slope (i.e., from estimate/SE) tells us directly that the fixed linear slope significantly improved model fit.

After including the fixed linear effect of time γ_{10}, the other model parameters (as seen in Table 5.1) and predicted trajectories (as shown in the bottom panel of Figure 5.3a) have changed. The fixed intercept is now $\gamma_{00} = 10.27$ because it is *conditional* on time, such that 10.27 is the predicted outcome specifically when time = 0 (at the first occasion here). Note that γ_{00} will not be the *actual* mean outcome at time 0—it will be the *predicted* mean outcome at time 0 based on a linear model of change over time. The fixed intercept in the previous model without the fixed linear effect of time was $\gamma_{00} = 12.85$, which was the (unconditional) grand mean of the person means instead. After adding a fixed linear effect of time, the means over time are predicted to increase linearly from $\gamma_{00} = 10.27$ at time 0 at a rate of $\gamma_{10} = 1.72$/year (as shown by the slope of the heavy dashed line). Furthermore, by predicting each person's trajectory using an intercept of $\gamma_{00} + U_{0i}$ and the fixed slope γ_{10}, the residual variation around each person's line in total is reduced from $\sigma_e^2 = 7.06$ in the empty means, random intercept model to $\sigma_e^2 = 2.17$ in the fixed linear time, random intercept model, for a 69% reduction of the level-1 residual variance, as calculated from $(7.06 - 2.17) / 7.06$. This is because adding the fixed linear time slope made the individual lines fit better, resulting in less residual e_{ti} variation. Said differently, because time is a within-person (level-1) effect, it can explain the level-1 σ_e^2 residual variance. But the predicted trajectories are still assumed to be parallel because persons are only allowed to differ in their intercept, and as a result, the total variance over time and covariance over time are still predicted to be constant (i.e., $\tau_{U_0}^2$ would be the same at any occasion because U_{0i} would be the same at any occasion).

Curiously, the random intercept variance actually increased after adding the fixed linear effect of time, from $\tau_{U_0}^2 = 2.88$ to 4.10. In reality, though, this increase in $\tau_{U_0}^2$ is an expected artifact and stems from the process by which $\tau_{U_0}^2$ is estimated, perhaps best explained with an analogy. Let's say 100 stones of varying weight were randomly assigned to 10 different people, and the mean weight of the stones each person received is computed. Because the stones were randomly assigned, we would not expect significant mean differences in their weight across persons. We would, however, expect the mean weight of the stones to differ across persons by a small extent numerically because of random fluctuation in the specific stones given to each person. In order to see that the *true* between-person variation in the mean weight of the stones is actually 0, we would have to remove the influence of this random (within-person) fluctuation across stones from the *observed* between-person variation in the mean weight of the stones.

The same logic applies to occasions sampled within persons. That is, even in the absence of true mean differences between persons, some differences would be expected simply because the person mean is an aggregate of multiple data points collected over time (that should have at least some random fluctuation). So, the estimate of *true* between-person mean differences needs to be corrected for the *expected* between-person mean differences, as shown in Equation (5.4):

$$
\text{Observed } \tau_{U_0}^2 = \text{True } \tau_{U_0}^2 + \left(\sigma_e^2 / n \right)
$$
$$
\text{True } \tau_{U_0}^2 = \text{Observed } \tau_{U_0}^2 - \left(\sigma_e^2 / n \right)
$$

(5.4)

in which n is the number of occasions per person (or $n = 4$, here). As shown, we would expect the observed level-2 random intercept variance $\tau_{U_0}^2$ for the extent of between-person differences in the mean outcome over time to reflect a contribution of both true between-person variability and time-specific sampling fluctuation, the latter of which is approximated by the level-1 residual variance divided by the number of occasions (σ_e^2 / n). To get the *true* estimate of $\tau_{U_0}^2$ that is reported by multilevel software programs, the correction of (σ_e^2 / n) is subtracted from the *observed* estimate of $\tau_{U_0}^2$ from the data. Thus, whenever a level-1 predictor such as linear time reduces the $\tau_{U_0}^2$ residual variance, it also changes the (σ_e^2 / n) correction used in estimating true $\tau_{U_0}^2$. In this case, because time is perfectly balanced across persons, the inclusion of a fixed linear effect of time will not reduce the level-2 random intercept variance $\tau_{U_0}^2$, but its reduction of σ_e^2 does create a smaller correction of (σ_e^2 / n), which then makes $\tau_{U_0}^2$ appear to increase. This is indeed what happened in our four-occasion example. Using the $\tau_{U_0}^2$ estimates reported in Table 5.1, we can calculate the original *observed* $\tau_{U_0}^2 = 4.65$, which then was reduced in the empty means, random intercept model to true $\tau_{U_0}^2 = 4.65 - (7.06 / 4) = 2.88$, but reduced in the fixed linear time, random intercept model to true $\tau_{U_0}^2 = 4.65 - (2.17 / 4) = 4.10$, thus creating a net increase in true $\tau_{U_0}^2$ just by reducing (σ_e^2 / n).

To summarize, adding fixed effects of time that decrease the σ_e^2 residual variance will result in an increase in the true $\tau_{U_0}^2$ random intercept variance, creating the impression of larger individual differences between persons than would have been indicated by the unconditional ICC from the empty means, random intercept model. For this reason, some authors (e.g., Hox, 2010) recommend that the ICC reflecting the proportion of outcome variation due to $\tau_{U_0}^2$ should only be calculated after including a fixed effect of time, such that the ICC would then be interpreted as *conditional* on time (i.e., as the proportion of outcome variance due to person mean differences after controlling for time). In our example data, this would increase the ICC from .29 to .65, resulting in a large difference in the interpretation of the ICC. In practice, this suggestion leaves some gray area, in that it does not consider exactly *which* fixed effects of time should be included before computing an ICC— in addition to linear effects of time, there may be higher-order time effects (e.g., quadratic, cubic), or many other possible nonlinear effects of time, as we'll see in chapter 6. Is it enough to control for just the fixed linear effect of time to calculate an ICC, or should all possible fixed effects of time be controlled for? Because of this ambiguity, the position taken in this text is that when possible we will calculate the *unconditional* ICC (i.e., before controlling for *any* effects of time) and thus interpret it as the proportion of outcome variance that is between persons on average before examining any within-person change.

However, when most of the outcome variation is within persons (due to σ_e^2), it is possible that the correction of (σ_e^2 / n) in an empty means, random intercept model may push true $\tau_{U_0}^2$ to be estimated as 0, with the result that it would not be possible to calculate an unconditional ICC at all. In those situations, I would advise you to report a *conditional* ICC, controlling for the fixed effect of time instead, but to be very specific about which fixed effects of time were included when interpreting the resulting conditional ICC (i.e., as the proportion of outcome variance due to person mean differences after controlling for whichever fixed effects of time were included). This also implies that a model that allows for within-person covariance (e.g., constant covariance through a random intercept variance in the G matrix) should still be used for longitudinal data even when the unconditional ICC ≈ 0, given that the conditional ICC for the between-person variance after including fixed effects for within-person change over time may become greater than 0.

The first section in this chapter discussed two different questions related to the roles that *time* can play in a longitudinal model for within-person change. So far, we have only answered the first of these two questions—whether there is change over time on average—by adding a *fixed* linear effect of time to our model. Accordingly, we can now answer the second question about the role of time—whether people differ in their rates change over time—by adding a **random linear effect of time** to the model, as shown in Equation (5.5):

Level 1: $y_{ti} = \beta_{0i} + \beta_{1i}(\text{Time}_{ti}) + e_{ti}$

Level 2: $\beta_{0i} = \gamma_{00} + U_{0i}$ (5.5)

$\beta_{1i} = \gamma_{10} + U_{1i}$

Composite: $y_{ti} = (\gamma_{00} + U_{0i}) + (\gamma_{10} + U_{1i})(\text{Time}_{ti}) + e_{ti}$

in which a new term, the random linear effect of time U_{1i}, has been added to the level-2 equation for β_{1i}, by which each person can now receive his or her own random deviation from the fixed linear effect of time γ_{10}. The composite model in the last line (in which the contents of the β_{0i} and β_{1i} placeholders are shown directly instead) indicates how the addition of the fixed and random linear slopes creates a new slope for each person that is then multiplied by the time predictor. In other words, by including both U_{0i} and U_{1i}, each person now gets his or her own intercept *and* own slope for time, whose variances are estimated in the **G** matrix as $\tau^2_{U_0}$ and $\tau^2_{U_1}$, respectively. Although not shown in Equation 5.5 because it does not directly predict the y_{ti} outcome, also now estimated in the **G** matrix is a $\tau_{U_{01}}$ covariance that allows a between-person relationship for the predicted outcomes at time 0 (random intercepts) and the linear rates of change over time (random linear slopes). Thus, **G** is now a 2x2 matrix with $\tau^2_{U_0}$ and $\tau^2_{U_1}$ on the diagonal and $\tau_{U_{01}}$ on the (2, 1) and (1, 2) off-diagonals, such that the **G** matrix has only three unique parameters.

The model in Equation (5.5) can simply be called a **random linear time model** because the fixed linear time slope is already implied as what the random linear time slope is deviating from. Likewise, the random intercept variance is also already implied because the random linear time slope variance is a higher-order term, requiring the random intercept variance to already be included for proper interpretation of each term. Thus, our model is now symmetric, with an intercept and a linear time slope on both sides of the model (as fixed effects in the model for the means, and as random effects in the model for the variance). In the results for our example data shown in the third column of Table 5.1, the variance of the U_{1i} random linear slopes for time was estimated as $\tau^2_{U_1} = 0.91$ with an intercept–slope covariance of $\tau_{U_{01}} = 0.05$.

So how do we know if adding the random linear time slope variance ($\tau^2_{U_1}$) improves model fit? Although a Wald test *p*-value (i.e., from estimate/SE) for the significance of $\tau^2_{U_1}$ is often provided in program output, its use for assessing the significance of a new random effect variance is generally not recommended. Unlike fixed effects that could be positive or negative, variances can't be negative, such that the lower end of their sampling distribution must be truncated at 0. So, Wald tests of their significance based on the idea of a normal, two-sided continuous sampling distribution for the possible estimated variance may not work very well.

Instead, to test whether the random linear time slope variance $\tau^2_{U_1}$ significantly improves model fit, we can conduct a $-2\Delta LL$ likelihood ratio test, given that the fixed linear time, random intercept model in Equation (5.3) is nested within the random linear time model in Equation (5.5). Their difference in fit is $-2\Delta LL(\sim 2) = 48.4$, $p < .0001$, indicating that the addition of $\tau^2_{U_1}$ did significantly improve model fit, or that people need their own random linear time slopes in addition to their own random intercepts (and the smaller AIC and BIC for the random linear time model concur). As indicated by the $df = 2$ for their comparison of model fit, the fixed linear time, random intercept model and the random linear time model will differ by two **G** matrix parameters: the random slope variance $\tau^2_{U_1}$ and the intercept–slope covariance $\tau_{U_{01}}$. Furthermore, although it is not the default in most software programs, the intercept–slope covariance $\tau_{U_{01}}$ (as well as covariances among any other additional random effects) should always be included because its estimate is strongly dependent on where time 0 is (as described shortly). Finally, the ~ is again used because the random slope variance cannot be negative and thus a $-2\Delta LL$ test using $df = 2$ will be overly conservative—although we don't need to worry about this problem here given the significant improvement in model fit despite the conservative test.

The role of each term in the random linear time model in Equation (5.5) is illustrated in the top panel of Figure 5.3b. Given the random linear time slope, the fixed linear time slope is now interpreted as the mean of the person slopes; the fixed intercept is the mean of the person means expected at time 0. The means over time are still predicted to increase linearly from $\gamma_{00} = 10.27$ at time 0 by a rate of $\gamma_{10} = 1.72$/year (as shown by the slope of the heavy dashed line). The predicted slope for the sample means over time is the same because the model for the means is still the same—we did not add any new fixed effects in the model for the means, but we did add a new random effect (of linear time) in the model for the variance. As a result, the predicted individual trajectories are no longer parallel because each person's linear time slope is now created by $\beta_{1i} = \gamma_{10} + U_{1i}$. That is, because person A's slope is steeper than $\gamma_{10} = 1.72$, U_{1A} will be positive; because person B's slope is less steep than $\gamma_{10} = 1.72$, U_{1B} will be negative.

In addition, because the individual trajectories are no longer parallel, the estimate for and the interpretation of the random intercept variance $\tau^2_{U_0}$ will change as well. In the previous fixed linear time, random intercept model (as seen in the bottom panel of Figure 5.3a), $\tau^2_{U_0}$ was the amount of individual differences in the *predicted person mean outcome over time*. That is, $\tau^2_{U_0}$ would have been the same at any point in time because the individual trajectories were parallel over time. But just as the fixed intercept becomes conditional on time 0 after adding the fixed linear time slope, the random intercept variance also becomes conditional on time 0 after adding the random linear time slope variance, changing from $\tau^2_{U_0} = 4.10$ in the fixed linear time, random intercept model to $\tau^2_{U_0} = 2.26$ in the random linear time model. But $\tau^2_{U_0}$ isn't smaller because it was "explained"—instead, $\tau^2_{U_0}$ changed because it now refers to the amount of individual differences in the expected outcome *specifically at time 0*. This can be seen in the top panel of Figure 5.3b, in which U_{0A} and U_{0B} would each have to take on different values if time 0 was not the first occasion in order to still capture the difference between the predicted sample and individual trajectories (given that they are no longer parallel). More specifically, the random linear time model for these data predicts $\tau^2_{U_0}$ to increase systematically over time—exactly why and how will be explained shortly. Furthermore, an ICC is not typically computed for models with random slopes for time (i.e., in which $\tau^2_{U_0}$ will differ over time, which would cause the ICC to then differ over time as well).

Lastly, the e_{ti} residuals (i.e., the remaining deviations between the actual outcome at each occasion and each person's predicted trajectory) are now smaller (i.e., now $\sigma^2_e = 0.70$, down from 2.17) because each person's outcomes are predicted more closely after allowing each person both a unique U_{0i} intercept deviation and a unique U_{1i} linear slope deviation. But we still wouldn't say that the level-1 residual variance σ^2_e has been "explained" by including the level-2 random linear time slope variance $\tau_{U_1}^2$. This is because only fixed effects (e.g., fixed linear time) can explain outcome variance—the addition of random effects simply serves to re-partition the existing variance instead, so that each variance then has a different interpretation, as discussed next.

2.B. Modeling Dependency Through Piles of Variance

The result of this partitioning into **piles of variance** is illustrated in the bottom panel of Figure 5.3b. The left column shows all outcome variation as originally contained in just one pile as the residual variance σ_e^2 (i.e., as in a between-person model from chapter 2). The middle column shows what happens to that total variation upon adding the random intercept U_{0i} into the level-2 model for β_{0i}, in which the outcome variation splits into two piles: between-person variation in the predicted person means across time (level-2 $\tau_{U_0}^2$ in the G matrix) and within-person variation around those person means (level-1 σ_e^2 in the R matrix). No outcome variation has been explained in adding U_{0i} to the model; the total outcome variation has simply been partitioned. In contrast, adding a fixed linear slope for time should actually reduce the level-1 σ_e^2 (and also the level-2 $\tau_{U_0}^2$ if time has between-person variation, as will be seen in chapter 10).

Finally, as indicated on the right column in the bottom panel of Figure 5.3b, adding the random linear time slope U_{1i} into the level-2 model for β_{1i} does not "explain" variance—it again partitions the σ_e^2 residual variance into two piles: between-person variance in the predicted linear slopes across time (level-2 $\tau_{U_1}^2$ in the G matrix), and within-person variation around the predicted linear slopes (level-1 σ_e^2 in the R matrix). In other words, part of the reason for the e_{ti} residual deviations in the previous model (in which the effect of time was just fixed) was because using the same linear slope for everyone just didn't fit—once people are allowed their own U_{1i} linear slopes in the random linear time model, the e_{ti} deviations should be smaller, thereby reducing level-1 σ_e^2. However, because we still don't know *why* each person needs his or her own U_{1i} linear time slope, the variance in the random linear slopes $\tau_{U_1}^2$ is still conceptually a type of error variance. But because we know that this error variance results from a random interaction between persons and the effect of time, it can be moved to the level-2 G matrix. The three piles of variance (or **variance components**) that result at the end of this partitioning variance process are enclosed in the box with dashed lines in the right column of the bottom panel of Figure 5.3b.

This idea of *piles of variance* is related to the three sources of dependency that are often present in the residuals for longitudinal outcomes (as originally introduced in chapter 1): (1) constant mean differences between persons, (2) differences between persons in the effects of predictors (such as time), and (3) non-constant within-person correlation over time for unknown reasons. The G matrix for a random linear time model in Equation (5.5) explicitly represents the first two kinds of dependency via $\tau_{U_0}^2$ and $\tau_{U_1}^2$, respectively. In other words, the way dependency is incorporated into the model is by partitioning the outcome variance into piles that reflect each source of dependency. Upon doing so, the variation at level 1 (σ_e^2) should then be independent of the variation at level 2 ($\tau_{U_0}^2$ and $\tau_{U_1}^2$), although random effects are allowed to covary within a level ($\tau_{U_{01}}$). So far, we have only considered a single random linear slope for the effect of time, but other predictors that vary over time could also have random slopes, thus allowing for any additional dependency created by differences between persons in the effects of those predictors, too. In essence, the goal of random effects models is to keep partitioning the level-1 residual variance into new level-2 random effects variances until independence across levels is achieved. Other sources of non-constant within-person correlation can be addressed by combining random effects models with alternative covariance structures in the **R** matrix, as we'll see shortly.

2.C. Interpreting Random Effect Variances and Covariances

Earlier we found that including both U_{0i} and U_{1i} in the level-2 model significantly improved model fit, but what does that really mean? That is, we know that the variance of the U_{0i} random intercepts ($\tau_{U_0}^2 = 2.26$) and the variance of the U_{1i} random linear time slopes ($\tau_{U_1}^2 = 0.91$) are significantly greater than 0, but is there a more meaningful way to think about these values? Yes—as also described by Snijders and Bosker (2012), a useful descriptive statistic that can be calculated from random effects models is a *random effect 95% confidence interval (CI)* that conveys the predicted range around each fixed effect in which 95% of the sample individuals are predicted to fall, as shown in Equation (5.6):

$$\text{Random Effect 95\% CI} = \text{fixed effect} \pm \left(1.96 * \sqrt{\text{Random Variance}}\right)$$

$$\text{Intercept 95\% CI} = \gamma_{00} \pm \left(1.96 * \sqrt{\tau_{U_0}^2}\right) \rightarrow 10.27 \pm \left(1.96 * \sqrt{2.26}\right) = 7.33 \text{ to } 13.22 \quad (5.6)$$

$$\text{Linear Time Slope 95\% CI} = \gamma_{10} \pm \left(1.96 * \sqrt{\tau_{U_1}^2}\right) \rightarrow 1.72 \pm \left(1.96 * \sqrt{0.91}\right) = -0.15 \text{ to } 3.59$$

for the random intercept and linear time slope. The ±1.96 value is based on the points on the *t*-distribution within which 95% of its area should fall (e.g., a 90% CI would use ±1.65 instead). Please note that the results of the calculations that follow were based on the actual estimated values; small differences may appear when using the rounded estimates reported in the text instead.

It is important to distinguish this new **random effect** CI from a traditional **fixed effect** CI, which instead conveys the uncertainty of a fixed effect estimate using its SE. For instance, a *fixed effect CI* for the intercept would be calculated as: $\gamma_{00} \pm (1.96*\text{SE}) = 10.27 \pm (1.96*0.33) = 9.59 \text{ to } 10.96$, indicating that if the study was replicated many times, the interval between 9.59 and 10.96 should include the *fixed intercept estimate* approximately 95% of the time. In contrast, the *random effect CI* replaces the SE of the fixed effect with the standard deviation (via the square root) of the random effect variance that goes with it (e.g., $\tau_{U_0}^2$ for the intercept; $\tau_{U_1}^2$ for the linear slope) so that the 95% CI for the random effect is based on around approximately ±2 SD of the *expected individual random variation* around its fixed effect. Accordingly, *the random effect CI for the intercept, as calculated in Equation (5.6), indicates that 95% of the sample* is predicted to have outcomes at time 0 between 7.33 and 13.22

(with a mean across persons of the fixed intercept $\gamma_{00} = 10.27$). It is important to note, however, that random effect CIs assume a normal, symmetric distribution of random effects, which may not always hold in real data. If the random intercept CI extends below 0 when the scale of the outcome variable cannot, this likely indicates a skewed rather than symmetric distribution of the individual random intercepts. In such cases, the random effect CI for the intercept should be truncated at 0 and interpreted very cautiously as a result.

Also as calculated in Equation (5.6), the random effect CI for the linear time slope indicates that 95% of the sample is predicted to have linear rates of change between –0.15 and 3.59 per year (with a mean across persons of the fixed linear time slope $\gamma_{10} = 1.72$). The fact that the random effect CI for the linear time slope overlaps 0 does *not* mean that the fixed linear time slope is not significant (because $\gamma_{10} = 1.72$ is indeed significantly larger than 0, with a *fixed effect CI* for the linear time slope calculated from $\gamma_{10} \pm [1.96*SE] = 1.72 \pm [1.96*0.20] = 1.29$ to 2.14). Instead, the overlap with 0 of the *random effect CI* for the linear time slope means that the size of the variation in the random U_{1i} linear slope deviations predicts that some people should actually decrease or not change at all (while most others should increase over time).

Thus, to summarize, the Wald test for the fixed linear time slope tells us whether people change on average, the $-2\Delta LL$ test for the random linear time slope variance tells us whether there is significant individual variation in those linear time slopes, and the random effect CIs then provide meaningful effect sizes for the amounts of random intercept and random linear time slope variation across persons using the original scale of the time predictor and the outcome. Although we can do the same for any random effect, by definition we cannot compute a random effect CI for an effect that is only fixed—if everybody gets the same effect, there is no random effect interval (although a traditional fixed effect interval could still be calculated, of course).

Finally, in addition to the random effects variances, you may wish to interpret the covariance among the random intercepts and random linear time slopes ($\tau_{U_{01}} = 0.05$), which can be converted to a correlation as: $Cor_{01} = \frac{\tau_{U_{01}}}{\sqrt{\tau_{U_0}^2} * \sqrt{\tau_{U_1}^2}} = \frac{0.05}{\sqrt{2.26} * \sqrt{0.91}}$ = .04. Although, based on this result, you might be tempted to conclude there is no correlation between the intercepts and slopes, this is not strictly correct when stated this way. This is because the intercept–slope covariance and correlation are dependent on where time 0 is given that the intercept is the expected outcome specifically at time 0. This dependency on time 0 is illustrated in Figure 5.4 by showing random linear trajectories for four hypothetical individuals. If time 0 was located at the dashed line on the left, we would see a perfect *negative correlation* between the intercepts and slopes, because those lowest on the y-axis at that point in time have the steepest rates of change. In contrast, if time 0 was located at the dashed line in the center, we would see *no correlation* between the intercepts and slopes. Finally, if time 0 was located at the dashed line on the right, we would see a perfect *positive correlation* between the intercepts and slopes, because those highest on the y-axis at that later point in time would now have the steepest rates of change.

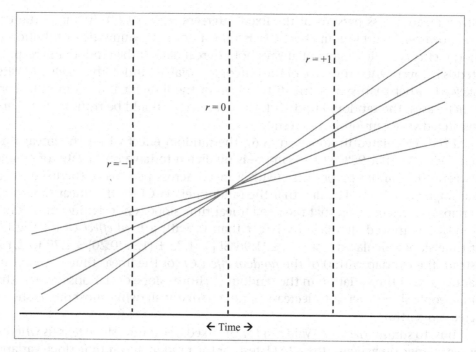

Figure 5.4 Sensitivity of intercept–slope correlation (*r*) to the centering of time.

So of these three (and infinitely many more) possible intercept–slope correlations, which one is correct? They all are—the covariance (and correlation) between the random intercept and random slope depends on where the intercept is with respect to the random slope—in this case, where time 0 is. This is why we will always estimate the covariances among the random intercept and any random slopes—because these covariances can change with the centering of the predictors with the random slope, and thus could be significant or nonsignificant across equivalent (but re-centered) versions of the same model. In summary, the correct way to interpret any estimated covariance or correlation between the intercepts and any slopes is as *conditional* on the location of the intercept with respect to the random slope. So, for our example data, we would say that .04 is the correlation (or that 0.05 is the covariance) of the individual linear rates of change over time with the individual expected outcomes *at baseline specifically.* If we wished to find the correlation between the individual linear rates of change over time and the individual expected outcomes at another point in time instead (e.g., at the end of the study), we could do so from a model in which time 0 is at that point of interest instead.

2.D. Predicted Variances and Covariances Over Time From a Random Linear Time Model

So far the models for within-person change we've examined have included both fixed linear change over time (i.e., change on average) and random linear change over time (i.e., individual differences in the rate of change as well as in the intercept).

Assessing the extent of these individual differences (and later, the predictors of these differences) can be substantively important. But at the same time, the other, more statistical purpose of random effects of time is to allow the outcome variance and covariance to change over time as needed. That is, models including random effects of time serve as another kind of "happy medium" on the spectrum of models for the variance ranging from least to most complex (i.e., *compound symmetry* to *unstructured*), but without requiring complete data or balanced time data to do so. Using our example random linear model of change over time, the next section now describes exactly how random effects translate into flexible patterns of predicted variances and covariances over time.

There are two ways to explain this: via **scalar notation** (predicting a single value) or via **matrix notation** (predicting many values at once). We'll begin with the former but continue to the latter. Scalar notation is a good starting point to describe how models with random effects of time predict the variance at a given occasion and the covariance across occasions as a direct function of time. But what scalar notation does not readily convey is how random effects models adapt to be able to include unbalanced time or incomplete data across persons—so to describe how the model keeps track of time at the individual level, we will eventually need matrix notation instead.

First, using the algebra of expectations (the logic of which for this instance is explained thoroughly below), we can show how the random linear time model uses the four parameters in its model for the variance (σ_e^2, $\tau_{U_0}^2$, $\tau_{U_1}^2$, and $\tau_{U_{01}}$) to form the *predicted* or *expected* total outcome variance across persons at a specific time occasion as shown in Equation (5.7):

$$
\begin{aligned}
\text{Var}[y_{ti}] &= \text{Var}\big[(\gamma_{00} + U_{0i}) + (\gamma_{10} + U_{1i})(\text{Time}_i) + e_{ti}\big] \\
&= \text{Var}\big[(U_{0i}) + (U_{1i} * \text{Time}_i) + e_{ti}\big] \\
&= \{\text{Var}(U_{0i})\} + \{\text{Var}(U_{1i} * \text{Time}_i)\} + \{2 * \text{Cov}(U_{0i}, U_{1i} * \text{Time}_i)\} + \{\text{Var}(e_{ti})\} \\
&= \{\text{Var}(U_{0i})\} + \{\text{Time}_i^2 * \text{Var}(U_{1i})\} + \{2 * \text{Time}_i * \text{Cov}(U_{0i}, U_{1i})\} + \{\text{Var}(e_{ti})\} \\
&= \{\tau_{U_0}^2\} + \{\text{Time}_i^2 * \tau_{U_1}^2\} + \{2 * \text{Time}_i * \tau_{U_{01}}\} + \{\sigma_e^2\} \\
&= \{2.26\} + \{\text{Time}_i^2 * 0.91\} + \{2 * \text{Time}_i * 0.05\} + \{0.70\}
\end{aligned}
\tag{5.7}
$$

in which the first line writes the expected total variance across persons at a specific time *t*, Var[y_{ti}], using the composite random linear time model from Equation (5.5). Time$_i$ has a subscript *i* to indicate that although the variance is conditional on time *t*, time can be unbalanced across persons (i.e., each person can have his or her own time values). The second line removes the fixed effects because they are constants that won't contribute to the expected variance (i.e., because adding a constant to a variable changes its mean but not its variance).

The third line (now including braces to help visually separate each term) distributes the expected variance across each of the three additive terms, and so must now include any estimated covariances among U_{0i}, U_{1i}, and e_{ti}. It does not include the covariance terms of Cov(U_{0i}, e_{ti}) and Cov($U_{1i} *$ Time$_i$, e_{ti}) because no relationships are permitted across residual terms at different levels by definition of the multilevel model. But given that the U_{0i} random intercepts and U_{1i} random linear time slopes are both at level 2 and thus can (and should) be allowed to be related, the covariance term of $Cov(U_{0i}, U_{1i}*Time_i)$ is included, and it gets multiplied by 2. One way to remember the "2" part is that covariances will appear twice in the off-diagonals of the symmetric $\mathbf{G}$ matrix (whereas each variance will appear only once on the $\mathbf{G}$ matrix diagonal). The fourth line extracts the constant $Time_i$ from the variance and covariance terms. Note that $Time_i$ becomes $Time_i^2$ when extracted from the variance term of $Var(U_{1i}*Time_i)$. This is because $Var(U_{1i}*Time_i)$ is equivalent to the covariance term $Cov(U_{1i}*Time_i, U_{1i}*Time_i)$ in which $Time_i$ appears twice, and thus $Time_i$ must be squared when extracted from it. The fifth line substitutes our general notation for the level-2 and level-1 variances and covariances. The sixth line then substitutes the estimates from our example, in which the total outcome variance at $Time_i = 0, 1, 2,$ or 3 is predicted to be 2.96, 3.98, 6.82, or 11.47, respectively.

More generally, Equation (5.7) shows how the random linear time model predicts the total variance to change over time in a symmetric, quadratic (i.e., U-shaped) form due to the contribution of $Time^2$. Furthermore, using the function in the fifth line in Equation (5.7), we can calculate the **aperture**, which is the occasion at which the variance will be at a minimum (see Hancock & Choi, 2006; Preacher & Hancock, 2012) by finding when the first derivative with respect to Time will be 0, in this example as $Time = -\tau_{U_{01}}/\tau_{U_1}^2 = -0.05/0.91 = -0.06$. Thus, because our occasions of 0, 1, 2, and 3 are past the variance minimum at -0.06 years (i.e., they are located on the right side of the predicted U-shaped variance function), the total variance is predicted to increase quadratically over the observed time occasions in our data.

The random linear time model also directly predicts the expected time-dependent covariance between any two occasions (e.g., Time A_i and Time B_i), as shown in Equation (5.8):

$$
\begin{aligned}
Cov[y_{Ai}, y_{Bi}] &= Cov\left[\{(\gamma_{00} + U_{0i}) + (\gamma_{10} + U_{1i})(A_i) + e_{Ai}\}, \{(\gamma_{00} + U_{0i}) + (\gamma_{10} + U_{1i})(B_i) + e_{Bi}\}\right] \\
&= Cov\left[\{U_{0i} + (U_{1i}A_i)\}, \{U_{0i} + (U_{1i}B_i)\}\right] \\
&= Cov[U_{0i}, U_{0i}] + Cov[U_{0i}, U_{1i}B_i] + Cov[U_{0i}, U_{1i}A_i] + Cov[U_{1i}A_i, U_{1i}B_i] \\
&= \{Var(U_{0i})\} + \{(A_i + B_i)*Cov(U_{0i}, U_{1i})\} + \{(A_iB_i)Var(U_{1i})\} \\
&= \{\tau_{U_0}^2\} + \{(A_i + B_i)\tau_{U_{01}}\} + \{(A_iB_i)\tau_{U_1}^2\} \\
&= \{2.26\} + \{(A_i + B_i)0.05\} + \{(A_iB_i)0.91\}
\end{aligned}
\tag{5.8}
$$

in which the first line writes the expected covariance between Time A_i and Time B_i, $Cov[y_{Ai}, y_{Bi}]$ from the composite random linear time model from Equation (5.5). The second line removes the terms that will not contribute to the covariance: the fixed effects (i.e., that are constants) and the e_{Ai} and e_{Bi} residuals (i.e., that are uncorrelated in the model). The third line unpacks the terms within the covariance using the FOIL method (First, Outer, Inner, Last—because algebra is actually useful sometimes). The fourth line combines the covariances and re-writes the other terms as variances. The fifth line substitutes our general notation for the level-2 variances and covariances. The sixth line then substitutes the variance and covariance estimates from our example model, and the resulting predictions will be shown momentarily in Table 5.2.

But to better understand the level-1 **R** matrix, the level-2 **G** matrix, and how they fit together to create the overall predicted **V** matrix, we'll now go through the exact same process of finding the model-predicted variances and covariances over time using these matrices instead. In doing so, we will also see how a new **Z** matrix incorporates the necessary information about which specific time observations are available for each person.

Thus, when expressed in matrix notation, the model for the variance is constructed from two symmetric matrices: the **level-2 G matrix** that holds the variances and covariances of the random effects (in a random linear time model, this includes $\tau^2_{U_0}$, $\tau^2_{U_1}$, and $\tau_{U_{01}}$), and the **level-1 R matrix** that holds the variances and covariances of the e_{ti} residuals over time (just σ^2_e so far). More specifically, in a random linear time model for $n = 4$ occasions, for a single person, **G** will be a 2x2 matrix (for the u by u number of random effects—the intercept and linear slope here) and **R** will be a 4x4 matrix (for the n by n number of occasions), as shown in Equation (5.9):

$$\text{Level-2 } \mathbf{G} = \begin{bmatrix} \tau^2_{U_0} & \tau_{U_{01}} \\ \tau_{U_{01}} & \tau^2_{U_1} \end{bmatrix}, \text{ Level-1 } \mathbf{R} = \begin{bmatrix} \sigma^2_e & 0 & 0 & 0 \\ 0 & \sigma^2_e & 0 & 0 \\ 0 & 0 & \sigma^2_e & 0 \\ 0 & 0 & 0 & \sigma^2_e \end{bmatrix} \tag{5.9}$$

in which the form of the level-2 **G** matrix is **unstructured** (i.e., each random effect variance and covariance is estimated separately), but the form of the level-1 **R** matrix is **diagonal** or **variance components** (i.e., for an independence model of the e_{ti} residuals over time with constant variance and no covariance). A diagonal **R** matrix reflects the idea that the only reason why the outcomes were correlated over time to begin with was because of systematic differences between persons in their intercepts and linear slopes for time—after moving those sources of person-related correlation (i.e., person-related dependency) into the level-2 **G** matrix, the e_{ti} residuals should then have no correlation over time within a person (i.e., as indicated by the 0's in the off-diagonals for the residual covariances in the level-1 **R** matrix). Furthermore, although these **G** and **R** matrices are just for one person, the estimated model parameters they contain ($\tau^2_{U_0}$, $\tau^2_{U_1}$, $\tau_{U_{01}}$, and σ^2_e) are assumed to be the same across persons (i.e., unless specified otherwise, such as in heterogeneous variance models, as will be discussed in chapters 7 and 8).

The **G** and **R** matrices work together to create the **V matrix** of the total predicted outcome variance and covariance over time, which will be a symmetric n by n matrix (a 4x4 matrix here). However, the 2x2 **G** and 4x4 **R** matrices cannot be combined directly into the **V** matrix given their differing dimensions. Furthermore, they also do not contain any direct information about which occasions of measurement were observed for each person, as needed in the event of unbalanced and/or incomplete data. To solve these two problems, we need a new and asymmetric matrix, commonly referred to as the **Z** matrix, which for each person will have dimensions of rows = n occasions and columns = u random effects. For our example with time values of 0, 1, 2, and 3, the $\mathbf{Z}$ matrix for a single individual, as well as its transposed version labeled $\mathbf{Z}^T$ (in which the matrix rows and columns have been interchanged), are shown in Equation (5.10):

$$\text{Level-1 } \mathbf{Z} = \begin{bmatrix} 1 & 0 \\ 1 & 1 \\ 1 & 2 \\ 1 & 3 \end{bmatrix}, \quad \text{Level-1 } \mathbf{Z}^T = \begin{bmatrix} 1 & 1 & 1 & 1 \\ 0 & 1 & 2 & 3 \end{bmatrix} \tag{5.10}$$

in which the first column in the $\mathbf{Z}$ matrix (or the first row in $\mathbf{Z}^T$) of just 1's is for the random intercept, and the second column in the $\mathbf{Z}$ matrix (or the second row in $\mathbf{Z}^T$) holds the observed values for that person's linear time variable. The $\mathbf{Z}$ matrix is labeled as a level-1 matrix because, in addition to the intercept column of 1's, it can only contain values for predictors that vary over time, and only values for those time-varying predictors that have random effects in the model. For instance, the $\mathbf{Z}$ matrix would not include the second column for time if the linear effect of time was just fixed and not random (as in a fixed linear time, random intercept model instead).

Using the $\mathbf{Z}$ and $\mathbf{Z}^T$ matrices, the level-2 $\mathbf{G}$ matrix is combined with the level-1 $\mathbf{R}$ matrix to create the $\mathbf{V}$ matrix for the total variance and covariance over time as: $\mathbf{V} = \mathbf{Z}\mathbf{G}\mathbf{Z}^T + \mathbf{R}$. For our random linear time model, the pre-multiplication of the $\mathbf{G}$ matrix by the $\mathbf{Z}$ matrix and post-multiplication by the $\mathbf{Z}^T$ matrix is needed for two reasons. First, it squares the time values as needed to contribute to the predicted variance at a given occasion—as we saw happen in the scalar formula for the predicted variance in Equation (5.7). Second, it changes the dimensions of the 2x2 $\mathbf{G}$ matrix to a 4x4 matrix so that it can be added directly to the 4x4 $\mathbf{R}$ matrix. Importantly, because the individual-specific $\mathbf{Z}$ and $\mathbf{Z}^T$ matrices hold the time values observed for each person, this means that we can create a predicted $\mathbf{V}$ matrix for the total variance and covariance at each occasion for each person regardless of the specific time values that person has, as we'll see shortly. This feature is especially useful for unbalanced and/or incomplete data.

To begin, we can compute the predicted $\mathbf{V}$ matrix based on our example random linear time model for any individual with complete data and time values of 0, 1, 2, and 3, as shown in Table 5.2, which first lists the four original matrices. The second row of matrices then substitutes in the time values and estimated parameters from our example data. The third row of matrices pre-multiplies $\mathbf{G}$ by $\mathbf{Z}$, the fourth row of matrices then post-multiplies $\mathbf{Z}\mathbf{G}$ by $\mathbf{Z}^T$, and the fifth row of matrices then provides the resulting $\mathbf{V}$ matrix from adding $\mathbf{Z}\mathbf{G}\mathbf{Z}^T$ to $\mathbf{R}$. Although perhaps more intimidating initially, the matrix expression $\mathbf{V} = \mathbf{Z}\mathbf{G}\mathbf{Z}^T + \mathbf{R}$ neatly conveys all the predicted variances and covariances that we calculated previously using scalar notation instead. Furthermore, in reality we don't actually have to calculate anything ourselves—the $\mathbf{G}$, $\mathbf{R}$, and $\mathbf{V}$ matrices can usually be requested as part of software program output, as well as their standardized, correlation versions that show 1's on the diagonal and predicted correlations on the off-diagonals instead (i.e., the **GCORR**, **RCORR**, and **VCORR** matrices, respectively, in SAS MIXED).

Table 5.2 Predicted V matrix for a single individual for the four-occasion example data from a random linear time model.

$$\mathbf{V} = \mathbf{Z} \quad * \quad \mathbf{G} \quad * \quad \mathbf{Z}^{\mathrm{T}} \quad + \quad \mathbf{R}$$

$$\mathbf{V} = \begin{bmatrix} 1 & 0 \\ 1 & 1 \\ 1 & 2 \\ 1 & 3 \end{bmatrix} \begin{bmatrix} \tau^2_{U_0} & \tau_{U_{01}} \\ \tau_{U_{01}} & \tau^2_{U_1} \end{bmatrix} \begin{bmatrix} 1 & 1 & 1 & 1 \\ 0 & 1 & 2 & 3 \end{bmatrix} + \begin{bmatrix} \sigma^2_e & 0 & 0 & 0 \\ 0 & \sigma^2_e & 0 & 0 \\ 0 & 0 & \sigma^2_e & 0 \\ 0 & 0 & 0 & \sigma^2_e \end{bmatrix}$$

$$\mathbf{V} = \begin{bmatrix} 1 & 0 \\ 1 & 1 \\ 1 & 2 \\ 1 & 3 \end{bmatrix} \begin{bmatrix} 2.26 & 0.05 \\ 0.05 & 0.91 \end{bmatrix} \begin{bmatrix} 1 & 1 & 1 & 1 \\ 0 & 1 & 2 & 3 \end{bmatrix} + \begin{bmatrix} 0.70 & 0 & 0 & 0 \\ 0 & 0.70 & 0 & 0 \\ 0 & 0 & 0.70 & 0 \\ 0 & 0 & 0 & 0.70 \end{bmatrix}$$

$$\mathbf{V} = \quad\quad \mathbf{ZG} \quad * \quad \mathbf{Z}^{\mathrm{T}} \quad + \quad\quad \mathbf{R}$$

$$\mathbf{V} = \begin{bmatrix} 2.26 & 0.05 \\ 2.32 & 0.96 \\ 2.37 & 1.87 \\ 2.43 & 2.78 \end{bmatrix} \begin{bmatrix} 1 & 1 & 1 & 1 \\ 0 & 1 & 2 & 3 \end{bmatrix} + \begin{bmatrix} 0.70 & 0 & 0 & 0 \\ 0 & 0.70 & 0 & 0 \\ 0 & 0 & 0.70 & 0 \\ 0 & 0 & 0 & 0.70 \end{bmatrix}$$

$$\mathbf{V} = \quad\quad\quad \mathbf{ZGZ}^{\mathrm{T}} \quad\quad + \quad\quad\quad \mathbf{R}$$

$$\mathbf{V} = \begin{bmatrix} 2.26 & 2.32 & 2.37 & 2.43 \\ 2.32 & 3.28 & 4.25 & 5.21 \\ 2.37 & 4.25 & 6.12 & 7.99 \\ 2.43 & 5.21 & 7.99 & 10.77 \end{bmatrix} + \begin{bmatrix} 0.70 & 0 & 0 & 0 \\ 0 & 0.70 & 0 & 0 \\ 0 & 0 & 0.70 & 0 \\ 0 & 0 & 0 & 0.70 \end{bmatrix}$$

$$\mathbf{V} = \begin{bmatrix} 2.96 & 2.32 & 2.37 & 2.43 \\ 2.32 & 3.98 & 4.25 & 5.21 \\ 2.37 & 4.25 & 6.82 & 7.99 \\ 2.43 & 5.21 & 7.99 & 11.47 \end{bmatrix}$$

Although following these matrix operations can be quite tedious, it is important not to lose track of their overall purpose, which can be summarized as follows: *By adding a random effect of time by which each person gets his or her own slope for time, the total variances and covariances are then predicted to change over time, rather than assuming they are constant over time instead* (i.e., as in a random intercept only model). The way this occurs, however, is *not* by estimating a separate variance at each specific occasion or different pattern of covariance based on the idea of a time lag, as in the alternative covariance structure models for the **R** matrix in chapter 4. Instead, the random linear time model predicts the change in the total variance and covariance *directly as a function of the change in time,* meaning that model predictions can adapt to the specific time values observed for any given person—even if that person has unbalanced or incomplete outcome data over time. This is why the predictor variable for *time* gets both *t* and *i* subscripts, because each person can have his or her own set of time observations that go into the random linear time model (and into other random effects models more generally). No data are imputed—the model simply uses whatever data each person has, although persons with fewer occasions will have less reliable individual random slopes, as discussed later in the chapter.

Furthermore, the way that random effects models handle unbalanced time is by building each person his or her own $\mathbf{Z}$ matrix that predicts whatever outcomes that person has, whenever they were obtained. This is illustrated in Table 5.3, which shows the predicted matrices from our four-occasion example combined for two hypothetical people at once. Table 5.3 illustrates unbalanced time, in that the first person was observed at time 0, 1, 2, and 3 as scheduled, but the second person was actually observed only at time 0.2, 1.4, and 3.5, missing her third session. Accordingly, the $\mathbf{Z}$ matrix now has seven rows, given four occasions for the first person but three occasions for the second person, as well as four columns given 2 persons * 2 random effects each (because each person gets his or her own intercept

Table 5.3 Predicted V matrix for two hypothetical individuals with unbalanced time observations from a random linear time model for the four-occasion example data.

$$\mathbf{V} = \mathbf{Z} * \mathbf{G} * \mathbf{Z}^T + \mathbf{R}$$

$$\mathbf{V} = \begin{bmatrix} 1 & 0.0 & 0 & 0 \\ 1 & 1.0 & 0 & 0 \\ 1 & 2.0 & 0 & 0 \\ 1 & 3.0 & 0 & 0 \\ 0 & 0 & 1 & 0.2 \\ 0 & 0 & 1 & 1.4 \\ 0 & 0 & 1 & 3.5 \end{bmatrix} \begin{bmatrix} \tau^2_{U_0} & \tau_{U_{01}} & 0 & 0 \\ \tau_{U_{01}} & \tau^2_{U_1} & 0 & 0 \\ 0 & 0 & \tau^2_{U_0} & \tau_{U_{01}} \\ 0 & 0 & \tau_{U_{01}} & \tau^2_{U_1} \end{bmatrix} \begin{bmatrix} 1 & 1 & 1 & 1 & 0 & 0 & 0 \\ 0.0 & 1.0 & 2.0 & 3.0 & 0 & 0 & 0 \\ 0 & 0 & 0 & 0 & 1 & 1 & 1 \\ 0 & 0 & 0 & 0 & 0.2 & 1.4 & 3.5 \end{bmatrix} + \begin{bmatrix} \sigma^2_e & 0 & 0 & 0 & 0 & 0 & 0 \\ 0 & \sigma^2_e & 0 & 0 & 0 & 0 & 0 \\ 0 & 0 & \sigma^2_e & 0 & 0 & 0 & 0 \\ 0 & 0 & 0 & \sigma^2_e & 0 & 0 & 0 \\ 0 & 0 & 0 & 0 & \sigma^2_e & 0 & 0 \\ 0 & 0 & 0 & 0 & 0 & \sigma^2_e & 0 \\ 0 & 0 & 0 & 0 & 0 & 0 & \sigma^2_e \end{bmatrix}$$

$$\mathbf{V} = \begin{bmatrix} 1 & 0.0 & 0 & 0 \\ 1 & 1.0 & 0 & 0 \\ 1 & 2.0 & 0 & 0 \\ 1 & 3.0 & 0 & 0 \\ 0 & 0 & 1 & 0.2 \\ 0 & 0 & 1 & 1.4 \\ 0 & 0 & 1 & 3.5 \end{bmatrix} \begin{bmatrix} 2.26 & 0.05 & 0 & 0 \\ 0.05 & 0.91 & 0 & 0 \\ 0 & 0 & 2.26 & 0.05 \\ 0 & 0 & 0.05 & 0.91 \end{bmatrix} \begin{bmatrix} 1 & 1 & 1 & 1 & 0 & 0 & 0 \\ 0.0 & 1.0 & 2.0 & 3.0 & 0 & 0 & 0 \\ 0 & 0 & 0 & 0 & 1 & 1 & 1 \\ 0 & 0 & 0 & 0 & 0.2 & 1.4 & 3.5 \end{bmatrix} + \begin{bmatrix} 0.70 & 0 & 0 & 0 & 0 & 0 & 0 \\ 0 & 0.70 & 0 & 0 & 0 & 0 & 0 \\ 0 & 0 & 0.70 & 0 & 0 & 0 & 0 \\ 0 & 0 & 0 & 0.70 & 0 & 0 & 0 \\ 0 & 0 & 0 & 0 & 0.70 & 0 & 0 \\ 0 & 0 & 0 & 0 & 0 & 0.70 & 0 \\ 0 & 0 & 0 & 0 & 0 & 0 & 0.70 \end{bmatrix}$$

$$\mathbf{V} = \mathbf{ZG} * \mathbf{Z}^T + \mathbf{R}$$

$$\mathbf{V} = \begin{bmatrix} 2.26 & 0.05 & 0 & 0 \\ 2.32 & 0.96 & 0 & 0 \\ 2.37 & 1.87 & 0 & 0 \\ 2.43 & 2.78 & 0 & 0 \\ 0 & 0 & 2.28 & 0.24 \\ 0 & 0 & 2.34 & 1.33 \\ 0 & 0 & 2.46 & 3.24 \end{bmatrix} \begin{bmatrix} 1 & 1 & 1 & 1 & 0 & 0 & 0 \\ 0.0 & 1.0 & 2.0 & 3.0 & 0 & 0 & 0 \\ 0 & 0 & 0 & 0 & 1 & 1 & 1 \\ 0 & 0 & 0 & 0 & 0.2 & 1.4 & 3.5 \end{bmatrix} + \begin{bmatrix} 0.70 & 0 & 0 & 0 & 0 & 0 & 0 \\ 0 & 0.70 & 0 & 0 & 0 & 0 & 0 \\ 0 & 0 & 0.70 & 0 & 0 & 0 & 0 \\ 0 & 0 & 0 & 0.70 & 0 & 0 & 0 \\ 0 & 0 & 0 & 0 & 0.70 & 0 & 0 \\ 0 & 0 & 0 & 0 & 0 & 0.70 & 0 \\ 0 & 0 & 0 & 0 & 0 & 0 & 0.70 \end{bmatrix}$$

$$\mathbf{V} = \mathbf{ZGZ}^T + \mathbf{R}$$

$$\mathbf{V} = \begin{bmatrix} 2.26 & 2.32 & 2.37 & 2.43 & 0 & 0 & 0 \\ 2.32 & 3.28 & 4.25 & 5.21 & 0 & 0 & 0 \\ 2.37 & 4.25 & 6.12 & 7.99 & 0 & 0 & 0 \\ 2.43 & 5.21 & 7.99 & 10.77 & 0 & 0 & 0 \\ 0 & 0 & 0 & 0 & 2.32 & 2.61 & 3.10 \\ 0 & 0 & 0 & 0 & 2.61 & 4.20 & 6.99 \\ 0 & 0 & 0 & 0 & 3.10 & 6.99 & 13.78 \end{bmatrix} + \begin{bmatrix} 0.70 & 0 & 0 & 0 & 0 & 0 & 0 \\ 0 & 0.70 & 0 & 0 & 0 & 0 & 0 \\ 0 & 0 & 0.70 & 0 & 0 & 0 & 0 \\ 0 & 0 & 0 & 0.70 & 0 & 0 & 0 \\ 0 & 0 & 0 & 0 & 0.70 & 0 & 0 \\ 0 & 0 & 0 & 0 & 0 & 0.70 & 0 \\ 0 & 0 & 0 & 0 & 0 & 0 & 0.70 \end{bmatrix}$$

$$\mathbf{V} = \begin{bmatrix} 2.96 & 2.32 & 2.37 & 2.43 & 0 & 0 & 0 \\ 2.32 & 3.98 & 4.25 & 5.21 & 0 & 0 & 0 \\ 2.37 & 4.25 & 6.82 & 7.99 & 0 & 0 & 0 \\ 2.43 & 5.21 & 7.99 & 11.47 & 0 & 0 & 0 \\ 0 & 0 & 0 & 0 & 3.02 & 2.61 & 3.10 \\ 0 & 0 & 0 & 0 & 2.61 & 4.90 & 6.99 \\ 0 & 0 & 0 & 0 & 3.10 & 6.99 & 14.48 \end{bmatrix}$$

and slope, this means that people can't share columns). Thus, $\mathbf{Z}$ is a 7x4 matrix and its transpose $\mathbf{Z}^T$ is a 4x7 matrix. $\mathbf{G}$ is now a 4x4 matrix for 4 = 2 persons*2 random effects each. Finally, $\mathbf{R}$ and $\mathbf{V}$ are now 7x7 matrices (because the first person has four occasions but the second person has three occasions). If everyone had complete data, in the combined matrices for $N = 25$ persons in our sample across $n = 4$ occasions (which is what some programs like SAS MIXED would use for estimation), $\mathbf{Z}$ would be a 100x50 matrix, $\mathbf{G}$ would be a 50x50 matrix, and $\mathbf{R}$ and $\mathbf{V}$ would be 100x100 matrices. But if persons have differing numbers of occasions, then the dimensions of $\mathbf{R}$ and $\mathbf{Z}$ will differ per person (with a different total).

The pattern of the matrices seen in Table 5.3 is known as **block diagonal**, in which the main diagonal first holds the 4x4 matrices for the first person, then for the second person, and so on. The 0 values in the block off-diagonals mean that no covariance is allowed between persons (thus, persons are treated as independent). If persons were in fact related (e.g., persons were nested within groups), those off-diagonals could be modified to allow a relationship due to group membership via random group effects (i.e., a three-level model of time within person within group), as we'll see in chapter 11. Furthermore, the matrices in Table 5.3 show how each unique time value is used in the unique $\mathbf{Z}$ and $\mathbf{Z}^T$ matrices for each person's data. After computing $\mathbf{V} = \mathbf{ZGZ}^T + \mathbf{R}$ as before, we see that the same random linear time model with just four parameters in the model for the variance ($\tau^2_{U_0}$, $\tau^2_{U_1}$, $\tau_{U_{01}}$, and σ^2_e) can predict the variance and covariance across all persons and occasions no matter which occasions are actually included for each person. Thus, rather than treating time as a fixed and discrete set of occasions, the random linear time model predicts variances and covariances directly as a function of continuous time instead, which then renders the model capable of extrapolating between occasions as needed for each person.

Finally, as seen in Table 5.4, we can use matrices to write the more general single-level version of the random linear time model equation that is often seen

Table 5.4 Matrix equation for predicted values from a random linear time model for the four-occasion example data.

$$\mathbf{Y}_i = \mathbf{X}_i * \boldsymbol{\gamma} + \mathbf{Z}_i * \mathbf{U}_i + \mathbf{E}_i$$

$$\begin{bmatrix} y_{0i} \\ y_{1i} \\ y_{2i} \\ y_{3i} \end{bmatrix} = \begin{bmatrix} 1 & 0 \\ 1 & 1 \\ 1 & 2 \\ 1 & 3 \end{bmatrix} \begin{bmatrix} \gamma_{00} \\ \gamma_{10} \end{bmatrix} + \begin{bmatrix} 1 & 0 \\ 1 & 1 \\ 1 & 2 \\ 1 & 3 \end{bmatrix} \begin{bmatrix} U_{0i} \\ U_{1i} \end{bmatrix} + \begin{bmatrix} e_{0i} \\ e_{1i} \\ e_{2i} \\ e_{3i} \end{bmatrix}$$

$$\begin{bmatrix} y_{0i} \\ y_{1i} \\ y_{2i} \\ y_{3i} \end{bmatrix} = \begin{bmatrix} \gamma_{00} + \gamma_{10}(0) \\ \gamma_{00} + \gamma_{10}(1) \\ \gamma_{00} + \gamma_{10}(2) \\ \gamma_{00} + \gamma_{10}(3) \end{bmatrix} + \begin{bmatrix} U_{0i} + U_{1i}(0) \\ U_{0i} + U_{1i}(1) \\ U_{0i} + U_{1i}(2) \\ U_{0i} + U_{1i}(3) \end{bmatrix} + \begin{bmatrix} e_{0i} \\ e_{1i} \\ e_{2i} \\ e_{3i} \end{bmatrix}$$

$$\begin{bmatrix} y_{0i} \\ y_{1i} \\ y_{2i} \\ y_{3i} \end{bmatrix} = \begin{bmatrix} \gamma_{00} + \gamma_{10}(0) + U_{0i} + U_{1i}(0) + e_{0i} \\ \gamma_{00} + \gamma_{10}(1) + U_{0i} + U_{1i}(1) + e_{1i} \\ \gamma_{00} + \gamma_{10}(2) + U_{0i} + U_{1i}(2) + e_{2i} \\ \gamma_{00} + \gamma_{10}(3) + U_{0i} + U_{1i}(3) + e_{3i} \end{bmatrix}$$

in textbooks on mixed models. Using the notation introduced in this chapter, the matrix equation for the predicted outcomes for a single person would be $\mathbf{Y}_i = \mathbf{X}_i\gamma + \mathbf{Z}_i\mathbf{U}_i + \mathbf{E}_i$, which is expanded in Table 5.4 to show what it would look like given a random linear time model for four occasions. More generally, though, for each person: $\mathbf{Y}_i$ is a column vector (i.e., one column with multiple rows) that holds the y_{ti} outcomes across occasions, $\mathbf{X}_i$ is a matrix that holds the values of the predictors that have fixed effects (including a column of 1's for the fixed intercept), γ is a column vector that holds the fixed effect estimates, $\mathbf{Z}_i$ is a matrix that holds the values of the predictors that have random effects, $\mathbf{U}_i$ is a column vector that holds the random effect estimates, and $\mathbf{E}_i$ is a column vector that holds the e_{ti} residuals across occasions. Subscripts of i are included purposefully for all matrices that can vary across persons, which excludes γ because its fixed effects are the same for everyone. In Table 5.4, the matrix multiplication in line

Table 5.5 Predicted means, variances, covariances, and correlations by model for the four-occasion example data.

Fixed Linear Time, Random Intercept Model				
Time	0	1	2	3
0	6.28	4.10	4.10	4.10
1	.65	6.28	4.10	4.10
2	.65	.65	6.28	4.10
3	.65	.65	.65	6.28
Mean	10.27	11.99	13.71	15.42
SE	0.47	0.44	0.44	0.47

Random Linear Time Model				
Time	0	1	2	3
0	2.96	2.32	2.37	2.43
1	.68	3.98	4.24	5.21
2	.53	.82	6.81	7.99
3	.42	.77	.90	11.47
Mean	10.27	11.99	13.71	15.42
SE	0.33	0.37	0.50	0.67

Saturated Means, Unstructured Variance Model				
Time	0	1	2	3
0	2.36	2.79	1.96	2.42
1	.82	4.89	4.04	5.55
2	.51	.73	6.22	7.80
3	.46	.73	.91	11.74
Mean	10.40	11.86	13.58	15.55
SE	0.31	0.44	0.50	0.69

2 followed by the matrix addition in line 3 yields the combined random linear time model from Equation (5.5).

Returning to the balanced data across persons in our current example, Table 5.5 now compares more directly the predicted means, variances, and covariances for times 0, 1, 2, and 3 based on the parameters reported in Table 5.1 for two alternative models for change: the fixed linear time, random intercept model from Equation (5.3) and the random linear time model from Equation (5.5). As in chapter 4, to save space, in the predicted **V** matrices as shown in Table 5.5, the variances are on the diagonal, the covariances are above the diagonal, and the corresponding correlations from the **VCORR** matrix are below the diagonal. Because this example contains perfectly balanced data (i.e., the same time observations across persons), Table 5.5 also includes the results from a saturated means, unstructured variance model (as introduced in chapter 3), in which all means, variances, and covariances are estimated separately, and thus that can be used as the "answer key" with which to compare the two sets of model predictions. If we did not have balanced time data, then a saturated means, unstructured variance model would not have been estimable.

With regard to the predicted means as created by $\gamma_{00} + \gamma_{10}(\text{Time}_{ti})$, we see that a fixed linear effect of time (as included in both models) does a pretty good job describing the overall pattern of increase over time (that we also saw previously in Figure 5.3). However, the models diverge with respect to how accurately they predict the variance over time, as illustrated in the top panel of Figure 5.5. In the fixed linear time, random intercept model, the total variance at each occasion is predicted to be constant at $\tau_{U_0}^2 + \sigma_e^2 = 4.10 + 2.17 = 6.28$, an overestimate for three of the four variances in the original data (as given by the unstructured variance model). In contrast, in the random linear time model, the predicted variances match more closely those in the original data. The same can be said of the predicted correlations over time, as illustrated in the bottom panel of Figure 5.5. As shown, the fixed linear time, random intercept model predicts a constant correlation of $r = .65$, but in reality the correlations generally tended to decline with increasing time lags, as also better captured by the random linear time model.

2.E. Combining a Random Slope With Alternative Covariance Structure Models

So far we have seen how models for within-person change that include fixed and random effects of time (in addition to fixed and random intercepts) can be used to predict a pattern of means, variances, covariances, and correlations that change systematically as a function of time. Random effects models can provide such predictions even for unbalanced time in which the same time occasions are not observed across persons—a significant advantage in real-world data.

Furthermore, as explained earlier, random effects (or *piles of variance*) are used to address two kinds of dependency often present in longitudinal data. The first is dependency due to constant mean differences over time between persons, which

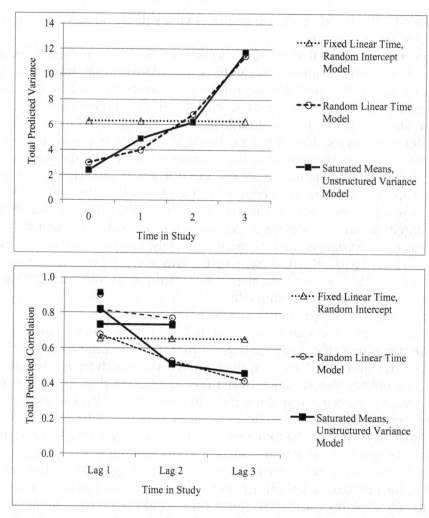

Figure 5.5 Predicted variances (top panel) correlations (bottom panel) by model for the four-occasion example data.

can be captured by the random intercept. The second is dependency due to differences between persons in the effects of time-varying predictors (such as in the linear effect of time), which can be captured by the random linear time slope. Dependency resulting from differences in the effects of other time-varying predictors can similarly be captured by including random slopes for those as well, as we'll see later in the text.

Finally, to account for the third kind of dependency, non-constant within-person correlation for unknown reasons, we can combine random effects with the alternative covariance structure (ACS) models from chapter 4. That is, after examining fixed and random effects related to time (of whatever type of model for change over time is warranted by the data, as elaborated in chapter 6), we might examine whether allowing some pattern of residual covariances can improve model fit rather than simply assuming that all within-person residual covariances in the **R** matrix should be 0. To illustrate, we will use our 4-occasion example data to examine two models that include additional relationships in the **R** matrix. Although we could also potentially allow heterogeneous *residual* variances over time in the **R** matrix as well, given that the random effects already predict different *total* variances across occasions in the **V** matrix, the estimation of separate residual variances per occasion is likely to be problematic given only four occasions.

First, we might consider adding a **first-order autoregressive structure** (AR1) to the within-person e_{ti} residuals in the **R** matrix. As presented in chapter 4, an AR1 model predicts the correlation at increasing time lags as an exponential function of an r auto-correlation parameter, such that occasions one unit apart in time are cor-related at r^1, those two units apart in time are correlated at r^2, and so forth. We can add this residual auto-correlation parameter directly for balanced data using an AR1 model for the **R** matrix, or indirectly for unbalanced data via a spatial covariance model in which the correlation decays exponentially as a function of continuous time instead of discrete time [e.g., SAS MIXED with TYPE = SP(POW)(Time)]. The predicted **V** matrix from combining a random linear time model in the **G** matrix with an AR1 model in the **R** matrix is shown in the top panel of Table 5.6. The AR1 residual correlation was estimated as $r_e = 0.0256$, and thus the **R** matrix is given to the fourth decimal place to show the predicted residual covariance across lags (as calculated by $r_e^1 * \sigma_e^2$ for lag-1, $r_e^2 * \sigma_e^2$ for lag-2, and $r_e^3 * \sigma_e^2$ for lag-3), which do not appear much different than the 0 values assumed before. So, does the extra AR1 residual auto-correlation parameter help model fit? The previous random linear time model is nested within this model also including an AR1 structure in the **R** matrix, and a comparison of their fit yields $-2\Delta LL(1) = 0.0$, $p = 1.0$, indicating that the extra AR1 correlation appears unnecessary (and the higher AIC and BIC for the model with the AR1 **R** matrix agree).

Second, we might instead consider adding a reduced Toeplitz structure (TOEP) to the **R** matrix, by which occasions with the same time lag would have the same residual covariance (thus requiring balanced, equal interval time observations). As in chapter 4, we could then test the number of additional lagged relationships needed by comparing alternative models. The predicted **V** matrix from combin-ing a random linear time model in the **G** matrix with a 1-lag Toeplitz model (e.g., TOEP2) in the **R** matrix is shown in the bottom panel of Table 5.6. This model adds a residual covariance in the **R** matrix for occasions 1-lag apart estimated as $c_{e1} = 0.0126$, but no extra covariances for occasions further apart (shown as exactly 0). This residual lag-1 covariance also appears unnecessary, as confirmed by com-paring the fit of this model to the nested original random linear time model, $-2\Delta LL(1) = 0.0$, $p = 1.0$ (with a higher AIC and BIC as well). If no residual relation-ship remains among adjacent occasions, it seems unlikely that a residual relation-ship might exist among lag-2 occasions (e.g., as tested by a TOEP3 **R** matrix), and so we do not proceed further with Toeplitz models that include additional lagged covariances.

Thus, to summarize, in our four-occasion example data, the pattern of change on average predicted by the fixed linear effect of time appears adequate. Furthermore,

Table 5.6 Predicted **V** matrix for a single individual for the four-occasion example data from a random linear time model after adding additional within-person auto-regressive (top panel) or 1-lag Toeplitz (bottom panel) covariance structures in the **R** matrix.

$$\mathbf{V} = \mathbf{Z} * \mathbf{G} * \mathbf{Z}^T + \mathbf{R}$$

$$\mathbf{V} = \begin{bmatrix} 1 & 0 \\ 1 & 1 \\ 1 & 2 \\ 1 & 3 \end{bmatrix} \begin{bmatrix} \tau^2_{U_0} & \tau_{U_{01}} \\ \tau_{U_{01}} & \tau^2_{U_1} \end{bmatrix} \begin{bmatrix} 1 & 1 & 1 & 1 \\ 0 & 1 & 2 & 3 \end{bmatrix} + \begin{bmatrix} \sigma^2_e & r^1_e\sigma^2_e & r^2_e\sigma^2_e & r^3_e\sigma^2_e \\ r^1_e\sigma^2_e & \sigma^2_e & r^1_e\sigma^2_e & r^2_e\sigma^2_e \\ r^2_e\sigma^2_e & r^1_e\sigma^2_e & \sigma^2_e & r^1_e\sigma^2_e \\ r^3_e\sigma^2_e & r^2\sigma^2_e & r^1_e\sigma^2_e & \sigma^2_e \end{bmatrix}$$

$$\mathbf{V} = \begin{bmatrix} 1 & 0 \\ 1 & 1 \\ 1 & 2 \\ 1 & 3 \end{bmatrix} \begin{bmatrix} 2.22 & 0.07 \\ 0.07 & 0.90 \end{bmatrix} \begin{bmatrix} 1 & 1 & 1 & 1 \\ 0 & 1 & 2 & 3 \end{bmatrix} + \begin{bmatrix} 0.7193 & 0.0181 & 0.0005 & 0.0000 \\ 0.0181 & 0.7193 & 0.0181 & 0.0005 \\ 0.0005 & 0.0181 & 0.7193 & 0.0181 \\ 0.0000 & 0.0005 & 0.0181 & 0.7193 \end{bmatrix}$$

$$\mathbf{V} = \begin{bmatrix} 2.94 & 2.31 & 2.36 & 2.43 \\ 2.31 & 3.98 & 4.25 & 5.20 \\ 2.36 & 4.25 & 6.82 & 8.00 \\ 2.43 & 5.20 & 8.00 & 11.47 \end{bmatrix}$$

$$\mathbf{V} = \mathbf{Z} * \mathbf{G} * \mathbf{Z}^T + \mathbf{R}$$

$$\mathbf{V} = \begin{bmatrix} 1 & 0 \\ 1 & 1 \\ 1 & 2 \\ 1 & 3 \end{bmatrix} \begin{bmatrix} \tau^2_{U_0} & \tau_{U_{01}} \\ \tau_{U_{01}} & \tau^2_{U_1} \end{bmatrix} \begin{bmatrix} 1 & 1 & 1 & 1 \\ 0 & 1 & 2 & 3 \end{bmatrix} + \begin{bmatrix} \sigma^2_e & c_{e1} & 0 & 0 \\ c_{e1} & \sigma^2_e & c_{e1} & 0 \\ 0 & c_{e1} & \sigma^2_e & c_{e1} \\ 0 & 0 & c_{e1} & \sigma^2_e \end{bmatrix}$$

$$\mathbf{V} = \begin{bmatrix} 1 & 0 \\ 1 & 1 \\ 1 & 2 \\ 1 & 3 \end{bmatrix} \begin{bmatrix} 2.23 & 0.06 \\ 0.06 & 0.90 \end{bmatrix} \begin{bmatrix} 1 & 1 & 1 & 1 \\ 0 & 1 & 2 & 3 \end{bmatrix} + \begin{bmatrix} 0.7127 & 0.0126 & 0 & 0 \\ 0.0126 & 0.7127 & 0.0126 & 0 \\ 0 & 0.0126 & 0.7127 & 0.0126 \\ 0 & 0 & 0.0126 & 0.7127 \end{bmatrix}$$

$$\mathbf{V} = \begin{bmatrix} 2.95 & 2.31 & 2.36 & 2.43 \\ 2.31 & 3.98 & 4.25 & 5.21 \\ 2.36 & 4.25 & 6.82 & 7.99 \\ 2.43 & 5.21 & 7.99 & 11.47 \end{bmatrix}$$

the predicted pattern of variance and covariance (in the **V** matrix) from a random intercept variance, random linear slope variance, and their covariance (in the **G** matrix) paired with a single residual variance with no remaining covariances (in the **R** matrix) also appears adequate. Thus, if these were our data to be analyzed further, we could now proceed to add effects of predictors, and have better confidence in the accuracy of their standard errors (and thus *p*-values) than if we had never examined the pattern of variance and covariance over time (on which those standard errors and thus *p*-values are based). However, a simple random linear time model may not always be sufficient when encountering more complex patterns of change, and so alternative models may need to be considered instead, as we'll see in chapter 6. For now, though, we'll use this random linear time model as a specific working example to present a more detailed explanation of the process of likelihood estimation and subsequent prediction of individual random effects, as described next.

3. Likelihood-Based Estimation of Random Effects Models

I'd like to begin this section with an honest disclaimer—I know that, like me, some of you reading this text may not have had much training in advanced mathematics (e.g., matrix algebra and calculus). As a result, I know firsthand how frustrating it can be to try to understand technical descriptions of likelihood-based estimation processes that rely heavily on these somewhat foreign concepts. So, as tempting as it may be to skip this section on estimation, please keep this in mind: In order to be informed consumers and responsible users of longitudinal models, we have to understand enough about estimation to at least recognize in our own data when things have gone wrong, why they probably went wrong, and what we should do instead. Accordingly, the purpose of this next section describing the processes of likelihood estimation in random effects models is to facilitate these more practical analytic goals. These estimation processes will still apply to the more complex models to follow in the rest of the text, and so I have chosen to present them here (i.e., in the context of estimating parameters for a random linear time model) in order to try and present this material as clearly as possible.

Thus, we will now examine how these likelihood functions are constructed and how the model parameter estimates are then obtained, referring to our random linear time model as a specific example to help make these operations more concrete. We'll start with the normal distribution and how it relates to maximum likelihood estimation specifically, and later we'll examine the difference between the maximum likelihood and restricted maximum likelihood functions. Before diving in, though, it is important to review the five specific assumptions about the model residuals by which the likelihood estimation process will proceed for random effects models in general (and for our random linear time model in particular).

First, the level-1 e_{ti} residuals are assumed to have a normal distribution with a 0 mean and σ_e^2 variance in the **R** matrix (unless we choose another form of the **R** matrix besides diagonal, which would then be what we assume instead). Second, the set of level-2 U_i random effects are assumed to have a multivariate normal distribution with **0** means and an unstructured **G** matrix of variances and covariances. In the context of our random linear time model specifically, this means that the U_{0i} random intercepts and U_{1i} random linear time slopes at level 2 are assumed to have a multivariate normal distribution with 0 means, and with $\tau_{U_0}^2$ and $\tau_{U_1}^2$ variances and a $\tau_{U_{01}}$ covariance in the **G** matrix. For our random effects model, the **G** and **R** matrices together with the **Z** matrix of individual intercept and time values create the **V** matrix as: $\mathbf{V} = \mathbf{ZGZ}^{\mathrm{T}} + \mathbf{R}$. This person-specific $\mathbf{V}_i$ matrix (with rows and columns equal to the n occasions per person, now deliberately subscripted i to sync with what follows) will reappear frequently throughout this section. Third, all persons are assumed conditionally independent (e.g., no relationships *within* each of the U_{0i}, U_{1i}, or e_{ti} values across persons after including the model predictors). Fourth, no covariances are allowed for the variance terms across levels (e.g., the e_{ti} values are uncorrelated with both the U_{0i} and U_{1i} values). Finally, all variances and covariances are assumed constant over persons (e.g., $\tau^2_{U_0}$, $\tau^2_{U_1}$, $\tau_{U_{01}}$, and σ^2_e in the random linear time model). These five assumptions will allow us to utilize the multivariate normal distribution, as shown next.

3.A. Univariate and Multivariate Normal Distributions

The first step in understanding likelihood-based estimation is to recognize how the normal distribution tells us how *likely* each person's outcomes are given the model parameters. If the outcome is a continuous random variable, its **univariate normal probability density function** (the PDF for one outcome for one person using scalar values) and corresponding **multivariate normal probability density function** (the PDF using matrix values for the set of n y_i outcomes per person in the $\mathbf{Y}_i$ vector instead of a single y_i scalar value) are shown in Equation (5.11):

$$\text{Univariate Normal PDF}: \ f(y_i) = \frac{1}{\sqrt{2\pi\sigma^2_e}} * \exp\left[-\frac{1}{2} * \frac{(y_i - \hat{y}_i)^2}{\sigma^2_e}\right]$$

$$\text{Univariate Normal PDF}: \ f(y_i) = \left(2\pi\sigma^2_e\right)^{-1/2} * \exp\left[-\frac{1}{2} * (y_i - \hat{y}_i)(\sigma^2_e)^{-1}(y_i - \hat{y}_i)\right] \quad (5.11)$$

$$\text{Multivariate Normal PDF}: \ f(\mathbf{Y}_i) = (2\pi)^{-n/2} * |\mathbf{V}_i|^{-1/2} * \exp\left[-\frac{1}{2} * (\mathbf{Y}_i - \mathbf{X}_i\gamma)^{\mathsf{T}}(\mathbf{V}_i)^{-1}(\mathbf{Y}_i - \mathbf{X}_i\gamma)\right]$$

in which the first line writes the univariate normal PDF for a single outcome y_i in familiar terms, which from left to right includes the constant π (3.141 . . .), the σ^2_e residual variance, and the conditional mean of y_i, $\hat{y}_i$, as predicted from the fixed effects. The term "exp" indicates that the constant e (2.71 . . .) should be raised to the power of the terms in [ ] that follow. The univariate normal PDF returns the **likelihood** (the height of the y-axis) of obtaining that specific y_i value (the location on the x-axis) given the model parameters (σ^2_e and the fixed effects that create $\hat{y}_{ti}$ as the predicted value of y_i). Although the term *likelihood* is analogous to the idea of the *probability* of observing y_i (which would be used for categorical outcomes instead), the term *likelihood* is more correct for continuous outcomes because the probability of any specific point on a continuous distribution is technically 0 (and also because likelihood values can be greater than 1 for some y_i values depending on the shape of the likelihood distribution).

The second line re-writes the univariate normal PDF to look more similar to the multivariate normal PDF that follows. This includes raising $2\pi\sigma^2_e$ to the $-1/2$ power: given that the -1 power would indicate $(1/2\pi\sigma^2_e)$, the $-1/2$ power adds the missing square root. In the exp[ ] part, σ^2_e was originally in the denominator, and so it can be written equivalently as σ^2_e to the -1 power. The third line then writes the **multivariate normal PDF** that describes the likelihood of observing all of that person's n outcomes simultaneously (i.e., the height of the y-axis in n-dimensional space rather than in one univariate dimension). Accordingly, several modifications have been made given that we now need matrices or vectors that can hold multiple values (rather than just scalar or single values in the univariate normal PDF). For our random linear time model with 4 occasions, the 4x1 column vector $\mathbf{Y}_i$ would hold that person's four y_{ti} outcomes, the 4x2 $\mathbf{X}_i$ matrix would hold each person's values for the predictors with fixed effects (for the intercept and time slope here), the 2x1 γ column vector would hold the two fixed effects (γ_{00} and γ_{10}), and the 4x4 $\mathbf{V}_i$ matrix would hold that person's predicted variance and covariance across occasions (from $\mathbf{V}_i = \mathbf{Z}_i\mathbf{G}_i\mathbf{Z}_i^T + \mathbf{R}_i$). The term $\mathbf{Y}_i - \mathbf{X}_i\gamma$ in the multivariate normal PDF is analogous to the $y_i - \hat{y}_i$ term in the univariate normal PDF, in which $\hat{y}_i$ is created by $\mathbf{X}_i\gamma$. The pre-multiplication of the ($\mathbf{Y}_i - \mathbf{X}_i\gamma$) term by its transpose ($\mathbf{Y}_i - \mathbf{X}_i\gamma)^T$ creates the squared deviations between each original y_i and the $\hat{y}_i$ predicted from $\mathbf{X}_i\gamma$ (like $[y_i - \hat{y}_i]^2$ in the univariate normal PDF).

In addition, although the univariate normal PDF could include $(\sigma_e^2)^{-1}$ given that σ_e^2 was just a single number, in the multivariate normal PDF, σ_e^2 is replaced by the $\mathbf{V}_i$ matrix, requiring two other changes. First, the term $(2\pi\sigma_e^2)^{-1/2}$ is replaced by $(2\pi)^{-n/2}$ because there will be n of them, which then gets multiplied by $|\mathbf{V}_i|^{-1/2}$. The term $|\mathbf{V}_i|$ is the **determinant** of the $\mathbf{V}_i$ matrix, which is a matrix operation that summarizes the information contained in the matrix into a single number, sometimes referred to as its **generalized variance**, that takes into account the total variance across terms minus any redundancies across terms (i.e., it essentially reflects the total of the variances across occasions controlling for covariances across occasions). Second, because matrix division doesn't work like regular division, to "divide" the quantity $(\mathbf{Y}_i - \mathbf{X}_i\gamma)^T(\mathbf{Y}_i - \mathbf{X}_i\gamma)$ by the $\mathbf{V}_i$ matrix, instead we have to multiply by its **matrix inverse** (written as $\mathbf{V}_i^{-1}$), which is the matrix needed to solve for $(\mathbf{V}_i)(\mathbf{V}_i^{-1})$ = $\mathbf{I}$ (in which $\mathbf{I}$ is an *identity matrix* of 1's on the diagonal and 0's everywhere else). So, $\mathbf{V}_i^{-1}$ is conceptually like the reciprocal of $\mathbf{V}$ (e.g., 2*1/2 = 1), but in actuality it is much more complicated in order to account for all the of the matrix elements.

Notably, in finding a matrix inverse (e.g., $\mathbf{V}_i^{-1}$), each matrix element gets divided by its matrix determinant (e.g., $|\mathbf{V}_i|$). Therefore, in order to invert a matrix, it must be **positive definite**, which means the determinant summarizing its contents must be greater than 0: Because division by 0 is undefined, a matrix that is not positive definite cannot be inverted. Accordingly, whether $|\mathbf{V}_i|$ is greater than 0 is a direct assessment of whether the $\mathbf{V}$ matrix can be inverted (i.e., whether $\mathbf{V}_i^{-1}$ exists). If not, this presents a problem (and will result in an error message from the software program), as the matrix inverse $\mathbf{V}_i^{-1}$ will be needed in several places in the likelihood-based formulas that follow. If $\mathbf{V}_i^{-1}$ can't be found, then a *generalized inverse* will often be used instead to obtain model estimates, but these results are likely to be questionable. The likely reasons for such estimation problems due to $\mathbf{V}_i^{-1}$ will be addressed at the end of this section.

Although it is easy to get lost in the world of matrix inverses and determinants, the important thing to remember is this—*the multivariate normal PDF returns a single likelihood value that indicates how likely each person's set of outcomes are given a specific set of values for the model parameters.* These likelihood values provide us with a means by which to compare models with different parameters (i.e., with effects added or removed) and thus to evaluate empirically which model results in a greater likelihood of observing each person's outcomes.

3.B. Likelihood and Log-Likelihood Functions for the Total Sample

The process of combining these likelihoods across all persons in the sample results in a **likelihood function**, whose original and log-transformed versions are shown in Equation (5.12):

$$L = \prod_{i=1}^{N} \left\{ (2\pi)^{-n/2} * |\mathbf{V}_i|^{-1/2} * \exp\left[-\frac{1}{2}(\mathbf{Y}_i - \mathbf{X}_i\gamma)^T (\mathbf{V}_i)^{-1}(\mathbf{Y}_i - \mathbf{X}_i\gamma)\right] \right\}$$

$$LL = \sum_{i=1}^{N} \left\{ \left[-\frac{n}{2}\log(2\pi)\right] + \left[-\frac{1}{2}\log|\mathbf{V}_i|\right] + \left[-\frac{1}{2}(\mathbf{Y}_i - \mathbf{X}_i\gamma)^T (\mathbf{V}_i)^{-1}(\mathbf{Y}_i - \mathbf{X}_i\gamma)\right] \right\} \quad (5.12)$$

$$LL = \left[-\frac{T}{2}\log(2\pi)\right] + \left[-\frac{1}{2}\sum_{i=1}^{N}\log|\mathbf{V}_i|\right] + \left[-\frac{1}{2}\sum_{i=1}^{N}(\mathbf{Y}_i - \mathbf{X}_i\gamma)^T (\mathbf{V}_i)^{-1}(\mathbf{Y}_i - \mathbf{X}_i\gamma)\right]$$

in which the overall sample **likelihood** (L) is created by multiplying the likelihood of each person's n outcomes across all N persons (because persons are assumed independent). However, because likelihood values can get very small after multiplying across persons, they can become numerically unstable (i.e., too much potential for rounding error). Thus, it is easier to find the **natural log of the likelihood**, or **log-likelihood** (LL), by which log-likelihoods of separate persons can then be added together rather than multiplied, as seen by the summation at the front of the second line of Equation (5.12). As shown, the log transformation is then applied to each of the three parts of the original equation, with the result that they can also be added rather than multiplied. In further simplifying in the second line using the rules of log transformations, the exponents of –1/2 in the first two parts became constant multipliers of the log term, and the log of the quantity exp[ ] simply becomes the [ ] part. Finally, the third line distributes the summation over persons across terms, and the first part that is constant over persons becomes T = N*n in the numerator (for T total observations from N persons by n occasions).

3.C. Obtaining Estimates of Fixed Effects

The point of the overall sample log-likelihood (LL) value is to summarize how likely the total set of the observed y_{ti} outcomes are given the model parameters, and through this process to find the most likely estimates of those parameters. For example, the log-likelihood for a random linear time model as in Equation (5.5) is calculated given its six parameters: the fixed intercept and linear time slope γ_{00} and γ_{10} in the model for the means (in the γ column vector), and $\tau_{U_0}^2$, $\tau_{U_1}^2$, $\tau_{U_{01}}$, and σ_e^2 in the model for the variance (that together create the $\mathbf{V}_i$ matrix). This brings us to two important (but not immediately obvious) points as to which parameters in random effects models actually need to be estimated through the log-likelihood construction itself.

First, to calculate a log-likelihood for each person (and thus a total log-likelihood for the sample), we do not need to know what the U_{0i} random intercept and U_{1i}

random linear time slope values should be for each person—they are not in the log-likelihood formula above. Instead, it is *their variances and covariance across persons* ($\tau_{U_0}^2$, $\tau_{U_1}^2$, $\tau_{U_{01}}$) combined with σ_e^2 that are used to predict an individual $\mathbf{V}_i$ matrix using each person's observed time values, and it is that individual $\mathbf{V}_i$ matrix that actually goes into the log-likelihood function. Although the individual U_{0i} and U_{1i} values can be predicted after the fact if desired (as shown later in the chapter), we don't actually need to know what each U_{0i} and U_{1i} would be to estimate a model—it is sufficient to assume that they have means of 0 and a multivariate normal distribution with constant variance across persons (i.e., the $\mathbf{G}$ matrix contains the sufficient statistics for describing the $\mathbf{U}_i$ values). Furthermore, although the conditional outcome distribution (i.e., the level-1 e_{ti} residuals) could be non-normal (i.e., as in generalized mixed models), the distribution of the level-2 random effects is almost always assumed to be multivariate normal (and few software programs allow otherwise).

Second, the fixed effects in the γ matrix are determined entirely by the values in the $\mathbf{Y}_i$ column vector and the $\mathbf{X}_i$ and $\mathbf{V}_i$ matrices. That is, we already have the predictors in $\mathbf{X}_i$ and the outcomes in $\mathbf{Y}_i$. Once we obtain estimates of the variance parameters that create $\mathbf{V}_i$, the fixed effects and their standard errors (SE) are then a direct byproduct, as shown in Equation (5.13):

$$\gamma = \left\{ \sum_{i=1}^{N} \left(\mathbf{X}_i^T \mathbf{V}_i^{-1} \mathbf{X}_i \right) \right\}^{-1} \sum_{i=1}^{N} \left(\mathbf{X}_i^T \mathbf{V}_i^{-1} \mathbf{Y}_i \right), \quad \mathbf{Cov}(\gamma) = \left\{ \sum_{i=1}^{N} \left(\mathbf{X}_i^T \mathbf{V}_i^{-1} \mathbf{X}_i \right) \right\}^{-1} \quad (5.13)$$

in which substituting in the predicted $\mathbf{V}_i$ matrix leads to a generalized least squares estimate of the fixed effects in the γ matrix and their sampling variance and covariance in Cov(γ). The SE for each fixed effect is then given by the square root of the variances on the diagonal of Cov(γ). Because γ can be found from $\mathbf{X}_i$, $\mathbf{Y}_i$, and $\mathbf{V}_i$, sometimes the γ matrix in the [ ] part of the log-likelihood function in Equation (5.12) is replaced by the matrix solution for γ in Equation (5.13) (although I did not do so because I thought the log-likelihood looked scary enough as it was).

Even though the expressions in Equation (5.13) for the fixed effects in the general linear mixed model (i.e., multilevel model) may look unfamiliar initially, each has its origins in general linear models (e.g., regression, as seen in chapter 2) as found through ordinary least squares (OLS). Because the least squares and maximum likelihood fixed effect solutions for these models are the same given complete data, these solutions map onto each other directly (and the same is true for incomplete data under the assumption of missing at random). Thus, to show the parallel with the general linear model (GLM), its matrix solution for the fixed effects and their SEs, as well as for its scalar solution for a single fixed effect and its SE are given in Equation (5.14):

$$\text{GLM matrix solution}: \ \beta = \left(\mathbf{X}^T \mathbf{X} \right)^{-1} \left(\mathbf{X}^T \mathbf{X} \right), \qquad \text{Cov}(\beta) = \left(\mathbf{X}^T \mathbf{X} \right)^{-1} \sigma_e^2$$

$$\text{GLM scalar solution}: \ \beta = \frac{\sum_{i=1}^{N}(x_i - \bar{x})(y_i - \bar{y})}{\sum_{i=1}^{N}(x_i - \bar{x})^2}, \qquad \text{Cov}(\beta) = \frac{\sigma_e^2}{\sum_{i=1}^{N}(x_i - \bar{x})^2} \qquad (5.14)$$

in which β is used instead of γ to help distinguish the GLM solutions for fixed effects (for matrix β or scalar β) from the mixed model solutions for fixed effects (for matrix γ). A few relationships can be found between these sets of solutions, however.

First, summation over persons is included for γ in Equation (5.13) because the $\mathbf{X}_i$ matrix and $\mathbf{Y}_i$ column vector contain data for just one person. But in the GLM matrix solution for β in Equation (5.14), because each person has only one X and one Y value, the $\mathbf{X}$ and $\mathbf{Y}$ matrices in Equation (5.14) contain all sample values already, and thus no summation over persons is necessary. But in the GLM scalar solution for β in Equation (5.14) because x_i and y_i are again just for one person, summation over persons is again needed.

Second, the denominator in the scalar solution for β in Equation (5.14) contains the squared x_i deviations, which also appears in the matrix solution for β in Equation (5.14) as $(\mathbf{X}^T\mathbf{X})^{-1}$ and for γ in Equation (5.13) as $(\mathbf{X}_i^T\mathbf{V}_i^{-1}\mathbf{X}_i)^{-1}$ (recall that the matrix inverse $^{-1}$ is how matrices go into a denominator, and so taking the inverse of the whole quantity puts the $\mathbf{X}_i$ matrices in the denominator instead). Likewise, the numerator in the scalar solution for β in Equation (5.14) contains the product of the x_i and y_i mean deviations, which also appears in the matrix solution for β in Equation (5.14) as $(\mathbf{X}^T\mathbf{Y})$ and for γ in Equation (5.13) as $(\mathbf{X}_i^T\mathbf{V}_i^{-1}\mathbf{Y}_i)$.

Third, the inverse V matrix $(\mathbf{V}_i^{-1})$ is necessary in each part of the matrix solution for γ in Equation (5.13) to serve as a weight, given that the outcome variance is not constant across observations as it is assumed to be in general linear models (and thus in which no such variance-related weight is necessary for β or β). Finally, with respect to the fixed effect SEs [the square roots of the diagonals in Cov(β) or Cov(β) in Equation (5.14)], the numerator of their solution includes σ_e^2, whose analog for Cov(γ) in Equation (5.13) is the $\mathbf{V}_i$ matrix (e.g., built from $\tau_{U_0}^2$, $\tau_{U_1}^2$, $\tau_{U_{01}}$, and σ_e^2) that results after resolving $(\mathbf{V}_i^{-1})^{-1}$. The denominator in the Cov(β), Cov(β), and Cov(γ) equations is then based on the x_i, $\mathbf{X}$, or $\mathbf{X}_i$ values, respectively.

Thus, to summarize, in both cross-sectional and longitudinal models, the fixed effects and their SEs are determined by the predictor variables, the outcome variables, and the amount of outcome variance that remains. This latter variance term is necessarily more complicated in longitudinal models in order to accurately reflect the dependency of observations within persons. Finally, it is important to note that the accuracy of the SEs for the fixed effects depends on having the "right" model for the variance, and we've discussed this issue repeatedly with respect to which terms need to be included in the $\mathbf{V}_i$ matrix in order to best match the original data. But another critical issue is the potential for non-normality of the terms in the $\mathbf{V}_i$ matrix, which is an important consideration given that the likelihood function is based on the multivariate normal distribution. We will re-consider the issue of outcome non-normality in chapter 13.

3.D. Obtaining Estimates of Variance Parameters

The fact that the fixed effects can be solved for directly will be important as we consider the next logical question: how do we get estimates for the rest of the model parameters in the first place? That is, we need to find values for all parameters in the model for the variance (e.g., the $\tau_{U_0}^2$, $\tau_{U_1}^2$, $\tau_{U_{01}}$, and σ_e^2 parameters that create the $\mathbf{V_i}$ matrix in the random linear time model) that will result in the highest possible log-likelihood value across persons. This is how estimation problems can arise, because each additional parameter in the model for the variance adds another dimension to this simultaneous search for the estimates of all other variance parameters. Fortunately, because they are determined as shown in Equation (5.13), fixed effects do not add to this search-related complexity. So, unlike random effects, additional fixed effects can almost always be added without creating any new estimation problems.

Much attention in the statistical literature has been given to the problem of how to find the optimal estimates for all variance parameters simultaneously (i.e., that result in the highest log-likelihood across persons). An intuitive approach would be to specify a range of possible values for each variance parameter and to then calculate the sample log-likelihood for every possible combination of parameter values (e.g., over four dimensions of $\tau_{U_0}^2$, $\tau_{U_1}^2$, $\tau_{U_{01}}$, and σ_e^2 in a random linear time model). Eventually you would find the combination of values that leads to the highest possible log-likelihood across persons, and those values would be your best estimates of the variance parameters (which would then be used to calculate the fixed effects). This parameter search approach, known as a *grid search*, is usually inefficient at best or infeasible at worst due to the sheer volume of computations it would require. Instead, the search for estimates of the variance parameters more often occurs through the use of derivatives based on differential calculus. An excellent and readable introduction to likelihood estimation and obtaining parameter estimates through the use of derivatives can be found in Enders (2010); the main concepts involved will be summarized broadly here.

The general idea is that the range of possible log-likelihood values that could be obtained through different sets of parameter estimates should form a mountain-like function that has a peak at some point along each of its dimensions (i.e., one dimension for each estimated variance or covariance parameter). The **first derivative** of the mountain-like function of possible log-likelihood values provides the instantaneous linear rate of change at that point (or more specifically, it is the slope of the tangent line to the curve of the function at that point). There is a first derivative with respect to each parameter value to be found (i.e., with respect to each dimension), which is thus known as a **partial first derivative** when there is more than one dimension to consider. The resulting matrix of partial first derivatives is also known as the **score function** or **gradient**. The partial first derivative with respect to each parameter will be 0 at the peak of the function where there is no more linear change (i.e., the function has finished increasing up one side and has not yet started decreasing down the other, so the tangent line to the curve at the peak will be flat). The parameter values at the peak of the log-likelihood mountain where are all first derivatives are 0 simultaneously are their *most likely* estimates.

Although in theory the first derivative could also be 0 at the bottom of the likelihood function, too (i.e., the *lowest* log-likelihood where the *least* likely parameter estimates would be found), this won't happen in these models that are part of the exponential family of models, because the likelihood function will always be convex with a single peak. This can be demonstrated by finding the **partial second derivative** with respect to each parameter, which is the **change in the linear rate of change,** or the rate of acceleration or deceleration of the function at that point. Because the rate of increase should slow down (decelerate) as we get to the top of the log-likelihood function, if we are really at the top, the partial first derivatives will be 0 *and* the partial second derivatives will be negative.

When the log-likelihood function is fairly simple (e.g., a random intercept model), it can be straightforward to find its peak based on expected first and second partial derivatives. More elaborate parameter search processes are needed for more complex functions, but these processes also work with first and second partial derivatives to determine which parameter values should be tried next. To illustrate, let's say the current guess for one of our variance parameters is too low. The partial first derivative at that point will be *positive* (because it is still heading toward the peak), but the partial second derivative will be negative. The ratio of the (+first/−second) partial derivatives will be a *negative* number that indicates the next parameter value tried should be *higher* (i.e., a larger number than our current guess will be needed to get to the peak where the partial first derivative for that parameter is 0). In contrast, if our current parameter guess was too high, the partial first derivative at that point will instead be *negative* (because we are heading away from the peak), but the partial second derivative at that point will still be negative. So then, the ratio of (−first/−second) partial derivatives will be a *positive* number that indicates that the next parameter value tried should be *lower* (i.e., a smaller number will be needed than our current guess to get to the peak where the partial first derivative for that parameter is 0). In addition, the absolute value for the magnitude of the ratio of the (first/second) partial derivatives indicates how much to adjust the next guess for the most likely variance parameter (i.e., values that are closer to the top should have smaller ratios in absolute value). This general process falls under the heading of **Newton-Raphson procedures** when the actual partial derivatives are used and under **Fisher Scoring** when the expected partial derivatives are used instead.

One benefit of Newton-Raphson procedures in particular is that they result in an observed matrix of partial second derivatives (known as the **Hessian matrix**) that plays another useful role in and of itself. That is, once we have obtained the values of the variance parameters that result in the highest possible log-likelihood for the sample, the Hessian matrix of partial second derivatives can be used to indicate just how good those variance parameter estimates really are. Conceptually, we want our log-likelihood mountain to be as steep as possible so it is clear which set of parameter estimates are really most likely. This idea is shown mathematically by partial second derivatives that are *more negative,* indicating steeper deceleration toward the peak. Otherwise, a flatter log-likelihood function (represented by partial second derivatives that are *less negative* instead) would indicate that one set of parameter estimates is just as likely as the next (meaning that in our data none of them is really very likely at all, which is not good).

For these reasons, through two steps the Hessian matrix of partial second derivatives gets transformed into the sampling variance and covariance matrix for the variance parameters (from which SEs reflecting their precision can be found). First, because SEs are positive, the Hessian matrix (which holds negative values) is multiplied by –1: this positive result is then called the **information matrix.** At this point, larger information matrix values now reflect a steeper peak indicating *more precise* estimates, but this is backwards in terms of indexing standard error (for which larger values actually mean *less* precision). Thus, the second step is to find the inverse (i.e., reciprocal) of the information matrix so that larger values then represent *less* precision. The inverse of the information matrix is the **sampling variance and covariance matrix** for the variance parameters (in which the square root of its diagonal is then the SE for each parameter).

To summarize, the process of likelihood estimation proceeds in six steps. (1) For a given set of possible values for the variance parameters, calculate the log-likelihood (LL) for each person using his or her set of X_i, Y_i and V_i values, and sum those LL values across persons. (2) Repeat this process with different sets of possible parameter values (as suggested by the first and second partial derivatives of the LL function) until the most likely parameter values are found. In practice this point is defined by meeting **convergence criteria** for how much the LL values have to change for each new set of possible parameter values to be considered an improvement. (3) Once the model has reached convergence (i.e., no real improvements can be found), the height of the *y*-axis at that multidimensional peak is the model's summary LL value that can then be used as the basis of relative model fit comparisons. (4) Using the variance parameters values found to be most likely, calculate the fixed effect estimates and their standard errors. (5) Using the partial second derivatives, calculate the SEs of the variance parameter estimates. (6) Be ecstatic that modern statistical software packages will do all of this for you in just seconds!

3.E. Estimation via Maximum Likelihood Versus Restricted Maximum Likelihood

So far we have examined the process of likelihood estimation without considering the two different likelihood functions by which LL values can be derived: maximum likelihood (ML) or restricted maximum likelihood (REML). As introduced in chapter 3, the differences between ML and REML estimation result from differences in how they account for the fact that fixed effects are being estimated simultaneously with the variance parameters. That is, REML estimates of variance parameters account for the uncertainty that arises from also estimating the fixed effects simultaneously, whereas ML estimates of variance parameters do not.

Before diving into the actual ML and REML log-likelihood functions, though, it may be helpful to consider what the phrase *uncertainty from also estimating the fixed effects* means using a simpler context. Consider a univariate normal distribution for an outcome y_i. The formulae for the population and sample estimates of its variance are given in Equation (5.15):

$$\text{Population}: \quad \sigma_e^2 = \frac{\sum\limits_{i=1}^{N}(y_i - \mu)^2}{N} \qquad \text{Sample}: \quad \sigma_e^2 = \frac{\sum\limits_{i=1}^{N}(y_i - \bar{y})^2}{N-1} \qquad (5.15)$$

in which the numerator is the sum over persons of the squared deviations of each y_i value from the predicted $\hat{y}_i$ (from just the mean of y_i here) and N is the number of persons. In the sample estimate of σ_e^2, $N-1$ is used as the denominator instead of N because 1 fixed effect for the sample mean was estimated, resulting in a loss of 1 degree of freedom.

This difference of N versus $N-1$ corresponds exactly to the distinction between ML and REML estimates of variance parameters, respectively. That is, ML variance estimates will be downwardly biased (too small) because their denominator does not reflect that the fixed effects were also estimated in the model, whereas REML variance estimates that do use the correct denominator will be unbiased (i.e., will be correct). In general, ML variance estimates will be downwardly biased by a factor of $(N-k)/N$, where k is the number of fixed effects including the fixed intercept. Figure 5.6 illustrates this relationship between the sample size N on the x-axis and the ML predicted variance (assuming a true value from REML of 100) on the y-axis as a function of either $k = 2$, 5, or 8 fixed effects. As shown, more persons are required as the number of fixed effects increases to counteract the downward bias in the ML variance estimates.

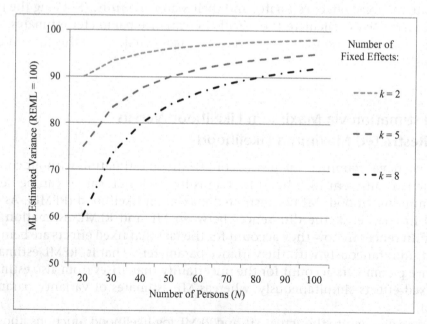

Figure 5.6 Predicted maximum likelihood (ML) variances across sample size (N) and number of fixed effects (k) given a restricted maximum likelihood (REML) variance of 100.

We can now examine the differences in the ML and REML log-likelihood functions that correspond to this difference. Unfortunately, the translation of this idea when many variance parameters are to be estimated at once (i.e., as in models with additional random effects) is not as straightforward as we would like. Nevertheless, the differences between ML and REML all result from modifications to REML to account for the simultaneous estimation of fixed effects.

The log-likelihood (LL) functions for ML and REML can be seen in Equation (5.16):

$$\text{ML}: \quad \text{LL} = \left[-\frac{T-0}{2}\log(2\pi) \right] + \left[-\frac{1}{2}\sum_{i=1}^{N}\log|\mathbf{V}_i| \right] + \left[-\frac{1}{2}\sum_{i=1}^{N}(\mathbf{Y}_i - \mathbf{X}_i\gamma)^{\text{T}}\mathbf{V}_i^{-1}(\mathbf{Y}_i - \mathbf{X}_i\gamma) \right]$$

$$\text{REML}: \quad \text{LL} = \left[-\frac{T-k}{2}\log(2\pi) \right] + \left[-\frac{1}{2}\sum_{i=1}^{N}\log|\mathbf{V}_i| \right] + \left[-\frac{1}{2}\sum_{i=1}^{N}(\mathbf{Y}_i - \mathbf{X}_i\gamma)^{\text{T}}\mathbf{V}_i^{-1}(\mathbf{Y}_i - \mathbf{X}_i\gamma) \right]$$

$$+ \left[-\frac{1}{2}\log\left| \sum_{i=1}^{N}\mathbf{X}_i^{\text{T}}\mathbf{V}_i^{-1}\mathbf{X}_i \right| \right] \tag{5.16}$$

$$\text{where}: \quad \left[-\frac{1}{2}\log\left|\sum_{i=1}^{N}\mathbf{X}_i^{\text{T}}\mathbf{V}_i^{-1}\mathbf{X}_i\right| \right] = \left[\frac{1}{2}\log\left|\left(\sum_{i=1}^{N}\mathbf{X}_i^{\text{T}}\mathbf{V}_i^{-1}\mathbf{X}_i\right)^{-1}\right| \right] = \left[\frac{1}{2}\log|\text{Cov}(\gamma)| \right]$$

in which two main differences between the ML and REML functions can be seen. First, in the first part that is constant over persons, $T - k$ is used instead of T, in which T is the total number of observations and k is the number of fixed effects (so $k = 2$ in a random linear time model). Second, in the third line of Equation (5.16) there is an extra matrix determinant (as indicated by the | |) at the end of the REML function that is not present in the ML function. The fourth line shows how the interior of this matrix determinant can be re-written (as seen in Fitzmaurice, Laird, & Ware, 2004) to resemble something we've already seen—the sampling variance-covariance matrix of the fixed effects, $\text{Cov}(\gamma)$, from which their SEs can be found. Although not at all obvious, this extra determinant term found in REML is the multivariate analog to correcting the variance estimates by the factor of $(N - k)/N$. From a conceptual standpoint, the extra determinant puts the amount of uncertainty found in estimating the fixed effects (as summarized by the determinant of the sampling variance and covariance matrix for the fixed effects) back into the REML log-likelihood function so that it can be properly accounted for.

There are two equivalent ways to think about this correction process from the literature about REML estimation. First, the REML estimation approach was first described by Patterson and Thompson (1971), who transformed the $\mathbf{Y}$ column vector (the total $\mathbf{Y}_i$ summed over persons) into a matrix of residuals using an $\mathbf{A}$ matrix of T by $T - k$ linearly independent contrasts that are orthogonal to the $\mathbf{X}$ matrix of predictors (the total $\mathbf{X}_i$ matrix summed over persons). They then created a new column vector $\mathbf{A}^{\text{T}}\mathbf{Y}$ (with a mean of 0 and a variance of $\mathbf{A}^{\text{T}}\mathbf{V}\mathbf{A}$) to replace the original $\mathbf{Y}$ column vector. This is the reason why the difference between ML and REML is often described such that ML maximizes the likelihood of the original data (in $\mathbf{Y}$) whereas REML maximizes the likelihood of the residuals instead (in $\mathbf{A}^{\text{T}}\mathbf{Y}$). Second, Harville (1974, 1977) showed how an equivalent but computationally easier result could be obtained simply by including the extra determinant term in the REML function in Equation (5.16) (although there was also a second determinant term that involved only the **X** matrix, it could be ignored given that it contains no unknown model parameters). For this reason, the REML function in Equation (5.16) is how the approach of maximizing the residuals of **Y** instead of the original **Y** is actually implemented in most statistical software for random effects models (e.g., SAS MIXED).

Now that the difference between ML and REML is hopefully a little more concrete, we can revisit the use of their log-likelihood values in comparing the fit of nested models, as originally introduced in less detail in chapter 3. There are three different ways this same process of comparing nested models has been described, corresponding to summary values in the form of likelihoods (L), log-likelihoods (LL), or deviances (–2LL). First, a **likelihood ratio test** (LR) can be computed as: LR = $-2*\log (L_{fewer}/L_{more})$, in which L_{fewer} denotes the likelihood from the model with fewer parameters and L_{more} denotes the likelihood from the model with more parameters. Second, because quantities that were divided get subtracted instead once they are log-transformed, the likelihood ratio test is also described as LR: $-2*(LL_{fewer} - LL_{more})$. Third, if the LL values are multiplied by –2 beforehand to compute *deviance* values instead as –2LL, then the LR (labeled a **deviance difference test**) = $(-2LL_{fewer}) - (-2LL_{more})$ directly. To be clear, please note that although the term *deviance* is sometimes used in other contexts to refer to a *difference* in –2LL values, we are using the term *deviance* to refer to the –2LL value itself.

The reason for multiplying by –2 in each version of a nested model comparison process just described is so that the –2LL difference between models (written as $-2\Delta LL$) will be chi-square (χ^2) distributed (in which the χ^2-distribution ranges from 0 to ∞, with a mean equal to its degrees of freedom, or *df*, the difference in the number of model parameters, or Δdf). The reason it is –2 instead of just 2 is because, as seen in Equation (5.16), each part of the LL functions starts off with a negative number, which means the overall LL is likely to be negative. More specifically, the first part involving *T*, *k*, and $\log(2\pi)$ will be negative, the second part involving $|V_i|$ will also be negative (because the determinant must be positive), and the fourth part (the extra determinant found only in REML) will also be negative. Accordingly, the overall model LL value will usually be negative, although in practice this will depend on the scale of X_i and Y_i from the third part of the LL function. Either way, multiplying the difference between nested models of $LL_{fewer} - LL_{more}$ by –2 ensures the result will be a positive number as needed.

The practice we have followed in the text is to use the difference between model –2LL values directly to conduct a significance test to see if the model with more parameters fits better (i.e., a $-2\Delta LL$ likelihood ratio test as introduced in chapter 3). The model with the smaller –2LL deviance value (but with the larger LL value) fits better. The fit of models that are non-nested can be compared using the *Akaike Information Criterion*, or AIC = –2LL + 2*(#parameters), or the *Bayesian Information Criterion*, or BIC = –2LL + log(N)*(#parameters). The AIC and BIC indices account for differences in parsimony based on the number of parameters (and the natural log of the number of persons *N* in the BIC). Smaller AIC and BIC values indicate a better model, although there is no cutoff after which we can say that one model is "significantly better" given that the differences between their values across models do not follow any known distribution.

The differences in how ML and REML functions are constructed as shown in Equation (5.16) provide some insight as to why only certain nested model comparisons are permitted under REML. That is, the LL (and –2LL, AIC, and BIC) values provided by ML can be used to compare models that differ in their model for the means (i.e., in fixed effects), in their model for the variance (i.e., in random effects), or that differ in both sides at once. Unfortunately, the resulting ML estimates of variance parameters will be downwardly biased by a factor of $(N - k)/N$ because they do not account for the fact that k fixed effects were also estimated. Furthermore, because these same variances are utilized in finding the SEs of the fixed effects, the SEs under ML may also be downwardly biased, resulting in p-values that may be too liberal (too small).

In contrast, the REML function does explicitly account for estimation of k fixed effects (in the $T - k$ term in the first part and through the extra determinant in the fourth part), and so the REML estimates of variance parameters (and thus the fixed effect SEs and p-values) will be unbiased. However, if the models to be compared have different fixed effects (in addition to or instead of different variance parameters), this will require different sets of $(T - k)$ error contrasts to create $\mathbf{A^T Y}$ (or equivalently, a different correction factor in the fourth part of the REML function). In other words, because REML maximizes the likelihood of the model residuals specifically, and because the residuals from models with different fixed effects are defined differently, REML functions including different fixed effects will no longer be comparable—essentially, they will be on different scales. For this reason, the LL (and –2LL, AIC, and BIC) values provided by REML will only index the fit of the variance side of the model, and so cannot be used to compare the fit of models with different fixed effects. That is, REML indices can only be used to compare models differing on their variance side. Fortunately, because the contribution of each fixed effect to a model can be evaluated directly from its Wald test (from estimate/SE), we don't have to test fixed effects via –2ΔLL tests. If you wish to test the contribution of multiple fixed effects simultaneously using the –2ΔLL test, though, then only the –2ΔLL test under ML can be used for this purpose, and not the –2ΔLL test under REML. However, multiple fixed effects can be tested simultaneously via a multivariate Wald test (e.g., omnibus ANOVA tests) within ML or REML. Furthermore, either ML or REML can be used to compare the fit of models with different variance parameters, but REML is preferred given that its estimates of those variance parameters themselves will be unbiased.

3.F. Adjustments to the Chi-Square Test P-Value When Testing Variance Components

As also introduced in chapter 3, there is one additional wrinkle in conducting likelihood ratio or deviance difference tests that pertains to the χ^2 critical values against which the –2ΔLL values are compared. As noted by several authors (e.g., Stoel, Garre, Dolan, & van den Wittenboer, 2006; Verbeke & Molenberghs, 2000), the $-2\Delta LL$ between two nested models follows a χ^2-distribution (with $df = \Delta df$ for the difference in the number of parameters between models) only when the added parameters do not have a boundary (i.e., they could be estimated as any positive or negative value). As a result, the $-2\Delta LL$ is not χ^2-distributed when testing the significance of new random intercept variances or random slope variances that cannot be negative. This is also why we should not assess the significance of new variances by using their SEs to form a Wald test (i.e., because the sampling distribution of any random effect variance is bounded at 0, which means that its sampling distribution cannot be normal when the variance estimate is close to 0).

More formally, when testing whether a parameter that can't be negative is 0, that null hypothesis is referred to as being on the **boundary of the parameter space**. In these cases, the $-2\Delta LL$ from adding a parameter that is bounded at 0 will follow a **mixture of two or more χ^2-distributions** instead of just a single χ^2-distribution. For example, in comparing a model with σ_e^2 to a model with both σ_e^2 and $\tau_{U_0}^2$, the critical χ^2 for $\Delta df = 1$ at $\alpha < .05$ should be 3.84. But because $\tau_{U_0}^2$ can't be negative, the distribution for the $-2\Delta LL$ value under the null hypothesis will be a mixture of χ^2-distributions with $\Delta df = 0$ (χ_0^2 when $\tau_{U_0}^2$ would have been estimated as negative, which will always be 0) and $\Delta df = 1$ (χ_1^2 when $\tau_{U_0}^2$ is estimated as positive). The same principle applies in adding a single random slope variance that also can't be negative.

In situations like these in which only one of the added model parameters has a boundary, the correct p-value from a **mixture χ^2-distribution** can be calculated as shown in Equation (5.17):

$$\text{Mixture } p\text{-value} = 0.5 * \text{prob}(\chi^2_{\Delta df-1} > -2\Delta LL)$$
$$+ 0.5 * \text{prob}(\chi^2_{\Delta df} > -2\Delta LL) \tag{5.17}$$

in which Δdf is the number of new variance parameters by which the models differ. If $\Delta df = 1$ (e.g., comparing a model with σ_e^2 to a model with both σ_e^2 and $\tau_{U_0}^2$), χ_0^2 will always be 0 and would not contribute regardless of the obtained $-2\Delta LL$. In that case, the correct mixture p-value would just be half of that from χ_1^2 only, such that $p < .10$ could be obtained for the $-2\Delta LL$ test to still be significant at the $\alpha < .05$ level. Thus, the critical value for the mixture χ_0^2 and χ_1^2 distributions when adding $\tau_{U_0}^2$ ($\Delta df = 1$) is 2.71, not 3.84 for $df = 1$. Similarly, in then testing the contribution from adding a random linear time slope variance and its covariance with the random intercept ($\tau_{U_0}^2$ and $\tau_{U_{01}}$ so $\Delta df = 2$), the distribution for the $-2\Delta LL$ will be a mixture of χ_1^2 and χ_2^2, such that the critical value is 5.14, not 5.99 from $df = 2$. A table of critical values for mixture chi-square distributions can be found in Appendix C of Fitzmaurice, Laird, and Ware (2004).

However, these approximations assume equal weighting of the separate χ^2 distributions in creating the mixture χ^2-distribution, and thus do not take into account the potential relationships among the estimates for the random effects variances and covariances (i.e., they assume the information matrix for those estimates is diagonal with no covariances). This problem becomes intractable in more complex models, in which simulation is then required to determine the actual mixture

χ^2-distribution by which the test should be conducted (see Stoel et al., 2006). A compromise that takes considerably less effort that has been suggested by several authors (e.g., Fitzmaurice, Laird, & Ware, 2004; Hedeker & Gibbons, 2006) is to use $\alpha < .10$ rather than $\alpha < .05$ when testing random effects variances to avoid an unduly conservative test.

Fortunately, not all tests for additions to the model for the variance are subject to these boundary issues. For instance, in comparing the fit of a compound symmetry model for the **R** matrix (i.e., CS with equal variances and equal covariances across occasions) to the fit of an unstructured model for the **R** matrix (i.e., UNn with separate variances and covariances across all occasions), the extra parameters in the UNn model can be viewed as deviations from the average variance and average covariance across occasions estimated in the CS model. These extra deviations are unbounded, and thus the $-2\Delta LL$ between the CS and UNn models should be χ^2-distributed with $df = \Delta df$. The same would be true for tests of variance heterogeneity or lagged covariances or correlations in the **R** matrix. In general, the $-2\Delta LL$ test will be conservative for asking whether a new parameter with a boundary is different from that boundary (e.g., $\tau_{U_0}^2 > 0$), but it will be accurate when asking if new parameters differ from existing parameters (e.g., whether σ_e^2 differs across occasions), or when asking whether unbounded parameters differ from 0 (e.g., in testing fixed effects that could take on any value).

To summarize, the main point is this: when using $-2\Delta LL$ tests to assess the contribution of new random effect variances that cannot be negative (and their associated covariances), use of a critical χ^2 value for $df = \Delta df$ will result in p-values that are too conservative. But if the $-2\Delta LL$ test is significant under this overly conservative approach, then it will also be significant using a more correct mixture p-value instead. So, for cases in which the $-2\Delta LL$ test is *not* significant, it's probably a good idea to determine the more correct mixture p-value to avoid a Type II error.

3.G. Adjustments to the Denominator Degrees of Freedom When Testing Fixed Effects

Just as the process of assessing the significance of new random effects variances turned out to be not quite as simple as it first seemed, the same can be said about the process of testing the significance of fixed effects. Although so far we have described the process of evaluating the Wald test statistic (for each fixed effect estimate divided by its SE) relative to a t-distribution, there are several variations of this approach that are actually used in practice. Recall that the significance of a Wald test statistic is evaluated relative to a critical $\pm t$-value for a given denominator degrees of freedom (usually based on $N - k$, in which N is the sample size and k is the number of fixed effects in the model). For testing the significance of multiple fixed effects simultaneously (i.e., a multivariate Wald test), a test statistic based on the F-distribution is used instead (given that $t^2 = F$ for a single degree of freedom test), which then requires both a numerator degrees of freedom (based on the number of parameters being tested simultaneously) and a denominator degrees of freedom (again based on $N - k$). If the denominator degrees of freedom are considered infinite instead, then the analog to the t-distribution is the z-distribution, and the analog to the F-distribution is the χ^2-distribution. Accordingly, software programs differ in how they evaluate their Wald test statistics (or multiple degree of freedom multivariate versions) to obtain p-value for the tests of significance of the model fixed effects. Some programs (e.g., STATA MIXED and M*plus*) use the z-distribution and χ^2-distribution in which denominator degrees of freedom are not applicable. In contrast, other programs (e.g., SPSS and SAS MIXED) use approximate t-distribution and F-distribution in which denominator degrees of freedom are then relevant, but they may be difficult to determine in unbalanced data.

SAS MIXED has several options for estimating **denominator degrees of freedom** (**DDF**), the most applicable for longitudinal analysis are the between-within, Satterthwaite, and Kenward-Roger methods. First, the **between-within** DDF method uses an ANOVA-like approach in which the total DDF (based on the total number of observations) are divided into between-person (level-2) and within-person (level-1) parts, and thus is only available for models with one type of nesting. The DDF for level-2 fixed effects is based on the number of persons minus the number of level-2 fixed effects; the DDF for level-1 or cross-level interaction fixed effects is based on the remainder of the total DDF minus the total number of level-1 or cross-level fixed effects.

Second, the considerably more complex **Satterthwaite** DDF method (Satterthwaite, 1946; see also Appendix A of Verbeke & Molenberghs, 1997) is currently the only method available in SPSS MIXED and is based on the formula for a two-group t-test given unequal residual variances and unequal sample sizes between groups. Usually the numerator of the t-statistic (i.e., the fixed effect estimate for the group mean difference) is a normally distributed random variable, and its denominator (i.e., the SE of group mean difference) is a χ^2-distributed random variable (from the pooled residual variance across observations divided by the sample size) with an exact degrees of freedom based on $N - k$. But given unequal residual variances and unequal sample sizes between groups, the SE in the denominator of the t-statistic must instead weight the residual variance of each group by the sample size in each group. In that case, the degrees of freedom are no longer exact, and must be estimated taking into account the varying residual variances and sample sizes across groups. The Satterthwaite DDF method follows a parallel process in longitudinal data, in which the DDF are estimated by taking into account the contribution of the variance components at each level of the model (e.g., σ_e^2, $\tau_{U_0}^2$, and $\tau_{U_1}^2$) along with the level-2 and level-1 sample sizes. DDF for level-2 fixed effects will generally resemble the number of persons minus the number of level-2 fixed effects, whereas DDF for level-1 or cross-level interaction fixed effects will generally resemble the remainder of the total DDF minus the total number of level-1 or cross-level fixed effects when the level-1 effect is fixed, but will resemble the level-2 DDF instead when the level-1 effect has a random slope. Because of its availability (e.g., in both SAS and SPSS MIXED), results using the Satterthwaite DDF method are reported in this text so that results stay as similar across programs as possible.

Finally, the **Kenward-Roger** DDF method (Kenward & Roger, 1997; designed for small samples and currently available only in SAS MIXED) uses a slightly inflated estimate of the sampling covariance matrix of the fixed effects and variance components. This adjusted sampling covariance matrix (as then provided in the output) better reflects the uncertainty introduced by estimating the variance and covariance parameters in small samples using ML or REML (whose asymptotic properties generally only hold in large samples). The Kenward-Roger adjusted sampling covariance matrix is then used within the Satterthwaite DDF.

A few caveats are worth noting with respect to these choices for degrees of freedom, however. First, given an unstructured V matrix, each fixed effect is tested using the level-2 DDF such that these choices do not apply. Second, given enough observations, the difference in the obtained p-values from these different methods of calculating DDF (or using a z-distribution instead) are likely to be very minor. For instance, the critical t-value for $p < .05$ at DDF = 20 is 2.086, whereas the critical z-value at $p < .05$ when assuming infinite DDF instead is 1.960. So, only in very small samples will these different DDF methods potentially change the substantive conclusions drawn about the significance of the fixed effects. A conservative approach would be to use the Kenward-Roger DDF as a first choice, the Satterthwaite DDF as a second choice, and a traditional Wald test based on the z-distribution assuming infinite DDF in larger samples.

3.H. When Likelihood Estimation Goes Awry

Up to this point we have assumed there will be no difficulty in achieving convergence of the model, at which point model parameter estimates, standard errors, and −2LL, AIC, and BIC values would then be provided in your output. But what if this doesn't happen? That is, what if you receive an incomplete set of results with an error message such as *covariance parameters at last iteration* instead? When this happens, it means that the estimation routine could not find an acceptable simultaneous solution for all the variance parameters, and it gave up trying once it went through the maximum number of iterations (which is usually set by the program). It is possible that increasing the number of iterations could help in some cases. In addition, although it is also possible to adjust the convergence criteria set within the program, this can be dangerous, as those values were most likely set as they are for good reason!

Even if the model appears to converge (i.e., you find a full set of output as anticipated), you may still find that some of your parameters are missing (e.g., variances that are estimated as exactly 0, with no standard errors given). These missing parameters will usually be accompanied by an angry error message stating something like "the estimated G matrix is not positive definite; the asymptotic variance matrix of covariance parameter estimates has been found to be singular and a generalized inverse was used"—this is not good. What it means is that the estimation routine could not find an acceptable positive value for that variance estimate, such that the entire G matrix of random effects and covariances is suspect. By default most programs do not allow variance parameters to have negative values at any point in the estimation (although this option can sometimes be overridden for troubleshooting purposes). So, what happened is that the highest log-likelihood values for that variance estimate were found so close to 0 that the algorithms could not figure out what its value should be (and gave up trying).

The term **non-positive definite G matrix** more generally refers to a **G** matrix in which at least one of its random effects variances are estimated at 0 and/or at least one of its covariances are out of bounds (i.e., leading to a correlation between random effects greater than 1 or less than –1). A non-positive definite **G** matrix will result in a determinant for the **V** matrix that is not greater than 0, which it needs to be in order to invert the **V** matrix (recall that $\mathbf{V}^{-1}$ appears frequently in the log-likelihood functions). So, the program used a different tactic to find $\mathbf{V}^{-1}$ instead, creating a *generalized inverse* as referred to in the second part of the angry error message, which essentially provides a work-around solution so that the log-likelihood values can still be found (although they may not be trustworthy as a result).

To summarize, problems in estimation are far more likely to occur when adding parameters in the model for the variance (e.g., new random slope variances and covariances), given that they will require additional dimensions in the log-likelihood functions across which the parameter search must proceed simultaneously. If the model does not converge or a random variance is estimated as exactly 0, it is highly likely that the parameter does not need to have a random effect (or there is not enough variability in the data with which to estimate it). For instance, in the example from this chapter, if the variance across persons in the random linear time slopes was estimated as exactly 0, this would imply that each person does not need his or her own slope, and thus the random time slope variance (and covariance with the random intercept) should not be retained. Notably, this is the case even if the model –2LL appears to go down significantly after adding a random effect that was estimated as 0. Rather than reflecting a true increase in model fit, a "significant" –2ΔLL test may occur simply because a proper matrix inverse was used for **V** in the model without the random effect but a generalized matrix inverse was used for **V** in the model with the extra (but non-estimable) random effect (as should be indicated by an error message from the software), such that their log-likelihoods are then not comparable. Thus, the bottom line is that if a variance parameter is estimated as exactly 0, then it doesn't belong in your model.

3.I. Prediction of Individual Random Effects

Last, but not least, a full description of estimation in random effects models needs to describe how the set of individual $\mathbf{U}_i$ random effects may be predicted. As discussed previously, although they appear in the y_{ti} equation, the individual $\mathbf{U}_i$ values are not the estimated model parameters—it is their variances and covariances across persons in the **G** matrix that are estimated instead. Given a solution for those variances and covariances, though, we can predict each individual $\mathbf{U}_i$ value after the fact. But because they are not directly estimated in the model, the term *predict* is used instead of the term *estimate* to describe how the U_i values are obtained. These U_i values are known as **empirical Bayes estimates** or **best linear unbiased predictors (BLUP)**. Although what follows applies to random effects models more generally, we will again use the example random linear time model as the basis for explaining this process.

Earlier you read that the individual U_{0i} random intercept for person *i* was the difference between the fixed intercept (i.e., predicted by the fixed effects in the model at time = 0) and that person's predicted individual intercept. Likewise, the individual U_{1i} random linear time slope was described as the difference between the fixed linear time slope predicted by the model and that person's predicted individual linear time slope. Although these definitions work at a conceptual level, they are not strictly correct when used to describe how the U_{0i} and U_{1i} values would actually be predicted. The discrepancy arises when considering the source of information that goes into estimating each U_i value—from just each individual versus the full sample.

On the one hand, a straightforward way to estimate an intercept and linear time slope for each person would be to conduct a regression analysis per person using just that person's data. The ordinary least squares (or OLS) intercept and slope estimates could then be saved to be used as variables in a secondary analysis. This approach, known as **slopes-as-outcomes**, was popular prior to the widespread availability of software with which to estimate random effects models. It has the advantage that the OLS estimates will be completely unbiased because they are based only on that person's data. On the other hand, there are three serious drawbacks to the slopes-as-outcomes approach. First, the OLS estimates will be very imprecise when based on very few data points per person. Second, using the OLS estimates in a secondary analysis ignores the variability around the regression line for each person, treating the OLS estimates as if they were perfectly reliable instead. Third, the OLS estimates would also be treated as equally reliable across persons, which is especially unreasonable when the number of data points available with which to estimate each person's OLS intercept and slope differs across persons. In addressing these problems, however, random effects models like that in Equation (5.5) end up creating different intercept and slope estimates for each person (i.e., through $\beta_{0i} = \gamma_{00} + U_{0i}$ and $\beta_{1i} = \gamma_{10} + U_{1i}$, respectively) than the OLS estimates that would be found from an individual regression.

The individual U_i predicted random effects can be found through Equation (5.18):

$$\mathbf{U}_i = \mathbf{G}_i \mathbf{Z}_i^T \mathbf{V}_i^{-1}(\mathbf{Y}_i - \mathbf{X}_i\gamma) \tag{5.18}$$

in which the deviations of the y_{ti} outcomes from the $\hat{y}_{ti}$ outcomes (predicted from $\mathbf{X}_i\gamma$) are standardized against the amount of the total variance in $\mathbf{V}_i$ (given that multiplying by the matrix inverse $\mathbf{V}_i^{-1}$ is analogous to dividing by the standard deviation to form a *z*-score). $\mathbf{Z}_i^T$ then projects the part of those standardized residuals that should be due to each random effect; $\mathbf{G}_i$ then rescales those projections to have variances and covariances as estimated for the random effects.

What Equation (5.18) does not show as directly is how the composite individual intercept and slope estimates (i.e., the values for the β_i placeholders, which here include $\beta_{0i} = \gamma_{00} + U_{0i}$ and $\beta_{1i} = \gamma_{10} + U_{1i}$, respectively) are created, as shown more directly in Equation (5.19):

Composite Individual Effects : $\beta_i = W_i \beta_{OLSi} + (I - W_i)\gamma$

where : $W_i = G_i \left[G_i + R_i \left(Z_i^T Z_i \right)^{-1} \right]^{-1}$
(5.19)

and as interpreted for a random linear time model as follows. The model-predicted composite intercept and slopes for each person are based on a weighted function of that person's OLS estimates of his or her intercept and slope (β_{OLSi}) and the model fixed effects for the intercept and slope in γ (here, γ_{00} and γ_{10}). The individual weighting matrix W_i will have the same dimensions as the G_i matrix (here, 2x2) but is quite complex. The W_i weight matrix essentially provides a ratio for the proportion of total variance that is due to individual differences in the intercepts and slopes (in the G_i matrix) rather than residual variation around the individual trajectories (in the R_i matrix). Thus, the more variation in the outcome that is due to individual differences in the intercepts and slopes, the more weight (through W_i) is given to that person's OLS intercept and slope estimates in predicting his or her composite intercepts and slopes. In contrast, if there is relatively more unexplained residual variation (in the R_i matrix) around the individual predicted trajectories than variation due to individual differences in those trajectories themselves, the less reliable those individual predicted trajectories are considered to be. So then less weight would be given to the individual OLS estimates and more weight would be given to the fixed effects instead (through $I - W_i$ that reflects the contribution of the R_i matrix). Notably, a W_i weight matrix is predicted using each person's Z_i matrix of intercept and time observations, so it also adjusts for the amount of data each person has—people who have less data (e.g., incomplete data) will have their intercepts and slopes pushed more towards the fixed effects.

For these reasons the U_i empirical Bayes or BLUP values are called **shrunken estimates** because this weighting process (reflecting the unreliability of the intercepts and slopes in the sample and the unreliability of each person's data) will reduce their overall variability. In general when comparing the results from different methods for assessing the variability across persons in intercepts or slopes, the variance of the OLS intercept or slope estimates will be greatest, followed by their corresponding random effects variances in the estimated G matrix, followed by the variance of the predicted (and shrunken) β_i values. Thus, using the predicted individual β_i values as observed variables in a secondary analysis cannot be recommended any more readily than the original OLS slopes-as-outcomes approach, not only because of their shrinkage, but for two other reasons as well. First, although the β_i values will be corrected for differential reliability across persons, the e_{ti} residuals around the individual trajectories (that reflect their imprecision in actually describing each person's data) would not be properly included in the secondary analysis.

variance and covariance over time in the **V** matrix), new fixed effects can usually be included without creating problems of estimation. In contrast, each new parameter in the model for the variance (e.g., new random effects variances and covariances) adds another dimension to the multidimensional log-likelihood function that is trying to find the optimal values of all of these variance parameters simultaneously (i.e., using search techniques based on its first and second partial derivatives), which could lead to problems of estimation. When random effects variances are estimated as exactly 0 and/or when the **G** matrix is reported as non-positive definite, this indicates that the model is not viable and should not be retained.

Armed with this more thorough view of likelihood functions, the chapter then revisited the differences between estimation using maximum likelihood (ML) or restricted (residual) maximum likelihood (REML). Because ML estimates of variance parameters do not account for the uncertainty from also estimating the model's fixed effects, they will be downwardly biased (too small) by a factor of $(N - k)/N$. In contrast, REML estimates of variance parameters do account for the uncertainty in estimating the model's fixed effects and will be unbiased. Furthermore, because ML maximizes the likelihood of the original y_{ti} outcomes, its $-2LL$, AIC, and BIC indices can be used to compare models that differ in their model for the means (i.e., in fixed effects), in their model for the variance (i.e., in random effects), or models that differ in both sides at once. In contrast, because REML maximizes the likelihood of the model *residuals,* its $-2LL$, AIC, and BIC indices will only index the fit of the variance side of the model, and thus cannot be used to compare the fit of models with different fixed effects (for which the model residuals would be defined differently, putting their REML $-2LL$ values on a different scale).

This chapter also revisited the *likelihood ratio test* or *deviance difference test* for comparing two nested models. When testing the contribution of a new random effects variance that can't be negative (or any other bounded parameters), the resulting $-2\Delta LL$ model comparison value will be a mixture of χ^2-distributions with degrees of freedom equal to the number of added parameters or to one fewer parameter (e.g., testing a random linear slope variance and its covariance with the random intercept would result in the $-2\Delta LL$ following a mixture χ^2-distribution with 2 degrees of freedom when the random linear slope variance was estimated as positive or 1 degree of freedom when it would have been estimated as negative). This chapter described a few ways to obtain a corrected *p*-value for the model comparison, but noted that a traditional χ^2-test will simply lead to a more conservative result (and thus the χ^2 correction would only be relevant for nonsignificant model comparisons for bounded parameters). The chapter then addressed different methods for computing denominator degrees of freedom in testing the significance of fixed effects via Wald tests (and why not all programs report such information).

Finally, this chapter described how the individual intercepts and slopes (i.e., created by $\beta_{0i} = \gamma_{00} + U_{0i}$ and $\beta_{1i} = \gamma_{10} + U_{1i}$) can be predicted using a weighted combination of the random effects variances and covariances and the individual OLS intercept and slope estimates. However, these predictions should *not* be used as observed variables in a secondary analysis for three reasons: they will not carry with them the existing e_{ti} residual variability around them, they will be shrunken (i.e., pushed towards the model fixed effects based on the reliability of the individual trajectories over time as well as how much data each person has), and they are really only measures of central tendency from a distribution of possible values for each person. Instead, the between-person variability in the individual intercepts and slopes can be predicted within the same model in which this variability is quantified directly, as we will see beginning in chapter 7.

5. Sample Results Section

Multilevel models in which occasions at level 1 were nested within persons at level 2 were estimated to examine the overall pattern of and individual differences in linear change in an outcome measured over four annual occasions ($M = 12.85$, $SD = 3.14$, range = 6.96 to 22.41). The time observations were balanced across persons with no missing data, and time was centered such that 0 indicated the first observation. The 95% confidence interval (CI) for the random variation around each fixed effect was calculated as ± 1.96 standard deviations of its accompanying random variance term. Parameters from each model reported below as obtained through restricted maximum likelihood (REML) are provided in Table 5.1.

An empty means, random intercept model was estimated first, in which the fixed intercept for the grand mean outcome over time was estimated as 12.85. The intraclass correlation (for the proportion of random intercept variance relative to the total variance) was estimated as .29, indicating that 29% of the variance was between persons in the mean outcome over time. A fixed linear effect of time was then added to the model, which was significant as indicated by a Wald test ($p < .05$) and accounted for 69% of the level-1 residual variance relative to the empty means, random intercept model, such that the outcome increased from a predicted value of 10.27 at the first occasion by 1.72 per year. The addition of a random linear time slope variance (as well as a covariance between the random intercept and random linear time slope) significantly improved the fit of the model, $-2\Delta LL(\sim2) = 48.4$, $p < .001$. The 95% random effects confidence intervals for the intercept and linear time slope indicated that 95% of the sample was expected to have individual intercepts ranging from 7.33 to 13.22 and individual linear time slopes ranging from -0.15 to 3.59. Thus, while there was a significant rate of linear increase in the outcome on average, the random variation around the linear time slope indicated that not all persons were expected to improve over time.

As shown in Table 5.5, there was good correspondence between the model-predicted means, variances, and covariances across the four occasions with those in the observed data (as estimated from a saturated means, unstructured variance model). Furthermore, the assumption of no residual covariance across time after accounting for the random intercept and random linear time slope was tested by comparing the fit of a random linear time model without within-person residual correlations to that of a random linear time model with within-person residual correlations. Neither a first-order auto-regressive correlation nor a lag-1 Toeplitz residual covariance resulted in significant improvement in model fit, $-2\Delta LL(1) < 1$,

$p > .05$, and so the random linear time model without within-person residual correlation over time was retained.

Review Questions

1. What is the purpose of fixed effects of time and of random effects of time?
2. How is dependency of residuals modeled by adding random effects? Can adding random effects "explain" the variance in an outcome? Why or why not?
3. What are the relationships among and the contents of the **Z**, **G**, **R**, and **V** matrices?
4. What is a likelihood function? What is the difference in how the estimates and standard errors are obtained for the fixed effects and for the random effects variances?
5. Why aren't the same kinds of $-2LL$ comparisons permitted within REML as in ML?
6. Why shouldn't predicted individual intercepts and slopes be used in secondary analyses?

References

Biesanz, J. C., Deeb-Sossa, N., Papadakis, A. A., Bollen, K. A., & Curran, P. J. (2004). The role of coding time in estimating and interpreting growth curve models. *Psychological Methods, 9*, 30–52.

Enders, C. K. (2010). *Applied missing data analysis*. New York, NY: Guilford.

Fitzmaurice, G. M., Laird, N. M., & Ware, J. H. (2004). *Applied longitudinal analysis* (Wiley series in probability and statistics). Hoboken, NJ: Wiley.

Hancock, G. R., & Choi, J. (2006). A vernacular for linear latent growth models. *Structural Equation Modeling: A Multidisciplinary Journal, 13*, 352–377.

Harville, D. A. (1974). Bayesian inference for variance components using only error contrasts. *Biometrika, 61*, 383–385.

Harville, D. A. (1977). Maximum likelihood approaches to variance component estimation and to related problems. *Journal of the American Statistical Association, 72*, 320–338.

Hedeker, D., & Gibbons, D. (2006). *Longitudinal data analysis* (Wiley series in probability and statistics). Hoboken, NJ: Wiley.

Hox, J. J. (2010). *Multilevel analysis: Techniques and applications* (2nd ed.). New York, NY: Routledge.

Kenward, M. G., & Roger, J. H. (1997). Small sample inference for fixed effects from restricted maximum likelihood. *Biometrics, 53*, 983–997.

Preacher, K. J., & Hancock, G. R. (2012). On interpretable reparameterizations of linear and nonlinear latent growth curve models. In J. Harring & G. Hancock (Eds.), *Advances in longitudinal methods in the social and behavioral sciences* (pp. 25–58). Charlotte, NC: Information Age Publishing.

Patterson, H. D., & Thompson, R. (1971). Recovery of inter-block information when block sizes are unequal. *Biometrika, 58*, 545–554.

Satterthwaite, F. E. (1941). Synthesis of variance. *Psychometrika, 6*, 309–316.

Satterthwaite, F. E. (1946). An approximate distribution of estimates of variance components. *Biometrics Bulletin, 45*, 111–129.

Snijders, T. A. B., & Bosker, R. (2012). *Multilevel analysis* (2nd ed.). Thousand Oaks, CA: Sage.

Stoel, R. D., Garre, F. G., Dolan, C., & van den Wittenboer, G. (2006). On the likelihood ratio test in structural equation modeling when parameters are subject to boundary constraints. *Psychological Methods, 11,* 439–455.

Verbeke, G., & Molenberghs, G. (1997). *Linear mixed models in practice: A SAS-oriented approach* (Lecture notes in statistics series #126). New York, NY: Springer-Verlag.

Verbeke, G., & Molenberghs, G. (2000). *Linear mixed models for longitudinal data* (Springer series in statistics). New York, NY: Springer.

DESCRIBING WITHIN-PERSON CHANGE OVER TIME

The current section of the text (chapters 4–6) focuses on describing the effects of time in *unconditional* models (i.e., in which *time* is the only predictor variable). Chapter 4 presented models for describing patterns of outcome variance and covariance arising primarily from within-person fluctuation over time. Chapter 5 then introduced the ideas of fixed and random effects of time using a simple linear model for within-person change, as well as the likelihood-based methods by which longitudinal models can be estimated more generally. Chapter 6 will expand on chapter 5 to show how other families of models including fixed and random effects can be used to describe more complex trajectories of within-person change over time. As in chapter 5, throughout this chapter we are assuming that we have already chosen a meaningful time metric by which to index change, and in each model to be presented the predictors related to *time* will be centered such that time 0 is observed within the study (i.e., so that the model intercept and the main effects of any interacting predictors will have meaningful values).

 The purpose of this chapter is to present several options for describing nonlinear change over time and individual differences therein, including models of *continuous* change (e.g., polynomial, exponential, and logistic models) and *discontinuous* change (e.g., piecewise slopes models). The first section in this chapter provides an overview of continuous and discontinuous models of change and then reviews the general rules and strategies by which fixed and random effects of time can be included in longitudinal models. The second section of this chapter presents an extended working example of how a nonlinear pattern of change could be described by three different types of models. The third section of this chapter then presents some options for outcomes that show more complex forms of nonlinear change (i.e., in which the rate of change shifts at multiple points, or in which there are multiple "bends" over time) and describes how to interpret the parameters in those more complex models. Finally, the chapter concludes with a summary section, a sample results section for the extended example, and an appendix that summarizes the material from chapters 4, 5, and 6 to guide the overall process of describing the pattern of within-person fluctuation or within-person change over time in unconditional models.

1. Considerations in Modeling Nonlinear Change Over Time

1.A. Families of Models for Nonlinear Change Over Time

In choosing amongst alternative models for describing nonlinear change over time, it can be useful to distinguish between two major families: models for *continuous* change versus models for *discontinuous* change. To begin, in many instances change over time can be characterized by a trajectory that may be nonlinear, but that is nevertheless **continuous** across the range of time observed. Continuous trajectories are especially likely to occur when change over time is simply measured (e.g., as in observational studies of human development), rather than when change is intentionally created or modified (e.g., as in intervention or experimental designs). This chapter will describe several options for such continuous trajectories, including **polynomial** models (i.e., in which linear, quadratic, cubic, and higher-order effects of time combine linearly and additively to describe nonlinear change) as well as truly **nonlinear** models (i.e., in which the time-related parameters do not combine linearly and additively, and may instead be used to characterize a standard but nonlinear functional form, such as in exponential or logistic models of change). The difference between polynomial models and truly nonlinear models is in where their nonlinearity lies—in their *predictor variables* or in their *model parameters*, respectively.

As we'll see in more detail later, in models with polynomial effects of time (e.g., $time^2$, $time^3$), although the predictors used to describe change are nonlinear transformations of the time variable, each is still multiplied by a single fixed effect (slope) coefficient, and those products are still added together to create a predicted outcome, just like in any other linear model. That is, although polynomial models of change over time are nonlinear with respect to their time *predictor variables*, they are still linear with respect to how their *model parameters* relate to those time predictor variables. In contrast, in truly nonlinear models, the products of their model parameters and time predictor variables do not combine linearly and additively, such that the model is nonlinear with respect to how its *parameters* relate to its time predictor variables. For instance, in an exponential model, nonlinear change over time is created by multiplying an *amount* parameter by an exponential effect of a *rate* parameter, as *amount*exp(rate*time)*, or *amount*$e^{rate*time}$*. Although given their complexity truly nonlinear models usually require more data per person in order to be estimated, they can be more useful than polynomial models when modeling continuous change that appears to "level off" over time (i.e., to reach an asymptote).

In other types of longitudinal designs, however, the goal may be to assess the extent to which an intervention or manipulation creates a different intercept and/

or slope over time, thus creating a discontinuous trajectory over time instead. In such models for **discontinuous** change, known as **piecewise** or **spline** models, nonlinearity in the overall trajectory is described by separate linear (or perhaps nonlinear) trajectories corresponding to distinct phases of time with inherent meaning (e.g., pre- and post-intervention). In addition to their use in experimental or intervention designs, discontinuous change models can also be useful when a study includes a naturally occurring breakpoint, such as when modeling change in adolescent behavior across the transition from middle school to high school, or when modeling economic indicators before and after new business regulations go into effect. In most cases, the use of discontinuous piecewise models of change is motivated by a known breakpoint that could result in an abrupt shift in the level and/or change in an outcome over time. But the use of discontinuous change models may also be empirically driven, in which the location of a non-theoretical breakpoint is based by the data simply as a means to approximate a nonlinear trajectory. This chapter will address both theoretically motivated and empirically motivated uses of discontinuous change models.

1.B. General Rules for the Use of Fixed and Random Effects to Describe Change Over Time

As introduced in chapter 5, models for within-person change will usually include both fixed and random effects of time, which mean different things and accomplish different goals. Because they will appear in every model in this chapter, it will be critical for you to understand the basic differences between fixed and random effects, as well as the general rules for their order of inclusion and tests of significance in longitudinal models, as reviewed below.

On one side of the model are the fixed effects, which belong to the model for the means. The term **fixed effect** means everybody gets the *same* effect. Fixed effects always come first—their purpose is to describe the *average* pattern of change over time, potentially explaining some of the outcome variance in doing so. Most models for the means have a fixed intercept (i.e., that allows the mean outcome to differ from 0), but whether additional fixed effects are needed is a testable hypothesis. The significance of a fixed effect can always be tested via a Wald test (i.e., the p-value resulting from the t-statistic or z-statistic formed from the ratio of the fixed effect estimate to its standard error), regardless of whether the model was estimated using maximum likelihood (ML) or restricted (residual) maximum likelihood (REML). However, REML estimation is preferred in samples of fewer persons, for which the standard errors of the fixed effects will show less downward bias when produced by REML than ML. Although the addition of a new fixed effect (or a set of multiple fixed effects) could also be tested by a $-2\Delta LL$ deviance difference test, such comparisons are only valid under ML, and NOT under REML. This is because the $-2LL$, AIC, and BIC values are not on the same scale for REML-estimated models with different fixed effects (and thus have different residuals whose likelihood is being maximized).

In interpreting the fixed effects in the model for the means, the fixed intercept is always conditional on the 0 value of all predictors with fixed effects. For instance, in the unconditional random linear time model we saw in chapter 5 (i.e., with no predictors besides a linear time slope), the *fixed intercept* is the predicted mean outcome at time 0, and the *fixed linear time slope* is the mean rate of change in the outcome per unit change in time. Together the fixed intercept and any fixed effects for time will create an *average* trajectory over time that may explain some of the outcome variation (e.g., a trajectory of constant linear change over time will explain any outcome variation caused by the outcome means changing linearly over time).

On the other side of the model are the random effects, which belong to the model for the variance rather than the model for the means. In these longitudinal models the term **random effect** means everybody gets his or her *own* effect. Because random effects are specified as deviations from their corresponding fixed effects, random effects always come second—they are added only after their corresponding fixed effects have already been included. In the same unconditional random linear time model, the *random intercept* is the *deviation* at time 0 between the fixed intercept and that person's predicted intercept, and the *random linear time slope* is the *deviation* between the fixed linear time slope and that person's predicted linear time slope. Thus, by combining the fixed effect (that everyone gets) with the random effect (the person-specific deviation), each person can obtain his or her own version of the intercept and of the effect of any predictor that varies over time (such as the linear time slope in a random linear time model).

But rather than estimating each individual random effect separately (i.e., as per-person fixed effects in the model for the means), the variance and covariance of these random effects across persons are estimated as part of the model for the variance in the level-2 $\mathbf{G}$ matrix. The variance (and perhaps covariance; see chapters 4 and 5) of the within-person e_{ti} time-specific deviations between the observed outcomes and the outcomes predicted by the fixed and random effects are then estimated in the level-1 $\mathbf{R}$ matrix. As shown in chapter 5, the $\mathbf{G}$ and $\mathbf{R}$ matrices combine with an individual-specific $\mathbf{Z}$ matrix that holds the values of the intercept and of any predictors with a random effect to form the individual-specific total predicted variance and covariance over each person's outcomes as $\mathbf{V} = \mathbf{Z}\mathbf{G}\mathbf{Z}^T + \mathbf{R}$.

All models for the variance have at least an e_{ti} residual, but whether or not any random effect variances are needed (including whether a random intercept variance is needed) is a testable hypothesis. Recall that fixed effects can be estimated as positive or negative, and so a Wald test based on a symmetric and unbounded sampling distribution is appropriate for testing fixed effects. But a Wald test will not be appropriate when testing the contribution of new variances that cannot be negative, and thus whose sampling distributions are bounded at 0. Instead, the contribution of the variance of a new random effect (and its covariances with any other random effects already in the model) can be tested with a $-2\Delta LL$ deviance difference test under ML or REML. However, as discussed in chapter 5, REML is preferred over ML, especially in samples with fewer persons, because REML variance estimates will be less biased than those of ML by a factor of $[N - k] / N$, in which N is the number of persons and k is the number of fixed effects. Also as discussed in chapter 5, using a critical χ^2-value with degrees of freedom (*df*) equal to the number of new random effects variances and covariances will result in a slightly conservative –2ΔLL test under either REML or ML (as will be recognized by the ~ we'll place next to the actual degrees of freedom for the model comparison in those instances).

Finally, it is important to note that unlike fixed effects of time, the goal of including random effects of time is NOT to explain variance in the outcome. Instead, random effects simply partition the outcome variance into different piles (or *variance components*, as discussed in chapter 5) that each in turn represent a source of person-related dependency. For instance, person dependency in predicted mean level is represented by the random intercept variance, and person dependency in predicted rates of linear change is represented by the random linear time slope variance. The goal of building conditional models (i.e., with predictors besides time) will be to try to *explain* each pile of variance. Thus, we need to assess each potential source of person dependency with respect to *all* linear or nonlinear effects of time prior to considering which fixed effects of predictors might explain each source of variance. That is, we need to know what kinds of outcome variance are present to start with before we can see what predicts them!

In each example that follows, there may be multiple viable strategies with which to add fixed and random effects in sequential models. For instance, we could add all possible fixed effects to the model at once, followed by each corresponding random effect in sequential models. Alternatively, we could add the fixed and random parts of each effect before continuing to add those of a new effect. Although the rationale behind these choices will be explained where relevant, our general approach to model building will follow four basic principles informed by the preceding review of the roles of fixed and random effects in longitudinal models:

1. Fixed effects will always be added *before* their corresponding random effects are added, given that the fixed effects are what those random effects would be deviating from.
2. Random effects will be tested (when possible) even if the corresponding fixed effect was not significant. That is, a nonsignificant fixed effect would mean there is no effect *on average*, but this does not preclude finding significant random *individual differences* in that effect.
3. Although multiple fixed effects may be added to the model simultaneously given that the significance of each can be evaluated directly via its Wald test *p*-value, variances of random effects (and their covariances with random effects already in the model) will be added one at a time so that the unique contribution of each can be evaluated with a –2ΔLL test.
4. For the same reason, fixed effects and random effects will be added in sequential models, rather than adding both at the same time. For instance, if we compared an empty means, random intercept model directly to a random linear time model, those models would differ by the fixed effect of time and by the variance of the random effect of time (and by its covariance with the random intercept). Thus, if the random linear time model fit significantly better than the empty means, random intercept model via a –2ΔLL test (using ML but not

REML, given that the models differ in their fixed effects), we couldn't be sure whether the improvement in fit was due to the new random effect or just to the new fixed effect. Adding fixed and random effects in separate models resolves this ambiguity.

1.C. Considering Potential Models of Change

With these guidelines in mind, we will continue by examining a plethora of options for continuous and discontinuous models for nonlinear change over time—although before doing so it is important to note two caveats. First, we will use a specific working example to introduce the families of models and to highlight their similarities and differences, with the result that our model evaluation and comparison process may seem largely exploratory. In practice, however, the appropriate family (or families) of nonlinear models should be selected using both empirical data and consideration of the theoretical process responsible for the observed change. Combining both sources of information can sometimes be more art than science, but I'll try to highlight the kinds of situations in which each family of model can be most useful as we go. Second, although we will begin with polynomial models, this is not meant to imply that they should always be considered first (or at all). Polynomial models are perhaps the most common approach to modeling nonlinear change because of their relatively low data requirements, ease of estimation, and wide-spread availability across software programs, and so it is important to understand exactly how to interpret their parameters. However, because polynomial models do have limited theoretical utility, it is equally important to be aware of alternative models whose parameters might be more meaningful and therefore useful in describing change over time.

2. Models for Outcomes With a Single Bend in the Rate of Change Over Time

This section presents three options for modeling nonlinear trajectories that appear to have a single *bend*—trajectories in which the rate of change appears to change only once. For each model, we will first examine how it is specified and how its fixed and random effects are interpreted more generally, followed by an example. We will use the same six-occasion example data from the *Cognition, Health, and Aging Project* as used in chapter 3, in which 101 older adults were measured on six occasions (once per day) during a two-week span (with no missing data). The outcome variable was a measure of processing speed—the average response time (RT) across trials (in milliseconds) needed to accurately judge whether two series of three numbers were the same or different. The goal of the study was to assess individual differences in short-term learning via the change in RT across the six practice sessions. As was seen in Table 3.2 and Figure 3.4, the means over time appear to decrease (i.e., RT improves across sessions), but the rate of the decrease appears to slow down after the second session. We will examine three different models that might predict this kind of trajectory, starting with a quadratic model of change, followed by a two-slope piecewise model, and then a truly nonlinear exponential model.

2.A. A Quadratic Model of Change

Our first option lies within the polynomial family of models for continuous change. A **quadratic model of change** includes a quadratic effect of time (i.e., as time^2, otherwise known as the *quadratic rate of change,* or the *quadratic slope for time*) in addition to an intercept and a linear effect of time (i.e., time^1, otherwise known as the *linear rate of change,* or the *linear slope for time*). A quadratic effect of time implies a *change* in the linear rate of change over time, such that the linear time slope either **accelerates** (speeds up) or **decelerates** (slows down) over time.

Figure 6.1 illustrates how positive or negative linear and quadratic effects of time can work together to create many possible patterns of nonlinear change. First, the top left shows how a *positive* linear effect of time and a *positive* quadratic effect of time create an **accelerating positive function,** or a mean trajectory in which the rate of increase speeds up over time. Second, the top right shows how a *positive*

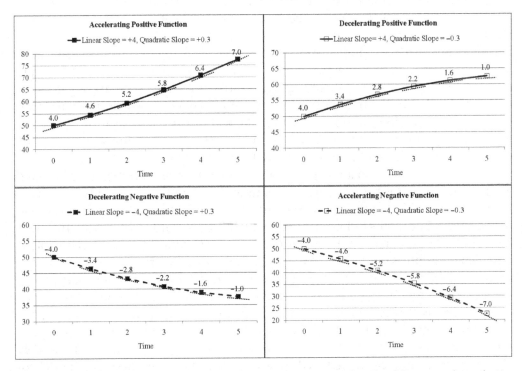

Figure 6.1 Predicted mean trajectories from positive or negative fixed linear and quadratic effects of time. The values above the points are the predicted instantaneous linear slopes for change over time (shown by small dashes lines) as evaluated at that occasion.

linear effect of time and a *negative* quadratic effect of time create a **decelerating positive function,** or a mean trajectory in which the rate of increase slows down over time instead. Third, the bottom left shows how a *negative* linear effect of time and a *positive* quadratic effect of time create a **decelerating negative function,** or a mean trajectory in which the rate of decrease slows down over time. Finally, the bottom right shows how a *negative* linear effect of time and a *negative* quadratic effect of time create an **accelerating negative function,** or a mean trajectory in which the rate of decrease speeds up over time. We cannot determine just from its sign if a quadratic effect creates acceleration or deceleration. A *positive* quadratic effect of time can make a positive linear effect of time *more positive* (acceleration), or it can make a negative linear effect of time *less negative* (deceleration). Similarly, a *negative* quadratic effect of time can make a positive linear effect of time *less positive* (deceleration), or it can make a negative linear effect of time *more negative* (acceleration).

Furthermore, just like any other predictor that varies over time, a quadratic effect of time can have both a fixed effect and a random effect. That is, a **fixed quadratic effect of time** in the model for the means implies a change in the linear rate of change *on average.* More specifically, for reasons to be explained shortly, the fixed quadratic effect of time is actually *half* the rate of acceleration or deceleration of the fixed linear time slope over time. A **random quadratic effect of time** is a person-specific deviation from the fixed quadratic effect, such that a **random quadratic slope variance** in the model for the variance represents *individual differences* across persons in half the rate of acceleration or deceleration of the linear rate of change over time.

Although quadratic models of change are used quite frequently to describe nonlinear trajectories, their model parameters are sometimes perceived as "too difficult" to interpret. Not so—any difficulty can be resolved using the same principles we practiced in chapter 2 about conditionality of effects when including both main effects and interactions among predictors. We will utilize the trajectories shown in Figure 6.1 to explain how fixed linear and quadratic effects of time are interpreted once they are combined in the same model for the means.

To begin, recall that in an empty means model, the fixed intercept is interpreted as the grand mean over time. Once a fixed linear effect of time is included, the fixed intercept becomes conditional, such that the intercept is the outcome at time 0 predicted from a linear effect of time. This is why it is important to center the time predictor so that 0 has a meaningful value (i.e., at the first occasion here, or at any other observed occasion as desired). When it is the highest-order term in the model for the means, the fixed linear effect of time (i.e., the main effect of time) is *unconditional,* as a linear model for change predicts constant change over time. But once a quadratic effect of time is also included, this is no longer the case, and two things happen.

First, in a quadratic model of change, although the fixed intercept is still conditional on time = 0, its estimate for the predicted outcome at time 0 will probably change because it is now predicted by a different model—a quadratic model for change rather than a linear model. In each panel of Figure 6.1, the fixed intercept was 50.0, which can be seen as the outcome specifically at time = 0, as predicted by the fixed linear and quadratic effects of time within each panel.

Second, after including a fixed quadratic effect of time, the fixed linear effect of time is now also conditional, such that it becomes the *instantaneous linear rate of change specifically at time 0*. The origin of the term *instantaneous* will be explained momentarily, but otherwise the reason for the change in interpretation is exactly the same as was explained in chapter 2—when a predictor becomes part of an interaction term, its main effect becomes its *simple* effect evaluated specifically when the interacting predictor = 0. Thus, in a quadratic model of change, because time is interacting with itself (i.e., time² = time*time), the fixed linear effect of time (main effect) becomes the fixed linear effect of time specifically when time = 0 (simple effect). In other words, because a fixed quadratic effect of time causes the linear rate of change to change over time, it is no longer sufficient to refer to "the fixed linear effect of time" as a single, unconditional entity—the fixed linear effect of time now depends on time. In Figure 6.1, the values shown above the points are the instantaneous linear rates of change as evaluated at each occasion from each set of fixed effects. As shown, the only occasion at which the linear rate of change matches that in its title (i.e., a linear slope = ±4) is at time 0. After that, the linear rate of change either speeds up or slows down depending on the fixed quadratic effect of time, as explained next.

Although the quadratic effect of time is often labeled as the rate of acceleration or deceleration, its estimated coefficient is actually only *half* of the rate. There are two ways to think about this—the first reason is based on calculus, but fortunately the second reason is not. More specifically, the first rationale for why the quadratic effect of time is only half the rate of acceleration is based on the first and second derivatives with respect to time of the quadratic function. This is shown using the fixed effects from the top left of Figure 6.1 in Equation (6.1):

Intercept (Position) at Time T: $\hat{y}_T = 50.0 + 4.0T + 0.3T^2$

First Derivative (Velocity) at Time T: $\dfrac{d\hat{y}_T}{d(T)} = 4.0 + 0.6T$

$$(6.1)$$

Second Derivative (Acceleration) at Time T: $\dfrac{d^2\hat{y}_T}{d(T)} = 0.6$

in which the first line writes the quadratic model for change predicting the outcome $\hat{y}_T$ at time T (also known as the **position** of the function at that occasion) from the fixed intercept (50.0), fixed linear effect of time (4.0), and fixed quadratic effect of time (0.3). The second line writes the **first derivative with respect to time**, in which the intercept (a constant not involving time) drops out, the linear effect of time becomes a constant, and the exponent of 2 for time² is multiplied by the quadratic effect of time (which is multiplied by just time¹ after differentiation). Earlier we referred to the first derivative with respect to time as the **instantaneous linear rate of change over time**, which more technically is the slope of the tangent line to the function at that occasion (as shown in Figure 6.1 by the small dashed lines through each point), also known as the **velocity** of the function at that occasion. The term *instantaneous* is used to denote that the tangent line is only for a single point on the overall quadratic function. Although the instantaneous linear rate of change reported by the model will be specifically as evaluated at time 0, as shown in the second line of Equation (6.1), it can be calculated for any occasion as the linear effect of time plus *twice* the quadratic effect of time *per unit time* (or 4.0 + 0.3*2*time here). Finally, the third line writes the **second derivative with respect to time**, which is the **rate of acceleration or deceleration** of the function. We can think of acceleration or deceleration as how the fixed linear effect of time *changes* per unit time, which is given by *twice* the fixed quadratic effect of time. The rate of acceleration or deceleration will be constant (unconditional) across time if the quadratic term is the highest-order fixed effect (i.e., a constant slope for how the slope of the line tangent to the curve changes over time), but the rate of acceleration will become conditional on time 0 if higher-order polynomial fixed effects of time are included (e.g., a cubic effect via time^3).

Besides the previous calculus-based explanation, there is another way to explain why twice the quadratic effect of time is how the linear time slope changes per unit time that is based on more general concepts of main effects and interactions, as illustrated in Equation (6.2):

$$\hat{y} = \beta_0 + \beta_1 X + \beta_2 Z + \beta_3 XZ$$
$$\text{Effect of } X = \beta_1 + \beta_3 Z$$
$$\text{Effect of } Z = \beta_2 + \beta_3 X \tag{6.2}$$
$$\hat{y}_T = \beta_0 + \beta_1 \text{Time}_T + \underline{\quad} + \beta_3 \text{Time}_T^2$$
$$\text{Effect of Time}_T = \beta_1 + 2\beta_3 \text{Time}_T$$

in which the first line shows the predicted outcome $\hat{y}_i$ for each individual i from an intercept, simple main effects of X and Z, and their interaction. The second and third lines show (as described in chapter 2) how the simple effect of each predictor can be calculated as its main effect plus the interaction term multiplied by its interacting predictor. Accordingly, the XZ interaction coefficient β_3 thus plays two roles—it describes how the effect of X is moderated as a function of Z, and it also describes how the effect of Z is moderated as a function of X. But in writing an analogous model in the fourth line including linear and quadratic effects of time, we see there is only one main effect—because time interacts with itself, there is no other main effect to be included (i.e., time is like X, but there is no analog to Z). So, because the time*time interaction coefficient β_3 has only one main effect to modify instead of two separate main effects, it needs to be included *twice* to indicate how the linear (main) effect of time changes as a function of its interacting predictor of time. So *twice* the quadratic time slope is how the linear time slope changes per unit time, as shown in the last line.

To see how a twice the quadratic effect of time translates into the rate of acceleration or deceleration, we can again examine Figure 6.1. In the top left, the instantaneous linear effect of time is 4.0 at time 0. By time 1, due to the positive quadratic effect of time = 0.3, the positive linear effect of time will become *more positive* by 0.6 (the quadratic effect of time 0.3*2), such that the linear rate of change will be 4.6 at time 1. Similarly, by time 2, the positive linear effect of time will be 5.2. In the top right, the negative quadratic effect of time will make the instantaneous positive linear effect of time *less positive* by 0.3*2 per unit time (i.e., from 4.0 at time 0 to 3.4 at time 1). In the bottom left, the positive quadratic effect will make the negative linear effect of time *less negative* by 0.3*2 per unit time (i.e., from −4.0 at time 0 to −3.4 at time 1). Finally, in the bottom right, the negative quadratic effect makes the negative linear effect of time *more negative* by 0.3*2 per unit time (i.e., from −4.0 at time 0 to −4.6 at time 1).

The same principles for the hierarchy and conditionality of polynomial terms also hold for their random effects on the variance side of the model. Regardless of what fixed effects are included in the model for the means, if the random intercept variance is the only term in the model for the variance (besides the residual variance), then the random intercept variance reflects the amount of individual differences between the predicted trajectories *at any occasion* (unconditionally across time). After including the variance of the random linear time slope (and its covariance with the random intercept), the random intercept variance then reflects the amount of individual differences between the predicted trajectories *conditionally at time 0*. When the random linear slope variance is the highest-order term in the model for the variance (again, regardless of what fixed effects are included), the random linear slope variance will reflect the amount of individual differences in the linear rate of change unconditionally across time.

Similarly, once the variance of the random quadratic time slope (and its covariances with the random intercept and the random linear time slopes) are also included, then the random linear time slope variance is also conditional on time 0. That is, because people are now allowed their own quadratic deviations (i.e., for how their rate of change changes over time), this implies that the random linear time slope variance (for the amount of individual differences in the linear rate of change) will also change systematically over time, as we'll see in our example data. However, when it is the highest-order term in the model for the variance, the random quadratic slope variance will represent the amount of individual differences in half the rate of acceleration or deceleration over time *unconditionally* across time.

Finally, we note that the hierarchy of fixed and random effects (as reviewed earlier) also applies to polynomial models of change. That is, because a random effect is specified as a person-specific deviation from its corresponding fixed effect, a random quadratic effect of time requires that a fixed quadratic effect of time is also included regardless of its significance (and a random linear effect of time requires that a fixed linear effect of time is also included). In addition, a unique feature of polynomial models is that they are hierarchical with respect to their terms on each side of the model, such that the quadratic effect ($time^2$) is higher-order than the linear effect ($time^1$), and the intercept is the lowest-order term in the model. Thus, for a *fixed* quadratic effect of time to be interpreted properly, a fixed intercept and a fixed linear effect of time must also be included in the model for the means, regardless of their significance. Likewise, for a *random* quadratic slope variance to be interpreted properly, a random intercept variance and a random linear slope variance must also be included in the model for the variance, regardless of their significance. The reason for this is that each higher-order term reflects its specific incremental contribution only if its lower-order terms are included—otherwise, its estimated coefficient would be conflated with the missing lower-order terms (i.e., a quadratic effect really only represents just the quadratic effect when its corresponding linear effect is also included).

These hierarchies (random effects over fixed effects, higher-order over lower-order polynomial effects of time) allow for convenient labeling of polynomial models. For instance, a *random quadratic time model* includes all lower-order terms (i.e., the model has all fixed and random intercepts, linear time slopes, and quadratic time slopes), whereas a *fixed quadratic, random linear time model* includes all fixed and random intercepts and linear time slopes, but only has a fixed quadratic time slope (i.e., no random quadratic time slope is included).

We will now examine a quadratic model using an example describing change in response time (RT) across six sessions in 101 older adults, as described earlier. The time variable of *session* will be centered at 1 so that time 0 represents the initial observation (i.e., *Time* = Session – 1). REML estimation will be used, so the contribution of new fixed effects will be assessed via their Wald test *p*-values rather than –2ΔLL tests. The contribution of new random effects will be assessed via –2ΔLL tests between models with the same fixed effects.

Because these data are balanced such that each person has the same sessions 1 to 6, we can begin by examining the "answer key" for the data our model will be trying to predict—the results of the **saturated means, unstructured variance** model (which we'll call *model 0*), as seen in Table 6.1. As discussed in chapter 3, a *saturated* means model has a fixed intercept and $n – 1$ fixed effects for the n different means over time. Analogously, an *unstructured* variance model estimates all

Table 6.1 Predicted V matrix (with variances on the diagonal, covariances above the diagonal, and correlations below the diagonal), and means (with SE = standard errors) from the saturated means, unstructured variance model (0) for the six-session response time data (in which n = number of occasions).

Model Description and Parameters		V Matrix					
	Session	1	2	3	4	5	6
Saturated Means, Unstructured Variance Model: 27 total parameters (Model 0)							
	1	301,985	235,659	217,994	202,607	192,154	195,360
	2	.84	259,150	230,217	213,232	202,092	193,268
$n*(n + 1) / 2 + n = 27$	3	.82	.94	233,368	205,209	196,919	188,604
total parameters:	4	.79	.90	.91	217,544	193,676	185,321
6 means	5	.76	.86	.89	.90	212,098	187,840
6 total variances	6	.80	.86	.88	.90	.92	196,733
15 total covariances	Mean	1961.89	1815.17	1750.03	1717.80	1707.18	1672.14
	SE	54.68	50.65	48.07	46.41	45.83	44.13

possible total variances and covariances over time, and as such will have the best absolute fit. The solid lines with squares in the top and bottom panels of Figure 6.2 show the estimated means and variances, respectively, for the six sessions from the saturated means, unstructured variance model (as well as the predicted means and

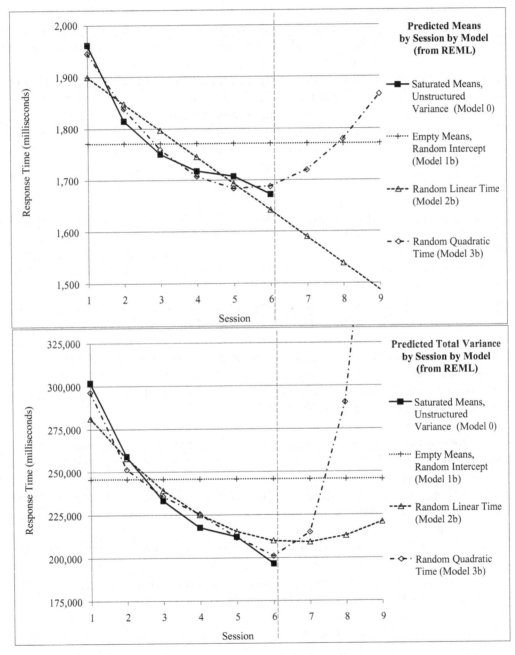

Figure 6.2 Predicted means (top panel) and variances (bottom panel) by polynomial model for the six-session response time data (with three extra sessions predicted after the vertical line).

variances from the models we'll examine for the actual six sessions and for three hypothetical future sessions). As shown, both the RT mean and variance appear to form a decelerating negative function across sessions (i.e., they both decrease over time, but the rate of the decrease appears to slow down over time).

Although in the analysis of variance models in chapter 3 the results from the saturated means, unstructured variance model matched the observed data perfectly, this may not be the case when some persons have incomplete data over time. That is, the model will return the means, variances, and covariances across time that would be expected if the data were complete under the assumption of **missing at random**, in which the pattern of missingness is truly random only after taking into account the person's other data (for a more thorough treatment see Enders, 2010). Because the results from the saturated means, unstructured variance model are what other alternative unconditional models for time will be trying to reproduce, it can be a useful baseline when it is estimable (which is only for balanced data on a sufficient number of persons with which to estimate all possible means, variances, and covariances across occasions).

For ease of comparison, Table 6.2 summarizes the polynomial models to be evaluated. The first column provides the name and number of estimated parameters for each model, the second column shows the multilevel equations for each model (in which *level 1* is *within persons over time* and *level 2* is *between persons*), and the third column shows the level-2 **G** matrix of random effects variances and covariances for each model. In all the models to follow for the six-session response time (RT) data, the level-1 **R** matrix will be a 6x6 diagonal matrix (i.e., an n by n matrix for the $n = 6$ sessions with constant residual variance σ_e^2 over time on the diagonal and no residual covariance over time in the off-diagonals). Finally, the fourth column summarizes the purpose or question answered by the new parameters in each model, as elaborated below. Model estimates are presented in the text below, and those from 2b and 3b are given in Table 6.3. As before, small differences may occur in results of the calculations given that they were based on the original values instead of the rounded values reported below.

The first model is the simplest (and worst-fitting) possible model (1a), a 2-parameter **empty means**, σ_e^2 **only model**, which predicts no change over time (fixed intercept $\gamma_{00} = 1,770.7$) and no correlation among the e_{ti} residuals from the same person (total variance at each session of $\sigma_e^2 = 244,123$; no predicted covariance over time). Although highly unrealistic for longitudinal data, this model does provide us with a comparison for assessing whether there are significant mean differences in the RT outcome across persons, as then included in model (1b).

The 3-parameter **empty means, random intercept model** (1b) still predicts a constant mean over time (from the fixed intercept $\gamma_{00} = 1,770.7$) but separates outcome variance due to *between-person variation* in mean RT (level-2 random intercept variance in the **G** matrix of $\tau_{U_0}^2 = 200,883$) from outcome variance due to *within-person, time-specific variation* (level-1 residual variance in the **R** matrix of $\sigma_e^2 = 44,900$). It predicts (in the **V** matrix) that the total variance at each occasion is constant at $\tau_{U_0}^2 + \sigma_e^2 = 245,783$ and that the total covariance across occasions is constant at $\tau_{U_0}^2 = 200,883$. (Note that in this example the total variance is close to, but not exactly the same as, the original outcome variance.) We can calculate an intraclass correlation as ICC $\tau_{U_0}^2/(\tau_{U_0}^2 + \sigma_e^2) = 200,883/(200,883 + 44,900) = .82$,

Table 6.2 Polynomial model equations and level-2 G matrix for the six-session response time data (in which *time* = session − 1).

Model (# Total Parameters)	Model Equation	Level-2 G Matrix	Purpose (New Parameters)
1a Empty Means, σ^2_e only (2)	**Level 1:** $y_{ti} = \beta_{0i} + e_{ti}$ **Level 2: Intercept:** $\beta_{0i} = \gamma_{00}$	none	Simplest Baseline Model (none)
1b Empty Means, Random Intercept (3)	**Level 1:** $y_{ti} = \beta_{0i} + e_{ti}$ **Level 2: Intercept:** $\beta_{0i} = \gamma_{00} + U_{0i}$	$G = \begin{bmatrix} \tau^2_{U_0} \end{bmatrix}$	Is the ICC for the proportion of person dependency greater than 0? ($\tau^2_{U_0}$)
2a Fixed Linear Time, Random Intercept (4)	**Level 1:** $y_{ti} = \beta_{0i} + \beta_{1i}(\text{Time}_{ti}) + e_{ti}$ **Level 2: Intercept:** $\beta_{0i} = \gamma_{00} + U_{0i}$ **Linear Time:** $\beta_{1i} = \gamma_{10}$	$G = \begin{bmatrix} \tau^2_{U_0} \end{bmatrix}$	Is there linear change over time on average? (γ_{10})
2b Random Linear Time (6)	**Level 1:** $y_{ti} = \beta_{0i} + \beta_{1i}(\text{Time}_{ti}) + e_{ti}$ **Level 2: Intercept:** $\beta_{0i} = \gamma_{00} + U_{0i}$ **Linear Time:** $\beta_{1i} = \gamma_{10} + U_{1i}$	$G = \begin{bmatrix} \tau^2_{U_0} & \tau_{U_{01}} \\ \tau_{U_{01}} & \tau^2_{U_1} \end{bmatrix}$	Are there individual differences in linear change over time? ($\tau^2_{U_1}$ and $\tau_{U_{01}}$)
3a Fixed Quadratic, Random Linear Time (7)	**Level 1:** $y_{ti} = \beta_{0i} + \beta_{1i}(\text{Time}_{ti}) + \beta_{2i}(\text{Time}_{ti})^2 + e_{ti}$ **Level 2: Intercept:** $\beta_{0i} = \gamma_{00} + U_{0i}$ **Linear Time:** $\beta_{1i} = \gamma_{10} + U_{1i}$ **Quadratic Time:** $\beta_{2i} = \gamma_{20}$	$G = \begin{bmatrix} \tau^2_{U_0} & \tau_{U_{01}} \\ \tau_{U_{01}} & \tau^2_{U_1} \end{bmatrix}$	Is there quadratic change over time on average? (γ_{20})
3b Random Quadratic Time (10)	**Level 1:** $y_{ti} = \beta_{0i} + \beta_{1i}(\text{Time}_{ti}) + \beta_{2i}(\text{Time}_{ti})^2 + e_{ti}$ **Level 2: Intercept:** $\beta_{0i} = \gamma_{00} + U_{0i}$ **Linear Time:** $\beta_{1i} = \gamma_{10} + U_{1i}$ **Quadratic Time:** $\beta_{2i} = \gamma_{20} + U_{2i}$	$G = \begin{bmatrix} \tau^2_{U_0} & \tau_{U_{01}} & \tau_{U_{02}} \\ \tau_{U_{01}} & \tau^2_{U_1} & \tau_{U_{12}} \\ \tau_{U_{02}} & \tau_{U_{12}} & \tau^2_{U_2} \end{bmatrix}$	Are there individual differences in quadratic change over time? ($\tau^2_{U_2}$, $\tau_{U_{02}}$, and $\tau_{U_{12}}$)

Table 6.3 Polynomial model parameters for the six-session response time data (in which *time* = session − 1). Bold values are *p* < .05.

Model Parameter	Model 2b Random Linear Time (Time 0 = Session 1)			Model 3b Random Quadratic Time (Time 0 = Session 1)			Model 3b Random Quadratic Time (Time 0 = Session 6)		
	Est	SE	p <	Est	SE	p <	Est	SE	p <
Model for the Means									
γ₀₀ Intercept	**1,899.6**	51.5	.001	**1,945.9**	53.9	.001	**1,688.0**	44.2	.001
γ₁₀ Linear	**−51.6**	6.2	.001	**−120.9**	20.0	.001	17.8	16.0	.271
γ₂₀ Quadratic				**13.9**	3.4	.001	**13.9**	3.4	.001
Model for the Variance									
$\tau^2_{U_0}$ Intercept Variance	**253,258.0**	37,897.0	.001	**276,206.0**	41,442.0	.001	**180,678.0**	27,943.0	.001
$\tau_{U_{01}}$ Intercept-Linear Covariance	**−12,701.0**	3,622.0	.001	**−35,734.0**	11,941.0	.003	−1,645.7	7,298.4	.822
$\tau^2_{U_1}$ Linear Slope Variance	**2,233.8**	552.9	.001	**25,840.0**	5,864.4	.001	**11,221.0**	3,863.8	.002
$\tau_{U_{02}}$ Intercept-Quadratic Covariance				**3,902.0**	1,949.1	.045	247.2	1,545.7	.873
$\tau_{U_{12}}$ Linear-Quadratic Covariance				**−3,903.3**	982.6	.001	**2,441.4**	788.1	.002
$\tau^2_{U_2}$ Quadratic Slope Variance				**634.5**	172.4	.001	**634.5**	172.4	.001
σ^2_e Residual Variance	**27,905.0**	1,963.4	.001	**20,298.0**	1,649.1	.001	**20,298.0**	1,649.1	.001
REML Model Fit									
Total Number of Parameters	6			10			10		
−2LL	8,372.1			8,302.7			8,302.7		
AIC	8,380.1			8,316.7			8,316.7		
BIC	8,390.6			8,335.1			8,335.1		

which indicates that 82% of the variance in the RT outcome is between-person $\tau_{U_0}^2$ variance in meant RT, whereas 18% is within-person σ_e^2 variance over time (or equivalently, the average correlation of the residuals from the same person over time is .82). We can test whether the ICC = .82 is significantly greater than 0 by comparing the –2LL values from the empty means, σ_e^2 only model (1a) and the empty means, random intercept model (1b) given that they differ only in $\tau_{U_0}^2$. This test yields $-2\Delta LL(\sim1) = 691.7$, $p < .001$ (with a much smaller AIC and BIC as well), indicating that including the random intercept variance $\tau_{U_0}^2$ did significantly improve the model fit, or equivalently, that the ICC = .82 for the proportion of between-person variance is indeed significantly greater than 0. However, as seen in Figure 6.2, the predicted constant mean and variance over time don't really match the "answer key" from model (0) at all, so we'll continue by evaluating alternative models including polynomial effects of time that might do a better job in both respects. Given that polynomial effects of time are hierarchical on each side of the model, our model-building strategy will be to evaluate the fixed and random parts of each new effect before continuing to the next effect.

Accordingly, the next model (2a) in Table 6.2 is the 4-parameter **fixed linear time, random intercept model**, which has the same model for the variance with just $\tau_{U_0}^2$ and σ_e^2, but whose model for the means now predicts a mean trajectory for RT that starts at fixed intercept of $\gamma_{00} = 1{,}899.6$ at session 1 and decreases linearly over time by fixed linear slope of $\gamma_{10} = -51.6$ per session. The Wald test p-value for the fixed linear slope is significant, and the level-1 residual variance was reduced to $\sigma_e^2 = 35{,}662$ from $\sigma_e^2 = 44{,}900$ in the empty means, random intercept model (1b), or a reduction of $(44{,}900 - 35{,}662) / 44{,}900 = 20.6\%$. Because only the intercept is random, model (2a) still predicts constant total covariance ($\tau_{U_0}^2 = 202{,}422$) and constant total variance ($\tau_{U_0}^2 + \sigma_e^2 = 202{,}422 + 35{,}662 = 238{,}804$) over time. Finally, we note that although the level-2 random intercept variance increased to $\tau_{U_0}^2 = 202{,}422$ from $\tau_{U_0}^2 = 200{,}883$ in model (1b), as explained in chapter 5, this increase in $\tau_{U_0}^2$ is an artifact of decreasing the level-1 σ_e^2 variance. Because the "true" value of $\tau_{U_0}^2$ (that appears in the output) is estimated as: (observed $\tau_{U_0}^2$) – (σ_e^2 / n), $\tau_{U_0}^2$ will increase whenever σ_e^2 is reduced, such as when adding a fixed linear time slope here. But because our *time* predictor is purely within persons, it could not possibly cause a decrease in $\tau_{U_0}^2$. Consequently, we observe only an artificial increase in $\tau_{U_0}^2$ that results from reducing σ_e^2.

So far we know that people decrease linearly in RT across sessions on average, but does each person change the same? To answer this, we examine the next model (2b) in Table 6.2, the 6-parameter **random linear time model**, whose results are shown in the first set of columns in Table 6.3. The estimates for the fixed effects in the model for the means are the same as in model (2a), as expected given that we added only to the model for the variance. To test the significance of the addition of the $\tau_{U_1}^2$ variance of the random linear time slope (and its $\tau_{U_{01}}$ covariance with the random intercept), we can do a $-2\Delta LL$ test against the fixed linear time, random intercept model (2a, which differs from 2b by $\tau_{U_1}^2$ and $\tau_{U_{01}}$). This test yields $-2\Delta LL(\sim2) = 42.6$, $p < .001$ (with a much smaller AIC and BIC as well), indicating that the random linear time slope variance significantly improved model fit, or that each person needs his or her own linear time slope deviation (as represented by the U_{1i} term in model 2b in Table 6.2). Furthermore, we note that although the level-1 σ_e^2 residual variance is smaller than in the previous model (2a), σ_e^2 has *not* been reduced—instead, the total outcome variance has now been partitioned into three piles ($\tau_{U_0}^2$, $\tau_{U_1}^2$, and σ_e^2) rather than just two piles ($\tau_{U_0}^2$ and σ_e^2). Likewise, although the level-2 random intercept variance $\tau_{U_0}^2$ is now larger than in previous models (1b or 2a), this is because $\tau_{U_0}^2$ means something different—it is now the amount of individual differences in the intercept *specifically at time 0* (session 1 here), rather than at any occasion (i.e., conditional rather than unconditional).

As shown in chapter 5, the four parameters in the model for the variance in the random linear time model ($\tau_{U_0}^2$, $\tau_{U_1}^2$, and $\tau_{U_{01}}$ in the **G** matrix and σ_e^2 in the **R** matrix) combine with a **Z** matrix that holds each person's values for the predictors with random effects (with rows = n occasions and columns = u number of random effects, or **Z** = 6x2 here). These form the **V** matrix for the total predicted variances and covariances over time as $\mathbf{V} = \mathbf{ZGZ}^T + \mathbf{R}$. The predicted **V** matrix for the random linear time model is shown in the first row of Table 6.4, in which, as in previous chapters, the total variances are on the diagonal, the total covariances are above the diagonal, and the corresponding total correlations are below the diagonal (i.e., as would be found in **VCORR**). Also given are the scalar formulas to predict the total variance and covariance across time (as derived in chapter 5), which show how the total variance is predicted to change over time as a quadratic function of time, as seen in the bottom of Figure 6.2, in which the minimum variance (i.e., aperture) will be observed at $time = -\tau_{U_{01}}/\tau_{U_1}^2 = 12{,}701/2{,}234 = 5.69$, which is session 6.69 here. As seen in the top of Figure 6.2, though, a linear trend doesn't really capture the mean trajectory over time. Furthermore, the prediction that RT will keep decreasing at a constant rate through additional practice sessions may not be realistic. So, we can see if adding fixed and random quadratic effects of time might result in better fit and predictions.

Thus, the next model (3a) in Table 6.2 is the 7-parameter **fixed quadratic, random linear time model,** which has the same model for the variance ($\tau_{U_0}^2$, $\tau_{U_1}^2$, $\tau_{U_{01}}$, and σ_e^2), but whose model for the means now includes a fixed quadratic time slope γ_{20}. Specifically, the level-1 model now has a third placeholder for the individual quadratic effect of time, β_{2i}, which is then defined in the level-2 model by its own equation (with just the fixed quadratic time effect γ_{20} so far). The fixed quadratic time slope γ_{20} is significant, as indicated by its significant Wald test p-value, and the level-1 residual variance was reduced to $\sigma_e^2 = 26{,}176$ from $\sigma_e^2 = 27{,}905$ in the previous model (2b), or a reduction of $(27{,}905 - 26{,}176) / 27{,}905 = 6.2\%$ of σ_e^2 that remained after accounting for individual differences in linear change over time. We know this further reduction of 6.2% is significant via the p-value for the new quadratic time slope. However, we can't calculate an estimate of the total residual variance accounted for so far by comparing σ_e^2 from our current model (3a) that has three piles of variance ($\tau_{U_0}^2$, $\tau_{U_1}^2$, and σ_e^2) back to σ_e^2 from the empty means, random intercept model (1b, which did not have the random linear slope variance $\tau_{U_1}^2$).

Table 6.4 Predicted V matrix (with variances on the diagonal, covariances above the diagonal, and correlations below the diagonal, and means (with SE = standard errors) from the polynomial models for the six-session response time data (*time* = session − 1).

Model Description and Parameters	Session	V Matrix					
		1	2	3	4	5	6
Random Linear Time: 6 total parameters (Model 2b)							
2 fixed effects (intercept γ_{00}, linear slope γ_{10})	1	281,163	240,557	227,856	215,155	202,455	189,754
	2	.89	257,995	219,623	209,156	198,689	188,222
	3	.88	.88	239,295	203,157	194,924	186,691
	4	.86	.87	.88	225,063	191,158	185,159
	5	.82	.84	.86	.87	215,298	183,627
	6	.78	.81	.83	.85	.86	210,001
	Mean	1899.63	1848.06	1796.92	1744.92	1693.34	1641.77
	SE	51.50	48.58	46.29	44.74	44.01	44.13

Intercept Variance $\tau^2_{U_0}$ = 253,258

Intercept-Linear Covariance $\tau_{U_{01}}$ = −12,701

Linear Time Slope Variance $\tau^2_{U_1}$ = 2,233

Residual Variance σ^2_e = 27,905

Predicted Variance at Time T: $\mathrm{Var}(y_T) = \sigma^2_e + \tau^2_{U_0} + 2{*}T{*}\,\tau_{U_{01}} + T^2{*}\,\tau^2_{U_1}$

Predicted Covariance between Time A and B: $\mathrm{Cov}(y_A, y_B) = \tau^2_{U_0} + (A+B){*}\,\tau_{U_{01}} + (AB){*}\,\tau^2_{U_1}$

Model Description and Parameters	Session	V Matrix					
		1	2	3	4	5	6
Random Quadratic Time: 10 total parameters (Model 3b)							
3 fixed effects (intercept γ_{00}, linear γ_{10}, quadratic γ_{20})	1	296,504	244,374	220,346	204,122	195,702	195,085
	2	.89	251,508	219,312	208,680	199,315	191,215
	3	.83	.90	235,842	209,043	199,808	187,840
	4	.79	.88	.91	225,508	197,182	184,958
	5	.78	.86	.89	.90	211,735	182,571
	6	.80	.85	.86	.87	.89	200,977
	Mean	1945.82	1838.82	1759.51	1707.94	1684.10	1687.99
	SE	53.85	48.49	47.00	45.86	44.24	44.20

Intercept Variance $\tau^2_{U_0}$ = 276,206

Intercept-Linear Covariance $\tau_{U_{01}}$ = −35,734

Linear Time Slope Variance $\tau^2_{U_1}$ = 25,840

Intercept-Quadratic Covariance $\tau_{U_{02}}$ = 3,902

Linear-Quadratic Covariance $\tau_{U_{12}}$ = −3,903

Quadratic Time Slope Variance $\tau^2_{U_2}$ = 634

Residual Variance σ^2_e = 20,298

Predicted Variance at Time T:

$\mathrm{Var}(y_T) = \sigma^2_e + \tau^2_{U_0} + T^2{*}\,\tau^2_{U_1} + 2{*}T{*}\,\tau_{U_{01}} + 2{*}T^2{*}\,\tau_{U_{02}} + 2{*}T^3{*}\,\tau_{U_{12}} + T^4{*}\,\tau^2_{U_2}$

Predicted Covariance between Time A and B:

$\mathrm{Cov}(y_A, y_B) = \tau^2_{U_0} + (A+B){*}\,\tau_{U_{01}} + (AB){*}\,\tau^2_{U_1} + (A^2+B^2){*}\,\tau_{U_{02}} + (AB^2 + A^2B){*}\,\tau_{U_{12}} + (A^2B^2){*}\,\tau_{U_2}$

Because these models define σ_e^2 differently, their estimates of σ_e^2 are not meaningfully comparable.

In interpreting the fixed effects from model (3a), we see that the fixed intercept for the predicted RT at session 1 is now $\gamma_{00} = 1{,}945.9$ rather than $\gamma_{00} = 1{,}899.6$ from the random linear model (2b). The fixed linear slope has also changed to $\gamma_{10} = -120.9$ from $\gamma_{10} = -51.6$ in the random linear model—it had to change, because γ_{10} now means something different. In a linear model the fixed linear time slope is the *constant* rate of change over time, but in a quadratic model it becomes the *instantaneous* linear rate of change *at time 0*. Thus, *at session 1*, RT decreases by $\gamma_{10} = -120.9$ per session. The positive fixed quadratic time slope creates a decelerating negative trajectory, such that the negative linear rate of change will become *less negative* per session by twice the quadratic time slope of $\gamma_{20} = 13.9$. Thus, the linear rate of change at session 1 of $\gamma_{10} = -120.9$ per session will become less negative by 27.8 per session.

Programming statements (e.g., ESTIMATE in SAS, TEST in SPSS, LINCOM in STATA, or NEW in M*plus*) can be used to request the model-implied estimates of the instantaneous linear rate of change at each occasion and the standard errors by which to assess their significance. In doing so here, we find that the linear rate of change is significantly negative through session 4, but by session 5 it is nonsignificantly negative (and is nonsignificantly positive at session 6). Thus, the improvement predicted by the quadratic model appears to "shut off" after session 4. We can also use these results to calculate the exact occasion at which the linear time slope is predicted in the quadratic model to become 0 as: $time = -\gamma_{10} / 2\gamma_{20} = 120.9 / (2*13.9) = 4.35$, or at approximately session 5.35 here (given that $time = $ session $- 1$).

So far we know that the rate of decline in RT slows down across sessions on average, but do people differ in their rates of deceleration? To answer this, we examine the last model (3b) in Table 6.2, the 10-parameter **random quadratic time model**, whose results are shown in the second set of columns in Table 6.3. The estimates for the fixed effects in the model for the means are the same as in model (3a), as expected given that we only added to the model for the variance. To test the significance of the addition of the $\tau_{U_2}^2$ variance of the random quadratic time slope (and its $\tau_{U_{02}}$ and $\tau_{U_{01}}$ covariances with the random intercept and random linear time slope), we can do a $-2\Delta LL$ test against the fixed quadratic, random linear time model (3a, which differs from 3b by $\tau_{U_2}^2$, $\tau_{U_{02}}$ and $\tau_{U_{12}}$). This test yields $-2\Delta LL(\sim3) = 38.7$, $p < .001$ (with a much smaller AIC and BIC as well), indicating that the random quadratic time slope variance significantly improved model fit, or that each person needs his or her own quadratic time slope deviation (as represented by the U_{2i} term in model 3b in Table 6.2). Although σ_e^2 is smaller than in model (3a), it has *not* been reduced—instead, the total variance has now been partitioned into four piles ($\tau_{U_0}^2$, $\tau_{U_1}^2$, $\tau_{U_2}^2$, and σ_e^2) rather than just three piles ($\tau_{U_0}^2$, $\tau_{U_1}^2$ and σ_e^2). Although the level-2 random linear time slope variance $\tau_{U_1}^2$ is now larger than in previous models (2b and 3a), this is because it means something different—it is now the amount of individual differences in the linear time slopes *specifically at time 0* (session 1), rather than at any occasion as in model (2b) or (3a).

We can further interpret the fixed and random effects by constructing **95% random effects confidence intervals**, as introduced in chapter 5 and as illustrated in Equation (6.3):

Random Effect 95% CI = fixed effect $\pm \left(1.96*\sqrt{\text{Random Variance}}\right)$

Intercept 95% CI = $\gamma_{00} \pm \left(1.96*\sqrt{\tau_{U_0}^2}\right) \rightarrow 1{,}945.9 \pm \left(1.96*\sqrt{276{,}209}\right)$

    = 916 to 2,976

Linear Time Slope 95% CI = $\gamma_{10} \pm \left(1.96*\sqrt{\tau_{U_1}^2}\right) \rightarrow -120.9 \pm \left(1.96*\sqrt{25{,}840}\right)$ (6.3)

    = -436 to 194

Quadratic Time Slope 95% CI = $\gamma_{20} \pm \left(1.96*\sqrt{\tau_{U_2}^2}\right) \rightarrow 13.9 \pm \left(1.96*\sqrt{634}\right)$

    = -36 to 63

in which 95% random effects confidence intervals (CI) are computed for each effect that has both a fixed and a random part. First, the intercept 95% CI indicates that 95% of the sample is predicted to have individual intercepts for the predicted RT at session 1 between 916 and 2,976 msec. Second, 95% of the sample is predicted to have individual linear rates of change at session 1 between −436 and 194 per session, indicating that although there is linear change at session 1 on average (because the fixed linear time slope γ_{10} = −120.9 was significantly different from 0), not everyone is predicted to decline (i.e., to improve in RT) right away—some people are predicted to increase in RT at session 1 instead. Third, 95% of the sample is predicted to have individual quadratic rates of change between −36 to 63, indicating that although there is quadratic change on average (because the fixed quadratic time slope γ_{20} = 13.9 was significantly different than 0), not everyone is predicted to decelerate over time—some persons are predicted to accelerate instead (i.e., if a negative linear slope is paired with a negative quadratic slope).

To highlight the impact of centering time on the random quadratic model parameters, the same model in which time 0 is set to session 6 instead (i.e., in which *time* = session − 6) is shown in the third set of columns in Table 6.3. The model parameters that were conditional on *session 1* as time 0 have changed because they are now conditional on *session 6* as time 0, including the fixed intercept γ_{00}, fixed linear time slope γ_{10}, random intercept variance $\tau_{U_0}^2$, random linear time slope variance $\tau_{U_1}^2$, intercept–linear slope covariance $\tau_{U_{01}}$, intercept–quadratic slope covariance $\tau_{U_{02}}$, and the linear–quadratic slope covariance $\tau_{U_{12}}$. Both the fixed quadratic time slope γ_{20} and the random quadratic time slope variance $\tau_{U_2}^2$ are the same because they are the highest-order term on their side of the model (means and variances, respectively), and are thus unconditional. The residual variance σ_e^2 and the model fit are the same because it is the same model that makes the same predictions (just with a few parameters re-arranged based on when time = 0).

Just as with the random linear time model, the parameters in the model for the variance in the random quadratic time model (now $\tau_{U_0}^2$, $\tau_{U_{01}}$, $\tau_{U_1}^2$, $\tau_{U_{02}}$, $\tau_{U_{12}}$, and $\tau_{U_2}^2$ in the G matrix and σ_e^2 in the R matrix) combine with an individual **Z** matrix that holds each person's values for the predictors with random effects (with rows = n occasions and columns = u number of random effects, or Z = 6x3 now). The predicted V matrix for the random quadratic time model from $V = ZGZ^T + R$ is shown in the second row of Table 6.4 along with the scalar formulas to predict the total variance and covariance across time from a random quadratic model (as derived using the same algebra of expectations as was derived for the random linear time model in chapter 5). In contrast to the random linear model in which the variance is predicted to change as a quadratic function of time, the variance in a random quadratic model is predicted to change as a *quartic* function of time (which occurs because time^2 itself becomes a squared term).

As seen in Figure 6.2, the random quadratic model better captures the change in the RT mean trajectory and the change in the RT total variance over the observed sessions (i.e., as given by the saturated means, unstructured variance model 0) than do the random intercept or random linear time models. However, if we extrapolate to what these models would predict for three additional practice sessions, we see that the random quadratic model predicts that mean RT should begin to *increase,* or that performance should worsen with more practice (with a sharply increasing RT total variance over time as well). This is why polynomial models of change (and quadratic models in particular) are often met with criticism, because their predictions—that what goes up must come down, and that what goes down must come up—may not be realistic when studying practice effects, learning, or other processes whose effects that should not logically reverse. There are other truly nonlinear models that explicitly account for rates of change that should "level off" over time—one example is the *exponential* model, as we will see shortly. For now, though, we'll turn to the second in our three options for modeling change with a single bend—a *two-slope, piecewise discontinuous model of change,* as presented next.

2.B. A Two-Piece Discontinuous Model of Change

A trajectory with a single bend can also be approximated with a **piecewise model**, in which change is described using a *discontinuous* rather than continuous trajectory with separate slopes through distinct phases of time. As discussed earlier, piecewise models are useful for data with a known breakpoint (i.e., to distinguish change before and after a naturally occurring event, intervention, or manipulation). However, piecewise models can also be used to approximate a nonlinear continuous trajectory, in which a breakpoint could be selected based on the observed data. This empirically based use of a piecewise model will be demonstrated using our current example. As seen in Figure 6.3 for our six-session RT data, it appears the decelerating decline in RT across sessions (that we previously predicted using a quadratic model) could also be captured by a negative linear slope from session 1 to 2, and a second, less negative linear slope from session 2 to 6. Accordingly, this section will use the RT data to describe two parameterizations of piecewise models with two separate linear slopes: either to specify the slope during each time period directly, or to specify the difference between the two slopes directly.

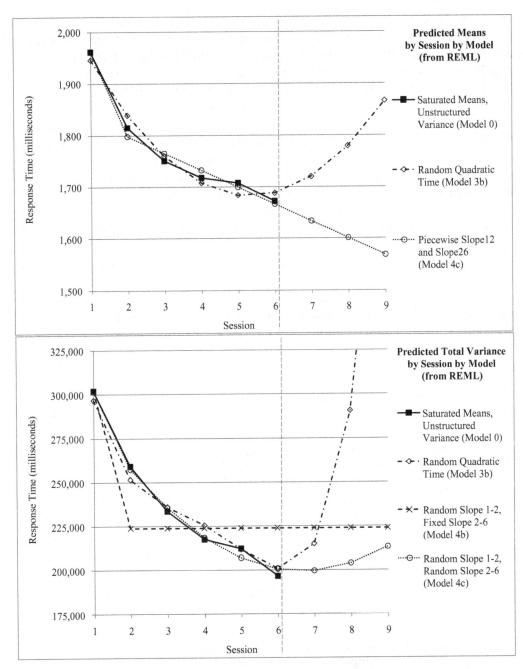

Figure 6.3 Predicted means (top panel) and variances (bottom panel) by model for the six-session response time data (with three extra sessions predicted after the vertical line).

Before we begin, we note that although breakpoints can be selected manually based on the observed pattern of mean differences, it is also possible to estimate a **latent change point model,** in which the location of an unknown breakpoint is estimated within the model. Although purely empirically derived, the estimated latent breakpoints are sometimes interpreted theoretically. For instance, change in cognitive abilities across adulthood could potentially be described with a flat slope across age for normal functioning up to some estimated breakpoint age, after which cognitive decline begins. Although most applications of latent change point models include an estimated breakpoint that is fixed across persons, it is also technically possible to estimate a random variance for individual differences in the location of the breakpoint across persons. However, given that both the slopes and the breakpoint at which the slopes differ would need to be estimated simultaneously, these latent change point models can be highly unstable and typically require large amounts of within-person data (especially to estimate a random latent change point), which limits their practical utility. For this reason we do not demonstrate this approach here, and instead present piecewise models with fixed, non-estimated breakpoints, as chosen based on the design of the study or as a means of describing nonlinear patterns of change.

A good place to begin is to explain how the two predictor variables (called *slope12* and *slope26* here) for the two piecewise slopes would be formed, both for our six-session example with balanced time and more generally for unbalanced time, as seen in Table 6.5. To illustrate how piecewise slopes would be created more generally, three different scenarios are given for creating piecewise slopes using

Table 6.5 Calculation of piecewise slopes given balanced and unbalanced time with different locations for time 0.

Session	Scenario A:			Scenario B:			Scenario C:		
	Intercept at Session 1, Breakpoint at Session 2			Intercept at Session 2, Breakpoint at Session 2			Intercept at Session 6, Breakpoint at Session 2		
	Time	Slope12	Slope26	Time	Slope12	Slope26	Time	Slope12	Slope26
1	0	0	0	−1	−1	0	−5	−1	−4
2	1	1	0	0	0	0	−4	0	−4
3	2	1	1	1	0	1	−3	0	−3
4	3	1	2	2	0	2	−2	0	−2
5	4	1	3	3	0	3	−1	0	−1
6	5	1	4	4	0	4	0	0	0

Scenario A (Intercept at **Session 1**, Breakpoint at Session 2):
IF (session ≤ 2) THEN DO; **slope12 = session − 1**; slope26 = 0; END;
ELSE IF (session > 2) THEN DO; slope12 = 1; slope26 = session − 2; END;

Scenario B (Intercept at **Session 2**, Breakpoint at Session 2):
IF (session ≤ 2) THEN DO; **slope12 = session − 2**; slope26 = 0; END;
ELSE IF (session > 2) THEN DO; slope12 = 0; slope26 = session − 2; END;

Scenario C (Intercept at **Session 6**, Breakpoint at Session 2):
IF (session ≤ 2) THEN DO; slope12 = session − 2; slope26 = −4; END;
ELSE IF (session > 2) THEN DO; slope12 = 0; **slope26 = session − 6**; END;

different locations for the intercept (i.e., when time = 0 across all slopes), but in which session 2 is the breakpoint for the two slopes in each scenario. In scenario A (which we will use for our example), the intercept is session 1, as indicated by the 0 values for both slope12 and slope26 at session 1. From there, slope12 indexes the change to session 2, but then "shuts off" after session 2 by keeping the same value it had at session 2 for the rest of the sessions. Meanwhile, slope26 is inactive during sessions 1 and 2 because of the codes of 0, but then "turns on" after session 2 to index change from session 2 to 6. The slope12 and slope26 predictor variables can be created with integers in this fashion in balanced data (i.e., in which everyone has the same sessions), but not in unbalanced data (i.e., in which the values for the slope predictors will need to differ based on the exact occasions observed for each person). Conditional logic statements are given in the bottom of Table 6.5 to show how the slope12 and slope26 predictor variables would be created more generally using any values of *session*.

The same process would be followed for the other scenarios in Table 6.5, in which time is centered such that the intercept is session 2 or 6 instead (i.e., as the occasion at which both slope12 and slope26 are set to 0). As shown by the bold text in each scenario, the slope closest to the intercept occasion is activated first and is created by subtracting the centering point for time. During that period, the other slope is inactive at 0. After the breakpoint (at session 2 in each scenario), the slope that was inactive (i.e., was held constant at 0) turns on to index change relative to session 2 (i.e., the previously inactive slope is then created by subtracting 2), whereas the previously active slope shuts off, such that its value after the breakpoint will be that held last.

As in the quadratic models of change, we will use session 1 as our intercept and examine a series of piecewise models for the RT data. For ease of comparison, the piecewise models to be examined are shown in Table 6.6. For each model the first column provides the name and number of estimated parameters, the second column shows the multilevel equations, the third column provides the level-2 G matrix, and the fourth column lists the question to be answered. As before, in all models the level-1 **R** matrix will be a 6x6 diagonal matrix for the n = 6 sessions (in which is constant with no covariance over time). Model estimates will be presented in the text below, and those from models 4c, 5b, and 5c are given in Table 6.7.

REML estimation will again be used, such that the significance of new fixed or random effects will be assessed via their Wald test p-values or -2ΔLL tests, respectively. For our model-building strategy, because both piecewise slopes will be needed to describe the trajectory (i.e., they are not hierarchical), we will begin with both fixed slopes, and then examine the random effect of each in separate models. There are two possible parameterizations of piecewise models—we'll start by specifying the slope during each time period directly, and follow by specifying the *difference* between the slopes directly.

In our first **direct slopes model**, the 5-parameter **fixed slope12, fixed slope26, random intercept model** (4a), the goal is to test whether there is significant linear change on average before and after the breakpoint at session 2. In our six-session RT data, the fixed intercept for RT at session 1 predicted by the piecewise linear slopes

Table 6.6 Piecewise model equations and level-2 G matrix for the six-session response time data (in which *slope12* = change between sessions 1 and 2, *slope26* = linear change between sessions 2 and 6, and *time* = session − 1).

Model (# Total Parameters)	Model Equation	Level-2 G Matrix	Purpose (New Parameters)
4a Fixed Slope12, Fixed Slope 26, Random Intercept (5)	Level 1: $y_{ti} = \beta_{0i} + \beta_{1i}(\text{Slope12}_{ti}) + \beta_{2i}(\text{Slope26}_{ti}) + e_{ti}$ Level 2: Intercept: $\beta_{0i} = \gamma_{00} + U_{0i}$ Slope12: $\beta_{1i} = \gamma_{10}$ Slope26: $\beta_{2i} = \gamma_{20}$	$\mathbf{G} = \begin{bmatrix} \tau_{U_0}^2 \end{bmatrix}$	Is there linear change during each time period on average? (γ_{10} and γ_{20})
4b Random Slope12, Fixed Slope26 (7)	Level 1: $y_{ti} = \beta_{0i} + \beta_{1i}(\text{Slope12}_{ti}) + \beta_{2i}(\text{Slope26}_{ti}) + e_{ti}$ Level 2: Intercept: $\beta_{0i} = \gamma_{00} + U_{0i}$ Slope12: $\beta_{1i} = \gamma_{10} + U_{1i}$ Slope26: $\beta_{2i} = \gamma_{20}$	$\mathbf{G} = \begin{bmatrix} \tau_{U_0}^2 & \tau_{U_{01}} \\ \tau_{U_{01}} & \tau_{U_1}^2 \end{bmatrix}$	Are there individual differences in linear change between sessions 1 and 2? ($\tau_{U_1}^2$ and $\tau_{U_{01}}$)
4c Random Slope12, Random Slope26 (10)	Level 1: $y_{ti} = \beta_{0i} + \beta_{1i}(\text{Slope12}_{ti}) + \beta_{2i}(\text{Slope26}_{ti}) + e_{ti}$ Level 2: Intercept: $\beta_{0i} = \gamma_{00} + U_{0i}$ Slope12: $\beta_{1i} = \gamma_{10} + U_{1i}$ Slope26: $\beta_{2i} = \gamma_{20} + U_{2i}$	$\mathbf{G} = \begin{bmatrix} \tau_{U_0}^2 & \tau_{U_{01}} & \tau_{U_{02}} \\ \tau_{U_{01}} & \tau_{U_1}^2 & \tau_{U_{12}} \\ \tau_{U_{02}} & \tau_{U_{12}} & \tau_{U_2}^2 \end{bmatrix}$	Are there individual differences in linear change between sessions 2 and 6? ($\tau_{U_2}^2$, $\tau_{U_{02}}$, and $\tau_{U_{12}}$)
5a Fixed Slope, Fixed Deviation Slope, Random Intercept (5)	Level 1: $y_{ti} = \beta_{0i} + \beta_{1i}(\text{Time}_{ti}) + \beta_{2i}(\text{Slope26}_{ti}) + e_{ti}$ Level 2: Intercept: $\beta_0 = \gamma_{00} + U_{0i}$ Time: $\beta_{1i} = \gamma_{10}$ Slope26: $\beta_{2i} = \gamma_{20}$	$\mathbf{G} = \begin{bmatrix} \tau_{U_0}^2 \end{bmatrix}$	Is there *differential* linear change after session 2 on average? (γ_{20})
5b Random Slope, Fixed Deviation Slope (7)	Level 1: $y_{ti} = \beta_{0i} + \beta_{1i}(\text{Time}_{ti}) + \beta_{2i}(\text{Slope26}_{ti}) + e_{ti}$ Level 2: Intercept: $\beta_{0i} = \gamma_{00} + U_{0i}$ Time: $\beta_{1i} = \gamma_{10} + U_{1i}$ Slope26: $\beta_{2i} = \gamma_{20}$	$\mathbf{G} = \begin{bmatrix} \tau_{U_0}^2 & \tau_{U_{01}} \\ \tau_{U_{01}} & \tau_{U_1}^2 \end{bmatrix}$	Are there individual differences in linear change between sessions 1 and 6? ($\tau_{U_1}^2$ and $\tau_{U_{01}}$)
5c Random Slope, Random Deviation Slope (10)	Level 1: $y_{ti} = \beta_{0i} + \beta_{1i}(\text{Time}_{ti}) + \beta_{2i}(\text{Slope26}_{ti}) + e_{ti}$ Level 2: Intercept: $\beta_{0i} = \gamma_{00} + U_{0i}$ Time: $\beta_{1i} = \gamma_{10} + U_{1i}$ Slope26: $\beta_{2i} = \gamma_{20} + U_{2i}$	$\mathbf{G} = \begin{bmatrix} \tau_{U_0}^2 & \tau_{U_{01}} & \tau_{U_{02}} \\ \tau_{U_{01}} & \tau_{U_1}^2 & \tau_{U_{12}} \\ \tau_{U_{02}} & \tau_{U_{12}} & \tau_{U_2}^2 \end{bmatrix}$	Are there individual differences in *differential* linear change after session 2? ($\tau_{U_2}^2$, $\tau_{U_{02}}$, and $\tau_{U_{12}}$)

Table 6.7 Piecewise model parameters for the six-session response time data in which *slope12* = change between sessions 1 and 2, *slope26* = change between sessions 2 and 6, and *time* = session − 1 is included for *slope12* in model 5c. Bold values are $p < .05$.

Model Parameter		Model 4b Random Slope12, Fixed Slope26 (Time 0 = Session 1)			Model 4c Random Slope12, Random Slope26 (Time 0 = Session 1)			Model 5c Random Time, Random Slope26 (Time 0 = Session 1)		
		Est	SE	p <	Est	SE	p <	Est	SE	p <
Model for the Means										
γ_{00}	Intercept	**1,961.9**	54.7	.001	**1,961.9**	54.7	.001	**1,961.9**	54.7	.001
γ_{10}	Linear Slope12/Time	**−163.6**	31.2	.001	**−163.6**	30.2	.001	**−163.6**	30.2	.001
γ_{20}	Linear Slope26	**−32.9**	4.9	.001	**−32.9**	6.6	.001	**130.8**	32.6	.001
Model for the Variance										
$\tau^2_{U_0}$	Intercept Variance	**277,818.0**	42,471.0	.001	**284,312.0**	42,731.0	.001	**284,312.0**	42,731.0	.001
$\tau_{U_{01}}$	Intercept–Slope12 Covariance	**−69,063.0**	18,932.0	.001	**−54,270.0**	18,230.0	.003	**−54,270.0**	18,230.0	.003
$\tau^2_{U_1}$	Linear Slope12/Time Variance	**59,941.0**	12,743.0	.001	**63,954.0**	13,244.0	.001	**63,954.0**	13,244.0	.001
$\tau_{U_{0z}}$	Intercept–Slope26 Covariance				**−10,644.0**	3,791.3	.001	**43,626.0**	19,049.0	.022
$\tau_{U_{1z}}$	Slope12–Slope26 Covariance				−1,672.3	2,097.0	.425	**−65,626.0**	14,154.0	.001
$\tau^2_{U_2}$	Linear Slope26 Variance				**2,617.3**	636.5	.001	**69,916.0**	15,434.0	.001
σ^2_e	Residual Variance	**24,168.0**	1,702.5	.001	**17,673.0**	1,435.8	.001	**17,673.0**	1,435.8	.001
REML Model Fit										
	Total Number of Parameters	7			10			10		
	−2LL	8,319.6			8,275.4			8,275.4		
	AIC	8,327.6			8,289.4			8,289.4		
	BIC	8,338.1			8,307.7			8,307.7		

was γ_{00} = 1,961.9, the linear rate of change between sessions 1 and 2 (via slope12) was γ_{10} = –163.6 per session, and the linear rate of change between sessions 2 and 6 (via slope26) was γ_{20} = –32.9 per session. The Wald test p-values for each fixed slope indicated a significant decrease (improvement) in RT during each phase on average, and these two piecewise slopes do appear to reasonably approximate the observed mean RT trajectory over time (from model 0), as seen in the top of Figure 6.3. Further, relative to the empty means, random intercept model (1b), the two piecewise slopes reduced the level-1 residual variance by 24%, as calculated from (44,900 – 34,098) / (44,900) = .24.

However, only the intercept is random in model (4a), which thus predicts constant total variance ($\tau_{U_0}^2 + \sigma_e^2$ = 202,683 + 34,098 = 236,781) and constant covariance ($\tau_{U_0}^2$ = 202,683) over time, but we know from Table 6.1 that the total variance and covariance decrease over time instead. Accordingly, in addition to their *fixed* effects, we can test whether each of the piecewise slopes should also have a *random* effect, by which each person would be allowed his or her own random slope deviation, and by which the total variances and covariances would then be predicted to change over time. But unlike the linear and quadratic effects of time in which the linear effect was lower-order relative to the quadratic effect, the two piecewise slopes are not hierarchical, and thus there is no required order in which their random effects should be tested.

We continue with model (4b) in Table 6.6, the 7-parameter **random slope12, fixed slope26 model**, which contains the same fixed effects but adds a random effect for the change between sessions 1 and 2 (slope12), and whose results are shown in the first set of columns in Table 6.7. The estimates for the fixed effects in the model for the means are the same as in model (4a), as expected given that we added only to the model for the variance. To test the significance of the addition of the $\tau_{U_1}^2$ variance of the random slope12 (and its $\tau_{U_{01}}$ covariance with the random intercept), we can do a –2ΔLL test against the fixed slope12, fixed slope26, random intercept model (4a, which differs from 4b by $\tau_{U_1}^2$ and $\tau_{U_{01}}$). This test yields –2ΔLL(~2) = 63.1, p < .001 (with a smaller AIC and BIC as well), indicating that the random slope12 variance significantly improved model fit, or that each person needs his or her deviation for the rate of change between sessions 1 and 2 (as represented by the U_{1i} term in model 4b in Table 6.6).

As in the polynomial models, although σ_e^2 is now smaller than in model (4a), this is because the total RT variance has now been partitioned into three piles ($\tau_{U_0}^2$, $\tau_{U_1}^2$, and σ_e^2) rather than just two piles ($\tau_{U_0}^2$ and σ_e^2). Likewise, $\tau_{U_0}^2$ is now larger than in model (4a) because it is now the amount of individual differences in the intercept *specifically at time 0* (session 1 here), rather than at any occasion. The predicted **V** matrix for model (4b) is shown in the first row of Table 6.8, constructed as described previously from $V = ZGZ^T + R$ (in which **Z** is a 6x2 matrix with two columns for the random intercept and random slope12), along with the scalar equations for the total predicted variance and covariance over time. Because only the first slope is random, the total variance and covariance are predicted to be constant from session 2 to 6, a pattern that does not match the original data given by model (0), as shown in the bottom of Figure 6.3.

Table 6.8 Predicted **V** matrix (with variances on the diagonal, covariances above the diagonal, and correlations below the diagonal, and means (with SE = standard errors) from the piecewise models for the six-session response time data (in which *slope12* = change between sessions 1 and 2, *slope26* = linear change between sessions 2 and 6).

Model Description and Parameters		V Matrix					
	Session	1	2	3	4	5	6
Random Slope12, Fixed Slope26: 7 total parameters (Model 4b)							
	1	301,985	208,755	208,755	208,755	208,755	208,755
	2	.80	223,800	199,632	199,632	199,632	199,632
3 fixed effects (intercept γ_{00}, slope12 γ_{10}, slope26 γ_{20})	3	.80	.89	223,800	199,632	199,632	199,632
	4	.80	.89	.89	223,800	199,632	199,632
Intercept Variance $\tau^2_{U_0} = 277{,}818$	5	.80	.89	.89	.89	223,800	199,632
Intercept-Linear Covariance $\tau_{U_{01}} = -69{,}063$	6	.80	.89	.89	.89	.89	223,800
Linear Slope12 Variance $\tau^2_{U_1} = 59{,}941$	Mean	1961.89	1798.25	1765.36	1732.46	1699.57	1666.68
Residual Variance $\sigma^2_e = 24{,}168$	SE	54.68	46.04	45.26	44.99	45.26	46.04

Predicted Variance at Time T (from just the random *slope12*):– $Var(y_T) = \sigma^2_e + \tau^2_{U_0} + 2 T_{12} {}^* \tau_{U_{01}} + T_{12}^{2 *} \tau^2_{U_1}$

Predicted Covariance between Time A and B (from just the random *slope12*): $Cov(y_A, y_B) = \tau^2_{U_0} + (A_{12}+B_{12})^* \tau_{U_{01}} + (A_{12}B_{12})^* \tau^2_{U_1}$

Model Description and Parameters		V Matrix					
Random Slope12, Random Slope26: 10 total parameters (Model 4c)							
	1	301,985	230,042	219,399	208,755	198,111	187,467
	2	.83	257,400	227,410	215,094	202,778	190,462
3 fixed effects (intercept γ_{00}, slope12 γ_{10}, slope26 γ_{20})	3	.82	.92	235,385	208,013	198,314	188,615
	4	.81	.91	.92	218,604	193,850	186,768
Intercept Variance $\tau^2_{U_0} = 284{,}312$	5	.79	.88	.90	.91	207,059	184,921
Intercept-Slope12 Covariance $\tau_{U_{01}} = -354{,}270$	6	.76	.84	.87	.90	.91	200,747
Linear Slope12 Variance $\tau^2_{U_1} = 63{,}954$							
Intercept-Slope26 Covariance $\tau_{U_{02}} = -10{,}644$							
Slope12-Slope26 Covariance $\tau_{U_1} = -1{,}672$	Mean	1961.89	1798.25	1765.36	1732.46	1699.57	1666.68
Linear Slope26 Variance $\tau^2_{U_2} = 2{,}617$	SE	54.68	49.78	46.99	44.99	43.90	43.79
Residual Variance $\sigma^2_e = 17{,}673$							

Predicted Variance at Time T (from both slopes):

$Var(y_T) = \sigma^2_e + \tau^2_{U_0} + 2 T_{12} {}^* \tau_{U_{01}} + 2 T_{26} {}^* \tau_{U_{02}} + T_{12}^{2 *} \tau^2_{U_1} + 2 T_{12} {}^* T_{26} {}^* \tau_{U_{12}} + T_{26}^{2 *} \tau^2_{U_2}$

Predicted Covariance between Time A and B (from both slopes):

$Cov(y_A, y_B) = \tau^2_{U_0} + (A_{12}+B_{12})^* \tau_{U_{01}} + (A_{26}+B_{26})^* \tau_{U_{02}} + (A_{12}B_{12})^* \tau^2_{U_1} + (A_{12}B_{26} + A_{26}B_{12})^* \tau_{U_{12}} + (A_{26}B_{26})^* \tau^2_{U_2}$

We continue by examining model (4c) in the third row of Table 6.6, the 10-parameter **random slope12, random slope26 model**, which now includes a random effect for the linear change between sessions 2 and 6 (slope26), and whose results are shown in the second set of columns in Table 6.7. To test the significance of the addition of the random slope26, we can do a $-2\Delta LL$ test against the random slope12, fixed slope26 model (4b, which differs from 4c by $\tau_{U_2}^2$, $\tau_{U_{02}}$, and $\tau_{U_{12}}$). This test yields $-2\Delta LL(\sim3) = 44.2$, $p < .001$ (with a smaller AIC and BIC as well), indicating that the random slope26 variance significantly improved model fit, or that each person needs his or her deviation for the rate of change between sessions 2 and 6 (as represented by the U_{2i} term in model 4c in Table 6.6). The predicted $\mathbf{V}$ matrix is shown in the second row of Table 6.8, as constructed from $\mathbf{V} = \mathbf{ZGZ}^T + \mathbf{R}$ (in which $\mathbf{Z}$ is a 6x3 matrix now), along with the scalar equations for the total predicted variance and covariance over time. As seen in the bottom of Figure 6.3, the U-shaped variance pattern better matches the "answer key" given by model (0).

To interpret the model parameters with both fixed and random effects, we can again calculate 95% random effects confidence intervals, as shown in Equation (6.4):

$$\text{Random Effect 95\% CI} = \text{fixed effect} \pm \left(1.96 * \sqrt{\text{Random Variance}}\right)$$

$$\text{Intercept 95\% CI} = \gamma_{00} \pm \left(1.96 * \sqrt{\tau_{U_0}^2}\right) \rightarrow 1{,}961.9 \pm \left(1.96 * \sqrt{284{,}312}\right)$$

$$= 917 \text{ to } 3{,}007$$

$$\text{Slope12 95\% CI} = \gamma_{10} \pm \left(1.96 * \sqrt{\tau_{U_1}^2}\right) \rightarrow -163.6 \pm \left(1.96 * \sqrt{63{,}954}\right) \qquad (6.4)$$

$$= -659 \text{ to } 322$$

$$\text{Slope26 95\% CI} = \gamma_{20} \pm \left(1.96 * \sqrt{\tau_{U_2}^2}\right) \rightarrow -32.9 \pm \left(1.96 * \sqrt{2{,}617}\right)$$

$$= -133 \text{ to } 67$$

First, the intercept 95% CI indicates that 95% of the sample is predicted to have individual intercepts for the predicted RT at session 1 between 917 and 3,007 msec. Second, 95% of the sample is predicted to have individual linear rates of change between sessions 1 and 2 of −659 to 322 per session, indicating that although there is a decline from session 1 to 2 on average (because the fixed slope12 $\gamma_{10} = -163.6$ was significantly different from 0), not everyone is predicted to improve initially from session 1 to 2. Third, 95% of the sample is predicted to have individual linear rates of change from sessions 2 to 6 of −133 to 67, indicating that although there is a decline on average (because the fixed slope26 $\gamma_{20} = -32.9$ was significantly different than 0), not everyone is predicted to improve (decline) in RT after session 2.

It is important to note that because piecewise slopes are not hierarchical, we could have tested the random slope26 variance regardless of whether the random slope12 variance was significant. In this case, however, we already knew that the random slope12 variance improved the model, so it made sense to continue by adding the random slope26 variance, rather than by removing the random slope12 variance and testing the random slope26 variance by itself (although we could have tested a random slope26 before a random slope12 instead). Finally, we note that although piecewise slopes are usually specified as linear slopes, a quadratic effect could also be tested for piecewise slopes that span three or more occasions. For instance, the change from session 2 to 6 could be described by both fixed linear and quadratic effects of slope26. However, adding a fixed quadratic effect for slope26^2 (not shown) did not significantly improve our model (Est = 5.8, SE = 3.5, p = .10), indicating that a linear effect of slope26 is sufficient.

So far we have examined piecewise models containing two slopes that directly represent the change in RT from session 1 to 2 (slope12) and between sessions 2 and 6 (slope26), and found significant average decline (and individual differences therein) during each phase. But we don't yet know whether the slopes *differ* across phases. Although we could calculate the numeric difference between the two slopes, we would not have a standard error (and thus a p-value) to assess whether the slopes were significantly different. So, to obtain a model parameter that would directly answer this question (as well as to be able to test whether persons differ randomly in their *differences between slopes*), we can use an alternative specification of the piecewise model, the **slope and deviation slope model,** in which a single continuous linear slope is specified during the entire time period (i.e., via a predictor of *time*), and then a second piecewise slope is specified that turns on before or after the breakpoint. The slope and deviation slope model can be made equivalent to the previous direct slopes models, but each provides slightly different information and thus may be more or less useful given the questions to be answered.

For instance, consider a study examining growth in children's learning before a new instruction method went into effect and then afterwards. If the new method was not more effective than the old method, this would be evidenced by children continuing on the same learning trajectory they were already on before the new method was implemented. In contrast, if the new method increased the rate of learning, then the slope representing the rate of learning over time should be *more positive* after the new method was implemented than before. Thus, in this situation, the investigators would *not* want to know if the slope for each phase was significantly positive—this is what they would have expected to begin with. Instead they would want to know if there is a *difference* between the positive slopes before and after the new method of instruction went into effect. Although the model-implied difference in the slopes could have been estimated using an additional programming statement, only by making the slope difference a direct model parameter could we examine individual random variation in the difference between the slopes (e.g., for differences in how children respond to the new instruction method).

To illustrate how the slope and deviation slope models can directly assess the difference between slopes using our RT data, we will replace slope12 by a predictor of time, as shown in the last three rows of Table 6.6. The result of this modification can be understood by revisiting how each predictor was originally created (as seen in Table 6.5). In each scenario, the time predictor is active across all six sessions, but the slope26 predictor is only active after session 2. Thus, *after controlling for the effect of slope26*, the effect of time becomes the *unique* effect for the change only between sessions 1 and 2. Likewise, *after controlling for the effect of time*, the effect of slope26 becomes the *unique* effect for how the linear slope differs after session 2.

In our first slope and deviation slope model (5a), a 5-parameter **fixed slope, fixed deviation slope, random intercept model,** the fixed intercept for the predicted RT at session 1 was still estimated as γ_{00} = 1,961.9 and the linear rate of change from session 1 to 2 was still estimated as γ_{10} = –163.6 per session (which is now indexed by time after controlling for slope26). The fixed effect of slope26 of γ_{20} = 130.8 per session is the new information—after controlling for time, it is the *difference* between the linear rates of change before and after session 2. That is, the linear rate of change before session 2 is γ_{10} = –163.6 per session, and the linear rate of change after session 2 is γ_{20} = 130.8 *less negative,* such that the rate of change after session 2 could be calculated as $\gamma_{10} + \gamma_{20}$ = –163.6 + 130.8 = –32.9, which is exactly what we obtained for the effect of slope26 in the previous direct slopes models. This is because the direct slopes model (4a) and the slope + deviation slope model (5a) are equivalent.

In model (5b), a 7-parameter **random slope, fixed deviation slope model,** a random effect of time has been added, and the $\tau_{U_1}^2$ variance of the random time slope (and its $\tau_{U_{01}}$ covariance with the random intercept) was a significant improvement over model (5a), $-2\Delta LL(\sim 2)$ = 49.3, $p < .001$ (with a smaller AIC and BIC as well). The interpretation of the random effect of time is somewhat strange, however. Although the fixed effect of time becomes the change between sessions 1 and 2 after controlling for slope26, in model (5b) the random effect of time has not yet been controlled for slope26. So, the model is asymmetric—the random effect of time represents individual differences in the linear rate of change *across all six sessions.*

Thus, we also need a random effect of slope26, as in the 10-parameter **random slope, random deviation slope model** (5c), in which the *difference* in the slope after session 2 can also vary across persons. The three new parameters (the variance $\tau_{U_2}^2$ of the random slope26 and its $\tau_{U_{02}}$ and $\tau_{U_{12}}$ covariances with the random intercept and random time slope) resulted in a significant improvement over model (5b), $-2\Delta LL(\sim 3)$ = 58.0, $p < .001$ (with a smaller AIC and BIC as well), indicating significant between-person variation in how the rate of decline in RT *changed* after session 2. But had model fit *not* improved, this would have meant that although there were individual differences in the rate of change during the whole period (given by time), the difference between the slopes (given by slope26) would have been the same across persons.

The results for model (5c) are shown in the third set of columns in Table 6.7. The 95% random effect CI for slope26 (as calculated from 130.8 ± 1.96*$\sqrt{69,916}$) indicates that 95% of the sample is predicted to differ in their rates of change after session 2 by –388 to 649. So, although the rate of change is *less negative* after session 2 on average (as shown by the positive significant fixed slope26 γ_{20} = 103.8), the negative values in the 95% slope26 random effect CI indicate that some people are instead predicted to have *more negative* rates of change after session 2. After controlling for the random effect of slope26, the random time slope variance now represents individual differences in the rate of change only between sessions 1 and 2 as before, and so the random slope and random deviation slope model (5c) is fully equivalent to the random direct slopes model (4c), just with re-arranged parameters.

Finally, we note that the choice to make the second slope the "deviation" slope was arbitrary. That is, the model could have also been specified using *time* and *slope12* instead, in which case slope12 would be the "deviation" slope. In that case, the effect of time after controlling for slope12 would become the linear slope from sessions 2 to 6, and the effect of slope12 after controlling for time would become the *difference* in the linear slope before session 2. So long as both slopes are random, these alternative models will have equivalent fit, just with re-arranged parameters. Whether any deviation slope has a fixed or random effect is always a testable hypothesis, so you should feel free to choose the one that best maps onto your questions.

In considering our original RT data to be modeled, although the random quadratic and random piecewise slope models both approximate the change in the mean and total variance of RT over the six sessions reasonably well, as seen in Figure 6.3, neither model makes a plausible prediction for the additional practice sessions. The random quadratic model predicts that RT should increase (or worsen) with additional practice (and show sharply increasing total variance over time), whereas the piecewise model predicts a constant decline in RT indefinitely (with total RT variance that also begins to increase over time). To address these limitations, we now turn to a third option that can explicitly account for change that "levels off" over time (as would be expected for such learning behavior), the exponential model of change, as described next.

2.C. An Exponential Model of Change

The **exponential model** is our first truly nonlinear model of change, in that it is nonlinear in its *parameters* rather than its *variables*. Because it is very different from the previous polynomial and piecewise slopes models, we will first examine the exponential model parameters more generally. For these data we will need a negative exponential model, so-named because the rate of change decreases over time. As illustrated in Figure 6.4, the negative exponential model we will be estimating for the six-session RT data contains three parameters: an *asymptote*, an *amount of change*, and a *rate of approach to asymptote*, such that y = *asymptote* + *amount**exp(*rate**time). The role of each parameter will be explained in turn.

First, the **asymptote** is the optimal level of performance to which the function of change over time is heading. In our example, because RT is decreasing over time, the asymptote will be a *lower* asymptote; for outcomes that should increase up to a maximum point, the asymptote would be an *upper* asymptote instead. Either way, the asymptote is the value of the outcome at which the function is predicted to level off across time. The functions of change over time in the top panel of Figure 6.4 have the same *amount* and *rate* parameters but differ in the *asymptote* that describes their optimal level of performance. Although it can be estimated from data, the asymptote is a theoretical parameter—it is defined as the tangent line to the function at infinity—and so the asymptote may not always be observed within the time frame of the data collected.

Second, the parameter for **amount of change** is the distance from the predicted outcome at asymptote to the predicted outcome at time 0 (session 1 here).

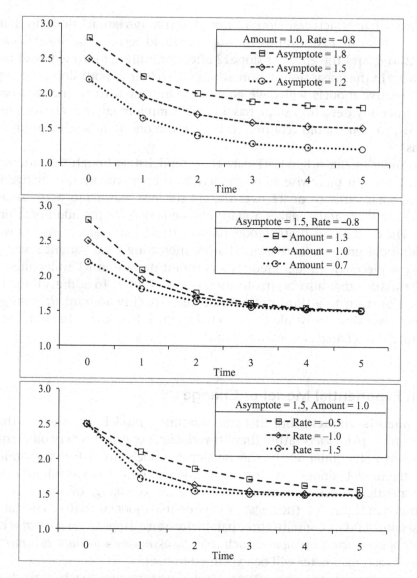

Figure 6.4 Example negative exponential model parameters.

To facilitate estimation, the form of our model takes into account the fact that RT is decreasing towards a lower asymptote as y = *asymptote* + *amount**exp(*rate**time), such that the *asymptote* is the intrinsic reference point of the model, and *not* time 0. Therefore, our amount parameter—for how far away the predicted outcome at time 0 is from the asymptote—will be a positive value. The functions in the middle panel of Figure 6.4 have the same *asymptote* and *rate* parameters but differ in their *amounts of change*. As shown, given the same asymptote and rate, different amounts of change translate into different predicted values at time 0. For this reason, the negative exponential model is sometimes modified to include a parameter for the *intercept* rather than for the *amount of change* (in which the intercept would simply be calculated as *asymptote + amount of change* here).

The third parameter is the **rate of approach to asymptote**, which appears in the nonlinear, exponential part of the function. The functions in the bottom panel of Figure 6.4 have the same *asymptote* and *amount* parameters but differ in their *rates of approach to asymptote*. As shown, the functions start at the same value at time 0, show the same amount of change, and will end at the same asymptote, but they differ in how quickly they get to asymptote—the function with the largest rate parameter (in absolute value) will get to the asymptote the fastest. In this plot, the line for rate = –0.5 doesn't yet hit asymptote, although the other lines at rate = –1.0 or –1.5 do.

The name of the exponential model is derived from the sign of its rate parameter, and *not* the direction of its change. That is, a *negative* exponential model could describe a *positive* rate of change that is slowing down as it approaches an *upper* asymptote or a *negative* rate of change that is slowing down as it approaches a *lower* asymptote (as we will see in our RT data). In contrast, a positive exponential model would include a *positive* rate parameter to describe a function that is moving *away* from the asymptote instead (i.e., the function is speeding up). Positive exponential functions are more commonly see in biological applications (e.g., exponential growth of bacteria over time), although they may have other applications as well.

As with other models of change we've examined, each parameter of our negative exponential model can have both a fixed part and a random part. The **fixed asymptote** is the optimal level of performance on average, whereas the **random asymptote** is an individual deviation from the fixed asymptote, such that the *random asymptote variance* would then capture the amount of individual differences in the asymptote. Likewise, the **fixed amount** is the amount of change from the outcome at asymptote to the outcome at time 0 to on average, whereas the **random amount** is an individual deviation from the fixed amount, such that the *random amount variance* would then capture the amount of individual differences in the amount of change over time. Finally, the **fixed rate** can be thought of as the rate of approach to asymptote on average, whereas the **random rate** is an individual deviation from the fixed rate, such that the *random rate variance* would then capture the amount of individual differences in the rate over time. However, the random rate variance may not always be possible to estimate (as we'll see shortly).

For ease of comparison, the negative exponential models to be examined for our six-session RT data are shown in Table 6.9. For each model, the first column provides the name and number of estimated parameters, the second column shows the multilevel equations, the third column provides the level-2 **G** matrix, and the fourth column lists the question to be answered. As before, in all models the level-1 **R** matrix will be a 6x6 diagonal matrix for the $n = 6$ sessions (in which σ_e^2 is constant with no covariance over time). Model estimates will be presented in the text below and given in Table 6.10. Because the exponential model is nonlinear, the total variance at each occasion will be predicted by a different function than $\mathbf{V} = \mathbf{ZGZ}^T + \mathbf{R}$, but can still be determined by the model, as shown in Table 6.11.

Table 6.9 Negative exponential model equations and level-2 G matrix for the six-session response time data (in which *time* = session − 1).

Model (# Total Parameters)	Model Equation	Level-2 G Matrix	Purpose (New Parameters)
6a Fixed Asymptote, Fixed Amount, Fixed Rate (4)	**Level 1:** $y_{ti} = \beta_{0i} + \beta_{1i} * \exp(\beta_{2i} * \text{Time}_{ti}) + e_{ti}$ **Level 2:** Asymptote: $\beta_{0i} = \gamma_{00}$ Amount: $\beta_{1i} = \gamma_{10}$ Rate: $\beta_{2i} = \gamma_{20}$	none	Obtain start values for fixed effects and σ_e^2
6b Random Asymptote, Fixed Amount, Fixed Rate (5)	**Level 1:** $y_{ti} = \beta_{0i} + \beta_{1i} * \exp(\beta_{2i} * \text{Time}_{ti}) + e_{ti}$ **Level 2:** Asymptote: $\beta_{0i} = \gamma_{00} + U_{0i}$ Amount: $\beta_{1i} = \gamma_{10}$ Rate: $\beta_{2i} = \gamma_{20}$	$\mathbf{G} = \left[\tau_{U_0}^2 \right]$	Are there individual differences in the asymptote? ($\tau_{U_0}^2$)
6c Random Asymptote, Random Amount, Fixed Rate (7)	**Level 1:** $y_{ti} = \beta_{0i} + \beta_{1i} * \exp(\beta_{2i} * \text{Time}_{ti}) + e_{ti}$ **Level 2:** Asymptote: $\beta_{0i} = \gamma_{00} + U_{0i}$ Amount: $\beta_{1i} = \gamma_{10} + U_{1i}$ Rate: $\beta_{2i} = \gamma_{20}$	$\mathbf{G} = \begin{bmatrix} \tau_{U_0}^2 & \tau_{U_{01}} \\ \tau_{U_{01}} & \tau_{U_1}^2 \end{bmatrix}$	Are there individual differences in the amount of change over time? ($\tau_{U_1}^2$ and $\tau_{U_{01}}$)
6d Random Asymptote, Random Amount, Random Rate (10)	**Level 1:** $\beta_{0i} + \beta_{1i} * \exp(\beta_{2i} * \text{Time}_{ti}) + e_{ti}$ **Level 2:** Asymptote: $\beta_{0i} = \gamma_{00} + U_{0i}$ Amount: $\beta_{1i} = \gamma_{10} + U_{1i}$ Rate: $\beta_{2i} = \gamma_{20} + U_{2i}$	$\mathbf{G} = \begin{bmatrix} \tau_{U_0}^2 & \tau_{U_{01}} & \tau_{U_{02}} \\ \tau_{U_{01}} & \tau_{U_1}^2 & \tau_{U_{12}} \\ \tau_{U_{02}} & \tau_{U_{12}} & \tau_{U_2}^2 \end{bmatrix}$	Are there individual differences in the rate of approach to asymptote? ($\tau_{U_2}^2$, $\tau_{U_{02}}$, and $\tau_{U_{12}}$)

Table 6.10 Negative exponential model parameters for the six-session response time data in which *time* = session − 1. Bold values are $p < .05$.

Model Parameter		Model 6a			Model 6b			Model 6c		
		Fixed Asymptote, Fixed Amount, Fixed Rate (Time 0 = Session 1)			*Random Asymptote, Fixed Amount, Fixed Rate (Time 0 = Session 1)*			*Random Asymptote, Random Amount, Fixed Rate (Time 0 = Session 1)*		
		Est	*SE*	*p <*	*Est*	*SE*	*p <*	*Est*	*SE*	*p <*
Model for the Means										
γ_{00}	Asymptote	**1,675.3**	54.8	.001	**1,675.3**	49.2	.001	**1,683.5**	45.5	.001
γ_{10}	Amount of Change	**284.7**	64.6	.001	**284.7**	24.5	.001	**279.9**	33.6	.001
γ_{20}	Rate of Approach to Asymptote	**-0.670**	0.42	.115	**-0.670**	0.16	.001	**-0.753**	0.12	.001
Model for the Variance										
$\tau^2_{U_0}$	Asymptote Variance				**200,656.0**	29,033.0	.001	**190,823.0**	27,870.0	.001
$\tau_{U_{01}}$	Asymptote-Amount Covariance							6,649.4	14,780.0	.654
$\tau^2_{U_1}$	Amount of Change Variance							**77,254.0**	15,828.0	.001
σ^2_e	Residual Variance	**234,532.0**	13,474.0	.001	**33,875.0**	2,131.8	.001	**23,039.0**	1,621.8	.001
ML Model Fit										
	Total Number of Parameters	4			5			7		
	–2LL	9,213.2			8,404.0			8,327.3		
	AIC	9,221.2			8,414.0			8,341.3		
	BIC	9,238.8			8,427.1			8,359.6		

Table 6.11 Predicted **V** matrix (with variances on the diagonal, covariances above the diagonal, and correlations below the diagonal), and means (with SE = standard errors) from the negative exponential models for the six-session response time data (in which time = session − 1).

Model Description and Parameters

			V Matrix			
Session	1	2	3	4	5	6

Random Asymptote, Random Amount, Fixed Rate: 7 total parameters (Model 6c)

	1	2	3	4	5	6
1	304,406	236,968	216,065	206,224	201,590	199,409
2	.88	237,243	203,487	198,441	196,065	194,947
3	.83	.89	220,604	194,776	193,464	192,846
4	.80	.88	.89	216,090	192,239	191,857
5	.79	.87	.89	.89	214,701	191,391
6	.78	.86	.89	.89	.89	214,211
Mean	1963.43	1815.29	1745.54	1712.70	1697.24	1689.96
SE	54.74	47.24	45.04	44.31	44.39	44.71

3 fixed effects (asymptote γ_{00}, amount γ_{10}, rate γ_{20})
Asymptote Variance $\tau_{U_0}^2 = 190,823$
Asymptote-Amount Covariance $\tau_{U_{01}} = 6,644.8$
Amount of Change Variance $\tau_{U_1}^2 = 77,254$
Residual Variance $\sigma_e^2 = 23,039$

Predicted Variance at Time *T*:
$$Var(y_T) = \sigma_e^2 + \tau_{U_0}^2 + 2*exp[\gamma_{20}*T]*\tau_{U_{01}} + (exp[\gamma_{20}*T])^{2*}\tau_{U_1}^2$$
Predicted Covariance between Time *A* and *B*:
$$Cov(y_A, y_B) = \tau_{U_0}^2 + (exp[\gamma_{20}*T_A] + exp[\gamma_{20}*T_B])*\tau_{U_{01}} + (exp[\gamma_{20}*T_A]*exp[\gamma_{20}*T_B])*\tau_{U_1}^2$$

In addition, because nonlinear models require special software (e.g., SAS NLMIXED), only ML estimation is available for these models, but the significance of new fixed or random effects will still be tested via Wald test p-values or -2ΔLL tests, respectively. For our model building strategy, because all three negative exponential parameters will be needed to describe the trajectory (i.e., they are not hierarchical), we will begin with fixed effects for the asymptote, amount, and rate, and then examine their random effects in separate sequential models.

Truly nonlinear models like the negative exponential can be very challenging to estimate, and often will not estimate at all without reasonable starting values (i.e., parameter values at which the likelihood-based algorithms can begin searching for the most likely estimates). Furthermore, because estimating the large values for the residual and random effects variances in our example data may lead to estimation problems, the example code provided will estimate their standard deviations, and then square those values to obtain the actual variances for reporting the model results. As a result of these issues, the sole purpose of the first model is to obtain starting values for our subsequent models, and at each step we will use the estimates from the previous model as starting values for the next model. Thus, we begin with the simplest possible model (6a), the 4-parameter **fixed asymptote, fixed amount, and fixed rate model,** as shown in the first row of Table 6.9, which includes no random effects and thus ignores the dependency of the residuals from the same person. It provides us with estimates for the fixed asymptote of $\gamma_{00} = 1675.3$, for the fixed amount of change of $\gamma_{10} = 284.7$, for the fixed rate of approach to asymptote of $\gamma_{20} = -0.67$, and for the residual variance (which is currently all of the outcome variance, not just the level-1 residual variance) of $\sigma_e^2 = 234,532$. Putting these together, the model predicts the function for change in RT over time on average to asymptote at $\gamma_{00} = 1675.3$, which is lower than the predicted RT at time 0 (session 1) by the amount $\gamma_{10} = 284$, such that the predicted intercept at time 0 should be $\gamma_{00} + \gamma_{10} = 1675.3 + 284.7 = 1960.0$.

We can now estimate model (6b) in Table 6.9, the 5-parameter **random asymptote, fixed amount, fixed rate model,** which now includes a U_{0i} term for a random asymptote in the level-2 equation for β_{0i}, by which people are allowed to differ in their asymptotes, which here represent the theoretical optimal level of RT for performing this task given infinite practice. Testing the addition of the random asymptote variance $\tau_{U_0}^2$ relative to model (6a) with no random effects yields -2ΔLL($\sim$1) = 809.1, $p < .001$ (with a smaller AIC and BIC as well), or a significant improvement in fit by allowing each person his or her own asymptote. However, only allowing a random asymptote is like allowing only a random intercept, in that the model then predicts constant total variance (of $\tau_{U_0}^2 + \sigma_e^2$) and constant total covariance (of $\tau_{U_0}^2$) over time, or parallel trajectories across persons. We already know that the variance in RT declines over time, and as such, that additional random effects that incorporate change over time will likely be needed.

Accordingly, we continue with model (6c) in Table 6.9, the 7-parameter **random asymptote, random amount, fixed rate model,** which now includes a U_{1i} term for a random amount of change in the level-2 equation for β_{1i}, by which people are allowed to differ in the overall amount of change between the asymptote and the predicted outcome at time 0. Testing the addition of the $\tau_{U_1}^2$ variance for the random amount parameter (and its $\tau_{U_{01}}$ covariance with the random asymptote) relative to model (6b) with only a random asymptote variance yields $-2\Delta LL(\sim2) = 76.7$, $p < .001$ (with a smaller AIC and BIC as well), or a significant improvement in fit by allowing each person his or her own amount of change. Finally, we consider model (6d), the 10-parameter **random asymptote, random amount, random rate model**, which now includes a U_{2i} term for a random rate of approach to asymptote in the level-2 equation for β_{2i}, in which the rate of approach to asymptote was also allowed to have a random variance. However, model (6d) would not estimate, even when using the parameter estimates from model (6c) as starting values or changing the scale of the RT outcome, and thus its improvement in fit could not be evaluated. Random effects are usually more difficult to estimate for parameters in the nonlinear part of the function; here the six occasions likely do not provide enough information with which to estimate a random rate variance. Consequently, we must assume a fixed rate across persons instead.

Thus, our best-fitting negative exponential model (6c) contains a random asymptote and a random amount of change, but a fixed rate of approach to asymptote. As shown in the top of Figure 6.5 and in Table 6.10, the negative exponential model predicts an average function with an *asymptote* for an optimal value of $\gamma_{00} = 1683.5$, which is lower than the predicted RT at time 0 (session 1) by the *amount* of $\gamma_{10} = 279.9$, such that the predicted intercept at session 1 is $\gamma_{00} + \gamma_{10} = 1,683.5 + 279.9 = 1963.4$. The function reaches asymptote at a *rate* of $\exp(-0.75*time)$. As shown in Table 6.11, the total variance and covariance over time in the **V** matrix is predicted to change as a function of the exponential part of the equation for change over time, $\exp(rate*time)$.

To describe the random individual variation, we can again compute 95% random effects confidence intervals for the parameters with random effects, as shown in Equation (6.5):

Random Effect 95% CI = fixed effect $\pm \left(1.96*\sqrt{\text{Random Variance}}\right)$

$$\text{Asymptote 95\% CI} \quad = \gamma_{00} \pm \left(1.96*\sqrt{\tau_{U_0}^2}\right) \rightarrow 1,683.5 \pm \left(1.96*\sqrt{190,823}\right)$$

$$= 827 \text{ to } 2,540 \tag{6.5}$$

$$\text{Amount 95\% CI} \quad = \gamma_{10} \pm \left(1.96*\sqrt{\tau_{U_1}^2}\right) \rightarrow 279.9 \pm \left(1.96*\sqrt{77,254}\right)$$

$$= -265 \text{ to } 825$$

The model predicts that 95% of the sample should have individual asymptotes for optimal performance between 827 and 2,540 msec, and that 95% of the sample should have individual amounts of change between –265 and 825 msec. Recall that the amount of change in this model is *from* the asymptote *to* the predicted outcome at time 0 (and thus the parameter for the amount of change should be positive given that RT is higher—meaning slower—at time 0 than at asymptote). So, the fact negative amount values are included in the 95% random effect CI means that some people are expected have *lower* outcomes at time 0 than at their asymptote, or more simply, that RT is actually predicted to increase over time for those persons. This is an unexpected and potentially suspicious result worthy of some troubleshooting, as described next.

One issue in estimating nonlinear models is that their results can be sensitive to the starting values used, such that different starting values may lead to different results. In our case, specifying different starting values did not change the model estimates, suggesting they were stable. Furthermore, the *gradient* value listed for each parameter (i.e., its partial first derivative, or the rate of change in the likelihood function at that parameter value; see chapter 5) was near 0 as needed, indicating that the ML estimation routine did appear to have converged on the most likely value for each parameter. Another issue to consider is that 95% random effects CIs assume a symmetric and normal distribution of the random effects. If this is not the case (e.g., U_{1i} has a skewed distribution instead), then the CI may not be a useful descriptor of the distribution of the random effect. In examining the empirical Bayes predictions for the random effects from this model, however, their distributions did appear normal, so skewness of the U_{1i} random amount of change parameter was also not responsible for the strange CI. In examining the data of individuals with positive predicted amounts of change, however, they did indeed show an increase (worsening) of RT from session 1 to 6. Thus, this strange result appears to be real!

2.D. Comparing Model Predictions and Fit Across Families of Models for Change Over Time

The predicted means and total variances over time from model (6c) as compared with those from the previous best models from each family are shown in Figure 6.5, in which all predictions are provided using ML estimation so that they are directly comparable. As shown in the top of Figure 6.5, similar to the random quadratic and random two-slope piecewise model, the negative exponential model (with a random asymptote and random amount, but a fixed rate) does a good job describing the mean trajectory of RT across the six sessions given by model (0). But unlike the other models, the negative exponential model predicts that mean RT should "level off" over time (i.e., it should approach a lower asymptote), which is more realistic than predicting future sessions in which mean RT would begin increasing (by the quadratic model) or continue decreasing at a constant rate indefinitely (by the two-slope piecewise model). Similarly, as shown in the bottom of Figure 6.5, the negative exponential model predicts the total RT variance to decrease and eventually become constant over time (i.e., once people are at their asymptotes, their predicted trajectories will be parallel), which seems more reasonable than predicting that the RT variance should begin to increase over time in a quartic trend (by the quadratic model) or a quadratic trend (by the two-slope piecewise model). But the negative exponential model does not seem to predict the total variance across the observed sessions as well as the other models.

So how can we decide which option we should consider as our "best" unconditional model to describe the effects of time (to which we would then add effects of other predictors)? Recall from chapter 5 that the fit of models that differ in the

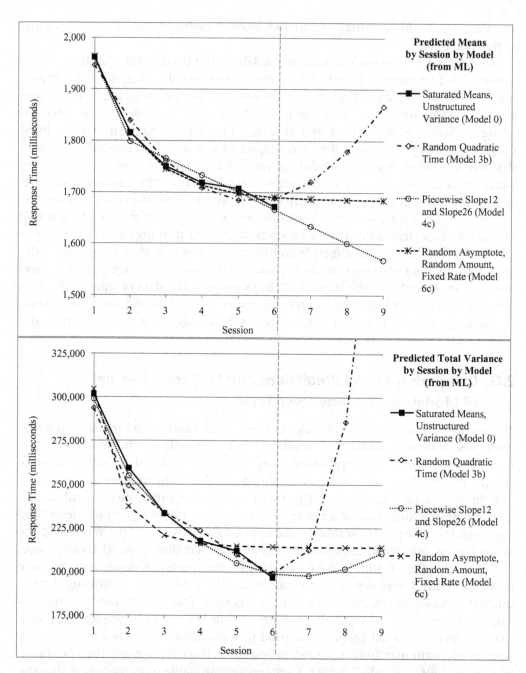

Figure 6.5 Predicted means (top panel) and variances (bottom panel) by model for the six-session response time data (with three extra sessions predicted after the vertical line).

fixed effects in their model for the means can only be compared via –2LL, AIC, and BIC values from ML, and not from REML. Accordingly, the ML model fit indices (in which smaller values indicate a better-fitting model) are shown in Table 6.12 for five models organized from most to least parsimonious (i.e., starting with the

Table 6.12 Comparison of ML model fit across families of models for the six-session response time data.

Model	Total # Parameters	ML −2LL	ML AIC	ML BIC
1b Most Parsimonious Baseline: Empty Means, Random Intercept	3	8546.3	8552.3	8560.2
6c Negative Exponential: Random Asymptote, Random Amount, Fixed Rate	7	8327.3	8341.3	8359.6
3b Polynomial: Random Quadratic Time	10	8321.8	8341.8	8367.9
4c Piecewise: Random Slope12, Random Slope26	10	8298.9	**8318.9**	**8345.1**
0 Least Parsimonious Baseline: Saturated Means, Unstructured Variance	27	**8278.1**	8332.1	8402.7
1b Fit better than Empty Means, Random Intercept Model?	Δdf	ML −2ΔLL	$p <$	
6c Negative Exponential: Random Asymptote, Random Amount, Fixed Rate	4	219.0	.001	
3b Polynomial: Random Quadratic Time	7	224.6	.001	
4c Piecewise: Random Slope12, Random Slope26	7	247.4	.001	
0 Least Parsimonious Baseline: Saturated Means, Unstructured Variance	24	268.2	.001	
0 Fit worse than Saturated Means, Unstructured Variance Model?	Δdf	ML −2ΔLL	$p <$	
1b Most Parsimonious Baseline: Empty Means, Random Intercept	24	268.2	.001	
6c Negative Exponential: Random Asymptote, Random Amount, Fixed Rate	20	49.3	.001	
3b Polynomial: Random Quadratic Time	17	43.7	.001	
4c Piecewise: Random Slope12, Random Slope26	17	20.9	.233	

fewest total number of parameters). As expected, the worst absolute fit (as indicated by the largest −2LL) belongs to the empty means, random intercept model (1b) that predicts no change and constant variance and covariance over time (and which is always estimable). The best absolute fit belongs to the saturated means, unstructured variance model (0) that perfectly describes the *n* means over time by estimating *n* fixed effects and also estimating all possible variances and covariances separately (and which is only estimable for outcomes with balanced time). As also shown in Table 6.12, the empty means, random intercept model (1b) fit significantly worse than every other model, while the saturated means, unstructured variance model (0) fit significantly better than every other model except the random two-slope piecewise model (4c; which thus had good *absolute* fit). The negative exponential, polynomial, and piecewise models are non-nested and thus can be compared only with their ML AIC and BIC values—both prefer the random two-slope piecewise model (1b).

Furthermore, we note that in every model the level-1 e_{ti} residuals were assumed to have equal variance and no covariance over time (i.e., a diagonal **R** matrix). As we saw in chapters 4 and 5, these assumptions are testable, such that additional parameters for correlation of the e_{ti} residuals (e.g., in an autoregressive or Toeplitz pattern) or heterogeneity of residual variance could also be tested for the polynomial and piecewise models (although this is limited by the software for estimating nonlinear models like the negative exponential). In these data, however, the addition of residual correlation parameters never improved model fit, and including heterogeneous residual variances over time lead to estimation problems. Thus, it appears reasonable to assume equal variance and no covariance for the e_{ti} residuals of the RT outcome over time in the level-1 **R** matrix (after including the random effects variances and covariances in the level-2 **G** matrix).

To summarize, in terms of empirical criteria, the piecewise model that includes separate random linear slopes between sessions 1 and 2 (slope12) and between sessions 2 and 6 (slope26) appears to be the most parsimonious model for describing the pattern of mean change over time and individual differences therein that still achieves reasonable fit to the data. However, it is also the most atheoretical, in that the breakpoint at session 2 is not inherently meaningful, but is used simply as a means to approximate a nonlinear pattern of decline over time. The second-place model according to the ML AIC and BIC would be negative exponential model, which is more theoretically appealing, but doesn't fit the observed data quite as well. Which model should be used to move forward may be debatable based on the relative importance the analyst places on these empirical versus theoretical criteria. A reasonable compromise may be to test the effects of predictors within both the two-slope piecewise model and the negative exponential model to see how the substantive conclusions might change based on how change over time is described.

Finally, there are many other nonlinear model variants that we might also consider, many of which also predict change to level off over time (see Singer & Willett, 2003, for models designed for learning data, or Sit & Poulin-Costello, 1994, for a large catalog of options for modeling curves). However, in many of these models the parameters related to change are embedded in a nonlinear function (e.g., 1 / slope*time in the hyperbolic model), and as such any random effects variances for these parameters can be challenging to estimate. The advantage of the exponential model is that it includes both the asymptote and the amount of change outside the nonlinear function, such that their random effects variances can be estimated more readily.

2.E. Options for Nonlinear Models by Number of Occasions

So far we've evaluated fixed and random effects related to time in three families of models for change (polynomial, piecewise, exponential) without considering the data requirements for estimating these effects. We do so now for two to five occasions of data.

In general, the goal of evaluating fixed effects of time is to reproduce the observed means over time using as few parameters as possible—that is, to predict (rather than just describe) the pattern of change over time on average. A general rule in evaluating how many *fixed effects for time* can be estimated in balanced data (i.e., in which everyone is on the same measurement schedule) is $n - 1$, in which n is the maximum number of occasions per person. The 1 extra parameter not available is reserved for estimating the fixed intercept (or for a similar parameter that would describe outcome level, such as an asymptote in the exponential model).

For example, given two occasions, you could only estimate a fixed intercept and a fixed linear effect of time, which would perfectly describe the two means over time. Given three occasions, you could estimate a polynomial model with three fixed effects for the intercept, linear time slope, and quadratic time slope, or a piecewise model with three fixed effects for the intercept and for two linear slopes, or an exponential model with three fixed effects for the asymptote, amount of change, and rate of approach to asymptote (although estimation of the latter model might be problematic with only three occasions). The three fixed effects estimated in each of those models would perfectly reproduce the mean at each of the three occasions. Given four occasions, you could estimate a polynomial model with four fixed effects for the intercept, linear, quadratic, and cubic (time^3) effects of time. Another possibility is a piecewise model with four fixed effects for the intercept and for three linear piecewise slopes, or for an intercept, one piecewise linear slope, and one piecewise linear and quadratic slope. The four fixed effects in each of these models would perfectly reproduce the mean at each of the four occasions. Likewise, given five occasions, up to four fixed effects for time could be estimated.

In balanced data, a model with as many fixed effects for time as there are $n - 1$ occasions will fit the means over time perfectly, and will thus be equivalent to a saturated means model. As discussed in chapter 10, however, exceptions to this rule can occur in unbalanced data, in which the pattern of change over time to be modeled results from aggregating the data across persons with distinct values of time. For instance, consider an accelerated longitudinal design in which persons ranging continuously in age from 20 to 50 years at baseline are sampled at four annual occasions. If *age* is used as the index of *time*, then the fixed effects in the model for the means must describe the overall pattern of change from age 20 to 53. Thus, even though each person's four outcomes would only contribute to a small portion of the overall trajectory, many more than three fixed effects for time could be estimated to predict all possible means from age 20 to 53. However, given the large number of possible distinct age values, a saturated means model (i.e., that would include a separate mean for each unique value of age) may not be estimable. In such cases, it may be useful *for descriptive purposes only* to temporarily round the time variable into convenient intervals, just for the sake of estimating a saturated means model with which to visualize the overall mean trajectory. For instance, we could estimate a saturated means model for age rounded into 2-year intervals to get a general sense of what the mean pattern from age 20 to 53 looks like before trying to predict it with a more parsimonious model. However, the rounded time predictor should *never* be used in subsequent analyses (and the fit of the saturated means model with rounded time should not be compared to the fit of subsequent models, either).

An alternative approach that may ultimately be more useful for such data is to model change within persons as a function of time (i.e., across the $n = 4$ occasions), but use age at the first occasion as a predictor. These options will be presented in more detail in chapter 10.

The preceding discussion focused on the number of fixed effects related to time that could be estimated in the model for the means given n occasions per person. We now consider the other side of the model—how many random effects can be estimated given n occasions per person. In general, the purpose of including random effects of time is twofold: to quantify individual differences related to the effects of time, and to predict the outcome variances and covariances over time using as few parameters as possible. A general rule for the number of *random effects related to time* that can be estimated is $n - 2$, in which n is the maximum number of occasions per person. The 2 extra parameters not available are reserved for estimating the level-1 residual variance and the level-2 random intercept variance that allows the residuals from the same person to be correlated (or for an analogous parameter to describe variance in outcome level, such as a level-2 random asymptote variance). This rationale is further illustrated in Table 6.13, which shows the degrees of freedom available with which to estimate the random effects variances and covariances as a function of the n occasions per person. This is the point at which you are likely to be sorely disappointed if you have only two or three occasions of data!

First, given two occasions, there are two variances and one covariance over time to be predicted, and thus three degrees of freedom with which to estimate the model for the variance. Accordingly, the only random effect that can be estimated is for the intercept, because individual differences in linear change *cannot* be distinguished from level-1 residual variance using only two occasions (as was illustrated in chapter 3). If the total variance differs between the two occasions, then an unstructured variance model that estimates each variance separately should be used instead. Second, given three occasions (for which there are three variances and three covariances to be predicted, creating six degrees of freedom), the **G** matrix can be extended to include a single random slope related to time in addition to a random intercept (and their covariance)—but only one random slope! Thus, the highest-order polynomial model that could be estimated for three occasions would be a fixed quadratic, random linear time model—a random quadratic effect of time cannot be distinguished from the level-1 residual variance. This restriction of only one random slope given three occasions is especially problematic for a two-slope piecewise model—what this means is that although one of the piecewise slopes could be random, the other slope cannot. But as we saw earlier, specifying one

Table 6.13 Degrees of freedom with which to estimate random effects variances and covariances by n occasions per person.

n	Variances and Covariances over Time for n Occasions	Degrees of Freedom Available	G Matrix of Random Effects Variances and Covariances (in addition to a diagonal R matrix with σ^2_e)	Total Parameters in the Model for the Variance
2	$\begin{bmatrix} \text{Var}_1 & \\ \text{Cov}_{21} & \text{Var}_2 \end{bmatrix}$	3	$\mathbf{G} = \begin{bmatrix} \tau^2_{U_0} \end{bmatrix}$	2: 1 parameter in **G** 1 parameter in **R**
3	$\begin{bmatrix} \text{Var}_1 & & \\ \text{Cov}_{21} & \text{Var}_2 & \\ \text{Cov}_{31} & \text{Cov}_{32} & \text{Var}_3 \end{bmatrix}$	6	$\mathbf{G} = \begin{bmatrix} \tau^2_{U_0} & \tau_{U_{01}} \\ \tau_{U_{01}} & \tau^2_{U_1} \end{bmatrix}$	4: 3 parameters in **G** 1 parameter in **R**
4	$\begin{bmatrix} \text{Var}_1 & & & \\ \text{Cov}_{21} & \text{Var}_2 & & \\ \text{Cov}_{31} & \text{Cov}_{32} & \text{Var}_3 & \\ \text{Cov}_{41} & \text{Cov}_{42} & \text{Cov}_{43} & \text{Var}_4 \end{bmatrix}$	10	$\mathbf{G} = \begin{bmatrix} \tau^2_{U_0} & \tau_{U_{01}} & \tau_{U_{02}} \\ \tau_{U_{01}} & \tau^2_{U_1} & \tau_{U_{12}} \\ \tau_{U_{02}} & \tau_{U_{12}} & \tau^2_{U_2} \end{bmatrix}$	7: 6 parameters in **G** 1 parameter in **R**
5	$\begin{bmatrix} \text{Var}_1 & & & & \\ \text{Cov}_{21} & \text{Var}_2 & & & \\ \text{Cov}_{31} & \text{Cov}_{32} & \text{Var}_3 & & \\ \text{Cov}_{41} & \text{Cov}_{42} & \text{Cov}_{43} & \text{Var}_4 & \\ \text{Cov}_{51} & \text{Cov}_{52} & \text{Cov}_{53} & \text{Cov}_{54} & \text{Var}_5 \end{bmatrix}$	15	$\mathbf{G} = \begin{bmatrix} \tau^2_{U_0} & \tau_{U_{01}} & \tau_{U_{02}} & \tau_{U_{03}} \\ \tau_{U_{01}} & \tau^2_{U_1} & \tau_{U_{12}} & \tau_{U_{13}} \\ \tau_{U_{02}} & \tau_{U_{12}} & \tau^2_{U_2} & \tau_{U_{23}} \\ \tau_{U_{03}} & \tau_{U_{13}} & \tau_{U_{23}} & \tau^2_{U_3} \end{bmatrix}$	11: 10 parameters in **G** 1 parameter in **R**

slope as random while the other is fixed means assuming compound symmetry for the occasions included in the fixed slope. So, if all three variances differ over time, an unstructured variance model is again recommended instead. Although there may be individual differences in both piecewise slopes, they cannot both be distinguished from level-1 residual variance at the same time given only three occasions.

Third, given four occasions (and ten degrees of freedom), a **G** matrix with two random slopes related to time is now possible. So, the highest-order polynomial model that could be estimated for four occasions would be a fixed cubic, random quadratic time model (but a random cubic effect could not be distinguished from the level-1 residual variance). Similarly, a two-slope piecewise model given four occasions could now include random effects for both slopes, even if one of the slopes is based only on two occasions. But if a piecewise model with three slopes were specified for the four occasions, then only two of the slopes could be random. Fourth, given five occasions (and fifteen degrees of freedom), a **G** matrix with three random slopes related to time is now possible. So, for five occasions, the highest-order polynomial model that could be estimated would be a fixed quartic (time^4), random cubic time model (although a random cubic effect may be highly unlikely in real data). Similarly, a piecewise model for five occasions could now include fixed effects for up to four fixed slopes, and random effects for up to three slopes.

If time is unbalanced across persons, exceptions to the rule of $n - 2$ random slopes related to time may occur in practice, such that additional random slopes may be able to be estimated to predict the total variances and covariances across occasions in the overall aggregated trajectory. But as discussed in chapter 5, though, models with additional random effects are more likely to have estimation problems because each new random effect variance and covariance adds another dimension to the problem of simultaneously finding the variance parameter values that result in the highest log-likelihood. This is true for both balanced and unbalanced data. So, just because a model with multiple random slopes *could* be estimated based on the number of occasions doesn't mean it *can* be estimated in a given data set. If a random slope variance is estimated as exactly 0 (or an error message says the **G** matrix is *not positive definite*), this means a trustworthy estimate of the random slope variance cannot be found, and so it should not be retained.

Finally, although you may be tempted to "save" degrees of freedom by not estimating all possible random effects covariances, this is *not* recommended. As seen in chapter 5, the values of these covariances are highly conditional on the centering of time (i.e., on where time 0 happens to be). So, just because a covariance was nonsignificantly different than 0 as evaluated at a particular occasion doesn't mean it would stay that way if evaluated at another time 0. Just as the main effects of an interaction should stay in the model, so should the covariances among the random effects. Ignoring the embedded covariances among the random effects may lead to a biased estimate of the generalized variance of the **V** matrix, which could then propagate to other model parameters or their standard errors. Therefore, all covariances among the random effects need to be estimated in the model, even if they happen to be nonsignificant.

3. Models for Outcomes With Multiple Bends in the Rate of Change Over Time

The previous RT data were examined as an example of how to model a nonlinear pattern of change with a single bend (i.e., with deceleration or acceleration that remained constant across the study). The section below presents three options for describing more complex patterns of nonlinear change that include multiple bends (i.e., in which the rate of change changes more than once): a cubic polynomial model, a logistic model, and a three-slope piecewise model. However, in this section, the interpretation of these model parameters will be presented generally rather than by using a single example to demonstrate all of them. This is for two reasons: because the patterns of change observed with this level of complexity are likely to be data-idiosyncratic, and because fitting these models to data will require the exact same procedures and concepts as were demonstrated for the RT example data in the previous section. A general sequence for examining their fixed and random effects in practice will be recommended for each model, though.

3.A. A Cubic Model of Change

The first model to be presented is another polynomial model of continuous change, the **cubic model**, in which fixed (and potentially random) effects of time^1, time^2, and time^3 are included to represent the linear, quadratic, and cubic rates of change, respectively. Predicted outcome trajectories over time given eight combinations of fixed positive or negative linear, quadratic, and cubic effects of time are shown in Figure 6.6, in which time 0 is located in the middle of the data and the fixed intercept is approximately 50 in each plot (but slightly offset in order to distinguish the lines in each). Note that the specific patterns of change created by a cubic model will depend on the exact values of the linear, quadratic, and cubic effects as estimated from the data, so Figure 6.6 is intended to illustrate just a few possibilities. Furthermore, although all three effects operate continuously along the trajectory, the cubic effects can be seen most readily at the occasions furthest from time 0 (in which time 0 is located in the data center in Figure 6.6). Positive and negative cubic effects are shown by the squares and triangles, respectively.

Earlier we described quadratic models of change as predicting a *constant* change over time in the *linear* slope itself, such that the linear slope becomes more/less positive/negative over time, creating acceleration or deceleration (i.e., as seen in Figure 6.1). Similarly, we can describe cubic models of change as predicting a *constant* change over time in the *quadratic* slope itself (i.e., the acceleration or deceleration becomes more/less positive/negative over time). For instance, as shown in the top left panel in Figure 6.6, in the *accelerating positive* trajectory (created by positive linear and quadratic effects at time 0), the *positive* cubic effect works with

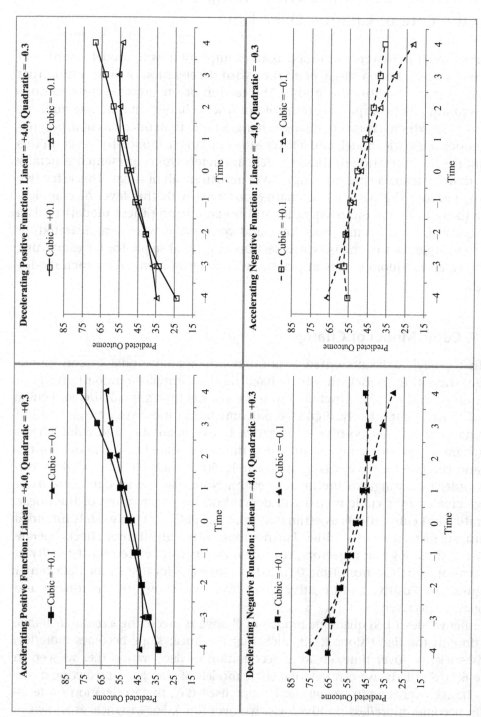

Figure 6.6 Predicted mean trajectories from positive or negative cubic effects of time in polynomial models of change.

the positive quadratic to create even more positive acceleration as time increases, whereas the *negative* cubic effect instead dampens the quadratic's positive acceleration as time increases. As shown in the top right panel, given a *decelerating positive* trajectory (created by positive linear and negative quadratic effects at time 0), the *positive* cubic effect works against the positive deceleration created by the negative quadratic, eventually creating positive acceleration (although not as much acceleration as if the quadratic were positive, as in the top left panel), whereas the *negative* cubic effect works with the negative quadratic to create even more positive deceleration as time increases. As shown in the bottom left panel, given a *decelerating negative* trajectory (with negative linear and positive quadratic effects at time 0), the *positive* cubic effect works with the positive quadratic to create even more negative deceleration as time increases, whereas the *negative* cubic effect works against the quadratic's positive deceleration as time increases, eventually creating negative acceleration. Finally, as shown in the bottom right panel, given an *accelerating negative* trajectory (with negative linear and quadratic effects at time 0), the *positive* cubic effect works against the negative acceleration created by the negative quadratic as time increases, eventually creating positive acceleration, whereas the *negative* cubic effect works with the negative quadratic to create even more negative acceleration as time increases.

Although the overall shape of change over time implied by a cubic model can be most easily explained through plots of model-predicted trajectories like those shown in Figure 6.6, the coefficients from a cubic polynomial model can be interpreted directly as well. A model with a random cubic effect of time (and its associated G matrix) is shown in Equation (6.6):

Level 1 : $y_{ti} = \beta_{0i} + \beta_1(\text{Time}_{ti}) + \beta_{2i}(\text{Time}_{ti})^2 + \beta_{3i}(\text{Time}_{ti})^3 + e_{ti}$

Level 2 : Intercept: $\qquad\qquad\qquad \beta_{0i} = \gamma_{00} + U_{0i}$

Linear Effect of Time: $\qquad \beta_{1i} = \gamma_{10} + U_{1i}$

Quadratic Effect of Time: $\beta_{2i} = \gamma_{20} + U_{2i}$

Cubic Effect of Time: $\qquad \beta_{3i} = \gamma_{30} + U_{3i}$

$$ \mathbf{G} = \begin{bmatrix} \tau^2_{U_0} & \tau_{U_{01}} & \tau_{U_{02}} & \tau_{U_{03}} \\ \tau_{U_{01}} & \tau^2_{U_1} & \tau_{U_{12}} & \tau_{U_{13}} \\ \tau_{U_{02}} & \tau_{U_{12}} & \tau^2_{U_2} & \tau_{U_{23}} \\ \tau_{U_{03}} & \tau_{U_{13}} & \tau_{U_{23}} & \tau^2_{U_3} \end{bmatrix} \tag{6.6} $$

First, just as in the quadratic polynomial model we saw previously, the *fixed intercept* γ_{00} is the model-predicted outcome at time 0, and the *random intercept variance* $\tau^2_{U_0}$ is the amount of individual differences among the predicted trajectories over time (based on the fixed effects and each person's random effects) at time 0. Second, just as in the quadratic model, the *fixed linear effect of time* (i.e., linear slope) γ_{10} is the instantaneous linear rate of change at time 0, and the random linear slope variance $\tau^2_{U_1}$ is the amount of individual differences in the linear rates of change at time 0. Third, because of the fixed cubic effect of time, the *fixed quadratic effect of time* (i.e., quadratic slope) γ_{20} is now conditional on time 0—it becomes half the instantaneous rate of acceleration or deceleration *specifically at time 0*. Furthermore, because of the random cubic effect of time, the random quadratic slope variance $\tau_{U_2}^2$ is also now conditional on time 0—it becomes the amount of individual differences in half the instantaneous rate of acceleration or deceleration specifically at time 0. The nine **G** matrix random effect covariances are all also conditional on time 0. Finally, the fixed cubic effect of time γ_{30} is the highest-order term in the model for the means and is thus unconditional—it is one-sixth the rate of change per unit time in the rate of acceleration over time, as explained below. Likewise, the random cubic slope variance $\tau_{U_3}^2$ is the highest-order term in the model for the variance and is also unconditional—it is the amount of individual differences in the cubic effect of time.

We can express how the higher-order polynomial effects of time work together to form cubic change using the same logic and process of differentiating the fixed effects with respect to time that was used previously used to describe the quadratic model, as seen in Equation (6.7):

Intercept (Position) at Time T: $\hat{y}_T = \gamma_{00} + (\gamma_{10}T) + (\gamma_{20}T^2) + (\gamma_{30}T^3)$

First Derivative (Velocity) at Time T: $\dfrac{d\hat{y}_T}{d(T)} = \gamma_{10} + (2\gamma_{20} + 3\gamma_{30}T)T$

$$(6.7)$$

Second Derivative (Acceleration) at Time T: $\dfrac{d^2\hat{y}_T}{d(T)} = 2(\gamma_{20} + 3\gamma_{30}T)$

Third Derivative (Jerk) at Time t: $\dfrac{d^3\hat{y}_T}{d(T)} = 6\gamma_{30}$

in which the first line writes the cubic model for change predicting the outcome $\hat{y}_T$ at time *T* (or *position*) from the model fixed effects, and the next three lines show the first, second, and third derivatives with respect to time that represent the function's velocity, acceleration, and jerk. As shown in the second line, the linear rate of change depends on both time and time²—twice the quadratic slope plus three times the cubic slope by time is how the model predicts the linear slope to change per unit time. As shown in the third line, the rate of acceleration of the change depends only on time—three times the cubic slope is how the model predicts the quadratic slope to change per unit time (which then gets multiplied by two to become the rate of acceleration). Finally, the change in the rate of acceleration (known in physics as the *jerk, surge,* or *jolt*) does not depend on time, as given by six times the cubic slope (the highest-order fixed effect of time).

The use of a cubic polynomial (which needs at least four occasions of data) is most likely to be driven by the shape of the mean trajectory (i.e., would be suggested by multiple bends). Therefore, a useful model-building strategy would be to test the fixed linear, quadratic, and cubic effects of time in a single model with a random effect only for the intercept. If the Wald test *p*-value for the fixed cubic effect is significant, then all lower-order fixed effects must remain in the model. From there, variances of the random linear, quadratic, and cubic slopes (and their covariances with the lower-order random effects at each step) should be added in sequential models (although at least five occasions of data are needed to test a random cubic slope). The model-predicted change over time in the total variance of the outcome can be derived as described earlier: A random linear slope implies variance that changes over time^2, a random quadratic slope implies variance that changes over time^4, and a random cubic slope implies variance that changes over time^9 (and may not be estimable even with five occasions of data). Fortunately, the model need not be symmetric on both sides—a fixed cubic effect of time could be paired with just a random intercept or just a random intercept and random linear time slope. However, all lower-order terms on the same side of the model must be included in order for each polynomial term to be properly interpreted—so if a random cubic slope variance was tested, this would require all three lower-order random variances for the intercept, linear slope, and quadratic slope to be included (i.e., a 4x4 **G** matrix), or else the random cubic slope variance won't represent just cubic slope variance.

An important consideration in testing higher-order random slope variances is where time 0 is located. Because the lower-order random slope variances are conditional on time 0, estimation problems may occur if time 0 is located in a region of the data with less variability. Estimation problems due to collinearity among the random effects may also occur when time 0 is at the beginning or the end of the data. For these reasons, it may be most feasible in estimating a cubic model to center time such that time 0 is in the middle of the data (e.g., as in Figure 6.6). Finally, to retain each model, its **G** matrix must be *positive definite*: all random effects variances must be positive; all random effects correlations as shown in **GCORR** must range from −1 to 1. Additional problematic patterns of covariance may also lead to non-positive definite **G** matrices.

Given that it can be specified as a linear model (and thus can be estimated using many traditional software programs for longitudinal models), the cubic polynomial model remains a popular option for modeling complex patterns of nonlinear change. Unfortunately, the cubic model suffers from some of the same limitations as the quadratic model, in that it will not make accurate predictions for change that should eventually "level off" by reaching a lower or upper asymptote—instead it will predict that the rate of change should eventually change directions. Furthermore, the polynomial fixed effects of time themselves do not readily correspond to theoretical notions of change. For instance, researchers don't often posit hypotheses about half the rate of acceleration (the quadratic coefficient) or one-sixth the rate of jerk (the cubic coefficient). Instead, researchers may have questions about specific aspects of the nonlinear growth process, such as the optimal level of performance that results after extended training, or the age at which the rate of improvement is the greatest.

Accordingly, we now consider two variants of another type of model that may provide more reasonable predictions in future occasions for how change should continue (or not), as well as more meaningful model parameters—the logistic model of change. Although many forms of logistic models have been described, we will examine two specific exemplars: the simpler (and easier to estimate) standard logistic model (as adapted from a model described by Choi, Harring, & Hancock, 2009), and the more flexible (but potentially harder to estimate) *Richards curve* logistic model (Richards, 1959; as described in Grimm & Ram, 2009).

3.B. A Logistic Model of Change

The **logistic model** predicts an S-shaped curve (also known as a *sigmoid* or *ogive* curve). A basic two-parameter version of the logistic model is shown in Equation (6.8):

Level 1: $y_{ti} = A_{Lower} + (A_{Upper} - A_{Lower}) * \dfrac{\exp[\beta_{0i} + \beta_{1i}(\text{Time}_{ti}) + e_{ti}]}{1 + \exp[\beta_{0i} + \beta_{1i}(\text{Time}_{ti}) + e_{ti}]}$

$$(6.8)$$

Level 2: Intercept: $\beta_{0i} = \gamma_{00} + U_{0i}$

Slope: $\beta_{1i} = \gamma_{10} + U_{1i}$

in which A_{Lower} is the lower asymptote for the lowest possible outcome and A_{Upper} is the upper asymptote for the highest possible outcome, both of which are assumed known here (and therefore are not represented using β placeholders with individual *i* subscripts). The level-1 placeholders of β_{0i} and β_{1i} represent the individual intercept and slope of the logistic function, each of which can potentially have a fixed and random effect, as seen in the level-2 model.

Although this logistic model is nonlinear in its parameters, it can be reparameterized to become a linear model so long as the lower and upper asymptotes can be set to known values—for example, if a test outcome is scored from 0% to 100% correct, then $A_{Lower} = 0$ and $A_{Upper} = 100$. More generally, the linear model version of the logistic model is shown in Equation (6.9):

Level 1: $\log\left[\dfrac{y_{ti} - A_{Lower}}{A_{Upper} - y_{ti}}\right] = \beta_{0i} + \beta_{1i}(\text{Time}_{ti}) + e_{ti}$

$$(6.9)$$

Level 2: Intercept: $\beta_{0i} = \gamma_{00} + U_{0i}$

Slope: $\beta_{1i} = \gamma_{10} + U_{1i}$

which now looks exactly like a random linear model of change, with one exception—it predicts a new transformed y_{ti} outcome instead of the original y_{ti} outcome. This transformation is known as the **logit** (or **log-odds**) **link** and is used in many other areas of statistics (e.g., logistic regression models, item response models). In this case, the new y_{ti} outcome being predicted is the natural log of the ratio for how far the outcome has moved from the lower asymptote ($y_{ti} - A_{Lower}$) to how far the outcome still is from the upper asymptote ($A_{Upper} - y_{ti}$). That is, the transformed outcome is the proportion of possible total change that has occurred by that occasion.

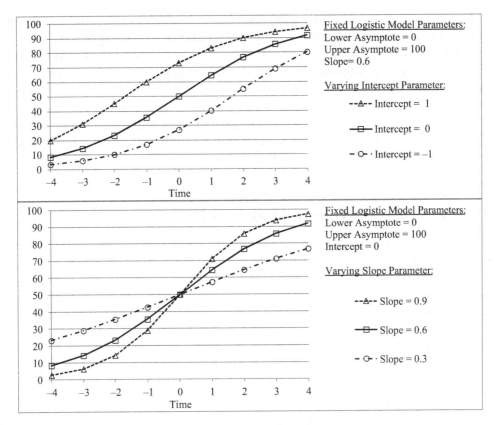

Figure 6.7 Predicted trajectories from standard logistic models of change.

The fixed intercept γ_{00} and fixed time slope γ_{10} then predict a straight line with respect to the logit-transformed y_{ti} outcome, which translates into a logistic, S-shaped function instead for the original y_{ti} outcome, as seen in Figure 6.7. The top panel illustrates variation in the intercept, in which the expected logit-transformed y_{ti} at time 0 of $\gamma_{00} = 1, 0,$ or -1 can be translated using Equation (6.8) into a predicted original y_{ti} outcome at time 0 of 73.1, 50.0, or 26.9, respectively. The bottom panel illustrates variation in the time slope, in which the expected increase in the logit-transformed y_{ti} per unit time is $\gamma_{10} = 0.9, 0.6,$ or 0.3, in which greater slopes predict more rapidly increasing functions over time (and more negative slopes would predict more rapidly decreasing functions over time). Critically, there is no direct translation of the fixed time slope γ_{10} as "per unit time" with respect to the original outcome, because the logistic model explicitly predicts that the expected outcome will "shut off" the closer it gets to either asymptote. That is, even though there is only one slope parameter, its effect is not constant over time in terms of the original outcome (although it is constant with respect to the logit-transformed outcome).

Although this logistic model may be useful in describing certain forms of non-linear growth, it does have some significant limitations. Namely, it assumes the upper and lower asymptotes can be set to known values for everyone. While this may be sufficient for outcomes with a known floor and ceiling (e.g., a test scored from 0%–100% correct), it would not be appropriate for unbounded outcomes, such as response time. Furthermore, it assumes the logistic function is symmetric, such that 50% of growth occurs before the point of inflection and 50% occurs after. Fortunately, these limitations can be overcome by augmenting the logistic model to include additional parameters, as described next.

3.C. A More Flexible Logistic Model of Change

Although many other variations of the logistic model of change exist, the version that is potentially the most flexible is the *Richards curve* (Richards, 1959), as described in Grimm and Ram (2009), and as shown in Figure 6.8. This logistic model has five parameters, each of which could potentially have fixed and random effects, as shown in Equation (6.10):

$$\text{Level 1}: \quad y_{ti} = \beta_{0i} + \frac{\beta_{1i}}{\left(1 + \beta_{4i} * \exp\left[-(\text{time}_{ti} - \beta_{2i}) * \beta_{3i}\right]\right)^{1/\beta_{4i}}} + e_{ti}$$

Level 2 : Lower Asymptote: $\beta_{0i} = \gamma_{00} + U_{0i}$

Amount of Change: $\beta_{1i} = \gamma_{10} + U_{1i}$ (6.10)

Time of Inflection: $\beta_{2i} = \gamma_{20} + U_{2i}$

Rate of Change: $\beta_{3i} = \gamma_{30} + U_{3i}$

Symmetry: $\beta_{4i} = \gamma_{40} + U_{4i}$

whose level-1 model for within-person change is the most complex function we've seen yet. Nevertheless, the structure of the level-2 model is exactly the same as the other model—the five β placeholders in the level-1 model are defined at level-2 by a fixed effect (the γ term) and potentially a random effect (the U term). Fortunately, not every parameter may need to be estimated for a given outcome—sometimes they may be set to known values, as described next.

First, β_{0i} is the placeholder for the **lower asymptote**, which is the lowest value of the outcome possible at any occasion. The lower asymptote may sometimes be a known value. For instance, if a test outcome was scored from 0% to 100% correct, then it may be reasonable to set the lower asymptote to 0 with no variance under the assumption that it is the same fixed value for everyone (i.e., γ_{00} and $\tau^2_{U_0}$ would not be estimated). But in other cases the lower asymptote may not be known (e.g., when the lower asymptote reflects the optimal RT after practice in a speeded task), and thus a fixed effect for the lower asymptote γ_{00} may need to be estimated. If individual differences in the lower asymptote are expected, then $\tau^2_{U_0}$ could be estimated, too.

Second, β_{1i} is the placeholder for the total possible **amount of change**. Given a lower asymptote β_{0i} and an amount of change β_{1i}, an upper asymptote could be

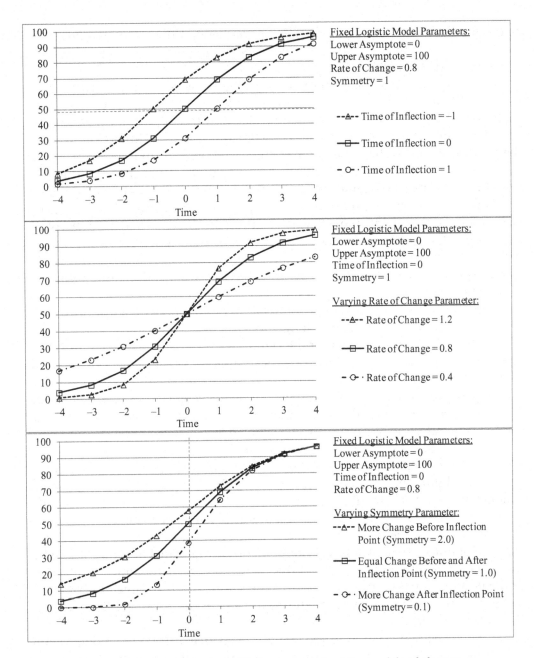

Figure 6.8 Predicted trajectories from Richards curve logistic models of change.

calculated as $\beta_{0i} + \beta_{1i}$, so another way to think of the amount of change is as the difference between the lower and upper asymptotes. As with the lower asymptote, the total possible amount of change could be a known value. For instance, if everyone was expected to begin at 0 and eventually reach a test ceiling of 100, then the amount of change could be set to 100 with no variance (i.e., γ_{10} and $\tau^2_{U_1}$ would not be estimated). But if all persons do not start and end at the same place, then the fixed amount of change γ_{10} and potentially its random variance across persons $\tau^2_{U_1}$ may need to be estimated.

The interpretation of the other three less-straightforward parameters is illustrated in Figure 6.8, in which for demonstration purposes all lower and upper asymptotes are fixed to 0 and 100, respectively, and in which time 0 is again in the middle of the data. The third parameter is β_{2i}, the placeholder for the **time of inflection**, which is the occasion at which the slope of the curve reaches its maximum before the curve "tips over" (i.e., goes from accelerating change to decelerating change). The functions in the top panel of Figure 6.8 have inflection times of $\beta_{2i} = -1$, 0, or 1, as indicated by the point on the curve where the slope is at its maximum. Fourth, β_{3i} is the placeholder for the **rate of change**, which controls the direction and steepness of the curve, such that *positive* rate values create *increasing* trajectories over time, whereas *negative* rate values create *decreasing* trajectories over time. The larger the rate of change is in absolute value, the steeper the trajectory will be: the steepest function in the middle panel of Figure 6.8 has the largest rate of change ($\beta_{3i} = 1.2$) and will reach asymptote the fastest, whereas the shallower functions with less positive rates of change ($\beta_{3i} = 0.8$ or 0.4) will take longer to reach asymptote.

Finally, β_{4i} is the placeholder for the **symmetry** parameter, which controls how much of the change occurs before the inflection point versus after. The functions in the bottom panel of Figure 6.8 have the same parameters for the time of inflection (β_{2i}) and rate (β_{3i}), but differ in their symmetry parameter (β_{4i}). In the middle function $\beta_{4i} = 1$, in which the same amount of change happens before and after the time of inflection. In other words, symmetry = 1 means perfect symmetry, as in the case in other logistic models in which the symmetry parameter is not estimated—the Richards version of the logistic model is unique in that it includes an estimated symmetry parameter instead. The absolute values for the symmetry parameter depend on the values of the other model parameters, but in general, the *greater* the symmetry value is than 1, the more change happens *before* the time of inflection; the *less* the symmetry value is than 1, the more change happens *after* the time of inflection. Consider for example the bottom panel of Figure 6.8. In the top function in which $\beta_{4i} = 2$, 60% of the change occurs by the time of inflection; in the bottom function in which $\beta_{4i} = 0.1$, only 40% of the change has happened by the time of inflection (as seen by the y-axis value at the point of inflection given the scale of 0–100).

As with the lower asymptote and amount of change, these other model parameters (time of inflection, rate of change, symmetry) could also differ across persons in theory. However, in practice their random effects variances and covariances may be challenging to estimate because they appear in the nonlinear part of the function. Therefore, a useful model-building strategy would be to first try to estimate all fixed effects (i.e., including the lower asymptote and amount of change if they are not already known). If estimation problems occur, it may be helpful to fix the symmetry parameter to 1 as well. Then, using the estimates from the previous model as starting values at each step, the random effects variances for each parameter could be estimated one at a time, starting with whichever parameter is most likely to show individual differences in the context of the data. This is why a **G** matrix was not shown for the logistic model in Equation (6.10)—because not all effects have to be random given that the model terms are not hierarchical (unlike those in the random cubic model). And as with the negative exponential model earlier, different starting values should be tried to ensure that the model converges onto as close to the same estimates as possible each time. If provided by the software (e.g., as in SAS NLMIXED), the gradient (i.e., the partial first derivative) value should also be examined for each parameter to ensure it is as close to 0 as possible. Otherwise, even if results appear, they may not be reliable.

Finally, we note that that many, many other models and model permutations have been developed to describe nonlinear change, including hybrid approaches (e.g., models that combine linear and exponential growth). More importantly, many truly nonlinear models can be re-parameterized as linear models in order to be estimated more easily (see Preacher & Hancock, 2012, and Sit & Poulin-Costello, 1994, for some examples). So, you need not feel that your data must follow one of these few example functions—there are literally hundreds more that could be used to describe continuous nonlinear change. But when trying to describe nonlinear change that is *discontinuous* instead, a piecewise linear model may be more fruitful, as described next.

3.D. A Piecewise Model for Discontinuity in Intercept and Slope

The cubic and logistic models presented thus far are continuous models of change, which are appropriate when there is no meaningful segregation of time (i.e., as in an observational study of development). But what about longitudinal studies in which the goal is to modify the intercept or rate of change, such as in interventions or experimental designs? Our final model of discontinuous change is well suited to capture change across meaningful, discrete phases of time.

Earlier we examined a two-slope piecewise model of discontinuous change, which fit the example RT data well, but which was limited in two respects. First, there was no theoretical reason for a change in the slope specifically at session 2—this breakpoint was chosen empirically and did not have any inherent meaning. Second, because the first slope only spanned two occasions, we could only test whether there was a different slope before and after the breakpoint, but not whether there was also a different intercept (which we will refer to as a *jump,* below).

To overcome these limitations, we consider a final hypothetical example of a three-phase intervention study designed to improve student learning, as illustrated in the top of Figure 6.9. This pretend study included both treatment and control groups, such that the distinction between phases was relevant for the treatment group only. First, a series of baseline observations was collected in phase 1 (time 0 to 3), in which the usual methods of instruction were utilized. Next, after phase 1, a new method of instruction was introduced, after which performance in phase 2 (time 4 to 7) was expected to improve immediately (i.e., a jump upon entering

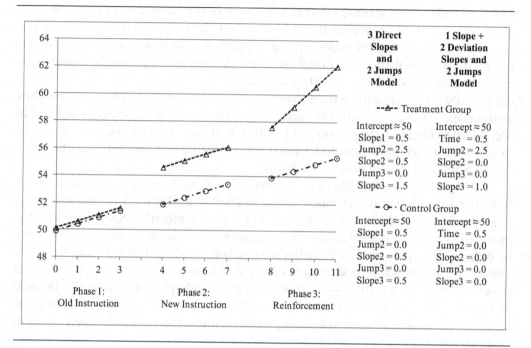

Model Predictors	Phase 1: Old Instruction				Phase 2: New Instruction				Phase 3: Reinforcement			
Time	0	1	2	3	4	5	6	7	8	9	10	11
Slope1	0	1	2	3	3	3	3	3	3	3	3	3
Jump2	0	0	0	0	1	1	1	1	1	1	1	1
Slope2	0	0	0	0	1	2	3	4	4	4	4	4
Jump3	0	0	0	0	0	0	0	0	1	1	1	1
Slope3	0	0	0	0	0	0	0	0	1	2	3	4

Conditional Logic Statements to Create Predictor Variables:
    IF (time ≥ 0 AND time < 4) THEN DO;
        slope1 = time; jump2 = 0; slope2 = 0; jump3 = 0; slope 3 = 0; END;
    ELSE IF (time ≥ 4 AND time < 8) THEN DO;
        slope1 = 3; jump2 = 1; slope2 = time − 3; jump3 = 0; slope 3 = 0; END;
    ELSE IF (time ≥ 8 AND time < 12) THEN DO;
        slope1 = 3; jump2 = 1; slope2 = 4; jump3 = 1; slope 3 = time − 7; END;

Figure 6.9 Example trajectories, predictor variable values, and conditional logic statements to create the predictor variable values from a piecewise model of change
with three slopes.

phase 2). Finally, during phase 3 (time 8 to 11), reinforcement was also provided
at each occasion, which was expected to create an increased rate of growth (i.e.,
a change in the phase 3 slope relative to the previous slopes), but no jump in the
intercept. The bottom panel of Figure 6.9 provides the coding for the jump and

slope predictor variables that will represent the shifts in the intercepts and slopes across phases (as well as the conditional logic statements to create those predictor variables). As with the two-slope piecewise models seen earlier, there are (at least) two different ways to specify this three-slope, two-jump piecewise model, as described next.

First, let's examine how the piecewise model could be specified to reflect the slopes for each phase directly, as well as the jumps in intercept between phases. An example **three direct slopes, two jumps model**, as estimated separately for each group in Figure 6.9, is shown in Equation (6.11):

Level 1: $y_{ti} = \beta_{0i} + \beta_1(\text{Slope1}_{ti}) + \beta_{2i}(\text{Jump2}_{ti}) + \beta_{3i}(\text{Slope2}_{ti})$
$$+ \beta_{4i}(\text{Jump3}_{ti}) + \beta_{5i}(\text{Slope3}_{ti}) + e_{ti}$$

Level 2: Intercept: $\beta_{0i} = \gamma_{00} + U_{0i}$

Slope1: $\beta_{1i} = \gamma_{10} + U_{1i}$

Jump2: $\beta_{2i} = \gamma_{20} + U_{2i}$ $\qquad$ (6.11)

Slope2: $\beta_{3i} = \gamma_{30} + U_{3i}$

Jump3: $\beta_{4i} = \gamma_{40} + U_{4i}$

Slope3: $\beta_{5i} = \gamma_{50} + U_{5i}$

Parameter values that would conform to the expected patterns for each group are given on the left-hand side of the legend in the top of Figure 6.9. Each group has a fixed intercept of $\gamma_{00} \approx 50$ for their predicted outcome at time 0 (offset slightly to better distinguish the lines). Let's begin by considering the treatment group, for which the distinctions between phases are relevant.

First, the predictor variable for *slope1* captures the slope specifically during phase 1 (i.e., the usual method of instruction): it starts at 0 and indexes the change in time during phase 1, but then shuts off afterwards (at its last value of 3). Here, the fixed effect for *slope1* of $\gamma_{10} = 0.5$ indicates that the outcome was predicted to increase by 0.5 per unit time during phase 1. If no other jump or slope parameters for the other phases were included, then the model would predict that the outcome value expected at time 3 should remain constant for the rest of the study.

The next two phases are each characterized by a *jump* and a *slope* that work together to describe the trajectory during each phase. The predictor variable for *jump2* represents the acute shift in the intercept at the beginning of phase 2 (i.e., immediately after receiving the new method of instruction): it has a value of 0 before phase 2 and a value of 1 afterwards. The predictor variable for *slope2* captures the slope specifically during phase 2: it is 0 until the end of phase 1, indexes the change in time during phase 2, and then turns off afterwards (at its last value of 4). The *jump2* variable is incremental to *slope2*—it is the shift in intercept above and beyond that created by *slope2*. So, putting these together, the fixed effect for *jump2* of $\gamma_{20} = 2.5$ and the fixed effect for *slope2* of $\gamma_{30} = 0.5$ indicate that at the first occasion in phase 2, the predicted outcome is higher than where it left off after phase 1 by $\gamma_{20} + \gamma_{30} = 2.5 + 0.5 = 3.0$, and the outcome is predicted to further increase during phase 2 by $\gamma_{30} = 0.5$ per unit time. Thus, if we consider the rate of growth in phase 1 (for *slope1*) of $\gamma_{10} = 0.5$ as a baseline for what would have been expected in phase 2, the new method of instruction appeared to create an acute shift in the intercept (because the jump to time 4 was 3.0 rather than the expected 0.5 given a one-unit change in time), but did not appear to modify the slope (i.e., because *slope1 = slope2*).

Continuing further along the trajectory for the treatment group, the predictor variable for *jump3* represents the acute shift in the intercept at the beginning of phase 3 (i.e., immediately after beginning reinforcement): It has a value of 0 before phase 3 and a value of 1 afterwards. The predictor variable for *slope3* captures the slope specifically during phase 3: It is 0 until the end of phase 2 and then indexes the change in time during phase 3. Putting these together, the fixed effect for *jump3* of $\gamma_{40} = 0.0$ and the fixed effect for *slope3* of $\gamma_{50} = 1.5$ indicate that at the first occasion in phase 3, the predicted outcome is higher than where it left off after phase 2 by $\gamma_{40} + \gamma_{50} = 0.0 + 1.5 = 1.5$, and the outcome is predicted to further increase during phase 3 by $\gamma_{50} = 1.5$ per unit time. Thus, upon entering phase 3, the jump to time 8 of 1.5 was exactly as expected based on the new slope during phase 3, but the new reinforcement did result in a greater rate of change (*slope3* of $\gamma_{50} = 1.5$ vs. *slope2* of $\gamma_{30} = 0.5$).

Although so far we have focused only on interpreting the fixed effects related to the jumps and slopes, each of these effects can potentially show random variation across persons as well, as indicated by the U terms in each level-2 equation. But as with the two-slope piecewise models for the RT data we saw before, these three piecewise slopes are not hierarchical, and thus random variances could be examined for any or all of the jumps and slopes, data permitting.

In considering the control group, however, because the distinctions between phases are irrelevant, a continuous trajectory across phases would be expected instead. If so, as shown in Figure 6.9, the slopes during each phase would be 0.5, and the jump effects for the acute shift in intercept between phases would be 0.0 (e.g., the next phase would begin 0.5 higher than the previous occasion as expected from a constant rate of change and no acute shifts in intercept). Thus, for the control group, a one-slope linear model would suffice.

But the inclusion of the control group does highlight some important information that is currently lacking. That is, the direct slopes version of the piecewise model tells us whether there was growth in each phase *per se*. But if we want to test the *difference in growth* across phases instead (and individual differences in the difference in growth across phrases), then we need a different version of the model, a **slope and two deviation slopes, two jumps model**, which would include a continuous slope and two deviation slopes to distinguish among the three phases. To do so, in Equation (6.11) the predictor variable for *slope1* would be replaced by the predictor of continuous *time*, which indexes the change in time across all twelve occasions, as seen in the bottom of Figure 6.9. Although the other predictor variables would stay the same, they would be interpreted differently in creating the same overall model trajectory.

First, beginning with the treatment group, the fixed effect of *time* would be $\gamma_{10} = 0.5$, which is the slope specifically during phase 1 after controlling for the other fixed effects (*jump2, slope2, jump3,* and *slope3*). However, unlike *slope1*, the *time* predictor doesn't shut off by taking a constant value of 3 across phases 2 and 3. As a result, the slope for phase 2 must now be interpreted as *incremental*—as the effect *after* controlling for a continuous linear time slope that operates throughout the study. Accordingly, the fixed effect of *slope2* is now $\gamma_{30} = 0.0$ rather than 0.5, because there is no difference in the rate of change between phase 2 (via *slope2*) and phase 1 (via *time*). In addition, the slope for phase 3 is incremental with respect to both time and the slope for phase 2. Thus, the fixed effect of *slope3* is now $\gamma_{50} = 1.0$ rather than 1.5, because the rate of change during phase 3 (via *slope3*) is more positive by 1 than the rate of change of 0.5 during phase 2 (via *time + slope2*). The jumps are estimated and interpreted the same as before because they still represent the incremental acute shift in intercept during each phase after considering the slope in each phase. Furthermore, any random effects for individual differences in the slope, deviation slopes, and jumps will mirror the interpretations of their fixed effects.

Second, for the control group, the fixed effect of *time* would be $\gamma_{10} = 0.5$, which is the slope specifically during phase 1 after controlling for the other fixed effects (*jump2, slope2, jump3,* and *slope3*). But because the rest of the trajectory follows the same slope of 0.5 per unit time, the other fixed effects will each be 0, meaning no incremental shift in phases 2 and 3 in the intercepts (via *jump2* and *jump3*) or in the slopes (via *slope2* and *slope3*) beyond what would have been expected based on phase1 (via *time*).

As with the two-slope piecewise model demonstrated with the RT data, any slope within a three-slope (or larger) piecewise model could logically be "the slope" as indicated by *time,* with the other slopes becoming slope deviations for the other phases. In such complex data many other possibilities may exist as well—ultimately the model specification should be chosen on the basis of creating interpretable parameters that most directly map onto the questions of interest.

4. Chapter Summary

The purpose of this chapter was to provide a plethora of options for describing nonlinear trajectories of within-person change. In each type of model, the parameters related to the level of the outcome or to change in the outcome over time can have *fixed effects* (which are included first and represent their average value in the sample) and potentially *random effects* (which are included second to represent individual differences in each parameter). In general for balanced data, a total of $n - 1$ fixed effects and $n - 2$ random effects related to time can be included in a model, in which n is the number of occasions per person. The options presented in this chapter within the general families of *continuous* or *discontinuous* change can be summarized as follows.

First, continuous models of change can be nonlinear in their variables and/or in their parameters. As a very common example of the first type, *polynomial models* use polynomial transformations of time to describe nonlinear trajectories. Quadratic models (i.e., with $time^1$ and $time^2$) can describe trajectories with a single bend, whereas cubic models (i.e., with $time^1$, $time^2$, and $time^3$) can describe trajectories with two bends. Polynomial models are hierarchical in both their fixed and random effects, such that all lower-order terms must be included for the higher-order terms to be interpreted properly. Although commonly used and easily estimated, the utility of polynomial models is limited when the predictions they make for what should happen on future occasions are not reasonable. For instance, linear models predict that the mean outcome should continue to change at a constant rate (i.e., either a constant increase or decrease) with variance that changes quadratically over time, whereas quadratic models predict that the mean outcome should eventually head in the opposite direction (i.e., what comes up must go down, what goes down must come up), with variance that changes quartically over time. In addition, polynomial model parameters do not readily lend themselves to theoretical interpretations.

In contrast, truly nonlinear models (i.e., that are nonlinear in their parameters rather than in their variables) may be more useful in describing change that is expected to "level off" over time. The *exponential* model is appropriate for patterns of continuous change that show a single bend over time and includes three parameters: as *asymptote* for the optimal level of performance, an *amount of change* for the difference between the outcome at asymptote and at time 0, and a *rate* for how quickly the trajectory approaches its asymptote. Although each parameter could show individual variability, a random variance for the rate parameter may be more challenging to estimate given that it occurs in the exponential part of the function (i.e., as exp[*rate**time]).

Logistic models are appropriate for patterns of continuous change that may show more than one bend. In a standard logistic model, change occurs in a symmetric, S-shaped pattern between fixed lower and upper asymptotes. The logistic model can be specified using parameters for an *intercept* (for the y-axis location of the curve at time 0) and *slope* (for how quickly the curve rises), which describe linear change in the transformed outcome, but nonlinear change in the original outcome. The more flexible Richards version of the logistic model also contains a parameter for rate of change and for the lower and upper asymptotes (that may be estimated instead of fixed to known values), as well as two other parameters: a *time of inflection* (i.e., the time at which the maximum slope occurs) and the *symmetry of the curve* (i.e., how much of the change occurs before the time of inflection). Each of these parameters could also show individual differences, although random effects variances may be more difficult to estimate for the parameters included in the nonlinear part of the model. Because truly nonlinear models can be more challenging to estimate in general, the stability of their results should be examined carefully (e.g., results are stable if the same estimates are obtained when using different starting values, and if the gradient value for each parameter is close to 0 as it should be).

In addition to models of continuous change, another method of approximating nonlinear trajectories is through discontinuous models of change. In piecewise slopes models, one or more theoretically or empirically derived breakpoints are used to divide the overall trajectory into distinct regions, across which discontinuities in intercept and/or slope may then be evaluated. There are two equivalent and complementary ways to specify a piecewise model. First, the slope during each distinct phase can be specified directly, which is useful in evaluating whether or not significant change occurred in each phase *per se*. Second, one of the piecewise slopes could be replaced with a continuous slope that indexes change across the entire trajectory, which is more useful in evaluating the *differences* between the slopes across phases instead (and individual differences in the differences between slopes across phases). Acute differences in intercepts between phases (i.e., jumps) can also be examined as needed in either model given at least three occasions per slope. Finally, piecewise models are not hierarchical, and so random effects of any of its jumps or slopes can be examined as needed (data permitting, of course).

5. Sample Results Section

The process of building an unconditional model to describe change over time before adding predictors is often greatly summarized in published work, and rarely would someone report examining as many models as we did for the RT data! That said, a complete summary of the results from each set of models presented for the RT example data would read as follows:

A series of unconditional longitudinal models were examined to describe the overall pattern of and individual differences in change in response time (RT in milliseconds) over six sessions in 101 older adults. Session was centered at 1 so that time 0 represented the first session in each model. An intraclass correlation (as calculated from an empty means, random intercept only model) was .82, indicating that 82% of the RT variance was due to person mean differences (i.e., random intercept variation), whereas 18% was due to within-person residual variation over time. Table 6.1 provides the results from a saturated means, unstructured variance baseline model in which each mean, variance, and covariance across the six occasions was estimated separately. We then evaluated the extent to which three types of models (polynomial, piecewise, and negative exponential models) could describe the patterns in Table 6.1 as parsimoniously but accurately as possible. All models were estimated using restricted maximum likelihood (REML) unless stated otherwise. Accordingly, the significance of fixed effects was evaluated via their Wald test p-values, and the significance of random effects was evaluated via $-2\Delta LL$ tests (i.e., likelihood ratio tests using degrees of freedom equal to the difference in the number of estimated parameters) and information criteria (AIC and BIC) between models with the same fixed effects. To describe the size of the random variation around each effect, 95% confidence intervals were computed as: fixed effect ±1.96*SQRT(random variance). Finally, in all models the within-person residual variance was specified as constant over time with no residual covariance over time after accounting for any between-person random effects variances and covariances.

We first examined polynomial models of change, with an empty means, random intercept model as a baseline. The addition of a fixed linear time slope was significant ($p < .001$), such that after a predicted value of 1,899.6 msec at session 1, RT declined by –51.6 msec per session on average. Adding a variance of the random linear time slope (and its covariance with the random intercept) also significantly improved model fit, –2ΔLL(~2) = 42.6, $p < .001$ (with a smaller AIC and BIC), indicating significant individual differences in the linear rate of change.

Next, a fixed quadratic time slope was significant ($p < .001$), indicating a significant deceleration in the rate of improvement in RT on average. More specifically, the instantaneous linear rate of decline at session 1 of –120.9 msec per session became less negative by 38.8 msec per session (i.e., twice the quadratic coefficient of 13.9 msec per session^2). The instantaneous linear rate of change at each session was significantly negative through session 4, after which it became nonsignificant. Finally, adding a variance for the random quadratic time slope (and its covariance with the random intercept and random linear time slope) also significantly improved model fit, –2ΔLL(~3) = 38.7, $p < .001$ (with a smaller AIC and BIC), indicating significant individual differences in quadratic change. As shown in Figure 6.2, the RT mean and variance predicted by the random quadratic model closely approximated those from the saturated means, unstructured variance baseline model, so higher-order polynomial effects were not examined.

The parameters of the best-fitting polynomial model included a fixed intercept for the predicted RT at session 1 of 1,945.9 msec, a fixed instantaneous linear rate of change at session 1 of –120.9 msec per session, and a fixed quadratic rate of change (i.e., half the rate of deceleration) of 13.9 msec per session^2. In computing 95% random effects confidence intervals as described previously, 95% of the sample was expected to have individual intercepts for the predicted RT at session 1 of 916 to 2,976 msec, to have individual instantaneous linear rates of change at session 1 of –436 to 194 msec per session, and to have individual quadratic rates of change of –36 to 63 msec per session^2. Thus, not everyone was predicted to initially improve in RT, or to show decelerating improvement in RT over time.

Second, because there appeared to be a breakpoint in the RT trajectory after session 2, we then examined a piecewise model of change in which the change before and after session 2 was described by two separate linear slopes. Each slope was significant ($p < .001$), such that after a predicted RT of 1961.9 msec at session 1, RT declined by –163.3 per session until session 2, and then by –32.9 per session after session 2. Adding a variance for the random slope before session 2 (and its covariance with the random intercept) significantly improved model fit, –2ΔLL(~2) = 63.1, $p < .001$ (with a smaller AIC and BIC). Likewise, adding a variance for the random slope after session 2 (and its covariance with the random intercept and random slope before session 2) significantly improved model fit, –2ΔLL(~3) = 44.2, $p < .001$ (with a smaller AIC and BIC). Thus, there were significant individual differences in the linear change both before and after session 2. The addition of a fixed quadratic slope after session 2 did not improve model fit ($p = .09$), suggesting that a linear slope after session 2 was sufficient. Finally, to examine whether the slopes before and after session 2 were significantly different, the model was re-specified to include a continuous linear time slope and a slope after session 2, the latter of which then represented the difference between the slopes. The difference in the slopes was indeed significant ($p < .001$); the slope after session 2 was significantly less negative by 130.8 msec per session.

The parameters of the best-fitting piecewise slope model included a fixed intercept for the predicted RT at session 1 of 1,961.9 msec, a fixed linear rate of change before session 2 of –163.3 msec per session, and a fixed linear rate of change after session 2 of –32.9 msec per session. In computing 95% random effects confidence intervals as described previously, 95% of the sample was expected to have individual intercepts for the predicted RT at session 1 of 917 to 3,007 msec, to have individual linear rates of change before session 2 of –659 to 322 msec per session, and to have individual linear rates of change after session 2 of –133 to 67 msec per session. Thus, not everyone was predicted to improve in RT before and after session 2. The mean and variance for RT predicted by the two-slope model also closely approximated those from the saturated means, unstructured variance baseline model, as seen in Figure 6.3.

Our last candidate model to describe the decline in RT across six sessions was the negative exponential model, which was specified as RT = *asymptote* + *amount***exp(*rate***time). That is, the model included a *lower asymptote* for the optimal value of RT, an *amount of change* for the difference between RT at the lower asymptote and at session 1, and a nonlinear *rate of approach to asymptote*. Fixed effects of each parameter were specified first to obtain starting values, and maximum likelihood was used to estimate each model. A random asymptote variance was significant, $-2\Delta LL(\sim 1) = 809.2$, $p < .001$ (with a smaller AIC and BIC as well), indicating significant individual differences in the lower asymptote. Likewise, adding a random variance for the amount of change (and its covariance with the random asymptote) was also significant, $-2\Delta LL(\sim 2) = 76.7$, $p < .001$ (with a smaller AIC and BIC), indicating significant individual differences in the amount of change. A model with a random rate variance would not converge, however, and as such the rate of approach to asymptote remained constant (fixed) across persons.

The parameters of the best-fitting negative exponential model included a fixed lower asymptote for the optimal value of RT of 1,683.5 msec, a fixed amount of change in RT from asymptote to session 1 of 279.9 msec, and a fixed rate of approach to asymptote of –0.75 per session. In computing 95% random effects confidence intervals as described previously, 95% of the sample was expected to have individual lower asymptotes for the optimal value of RT of 827 to 2,540 msec and to have individual amounts of change of –265 to 825 msec. Thus, not everyone was predicted to improve in RT across the six sessions. Overall, the mean and variance for RT predicted by the negative exponential model less closely approximated those from the saturated means, unstructured variance baseline model or the other models, as seen in Figure 6.5.

To determine the best-fitting model, each baseline model and candidate model was re-estimated using maximum likelihood in order to compare their fit to the random asymptote, random amount, and fixed rate negative exponential model. As seen in Table 6.12, the two-slope piecewise model was preferred by the AIC and BIC, and was the only model that did not fit significantly worse than the saturated means, unstructured variance model. Thus, despite its lack of theoretical appeal, the two-slope piecewise model appears to have the best fit to the six-session RT data, followed by the negative exponential model and the random quadratic model.

Review Questions

1. Describe the roles that fixed and random effects of time play in each of the models presented. Which of these two types of effects should be included in the model before the other, and why?
2. What are the general rules for the number of fixed and random effects related to time that can be included in a model? What potential problems arise in modeling change across only three occasions?
3. What is the difference between models for continuous change and models for discontinuous change? When might one family of models be more useful than the other?
4. Using the models presented in this chapter as an example, describe the differences between models that are nonlinear in their variables versus nonlinear in their parameters. What special concerns apply in estimating the latter?
5. Describe the two alternative specifications of piecewise models of discontinuous change that were discussed. Provide an example of when each might be more useful than the other.

References

Choi, J., Harring, J. R., & Hancock, G. R. (2009). Latent growth modeling for logistic response functions. *Multivariate Behavioral Research, 44,* 620–645.

Enders, C. K. (2010). *Applied missing data analysis.* New York, NY: Guilford.

Grimm, K. J., & Ram, N. (2009). Nonlinear growth models in M*plus* and SAS. *Structural Equation Modeling, 16,* 676–701.

Preacher, K. J., & Hancock, G. R. (2012). On interpretable reparameterizations of linear and nonlinear latent growth curve models. In J. Harring & G. Hancock (Eds.), *Advances in longitudinal methods in the social and behavioral sciences* (pp. 25–58). Charlotte, NC: Information Age Publishing.

Richards, F. J. (1959). A flexible growth function for empirical use. *Journal of Experimental Botany, 10,* 290–301.

Singer, J. D., & Willett, J. B. (2003). *Applied longitudinal data analysis.* New York, NY: Oxford University Press.

Sit, V., & Poulin-Costello, M. (1994, March). *Catalog of curves for curve fitting.* In W. Bergerud & V. Sit (Eds.), *Biometrics information handbook series* (Vol. 4). Retrieved from Province of British Columbia Ministry of Forests, www.for.gov.bc.ca/hfd/pubs/docs/bio/bio04.htm

Appendix 6.A: Checklist for Building Unconditional Models of Change

Following is a checklist that summarizes the sequence of decision points in building an unconditional model of change, as derived from the material in chapters 4, 5, and 6.

1. *Carefully consider issues related to time (see also chapter 10):*
   a. Decide what your metric of time will be—which index of change over time most closely aligns with the theoretical cause of the observed change?
   b. Decide at what occasion time 0 should be located—to avoid estimation problems, this should be an occasion in which individual variability is observed in your data.
2. *Continue with data description:*
   a. Compute an intraclass correlation (ICC) from an empty means, random intercept model for the proportion of outcome variance due to between-person mean differences, or how much longitudinal outcome variation is actually cross-sectional.
      i. If the random intercept variance is not estimable, add fixed effects of time (see step 4a) and then compute a *conditional* ICC for the proportion of between-person mean differences after controlling for the effects of time.
      ii. Is your ICC at or very close to 1? If so, you do not have within-person, longitudinal variation to model—game over!
   b. Plot individual trajectories over time (or a random subsample thereof).
      i. What kind of change, if any, do you see on average?
      ii. Do you see individual differences in that pattern of change?
   c. Check the "answer key" for the means (and variances) the models will try to describe.
      i. Do you have balanced data? Estimate a saturated means, unstructured variance model directly if possible (or just a saturated means, random intercept model if not).
      ii. Do you have unbalanced data? Round time into convenient intervals and estimate a saturated means model, unstructured variance model if possible (or just a saturated means, random intercept model if not).
3. *If you do* not *have systematic change over time on average or at the individual level (i.e., you have within-person fluctuation rather than within-person change over time):*
   a. Are you sure? Consider other ways that systematic effects of time could be present (e.g., day of the week and day of study). If you do find any effects related to time you weren't expecting, go to step 4.
   b. If you do only have within-person fluctuation over time, include a fixed intercept in the model for the means and then evaluate alternative

covariance structures to parsimoniously but accurately describe the pattern of outcome variance and covariance over time. These may include **R**-only models (in which the total variance and covariance is specified through a single **R** matrix), or **G** and **R** combination models (in which a random intercept variance is estimated in the **G** matrix and any within-person residual variance and covariance is estimated in the **R** matrix). The choices for the **R** matrix available for unbalanced data will be more limited, though.

4. *If you* do *have systematic change over time on average or at the individual level:*

   a. What *fixed effects* related to time will be most useful in describing the pattern of *average change* in your outcome over time?

   i. The number of fixed effects related to time that can be included for balanced data is generally $n - 1$ (more effects can be included for unbalanced data in which the mean trajectory is aggregated across persons at different points).

   ii. Does your study include discrete phases of time (e.g., pre- and post-intervention)? If so, discontinuous piecewise models may be useful. Each phase that has three or more occasions may show differences in the intercept and/or slopes (and the slopes can be either linear or nonlinear as needed).

   iii. Does your study include continuous time instead? If so, continuous models may be useful (although piecewise models may still be used to capture nonlinearity if there is a visible breakpoint in the trajectory).

   iv. Do you expect the effects of time to level off in your study (i.e., to reach asymptote)? If so, then nonlinear models that include lower and/or upper asymptotes (e.g., exponential or logistic models) may be more useful than polynomial models that predict that change should continue over time.

   b. What *random effects* for individual differences related to time will be most useful in describing the pattern of outcome *variance and covariance* over time?

   i. All models require a within-person residual variance, and most models will also require a random variance for individual differences in the outcome level (e.g., a random intercept or random asymptote). So, the number of random effects related to time that can be included for balanced data is usually $n - 2$.

   ii. In polynomial models, random effects variances must be added hierarchically, but this is usually not required in other models.

   iii. Random effects variances for nonlinear effects will be harder to estimate.

   iv. All covariances among the random effects should be estimated.

   c. After accounting for the random effects variances and covariances, is there any evidence for additional within-person residual covariance (e.g., auto-regressive or Toeplitz lagged relationships in the **R** matrix for the occasions nearest in time)?

5. *Understand the point of what you've done so far:*

a. The fixed effects of time are what the random effects of time vary around.

b. The random effects of time comprise the between-person variances (i.e., piles of variance) that the person-level, time-invariant predictors will account for.

c. The effects of time-varying predictors will account for any within-person residual variance (i.e., variance leftover after accounting for the effects of time and person-level predictors thereof).

d. Therefore, what fixed and random time effects related to time are included in the model constrain the sources of variance to be predicted, as well as how the standard errors for any fixed effects of predictors will be formulated.

e. There is little point in trying to predict between-person differences in change over time (and within-person deviations thereof) if the model for change is mis-specified. That's why it is critically important to get *time* right on both sides of the model first!

f. However—because the model for the variance describes the leftover variation at each level (between persons and within persons), the model for time should be reconsidered after testing the effects of predictors to ensure that it is still appropriate. For instance, fixed effects related to time that become nonsignificant and that are not involved in any higher-order interactions may be eliminated. You might also consider testing whether the random slope variances that remain after including predictors are significantly different than 0—this is a formal way of testing to what extent you have explained individual differences in change over time, as discussed in chapter 7.

MODELING THE EFFECTS OF PREDICTORS

CHAPTER 7

TIME-INVARIANT PREDICTORS IN LONGITUDINAL MODELS

The first section of this text (chapters 1–3) presented some necessary building blocks for conducting longitudinal analysis. The second section then utilized those building blocks to fit *unconditional* longitudinal models for describing within-person fluctuation over time (chapter 4) and systematic within-person change over time (chapters 5 and 6). Finding a plausible model for the means and variance with respect to time is a necessary precursor to examining the effects of other predictor variables because the accuracy of their standard errors depends on having the correct model for the variance (where *correct* in reality means *least wrong* or *most plausible*). Building on this previous material, the third section of this text will focus on *conditional* models, which include predictors that are time-invariant (chapter 7) and time-varying (chapters 8 and 9).

The purpose of chapter 7 is to describe the examination of time-invariant predictors, or person-related predictors that are constant over time, within models of within-person fluctuation and models of within-person change over time. The chapter begins with some practical issues in modeling time-invariant predictors, including what happens when they have missing data, decisions for their centering, the potential roles they can play in longitudinal models, and how to assess their effect sizes. The second and third sections illustrate time-invariant predictors in models of within-person fluctuation and within-person change, respectively—we will expand on these examples to consider effects of time-varying predictors in chapters 8 and 9. As in previous chapters, this chapter concludes with summary and sample results sections. Finally, the chapter appendix describes the assumptions that underlie longitudinal models (i.e., residual normality, constant variance, and independence across predictors and sampling units) and presents some general strategies for identifying and remedying such violations.

1. Considering Time-Invariant Predictors in Longitudinal Models

As initially discussed in chapter 1, there are two main types of predictors to be included in longitudinal models: time-invariant or time-varying. The focus of this chapter will be **time-invariant predictors**, also known as **person-level** predictors, or as **level-2** predictors in multilevel models for longitudinal data in which occasions (at level 1) are nested within persons (at level 2). Although by definition time-invariant predictors are those measured only once during a study, in reality there is a continuum for just how invariant over time they actually are. At one end of the spectrum are time-invariant predictors that will *never* change over time. For instance, variables like biological sex or race will not change over time, and so there is no point in assessing them repeatedly (except for data verification). In the middle of the spectrum are time-invariant predictors that are *not likely* to change during a study, and so may be assessed only once to save time. For example, in a study of daily behavior, personality variables might be measured only once under the assumption that, although personality may change over a lifetime, it is not likely to change over a week of data collection. The same may be true of person-level variables like educational attainment (in working adults), socioeconomic status, or religious affiliation.

At the other end of spectrum are time-invariant predictors that are *likely* to change over time, but nevertheless for which only one measurement is available (i.e., longitudinal variables that are measured cross-sectionally). Consider, for example, the effects of parental attitudes in a study of adolescent development. If parental attitudes were measured at only one occasion (e.g., when their child is 12 years old), then parental attitudes is still a time-invariant predictor, even though parental attitudes are likely to change as their child ages. In such scenarios, it is important to interpret the effects of the time-invariant predictor conditionally on when it was measured. In this example, rather than saying you have examined the effect of *parental attitudes,* a more accurate statement is that you have examined the effect of *parental attitudes at age 12*. The latter phrasing acknowledges that the effects of parental attitudes may have been different if they had been measured at a different occasion. An analogous scenario happens when *time in study* is used to index within-person change (i.e., change is assessed relative to the first occasion), but in which moderation of that within-person change is examined as a function of other time-related variables that vary between persons, such as age or time to event. In this case, even though they are inherently time-varying, age or time to event will need to be modeled as time-invariant instead (i.e., as age or time to event *at baseline*) given that are perfectly correlated within-persons with *time in study*. But we will forgo these more complex examples until chapter 10.

1.A. Time-Invariant Predictors With Missing Data

Before continuing any further, we must consider what happens to persons with missing time-invariant predictors when estimating longitudinal models via software for multilevel models or for structural equation models. An excellent and more general treatment of missing data can be found in Enders (2010); only the major issues will be highlighted here. It is commonly stated that multilevel models "handle" missing data, often without realizing what this actually implies. As described in chapter 1, estimating longitudinal models as multilevel models requires a *stacked* or *long* data format in which a case (or row) holds the data at *one* occasion for *one* person. This stacked data format is advantageous because, even if a person missed some occasions, the cases for his or her other occasions can still be included in the model. Multilevel models use likelihood-based estimation (as presented in chapter 5) that does not necessarily require listwise deletion (i.e., they do not automatically remove persons with any incomplete outcome data from the analysis), which is a significant advantage over alternatives based on least squares estimation that do require listwise deletion (e.g., traditional analysis of variance, as discussed in chapter 3).

There is a downside, however. Simply stated, most software for multilevel models requires that each case (a time-specific row within a person) must be *complete*—it must contain *all* predictors and outcomes that are included in a model. We haven't worried about this so far (i.e., in fitting unconditional models for the effects of time only) because any case that has an outcome almost always has a corresponding time value that indicates when it occurred. But in conditional models, each case must be complete with respect to *all* predictors, not just time. This means that a person missing a time-invariant predictor will not have *any* of his or her data used when that predictor is included in the model. That is, because the person's time-invariant predictor will be missing at each occasion, all of his or her cases will be incomplete and thus will be deleted from the analysis—that is how multilevel models actually "handle" missing data!

The fact that persons with missing time-invariant predictors will be deleted when estimating longitudinal models using multilevel modeling software creates three problems. First, the likelihood-based model fit indices (–2LL, AIC, and BIC) are only comparable for models that include the exact same set of cases. Consider, for example, an ML –2ΔLL test to compare a model that includes predictor A to a model that includes predictors A and B. The model log-likelihood (LL) value is literally the sum over persons of the results from their individual log-likelihood functions. Accordingly, if some people are missing predictor B, the –2LL value for the latter model will be smaller simply because it includes fewer persons—regardless of whether predictor B actually improved the model. A correct model comparison would be achieved by including only those cases that are complete with respect to predictors A and B in *both* models, and then comparing their model fit via their –2LL, AIC, and BIC values.

The other two more insidious problems created by deletion of persons with missing time-invariant predictors in software for multilevel models are not unique to longitudinal data. The second problem is that a reduction of sample size leads to a reduction in statistical power. This problem will get even worse to the extent that multiple time-invariant predictors with different patterns of missingness are included in the same model. Third, including only those persons with all time-invariant predictors may result in biased model effects, given that the people with complete data for the model predictors may not be a random subset of the overall sample (which in turn may not represent its intended population). More formally, the deletion of persons with missing time-invariant predictors will result in biased effects whenever the missingness is not *completely at random* (MCAR; a condition in which the reason for the missingness is completely unrelated to what the missing values would have been). Fortunately, though, all is not lost. As will be addressed in chapter 9, estimating longitudinal models via software for structural equation models instead can allow persons with missing time-invariant predictors to stay in the model given specific assumptions about the distributions of and reasons for missingness of the time-invariant predictors. This chapter will address the examination of the effects of time-invariant predictors more generally, but these issues related to missing data for time-invariant predictors will be important when deciding how to estimate longitudinal models in practice.

1.B. Centering or Coding of Time-Invariant Predictors

As presented in chapter 2, the scale of all model predictors should have a meaningful 0 value in order for the model intercept (and the main effects of any interacting predictors) to be meaningful. If the original scale of the predictor does not include 0, then a constant should be subtracted or added so that 0 is a meaningful value, a procedure known as **centering**. Although the predictor's sample mean is most often used as its centering constant, a useful alternative is to choose a centering point that has a meaningful value within the original scale of the predictor. For example, if a predictor of *stress* was created as a mean across items whose value could range from 1 to 9, centering at 5 would create a reference point as someone who tends to respond at 5. However, if the same predictor were skewed such that most responses were between 1 and 3, a centering at a constant of 2 might be more reasonable than a centering constant of 5. In that case, although 5 would be in the predictor's *possible* scale, creating a reference point as someone who answered 5 extrapolates beyond the predictor's *observed* scale. It is important to stay within the possible scale (and preferably within the observed scale) when plotting predictor effects as well.

The same centering issues also apply to categorical predictors. For instance, consider biological sex as a predictor: how should we represent men and women with numeric values? A natural option is to designate one group as the reference by giving them a value of 0, and the other group as the alternative group by giving them a value of 1. For instance, if men were the reference group (coded sex = 0) and women were the alternative group (coded sex = 1), the intercept would then become the expected outcome *specifically for men*, and the main effect of sex would represent the difference in the outcome for women (i.e., a one-unit difference in sex). Given this pattern of coding, it would be helpful to rename the predictor for sex using a name like *women* that conveys the direction of the additional effect for women instead of the neutral and unhelpful label *sex* that does not convey the direction of the effect. If the variable coding was switched to designate women as the reference group (sex = 0) and men as the alternative group (sex = 1), then the intercept would be the expected outcome for women, and the main effect of sex would be exactly backwards—the difference for men (in which the variable for *sex* should then be named *men* instead). Recall from chapter 2 that representing a categorical predictor with three or more levels proceeds similarly, such that the differences among three groups would be represented using two dummy codes, four groups using three dummy codes, and so forth.

Another popular alternative is to code sex such that 0 becomes the average of the two groups. In this approach called *effects coding,* the fixed intercept would then represent the mean outcome for the sample. For instance, if half the sample was comprised of men, one method of coding sex is to give men a value −0.5 and women a value of 0.5. (Note that ± 0.5 would be used so as to maintain the one-unit difference between the groups as the direct interpretation of the group main effect. If ±1 were used instead, the resulting effect for sex would then be twice the group difference.) The disadvantage of using effects coding for sex is that the intercept becomes the expected value for someone with sex = 0, or the "average" person. But given that such a person does not exist, the intercept has no real-world counterpart. The same can be said for the naïve practice of including sex in whatever manner it was entered into the dataset (i.e., men = 1 and women = 2). In using this 1 versus 2 coding, the effect of sex will still be estimated correctly as the difference between men and women, but the fixed intercept again will have no real-world counterpart—it becomes the expected value for someone with sex = 0, and given the coding of 1 versus 2, that person does not exist. In essence, such alternative methods of coding are not wrong but they can be weird, in that they can result in nonsensical interpretations of the intercept.

The different methods of centering or coding also become relevant when interpreting the main effects of predictors that are part of an interaction term. As presented in chapter 2, when a predictor is not part of an interaction, its main effect applies equally across all levels of the other model predictors. For instance, if predictors of stress and sex had main effects only, the effect of stress would apply equally to men and women, and the sex difference would apply to all stress levels. When a predictor is part of an interaction, however, its main effect becomes its simple effect, interpreted *specifically when its interacting predictor is 0,* whomever that reference group happens to be. For instance, given an interaction of sex by stress, depending on the coding of sex, the simple main effect of stress could be the stress slope specifically for men, specifically for women, or specifically for no real person. Likewise, depending on the coding of stress, the simple main effect of sex could be the difference specifically between men and women with a stress level that corresponds to *never, sometimes, always,* or to no possible scale response. In any event, models using different centering constants will always be equivalent—they will result in the same predicted values and the same model fit. So, there is no wrong constant with which to center predictor variables, only values that make more or less sense for representing the intercept and main effects of their interacting predictors. But it will make the task of interpreting your parameters easier if the model reference point is someone who actually exists in your sample!

No matter how they are centered, time-invariant predictors have a few distinct roles they can play in a longitudinal model. The next sections describe their roles within the model for the means and within the model for the variance in general terms. If the text below does not make perfect sense immediately, don't worry—these concepts will be demonstrated more concretely in the examples that follow and repeatedly throughout the rest of the text as well.

1.C. The Role of Time-Invariant Predictors in the Model for the Means

In chapters 4–6 we saw how longitudinal models can be described as multilevel models, in which *within-person variation over time* is described in the **level-1** model, and *between-person variation* is described in the **level-2** model. Each level-1 β placeholder (e.g., for the intercept or asymptote and for any effects for time) is then defined by a level-2 equation containing at least a *fixed effect* for its expected value in the sample (indicated by a γ), and potentially a *random effect* that allows that effect to vary over persons (indicated by a U_i). Because time-invariant predictors describe person-level characteristics that are measured at level 2, they cannot be included in the level-1 model for within-person variation over time. That is, by themselves (i.e., as main effects or as part of interactions with other time-invariant predictors, known as **level-2 interactions**), time-invariant predictors cannot account for time-specific, within-person (level-1) residual variance because they do not vary within persons. However, main effects of and interactions among time-invariant predictors can be included in the level-2 equation for each β placeholder, in which their purpose would be to modify the γ fixed effect within that level-2 equation and to explain (or account for) the random effect variance represented by the corresponding U_i term.

For example, consider the addition of a time-invariant predictor of sex to a random quadratic model of change, in which the level-1 β placeholders for the individual intercepts, linear time slopes, and quadratic time slopes are each defined by a separate level-2 equation that includes a fixed effect, an effect of sex, and a random effect, as shown in Equation (7.1):

$$\textbf{Level 1:}\ \ y_{ti} = \beta_{0i} + \beta_{1i}(\text{Time}_{ti}) + \beta_{2i}(\text{Time}_{ti})^2 + e_{ti}$$

$$\textbf{Level 2:}\ \text{Intercept:}\qquad \beta_{0i} = \gamma_{00} + \gamma_{01}(\text{Sex}_i) + U_{0i}$$

$$\text{Linear Time:}\qquad \beta_{1i} = \gamma_{10} + \gamma_{11}(\text{Sex}_i) + U_{1i}$$

$$\text{Quadratic Time:}\ \ \beta_{2i} = \gamma_{20} + \gamma_{21}(\text{Sex}_i) + U_{2i} \qquad (7.1)$$

$$\textbf{Composite:}\ \ y_{ti} = \{\gamma_{00} + \gamma_{01}(\text{Sex}_i) + U_{0i}\} +$$
$$\{\gamma_{10} + \gamma_{11}(\text{Sex}_i) + U_{1i}\}(\text{Time}_{ti}) +$$
$$\{\gamma_{20} + \gamma_{21}(\text{Sex}_i) + U_{2i}\}(\text{Time}_{ti})^2 + e_{ti}$$

and in which the composite equation substituting for the β placeholders is also shown. First, the fixed effect of Sex_i γ_{01} in the level-2 equation for the intercept is the *main effect* of Sex_i. As a result, the fixed intercept γ_{00} will become the expected mean outcome at $Time_{ti} = 0$ specifically for persons in which $Sex_i = 0$. The fixed effect of Sex_i on the intercept γ_{01} is the difference in the intercept between men and women, such that the intercept for persons in which $Sex_i = 1$ can then be found as $\gamma_{00} + \gamma_{01}$. For each γ fixed effect, the first subscript indicates which β the effect applies to in the level-1 equation, whereas the second subscript indicates its order in the level-2 equation. Thus, for the main effect of Sex_i γ_{01}, the 0 indicates that it predicts β_{0i} in the level-1 equation, and the 1 indicates it is the first predictor in that level-2 equation for β_{0i}. The main effect of the next time-invariant predictor (e.g., years of education, not shown) to modify the intercept would be γ_{02}. Also modifying the intercept would be level-2 interactions among two or more time-invariant predictors (e.g., sex by education, which would then be γ_{03}, not shown).

Second, the fixed effect of Sex_i γ_{11} in the level-2 equation for the individual linear time slope is the interaction of Sex_i by $Time_{ti}$. This is shown more clearly in the composite equation, in which $Time_{ti}$ is directly multiplied by each term in the β_{1i} equation. As a result, the fixed linear time slope γ_{10} will become the expected mean instantaneous linear rate of change at $Time_{ti} = 0$ (given the fixed quadratic time slope) specifically for persons in which $Sex_i = 0$. The fixed effect of Sex_i on the linear time slope γ_{11} is the difference in the linear time slope between men and women, such that the linear time slope for persons in which $Sex_i = 1$ can then be found as $\gamma_{10} + \gamma_{11}$. The interaction of Sex_i by $Time_{ti}$ γ_{11} is known as a **cross-level interaction** because it occurs between the level-1 predictor of $Time_{ti}$ and the level-2 predictor of Sex_i. Cross-level interactions of $Time_{ti}$ with one or more other time-invariant predictors (which would be indicated by γ_{12}, γ_{13}, and so on) would also modify the linear time slope as a function of those person predictors.

Third, the fixed effect of sex in the level-2 equation for the individual quadratic time slope is the cross-level interaction of Sex_i by $Time_{ti}^2$. As a result, the fixed quadratic time slope γ_{20} will become half the expected mean rate of acceleration or deceleration per unit time specifically for persons in which $Sex_i = 0$. The fixed effect of Sex_i on the quadratic time slope γ_{21} is the difference in the quadratic time slope between men and women, such that the quadratic time slope for persons in which $Sex_i = 1$ can then be found as $\gamma_{20} + \gamma_{21}$. Cross-level interactions of $Time_{ti}^2$ with one or more other time-invariant predictors (which would be indicated by γ_{22}, γ_{23}, and so on) would also modify the quadratic time slope as a function of those person predictors.

The same pattern would apply to other types of models of change over time. For instance, in a piecewise model for discontinuity in intercept and/or change (as captured by *jumps* and *slopes*, respectively), a time-invariant predictor could modify the intercept (as a main effect) and each jump or slope (through its cross-level interactions with each level-1 predictor defining the jump or slope). In a negative exponential model of change over time, a time-invariant predictor could modify the asymptote (as a main effect), the amount of change (through its cross-level interaction with the amount parameter), and the rate of approach to asymptote (through its cross-level interaction with the rate parameter). But in models for within-person fluctuation over time, if the level-1 model includes an intercept but no other level-1 effects for time (and no other time-varying predictors), then time-invariant predictors could only contribute to the level-2 equation for the intercept (e.g., the average outcome over time could differ between men and women).

1.D. The Role of Time-Invariant Predictors in the Model for the Variance

Testing the fixed effects of time-invariant predictors in the model for the means as just described is usually of primary interest. It is important to note, though, that in purely longitudinal models, *time-invariant predictors cannot have random effects* in the model for the variance (i.e., each person cannot have his or her own effect). This is because time-invariant predictors by definition do not vary within persons, and therefore they have no possible within-person effect that could vary over persons (e.g., each person cannot have his or her own *effect* of sex because sex is constant within a person over time). As will be discussed in chapter 11, though, if persons are nested in groups (i.e., a clustered longitudinal study), then it is possible for time-invariant predictors to have a random effect over *groups* (but still not a random effect over *persons*).

What is less well known (given that it is not always easy or even possible to do within many software programs) is how time-invariant predictors *can* be included in the model for the variance—not as random effects, but instead to predict **heterogeneity of variance.** That is, rather than just *explaining* variation through their fixed effects in the model for the means (e.g., why some people need different intercepts or time slopes), time-invariant predictors can also be used to predict how the *amount* of variation may differ systematically across persons.

Consider a time-invariant predictor of sex in describing within-person fluctuation in negative mood over time, in which the model for the variance contains a random intercept variance and a residual variance. Sex could be included as a main effect in the model for the means to examine whether the *mean level* of negative mood over time differs between men and women, potentially reducing the size of the random intercept variance (as explained in the next section). But sex could also be included in the model for the variance as a predictor of the *amount* of level-2 random intercept variance—whether the *amount* of between-person variability in mean negative mood over time is greater in men than in women (or vice-versa). Similarly, sex could also be included in the model for the variance as a predictor of the *amount* of level-1 residual variance—whether the *amount* of within-person fluctuation in negative mood over time (e.g., degree of "moodiness") is greater in men than in women (or vice-versa).

The same options for predicting heterogeneity of variance by time-invariant predictors are available in models of within-person change as well. For instance, in the level-2 model for the variance, sex could predict whether the *amount* of between-person variance in the intercept, asymptote, and/or any random effects related to time differs between men and women. In the level-1 model for the variance, sex could predict whether the *amount* of residual within-person variance (i.e., the remaining variation after predicting individual change over time) differs between men and women. Thus, although time-invariant predictors cannot have random effects in two-level longitudinal models, they have many other roles to play—as level-2 predictors in the model for the means (as main effects, as part of level-2 interactions, or as part of cross-level interactions), or in describing heterogeneity of variance at each level of the model.

1.E. Assessing the Effect Size of Time-Invariant Predictors

The results for fixed effects in the model for the means will include a parameter estimate, a standard error, and *p*-value with which to assess statistical significance (using a *Wald test* for the ratio of each estimate to its standard error). These fixed effect estimates are unstandardized, and thus their absolute magnitude is based on the scale of the predictor and outcome variables. Unfortunately, it is not usually possible to calculate standardized fixed effect estimates given that having multiple variance components (i.e., piles of variance) in a longitudinal model does not provide a clear basis for standardization. So, beyond assessing levels of statistical significance, how do we know whether the absolute size of a given effect is "small" or "large"? A common way of expressing standardized effect size (e.g., Hox, 2010; Raudenbush & Bryk, 2002; Singer & Willett, 2003) is the **proportion reduction in variance**, known as **pseudo-R²**, which can be calculated using the variance estimated from a comparison model with *fewer* parameters relative to the variance estimated from a model with *more* parameters, as shown in Equation (7.2):

$$\text{Pseudo-R}^2 = \frac{\text{Variance}_{\text{fewer}} - \text{Variance}_{\text{more}}}{\text{Variance}_{\text{fewer}}} \tag{7.2}$$

We have already used this basic pseudo-R² formula a few times in the text to assess the reduction in the level-1 residual variance after including fixed effects of time, but now the full complexity of this issue is given a more thorough treatment.

Pseudo-R² is like the traditional R² used in general linear models, in that its purpose is to describe the proportion of outcome variance accounted for by the fixed effects of predictors in the model for the means. But given that there are multiple variance components in longitudinal models, we will have a pseudo-R² value for *each* pile of variance (as well as a pseudo-R² value for each occasion when the total or residual variance is allowed to differ over time). These R² values are called *pseudo* because they are inexact and interdependent approximations with some quirky properties. In general, a reduction in any level-2 random effects variance (e.g., a random intercept or random time slope variance) will not affect the level-1 residual variance, but the reverse is not true. That is, as we saw in chapters 5 and 6, a reduction in the level-1 residual variance σ_e^2 causes an increase in the level-2 random intercept variance $\tau_{U_0}^2$. This is because the "true" value of $\tau_{U_0}^2$ (that appears in the output) is estimated as (observed $\tau_{U_0}^2$) − (σ_e^2 / *n*), in which *n* is the number of occasions per person. So, the estimate of $\tau_{U_0}^2$ will appear to increase whenever σ_e^2 is reduced but $\tau_{U_0}^2$ is not, such as when adding a level-1 fixed effect that varies purely within persons (like an effect of *time* when *time* has no between-person variation).

Although there are other versions of pseudo-R^2 based on reduction of variance at each level of the model (e.g., Snijders & Bosker, 2012), they do not generalize readily to models with random slopes.

Given the potential for a reduction in each variance component, we now consider *which* of these piles should be reduced for *each* potential effect of a level-2 time-invariant predictor. As explained earlier, time-invariant predictors can modify the level-1 fixed effect within each level-2 equation (i.e., they can moderate the effects that describe the expected level of the outcome and its pattern of change over time). But which source of variance is accounted for by the effects of time-invariant predictors depends on whether the level-1 effect they are modifying (predicting) has been specified as *randomly varying* across persons. If so, then the time-invariant predictor can reduce the random variation around the level-1 effect in each level-2 equation, and a pseudo-R^2 value due to the added effect of the time-invariant predictor would be calculated accordingly.

Consider, for example, the same random quadratic model from Equation (7.1). Including sex in the level-2 equation for the *intercept* ($\beta_{0i} = \gamma_{00} + \gamma_{01}\text{Sex}_i + U_{0i}$) may reduce the *random intercept variation* (as indexed by pseudo-R^2 for $\tau^2_{U_0}$), including sex in the level-2 equation for the *linear time slope* ($\beta_{1i} = \gamma_{10} + \gamma_{11}\text{Sex}_i + U_{1i}$) may reduce the *random linear time slope variation* (as indexed by pseudo-R^2 for $\tau^2_{U_1}$), and including sex in the level-2 equation for the *quadratic time slope* ($\beta_{2i} = \gamma_{20} + \gamma_{21}\text{Sex}_i + U_{2i}$) may reduce the *random quadratic time slope variation* (as indexed by pseudo-R^2 for $\tau^2_{U_2}$). In each case, part of the reason why people need their own effect (e.g., their own U_{0i} intercept, U_{1i} linear time slope, or U_{2i} quadratic time slope) would be because of sex differences. The same is true for any other model of change over time (e.g., piecewise, exponential)—when included in a level-2 equation, a time-invariant predictor explains any between-person level-2 random variance in that specific level-1 effect.

But what if the level-2 equation for a level-1 effect does *not* contain a random effect? For instance, what if an unconditional polynomial model included fixed quadratic time, but not random quadratic time (i.e., the quadratic time slope is given by $\beta_{2i} = \gamma_{20}$ without U_{2i})? In that case, if sex is included in the level-2 equation for the individual quadratic time slope (as $\beta_{2i} = \gamma_{20} + \gamma_{21}\text{Sex}_i$), the quadratic time slope would be called **systematically** or **non-randomly varying** rather than fixed. The idea of a *systematically varying* effect is essentially a compromise between the two extremes of fixed and random—it's not that everyone should get exactly the same fixed level-1 effect (e.g., the same fixed quadratic time slope), or that everyone should get their own random level-1 effect (e.g., individually varying quadratic time slopes), but that the level-1 effect can vary *deterministically* as a function of model predictors, but not randomly otherwise (e.g., quadratic time slopes differ only between men and women, but are the same within sex groups).

Evaluating systematically varying effects can be a little tricky, as will be discussed in the within-person change example later in the chapter. But for now, the possible kinds of level-1 effects can be summarized as follows (again using an example of a quadratic time slope as the level-1 effect). If the level-2 equation for a quadratic time slope includes just a fixed slope ($\beta_{2i} = \gamma_{20}$), the quadratic time slope would be considered *fixed* across persons. If the level-2 equation for a quadratic time slope includes a fixed slope and one or more level-2 predictors ($\beta_{2i} = \gamma_{20} + \gamma_{21}\text{Sex}_i$), then the quadratic time slope would be considered *systematically varying* across persons. Finally, if the level-2 equation for a quadratic time slope includes a random slope (regardless of whether other predictors are included, so $\beta_{2i} = \gamma_{20} + U_{2i}$ *or* $\beta_{2i} = \gamma_{20} + \gamma_{21}\text{Sex}_i + U_{2i}$), then the quadratic time slope would be considered *randomly varying* across persons.

Although it may seem strange, when including interactions of time-invariant predictors with level-1 predictors that do not have random effects (i.e., adding sex*time^2, if time^2 did not have a no random effect, or $\beta_{2i} = \gamma_{20} + \gamma_{21}\text{Sex}_i$), the relevant variance component for calculating pseudo-R^2 is actually the level-1 residual variance σ_e^2. The reason for this can be understood as follows. Recall from chapter 5 our partitioning *piles of variance*: We start with all the variation in the outcome represented by e_{ti}, thus residing in one pile we call *residual variance* (σ_e^2). In building an unconditional model for change over time, we examine whether each level-1 effect for the intercept or change over time should be treated as *fixed*, in which the level-1 effect is the same for everybody, or as *randomly varying*, in which each person gets his or her own level-1 effect. Each random effect variance is partitioned from the level-1 residual variance σ_e^2, forming a new level-2 pile of variance specific to the effect of that level-1 predictor (e.g., $\tau_{U_2}^2$ for time^2). But if a level-1 effect is fixed only, then any between-person variation in it still resides in the level-1 σ_e^2. So, if the fixed quadratic time slope does in fact vary systematically by sex, a sex by time^2 interaction must explain the level-1 σ_e^2 because the level-2 $\tau_{U_2}^2$ variance specific to time^2 that sex *would* have explained was not distinguished from level-1 σ_e^2 ahead of time. As reported by Hoffman and Templin (2011), this would be problematic if $\tau_{U_2}^2$ should have been in the model but was omitted, but not if $\tau_{U_2}^2$ did not significantly improve model fit when tested beforehand.

The same would be true of any model that does not use random effects of time to describe the pattern of variance and covariance over time. For instance, if fixed effects for the intercept, time, and time^2 in the model for the means were paired with just a level-2 random intercept variance $\tau_{U_0}^2$ and a level-1 residual variance σ_e^2 (i.e., compound symmetry), then the main effect of sex would reduce $\tau_{U_0}^2$ (because the intercept has its between-person level-2 variance explicitly in the model to be reduced). But the interactions of sex with time or time^2 would reduce σ_e^2 instead if time and time^2 didn't have their own random slope variances.

So, to summarize, the process of calculating pseudo-R^2 values in a model with at least one random effect variance should theoretically proceed as follows:

- Any fixed main effect of a level-1 time-varying predictor, or any interactions among level-1 predictors (e.g., time or time^2) will reduce the level-1 residual variance.
- Any fixed main effects or interactions among level-2 time-invariant predictors will reduce the level-2 variance pertaining to the expected level of the outcome across time (e.g., the random intercept variance or random asymptote variance).
- Any fixed effects for cross-level interactions of a level-1 predictor with a level-2 predictor will reduce that level-1 predictor's random effect variance when present, or the level-1 residual variance if the level-1 predictor is fixed or systematically varying.

In addition, it is important to note the following:

- If the model for the variance has no random effects (i.e., an **R**-only model in which the **R** matrix directly becomes the **V** matrix for the total variance and covariance over time), then including any predictor will reduce the *total variance* (whose amount may differ by occasion), given that an **R**-only model would not distinguish *any* sources of between-person level-2 variance in the **G** matrix.
- Pseudo-R^2 will never be calculated when adding new random effects variances because only *fixed* effects can explain variance—random effects partition existing variance into different piles instead. Furthermore, the variance components in the new model cannot be meaningfully compared to the variance components in previous models because their interpretations will have changed after creating a new random effect variance.

As seen in Equation (7.2), working with pseudo-R^2 values in practice requires a baseline model (with *fewer* parameters) against which to compare an alternative model (with *more* parameters) in order to assess the proportion of variance accounted for by the added fixed effects. But what should the baseline model be? On this point reasonable people may disagree, and different strategies for assessing effect size may each be useful, as described below.

One strategy is to specify the baseline as a model with *no* predictors for the specific pile of variance of interest. For example, in calculating pseudo-R^2 for a reduction in random intercept variance, a useful baseline model is an unconditional model of change (i.e., that includes any fixed and random effects needed to describe change over time), but without *any* effects of time-invariant predictors. This is because main effects of time-invariant predictors will account for the random intercept variance, and thus a useful baseline model for assessing their effect size should include all random intercept variance available to be predicted. Likewise, in calculating pseudo-R^2 for a reduction in random linear time slope variance, a useful baseline would include *main effects* of time-invariant predictors only, which then still includes all random linear time slope variance available to be predicted. This baseline main effects model would then be compared to an alternative model that includes cross-level interactions of linear time with the time-invariant predictors (which then reduce the random linear time slope variance). The same logic would apply to forming baseline models for a reduction in any other level-2 random effects variances.

However, because individual random effects should be allowed to correlate (i.e., through covariances estimated in the level-2 **G** matrix), sometimes adding fixed effects of time-invariant predictors will reduce other level-2 piles of variance in addition to the pile they *should* reduce. For instance, in a random quadratic model, adding a cross-level interaction of a time-invariant predictor with linear time should reduce the level-2 variance for the random effect of linear time, but it may also reduce the level-2 variance for the random effect of quadratic time given a correlation between the linear and quadratic random time slopes. So, from this perspective, it may be useful to add simultaneously all time-relevant effects of a time-invariant predictor (i.e., its main effect, interaction with linear time, and interaction with quadratic time) to an unconditional baseline model in order to assess all effect sizes of that time-invariant predictor.

Another important to thing to remember in calculating pseudo-R^2 values is to interpret the proportion of explained variance in the context of how much of that type of variance existed in the first place. For instance, consider a model for the variance that includes a level-1 residual variance (σ_e^2) and a level-2 random intercept variance ($\tau_{U_0}^2$) such that $\sigma_e^2 + \tau_{U_0}^2 = 10$. Let's say you added the main effect of a time-invariant predictor, which resulted in a 25% reduction of the random intercept variance. In considering the original total variance to be accounted for, if 80% was between-persons (original $\tau_{U_0}^2 = 8$), you would have explained an *absolute* amount of variance of $R^2 = 8*0.25 = 2$, or 20% of the *total* original outcome variance. But if only 10% of the total variance was between-persons (original $\tau_{U_0}^2 = 1$), in that case you would have explained an *absolute* amount of variance of $R^2 = 1*0.25 = 0.25$, or 2.5% of the *total* original outcome variance, which is not nearly as impressive. This is why pseudo-R^2 values should be interpreted in the context of the original size of the variance components (e.g., "of the 80% of the original outcome variation that was between persons, 25% of it was explained by the predictor").

However, this practice of referring to the original amount of variation no longer applies once random effects of other level-1 predictors (e.g., random linear time slopes) are included (which is why the appropriate baseline for assessing effect size of time-invariant predictors is the unconditional model for change with any needed fixed and random effects of time, and not the original empty means, random intercept model). Because random effects are correlated, their variances cannot be directly combined to describe the reduction in the original total variance without also taking into account the covariances among the random effects. Furthermore, as noted earlier, pseudo-R^2 values cannot be computed across models with different models for the variance (e.g., after including additional random effects variances) because the interpretation of each variance component will differ as a result of the new variance partitioning.

As this discussion has illustrated, the process of calculating pseudo-R^2 values can be fraught with difficulty and inconsistency. However, a simple solution to these problems is to treat the variance in the outcome across time as a *single* entity for the purpose of calculating **proportion of explained total outcome variance**. That is, for each observation we can generate a predicted outcome using the fixed effects in the model for the means. We can correlate the predicted outcome with the actual outcome—the square of that correlation is R^2—which is then a single number that describes how much of the *total* outcome variance was accounted for by the fixed effects. This approach creates a true R^2 given that it is based on the total original outcome variance, which can simplify interpretation in models with many piles of variance. The drawback is that we lose the ability to describe how well each part of the model works (i.e., how much of *each* pile of variance was predicted by its relevant fixed effects). But this may be an acceptable compromise given how useful a single R^2 value can be, as we'll see in the examples that follow.

2. Time-Invariant Predictors in Models for Within-Person Fluctuation

Our first example comes from the first measurement burst of the Cognition, Health, and Aging Project (as described in chapter 1), in which six assessments were collected over two weeks. Because of concerns about initial reactivity to the assessments, only sessions 2 to 6 when occurring within a two-week period were used in the analyses below. The analysis sample of 509 observations was obtained from 105 older adults age 69 to 95 years ($M = 80.13$, $SD = 6.11$), approximately 27% of which were men, who had complete data on all predictors to be included (just sex and age in chapter 7, as well as daily negative mood and daily stressors in chapter 8). The outcome was the number of physical symptoms participants reported experiencing in the past 24 hours, including aches/pain, gastrointestinal, cardiovascular, upper respiratory, and "other" symptoms. Few symptoms were reported on average per day ($M = 1.27$, $SD = 1.32$, range = 0 to 5).

Although up to this point we've used restricted maximum likelihood (REML) to estimate our example models when possible, the examples in this chapter use maximum likelihood (ML) instead. This is for a few reasons. First, although variance components can be under-estimated in ML, an empty means, random intercept model for these data revealed only a 1% downward bias in the size of the random intercept variance when using ML rather than REML, suggesting the results should be highly comparable with either estimator. Second, the models for prediction of heterogeneity of variance are not currently able to be estimated using REML (i.e., REML is not available in SAS NLMIXED). Finally, this chapter focuses primarily on fixed effects in the model for the means, and REML model fit statistics ($-2\Delta LL$, AIC, BIC) cannot be used to compare the fit of models that differ in fixed effects. Thus, the significance of a set of multiple fixed effects or of new variance model parameters will be tested by ML deviance difference tests (i.e., $-2\Delta LL$ likelihood ratio tests, as introduced in chapter 3), whereas the significance of individual fixed effects will be tested by their Wald test p-values as usual.

Our process of model building and evaluation will proceed as follows. We will first obtain an unconditional model to describe the variation and covariation of physical symptoms across days. We will then examine fixed effects for the time-invariant predictors of sex, age, and their interaction in the model for the means. Finally, we will examine heterogeneity of variance both between-persons and within-persons as a function of sex and age. The findings from this example will be summarized in a sample results section presented at the end of chapter.

2.A. Unconditional Model of Within-Person Fluctuation Over Time

We begin our examination of reported daily physical symptoms using an *empty means, random intercept* model as our most parsimonious baseline, as shown in Equation (7.3):

$$\textbf{Level 1}: \text{Symptoms}_{ti} = \beta_{0i} + e_{ti}$$
$$\textbf{Level 2}: \text{Intercept}: \beta_{0i} = \gamma_{00} + U_0 \tag{7.3}$$

Table 7.1 Results for the effects of time-invariant predictors in the model for the means for the 5-day physical symptom data. Bold values are $p < .05$.

Model Effects		Equation 7.3			Equation 7.4		
		Est	SE	p <	Est	SE	p <
Model for the Means							
γ_{00}	Intercept	**1.294**	0.112	.001	**1.713**	0.211	.001
γ_{01}	Sex (Men = 0, Women = 1)				**−0.531**	0.245	.033
	Age (0 = 80 years)						
γ_{02}	Age Slope in Men				**0.100**	0.037	.008
$\gamma_{02} + \gamma_{03}$	Age Slope in Women				−0.010	0.020	.607
γ_{03}	Sex by Age Interaction				**−0.110**	0.042	.010
Model for the Variance							
$\tau^2_{U_0}$	Random Intercept Variance	**1.189**	0.184	.001	**1.073**	0.167	.001
	Pseudo-R^2				.098		
σ^2_e	Residual Variance	**0.616**	0.043	.001	**0.615**	0.043	.001
	Pseudo-R^2				.002		
ML Model Fit							
	Number of Parameters	3			6		
	−2LL	1443.0			1432.6		
	AIC	1449.0			1444.6		
	BIC	1456.9			1460.5		

in which the level-1 model describes within-person daily variation in symptoms as a function of a person-specific intercept β_{0i} and a time-specific and person-specific deviation e_{ti}. Because there are no predictors in this empty means model, the β_{0i} individual intercept represents each person's mean symptoms across days. In the level-2 model for β_{0i}, each person's mean symptoms is then described by a fixed intercept γ_{00} (the grand mean of the person means) plus a person-specific random intercept U_{0i} (the difference between the grand mean and person i's mean across days).

Results from this model can be seen in the first set of columns in Table 7.1. The sample mean of physical symptoms is $\gamma_{00} = 1.294$ with a level-2 random intercept variance of $\tau^2_{U_0} = 1.189$ and a level-1 residual variance of $\sigma^2_e = 0.616$. As in previous chapters, we can use these results to calculate an intraclass correlation as ICC = $\tau^2_{U_0}$ / $(\tau^2_{U_0} + \sigma^2_e)$ = 1.189 / (1.189 + 0.616) = .659. Thus, 66% of the variance in symptoms is due to person mean differences, and 34% is due to within-person variation across days. We can also calculate a 95% random intercept confidence interval for the individual intercepts as CI = $\gamma_{00} \pm 1.96*\sqrt{\tau^2_{U_0}}$ = 1.294 ± 1.96*$\sqrt{1.189}$ = −0.843 to 3.431. This confidence intervals assumes a normal, symmetric distribution of the intercepts, such that 95% of the sample is predicted to have individual intercepts representing their person mean symptoms between –0.843 and 3.431 (on a 0 to 5 scale). The lower bound below 0 is likely due to positive skewness of the distribution of daily symptoms, and thus of person mean symptoms (as also indicated by the sample mean of only 1.294 symptoms). Accordingly, in reporting this confidence interval, we would truncate the lower bound at 0, the lowest possible of the outcome, and explicitly acknowledge the likely asymmetry of the random intercept distribution.

Here, *time* is unbalanced given that each person's five observations were collected during 14 possible days. Accordingly, it will not be possible to fit an unstructured variance model as the "answer key" because there is not enough data per person to estimate all possible variances and covariances across 14 days. Unfortunately, the options for alternative covariance structures when time is unbalanced are limited because most operate on the concept of a time-lag that implies equidistant occasions (see chapter 4). Although one option is to add an auto-regressive residual correlation, when attempted with these data it did not estimate properly. Therefore, in the model for the variance with respect to time, we will assume a constant correlation across days due to person mean differences via the random intercept variance $\tau_{U_0}^2$ in the level-2 **G** matrix, and constant residual variance σ_e^2 with no additional covariance across days in the level-1 **R** matrix.

In the model for the means, however, we can examine mean differences across time for two different metrics of time (but in which each person will contribute up to 5 days towards the overall mean trajectory spanning 14 possible days). First, reported physical symptoms might vary by *day of study* (i.e., reactivity effects such that fewer symptoms are reported at later occasions). In fitting a saturated means model for day of study 1 to 14, although no significant omnibus mean differences across days was found, $F(13, 416) = 0.62$, $p = .839$, there did appear to be somewhat of a decrease in the mean number of symptoms reported as the study progressed. However, a fixed linear effect of day of study did not contribute significantly to the model, as indicated by a Wald test $p = .369$, nor were there significant individual differences in the linear effect of day of study (i.e., no significant random linear effect of day of study), $-2\Delta LL(\sim 2) = 2.00$, $p = .371$. Thus, no fixed or random effects related to day of study were retained. Second, reported physical symptoms might vary systematically by *day of the week*. In fitting a saturated means model, though, no significant omnibus mean differences across day of the week were found, $F(6, 418) = 0.11$, $p = .995$. Furthermore, there was no significant differences on average between weekdays and weekends, as indicated by a fixed effect Wald test $p = .526$, and a model with a random weekend effect resulted in a 0 estimate of its random slope variance. Thus, no fixed or random effects related to day of week were retained—these decisions with respect to omitting fixed effects of time will be reconsidered in the chapter appendix as well.

2.B. Predicting Individual Differences in Outcome Level Over Time

We are now ready to examine the effects of the time-invariant predictors of sex and age on physical symptoms. Because no effects related to time are needed in the model for the means, the only individual effect to be predicted at level 2 is the intercept, as shown in Equation (7.4):

Level 1 : $\text{Symptoms}_{ti} = \beta_{0i} + e_{ti}$

Level 2 :

$$\text{Intercept: } \beta_{0i} = \gamma_{00} + \gamma_{01}(\text{Women}_i) + \gamma_{02}(\text{Age}_i - 80)$$
$$+ \gamma_{03}(\text{Women}_i)(\text{Age}_i - 80) + U_{0i}$$

(7.4)

in which the level-1 model is the same as in the empty means, random intercept model of Equation (7.3), but the level-2 equation for the intercept β_{0i} now contains three new fixed effects. The predictor for sex is labeled Women_i given that men = 0 and women = 1, and the predictor for age is written as $(\text{Age}_i - 80)$ to indicate that 80 years is the centering point (i.e., age 80 is the new 0). Thus, the reference point for the model intercept is an 80-year-old man (i.e., $\text{Women}_i = 0$ and $\text{Age}_i - 80 = 0$). The time-invariant predictors of Women_i and Age_i have subscripts of i to indicate that they vary over persons, but they do not have a subscript of t because they do not vary over time (as would be the case for any time-invariant predictor in the level-2 model). Results from this model can be seen in the second set of columns in Table 7.1. In addition to their significant individual coefficients discussed next, as a whole the three fixed effects for women, age, and their interaction significantly improved model fit relative to the empty means, random intercept only model, as evaluated by an ML likelihood ratio test, $-2\Delta LL(3) = 10.4$, $p < .015$. The smaller AIC value concurs, although the larger BIC value does not.

Given the predictor centering, the fixed intercept $\gamma_{00} = 1.713$ is the expected mean symptoms across days for an 80-year-old man (on any day because there are no effects for time in the model for the means). The main effects of women and age are conditional given their interaction term. Accordingly, the *simple main effect of women* of $\gamma_{01} = -0.531$ indicates that specifically among 80-year-olds, women report 0.531 fewer mean symptoms across days than men. The *simple main effect of age* of $\gamma_{02} = 0.100$ indicates that specifically in men, the number of mean symptoms across days is higher by 0.100 per additional year of age. The *women by age interaction* of $\gamma_{03} = -0.110$ can be interpreted two ways: For every additional year of age, the sex difference in mean symptoms across days in which men report more symptoms becomes larger (more negative) by -0.110, or the effect of age on mean symptoms across days is smaller (less positive) by -0.110 in women than in men. The simple effect of age in women of $\gamma_{02} + \gamma_{03} = 0.100 - 0.111 = -0.010$ was nonsignificant (as can be obtained by coding women = 0 instead, or via statements like ESTIMATE in SAS, TEST in SPSS, LINCOM in STATA, or NEW in Mplus).

The coefficient for the interaction of sex by age tells us that the simple effect of sex in which men report more mean symptoms grows by $\gamma_{03} = -0.110$ per year of age, and we can further decompose the simple effect of sex by calculating **regions of significance**, as originally described in chapter 2. The example calculations using the covariance matrix of the parameter estimates (i.e., the square of the fixed effect standard errors and their covariances) are available in the online resources for the text. The upper and lower boundaries for age as the moderator of the sex difference are -0.478 and -19.836, respectively, which translate into ages of 79.522

and 60.164 years given the centering such that age 0 = 80 years. Thus, at age 79.522 or older, women are expected to report significantly *fewer* mean symptoms across days than men. Between 60.164 and 79.522 years there is no significant sex difference. At 60.164 years or younger, women are expected to report significantly *more* mean symptoms across days than men. However, the latter effect would not occur in this sample, in which age ranges from 69 to 95 years, such that approximately 50% of these persons are older than 80. Therefore, we would expect a significant sex difference (with women reporting fewer mean symptoms) for about half the sample.

Relative to the previous unconditional baseline model with no fixed effects of sex or age, the proportion reduction in the level-2 random intercept variance $\tau_{U_0}^2$ was pseudo-R^2 = (1.189 − 1.073) / 1.189 = .098. Therefore, of the 65.9% of the variance in reported daily physical symptoms that was originally due to between-person mean differences, approximately 9.80% of it can be explained by the effects of women, age, and their interaction (which translates to .659*.098 = .065, or 6.50% of the *total* symptoms variance). Accordingly, in Equation (7.4), U_{0i} is now the deviation between each person's own intercept and the fixed intercept predicted by the model from effects of women, age, and their interaction—that is, U_{0i} represents the 90.2% of the random intercept variance that still remains. As expected given no cross-level interactions with any time-varying level-1 predictors, the pseudo-R^2 for the level-1 residual variance σ_e^2 was $\approx$ 0%.

Finally, we could also determine the proportion reduction of the *total* symptoms variance by calculating predicted outcomes from the fixed effects in the model for the means. The Pearson correlation between the predicted and actual outcomes for the 509 observations was r = .220, or R^2 = .048, or a reduction of $\approx$ 4.8% of the total daily symptoms variance (which is not "pseudo" because it is based on the original symptoms variance and not model-estimated partitions thereof). To summarize, it appears only 5% to 6% of the total variance in daily physical symptoms was related to person mean differences predictable by sex, age, and their interaction—a small effect size at best. As this example illustrates, though, the methods for calculating the proportion reduction in variance may not converge on the same estimates—and this is why it will be important to always describe exactly how any R^2 values were obtained in reporting your results.

2.C. Predicting Individual Differences in Variation

In addition to their roles in the model for the means, time-invariant predictors may also contribute to the model for the variance by predicting heterogeneity of variance across persons at level 2, as well as across time at level 1. Accordingly, we continue by examining whether the *amount* of variance at each level of the longitudinal model differs by sex, age, and their interaction, beginning with the level-2 random intercept variance $\tau_{U_0}^2$, as seen in Equation (7.5):

Level 1:

Symptoms$_{ti}$ = β_{0i} + e$_{ti}$

Residual Variance: $\sigma^2_{e_{ti}}$ = exp$[\eta_{0i}]$

Level 2:

Intercept: β_{0i} = γ_{00} + γ_{01}(Women$_i$) + γ_{02}(Age$_i$ − 80) + γ_{03}(Women$_i$) $\qquad$ (7.5)
(Age$_i$ − 80) + U$_{0i}$

Random Intercept Variance $\tau^2_{U_{0i}}$ = exp$\begin{bmatrix} \upsilon_{00} + \upsilon_{01}(\text{Women}_i) + \upsilon_{02}(\text{Age}_i - 80) \\ + \upsilon_{03}(\text{Women}_i)(\text{Age}_i - 80) \end{bmatrix}$

Residual Variance: η_{0i} = ε_{00}

in which the amount of random intercept variance $\tau^2_{U_0}$ itself is now predicted as a function of Women$_i$, Age$_i$, and their interaction, and thus is now written as $\tau^2_{U_{0i}}$ given that it varies over persons. The predictor effects on the level-2 random intercept variance $\tau^2_{U_0}$ are indicated here by the υ terms (pronounced "upsilon"), which have the same subscripts as their corresponding fixed effects in the model for the means. Although there is currently no general accepted notation for heterogeneous variance models like this, the symbol υ was chosen based on its visual similarity to U$_{0i}$ to help us remember that the U$_{0i}$ variance is what the υ terms are predicting. But because variances can't be negative, the exp[ ] term (or e$^{[\ ]}$) is used so that the υ terms predict the natural log of $\tau^2_{U_{0i}}$ (rather than the original $\tau^2_{U_{0i}}$), ensuring positive predicted values for $\tau^2_{U_{0i}}$. The values for the υ terms are scaled such that log($\tau^2_{U_{0i}}$) = the prediction given by the [ ] terms.

The υ_{00} term functions like an intercept for the variance equation—it is the expected log of the random intercept variance specifically for 80-year-old men. The other υ effects are similar to simple main effects and interactions, but they predict the *amount* of log $\tau^2_{U_{0i}}$ (rather than the person mean differences themselves as in the model for the means). That is, they don't explain $\tau^2_{U_{0i}}$ variance; they predict how much $\tau^2_{U_{0i}}$ variance exists in reported symptoms from different kinds of people. Thus, υ_{01} is the difference in log $\tau^2_{U_{0i}}$ specifically between 80-year-old men and women, υ_{02} is the effect on log $\tau^2_{U_{0i}}$ of a one-unit difference in age specifically in men, and υ_{03} is how the age effect on log $\tau^2_{U_{0i}}$ differs between men and women (or how the sex difference in log $\tau^2_{U_{0i}}$ differs by age). Finally, although it is not yet predicted by anything, for similarity of scale, the natural log of the level-1 residual variance σ^2_e is now also modeled rather than the original σ^2_e, and it is now labeled as $\sigma^2_{e_{ti}}$ given that it could vary over both persons and days. The symbol ε (pronounced "epsilon") was chosen for the effects of the predictors on log $\sigma^2_{e_{ti}}$ based on its visual similarity to e$_{ti}$ to help us remember that the e$_{ti}$ variance is what the ε terms will be predicting (although ε_{00} is just the expected natural log of $\sigma^2_{e_{ti}}$ for all persons and days so far).

The model in Equation (7.5) must be estimated with software that allows user-defined variance terms, such as SAS NLMIXED, in which good starting values for all parameters are essential. Starting values for the model for the means (and for the υ_{00} and ε_{00} "intercepts" of the predicted variance terms) can be obtained from the previous results, and starting values of 0 are likely to be reasonable for the other effects of predictors on the random intercept and residual variances (i.e., the other υ and ε effects, which could conceivably be positive or negative). As in the nonlinear models from chapter 6, different starting values should be tried to ensure that the model converges onto the same set of estimates. Acceptable convergence is also indicated by gradient values for the partial first derivatives with respect to each parameter that are close to 0, as can be requested in some programs (such as SAS NLMIXED).

The results for the model in Equation (7.5) are shown in the first set of columns in Table 7.2. The intercept-like term for the expected natural log of the random intercept variance $\tau^2_{U_{0i}}$ for an 80-year-old man was estimated as $\upsilon_{00} = 0.481$, such that $\tau^2_{U_{0i}} = \exp[0.481] = 1.618$. The simple main effect of sex on log $\tau^2_{U_{0i}}$ of $\upsilon_{01} = -0.594$ indicates nonsignificantly less between-person variability in mean physical symptoms in 80-year-old women (in which log $\tau^2_{U_{0i}} = 0.481 + -0.594[1] = -0.113$) than in 80-year-old men (in which log $\tau^2_{U_{0i}} = 0.481$). The simple main effect of age on log $\tau^2_{U_{0i}}$ of $\upsilon_{02} = 0.068$ indicates a nonsignificant expected increase of 0.068 in log $\tau^2_{U_{0i}}$ per year older age specifically in men (so nonsignificantly greater between-person variability in mean physical symptoms in older men than in younger men). Finally, the women by age interaction on log $\tau^2_{U_{0i}}$ of $\upsilon_{03} = -0.077$ indicates that the sex difference in log $\tau^2_{U_{0i}}$ (in which women were less variable) grows nonsignificantly by -0.077 per year of age, or that the age effect on log $\tau^2_{U_{0i}}$ is less positive by -0.077 in women. Just as we did for the fixed effects, we can also obtain the simple effect of age for women on log $\tau^2_{U_{0i}}$ as $\upsilon_{02} + \upsilon_{03} = 0.068 - 0.077 = -0.008$, which is also not significant, as reported in Table 7.2. Not surprisingly given their lack of individual significance, as a set the υ_{01}, υ_{02}, and υ_{03} effects on log $\tau^2_{U_{0i}}$ for women, age, and their interaction did not significantly improve the model, $-2\Delta LL(3) = 4.4$, $p = .224$. The main effects of women and age on log $\tau^2_{U_{0i}}$ remained nonsignificant when their interaction on log $\tau^2_{U_{0i}}$ was removed from the model, and so all three effects on log $\tau^2_{U_{0i}}$ were removed from the model. Thus, the amount of between-person variability in mean physical symptoms reported across days does not appear to differ systematically between men and women or by age.

However, it is still possible for the amount of *within-person* variability in physical symptoms to show systematic individual differences (some of which may be predictable by person-level variables like sex and age). That is, the *amount of daily fluctuation* in reported symptoms may differ randomly across persons, as now permitted in Equation (7.6):

Level 1:

$\text{Symptoms}_{ti} = \beta_{0i} + e_{ti}$

Residual Variance: $\sigma^2_{e_{ti}} = \exp[\eta_{0i}]$

Level 2:

Intercept: $\beta_{0i} = \gamma_{00} + \gamma_{01}(\text{Women}_i) + \gamma_{02}(\text{Age}_i - 80)$ (7.6)

$\qquad\qquad + \gamma_{03}(\text{Women}_i)(\text{Age}_i - 80) + U_{0i}$

Random Intercept Variance $\tau^2_{U_{0i}} = \exp[\upsilon_{00}]$

Residual Variance: $\eta_{0i} = \varepsilon_{00} + \omega_{0i}$

Table 7.2 Results for the effects of time-invariant predictors in the model for the means and the model for the variances for the 5-day physical symptom data. Bold values are $p < .05$.

Model Effects		Equation 7.5			Equation 7.7		
		Est	SE	p <	Est	SE	p <
Model for the Means							
γ_{00}	Intercept	**1.701**	0.269	.001	**1.710**	0.211	.001
γ_{01}	Sex (Men = 0, Women = 1)	−0.517	0.293	.080	**−0.528**	0.245	.034
	Age (0 = 80 years)						
γ_{02}	Age Slope in Men	0.091	0.047	.054	**0.099**	0.037	.009
$\gamma_{02} + \gamma_{03}$	Age Slope in Women	−0.012	0.020	.542	−0.010	0.020	.613
γ_{03}	Sex by Age Interaction	**−0.103**	0.051	.045	**−0.109**	0.042	.011
Model for the Variance^							
υ_{00}	Random Intercept Variance	0.481	0.296	.107	0.065	0.156	.679
υ_{01}	Sex (Men = 0, Women = 1)	−0.594	0.349	.091			
	Age (0 = 80 years)						
υ_{02}	Age Slope in Men	0.068	0.060	.258			
$\upsilon_{02} + \upsilon_{03}$	Age Slope in Women	−0.008	0.035	.813			
υ_{03}	Sex by Age Interaction	−0.077	0.069	.273			
ε_{00}	Residual Variance	**−0.487**	0.070	.001	**−0.421**	0.146	.005
ε_{01}	Sex (Men = 0, Women = 1)				−0.085	0.167	.610
	Age (0 = 80 years)						
ε_{02}	Age Slope in Men				0.012	0.024	.616
$\varepsilon_{02} + \varepsilon_{03}$	Age Slope in Women				0.008	0.014	.601
ε_{03}	Sex by Age Interaction				−0.004	0.028	.872
ML Model Fit							
	Number of Parameters	9			9		
	−2LL	1428.2			1431.9		
	AIC	1444.6			1449.9		
	BIC	1470.1			1473.8		

^ The terms in the model for the variance are each contained within an exponent as exp[ ], and as such predict the natural log of the random intercept or residual variance.

in which the natural log of the level-2 random intercept variance $\tau^2_{U_{0i}}$ is now constant across persons (i.e., predicted only by exp[υ_{00}], given the results of the previous model), but in which the natural log of the level-1 residual variance $\sigma^2_{e_{ti}}$ is now decomposed into a two-level equation. This is necessary because $\sigma^2_{e_{ti}}$ includes variance over both persons and days (and thus log $\sigma^2_{e_{ti}}$ can have predictors at level 1 or level 2, whereas log $\tau^2_{U_{0i}}$ only required a single-level model given that it could only have predictors at level 2). As before, the exp[ ] term predicts log $\sigma^2_{e_{ti}}$ rather than the original $\sigma^2_{e_{ti}}$ so that the predicted values for its variance stay positive.

In the level-1 model, log $\sigma^2_{e_{ti}}$ is predicted by a placeholder η_{0i} for person i's residual variance (analogous to β_{0i} in the level-1 model for symptoms) that is then decomposed at by its level-2 equation with two terms. First is the intercept-like ε_{00} term for the mean log $\sigma^2_{e_{ti}}$ for the sample (as in the previous model). The second ω_{0i} term is known as a **scale factor** (see Hedeker, Mermelstein, & Demirtas, 2008), that represents person i's deviation from the mean value of log $\sigma^2_{e_{ti}}$ (analogous to the random intercept U_{0i} in the level-2 model for β_{0i}), or the extent to which persons differ randomly from each other in the amount of their daily *fluctuation* in reported symptoms. The person-specific scale factor ω_{0i} becomes a random effect with a log-normal distribution whose variance (labeled $\tau^2_{\omega_0}$) and covariance with any other random effects are then estimated in the model. Time-invariant predictors can then be included in the level-2 model for η_{0i} to predict individual differences the amount of within-person fluctuation in daily reported symptoms, thereby reducing the scale factor variance $\tau^2_{\omega_0}$ (and time-varying predictors could also be included in the level-1 model for $\sigma^2_{e_{ti}}$, as we'll see in chapter 8). Finally, note that there is no analogous e_{ti} residual term in the level-1 model for log $\sigma^2_{e_{ti}}$ because ε_{00} is already the expected residual variance (i.e., there are no further deviations in physical symptoms to be considered).

In estimating the model in Equation (7.6) to our example data, however, the variance of the scale factor ω_{0i} could not be estimated, and thus we cannot retain it in the model. These types of heterogeneous variance models are recent developments, and empirical study of their properties is still ongoing. In this case, however, there are several possibilities for the lack an estimable individual scale factor variance. One possibility is that there truly are no individual differences in the amount of within-person variability in daily reported symptoms. A more likely possibility is that five observations per person do not provide sufficient information with which to reliable capture individual differences in within-person symptom variability. If quantifying and predicting differential within-person variability is of interest, then it would be advantageous to have as many level-1 observations as possible to have as much power to do so as possible.

Nevertheless, for the sake of illustration, we can examine if within-person fluctuation differs systematically across persons as a function of sex and age (although not randomly across persons otherwise), as seen in one final model for these example data in Equation (7.7):

Level 1:

$$\text{Symptoms}_{ti} = \beta_{0i} + e_{ti}$$
$$\text{Residual Variance: } \sigma^2_{e_{ti}} = \exp[\eta_{0i}]$$

Level 2:

$$\text{Intercept: } \beta_{0i} = \gamma_{00} + \gamma_{01}(\text{Women}_i) + \gamma_{02}(\text{Age}_i - 80)$$
$$+ \gamma_{03}(\text{Women}_i)(\text{Age}_i - 80) + U_{0i}$$

(7.7)

$$\text{Random Intercept Variance } \tau^2_{U_{0i}} = \exp[\upsilon_{00}]$$
$$\text{Residual Variance: } \eta_{0i} = \varepsilon_{00} + \varepsilon_{01}(\text{Women}_i) + \varepsilon_{02}(\text{Age}_i - 80)$$
$$+ \varepsilon_{03}(\text{Women}_i)(\text{Age}_i - 80)$$

in which the log of $\sigma^2_{e_{ti}}$ (as represented by the level-1 placeholder η_{0i}) is now predicted at level 2 by Women$_i$, Age$_i$, and their interaction, but no random scale factor ω_{0i} is included.

The results for the model in Equation (7.7) are shown in the second columns of Table 7.2. The intercept-like term for the expected natural log of the level-1 residual variance $\sigma^2_{e_{ti}}$ for an 80-year-old man was $\varepsilon_{00} = -0.421$, such that $\sigma^2_{e_{ti}} = \exp[-0.421] = 0.656$. The simple main effect of sex on log $\sigma^2_{e_{ti}}$ of $\varepsilon_{01} = -0.085$ indicates nonsignificantly less within-person fluctuation in daily symptoms in 80-year-old women (in which log $\sigma^2_{e_{ti}} = -0.421 - 0.085[1] = -0.506$) than in 80-year-old men (in which log $\sigma^2_{e_{ti}} = -0.421$). The simple main effect of age on log $\sigma^2_{e_{ti}}$ of $\varepsilon_{02} = 0.012$ indicates a nonsignificant difference of 0.012 in log $\sigma^2_{e_{ti}}$ per year older specifically in men (so nonsignificantly greater within-person daily fluctuation in symptoms in older men). Finally, the women by age interaction on log $\sigma^2_{e_{ti}}$ of $\varepsilon_{03} = -0.004$ indicates that the sex difference in log $\sigma^2_{e_{ti}}$ (in which women were less variable across days) grows nonsignificantly by -0.004 per year of age, or that the age effect on log $\sigma^2_{e_{ti}}$ is less positive by -0.004 in women. We can also obtain the simple effect of age for women on log $\sigma^2_{e_{ti}}$ as $\varepsilon_{02} + \varepsilon_{03} = 0.012 - 0.004 = 0.008$, which is also not significant, as reported in Table 7.2. Not surprisingly given their lack of individual significance, as a set the effects on log $\sigma^2_{e_{ti}}$ for women, age, and their interaction did not significantly improve the model, $-2\Delta LL(3) = 0.7$, $p = .873$. The main effects of women and age on log $\sigma^2_{e_{ti}}$ remained nonsignificant when their interaction on log $\sigma^2_{e_{ti}}$ was removed, and so all effects on log $\sigma^2_{e_{ti}}$ were removed. Thus, the amount of within-person daily symptom fluctuation does not appear to differ systematically between men and women or by age.

2.D. Summary

The previous example served to illustrate the role of time-invariant predictors (e.g., sex, age) in longitudinal models for outcomes that show within-person fluctuation over time (e.g., daily reported physical symptoms). In the model for the means, we found that sex and age combined interactively to predict individual differences in mean symptoms across days, such that greater mean symptoms were reported with age in men, but not in women; women reported significantly fewer mean symptoms than men only after age 79. The effects of sex, age, and their interaction accounted for $\approx 9.8\%$ of the random intercept variance in symptoms, or $\approx 4.8\%$ of the total symptoms variance. In the model for the variance, we found that sex and age were unrelated to both the amount of between-person variation in mean symptoms and the amount of within-person fluctuation in daily symptoms (i.e., no moderation by sex or age of the size of the level-2 random intercept or level-1 residual variances, respectively). The lack of prediction for the amount of within-person fluctuation is not too surprising given that we could not estimate a variance to quantify those individual differences in the first place, though. In chapter 8 we will continue with this example but include only those effects that were significant here (e.g., a homogeneous variance model with fixed effects for sex, age, and their interaction in the model for the means only). But for now, we turn to our second example, the goal of which is to illustrate the role of time-invariant predictors in models of within-person change over time.

3. Time-Invariant Predictors in Models for Within-Person Change

Our second example features simulated data based on The Pennsylvania State University Family Relationships Project (as described in chapter 1), in which seven (approximately annual) assessments were collected from 200 adolescent girls age 12 to 18 ($M = 15.00$, $SD = 2.00$, range = 11.53 to 18.34 years; 1,400 total observations). The outcome variable was a sum of 10 items indexing frequency of risky behavior (e.g., smoking, drinking, shoplifting, skipping school), in which each item response ranged from 1 to 5 (for a possible range of 10 to 50; $M = 19.38$, $SD = 5.30$, observed range 10.00 to 36.28). The time-invariant predictor of interest is an index of their mothers' attitudes about smoking and drinking, as measured by the mean across 26 items on a 1 to 5 scale, where higher values indicate more conservative attitudes ($M = 3.95$, $SD = 0.60$, observed range = 2.44 to 5.00). Although mothers' attitudes may indeed change over time, the attitudes variable is a time-invariant predictor given that it was only assessed at age 12.

ML will again be used instead of REML to estimate the models that follow given a <1% downward bias in the random intercept variance under ML relative to REML and the need to compare models differing in fixed effects. Accordingly, the significance of a set of multiple fixed effects or random effects variances and covariances will be tested by ML $-2\Delta LL$ tests, whereas the significance of individual fixed effects will be tested by their Wald test p-values. As usual, we will first obtain an unconditional model of within-person change to describe the overall pattern of and individual differences in change in risky behavior across age; random effect variability will be described using 95% random effects confidence intervals (calculated as the fixed effect $\pm1.96*SQRT$(random effect variance). We will then examine fixed effects for the time-invariant predictor of parent attitudes at age 12 about smoking and drinking.

3.A. Unconditional Model of Within-Person Change Over Time

As usual, we begin with an empty means, random intercept model for risky behavior. The model-predicted mean risky behavior across age was $\gamma_{00} = 19.38$, with a level-2 random intercept variance of $\tau_{U_0}^2 = 10.84$ and a level-1 residual variance of $\sigma_e^2 = 17.24$. The intraclass correlation was ICC = $\tau_{U_0}^2 / (\tau_{U_0}^2 + \sigma_e^2) = 10.84 / (10.84 + 17.24) = .39$, indicating that 39% of the variation in risky behavior resulted from constant mean differences between persons. The ICC = .39 was significantly greater than 0, as indicated by $-2\Delta LL(\sim1) = 345.7$, $p < .001$, relative to a model without the random intercept variance. Observed individual trajectories are shown in the top panel of Figure 7.1. Although exact age was not completely balanced across persons, for descriptive purposes, a balanced age variable was created by rounding age to the nearest year in order to estimate a saturated means, unstructured variance model (i.e., in which the mean, variance, and covariance across each age was estimated). A significant omnibus effect of age was obtained, $F(6, 200) = 55.47$, $p < .001$, such that risky behavior increased from a mean of 16.72 at age 12 to 23.52 at age 18, as shown in the bottom panel of Figure 7.1. The variances and covariances for risky behavior also increased across time (not shown).

Because there was no theoretical or observed breakpoint for a change in the age slope (i.e., that might suggest a piecewise model), and because change in risky behavior did not appear to level off over time (i.e., that might suggest a negative exponential model) or to accelerate dramatically (i.e., that might suggest a positive exponential model), polynomial random effects models will be used to describe

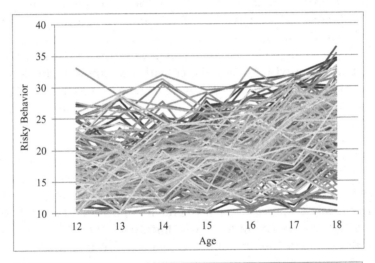

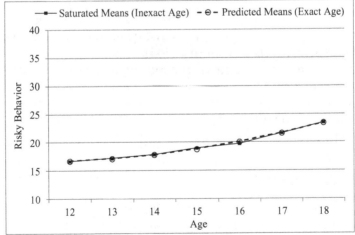

Figure 7.1 Individual trajectories for risky behavior across age (top panel); observed and model-predicted mean trajectories for risky behavior across age (bottom panel).

continuous change in risky behavior across exact age. Unlike previous examples, however, the reference point for exact age will not be the beginning of the study—it will be the end instead (i.e., via $Age_{ti} - 18$). This is for two reasons. First, this example study is focused on predicting longitudinal outcomes given earlier information (i.e., behavior at age 18 given parent attitudes at age 12), and centering at age 18 will allow us to test the age 18 outcome specifically via the main effects in the conditional model (i.e., after adding predictors besides age). Second, there is more variability in risky behavior at age 18 than at age 12 (as seen in Figure 7.1), and so the random intercept variance should be easier to estimate when it is conditional on age 18 than on age 12. Although this may not be a problem here, for purposes of demonstration for similar studies, our intercept will be conditional on (exact) age 18.

To begin, a fixed linear effect of age centered at 18 years ($Age_{ti} - 18$) was entered into the empty means, random intercept model. It was significant as indicated by its Wald test ($p < .001$) and accounted for 34.0% of the level-1 residual variance. Risky behavior increased by an average of 1.12 per year, creating a predicted average of 22.74 by age 18. Given these fixed effects, the intercept at age 12 is predicted to have been $22.74 + (-6*1.12) = 16.03$. Next, a variance for the random linear age slope was added (along with its covariance with the random intercept), resulting in a significant improvement in model fit, $-2\Delta LL(\sim 2) = 120.8$, $p < .001$, indicating significant individual differences in the linear rate of increase in risky behavior across age. A fixed quadratic effect of age ($Age_{ti} - 18)^2$ was then entered into the random linear age slope model. It was also significant as indicated by its Wald test ($p < .001$) and accounted for 4.2% of the remaining level-1 residual variance. The linear age slope became more positive by twice the quadratic coefficient of 0.14 per year, resulting in an instantaneous linear age slope of 1.99 per year as evaluated at age 18. Thus, the rate of increase in risky behavior appeared to accelerate across age on average. A variance for the random quadratic age slope was then added (along with its covariances with the random intercept and random linear age slope), but did not significantly improve model fit, $-2\Delta LL(\sim 3) = 5.3$, $p = .153$, indicating no individual differences in acceleration of risky behavior across age. Finally, a fixed cubic effect of age was then added to the fixed quadratic, random linear age slope model, but it was also not significant ($p = .444$).

Based on these results, our final unconditional growth model is shown in Equation (7.8):

$$
\begin{aligned}
\textbf{Level 1:} \quad & \text{Risky Behavior}_{ti} = \beta_{0i} + \beta_{1i}(Age_{ti} - 18) + \beta_{2i}(Age_{ti} - 18)^2 + e_{ti} \\
\textbf{Level 2:} \quad & \text{Intercept:} \quad \beta_{0i} = \gamma_{00} + U_{0i} \\
& \text{Linear Age:} \quad \beta_{1i} = \gamma_{10} + U_{1i} \\
& \text{Quadratic Age:} \quad \beta_{2i} = \gamma_{20} \\
\textbf{Composite:} \quad & y_{ti} = (\gamma_{00} + U_{0i}) + (\gamma_{10} + U_{1i})(Age_{ti} - 18) \\
& \quad\quad + (\gamma_{20})(Age_{ti} - 18)^2 + e_{ti}
\end{aligned}
\tag{7.8}
$$

which includes a fixed quadratic age slope but a random linear age slope. Results are given in the first set of columns in Table 7.3 and can be interpreted as follows.

Table 7.3 Results for the effects of the time-invariant mother's attitudes predictor for the risky behavior data. Bold values are $p < .05$.

Parameters		Unconditional Growth Model (7.8)			Attitudes by Intercept (7.9)			Attitudes by Intercept and Linear Age (7.9)			Attitudes by Intercept, Linear Age, and Quadratic Age (7.9)		
		Est	SE	p <	Est	SE	p <	Est	SE	p <	Est	SE	p <
Model for the Means													
γ_{00}	Intercept	**23.47**	0.37	.001	**23.40**	0.36	.001	**23.31**	0.35	.001	**23.30**	0.35	.001
γ_{10}	Linear Age Slope (0 = 18)	**1.99**	0.15	.001	**1.99**	0.15	.001	**1.96**	0.15	.001	**1.95**	0.15	.001
γ_{20}	Quadratic Age Slope	**0.14**	0.02	.001	**0.14**	0.02	.001	**0.15**	0.02	.001	**0.14**	0.02	.001
γ_{01}	Mothers' Attitudes (0 = 4)				**-1.33**	0.41	.001	**-3.16**	0.55	.001	**-3.48**	0.58	.001
γ_{11}	Attitudes by Linear Age							**-0.52**	0.10	.001	**-0.90**	0.24	.001
γ_{21}	Attitudes by Quadratic Age										-0.06	0.04	.078
Model for the Variance													
$\tau^2_{U_0}$	Random Intercept Variance	**21.69**	2.56	.001	**19.30**	2.39	.001	**18.08**	2.20	.001	**18.08**	2.20	.001
	Pseudo-R²				.11			.06			.00		
$\tau^2_{U_1}$	Linear Age Slope Variance	**0.58**	0.09	.001	**0.58**	0.09	.001	**0.49**	0.08	.001	**0.49**	0.08	.001
	Pseudo-R²				0.00			.17			.00		
$\tau_{U_{01}}$	Intercept-Linear Age Slope Covariance	**2.48**	0.41	.001	**2.23**	0.40	.001	**1.88**	0.36	.001	**1.89**	0.36	.001
σ^2_e	Residual Variance	**8.35**	0.37	.001	**8.35**	0.37	.001	**8.35**	0.37	.001	**8.33**	0.37	.001
	Pseudo-R²				.00			.00			.00		
	Total R²	.19			.22			.24			.24		
ML Model Fit													
	Number of Parameters	7			8			9			10		
	−2LL	7634.8			7625.6			7602.5			7599.4		
	AIC	7648.8			7641.6			7620.5			7619.4		
	BIC	7671.9			7667.9			7650.2			7652.4		

Mean risky behavior at age 18 was predicted as $\gamma_{00} = 23.47$, which is moderate risky behavior. We can calculate a 95% random intercept confidence interval as CI = $\gamma_{00} \pm 1.96*\text{SQRT}[\tau_{U_0}^2]$ = 23.47 ± 1.96*SQRT[21.69] = 14.34 to 32.59. This CI assumes a normal, symmetric random intercept distribution, such that 95% of the sample is predicted to have individual intercepts representing their risky behavior at age 18 between 14.34 and 32.59 (on a 10 to 50 scale). The instantaneous linear rate of change per year at age 18 was predicted as $\gamma_{10} = 1.99$, with a 95% random linear age slope confidence interval as CI = $\gamma_{10} \pm 1.96*\text{SQRT}[\tau_{U_1}^2]$ = 1.99 ± 1.96*SQRT[0.58] = 0.49 to 3.49, such that 95% of the sample is predicted to have individual linear age slopes at age 18 for their change in risky behavior per year between 0.49 and 3.49. Thus, while risky behavior is still increasing on average at age 18, the linear age slope variance around it (which is unconditional across age) suggests that the extent of this increase at age 18 varies across girls. Finally, the fixed quadratic age slope was $\gamma_{20} = 0.14$, with no 95% random confidence interval given the lack of significant individual variation. Thus, the linear age slope was predicted to become more positive by 0.28 per year for all girls. Given these fixed effects, the linear age slope at age 12 is predicted to be 1.99 + (–6*0.28) = 0.25, which was marginally significant (SE = 0.15, $p = .088$).

Finally, as shown in the bottom panel of Figure 7.1, the model-predicted means closely approximate the means from the saturated means (inexact) age model, suggesting that a quadratic model successfully summarizes the overall mean pattern of change in risky behavior across age. However, the fixed linear and quadratic effects of age predicted only 19% of the total variance in risky behavior (i.e., as computed from the square of the correlation between the actual and age-predicted outcome), suggesting that other variables besides age will need to be considered.

3.B. Predicting Individual Differences in the Intercept and Rates of Change Over Time

The next step in our example analysis is to examine how mothers' attitudes about smoking and drinking at age 12 might predict change in risky behavior from age 12 to age 18. Although the construct of risky behavior is more broad, it may be reasonable to infer that girls whose mothers are more conservative about smoking and drinking may engage in those behaviors (as well as other related risky behaviors) at a lower rate—this will be our empirical question. The full model we will eventually examine is shown in Equation (7.9):

Level 1 : Risky Behavior$_{ti}$ = $\beta_{0i} + \beta_{1i}(\text{Age}_{ti} - 18) + \beta_{2i}(\text{Age}_{ti} - 18)^2 + e_{ti}$

Level 2 : Intercept: $\beta_{0i} = \gamma_{00} + \gamma_{01}(\text{Attitudes12}_i - 4) + U_{0i}$

Linear Age: $\beta_{1i} = \gamma_{10} + \gamma_{11}(\text{Attitudes12}_i - 4) + U_{1i}$

Quadratic Age: $\beta_{2i} = \gamma_{20} + \gamma_{21}(\text{Attitudes12}_i - 4)$ (7.9)

Composite : $y_{ti} = \{\gamma_{00} + \gamma_{01}(\text{Attitudes12}_i - 4) + U_{0i}\} +$

$\{\gamma_{10} + \gamma_{11}(\text{Attitudes12}_i - 4) + U_{1i}\}(\text{Age}_{ti} - 18) +$

$\{\gamma_{20} + \gamma_{21}(\text{Attitudes12}_i - 4)\quad\}(\text{Age}_{ti} - 18)^2 + e_{ti}$

which includes a time-invariant predictor of mothers' attitudes at age 12 (centered at the scale mean of 4 out of 5) in each level-2 equation. To illustrate the impact of *each* new fixed effect, though, we will examine each incrementally, as reported in Table 7.3 and discussed below.

The first effect to be examined of mothers' attitudes collected at age 12 is a main effect (γ_{01}), which will predict individual differences in the intercept. As shown in the second set of columns in Table 7.3, the main effect of attitudes indicated that for every one-unit higher (more conservative) a mother's attitude is about smoking and drinking taken at age 12, her daughter is predicted to have significantly lower risky behavior *on average* by $\gamma_{01} = -1.33$. Although the main effect of attitudes does apply to the intercept at age 18 specifically, the lack of any included interactions of age (so far) means that the model predicts a constant effect of attitudes across age.

After including the main effect of mothers' attitudes, U_{0i} now represents the remaining deviation between each girl's intercept and the intercept predicted by her mother's attitudes. As shown in Table 7.3, approximately 11% of the random intercept variance was accounted for by the main effect of attitudes (Pseudo-R^2 for $\tau^2_{U_0} = .11$); as expected, the other variance components were not reduced (Pseudo-R^2 values $\approx .00$). The total variance accounted for in risky behavior rose to 22% (i.e., as computed from the square of the Pearson correlation between the actual outcome and the outcome predicted from the fixed effects of age and attitudes).

Next, the results when predicting both the intercept and linear age slope are shown in the third set of columns in Table 7.3. Given its interaction with age, the main effect of attitudes is now conditional on age 18 (i.e., when $Age_{ti} - 18 = 0$). Accordingly, for every one-unit higher (more conservative) a mother's attitude about smoking and drinking taken at age 12, her daughter is predicted to have significantly lower risky behavior at age 18 by $\gamma_{01} = -3.16$, and a significantly less positive linear age change in risky behavior per year by $\gamma_{11} = -0.52$. These effects are illustrated in Figure 7.2, which

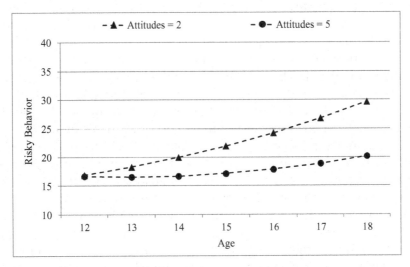

Figure 7.2 Predicted trajectories for risky behavior across age by mothers' attitudes about smoking and drinking taken at age 12. Higher values indicate more conservative attitudes.

plots predicted trajectories across age for girls whose mothers had values of 2 or 5 on the attitudes scale (top and bottom lines, respectively). Thus, more conservative attitudes in mothers taken at age 12 appear to relate to more conservative actions in daughters at age 18, as well as a lesser linear increase in risky behaviors across age.

After including both the main effect of attitudes and its cross-level interaction with age, U_{0i} still represents the remaining deviation between each girl's intercept and the intercept predicted by her mother's attitudes, and U_{1i} now represents the remaining deviation between each girl's linear slope at age 18 and the linear slope predicted by her mother's attitudes. As shown in Table 7.3, approximately 17% of the random linear age slope variance was accounted for by the linear age by attitudes cross-level interaction (Pseudo-R^2 for $\tau^2_{U_1}$ = .17). Unexpectedly, the random intercept variance was also further reduced (Pseudo-R^2 for $\tau^2_{U_0}$ = .06, cumulative Pseudo-R^2 for $\tau^2_{U_0}$ = .17), highlighting the "pseudo" nature of pseudo-R^2 values. As expected, though, the residual variance was not reduced (Pseudo-R^2 for $\sigma^2_e \approx .00$). So, it appears mothers' attitudes are a small part of the story behind risky behavior—more specifically, the total variance in risky behavior explained by the fixed effects for age and mothers' attitudes was $\approx 24\%$ (an increment of $\approx 5\%$ from attitudes).

Thus far we have examined to what extent individual differences in the intercept and linear age slopes were predictable by mothers' attitudes, but what about the quadratic age slopes? Recall from our previous unconditional model evaluation that no significant random variation in the quadratic age slopes was detected. Does this mean that we cannot examine whether the quadratic age slope is also moderated by attitudes? The short answer is no—we still can. As discussed earlier in the chapter, level-1 effects can be classified three different ways: A *fixed* effect means that everyone gets the same effect, whereas a *random* effect means that each person gets his or her own effect (i.e., via a combination of a fixed effect and a random effect deviation). In the middle of these two extremes is a compromise known as *systematically* or *non-randomly* varying, in which the level-1 effect is allowed to vary deterministically as a function of other model predictors, but not randomly otherwise. In this case, by adding a cross-level interaction of age^2 by attitudes, the quadratic age slope would then vary systematically based on mothers' attitudes, but it would still be predicted to be constant in daughters whose mothers feel similarly.

The results from a model including mothers' attitudes as a predictor of the intercept, linear age slope, and quadratic age slope are shown in the fourth set of columns in Table 7.3. The cross-level interaction of attitudes by quadratic age of γ_{21} = –0.06 was not significant, indicating that half the rate of acceleration was nonsignificantly less positive by 0.06 for every one-unit higher (more conservative) mothers' attitudes. Recall that because the quadratic age slope had no level-2 random variance, any cross-level interactions with the quadratic age slope must explain the level-1 residual variance instead. But in this case, it explained <1% (Pseudo-R^2 for $\sigma^2_e \approx .00$). Thus, it appears so far that the quadratic age slope really is fixed—although it is significant on average, it does not vary randomly across persons, and it does not vary systematically as a function of mothers' attitudes (i.e., unlike the intercept and linear age slope, which were moderated by mothers' attitudes, albeit with significant random variation remaining).

The results from this example may not be too surprising—given the lack of detectable between-person differences in the quadratic age slopes, it seems unlikely to find significant predictors (through cross-level interactions) of that non-variation. In reality, though, statistical power to detect fixed effect interactions will usually be greater than the power to detect random effects variances (Snijders & Bosker, 2012). Consequently, systematically varying effects may be more possible in smaller samples that have enough power to detect the cross-level interaction, but yet not enough power to detect the corresponding random variance of the level-1 effect (e.g., as would be the case here if we had found a significant attitudes by quadratic age interaction without a significant random quadratic age slope variance). In such low power cases, Type I error rates for the cross-level interaction may be slightly inflated if omitting the corresponding random effects variance is likely to be a Type II error. However, Type I error rates should be within acceptable levels if the random effect variance truly does not belong in the model (see Hoffman & Templin, 2011). A safe strategy is to always test for the random variance of a level-1 effect prior to including any cross-level interactions with the level-1 effect in the model. In small samples it may also be beneficial to adopt a more lenient criterion for significance of the random effect variance (e.g., test at $p < .10$) to ensure that it really is unnecessary in the model.

3.C. Predicting Individual Differences in Variation in Models of Within-Person Change

Thus far our example predicting within-person change in risky behavior across age has examined the role of a time-invariant predictor of mothers' attitudes in the model for the means only. As explained earlier in the chapter, time-invariant predictors cannot have random effects in two-level models because there is no third level for their effects to be random over. However, time-invariant predictors can potentially predict heterogeneity of level-2 or level-1 variance, just as we saw in the first example of within-person fluctuation in physical symptoms, in which differential variability was examined as function of sex and age. In models of within-person change, though, while heterogeneous variance models may be possible to imagine, they can be problematic in practice. For instance, in the current example, although the prediction of the entire **G** matrix of random intercept variance, random linear age slope variance, and their covariance could be specified as varying across mothers' attitudes, this may be difficult to estimate, especially when a slope variance is based on relatively few longitudinal occasions per person. Furthermore, the meaning of the level-1 residual variance is somewhat different in a model of within-person fluctuation than it is in a model of within-person change, in which it represents not only time-specific fluctuation, but also potential misfit of each individual to his or her predicted trajectory of change over time. For these reasons, we do not pursue heterogeneous variance models here, but note that the models in section 2C could be modified for this purpose including any needed fixed and random effects of time while predicting heterogeneity of variance.

3.D. Summary

The previous example served to illustrate the role of time-invariant predictors (e.g., mothers' attitudes about smoking and drinking) in longitudinal models for outcomes that show within-person change over time (e.g., risky behavior across adolescence). We first obtained an unconditional baseline growth model that described accelerating growth in risky behavior across age (with significant individual variation in the intercept and linear age slopes). In the model for the means, we then found that the daughters of mothers with more conservative attitudes at age 12 engaged in less risky behavior at age 18 and also increased linearly in risky behavior at a slower rate across adolescence; these fixed effects of age and attitudes accounted for ≈ 24% of the total variance in risky behavior. In chapter 9 we will continue with this example in order to also examine a time-varying predictor of mothers' monitoring behavior at each age.

4. Chapter Summary

The purpose of this chapter was to describe and illustrate the roles that time-invariant predictors (i.e., person-level or level-2 predictors) can play in a longitudinal model. Regardless of whether a predictor is expected to change over time, if it is only measured once, it will be a time-invariant predictor. As in previous chapters, time-invariant predictors should always be centered or coded such that 0 is a meaningful value in order to maintain interpretability of the model intercept and of the simple main effects of any interacting predictors. Unfortunately, because software for multilevel models usually requires each occasion within a person to have all model predictors and outcomes, persons without all time-invariant predictors included in the model would be listwise-deleted from the analysis (because all of their occasions will be incomplete); such missingness will be assumed to be completely at random. Chapter 9 will describe some potential remedies for this problem (and their potential drawbacks).

This chapter then described the multiple roles time-invariant predictors can play on each side of the model. In the model for the means, time-invariant predictors can modify each level-1 fixed effect (e.g., intercepts, asymptotes, and effects for change over time) within its level-2 equation. In the process, time-invariant predictors will then account for the corresponding between-person random variance included in each level-2 equation (e.g., a main effect would predict random intercept variance; a cross-level interaction with linear time would predict the random linear time slope variance). As main effects or as part of level-2 interactions, time-invariant predictors cannot predict level-1 residual within-person variance because they do not vary within persons. However, they can predict level-1 residual variance as part of a cross-level interaction with a non-random (systematically varying) level-1 effect. In models without any random effects variances, time-invariant predictors will account for the total variance(s) instead. The chapter also provided a more formal treatment of computing pseudo-R^2 values for the proportion reduction in each variance component, including the potential complications in doing so. A useful and more generalizable alternative is to compute a total true R^2 value as the squared correlation between the actual outcome and the outcome predicted by the fixed effects.

Finally, with respect to the model for the variance, time-invariant predictors cannot have random effects over persons because they do not vary within persons (i.e., each person cannot have his or her own effect of sex because sex is constant over time for each person). But time-invariant predictors can be included in the model for the variance to predict differential variation at each level of the model. That is, time-invariant predictors can predict differential *amounts* of between-person random variation in the expected level of the outcome and/or its change over time, and they can also predict differential *amounts* of within-person residual variation over time. Heterogeneous variance models may be more useful in models of within-person fluctuation than in models of within-person change (which tend to have more complex variance models, and in which the residual variance represents both time-specific fluctuation and misfit of the individual predicted time trajectories). Unfortunately, these options for predicting heterogeneous variances are not as widely known or readily available in software at this time.

5. Sample Results Sections

5.A. Within-Person Fluctuation

General linear mixed models (i.e., multilevel models in which occasions were modeled as nested within persons) were used to examine predictors of daily fluctuation in physical symptoms. A sample of 509 observations was obtained from 104 older adults age 69 to 95 years ($M = 80.13$, $SD = 6.11$), 27% of whom were men. Five observations were collected during a 14-day period for the number of physical symptoms participants reported experiencing in the past 24 hours, including aches/pain, gastrointestinal, cardiovascular, upper respiratory, and "other" physical symptoms ($M = 1.27$, $SD = 1.32$, possible range = 0 to 5). All models were estimated using maximum likelihood (ML). The significance of individual fixed effects was tested by their Wald test p-values, whereas the significance of a set of multiple fixed effects or of new variance model parameters (e.g., random effects) was tested by the ML $-2\Delta LL$ between nested models as evaluated by the difference in the model degrees of freedom. Results are shown in Table 7.1.

An intraclass correlation as calculated from an empty means, random intercept model indicated that 66% of the variation in symptoms was between persons (i.e., individual differences in mean symptoms over time), whereas 34% was within persons (i.e., time-specific deviations or daily fluctuation about one's usual level). A 95% random effects confidence interval suggested person mean symptoms were expected to range from -0.843 and 3.431 with a sample mean of 1.294 (on a 0 to 5 scale), indicating positive skewness in symptoms. Preliminary examination revealed no significant effects pertaining to day in study or day of the week either on average or at the individual level, and thus no fixed or random effects related to time were included.

Fixed effects of a time-invariant predictor for sex (coded such that men = 0 and women = 1), for age (centered such that age 0 = 80 years), and for their interaction were then included in the model for the means as shown in Equation (7.4), each of which was significant, resulting in a significant improvement over the empty means, random intercept model, $-2\Delta LL(3) = 10.4$, $p < .015$. As seen in Table 7.1, the fixed intercept $\gamma_{00} = 1.713$ is the expected mean symptoms across days for an 80-year-old man. The simple main effect of women of $\gamma_{01} = -0.531$ indicates that specifically among 80-year-olds, women report 0.531 fewer mean symptoms across days than men. The simple main effect of age of $\gamma_{02} = 0.100$ indicates that specifically in men, mean symptoms are 0.100 higher per additional year of age. The women by age interaction of $\gamma_{03} = -0.110$ indicates that for every additional year of age, the sex difference in mean symptoms across days in which men report more symptoms becomes larger by -0.110, as well as that the effect of age on mean symptoms across days is smaller (less positive) by -0.110 in women than in men. As obtained via an additional requested contrast, the simple effect of age in women of $\gamma_{02} + \gamma_{03} = 0.100 - 0.110 = -0.010$ was nonsignificant. Calculation of regions of significance for the sex difference in mean symptoms as moderated by age indicated that at age 79.522 or older, women are expected to report significantly fewer mean symptoms across days than men (which is about 50% of the sample), whereas the sex difference is expected to be nonsignificant between 60.164 and 79.522 years (and to be significant in the reverse direction below 60.164 years).

As shown in Table 7.1, the proportion reduction in the random intercept variance relative to the empty means, random intercept model was pseudo-$R^2 = (1.189 - 1.073) / 1.189 = .098$. The R^2 for the total symptoms outcome as calculated by the square of the Pearson correlation between the actual outcome and the outcome predicted from the fixed effects was $r = .219$, or $R^2 = .048$. Thus, approximately 5% to 6% of the total variance in daily physical symptoms was related to person mean differences predictable by sex, age, and their interaction—a small effect size at best.

The extent to which sex, age, and their interaction could moderate the amount of random intercept variance and residual variance was then examined in separate models. No significant effects were found, indicating that neither the amount of between-person variability in mean symptoms nor the amount of within-person fluctuation in daily symptoms varied by sex or age.

5.B. Within-Person Change

General linear mixed models (i.e., multilevel models in which occasions are nested within persons) were used to examine predictors of age-related change in risky behavior, in which seven (approximately annual) assessments were collected from 200 adolescent girls age 12 to 18 years ($M = 15.00$, $SD = 2.00$, range = 11.53 to 18.34 years; 1,400 total observations). Risky behavior was indicated by the sum of 10 items in which each item response ranged from 1 to 5 ($M = 19.38$, $SD = 5.30$, observed range 10.00 to 36.28). All models were estimated using maximum likelihood (ML). The significance of individual fixed effects was tested by their Wald test *p*-values; the significance of random effects variances and covariances was tested by the ML $-2\Delta LL$ between nested models given the difference in model degrees of freedom. Results are shown in Table 7.3; individual and predicted mean age trajectories are shown in Figure 7.1.

An intraclass correlation as calculated from an empty means, random intercept model indicated that 39% of the variation in risky behavior was between persons (i.e., individual mean differences across age), whereas 61% was within persons (i.e., time-specific deviations or daily fluctuation about one's mean level). Polynomial models were then used to describe the overall pattern of and individual differences in change in risky behavior across age centered at 18 years. A fixed linear effect of age and its random variance across girls were each significant ($p < .001$, $-2\Delta LL(\sim2) =$ 120.8, $p < .001$, respectively), indicating a significant increase with age on average and individual differences therein. Although a fixed quadratic effect of age indicated significant acceleration of change on average, its corresponding random effect was not significant (i.e., no individual differences in the quadratic effect of age were found).

Thus, the best-fitting unconditional growth model as shown in Equation (7.8) included a fixed intercept for the expected amount of risky behavior at age 18 of 23.47 with a 95% random intercept confidence interval of 14.34 to 32.59. The significant instantaneous fixed linear effect of age at age 18 of 1.99 per year had a 95% random linear age slope confidence interval of 0.49 to 3.49, indicating that not all girls were predicted to continue increasing in risky behavior at age 18. Finally, the significant fixed quadratic effect of age of 0.14 per year^2 indicated that the linear effect of age became more positive by 0.28 per year; the quadratic age slope did not vary significantly across girls. The fixed effects of linear and quadratic age accounted for approximately 19% of the total variance in risky behavior (i.e., as computed from the square of the correlation between the actual outcome and the outcomes predicted by the fixed effects).

We then examined the effects of a time-invariant predictor of mothers' attitudes about smoking and drinking assessed when her daughter was 12 (a mean of 26 items on a scale of 1 to 5, in which higher values indicate more conservative attitudes, $M = 3.95$, $SD = 0.60$, observed range = 2.44 to 5.00). The full model examined is shown in Equation (7.9). Although attitudes did not significantly moderate the quadratic age effect, significant moderation of the intercept at age 18 and linear age effect were found. Specifically, for every one-unit more conservative a mother's attitude about smoking and drinking as assessed at age 12, her daughter is predicted to have significantly lower risky behavior at age 18 by 3.16, and a significantly less positive linear age change in risky behavior per year by 0.52. Thus, more conservative attitudes in mothers appear to relate to more conservative actions in daughters at age 18, as well as a lesser increase in risky behaviors across age, as shown in Figure 7.2. The effects of mothers' attitudes taken at age 12 accounted for an additional 5% of the total variance in risky behavior, including 17% of the random intercept variance and 17% of the random linear age slope variance.

Review Questions

1. What are the roles of time-invariant predictors in the model for the means in a longitudinal analysis?
2. Can time-invariant predictors have random effects in a two-level longitudinal model? Why or why not?
3. What other roles can time-invariant predictors potentially play in the model for the variance in a longitudinal analysis?
4. Describe how pseudo-R^2 values are computed. How do we know which level-2 variance component each effect of a time-invariant predictor should reduce?
5. Can time-invariant predictors ever account for level-1 residual variance? If so, give an example of when this might happen.

References

Enders, C. K. (2010). *Applied missing data analysis*. New York, NY: Guilford.

Hedeker, D., Mermelstein, R. J., & Demirtas, H. (2008). An application of a mixed-effects location scale model for analysis of ecological momentary assessment (EMA) data. *Biometrics, 64*, 627–634.

Hoffman, L., & Templin, J. L. (October, 2011). *Systematically varying effects in multilevel models: Permissible or problematic?* Paper presented at the annual meeting of the Society for Multivariate Experimental Psychology, Norman, OK.

Hox, J. J. (2010). *Multilevel analysis: Techniques and applications* (2nd ed.). New York, NY: Routledge.

Mardia, K. V. (1970). Measures of multivariate skewness and kurtosis with applications. *Biometrika, 57*, 519–530.

Raudenbush, S. W., & Bryk, A. S. (2002). *Hierarchical linear models: Applications and data analysis methods* (2nd ed.). Thousand Oaks, CA: Sage.

Singer, J. D., & Willett, J. B. (2003). *Applied longitudinal data analysis*. New York, NY: Oxford University Press.

Snijders, T. A. B., & Bosker, R. (2012). *Multilevel analysis* (2nd ed.). Thousand Oaks, CA: Sage.

Appendix 7.A: Evaluating Assumptions About Model Residuals

Let's say by now you've painstakingly collected your data, checked your data for errors, formulated all of your research questions, estimated all of your models, and carefully interpreted all of your results. Perhaps you have even obtained the answers you wanted—hooray! But before the celebration (and the manuscript) gets underway, there is one more step to consider—the tenability of your model's assumptions. Depending on your background, model assumptions may have been presented as something of paramount importance (more common among statisticians) or simply as a brief aside (more common among social scientists). Some may think of checking model assumptions as a task akin to flossing your teeth—you know you should, but too often, you just don't often bother. (I am admittedly as guilty of this as any reader, although after years of accumulation of expensive dental work I have now seen the error of my non-flossing ways.)

The most common reasons for this oversight are simple: you may not know what your model assumptions actually are, how to check whether they appear reasonable for your data, or what to do if they appear to be violated. It's true that many graphical techniques for checking the tenability of model assumptions do not have rigid standards for acceptance or rejection, except in the most egregious violations. But it is still better to know what might be lurking in your data than to hope naively that everything is fine. In general, violations concerning the *model for the means* can bias in model parameter *estimates,* whereas violations concerning the *model for the variance* can bias the *standard errors* of the parameter estimates. That is, problems with the fixed effects can affect the answers you seek; problems with the random effects and residuals can affect the quality and associated significance tests of those answers. Conveniently, though, we aren't left just hoping that the model assumptions appear to be met. Instead, the longitudinal models we've been using have many extensions and permutations by which you can *change their assumptions into something more tenable for your data.* So, contrary to how they are sometimes presented, model assumptions are not set in stone—they are quite literally what you make them.

To evaluate the tenability of model assumptions, this section outlines a general approach of (1) conducting statistical tests where possible for potential problems identified on the basis of study design, and (2) inspection of graphical displays where possible to detect any egregious remaining violations. But just as your dentist cannot promise that flossing will save you from fillings (or crowns, or root canals), I cannot promise these solutions will always point towards the "right" model. Instead, these practices will hopefully result in selecting the model that appears to be "least wrong" for your data. If nothing else, I hope that these suggestions may keep you from accidentally reporting models with egregious violations and regretting it later!

In order to examine assumptions about the model residuals, we need to obtain some indication of what the models residuals would be at each level, which is made more difficult by the fact that level-2 residuals are really random distributions for each person, not single values. However, for the purposes of examining model assumptions, we can generate Empirical Bayes Estimates for the residuals, as were originally described in chapter 5, keeping in mind that they are approximations of the U_i values that would have been observed for each individual. That is, these U_i estimates will be shrunken to the conditional mean predicted by the fixed effects based on the extent of unreliability and extremeness of each individual's data, as well as the amount of random effect variance relative to residual variance in the sample. Nevertheless, the U_i estimates do provide us with a mechanism with which to identify potential model mis-specification.

Although the specific assumptions that underlie the example models have been identified when relevant throughout the text, they are presented more formally and generally in this section. Assumptions for the general linear mixed (i.e., multilevel) models are often described via three ideas: *normality, independence,* and *constant variance* (also known as *homoscedasticity* or *homogeneity of variance,* with *non-constant variance* referred to as *heteroscedasticity* or *heterogeneity of variance*). The assumption of normality is comparatively easy to consider, but the assumptions regarding independence and constant variance are more complex given that they fall into two distinct sets. As such, the remainder of this section is organized by first discussing normality of residuals, followed by independence and constant variance with respect to sampling units, and then independence and constant variance with respect to predictors. For each category, the model assumption is presented along with how it is likely to be violated. Some ways of testing or visualizing your data for violations are then presented. For the latter, some hypothetical examples of "good" and "bad" plots are included to illustrate each point where possible. Finally, model-based alternatives for addressing each kind of violation are also provided where possible.

Normality

The models in this text are *general linear models* or *general linear mixed models.* To review, "linear" refers to the additive equation that generates expected outcomes. "Mixed" refers to the presence of both fixed and random effects (i.e., more than one pile of variance besides residual). Most pertinent to us now, "general" refers to the first major assumption: *all model residuals should have a normal distribution.* It's important to note that the normality assumption applies to the *model residuals,* not the *original outcomes* (although plots of the original outcomes may sometimes foreshadow potential problems for their residuals). In addition, we note that so far we have used the term "residual" specifically to describe the e_{ti} level-1, time-specific residuals. Within the context of model assumptions, however, the idea of normally distributed residuals pertains to *any* leftover variance term in the model—so the U_i level-2, person-specific random effects should have normal distributions as well. In addition, residuals at the same level (i.e., intercepts and slopes at level 2) should have a multivariate normal distribution.

The rationale for these normality assumptions—as well as the remedy for their failures—can be understood by considering the overall log-likelihood function that determines the most likely estimates of the random effects variances and covariances (which then determine the most likely estimates for the fixed effects in general linear mixed models). The quality of all of these estimates (i.e., just how likely they really are) as indexed by their standard errors is a by-product of the estimation process. In chapter 5 we saw how the level-1 and level-2 variance terms get re-assembled into an individual **V** matrix that is thought to follow a multivariate normal distribution. Although the general process of likelihood estimation can be used for any kind of data, our choice of a multivariate normal distribution as the basis of this function is predicated on the idea that it should indeed fit the model residuals. Otherwise, we are essentially using the wrong formula to find the most likely estimates and their standard errors. Unfortunately, multivariate normality can be tricky to evaluate (although formal tests exist, e.g., Mardia, 1970). However, if univariate normality fails, then so will multivariate normality, which means that examining univariate normality of all random effects and residuals is a good place to start.

Evaluation of univariate normality can be done with traditional diagnostic plots such as histograms and normal probability plots, as shown in Figure 7.3. The top panels show a "good" result in which the residuals appear normally distributed, whereas the bottom panels show a "not so good" result in which the residuals are positively skewed. The left panels display histograms with an overlaid normal curve, in which the bottom left panel shows an apparent floor effect. The right panels show *normal probability plots* of the residuals on the y-axis against their associated percentiles from a normal distribution on the *x*-axis. If the residuals are normally distributed, the data should follow a diagonal line (as in the top right

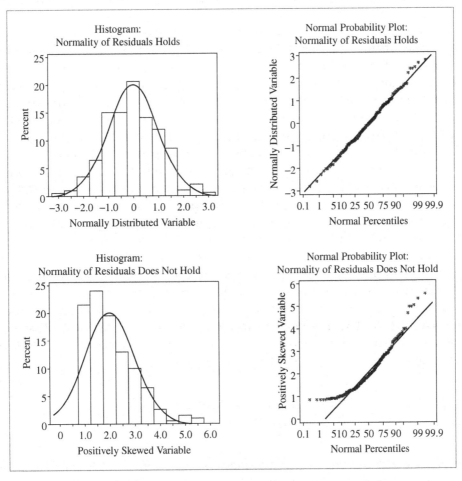

Figure 7.3 Inspection of residual normality using histograms (left) and normal probability plots (right). Top panel: Example of desired result. Bottom panel: Example of less desired result.

panel). Non-normality is indicated by deviation from the diagonal line, such as in the bottom right panel in which the residuals on the lower end fall closer to center than expected, suggesting the left side of the distribution is truncated, but fall further away from center on the right side, indicating positive skewness.

For continuous outcomes, residual normality may be a reasonable assumption, or at least within the ballpark given some modification (e.g., skewed residuals may be normally distributed after log-transforming the outcome). But for other kinds of outcomes, such as binary, categorical, count, or zero-inflated data, residual normality may never be possible. Fortunately, though, other distributions can be used in log-likelihood functions to create *generalized* linear mixed models. Chapter 13 presents a brief overview of generalized models, which include a *link function* to transform a conditional mean into a more continuous outcome to be predicted by a linear model; they also specify an appropriate non-normal conditional outcome distribution. For instance, binary longitudinal outcomes can be predicted via a logit link (the natural log of the odds of the probability of a 1), using a Bernoulli distribution for the binary outcomes. Generalized linear mixed models permit many alternative distributions (e.g., Binomial, Multinomial, Poisson, and Negative Binomial). But as of this writing, their level-2 random effects are still restricted to have a multivariate normal distribution in most software programs. Without the convenience of an overall multivariate normal distribution, generalized linear mixed models are more complex to estimate, as also discussed in chapter 13. Nevertheless, many of the model-building concepts presented in this text for general models will still apply to generalized longitudinal models.

We now switch our focus to evaluations of independence and constant variance. As discussed earlier, two distinct sets of assumptions are embedded within each of these terms. The first is *independence and constant variance with respect to sampling:* the residuals within a single variance component (i.e., that form a specific pile of variance) have no relationship across sampling units, with equal variance across sampling units. Similarly, the second assumption is *independence and constant variance with respect to predictors:* predictors and residuals should be independent, and residuals should have equal variance across levels of the predictors. Because violations of these two sets of assumptions can result from different causes and will also have different remedies, we will present each in turn. Furthermore, because problems with the level-1 within-person model can propagate to the level-2 between-person model, assumptions for the level-1 model should be addressed first, followed by assumptions for the level-2 model.

Independence and Constant Variance With Respect to Sampling

At level 1 (within persons over time), *independence with respect to sampling* means that the level-1 residuals are unrelated across persons, which was the goal of partitioning the residual variance into level-2 piles as needed. That is, after forming level-2 random effects variances by extracting between-person covariance arising from mean differences over time (which becomes random intercept variance), as well as between-person covariance due to individual differences in effects of predictors (which becomes random slope variance), the remaining level-1 residual variance should no longer contain person-specific covariance. In general, the process of testing for random effects can help indicate the presence or absence of these specific sources of person dependency, but it is not a guarantee, as person covariance could still lurk for unknown reasons.

Also at level 1, the assumption of *constant variance with respect to sampling* means that the variance of the level-1 residuals should be homogeneous across persons: this translates to *equal fluctuation over time* across persons in models of within-person fluctuation, or equal *residual deviation from predicted change over time* across person in models of within-person change. Although a default in most longitudinal models, this expectation of constant level-1 residual variance across persons may be unreasonable for some outcomes. For instance, in a study of daily fluctuation in negative mood, specifying constant level-1 residual variance across persons implies that all persons should be equally "moody" (which seems highly unlikely).

A test of constant level-1 residual variance was presented by Raudenbush and Bryk (2002 pp. 263–264; see also Snijders & Bosker, 2012, pp. 159–161; Hoffman, 2007). Briefly, this test involves estimating a single-level regression per person using the predictors in the level-1 model to obtain an individual residual variance; these variances are combined through intermediate calculations into an H-statistic for the sample that can be compared to a χ^2 distribution. However, this test is only recommended for studies with $n > 10$ occasions, which limits its utility for most longitudinal data. Furthermore, such tests for between-person heterogeneity of level-1 residual variance say nothing about the possible *reasons* for the heterogeneity, only whether or not it exists. Consequently, the process of testing predictors for heterogeneity of variance is likely to be more informative, as was illustrated in this chapter and will also be shown in chapter 8.

At level 2, given that the random intercepts and slopes are thought to have a multivariate normal distribution, their covariance does imply a relationship between the random intercepts and the random slopes (e.g., where people start is related to how much they change over time). However, the assumption of *independence with respect to sampling* at level 2 means there is no correlation across persons *within* the random intercepts or *within* any random slopes. In practice, this assumption means *no clustering or grouping of individuals,* which could be violated in some sampling designs. For instance, if children are sampled from different schools, the random intercepts of children from the same school may be more alike than the random intercepts of children from different schools. If this dependency is not built into the model, the standard errors for the estimates of the level-2 fixed effects may be downwardly biased. The same problem can occur for random slopes—unmodeled correlation in the slopes across children from the same school could result in too-small standard errors for the estimates of any cross-level interactions involving the random slopes. The reason for these biases more generally is that dependency results in a loss of information: if the children are not really independent, then they do not provide as much unique information as would be expected based on their actual sample size.

Fortunately, dependency due to sampling design can easily be included in the model by adding additional effects that account for those levels of sampling. This may be as simple as adding a few fixed effects for school differences to the model for the means (i.e., if only a few different schools are sampled) or as complex as adding another level of random effects to the model for the variance (i.e., if many schools are sampled). Chapter 11 discusses this problem and presents both strategies for tackling it. Unfortunately, though, if you do not have any *a priori* reasons why the persons in your sample might show dependency, you are likely to be left making the assumption of independence with respect to sampling without any definitive way of testing it.

Also at level 2, the assumption of *constant variance with respect to sampling* means that the distribution of random effects should be homogeneous across persons. In reality this usually translates to finding no groupings of persons who are more or less variable in their random intercepts and/or random slopes, and this can be evaluated by including level-2 predictors of heterogeneity in the model for variances, as already demonstrated in this chapter.

Independence and Constant Variance With Respect to Predictors

The previous section presented assumptions about independence and constant variance with respect to *sampling*. We now turn to its counterpart of independence and constant variance with respect to *predictors*, first for level-2 random effects and then for level-1 residuals.

At level 2, we assume two things about the individual random effects: that they are unrelated to (independent of) any model predictors, and that they have constant variance across model predictors. In other words, the U_i random intercept and slope terms represent *variance left over* after accounting for all systematic relationships with level-2 predictors via those predictors' fixed effects in the model for the means. If a predictor is not included in the model for the means, then we assume the true form of the relationship is, in fact, no relationship—this is testable for predictors that were actually collected, but of course we have no way of knowing if systematic effects exist for unmeasured variables. Another way in which the assumption of independence could be violated is if a linear effect is specified for a predictor, but in reality the relationship is nonlinear. For instance, an effect of a predictor that abates at higher levels of the predictor could be modeled with a negative quadratic fixed effect (e.g., Age_i^2) in addition to the positive linear effect (Age_i). Other kinds of nonlinear effects as discussed in chapter 6 for modeling change over time (e.g., piecewise slopes, exponential functions) could similarly be specified for any predictor to more fully capture nonlinear relationships. Furthermore, in addition to problems of independence with respect to predictors, the assumption of constant variance with respect to predictors could be violated because of missing interaction terms. That is, the problem is not that the effect of the predictor by itself is misspecified, but that its *total* effect in the model is incomplete.

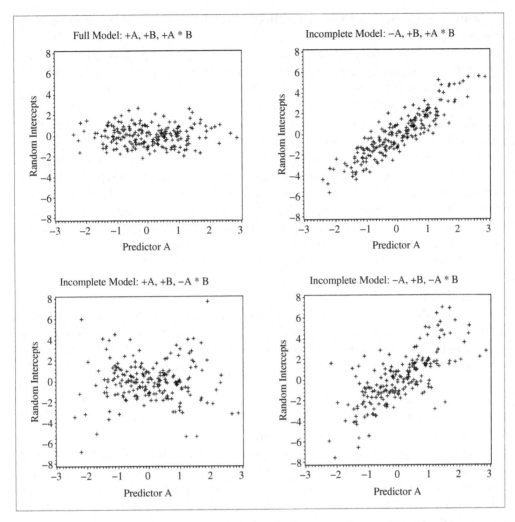

Figure 7.4 Inspection of the independence and constant variance at level 2 with respect to predictors via scatterplots of level-2 random intercepts (*y*-axis) by a level-2 predictor (*x*-axis).

Figure 7.4 illustrates violations in the assumptions of independence and constant variance in the random intercept for a hypothetical model including two level-2 predictors, denoted *A* (as shown on the *x*-axis) and *B*. The true model—as shown in the top left panel—includes positive main effects of both predictors, as well as a positive interaction. The true model plot shows the desired pattern of residuals (here, leftover random intercepts in the level-2 model) that are *flat* and *even*. *Flat* residuals indicate independence—that no sizeable relationships with predictor *A* have been left out of the model. *Even* residuals indicate *constant variance*—that the model works equally well at all levels of predictor *A*. The other three panels in Figure 7.4 show the deviations from *flat* and *even* that would be expected as a result of each type of model mis-specification.

For instance, when just the main effect of predictor A is missing (top right, as indicated by the $-A$), the random intercept residuals appear *even*, but they are not *flat*—a positive linear trend is still observed because predictor A is still systematically related to the random intercepts given its missing main effect. (Of course we would almost always include the main effects of an interaction in the model to begin with, so this panel is included for the sake of demonstration.) Furthermore, when the main effect of predictor A has been included but its interaction with predictor B is missing (bottom left, as indicated by $-A*B$), the residuals are *flat*, but they are not *even*—the model works well for midrange values of predictor A, but works less well at the extreme values, as indicated by the greater intercept variability when moving away from center. The missing $A*B$ interaction would have allowed persons with differing values of predictor B to have different predictor A slopes, so the effect of this missing interaction can be seen predominantly at extreme values of predictor A. Finally, when both the main effect of predictor A and its interaction with predictor B are missing (bottom right panel), the residuals are not *flat* or *even*—they are not *flat* because of the missing main effect, and they are not *even* because of the missing interaction.

Plots like those in Figure 7.4 should be examined for the level-2 random intercept with each level-2 predictor to check for model mis-specification with respect to level-2 main effects and level-2 interactions. Likewise, plots should be examined for every pair of level-2 random slopes and level-2 predictors to check for model mis-specification with respect to cross-level interactions between level-2 predictors and the level-1 predictor with the random slope. Furthermore, although the assumption of independence and constant variance has been discussed so far for level-2 random effects and level-2 predictors, the same is true for level-2 random effects and level-1 predictors—there should be no remaining systematic relationship and the random effects should be evenly distributed across levels of the level-1 predictor. Violations of this assumption could result if the between-person portion of the total effect of a level-1 predictor is not properly represented in the level-2 model for the means. This problem of "smushing" and its remedies will be discussed more broadly in chapters 8 and 9. Finally, level-2 random effects and level-1 residuals are supposed to be uncorrelated; testing for random slopes for all level-1 predictors may address this issue, although it could also result from any of the aforementioned problems.

Turning to the level-1 model, we also assume the level-1 residuals are independent of and have constant variance across all level-1 predictors. Relationships between level-1 residuals and level-1 predictors can remain if the total effect of a predictor is not properly specified through its main effect or interactions. For this problem, inspection of plots like Figure 7.4 may indicate when testing additional fixed effects may be warranted by residuals that are not *flat* or *even*.

In considering independence and constant variance for cross-level relations, fortunately we do not have to worry about correlations of level-1 residuals with level-2 predictors, because level-2 predictors on their own do not directly account for level-1 variance (e.g., being a man or a woman cannot explain why today is worse than yesterday). But we do have to worry about non-constant variance of level-1 residuals across level-2 predictors, which could arise for a few different reasons. One cause may be a missing cross-level interaction. As shown earlier, missing interactions in general can result in non-constant variance, but the only way for level-2 predictors to be related to level-1 residuals is for the missing interaction term to be cross-level.

Besides missing interactions, non-constant level-1 residual variance could reflect real differences in within-person variation as a function of a level-2, between-person predictor. For instance, men and women may differ in their amount of fluctuation of mood over time (i.e., be differentially "moody"). The reasons behind non-constant within-person variance can be tested by including level-2 predictors of heterogeneity of the level-1 residual variance, also shown in this chapter, or by including level-1 predictors of heterogeneity, as will be shown in chapter 8. In either case, if the predictors of heterogeneity improve model fit, we then assume heterogeneity of variance as a function of those predictors, but constant residual variance otherwise. One caveat is that these kinds of heterogeneous variance models can often be hard to estimate, and thus you should proceed cautiously when adding multiple terms for heterogeneity, making sure to watch for potential problems of estimation while doing so (i.e., as was presented in chapters 5–6).

Finally, we note the assumptions regarding the level-1 residuals with respect to time. Although these assumptions are often given special attention, the possible concerns fall into the same categories as before, because "time" is just (another) level-1 predictor. Specifically, we assume the pattern of residual correlation and the magnitude of variation across occasions is *as specified by the model*. As described in chapters 4–6, concerns about time would have already been addressed in constructing an unconditional model before considering additional predictors. So, after the inclusion of whatever fixed effects were necessary to describe change over time, the pattern of residuals should be *flat* across occasions. Likewise, after the inclusion of any random effects needed to describe individual differences in change, and/or the inclusion of alternative covariance structures to describe fluctuation, the residuals that remain should show the pattern of variation and covariation predicted in the **R** matrix. Thus, the residuals should be *even* across occasions if the **R** matrix is predicted to have homogeneous variance (e.g., AR1 or TOEP), but not if a heterogeneous structure was used (e.g., ARH1 or TOEPH). The same should be true after including all model predictors; otherwise, the model for time itself may need to be re-considered. The point is that the assumptions we make about the correlations among and the variance of the residuals over time is *whatever the model says it should be*, and we have many choices for what the model can include in order to approximate the actual data as "least wrongly" as possible.

Summary

The assumptions we make in estimating any model—and especially when believing the results that it provides—are all predicated on the idea that the model fits the data. But rather than making default assumptions and simply hoping they are tenable, our goal should be to *modify the model as needed to change the assumptions to be more plausible.* For instance, level-1 residuals should be normally distributed, but if they aren't, we can transform the data, or better yet, choose a generalized longitudinal model instead. Residuals at each level (i.e., level-2 random intercepts and slopes, level-1 residuals) should have whatever form of dependency across persons and occasions is predicted by the model, but none otherwise. Model residuals should have *flat* and *even* distributions across predictors at both levels; the remedies for any violations observed will depend on which level of residual and which level of predictor are involved. Finally, please note that although an understanding of these principles may help avoid egregious errors, it cannot guarantee that the "right model" will ever be selected (or that such a model even exists).

CHAPTER 8

TIME-VARYING PREDICTORS IN MODELS OF WITHIN-PERSON FLUCTUATION

The third section of this text focuses on *conditional* models, which so far has included predictors collected at only one occasion. In chapter 7 we examined the roles of those **time-invariant predictors** in modifying each aspect of a trajectory of within-person change over time (as fixed effects in the model for the means), as well as in predicting systematic heterogeneity of between-person and within-person variance (in the model for the variance). We now turn to the inclusion of predictors that are collected at *each* occasion. Chapter 8 will focus on these **time-varying predictors** in models of *within-person fluctuation* over time, whereas chapter 9 will focus on including time-varying predictors in models of *within-person change* over time instead.

Accordingly, the first part of this chapter overviews the same practical issues that were addressed for time-invariant predictors in chapter 7, including what happens when time-varying predictors have missing data, the levels of variation they contain and the corresponding effects they can show, their potential roles in longitudinal models, and how their effect sizes can be assessed. As we will see shortly, issues related to centering are paramount in properly specifying the effects of time-varying predictors, and historically have been one of the most complex and confusing topics in longitudinal analysis. The primary source of confusion arises from the use of two different methods for centering time-varying predictors: *person-mean-centering* and *grand-mean-centering*. The person-mean-centering approach has important interpretational advantages within longitudinal analysis, and so the second part of this chapter begins with an example of time-varying predictors from this perspective, followed by the more commonly used approach of grand-mean-centering. We will see when the two methods of centering continuous time-varying predictors will or will not result in equivalent models, and we will consider categorical time-varying predictors as well. The third part of this chapter demonstrates three types of interactions involving time-varying predictors, and then discusses some additional roles of time-varying predictors, including as lagged effects and predictors of heterogeneity of variance. Finally, as in previous chapters, this chapter concludes with a summary section and a sample results section.

1. Considering Time-Varying Predictors in Longitudinal Models

As initially discussed in chapter 1, there are two main types of predictors to be included in longitudinal models: time-invariant or time-varying. The focus of this chapter will be **time-varying predictors**, also known as **longitudinal** predictors, **dynamic** predictors, or as **level-1** predictors in multilevel models for longitudinal data in which occasions (at level 1) are nested within persons (at level 2). The models examined in this chapter are for time-varying predictors and outcomes that show only within-*person fluctuation* over time; time-varying predictors that show systematic *within-person change* over time instead will be addressed in chapter 9.

Time-varying predictors are usually measured at the same occasions as the outcome variable, although this need not be the case. For instance, if a lagged effect of a time-varying predictor is of interest, then a researcher may deliberately off-set collection of the corresponding outcome data by a pre-determined time lag in order to examine the expected temporally specific relationship. However, it will be most useful to have a direct time correspondence between predictors and outcomes that vary over time. For instance, if a predictor is assessed daily but an outcome is assessed only weekly, then the values of the daily predictor would have to be somehow aggregated or summarized to the nearest week in order for its effect on a weekly outcome to be examined. In considering the reverse scenario in which a predictor is assessed weekly but an outcome is assessed daily, the predictor could only have an effect at the week level (e.g., it could predict the mean outcome across days during the week in which the predictor was measured). So, in general, although time-varying predictors and outcomes do not necessarily need to be collected at the same exact *time*, they should be sampled within the same time *frame*.

1.A. Time-Varying Predictors With Missing Data

Before continuing, we must recognize the impact of missing time-varying predictors when estimating longitudinal models. As described in chapter 7, the way that most software for multilevel models "handles" missing data is to require that a case must be *complete*—it must include *all* model predictors and outcomes—for the case to be included in the model. Multilevel models utilize a stacked data format in which a case contains the data for a single occasion from a single person. This is good news when faced with persons who are missing time-varying predictors at some occasions, in that a person's complete cases for the other occasions can still be included. But the deletion of cases missing any time-varying predictors or outcomes still creates three problems, as discussed in chapter 7: incomparable fit statistics if the models are based on different cases, a reduction in statistical power, and a potential for biased model results. As will be addressed in chapter 9, the first two problems can be addressed by estimating longitudinal models via software for structural equation models—these models will allow cases with missing time-varying predictors to remain in the model given specific assumptions about the distributions of the time-varying predictors and the reasons for their incomplete data.

With regard to the third problem of potential bias, the deletion of cases with missing time-varying predictors or outcomes (as well as the inclusion of persons with any incomplete data in a structural equation model) will result in biased effects if the data are not **missing at random** (MAR), a condition in which the missingness is predictable from the person's other data (see Enders, 2010, for a more thorough treatment). Although it is a cornerstone of most modern methods for addressing missing data, unfortunately the assumption of MAR is not testable, but including the person's other complete occasions as well as any predictors related to missingness (i.e., even if not related to the outcome) should make the assumption of MAR more plausible.

As in chapter 7, this chapter will address the examination of the effects of time-varying predictors more generally, but these issues related to missing data will be important when deciding how to estimate such conditional longitudinal models in practice.

1.B. Time-Varying Predictors Contain Between-Person and Within-Person Information

Chapter 7 revisited the process of centering continuous predictors and coding categorical predictors—all time-invariant predictors must have meaningful 0 value for the model intercept (and for the main effects of any interacting predictors) to be interpretable. The same requirement of a meaningful 0 value will also apply in modeling the effects of time-varying predictors, except that decisions related to centering can be much more complicated when applied to time-varying predictors. The reason for this, as explained below, is that although time-varying predictors are measured at the time level (i.e., at each occasion), they usually contain systematic variation at higher levels of sampling as well (i.e., time-invariant variation). That is, *time-varying predictors contain both between-person and within-person information.* Accordingly, both sources of variation must be represented explicitly (and centered appropriately) within a longitudinal model.

Consider the example mentioned in chapter 1: stress predicting negative mood. Although stress levels will vary across days, to the extent that some people tend to report more stress every day, stress will also vary systematically across *people*. That is, even though time-varying stress is measured at level 1 (across time), it will most likely contain **between-person variation** (i.e., person-to-person differences in mean stress levels across days that belongs in the *level-2* model) as well as **within-person variation** (i.e., variation around a person's mean level—having more or less stress than usual at a given time, which belongs in the *level-1* model). Because longitudinal variables usually contain both between-person and within-person variation, as a result they are usually really two variables instead of one. Each source of variation (person-to-person variation at level 2, time-to-time variation at level 1) can have a different effect on the outcome—a **between-person effect** and a **within-person effect**, respectively. In the example of stress and negative mood, people with *higher stress on average* (than other people) may report *greater negative mood on average;* this between-person effect at level 2 would be thought of as a **trait** or chronic effect. Furthermore, at times when *stress is higher than usual,* negative mood may be *greater than usual* as well; this within-person effect at level 1 would be thought of as a **state** or acute effect.

A logical precursor to examining a time-varying predictor's between-person and within-person effects is to estimate just how much of its variation is due to each source. To determine this, we can treat the time-varying predictor as an outcome and use an empty means, random intercept model to quantify its amount of between-person variation (as the level-2 random intercept variance $\tau^2_{U_0}$) and within-person variation (as the level-1 residual variance σ^2_e) in order to calculate an intraclass correlation as ICC = $\tau^2_{U_0} / (\tau^2_{U_0} + \sigma^2_e)$. The ICC provides the proportion of total variance that is between persons in their mean levels of the outcome over time (i.e., due to $\tau^2_{U_0}$). Whether that between-person variation ($\tau^2_{U_0}$) is significantly greater than 0 can be assessed via a likelihood ratio test (i.e., the $-2\Delta LL$ relative to an σ^2_e-only model).

The size of its ICC will dictate which effects the time-varying predictor can potentially show. First (and most likely), if there is significant between-person variance in the time-varying predictor (i.e., $\tau^2_{U_0} > 0$), then that between-person variation can potentially show a corresponding between-person effect. Alternatively, if the time-varying predictor does *not* have significant between-person variance (i.e., $\tau^2_{U_0} \approx 0$), this means it has only within-person variation, and thus the time-varying predictor could only show a within-person effect. An example of when the latter is likely to occur is when modeling change across balanced time. If everyone in the sample has the same set of balanced time observations, then the predictor of *time* will only have within-person variance and thus can only show a within-person effect. But when *time* is unbalanced such that its ICC is greater than 0 (e.g., persons differ at the beginning of a study in age or grade level), then that unbalanced *time* predictor for time (e.g., age or grade) has the potential to show differential between-person and within-person effects—this will be the topic of chapter 10. Finally, it is also possible for a time-varying predictor to have an ICC ≈ 1, indicating little to no within-person variation (and in which case it is essentially a time-*invariant* predictor instead). Unfortunately there are usually no straightforward provisions in most software for multilevel models for testing whether the amount of within-person variance is significantly greater than 0 (i.e., $\sigma^2_e > 0$ and ICC < 1). But if its ICC ≈ 1, the time-varying predictor should be treated as a time-invariant predictor instead, such as by including only its value at time 0.

1.C. Time-Varying Predictors Can Have Between-Person and/or Within-Person Effects

The kinds of variance a time-varying predictor has (between-person and/or within-person) will dictate the kinds of effects it can show. To better illustrate these different effects, four sets of hypothetical effects of time-varying stress (on the *x*-axis) predicting time-varying negative mood (on the *y*-axis) are shown in Figure 8.1. Here stress and negative mood are both continuous variables with a mean of 5 for ease of explanation, and separate trajectories are plotted for persons with a mean stress score across time of 4, 5, or 6. Note that *time* is not needed in Figure 8.1: Once any necessary fixed and random effects related to time have been included in the model, it likely will no longer matter which occasion it is when considering the effects of time-varying predictors. Here, what we need to know is what the stress value was at each occasion, and not necessarily *when* that stress value was reported (which occasion it is may matter if the effect of the time-varying predictor changes over time, however). Critically, both stress and negative mood have some between-person variation and some within-person variation, and thus there is the potential for stress to show both a between-person and within-person effect—Figure 8.1 was designed to illustrate different patterns of these effects.

To begin, the top-left panel of Figure 8.1 shows an effect of stress that is entirely *between persons:* There is a positive slope of 1 through the person means of stress (as shown by the dashed line through the center of the individual trajectories), indicating that for every one-unit higher *person mean stress,* mean negative mood is expected to be higher by 1. Or stated more simply, people who report more stress on average than other people tend to be grumpier on average than other people. However, there is no effect of stress within persons (the individual trajectories have a slope of 0), indicating that reporting *more stress than your own mean* has no effect on that occasion's negative mood. This means that the effect of stress in the top left

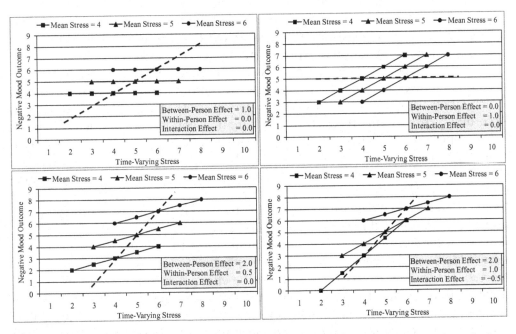

Figure 8.1 Hypothetical between-person effects (as the slope of the dashed line through the person means) and within-person effects (as the slope of the individual line for mean = 5; triangle markers) of time-varying stress on time-varying negative mood.

panel is entirely *cross-sectional:* The individual differences in mean stress over time relate to mean negative mood, but the intraindividual variation in stress does not relate to that occasion's negative mood.

Next consider the top right panel of Figure 8.1, which shows an effect of stress that is entirely *within persons:* There is a positive slope of 1 in each individual stress trajectory, indicating that for every one-unit *more stress than your own mean* (whatever your own mean is), that occasion's negative mood is expected to be higher by 1. Or stated more simply, negative mood is predicted to be higher than usual on days when people report more stress than usual. However, this time there is no effect of stress between persons: person mean stress does not predict person mean negative mood. So, the effect of stress in top right panel is entirely *longitudinal:* It's not that chronically stressed people are grumpier than other people, it's that whenever people report more stress than usual (regardless of what "usual" is, as indicated by their person mean stress), they are grumpier than usual, too.

But rarely do we find only a between-person effect or only a within-person effect of a time-varying predictor—it is more likely that both effects would be observed to some extent. To illustrate, consider the bottom left panel of Figure 8.1, which shows positive stress effects of both types. But here the between-person effect of 2.0 is larger than the within-person effect of 0.5: The slope of the line through the person means is steeper by 1.5 than the slope of the individual stress trajectories. Accordingly, for every one-unit higher *person mean stress than other people,* mean negative mood is expected to be higher by 2.0, but for every one-unit *more stress than your own mean,* that occasion's negative mood is expected to be higher by 0.5. Given equal variability at level 2 and level 1 for both stress and negative mood (i.e., ICCs of .50 for each variable), this result would mean that being a more stressed-out person (than other people) matters more for predicting negative mood than does having a more stressful occasion (than usual), but here both individual differences and intraindividual variation in stress do matter to some extent.

So far the hypothetical effects of stress have been additive across levels, but this need not be the case. To illustrate, consider the bottom right panel of Figure 8.1 in which a between-person stress by within-person stress interaction is also present. Accordingly, the two main effects of stress are now conditional on each other: the between-person stress effect of 2.0 applies *specifically when people are at their own mean levels of stress* (e.g., as shown by the dashed line through the person means of stress), and the within-person stress effect of 1.0 applies *specifically for persons at the centering value of person mean stress* (e.g., person mean stress = 5 here, as indicated by the triangles). The between-person stress by within-person stress interaction of –0.5 can be interpreted two equivalent ways. First (and more intuitively), it means that the *within-person effect* of reporting more stress than usual on a given occasion (which was 1.0 given a person mean stress = 5) *becomes less positive by 0.5 for every one-unit higher person mean stress:* the effect of reporting more stress than usual matters *less* for people who have more stress in general. Alternatively, the between-person stress by within-person stress interaction of –0.5 also means that the *between-person effect* of reporting greater mean stress than other people (which was 2.0 when time-varying stress is at the person's mean) *becomes less positive by*

0.5 for every one-unit more stress than usual: differences between people due to mean stress are less pronounced whenever people are more stressed than usual.

To summarize, time-varying predictors are likely to be informative at multiple levels of analysis because they almost always contain both between-person and within-person variance, and each source of variation is likely to have a different effect (a level-2 between-person effect and a level-1 within-person effect, respectively) on the outcome. These effects can be additive or interactive (and they can each interact with other predictors as well). Experience suggests *it is the rule, rather than the exception, that the between-person and within-person effects of time-varying predictors will differ from each other,* and there are (at least) two reasons for this. The first reason pertains to the theoretical constructs measured by the predictor at each level of analysis. In the example of stress, a confluence of various chronic factors can result in a given individual being a "high stress" or "low stress" person, such as personality variables, lifestyle differences, and so forth. Yet different, more acute factors are likely to be the reason why some days are more stressful than others, such as temporally specific deviations from normal routines of work, family, or health. Thus, given that between-person and within-person variation likely represent two different theoretical constructs, their effects on a given outcome will often be of different magnitudes or even different directions. But in addition to differences in the constructs they reflect, however, the second reason why between-person and within-person effects will likely differ from each other is simply because they are unstandardized coefficients. That is, unequal amounts of between-person versus within-person variation will result in fixed effects that are estimated on different numeric scales—this will be illustrated in the chapter example.

1.D. The Role of Time-Varying Predictors in the Model for the Means

We now consider the potential roles time-varying predictors can play in each side of the model. It is commonly believed that the role of fixed effects of time-varying predictors in the model for the means is to account for within-person level-1 residual variance (σ_e^2). While this is true, it is not the whole story, because time-varying predictors will need to be represented by two separate predictors that distinguish their between-person and within-person sources of variance in order to properly distinguish their potential between-person and within-person effects on a longitudinal outcome. Therefore, to be more specific, it is the *within-person part of the time-varying predictor* that could potentially account for the level-1 within-person σ_e^2 variance. Similarly, interactions among the within-person parts of two or more time-varying predictors would also reduce σ_e^2. In contrast, the *between-person part of the time-varying predictor* is actually a time-*invariant* predictor. And as presented in chapter 7, time-invariant predictors can modify any level-1 term for the intercept, asymptote, change over time, or the effect of any time-varying predictor. In doing so they explain the level-2 random variance in the level-1 effect if the level-1 effect is random, or else the level-1 residual variance if the level-1 effect is not random.

1.E. The Role of Time-Varying Predictors in the Model for the Variance

In addition to fixed effects in the model for the means that can explain outcome variance, a time-varying predictor can contribute to the model for the variance in two ways. First, just as we saw for level-1 effects related to time in chapters 5 and 6, because they are also measured at level 1, time-varying predictors can have *random effects*—that is, each person may need his or her own slope for the effect of the time-varying predictor. For instance, *the effect of having more stress than usual* on negative mood could differ randomly across persons. Individual differences in the stress slopes would then become another level-2 pile of variance to be predicted (i.e., by cross-level interactions of the time-varying predictor with the random slope with one or more time-invariant predictors, just as we saw in chapter 7).

Second, time-varying predictors can also be used to predict heterogeneity of variance in the outcome, but only at their corresponding level or lower. That is, the *between-person part* of a time-varying predictor can predict heterogeneity of between-person variance at level 2 (i.e., differential amounts of the random effects variances across persons) or heterogeneity of within-person residual variance at level 1 (i.e., differential amounts of within-person fluctuation across persons). But the *within-person part* of a time-varying predictor can only predict heterogeneity of within-person residual variance at level 1. In summary, as you've probably guessed by now, properly specifying and assessing the many contributions of a time-varying predictor (and all its additive and interactive parts) in a longitudinal model can be quite a complex endeavor!

1.F. Assessing the Effect Size of Time-Varying Predictors

Chapter 7 presented two methods for assessing effect size in conditional models, each of which can also be used with time-varying predictors. First, we can calculate the *pseudo-R^2 for the proportion reduction in each variance component* using the variances from two alternative models (with either *fewer* or *more* parameters) as Pseudo R^2 = (Variance$_{fewer}$ − Variance$_{more}$) / Variance$_{fewer}$. Each pile of variance in the model will have its own pseudo-R^2. As we will see, adding a main effect for the between-person part of a time-varying predictor to a model can reduce the level-2 random intercept variance $\tau_{U_0}^2$, whereas adding a main effect for the within-person part of a time-varying predictor can reduce the level-1 residual variance σ_e^2. Adding a cross-level interaction of a level-2 (between-person) predictor with a level-1 predictor that has a random slope will reduce the corresponding level-2 random slope variance of the level-1 predictor, whereas a cross-level interaction will reduce the level-1 residual variance σ_e^2 instead if the level-1 effect is not random (i.e., it is fixed or systematically varying; see chapter 7).

Although straightforward in principle, there are a number of issues that plague the use of pseudo-R^2 in practice that can make it less useful for assessing effect size, especially in models with time-varying predictors. Most problematic is that, as we've seen previously, a reduction in level-1 residual variance σ_e^2 can cause the level-2 random intercept variance $\tau_{U_0}^2$ to increase, because the "true" value of $\tau_{U_0}^2$ (that appears in the output) is estimated as (observed $\tau_{U_0}^2$) − (σ_e^2 / n), in which n is the number of occasions per person. So, the level-2 $\tau_{U_0}^2$ will increase whenever the level-1 σ_e^2 is reduced but level-2 $\tau_{U_0}^2$ is not, which can happen when adding the within-person part of a time-varying predictor without its corresponding between-person part.

This inflation of the level-2 $\tau_{U_0}^2$ after explaining some of the level-1 σ_e^2 has caused some authors (e.g., Raudenbush & Bryk, 2002) to recommend that pseudo-R^2 should not be calculated for level-2 $\tau_{U_0}^2$ unless the models to be compared have the same level-1 fixed effects. However, this creates a problem when examining time-varying predictors that contain two levels of variation (as most of them tend to do). If the within-person part of the time-varying predictor is included by itself first, the level-2 $\tau_{U_0}^2$ will increase relative to the previous model. If the between-person part of the same time-varying predictor is then added second, there will be more level-2 $\tau_{U_0}^2$ to explain than there was to begin with, and so the pseudo-R^2 estimate for the between-person part will be artificially inflated as a result. Adding both parts of the same predictor simultaneously makes more sense, but that violates the "same level-1 effects" rule.

Another challenge is that pseudo-R^2 values cannot be computed across models with different parameters in the model for the variance (e.g., after adding a random slope for a time-varying predictor). This is for two reasons. First, the level-1 σ_e^2 will be smaller because some of its variation has reallocated to the level-2 random slope variance, but this is not a real reduction (i.e., adding a random effect repartitions the outcome variance, but does not explain it like adding a fixed effect would). Second, the level-2 $\tau_{U_0}^2$ will became conditional on the 0 value of the time-varying predictor with a random effect (e.g., just as $\tau_{U_0}^2$ became conditional on *time* = 0 after adding a random time slope), and so the estimate of $\tau_{U_0}^2$ may change in size after adding a random slope. So, once a time-varying predictor is given a random effect, we can no longer refer back to any model without that new random slope variance as a baseline for assessing effect size.

In light of these issues, the use of pseudo-R^2 as a measure of effect size will be limited in this chapter to just the few scenarios in which it is straightforward to compute. Instead, we will assess effect size using the more generalizable approach (as seen in chapter 7) of R^2 *for the proportion of explained total outcome variance*. This total R^2 value is calculated as the square of the Pearson correlation between the outcome predicted by the model fixed effects and the actual outcome. Because the proportion of explained outcome variance is based only on fixed effects, and only the model fixed effects can possibly explain outcome variance anyway, this total R^2 value can be computed across any models with different fixed effects no matter what level they belong to and regardless of the contents of their model for the variance. We will demonstrate this total R^2 method of assessing effect size throughout the chapter example, to which we now turn.

2. Examining the Multilevel Main Effects of Time-Varying Predictors

The example for this chapter will build on the same data that were used in chapter 7 to demonstrate the modeling of time-invariant predictors for outcomes that show within-person fluctuation over time. To review, five assessments were collected over a two-week period from 105 older adults ages 69 to 95 years ($M = 80.13$, $SD = 6.11$), 27% of which were men. The outcome was a sum of the number of physical symptoms participants reported experiencing in the past 24 hours ($M = 1.27$, $SD = 1.32$, possible range = 0 to 5; ICC = .66). A total of 509 cases were complete with respect to the variables to be included (i.e., symptoms predicted by sex, age, daily negative mood, and daily stressors). Given our eventual interest in models with heterogeneous variances as estimated in SAS NLMIXED, we will again estimate all models using maximum likelihood (ML). The significance of individual fixed effects will be tested by their Wald test p-values (i.e., from the test statistic that results from a parameter estimate divided by its standard error); the significance of a set of multiple new fixed effects or of new random effects will be tested by ML likelihood ratio ($-2\Delta LL$) tests. We will make the usual assumptions about the level-2 random effect (U_i) and level-1 residual (e_{ti}) terms unless otherwise noted—these include normality, as well as independence and constant variance across persons, days, and predictors.

In chapter 7 we determined that the best-fitting unconditional model for time had only a fixed intercept in the model for the means, with random intercept and residual variances in the model for the variance (i.e., no fixed or random effects of time were needed). We then examined the effects of time-invariant predictors for sex (coded such that men = 0 and women = 1, which will be referred to as $Women_i$) and age (centered such that age 0 = 80 years, which will be referred to as $Age80_i$). The best-fitting conditional model with respect to sex and age (that will serve as our new conditional baseline model) is shown in Equation (8.1):

Level 1: $Symptoms_{ti} = \beta_{0i} + e_{ti}$

Level 2:

$$\text{Intercept: } \beta_{0i} = \gamma_{00} + \gamma_{01}(Women_i) + \gamma_{02}(Age_i - 80) \quad (8.1)$$
$$+ \gamma_{03}(Women_i)(Age_i - 80) + U_{0i}$$

which includes in the model for the means the main effects of sex and age and their interaction (i.e., as predictors of the level-2 individual intercept); results are shown in the first set of columns in Table 8.1. Given the previous nonsignificant findings, our baseline model does not include sex or age as predictors of heterogeneity of variance in the model for the variance.

We now continue the example for daily physical symptoms by first examining a time-varying predictor of **daily negative mood** as computed as the mean of five items: *sad, annoyed, worried, irritated,* and *depressed,* each rated on a 5-point scale (from *not at all* to *extremely*). Low negative mood was reported overall ($M = 1.20$, $SD = 0.38$, range = 1.00 to 3.60). The intraclass correlation for daily negative mood (as calculated from the results of an empty means, random intercept model) was ICC = .36,

Table 8.1 Comparison of results from person-mean-centered (PMC) and grand-mean-centered (GMC) models for the main effects of daily negative mood on daily symptoms. Bold values are $p < .05$.

Model Effects	Equation 8.1: No Effects of Negative Mood				Equation 8.3 (PMC) and 8.7 (GMC): Level-1 and Level-2 Effects					Equation 8.5 (GMC): Convergence Effect			
	Term	Est	SE	$p <$	PMC	GMC	Est	SE	$p <$	Term	Est	SE	$p <$
Model for the Means													
Intercept	γ_{00}	**1.713**	0.211	.001	γ_{00}	γ_{00}	**3.266**	0.346	.001	γ_{00}	**1.976**	0.226	.001
Sex (Men = 0, Women = 1)	γ_{01}	**-0.531**	0.245	.033	γ_{01}	γ_{01}	**-0.518**	0.218	.019	γ_{01}	**-0.532**	0.237	.027
Age (0 = 80 years)	γ_{02}	**0.100**	0.037	.008	γ_{02}	γ_{02}	**0.067**	0.033	.049	γ_{02}	**0.095**	0.036	.009
Sex by Age	γ_{03}	**-0.110**	0.042	.010	γ_{03}	γ_{03}	**-0.092**	0.038	.017	γ_{03}	**-0.108**	0.041	.009
Negative Mood Effects:													
Level-2 Between-Person					γ_{04}	$\gamma_{04} + \gamma_{10}$	**1.970**	0.369	.001				
Level-2 Contextual Effect					$\gamma_{04} - \gamma_{10}$	γ_{04}	**1.811**	0.391	.001				
Level-1 Within-Person					γ_{10}	γ_{10}	0.159	0.128	.214				
Level-1 Convergence										γ_{10}	**0.330**	0.122	.007
Model for the Variance													
Random Intercept Variance	$\tau^2_{U_0}$	**1.073**	0.167	.001	$\tau^2_{U_0}$	$\tau^2_{U_0}$	**0.816**	0.131	.001	$\tau^2_{U_0}$	**0.996**	0.159	.001
Residual Variance	σ^2_e	**0.615**	0.043	.001	σ^2_e	σ^2_e	**0.613**	0.043	.001	σ^2_e	**0.615**	0.043	.001
ML Model Fit													
Number of Parameters	6				8					7			
-2LL	1432.6				1405.7					1425.5			
AIC	1444.6				1421.7					1439.5			
BIC	1460.5				1442.9					1458.1			

indicating that 36% of its variance was due to between-person mean differences, and 64% was due to within-person variation across days.

We will begin examining the effects of daily negative mood on daily physical symptoms with the more intuitive approach of person-mean-centering, followed by the more common alternative approach of grand-mean-centering. We will then see how these two centering methods can result in equivalent fixed effects, but non-equivalent random effects variances and covariances. At each step the new terms in the model equations have been underlined for emphasis. Finally, any fixed effect (and its SE and p-value) not provided directly by a model has been obtained using additional statements (e.g., ESTIMATE in SAS, TEST in SPSS, LINCOM in STATA, or NEW in M*plus*), as seen in the online materials for the text.

The previous section described how time-varying predictors that include both between-person variation and within-person variation are really two variables in one. Thus, our next step is to literally create the two predictor variables contained in the original time-varying predictor of negative mood, a method of model specification for time-varying predictors called **person-mean-centering**. A related term for the same idea is **group-mean-centering**, which is used in multilevel models in which persons at level 1 are nested within groups at level 2. To keep the terminology as applicable as possible, however, we will use the term *person-mean-centering*, given that we will center time-varying negative mood using its level-2 *person* mean (and not a *group* mean).

2.A. Person-Mean-Centering of Continuous Time-Varying Predictors

Thus, in order to separately represent between-person and within-person variation in negative mood, we compute two new predictor variables, using person-mean-centering to compute the level-1 predictor specifically, as shown in Equation (8.2):

$$\text{Level 2 Predictor: PMmood2}_i = \overline{\text{Mood}}_i - 2$$
$$\text{Level 1 Predictor: WPmood}_{ti} = \text{Mood}_{ti} - \overline{\text{Mood}}_i \tag{8.2}$$

in which Mood_{ti} is the time-varying negative mood predictor value at time t for person i, and $\overline{\text{Mood}}_i$ is the person mean of time-varying negative mood across days. As shown in the first line of Equation (8.2), **between-person variation in negative mood** will be represented by a level-2, time-*invariant* predictor of person mean negative mood (as indicated by its subscript of just i) for which a centering constant of 2 was chosen based on the observed distribution of $\overline{\text{Mood}}_i$ ($M = 1.20$, $SD = 0.26$, range = 1.00 to 2.52). To help us remember that person mean negative mood is centered at 2, we will refer to it as *PMmood2*$_i$ (and its construction as $\overline{\text{Mood}}_i - 2$ will be shown in the equations as well). So, the reference point for the intercept (and for the simple main effects of any predictors interacting with PMmood2$_i$) will be a person who responded with an average of 2 across days for negative mood ($\overline{\text{Mood}}_i = 2$ or PMmood2$_i = 0$). Any centering constant besides 2 could have been chosen for the level-2 predictor instead, including the grand mean, because the term *person-mean-centering* refers only to the level-1 predictor specifically, as explained next.

As shown in the second line of Equation (8.2), **within-person variation in negative mood** will be represented by the level-1, time-*varying* predictor of within-person negative mood (as indicated by its subscript of *ti*) that we will refer to as $WPmood_{ti}$. We do not add a constant to its name (such as the "2" in $PMmood2_i$) because it is not centered at a *constant*: under person-mean-centering, $WPmood_{ti}$ is centered at a *variable*—a person's usual level of daily negative mood, as represented by each person's mean across all of his or her occasions. By subtracting the original person mean negative mood ($\overline{Mood_i}$) from negative mood at each occasion ($Mood_{ti}$), *only the within-person part* of daily negative mood is included in the new $WPmood_{ti}$ predictor ($M = 0.00$, $SD = 0.27$, range $= -0.72$ to 1.28). Positive values for $WPmood_{ti}$ indicate higher-than-usual reported negative mood at time t for person i, whereas negative values represent lower-than-usual reported negative mood. As a result, the $WPmood_{ti}$ predictor (that contains only the *within-person* part of negative mood) will be uncorrelated with the $PMmood2_i$ predictor (that contains only the *between-person* part of negative mood) when based on the exact same data (i.e., no level-1 observations are absent in the model that contributed to the level-2 person mean). Thus, the effects of $PMmood2_i$ and $WPmood_{ti}$ can be evaluated simultaneously because they operate at separate levels of the model (level 2 between persons and level 1 within persons over time, respectively). Note that we are assuming no time-related individual variance or covariance in the within-person predictor of $WPmood_{ti}$—that it fluctuates (but not does change systematically) over time. We will need to consider other approaches for predictors that show individual change over time (i.e., that are not stationary), starting in chapter 9.

Another way to think about person-mean-centering is that it is a brute-force method for obtaining the same type of variance decomposition for a time-varying *predictor* that would be found by estimating a model for a time-varying *outcome*. That is, if daily negative mood were an outcome, then the between-person variance in $PMmood2_i$ would be a proxy for its level-2 random intercept variance, and the within-person variance in $WPmood_{ti}$ would be a proxy for its level-1 residual variance. Simultaneous model-based variance decomposition of time-varying predictors and outcomes is possible within multivariate longitudinal models, which often go by the name of **multilevel structural equation models** (MSEM). The upside of these multivariate longitudinal models is that the estimation of variance components for a time-varying predictor takes into account any differential unreliability of each person mean, whereas simply using the person mean as an observed predictor does not. Otherwise, the level-2 fixed effects of the person mean predictor in a univariate multilevel model may be downwardly biased. The downside is that multivariate longitudinal models can be much more computationally demanding, especially when considering interactions involving the level-2 part of a time-varying predictor (which then become latent variable interactions rather than observed variable interactions). Chapter 9 will elaborate on these concerns. For now our goal is to learn how to interpret the effects of time-varying predictors across levels of analysis more generally, because these fundamental concepts will carry forward into a multilevel structural equation modeling framework as well.

2.B. Between-Person and Within-Person Fixed Main Effects in Person-Mean-Centering

We are now ready to examine the effects of negative mood in the model for the means using person-mean-centering. The new terms in each model will be underlined for emphasis. We begin by simultaneously adding the between-person and within-person main effects of negative mood (via PMmood2$_i$ and WPmood$_{ti}$, respectively), as shown in Equation (8.3):

Level 1 : $\text{Symptoms}_{ti} = \beta_{0i} + \beta_{1i}\underline{\left(\text{Mood}_{ti} - \overline{\text{Mood}}_i\right)} + e_{ti}$

Level 2 :

Intercept: $\beta_{0i} = \gamma_{00} + \gamma_{01}\left(\text{Women}_i\right) + \gamma_{02}\left(\text{Age}_i - 80\right) + \gamma_{03}\left(\text{Women}_i\right)\left(\text{Age}_i - 80\right)$

$\qquad\qquad + \underline{\gamma_{04}\left(\overline{\text{Mood}}_i - 2\right)} + U_{0i}$

Within-Person Mood: $\beta_{1i} = \underline{\gamma_{10}}$

$$(8.3)$$

Composite :

$\text{Symptoms}_{ti} = \gamma_{00} + \gamma_{01}\left(\text{Women}_i\right) + \gamma_{02}\left(\text{Age}_i - 80\right) + \gamma_{03}\left(\text{Women}_i\right)\left(\text{Age}_i - 80\right)$

$\qquad + \underline{\gamma_{04}\left(\overline{\text{Mood}}_i - 2\right)} + \underline{\gamma_{10}\left(\text{Mood}_{ti} - \overline{\text{Mood}}_i\right)} + U_{0i} + e_{ti}$

in which the centering of *PMmood2*$_i$ (as $\overline{\text{Mood}}_i$ − 2) and *WPmood*$_{ti}$ (as Mood$_{ti}$ − Mood$_i$) is shown to aid our interpretation of these fixed effects. The *between-person* main effect of negative mood is given directly by γ_{04} for PMmood2$_i$ in the level-2 equation for the intercept β_{0i}. The *within-person* main effect of negative mood is first defined by the β_{1i} placeholder for WPmood$_{ti}$ in the level-1 model, and β_{1i} is then defined by a level-2 equation including just the fixed effect γ_{10}. So, as seen in the single-level composite model that results from replacing the β placeholders with their level-2 contents, we are assuming that the within-person effect of negative mood is *fixed*—that everybody gets the same effect for WPmood$_{ti}$ of just γ_{10}. The two new main effects significantly improved model fit over the baseline model, $-2\Delta LL(2) = 26.9$, $p < .001$; the smaller AIC and BIC values concur. However, only one of these effects is individually significant in examining the Wald test *p*-values. Results are reported in the second set of columns in Table 8.1.

The fixed intercept $\gamma_{00} = 3.266$ is now the expected number of physical symptoms when all predictors have a value of 0: for an 80-year-old man with a person mean negative mood of 2 on a day when he is at his average of 2 for negative mood. The fixed effects of sex, age, and their interaction are now their unique effects after controlling for person mean negative mood, but are otherwise interpreted the same way as in chapter 7. Accordingly, the significant simple main effect of $Women_i$ of $\gamma_{01} = -0.518$ indicates that among 80-year-olds, women report 0.518 fewer mean symptoms than men. The significant simple main effect of $Age80_i$ of $\gamma_{02} = 0.067$ indicates that among men, mean symptoms are expected to be higher by 0.067 per additional year of age. The significant $Women_i$ by $Age80_i$ level-2 interaction of $\gamma_{03} = -0.092$ indicates that the sex difference (in which men reported more mean symptoms) grows by 0.092 per year of age, or that the age slope is less positive by 0.092 in women. As also requested, the simple effect of age for women of $\gamma_{02} + \gamma_{03} = 0.067 - 0.092 = -0.025$ was nonsignificant (not reported in Table 8.1).

We now turn to the new effects in Equation (8.3). At level 2, the significant **between-person main effect** of negative mood for $PMmood2_i$ of $\gamma_{04} = 1.970$ indicates that for every one-unit higher *person mean negative mood*, the *mean* number of symptoms reported across days is expected to be higher by 1.970. At level 1, the nonsignificant **within-person main effect** of negative mood for $WPmood_{ti}$ of $\gamma_{10} = 0.159$ indicates that for every one-unit more negative mood *than usual* (i.e., relative to the person's mean), *that specific day's* symptoms are expected to be nonsignificantly higher by 0.159. In addition, we note that the main effects of $PMmood2_i$ and $WPmood_{ti}$ are each assumed to be *linear* (i.e., that a unit difference in each predictor has the same effect on negative mood across the entire range of the predictor, which we also assumed for the effect of $Age80_i$) and to be *additive* (i.e., not to depend on each other or on the other predictors). Each of these assumptions is of course testable, as shown later in this chapter.

In terms of effect size, relative to the baseline conditional model (in the first set of columns in Table 8.1), the between-person main effect of negative mood explained an additional 24% of the level-2 random intercept variance that remained after controlling for sex and age, pseudo-R^2 for $\tau_{U_0}^2 = (1.703 - 0.816) / 1.703 = .239$. As a result, U_{0i} now indicates the random intercept variance (i.e., between-person variation in mean physical symptoms) that remains after controlling for sex, age, and person mean negative mood. In addition, the within-person main effect of negative mood explained only 0.4% of the level-1 residual variance, pseudo-R^2 for $\sigma_e^2 = (0.615 - 0.613) / 0.615 = .004$. As a result, e_{ti} now indicates the within-person fluctuation in daily physical symptoms that remains after controlling for the within-person effect of negative mood (and after controlling for everything that predicts the individual intercept). Finally, we can also calculate a comprehensive R^2 value for the proportion reduction in total outcome variance by squaring the correlation of the outcome predicted from the fixed effects with the actual outcome. As reported in chapter 7, the correlation between the predicted outcome from just the fixed effects of sex and age in the baseline model was $r = .220$ or $R^2 = .048$. The correlation between the predicted outcome also including the between-person and within-person main effects of negative mood was $r = .442$ or $R^2 = .196$, such that the between-person and within-person parts of negative mood accounted for *another* 14.7% of the total variance in daily physical symptoms.

So, to summarize, the significant between-person main effect of negative mood and nonsignificant within-person main effect of negative mood indicate that grumpier people tend to report more symptoms across days than do less grumpy people, but being in a worse mood than usual doesn't predict reporting more physical symptoms that day. Thus, the between-person and within-person effects of the same variable appear to differ from each other. Furthermore, based on the size of their coefficients, it seems that between-person variation in negative mood matters much more for predicting physical symptoms than does within-person variation in negative mood. But as explained earlier in the chapter, another reason why they may differ is because their fixed effects are unstandardized coefficients on different scales, and are thus not directly comparable.

It would be nice if we could obtain standardized coefficients, such as in single-level regression, in which standardized coefficients can be calculated as $\beta_{unstd}*SD(X) / SD(Y)$. Unfortunately, fully standardized coefficients are not available in models with random effects given the ambiguity in what SD(Y) could be. However, we can calculate **pseudo-standardized coefficients** as: $\gamma_{STD} = \gamma*SD(X)/SD(Y)$, in which the X and Y variances are those relevant for the level of the fixed effect of interest (i.e., the term "pseudo" is used similarly here as when calculating proportion reduction in variance of a specific variance component). The pseudo-standardized between- and within-person effects of negative mood are shown in Equation (8.4):

$$BP_{std} = \left(BP_{unstd} * \frac{SD(x_i)}{SD(y_i)}\right) = \left(\gamma_{04} * \frac{SD(PMmood2_i)}{\sqrt{\tau^2_{U_0}}}\right) = 1.970 * \frac{0.267}{0.903} = .582$$

$$WP_{std} = \left(WP_{unstd} * \frac{SD(x_{ti})}{SD(y_{ti})}\right) = \left(\gamma_{10} * \frac{SD(WPmood_{ti})}{\sqrt{\sigma^2_e}}\right) = 0.159 * \frac{0.273}{0.783} = .055$$

(8.4)

in which X is standardized based on the original SD of the predictors at each level (PMmood2$_i$ at level 2; WPmood$_{ti}$ at level 1). The Y standardization is based on the SD (square root) of the level-2 random intercept variance $\tau^2_{U_0}$ and level-1 residual variance σ^2_e. As is shown in Equation (8.4), the pseudo-standardized between- and within-person negative mood effects are .582 and .055, respectively. So, in this example, even though they are less discrepant when placed on similar scales, the between-person and within-person main negative mood effects still differ. In general, to the extent that variation in the predictors and in the outcomes is not equally distributed across levels, the unstandardized fixed effects at each level are likely to differ numerically simply for this reason, above and beyond any theoretical sources for differences in the between-person and within-person effects of the same variable.

2.C. Grand-Mean-Centering of Continuous Time-Varying Predictors

Although others may disagree, the view presented in this text is that person-mean-centering of time-varying predictors is well suited for most longitudinal data and is relatively easy to understand. This is because by explicitly separating the between-person from the within-person parts of a time-varying predictor ahead of time, their effects are then directly represented in the model. Furthermore, this explicit separation provides a natural symmetry with the model for the variance in the outcome, in which between-person variation ($\tau_{U_0}^2$ at level 2) is also explicitly differentiated from within-person variation (σ_e^2 at level 1). And as we'll see in chapter 9, it also mirrors the estimation of variances for predictors in multivariate longitudinal models.

Despite these advantages for longitudinal data, *person-mean-centering* is used less often than *grand-mean-centering*, a different method of including effects of time-varying predictors. In *grand-mean-centering*, the time-varying predictor is simply rescaled so that 0 is a meaningful value, just like any other predictor. That is, rather than subtracting a *variable* (the person mean) from the time-varying predictor as in person-mean-centering, in grand-mean-centering a *constant* is subtracted instead. As indicated by its name, the grand mean of the time-varying predictor is usually the centering constant, but the term *grand-mean-centering* (and the interpretation of the model effects when using this method) will apply whenever any constant is used to simply rescale a time-varying predictor (or when the predictor is left uncentered as well). Here, the grand-mean-centered version of daily negative mood will be $Mood2_{ti} = Mood_{ti} - 2$ (so $Mood2_{ti} = 0$ when $Mood_{ti} = 2$). In this case, we had also centered the level-2 person mean negative mood predictor at 2, but the same centering constant does not have to be used for a given predictor at both levels (although doing so can make it easier to remember who the reference person will be).

So what happens when a time-varying predictor is centered at a *constant* (via grand-mean-centering) rather than centered at a *variable* (via person-mean-centering)? To illustrate, Table 8.2 shows two hypothetical occasions from two different persons. The first person (rows 1 and 2) has a person mean negative mood of 2 and the second person (rows 3 and 4) has a person mean negative mood of 4. The third column for $Mood_{ti}$ gives two daily negative mood values for each person. As seen in the fourth column, the person-mean-centered $WPmood_{ti}$ predictor only represents *relative* levels of negative mood (relative to the person's mean, whatever that happens to be), and thus only contains *within-person* variation. In contrast, as seen in the fifth column, the grand-mean-centered $Mood2_{ti}$ predictor still represents *absolute* levels of negative mood (just rescaled so that 2 is the new 0), and thus $Mood2_{ti}$ still contains *all* of its between-person and within-person variation. So, the $PMmood2_{ti}$ level-2 predictor will still be correlated with the grand-mean-centered $Mood2_{ti}$ level-1 predictor (but not with the person-mean-centered $WPmood_{ti}$ level-1 predictor, as noted earlier). This difference in how the level-1 predictors are formed

Table 8.2 Comparison of person-mean-centering and grand-mean-centering of time-varying negative mood. A centering constant of 2 was used to provide a meaningful 0 value for negative mood, but other centering constants will result in the same model fit and predicted values.

Level 2		Level 1		
$Mood_i$	$PMmood2_i =$ $\overline{Mood}_i - 2$	$Mood_{ti}$	*Person-Mean-Centering:* $WPmood_{ti} =$ $Mood_{ti} - \overline{Mood}_i$	*Grand-Mean-Centering:* $Mood2_{ti} =$ $Mood_{ti} - 2$
2	0	1	−1	−1
2	0	3	1	1
4	2	3	−1	1
4	2	5	1	3

Model Terms	Person-Mean-Centering	Grand-Mean-Centering
Variable Definition		
Level-2 Predictor	$PMmood2_i = \overline{Mood}_i - 2$	$PMmood2_i = \overline{Mood}_i - 2$
Level-1 Predictor	$WPmood_{ti} = Mood_{ti} - \overline{Mood}_i$	$Mood2_{ti} = \overline{Mood}_i - 2$
Model Specification		
Level-2 predictor only:		
Level-2 interpretation?	Between-person effect	Between-person effect
Level-1 predictor only:		
Level-1 interpretation?	Within-person effect	Convergence ("smushed") effect across levels
Assumption in leaving out the level-2 predictor?	Between-person effect = 0	Between-person effect = Within-person effect
Level-1 and level-2 predictors:		
Level-2 interpretation?	Between-person effect	Contextual effect (difference of Between-person and Within-person effects)
Level-1 interpretation?	Within-person effect	Within-person effect

will result in important differences in how their effects are interpreted, as summarized in the bottom of Table 8.2 and as explained next using our example of time-varying negative mood.

2.D. Convergence (Smushed) Effects in Grand-Mean-Centering

To demonstrate the most typical—but usually incorrect—specification of time-varying predictors via grand-mean-centering, we will modify the previous best-fitting model in Equation (8.3) to replace the person-mean-centered level-1 predictor (of WPmood$_{ti}$ = Mood$_{ti}$ − $\overline{\text{Mood}}_i$) with the grand-mean-centered *Mood2$_{ti}$* (as Mood$_{ti}$ − 2), as seen in Equation (8.5):

Level 1: Symptoms$_{ti}$ = β_{0i} + $\underline{\beta_{1i}(\text{Mood}_{ti} - 2)}$ + e_{ti}

Level 2:

Intercept: β_{0i} = γ_{00} + $\gamma_{01}(\text{Women}_i)$ + $\gamma_{02}(\text{Age}_i - 80)$
$\qquad\qquad$ + $\gamma_{03}(\text{Women}_i)(\text{Age}_i - 80)$ + U_{0i}

Time-Varying Mood: $\beta_{1i} = \gamma_{10}$

$$(8.5)$$

Composite:

Symptoms$_{ti}$ = γ_{00} + $\gamma_{01}(\text{Women}_i)$ + $\gamma_{02}(\text{Age}_i - 80)$
$\qquad\qquad$ + $\gamma_{03}(\text{Women}_i)(\text{Age}_i - 80)$ + $\underline{\gamma_{10}(\text{Mood}_{ti} - 2)}$ + U_{0i} + e_{ti}

in which the effect of Mood2$_{ti}$ is first defined by the β_{1i} placeholder in the level-1 model, and β_{1i} is then defined by a level-2 equation including just the fixed effect γ_{10}. Note that so far, no effect of person mean negative mood is included in the level-2 equation for the intercept β_{0i}, which is exactly why this model specification is usually incorrect.

We previously found between-person and within-person main effects of negative mood of 1.970 ($p < .001$) and 0.159 ($p = .214$), respectively. As shown in the third set of columns in Table 8.1, the fixed main effect of Mood2$_{ti}$ is now γ_{10} = 0.330 ($p = .007$), but what does it mean? Given that Mood2$_{ti}$ still contains all of its between-person and within-person variation, its grand-mean-centered level-1 main effect—when included by itself, as in Equation (8.5)—is neither the between-person nor within-person main effect, but a weighted blend of the two effects **smushed** together, more formally known as a **convergence effect** or a **conflated effect**. That is, although there are two different effects of negative mood to be estimated, there is only one fixed effect (for Mood2$_{ti}$) included in the model. As a result, the model assumes *convergence* of the between-person and within-person main effects of negative mood—that they are equivalent, such that they can both be represented by the single (smushed) level-1 fixed effect of γ_{10} = 0.330 for grand-mean-centered Mood2$_{ti}$. As seen in Table 8.1, the level-1 effect of Mood2$_{ti}$ resulted in a pseudo-R^2 for $\sigma_e^2 \approx 0$. However, the fact that Mood2$_{ti}$ also has an implied level-2 between-person effect of 0.330 is indicated by the 7.1% reduction in the level-2 $\tau_{U_0}^2$ relative to the baseline model with no effects of mood, pseudo-R^2 for $\tau_{U_0}^2$ = (1.073 − 0.996) / 1.073 = .071. This 7.1% reduction due to a between-person effect = .330 is much less than the 23.9% reduction that would have been due to the *full* between-person effect = 1.970. Furthermore, whenever the between-person and within-person effects are in opposite directions, a convergence effect that forces them to be the same can actually cause an *increase* in the level-2 random intercept variance! These consequences of smushed effects on model variance components will also be revisited in chapter 9.

The between-person and within-person effects will not be weighted equally in creating a single (smushed) convergence effect—Raudenbush and Bryk (2002, p. 138) describe how a convergence effect can be approximated by the between-person (BP) and within-person (WP) fixed main effect estimates and the square of their standard errors (SE), as shown for negative mood in Equation (8.6):

$$\text{Convergence Effect: } \gamma_{conv} \approx \frac{\dfrac{\gamma_{BP}}{SE_{BP}^2} + \dfrac{\gamma_{WP}}{SE_{WP}^2}}{\dfrac{1}{SE_{BP}^2} + \dfrac{1}{SE_{WP}^2}} = \frac{\dfrac{1.970}{0.369^2} + \dfrac{0.159}{0.128^2}}{\dfrac{1}{0.369^2} + \dfrac{1}{0.128^2}} = 0.353 \qquad (8.6)$$

in which the predicted convergence effect is 0.353, which is close to the obtained convergence effect of $\gamma_{10} = 0.330$ for grand-mean-centered Mood2$_{ti}$. Because the WP effect usually has a smaller SE than the BP effect due to the exclusion of $\tau_{U_0}^2$ (see chapter 3), the convergence effect will usually be more heavily weighted towards the WP effect, as it is here. But if the BP and WP effects differ from each other (as they do here), then the convergence effect as obtained from the grand-mean-centered time-varying predictor by itself will not be meaningful at all.

2.E. Contextual and Within-Person Fixed Main Effects in Grand-Mean-Centering

Fortunately, the assumption of convergence of the between-person and within-person main effects of negative mood (i.e., that they both equal a single effect of 0.330) is testable by adding the level-2 main effect of person mean of negative mood via PMmood2$_i$ to the previous model with the level-1 grand-mean-centered Mood2$_{ti}$, as seen in Equation (8.7):

Level 1: $\text{Symptoms}_{ti} = \beta_{0i} + \beta_{1i}(\text{Mood}_{ti} - 2) + e_{ti}$

Level 2:

Intercept: $\beta_{0i} = \gamma_{00} + \gamma_{01}(\text{Women}_i) + \gamma_{02}(\text{Age}_i - 80)$
$+ \gamma_{03}(\text{Women}_i)(\text{Age}_i - 80) + \gamma_{04}\left(\overline{\text{Mood}}_i - 2\right) + U_{0i}$

Within-Person Mood: $\beta_{1i} = \gamma_{10}$

Composite: $\qquad\qquad\qquad\qquad\qquad\qquad\qquad\qquad\qquad (8.7)$

$\text{Symptoms}_{ti} = \gamma_{00} + \gamma_{01}(\text{Women}_i) + \gamma_{02}(\text{Age}_i - 80)$
$+ \gamma_{03}(\text{Women}_i)(\text{Age}_i - 80) + \gamma_{04}\left(\overline{\text{Mood}}_i - 2\right)$
$+ \gamma_{10}(\text{Mood}_{ti} - 2) + U_{0i} + e_{ti}$

in which an effect for PMmood2$_i$ of γ_{04} has now been included in the level-2 equation for β_{0i}. In grand-mean-centering it is often helpful for simplicity of interpretation (but not required) to use the same centering constant for both predictors, as we have done here for negative mood. But before diving into how these level-1 and level-2 main effects of negative mood (γ_{10} and γ_{04}, respectively) would now be interpreted, let us briefly revisit their construction, as illustrated in the top of Table 8.2. Because the level-1 grand-mean-centered predictor of $Mood2_{ti}$ has only been rescaled, it will still be correlated with the level-2 predictor of $PMmood2_i$—as a result, their effects will be different when estimated simultaneously than when estimated in separate models.

To explain why this is the case, we draw from the logic of multiple regression. If a single predictor X is included in a regression model, its effect on Y will be its *total* effect reflecting its bivariate relationship with Y. But once another predictor Z is added to the model, the effect of X will no longer be its total effect—it will become its *unique* effect after controlling for Z. In other words, only the variance in X that is related to Y, but that is not related to Z, counts towards the unique effect of X in the model. Only when X and Z are completely uncorrelated would their simultaneous effects reflect their total effects—if there is no shared variance between X and Z, then there will be no difference between their total effects and their unique effects on Y.

We can extend this idea to reiterate what happens when person-mean-centering (PMC) the time-varying predictor of negative mood (followed by what happens in the new grand-mean-centering approach below). In PMC, the subtraction of the person mean in creating the level-1 predictor renders level-1 $WPmood_{ti}$ and level-2 $PMmood2_i$ uncorrelated. Thus, their effects will not compete in the model, and each will retain its *total* possible effect for each level. Given that $PMmood2_i$ contains only level-2 between-person variance, it carries the *total between-person mood main effect* and will only account for level-2 random intercept variance $\tau_{U_0}^2$. Furthermore, given that $WPmood_{ti}$ contains only level-1 within-person variance, it carries the *total within-person mood main effect* and will only account for level-1 residual variance. As shown in the bottom of Table 8.2 under PMC, each predictor retains its own effect regardless of whether the other predictor is in the model. Their effects do not compete with each other.

A different pattern of relationship is found when grand-mean-centering (GMC), however. Because the level-1 $Mood2_{ti}$ predictor still contains between-person and within-person variation, it will be correlated with $PMmood2_i$, and so their effects will be different when together in the same GMC model than when each is by itself. Thus, once $PMmood2_i$ is included in the level-2 model, the level-1 effect for $Mood2_{ti}$ of γ_{10} is no longer the convergence (smushed) effect—it must become its *unique* effect after controlling for $PMmood2_i$. And because $PMmood2_i$ contains only level-2 between-person variation, what is left for $Mood2_{ti}$ to contribute uniquely is based on its level-1 *within-person* variation. So, the level-1 effect of $Mood2_{ti}$ changes from the (smushed) *convergence* effect to the (unique) *within-person* effect after controlling for $PMmood2_i$. As seen in the second set of columns in Table 8.1, the level-1 effect for $Mood2_{ti}$ of $\gamma_{10} = 0.159$ is now the same within-person effect of negative mood as found for the level-1 effect of $WPmood_{ti}$ in PMC.

So what about the level-2 effect of $PMmood2_i$ when included with GMC $Mood2_{ti}$? In contrast to its effect of $\gamma_{04} = 1.970$ as seen in the PMC model, the main effect of PMmood2$_i$ was estimated as γ_{04} = 1.811 in the GMC model. The reason why PMmood2$_i$ doesn't have the same between-person effect in GMC as in PMC is that PMmood2$_i$ must also carry its unique effect after controlling for Mood2$_{ti}$. That is, to the extent that daily negative mood is higher for a given person than for the rest of the sample, we would expect that person's mean negative mood to be higher than the rest of the sample as well. As a result, *part* of the between-person effect can be captured just by including time-varying Mood2$_{ti}$. But if the between-person and within-person effects differ, then the level-2 effect of PMmood2$_i$ is still needed—its effect in GMC represents the *difference* needed to get from the part of the between-person effect carried by just time-varying Mood2$_{ti}$ to the *total* between-person effect that belongs in the level-2 model.

Thus, the *unique* between-person main effect for PMmood2$_i$ in GMC (after controlling for level-1 Mood2$_{ti}$) is called the level-2 **contextual** (or **incremental between-person**) **main effect**. The term *contextual effect* is derived from multilevel models for clustered data, in which the context of the group to which a person belongs provides some additional effect on a person's outcome. In longitudinal models, we can think of **persons as contexts**, such that contextual effects in our models will reflect the incremental effects of general person characteristics (like person mean negative mood) over and above the characteristics of a specific occasion. Here, the contextual effect of PMmood2$_i$ is γ_{04} = 1.811 ($p < .001$), which indicates that mean symptoms are expected to be higher by 1.811 for every one-unit higher PMmood2$_i$ *after controlling for that day's negative mood*. It also means that the between-person effect (of 1.970 from PMmood2$_i$ in PMC) is more positive by 1.811 than the within-person effect (of 0.159 for WPmood$_{ti}$ in PMC, or for Mood2$_{ti}$ in GMC after controlling for PMmood2$_i$). That the level-2 contextual main effect of PMmood2$_i$ (i.e., when included with GMC level-1 Mood2$_i$) reflects an *incremental* between-person main effect can be seen in the additional 18.1% reduction in the level-2 $\tau^2_{U_0}$ relative to the model with just the convergence level-1 main effect of Mood2$_{ti}$ in Equation (8.5).

The three different effects of negative mood (level-1 within-person, level-2 between-person, and level-2 contextual or incremental between-person) are shown in the top of Figure 8.2, in which the x-axis is daily negative mood and the y-axis is daily physical symptoms. Given that sex and age were not included in the figure, the predicted outcomes are for an 80-year-old man (i.e., at Women$_i$ = 0 and Age80$_i$ = 0). The individual lines display the predictions for hypothetical individuals with a person mean negative mood of 2 or 3 and within-person values of negative mood of –1, 0, or 1 relative to their person mean (so daily negative mood of 1, 2, or 3 given a person mean of 2, or daily negative mood of 2, 3, or 4 given a person mean of 3). The level-2 between-person main effect = 1.970 is the slope of the dashed line through the person means. The level-1 within-person main effect = 0.159 is the slope of the individual lines (which are parallel here given the lack of a cross-level interaction). The new effect, the level-2 contextual main effect (i.e., incremental between-person main effect), is represented by the vertical distance in the straight line at daily negative mood = 2 and can be understood as follows.

In the GMC model from Equation (8.7) with Mood2$_{1i}$ and PMmood2$_i$, the GMC level-1 Mood2$_{ti}$ predictor still contains the *absolute* amount of daily mood—for example, Mood2$_{ti}$ = 0 represents a daily negative mood score of 2, regardless of what

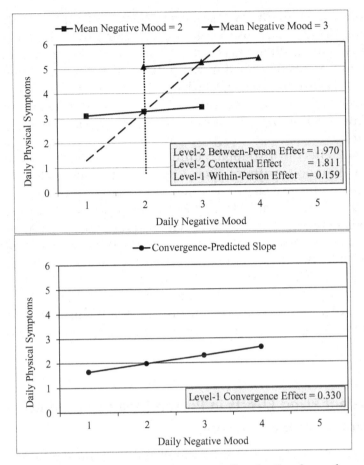

Figure 8.2 Top: The between-person effect (as the slope of the dashed line through the person means), the contextual effect (as the vertical distance between the lines at $x = 2$), and the within-person effect (as the slope of the individual lines) for daily negative mood predicting daily physical symptoms. Bottom: The convergence effect (single slope) for daily negative mood predicting daily physical symptoms.

person mean negative mood is. So, after controlling for the *absolute amount* of time-varying negative mood, the incremental (unique) effect of PMmood2$_i$ is given by its level-2 contextual effect. So, in the top of Figure 8.2, after holding daily negative mood constant at 2, for every unit higher person mean mood, mean daily symptoms are expected to be higher by the level-2 contextual effect = 1.811—the vertical distance between the lines at daily negative mood = 2. In summary, the level-2 contextual effect provided by PMmood2$_i$ tells us two things: (1) being a grumpier person on average has an *additional* impact on mean symptoms after controlling for (over and above) that day's negative mood, and (2) the between-person effect is more positive than the within-person effect.

In contrast, this idea of "over and above" does not apply to PMC time-varying predictors. That is, because WPmood$_{ti}$ is created by subtracting the person mean negative mood, WPmood$_{ti}$ then contains only the *relative* amount of daily negative mood. So, as described in the bottom of Table 8.2, PMmood2$_i$ carries the *total level-2 between-person effect* when with PMC WPmood$_{ti}$ (*not* controlling for today's negative mood), but PMmood2$_i$ carries the *unique level-2 contextual effect* (incremental between-person effect) when paired with GMC Mood2$_{ti}$ (*after* controlling for today's negative mood). Thus, what it means to leave out the level-2 effect of PMmood2$_i$ differs between models. By including only PMC level-1 WPmood$_{ti}$ without level-2 PMmood2$_i$, you would be assuming *no* between-person effect of negative mood at all. In contrast, by including only GMC level-1 Mood2$_{ti}$ without level-2 PMmood2$_i$, you would instead be assuming convergence: equivalent between-person and within-person effects of negative mood. Neither of these assumptions is likely to be reasonable, although both are testable. But once PMmood2$_i$ is included at level 2 in either the PMC or GMC model (with WPmood$_{ti}$ or Mood2$_{ti}$, respectively), the level-1 effect is the same within-person effect in either model. Without PMmood2$_i$, though, the level-1 effect of GMC Mood2$_{ti}$ is the convergence (smushed) effect, as shown in the bottom of Figure 8.2, which doesn't accurately reflect any of the effects of negative mood.

2.F. Equivalent Fixed Effects in Person-Mean-Centering and Grand-Mean-Centering

As you might have already guessed from examining the second set of columns in Table 8.1, the PMC model from Equation (8.3) and the GMC model from Equation (8.7) that both contain a level-2 main effect of PMmood2$_i$ are in fact equivalent: they have the same model fit and will create the same predicted values. Their level-2 main effects of negative mood are simply re-arrangements of each other, as can be seen by writing the PMC model in terms of the GMC model in **single-level composite form** (i.e., filling in the β placeholders) as in Equation (8.8):

PMC: Symptoms$_{ti}$

$$= \gamma_{00}\cdots + \gamma_{04}\left(\overline{\text{Mood}}_i\right) + \gamma_{10}\left(\text{Mood}_{ti} - \overline{\text{Mood}}_i\right) + U_{0i} + e_{ti}$$

$$= \gamma_{00}\cdots + \gamma_{04}\left(\overline{\text{Mood}}_i\right) + \gamma_{10}\left(\text{Mood}_{ti}\right) - \gamma_{10}\left(\overline{\text{Mood}}_i\right) + U_{0i} + e_{ti} \qquad (8.8)$$

$$= \gamma_{00}\cdots + \left(\gamma_{04} - \gamma_{10}\right)\left(\overline{\text{Mood}}_i\right) + \gamma_{10}\left(\text{Mood}_{ti}\right) + U_{0i} + e_{ti}$$

GMC: Symptoms$_{ti}$

$$= \gamma_{00}\cdots + \gamma_{04}\left(\overline{\text{Mood}}_i\right) + \gamma_{10}\left(\text{Mood}_{ti}\right) + U_{0i} + e_{ti}$$

in which the other effects of sex and age that are unrelated to the effects of negative mood have been excluded and the centering constant of 2 has been dropped for clarity (given that models with different centering constants are already equivalent). The first line for the PMC model shows the original between-person and within-person effects of negative mood (γ_{04} and γ_{10}, respectively). The within-person effect γ_{10} is then distributed across its constituent variables in the second line, and the terms are combined based on their common variables in the third line to be directly comparable to the fixed effects of the GMC model in the fourth line. Thus, as seen in the second set of columns of Table 8.1, the level-2 contextual effect (incremental or unique between-person effect) for $\overline{\text{Mood}}_i$ is given directly by γ_{04} in the GMC model, but by $(\gamma_{04} - \gamma_{10})$ in the PMC model. Translating the other way, the level-2 total between-person effect for $\overline{\text{Mood}}_i$ is given directly by γ_{04} in the PMC model, but by $(\gamma_{04} + \gamma_{10})$ in the GMC model. Finally, the level-1 within-person effect is given directly by γ_{10} for Mood_{ti} in either model.

2.G. Nonequivalent Random Effects in Person-Mean-Centering and Grand-Mean-Centering

At this point you might wondering why the difference between person-mean-centering and grand-mean-centering of time-varying predictors is such a big deal—if they are equivalent in their fixed effects (so long as the person mean of the time-varying predictor is included at level 2), then why does it matter which is used? The reason we were able to create equivalent PMC and GMC models is that all of our examples so far have dealt with level-1 negative mood as a *fixed* effect. But if the level-1 effect is allowed a random slope (to vary over persons), then the PMC and GMC models cannot be made equivalent. To demonstrate, we consider an otherwise equivalent set of PMC and GMC models in which a random slope for the within-person main effect of mood has now been added (U_{1i} in the level-2 equation for β_{1i}), as seen in Equation (8.9):

PMC Level 1 : $\text{Symptoms}_{ti} = \beta_{0i} + \beta_{1i}\left(\text{Mood}_{ti} - \overline{\text{Mood}}_i\right) + e_{ti}$

GMC Level 1 : $\text{Symptoms}_{ti} = \beta_{0i} + \beta_{1i}\left(\text{Mood}_{ti} - 2\right) + e_{ti}$

PMC or GMC Level 2 :

Intercept: $\beta_{0i} = \gamma_{00} + \gamma_{01}\left(\text{Women}_i\right) + \gamma_{02}\left(\text{Age}_i - 80\right) + \gamma_{03}\left(\text{Women}_i\right)\left(\text{Age}_i - 80\right)$
$$+ \gamma_{04}\left(\overline{\text{Mood}}_i - 2\right) + U_{0i} \qquad (8.9)$$

Within-Person Mood: $\beta_{1i} = \gamma_{10} + \underline{U_{1i}}$

Composite :

PMC: $\text{Symptoms}_{ti} = \left(\text{fixed effects}\right) + U_{0i} + U_{1i}\left(\text{Mood}_{ti} - \overline{\text{Mood}}_i\right) + e_{ti}$
$$= \left(\text{fixed effects}\right) + U_{0i} + U_{1i}\left(\text{Mood}_{ti} - 2\right) - U_{1i}\left(\overline{\text{Mood}}_i\right) + e_{ti}$$

GMC: $\text{Symptoms}_{ti} = \left(\text{fixed effects}\right) + U_{0i} + U_{1i}\left(\text{Mood}_{ti} - 2\right) + e_{ti}$

in which the model for the means is the same, but in which the within-person effect of negative mood (as defined by the level-2 equation for β_{1i}) is now a function of a fixed effect γ_{10} and of a person-specific deviation from that fixed effect, the random slope U_{1i}. That is, U_{1i} represents how far off person i's within-person slope for negative mood is from the fixed slope γ_{10}. As before, rather than estimate the individual U_{1i} random slopes directly, we estimate the variance of the U_{1i} random slopes ($\tau_{U_1}^2$) and their covariance with the random intercept ($\tau_{U_{01}}$) as two new parameters in the model for the variance. The level-2 U_{0i} random intercepts and U_{1i} random slopes are assumed to have a multivariate normal distribution and to be unrelated to the level-1 e_{ti} time-specific residuals. Although we allow the U_{0i} and U_{1i} terms to be correlated, no correlation is assumed *within* the U_{0i} random intercepts and *within* the U_{1i} random slopes (i.e., persons are independent).

As shown in the last two lines, the resulting PMC and GMC composite models now have different models for the variance. In the PMC model, the U_{1i} random slope applies only to the within-person part of negative mood (i.e., the between-person part is removed via the subtraction of $\overline{Mood_i}$), whereas in the GMC model, the U_{1i} random slope still applies to both parts of negative mood contained in $Mood_{ti}$. This difference in how the U_{1i} random slopes are defined in using PMC versus GMC translates into conceptually different models for the variance in two respects. Results from these models are not reported in Table 8.1 but instead are presented in the text below.

First, although the level-1 *fixed* effect is the within-person main effect of negative mood in both models, the interpretation of its corresponding *random* effect (i.e., for which we estimate a level-2 random slope variance $\tau_{U_1}^2$) differs across models. In the PMC model, the *relative* effect of negative mood is random: what varies over persons is the effect of greater negative mood *than usual* (based on just within-person variation). But in the GMC model, the *absolute* effect of negative mood is random: what varies over persons is the effect of greater negative mood, *period* (based on both between-person and within-person variation). Thus, the random slope variances may differ between the PMC and GMC models because they represent different things, although here they differ only slightly: PMC $\tau_{U_1}^2 = 0.062$ (SE = 0.140); GMC $\tau_{U_1}^2 = 0.063$ (SE = 0.138).

Second, the level-2 random intercept variance $\tau_{U_0}^2$ is also now interpreted differently across models. Recall that $\tau_{U_0}^2$ represents individual differences in the intercept (after accounting for the fixed effects) when all predictors with a random slope = 0 (e.g., at time = 0 in earlier chapters). But in this case, when level-1 negative mood = 0 differs across models. In the PMC model, $\tau_{U_0}^2$ represents intercept differences *specifically when people are at their person mean negative mood* (WPmood$_{ti}$ = 0). But in the GMC model, $\tau_{U_0}^2$ represents intercept differences *specifically when people are at a daily negative mood of 2* (Mood2$_{ti}$ = 0). Thus, the random intercept variances may also differ between models because they, too, represent different things. Here, PMC $\tau_{U_0}^2 = 0.817$ (SE = 0.132), while GMC $\tau_{U_0}^2 = 1.100$ (SE = 0.284). In addition, the level-1 residual variance (of PMC $\sigma_e^2 = 0.607$, SE = 0.045; of GMC $\sigma_e^2 = 0.608$, SE = 0.045) will be smaller in either random slope model because part of the unexplained time-specific variation is now allocated to a separate pile of variance—the level-2 $\tau^2_{U_1}$ random slope variance for the individual differences in the level-1 effect of negative mood (and σ^2_e may also differ across models given that $\tau^2_{U_0}$ and $\tau^2_{U_1}$ may differ). Finally, because they are derived using the estimated random effect and residual variances and covariances, the fixed effect estimates—even if conceptually equivalent—may differ across the PMC and GMC random slope models as well.

As a result of these different level-1 random slopes, the overall PMC and GMC models cannot be made equivalent, regardless of their fixed effects. Accordingly, although the previous PMC and GMC models without U_{1i} (as reported in Table 8.1) had the same fit of –2LL = 1405.7 (AIC = 1421.7, BIC = 1442.9), after adding the U_{1i} random slope in Equation (8.9), the fit of the PMC model is –2LL = 1404.2 (AIC = 1424.2, BIC = 1450.7), while the fit of the GMC model is –2LL = 1403.4 (AIC = 1423.4, BIC = 1449.9). However, neither is a significant improvement over the model without $\tau^2_{U_1}$ and $\tau_{U_{01}}$, PMC –2ΔLL(~2) = 1.5, p = .467, and GMC –2ΔLL(~2) = 2.3, p = .321. The PMC and GMC random slope models are non-nested but can be compared with their AIC and BIC values under ML; AIC and BIC slightly prefer the GMC model in this instance (although based on the –2ΔLL test the fixed slope model from Equation 8.3 or 8.5 is still preferred overall).

In general, the multilevel literature provides little recommendation as to how to choose between the PMC and GMC models in considering a random slope for a time-varying predictor. You might decide on a substantive basis which model specification maps onto the random effect of theoretical interest. For instance, individual differences in the PMC random slope correspond to the idea of "frog-pond" effect: the idea that where you are *currently* only matters relative to where you *usually* are. The interpretation of individual differences in the GMC random slope is less clear, but presumably would be more useful whenever grand-mean-centering is more useful (i.e., when used to control for the absolute amount of a time-varying predictor before examining the incremental fixed effects of person characteristics). On an empirical basis, AIC and BIC could also be used to decide between PMC and GMC versions of a random level-1 effect.

Finally, there is some evidence that the random slope variance (e.g., $\tau^2_{U_1}$) in GMC models may be downwardly biased relative to that obtained in PMC models due to the difference in the random intercepts from each model. Recall that $\tau^2_{U_0}$ represents individual intercept differences *when people are at their person mean* of the time-varying predictor in PMC (e.g., WPmood$_{ti}$ = 0), but $\tau^2_{U_0}$ represents individual intercept differences *when people are at the centering constant* of the time-varying predictor in GMC (e.g., Mood2$_{ti}$ = 0). The intercept in GMC will require greater extrapolation for those cases in which 0 is not observed, creating lower reliability and greater shrinkage of the random intercept towards the fixed intercept. That intercept shrinkage can cause the individual slopes to become homogenized, with the result that the slope variance for the level-1 random effect could be smaller than it should be in the GMC model, but more accurately estimated in the PMC model. This may be especially likely given greater between-person variation in the time-varying predictor, and thus in which persons are relatively more spread-out in their individual distributions of the time-varying predictor (see Raudenbush & Bryk, 2002, pp. 143–149). However, this conjecture has received little empirical study, and so the extent of the problem and the factors that exacerbate it are not yet well understood.

2.H.   Summary and Advice for Model Building

To summarize, time-varying predictors usually contain both between-person variation (i.e., person-to-person differences in mean predictor over time) and within-person variation (i.e., variation around a person's mean of the predictor over time). So far, we have seen two different ways of representing the effects of these two sources of variation in our models with a time-varying predictor of daily negative mood. First, we utilized *person-mean-centering*, in which the resulting level-1 predictor (e.g., $WPmood_{ti} = Mood_{ti} - \overline{Mood_i}$) contains only the within-person part of the time-varying predictor, and so its main effect in the level-1 model directly represents the predictor's within-person effect. The person mean of the predictor, centered at a constant so that 0 is meaningful (e.g., $PMmood2_i = \overline{Mood_i} - 2$) contains only the between-person part of the time-varying predictor, and so its main effect in the level-2 model directly represents the predictor's between-person effect. We then examined their fixed main effects and found that greater than usual negative mood did not significantly predict that day's symptoms (no fixed *level-1 within-person main effect*), but that higher person mean negative mood significantly predicted greater mean symptoms across days (a fixed *level-2 between-person main effect*).

Second, we utilized *grand-mean-centering* (GMC), in which the level-1 predictor is simply rescaled by subtracting a constant (e.g., $Mood2_{ti} = Mood_{ti} - 2$). As a result, the GMC level-1 predictor still contains all of its original between-person and within-person variation. When included by itself, its effect will be a *(smushed) convergence effect*, a weighted blend of the between-person and within-person main effects of the time-varying predictor (but usually more heavily weighted towards the within-person main effect). The (smushed) convergence effect assumes equivalent between-person and within-person main effects, which is testable by adding the person mean of the time-varying predictor (centered with a constant so that 0 is meaningful), which then becomes the *level-2 contextual main effect*. This contextual main effect can be interpreted in two equivalent ways: (1) as the incremental between-person main effect after controlling for that occasion's absolute amount of the time-varying predictor, or (2) as the difference of the time-varying predictor's between-person and within-person main effects. In our example, the level-2 contextual effect was 1.811, indicating that the between-person main effect of 1.970 was significantly larger by 1.811 than the within-person main effect of 0.159 (i.e., the main effects of negative mood across levels did not converge onto the same numeric estimate).

Grand-mean-centered (GMC) and person-mean-centered (PMC) models for time-varying predictors can be made equivalent in their fixed main effects so long as the person mean of the time-varying predictor is included as a level-2 main effect. In that case, the level-1 GMC effect becomes the within-person main effect (the same as in PMC) instead of the convergence effect. The difference between the GMC and PMC models occurs in which effects are given at level 2: GMC provides the level-2 *contextual* main effect (that *does* control for that occasion's absolute level of the time-varying predictor), whereas PMC provides the level-2 *between-person* main effect (that does *not* control for that occasion's absolute level of the time-varying predictor).

At this point you might be wondering what happens if the level-2 contextual main effect of a time-varying predictor is not significant. That is, if its between-person and within-person effects are not significantly different from each other, is it then acceptable to smush them together by estimating a single convergence effect instead? In that case, although there may be nothing wrong technically with doing so, estimating only a single convergence effect across levels still cannot be recommended in practice for several reasons. First is an interpretational issue—what does a "one-unit" difference in the time-varying predictor then mean? For instance, consider a convergence effect of daily negative mood—a one-unit difference in daily negative mood does not map onto higher negative mood than usual or to higher negative mood than other people, but to some mixture of both without a clear reference point. Second, the between-person and within-person main effects of a time-varying predictor may be equivalent when they are first examined, but the addition of other fixed effects into the model may then ruin their equivalence. For instance, if we added another level-2 predictor that was related to PMmood2$_i$, then the effect of PMmood2$_i$ must be adjusted (relative to what it was before adding the other level-2 predictor) in order to remain the *unique* effect of PMmood2$_i$ after controlling for *all* other predictors. As a result, that *controlled* between-person effect may then differ from the *uncontrolled* within-person effect (given that level-1 WPmood$_{ti}$ would not be related to the other level-2 predictor). If you had estimated a convergence effect after examining only the contextual main effect of negative mood, you would not have seen this adjustment—and created non-convergence—happen.

Finally, just as the main effects at each level should not be smushed together, nor should any interaction terms. That is, just as including only the GMC convergence effect assumes equal of between-person and within-person *main* effects, including interactions with only a level-1 GMC predictor assumes equal *moderation* of the between-person and within-person effects. For instance, an interaction of sex with the level-1 GMC effect of negative mood would imply equal moderation of the between-person and within-person effects of negative mood by sex—that is, the resulting interaction would be smushed across levels. But just as the main effects of negative mood were allowed to differ across levels after including a level-2 main effect of the person mean, adding level-2 interactions with the person mean would then allow moderation by the interacting predictor to differ across levels as well, as we will see in much more detail shortly.

The choice between PMC and GMC with respect to their fixed effects can be based on convenience (given that they can be made equivalent). But after including a random slope for the time-varying predictor, the GMC and PMC models will no longer be equivalent: its *absolute* effect is random over persons in GMC, but only its *relative* effect is random over persons in PMC. The AIC and BIC values from ML could be used to decide between them, but the random slope variance in the PMC model may show less downward bias if the time-varying predictor has a large ICC. In our example, though, neither level-1 effect showed random variation between persons; the random slope variances across PMC and GMC were largely similar as well.

2.1. Fixed and Random Effects of a Dichotomous Time-Varying Predictor

So far we have only considered how to examine the effects of a *continuous* time-varying predictor of negative mood. We now continue our example by examining a *categorical* time-varying predictor: *presence of a daily stressor* ($Stressor_{ti}$), which was assessed as a dichotomous variable for whether any of five questions about stressors relating to relationships, events, and health had been endorsed (0 = stressor-free day; 1 = stressor day). A stressor was reported on 45% of the total sample days; 20% of the persons in the sample reported no stressors on any day, and 14% reported a stressor on each day. The intraclass correlation for presence of a daily stressor (as calculated from an empty means, random intercept model) was ICC = .32, indicating that 32% of its variance was due to between-person mean differences, and 68% was due to within-person variation across days. However, because the presence of a daily stressor is a dichotomous variable, the assumptions of normality and constant variance of the level-1 e_{ti} residuals will not hold, and thus this ICC value is likely inaccurate. Instead, we should use a multilevel model for logistic outcomes (i.e., with a logit transformation of the 0/1 stressor values and a Bernoulli distribution; see chapter 13). An empty means, random intercept logistic model for the presence of a daily stressor yielded an ICC = .44 instead.

Although person-mean-centering (PMC) can be an intuitive way to examine the within-person and between-person effects of continuous time-varying predictors, it is less useful for categorical predictors that already have a natural 0 point and a limited range of possible values, such as for the presence of a daily stressor in continuing our example. In this binary predictor, 0 indicates no stressors and 1 indicates a stressor, so the person mean ($\overline{Stressor_i}$) indicates the proportion of days in which a stressor was reported ($M = 0.45$, $SD = 0.34$, range = 0 to 1). But PMC would create strange values for the level-1 predictor of stressors. For instance, if a stressor was reported on 50% of a person's days, the PMC level-1 predictor would be calculated as $WPstressor_{ti} = Stressor_{ti} - \overline{Stressor_i}$, so $WPstressor_{ti} = -0.5$ on no-stressor days or $WPstressor_{ti} = 0.5$ on stressor days, which are non-meaningful values given possible values of 0 or 1 for the daily stressor variable. Although PMC in this case wouldn't be wrong, it would be weird, in that the intercept (and any main effects of predictors that interact with $WPstressor_{ti}$) would be conditional on a 0 value that does not exist. But in considering grand-mean-centering (GMC) instead, no centering constant is needed given that 0 is already meaningful for daily stressors.

However, to prevent smushing (assuming convergence of the between-person and within-person effects) of the effects of stressors across levels, we still need to include the person mean of stressors (which will be centered at 0.40 so that 0 represents someone who reported a stressor on 40% of their days, to be referred to as *PMstressor40$_i$*). The effect of PMstressor40$_i$ will then provide the level-2 contextual effect of stressors (controlling for that day's stressors). The *within-person* level-1 effect (of uncentered Stressor$_{ti}$) can be differentiated from the *convergence* level-1 effect by noting that the within-person effect of Stressor$_{ti}$ controls for the proportion of stressor days (i.e., it holds PMstressor40$_i$ constant), whereas the convergence effect of Stressor$_{ti}$ does not.

To illustrate, we will build on the previous results including the effects of sex, age, and both parts of person-mean-centered daily negative mood to examine the effects of daily stressors on daily physical symptoms across levels, in which new terms are underlined in Equation (8.10):

Level 1 : $\text{Symptoms}_{ti} = \beta_{0i} + \beta_{1i}\left(\text{Mood}_{ti} - \overline{\text{Mood}}_i\right) + \underline{\beta_{2i}\left(\text{Stressor}_{ti}\right)} + e_{ti}$

Level 2 :

Intercept: $\beta_{0i} = \gamma_{00} + \gamma_{01}\left(\text{Women}_i\right) + \gamma_{02}\left(\text{Age}_i - 80\right) + \gamma_{03}\left(\text{Women}_i\right)\left(\text{Age}_i - 80\right)$
$\qquad\qquad + \gamma_{04}\left(\overline{\text{Mood}}_i - 2\right) + \underline{\gamma_{08}\left(\overline{\text{Stressor}}_i - 0.40\right)} + U_{0i}$

Within-Person Mood: $\beta_{1i} = \gamma_{10}$

Within-Person Stressor: $\underline{\beta_{2i} = \gamma_{20}}$
$\qquad\qquad\qquad\qquad\qquad\qquad\qquad\qquad\qquad\qquad\qquad\qquad (8.10)$

Composite :

$\text{Symptoms}_{ti} = \gamma_{00} + \gamma_{01}\left(\text{Women}_i\right) + \gamma_{02}\left(\text{Age}_i - 80\right) + \gamma_{03}\left(\text{Women}_i\right)\left(\text{Age}_i - 80\right)$
$\qquad\qquad + \gamma_{04}\left(\overline{\text{Mood}}_i - 2\right) + \underline{\gamma_{08}\left(\overline{\text{Stressor}}_i - 0.40\right)}$
$\qquad\qquad + \gamma_{10}\left(\text{Mood}_{ti} - \overline{\text{Mood}}_i\right) + \underline{\gamma_{20}\left(\text{Stressor}_{ti}\right)} + U_{0i} + e_{ti}$

in which the within-person effect of *Stressor$_{ti}$* is represented by the β_{2i} placeholder in the level-1 model, and β_{2i} is then defined by a level-2 equation including just the fixed effect γ_{20}. The level-2 contextual main effect of PMstressor40$_i$ is given by γ_{08}. Note that γ_{08} is used for consistency in the notation: because fixed effects of Women$_i$, Age80$_i$, and Women$_i$ by Age80$_i$ were included first (γ_{01}, γ_{02}, and γ_{03}, respectively), after the introduction of PMmood2$_i$ as γ_{04}, the next three fixed effects would be reserved for the potential interactions of PMmood2$_i$ by Women$_i$ (γ_{05}), PMmood2$_i$ by Age80$_i$ (γ_{06}), and PMmood2$_i$ by Women$_i$ by Age80$_i$ (γ_{07}).

Results for the model in Equation (8.10) are shown in the first set of columns in Table 8.3 in a new format. Rather than listing just the fixed effects directly estimated in the model, Table 8.3 provides each simple effect for men and for women, as well as the sex differences thereof. This will help us keep track as we add higher-order interactions with sex in subsequent models.

Accordingly, the fixed intercept for men as the reference group is given by γ_{00}, how the intercept differs for women is given by the simple main effect of Women$_i$ γ_{01}, and so the intercept for women is created from $\gamma_{00} + \gamma_{01}$. Given the other main effects in the model, the intercepts for men and women are also the predicted

Table 8.3 Results for effects of daily negative mood and stressors on physical symptoms moderated by sex. Bold values are $p < .05$.

Model Effects	Equation 8.10: Main Effects of Negative Mood and Stressors				Equation 8.11: Interactions of Negative Mood and Stressors with Sex			
	Term	Est	SE	p <	Term	Est	SE	p <
<u>Model for the Means</u>								
Intercept								
For Men (= 0)	γ_{00}	**2.784**	0.352	.001	γ_{00}	**2.916**	0.766	.001
For Women (= 1)	$\gamma_{00} + \gamma_{01}$	**2.271**	0.323	.001	$\gamma_{00} + \gamma_{01}$	**2.242**	0.339	.001
Sex Difference	γ_{01}	**−0.513**	0.205	.014	γ_{01}	−0.674	0.837	.422
Age (0 = 80 years)								
For Men (= 0)	γ_{02}	**0.073**	0.032	.023	γ_{02}	0.064	0.034	.059
For Women (= 1)	$\gamma_{02} + \gamma_{03}$	−0.021	0.017	.229	$\gamma_{02} + \gamma_{03}$	−0.020	0.017	.227
Sex Difference	γ_{03}	**−0.094**	0.036	.010	γ_{03}	**−0.084**	0.037	.027
Negative Mood Effects (PMC):								
Level-2 Between-Person	γ_{04}	**1.477**	0.374	.001				
For Men (= 0)					γ_{04}	1.814	0.921	.051
For Women (= 1)					$\gamma_{04} + \gamma_{05}$	**1.383**	0.395	.001
Sex Difference					γ_{05}	−0.432	1.002	.667
Level-2 Contextual	$\gamma_{04} - \gamma_{10}$	**1.343**	0.397	.001				
For Men (= 0)					$\gamma_{04} - \gamma_{10}$	**1.970**	0.953	.041
For Women (= 1)					$\gamma_{04} - \gamma_{10} + \gamma_{05} - \gamma_{11}$	**1.153**	0.424	.007
Sex Difference					$\gamma_{05} - \gamma_{11}$	−0.817	1.043	.435
Level-1 Within-Person	γ_{10}	0.134	0.131	.306				
For Men (= 0)					γ_{10}	−0.156	0.273	.569
For Women (= 1)					$\gamma_{10} + \gamma_{11}$	0.230	0.148	.122
Sex Difference					γ_{11}	0.386	0.311	.215
Daily Stressor Effects (GMC):								
Level-2 Between-Person	$\gamma_{08} + \gamma_{20}$	**1.029**	0.287	.001				
For Men (= 0)					$\gamma_{08} + \gamma_{20}$	**2.229**	0.644	.001
For Women (= 1)					$\gamma_{08} + \gamma_{20} + \gamma_{09} + \gamma_{21}$	**0.718**	0.310	.022
Sex Difference					$\gamma_{09} + \gamma_{21}$	**−1.511**	0.714	.037
Level-2 Contextual	γ_{08}	**0.943**	0.303	.002				
For Men (= 0)					γ_{08}	**1.985**	0.667	.003

For Women (= 1)					$\gamma_{08} + \gamma_{09}$	**0.708**	0.331	.034
Sex Difference					γ_{09}	−1.277	0.744	.089
Level-1 Within-Person	γ_{20}	0.086	0.097	.378				
For Men (= 0)					γ_{20}	0.244	0.172	.158
For Women (= 1)					$\gamma_{20} + \gamma_{21}$	0.010	0.117	.932
Sex Difference					γ_{21}	−0.234	0.208	.262

Model for the Variance

Random Intercept Variance	$\tau^2_{U_0}$	0.713	0.117	.001	$\tau^2_{U_0}$	0.663	0.110	.001
Residual Variance	σ^2_e	0.612	0.043	.001	σ^2_e	0.608	0.043	.001

ML Model Fit

Number of Parameters	10	14
−2LL	1392.8	1383.9
AIC	1412.8	1411.9
BIC	1439.3	1449.0

physical symptoms specifically for 80-year-olds (Age80$_i$ = 0) with a person mean negative mood of 2 (PMmood2$_i$ = 0) on days when they are at their person mean negative mood (WPmood$_{ti}$ = 0), and for persons who reported stressors on 40% of their days (PMstressor40$_i$ = 0) on a non-stressor day (Stressor$_{ti}$ = 0). Furthermore, the simple main effect of age for men as the reference group is given directly by γ_{02}, how the simple main effect of age differs for women is given by the Women$_i$ by Age80$_i$ interaction γ_{03}, and so the simple main effect of age for women is created from γ_{02} + γ_{03}. However, because age does not interact with negative mood or stressors, these age slopes are conditional on sex only. Likewise, the sex difference is conditional on age only. Table 8.3 also provides the additional level-2 effects not given directly by the model (e.g., level-2 contextual effect for PMC daily negative mood; the level-2 between-person effect for GMC daily stressors). Because only the main effects of negative mood and stressors are included, they are all unconditional on age, sex, and each other. The fixed effects of sex, age, and PMC negative mood are interpreted the same as previously, but now also control for the effects of daily stressors.

The new within-person effect for Stressor$_{ti}$ of γ_{20} = 0.086 (p = .378) indicates that, *holding the proportion of stressor days constant*, symptoms were expected to be non-significantly higher by 0.086 on days when a stressor was reported as compared to a day with no stressors. This level-1 stressor effect accounted for ≈ 0% of the level-1 σ^2_e, pseudo-R^2 for = (0.613 − 0.612) / 0.613 = .002. The new level-2 contextual effect for PMstressor40$_i$ of γ_{08} = 0.943 (p = .002) indicates that *after controlling for that day's stressors*, mean symptoms were expected to be significantly higher by 0.943 for every unit of PMstressor40$_i$. However, PMstressor40$_i$ is the proportion of stressor days, and so a one-unit difference in PMstressor40$_i$ is the difference between reporting a stressor on no days (PMstressor40$_i$ = 0) or on all days (PMstressor40$_i$ = 1). Given that each person had up to five days of data, we can convert its effect to reflect the difference in mean symptoms per additional stressor day as γ_{08} = 0.943 / 5 = 0.189. In addition, the implied level-2 between-person stressor effect of $\gamma_{08} + \gamma_{20}$ = 0.943 + 0.085 = 1.029 was also significant, and accounted for another 12.6% of the level-2 $\tau^2_{U_0}$, pseudo-R^2 for $\tau^2_{U_0}$ = (0.816 − 0.713) / 0.816 = .126. The two effects significantly improved model fit over the previous model with sex, age, and negative mood, −2ΔLL(2) = 12.9, p = .002, and accounted for another 5.7% of the total symptoms variance (total R^2 = .253 after including all fixed effects). In case you are curious, the level-1 *convergence* effect of Stressor$_{ti}$ (without PMstressor40$_i$ at level 2) is 0.175 (p = .059), a weighted combination of its within-person effect = 0.085 and its between-person effect = 1.029, but again more heavily weighted towards the within-person effect.

Although the within-person fixed effect of stressors is not significant, this within-person effect could still vary across persons. We can test this by comparing the model in Equation (8.10) to one in which the equation for β_{2i} is replaced by β_{2i} = $\gamma_{20} + U_{2i}$, in which U_{2i} represents a random slope for the stressor effect. However, the variance of the U_{2i} random slopes was estimated as $\tau^2_{U_2}$ = 0, such that the **G** matrix of random effects variances and covariances was not positive definite. As such, the model cannot be retained. Thus, whether a stressor occurs on a given day does not appear to relate to that day's physical symptoms (i.e., no fixed within-person effect), and the difference between stressor and non-stressor days is the same across individuals (i.e., no random level-1 effect). However, persons who experience stressors on a higher proportion of days are more likely to report greater mean symptoms (i.e., a fixed between-person effect), even after controlling for that day's stressors (i.e., a fixed contextual effect).

2.J. Other Types of Categorical Time-Varying Predictors

Although our model for the effects of a dichotomous predictor of daily stressors was very similar to our model for the effects of a continuous predictor of daily negative mood, not all effects of categorical time-varying predictors can or should be specified in the same way. Some, like our predictor of daily stressors, describe transient states— a stressor can be reported one day but not the next. So, calculating a person mean across time for such transient categorical time-varying predictors (e.g., the proportion of stressor days) to represent between-person variance in the level-2 model makes sense. In other cases, though, the effects of a categorical time-varying predictor may not be as conveniently represented across levels, and may require some creativity.

One potential complication is that time-varying predictors with three (or more) categories will require two (or more) dummy codes to represent their within-person effects in the level-1 model. For instance, what if we had also collected data on types of responses to daily stressors as a predictor of symptoms, and had coded those behaviors into three categories of *no distinct response*, *adaptive response*, or *maladaptive response*, with *no distinct response* as the reference. There may be several reasonable options for how to represent between-person variance related to the three-category predictor in the level-2 model. One option might be to calculate the person mean of each dummy code for inclusion in the level-2 model as the proportion of occasions in which *adaptive* or *maladaptive* responses were observed (as opposed to *no distinct response* for each). But what if persons tend to report the same kind of coping behavior across days, such that those dummy codes were essentially constants? If so, it may be more useful to conceptualize between-person variance for the level-2 model as a new multiple-category variable based on the patterns in the daily data (e.g., non-responder, adaptive responder, maladaptive responder, mixed responder). In that case, the effects of stress response at each level could not be strictly labeled as *within-person* or *(incremental) between-person,* but a coarse distinction could still be made for effects that arise from differences between persons (at level 2) versus effects that arise from daily variation within persons (at level 1). Note that in this example, only the mixed responder group could logically show an effect of within-person variability in stress responding, because the other groups by definition would not have any within-person variability in stress responding. This is another example of why we must consider the effects of time-varying predictors between persons as well as within persons—not all persons may be able to show a within-person effect of a time-varying predictor. This is true for continuous time-varying predictors as well, and so we will return to this idea shortly.

Another complication occurs when nonlinear effects of a continuous predictor might be better captured using one or more categories. For instance, what if we had wished to consider the number of stressors reported each day, rather than simply whether or not a stressor was reported? Is it reasonable to posit a linear relationship between the number of stressors and physical symptoms, such that a one-unit increase in the number of stressors has the same impact for *every* increment of stressors? Or might there be a *qualitative* difference between a no-stressor day and a day with at least one stressor, as well as an additional *quantitative* difference across days with varying numbers of stressors? This idea could be implemented by examining a **piecewise effect** of stressors, with one predictor to capture the effect of whether or not at least one stressor had occurred (a categorical difference), and a second predictor to capture the effect of the number of stressors if at least one occurred (a continuous slope). The person means of each time-varying predictor (the stressor difference and the slope for the number of stressors) would then be examined in the level-2 model, or persons could be described via a more categorical representation as warranted by the within-person variability in number of stressors (or lack thereof, as discussed previously).

Finally, some time-varying predictors capture a more permanent change in state, such as the occurrence of a critical event (e.g., stroke, death of a spouse, a move to assisted living) that cannot be undone. In those cases a different approach may be needed to adequately represent the between-person characteristics embedded in the time-varying predictor, such as a distinction of *ever happened* as a level-2 predictor rather than the person mean of occurrence.

To summarize, although categorical time-varying predictors also generally include both between-person and within-person variation, person-mean-centering and grand-mean-centering may not be applicable. Given that 0 is already a meaningful value (e.g., as the reference group), differences between categories of a time-varying predictor can be represented directly in the level-1 model (via dummy codes equal to the number of categories – 1, as in any linear model). The challenge arises in deciding how to represent the presence of between-person variability in the level-2 model. If a person mean of the level-1 dummy codes can be calculated meaningfully, then their main effects will represent level-2 contextual effects, the same as in grand-mean-centering. But if other specifications are used instead (e.g., between-person variability as distinct kinds of people), then a formal separation of within-person effects from between-person effects may not be possible. Furthermore, categorical time-varying predictors highlight how within-person effects are only possible for those persons who show within-person variability of a time-varying predictor in the first place, a tenet that holds for continuous time-varying predictors as well.

3. Examining More Complex Effects of Time-Varying Predictors

To recap our example models thus far, we have examined the effects of two time-varying predictors (daily negative mood and presence of a daily stressor) to illustrate how to interpret the effects of time-varying predictors in person-mean-centering (PMC) or in grand-mean-centering (GMC). We will continue in this fashion in order to demonstrate interpretation of higher-order interactions among time-varying predictors. The models to be presented will use only PMC for negative mood (in which $PMmood2_i$ provides its level-2 between-person effect and $WPmood_{ti}$ provides its level-1 within-person effect), and stressors will be left uncentered at level 1 but its centered person mean will be included at level 2 (such that $PMstressor40_i$ provides its level-2 contextual effect and $Stressor_{ti}$ provides its level-1 within-person effect, the same as in GMC).

So far we have found that the level-1 effects of negative mood and stressors are fixed—they did not vary randomly over individuals. So, what does this imply about testing moderation of these within-person effects via cross-level interactions with level-2 predictors? On the one hand, a nonsignificant random effect implies a lack of quantifiable level-2 between-person variance in the within-person effect for a cross-level interaction with a level-2 predictor to then explain. On the other hand, as discussed in chapter 7, level-1 time-varying predictors can show three kinds of effects: **fixed, random,** or **systematically varying.** That is, although each person did not need his or her own random slope for the within-person effects of negative mood and stressors, these effects could still vary *systematically* as a function of other predictors. For example, the effect on that day's symptoms of reporting greater negative mood than usual or reporting a stressor could differ between men and women, or could differ by age—systematically, but not randomly otherwise.

Furthermore, we have also assumed that the level-2 between-person effect of negative mood and the level-2 contextual effect of stressors (as represented by their person means over time) are fixed as well. However, we do not need to examine their random effects given that person means are constant within a person over time (and thus each person can't have his or her own effect of a constant). However, it is still possible for level-2 effects to vary *systematically* as a function of other predictors. For example, the effect on mean symptoms of being a grumpier person or reporting more stressor days than other people could differ between men and women (or by age).

Accordingly, the following section will demonstrate how to examine systematically varying effects (*aka*, moderation) across levels. More specifically, examples are provided for three general kinds of interactions involving time-varying predictors that you are likely to encounter: among time-varying and time-invariant predictors, among time-varying predictors, and cross-level interactions among the multilevel parts of the same time-varying predictor (the latter of which will also be featured in chapter 10 in discussing alternative metrics of time).

3.A. Interactions of Time-Varying Predictors With Time-Invariant Predictors

The equality of the PMC and GMC models given fixed main effects at both levels is well known in the multilevel modeling literature (Kreft, de Leeuw, & Aiken, 1995; Snijders & Bosker, 2012; Raudenbush & Bryk, 2002), but what is less well known is that the PMC and GMC models for a time-varying predictor can still be made equivalent given more complex fixed effects so long as all interactions are included with both parts of the time-varying predictor. To illustrate this equivalence, as well as the idea of systematically varying effects at both levels, we consider a more complex model in which four interactions with sex have been added at each level with the effects of PMC negative mood and GMC stressors, as seen in Equation (8.11):

Level 1 : $\text{Symptoms}_{ti} = \beta_{0i} + \beta_{1i}\left(\text{Mood}_{ti} - \overline{\text{Mood}_i}\right) + \beta_{2i}\left(\text{Stressor}_{ti}\right) + e_{ti}$

Level 2 :

Intercept: $\beta_{0i} = \gamma_{00} + \gamma_{01}\left(\text{Women}_i\right) + \gamma_{02}\left(\text{Age}_i - 80\right) + \gamma_{03}\left(\text{Women}_i\right)\left(\text{Age}_i - 80\right)$
$$+ \gamma_{04}\left(\overline{\text{Mood}_i} - 2\right) + \gamma_{05}\left(\text{Women}_i\right)\left(\overline{\text{Mood}_i} - 2\right)$$
$$+ \gamma_{08}\left(\overline{\text{Stressor}_i} - 0.40\right) + \gamma_{09}\left(\text{Women}_i\right)\left(\overline{\text{Stressor}_i} - 0.40\right) + U_{0i}$$

Within-Person Mood: $\beta_{1i} = \gamma_{10} + \gamma_{11}\left(\text{Women}_i\right)$

Within-Person Stressor: $\beta_{2i} = \gamma_{20} + \gamma_{21}\left(\text{Women}_i\right)$

$$(8.11)$$

Composite :

$\text{Symptoms}_{ti} = \gamma_{00} + \gamma_{01}\left(\text{Women}_i\right) + \gamma_{02}\left(\text{Age}_i - 80\right) + \gamma_{03}\left(\text{Women}_i\right)\left(\text{Age}_i - 80\right)$
$$+ \gamma_{04}\left(\overline{\text{Mood}_i} - 2\right) + \gamma_{05}\left(\text{Women}_i\right)\left(\overline{\text{Mood}_i} - 2\right)$$
$$+ \gamma_{08}\left(\overline{\text{Stressor}_i} - 0.40\right) + \gamma_{09}\left(\text{Women}_i\right)\left(\overline{\text{Stressor}_i} - 0.40\right)$$
$$+ \gamma_{10}\left(\text{Mood}_{ti} - \overline{\text{Mood}_i}\right) + \gamma_{11}\left(\text{Women}_i\right)\left(\text{Mood}_{ti} - \overline{\text{Mood}_i}\right)$$
$$+ \gamma_{20}\left(\text{Stressor}_{ti}\right) + \gamma_{21}\left(\text{Women}_i\right)\left(\text{Stressor}_{ti}\right) + U_{0i} + e_{ti}$$

for which results are given in the second set of columns in Table 8.3. As a set the four interaction terms with sex only marginally improved model fit, $-2\Delta LL(4) = 8.9$, $p = .063$, and accounted for another 2.8% of the total variance in physical symptoms (for a cumulative $R^2 = .281$).

Because no new predictors have been added, the fixed intercept $\gamma_{00} = 2.916$ is interpreted the same as in the previous model in Equation (8.10) that included effects of negative mood and stressors at each level: as the expected symptoms when all predictors = 0. The nonsignificant simple main effect of Women$_i$ of $\gamma_{01} = -0.674$ was conditional on age but is now also conditional on negative mood and stressors given the four new interaction terms. Thus, the women who report 0.674 fewer mean symptoms than men are those specifically at the 0 value of all five interacting predictors: 80-year-olds with a person mean negative mood of 2 who reported stressors on 40% of their days, specifically on non-stressor days when they are at their person mean negative mood. The marginally significant simple main effect of Age80$_i$ of $\gamma_{02} = 0.064$ indicates that mean symptoms are expected to be higher by 0.064 per additional year of age (specifically in men, but not conditional on negative mood or stressors without those interaction terms). The significant Women$_i$ by Age80$_i$ interaction of $\gamma_{03} = -0.084$ (also not conditional on negative mood or stressors) indicates that the sex difference in which men report more symptoms grows by 0.084 per year of age, or that the age slope for symptoms is less positive by 0.084 in women (and the age slope for women is then $\gamma_{02} + \gamma_{03} = 0.064 - 0.084 = -0.020$, which is also nonsignificant as requested by a separate statement). The same practice will be used to decompose the effects of negative mood and stressors: in this model, their main effects will be the simple main effects for men, their interaction with Women$_i$ will be how each effect differs for women, and adding the main and interaction effects will yield the simple effect for women.

Accordingly, we continue by examining the effects of negative mood at each level. First, the level-1 *within-person simple main effect* for WPmood$_{ti}$ of $\gamma_{10} = -0.156$ indicates that in men, for every one-unit more negative mood *than usual, that day's* symptoms are expected to be nonsignificantly lower by 0.156. The Women$_i$ by WPmood$_{ti}$ cross-level interaction of $\gamma_{11} = 0.386$ indicates that the within-person effect of negative mood is nonsignificantly more positive by 0.386 in women (and the within-person effect in women is then $\gamma_{10} + \gamma_{11} = -0.156 + 0.386 = 0.230$, which is also not significant). Thus, neither men nor women show an effect on that day's physical symptoms of greater negative mood than usual; this null result is equivalent across sex.

Second, the level-2 *between-person simple main effect* for PMmood2$_i$ of $\gamma_{04} = 1.814$ indicates that in men, for every one-unit higher *person mean* negative mood, *mean* symptoms are expected to be (marginally) nonsignificantly higher by 1.814. The Women$_i$ by PMmood2$_i$ level-2 interaction of $\gamma_{05} = -0.432$ indicates that the between-person effect of negative mood is nonsignificantly less positive by 0.432 in women (and the between-person effect in women is then $\gamma_{04} + \gamma_{05} = 1.814 - 0.432 = 1.383$, which is significant). Thus, grumpier women report greater mean symptoms to the same extent as grumpier men (although this between-person effect is only marginally significant in men, likely due to 27% men vs. 73% women in this study).

However, these between-person effects do not control for current negative mood—would being a grumpier person still matter if we did? To answer this question, we can obtain the model-implied level-2 *contextual effect* for negative mood and how it differs by sex, as would have been provided directly if we had used GMC for level-1 negative mood instead. But given that we used PMC instead, the level-2 contextual main effect of negative mood for men is given by the difference of its between-person and within-person simple main effects, or $\gamma_{04} - \gamma_{10} = 1.814 + 0.156 = 1.970$ (which is significant). How the level-2 contextual effect of negative mood differs for women is given by the difference of the between-person and within-person negative mood interactions with Women$_i$, or $\gamma_{05} - \gamma_{11} = -0.432 - 0.386 = -0.817$ (which is not significant). Finally, the level-2 contextual effect of negative mood for women is given by the contextual effect for men ($\gamma_{04} - \gamma_{10}$) plus how it differs for women ($\gamma_{05} - \gamma_{11}$) as 1.153 (which is significant). Thus, *after controlling for that day's negative mood, for every one-unit higher person mean negative mood, mean symptoms are expected to be significantly higher by 1.970 in men and by 1.153 in women; alternatively, we could say that the between-person effect of negative mood is significantly larger than the within-person effect of negative mood by 1.970 in men and by 1.153 in women. Furthermore, these level-2 contextual effects of negative mood are equivalent across sex.

Next we turn to the effects of stressors at each level, whose simple effects are also conditional on men given their interactions with sex. First, the level-1 *within-person simple main effect* for Stressor$_{ti}$ of $\gamma_{20} = 0.244$ indicates that in men, holding the proportion of stressor days constant, symptoms on stressor days are expected to be nonsignificantly higher by 0.244. The Women$_i$ by Stressor$_{ti}$ cross-level interaction of $\gamma_{21} = -0.234$ indicates that the within-person effect of stressors is nonsignificantly less positive by 0.234 in women (and the within-person effect in women is then $\gamma_{20} + \gamma_{21} = 0.244 - 0.234 = 0.010$, which is not significant). Thus, neither men nor women show an effect on that day's physical symptoms of reporting a stressor (and this null result is equivalent across sex). Second, given that we did not use PMC for level-1 stressors, the model-estimated level-2 effect for PMstressor40$_i$ of $\gamma_{08} = 1.985$ is the *contextual simple main effect,* which indicates that in men, after controlling for that day's stressors, for every one-unit higher *proportion of stressor days,* mean symptoms are expected to be significantly higher by 1.985 (or 0.397 per stressor day). The Women$_i$ by PMstressor40$_i$ level-2 interaction of $\gamma_{09} = -1.277$ indicates that the contextual effect of stressors is nonsignificantly less positive by 1.277 in women (and the contextual effect in women is then $\gamma_{08} + \gamma_{09} = 1.985 - 1.277 = 0.708$, which is significant). Thus, after controlling for that day's stressors, men and women who report more stressor days report greater mean physical symptoms to (marginally) the same extent.

Finally, we can obtain the model-implied level-2 between-person stressor effect and how it differs by sex (i.e., the effects that would have been given directly if we had used PMC for stressors instead). The level-2 between-person effect of stressors for men is given by the addition of its contextual and within-person main effects, $\gamma_{08} + \gamma_{20} = 1.985 + 0.244 = 2.229$ (which is significant). How the level-2 between-person effect differs for women is given by the addition of the contextual and within-person stressor interactions with Women$_i$, $\gamma_{09} + \gamma_{21} = -1.277 - 0.234 = -1.511$ (which is significant). Finally, the level-2 between-person effect of stressors for women is given by the addition of the contextual and within-person main effects for men ($\gamma_{08} + \gamma_{20}$) plus how they differ for women ($\gamma_{09} + \gamma_{21}$), or 0.718 (which is significant). Thus, *not* controlling for that day's stressors, for every one-unit higher proportion of stressor days, mean physical symptoms are expected to be significantly higher by 2.229 in men and by 0.718 in women, and this between-person effect is significantly bigger in men.

Phew! The previous model illustrates why the interpretation of interaction terms is an absolutely critical skill for longitudinal analysis—and thus why most of chapter 2 was devoted to that topic! However, the previous model is still missing many other possible interactions of the time-varying predictors (both parts) with the time-invariant predictors—these include the two-way interactions of negative mood or stressors (at each level) by age, and the three-way interactions of negative mood or stressors (at each level) by women by age. Feel free to examine these additional interactions on your own for practice using the data available online.

3.B. Interactions Among Time-Varying Predictors

So far we have seen how to examine interactions of the parts of time-varying predictors (negative mood, stressors) with a time-invariant predictor (sex). Based on our previous results, we can simplify the model by removing both of the nonsignificant interactions of negative mood with sex. But given that the level-2 interaction of PMstressor40$_i$ by sex was significant, we will retain the stressor interactions with sex at both levels to maintain the symmetric interpretation of the stressor effects (i.e., as within-person effects at level 1 and contextual effects at level 2).

Our next model demonstrates how to examine interactions among the time-varying predictors of negative mood and stressors. That is, within persons, does the effect on that day's symptoms of reporting more negative mood than usual differ on stressor and no-stressor days? But just as we've seen previously, in doing so we also need to consider potential moderation of the effects of negative mood and stressors at level 2 and across levels, as seen in Equation (8.12):

Level 1: $\text{Symptoms}_{ti} = \beta_{0i} + \beta_{1i}\left(\text{Mood}_{ti} - \overline{\text{Mood}}_i\right) + \beta_{2i}\left(\text{Stressor}_{ti}\right)$

$$+ \beta_{3i}\left(\text{Mood}_{ti} - \overline{\text{Mood}}_i\right)\left(\text{Stressor}_{ti}\right) + e_{ti}$$

Level 2:

Intercept: $\beta_{0i} = \gamma_{00} + \gamma_{01}\left(\text{Women}_i\right) + \gamma_{02}\left(\text{Age}_i - 80\right)$

$$+ \gamma_{03}\left(\text{Women}_i\right)\left(\text{Age}_i - 80\right)$$

$$+ \gamma_{04}\left(\overline{\text{Mood}}_i - 2\right) + \gamma_{08}\left(\overline{\text{Stressor}}_i - 0.40\right) + \gamma_{09}\left(\text{Women}_i\right)\left(\overline{\text{Stressor}}_i - 0.40\right)$$

$$+ \gamma_{0,12}\left(\overline{\text{Mood}}_i - 2\right)\left(\overline{\text{Stressor}}_i - 0.40\right) + U_{0i}$$

Within-Person Mood: $\qquad \beta_{1i} = \gamma_{10} + \gamma_{18}\left(\overline{\text{Stressor}}_i - 0.40\right)$

Within-Person Stressor: $\qquad \beta_{2i} = \gamma_{20} + \gamma_{21}\left(\text{Women}_i\right) + \gamma_{24}\left(\overline{\text{Mood}}_i - 2\right)$

Within-Person Mood by Stressor: $\beta_{3i} = \gamma_{30}$

Composite :

$$
\begin{aligned}
\text{Symptoms}_{ti} = {} & \gamma_{00} + \gamma_{01}\left(\text{Women}_i\right) + \gamma_{02}\left(\text{Age}_i - 80\right) \\
& + \gamma_{03}\left(\text{Women}_i\right)\left(\text{Age}_i - 80\right) \\
& + \gamma_{04}\left(\overline{\text{Mood}}_i - 2\right) + \gamma_{08}\left(\overline{\text{Stressor}}_i - 0.40\right) \\
& + \gamma_{09}\left(\text{Women}_i\right)\left(\overline{\text{Stressor}}_i - 0.40\right) \\
& + \gamma_{0,12}\left(\overline{\text{Mood}}_i - 2\right)\left(\overline{\text{Stressor}}_i - 0.40\right) \\
& + \gamma_{10}\left(\text{Mood}_{ti} - \overline{\text{Mood}}_i\right) \\
& + \gamma_{18}\left(\overline{\text{Stressor}}_i - 0.40\right)\left(\text{Mood}_{ti} - \overline{\text{Mood}}_i\right) \\
& + \gamma_{20}\left(\text{Stressor}_{ti}\right) + \gamma_{21}\left(\text{Women}_i\right)\left(\text{Stressor}_{ti}\right) \\
& + \gamma_{24}\left(\overline{\text{Mood}}_i - 2\right)\left(\text{Stressor}_{ti}\right) + U_{0i} + e_{ti}
\end{aligned}
\tag{8.12}
$$

in which four new interaction terms have been added. Note that $\gamma_{0,12}$ is used for consistency in notation because the next two level-2 interactions after γ_{09} would have been PMstressor40$_i$ by Age80$_i$ ($\gamma_{0,10}$) and PMstressor40$_i$ by Women$_i$ by Age80$_i$ ($\gamma_{0,11}$). The new comma between the subscripts is needed to separate the second subscript that requires two digits. However, none of these new interactions was significant. As a set they did not improve model fit over the model with interactions for just sex by stressors, $-2\Delta LL(4) = 3.0$, $p = .556$, and accounted for another 0.6% of the total symptoms variance (cumulative $R^2 = .286$). If this was the result of a real data analysis we would likely remove these nonsignificant interactions, but we will still interpret them here for the sake of practice (just in case you ever need to do so!). We will forgo interpreting the previous model parameters, however, except for a few of the simple main effects as still needed.

We will begin with the most straightforward interaction: within-person negative mood and within-person stressors are purely level-1 variables, and so their interaction is represented by the β_{3i} placeholder in the level-1 model, and β_{3i} is then defined by a level-2 equation of just the fixed effect γ_{30}. The WPmood$_{ti}$ by Stressor$_{ti}$ level-1 interaction of $\gamma_{30} = 0.059$ means that the within-person effect of greater negative mood than usual (of $\gamma_{10} = -0.003$ for PMstressor40$_i$ = 0 and Stressor$_{ti}$ = 0) becomes *less negative* by $\gamma_{30} = 0.059$ on stressor days, or that the within-person effect of a daily stressor (of $\gamma_{20} = 0.223$ for Women$_i$ = 0, PMmood2$_i$ = 0, and WPmood$_{ti}$ = 0) becomes *more positive* by $\gamma_{30} = 0.059$ for every one-unit more negative mood than usual.

The remaining interactions will be more complicated to interpret due to the use of PMC for level-1 negative mood but GMC for level-1 stressors. That is, because their level-2 effects are different (i.e., the between-person effect of PMC mood; the contextual effect of GMC stressors), the interactions involving these level-2 terms will be asymmetric across predictors. But just as we've been able to reconstruct the other level-2 term not directly given by the model (i.e., the implied contextual effect for PMC mood; the implied between-person effect for GMC stressors), we can do so for these interactions as well. As seen in Table 8.4 and explained below, there are actually *nine* different interaction effects implied by the *four* interactions directly provided by the model. Rather than showing the specific model symbols, Table 8.4 uses the more transparent labels of "1" or "2" for the effects at level 1 or level 2, and "m" for negative mood and "s" for stressors.

First, we consider the other three interactions directly provided by our current model—using PMC negative mood and GMC stressors—as underlined in the first column of Table 8.4. The PMmood2$_i$ by PMstress40$_i$ level-2 interaction of $\gamma_{0,12}$ = –1.470 can be interpreted two different ways. One way uses contextual stressors as the moderator: the between-person effect of reporting greater negative mood than other people (of γ_{04} = 1.828 for PMstressor40$_i$ = 0 and Stressor$_{ti}$ = 0) becomes *less positive* by $\gamma_{0,12}$ = –1.470 for every one-unit higher proportion of stressor days (controlling for that day's stressors). The other way uses between-person negative mood as the moderator: the contextual effect of reporting more stressor days than other people (of γ_{08} = 0.871 for Women$_i$ = 0, PMmood2$_i$ = 0, and WPmood$_{ti}$ = 0) becomes *less positive* by $\gamma_{0,12}$ = –1.470 for every one-unit higher person mean negative mood (not controlling for that day's negative mood). The PMmood2$_i$ by PMstress40$_i$ interaction thus demonstrates what is meant by the phrase *asymmetric:* the level-2 contextual effect for stressors is controlled for that day's stressors, but the level-2 between-person effect for negative mood is *not* controlled for that day's negative mood. Similarly, the WPmood$_{ti}$ by PMstressor40$_i$ cross-level interaction of γ_{18} = 0.443 describes how the within-person effect of negative mood varies by proportion of stressor days (controlling for that day's stressors), but the Stressor$_{ti}$ by PMmood2$_i$ cross-level interaction of γ_{14} = 0.012 describes how the within-person effect of a daily stressor varies by person mean negative mood (*not* controlling for that day's negative mood). There is nothing inherently wrong with this asymmetry, but it can make interpreting such interactions even more challenging.

Fortunately, so long as all relevant interactions are included at each level, the symmetric (and more interpretable) versions of the interactions can be calculated as shown in Table 8.4. For example, the level-2 interaction of between-person negative mood by between-person stressors does not control for the current day's value of either predictor, whereas the level-2 interaction of contextual negative mood by contextual stressors controls for the current day's value of both predictors. As also shown in Table 8.4, symmetric interactions could be provided automatically by using PMC for both variables (in the second column, resulting in interactions among level-2 between-person and level-1 within-person effects exclusively), or by using GMC instead for both variables (in the third column, resulting in interactions among level-2 contextual and level-1 within-person effects exclusively). For completeness, the fourth column shows the computations for the reverse of our current model (for GMC for negative mood and PMC for stressors instead).

However, if PMC was used for stressors instead (i.e., WPstressor$_{ti}$ instead of Stressor$_{ti}$), the fixed intercept and any main effects interacting with level-1 stressor effect would then differ because of the change in what a value of 0 means for the

Table 8.4 Within-level and cross-level interactions between daily negative mood (m) and daily stressors (s) using all combinations of person-mean-centering (PMC) or grand-mean-centering (GMC). The underlined interactions are those given directly by each model.

Interaction Term	PMC Mood by GMC Stressors	PMC Mood by PMC Stressors	GMC Mood by GMC Stressors	GMC Mood by PMC Stressors	Est	SE	p <
Level-2 Between-Person Mood by Level-2 Between-Person Stressors	2m*2s + 2m*1s	<u>2m*2s</u>	2m*2s + 1m*2s + 2m*1s + 1m*1s	2m*2s + 1m*2s	−1.458	1.148	.207
Level-2 Between-Person Mood by Level-2 Contextual Stressors	<u>2m*2s</u>	2m*2s – 2m*1s	2m*s2 + 1m*s2	2m*2s + 1m*2s – 2m*1s – 1m*1s	−1.470	1.237	.237
Level-2 Between-Person Mood by Level-1 Within-Person Stressors	<u>2m*1s</u>	<u>2m*1s</u>	2m*1s + 1m*1s	2m*1s + 1m*1s	0.012	0.439	.979
Level-2 Contextual Mood by Level-2 Between-Person Stressors	2m*2s – 1m*2s + 2m*1s – 1m*1s	2m*2s – 1m*2s	2m*2s + 2m*1s	<u>2m*2s</u>	−1.960	1.223	.111
Level-2 Contextual Mood by Level-2 Contextual Stressors	2m*2s – 1m*2s	2m*2s – 2m*1s – 1m*2s + 1m*1s	<u>2m*2s</u>	2m*2s – 2m*1s	−1.913	1.341	.155
Level-2 Contextual Mood by Level-1 Within-Person Stressors	2m*1s – 1m*1s	2m*1s – 1m*1s	<u>2m*1s</u>	<u>2m*1s</u>	−0.047	0.541	.930
Level-1 Within-Person Mood by Level-2 Between-Person Stressors	1m*2s + 1m*1s	<u>1m*2s</u>	1m*2s + 1m*1s	<u>1m*2s</u>	0.502	0.425	.238
Level-1 Within-Person Mood by Level-2 Contextual Stressors	<u>1m*2s</u>	1m*2s – 1m*1s	<u>1m*2s</u>	1m*2s – 1m*1s	0.443	0.534	.408
Level-1 Within-Person Mood by Level-1 Within-Person Stressors	<u>1m*1s</u>	<u>1m*1s</u>	<u>1m*1s</u>	<u>1m*1s</u>	0.059	0.403	.884

level-1 stress predictor (i.e., 0 = a day at the person mean of stressors for WPstressor$_{ti}$; 0 = a no-stressor day for Stressor$_{ti}$), but the models would still be equivalent in terms of their fit and predicted values. In general, all fixed effects will be identical across PMC and GMC models for the same time varying-predictor only if the same centering constant was used at both levels—this is another reason we had used a centering constant of 2 for both levels of the negative mood predictors when originally introducing GMC.

Table 8.4 also helps explain what happens if some interactions were omitted. For instance, for PMC negative mood, if the WPmood$_{ti}$ by PMstress40$_i$ cross-level interaction was included without the matching PMmood2$_i$ by PMstress40$_i$ level-2 interaction, this would imply that the within-person effect of negative mood—but not the between-person effect—differs by proportion of stressor days. In English, this would mean that the effect of greater negative mood *than usual* depends on one's proportion of stressor days, but that the effect of one's usual amount of negative mood does not. In contrast, for GMC stressors, including the Stressor$_{ti}$ by PMmood2$_i$ cross-level interaction without the same matching PMstress40$_i$ by PMmood2$_i$ level-2 interaction would have a different result—it would imply that the within-person and between-person effects of stressors are moderated by person mean negative mood *to the same extent* (i.e., the Stressor$_{ti}$ by PMmood2$_i$ cross-level interaction would then be smushed across levels). In summary, when examining cross-level interactions involving a time-varying predictor, the corresponding level-2 interaction should be examined as well to avoid assuming that a moderation effect exists at one level but not the other (PMC), or that a moderation effect is equal across levels (GMC). We will return to this idea in the summary section following the next set of intra-variable interactions.

3.C. Cross-Level Interactions Among the Parts of a Time-Varying Predictor

So far we have seen how to examine interactions of the parts of time-varying predictors (negative mood, stressors) with a time-invariant predictor (sex), as well as how to examine interactions among time-varying predictors (and thus among their time-invariant parts as well). Based on our previous results, we can simplify the model by removing the four nonsignificant interactions of negative mood with stressors before continuing to our last type of interaction.

As you might have guessed, the same general principles on inclusion across levels apply when examining cross-level interactions among the parts of a single time-varying predictor. For example, we could test the cross-level interaction of PMmood2$_i$ by WPmood$_{ti}$ within PMC to see whether the effect of reporting greater negative mood than usual depends on how much negative mood a person has in general. However, this interaction would only allow the *within-person* negative mood effect to depend on person mean negative mood—we also need a PMmood2$_i$ by PMmood2$_i$ level-2 interaction (i.e., PMmood2$_i^2$) to then allow the *between-person* effect to depend on person mean negative mood as well. An analogous problem would occur for the cross-level interaction of PMstressor40$_i$ by Stressor$_{ti}$ in GMC. When added by itself, the interaction will be smushed— it would assume equal moderation of the within-person and between-person stressor effects by person mean stressors, and so we need to add PMstressor40$_i^2$ to allow differential moderation at each level instead. Thus, when estimating a cross-level interaction among the parts of a time-varying predictor in either PMC or GMC, we should also examine a quadratic level-2 effect of its person mean in order to allow moderation by the person mean at both levels. This will also allow us to calculate the implied level-2 effects not directly provided (i.e., the contextual effects in PMC or the between-person effects in GMC). Finally, although not strictly necessary, so long as we are considering a quadratic level-2 effect, we should also consider a quadratic level-1 effect. In this case, though, it will only be possible to examine a quadratic effect of the continuous predictor WPmood$_{ti}$, and not for the dichotomous predictor Stressor$_{ti}$ (given that its possible values of 0 or 1 create only one linear difference).

Accordingly, the resulting intra-variable interactions model is seen in Equation (8.13)

Level 1: $\text{Symptoms}_{ti} = \beta_{0i} + \beta_{1i}\left(\text{Mood}_{ti} - \overline{\text{Mood}}_i\right) + \beta_{2i}\left(\text{Stressor}_{ti}\right)$

$$+ \beta_{4i}\left(\text{Mood}_{ti} - \overline{\text{Mood}}_i\right)^2 + e_{ti}$$

Level 2:

Intercept: $\beta_{0i} = \gamma_{00} + \gamma_{01}\left(\text{Women}_i\right) + \gamma_{02}\left(\text{Age}_i - 80\right) + \gamma_{03}\left(\text{Women}_i\right)\left(\text{Age}_i - 80\right)$

$$+ \gamma_{04}\left(\overline{\text{Mood}}_i - 2\right) + \gamma_{08}\left(\overline{\text{Stressor}}_i - 0.40\right)$$

$$+ \gamma_{09}\left(\text{Women}_i\right)\left(\overline{\text{Stressor}}_i - 0.40\right)$$

$$+ \gamma_{0,16}\left(\overline{\text{Mood}}_i - 2\right)^2 + \gamma_{0,21}\left(\overline{\text{Stressor}}_i - 0.40\right)^2 + U_{0i}$$

Linear Within-Person Mood: $\beta_{1i} = \gamma_{10} + \gamma_{14}\left(\overline{\text{Mood}}_i - 2\right)$

Within-Person Stressor: $\beta_{2i} = \gamma_{20} + \gamma_{21}\left(\text{Women}_i\right) + \gamma_{28}\left(\overline{\text{Stressor}}_i - 0.40\right)$ (8.13)

Quadratic Within-Person Mood: $\beta_{4i} = \gamma_{40}$

Composite:

$\text{Symptoms}_{ti} = \gamma_{00} + \gamma_{01}\left(\text{Women}_i\right) + \gamma_{02}\left(\text{Age}_i - 80\right) + \gamma_{03}\left(\text{Women}_i\right)\left(\text{Age}_i - 80\right)$

$$+ \gamma_{04}\left(\overline{\text{Mood}}_i - 2\right) + \gamma_{08}\left(\overline{\text{Stressor}}_i - 0.40\right)$$

$$+ \gamma_{09}\left(\text{Women}_i\right)\left(\overline{\text{Stressor}}_i - 0.40\right)$$

$$+ \gamma_{0,16}\left(\overline{\text{Mood}}_i - 2\right)^2 + \gamma_{0,21}\left(\overline{\text{Stressor}}_i - 0.40\right)^2$$

$$+ \gamma_{10}\left(\text{Mood}_{ti} - \overline{\text{Mood}}_i\right) + \gamma_{14}\left(\overline{\text{Mood}}_i - 2\right)\left(\text{Mood}_{ti} - \overline{\text{Mood}}_i\right)$$

$$+ \gamma_{20}\left(\text{Stressor}_{ti}\right) + \gamma_{21}\left(\text{Women}_i\right)\left(\text{Stressor}_{ti}\right)$$

$$+ \gamma_{28}\left(\overline{\text{Stressor}}_i - 0.40\right)\left(\text{Stressor}_{ti}\right) + U_{0i} + e_{ti}$$

in which quadratic level-1 and level-2 effects of negative mood, a cross-level inter-action between the (linear) parts of negative mood, a quadratic level-2 effect of stressors, and a cross-level interaction between the (linear) parts of stressors have been added. The new quadratic within-person effect of $WPmood_{ti}^2$ is represented by the β_{4i} placeholder in the level-1 model, and β_{4i} is then defined by a level-2 equation including just the fixed effect γ_{40}. The new level-2 quadratic between-person effect for $PMmood2_i^2$ is given by $\gamma_{0,16}$ (because $\gamma_{0,13}$, $\gamma_{0,14}$, and $\gamma_{0,15}$ would have been used for the interactions of $PMmood2_i$ by $PMstressor40_i$ with $Women_i$, with $Age80_i$, and with $Women_i$ by $Age80_i$). Similarly, the new level-2 quadratic contextual effect for $PMstressor40_i^2$ is given by $\gamma_{0,21}$ (because $\gamma_{0,17}$, $\gamma_{0,18}$, $\gamma_{0,19}$, and $\gamma_{0,20}$ would have been used for the interactions of $PMmood2_i^2$ with $Women_i$, with $Age80_i$, with $Women_i$ by $Age80_i$, and with $PMstressor40_i$). Finally, the cross-level intra-variable interac-tions for negative mood and for stressors are given by γ_{14} and γ_{28}, respectively. Even though this practice of reserving level-2 subscripts for unmodeled interactions is somewhat unconventional and quickly becomes unwieldy, it does illustrate just how many interactions could possibly be considered!

Although as a set they did not improve model fit over the model with two interactions for just sex by stressors, $-2\Delta LL(5) = 7.3$, $p = .201$, and accounted for another 2.4% of the total symptoms variance (cumulative $R^2 = .304$), one new effect was indeed significant. As we did for the last model, we will forgo presenting and interpreting the previous model parameters and instead focus on the interpretation of the new parameters as seen in Table 8.5, which is similar to Table 8.4 in that it provides both the direct and model-implied effect if using PMC or GMC.

Beginning with the effects of stressors, the level-1 effect for $Stressor_{ti}$ of $\gamma_{20} = 0.198$ is still the within-person effect for men (the nonsignificant difference between no-stressor and stressor days holding proportion of stressor days constant), but is now conditional on $PMstressor40_i = 0$ (40% stressor days). The cross-level, intra-variable interaction $PMstressor40_i$ by $Stressor_{ti}$ of $\gamma_{28} = 0.176$ indicates that the symptom difference between no-stressor and stressor days becomes nonsignificantly more positive by $\gamma_{28} = 0.176$ for every one-unit higher proportion stressor days (or alterna-tively, that the significant linear contextual effect of proportion stressor days of $\gamma_{08} = 1.890$ for men for no-stressor days becomes nonsignificantly more positive by $\gamma_{28} = 0.176$ on stressor days). As shown in Table 8.5, the level-1 within-person effect of $Stressor_{ti}$ and its cross-level interaction with $PMstressor40_i$ would be the same using GMC or PMC for level-1 stressors. The level-2 effects for $PMstressor40_i$ of $\gamma_{08} = 1.890$ and for $PMstressor40_i^2$ of $\gamma_{0,21} = -0.386$ directly represent the linear and qua-dratic contextual effects of stressors (controlling for that day's stressors); the total between-person effects (i.e., not controlling for that day's stressors that would have been directly provided using PMC for level-1 stressors) can still be calculated as shown in Table 8.5. The linear contextual and linear between-person stressor effects are both significant and conditional on men with $PMstress40_i = 0$ and $Stressor_{ti} = 0$ (and thus would differ if the level-1 stressors predictor was centered differently). However, neither of the quadratic level-2 effects of stressors (contextual or between-person) was significant.

Table 8.5 Cross-level interactions among the parts of daily negative mood and daily stressors using all combinations of person-mean-centering (PMC) or grand-mean-centering (GMC). Bold values are $p < .05$. * Indicates effects were obtained from a model with a level-1 effect of $Stressor_{ti}$ specifically.

Model Fixed Effects	GMC	PMC	Est	SE	$p <$
Daily Stressor Effects:					
Level-2 Linear Between-Person*	$\gamma_{08} + \gamma_{20}$	γ_{08}	**2.088**	0.620	.001
Level-2 Quadratic Between-Person	$\gamma_{0,21} + \gamma_{28}$	$\gamma_{0,21}$	−0.210	0.857	.807
Level-2 Linear Contextual*	γ_{08}	$\gamma_{08} - \gamma_{20}$	**1.890**	0.633	.003
Level-2 Quadratic Contextual	$\gamma_{0,21}$	$\gamma_{0,21} - \gamma_{28}$	−0.386	0.984	.696
Level-1 Within-Person	γ_{20}	γ_{20}	0.198	0.175	.259
Level-2 Between-Person by Level-1 Within-Person	γ_{28}	γ_{28}	0.176	0.486	.718
Level-2 Contextual by Level-1 Within-Person	γ_{28}	γ_{28}	0.176	0.486	.718
Daily Negative Mood Effects:					
Level-2 Linear Between-Person	$\gamma_{04} + \gamma_{10}$	γ_{04}	−0.298	0.802	.711
Level-2 Quadratic Between-Person	$\gamma_{0,16} + \gamma_{40} + \gamma_{14}$	$\gamma_{0,16}$	**−1.837**	0.717	.012
Level-2 Linear Contextual	γ_{04}	$\gamma_{04} - \gamma_{10}$	−0.671	0.849	.430
Level-2 Quadratic Contextual	$\gamma_{0,16}$	$\gamma_{0,16} - \gamma_{14} + \gamma_{40}$	**−2.379**	0.931	.011
Level-1 Linear Within-Person	γ_{10}	γ_{10}	0.373	0.260	.151
Level-1 Quadratic Within-Person	γ_{40}	γ_{40}	−0.266	0.313	.397
Level-2 Between-Person by Level-1 Within-Person	$\gamma_{14} + 2\gamma_{40}$	γ_{14}	0.277	0.397	.486
Level-2 Contextual by Level-1 Within-Person	γ_{14}	$\gamma_{14} - 2\gamma_{40}$	0.808	0.763	.290

Turning to the effects of negative mood, let's begin with its level-1 linear and quadratic within-person effects, which we learned how to interpret for change over time in chapter 6. The nonsignificant instantaneous linear effect for WPmood$_{ti}$ of $\gamma_{10} = 0.373$ (conditional on WPmood$_{ti}$ = 0 and PMmood2$_i$ = 0) becomes nonsignificantly less positive by *twice* the quadratic within-person effect for WPmood$_{ti}^2$ of $\gamma_{40} = -0.266$ *per one-unit greater negative mood than usual.* As seen in Table 8.5, both the linear and quadratic level-1 effects would have been the same using either PMC or GMC for level-1 negative mood. The cross-level, intra-variable interaction WPmood$_{ti}$ by PMmood2$_i$ of $\gamma_{14} = 0.277$ in PMC is the interaction of linear between-person by linear within-person negative mood: the linear *within-person* effect of negative mood is expected to be nonsignificantly more positive by 0.277 for every one-unit higher *person mean* negative mood, or the linear *between-person effect* of negative mood is expected to be nonsignificantly more positive by

0.277 for every one-unit more negative mood *than usual*. After controlling for that day's negative mood, the cross-level, intra-variable interaction of the linear contextual by linear within-person negative mood effects can be calculated as shown in Table 8.5 (as would have been provided directly using GMC level-1 negative mood instead of PMC).

The level-2 effects from the PMC model for $PMmood2_i$ directly represent the linear and quadratic between-person effects of negative mood (i.e., not controlling for that day's negative mood). Accordingly, the instantaneous linear between-person effect for $PMmood2_i$ of $\gamma_{04} = -0.298$ (conditional on $PMmood2_i = 0$ and $WPmood_{ti} = 0$) becomes significantly more negative by twice the quadratic effect of $\gamma_{0,16} = -1.837$ per *one-unit higher person mean negative mood*. But because the distribution of person mean negative mood was positively skewed ($M = 1.20$, $SD = 0.26$, range = 1.00 to 2.52), we should interpret the quadratic effect per one-unit *lower* instead: At $PMmood2_i = -1$ (at person mean negative mood = 1), the instantaneous linear effect for $PMmood2_i$ of $\gamma_{04} + (2*\gamma_{08}*PMmood2_i) = -0.298 + (2*-1.837*-1) = 3.375$ is significant. But the linear effect of being a grumpier person on mean symptoms appears to level off quickly. The corresponding level-2 linear and quadratic contextual effects (after controlling for that day's negative mood, from the GMC model as shown in Table 8.5) reveal the same pattern.

The need for a nonlinear effect was foreshadowed in the top panel of Figure 8.2, in which the predicted outcomes at person mean negative mood = 3 went out of bounds for the 1 to 5 symptoms scale. Although we could have plotted person mean negative mood = 1 instead, this creates a logical dilemma—given that daily negative mood ranges from 1 to 5, the only way to obtain a person mean negative mood = 1 is to report 1 on each day. But persons who do not show any within-person mood variability then cannot show a within-person mood effect (i.e., they would have had only a single point to plot in Figure 8.2 rather than an individual line). The same problem could occur for daily stressors—only persons with a proportion of stressor days greater than 0 but less than 1 can possibly show a within-person effect of reporting a stressor. Thus, a cross-level interaction among the parts of a time-varying predictor may be necessary because individuals with person means near the top or bottom of the scale will have limited within-person variability, which will limit the size of the within-person effect those persons can show.

However, there is no evidence of this problem with respect to negative mood or stressors here: their within-person effects did not vary significantly over persons (i.e., no random slope variance), and their cross-level intra-variable interactions were not significant. Additional cross-level interactions of level-1 by quadratic level-2 effects (i.e., that would allow a smaller within-person effect near the floor and the ceiling of the person means) were also not significant (not reported). Thus, although both time-varying predictors showed within-person variability (i.e., the negative mood ICC = .36 and the stressors ICC = .44 both indicate more than 50% within-person variation), in our example data that within-person variation did not predict within-person variation in physical symptoms.

3.D. Summary and Advice for Model Building

The last three models were designed to illustrate how to specify and interpret three types of interactions involving time-varying predictors across levels of analysis: (1) interactions of time-varying with time-invariant predictors (e.g., two interactions for negative mood by sex, two interactions for stressors by sex), (2) interactions among time-varying predictors (including one level-1 interaction, one level-2 interaction, and two cross-level interactions), and (3) intra-variable interactions among the parts of a time-varying predictor (for negative mood including level-1 and level-2 quadratic effects and one intra-variable cross-level interaction; for stressors including one level-2 quadratic effect and one intra-variable cross-level interaction). Although few of the interactions were actually statistically significant, these examples were hopefully still useful in demonstrating an important model-building principle: that the need to distinguish *within-person* variation (and its potential *level-1* effects in the model) from *between-person* variation (and its potential *level-2* effects in the model) applies not only when examining the main effects of time-varying predictors, but also when examining their interactions with other variables (including with themselves). The way to distinguish these two levels of effects is to explicitly represent between-person variance in a time-varying predictor by including its person mean as a predictor in the model (centered at a constant such that 0 is meaningful)—not only as a main effect, but also as part of an interaction with any predictors that interact with the time-varying predictor. How the simple main effects and interactions involving the person mean then get interpreted depends on how the time-varying predictor is specified, as summarized below.

Although we first presented the two options of person-mean-centering (PMC) and grand-mean-centering (GMC) for time-varying predictors, the only distinction that really matters is *PMC or not PMC*—this is for two reasons. First, *PMC* is a fundamentally different type of centering that involves centering with a *variable* (the person mean) instead of a *constant*. Second, with respect to the *not PMC* label, because models with different centering constants (or with no centering constant at all) will always be equivalent, the effects of a time-varying predictor will be the same whether it has been grand-mean-centered (so that 0 is meaningful) or left uncentered (when 0 is already meaningful). Furthermore, as we saw earlier, if the level-1 effect of the time-varying predictor has a random slope (i.e., a level-2 random slope variance over persons is estimated), then *PMC or not PMC* will result in truly nonequivalent models. Otherwise, the differences between *PMC or not PMC* are purely cosmetic if the main and interaction effects of the time-varying predictor are represented at both levels (as illustrated throughout the chapter). So, which should be used? Let us consider the relative advantages and disadvantages of each.

As stated earlier, the view presented in this text is that *PMC* of continuous time-varying predictors is well suited for most longitudinal data and is easier to understand (than *not PMC*). By explicitly separating the time-varying predictor's between-person variance (via the person mean) from its within-person variance (via the deviation from the person mean) ahead of time, the model predictors are uncorrelated. As a result, the main effects and interactions at each level (level-1 within persons, level-2 between persons) can be interpreted the same way regardless of whether the other effect is included in the model. This is very convenient when keeping track of the conditionality of simple effects in complex models. It also results in (relatively) more easily described interpretations in which a level-2 *between-person* effect reflects the result of more of a predictor *than other people*, and a level-1 within-person effect reflects the result of more of a predictor *than usual* (than a person's mean). The drawback to *PMC* is that the level-2 effects of the person mean do not control for each occasion's absolute value of the time-varying predictor.

In contrast, specifying the effects of time-varying predictors using *not PMC* (either GMC or uncentered) has a few potential difficulties. The still-common approach of omitting a main effect of the person mean at level 2 will result in a convergence (smushed) level-1 effect of the time-varying predictor that assumes equivalent within-person and between-person main effects. Furthermore, omitting the corresponding level-2 interactions with the person mean will result in a convergence (smushed) cross-level interaction. For example, if our model included effects of $Stressor_{ti}$, $Women_i$, and $Stressor_{ti}$ by $Women_i$, we would be assuming equivalent between-person and within-person effects of a daily stressor (a convergence level-1 main effect or equivalently, no contextual effect) as well as equivalent moderation of those effects by sex (a convergence cross-level interaction). Adding a main effect of $PMstressor40_i$ separates the within-person and contextual main effects; adding an interaction of $PMstressor40_i$ by $Women_i$ separates the interactions of sex by the within-person effect and sex by the contextual effect. The resulting contextual main effects and interactions represent the difference of the between-person and within-person main effects and interactions while controlling for each occasion's absolute value of the time-varying predictor. However, my experience suggests that the *not PMC* models offer greater potential for misinterpretation given that their level-1 and level-2 effects mean different things when included by themselves than when paired together in the same model.

So which centering approach should be used, *PMC* or *not PMC*? Although I personally prefer *PMC* whenever possible, my recommendation is to use whichever approach more closely corresponds to your research questions: *PMC* models directly represent the *total* effect at each level, whereas GMC or *uncentered* models directly represent the *incremental* effects across levels (i.e., the differences in effects across levels). Regardless, I would also recommend that the main effects and interactions of a time-varying predictor be included at both levels to allow effects to exist at each level (in *PMC*) or to prevent the smushing of effects across levels (in *GMC* or *uncentered*). If desired, the missing model-implied level-2 effect (contextual effect in *PMC*; between-person effect in *GMC or uncentered*) can be obtained with additional syntax statements (e.g., ESTIMATE in SAS, TEST in SPSS, LINCOM in STATA, or NEW in M*plus*).

A more challenging set of decisions is which interaction terms to estimate, and in which order they should be included. Unfortunately, there is usually not a single "right" model to be found; such efforts to find "The Model" may be futile and frustrating, in that you may end up at a different place depending on which effects you examine first. In general, model-building should follow two main principles. First, it should be hypothesis-driven or question-driven, and second, it should take into account the multilevel nature of the predictors and the outcomes. In many cases the purpose of an analysis is to demonstrate the effect of a newly considered predictor variable net of previously considered predictor variables. Such substantive interpretation of the "old" variables as control variables necessarily dictates that their effects be included first.

For example, one hypothesis for why stressors may relate to physical symptoms is that stressors create negative mood, and it is actually this increased negative mood that manifests in increased physical symptoms. To examine this conjecture, we should have specified the effects of stressors first, followed by the effects of negative mood, to see if the stressor effects were diminished after controlling for negative mood. Furthermore, control variables may need to have both main effects and interactions. For example, if we expected sex differences in how the effects of stressors were diminished by controlling for negative mood, we should first include stressor main effects and interactions with sex, followed by negative mood main effects and interactions with sex. But to follow the second principle in doing so, we should examine the main effects and interactions of stressors and negative mood *at both levels* in order to acquire their entire story, not just the story of one level (or the smushed story across levels). That is, not having hypotheses or questions about what happens at each level does not free you from the responsibility and need to examine the relationships among your time-varying predictors at each level! This is especially noteworthy in our example, given that our goal was to observe how level-1 effects of daily negative mood and daily stressors related to daily physical symptoms, but in actuality only their level-2 effects—that reflect between-person differences over time instead—were significant!

The ideas of collinearity and total versus unique effects from multiple regression readily apply to longitudinal models as well, albeit at multiple levels simultaneously (e.g., collinearity among level-1 predictors, among level-2 predictors). So, in the absence of questions that imply an explicit order of entry for predictors, it may be useful to examine their effects (at both levels) in separate models for each predictor prior to examining their effects in a combined model. That way if a given predictor's effect is not significant in a combined model, you would know whether this was due to a lack of any effect at all (as shown in a separate model with just that predictor) or is a result of collinearity between predictors (nonsignificant effects only after including other predictors). The conditionality of main and interaction effects still applies—all lower-order main effects and interactions must also be included when examining a higher-order interaction. For clarity of interpretation, it is helpful to include all relevant interactions across levels to distinguish moderation of within-person effects from moderation of between-person effects. An abundance of fixed effects will not generally lead to estimation problems, and so including the additional interactions needed to maintain separation across levels may be well worth the trouble when it comes to interpreting those interaction terms, especially for *not PMC* models!

Finally, the most helpful description of interaction effects of any kind is likely to include a figure (i.e., of hypothetical persons and/or occasions, as introduced in chapter 2). However, the type of figure needed will depend on the kind of inter-action that is to be displayed. For outcomes that show within-person fluctuation rather than within-person change, *time* may not be relevant, and thus using *time* as the *x*-axis may not be useful. Instead, if a within-person effect is to be displayed, using the time-varying predictor as the *x*-axis (e.g., as in Figure 8.1) will be more useful. Whether to use the time-varying predictor's original scale (e.g., $Mood_{ti} = 1$ to 5) or within-person scale (e.g., $WPmood_{ti} = \pm 2$) is up to you, but it may be easiest to use the original scale for GMC time-varying predictors and a within-person scale for PMC predictors. Different lines would then be shown for different values of the interacting predictor (e.g., for men and women, and/or low and high person mean negative mood). If no within-person effects are of interest, then the *x*-axis could be a time-invariant predictor instead. Remember to use the centered values for your model predictors when calculating predicted outcomes (although the original val-ues of the predictors should still be used in the figure labels).

But enough about interactions—this section will now change gears to present a few less commonly seen ways that time-varying predictors can contribute to a longitudinal model: as lagged effects in the model for the means, or as predictors of heterogeneity of variance.

3.E. Lagged Effects of Time-Varying Predictors

Although our example time-varying predictors were measured at the same occasion as the outcome, in some scenarios it may be more reasonable to postulate delayed effects instead. For example, it may take some time before the impact of stressors translates into physical symptoms. In examining within-person lagged effects, it is usually necessary to control for within-person contemporaneous (simultaneous) effects. So, in our example, we could include a predictor for the previous occasion's stressors in addition to current stressors. This would allow us to test whether *yester-day's* stressors predict *today's* symptoms over and above *today's* stressors. In exam-ining the between-person effect, the person mean constructed from all occasions should be used when models of varying time lags are to be compared. Otherwise, between-person effects will not be comparable across models. The current and lagged effects of time-varying predictors will likely be easiest to understand using PMC, but GMC or uncentered predictors can also be used as needed so long as the person mean of the time-varying predictor is in the level-2 model as well.

An important caveat for implementing lagged models is to ensure the appro-priate data structure. The data file needs to include a new predictor variable that represents the lagged occasion's value in the same row as the current outcome (i.e., day 1 stressors in the same row as day 2 symptoms, day 2 stressors in the same row as day 3 symptoms, and so forth). This means you must be careful not to lag across persons—that is, you must ensure that the last observation for person 1 does not inadvertently get transferred into the first observation for person 2!

A limitation of examining lagged effects via multilevel models is that occasions with missing predictors will not be included. Therefore, if examining a lagged effect for the prior occasion, the first occasion will not be used because it does not have the previous occasion's predictor. Likewise, if examining lagged effects for two occasions prior, the first and second occasions will not be included. Fortunately, there are alternative ways of specifying lagged effects within multilevel structural equation models, as will be discussed in chapter 9.

3.F. Predicting Individual and Intraindividual Differences in Variation

The role of time-varying predictors in longitudinal analysis can be multifaceted. To summarize what we've seen so far, in the model for the means, time-varying predictors can show within-person, time-specific effects on an outcome measured at the same occasion (or lagged across occasions) as well as between-person effects on the average outcome over time. Each of these sources of variation may interact with each other or with other model predictors. In addition, in the model for the variance, time-varying predictors can have random slopes that allow between-person variance in their effects (which in turn allows heterogeneity in the random intercept variance as a function of time-varying predictors with random effects).

We now turn to one final set of models that will demonstrate yet another role that time-varying predictors can play: as predictors of heterogeneity of variance. That is, our models so far have assumed that the level-2 random intercept variance $\tau^2_{U_0}$ and the level-1 residual variance σ^2_e are homogeneous across persons, occasions, and all predictors after controlling for the effects of model predictors. We will relax this assumption for each variance in turn, beginning with the random intercept variance. Our new variance–predicting model (in which only previously significant fixed effects are included) is shown in Equation (8.14):

Level 1:

$$\text{Symptoms}_{ti} = \beta_{0i} + \beta_{1i}\left(\text{Mood}_{ti} - \overline{\text{Mood}}_i\right) + \beta_{2i}\left(\text{Stressor}_{ti}\right) + e_{ti}$$

Residual Variance: $\sigma^2_{e_{ti}} = \exp[\eta_{0i}]$

Level 2:

Intercept: $\beta_{0i} = \gamma_{00} + \gamma_{01}(\text{Women}_i) + \gamma_{02}(\text{Age}_i - 80) + \gamma_{03}(\text{Women}_i)(\text{Age}_i - 80)$

$$+ \gamma_{04}\left(\overline{\text{Mood}}_i - 2\right) + \gamma_{08}\left(\overline{\text{Stressor}}_i - 0.40\right)$$

$$+ \gamma_{09}(\text{Women}_i)\left(\overline{\text{Stressor}}_i - 0.40\right) \tag{8.14}$$

$$+ \gamma_{0,16}\left(\overline{\text{Mood}}_i - 2\right)^2 + U_{0i}$$

Within-Person Mood: $\quad \beta_{1i} = \gamma_{10} + \gamma_{14}\left(\overline{\text{Mood}}_i - 2\right)$

Within-Person Stressor: $\beta_{2i} = \gamma_{20} + \gamma_{21}(\text{Women}_i)$

Random Intercept Variance: $\tau^2_{U_{0i}} = \exp\begin{bmatrix} \upsilon_{00} + \upsilon_{01}(\text{Women}_i) + \upsilon_{02}(\text{Age}_i - 80) \\ + \upsilon_{04}\left(\overline{\text{Mood}}_i - 2\right) + \upsilon_{08}\left(\overline{\text{Stressor}}_i - 0.40\right) \end{bmatrix}$

Residual Variance: $\eta_{0i} = \varepsilon_{00}$

in which the amount of level-2 $\tau^2_{U_0}$ (now denoted as $\tau^2_{U_{0i}}$ given that it varies over persons) and level-1 σ^2_e (now denoted as $\sigma^2_{e_{ti}}$ given that it varies over persons and days) are each predicted using the notation introduced in chapter 7. To review, the predictor effects on the *amount* of level-2 $\tau^2_{U_{0i}}$ and level-1 $\sigma^2_{e_{ti}}$ are indicated by the υ and ε terms, respectively (which will have the same subscripts as their corresponding fixed effects in the model for the means). The exp[ ] term is again used to predict the natural log of $\tau^2_{U_{0i}}$ and $\sigma^2_{e_{ti}}$ to ensure positive predicted variances; thus, the values for the υ and ε terms are scaled such that $\log(\tau^2_{U_{0i}}) = [\ ]$ and $\log(\sigma^2_{e_{ti}}) = [\ ]$. Recall from chapter 7 that a model with a ω_{0i} scale factor for remaining individual differences in within-person variation would not converge, and so this term is also not included here.

Results from the model for the variance only in Equation (8.14) predicting a differential amount of level-2 $\tau^2_{U_{0i}}$ across persons (from main effects of Women$_i$, Age80$_i$, PMmood2$_i$, and PMstressor40$_i$) are shown in the second set of columns in Table 8.6. Although the effects of sex and age on log $\tau^2_{U_{0i}}$ were tested in chapter 7, they will be re-examined given that $\tau^2_{U_{0i}}$ is now defined differently (i.e., as random intercept variance now also controlling for all level-2 effects of negative mood and stressors). Results from a comparison model with homogeneous variance instead (i.e., with just the υ_{00} and ε_{00} terms) are shown in the first set of columns in Table 8.6. The four new predictors of heterogeneous level-2 $\tau^2_{U_{0i}}$ marginally improved model fit as a set, $-2\Delta LL(4) = 8.2$, $p = .085$, but only one effect was significant individually, as described next.

The υ_{00} and ε_{00} terms are like the intercepts of their respective variances. So, in the model in Equation (8.14), $\upsilon_{00} = -1.103$ is the expected log $\tau^2_{U_{0i}} = \exp[-1.103] = 0.332$) specifically for 80-year-old men with a person mean for negative mood of 2 who reported stressors on 40% of their days, whereas $\varepsilon_{00} = -0.497$ is the expected log $\sigma^2_{e_{ti}}$ (such that $\sigma^2_{e_{ti}} = \exp[-0.497] = 0.609$) for any person on any day (given that $\sigma^2_{e_{ti}}$ is not yet predicted by anything). The other υ effects are like between-person main effects that predict the *amount* of log $\tau^2_{U_{0i}}$ (rather than reducing the amount of $\tau^2_{U_{0i}}$ that remains as their γ fixed effects did in the model for the means). The main effect of sex on log $\tau^2_{U_{0i}}$ of $\upsilon_{01} = -0.178$ indicates nonsignificantly less between-person variability in mean symptoms in women than in men. The main effect of age on log $\tau^2_{U_{0i}}$ of $\upsilon_{02} = 0.039$ indicates that log $\tau^2_{U_{0i}}$ is expected to be nonsignificantly higher by 0.039 per additional year of age. The main effect of PMmood2$_i$ on log $\tau^2_{U_{0i}}$ of $\upsilon_{04} = -0.710$ indicates that log $\tau^2_{U_{0i}}$ is expected to be nonsignificantly lower by 0.710 for every one-unit higher person mean negative mood. Finally, the main effect of PMstressor40$_i$ on log $\tau^2_{U_{0i}}$ of $\upsilon_{08} = 1.581$ indicates that log $\tau^2_{U_{0i}}$ is expected to be significantly higher by 1.581 for every one-unit higher person mean stressors (or higher by 1.581 / 5 = 0.316 for every additional stressor day reported). Note that because Stressor$_{ti}$ is not included as a predictor of log $\tau^2_{U_{0i}}$, the level-2 stressor effect is its between-person effect, not its contextual effect as in the model for the means. To summarize, the amount of between-person differences in mean physical symptoms does not vary by sex, age, or mean negative mood, but there is more between-person symptom variability among persons who reported a higher

Table 8.6 Results for tests of heterogeneity of daily physical symptoms variance. Bold values are $p < .05$.

Model for the Variance: EXP[ ]	Baseline Fixed Effects: Homogeneous Variances			Equation 8.14: Add Level-2 Heterogeneity			Equation 8.15: Add Level-1 Heterogeneity		
	Est	SE	p <	Est	SE	p <	Est	SE	p <
v_{00} Level-2 Random Intercept Variance	**−0.473**	0.168	.006	−1.103	0.790	.166	−1.081	0.806	.183
v_{01} Sex (Men = 0, Women = 1)				−0.178	0.385	.646	−0.153	0.384	.692
v_{02} Age (0 = 80 years)				0.039	0.033	.244	0.039	0.032	.224
v_{04} Level-2 Between-Person Negative Mood				−0.710	0.848	.404	−0.698	0.872	.425
v_{08} Level-2 Between-Person Stressors				**1.581**	0.603	.010	**1.425**	0.587	.017
ε_{00} Level-1 Residual Variance	**−0.496**	0.070	.001	**−0.497**	0.070	.001	−0.084	0.308	.786
ε_{01} Sex (Men = 0, Women = 1)							0.071	0.166	.672
ε_{02} Age (0 = 80 years)							−0.003	0.013	.807
ε_{04} Level-2 Between-Person Negative Mood							**0.697**	0.337	.041
ε_{08} Level-2 Contextual Stressors							**0.698**	0.315	.029
ε_{10} Level-1 Within-Person Negative Mood							0.026	0.310	.933
ε_{20} Level-1 Within-Person Stressors							−0.009	0.218	.967
ML Model Fit									
Number of Parameters	14			18			24		
−2LL	1379.3			1371.0			1346.3		
AIC	1407.3			1407.0			1394.3		
BIC	1444.5			1454.9			1458.0		

proportion of stressor days. But because we will be examining their effects on the level-1 $\sigma^2_{e_{ti}}$ next, for now we will retain each of these effects on level-2 $\tau^2_{U_{0i}}$.

Finally, differential amounts of within-person fluctuation (i.e., heterogeneity of level-1 $\sigma^2_{e_{ti}}$) can be predicted by level-2 time-invariant predictors *or* by the between-person and within-person parts of level-1 time-varying predictors, as shown in Equation (8.15):

Level 1:

$$\text{Symptoms}_{ti} = \beta_{0i} + \beta_{1i}\left(\text{Mood}_{ti} - \overline{\text{Mood}}_i\right) + \beta_{2i}\left(\text{Stressor}_{ti}\right) + e_{ti}$$

Residual Variance: $\sigma^2_{e_{ti}} = \exp\left[\eta_{0i} + \underline{\eta_{1i}\left(\text{Mood}_{ti} - \overline{\text{Mood}}_i\right)} + \underline{\eta_{2i}\left(\text{Stressor}_{ti}\right)}\right]$

Level 2:

Intercept: $\beta_{0i} = \gamma_{00} + \gamma_{01}\left(\text{Women}_i\right) + \gamma_{02}\left(\text{Age}_i - 80\right)$
$\qquad\qquad + \gamma_{03}\left(\text{Women}_i\right)\left(\text{Age}_i - 80\right)$
$\qquad\qquad + \gamma_{04}\left(\overline{\text{Mood}}_i - 2\right) + \gamma_{08}\left(\overline{\text{Stressor}}_i - 0.40\right)$
$\qquad\qquad + \gamma_{09}\left(\text{Women}_i\right)\left(\overline{\text{Stressor}}_i - 0.40\right)$
$\qquad\qquad + \gamma_{0,16}\left(\overline{\text{Mood}}_i - 2\right)^2 + U_{0i}$

Within-Person Mood: $\beta_{1i} = \gamma_{10} + \gamma_{14}\left(\overline{\text{Mood}}_i - 2\right)$

Within-Person Stressor: $\beta_{2i} = \gamma_{20} + \gamma_{21}\left(\text{Women}_i\right)$

Random Intercept Variance: $\tau^2_{U_{0i}}$

$$= \exp\left[\begin{array}{l} \upsilon_{00} + \upsilon_{01}\left(\text{Women}_i\right) + \upsilon_{02}\left(\text{Age}_i - 80\right) \\ + \upsilon_{04}\left(\overline{\text{Mood}}_i - 2\right) + \upsilon_{08}\left(\overline{\text{Stressor}}_i - 0.40\right) \end{array}\right]$$

Residual Variance:

$\eta_{0i} = \varepsilon_{00} + \underline{\varepsilon_{01}\left(\text{Women}_i\right)} + \varepsilon_{02}\left(\text{Age}_i - 80\right)$
$\qquad + \varepsilon_{04}\left(\overline{\text{Mood}}_i - 2\right) + \varepsilon_{08}\left(\overline{\text{Stressor}}_i - 0.40\right)$

$\eta_{1i} = \varepsilon_{10}$

$\eta_{2i} = \varepsilon_{20}$

(8.15)

in which the same level-2 predictors of log $\tau^2_{U_{0i}}$ have been retained along with six new predictors of log $\sigma^2_{e_{ti}}$. The prediction of log $\sigma^2_{e_{ti}}$ through exp[ ] operates similarly to the level-1 model for the means. That is, the level-1 model for log $\sigma^2_{e_{ti}}$ includes three placeholders for the intercept-like term (η_{0i}) and for the effects of the two time-varying predictors (η_{1i} and η_{2i}), which are each then defined by their own level-2 equation including the actual predictor effects (the ε terms). All subscripts for the η_i placeholders and ε terms match those from the model for the means.

Results from the model for the variance only in Equation (8.15) predicting a differential amount of level-2 $\tau^2_{U_{0i}}$ across persons and a differential amount of level-1 $\sigma^2_{e_{ti}}$ across persons and days are shown in the third set of columns in Table 8.6.

The υ terms predicting level-2 $\log \tau^2_{U_{0i}}$ are interpreted as before; the main effect of PMstressor40$_i$ ($\upsilon_{08} = 1.425$) is still significant. The six new predictors of heterogeneity in the level-1 $\sigma^2_{e_{ti}}$ significantly improved model fit as a set, $-2\Delta LL(6) = 24.8$, $p = .004$, but only two effects were significant individually, as described next.

The intercept-like term $\varepsilon_{00} = -0.084$ is now the expected $\log \sigma^2_{e_{ti}}$ (or $\sigma^2_{e_{ti}} = \exp[-0.084] = 0.920$) specifically for 80-year-old men with a person mean for negative mood of 2 who reported stressors on 40% of their days, and on days when WPmood$_{ti} = 0$ (at person mean negative mood of 2) and Stressor$_{ti} = 0$ (a no-stressor day). The other ε effects are like main effects that predict the *amount* of $\log \sigma^2_{e_{ti}}$ (rather than reducing $\sigma^2_{e_{ti}}$ as did their γ fixed effects in the model for the means). The main effect of sex on $\log \sigma^2_{e_{ti}}$ of $\varepsilon_{01} = 0.071$ indicates nonsignificantly more within-person symptom fluctuation in women than in men. The main effect of age on $\log \sigma^2_{e_{ti}}$ of $\varepsilon_{02} = -0.003$ indicates that $\log \sigma^2_{e_{ti}}$ is expected to be nonsignificantly lower by 0.003 per additional year of age. The between-person main effect of PMmood2$_i$ on $\log \sigma^2_{e_{ti}}$ of $\varepsilon_{04} = 0.697$ indicates that $\log \sigma^2_{e_{ti}}$ is expected to be significantly higher by 0.697 for every one-unit higher person mean negative mood. The contextual main effect of PMstressor40$_i$ on $\log \sigma^2_{e_{ti}}$ of $\varepsilon_{08} = 0.698$ indicates that $\log \sigma^2_{e_{ti}}$ is expected to be significantly higher by 0.698 for every one-unit higher person mean stressor (or higher by 0.140 for every additional stressor day reported). Thus, persons with greater mean negative mood and who report more stressor days (after controlling for current stressors) are expected to show greater within-person symptom fluctuation. At level 1, the main within-person effect of WPmood$_{ti}$ on $\log \sigma^2_{e_{ti}}$ of $\varepsilon_{10} = 0.026$ indicates that $\log \sigma^2_{e_{ti}}$ is expected to be nonsignificantly higher by 0.026 for every one-unit higher negative mood than usual, and the main within-person effect of Stressor$_{ti}$ on $\log \sigma^2_{e_{ti}}$ of $\varepsilon_{20} = -0.009$ indicates that $\log \sigma^2_{e_{ti}}$ is expected to be nonsignificantly lower by 0.009 on stressor days than on non-stressor days. Thus, within-person symptom fluctuation does not differ by daily stressors or within-person variation in negative mood. We will retain only the significant heterogeneity of variance effects in reporting our final model, as summarized in the sample results section in the next section.

In this example we have only examined main effect of our predictors on heterogeneity of variance, but we could also examine the effects of the same interactions we included in the model for the means. That is, interactions among level-2 time-invariant predictors could also predict differential level-2 between-person or level-1 within-person variance, but interactions among level-1 time-varying predictors or cross-level interactions could only predict differential level-1 within-person variance. These investigations are left to you to pursue on your own.

But in addition to keeping track of which variables can potentially predict differential variability at each level, there are a few other caveats worth noting. One is to make sure that all predictors of heterogeneous variance have also been included as fixed effects in the model for the means. That is, while it is acceptable to include a predictor in the model for the *means* only, it is not acceptable to include a predictor in the model for the *variance* only. This rule is similar to the previous rule from chapters 4–6 that all random effects must also have their corresponding fixed effect in the model, and both are for the same reason: because the model for the variance is specified through deviations from the fixed effects in the model for the means. Finally, unlike fixed effects that are determined by the variance components, the heterogeneity effects are found through the same joint likelihood estimation process as the variance components—thus adding heterogeneity effects to the model for the variance may lead to estimation problems. The convergence of any heterogeneous variance model should always be checked carefully.

3.G. Measurement of Person Characteristics With Time-Varying Predictors

One final, more philosophical issue to consider with respect to models including time-varying predictors concerns their between-person effects. Throughout the chapter we have assumed that the person mean of a time-varying predictor can be used as a proxy for constant individual differences. For example, the person mean of daily negative mood served as a trait index of how grumpy a person is overall relative to other people. But for some constructs, a more direct measurement of individual differences might lead to a different variable with different results. For instance, what if we had asked persons about their general grumpiness relative to other people using a scale designed to measure this trait directly? How correlated would that *direct* index of overall negative mood be with the *indirect* index from the person mean of daily negative mood, and would their between-person effects differ as well? These are fundamentally questions of measurement, not analysis, and the extent to which person mean aggregation can adequately represent stable individual differences is likely to depend on the particular construct under study. However, if a non-aggregated direct index of individual differences is to be used in the level-2 model instead of the indirect person mean index, then examining the level-1 effects of the time-varying predictor with PMC will ensure that they represent pure within-person effects, whereas GMC may result in convergence (smushed) effects given that the person mean would not be present as needed to transform the level-1 convergence effects into within-person effects.

4. Chapter Summary

This chapter described the evaluation of effects of time-varying predictors (i.e., level-1 predictors measured at each occasion) on outcomes that show within-person fluctuation over time. Examination of time-varying predictors can be complicated because they almost always contain both level-2 between-person variation and level-1 within-person variation. Each of these parts of a time-varying predictor may have separate additive or interactive effects: a *between-person, general effect* of reporting more of the predictor than other people that accounts for level-2 random intercept variance; a *within-person, time-specific effect* of reporting more of the predictor than usual that accounts for level-1 residual variance. The between-person and within-person effects in the model for the means (or as predictors of variance heterogeneity in the model for the variance) will usually differ from each other because they refer to different constructs and because they are unstandardized coefficients on different scales. In two-level models for longitudinal data, level-1 within-person effects can be fixed, systematically varying, or random, but level-2 between-person (or contextual) effects can only be fixed or systematically varying.

The chapter then introduced two methods of including a time-varying predictor in order to distinguish its effects across levels: person-mean-centering (which involves centering at a variable) and grand-mean-centering (which involves centering at a constant). More specifically, in *person-mean-centering* (PMC), the between-person variance in a time-varying predictor is represented in the level-2 model by its person mean across time (centered at a constant so that 0 is meaningful), whereas its within-person variance is represented in the level-1 model by the within-person deviation of the time-varying predictor around the person's mean (in which 0 then represents the person's mean across time). Because these two new orthogonal predictors carry their total effects at each level regardless of whether the other predictor is in the model, their effects are relatively easy to understand: the level-2 (centered) person mean directly represents the total between-person effect, and the level-1 within-person deviation directly represents the total within-person effect. This *a priori* separation of the sources of variance in a time-varying predictor in PMC parallels the model-based decomposition of variance in the outcome.

In the alternative approach known as *grand-mean-centering* (GMC), the mean of the time-varying predictor is relocated—most often using the grand mean, but any centering constant (or none at all) will result in the same model effects. When included by itself, the GMC level-1 predictor will represent the *smushed* or *convergence effect*, which is a weighted combination of its between-person and within-person effects that assumes they are equivalent. This assumption can be tested by including the same level-2 predictor as in PMC—the centered person mean. Once both predictors are included, the GMC level-1 predictor then represents the total within-person effect (the same as the PMC level-1 predictor). But the GMC level-2 predictor represents the *incremental between-person effect*, or the *contextual effect*, which can be interpreted in two ways: as the between-person effect after controlling for the absolute amount of the time-varying predictor at that occasion, or as the difference of the between-person and within-person effects.

Fortunately, the GMC and PMC models can be made equivalent if their level-1 effects are fixed or systematically varying, and so the choice between them boils down to which more conveniently answers your research questions, given that different but complementary level-2 effects are provided directly from each (i.e., after controlling for the current value of the time-varying predictor in GMC, but not in PMC). However, the GMC and PMC models will not be equivalent if their level-1 effects have random slopes; in that case, the choice between them can be made on theoretical considerations (i.e., whether a relative or absolute random effect is more logical) or empirical grounds (e.g., ML AIC and BIC; avoiding downward bias in the

GMC slope variance). Finally, those with categorical time-varying predictors will still need to consider their possible between-person and within-person effects, but may need to be more creative in doing so given that the PMC or GMC methods are more applicable to continuous time-varying predictors.

The chapter then demonstrated how to examine three types of interactions (using PMC or GMC): among time-varying and time-invariant predictors, among time-varying predictors, and cross-level interactions among the multilevel parts of the same time-varying predictor. Although the specific interactions examined should be guided by your research questions, it is important to remember the multilevel nature of time-varying predictors in doing so. That is, interactions should be specified at each level in order to prevent assuming that moderation occurs at one level only (PMC) or to prevent assuming equal (smushed) moderation across levels (GMC). All lower-order main effects and interactions should always be included as well. Finally, although in this chapter we interpreted these interactions using just their coefficients, the other techniques demonstrated in chapter 2 for decomposing interactions (e.g., examining simple effects or regions of significance) in cross-sectional models may also be useful in longitudinal models. Figures can be especially helpful, as will be shown in the summary results section to follow.

Lastly, this chapter discussed some less commonly used models with time-varying predictors, including *lagged effects* (e.g., yesterday's stressors as a predictor of today's symptoms) and effects on *heterogeneity of variance* (i.e., on the amount of between-person mean variation at level 2 or the amount of within-person fluctuation at level 1). In these models, predictors can only allow for variance heterogeneity at the same level or lower. Thus, time-invariant predictors (and the between-person part of time-varying predictors) can predict heterogeneity of level-2 or level-1 variance, but the within-person part of time-varying predictors (or cross-level interactions thereof) can only predict heterogeneity of level-1 variance. Finally, it is important to consider issues of measurement when conceptualizing the trait (between-person) and state (within-person) effects of time-varying predictors. Aggregating across occasions to form a person mean is an indirect assessment of trait variance that may differ from a direct assessment—which is more appropriate will depend on the constructs and questions under study.

5. Sample Results Section

The analyses in this chapter could be summarized into the beginning of a results section as follows (which would then need to be expanded to capture the substantively meaningful story, theoretical framework, or set of research hypotheses to be tested). The amount of detail provided about the process of arriving at the final reported model(s) will usually be far less than the exposition in the chapter, but will vary depending on the goals of the study and the space available. The results section that follows refers to only some of the intermediate models as benchmarks before describing the final model in more detail, including a new table and figure to do so.

Furthermore, the results section begins where the example data analysis ended in chapter 7 (which presented the modeling approach, outcome data, unconditional models, and the effects of sex and age), although the first two paragraphs may be included in a method section instead:

Daily negative mood was computed as the mean of five items: *sad, annoyed, worried, irritated,* and *depressed,* each rated on a 5-point scale (from *not at all* to *extremely;* $M = 1.20$, $SD = 0.38$, range $= 1.00$ to 3.60). The intraclass correlation for daily negative mood (as calculated from the results of an empty means, random intercept model) was ICC $= .36$, indicating that 36% of its variance was due to between-person mean differences, and 64% was due to within-person variation around the person means across days. For inclusion as a predictor of daily symptoms in the models, daily negative mood was person-mean-centered, such that its within-person (level-1) effect was represented by the deviation from the person's mean negative mood across days of daily negative mood (i.e., as $\text{Mood}_{ti} - \overline{\text{Mood}}_i$; $M = 0.00$, $SD = 0.27$, range $= -0.72$ to 1.28), whereas its between-person (level-2) effect was represented by the person's mean negative mood across days ($M = 1.20$, $SD = 0.26$, range $= 1.00$ to 2.52) centered at 2 (i.e., $\overline{\text{Mood}}_i - 2$).

Presence of a daily stressor (Stressor_{ti}) was assessed as whether or not a stressor relating to relationships, events, and health occurred had been endorsed on each day ($0 =$ no, $1 =$ yes). A stressor was reported on 45% of the total sample days; 20% of the persons in the sample reported no stressors on any day, and 14% reported a stressor on each day. The intraclass correlation for presence of a daily stressor (as calculated from an empty means, random intercept logistic model for dichotomous outcomes) was ICC $= .44$, indicating that 44% of its variance was due to between-person mean differences, and 56% was due to within-person variation around the person means across days. Because 0 was already a meaningful value, its within-person (level-1) effect was represented by the original Stressor_{ti} predictor, whereas its contextual (incremental between-person, level-2) effect was represented by the person's proportion of stressor days ($M = 0.45$, $SD = 0.34$, range $= 0$ to 1) centered at 40% (i.e., $\overline{\text{Stressor}}_i - .40$). Any additional model-implied level-2 effects (i.e., contextual effect of negative mood; between-person effect of stressors) and their standard errors were obtained via separate programming statements.

The prediction of daily physical symptoms from time-varying predictors of daily negative mood and daily stressors was then examined. First, main effects at each level for both predictors were examined, as seen in Equation (8.10) and reported in the first set of columns in Table 8.3. The four new main effects significantly improved model fit over the baseline model, $-2\Delta LL(4) = 39.8$, $p < .001$ (and the smaller AIC and BIC values concur), and accounted for an additional 19.5% of the total variance in physical symptoms (cumulative $R^2 = .253$). However, only the level-2 effects of each variable were significant individually. The significant between-person effect of negative mood indicates that persons who report greater negative mood on average also report higher mean symptoms (even after controlling for current negative mood, as indicated by a significant implied contextual effect). Likewise, the significant implied between-person effect of stressors indicates that persons who report a higher proportion of stressor days also report higher mean symptoms (even after controlling for current stressors, as indicated by a significant contextual effect). However, the nonsignificant within-person (level-1) effect of negative mood indicates that reporting greater negative mood than usual was not related to that day's symptoms. The nonsignificant within-person effect of stressors indicates there is no difference in symptoms between stressor and non-stressors days, holding proportion of stressor days constant.

We then examined potential moderation of the effects of negative mood and stressors at each level by sex, as seen by the four new interaction terms in Equation (8.11), and as reported in the second set of columns in Table 8.3. As a set the four new sex interaction terms marginally improved model fit, $-2\Delta LL(4) = 8.9$, $p = .064$, and accounted for another 2.8% of the total variance in physical symptoms (cumulative $R^2 = .281$). However, only the implied between-person effect of stressors differed significantly by sex, such that the total effect of proportion of stressor days on mean symptoms was less positive for women than men (although this sex difference was lower after controlling for current stressors, as indicated by the nonsignificant contextual stressors by sex interaction). Both interactions of stressors with sex were retained to properly distinguish moderation by sex across levels, whereas the nonsignificant interactions of negative mood with sex were removed. We then examined moderation of the effects of negative mood by stressors at each level, as shown in Equation (8.12). However, the four interactions did not improve model fit, $-2\Delta LL(4) = 3.0$, $p = .556$, and they only accounted for another 0.6% of the total symptoms variance (cumulative $R^2 = .286$). Thus, the effects of negative mood did not depend on the effects of stressors at any level (and vice-versa). As a result, the four nonsignificant interactions among negative mood and stressors were removed.

We then examined five intra-variable interactions within the effects of negative mood and within the effects of stressors, as seen in Equation (8.13) and reported in Table 8.5. As a set they did not improve model fit, $-2\Delta LL(5) = 7.3$, $p = .201$, although they accounted for another 2.4% of the total symptoms variance (cumulative $R^2 = .304$). For stressors, neither the within-person effect nor the between-person effect depended on proportion of stressor days. For negative mood, although the within-person effect did not depend on itself (i.e., no quadratic level-1 effect) or on person mean negative mood (i.e., no cross-level interaction), there was a significant quadratic between-person effect, such that the linear negative mood effect became less positive at higher levels of person mean negative mood (even after controlling for current negative mood, as indicated by the significant implied quadratic contextual effect). Given the significant level-2 interaction, the cross-level negative mood interaction was also retained so as to allow differential moderation of the effects of negative mood by person mean negative mood at each level.

Finally, we examined the extent to which the main effects of sex, age, person mean negative mood, and proportion of stressor days predicted differential between-person variation in mean symptoms (i.e., heterogeneity of level-2 random intercept variance $\tau^2_{U_{0i}}$) using a log-linear model for the variance, as shown in Equation (8.14) and reported in the second set of columns in Table 8.6. Although as a set the four new predictors of heterogeneous level-2 $\tau^2_{U_{0i}}$ marginally improved model fit, $-2\Delta LL(4) = 8.2$, $p = .085$, only the between-person effect of proportion of stressor days was significant individually, indicating greater heterogeneity in mean symptoms in persons who reported a higher proportion of stressor days. Temporarily retaining all four level-2 heterogeneity effects, we followed by examining the extent to which the six main effects of sex, age, person mean negative mood, proportion of stressor days, within-person negative mood, and within-person stressors predicted differential within-person variation in mean symptoms (i.e., heterogeneity of level-1 residual variance $\sigma_{e_{ti}}^2$), as shown in Equation (8.15) and reported in the third set of columns in Table 8.6. The six new predictors of heterogeneity in the level-1 $\sigma_{e_{ti}}^2$ significantly improved model fit as a set, $-2\Delta LL(6) = 24.8$, $p = .004$, but only two effects were significant individually—within-person, daily symptoms fluctuation was significantly greater in persons with higher mean negative mood or who reported a greater proportion of stressor days. In removing the nonsignificant heterogeneity effects, the quadratic between-person effect of negative mood became nonsignificant as well, and so it and the cross-level negative mood interaction were also removed. Parameters from the final model that accounted for 28.0% of the total variance in daily physical symptoms are provided in Table 8.7 and displayed in Figure 8.3.

In the model for the means, the fixed intercept $\gamma_{00} = 2.803$ is the expected daily physical symptoms for 80-year-old men (Women$_i$ = 0; Age80$_i$ = 0) with a person mean negative mood of 2 (PMmood2$_i$ = 0) on days when they are at their person mean negative mood (WPmood$_{ti}$ = 0), and for persons who reported stressors on 40% of their days (PMstressor40$_i$ = 0) on a non-stressor day (Stressor$_{ti}$ = 0). The nonsignificant simple main effect of sex of $\gamma_{01} = -0.343$ indicates that women report 0.343 fewer mean symptoms than men (conditional on 80-year-olds who reported stressors on 40% of their days on a non-stressor day). The significant simple main effect of age of $\gamma_{02} = 0.068$ indicates that among men, mean symptoms are expected to be higher by 0.068 per additional year of age. The significant sex by age level-2 interaction of $\gamma_{03} = -0.087$ indicates that the negative sex difference in which men reported more mean symptoms grows by 0.088 per year of age, or that the age slope is less positive by 0.087 in women (in which the age slope is $\gamma_{02} + \gamma_{03} = -0.020$, which was nonsignificant). Turning to the effects of daily negative mood, the nonsignificant within-person effect at level 1 of $\gamma_{10} = 0.102$ indicates that for every one-unit more negative mood than usual (i.e., relative to the person's mean), that day's symptoms are expected to be higher by 0.102. However, the significant between-person main effect of negative mood at level 2 of $\gamma_{04} = 1.658$ indicates that for every one-unit higher person mean negative mood, the mean number of symptoms reported across days is expected to be higher by 1.658 (even after controlling for current negative mood, as indicated by a significant implied contextual effect of $\gamma_{04} - \gamma_{10} = 1.556$ per unit higher person mean negative mood).

The effects of daily stressors and their interactions with sex are displayed in Figure 8.3, which shows model-predicted values for daily symptoms (one the y-axis) on a no-stressor or stressor day (on the x-axis) for men and women who reported a stressor on 1 day or 4 days (i.e., 20% or 80% of days). The slopes of the lines depict the within-person stressor effects, and the distances between the lines depict

Table 8.7 Results from final model of person-mean-centered daily negative mood and grand-mean-centered daily stressors predicting daily physical symptoms. Bold values are $p < .05$.

Model Effects		Est	SE	$p <$
Model for the Means				
γ_{00}	Intercept: Men (= 0)	**2.803**	0.368	.001
$\gamma_{00} + \gamma_{01}$	Intercept: Women (= 1)	**2.460**	0.342	.001
γ_{01}	Intercept: Sex Difference	−0.343	0.206	.100
γ_{02}	Age (0 = 80 years): Men (= 0)	**0.068**	0.030	.025
$\gamma_{02} + \gamma_{03}$	Age (0 = 80 years): Women (= 1)	−0.020	0.015	.198
γ_{03}	Age (0 = 80 years): Sex Difference	**−0.087**	0.033	.010
γ_{04}	Level-2 Between-Person Negative Mood	**1.658**	0.397	.001
$\gamma_{04} - \gamma_{10}$	Level-2 Contextual Negative Mood	**1.556**	0.424	.001
γ_{10}	Level-1 Within-Person Negative Mood	0.102	0.147	.489
Stressor Effects:				
$\gamma_{08} + \gamma_{20}$	Level-2 Between-Person: Men (= 0)	**2.250**	0.577	.001
$\gamma_{08} + \gamma_{20} + \gamma_{09} + \gamma_{21}$	Level-2 Between-Person: Women (= 1)	**0.709**	0.314	.026
$\gamma_{09} + \gamma_{21}$	Level-2 Between-Person: Sex Difference	**−1.542**	0.640	.018
γ_{08}	Level-2 Contextual: Men (= 0)	**2.045**	0.601	.001
$\gamma_{08} + \gamma_{09}$	Level-2 Contextual: Women (= 1)	**0.680**	0.333	.044
γ_{09}	Level-2 Contextual: Sex Difference	**−1.365**	0.671	.044
γ_{20}	Level-1 Within-Person: Men (= 0)	0.206	0.165	.215
$\gamma_{20} + \gamma_{21}$	Level-1 Within-Person: Women (= 1)	0.029	0.112	.797
γ_{21}	Level-1 Within-Person: Sex Difference	−0.177	0.198	.374
Model for the Variance EXP[ ]				
υ_{00}	Random Intercept Variance	**−0.573**	0.171	.001
υ_{08}	Level-2 Between-Person Stressors	**1.388**	0.535	.011
ε_{00}	Residual Variance	−0.011	0.277	.969
ε_{04}	Level-2 Between-Person Negative Mood	**0.723**	0.329	.030
ε_{08}	Level-2 Between-Person Stressors	**0.677**	0.225	.003

ML Model Fit

Number of Parameters	15
−2LL	1351.8
AIC	1381.8
BIC	1421.6

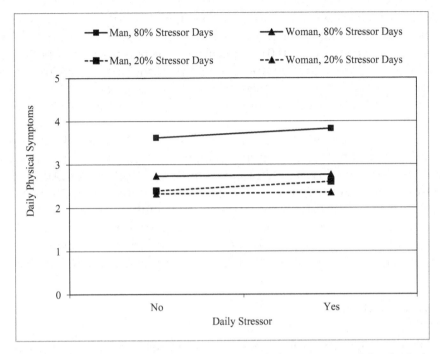

Figure 8.3 Moderation by sex of the effects of daily stressors on daily physical symptoms.

the between-person stressor effects. First, the nonsignificant level-1 within-person simple main effect of γ_{20} = 0.206 indicates that in men, holding the proportion of stressor days constant, symptoms on stressor days are expected to be higher by 0.206 than on non-stressor days. The nonsignificant within-person stressors by sex cross-level interaction of γ_{21} = −0.177 indicates that the within-person effect of daily stressors is less positive by 0.177 in women (and the within-person stressor effect in women is $\gamma_{20} + \gamma_{21}$ = 0.029, which is not significant). This nonsignificant interaction is shown in Figure 8.3 by the nearly parallel lines between men and women. Second, the significant level-2 contextual simple main effect of γ_{08} = 2.045 indicates that in men, after controlling for that day's stressors, for every one-unit higher proportion of stressor days, mean symptoms are expected to be higher by 2.045 (or 0.409 per stressor day). The significant contextual stressors by sex level-2 interaction of γ_{09} = −1.365 indicates that the contextual effect of stressors is less positive by 1.365 in women (and the contextual effect in women is $\gamma_{08} + \gamma_{09}$ = 0.680, which is significant). This interaction is shown in Figure 8.3 by the greater distance between the men than between the women. Though significant for both men and women, the implied between-person effects were more positive for men (as $\gamma_{08} + \gamma_{20}$ = 2.250) than for women (as $\gamma_{08} + \gamma_{20} + \gamma_{09} + \gamma_{21}$ = 0.709), as indicated by a significant implied between-person by sex level-2 interaction (of $\gamma_{09} + \gamma_{21}$ = −1.542).

Finally, in the log-linear model for the variance, the expected natural log of the level-2 random intercept variance (i.e., between-person in mean physical symptoms) is given by υ_{00} = −0.573 (specifically for persons who reported stressors on 40% of their days), which is predicted to be higher by υ_{08} = 1.388 for every one-unit higher proportion of stressor days (or 0.278 per day). Similarly, the expected natural log of the level-1 residual variance (i.e., within-person fluctuation in daily physical symptoms) is given by $e_{00} = -0.011$ (specifically for persons with a person mean negative mood of 2 who reported stressors on 40% of their days), which is predicted be higher by $\varepsilon_{04} = 0.723$ for every one-unit higher person mean negative mood, and higher by $\varepsilon_{08} = 0.677$ for every one-unit higher proportion of stressor days (or 0.135 per day).

Thus, to summarize all of these findings, persons who report being grumpier in general appear to have more physical symptoms in general and to show greater between-person variability in symptoms. Similarly, reporting stressor days more frequently also relates to reporting more physical symptoms in general (especially for men), as well as to greater between-person variability in symptoms and greater within-person fluctuation in symptoms. But these cross-sectional effects do not translate longitudinally—there is no effect of reporting greater than usual negative mood or of reporting a stressor on that day's amount or variability in symptoms.

Review Questions

1. Describe the sources of variance found in time-varying predictors, and the corresponding kinds of effects that can be shown for each source of variance.
2. What are some of the problems in using pseudo-R^2 to assess effect size in models with time-varying predictors?
3. Describe the roles of time-varying predictors in models of within-person variation, both in the model for the means and in the model for the variance.
4. Describe the assumption that is made when including a time-varying predictor directly in the level-1 model by itself. What can go wrong when doing so, and what are the two remedies?
5. Describe the difference between the level-2 main and interaction effects obtained under person-mean-centering or under grand-mean-centering of time-varying predictors. What is assumed when each effect level-2 is omitted from its corresponding model?
6. Will grand-mean-centering and person-mean-centering of time-varying predictors always result in equivalent models? When will these two approaches result in nonequivalent models?

References

Enders, C. K. (2010). *Applied missing data analysis*. New York, NY: Guilford Press.

Kreft, I.G.G., de Leeuw, J., & Aiken, L. S. (1995). The effect of different forms of centering in hierarchical linear models. *Multivariate Behavioral Research, 30,* 1–21.

Raudenbush, S. W., & Bryk, A. S. (2002). *Hierarchical linear models: Applications and data analysis methods* (2nd ed.). Thousand Oaks, CA: Sage.

Snijders, T.A.B., & Bosker, R. (2012). *Multilevel analysis* (2nd ed). Thousand Oaks, CA: Sage.

CHAPTER 9

TIME-VARYING PREDICTORS IN MODELS OF WITHIN-PERSON CHANGE

The third section of this text has focused on conditional models: chapter 7 featured time-invariant predictors collected at a single occasion, whereas chapter 8 featured time-varying predictors collected at the same (or similar) occasions as the outcomes. More specifically, the models that were presented in chapter 8 are best-suited for longitudinal studies in which both the predictors and outcomes show only within-person *fluctuation* over time. In contrast, the models in chapter 9 focus on time-varying predictors that show within-person *change* over time. Furthermore, although the example outcome in this chapter shows within-person change, the models in this chapter will still be relevant for outcomes that only show fluctuation over time instead.

This chapter will describe two strategies for examining the relationships between time-varying predictors and time-varying outcomes, which can be organized loosely as *univariate* versus *multivariate* approaches. **Univariate longitudinal modeling** with time-varying predictors that change over time will be presented first, in which the term "univariate" indicates that the model predicts a *single* longitudinal outcome from level-2 (time-invariant) and level-1 (time-varying) predictors. Many of the issues discussed in chapter 8 for time-varying predictors that fluctuate over time will still be relevant—although with some new twists, as described below.

Of greatest relevance here is that, just as in all of the univariate longitudinal models in the text so far, no *predictor* variables are part of the model log-likelihood function. As presented in chapter 5, the log-likelihood function contains the variance components (i.e., that build the **V** matrix) and predicted values only for the time-varying *outcome*. In contrast, the second section of the chapter describes **multivariate longitudinal modeling**, in which the time-varying predictor is formally specified as another outcome also included in the model log-likelihood. As a result, the variance components needed to build the **V** matrix for the "predictor" (e.g., its own random intercept, random slope, and residual variances) are estimated along with those of the "outcome." The benefit of a simultaneous estimation of longitudinal models for multiple variables is that their relationships at each level of the model can be estimated directly, as we'll see later.

Multivariate longitudinal models are conceptually very similar to univariate models, but specifying and estimating them can be more challenging. Consequently, the chapter example begins with univariate longitudinal models and then follows with multivariate longitudinal models for the same data. Multivariate longitudinal models can be estimated by "tricking" software for univariate longitudinal models (e.g., SPSS, SAS, or STATA MIXED), although such models are inherently less flexible given restrictions in the software. So, we will also examine how to estimate multivariate longitudinal models within "truly" multivariate software, as well as the extent to which comparable model parameters could be estimated using univariate models. The third section of the chapter then presents the pros and cons of univariate and multivariate approaches to time-varying predictors, as well how these issues relate to longitudinal mediation. Finally, the chapter concludes with a summary and results sections for the example models.

1. Univariate Modeling With Predictors That Show Within-Person Change Over Time

The example for this chapter began in chapter 7, in which seven (approximately annual) assessments were collected from 200 adolescent girls age 12 to 18 ($M = 15.00$, $SD = 2.00$, range = 11.53 to 18.34 years; 1,400 total observations). The outcome variable was a sum of 10 items indexing frequency of risky behavior (e.g., smoking, drinking, shoplifting, skipping school), in which each item response ranged from 1 to 5 (for a possible range of 10 to 50; $M = 19.38$, $SD = 5.30$, observed range 10.00 to 36.28). Maximum likelihood (ML) estimation will be again used instead of restricted maximum likelihood (REML) given our need to compare the $-2LL$, AIC, and BIC of models differing in fixed effects, which is only possible in ML. Accordingly, the significance of a set of multiple fixed effects or random effects variances and covariances will be tested by $-2\Delta LL$ tests with degrees of freedom equal to the number of added parameters, and the significance of individual fixed effects will be tested by their Wald test p-values.

Previously, we found that 39% of the variation in the risky behavior outcome was due to between-person mean differences (e.g., an ICC = .39 from an empty means, random intercept model), and that the best unconditional model included fixed quadratic and random linear effects of age. The overall pattern of change was an increase in risky behavior that accelerated across age, but in which girls differed from each other in only two ways: intercept and linear age slope (i.e., two kinds of between-person variance, or two kinds of person dependency to be represented by level-2 random effects). We then examined the effect of a time-invariant predictor (collected at the age 12 occasion) for mothers' attitudes about smoking and drinking, in which higher values indicated more conservative attitudes ($M = 3.95$, $SD = 0.60$, observed range = 2.44 to 5.00). We found that mothers' attitudes (centered such that 0 = 4) had a significant simple main effect at age 18 and a significant interaction with linear age, such that daughters whose mothers had more conservative attitudes (as measured at age 12) had lower risky behavior at age 18 and increased in risky behavior at a slower rate from age 12 to 18. These effects accounted for 17% of the intercept variance and 17% of the linear age slope variance, respectively, for a total model R^2 = .24 (as calculated from the square of the Pearson correlation between the original risky behavior outcome and the outcome predicted by the fixed effects of age and mothers' attitudes). The nonsignificant interaction of mothers' attitudes by quadratic age accounted for < 1% of the residual variance (given that the quadratic age slope it would have explained was not random).

We now turn to examine how girls' risky behavior might be predicted by mothers' monitoring behavior, as collected at the same occasions. Monitoring was measured as the mean across 10 items on a 1 to 5 scale, in which higher values indicated that mothers reported greater frequency of monitoring behaviors (M = 3.08, SD = 0.65, observed range = 1.00 to 5.00). Its ICC = .69 as calculated from the results of an empty means, random intercept model, indicating that 69% of the monitoring variance was due to between-person mean differences, which was significantly > 0, $-2\Delta LL(\sim 1)$ = 1,067.8, $p < .001$, relative to an empty means model without the random intercept variance. Although monitoring will be a time-varying predictor, given the developmental context of this study, it will be useful to examine to what extent monitoring itself shows individual change in interpreting its effects predicting risky behavior in the models that follow. More generally, examination of unconditional models of change is *always* recommended for any time-varying variable, regardless of whether it is labeled as a predictor or an outcome.

Accordingly, in fitting unconditional models for change in monitoring as an outcome, monitoring was expected to decrease on average nonsignificantly by −0.003 per year of age (SE = 0.004, p = .502), creating a predicted average of 3.065 by age 18. However, there were significant individual differences in the linear effect of age (i.e., significant random linear age slope variance), $-2\Delta LL(\sim 2)$ = 320.3, $p < .001$, although no fixed or random quadratic age effects were significant. As usual, we can compute 95% random effects confidence intervals as CI = fixed effect ± 1.96*SQRT[random effect variance] to quantify the random intercept and linear age slope variances more intuitively. In doing so, 95% of the sample is expected to have individual intercepts for monitoring at age 18 between 2.20 and 3.93 (as calculated from 3.065 ± 1.96*SQRT[0.195]), as well as individual linear rates of age change between −0.20 and 0.20 (as calculated from −0.003 ± 1.96*SQRT[0.010]). Thus, while on average there is no change with age in monitoring, some mothers are expected to increase while others are expected to decrease.

These results from the random linear age model for monitoring indicate that there are at least two sources of between-person variability that may be relevant in predicting risky behavior: differences in intercept (i.e., level of monitoring at a given age) and differences in the rate of change in monitoring across age. In addition, the residual variance (σ_e^2 = 0.081) indicates that even after allowing each person to have her own intercept and age slope, monitoring at each occasion is not predicted perfectly—it would be off by an expected average of ±SQRT[0.081] per occasion. Thus, these residuals represent yet another way that monitoring could predict risky behavior—through a within-person, time-specific relationship. Therefore, the more general issue to be addressed in this chapter, then, is how do we represent these three sources of variability—intercept, age slope, and residual—in specifying the effects of a given time-varying predictor? Next we consider our options within the most commonly used strategy, in which time-varying monitoring is included as a predictor in a univariate model for risky behavior. To foreshadow, though, we will soon encounter the significant limitations of these univariate approaches when the time-varying predictor itself contains individual differences in change over time.

1.A. Centering Within Univariate Models Including Predictors That Change Over Time

In chapter 8 we saw that even though time-varying predictors may be thought of as level-1 predictors given that they are measured at each occasion, they usually contain both within-person *and* between-person variation. That is, to the extent that some people tend to have higher or lower values than other people on average across time, the effects of time-varying predictors will also need to be represented in the level-2, between-person model. In chapter 8 we did so by calculating the person mean of a time-varying predictor, which is then centered at a constant C so that 0 is meaningful (e.g., $PMx_i = \bar{X}_i - C$). This new person-level predictor was then included in the level-2 equation defining each person's intercept, as well as in the level-2 equations for each person's slopes as needed. The time-varying predictor was then included in the level-1 model using one of two centering methods, as reviewed briefly below.

First, we examined *person-mean-centering*, in which the person mean (PM) is subtracted from the time-varying predictor to create a level-1 predictor with only within-person (WP) variation (e.g., $WPx_{ti} = x_{ti} - \bar{X}_i$). In person-mean-centering, the level-1 WPx_{ti} predictor carries only the within-person effect, whereas the level-2 PMx_i person-mean predictor carries only the between-person effect. The advantage of person-mean-centering lies in its clarity: because each predictor is uncorrelated with the other, their effects are interpreted the same way regardless of whether the predictor at the other level is included—PMx_i at level 2, WPx_{ti} at level 1—or not.

This is not the case in the second centering method we examined, known as *grand-mean-centering*, in which a constant is subtracted from the time-varying (TV) predictor, such that the level-1 predictor still has all of its original within-person and between-person variation (e.g., $TVx_{ti} = x_{ti} - C$). As implied by the name, although the constant is often the grand mean, the same interpretations will apply regardless of which constant is chosen (or if the level-1 predictor is left uncentered). So, in centering the level-1 predictor at a constant—rather than at a variable—the level-1 TVx_{ti} predictor *when included by itself* carries a weighted blend of the within-person and between-person effects, referred to in chapter 8 as the "smushed" (i.e., convergence, conflated) effect. But once the level-2 PMx_i person mean predictor is included, the level-1 TVx_{ti} predictor then carries the within-person effect—because these predictors are correlated, their effects have different interpretations depending on whether the other is in the model. Accordingly, when paired with the level-1 TVx_{ti} predictor, the level-2 PMx_i person mean predictor then carries the *contextual effect,* which can be described as the difference of the between-person and within-person effects, or the between-person effect after controlling for the time-specific original value of the time-varying predictor. Although more common, the disadvantage of using grand-mean-centering for level-1 predictors lies in its greater potential for model-misspecification (i.e., via "smushing") as well as greater difficulty in describing the person contextual effects it provides directly (relative to the between-person effects provided directly by person-mean-centering).

This chapter will also present a third method of centering that may be used in examining the effects of time-varying predictors that show change over time. In **baseline-centering**, the level-2 predictor is *not* created from the person mean. Instead, between-person variation is represented as the time-varying predictor at a specific "baseline" occasion—usually whenever time 0 is (i.e., predictor X at Time 0). The baseline–occasion predictor is then centered at a constant so that 0 is meaningful (e.g., $\text{BaselineX}_i = \text{XatTime0}_i - C$). A level-1 within-baseline (WB) predictor is then created from the difference at each occasion from the original baseline variable (e.g., $\text{WBx}_{ti} = x_{ti} - \text{XatTime0}_i$). So, if the first occasion was time 0, the level-2 BaselineX_i predictor would indicate initial status and the level-1 WBx_{ti} predictor would indicate *change* in the time-varying predictor from time 0. In other words, the level-1 predictor would capture having more or less of the predictor *than you started with* (as given by the level-2 BaselineX_i predictor), rather than more or less of the predictor *than usual* (as would be given by the person mean instead). Alternatively, if the last occasion was time 0 (such as in the chapter example), the level-1 WBx_{ti} predictor would indicate having more or less of the predictor *than you ended up with,* which itself would have been captured by the level-2 predictor for X_i at the last occasion.

Baseline-centering can be advantageous whenever the time 0 value of the time-varying predictor carries specifically useful information, such as in intervention studies in which a treatment is designed to impact both a time-varying predictor and a time-varying outcome. For instance, consider a study in which time 0 is the first occasion and a treatment is designed to improve time-varying parenting skills, which should in turn improve time-varying child outcomes. The effectiveness of the intervention could be indexed as how longitudinal *changes* in parenting skills *during the study* (as measured by the level-1 parenting) predict child outcomes incrementally beyond existing cross-sectional initial differences in parenting skills (as measured by level-2 parenting). In this case, *initial* parenting skills may be a more useful way to index between-person differences than *person mean* parenting skills, because the latter would reflect both existing initial parenting differences and within-person changes in parenting over time.

Returning to our current chapter example, how should we represent the effects of time-varying monitoring, keeping in mind that the monitoring predictor shows individual differences in age change over time? We begin with two univariate models for examining its effects in predicting risky behavior: person-mean-centering and baseline-centering from its age 18 value (i.e., at time 0). But please note the quotes in the titles of the next sections—these foreshadow that distinguishing between- and within-person effects will not be quite as easy as it seems!

1.B. "Between-Person" and "Within-Person" Effects of Predictors That Change Over Time

We continue our previous example by building on the last model from chapter 7, which included fixed effects of quadratic age and mothers' attitudes. Our new univariate longitudinal model to examine the between-person effects of mothers' monitoring on change across age in risky behavior is shown in Equation (9.1):

Level 1: Risky Behavior$_{ti}$ = β_{0i} + β_{1i} (Age$_{ti}$ − 18) + β_{2i} (Age$_{ti}$ − 18)^2 + e$_{ti}$

Level 2: Intercept : β_{0i} = γ_{00} + γ_{01} (Attitudes12$_i$ − 4) + γ_{02} (BPmonitor$_i$ − 3) + U$_{0i}$

Age : β_{1i} = γ_{10} + γ_{11} (Attitudes12$_i$ − 4) + γ_{12} (BPmonitor$_i$ − 3) + U$_{1i}$

Age^2 : β_{2i} = γ_{20} + γ_{22} (BPmonitor$_i$ − 3)

Composite : y$_{ti}$ = $\{\gamma_{00}$ + γ_{01} (Attitudes12$_i$ − 4) + γ_{02} (BPmonitor$_i$ − 3) + U$_{0i}\}$ + $\qquad$ (9.1)

$\{\gamma_{10}$ + γ_{11} (Attitudes12$_i$ − 4) + γ_{12} (BPmonitor$_i$ − 3) + U$_{1i}\}$(Age$_{ti}$ − 18) +

$\{\gamma_{20}$ + γ_{22} (BPmonitor$_i$ − 3) $\}$(Age$_{ti}$ − 18)^2 + e$_{ti}$

in which the level-1 model describes within-person variation in risky behavior via placeholders for the individual intercept (β_0), linear age slope (β_1), and quadratic age slope (β_2), as well as a time-specific residual (e$_{ti}$). In the level-2 model, each girl is predicted to have her own intercept and linear age slope (both conditional at age 18) as a function of a fixed effect (i.e., the intercept and fixed linear age slope for someone with attitudes and between-person (BP) monitoring at their centering constants; γ_{00}, γ_{10}), an increment to the intercept and linear age slope for a one-unit difference in attitudes (γ_{01} and γ_{11}), and an increment to the intercept and linear age slope for a one-unit difference in BP monitoring (γ_{02} and γ_{12}). Given their random effects (U$_{0i}$ and U$_{1i}$) that represent remaining intercept and linear age slope variation after controlling for attitudes and BP monitoring, both the intercept and linear age slope would be called *randomly varying*. However, given that the quadratic age effect (γ_{20} when BP monitoring = 0) differs only by γ_{22} per unit BP monitoring (and not randomly over girls otherwise), it would be called *systematically varying*.

The variable *BPmonitor*$_i$ in the level-2 model is a placeholder for the two different ways of creating this variable we will examine, each of which is centered at 3 to create a meaningful 0 point. Results are shown the first set of columns in Table 9.1 or Table 9.2, when using the person mean of monitoring or the age 18 (baseline) monitoring, respectively, to create the level-2 predictor. In both models, for every additional unit of BP monitoring, the intercept for risky behavior at age 18 is lower by its simple main effect (γ_{02}), the linear age slope at age 18 is more positive by its interaction with age (γ_{12}), and the quadratic age slope is more positive by its interaction with age^2 (γ_{22}). Although different in magnitude, these results generally indicate that girls whose mothers monitor them more closely than other girls (i.e., between persons) are predicted to engage in significantly less risky behavior at age 18, but they also are predicted to have increased in risky behavior at a faster rate with greater acceleration from age 12 to 18. The other way of interpreting the BP monitoring interactions is how its effect changes as a linear and quadratic function of age. As shown by the simple effects in Table 9.1 or Table 9.2, the negative

Table 9.1 Results for the effects of time-varying mothers' monitoring using person-mean-centering in predicting risky behavior. Bold values are $p < .05$.

Model Effects		Equation (9.1)			Equation (9.2)		
		Est	SE	p <	Est	SE	p <
Model for the Means							
γ_{00}	Intercept	**23.49**	0.33	.001	**23.47**	0.34	.001
γ_{10}	Linear Age Slope (0 = 18)	**1.93**	0.15	.001	**1.92**	0.14	.001
γ_{20}	Quadratic Age Slope	**0.14**	0.02	.001	**0.14**	0.02	.001
γ_{01}	Mothers' Attitudes (0 = 4)	**−3.32**	0.51	.001	**−3.30**	0.53	.001
γ_{11}	Attitudes by Linear Age	**−0.52**	0.10	.001	**−0.51**	0.11	.001
γ_{02}	Person Mean Monitoring (0 = 3)	**−2.59**	0.59	.001	**−1.73**	0.62	.006
γ_{12}	Person Mean Monitoring by Age	0.45	0.26	.089	**0.76**	0.26	.004
γ_{22}	Person Mean Monitoring by Age^2	**0.10**	0.04	.009	**0.12**	0.04	.002
γ_{30}	Within-Person Monitoring (0 = PM)				**2.55**	0.61	.001
γ_{40}	Within-Person Monitoring by Age				**−0.95**	0.46	.037
γ_{50}	Within-Person Monitoring by Age^2				**−0.22**	0.07	.004
Simple Effects of Person Mean Monitoring							
	At Age 12	**−1.53**	0.54	.005	**−1.89**	0.58	.001
	At Age 14	**−2.71**	0.43	.001	**−2.81**	0.44	.001
	At Age 16	**−3.07**	0.46	.001	**−2.76**	0.46	.001
	At Age 18	**−2.59**	0.59	.001	**−1.73**	0.62	.006
Model for the Variance							
$\tau^2_{U_0}$	Random Intercept Variance	**15.18**	1.91	.001	**16.58**	2.02	.001
	Pseudo-R^2	.160			−.092		
$\tau^2_{U_1}$	Linear Age Slope Variance	**0.48**	0.08	.001	**0.61**	0.09	.001
	Pseudo-R^2	.018			−.275		
$\tau_{U_{01}}$	Intercept-Linear Age Slope Covariance	1.69	1.72	0.33	**2.13**	0.37	.001
σ^2_e	Residual Variance	**8.30**	0.37	.001	**7.34**	0.33	.001
	Pseudo-R^2	.006			.115		
	Total R^2	.310			.321		
ML Model Fit							
	Number of Parameters	12			15		
	−2LL	7559.6			7460.0		
	AIC	7583.6			7490.0		
	BIC	7623.1			7539.4		

Table 9.2 Results for the effects of time-varying mothers' monitoring using baseline-centering in predicting risky behavior. Bold values are $p < .05$.

Model Effects		Equation (9.1)			Equation (9.2)		
		Est	SE	p <	Est	SE	p <
Model for the Means							
γ_{00}	Intercept	**23.41**	0.34	.001	**23.40**	0.35	.001
γ_{10}	Linear Age Slope (0 = 18)	**1.91**	0.15	.001	**1.94**	0.14	.001
γ_{20}	Quadratic Age Slope	**0.13**	0.02	.001	**0.14**	0.02	.001
γ_{01}	Mothers' Attitudes (0 = 4)	**−3.32**	0.53	.001	**−3.33**	0.54	.001
γ_{11}	Attitudes by Linear Age	**−0.53**	0.10	.001	**−0.54**	0.10	.001
γ_{02}	Age 18 Monitoring (0 = 3)	**−1.79**	0.60	.003	**−1.41**	0.62	.024
γ_{12}	Age 18 Monitoring by Age	**0.66**	0.26	.012	0.34	0.26	.189
γ_{22}	Age 18 Monitoring by Age^2	**0.15**	0.04	.001	**0.09**	0.04	.017
γ_{30}	Change in Monitoring (0 = Age 18)				**4.72**	0.86	.001
γ_{40}	Change in Monitoring by Age				**1.20**	0.47	.011
γ_{50}	Change in Monitoring by Age^2				0.09	0.06	.131
Simple Effects of Age 18 Monitoring							
	At Age 12	−0.16	0.56	.781	−0.11	0.59	.857
	At Age 14	**−1.94**	0.45	.001	**−1.29**	0.49	.009
	At Age 16	**−2.49**	0.47	.001	**−1.72**	0.50	.001
	At Age 18	**−1.79**	0.60	.003	**−1.41**	0.62	.024
Model for the Variance							
$\tau^2_{U_0}$	Random Intercept Variance	**16.17**	2.01	.001	**17.84**	2.16	.001
	Pseudo-R^2	.106			−.104		
$\tau^2_{U_1}$	Linear Age Slope Variance	**0.47**	0.08	.001	**0.52**	0.08	.001
	Pseudo-R^2	.038			−.104		
$\tau_{U_{01}}$	Intercept-Linear Age Slope Covariance	**1.69**	0.33	.001	**1.76**	0.35	.001
σ^2_e	Residual Variance	**8.23**	0.37	.001	**7.47**	0.34	.001
	Pseudo-R^2	.015			.092		
	Total R^2	.275			.240		
ML Model Fit							
	Number of Parameters	12			15		
	−2LL	7567.5			7503.5		
	AIC	7591.5			7533.5		
	BIC	7631.1			7583.0		

effect of BP monitoring initially becomes more negative as age increases, but at a diminishing rate, such that the negative BP effect eventually becomes less negative as age increases.

But why do the effects of the two versions of BP monitoring differ in size? One reason could be differences in scale given that these are unstandardized coefficients. However, the scale of these two BP monitoring variables is very similar (SD = 0.553 for person mean monitoring and SD = 0.556 for age 18 baseline monitoring); furthermore, models estimated using z-scored versions instead show the same pattern: person mean monitoring has a larger effect on the intercept but smaller effects on the linear and quadratic age slopes. Variance explained (i.e., Pseudo-R^2 relative to the previous attitudes-only model from chapter 7) tells the same story, as shown in Table 9.1 or Table 9.2. Contrasting person mean monitoring with age 18 baseline monitoring, the simple main effects explained 16.0% or 10.6% of the intercept variance, the interactions with age explained 1.8% or 3.8% of the linear age slope variance, and the interactions with age^2 explained 0.6% or 1.5% of the residual variance (given that quadratic age did not have a random slope variance that their interactions with age^2 could explain). In terms of total R^2, the models accounted for 31% or 28% of the overall variance in risky behavior. So, what is responsible for these differences? Figure 9.1 may help clarify why it matters whether BP variance in monitoring is indexed by the person mean across age or by the age 18 baseline.

Earlier we found that monitoring showed no significant linear or quadratic change across age on average. The left panel of Figure 9.1 shows example trajectories of change in monitoring that could result from such nonsignificant fixed age slopes—this pattern would imply parallel change. Accordingly, in this situation it shouldn't matter how we chose to index BP differences in monitoring (i.e., differences in the monitoring intercept) because the relative BP differences would be constant across age. But this is not the case in our data—although we found no age change in monitoring *on average*, we found significant *individual* differences in linear age change (i.e., no significant fixed age effects, but significant random age effects). This scenario is depicted in the right panel of Figure 9.1, which shows

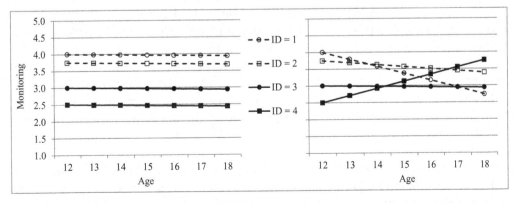

Figure 9.1 Individual trajectories for monitoring across age given a fixed slope (left panel) or a random slope (right panel).

example trajectories that include a random linear age slope. In this case, the non-parallel lines—created when each girl is given her *own* linear age slope—are predicted to eventually cross, such that the girls' relative ordering captured by the BP monitoring predictor will depend on age. Accordingly, it matters *when* we take an age-specific snapshot to index BP differences in monitoring, because those girls who were monitored relatively more at age 12 may not necessarily be monitored relatively more at age 18 or on average across age. In fact, the monitoring at age 12 and age 18 variables are correlated only $r = .52$; correlations with person mean monitoring are $r = .91$ at age 12 and $r = .74$ at age 18.

This idea of rank orders changing over time may sound familiar, because it was originally presented in chapter 5 when random time slopes were introduced. Specifically, we learned that a random intercept initially represents individual differences in outcome level *unconditionally* over time. But once a random time slope is included, the random intercept becomes *conditional*—it then indexes individual intercept differences *at time 0*. So, even though we are considering variation in a predictor rather than in an outcome, the same logic of conditionality must apply: Given the presence of individual differences in change in monitoring across age, the ordering of individual differences in monitoring will also change across age. In these data, it just so happens that the person mean of monitoring is a relatively better predictor of intercept variance in risky behavior at age 18, but monitoring specifically at age 18 better predicts linear and quadratic age change in risky behavior (through linear age slope variance and residual variance, respectively).

Considering how rank orders can change across time may resolve why different versions of BP monitoring could have different effects, but it highlights another complication: What do we mean by "between-person"? As we also learned in chapter 5, any variable that shows individual change has two kinds of BP variance—in intercept and in slope. Variables that show nonlinear patterns of change may have additional kinds of BP variance (e.g., BP quadratic slope variance too, as in chapter 6). But in examining the effects of time-varying predictors thus far, we have treated "between-person" as a single entity instead. This is because we began with time-varying predictors that *fluctuate* over time (i.e., that do not show BP slope differences), and in which only one source of BP variance is present. Accordingly, we used the person mean as a proxy for what would have been the predictor's level-2 random intercept variance if it were an outcome. Similarly, by person-mean-centering a level-1 predictor, we created an observed variable proxy for its level-1 residual variance. The same logic applies for time-varying predictors that show change on average, but that do not show individual differences in change. This is because the fixed effect of a level-1 person-mean-centered predictor will be estimated controlling for the variance of any time predictors in the model, and so we can still think of the level-1 predictor as a proxy for what its level-1 residual variance would be after controlling for fixed effects of time.

But as we will see next, this convention of representing "between-person" as a single entity will no longer be sufficient when time-varying predictors show individual differences in change over time, and in which *multiple* kinds of BP variance are then present. To illustrate the problem, let us examine the corresponding within-person effects for each version of the model. Building from the previous univariate longitudinal model, we will consider two ways of representing the level-1 variance in monitoring. When using person mean monitoring as the BP level-2 predictor, the level-1 predictor called "WP monitoring" will be created as the difference at each occasion from person mean monitoring: $\text{WPmonitor}_{ti} = \text{Monitor}_{ti} - \overline{\text{Monitor}_i}$. Alternatively, when using the age 18 baseline as the BP level-2 predictor, the level-1 predictor called "change in monitoring" will be created as the change at each occasion from monitoring at age 18: $\Delta\text{Monitor}_{ti} = \text{Monitor}_{ti} - \text{Monitor}18_i$. It is important to note that these two versions of the WP predictor are not the same—in fact, they are correlated only $r = .64$ in the stacked data. Furthermore, the predictor for WP deviation from person mean monitoring is completely uncorrelated with both BP predictors, whereas the predictor for WP change in monitoring from age 18 is correlated $r = -.28$ with age 18 monitoring and $r = .27$ with person mean monitoring.

As with BP monitoring, we will include not only the WP monitoring main effect, but also its interactions with linear and quadratic age. Although it might not always make sense to include these age interactions, we do so here given that from a theoretical standpoint, the importance of WP parental monitoring may change across age. For example, at older ages when risky behavior is more prevalent, it may be relatively more important for parents to monitor their children more closely. This idea can be operationalized by interactions of WP monitoring with age and with age^2 that allow the WP effect to differ across ages. Therefore, our univariate longitudinal model to examine the WP effect of monitoring on risky behavior across age is shown in Equation (9.2):

Level 1 : $\text{Risky Behavior}_{ti} = \beta_{0i} + \beta_{1i}(\text{Age}_{ti} - 18) + \beta_{2i}(\text{Age}_{ti} - 18)^2$
$+ \beta_{3i}(\text{Monitor}_{ti} - \text{BPmonitor}_i) + \beta_{4i}(\text{Monitor}_{ti} - \text{BPmonitor}_i)(\text{Age}_{ti} - 18)$
$+ \beta_{5i}(\text{Monitor}_{ti} - \text{BPmonitor}_i)(\text{Age}_{ti} - 18)^2 + e_{ti}$

Level 2 : Intercept : $\beta_{0i} = \gamma_{00} + \gamma_{01}(\text{Attitudes12}_i - 4) + \gamma_{02}(\text{BPmonitor}_i - 3) + U_{0i}$

Age : $\beta_{1i} = \gamma_{10} + \gamma_{11}(\text{Attitudes12}_i - 4) + \gamma_{12}(\text{BPmonitor}_i - 3) + U_{1i}$

Age^2 : $\beta_{2i} = \gamma_{20} \qquad\qquad\qquad\qquad + \gamma_{22}(\text{BPmonitor}_i - 3)$

WP Monitor : $\beta_{3i} = \gamma_{30}$ (9.2)

WP Monitor by Age : $\beta_{4i} = \gamma_{40}$

WP Monitor by Age^2 : $\beta_{5i} = \gamma_{50}$

Composite : $y_{ti} = \{\gamma_{00} + \gamma_{01}(\text{Attitudes12}_i - 4) + \gamma_{02}(\text{BPmonitor}_i - 3) + U_{0i}\} +$
$\{\gamma_{10} + \gamma_{11}(\text{Attitudes12}_i - 4) + \gamma_{12}(\text{BPmonitor}_i - 3) + U_{1i}\}(\text{Age}_{ti} - 18) +$
$\{\gamma_{20} + \gamma_{12}(\text{BPmonitor}_i - 3)\}(\text{Age}_{ti} - 18)^2 +$
$\{\gamma_{30} + \gamma_{40}(\text{Age}_{ti} - 18) + \gamma_{50}(\text{Age}_{ti} - 18)^2\}(\text{Monitor}_{ti} - \text{BPmonitor}_i) + e_{ti}$

in which three β placeholders have been added to the level-1 model. The simple main effect of WP monitoring (β_{3i}) is the effect of monitoring more than the BP baseline (either person mean monitoring or monitoring at age 18, depending on which level-2 effect it is paired with) as evaluated specifically at age 18; the interactions with linear and quadratic age (via β_{4i} and β_{5i}) then describe how the WP monitoring effect differs across age. So far, each β placeholder only has a fixed effect in the level-2 model, although we could also examine random effects for each level-1 predictor (e.g., U_{3i} for each girl to have her own effect of being monitoring relatively more). We could also examine interactions among the attitudes and monitoring predictors, although we forgo these complexities in this example so that we can focus just on interpreting the WP fixed effects for the time-varying monitoring predictors across age.

Results from the model in Equation (9.2) when the WP deviation from the person mean of monitoring is the level-1 predictor are shown the second set of columns in Table 9.1. The WP monitoring simple main effect of γ_{30} = 2.55 is the expected increase in risky behavior at age 18 for every unit greater monitoring than their person mean. In practical terms, this positive WP effect indicates that when girls are monitored more than usual, their risky behavior at age 18 is predicted to be *higher* than expected from the level-2 model (i.e., a positive e_{ti} residual). Furthermore, the WP interactions with linear and quadratic age indicate that although the positive WP effect initially became more positive from ages 12 to 18, it did so at a diminishing rate, such that it eventually became less positive at older ages. For instance, the WP effect was predicted to be 0.49 at age 12, 2.90 at age 14, 3.59 at age 16, and γ_{30} = 2.55 at age 18. The results are shown in Table 9.2 when the WP change from baseline monitoring is the level-1 predictor instead: the WP effect of the expected change in risky behavior for every unit greater monitoring than was observed at age 18 became significantly more positive across age, such that the WP effect was predicted to be 0.83 at age 12, 1.39 at age 14, and 2.69 at age 16, and γ_{30} = 4.72 at age 18.

Both models suggest that the WP effect of monitoring differs across age, but the direction of the WP effect itself is somewhat counterintuitive: More WP monitoring is associated with *greater* occasion-specific risky behavior, not less. Before coming to the conclusion that parental monitoring is a bad idea, though, we should remember that causal ordering cannot be inferred from two variables measured simultaneously. In this case, it may actually work the other way—mothers who observe greater misbehavior in their daughters may become stricter, such that greater monitoring is a consequence of relatively greater risky behavior, not a cause. It is important to remember that, even in longitudinal data, our observational study does not allow us to establish the direction of such effects—we would need a true experiment to do that. Before further considering the substantive interpretations these results may imply, though, it is important to consider in more detail some of the red flags raised by these results and their causes.

1.C. Problems Interpreting "Within-Person" Effects of Predictors That Change Over Time

There are several statistical and interpretational problems inherent in these WP results that all stem from the same problem: What do these WP predictor variables actually measure? To review, our models included an observed BP monitoring predictor variable to serve as a proxy for BP monitoring differences in intercept (either on average across age or specifically at age 18). But because we previously found that monitoring also shows individual differences in change across age, we know that monitoring actually contains two kinds of BP differences—in intercept *and* in age slope. So, although the WP monitoring predictors we created should have been free of BP variance, they aren't—they also still contain at least some of the BP variance in the rate of change in monitoring across age (along with the WP variance we thought we had).

One consequence of the embedded BP age slope variation in the WP predictor is that it creates differential scaling of predictors and their effects across age. To illustrate, let us examine more precisely two patterns that appeared in our results: that WP change in monitoring from age 18 has a bigger effect than WP deviation from person mean monitoring, and that the WP effect changes significantly across age (via their interactions with age and age^2). Given that these fixed effects are unstandardized, they partially reflect the scale of the predictor and outcome variables. So, let us consider the validity of each of these patterns after accounting for differences in scale by standardizing these fixed effects. In single-level models standardized coefficients would be calculated as $\beta_{STD} = \beta {*} SD(X)/SD(Y)$, although fully standardized effects are not used in models with random effects given the ambiguity in what SD(Y) could be. Instead, as introduced in chapter 8, we can calculate *pseudo-standardized estimates* as: $\gamma_{STD} = \gamma {*} SD(X)/SD(Y)$, in which the X and Y variances are those relevant for the level of the fixed effect of interest.

First, in order to more accurately compare the size of the WP effects across predictors, pseudo-standardized estimates can be calculated as: $\gamma_{STD} = \gamma {*} SD(X)/SD(Y)$, in which SD(X) = 0.334 for the WP deviation from person mean monitoring, SD(X) = 0.520 for the WP change from age 18 (baseline) monitoring, and SD(Y) = SQRT(σ_e^2 for risky behavior) from each model. Model-predicted WP effects across age are shown in Figure 9.2 by the solid gray lines: The top panel shows the effects for the WP deviation from person mean monitoring, and the bottom panel shows the effects for the WP change from age 18 monitoring. So, after controlling for the scale of each variable, the effects of change in monitoring from age 18 (bottom panel) are indeed still relatively larger than the effects of WP deviation from person mean monitoring (top panel).

But what about the second pattern, the change in the size of the WP effects across age? Although we have corrected for differences in scale between models using the SD of the predictors in the stacked data, we have not yet considered differences in scale *within models across age*. As we learned in chapter 5 (section 2.D), individual differences in linear change imply a quadratic pattern of changing variance over time—so if monitoring shows individually varying change across age, then its variance must change across age, too. To demonstrate, the SD for the WP monitoring predictor on average across age is shown by the gray dashed line in Figure 9.2, whereas the actual per-occasion SD is shown by the black dashed line. The WP effects re-standardized using these age-specific SDs are given by the solid black line. As shown in the top panel by the difference between the solid gray and solid black lines, after adjusting for the change in the WP predictor's SD across age, the change in the WP effect across age is somewhat mitigated (although both indicate a smaller effect at younger ages). However, the bottom panel shows a bizarre pattern, such that after correcting for changes in the WP predictor's SD across age, the WP effect increases only from age 12 to 17, after which point it actually becomes 0 rather than

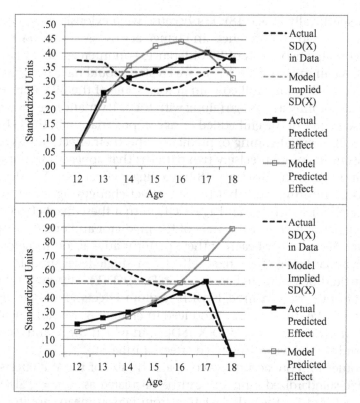

Figure 9.2 Model-predicted and scale-corrected standardized
level-1 effects across age for the within-person
predictor created as the deviation from the
person mean (top panel) or as the change from
the age 18 baseline predictor (bottom panel).

continues to increase as was predicted. This is because the WP predictor for change
in monitoring from age 18 is defined such that *there is no variance at age 18*—all
variance at age 18 was used to form the BP monitoring predictor instead. But the
model doesn't realize this and instead predicts continued acceleration of the WP
effect across age, even at age 18. This creates a problem in interpreting these results,
given that the simple main effect of WP change in monitoring from 18 is logically
impossible *as evaluated at age 18*. Indeed, if age were balanced instead, such that we
could treat age as a categorical variable in an interaction with the WP predictor, its
effect at age 18 could not have been estimated at all (when it was a constant).

We could rephrase the baseline-centered model to omit a WP effect at age 18
to obtain results that made more sense, but there is still a bigger interpretational
issue to be dealt with. That is, we can't be sure which aspect of monitoring is actually behind these WP effects—is it BP age slope differences in monitoring that predicts greater risky behavior, WP monitoring relatively more than expected, or some
amalgam of the two? This ambiguity in interpretation is also shown by the language used in describing the effect of the WP predictor across models. When using
person-mean-centering, describing WP effects as arising from "more monitoring

than usual" implies a residual effect. In contrast, when using baseline-centering at age 18, describing WP effects as arising from "change in monitoring from age 18" seems to imply an age slope effect instead. But without explicitly distinguishing the effects of these two different sources of variance, we can't be sure what the source of this single "WP effect" really is.

This idea that one predictor variable contains two different sources of variance, each of which may have a different effect, should sound familiar—this is the idea of a "smushed effect" from chapter 8 re-appearing in a new context. Previously we saw how adding a constant-centered time-varying predictor to the level-1 model only would result in an effect that was neither its BP effect nor its WP effect, but a weighted blend of the two, referred to as a smushed effect (i.e., a conflated or convergence effect). In this context of time-varying predictors that show individual change, we tried to distinguish (i.e., "unsmush") monitoring's BP variance by including person mean monitoring or age 18 monitoring. But those level-2 predictors could only represent BP intercept variance, not BP age slope variance. Consequently, the level-1 monitoring predictor still contained both BP age slope variance and WP residual variance.

This "smushing" problem may also explain our strange results for explained variance (that so far have gone unmentioned). Given that they are all level-1 effects, adding the WP effect of monitoring and its interactions with age and age^2 to the model should have reduced the residual variance—and it did, by pseudo-$R_e^2 = .115$ for WP monitoring in Table 9.1, and by pseudo-$R_e^2 = .092$ for change in monitoring from age 18 in Table 9.2. However, adding these level-1 effects also *increased* the level-2 random effects variances (i.e., negative pseudo-R^2 values). Although we would expect an increase in level-2 random intercept variance whenever the level-1 residual variance is reduced (see chapter 4), these increases of 9.2% and 10.4% across models would still be 7.7% and 9.5% after taking into account the smaller residual variance correction factor. Furthermore, the random age slope variance inexplicably also increased by 27.5% and 10.4%, and total R^2 for the model (i.e., the square of the correlation between the actual outcome and the outcome predicted by the fixed effects) actually went down upon adding change in monitoring from age 18, from $R^2 = .275$ to .240—this is not ever supposed to happen. So, what's going on?

1.D. Smushed Intercept, Slope, and Residual Effects in Predictors That Change Over Time

There are two main problems with interpreting our "between-person" and "within-person" results for the monitoring time-varying predictor as we have thus far, both stemming from the fact that two predictor variables are not enough to adequately capture three sources of variance. First, the fact that monitoring shows individual differences in change across age means that its relative order across girls (i.e., BP differences in their intercepts) is likely to change over time. This is why we saw that using a different level-2 predictor—person mean monitoring or age 18 monitoring—lead to different results. Second, both person-mean-centering and baseline-centering can be considered observed variable equivalents of a random intercept only model, such that the BP age slope variance would still be embedded in the residual variance, both of which are then contained in the observed WP predictor. So, we don't know whether the level-1 effects from either model are the result of greater changes in monitoring across age (BP age slope differences) or by greater monitoring than usual at that occasion (WP residual variation).

Figure 9.3 illustrates how these three sources of monitoring variance—intercept, age slope, and residual—are allocated into the two observed level-2 and level-1 predictors. First, let us consider the level-2 predictor when using baseline-centering—although the observed variance in monitoring at age 18 is the closest thing to a model-based random intercept variance, it's not exactly the same. This is because the random intercept creates a *predicted* monitoring outcome at age 18 based on the model for *all* of a person's data, not the *actual* value at age 18. As a result, a part of the observed variance in monitoring at age 18 would become residual variance

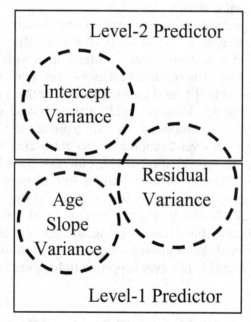

Figure 9.3 Conceptual illustration of variance partitioning when variables that show individual change over time are included as time-varying predictors. Observed predictor variables are shown in solid-line boxes; the random effects and residual variances contained in the original variable are shown in dashed-line circles.

instead. So, the level-2 predictor's effect will be a weighted blend of the intercept and residual effects, such that the "pure" intercept effect will not be adequately captured. In this case, although the level-2 effect was significantly negative as expected from the negative relationship between the random intercepts, it would have been positively biased by the positive residual relationship. Using person mean monitoring instead as a proxy for intercept differences appeared to work better, in that its effect was more negative, and thus closer to the actual intercept effect. In general the person mean should be a more reliable index of intercept differences (albeit on average across age rather than at a specific age) given that it is based on all of a person's data. However, the person mean is still treated as a perfectly reliable predictor, even though there may be differences in how variably girls are monitored across age. The observed person mean variable ignores these differences, whereas a model-estimated random intercept variance would take this into account.

Second, let us consider the level-1 predictor from either model—because it was more heavily composed of WP residual variance than BP age slope variance, the level-1 effect was much closer to the positive residual effect, and the residual variance did decrease as expected. However, the single level-1 effect assumed the same *positive* effect for both residual and age slope variance, whereas in reality the age slope effect was significantly *negative*. Unfortunately, there was nothing in the model to explicitly represent monitoring age slope differences to counter this misspecification, resulting in an increase in the risky behavior random slope variance.

The pattern of effects in these example data is somewhat unusual, in that the level-2 effects for the intercept and slope were of opposite sign from the level-1 residual effect. What would have happened if these effects were in the same direction instead—would we have known there was a problem? To provide an empirical answer to this question, consider the results of a small simulation study, in which two variables over seven occasions were each constructed from a fixed intercept = 50, a random intercept $\sim N(0, 75)$, and a residual $\sim N(0, 25)$. The time-varying outcome had a fixed age slope of 2 and a random age slope $\sim N(0, 2)$, whereas similar to our example, the time-varying predictor had a fixed age slope = 0 and a random age slope $\sim N(0, 2)$. A total of 75 conditions were created by fully crossing intercept correlations (−.4, −.2, 0, .2, .4), slope correlations (−.4, −.2, 0, .2, .4), and residual correlations (−.2, 0, .2). A series of univariate models were estimated for each of the 100 replications of each multivariate dataset using person-mean-centering or baseline-centering to examine the impact of representing these three distinct types of time-varying predictor effects using only two observed predictor variables.

Simulation results for changes in the outcome's random effects variances across models are shown in Figure 9.4, in which the solid or dashed lines show the results from the baseline-centered or person-mean-centered models, respectively. The top panel displays the decrease in the random intercept variance from fitting both level-2 and level-1 effects of the time-varying predictor (note that although the decrease in the random intercept variance is actually caused by the level-2 effect, the total change after also including the level-1 effect was plotted given that explaining residual variance will cause the random intercept variance to increase). As expected, a larger amount of random intercept variance was explained in the conditions with

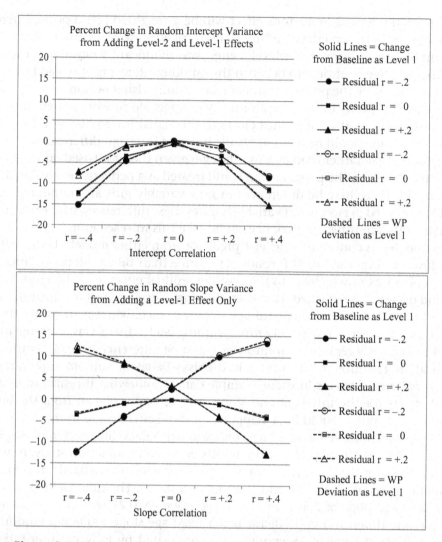

Figure 9.4 Changes in level-2 variance components from fitting univariate models to simulated data with varying intercept, slope, and residual correlation of a time-varying predictor and outcome.

stronger intercept correlations, but these decreases in random intercept variance were even larger when the residual correlation was in the same direction as the intercept correlation. For instance, an intercept $r = .4$ resulted in an ~8% decrease if the residual $r = -.2$, but a decrease of ~11% or ~15% if the residual $r = 0$ or $r = .2$. The reason for these differences in explained random intercept variance is that neither level-2 predictor represents only random intercept variance as intended—they also include residual variance, as discussed previously. Consequently, their observed effects are due not only to an intercept effect, but also partly to a residual effect as well.

The bottom panel of Figure 9.4 displays the results for changes in the estimated random slope variance after adding the level-1 time-varying predictor effect (after the corresponding level-2 effect was already included). As shown, when the random slope and residual correlations were in the same direction, the estimated random slope variance was lower, but when they were in opposite directions, the random slope variance was greater instead. Both of these patterns were exacerbated by stronger slope correlations. So, although these level-1 effects primarily reflected the residual effect, the concomitant changes in the estimated random slope variance demonstrate that a slope effect is also implicitly assumed by the level-1 effect. To the extent that this assumed slope effect is incorrect, the outcome's random slope variance will increase as a result.

These simulation results illustrate the rationale behind a more general recommendation: When a time-varying predictor contains random slope variance (i.e., due to individual differences in change over time or in the effect of another time-varying predictor), person-mean-centering, baseline-centering, or grand-mean-centering the level-1 predictor will result in an incomplete partitioning of between-person from within-person variance and cannot be recommended.

1.E. Two-Stage Univariate Models for Predictors That Change Over Time

So now what? Can a univariate model ever be made suitable for time-varying predictors that show individual differences in change over time? The fundamental problem in our univariate models so far has been the confounding of individual intercepts, age slopes, and residuals in our two observed predictors. Perhaps we can solve this problem by using three observed predictors instead of two to explicitly distinguish these three sources of variance. This strategy has been suggested by Curran and Bauer (2011), who provided an example in which they used individual regression models to create observed variables of intercept, age slope, and time-varying residual for a longitudinal predictor. The intercept and residual variables were then included as observed predictors in a longitudinal model in order to estimate the predictor's between- and within-person effects, respectively. The estimated effects were indeed comparable to the correct effects in their simulated data so long as the time range sampled was balanced across individuals (i.e., a non-accelerated longitudinal design; see chapter 10 in this text for more on that topic). However, their simulated data example did not address the situation in which the individual age slopes also had a unique relationship in predicting the time-varying outcome (i.e., the individual slopes were not included as a predictor in their model given that the simulated data did not include a slope predictive effect), so it is unclear whether this strategy may help remedy our current problem.

A two-stage approach of estimating individual intercepts, slopes, and residuals for use in subsequent models has an intuitive appeal, given that it should partition the variance in a time-varying predictor more accurately than did our inadequate (but also two-stage) approaches of person-mean-centering or baseline-centering. Unfortunately, two-stage estimation procedures (historically known as *slopes-as-outcomes* in this context) are statistically inefficient and are generally not recommended. Instead, models with random effects that partition multiple sources of variance and simultaneously allow for the direct prediction of each variance are almost always preferable. So, for now, we continue with multivariate longitudinal models, which will provide a model-based representation of the sources of varying in a predictor that shows change over time. Later in the chapter we will examine to what extent a two-stage, slopes-as-outcomes univariate model can provide comparable results to these simultaneous, model-based alternatives.

2. Multivariate Longitudinal Modeling of Predictors That Change Over Time

In *multivariate longitudinal modeling* the time-varying predictor is specified as another outcome, such that it also becomes part of the model log-likelihood. It would thus have whatever distributional assumptions are inherent in the log-likelihood formula—in this case, we would be assuming multivariate normality for both monitoring and risky behavior giving the likelihood function being used. In this section we will see two different ways of estimating these models.

2.A. Multivariate Longitudinal Modeling Using Univariate Longitudinal Software

In our first multivariate model, monitoring and risky behavior will each be modeled as longitudinal outcomes simultaneously by "tricking" univariate longitudinal software into thinking it is fitting a three-level model for outcomes within occasions within persons. For simplicity we will restrict our example to just the two variables of interest in this example; this approach can be generalized to more than two outcome variables if needed.

Our first task is to restructure our data from their original stacked format, in which each row was for one occasion for one person, into a "double-stacked" format, as illustrated in Table 9.3 for the first two persons in our example data. Syntax to conduct this data restructuring can be found in the electronic materials online. In this new "double-stacked" format, each row contains the data for *one outcome* at one occasion for one person. For example, each person now has 2 outcomes*7 occasions = 14 rows. As before, time-invariant variables (e.g., Person ID or Age 12 Attitudes) are copied across all rows *for that person*. Similarly, time-specific variables (e.g., age, monitoring, and risky behavior) are copied across all rows *for that occasion* (e.g., the variables' values are the same on rows 1 and 8, on rows 2 and 9, and so forth). The critical distinction is that both variables to be analyzed as outcomes *now reside in a single new column*. In this new Outcome column in Table 9.3, each person's first seven rows contain values for risky behavior, whereas the next seven rows contain values for monitoring. Accordingly, we also need an indicator variable to keep track of which outcome is which—this is the purpose of the string-variable *DV* column. Finally, two additional dummy-coded variables have been created, in

Table 9.3 Illustration of data structure for fitting multivariate models within univariate software.

Person ID	Age 12 Attitudes (4 = 0)	Occasion	Age (18 = 0)	Monitoring	Risky Behavior	DV	dvR	dvM	Outcome
1	1	12	−6.30	2.69	27.37	1R	1	0	27.37
1	1	13	−4.78	2.60	26.71	1R	1	0	26.71
1	1	14	−3.96	2.46	25.01	1R	1	0	25.01
1	1	15	−2.70	2.84	22.33	1R	1	0	22.33
1	1	16	−2.14	2.63	22.94	1R	1	0	22.94
1	1	17	−0.95	2.50	22.38	1R	1	0	22.38
1	1	18	−0.08	3.04	22.19	1R	1	0	22.19
1	1	12	−6.30	2.69	27.37	2M	0	1	2.69
1	1	13	−4.78	2.60	26.71	2M	0	1	2.60
1	1	14	−3.96	2.46	25.01	2M	0	1	2.46
1	1	15	−2.70	2.84	22.33	2M	0	1	2.84
1	1	16	−2.14	2.63	22.94	2M	0	1	2.63
1	1	17	−0.95	2.50	22.38	2M	0	1	2.50
1	1	18	−0.08	3.04	22.19	2M	0	1	3.04
2	−0.95	12	−6.11	3.82	15.04	1R	1	0	15.04
2	−0.95	13	−5.25	4.56	17.71	1R	1	0	17.71
2	−0.95	14	−4.13	3.76	13.87	1R	1	0	13.87
2	−0.95	15	−3.09	4.12	17.52	1R	1	0	17.52
2	−0.95	16	−2.22	3.72	21.02	1R	1	0	21.02
2	−0.95	17	−1.23	3.07	19.84	1R	1	0	19.84
2	−0.95	18	−0.02	3.98	30.04	1R	1	0	30.04
2	−0.95	12	−6.11	3.82	15.04	2M	0	1	3.82
2	−0.95	13	−5.25	4.56	17.71	2M	0	1	4.56
2	−0.95	14	−4.13	3.76	13.87	2M	0	1	3.76
2	−0.95	15	−3.09	4.12	17.52	2M	0	1	4.12
2	−0.95	16	−2.22	3.72	21.02	2M	0	1	3.72
2	−0.95	17	−1.23	3.07	19.84	2M	0	1	3.07
2	−0.95	18	−0.02	3.98	30.04	2M	0	1	3.98

which $dvR = 1$ and $dvM = 0$ for the risky behavior values, and in which $dvR = 0$ and $dvM = 1$ for the monitoring values. Although these variables may seem redundant with the DV column, all three of these variables will be used in different places in the syntax that estimates our new multivariate model.

Multivariate longitudinal models are too frequently presented using highly convoluted notation with multiple embedded summations in order to permit a general model representation. I will eschew this unnecessary complexity and instead present a more transparent version of a **multivariate longitudinal model** for risky behavior and monitoring, as shown in Equation (9.3):

Level 1:

$$y_{tid} = dvR\left[\beta_{0iR} + \beta_{1iR}\left(Age_{tiR} - 18\right) + \beta_{2iR}\left(Age_{tiR} - 18\right)^2 + e_{tiR}\right] +$$
$$dvM\left[\beta_{0iM} + \beta_{1iM}\left(Age_{tiM} - 18\right) \qquad\qquad + e_{tiM}\right]$$

Level 2:

Risky Intercept: $\qquad \beta_{0iR} = \gamma_{00R} + \gamma_{01R}\left(Attitudes12_i - 4\right) + U_{0iR}$

Risky Age: $\qquad\qquad \beta_{1iR} = \gamma_{10R} + \gamma_{11R}\left(Attitudes12_i - 4\right) + U_{1iR}$

Risky Age^2: $\qquad\quad \beta_{2iR} = \gamma_{20R}$

Monitor Intercept: $\;\; \beta_{0iM} = \gamma_{00M} + U_{0iM}$ $\qquad\qquad\qquad\qquad\qquad\qquad$ (9.3)

Monitor Age: $\qquad\; \beta_{1iM} = \gamma_{10M} + U_{1iM}$

Composite:

$$y_{tid} = dvR\left\{\gamma_{00R} + \gamma_{01R}\left(Attitudes12_i - 4\right) + U_{0iR} + e_{tiR}\right\} +$$
$$dvR\left\{\gamma_{10R} + \gamma_{11R}\left(Attitudes12_i - 4\right) + U_{1iR}\right\}\left(Age_{tiR} - 18\right) +$$
$$dvR\left\{\gamma_{20R}\right\}\left(Age_{tiR} - 18\right)^2 +$$
$$dvM\left\{\gamma_{00M} + U_{0iM} + e_{tiM}\right\} +$$
$$dvM\left\{\gamma_{10M} + U_{1iM}\right\}\left(Age_{tiM} - 18\right)$$

in which y_{tid} is the new single column outcome at time t for individual i for dependent variable d (in which R = risky behavior and M = monitoring). Based on our previous univariate results for each variable as an outcome, risky behavior is predicted by a fixed quadratic, random linear effect of age, but monitoring is predicted by only a random linear effect of age. In general, it is recommended to examine univariate models for each outcome first to guide the form of the multivariate model, given how much extra estimation time multivariate models may require. In addition, the intercept and age slope for risky behavior is also predicted by mothers' attitudes about smoking and drinking. Although effects of mothers' attitudes were also initially included for the monitoring intercept and linear age slope as well, both were nonsignificant and were thus removed. Results for the multivariate longitudinal model are shown in Table 9.4.

Table 9.4 also lists the fixed (and random) effects that would be specified in the software program for this multivariate longitudinal model and how they correspond to the fixed effects in Equation (9.3). The global fixed intercept typically estimated by default must be removed (e.g., via NOINT in SAS/SPSS MIXED or NOCONSTANT in STATA). The key to understanding how to interpret the parameters in this model lies in role of the *dvR* and *dvM* dummy codes. In the absence of a global fixed intercept, the main effects of *dvR* and *dvM* will become the fixed intercepts for risky behavior and monitoring, respectively. And although the other effects then look like interaction terms, they aren't—instead, the *dvR* and *dvM* indicator variables act

Table 9.4 Model fit and results for the model for the means when using univariate software to estimate multivariate longitudinal models. Bold values are $p < .05$.

Model Effects		Predictor Variables	Equation (9.3) and (9.4)			
			Est	SE	p <	STD
Risky Behavior Model for the Means						
γ_{00R}	Intercept	dvR	**23.31**	0.35	.001	
γ_{10R}	Linear Age Slope (0 = 18)	dvR*age	**1.97**	0.14	.001	
γ_{20R}	Quadratic Age Slope	dvR*age*age	**0.15**	0.02	.001	
γ_{01R}	Mothers' Attitudes (0 = 4)	dvR*att	**−3.33**	0.51	.001	
γ_{11R}	Attitudes by Linear Age	dvR*att*age	**−0.53**	0.10	.001	
Monitoring Model for the Means						
γ_{00M}	Intercept	dvM	**3.07**	0.03	.001	
γ_{10M}	Linear Age Slope (0 = 18)	dvM*age	0.00	0.01	.688	
Risky Behavior Model for the Variance						
$\tau^2_{U_{0R}}$	Random Intercept Variance	dvR	**18.06**	2.20	.001	
$\tau^2_{U_{1R}}$	Linear Age Slope Variance	dvR*age	**0.49**	0.08	.001	
$\tau_{U_{0R,1R}}$	Intercept-Age Slope Covariance		**1.88**	0.36	.001	.63
σ^2_{eR}	Residual Variance		**8.35**	0.37	.001	
Monitoring Model for the Variance						
$\tau^2_{U_{0M}}$	Random Intercept Variance	dvM	**0.20**	0.02	.001	
$\tau^2_{U_{1M}}$	Linear Age Slope Variance	dvM*age	**0.01**	0.00	.001	
$\tau_{U_{0M,1M}}$	Intercept-Age Slope Covariance		−0.00	0.00	.916	−.01
σ^2_{eM}	Residual Variance		**0.08**	0.00	.001	
Cross-Variable Covariances						
$\tau_{U_{0R,0M}}$	Random Intercepts		**−0.86**	0.17	.001	−.46
$\tau_{U_{1R,1M}}$	Random Linear Age Slopes		**−0.02**	0.01	.013	−.25
$\sigma_{eR,eM}$	Residuals		**0.29**	0.03	.001	.35
$\tau_{U_{1R,0M}}$	Monitoring Intercept, Risky Behavior Age Slope		**−0.11**	0.03	.001	−.35
$\tau_{U_{0R,1M}}$	Monitoring Age Slope, Risky Behavior Intercept		0.04	0.04	.294	.09
ML Model Fit						
	Number of Parameters		20			
	−2LL		8784.5			
	AIC		8824.5			
	BIC		8890.5			

like switches that determine which effects actually get used to predict each outcome (otherwise known as a nested effect). Only the terms with an R (predicting risky behavior) are multiplied by dvR; likewise, only the terms with an M (predicting monitoring) are multiplied by dvM. So, for a row in which $dvR = 1$, the terms with an R subscript are "switched on" to predict that *risky behavior* outcome, but the terms with an M subscript are "switched off" by $dvR = 0$. Similarly, for a row in which $dvM = 1$, the terms with an M subscript are "switched on" to predict that *monitoring* outcome, but the terms with an R subscript are "switched off" by $dvM = 0$. So, in terms of the syntax, there are no "main effects" in this model—all predictor effects are explicitly tied to one outcome or the other via their "interaction" with dvR or dvM, as shown in Table 9.4.

However, after considering the role of the dvR and dvM switching terms, all parameters can be interpreted the same as in a univariate two-level model—the level-1 β placeholders hold the individual intercepts and slopes, each of which is defined by a level-2 model with γ fixed effects and U_i random effects. As noted earlier, this multivariate two-level model is sometimes described as a three-level model for outcome within occasion within person. However, there is no residual at the outcome level 1—given the values of the dvR and dvM predictors, there can be no error with respect to which outcome is being predicted. So, this is still a two-level model, given that it still has only two orthogonal sets of variance components related to time and to persons.

Turning to Table 9.4, as you might have guessed, the results are nearly identical to what we would have obtained through separate univariate longitudinal models. Given that the same data are used in separate univariate longitudinal models as in a joint multivariate longitudinal model, this will generally be the case. So, why bother? In general, there are two types of research questions that are best answered using multivariate models. One question concerns differences in effect size across outcomes—for instance, is the age slope greater in one outcome than in another? A description of how to use multivariate longitudinal models to answer this type of question will be given in chapter 11 in the context of dyadic or family data (in which the multivariate outcomes would be the responses to the same variable from multiple family members over time). For now, we turn to the other type of question answered by multivariate longitudinal models—about the relationships between outcomes at each level of analysis.

2.B. Between-Person and Within-Person Covariances Across Longitudinal Outcomes

Given that there are three piles of variance for each outcome—random intercept, random linear age slope, and residual—there are three ways that monitoring and risky behavior could relate to each other. To make this discussion more concrete, the **G** and **R** matrices for the unconditional multivariate longitudinal model from Equation (9.3) are shown in Equation (9.4):

$$
G = \begin{array}{l}
\\
\text{Risky Random Intercept} \\
\text{Monitor Random Intercept} \\
\text{Risky Random Age Slope} \\
\text{Monitor Random Age Slope}
\end{array}
\overset{\text{Int-R \quad Int-M \quad Age-R \quad Age-M}}{
\begin{bmatrix}
\tau^2_{U_{0R}} & \tau_{U_{0R,0M}} & \tau_{U_{0R,1R}} & \tau_{U_{0R,1M}} \\
\tau_{U_{0M,0R}} & \tau^2_{U_{0M}} & \tau_{U_{0M,1R}} & \tau_{U_{0M,1M}} \\
\tau_{U_{1R,0R}} & \tau_{U_{1R,0M}} & \tau^2_{U_{1R}} & \tau_{U_{1R,1M}} \\
\tau_{U_{1M,0R}} & \tau_{U_{1M,0M}} & \tau_{U_{1M,1R}} & \tau^2_{U_{1M}}
\end{bmatrix}}
\quad (9.4)
$$

$$
R = \begin{array}{l}
\\
\text{Risky Residual} \\
\text{Monitor Residual}
\end{array}
\overset{\text{Res-R \quad Res-M}}{
\begin{bmatrix}
\sigma^2_{eR} & \sigma_{eR,eM} \\
\sigma_{eM,eR} & \sigma^2_{eM}
\end{bmatrix}}
$$

the estimates for which are listed in Table 9.4. Given the two outcomes, **G** is a 4x4 matrix that holds the variances and covariances for the level-2 random intercepts and random age slopes for each outcome. As with the fixed effects, a global random intercept variance would not be estimated; instead, outcome-specific random effects variances would be specified using the same *dvR* and *dvM* indicators (e.g., the random effects would be *dvR, dvM, dvR*age,* and *dvM*age*).

Previously, **R** was defined as an *nxn* matrix of *n* occasions within persons; given 2 outcomes and 7 occasions, **R** here would be a 14x14 matrix per person instead. Fortunately, we can simplify **R** because this model assumes that each outcome has equal residual variance and no residual covariance across occasions within a person. Accordingly, the first 7 diagonal elements in the 14x14 within-person **R** matrix would be the residual variance for risky behavior (σ^2_{eR}) with 0's in the off-diagonals, and the next 7 diagonal elements would be the residual variance for monitoring (σ^2_{eM}), again with 0's in the off-diagonals. So, because **R** really only holds two unique elements (σ^2_{eR} and σ^2_{eM}), for simplicity we can just consider the **R** matrix *within occasions and persons*, resulting in a 2x2 version of the **R** matrix for *outcomes × outcomes* in Equation (9.4).

Let us now examine what these **G** and **R** matrices tell us about the different ways in which risky behavior relates to monitoring. To begin, the level-2 random effects variances in the **G** matrix represent individual differences, and so the covariances in the **G** matrix quantify between-person relationships. As before, the **G** matrix includes covariances of random effects within the same outcome, such as between the outcome's random intercept and linear age slope (e.g., $\tau_{U_{0R,1R}}$ in row 3, column 1 for risky behavior; $\tau_{U_{0M,1M}}$ in row 4, column 2 for monitoring). But more importantly, the **G** matrix also contains the covariances for the random effects *across* outcomes; likewise, the **R** matrix contains the covariance of the age-specific residuals across outcomes. These cross-variable covariances are the primary reason to conduct this multivariate analysis. However, to interpret them more easily, these covariances can be converted into correlations, as also reported in Table 9.4. Unfortunately, not all programs will report a standard error and *p*-value for correlations calculated from the **G** or **R** matrices. But most will provide a *p*-value for the Wald test for the covariances, which can be used to judge their significance given that covariances can be negative or positive (unlike variances, which can only be negative).

Turning to our results, $\tau_{U_{0R,0M}}$ in row 1, column 2 of the **G** matrix is the covariance between the random intercepts, which can be converted into an intercept correlation as: $(\tau_{U_{0R,0M}}) / [SQRT(\tau_{U_{0R}}^2)*SQRT(\tau_{U_{0M}}^2)] = (-0.86) / [SQRT(18.06)*SQRT(0.20)] =$ $-.46$. Likewise, $\tau_{U_{1R,1M}}$ in row 3, column 4 of the **G** matrix is the covariance between the random linear age slopes, which can be converted into an age slope correlation as: $(\tau_{U_{1R,1M}}) / [SQRT(\tau_{U_{1R}}^2)*SQRT(\tau_{U_{1M}}^2)] = (-0.02) / [SQRT(0.49)*SQRT(.01)] = -.25$. Finally, row 1, column 2 of the **R** matrix predicts a constant covariance between residuals from different outcomes at the same occasion, which can be converted into a residual correlation as: $(\sigma_{eR,eM}) / [SQRT(\sigma_{eR}^2)*SQRT(\sigma_{eM}^2)] = (0.29) / [SQRT(8.35)*SQRT(0.08)] =$ $.35$. Now let us interpret each correlation more specifically.

First, in the presence of a random linear age slope for each outcome, each random intercept is conditional on age 18. So, the random intercept correlation $r = -.46$ indicates that girls who are monitored *more* than other girls at age 18 are predicted to report *lower* risky behavior than other girls at age 18. However, in re-estimating the model with time 0 at different ages, the same pattern was observed (e.g., an intercept correlation $r = -.46$ at age 15, $r = -.45$ at age 12). Second, because there is no random quadratic age slope for either outcome, the random linear age slopes are not conditional on age. So, the random linear age slope correlation $r = -.25$ indicates that girls whose mothers increase their monitoring across age *more* than other girls are predicted to increase across age in risky behavior *less* than other girls. The key phrase for both correlations is *more or less than other girls*—these are level-2, between-person relationships.

Although relationships among intercepts and slopes are often of primary focus when examining if two variables are related "over time," they may not tell the full story. The residual correlation from the **R** matrix describes another type of relationship—a within-person, level-1 relationship for how age-specific deviations from the individually predicted trajectories are related across outcomes. In our example, the residual correlation $r = .35$ means that at any age when a girl is monitored *more* than was predicted, her risky behavior is expected to be *greater* than was predicted at that age. They key phrase here is *more/less than predicted*—after controlling for individual change in each variable, a positive residual correlation indicates that the time-specific deviations from the predicted trajectory for each variable are likely to go in the same direction. Such within-person residual relationships are sometimes described as how two variables "travel together" over time (or more specifically, the time-specific leftover parts of the variables "travel together" after controlling for everything in the model, as usual).

To recap, so far in the chapter we've seen how including a time-varying predictor in a univariate model results in an incomplete distinction of its intercept, age slope, and residual variance. We've now examined one model-based solution to this problem—a multivariate model in which all sources of variance for the time-varying outcome and for the time-varying predictor are properly modeled, which can be estimated by "tricking" univariate longitudinal software. In estimating this model, we have found negative relationships between the intercepts and between the age slopes for monitoring and risky behavior but a positive relationship between their age-specific residuals. Unfortunately, in univariate software all of the relationships between the time-varying predictor and outcome are expressed as covariances. Consequently, it is somewhere between difficult and impossible to implement certain model extensions that would otherwise be readily available in a univariate model, such as random effects of within-person relationships or moderator effects. Fortunately, these are software limitations only. We continue by examining multivariate models using **truly multivariate software**—which is distinguished by its capacity to allow variables to serve as both predictors and outcomes simultaneously. In this example, monitoring and risky behavior are both outcomes with respect to age, but monitoring also predicts risky behavior. So, even though monitoring should be a predictor and an outcome simultaneously, our models so far have only managed one or the other. That is, we examined change across age in monitoring *as an outcome only* in univariate models, monitoring *as a predictor only* of risky behavior in univariate models, and how monitoring and risky behavior *as outcomes only* covary between persons and within persons. Truly multivariate software will allow us to put all of these models together and offer greater flexibility in doing so.

2.C. Multivariate Longitudinal Models in Truly Multivariate Software

First, a note about terminology—truly multivariate models and their dedicated software are often regarded as synonymous with structural equation modeling (SEM). However, the more specific purpose of SEM is to construct measurement models in which **latent variables** are used to represent the covariance among observed variables thought to measure the same construct. Relationships are then specified amongst the latent variables (which can be predictors and outcomes simultaneously, such as when examining mediation). In this text, we've been using the term **random effect** to convey the same basic idea—an unobserved entity whose purpose is to represent covariance among observed variables (i.e., outcomes over time in our context). Statistically speaking, latent variables and random effects are indeed the same thing—that means that multilevel models could also be written as structural equation models (for elaboration see Bauer, 2003; Curran, 2003). Furthermore, once estimated within truly multivariate software, longitudinal multivariate models in which variables can serve as both predictors and outcomes simultaneously are sometimes called **multilevel structural equation models** (MSEM; e.g., Preacher, Zyphur, & Zhang, 2010; see also Lüdtke et al., 2008 for related terminology).

In practice, the semantic distinction in using one label or the other often coincides with the purpose of including the unobserved entities. That is, multilevel models include *random effects* to "account for dependency," whereas structural equation models use *latent variables* to "create latent constructs through measurement models." So when latent variable measurement models are not used (i.e., there are no latent variables present beyond just the random effects needed to describe longitudinal data), the term MSEM—that implies a model with both random effects *and* latent variable measurement models—can be potentially misleading. Therefore, we'll stick with the sufficiently descriptive term "multivariate longitudinal model" instead.

Although perhaps initially overwhelming to think about, the good news is that there are no new concepts in estimating a conditional multivariate longitudinal model within "truly" multivariate software, although it is an order of complexity higher. Figure 9.5 provides an overall multivariate equation and diagram that corresponds to our previous multivariate model. The diagram uses some of the typical conventions of SEM diagrams, such as using boxes for observed variables, circles for residual and random effects variances, two-headed arrows for covariances, and

Level 1: $\text{Monitor}_{ti} - 3 = \beta_{00M} + \beta_{10M}\left(\text{Age}_{tiM} - 18\right) + e_{tiM}$

$\text{Risky}_{ti} = \beta_{00R} + \beta_{10R}\left(\text{Age}_{tiR} - 18\right) + \beta_{20R}\left(\text{Age}_{tiR} - 18\right)^2 + \beta_{30R}\left(e_{tiM}\right) + e_{tiR}$

Level 2:

Monitor Intercept: $\beta_{00M} = \gamma_{00M} + U_{0iM}$

Monitor Age: $\beta_{10M} = \gamma_{10M} + U_{1iM}$

Risky Intercept: $\beta_{00R} = \gamma_{00R} + \gamma_{01R}\left(\text{Age12Attitudes}_i - 4\right) + \gamma_{02R}\left(U_{0iM}\right) + \gamma_{03R}\left(U_{1iM}\right) + U_{0iR}$

Risky Age: $\beta_{10R} = \gamma_{10R} + \gamma_{11R}\left(\text{Age12Attitudes}_i - 4\right) + \gamma_{12R}\left(U_{0iM}\right) + \gamma_{13R}\left(U_{1iM}\right) + U_{1iR}$

Risky Age^2: $\beta_{20R} = \gamma_{20R}$

Risky WP Monitor: $\beta_{30R} = \gamma_{30R}$

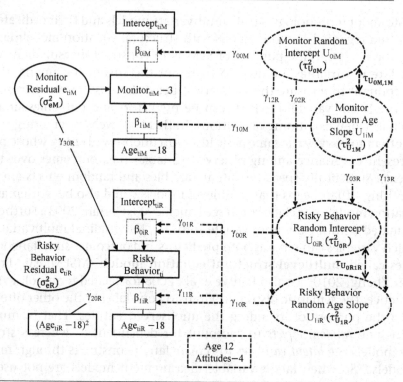

Figure 9.5 Multivariate longitudinal model when using truly multivariate software.

single-headed arrows for regression effects (i.e., fixed effects in which the arrow points from the predictor to the outcome). Unique to this example, solid lines and arrows are used for the level-1 model, whereas dashed lines and arrows are used for the level-2 model. The idea that the level-2 effects indirectly predict the actual outcomes through their direct prediction of the level-1 β placeholders (which then directly predict the outcomes) is shown by the arrows from the level-2 variables terminating at the dashed boxes for each β placeholders.

Our new multivariate longitudinal model does differ from our previous multivariate model that was estimated in univariate longitudinal software in a few ways. First, the variables of monitoring and risky behavior are now defined explicitly as separate outcomes through their level-1 models. This is indicated in the diagram by the separate boxes for these outcomes, as well as in the equation by the absence of the dummy-coded indicators used previously to distinguish their effects (i.e., when both variables were contained in a single outcome column). However, given that monitoring will be predicting risky behavior, monitoring was centered at 3 to keep the risky behavior intercept interpretable. Second, although the same random effects models have been estimated with respect to age (i.e., a fixed quadratic, random linear age model for risky behavior; a random linear age model for monitoring), it is now explicitly noted that the same ages do not need to be observed for each outcome, as indicated in the diagram and the equation by the separate age variables predicting each outcome with different outcome subscripts.

Third, and most importantly, the estimated variance components for monitoring are used *directly in constructing fixed effects* to predict risky behavior, rather than in covariances with those of risky behavior (as in the previous multivariate model), and instead of fitting fixed effects of their observed variable proxies (as in the univariate longitudinal models). That is, the within-person residual variance in monitoring is a level-1 predictor of risky behavior through β_{3i}; likewise, the between-person monitoring random intercepts and linear age slopes are predictors of the risky behavior random intercepts and random linear age slopes in the level-2 model.

Results for this multivariate longitudinal model as estimated via maximum likelihood in M*plus* v. 7.1 are shown in Table 9.5, in which the Wald test p-values are from a z-distribution (i.e., assuming infinite rather than estimated denominator degrees of freedom, as when using a t-distribution instead). Although the results with respect to age and mother's attitudes can be interpreted similarly to the previous multivariate longitudinal model, the estimated fixed effects for monitoring will require further explanation. Pseudo-standardized estimates were again calculated for the fixed effects as $\gamma_{STD} = \gamma^{*}SD(X)/SD(Y)$ to help convey absolute effect sizes.

First, the level-1 within-person monitoring effect was significantly positive, such that for every unit of monitoring at a given age *more than was predicted by one's individual trajectory,* risky behavior at that same age was expected to be higher by $\gamma_{30R} = 3.56$ *than was predicted by one's individual trajectory.* That is, a positive monitoring residual predicts a positive risky behavior residual. After considering the SD of the monitoring residuals as a predictor and the SD of the risky behavior residuals as the outcome, the standardized level-1 effect = .37, which is very similar to the previous residual correlation = .35 as expected. Before turning to the rest of the

Table 9.5 Results from multivariate longitudinal model using truly multivariate software.

Model Effects		Est	SE	p <	STD
Risky Behavior Model for the Means					
γ_{00R}	Intercept	**23.61**	0.33	.001	
γ_{10R}	Linear Age Slope (0 = 18)	**2.00**	0.14	.001	
γ_{20R}	Quadratic Age Slope	**0.15**	0.02	.001	
γ_{01R}	Mothers' Attitudes (0 = 4)	**−3.33**	0.51	.001	
γ_{11R}	Attitudes by Linear Age	**−0.53**	0.10	.001	
Monitoring Model for the Means					
γ_{00M}	Intercept	0.07	0.03	.057	
γ_{10M}	Linear Age Slope (0 = 18)	−0.00	0.01	.688	
Risky Behavior Model for the Variance					
$\tau^2_{U_{0R}}$	Random Intercept Variance	**14.17**	1.97	.001	
$\tau^2_{U_{1R}}$	Linear Age Slope Variance	**0.39**	0.08	.001	
$\tau_{U_{0R,1R}}$	Intercept-Age Slope Covariance	**1.48**	0.35	.001	
σ^2_{eR}	Residual Variance	**7.33**	0.33	.001	
Monitoring Model for the Variance					
$\tau^2_{U_{0M}}$	Random Intercept Variance	**0.20**	0.02	.001	
$\tau^2_{U_{1M}}$	Linear Age Slope Variance	**0.01**	0.00	.001	
$\tau_{U_{0M,1M}}$	Intercept-Age Slope Covariance	−0.00	0.00	.906	
σ^2_{eM}	Residual Variance	**0.08**	0.00	.001	
Cross-Variable Regressions					
	Monitoring Intercept → Risky Behavior Intercept				
γ_{02R}	Contextual Effect	**−7.93**	0.86	.001	
$\gamma_{02R} + \gamma_{30R}$	Total Effect	**−4.37**	0.78	.001	−0.51
	Monitoring Age Slope → Risky Behavior Age Slope				
γ_{13R}	Contextual Effect	**−5.32**	0.82	.001	
$\gamma_{13R} + \gamma_{30R}$	Total Effect	**−1.76**	0.72	.015	−0.29
γ_{30R}	Monitoring Residual → Risky Behavior Residual	**3.56**	0.30	.001	0.37
γ_{12R}	Monitoring Intercept → Risky Behavior Age Slope	**−0.55**	0.16	.001	−0.39
γ_{03R}	Monitoring Age Slope → Risky Behavior Intercept	3.69	3.49	.292	0.10

model, though, it is important to note that this level-1 effect was estimated using the original monitoring variable centered at a constant of 3 instead of at a variable (e.g., it was grand-mean-centered) so that its intercept and age slope random variances could be properly partitioned. So, although the level-1 effect is the true within-person effect, the level-2 effects among the intercepts and among the age slopes are actually contextual effects, which must be interpreted similarly as in grand-mean-centering of level-1 predictors (i.e., as seen in chapter 8).

Accordingly, the contextual effects provided directly by the model for the intercept and age slope are given in Table 9.5 as well as the total effects created by adding the level-1 effect to each. With respect to the random intercepts, for every unit greater predicted monitoring at age 18, predicted risky behavior at age 18 was expected to differ by $\gamma_{02R} + \gamma_{30R} = -7.93 + 3.56 = -4.37$. After considering the SD of the monitoring intercepts as a predictor and the SD of the risky behavior intercepts as the outcome, the standardized intercept effect $= -.51$, which is similar to the previous random intercept correlation $= -.46$ as expected, given the nonsignificant additional effect of the monitoring random age slope (standardized effect $= .10$). Similarly, with respect to the random linear age slopes, for every unit greater rate of age change per year in monitoring, the predicted rate of age change per year in risky behavior was expected to differ by $\gamma_{13R} + \gamma_{30R} = -5.32 + 3.56 = -1.76$. After considering the SD of the monitoring age slopes as a predictor and the SD of the risky behavior age slopes as the outcome, the standardized age slope effect $= -.29$, which is again similar to the previous random slope correlation $= -.25$ (even after controlling for the significant monitoring random intercept effect, standardized effect $= -.39$).

So, to summarize, our results from the conditional multivariate longitudinal model using "truly" multivariate software are strikingly similar to those from the conditional multivariate longitudinal model using univariate software—in fact, the model $-2LL$ value is exactly the same, because the same multivariate relationships have been specified. In this truly multivariate software we also could have replaced the fixed effects among the variance components with covariances (i.e., two-headed arrows instead of directed arrows), and we would have obtained the same model as when using univariate software. That is, the real difference between our multivariate models lies not in what software is used, but in *how* relationships across variables are specified—as fixed effects or as covariances. But the critical difference between univariate and multivariate models with time-varying predictors lies in whether the fixed effects are linked directly to the random effects (multivariate) or to their observed variable proxies (univariate).

3. Comparing Univariate and Multivariate Models for Time-Varying Predictors

We've just seen two types of multivariate longitudinal models, each of which provides a model-based partitioning of the sources of variance in predictors and outcomes that show individual change over time, and each of which allows relationships (either as fixed effects or covariances) among these variance components. These models revealed a negative relationship between the level-2 random intercepts, a negative relationship between the level-2 random age slopes, and a positive relationship between the level-1 residuals. Let us now revisit the idea of two-stage univariate models to see what extent they can be used to accomplish the same aim.

3.A. Two-Stage Univariate Models as a Proxy for Multivariate Models

As introduced in section 1, a two-stage approach of *slopes-as-outcomes* will involve estimating individual intercepts, age slopes, and time-varying residuals for monitoring for use as observed predictors of risky behavior. We have two options to do so. First, we can fit the unconditional random linear model predicting monitoring described in section 1, in which each girl's intercept can be predicted as: $\beta_{0i} = \gamma_{00} + U_{0i}$, each girl's age slope can be predicted as: $\beta_{1i} = \gamma_{10} + U_{1i}$, and the residual for each girl for each occasion can be predicted as: $e_{ti} = y_{ti} - [\beta_{0i} + \beta_{0i}(Age_{ti} - 18)]$. Alternatively, we can treat girls as fixed effects in estimating the same type of model, in which person ID would be considered a categorical (grouping) variable. The fixed intercept and fixed linear age slope would then be replaced by the main effect of person ID and a person ID by $(Age_{ti} - 18)$ interaction, which estimate per-person intercepts and linear age slopes as fixed effects instead. The time-varying residuals can then be predicted as before (i.e., using observed–predicted outcomes as each occasion). Treating persons as fixed effects is similar to using individual regression models, except that a common residual variance is used for all persons (as in our other models), and the model is estimated using ML instead of ordinary least squares (which is equivalent to REML instead given complete data).

The monitoring intercepts (centered at 3) and linear age slopes (left uncentered, given their mean ~0) can now be used as level-2 predictors, whereas the time-varying residuals (left uncentered, given their mean ~0) can be used as level-1 predictors, as shown in Equation (9.5):

Level 1 : Risky Behavior$_{ti} = \beta_{0i} + \beta_{1i}(Age_{ti} - 18) + \beta_{2i}(Age_{ti} - 18)^2 + \beta_{3i}(MonRes_{ti}) + e_{ti}$

Level 2 : Intercept : $\beta_{0i} = \gamma_{00} + \gamma_{01}(Attitudes12_i - 4)$
$\qquad\qquad\qquad\qquad + \gamma_{02}(MonInt_i - 3) + \gamma_{03}(MonSlope_i) + U_{0i}$

$\qquad$ Age : $\qquad\;\; \beta_{1i} = \gamma_{10} + \gamma_{11}(Attitudes12_i - 4)$
$\qquad\qquad\qquad\qquad + \gamma_{12}(MonInt_i - 3) + \gamma_{13}(MonSlope_i) + U_{1i}$

$\qquad$ Age^2 : $\qquad \beta_{2i} = \gamma_{20}$ $\hfill (9.5)$

$\quad$ WP Monitor : $\quad \beta_{3i} = \gamma_{30}$

Composite :

$y_{ti} = \{\gamma_{00} + \gamma_{01}(Attitudes12_i - 4) + \gamma_{02}(MonInt_i - 3) + \gamma_{03}(MonSlope_i) + U_{0i}\} +$
$\qquad \{\gamma_{10} + \gamma_{11}(Attitudes12_i - 4) + \gamma_{12}(MonInt_i - 3) + \gamma_{13}(MonSlope_i) + U_{1i}\}(Age_{ti} - 18) +$
$\qquad \{\gamma_{20}\}(Age_{ti} - 18)^2 + \{\gamma_{30}\}(MonRes_{ti}) + e_{ti}$

in which *MonInt*$_i$, *MonSlope*$_i$, and *MonRes*$_{ti}$ are the individual monitoring intercepts, linear age slopes, and time-varying residuals, respectively. Results are shown in Table 9.6, in which the first set of columns are for the slopes-as-outcomes model in which persons were random effects, and the second set of columns are for the slopes-as-outcomes model in which persons were fixed effects instead. Finally, Table 9.7 also presents the monitoring fixed effects from these slopes-as-outcomes models along with those of the multivariate longitudinal model using multivariate software, which is their direct model-based analog. Pseudo-standardized coefficients are again provided, as well as the predictor and outcome variances from which they were calculated.

Several things are noteworthy in comparing the results across models in Table 9.7. First are the differences in the estimated variances of the monitoring intercepts and

Table 9.6 Results from using slopes-as-outcomes for monitoring in predicting risky behavior.

Model Effects		Persons as Random Effects			Persons as Fixed Effects		
		Est	SE	p <	Est	SE	p <
Model for the Means							
γ_{00}	Intercept	23.60	0.33	.001	23.55	0.33	.001
γ_{10}	Linear Age Slope (0 = 18)	2.01	0.14	.001	1.99	0.14	.001
γ_{20}	Quadratic Age Slope	0.15	0.02	.001	0.15	0.02	.001
γ_{01}	Mothers' Attitudes (0 = 4)	−3.33	0.51	.001	−3.33	0.51	.001
γ_{11}	Attitudes by Linear Age	−0.53	0.10	.001	−0.53	0.10	.001
γ_{02}	Monitoring Intercept (0 = 3)	−4.36	0.77	.001	−3.35	0.65	.001
γ_{12}	Monitoring Intercept by Age	−0.55	0.15	.001	−0.31	0.13	.017
γ_{03}	Monitoring Age Slope	3.76	3.41	.272	7.47	2.69	.006
γ_{13}	Monitoring Age Slope by Age	−1.75	0.69	.012	−0.39	0.54	.468
γ_{30}	Monitoring Residual	3.56	0.30	.001	3.56	0.30	.001
Model for the Variance							
$\tau^2_{U_0}$	Random Intercept Variance	15.59	1.91	.001	15.62	1.91	.001
$\tau^2_{U_1}$	Linear Age Slope Variance	0.50	0.08	.001	0.50	0.08	.001
$\tau_{U_{01}}$	Intercept-Linear Covariance	1.80	0.33	.001	1.80	0.33	.001
σ^2_e	Residual Variance	7.33	0.33	.001	7.33	0.33	.001
	Total R^2	.337			.337		
ML Model Fit							
	Number of Parameters	14			14		
	−2LL	7430.8			7431.0		
	AIC	7458.8			7459.0		
	BIC	7505.0			7505.2		

Table 9.7 Comparison of results for the intercepts (int), age slopes (slope), and residuals (res) for monitoring (M) predicting risky behavior (RB) across models. Bold values are $p < .05$ for the unstandardized fixed effects.

Monitoring Effects	Multivariate Longitudinal Model with Fixed Effects of Monitoring				Slopes-as-Outcomes Model: Persons as Random Effects				Slopes-as-Outcomes Model: Persons as Fixed Effects			
	Var(X)	Var(Y)	Fixed Effect	STD Effect	Var(X)	Var(Y)	Fixed Effect	STD Effect	Var(X)	Var(Y)	Fixed Effect	STD Effect
M int → R int	0.195	14.17	**-4.37**	-0.51	0.168	15.59	**-4.36**	-0.45	0.233	15.62	**-3.35**	-0.41
M int → R slope	0.195	0.39	**-0.55**	-0.39	0.168	0.50	**-0.55**	-0.32	0.233	0.50	**-0.31**	-0.21
M slope → R int	0.010	14.17	3.69	0.10	0.008	15.59	3.76	0.09	0.013	15.62	**7.47**	0.22
M slope → R slope	0.010	0.39	**-1.76**	-0.29	0.008	0.50	**-1.75**	-0.23	0.013	0.50	**-0.39**	-0.06
M res → R res	0.081	7.33	**3.56**	0.37	0.062	7.33	**3.56**	0.33	0.058	7.33	**3.56**	0.32

age slopes. As to be expected, those predicted using per-person random effects (in the second set of columns) have *less* variability than their model-based counterparts (first set of columns), whereas those predicted using per-person fixed effects have *more* variability. As discussed in chapter 5, random effects are empirical Bayes estimates for the most likely value from each person's distribution of possible intercepts and slopes. However, these predictions are shrunken towards the mean of the overall intercept and slope distributions, the extent to which depends on the relative amount of random effect to residual variability and the reliability of each person's data. In contrast, the per-person fixed effects estimates reflect exactly what they would be using *only* that person's data, which means they are unbiased but less precise at the same time. Unfortunately, the precision with which each per-person fixed or random effect has been estimated is lost when using slopes-as-outcomes, because only the estimates themselves are included in subsequent models.

Second, the results using per-person random effects (second set of columns) appear to coincide fairly well with those of the multivariate model (first set of columns), just smaller in magnitude, as can be expected given the aforementioned shrinkage of the random effects. The same cannot be said when using per-person fixed effects (third set of columns). Despite their greater variability, the standardized effects for the monitoring intercept are smaller than in the other two models, although in the same direction. In contrast, the standardized effects for the monitoring age slope differ from the other models—the monitoring age slope appears to predict the risky behavior intercept, but not the risky behavior age slope. Finally, the residual relationship appears similar across models (although slightly larger in the multivariate model).

Given that this is only one set of data, we should be careful in generalizing these findings, but it appears for these data that the slopes-as-outcomes univariate models using per-person random effects provided the closest approximation to the truly multivariate model. Accordingly, in the next sections we consider more generally the three most optimal longitudinal models we've examined—univariate with slopes-as-outcomes random effects for the time-varying predictor, multivariate with covariances between variance components, and multivariate with fixed effects between variance components. More specifically, we will examine their pros and cons for how they address missing data, random effects of within-person relationships, moderation of between- and within-person relationships, and test hypotheses of mediation.

3.B. Missing Data for Time-Varying Predictors as Outcomes

Univariate and multivariate models differ significantly in what they do with cases that have missing data (in which a case is defined as an occasion within a person in longitudinal data). In univariate models with time-varying predictors, **each case must be complete**—it must include *all* model predictors and outcomes to be included in the model. When using slopes-as-outcomes for the effects of the time-varying predictor, the individual intercepts and slopes should be available for any person that has at least two occasions, although they will be less reliable to the extent that a person has fewer occasions. However, cases in which the time-varying residual predictor is missing for that occasion will be excluded from the model. Consequently, models may be estimated using different samples after including predictors with some missing data, resulting in non-comparable log-likelihoods (and thus non-comparable –2LL, AIC, and BIC model fit statistics). The effects from models with fewer cases may be detected with less statistical power; they may also be biased to the extent that the missing variables are not *missing at random* (i.e., a scenario in which the missingness is predictable from the person's other data).

Fortunately, some relief from the problems of missing data can be found in multivariate models in which time-varying predictors are modeled directly as outcomes instead, and in which every case that has at least one outcome will be included. Because the predictors are then included as part of the likelihood function, the missing observations are simply "skipped over" in the likelihood function under the same assumption of missing at random as for the outcomes. The flexibility inherent in this practice can solve many of the limitations found in univariate models with time-varying predictors. For instance, in multivariate lon-gitudinal models in truly multivariate software it is possible to estimate models in which the time-varying predictors and outcomes are measured on different time scales. Consider our current example—what if monitoring were measured only at ages 12, 15, and 18? A univariate longitudinal model would reduce risky behavior down to just those three occasions that also had the monitoring predictors. In contrast, a multivariate longitudinal model would use the risky behavior out-comes across all seven occasions, as well as change in monitoring across its three occasions, such that we could still examine relationships between the intercepts and age slopes across variables. Residual relationships, however, would only be estimable for the ages when both variables are measured. Similarly, in contrast to univariate longitudinal models, lagged relationships could be examined between "predictors" and outcomes without removing the outcome at the first occasion from the model (i.e., that would be missing its lag-1 predictor). Furthermore, in a multivariate longitudinal model lagged effects could be examined in both direc-tions simultaneously (i.e., a cross-lagged model in which lag-1 X predicts Y while lag-1 Y predicts X).

Unfortunately, this flexibility does not come for free. Making time-varying pre-dictors "outcomes" by including them in the likelihood function means that distri-butional assumptions are then made about their residuals at each level. As discussed in the chapter 7 appendix, if the likelihood function is based on the multivariate normal distribution, model assumptions include normality, independence, and constant variance of all residuals. While these assumptions may be at least plausible for a continuous time-varying predictor like monitoring, this may not always be the case more generally. And although other distributions are available for non-normal predictors within generalized longitudinal models, difficulty of estimation quickly escalates with the number of random effects variances needed (see chapter 13 for further discussion), such that estimation of truly multivariate models may be pro-hibitively complex in these cases.

3.C. Random Effects of Within-Person Relationships

Another point of contrast between the three models we've examined is their capacity to examine how multivariate relationships may differ across persons. One way this might happen is through a random effect for a within-person relationship. In our example, girls may differ in to what extent being monitored more than predicted relates to greater risky behavior than predicted. If this level-1 relationship were specified in a multivariate model through a residual covariance, then there is no easy way (in most software programs, at least) to test whether this covariance varies randomly over persons. But if this level-1 relationship were captured as a fixed effect instead in a univariate model, then we can test the corresponding random effect in the usual way. That is, we could have examined random level-1 effects in our last slopes-as-outcomes univariate models by adding U_{3i} to the level-2 equation for β_{3i} in Equation (9.5), which would result in a new random effect variance (τ_{U3}^2) and two covariances with the other level-2 random effects. In doing so, it appears these new effects significantly improved model fit in both the random effects model, $-2\Delta LL(\sim3) = 10.3$, $p = .016$, and in the fixed effects model, $-2\Delta LL(\sim3) = 11.8$, $p = .008$, although the G matrix was not positive definite in either model.

Given that both univariate slopes-as-outcomes model and the "truly" multivariate model can include fixed level-1 effects for the variance components of a time-varying predictor, we can also test the random level-1 effect using a "truly" multivariate model. In our example data this would entail adding a U_{3iR} random effect to the level-2 equation predicting β_{3iR} in Figure 9.5, which would require estimation of a new random effect variance (τ_{U3R}^2) and its covariances with the four other level-2 random effects (i.e., the monitoring and risky behavior intercepts and age slopes). In doing so, however, these five new terms did *not* significantly improve model fit, $-2\Delta LL(\sim5) = 6.1$, $p = .295$; neither did just τ_{U3R}^2 alone, $-2\Delta LL(\sim1) = 1.4$, $p = .229$. So, which set of results should we believe—does the WP effect of monitoring vary over girls or not? In this case, given that only the multivariate model simultaneously considers the imprecision in the random effects and residuals for both variables, its results are likely to be more trustworthy.

3.D. Moderators of Between-Person and Within-Person Effects

A third distinction along which univariate and multivariate longitudinal models differ is in their ease of incorporating moderation effects—that is, interaction terms that allow the multivariate relationships to differ systematically as a function of other observed variables. For instance, we might wish to see how the relationship between predicted monitoring and predicted risky behavior at age 18 differs by other factors—that is, moderation of the intercept relationship. Likewise, we might wish to see whether the relationship between the age slopes for monitoring and risky behavior depends on other factors as well. These types of moderation questions are straightforward to examine in univariate longitudinal models with time-varying predictors because the interactions would be specified as fixed effects of observed variables only.

Conversely, such moderation questions become exponentially more difficult to examine in multivariate longitudinal models when one or both of the interacting predictors is a random effect (*aka,* an unobserved latent variable). Estimating interactions involving latent variables has historically been a difficult problem, in which although many solutions have been proposed, few have been found to work well (see Schumacker & Marcoulides, 1998, for more discussion). Current state-of-the-art in estimating latent variable interactions (i.e., Klein & Moosbrugger, 2000, as implemented in M*plus*) uses numeric integration (as described briefly in chapter 13), which becomes exponentially more difficult with increasing numbers of random effects (and especially interactions thereof). Consequently, truly multivariate models estimated using maximum likelihood may be limited in practice to fewer interaction effects—and fewer model-partitioned level-1 variables in general—than what could be examined in a univariate model with observed time-varying predictors. Bayesian Markov-Chain Monte Carlo (MCMC) estimation is another possibility, but has not been well studied in estimation of latent variable interactions.

A simpler type of interaction that could be examined in our data is whether the WP monitoring effect differs by age (i.e., as was specified in the initial univariate models), which can be specified in a truly multivariate model using observed level-1 variables. However, adding this interaction highlights another situation in which the answer depends on which model you choose. The slopes-as-outcomes model using random effects detected a significant positive fixed effect for the interaction, such that the WP effect became more positive by 0.54 per year of age (Est = 0.54, SE = 0.17, p = .002). However, the same interaction in the truly multivariate model was not significant (Est = 0.17, SE = 0.13, p = .193). Once again, the results from the multivariate model—in which the monitoring residuals are not treated as observed variables—are likely to be more trustworthy.

3.E. Between-Person and Within-Person Mediation

Finally, let us consider briefly the topic of mediation analysis in longitudinal models. Mediation can be described generally as how the effect of a predictor on an outcome (X → Y) is reduced or otherwise altered after accounting for the effects of other "mediators" (M) that are related to both the predictor and the outcome, such that X → M → Y. Statistically, this question about the change in the X → Y effect after controlling for the M → Y effect is equivalent to evaluating the **indirect effect**, which is the product of the fixed effects of X → M and M → Y.

There is a large literature on testing mediation in cross-sectional data (see MacKinnon, 2008 for a thorough treatment). More recently, there is growing interest in assessing longitudinal mediation as well (e.g., Maxwell & Cole, 2007; Mitchell & Maxwell, 2013; Selig & Preacher, 2009). However, that despite the seemingly novel terms of *mediation* and *indirect effects,* such questions ultimately still concern fixed effects in predicting outcomes measured over time. Consequently, the same concerns and logic explicated in chapters 7, 8, and 9 for testing fixed and random effects will apply in testing mediation. That is, mediation should be examined for *all* sources of variance that are relevant, but only at the level(s) at which mediation can occur.

For instance, consider a question of mediation when all three variables (X, M, and Y) are time-varying, such that each variable is measured at level 1 (i.e., a 1 → 1 → 1 design; Preacher et al., 2010). Imagine that each variable has an intraclass correlation below 1 (i.e., it has both between-person intercept variation and within-person residual variation), but shows no individual differences in change over time. If we estimated a single indirect effect through the longitudinal variables (i.e., the product of the X → M and M → Y fixed effects), we would obtain a smushed (and thus likely useless) indirect effect. Instead, there are actually two kinds of mediation (or rather, indirect effects) to be examined in this scenario: between-person indirect effects through the three random intercepts at level 2, and within-person indirect effects through the three residuals at level 1. But what about the situation in which each variable also shows individual differences in change over time? In that case, we would then have to consider a third kind of indirect effect—a between-person indirect effect through their random time slopes at level 2. Assuming they were present for all three variables, random effects of other predictors besides time could similarly be examined for evidence of mediation at level 2.

More generally, it's essential to note what happens when the variables of interest are measured at different levels of analysis, and thus what kind of mediation is or is not theoretically possible. First, consider a design in which X is time-invariant but M and Y are time-varying (i.e., a 2 → 1 → 1 design). In this case, we may want to examine how the effect of time-invariant X on time-varying Y is mediated through time-varying M. But because X only varies between persons, the only way that mediation could occur is through the between-person effects of X on M—in other words, if X predicts the random intercepts and slopes for M, which in turn predict the random intercepts and slopes for Y. In this design, level-1 mediation is not possible (although the residual relationship of M → Y could still be examined). Similarly, given time-invariant X and M variables (a 2 → 2 → 1 design), mediation can only exist through prediction of the between-person variances of Y at level 2. Likewise, if the Y variable is time-invariant, but the X and M variables are time-varying (a 1 → 1 → 2 design), then again mediation is only possible at level 2 via the between-person variances in X and M (i.e., their level-1 variances would be irrelevant for assessing mediation). The point of the story is this—**mediation cannot cross levels of analysis**. A complete mediation analysis should always carefully consider all of the relevant variance components for the variables *at the level at which the indirect effects are estimated*, regardless of the level at which the variables appear to have been measured.

4. Chapter Summary

This chapter described univariate and multivariate longitudinal models for assessing relationships between time-varying predictors and outcomes that show individual differences in within-person change over time. That is, we examined models for data in which both predictors and outcomes should be partitioned into between-person intercept variance, between-person time slope variance, and within-person residual variance, at a minimum (i.e., any additional sources of between-person variance that are also present should then be modeled accordingly).

We began by considering two univariate models (i.e., in which the time-varying predictor is *not* part of the likelihood function) in which the variation in a time-varying predictor was represented using observed variables. First, *person-mean-centering* was used to create a "between-person" predictor to include in the level-2 model from the person mean of the time-varying predictor (centered at a constant to create a meaningful 0), along with a "within-person" predictor to include in the level-1 model as the occasion-specific deviation from the person mean. Second, we used *baseline-centering,* in which the predictor's value at a specific occasion (i.e., age 18 here; also centered at a constant to create a meaningful 0) was included in the level-2 model; the occasion-specific change from the baseline occasion was then included as a predictor in the level-1 model. Thus, the person means and the age 18 values should have been proxies for the time-varying predictor's between-person variance, whereas the within-person deviations and changes from baseline should have been proxies for the predictor's within-person variance.

In reality, though, these level-2 predictors were proxies for between-person *intercept* variance only—neither univariate approach included another level-2 predictor to serve as a proxy for between-person differences in change over time. As a result, the level-1 predictor still contained both within-person residual variance and between-person time slope variance, which had several negative consequences. These included changes in effect size artificially induced from changes in the level-1 predictor's variance over time, a not-possible-but-still-predicted level-1 effect conditional on the baseline occasion in the baseline-centering model, and fixed effects at both levels that were not what they should be. More specifically, the level-2 effect—that should have represented the negative between-person intercept relationship—was biased by the positive within-person residual relationship. The level-1 effect—that should have represented only the positive within-person relationship—was assumed to hold for the negative between-person slope relationship as well, resulting in another kind of "smushed" effect. The inflated random effects variances seen in the example data as a consequence of these model misspecifications were shown to occur more generally in a simulation study as well.

To summarize, just as random intercept only models are likely to be insufficient in modeling individual change in time-varying *outcomes,* person-mean-centering and baseline-centering are likely to be insufficient for time-varying *predictors* that also show individual change. Only through model-based partitioning of the three sources of variance within the time-varying predictor (intercept, slope, and residual) can these three distinct effects on an outcome be properly distinguished. Accordingly, we examined two kinds of multivariate longitudinal models through which this partitioning in variance can occur—in which "multivariate" means that the time-varying "predictor" is included as another outcome in the model likelihood function.

First, we saw how it is possible to estimate multivariate longitudinal models by "tricking" univariate longitudinal software. In this approach, the data are re-structured so that both the time-varying predictor and time-varying outcome are contained in a single data column. Separate model effects are then specified for each outcome through "interactions" with dummy-coded indicator variables that act like switches to control whether the model term is applied to each outcome. Critically, relationships between the time-varying "predictor" and outcome are specified only in the model for the variance. That is, the level-2 **G** matrix covariances indicate between-person relationships among random intercepts and slopes, whereas the level-1 **R** matrix covariances indicate within-person relationships among the residuals.

While their capacity to examine these distinct kinds of relationships directly is a definite advantage over univariate longitudinal models, multivariate longitudinal models estimated in univariate longitudinal software can be of limited utility for examining how these relationships may differ across persons. Because the relationships are expressed through covariances instead of fixed effects, in most software it is not possible to examine their random or moderator effects. For these and other extensions we turned to a second type of multivariate model, which requires "truly" multivariate software in which a variable can be both a predictor and an outcome simultaneously. The primary advantage of these models is that multivariate relationships can be specified as fixed effects. That is, the residual variance for the time-varying outcome can be regressed on (predicted by) the residual variance for the time-varying predictor; similarly, the outcome's random effects variances can be regressed on those of the time-varying predictor. Although equivalent in terms of model fit, the use of fixed effects instead of covariances then allows more flexibility, such as random effects for within-person relationships, mediation effects, and moderator effects. However, it is important to note that testing moderation for variance components (i.e., latent variable interactions) is currently much more challenging in terms of estimation than is testing moderation for observed variables (i.e., as in univariate longitudinal models). Nevertheless, the capabilities of these types of "truly" multivariate models (and the range of software in which they can be estimated) are likely to continue expanding in the future.

Finally, given the current limitations of "truly" multivariate models, we also examined to what extent predicted per-person intercepts, slopes, and residuals could be used as observed predictors in a univariate model (i.e., a slopes-as-outcomes approach) in order to overcome the problems of person-mean-centering or baseline-centering. We saw that although their variances were shrunken relative to the model-based analogs, the results using the per-person predicted random effects were largely similar to their analogs in the multivariate models, whereas the results using the per-person predicted fixed effects were somewhat different. More research is needed to better understand observed variable strategies, but the current example suggests that using predicted random effects may provide more comparable results to a multivariate model.

5. Sample Results Section

The analyses in this chapter could be summarized into the beginning of a results section as follows (which would then need to be expanded to capture the substantively meaningful story, theoretical framework, or set of research hypotheses to be tested). In this chapter, however, the results from the univariate longitudinal models using person-mean-centering or baseline-centering will not be summarized. This is because these models were presented for a different purpose—for continuity with the previous chapter, and to explicitly show how their problems for use with time-varying predictors that show individual change. In addition, because they are likely to be inferior to the multivariate models, the slopes-as-outcomes univariate models are also not summarized. Furthermore, because the multivariate models are statistically equivalent, they both don't need to be presented. Consequently, only the results from the most general and most accurate "truly" multivariate model will be summarized below. The results section would begin where the example data analysis ended in chapter 7 (which presented the modeling approach, outcome data, unconditional models, and the effects of mothers' attitudes collected at age 12).

A time-varying predictor of mothers' monitoring was collected at the same age 12 to 18 occasions as the risky behavior outcome. Monitoring was measured by the mean across 10 items on a 1 to 5 scale, in which higher values indicated that mothers reported greater frequency of monitoring behaviors ($M = 3.08$, $SD = 0.65$). The intraclass correlation for monitoring indicated that 69% of its variation arose from between-person mean differences. In addition, although there was no significant linear or quadratic change across age on average, there were significant individual differences in linear change across age, $-2\Delta LL(\sim 2) = 320.3$, $p < .001$. To describe the random intercept and linear age slope variances, 95% random effects confidence intervals were computed as CI = fixed effect $\pm$ 1.96*SQRT[random effect variance]. In doing so, 95% of the sample is expected to have individual intercepts for their levels of monitoring at age 18 between 2.20 and 3.93, as well as individual linear rates of change between –0.20 and 0.20. Thus, while on average there is no change in monitoring across age, some mothers are expected to increase while others are expected to decrease in their monitoring.

Given the presence of individual differences in change in monitoring, a multivariate longitudinal model was estimated via maximum likelihood in M*plus* v. 7.1 to describe the mean and variance in both monitoring and risky behavior across age. This model is illustrated in Figure 9.5, in which boxes depict observed variables, circles depict residual and random effects variances, two-headed arrows depict covariances, and single-headed arrows depict regression effects. Solid lines and arrows are used for the level-1 model, whereas dashed lines and arrows are used for the level-2 model. The idea that the level-2 effects indirectly predict the actual outcomes through their direct prediction of the level-1 β placeholders is shown by the arrows from the level-2 variables terminating at the dashed boxes for each β placeholders.

Full results for this multivariate model are provided in Table 9.5. Based on previous univariate results, a fixed quadratic, random linear age model was estimated for risky behavior, whereas a random linear age model was estimated for monitoring (centered at 3 to create a meaningful 0). A predictor for mothers' attitudes about smoking and drinking was included for both random intercepts and random linear age slopes. After controlling for the effects of monitoring, more conservative attitudes were still related to lower predicted risky behavior with a less positive age slope as evaluated at age 18; attitudes did not significantly predict monitoring.

All three effects of monitoring in predicting risky behavior were significant. First, the level-1 within-person monitoring effect was significantly positive, such that for every unit of monitoring at a given age *more than was predicted by one's individual trajectory,* risky behavior at that same age was expected to be higher by $\gamma_{30R} = 3.56$ *than was predicted by one's individual trajectory.* That is, a positive monitoring residual predicted a positive risky behavior residual. Second, with respect to the random intercepts, for every unit greater predicted monitoring at age 18, predicted risky behavior at age 18 was expected to differ by a total effect of -4.37 (or by a contextual effect of -7.93 after controlling for age-specific monitoring). Third, with respect to the random linear age slopes, for every unit greater rate of age change per year in monitoring, the predicted rate of age change per year in risky behavior was expected to differ by a total effect of -1.76 (or by a contextual effect of -5.32 after controlling for age-specific monitoring). Thus, to summarize, there were negative between-person relationships of intercept and age slope at level 2 as anticipated, indicating better outcomes for girls who are monitored more closely as a function of age. However, there is also a positive within-person residual relationship at level 1 that indicated greater risky behavior on occasions where girls were monitored relatively more. It is important to note, however, that the directionality of this effect cannot be determined in this design (i.e., relatively more risky behavior could have been a cause of relatively more monitoring rather than a consequence as interpreted here).

Review Questions

1. Describe the three approaches for centering level-1 predictors you have learned so far. What do the level-2 and level-1 effects of each indicate? When might these centering methods for level-1 predictors be problematic?
2. Describe and interpret the three kinds of multivariate relationships examined in this chapter.
3. What is the difference between fixed effects of time-varying "predictors" as estimated using multivariate longitudinal models versus univariate longitudinal models?

References

Bauer, D. J. (2003). Estimating multilevel linear models as structural equation models. *Journal of Educational and Behavioral Statistics, 28*(2), 135–167.

Curran. P. J. (2003). Have multilevel models been structural equation models all along? *Multivariate Behavioral Research, 38*(4), 529–569.

Curran, P. J., & Bauer, D. J. (2011). The disaggregation of within-person and between-person effects in longitudinal models of change. *Annual Review of Psychology, 62*, 583–619.

Klein, A., & Moosbrugger, H. (2000). Maximum likelihood estimation of latent interaction effects with the LMS method. *Psychometrika, 65*(4), 457–474.

Lüdtke, O., Marsh, H. W., Robitzsch, A., Trautwein, U., Asparouhov, T., & Muthén, B. (2008). The multilevel latent covariate model: A new, more reliable approach to group-level effects in contextual studies. *Psychological Methods, 13*(3), 203–229.

MacKinnon, D. P. (2008). *Introduction to statistical mediation analysis*. New York, NY: Taylor & Francis.

Maxwell, S. E., & Cole, D. A. (2007). Bias in cross-sectional analyses of longitudinal mediation. *Psychological Methods, 12*(1), 23–44.

Mitchell, M. A., & Maxwell, S. E. (2013). A comparison of cross-sectional and sequential designs when assessing longitudinal mediation. *Multivariate Behavioral Research, 48*, 301–339.

Preacher, K. J., Zyphur, M. J., & Zhang, Z. (2010). A general multilevel SEM framework for assessing multilevel mediation. *Psychological Methods, 15*(3), 209–233.

Selig, J. P., & Preacher, K. J. (2009). Mediation models for longitudinal data in developmental research. *Research in Human Development, 6*(2–3), 144–164.

Schumacker, R. E., & Marcoulides, G. A. (1998). *Interaction and nonlinear effects in structural equation modeling*. New York, NY: Psychology Press.

SECTION IV

ADVANCED APPLICATIONS

CHAPTER 10

ANALYSIS OVER ALTERNATIVE METRICS AND MULTIPLE DIMENSIONS OF TIME

The first three sections of this text focused on the logic behind and procedures for longitudinal analysis. Our goal has been to describe and predict the multiple sources of variation that arise when measuring the same entities repeatedly over time. Notably, in every example, we have presupposed to know exactly what *time* should be. The idea that there may be multiple plausible ways of "clocking time" (i.e., of organizing individuals along a common time metric) has been mentioned briefly in a few places so far (e.g., chapter 1 section 3.C; chapter 4 section 1.A; chapter 5 section 1.A; chapter 7 section 2.A). In chapter 10 we will explore these issues of *time* in greater depth, focusing specifically on longitudinal designs in which there is more than one way to think about *time*. As discussed in the first section of this chapter, a critical distinction is whether the study design confines the effects of multiple metrics of time to be observed concurrently within persons or whether these effects of time can be observed separately. Two-level models for concurrently occurring alternative metrics of time will be presented in the second section, followed by three-level models for multiple separable dimensions of time in the third section. As usual, the chapter then concludes with summary and sample results sections.

1. Dimensions of Time in Longitudinal Data

1.A. Considering Alternative Metrics of Concurrent Within-Person Time

Longitudinal studies begin with the goal of observing how some phenomenon unfolds over time within persons. Inherent in longitudinal designs is the belief that more informative results will be obtained by measuring changes within persons than by measuring differences across people—otherwise, why go to the extra trouble to conduct a longitudinal study? Accordingly, it is essential that the metric of time used in a longitudinal model indexes the causal process thought to be responsible for the observed within-person changes as directly as possible. Notably, this is *not* just a concern of how to center time (i.e., what constant to subtract in order to create a time 0 intercept). Instead, two more general issues will be important.

The idea of alternative metrics of time comes into play whenever *persons differ in where they are in time at the beginning of the study*—such longitudinal designs have been called *overlapping cohort designs, sequential cohort designs, or accelerated longitudinal designs* (Bell, 1953; see Duncan & Duncan, 2012, or McArdle & Bell, 2000, for further elaboration). Such designs tend to be used when researchers want to do a longer-term longitudinal study than what is logically feasible. For instance, you may wish to study adult development, but not have the decades needed in order to follow a group of teenagers as they progress from younger to middle to older adulthood. Instead, you may choose to begin with individuals who are already at different ages (e.g., cohorts of younger, middle, and older adults) and follow each cohort over some shorter length of time. Similarly, in studying educational outcomes, it may be more feasible to begin with children already at different grade levels in school and follow each group as they progress through at least some of the possible grades. However, if the same children were measured with the goal of studying biological rather than educational outcomes, then perhaps age at each occasion may be a more relevant metric of time than grade in school.

The previous examples of development and learning focus on moving forward in time; these are based on the idea that the causal process of interest begins from a common starting point (i.e., birth, formal schooling) and unfolds differently from that point. But in other areas it may be more meaningful to index time relative to a common *ending* point instead. For instance, a study of changes in the quality of intimate partner relationships over time could be anchored on the beginning of a relationship. A fully longitudinal design would entail following couples who just started dating or a group of newlyweds over time; an accelerated longitudinal design would instead follow couples who have already been together for different amounts of time. Such designs would be useful for measuring the process of relationship development, in which a meaningful common "time 0" point is the beginning of a relationship. But what if changes in relationship satisfaction don't occur systematically as a function of relationship *development*, but instead occur as a function of relationship *dissolution?* Then given the same data, a more meaningful common "time 0" point may be the point of relationship separation, such that changes occurring towards to the end of a relationship may be more relevant and systematic than changes occurring from the beginning. Of course such alternative models can and should be evaluated empirically. But the main point is that in accelerated longitudinal designs, multiple metrics of time may be relevant to consider (see also Hoffman, 2012, for additional discussion).

There are two primary questions to consider in choosing a metric of time in accelerated longitudinal designs. The first question is more conceptual—what should *time* be? That is, given the presence of both pre-existing cross-sectional differences in time and longitudinal variation in time, how should we organize the data from different individuals onto a common time metric? As we will see in an example in the second section of this chapter, given an imperfect between-person correlation for the time metrics of interest (e.g., there are differences in age among the children in the same grade at school), the between-person effects of those different metrics of time can be distinguished statistically, although the within-person effects cannot. That is, for every additional year in a study, children are 1 year older and have been in school 1 year longer; likewise, a person will be 1 year farther from birth and 1 year closer to death. Thus, within persons, time is just time, and so within-person changes are agnostic as to what the metric of time should be. Consequently, *the question of what time should be is really focused on how to represent between-person differences* (i.e., in the starting points or ending points for *time*).

The second question is more statistical—given the presence of both between-person differences and within-person changes in time, how should each effect of *time* be specified in a model? Fortunately, we already have the tools to properly distinguish these different levels of time effects—we will have to address the exact same set of issues as when examining the effects of any time-varying predictor, because time is just another time-varying predictor. These issues of testing convergence (i.e., avoiding "smushing") have also been described elsewhere when combining longitudinal data across discrete cohorts (e.g., Mehta & West, 2000; Miyazaki & Raudenbush, 2000). In non-group-based accelerated longitudinal designs, however, the same problem of smushing often tends to go unrecognized, which is particularly troublesome in longitudinal studies that begin with a wide individual age range (see Sliwinski, Hoffman, & Hofer, 2010a, for elaboration). Furthermore, it is often not well understood how different model specifications in accelerated longitudinal designs can still lead to the same model predictions (e.g., using age vs. time in study; McArdle, Ferrer-Caja, Hamagami, & Woodcock; 2002). Thus, in addition to considering what *time* should be, this chapter pays special attention to these issues of properly distinguishing cross-sectional from longitudinal effects of accelerated time.

1.B. Considering Differentiable Dimensions of Within-Person Time

Thus far in the text we have only considered longitudinal designs with a unidimensional measurement schedule for within-person time, such as when persons are sampled once a day or once a year. But increasingly more common are designs that are multidimensional with respect to within-person time; these designs are sometimes called **intensive longitudinal designs**. One specific type we will examine is **measurement burst designs** (see Nesselroade, 1991; Sliwinski, 2008). Their key feature is that persons are sampled over multiple *distinct* intervals of time, such that both shorter-term and longer-term changes can each be observed within persons. For instance, Sliwinski, Hoffman, and Hofer (2010b) describe results from the Cognition, Health, and Aging Project (CHAP; see chapter 1), in which five bursts of six observations within a 2-week period were collected at 6-month intervals. One goal of this study was to differentiate practice effects in speeded tests measuring cognition (i.e., changes observed during a 2-week period) from longer-term, age-related changes in cognition (i.e., changes observed across bursts spanning several years). In another example, Almeida, Piazza, and Stawski (2009) describe results from the National Study of Daily Experience (NSDE; see chapter 1), in which multiple measures were collected within each day to examine how a person's within-day changes and variability in stress hormones were related to daily life experiences and individual differences.

As we will see in more detail in the third section of the chapter, these measurement burst designs may require three-level models to capture the two distinct dimensions of time nested within persons. For now, we continue with a two-level example that illustrates how to examine multiple concurrent metrics of unidimensional time within an accelerated longitudinal design.

2. Two-Level Models for Alternative Metrics of Concurrent Within-Person Time

Our first example comes from the Octogenarian Twin Study of Aging (OCTO; see chapter 1), in which up to five observations were collected over eight years (i.e., about every two years) from same-sex twin pairs. Only one twin was selected from each pair so that persons would be independent in this example (but see chapter 11 for models that can include multiple persons from the same family). The sample included 557 observations from 207 persons without a dementia diagnosis during the study period. The outcome variable was a measure of memory, prose recall, which was scored as the number of questions that were answered correctly about a previously heard story ($M = 10.19$, $SD = 3.83$, possible range = 0 to 16). In order to compare models with different predictors of time, maximum likelihood will be used to estimate all models. An empty means, random intercept model for prose recall provided a grand mean of $\gamma_{00} = 9.73$ (SE = 0.25), with variances of $\tau_{U_0}^2 = 10.46$ and $\sigma_e^2 = 5.16$. Thus, the ICC = .67, such that 67% of the variance in prose recall was due to constant person mean differences over time. This ICC = .67 was significantly greater than 0, $-2\Delta LL(\sim 1) = 217.3$, $p < .001$.

2.A. Time Is Just Another Time-Varying Predictor

With respect to what *time* should be, as in every study we can consider the theoretically naïve metric of **years in study** ($M = 2.67$, $SD = 2.60$, range = 0 to 8.50), in which 0 indicates the first occasion. Given that all persons in this sample have known dates of birth and death, we can also compare the utility of two accelerated metrics of time using those events as time 0: **years since birth** (i.e., age) and **years to death.** Years since birth ($M = 85.65$, $SD = 3.56$, range = 79.42 to 99.90) was centered at 84, which was near its mean at the first occasion ($M = 83.33$, $SD = 2.97$, range = 79.42 to 97.78). Years to death ($M = -5.87$, $SD = 3.66$, range = -15.91 to -0.05) was centered at -7, which was near its mean at the first occasion ($M = -7.17$, $SD = 3.98$, range = -15.91 to -0.05). Individual trajectories along each predictor of *time* (years in study, years since birth, and years to death) are shown in Figure 10.1, in which the black line shows the estimated sample mean trajectory from a saturated means, random intercept model using *time* rounded to the nearest year for

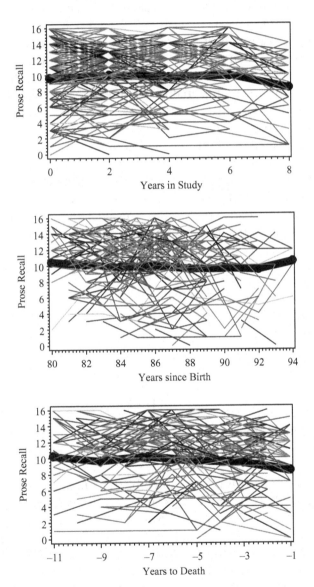

Figure 10.1 Individual trajectories for prose recall by years since birth, years to death, and years in study. The solid black line indicates estimated means per rounded unit of time.

each metric. Although the overall mean trajectories look mostly flat, the individual trajectories show considerable heterogeneity in level and change over time.

Because years since birth and years to death each vary both between and within persons, they can be treated the same as the time-varying predictors examined in chapters 8 and 9. That is, we can begin by examining their relative amount of between-person to within-person information from an empty means, random intercept model for each time predictor as an outcome. Both accelerated time metrics had significant between-person variance: ICC = .40 for years since birth, $-2\Delta LL(\sim 1) =$ 72.9, $p < .001$; ICC = .44 for years to death, $-2\Delta LL(\sim 1) = 87.5$, $p < .001$. Thus, we will need to consider the different effects arising from cross-sectional differences and longitudinal changes in each predictor of time. Notably, at the first occasion, years since birth and years to death were only correlated $r = .15$, indicating a minimal amount of between-person commonality in these accelerated time metrics. Finally, as expected, years in study (within-person time) had no between-person variation: ICC = 0, $-2\Delta LL(\sim 1) = 0$, $p = 1.0$.

We can begin as usual by choosing an unconditional model to best describe the overall pattern of mean change over time and individual differences therein, but here we do so for each metric of time (years since birth, years to death, and years in study). Based on the trajectories observed in Figure 10.1, polynomial models with linear and quadratic slopes for change per year were evaluated. After following the process in chapter 6 (i.e., beginning with a fixed linear time, random intercept model, then sequentially adding fixed and random effects), a fixed quadratic, random linear time model was selected for each metric of time, as shown in Equation (10.1):

Level 1 : $\text{Recall}_{ti} = \beta_{0i} + \beta_{1i}(\text{Time}_{ti} - C) + \beta_{2i}(\text{Time}_{ti} - C)^2 + e_{ti}$

Level 2 : Intercept: $\qquad \beta_{0i} = \gamma_{00} + U_{0i}$

$\qquad\qquad$ Linear Slope: $\qquad \beta_{1i} = \gamma_{10} + U_{1i}$

$\qquad\qquad$ Quadratic Slope: $\beta_{2i} = \gamma_{20}$ $\hfill (10.1)$

Composite : $\text{Recall}_{ti} = \gamma_{00} + \gamma_{10}(\text{Time}_{ti} - C) + \gamma_{20}(\text{Time}_{ti} - C)^2$

$\qquad\qquad\qquad + U_{0i} + U_{1i}(\text{Time}_{ti} - C) + e_{ti}$

in which Time_{ti} minus the constant C was replaced by each of the three metrics described above. No significant random quadratic effects were found in any model, and were thus not included.

Results from a model using years since birth as *time* are as shown in the first set of columns in Table 10.1. At 84 years since birth (regardless of years to death or years in study), the expected prose recall was $\gamma_{00} = 9.82$ with a nonsignificant instantaneous linear rate of decline of $\gamma_{10} = -0.08$ per year that became nonsignificantly less negative per year by twice the quadratic slope of $\gamma_{20} = 0.002$. The nonsignificant fixed quadratic slope was retained for comparability with the other models; without it, the linear slope was $\gamma_{10} = -0.09$ (SE = 0.04, $p = .046$). The linear and quadratic fixed effects of years since birth captured only 0.4% of the total variance in prose recall (i.e., the square of the correlation between the actual and fixed-effect-predicted outcomes). Significant individual differences in linear change were found relative to a fixed quadratic time model with only a random intercept, $-2\Delta LL(\sim 2) = 11.0$,

Table 10.1 Results for prose recall using the unconditional time metrics of years since birth, years to death, and years in study. Bold values are $p < .05$.

Model Effects	Years since Birth (0 = 84) Only			Years to Death (0 = –7) Only			Years in Study (0 = 0) Only		
	Est	SE	p <	Est	SE	p <	Est	SE	p <
Model for the Means									
γ_{00} Intercept	**9.82**	**0.27**	**.001**	**10.15**	**0.28**	**.001**	**9.64**	**0.29**	**.001**
γ_{10} Linear Slope	–0.08	0.06	.162	–0.09	0.05	.071	**0.28**	**0.11**	**.012**
γ_{20} Quadratic Slope	0.002	0.01	.795	**–0.02**	**0.01**	**.021**	**–0.05**	**0.01**	**.002**
Model for the Variance									
$\tau^2_{U_0}$ Intercept Variance	**11.26**	**1.47**	**.001**	**9.82**	**1.39**	**.001**	**13.07**	**1.65**	**.001**
$\tau^2_{U_1}$ Linear Slope Variance	**0.09**	**0.04**	**.005**	**0.12**	**0.04**	**.001**	**0.13**	**0.04**	**.001**
$\tau_{U_{01}}$ Intercept-Slope Covariance	–0.33	0.18	.064	–0.07	0.16	.654	**–0.66**	**0.23**	**.005**
σ^2_e Residual Variance	**4.26**	**0.39**	**.001**	**4.07**	**0.37**	**.001**	**3.96**	**0.36**	**.001**
Total R^2	.004			.012			.004		
ML Model Fit									
Number of Parameters	7			7			7		
–2LL	2839.6			2828.9			2827.8		
AIC	2853.6			2842.9			2841.8		
BIC	2876.9			2866.2			2865.2		

$p = .004$. Results from 95% random effects confidence intervals (i.e., as fixed effect $\pm 1.96*$SQRT[random effect variance]) indicate that 95% of the sample is predicted to have prose recall scores at age 84 from 3.25 to 16.40 with linear rates of change per year from –0.68 to 0.51. Thus, there is substantial heterogeneity in prose recall at 84 years since birth and in change across years since birth.

Next, results from a model using years to death as *time* are shown in the second set of columns in Table 10.1. At –7 years to death (regardless of years since birth or years in study), the expected prose recall was $\gamma_{00} = 10.15$ with a nonsignificant instantaneous linear rate of decline of $\gamma_{10} = -0.09$ per year that became significantly more negative per year by twice the quadratic slope of $\gamma_{20} = -0.02$. The linear and quadratic fixed effects of years to death explained only 1.2% of the total variance in prose recall. There were significant individual differences in linear change across years to death, again relative to a model with fixed quadratic time and a random intercept, $-2\Delta LL(\sim2) = 16.5$, $p < .001$. Results indicate that 95% of the sample is predicted to have prose recall scores at –7 years to death from 4.01 to 16.29, as well as linear rates of change per year from –0.77 to 0.59. Thus, there is also considerable heterogeneity in prose recall at –7 years to death and in linear change across years to death.

Finally, results from a model using years in study as *time* are shown in the third set of columns in Table 10.1. At the first occasion (regardless of years since birth or years to death), the expected prose recall was $\gamma_{00} = 9.64$ with a nonsignificant instantaneous linear rate of increase of $\gamma_{10} = 0.28$ per year that became significantly less positive (or more negative) per year by twice the quadratic slope of $\gamma_{20} = -0.05$. The linear and quadratic fixed effects of years in study captured only 0.4% of the total variance in prose recall. There were significant individual differences in linear change across years in study, again relative to a model with fixed quadratic time and a random intercept, $-2\Delta LL(\sim2) = 18.2$, $p < .001$. Results indicate that 95% of the sample is predicted to have prose recall scores at the first occasion from 2.55 to 16.72, as well as linear rates of change per year in study from -1.00 to 0.44. Thus, there is also heterogeneity in prose recall at the first occasion and in the subsequent rate of change during the study.

Thus, to summarize what we've learned so far, no matter which time metric we choose (i.e., which time predictor is included), there appears to be substantial variability between persons in both levels of prose recall and its linear rate of change over time. But this is far from the end of the story with respect to time—you may have noticed that in fitting two of these three models, I have committed the cardinal sin of smushing! That is, by including only level-1 effects of years since birth and years to death, I have assumed that their between-person and within-person effects are equivalent. Furthermore, a different problem arises in the third model: Because the time predictor of years in study only has within-person variance, it can only show within-person effects. So, while its effects are not smushed, the years in study model did assume any between-person cohort differences in time do not matter, which is highly unlikely to be true here.

Accordingly, we continue by exploring models to address these omissions, focusing first on the accelerated time metrics and continuing with the metric of years in study. To foreshadow, though, we will soon see how the differences between these models become largely cosmetic.

2.B. Evaluating Convergence of Time Effects in Accelerated Longitudinal Models

As originally described in chapters 8 and 9, there are multiple options for distinguishing the between- and within-person effects of a time-varying predictor. Using predictors for accelerated time (i.e., years since birth and years to death) in the level-1 model is akin to grand-mean-centering as presented in chapter 8. To review, this involves including the level-1 predictor centered at a constant rather than at a variable, and but then also including a predictor to represent its between-person variance in the level-2 model. Previously we had used the person mean of the predictor, and although we could do so here, too, this may not make the most sense.

In this context, between-person differences in years since birth and in years to death are not unobserved constructs that we need to derive using an aggregate of the level-1 data—here we have *known* dates of birth and death that we can use directly instead. Furthermore, because of the large quantity of incomplete data (i.e., only 557 observations rather than the 207*5 = 1,035 we would have had if each person had provided five observations), the person mean of the observed time predictors would be downwardly biased for those persons with fewer observations. For instance, consider two persons who each began the study at 84 years from birth: Completing three instead of five observations would result in a person mean age of 86 instead of 88 years. For this reason, between-person (cross-sectional) differences should be represented by year of birth or year of death. To preserve anonymity in this real data set, however, we will use their values at the first occasion (which is very closely, but not perfectly, related to birth year and death year).

These level-2 predictors will be referred to as *birth cohort* and *death cohort,* and for convenience each will be centered at the same constant as its level-1 counter-part (e.g., 84 years since birth or –7 years to death). In the models that follow, the cohort predictors will provide contextual effects that distinguish between-person from within-person effects of time. That is, a **cohort effect** means that it matters *when* you were at a given point in time, not just what point in time it was. For instance, would a person who was 84 years of age in 1950 have the same expected outcomes as a person who was 84 in the year 2000? If not, many possible factors could be responsible for these cohort effects that remain after controlling for age, such as generational differences in education, health care, working life, socialization, and so on. Our job here is not to determine the source of these cohort effects; instead, we aim to accurately describe the effects of cross-sectional differences and longitudinal changes within each accelerated metric of time.

If we consider the level-2 cohort predictors as moderators of the level-1 model of linear and quadratic change over *time,* then it is possible for cohort differences to explain individual variability, not only in intercept levels of prose recall but also in its rates of linear change over time. Accordingly, the model we will use is shown in Equation (10.2):

Level 1 : $\text{Recall}_{ti} = \beta_{0i} + \beta_{1i}(\text{Time}_{ti} - C) + \beta_{2i}(\text{Time}_{ti} - C)^2 + e_{ti}$

Level 2 : Intercept: $\quad \beta_{0i} = \gamma_{00} + \gamma_{01}(\text{Cohort}_i - C)$

$$+ \gamma_{02}(\text{Cohort}_i - C)^2 + U_{0i}$$

Linear Slope: $\quad \beta_{1i} = \gamma_{10} + \gamma_{11}(\text{Cohort}_i - C) + U_{1i}$

Quadratic Slope: $\beta_{2i} = \gamma_{20}$ $\hfill (10.2)$

Composite : $\text{Recall}_{ti} = \left\{ \gamma_{00} + \gamma_{01}(\text{Cohort}_i - C) + \gamma_{02}(\text{Cohort}_i - C)^2 + U_{0i} \right\}$

$$+ \left\{ \gamma_{10} + \gamma_{11}(\text{Cohort}_i - C) + U_{1i} \right\}(\text{Time}_{ti} - C)$$

$$+ \left\{ \gamma_{20} \right\}(\text{Time}_{ti} - C)^2 + e_{ti}$$

in which three effects of cohort have been added. Higher-order interactions (e.g., cohort and cohort^2 with quadratic time; cohort^2 with linear time) were not significant for any time predictor. Thus, the reported models include linear effect of cohort on the intercept and linear slope, as well as a quadratic effect of cohort on the intercept—the latter is necessary given the rules of interactions involving time-varying predictors, as presented in chapter 8 and explained below.

To review, a level-1 grand-mean-centered predictor *when included without its level-2 counterpart* will have a smushed main effect: here, the linear effect of $Time_{ti}$ γ_{10} would have implied equal between- and within-person linear effects of time. But after adding a linear effect of its level-2 predictor (γ_{01} for $Cohort_i$), the level-1 effect of $Time_{ti}$ γ_{10} becomes a purely within-person linear slope. Furthermore, the interaction of $Time_{ti}$ by $Cohort_i$ γ_{11} *when included without its level-2 counterpart* will result in a smushed interaction: Here, it would have implied equal moderation by cohort of the between- and within-person linear time slope. But after adding a quadratic effect of its level-2 predictor (γ_{02} for $Cohort_i^2$), the interaction of $Time_{ti}$ by $Cohort_i$ γ_{11} then becomes how cohort moderates the within-person linear time slope specifically. Similarly, the quadratic effect of $Time_{ti}^2$ γ_{20} *when included without its level-2 counterpart* would have implied equal between- and within-person quadratic effects of time. But after including γ_{02} for $Cohort_i^2$, the level-1 effect of $Time_{ti}^2$ γ_{20} becomes a purely within-person quadratic time slope.

So, what do these cohort effects then represent? The linear cohort effect γ_{01} is relatively straightforward—it is a contextual effect for the difference of the between-person from within-person linear effects of time. The quadratic cohort effect γ_{02} is more challenging to interpret because two other model terms already imply some between-person quadratic effect of time—γ_{11} for $Time_{ti}$ by $Cohort_i$ and γ_{20} for $Time_{ti}^2$. So, γ_{02} for $Cohort_i^2$ becomes a "double" contextual effect: It represents the difference of the between-person quadratic time effect already predicted in the model (by γ_{11} and γ_{20}) from the *total* between-person quadratic effect in the data.

Results from the model in Equation (10.2) using years since birth as *time* after controlling for birth cohort (i.e., years from birth at the first occasion) are given in the first set of columns in Table 10.2. Cohort effects are also shown in the top of Figure 10.2, in which the *x*-axis is years since birth and predicted trajectories are plotted for persons who began the study at 80, 84, or 88 years since birth. The intercept is highlighted with a vertical dashed line. Predicted time-specific values that could have been observed during the study are connected with solid lines, whereas the model-based extrapolations—as needed to actually understand the fixed effects—are connected with dotted lines. Finally, the predicted trajectory from the unconditional model for years since birth (not controlling for birth cohort) is shown by the gray, dashed line.

Understanding the contextual effects provided by cohort predictors in accelerated time models can be tricky, but the key is remembering what the intercept means. In this model, the reference point is 84 years since birth ($Time_{ti} - 84 = 0$) for a person who began the study at 84 years since birth ($Cohort_i - 84 = 0$). So, at that first occasion, an 84-year-old had an expected prose recall of $\gamma_{00} = 9.41$ with a significant instantaneous linear slope of $\gamma_{10} = 0.30$ per year that became significantly less positive per year by twice the quadratic slope of $\gamma_{20} = -0.05$; this reference trajectory is shown in the top of Figure 10.2 by the line with triangle markers.

Next, we consider the three contextual effects created by birth cohort—they significantly improved model fit relative to the unconditional model for years since birth, $-2\Delta LL(3) = 15.8$, $p < .001$, indicating that the between- and within-person effects of years since birth are not the same. More specifically, the contextual linear

Table 10.2 Results for prose recall using years since birth and years in study controlling for birth cohort. Bold values are $p < .05$.

Model Effects	Years since Birth (0 = 84) + Contextual Birth Cohort				Years in Study (0 = 0) + Total Birth Cohort			
	Term	Est	SE	p <	Term	Est	SE	p <
Model for the Means								
Intercept	γ_{00}	**9.41**	0.35	.001	γ_{00}	**9.34**	0.35	.001
Linear Slope	γ_{10}	**0.30**	0.11	.010	γ_{10}	**0.31**	0.11	.006
Quadratic Slope	γ_{20}	**-0.05**	0.02	.003	γ_{20}	**-0.05**	0.01	.003
Contextual Linear Birth Cohort on Intercept	γ_{01}	**-0.58**	0.15	.001	$\gamma_{01} - \gamma_{10}$	**-0.61**	0.16	.001
Contextual Quadratic Birth Cohort on Intercept	γ_{02}	**-0.08**	0.03	.012	$\gamma_{02} - \gamma_{11} + \gamma_{20}$	**-0.08**	0.03	.007
Contextual Linear Birth Cohort on Linear Slope	γ_{11}	**0.13**	0.03	.001	$\gamma_{11} - 2\gamma_{20}$	**0.14**	0.03	.000
Total Linear Birth Cohort on Intercept	$\gamma_{01} + \gamma_{10}$	**-0.28**	0.10	.007	γ_{01}	**-0.30**	0.11	.005
Total Quadratic Birth Cohort on Intercept	$\gamma_{02} + \gamma_{11} + \gamma_{20}$	0.00	0.02	.900	γ_{02}	0.01	0.02	.619
Total Linear Birth Cohort on Linear Slope	$\gamma_{11} + 2\gamma_{20}$	0.03	0.02	.087	γ_{11}	**0.04**	0.02	.035
Model for the Variance								
Intercept Variance	$\tau^2_{U_0}$	**11.15**	1.45	.001	$\tau^2_{U_0}$	**12.48**	1.60	.001
Linear Slope Variance	$\tau^2_{U_1}$	**0.09**	0.03	.004	$\tau^2_{U_1}$	**0.13**	0.04	.002
Intercept-Slope Covariance	$\tau_{U_{01}}$	-0.34	0.18	.053	$\tau_{U_{01}}$	**-0.60**	0.23	.008
Residual Variance	σ^2_e	**4.11**	0.37	.001	σ^2_e	**3.94**	0.36	.001
Total R²		.025				.026		
ML Model Fit								
Number of Parameters		10				10		
-2LL		2823.8				2818.5		
AIC		2843.8				2838.5		
BIC		2877.2				2871.9		

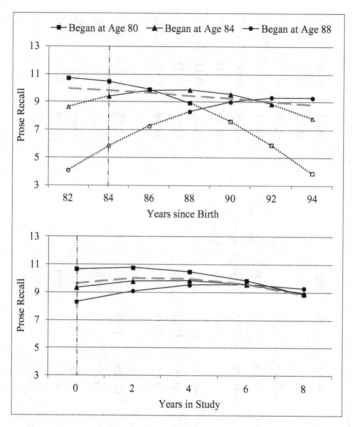

Figure 10.2 Predicted prose recall by birth cohort from models using years since birth and years in study. Solid black lines indicate possible predicted values by birth cohort; dotted black lines indicate model extrapolations to non-observed years since birth. The dashed gray horizontal line shows predictions not controlling for birth cohort; the dashed vertical line indicates the location of the model intercept (84 years since birth, or 0 years in study).

cohort effect on the intercept indicates that, after controlling for current years since birth, for every year older a person was at the first occasion, the difference in expected prose recall at age 84 was $\gamma_{01} = -0.58$ per year, which was significant as evaluated at age 84. That contextual linear cohort effect on the intercept became significantly more negative by twice the contextual quadratic cohort effect of $\gamma_{02} = -0.08$ per year (i.e., the difference between birth cohorts at age 84 became more pronounced in older cohorts). In addition, the contextual linear cohort effect on the linear slope indicates that, after controlling for current years since birth, for every year older a person was at the first occasion, the linear rate of change at 84 years since birth became significantly more positive by $\gamma_{11} = 0.13$. These cohort effects are shown in the top of Figure 10.2. Although persons who began the study farther from birth were expected to have much lower prose recall scores at age 84, their scores were predicted to actually grow over time, and at a greater rate than younger cohorts (again, at age 84). These findings may seem surprising, or at least a bit strange, especially for the linear slope. But it's important to keep in mind that in order to interpret these effects, we had to rely on predictions for outcomes that weren't actually observed—for instance, we did not have data at age 84 for persons who began the study at age 88. If we examine the observed predictions instead (i.e., the regions of solid lines for each cohort), then the cohort differences appear far less dramatic.

Strange results were also found from the model in Equation (10.2) using years to death as *time* while controlling for death cohort, as given in the first set of columns in Table 10.3 and as shown in the top panel of Figure 10.3 (in which the *x*-axis is now years to death). In this model, the reference point for the intercept is –7 years to death ($Time_{ti} + 7 = 0$) for a person who began the study at –7 years to death ($Cohort_i + 7 = 0$). So, at that first occasion, that person had an expected prose recall of $\gamma_{00} = 9.75$ with a nonsignificant instantaneous linear slope of $\gamma_{10} = 0.21$ per year that became significantly less positive per year by twice the quadratic slope of $\gamma_{20} = -0.06$; this reference trajectory is again shown by the line with triangle markers.

The contextual effects of death cohort significantly improved model fit relative to the unconditional model for years to death, $-2\Delta LL(3) = 8.7$, $p = .034$, indicating that the between- and within-person effects of years to death are also not the same. More specifically, the contextual linear cohort effect on the intercept indicates that, after controlling for current years to death, for every year closer to death a person was at the first occasion, the difference in expected prose recall at –7 years to death was $\gamma_{01} = -0.35$ per year, which was significant as evaluated at –7 years to death. That contextual linear cohort effect on the intercept became nonsignificantly more negative by twice the contextual quadratic cohort effect of $\gamma_{02} = -0.03$ per year. In addition, the contextual linear cohort effect on the linear slope indicates that after controlling for current years to death, for every year closer to death a person was at the first occasion, the linear rate of change at –7 years to death became significantly more positive by $\gamma_{11} = 0.08$. As shown in the top panel of Figure 10.3, these death cohort effects create a similar pattern as the birth cohort effects, with similar limitations in their real-world interpretability.

2.C. Time-in-Study Models via Baseline-Centering

At this point you might be wondering about the utility of these models using accelerated time, given that their parameters refer to extrapolations (e.g., a predicted value at a point in time that was not observed for all persons) and that the interpretation of their level-2 effects is convoluted at best. Fortunately, there is a solution to these quandaries—as presented in chapter 8, when between- and within-person effects diverge, a model that represents each type of effect specifically (rather than the differences between them) is likely to be more useful. We could use person-mean-centering (as in chapters 8 and 9) to create direct between- and within-person effects, except that in this context we aren't using a person mean for accelerated time.

Table 10.3 Results for prose recall using years to death and years in study controlling for death cohort. Bold values are $p < .05$.

Model Effects	Years to Death (0 = −7) + Contextual Death Cohort				Years in Study (0 = 0) + Total Death Cohort			
	Term	Est	SE	p <	Term	Est	SE	p <
Model for the Means								
Intercept	γ_{00}	**9.75**	0.37	**.001**	γ_{00}	**9.75**	0.39	**.001**
Linear Slope	γ_{10}	0.21	0.11	.062	γ_{10}	**0.24**	0.11	**.037**
Quadratic Slope	γ_{20}	**−0.06**	0.02	**.001**	γ_{20}	**−0.06**	0.02	**.001**
Contextual Linear Death Cohort on Intercept	γ_{01}	**−0.35**	0.13	**.007**	$\gamma_{01} - \gamma_{10}$	**−0.38**	0.13	**.003**
Contextual Quadratic Death Cohort on Intercept	γ_{02}	−0.03	0.02	.127	$\gamma_{02} - \gamma_{11} + \gamma_{20}$	−0.04	0.02	.079
Contextual Linear Death Cohort on Linear Slope	γ_{11}	**0.08**	0.03	**.007**	$\gamma_{11} - 2\gamma_{20}$	**0.09**	0.03	**.005**
Total Linear Death Cohort on Intercept	$\gamma_{01} + \gamma_{10}$	−0.14	0.07	.059	γ_{01}	**−0.15**	0.07	**.043**
Total Quadratic Death Cohort on Intercept	$\gamma_{02} + \gamma_{11} + \gamma_{20}$	−0.01	0.02	.707	γ_{02}	−0.01	0.02	.653
Total Linear Death Cohort on Linear Slope	$\gamma_{11} + 2\gamma_{20}$	−0.03	0.02	.124	γ_{11}	−0.02	0.02	.205
Model for the Variance								
Intercept Variance	$\tau^2_{U_0}$	**9.70**	1.37	**.001**	$\tau^2_{U_0}$	**12.71**	1.61	**.001**
Linear Slope Variance	$\tau^2_{U_1}$	**0.12**	0.04	**.001**	$\tau^2_{U_1}$	**0.13**	0.04	**.001**
Intercept-Slope Covariance	$\tau_{U_{01}}$	−0.06	0.16	.712	$\tau_{U_{01}}$	**−0.64**	0.23	**.005**
Residual Variance	σ^2_e	**4.00**	0.36	**.001**	σ^2_e	**3.92**	0.36	**.001**
Total R²		.026				.026		
ML Model Fit								
Number of Parameters		10				10		
−2LL		2820.2				2819.1		
AIC		2840.2				2839.1		
BIC		2873.5				2872.4		

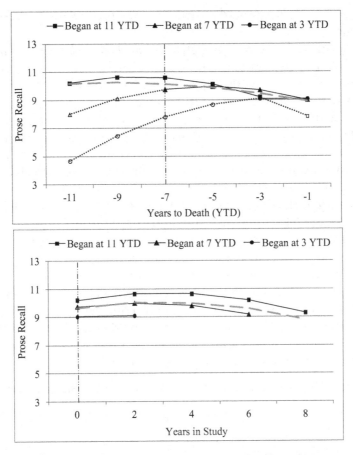

Figure 10.3 Predicted prose recall by death cohort from models using years to death and years in study. Solid black lines indicate possible predicted values by death cohort; dotted black lines indicate model extrapolations to non-observed years to death. The dashed gray horizontal line indicates predictions not controlling for death cohort; the dashed vertical line indicates the location of the model intercept (–7 years to death or 0 years in study).

Instead, we can use baseline-centering (as also presented in chapter 9) to create a level-1 time predictor for the within-baseline difference in *time* at each occasion from a baseline of *time* at the first occasion (i.e., $Birth1_i$ or $Death1_i$). For years since birth, the level-1 predictor for within-baseline time would be: $WBbirth_{ti} = Birth_{ti} - Birth1_i$; for years to death, it would be: $WBdeath_{ti} = Death_{ti} - Death1_i$. These level-1 within-baseline predictors would then contain solely within-person, longitudinal variation in time; the level-2 predictors for years at the first occasion since birth $(Birth1_i - C)$ or from death $(Death1_i - C)$ would then each contain solely between-person, cross-sectional variation in time. Thus, the level-2 predictors would provide the effects of *being further from birth* or *being closer to death* at the beginning of the study; the level-1 predictors would provide the effects of subsequent *changes in time* during the study.

It is important to remember, though, that *accelerated time metrics differ between persons only*. That is, within persons, time is just time—here, this means the level-1 predictors of WBbirth$_{ti}$ and WBdeath$_{ti}$ will always be equivalent. Furthermore, they are also equivalent to years in study (the naïve time metric we began with) that contains only within-person variation (i.e., ICC = 0). Thus, using years in study as the level-1 predictor is akin to baseline-centering, whereas using an accelerated time metric as a level-1 predictor is akin to grand-mean-centering (whose effects will be correctly un-smushed only after controlling for cohort). In chapter 9 we saw how baseline-centering can be problematic when used with time-varying predictors that show individual change over time if that individual time slope variance is not explicitly in the model (along with model-based intercept variance and residual variance). In this context, though, *time* cannot be another outcome—it can only be a predictor, and so these same concerns do not apply.

As shown in chapter 8, different ways of centering level-1 predictors can yield equivalent models with respect to their fixed effects given the inclusion of all relevant level-2 counterparts. The same is true in considering how the fixed effects from a model using years in study as the level-1 predictor can nevertheless recreate the fixed effects from a model using accelerated time as the level-1 predictor, as illustrated using years since birth in Equation (10.3):

Composite using Years in Study $(\text{YSB}_{ti} - \text{Cohort}_i)$ with Birth Cohort (Cohort_i) :

$$
\begin{aligned}
\text{Recall}_{ti} &= \gamma_{00} + \gamma_{10}(\text{YSB}_{ti} - \text{Cohort}_i) + \gamma_{20}(\text{YSB}_{ti} - \text{Cohort}_i)^2 + \gamma_{01}(\text{Cohort}_i) \\
&\quad + \gamma_{02}(\text{Cohort}_i)^2 + \gamma_{11}(\text{YSB}_{ti} - \text{Cohort}_i)(\text{Cohort}_i) \\
&\quad + U_{0i} + U_{1i}(\text{YSB}_{ti} - \text{Cohort}_i) + e_{ti} \\
&= \gamma_{00} + \gamma_{10}(\text{YSB}_{ti}) - \gamma_{10}(\text{Cohort}_i) + \gamma_{20}(\text{YSB}_{ti})^2 - 2\gamma_{20}(\text{YSB}_{ti})(\text{Cohort}_i) \\
&\quad + \gamma_{20}(\text{Cohort}_i)^2 + \gamma_{01}(\text{Cohort}_i) + \gamma_{02}(\text{Cohort}_i)^2 + \gamma_{11}(\text{YSB}_{ti})(\text{Cohort}_i) \\
&\quad - \gamma_{11}(\text{Cohort}_i)^2 + U_{0i} + U_{1i}(\text{YSB}_{ti}) - U_{1i}(\text{Cohort}_i) + e_{ti} \\
&= \gamma_{00} + \gamma_{10}(\text{YSB}_{ti}) + \gamma_{20}(\text{YSB}_{ti})^2 + (\gamma_{01} - \gamma_{10})(\text{Cohort}_i) \\
&\quad + (\gamma_{02} + \gamma_{20} - \gamma_{11})(\text{Cohort}_i)^2 + (\gamma_{11} - 2\gamma_{20})(\text{YSB}_{ti})(\text{Cohort}_i) \\
&\quad + U_{0i} + U_{1i}(\text{YSB}_{ti}) - U_{1i}(\text{Cohort}_i) + e_{ti}
\end{aligned}
\tag{10.3}
$$

Composite using Years Since Birth (YSB_{ti}) with Birth Cohort (Cohort_i) :

$$
\begin{aligned}
\text{Recall}_{ti} &= \gamma_{00} + \gamma_{10}(\text{YSB}_{ti}) + \gamma_{20}(\text{YSB}_{ti})^2 + \gamma_{01}^*(\text{Cohort}_i) \\
&\quad + \gamma_{02}^*(\text{Cohort}_i)^2 + \gamma_{11}^*(\text{YSB}_{ti})(\text{Cohort}_i) + U_{0i} + U_{1i}(\text{YSB}_{ti}) + e_{ti}
\end{aligned}
$$

in which both models are written in composite form (and in which centering constants have been omitted for clarity). The * superscripts denote fixed effects from the model for years since birth that get re-created from linear combinations of fixed effects from the model for years in study.

In the model for years in study, the first equation provides the original model, in which years in study is written explicitly as the difference in years since birth at each occasion (YSB$_{ti}$) from years since birth at the first occasion (Cohort$_i$). The second equation distributes the fixed effects across the predictors in parentheses, and the third equation combines the fixed effects by predictor. The results from estimating this years in study model controlling for birth cohort are given in the second set of columns in Table 10.2. Notably, the differences between the fixed effects from the two models are primarily because the effects of birth cohort from the years since birth accelerated time model are *contextual* effects (i.e., after controlling for current years since birth), whereas in the years in study model they are *total* effects (i.e., not controlling for current years since birth). Each set can be re-created from a linear combination of the other, although the estimates after doing so are not exactly the same, as explained shortly.

The total birth cohort effects are shown in the bottom panel of Figure 10.2, in which the *x*-axis is now years in study. The dashed gray line shows the predicted trajectory from the unconditional model (i.e., not controlling for birth cohort). The reference trajectory (as shown by the solid line with triangle markers) is the same as for the accelerated time model using years since birth: at the first occasion, an 84-year-old (Cohort$_i$ – 84 = 0) had an expected prose recall of γ_{00} = 9.34 with a significant instantaneous linear slope of γ_{10} = 0.31 per year that became significantly less positive per year by twice the quadratic slope of γ_{20} = –0.05. The three birth cohort effects significantly improved model fit relative to the unconditional years in study model, –2ΔLL(3) = 9.3, *p* = .026, but are interpreted differently than in the years since birth accelerated time model. This model for years in study provides the *total* linear cohort effect on the intercept. It indicates that for every year farther from birth a person was at the first occasion, expected prose recall *at the first occasion* (not at 84 years since birth) was significantly lower by γ_{01} = –0.30 per year. That total linear cohort effect on the intercept became nonsignificantly less negative per year by twice the total quadratic cohort effect on the intercept of γ_{02} = 0.01. In addition, the total linear cohort effect on the linear slope indicates that for every year farther from birth a person was at the first occasion, the linear slope *at the first occasion* became significantly more positive by γ_{11} = 0.04. So, as shown in the bottom of Figure 10.2, although persons who began the study farther from birth were expected to have lower prose recall, they were predicted to grow more over time.

As noted above, even after correcting for differences in contextual versus total birth cohort effects, the coefficients and predictions from the two models are not exactly the same. This is because once a random time slope is included, their models for the variance cannot be made equivalent, unlike their models for the means. Given a random time slope, the random intercept will have a different interpretation in each model: it will either indicate predicted individual differences in prose recall at 84 years since birth *or* at the first occasion. In addition, as shown in Equation (10.3), the part of the random linear slope variance that was due to cohort variance will be excluded from the model for years in study. And as discussed in chapter 5, our likelihood algorithm first searches for the random effects variances and covariances and then deterministically calculates the fixed effects using the estimated **V** matrix (and the values of the predictors). So, if the **V** matrix (as predicted per person by the random effect variances and covariances from the **G** matrix and the residual variances and covariances in the **R** matrix) is not the same across models, the fixed effects will also not be the same. In this case, relative to the accelerated time model using years since birth, in the years in study model, the random intercept variance is 12% larger, the random slope variance is 40% larger, and the residual variance is 4% smaller. Furthermore, although it explained only 0.1% more variance than the accelerated time model, the AIC and BIC prefer the years in study model (as does its relative ease of interpretation).

The point of the previous contrasting of the years in study model to the years from birth model was to show how they are or are not equivalent. As you may have already guessed, we can see the same scenario unfold in a years in study model after substituting years to death for years since birth, as shown in the second columns of Table 10.3 and in the bottom panel of Figure 10.3. Although there is still a significant total negative linear effect of death cohort on the intercept at the first occasion, the total linear effect of death cohort on the linear slope was nonsignificant. Relative to the accelerated time model using years to death, in the years in study model, the random intercept variance is 31% larger, the random slope variance is 13% larger, and the residual variance is 2% smaller. Finally, the AIC and BIC still prefer the years in study model (although it explained the same amount of variance as the accelerated time model).

To summarize, we have just seen how models using more theoretically driven accelerated time metrics of years since birth and years since death as level-1 predictors can nevertheless be re-created using the naïve level-1 predictor of years in study, which is equivalent within persons to any accelerated time metric. However, another useful feature of a years in study model is that it provides a neutral baseline with which to compare the contribution of different between-person effects of *time* (cohort). To illustrate, we can examine to what extent the birth and death cohort effects found in separate models persist when estimated simultaneously. Because the accelerated time metrics of years since birth and years to death only differ between persons, there is no information lost in introducing them into the level-2 model only, as shown in Equation (10.4):

Level 1: $\text{Recall}_{ti} = \beta_{0i} + \beta_{1i}(\text{YIS}_{ti}) + \beta_{2i}(\text{YIS}_{ti})^2 + e_{ti}$

Level 2: Intercept: $\beta_{0i} = \gamma_{00} + \gamma_{01}(\text{BirthCohort}_i - 84)$

$$+ \gamma_{02}(\text{BirthCohort}_i - 84)^2$$

$$+ \gamma_{03}(\text{DeathCohort}_i + 7)$$

$$+ \gamma_{04}(\text{DeathCohort}_i + 7)^2 + U_{0i}$$

Linear Slope: $\beta_{1i} = \gamma_{10} + \gamma_{11}(\text{BirthCohort}_i - 84)$

$$+ \gamma_{13}(\text{DeathCohort}_i + 7) + U_{1i}$$

Quadratic Slope: $\beta_{2i} = \gamma_{20}$

Composite:

$$\text{Recall}_{ti} = \begin{Bmatrix} \gamma_{00} + \gamma_{01}(\text{BirthCohort}_i - 84) + \gamma_{02}(\text{BirthCohort}_i - 84)^2 \\ + \gamma_{03}(\text{DeathCohort}_i + 7) + \gamma_{04}(\text{DeathCohort}_i + 7)^2 + U_{0i} \end{Bmatrix} +$$

$$\{\gamma_{10} + \gamma_{11}(\text{BirthCohort}_i - 84) + \gamma_{13}(\text{DeathCohort}_i + 7) + U_{1i}\}(\text{YIS}_{ti})$$

$$+ \{\gamma_{20}\}(\text{YIS}_{ti})^2 + e_{ti}$$

(10.4)

in which YIS$_{ti}$ indicates years in study directly, in which time 0 is the first occasion (as before).

Results are given in Table 10.4 and illustrated in Figure 10.4. The reference trajectory is now for someone who enters the study at both 84 years since birth and –7 years to death. That person had an expected prose recall at the first occasion of γ_{00} = 9.49 with a significant instantaneous linear slope of γ_{10} = 0.27 per year that became significantly less positive per year by twice the quadratic slope of γ_{20} = –0.05. For every year father from birth a person enters the study, prose recall at the first occasion was predicted to be significantly lower by γ_{01} = –0.28 (as evaluated at 84 years since birth); there was no significant deceleration in this effect across years since birth. Similarly, for every year closer to death a person enters the study, prose recall at the first occasion was predicted to be nonsignificantly lower by γ_{03} = –0.12

Table 10.4 Results for prose recall using years in study controlling for total effects of birth and death cohorts. Bold values are $p < .05$.

Model Effects	Years in Study (0 = 0) + Total Birth and Death Cohorts		
	Est	SE	p <
Model for the Means			
γ_{00} Intercept	**9.49**	0.43	.001
γ_{10} Linear Slope	**0.27**	0.11	.018
γ_{20} Quadratic Slope	**–0.05**	0.02	.001
γ_{01} Total Linear Birth Cohort on Intercept	**–0.28**	0.11	.009
γ_{02} Total Quadratic Birth Cohort on Intercept	0.01	0.02	.549
γ_{11} Total Linear Birth Cohort on Linear Slope	**0.05**	0.02	.027
γ_{03} Total Linear Death Cohort on Intercept	–0.12	0.07	.087
γ_{04} Total Quadratic Death Cohort on Intercept	–0.01	0.02	.540
γ_{13} Total Linear Death Cohort on Linear Slope	–0.03	0.02	.126
Model for the Variance			
$\tau^2_{U_0}$ Intercept Variance	**12.24**	1.57	.001
$\tau^2_{U_1}$ Linear Slope Variance	**0.13**	0.04	.002
$\tau_{U_{01}}$ Intercept-Slope Covariance	**–0.59**	0.22	.008
σ^2_e Residual Variance	**3.90**	0.35	.001
Total R^2	.043		
ML Model Fit			
Number of Parameters	13		
–2LL	2810.6		
– AIC	2836.6		
– BIC	2879.9		

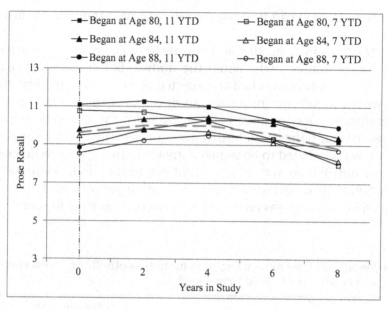

Figure 10.4 Predicted prose recall by birth and death cohort from models using years in study. The dashed gray horizontal line indicates predictions not controlling for birth or death cohort; the dashed vertical line indicates the location of the model intercept (0 years in study).

(as evaluated at –7 years to death); there was no significant deceleration in this effect across years to death. Finally, for every year father from birth a person enters the study, the linear slope at the first occasion was predicted to be more positive by $\gamma_{11} = 0.05$, but the effect of death cohort on the linear slope of $\gamma_{13} = -0.03$ was not significant. Thus, after controlling for years to death at the first occasion, years since birth at the first occasion was still related to a lower intercept but a less negative slope. We could continue by examining interactive rather than additive effects of birth and death cohort, but I will leave these now straightforward extensions to the ambitious reader!

2.D. Summary

The second section of this chapter illustrated two-level models for concurrently observed dimensions of time in accelerated longitudinal designs. In our example, because persons began the study at different points in *time*, there were significant between-person differences in *time*, both with respect to years since birth and years to death. Each person was measured every two years for up to five occasions, creating within-person variation in *time* as well. Accordingly, after an initial strawman model featuring smushed effects of accelerated time, we sought to properly distinguish the between-person from within-person effects of each metric of time.

We did so by including level-2 predictors for time cohort (e.g., years since birth or years to death *at the first occasion*). When paired with the accelerated time metric as the level-1 predictor (e.g., *current* years since birth or years to death), these level-2 cohort effects became *contextual* effects; when paired with the naïve time metric of years in study as the level-1 predictor, these level-2 cohort effects became *total* effects instead. Upon including all relevant level-2 effects, contextual or total effects of cohort can be provided from either model, although their estimates may not match exactly if the models have any random time slopes. That is, their random effects variances and covariances may differ given differences in what time 0 means in each model; these differences in variance components can translate into different fixed effects estimates as well.

This specific example was designed to illustrate two more fundamental tenets of what we can or cannot do with respect to *time* in accelerated longitudinal designs. First, although different ways of "clocking time" may diverge between persons, they are all equivalent within persons. So, there is nothing inherently more meaningful in using an "informative" accelerated time metric as a level-1 predictor (i.e., years from an event) relative to using a "naïve" time metric (i.e., years in study), because these two predictors contain the exact same information within persons (in which time is just time). Accelerated time metrics can differ between persons, but these differences then logically belong in the level-2 model instead. Second, we cannot ignore the fact that accelerated longitudinal designs create both between-person and within-person variation in time, each of which may have its own effects on a given outcome. As in previous chapters, whether the effects of a predictor are equivalent across levels is testable by including its contextual effects. When effects diverge across levels, estimating separate effects per level is likely to be more useful.

3. Three-Level Models for Analysis of Separable Dimensions of Within-Person Time

An important commonality in the longitudinal designs covered in this chapter so far is their unidimensionality with respect to *within-person* time. For instance, in our last example, persons were measured up to five times at two-year intervals. Thus, the only kind of within-person change that can have been observed is long-term change over two years or more; any shorter-term changes that might have happened between the two-year assessments would go undetected. This is the problem that *measurement burst designs*, as introduced in the beginning of this chapter, are designed to solve. These designs feature multidimensional measurement of time, such that two or more types of changes (i.e., over different time scales) can be observed within persons. As a result, two-level models that distinguish only one dimension of within-person variation due to time will no longer be sufficient. Accordingly, the example in the next section will introduce three-level models for separable dimensions of within-person time. How many levels are needed for a given design can be tricky to determine (as discussed further later and in chapter 11), but the key feature of this example is that the design includes two within-person time dimensions, which will require two levels beneath the highest level for persons.

Our example data come from the Cognition, Health, and Aging Project (see chapter 1), in which six assessments were collected over a two-week period, and in which this six-session measurement burst was repeated five times. The example featured in chapters 7 and 8 only used sessions 2 through 6 from the first measurement burst, but the analyses for this example will use all available occasions, for a possible total of 6 sessions*5 bursts = 30 observations per person. The study was designed such that bursts would be separated by six months, although in reality the timing of the observations was more variable than planned, especially towards the end of the study. Relative to burst 1 (0 months), burst 2 was collected an average of 6.25 months later (SD = 0.73, range = 4.90 to 9.03). Burst 3 was collected at an average of 12.84 months (SD = 0.80, range = 10.35 to 16.36), which was an average of 6.69 months after burst 2 (SD = 0.70, range = 5.22 to 9.49). Burst 4 was collected at an average of 19.30 months (SD = 1.17, range = 14.61 to 22.31), which was an average of 6.61 months after burst 3 (SD = 0.70, range = 4.99 to 8.94). Finally, burst 5 was collected at an average of 25.51 months (SD = 1.47, range = 21.85 to 28.75), which was an average of 6.25 months after burst 3 (SD = 1.05, range = 4.90 to 9.10).

Our sample was obtained from 108 older adults who were age 66 to 95 years (M = 80.34, SD = 6.41) at the first occasion; approximately 27% were men. As in the example in chapters 7 and 8, the outcome variable was a sum of the number of physical symptoms participants reported experiencing in the past 24 hours, including aches/pain, gastrointestinal, cardiovascular, upper respiratory, and "other" symptoms. Few symptoms were reported on average per day (N = 2,752, M = 1.66, SD = 1.43, range = 0 to 5). We will also examine how physical symptoms can be predicted by a simultaneously collected measure of positive affect, which was indicated by the mean across five items (happy, interested, energetic, content, and warmhearted) each rated on a scale of 0 = *not at all* to 4 = *very often* (N = 2,747, M = 2.58, SD = 0.73, range = 0 to 4).

Although our eventual goal is to examine how positive affect relates to reported physical symptoms, we don't yet know just how many types of relationships we will need to consider. This is because both variables may show individual differences in change across sessions and bursts, such that they could be related through their intercepts, slopes, residuals, and so on, as presented in chapter 9. So, we will need to assess the sources of time-related variation in each variable before we can examine their multivariate relationships. Accordingly, we will use the symptoms outcome to introduce three-level unconditional models for time, and then follow with comparable models using positive affect as a second outcome. As usual, we will start by partitioning variance with empty models as estimated using maximum likelihood, although with a three-level twist, as described next. For now we will focus the interpretation of each level of variance in a three-level model; how these estimated variances relate to the observed variances at each level will be examined in chapter 11.

Table 10.5 Results from empty means models for daily physical symptoms.

Quantity	Single-Level: Independent Observations	Two-Level: Session within Burst*Person	Three-Level: Session within Burst within Person
Fixed Intercept	1.66 (0.03)	1.67 (0.06)	1.71 (0.11)
Sum of Variances	2.04	2.06	2.13
Variance Estimates:			
Level-1 (L1) Residual Variance σ_e^2 for Session	2.04	0.63	0.63
Level-2 (L2) Intercept Variance $\tau_{U_{00}}^2$ for Burst	0	1.43	0.43
Level-3 (L3) Intercept Variance $\tau_{V_{00}}^2$ for Person	0	0	1.08
Percent of Total Variance:			
% Level-1 Residual Variance for Session	1	.31	.30
% Level-2 Intercept Variance for Burst	0	.69	.20
% Level-3 Intercept Variance for Person	0	0	.50
Intraclass Correlations (Variances):			
ICC_{L2} = (L3 + L2) / (L3 + L2 + L1)	0	.69	.70
ICC_{L3} = (L3) / (L3 + L2)	0	0	.72
Model –2LL for df = 1 Comparisons:	9,776.1	7,772.5	7,524.5
–2ΔLL for ICC_{L2} = .69 > 0: (Model 1 vs. 2) → Does burst + person matter (relative to all)?		2,003.6	
–2ΔLL for ICC_{L3} = .72 > 0: (Model 2 vs. 3) →Does person matter (relative to burst)?			248.0

3.A. A Three-Level Model for the Variance

We could begin with a two-level model for occasions nested within persons, in which t and i subscripts would indicate the level-1 model for time and the level-2 model for person, respectively. In this measurement burst design, though, a single index of t for time will not be sufficient, because we have to keep track of from which of the six sessions and from which of the five bursts each outcome was obtained, in addition to from which individual. This means we need a ***three-level model for the variance***, as shown in Equation (10.5):

Level 1 Sessions : $\text{Symptoms}_{sbi} = \beta_{0bi} + e_{sbi}$

Level 2 Bursts : $\beta_{0bi} = \delta_{00i} + U_{0bi}$

Level 3 Persons : $\delta_{00i} = \gamma_{000} + V_{00i}$

Composite : $\text{Symptoms}_{sbi} = \gamma_{000} + V_{00i} + U_{0bi} + e_{sbi}$

$$\text{ICC}_{\text{L2}} = \frac{\tau_{V_{00}}^2 + \tau_{U_{00}}^2}{\tau_{V_{00}}^2 + \tau_{U_{00}}^2 + \sigma_e^2} = \frac{1.08 + 0.43}{1.08 + 0.43 + 0.63} = .70$$

(10.5)

$$\text{ICC}_{\text{L3}} = \frac{\tau_{V_{00}}^2}{\tau_{V_{00}}^2 + \tau_{U_{00}}^2} = \frac{1.08}{1.08 + 0.43} = .72$$

in which there are three subscripts instead of two. Level 1 is now indicated by s for session, level 2 by b for burst, and level 3 by i for individual. Accordingly, the first subscript indexes the effect being predicted at level 1, the second subscript indexes the order of predictors in its level-2 equation, and the third subscript indexes the order of predictors in its level-3 equation. Although any three letters can be used for the subscripts in three-level models (i.e., ***ijk*** is a common choice), it can be helpful to use letters that clearly relate to the analysis (i.e., here, we use s sessions within b bursts within i individuals to help us remember the levels). In addition, instead of including the γ fixed effects at level 2, the three-level model contains an additional set of δ placeholders at level 2 instead, such that the fixed effects don't appear until level 3 for individuals, which is now the highest level of the model (where fixed effects belong).

As usual, the fixed intercept γ_{000} in an empty means model provides the outcome grand mean taking into account all levels of the model. To illustrate how the intercept estimates can change depending on which levels are modeled, Table 10.5 shows the results from single-level, two-level, and three-level empty means models for symptoms. As seen in the first row, the fixed intercept estimate differs across models, as does its interpretation. That is, the single-level model provides the grand mean across all sessions without regard to bursts or persons. The two-level model—in which level-1 sessions are nested within a collapsed level 2 of bursts by persons—provides the grand mean of the burst means without regard to persons. Finally, the three-level model—in which level-1 sessions are nested within level-2 bursts, which are nested in level-3 persons—provides the grand mean of the person means taken across each person's burst means. Although slight here, these intercept differences can become more pronounced when the data are more unbalanced (e.g., there is greater variation in the number of sessions per burst per person).

More generally, how many levels are needed is dictated *not* by the model for the means, but by the model for the variance—that is, the term **level** usually refers to an **orthogonal set of variance components**. For instance, we called our previous models "two-level" because they contained two sets of uncorrelated variance components: Level-1 σ_e^2 for within-person variation over time, and level-2 $\tau_{U_0}^2$ for between-person intercept variation. Other U_i random effect terms could also be included that would be correlated with the existing random effects in the level-2 model, but all U_i random effects would remain uncorrelated with the e_{ti} residuals in the level-1 model. So, our "three-level" model has three sets of uncorrelated variance components. To limit their confusion, we will keep e for level 1 and U for level 2, but add a new letter V for level 3.

All random effects in Equation (10.5) can be viewed as deviations from a predicted value (as created by the set of fixed effects or placeholders at each level). So, beginning at level 3, person i's intercept (δ_{00i}) is created from the fixed intercept (γ_{000}, the grand mean of the person means) plus person i's random intercept (V_{00i}), which is the difference from the grand mean to person i's mean (across bursts). That is, a *positive* value for V_{00i} indicates that person i reported *more* symptoms than other people; a *negative* value for V_{00i} indicates *fewer* symptoms than other people. Next, at level 2, the intercept at burst b for person i (β_{0bi}) is created from person i's intercept (δ_{00i}) plus burst b's random intercept (U_{0bi}), which is the difference from person i's overall mean to person i's mean for burst b (across sessions). Thus, a *positive* value for U_{0bi} indicates that person i reported *more* symptoms in burst b than during his or her other bursts; a *negative* value for U_{0bi} indicates relatively *fewer* symptoms. Finally, at level 1, the symptoms outcome at session s in burst b for person i is created from the intercept at burst b for person i (β_{0bi}) plus session s's residual (e_{sbi}), which is the difference from burst b's mean for person i to the current session s. Thus, a *positive* value for e_{sbi} indicates that person i reported more symptoms in session s of burst b than in his or her other sessions from that burst; a *negative* value for e_{sbi} indicates relatively *fewer* symptoms. In summarizing, the composite model shows more directly how, after substituting for the placeholders, there are only four unique estimated parameters: a fixed effect (γ_{000}) and three piles of variance (the uncorrelated $\tau^2_{V_{00}}$, $\tau^2_{U_{00}}$, and σ^2_e).

To help convey the partitioning of variance in a three-level model, Table 10.5 also shows the variance estimates, percentages at each level, and intraclass correlations from single-level, two-level, and three-level empty means models. Because each source of variance is uncorrelated, in these models we can just sum the variance components to create a total variance. Based on the total variance for the three-level model in the third column, 30% of the symptoms variance is across sessions at level 1, 20% is across bursts at level 2, and 50% is between persons at level 3. These percentages can be used to understand the different intraclass correlations (ICCs) that can be calculated from a three-level model, as shown in Equation (10.5) and reported in Table 10.5. Please note: The specific names of the ICCs presented next will vary by author, and so it will be critical to clearly define how each ICC is calculated when interpreting ICCs in results sections.

First is a level-2 intraclass correlation: *ICC_{L2} is the proportion of the total variance that is at or above level 2.* Although conceptually similar to the ICC we already know, ICC_{L2} is now the correlation of level-1 units within level-2 *and* level-3 units. As seen for the three-level model in Table 10.5, $ICC_{L2} = (.50 + .20) / (1.00) = .70$ is the correlation of sessions from the same burst (and from the same person, given that bursts are nested within persons). Not coincidentally, this is very close to the ICC_{L2} from the two-level model in the second column, which included a random intercept for bursts only, meaning that sessions were nested within bursts only. Whether $ICC_{L2} > 0$ can be tested by comparing the fit of a two-level model against a single-level σ_e^2-only model, just as we've done previously. A note of caution, however: if this comparison against the σ_e^2-only model is not significant, this may seem to indicate that $ICC_{L2} \approx 0$, such that there is no significant level-2 random intercept variance, and that a two-level model is *not* necessary. But because including level-1 predictors can reduce the residual variance, which will in turn *increase* the random intercept variance (due to the correction factor that links them together; see chapter 5), the random intercept variance may be larger in subsequent models. Therefore, the safest route is to include the level-2 random intercept variance regardless of ICC_{L2}, or at least until the point where you can be reasonably certain that no matter what, there really is no level-2 variance.

Next is a new level-3 intraclass correlation: ICC_{L3} *is the proportion of variance at or above level 2 that is actually due to level 3*. ICC_{L3} is the correlation of level-2 units within level-3 units—*but without regard to level-1 units,* whose variance is not part of the denominator in calculating ICC_{L3}. As seen for the three-level model in Table 10.5, $ICC_{L3} = (.50) / (.50 + .20) = .72$ for the correlation of bursts from the same person. Another way to think about the ICC_{L3} is as the *ICC for the intercept specifically*: Of the total *intercept* variance (at level 2 and 3), how much is at level 3? We will see later how this conceptualization of ICC_{L3} generalizes to random slope variances, but with respect to the random intercept here, whether $ICC_{L3} > 0$ can be tested by comparing the fit of the three-level model against the two-level model. In doing so, however, the same caution applies—the upper-level random intercept variances may grow larger after level-1 predictors reduce the residual variance, and as such should be retained so long as the **G** matrix is positive definite (i.e., the upper-level random intercept variances are estimable).

Table 10.5 also shows the implications with respect to the two ICCs for leaving a level out of the model. In first column, the single-level σ_e^2-only model has no random intercepts and thus predicts no correlation for sessions from the same burst ($ICC_{L2} = 0$) or bursts from the same person ($ICC_{L3} = 0$). In the second column, the two-level model for sessions within bursts predicts a correlation of sessions from the same burst ($ICC_{L2} > 0$) but still predicts no correlation of bursts from the same person ($ICC_{L3} = 0$). Only the three-level model in the third column predicts both kinds of correlations ($ICC_{L2} > 0$ and $ICC_{L3} > 0$), as are indeed present in these data. If both kinds of correlation are not predicted by the model, then the SEs and *p*-values for level-2 or level-3 predictors are likely to be too small (i.e., because all dependency has not been accounted for).

Previously we had calculated 95% random effect confidence intervals (CI) as: 95% CI = fixed effect ± 1.96*SQRT(random variance), and we can do so for each of the random intercepts here. The 95% CI for the level-3 random intercept indicates that 95% of the symptom person means are expected to range from –0.33 to 3.74, indicating some positive skewness in the person means. The 95% for the level-2 random intercept tends to be less directly interpretable because of the additional partitioning of variance. Here, the 95% CI for the level-2 random intercept means that, after controlling for person mean differences in symptoms, 95% of the burst symptom mean *deviations* are expected to range from 0.43 to 2.98.

As an aside, there is yet another type of intraclass correlation that can be calculated from three-level models that I will call ICC_{L3b}, which is the **proportion of total variance** (rather than the proportion of variance *at level 2 and 3*) *that is due to level 3*. For symptoms, $ICC_{L3b} = (.30) / (1.00) = .30$, which is the correlation of sessions that are from the same person, but *not* from the same burst. The fact that there is more than one type of level-3 ICC helps to illustrate the importance of explaining exactly how a given ICC is calculated in order to interpret it correctly!

Now that we have examined how many levels of random effects are needed for our symptoms outcome, let us do so for our eventual level-1 predictor of positive affect as well. Its single-level σ_e^2-only model fit significantly worse than its two-level model, $-2\Delta LL(\sim 1) = 2{,}105.6$, $p < .001$, which fit significantly worse than its three-level model, $-2\Delta LL(\sim 1) = 397.8$, $p < .001$. Its three-level model provided estimates of $\gamma_{000} = 2.54$, level-1 $\sigma_e^2 = 0.16$ (29% of total), level-2 $\tau_{U_{00}}^2 = 0.06$ (12% of total), and level-3 $\tau_{U_{00}}^2 = 0.16$ (59% of total). Thus, the correlation of positive affect in sessions from the same burst and person was $ICC_{L2} = (.12 + .59) / (1.00) = .71$, whereas the correlation of positive affect in sessions from the same person but *not* from the same burst was $ICC_{L3b} = .59$. Finally, the correlation of bursts from the same person was $ICC_{L3} = (.59) / (.59 + .12) = .83$, which is also the proportion of random intercept variance specifically at level 3 (meaning that 17% of the random intercept variation in positive affect was across bursts). The 95% random intercept CI for level-3 was 1.44 to 3.65; for level-2, the CI = 2.05 to 3.04.

3.B. Fixed Effects of Multidimensional Time

Our next step is to examine fixed and random effects of our two levels of time. Although changes in symptoms and positive affect across the six sessions within each 2-week burst were not expected, longer-term changes in symptoms between bursts (i.e., due to health changes) seemed plausible. And although the distances between bursts were unbalanced, it will still be helpful to see the overall pattern of means both within and between bursts. To obtain these means, our next model includes saturated means for session, burst, and their interaction (i.e., that will perfectly reproduce the 30 possible means), along with the previous random intercepts for burst and person (i.e., a three-level model), as shown in composite form in Equation (10.6):

$$
\begin{aligned}
\text{Symptoms}_{sbi} = {} & \gamma_{000} + \gamma_{100}\left(S1_{sbi}\right) + \gamma_{200}\left(S2_{sbi}\right) + \gamma_{300}\left(S3_{sbi}\right) + \gamma_{400}\left(S4_{sbi}\right) \\
& + \gamma_{500}\left(S5_{sbi}\right) + \gamma_{010}\left(B1_{bi}\right) + \gamma_{020}\left(B2_{bi}\right) + \gamma_{030}\left(B3_{bi}\right) + \gamma_{040}\left(B4_{bi}\right) \\
& + \gamma_{110}\left(S1_{sbi}\right)\left(B1_{bi}\right) + \gamma_{120}\left(S1_{sbi}\right)\left(B2_{bi}\right) + \gamma_{130}\left(S1_{sbi}\right)\left(B3_{bi}\right) \\
& + \gamma_{140}\left(S1_{sbi}\right)\left(B4_{bi}\right) + \gamma_{210}\left(S2_{sbi}\right)\left(B1_{bi}\right) + \gamma_{220}\left(S2_{sbi}\right)\left(B2_{bi}\right) \\
& + \gamma_{230}\left(S2_{sbi}\right)\left(B3_{bi}\right) + \gamma_{240}\left(S2_{sbi}\right)\left(B4_{bi}\right) + \gamma_{310}\left(S3_{sbi}\right)\left(B1_{bi}\right) \\
& + \gamma_{320}\left(S3_{sbi}\right)\left(B2_{bi}\right) + \gamma_{330}\left(S3_{sbi}\right)\left(B3_{bi}\right) + \gamma_{340}\left(S3_{sbi}\right)\left(B4_{bi}\right) \\
& + \gamma_{410}\left(S4_{sbi}\right)\left(B1_{bi}\right) + \gamma_{420}\left(S4_{sbi}\right)\left(B2_{bi}\right) + \gamma_{430}\left(S4_{sbi}\right)\left(B3_{bi}\right) \\
& + \gamma_{440}\left(S4_{sbi}\right)\left(B4_{bi}\right) + \gamma_{510}\left(S5_{sbi}\right)\left(B1_{bi}\right) + \gamma_{520}\left(S5_{sbi}\right)\left(B2_{bi}\right) \\
& + \gamma_{530}\left(S5_{sbi}\right)\left(B3_{bi}\right) + \gamma_{540}\left(S5_{sbi}\right)\left(B4_{bi}\right) + V_{00i} + U_{0bi} + e_{sbi}
\end{aligned}
\tag{10.6}
$$

in which the last value in each series—session 6 and burst 5—served as the reference category. The 30 fixed effects create all possible mean differences across sessions and bursts via the Sx and Bx dummy codes that distinguish each session and burst from its reference category.

Omnibus F-tests for symptoms revealed significant marginal main effects of session, $F(5, 2{,}291) = 15.35$, $p < .001$, and burst, $F(4, 355) = 9.78$, $p < .001$, but no significant interaction, $F(20, 2{,}291) = 1.32$, $p = .15$. The marginal means for session and burst are shown in the top panel of Figure 10.5, and the saturated means trajectory within each burst is shown in by the solid lines with squares in the bottom panel. Although there is some idiosyncrasy across bursts, the within-burst session means seem to suggest piecewise slopes by which symptoms are highest at the first session in each burst, but then decrease by the second session, with little change after that. Across bursts, however, symptoms seem to increase slightly from bursts 1–3, but then level off by bursts 4–5, perhaps suggesting quadratic change across bursts. To test these impressions, we will need to evaluate the fit of the fixed effects with respect to session and burst separately—we can do so by building a predictive model for each dimension, one level at a time.

First, we can test a piecewise model for change in symptoms across sessions while allowing different intercepts and piecewise slopes for each burst (i.e., keeping all differences across bursts saturated as before), as shown in composite form in Equation (10.7):

$$
\begin{aligned}
\text{Symptoms}_{sbi} = {}& \gamma_{000} + \gamma_{100}\left(\text{Slope12}_{sbi}\right) + \gamma_{200}\left(\text{Slope26}_{sbi}\right) \\
& + \gamma_{010}\left(\text{B1}_{bi}\right) + \gamma_{020}\left(\text{B2}_{bi}\right) + \gamma_{030}\left(\text{B3}_{bi}\right) + \gamma_{040}\left(\text{B4}_{bi}\right) \\
& + \gamma_{110}\left(\text{Slope12}_{sbi}\right)\left(\text{B1}_{bi}\right) + \gamma_{120}\left(\text{Slope12}_{sbi}\right)\left(\text{B2}_{bi}\right) \\
& + \gamma_{130}\left(\text{Slope12}_{sbi}\right)\left(\text{B3}_{bi}\right) + \gamma_{140}\left(\text{Slope12}_{sbi}\right)\left(\text{B4}_{bi}\right) \\
& + \gamma_{210}\left(\text{Slope26}_{sbi}\right)\left(\text{B1}_{bi}\right) + \gamma_{220}\left(\text{Slope26}_{sbi}\right)\left(\text{B2}_{bi}\right) \\
& + \gamma_{230}\left(\text{Slope26}_{sbi}\right)\left(\text{B3}_{bi}\right) + \gamma_{240}\left(\text{Slope26}_{sbi}\right)\left(\text{B4}_{bi}\right) \\
& + V_{00i} + U_{0bi} + e_{sbi}
\end{aligned}
\tag{10.7}
$$

in which Slope12_{sbi} (coded session 1 = –1 and sessions 2–6 = 0) indexes the change from session 1–2, and Slope26_{sbi} (coded sessions 1–2 = 0 and sessions 2–6 = session – 2) indexes the change from sessions 2–6. The intercept for mean symptoms at session 2 (when both slopes = 0) differed significantly across bursts, $F(4, 802) = 8.82$, $p < .001$; the intercepts still suggested a quadratic pattern of change across bursts. Slope12_{sbi} was negative as expected, and its effect did not differ significantly across bursts, $F(4, 2{,}292) = 0.37$, $p = .83$. However, the effect of Slope26_{sbi} did differ significantly across bursts, $F(4, 2{,}290) = 2.84$, $p = .02$, such that it appeared larger at bursts 3 and 4. However, of primary interest is that our piecewise session, saturated burst means model did not fit significantly worse than the previous fully saturated means model, $-2\Delta LL(15) = 9.4$, $p = .85$, indicating support for a piecewise model of mean change across sessions within bursts.

Continuing on, we can compare our piecewise session model to a further reduced model that replaces the saturated burst effects on the intercept and piecewise slopes

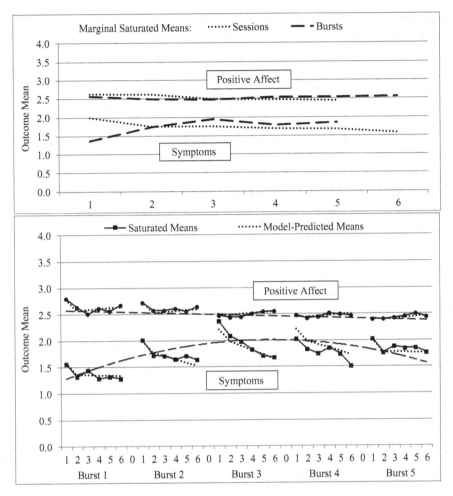

Figure 10.5 Observed and predicted daily physical symptoms and positive
affect. Top: saturated marginal means for burst and session.
Bottom: saturated means for burst by session (solid lines), and as
predicted from a piecewise model of within-burst change (dotted
lines across six sessions) and a quadratic model of between-burst
change (dashed line across five bursts).

with linear and quadratic burst slopes, centered at the first burst, as shown in composite form in Equation (10.8):

$$
\begin{aligned}
\text{Symptoms}_{sbi} = {}& \gamma_{000} + \gamma_{100}\left(\text{Slope12}_{sbi}\right) + \gamma_{200}\left(\text{Slope26}_{sbi}\right) \\
& + \gamma_{010}\left(\text{Burst}_{bi} - 1\right) + \gamma_{020}\left(\text{Burst}_{bi} - 1\right)^{2} \\
& + \gamma_{110}\left(\text{Slope12}_{sbi}\right)\left(\text{Burst}_{bi} - 1\right) + \gamma_{120}\left(\text{Slope12}_{sbi}\right)\left(\text{Burst}_{bi} - 1\right)^{2} \quad (10.8) \\
& + \gamma_{210}\left(\text{Slope26}_{sbi}\right)\left(\text{Burst}_{bi} - 1\right) + \gamma_{220}\left(\text{Slope26}_{sbi}\right)\left(\text{Burst}_{bi} - 1\right)^{2} \\
& + V_{00i} + U_{0bi} + e_{sbi}
\end{aligned}
$$

In fitting this model, the interactions of Slope12_{sbi} with Burst_{bi} and Burst_{bi}^2 were not significant and were thus removed. The resulting model did not fit significantly worse than our previous piecewise session, saturated burst means model from Equation (10.7), $-2\Delta LL(8) = 11.6$, $p = .17$, indicating that the changes across bursts in intercept and in the rate of change from sessions 2–6 could be approximated with a quadratic trend. Notably, this final model was not significantly worse than the original fully saturated means model from Equation (10.6), $-2\Delta LL(23) = 21.1$, $p = .57$, indicating that we have adequately predicted the original 30 session*burst symptom means with our seven fixed effects (whose interpretations will be provided after examining random effects).

This last model is now presented in three-level and composite form in Equation (10.9):

Level 1 Sessions: $\quad \text{Symptoms}_{sbi} = \beta_{0bi} + \beta_{1bi}(\text{Slope12}_{sbi}) + \beta_{2bi}(\text{Slope26}_{sbi}) + e_{sbi}$

Level 2 Bursts: $\quad$ Intercept: $\beta_{0bi} = \delta_{00i} + \delta_{01i}(\text{Burst}_{bi}-1) + \delta_{02i}(\text{Burst}_{bi}-1)^2 + U_{0bi}$

$\qquad\qquad\qquad$ Slope12: $\beta_{1bi} = \delta_{10i}$

$\qquad\qquad\qquad$ Slope26: $\beta_{2bi} = \delta_{20i} + \delta_{21i}(\text{Burst}_{bi}-1) + \delta_{22i}(\text{Burst}_{bi}-1)^2$

Level 3 Persons:

Intercept: $\delta_{00i} = \gamma_{000} + V_{00i}$ $\qquad$ Slope12: $\delta_{10i} = \gamma_{100}$ $\qquad\qquad$ Slope26: $\delta_{20i} = \gamma_{200}$ $\qquad$ (10.9)

$\quad$ Burst: $\delta_{01i} = \gamma_{010}$ $\qquad\qquad\qquad\qquad\qquad\qquad\qquad$ Slope26*Burst: $\delta_{21i} = \gamma_{210}$

$\quad$ Burst^2: $\delta_{02i} = \gamma_{020}$ $\qquad\qquad\qquad\qquad\qquad\qquad$ Slope26*Burst^2: $\delta_{22i} = \gamma_{220}$

Composite:

$\text{Symptoms}_{sbi} = \gamma_{000} + \gamma_{100}(\text{Slope12}_{sbi}) + \gamma_{200}(\text{Slope26}_{sbi}) + \gamma_{010}(\text{Burst}_{bi}) + \gamma_{020}(\text{Burst}_{bi})^2$

$\qquad\qquad + \gamma_{210}(\text{Slope26}_{sbi})(\text{Burst}_{bi}) + \gamma_{220}(\text{Slope26}_{sbi})(\text{Burst}_{bi})^2 + V_{00i} + U_{0bi} + e_{sbi}$

in which labels are provided for each equation in the level-2 and level-3 models to help us keep track of what each equation is actually predicting. The level-1 model has three level-2 β placeholders, each of which is then predicted by a level-2 equation. At level 2, there are then seven new level-3 placeholders, each of which requires its own level-3 equation. This system of placeholders may appear unnecessary here given that most of them are replaced with a single fixed effect in the level-3 model (as shown directly in the composite model). However, the three-level placeholder notation can be useful to distinguish the terms that have been included from what terms *could* be included (also indicated here by the blank spaces left in the level-3 model).

One other issue to be addressed is the unbalance in the time between bursts. Although convenient, using *burst* as our metric of level-2 time ignores the actual variability in the distance between bursts that was noted earlier. To address this unbalanced burst timing, two additional models were examined. First, the distance in time from when each burst was supposed to be (i.e., exactly 6 months apart) and when each burst actually began was calculated. This actual burst distance predictor was then included as a main effect and in interactions with the piecewise session slopes in our final fixed effects model, but none of these effects was close to significant. Second, the original distance in time between bursts was used in the final model instead of the even-interval burst predictor. However, this exact time model only accounted for 0.9% of the total symptoms variance (vs. 2.5%), and was not preferred by the AIC (4,725 vs. 4,761) or BIC (7,453 vs. 7,493). Thus, we will continue with the even-interval burst predictor that is at least equivalent to, if not better than, a predictor for the actual distance in time between bursts.

3.C. Random Effects of Multidimensional Time

Our next order of business is to examine which of our fixed effects of time may need to have random effects across higher levels. We will follow the same process as usual, except with added complexity given the three-level model. In our previous two-level models we examined whether persons needed their own slopes (e.g., for time or other time-varying predictors), which meant testing whether level-1 predictors should have random effects across level-2 units. Level-2 predictors could not have random effects, so we didn't worry about those. Now, however, it is possible for level-2 effects to vary randomly over level-3 persons—here, we need to examine whether persons (at level 3) need their own linear and quadratic burst slopes (level-2 predictors). To do so, we first add the level-3 random $Burst_{bi}$ slope V_{01i} to the level-3 equation predicting δ_{01i}. Note that this also entails also adding a covariance with the level-3 random intercept V_{00i}, but not with the level-2 random intercept U_{0bi} given that it is on a different (orthogonal) level. Model fit improved significantly, $-2\Delta LL(\sim 2) = 6.8$, $p = .03$. However, adding the level-3 random $Burst_{bi}^2$ slope V_{02i} to the level-3 equation predicting δ_{02i} (as well as its covariances with the level-3 random intercept V_{00i} and random $Burst_{bi}$ slope V_{01i}) did not improve model fit, $-2\Delta LL(\sim 3) = 2.9$, $p = .41$. Thus, although persons varied in the extent to which their symptoms changed linearly over bursts, they shared a common rate of quadratic change across bursts.

Next we address the level-1 predictors—we will need to examine in sequential models whether the piecewise slopes for session vary randomly across level-2 bursts, level-3 persons, or at both levels. Having random effects of the same predictor at two different levels of analysis may seem redundant, but it's actually not—the three possible outcomes are illustrated in Figure 10.6, which depicts negative slopes given the negative average piecewise slopes for session. Slopes for two hypothetical persons A and B are shown via black or gray lines, including dashed lines for their slopes per burst and solid lines for their mean slope across bursts. First, the left panel shows a *random slope across level-2 bursts only*: while there is slope variation across bursts, the mean slopes for persons A and B do not differ, indicating there is no commonality due to level-3 persons in the per-burst slopes. Next, the middle panel depicts a *random slope across level-3 persons only*: although it initially appears that the slopes differ across bursts, in actuality the slopes vary by person and not much by bursts otherwise. Finally, the right panel shows the hybrid result in which there is a *random slope at level 2 and level 3*—each level-3 person needs his or her own slope, and within persons, each level-2 burst needs its own slope as well.

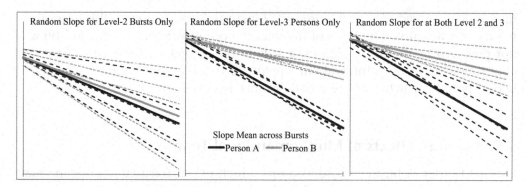

Figure 10.6 Illustration of random slopes at two levels, in which the dashed lines indicate per-burst slopes and the solid lines indicate person mean slopes for person A (black lines) and person B (gray lines).

So which of these scenarios will we see for symptoms? Although the piecewise slopes are not hierarchical, given that greater change was observed from sessions 1–2, we can start there. Furthermore, just as we originally proceeded from a single-level empty means model to a two-level model to a three-level model, we will follow the same logical sequence here. First, to allow Slope12$_{sbi}$ to vary across level-2 bursts, we add the random slope U$_{1bi}$ to the level-2 equation predicting β_{1bi}. Note that this also entails also adding a covariance with the level-2 random intercept U$_{0bi}$, but not with the level-3 random intercept V$_{00i}$ or random Burst$_{bi}$ slope V$_{01i}$ given that they are on a different level. Model fit improved significantly, $-2\Delta LL(\sim2) = 19.4$, $p < .001$, and provided a random level-2 Slope12$_{sbi}$ variance of $\tau^2_{U_{10}} = 0.25$. This indicates that the difference in symptoms from sessions 1–2 varies randomly over bursts (within persons). Next, to what extent does the Slope12$_{sbi}$ effect vary randomly over persons at level 3, in addition to over bursts at level 2? To answer this, we can continue by adding the random Slope12$_{sbi}$ slope V$_{10i}$ to the level-3 equation predicting δ_{10i}. This also entails adding a covariance with the random intercept V$_{00i}$ and random Burst$_{bi}$ slope V$_{01i}$ at the same level 3, but not with the random intercept U$_{0bi}$ and random Slope12$_{sbi}$ U$_{1bi}$ at level 2. However, the model with a random variance for Slope12$_{sbi}$ at both level 2 ($\tau^2_{U_{10}} = 0.20$) and level 3 ($\tau^2_{V_{10}} = 0.05$) did not fit significantly better than the model with a random variance for Slope12$_{sbi}$ at level 2 only, $-2\Delta LL(\sim3) = 5.5$, $p = .14$.

To help us understand what this means, we can use the same variance decomposition process by which we ended up with two levels of random intercepts in our empty means model. To review, after fitting a two-level model of sessions within bursts (and persons) and obtaining an ICC$_{L2}$ = .69, the next question was, of that 69% of the variance at level 2 or higher (i.e., of the random intercept variance), how much was actually due to person mean differences at level 3, rather than burst mean differences at level 2? The three-level model answered that question and provided an ICC$_{L3}$ = .72, indicating that 72% of the random intercept variance was actually at level 3, such that random intercepts were necessary at both levels. The level-3 random intercept is the difference from the fixed intercept to the person intercept, whereas the level-2 random intercept is the difference from the person intercept to the burst intercept.

Applying that same logic to the random Slope12$_{sbi}$ effects, the level-3 random Slope12$_{sbi}$ is the difference from the fixed slope to the person's mean slope over bursts, whereas the level-2 random Slope12$_{sbi}$ is the difference from that person mean slope to the slope for that burst. We can calculate a level-3 slope ICC to determine what proportion of the total Slope12$_{sbi}$ random variance (summed across levels 2 and 3) is actually at level 3. Using the slope variance estimates from the last model, slope ICC$_{L3}$ = ($\tau^2_{V_{10}}$) / ($\tau^2_{V_{10}}$ + $\tau^2_{U_{10}}$) = (0.05) / (0.05 + 0.20) = .20, indicating that 20% of the random Slope12$_{sbi}$ variance is at level 3 (and that 80% is at level 2). The fact that the level-3 random Slope12$_{sbi}$ variance did not improve model fit significantly means that the slope ICC$_{L3}$ = .20 $\approx$ 0, or that there is no significant commonality in the random slopes from the same person. So, it appears that Slope12$_{sbi}$ for symptoms best matches the pattern in the left panel of Figure 10.6. As an aside, although 20% may seem like it should be greater than 0, slopes will usually be estimated with greater imprecision than intercepts. Furthermore, although keeping the level-3 random Slope12$_{sbi}$ may seem like a conservative approach, models become more unlikely to converge with many random slopes, especially those whose variance approaches 0.

We can use the same process to test random effects of Slope26$_{sbi}$ on symptoms, keeping the random effect of Slope12$_{sbi}$ at level 2 only. Adding the random Slope26$_{sbi}$ U$_{2bi}$ to the level-2 equation for β_{2bi} (and its covariances with only the level-2 random intercept U$_{0bi}$ and random Slope12$_{sbi}$ U$_{1bi}$) significantly improved model fit, $-2\Delta LL(\sim 3) = 25.0$, $p < .001$. However, adding a random Slope26$_{sbi}$ V$_{20i}$ to the level-3 equation for δ_{20i} (and its covariances with the level-3 random intercept V$_{00i}$ and random Burst$_{bi}$ slope V$_{01i}$) did not significantly improve model fit, $-2\Delta LL(\sim 3) = 1.9$, $p = .60$. Only 13% of the random Slope26$_{sbi}$ variance was at level 3 (slope ICC$_{L3}$ = .13). Thus, while there is random variance in the difference in symptoms between sessions 1–2 and 2–6 across bursts, there is no significant commonality across persons for either.

Now are we finally done evaluating fixed and random effects of time for symptoms? The answer is probably, although other random effects are technically still possible. You may have noticed that each random effect variance has two subscripts instead of one—this is necessary because of the possible combinations in three-level models. In further considering the model in Equation (10.9), we have only examined random effects for the *main effects* in our model (Burst and Burst^2 at level 3; Slope12$_{sbi}$ and Slope26$_{sbi}$ at levels 2 and 3). But it is possible to also have random effects of interaction terms (although perhaps unlikely given the power that would be needed for these terms). For example, a cross-level interaction between level 1 and level 2 can have a random effect at level 3. So, here, we could also add person-level random effects V$_{21i}$ for Slope26$_{sbi}$*Burst and V$_{22i}$ for Slope26$_{sbi}$*Burst^2 to the level-3 equations predicting δ_{21i} and δ_{22i}, respectively. If we had any level-1 interactions, they could have random effects at level 2 and/or level 3; similarly, if we had level-2 interactions, they could have random effects at level 3. After including their random main effects, random interaction effects can also be tested via $-2\Delta LL$ tests, but watch for non-positive definite solutions (i.e., variances estimated as 0) in doing so!

Our final unconditional random effects model for symptoms is given in Equation (10.10):

Level 1 Sessions: $\text{Symptoms}_{sbi} = \beta_{0bi} + \beta_{1bi}\left(\text{Slope12}_{sbi}\right) + \beta_{2bi}\left(\text{Slope26}_{sbi}\right) + e_{sbi}$

Level 2 Bursts: Intercept: $\beta_{0bi} = \delta_{00i} + \delta_{01i}\left(\text{Burst}_{bi} - 1\right) + \delta_{02i}\left(\text{Burst}_{bi} - 1\right)^2 + U_{0bi}$

Slope12: $\beta_{1bi} = \delta_{10i}$ $\qquad\qquad\qquad\qquad\qquad + \underline{U_{1bi}}$

Slope26: $\beta_{2bi} = \delta_{20i} + \delta_{21i}\left(\text{Burst}_{bi} - 1\right) + \delta_{22i}\left(\text{Burst}_{bi} - 1\right)^2 + \underline{U_{2bi}}$

Level 3 Persons:

Intercept: $\delta_{00i} = \gamma_{000} + V_{00i}$ $\qquad$ Slope12: $\delta_{10i} = \gamma_{100}$ $\qquad\qquad\qquad$ Slope26: $\delta_{20i} = \gamma_{200}$

Burst: $\delta_{01i} = \gamma_{010} + \underline{V_{01i}}$ $\qquad\qquad\qquad\qquad\qquad$ Slope26*Burst: $\delta_{21i} = \gamma_{210}$

Burst^2: $\delta_{02i} = \gamma_{020}$ $\qquad\qquad\qquad\qquad\qquad\qquad$ Slope26*Burst^2: $\delta_{22i} = \gamma_{220}$

Composite: $\qquad\qquad\qquad\qquad\qquad\qquad\qquad\qquad\qquad\qquad\qquad\qquad$ (10.10)

$\text{Symptoms}_{sbi} = \gamma_{000} + \gamma_{100}\left(\text{Slope12}_{sbi}\right) + \gamma_{200}\left(\text{Slope26}_{sbi}\right) + \gamma_{010}\left(\text{Burst}_{bi}\right) + \gamma_{020}\left(\text{Burst}_{bi}\right)^2$

$\qquad\quad + \gamma_{210}\left(\text{Slope26}_{sbi}\right)\left(\text{Burst}_{bi}\right) + \gamma_{220}\left(\text{Slope26}_{sbi}\right)\left(\text{Burst}_{bi}\right)^2$

$\qquad\quad + V_{00i} + \underline{V_{01i}\left(\text{Burst}_{bi}\right)} + U_{0bi} + \underline{U_{1bi}\left(\text{Slope12}_{sbi}\right)} + \underline{U_{2bi}\left(\text{Slope26}_{sbi}\right)} + e_{sbi}$

$$\mathbf{G}\text{ Matrix} = \begin{bmatrix} \text{Level 3} & 0 \\ 0 & \text{Level 2} \end{bmatrix} = \begin{bmatrix} \tau^2_{V_{00}} & \tau_{V_{00,01}} & & & \\ \tau_{V_{01,00}} & \tau^2_{V_{01}} & & & \\ & & \tau^2_{U_{00}} & \tau_{U_{00,10}} & \tau_{U_{00,20}} \\ & & \tau_{U_{10,00}} & \tau^2_{U_{10}} & \tau_{U_{10,20}} \\ & & \tau_{U_{20,00}} & \tau_{U_{20,10}} & \tau^2_{U_{20}} \end{bmatrix}$$

in which the new random effects are underlined for emphasis. Also shown is the block-diagonal **G** matrix of random effects variances and covariances that contribute to a single person's data. Only the non-redundant part of the **G** matrix is shown Equation (10.10); in reality the level-2 block is repeated four more times given that each person has up to five bursts, creating a 17x17 **G** matrix. **R** would be a 30x30 matrix (given 6 sessions*5 bursts per person) with σ^2_e on the diagonal and 0's elsewhere, and thus **V** for each person would be a 30x30 matrix as well.

The symptoms means predicted by the model fixed effects are shown in the bottom panel of Figure 10.5, in which the piecewise slopes created the small dotted lines across sessions within bursts, and the quadratic effect of burst created the larger dashed line at session 2 across bursts. As shown, overall the mean differences due to sessions and bursts are fairly minimal, as also indicated by a total $R^2 = .025$ for symptoms from these effects of session and burst.

Results from the model in Equation (10.10) are given in the first set of columns of Table 10.6. The expected physical symptoms at session 2 of burst 1 was $\gamma_{000} = 1.36$. First, with respect to changes across bursts, symptoms increased significantly at a linear rate of $\gamma_{010} = 0.52$ per burst (as evaluated at session 2 of burst 1), although this rate of change became significantly less positive per burst by twice the quadratic burst effect of $\gamma_{020} = -0.10$ (as evaluated at session 2). There were also significant individual differences in the linear rate of change in symptoms across bursts; 95% random effects confidence intervals predicted per-person burst slopes from 0.30 to 0.74, suggesting most persons were predicted to report an increase in symptoms across the study. Note that we are not calculating 95% random intercept CIs or ICC_{L3} in this model, given that the intercept is defined differently (i.e., is conditional on different 0 points) across levels.

Next, with respect to changes across sessions, symptoms at session 1 were predicted to be significantly higher across bursts by $\gamma_{100} = -0.23$ (which becomes higher given that $Slope12_{sbi} = -1$). In contrast, symptoms were expected to decline from session 2–6 nonsignificantly at a rate of $\gamma_{200} = -0.005$ per session during burst 1. However, this $Slope26_{sbi}$ effect differed across bursts: it initially became significantly more negative by the $Slope26_{sbi}$ by $Burst_{bi}$ interaction $\gamma_{210} = -0.08$ (as evaluated at burst 1), but that rate became significantly less negative per burst by twice the $Slope26_{sbi}$ by $Burst_{bi}^2$ interaction of $\gamma_{220} = 0.02$. Estimated simple effects revealed that the predicted linear rate of the decline in symptoms from sessions 2–6 was significant only from bursts 2–4. There were significant random burst differences in both piecewise session slopes; 95% random effects CI predicted per-burst slopes of –1.11 to 0.65 from sessions 1–2 and –0.22 to 0.21 from sessions 2–6. However, the piecewise session slopes did not vary over persons.

Now that we've gained some practice with fixed and random effects of multi-dimensional time in three-level models, we can use these same models to examine changes in positive affect. The fully saturated means model from Equation (10.6) revealed significant marginal main effects of session, $F(5, 2{,}287) = 3.80$, $p = .002$, and burst, $F(4, 354) = 8.45$, $p < .001$, and a significant interaction, $F(20, 2{,}287) = 1.91$, $p = .009$. As shown in Figure 10.5, though, despite significant effects, there appears to be very little practically significant change either within or between bursts, with the exception of higher positive affect at session 1 during bursts 1 and 2, again suggesting a piecewise slopes model for session. In fitting the same model from Equation (10.7) for positive affect, its intercept for the session 2 mean differed significantly across bursts, $F(4, 1{,}032) = 3.98$, $p = .003$, such that the intercepts appeared to decline linearly across bursts. The effect of $Slope12_{sbi}$ differed significantly across bursts as well, $F(4, 2{,}287) = 3.63$, $p = .006$, such that it was significantly negative at bursts 1–2 (which were not different and significantly more negative than at bursts 3–5, which were also not different). $Slope26_{sbi}$ was positive and its effect did not differ across bursts, $F(4, 2{,}286) = 0.48$, $p = .75$. This piecewise session, saturated burst means model did not fit significantly worse than the fully saturated means model, $-2\Delta LL(15) = 15.9$, $p = .39$, indicating support for a piecewise model of sessions within bursts.

Based on these results, a model to replace the saturated burst effects will need to differ from the model in Equation (10.8) for symptoms, as shown in Equation (10.11):

$$\begin{aligned} \text{Positive Affect}_{sbi} = {} & \gamma_{000} + \gamma_{100}\left(Slope12_{sbi}\right) + \gamma_{200}\left(Slope26_{sbi}\right) \\ & + \gamma_{010}\left(Burst_{bi} - 1\right) + \gamma_{120}\left(Slope12_{sbi}\right)\left(B1or2_{bi}\right) \\ & + V_{00i} + U_{0bi} + e_{sbi} \end{aligned} \tag{10.11}$$

in which a linear slope for burst replaced the saturated burst effects on the intercept, and the effect of Slope26$_{sbi}$ was left equivalent across bursts (i.e., a main effect only). The new predictor B1or2$_{bi}$ is a contrast = 1 for bursts 1–2 and 0 for bursts 3–5 effect, such that the Slope12$_{sbi}$ effect γ_{100} is the change from sessions 1–2 during bursts 3–5, and the Slope12$_{sbi}$*B1or2$_{bi}$ interaction γ_{110} is the difference in the Slope12$_{sbi}$ effect for bursts 1–2. The new model did not fit significantly worse than our previous piecewise session, saturated burst means model from Equation (10.7), $-2\Delta LL(10) =$ 5.2, $p = .88$. It also did not fit significantly worse than the fully saturated means model from Equation (10.6), $-2\Delta LL(25) = 21.2$, $p = .68$, indicating that we have adequately predicted the original 30 session*burst positive affect means with our 5 fixed effects. Our last fixed effects model is now presented in three-level and composite form in Equation (10.12):

Level 1 Sessions : Positive Affect$_{sbi}$ = $\beta_{0bi} + \beta_{1bi}$ (Slope12$_{sbi}$) $+ \beta_{2bi}$ (Slope26$_{sbi}$) $+ e_{sbi}$

Level 2 Bursts :   Intercept: $\beta_{0bi} = \delta_{00i} + \delta_{01i}$ (Burst$_{bi}$ − 1) $+ U_{0bi}$

Slope12: $\beta_{1bi} = \delta_{10i} + \delta_{12i}$ (B1or2$_{bi}$)   Slope26: $\beta_{2bi} = \delta_{20i}$

Level 3 Persons :

Intercept: $\delta_{00i} = \gamma_{000} + V_{00i}$ Slope12: $\delta_{10i} = \gamma_{100}$ Slope26: $\delta_{20i} = \gamma_{200}$

Burst: $\delta_{01i} = \gamma_{010}$ Slope12*B1or2: $\delta_{12i} = \gamma_{120}$

Composite :

Positive Affect$_{sbi}$ = $\gamma_{000} + \gamma_{100}$ (Slope12$_{sbi}$) $+ \gamma_{200}$ (Slope26$_{sbi}$) $+ \gamma_{010}$ (Burst$_{bi}$ − 1)

$+ \gamma_{120}$ (Slope12$_{sbi}$)(B1or2$_{bi}$) $+ V_{00i} + U_{0bi} + e_{sbi}$

(10.12)

In addition, the two models that addressed the unbalance in bursts timing were also estimated for positive affect, but similarly did not indicate any improvement in considering the timing effects.

In turning to the random effects, adding a level-3 random Burst$_{bi}$ slope (V_{01i} in the level-3 equation for δ_{01i}) and its covariance with the level-3 random intercept V_{00i} significantly improved model fit, $-2\Delta LL(\sim2) = 23.5$, $p < .001$. Adding fixed and random Burst$_{bi}^2$ slopes did not improve model fit, $-2\Delta LL(\sim4) = 5.9$, $p = .21$; thus, a linear rate of change across bursts was sufficient.

Continuing with the piecewise session slopes, adding a level-2 random Slope12$_{sbi}$ (U_{1bi} in the level-2 equation for β_{1bi}) and its covariance with the level-2 random intercept U_{0bi} improved model fit significantly, $-2\Delta LL(\sim2) = 19.1$, $p < .001$. Adding a level-3 random Slope12$_{sbi}$ (V_{10i} in the level-3 equation for δ_{10i}) and its covariances with the level-3 random intercept V_{00i} and random Burst$_{bi}$ slope V_{01i} also improved model fit significantly, $-2\Delta LL(\sim3) = 27.2$, $p < .001$, resulting in a Slope12$_{sbi}$ ICC$_{L3}$ = .56. Adding a random interaction of Slope12$_{sbi}$* B1or2$_{bi}$ at level 3 (V_{12i} in the level-3 equation for δ_{12i}) and its three covariances with the other level-3 random effects did not significantly improve model fit, $-2\Delta LL(\sim4) = 4.6$, $p = .32$. Thus, there are burst and person differences in change from sessions 1–2, but not differentially so at burst 1 or 2.

Finally, adding a level-2 random Slope26$_{sbi}$ (U_{2bi} in the level-2 equation for β_{2bi}) and its two covariances with the level-2 random effects improved model fit significantly, $-2\Delta LL(\sim3) = 11.0$, $p = .01$. Adding a level-3 random Slope26$_{sbi}$ (V_{2bi} in the level-3 equation for δ_{20i}) and its three covariances with the other level-3 random effects also improved model fit significantly, $-2\Delta LL(\sim 4) = 13.3\ p = .01$, resulting in a Slope26$_{sbi}$ ICC$_{L3}$ = .48. Thus, there are both burst and person differences in change from sessions 2–6 as well. After retaining both random Slope26$_{sbi}$ effects, our final unconditional model for positive affect is shown in Equation (10.13):

Level 1 Sessions : $\quad$ Positive Affect$_{sbi} = \beta_{0bi} + \beta_{1bi}(\text{Slope12}_{sbi}) + \beta_{2bi}(\text{Slope26}_{sbi}) + e_{sbi}$

Level 2 Bursts : $\qquad$ Intercept: $\beta_{0bi} = \delta_{00i} + \delta_{01i}(\text{Burst}_{bi} - 1) \qquad\qquad + U_{0bi}$

$\qquad\qquad\qquad\qquad$ Slope12: $\beta_{1bi} = \delta_{10i} \qquad\qquad\qquad + \delta_{12i}(\text{B1or2}_{bi}) + U_{1bi}$

$\qquad\qquad\qquad\qquad$ Slope26: $\beta_{2bi} = \delta_{20i} \qquad\qquad\qquad\qquad\qquad + U_{2bi}$

Level 3 Persons :

Intercept: $\delta_{00i} = \gamma_{000} + V_{00i} \qquad\qquad$ Slope12: $\delta_{10i} = \gamma_{100} + \underline{V_{10i}}$ $\quad$ Slope26: $\delta_{20i} = \gamma_{200} + \underline{V_{20i}}$

$\qquad$ Burst: $\delta_{01i} = \gamma_{010} + \underline{V_{01i}}$ $\qquad$ Slope12*B1or2: $\delta_{12i} = \gamma_{120}$

Composite : $\hfill$ (10.13)

Positive Affect$_{sbi} = \gamma_{000} + \gamma_{100}(\text{Slope12}_{sbi}) + \gamma_{200}(\text{Slope26}_{sbi}) + \gamma_{010}(\text{Burst}_{bi} - 1)$

$\qquad\qquad + \gamma_{120}(\text{Slope12}_{sbi})(\text{B1or2}_{bi}) + V_{00i} + \underline{V_{10i}(\text{Slope12}_{sbi})} + \underline{V_{20i}(\text{Slope26}_{sbi})}$

$\qquad\qquad + \underline{V_{01i}(\text{Burst}_{bi} - 1)} + U_{0bi} + \underline{U_{1bi}(\text{Slope12}_{sbi})} + \underline{U_{2bi}(\text{Slope26}_{sbi})} + e_{sbi}$

$$\mathbf{G}\ \text{Matrix} = \begin{bmatrix} \text{Level 3} & 0 \\ 0 & \text{Level 2} \end{bmatrix} = \begin{bmatrix} \tau^2_{V_{00}} & \tau_{V_{00,10}} & \tau_{V_{00,20}} & \tau_{V_{00,01}} & & & \\ \tau_{V_{10,00}} & \tau^2_{V_{10}} & \tau_{V_{10,20}} & \tau_{V_{10,01}} & & & \\ \tau_{V_{20,00}} & \tau_{V_{20,10}} & \tau^2_{V_{20}} & \tau_{V_{20,01}} & & & \\ \tau_{V_{01,00}} & \tau_{V_{01,10}} & \tau_{V_{01,20}} & \tau^2_{V_{01}} & & & \\ & & & & \tau^2_{U_{00}} & \tau_{U_{00,10}} & \tau_{U_{00,20}} \\ & & & & \tau_{U_{10,00}} & \tau^2_{U_{10}} & \tau_{U_{10,20}} \\ & & & & \tau_{U_{20,00}} & \tau_{U_{20,10}} & \tau^2_{U_{20}} \end{bmatrix}$$

in which the new random effects are again underlined for emphasis. Also shown is the non-redundant part of the block-diagonal **G** matrix of random effects variances and covariances; in this model **G** is actually a 19x19 matrix after accounting for the four other repetitions of the level-2 block. **R** would again be a 30x30 matrix (given 6 sessions*5 bursts per person) with σ^2_e on the diagonal and 0's elsewhere, and thus **V** per person would again be a 30x30 matrix as well.

The positive affect means predicted by the fixed effects are shown in the bottom panel of Figure 10.5; the fixed effects accounted for only 0.5% of the total variance. Full results from the model in Equation (10.13) are given in the second column of Table 10.6. The predicted positive affect at session 2 of burst 1 was $\gamma_{000} = 2.57$. Positive affect decreased significantly at a linear rate of $\gamma_{010} = -0.05$ per burst. Given the significant individual differences in the linear rate of change across bursts, a 95% random effects CI predicted per-person burst slopes from -0.21 to 0.12, suggesting not everyone was predicted to decrease in positive affect across bursts.

Next, with respect to the piecewise changes across sessions, positive affect at session 1 (Slope12$_{sbi} = -1$) was predicted to be significantly higher by $\gamma_{100} + \gamma_{120} = -0.02 - 0.19 = -0.21$ during bursts 1–2, but nonsignificantly higher by $\gamma_{100} = 0.02$

Table 10.6 Results from three-level unconditional models predicting physical symptoms and positive affect. Bold values are $p < .05$.

Model Effects	Symptoms				Positive Affect			
	Term	Est	SE	$p <$	Term	Est	SE	$p <$
Model for the Means								
Intercept	γ_{000}	**1.36**	0.12	.001	γ_{000}	**2.57**	0.06	.001
Burst	γ_{010}	**0.52**	0.09	.001	γ_{010}	**−0.05**	0.01	.001
Burst²	γ_{020}	**−0.10**	0.02	.001				
Session 1–2 Slope (Slope12)	γ_{100}	**−0.23**	0.05	.001	γ_{100}	−0.02	0.03	.637
Slope12*Burst1 or 2					γ_{120}	**−0.19**	0.04	.001
Session 2–6 Slope (Slope26)	γ_{200}	0.005	0.02	.829	γ_{200}	**0.02**	0.01	.020
Slope26*Linear Burst	γ_{110}	**−0.08**	0.03	.004				
Slope26*Quadratic Burst	γ_{120}	**0.02**	0.01	.004				
Level-3 Model for the Variance								
Intercept Variance	$\tau^2_{v_{00}}$	**0.94**	0.17	.001	$\tau^2_{v_{00}}$	**0.31**	0.05	.001
Burst Slope Variance	$\tau^2_{v_{01}}$	0.01	0.01	.110	$\tau^2_{v_{01}}$	**0.01**	0.00	.001
Slope 12 Variance					$\tau^2_{v_{10}}$	**0.02**	0.01	.038
Slope 26 Variance					$\tau^2_{v_{20}}$	**0.00**	0.00	.031
Intercept–Burst Covariance	$\tau_{v_{00,01}}$	0.04	0.03	.174	$\tau_{v_{00,01}}$	−0.00	0.01	.543
Intercept–Slope12 Covariance					$\tau_{v_{00,02}}$	**0.04**	0.02	.042
Intercept–Slope26 Covariance					$\tau_{v_{00,03}}$	0.01	0.00	.142
Burst–Slope12 Covariance					$\tau_{v_{01,10}}$	−0.00	0.00	.984
Burst–Slope26 Covariance					$\tau_{v_{01,20}}$	0.00	0.00	.447
Slope12–Slope26 Covariance					$\tau_{v_{10,20}}$	0.00	0.00	.333

Level-2 Model for the Variance

		Estimate	SE	p	Estimate	SE	p
Intercept Variance	$\tau^2_{U_{00}}$	0.51	0.07	.001	0.06	0.01	.001
Slope12 Variance	$\tau^2_{U_{10}}$	0.20	0.08	.005	0.04	0.02	.047
Slope26 Variance	$\tau^2_{U_{20}}$	0.01	0.00	.006	0.00	0.00	.126
Intercept–Slope12 Covariance	$\tau_{U_{00,10}}$	0.10	0.05	.061	0.01	0.01	.372
Intercept–Slope26 Covariance	$\tau_{U_{00,20}}$	−0.05	0.01	.002	−0.01	0.00	.062
Slope12–Slope26 Covariance	$\tau_{U_{10,20}}$	0.01	0.01	.517	−0.00	0.00	.780
Level-1 Residual Variance	σ^2_e	0.54	0.02	.001	0.14	0.01	.001
ML Model Fit							
Number of Parameters		17			22		
−2LL		7345.5			3412.6		
−AIC		7388.5			3456.6		
−BIC		7434.2			3515.8		

during bursts 3–5. A 95% CI for the level-3 random Slope12$_\text{sbi}$ indicated that the person Slope12$_\text{sbi}$ means were expected to range from –0.30 to 0.27; after controlling for those person Slope12$_\text{sbi}$ differences, the burst Slope12$_\text{sbi}$ deviations were expected to range from –0.38 to 0.35. Finally, from sessions 2–6, at each burst positive affect was expected to increase significantly at a rate of $\gamma_{200} = 0.02$ per session. A 95% CI for the level-3 random Slope26$_\text{sbi}$ indicated that the person Slope26$_\text{sbi}$ means were expected to range from –0.06 to 0.09; after controlling for those person Slope26$_\text{sbi}$ differences, the burst Slope26$_\text{sbi}$ deviations were expected to range from –0.06 to 0.09.

3.D. A Multivariate Three-Level Model for Multidimensional Time

Now that we have painstakingly built unconditional models of multidimensional time for both variables, we finally get to tackle our original goal of examining the relationships between positive affect and physical symptoms across levels. To do so, we can use a multivariate three-level model in which all parameters in the model for symptoms in Equation (10.10) and in the model for positive affect in Equation (10.13) are estimated. As introduced in chapter 9, the advantage of a simultaneous estimation is that it directly provides cross-variable covariances at each level of analysis, while maintaining all relevant sources of variation in both variables. Our model can again be estimated by tricking univariate software—first, by restructuring (stacking) the data so that the two outcomes are in the same column, and then using the system of dummy code indicators to distinguish the model effects for each outcome. Truly multivariate software could also be used, so long as it is capable of representing all relevant sources of variance.

The fixed effects from the multivariate model were almost identical to those from the univariate models and so are not reported. Results from the multivariate model for the **G** and **R** matrices (and their correlation versions) are shown in Table 10.7, in which the variances are given on the diagonal, covariances are given above the diagonal, and correlations are given below the diagonal. We can use Wald tests for the covariances to assess the significance of these relationships, which should be appropriate given that the covariances are not bounded at 0 (the null hypothesis).

Only two cross-variable relationships were significant. First was a negative relationship between the level-3 random intercepts ($r = -.403$), which indicated that people who reported *more* symptoms than other people on average were likely to report *lower* positive affect than other people on average. That is, people who feel better are happier. This level-3 intercept relationship is conditional at burst 1 and session 2, although the nonsignificant relationships for the random slopes across variables suggest this effect would be similar if evaluated elsewhere. Second was a negative relationship between the level-1 residuals ($r = -.101$), which indicated that in sessions in which symptoms were higher than predicted (i.e., after taking into account all fixed and random effects), positive affect was lower than predicted. In other words, on days when you feel better than usual, you are

Table 10.7 Correlations from multivariate three-level model for symptoms and positive affect, in which variances are on the diagonal, covariances are above the diagonal, and correlations are below the diagonal. Bold correlations are for covariances significant at $p < .05$.

Level-3 G and GCORR Matrices

	Symptoms		Positive Affect			
	Intercept	Burst	Intercept	Burst	Slope12	Slope26
Symptoms Intercept	0.9359	0.0440	−0.2192	0.0212	−0.0159	0.0026
Symptoms Burst Slope	.402	0.0128	−0.0252	−0.0054	−0.0052	0.0011
Positive Affect Intercept	−.403	−.396	0.3167	−0.0063	0.0391	0.0050
Positive Affect Burst Slope	.256	−.557	−.131	0.0074	−0.0006	0.0008
Positive Affect Slope12	−.106	−.298	**.448**	−.044	0.0241	0.0014
Positive Affect Slope26	.075	.264	.246	.249	.254	0.0013

Level-2 G and GCORR Matrices

	Symptoms			Positive Affect		
	Intercept	Slope12	Slope26	Intercept	Slope12	Slope26
Symptoms Intercept	0.5110	0.0915	−0.0464	−0.0299	−0.0066	0.0032
Symptoms Slope12	.285	0.2013	0.0090	−0.0205	−0.0167	−0.0011
Symptoms Slope26	−.594	.184	0.0120	0.0075	−0.0023	−0.0013
Positive Affect Intercept	−.173	−.189	.282	0.0587	0.0082	−0.0059
Positive Affect Slope12	−.051	−.206	−.116	.186	0.0328	−0.0006
Positive Affect Slope26	.118	−.066	−.325	−.650	−.084	0.0014

Level-1 **R** and **RCORR** Matrices

	S	PA
Symptoms (S) Residual	0.5362	−0.0273
Positive Affect (PA) Residual	−.101	0.1371

a little happier than usual, too. Although small, this residual relationship was still significant because it was estimated using the level-1 observations ($N = 2,747$). A relationship of comparable size was obtained for the level-2 random intercepts ($r = −.173$, based on 462 bursts), but it was not significant, indicating that within persons, during bursts in which symptoms were higher than usual, positive affect was not lower than usual.

3.E. Additional Predictors in Three-Level Models

Whew! That's a lot of models considering all we really had is one predictor—*time!* Admittedly, although extremely complicated statistically, our final model was impoverished theoretically. This is because the primary goal of the previous example was to demonstrate three-level models for multiple dimensions of within-person time, and thus it focused mostly on fixed and random effects for each level of time. Although we did examine cross-variable relationships, there was nothing else to the story in terms of examining other predictors, moderators, and so forth. This executive decision to limit the scope of the example was made for two reasons.

First, there is an upper limit on the complexity of models that can be estimated using maximum likelihood in existing software. For instance, in preparing the last example, I also tried a truly multivariate model to examine moderation by gender of directed effects (i.e., paths) from positive affect to symptoms. But the model wouldn't estimate at all, likely due to the number of random effects already being estimated. It may be possible to estimate such a model through alternative ways of finding the parameter estimates, such as through Bayesian Markov-Chain Monte Carlo (MCMC) estimation. However, that topic requires another book in and of itself! How complex of a model can be estimated in practice cannot be determined easily ahead of time—instead, you may just have to try it and see if your chosen model will estimate for your data.

The second rationale for limiting the predictors examined in the last example is that once you understand how three-level models create piles of variance, the process of adding other predictors follows the same logic and procedures as for two-level models. For instance, level-3 person predictors (centered at a constant so that 0 is meaningful) can have fixed effects, but not random effects (because there would be no fourth level over which their effects could vary). Level-3 main effects and interactions among level-3 predictors explain level-3 random intercept variance. A cross-level interaction of a level-3 and level-1 predictor explains the level-3 random slope variance for that level-1 predictor if estimated. If not, it will explain the level-2 random slope for that level-1 predictor if estimated (because that is where the level-3 random slope variance would have come from had it been estimated). If the level-1 predictor does not have any random slopes, then a cross-level interaction of a level-3 and level-1 predictor will explain the level-1 residual variance. Likewise, a cross-level interaction of a level-3 and level-2 predictor explains that the level-3 random slope variance for that level-2 predictor if estimated. If not, it will explain the level-1 residual variance (where the level-3 random slope variance would have come from). Thus, all relevant random slope variances should still be examined before estimating cross-level interactions that would explain those variances, the same as before.

How to include a level-1 or level-2 predictor depends on whether it shows individual effects of time. If so, then for the same reasons discussed in chapter 9 (i.e., to avoid smushed effects of any kind), the predictor's variance should be properly partitioned by modeling it as an outcome. Its effects on other outcomes could then be examined via covariances in the model for the variance, as we did here, or by directed effects using truly multivariate software. If a level-1 or level-2 predictor has only fixed effects or no effects of time at all, then it may be sufficient to partition its variance through observed predictor variables instead (i.e., through person-mean-centering or grand-mean-centering), so long as its variability is represented at each level. This predictor approach will be demonstrated in chapter 11, but let us consider how this would have worked for our current example three-level model of sessions within bursts within persons.

For a level-2 predictor (x_{bi}) that has variance at both level 2 and 3, its within-person (WP) variability can be represented by an observed predictor as: level-2 $WP_{bi} = x_{bi} - \bar{x}_i$ (i.e., the burst-specific value centered at the person's mean across bursts). Its between-person (BP) variability can be represented by an observed predictor as: level-3 $BP_i = \bar{x}_i - C$ (i.e., the person's mean centered at a constant so that 0 is meaningful). Alternatively, the level-2 predictor's variance could be partitioned as an "outcome" in a truly multivariate model, such that its level-2 random intercept variance $\approx WP_{bi}$ and its level-3 random intercept variance $\approx BP_i$. Either way, the level-2 part is then a level-2 predictor, whose main effects and interactions with other level-2 predictors explain level-2 random intercept variance. A cross-level interaction of a level-2 and level-1 predictor explains the level-2 random slope variance for that level-1 predictor if estimated, or the level-1 residual variance if not. The level-2 predictor's effect can also vary randomly over level 3 persons. Finally, the level-3 part would become a level-3 predictor (as already described).

Let us also consider how to include effects of a level-1 predictor (x_{sbi}) that has variance at all three levels. Its within-burst (WB) variability can be represented by an observed predictor as: level-1 $WB_{sbi} = x_{sbi} - \bar{x}_{bi}$ (i.e., the session-specific value centered at the person's burst mean). Its within-person (WP) variability could be represented by an observed predictor as: level-2 $WP_{bi} = \bar{x}_{bi} - \bar{x}_i$ (i.e., the person's burst mean centered at the person's mean of their burst means). Its between-person (BP) variability could be represented by an observed predictor as: level-3 $BP_i = \bar{x}_i - C$ (i.e., the person's mean of their burst means centered at a constant for a meaningful 0). Alternatively, the level-1 predictor's variance could be partitioned as an "outcome" in a truly multivariate model, such that its level-1 residual variance $\approx WB_{sbi}$, its level-2 random intercept variance $\approx WP_{bi}$, and its level-3 random intercept variance $\approx BP_i$. Either way, the level-1 part is then a level-1 predictor, whose main effects and interactions with other level-1 predictors explain level-1 residual variance. The level-1 predictor's effect can also vary randomly over level-2 bursts and/or level-3 persons. Finally, the level-2 part would become a level-2 predictor, while the level-3 part would become a level-3 predictor (both with effects as already described).

3.F. Multidimensional Time: Two Levels or Three?

Finally, let us consider the modeling of multidimensional time more generally, as it is not always the case that a three-level model is the right choice. A three-level model was warranted for the last example because the measurement bursts were separated by about 6 months, such that a correlation of the last session of the previous burst with the first session of the next burst was highly unlikely. Accordingly, it made sense to think of burst as a discrete level of time—this notion is also testable empirically by comparing the fit of a two-level model (for all occasions at level 1 nested within persons at level 2) against the fit of the three-level model (of sessions at level 1 within bursts at level 2 within persons at level 3). That two-level model fit considerably worse for both symptoms, $-2\Delta LL(\sim 6) = 414.0$, $p < .001$, and positive affect, $-2\Delta LL(\sim 6) = 151.9$, $p < .001$, supporting the treatment of bursts as a separate level (i.e., that requires its own piles of variance to account for dependency of residuals from the same burst).

In contrast, consider an alternative scenario, such as in ecological momentary assessment designs, in which multiple outcomes are collected within a single day for several days in a row. A three-level model for this type of data would have within-day occasions at level 1, days at level 2, and persons at level 3, which at a minimum would entail random intercepts at levels 2 and 3. This would mean that some correlation would be predicted for occasions from the same day, as well as days from the same person. However, even after accounting for mean differences across days and persons via their random intercepts, there may still be a correlation of occasions from different days, such as between the last occasion of the previous night and the first occasion of the next morning. Such carryover effects may be more likely for some outcomes than others (such as for biological measures of stress hormones, or for affective measures of mood).

So what are the choices for modeling such additional relationships? One option is to use a same three-level model structure as just described but with a different **R** matrix. The default **R** matrix in many software programs predicts the residuals from all observations within a person to be uncorrelated once random effects are added. Instead, the **R** matrix can be specified to include a first-order auto-correlation for adjacent occasions, either by using an AR(1) model for equal-interval occasions as described in chapter 4, or through a spatial structure, such as in SAS MIXED, whose **R** matrix option TYPE = SP(POW)(*time*) predicts the first-order auto-correlation to decay exponentially by continuous time rather than across lags of discrete occasions.

A second option for modeling a correlation between occasions from different days is the two-level model described earlier, in which all occasions would be predicted at level 1 within persons at level 2 without regard to days. This two-level model would be useful to the extent that the demarcation of day is irrelevant, such that no additional correlation is expected for occasions from the same day beyond the correlation predicted for occasions from the same person. This two-level model of all occasions within persons can be compared to a three-level model of occasions within days within persons. To the extent that the level-2 random intercept variance for mean differences across days is close to 0 (i.e., ICC_{L3} approaches 1), the two-level model will not fit significantly worse than the three-level model, meaning that days don't matter (although other kinds of time-specific correlation may still exist). In general, the number of levels required to model multiple dimensions of within-person time will be guided by the specific measurement process, but ultimately, how many levels are needed for a given random intercept or slope is an empirical question that should be answered by comparisons of model fit whenever possible.

4. Chapter Summary

Until this chapter we have modeled change over time without thinking too hard about what *time* should be, because in the examples thus far there has been only one logical choice. But not anymore—this chapter focused on the analysis of data from longitudinal designs with greater complexity in their designation of *time*. The second section of the chapter was devoted to designs in which there is only one dimension of time *within* persons, but multiple possible dimensions of time *between* persons. When a given metric of time has between-person variability (i.e., people differ in *time* at the study beginning), there is potential for different between- and within-person effects of time. Because time is just another time-varying predictor, we can evaluate the effects of time at each level using the same techniques featured in chapters 8 and 9, such as grand-mean-centering, person-mean-centering, and baseline-centering. The critical element is that both between- and within-person variability in time is explicitly represented by the model predictors.

In these models focused on multilevel effects of time, contextual effects are known as *cohort effects*, which means that it matters *when* you were at a given point in time, not just what point in time it was. In our example data examining changes in prose recall in older adults, we found significant cohort effects, such that persons who began the study farther from birth or closer to death had different predicted trajectories at the same point in time (i.e., 84 years since birth or −7 years to death). Although more likely in some contexts than others, in general, cohort effects will be larger to the extent that between-person variability in time is larger and to the extent that non-random processes select which persons are available to be measured. In our example data, the people who were still able to begin the study at age 90 were likely not a random subset of the people who might have been available when they were age 80. Similarly, couples who begin a study of relationship satisfaction after being married for 20 years are likely not a random sample of the couples who could have been available when they were newlyweds (given that many of those couples will have separated or divorced before 20 years of marriage).

When contextual (cohort) effects are present, there are several reasons why it can be more useful to model level-1 change using a purely within-person metric of time, such as years in study in our example. One reason is that a model for years in study can be made equivalent to a model using accelerated time as a level-1 predictor with respect to its fixed effects. The years in study model provides total between-person effects, whereas the accelerated time models will provide contextual effects, but these effects are linearly related and thus can be estimated by either model, as shown earlier. When including random time slopes, though, the years in study model provides different results because of differences across models in what time 0 means. When time 0 is not observed for all persons in an accelerated time model, greater extrapolation is needed to predict each person's intercept, which can cause problems of interpretation as well as the potential for downwardly biased random slope variances, as described by Raudenbush and Bryk (2002; chapter 5). This problem does not usually occur in within-person time models like years in study, in which time 0 is defined as an observed occasion for each person (e.g., the first occasion). Furthermore, using years in study as the level-1 time predictor cannot be wrong—because it only contains within-person variance, the only effect of time it can show is a within-person effect, so there is no danger of smushing the effects of time across levels (i.e., ignoring cohort effects). Finally, the years in study model provides a neutral baseline with which to compare the predictive effects of different sources of between-person differences in time in the level-2 model.

Switching gears, the third section of the chapter presented three-level models for multiple dimensions of within-person time, such as are found in so-called *intensive longitudinal designs* (e.g., measurement burst and ecological momentary assessment designs). Although accelerated longitudinal designs may also have multiple relevant metrics of time to consider, these effects will be distinguishable only when their time effects are observed *separately within persons*. So, for instance, there is no way to distinguish the within-person effect of becoming one year farther from birth from the within-person effect of becoming one year closer to death because they co-occur in the same time interval. In other words, they are confounded within persons, in which time is just time. Although statistical solutions to distinguish multiple sources of time effects within persons have been proposed, they rely on an assumption of no cohort effects, which is not likely to be tenable in many contexts (see Hoffman, Hofer, & Sliwinski, 2011).

In contrast, the different sources of within-person changes can be distinguished when unconfounded by design instead. In our example, we could examine both short-term changes across sessions within a two-week period, as well as longer-term changes across bursts separated by six months because both shorter and longer time intervals were sampled within persons. To model these different effects, what used to be a single level of "time" at level 1 within persons at level 2 had to become two distinct levels within persons, who became level 3. We will see three-level models at work in chapter 11 as well, although the levels themselves will need to differ to reflect the specific designs covered in that chapter. More generally, the definition of a level is always design specific, because the term "level" usually refers generically to an orthogonal set of variance components. How many levels of random effects are needed for the data at hand will always be an empirical question, and intraclass correlations will be useful in conveying the relative amount of variance across levels. In the end, although admittedly more complex, three-level models are built using the same logic and principles as when building any two-level model.

5. Sample Results Sections

As in every previous example, the results sections below should be considered barebones summaries of what was found from each set of analyses. That is, this text would need to be embedded in a more theoretically motivated account of these results as part of a story or series of questions to be answered. In addition, to be more succinct, the order of the analyses presented below differs from the order they were presented in the chapter. Sample- and method-related details about the individual studies that would be found elsewhere have also been omitted.

5.A. Two-Level Models for Alternative Metrics of Concurrent Within-Person Time

The effects of between-person differences and within-person changes in time on a measure of story memory, prose recall, were examined in 207 persons measured up to five times at approximately two-year intervals. An initial empty means, random intercept model revealed that 67% of the variance in prose recall was due to between-person mean differences.

Of primary interest was the utility of two alternative metrics of time, years since birth and years to death, in describing individual changes in prose recall. Two-level longitudinal models (i.e., random effects models in which occasions were nested within persons) were estimated and compared using maximum likelihood. The level-1 predictors for years since birth and years to death were centered at 84 years and −7 years, respectively. Because each alternative metric of time had significant between-person variation (i.e., 46% of years since birth; 41% of years to death), the potential for differential effects across between-person and within-person levels of analysis was evaluated by including years from the first occasion of each time metric as a level-2 cohort predictor (also centered using the level-1 constants of 84 or −7 years).

First, an unconditional model using years since birth as the level-1 time predictor revealed significant linear decline at a rate of −0.09 per year (SE = 0.04, p = .046). Although there was no significant acceleration of change, a fixed quadratic effect of time was retained for comparability across models. Significant individual differences in linear change were found relative to a fixed quadratic time model with only a random intercept, $-2\Delta LL(\sim 2) = 11.0$, $p = .004$. However, adding three effects of birth cohort (i.e., years since birth at the first occasion) as shown in Equation (10.2) resulted in significantly better model fit, $-2\Delta LL(3) = 15.8$, $p < .001$, indicating that the between- and within-person effects of years since birth were not the same. As shown in the first set of columns in Table 10.2, significant linear and quadratic contextual effects of birth cohort were found for the intercept, as well as a significant linear contextual effect on the linear slope. As shown in the top panel of Figure 10.2, all of these effects are conditional on the intercept of 84 years since birth, which by definition was not observed for all birth cohorts.

Thus, to facilitate model interpretation, the accelerated time model was respecified as shown in Equation (10.3) to include only the within-person part of years since birth as the level-1 predictor (i.e., years in study), such that the level-2 birth cohort effects could then be interpreted as between-person total effects. Results are shown in the second set of columns in Table 10.2, in which the intercept now represents the first occasion. As shown in the bottom panel of Figure 10.2, persons who started the study farther from birth had significantly lower expected prose recall scores but more positive rates of change at the first occasion. Overall, however, the fixed effects of years since birth only accounted for 2.6% of the total variance in prose recall.

Second, turning to years to death as the time predictor instead, an unconditional model revealed that the linear slope of –0.09 per year became significantly more negative per year by twice the quadratic slope of –0.02. Significant individual differences in linear change were found relative to a fixed quadratic time model with only a random intercept, $-2\Delta LL(\sim 2) = 16.5$, $p < .001$. However, adding three effects of death cohort (i.e., years to death at the first occasion) as shown in Equation (10.2) resulted in significantly better model fit, $-2\Delta LL(3) = 8.7$, $p < .001$, indicating that the between- and within-person effects of years to death were also not the same. As shown in the first set of columns in Table 10.3, significant linear contextual effects of death cohort were found for the intercept and the linear slope. As shown in the top panel of Figure 10.3, all of these effects are conditional on the intercept of –7 years to death, which by definition was not observed for all death cohorts.

Thus, to facilitate model interpretation, the accelerated time model was again re-specified as shown in Equation (10.3) to include only the within-person part of years to death as the level-1 predictor (i.e., years in study), such that the level-2 death cohort effects could then be interpreted as between-person total effects. Results are shown in the second set of columns in Table 10.3, in which the intercept now represents the first occasion. As shown in the bottom panel of Figure 10.3, persons who started the study closer to death had significantly lower expected prose recall scores but similar rates of change at the first occasion. Overall, however, the fixed effects of years to death only accounted for 2.6% of the total variance in prose recall.

Finally, given their imperfect correlation of $r = .15$ at the first occasion, it was possible to examine the extent to which years since birth and years to death had unique between-person effects. The results from the model given in Equation (10.4) are displayed in Table 10.4 and depicted in Figure 10.4. As shown, persons who began the study farther from birth or closer to death had lower initial prose recall scores. Notably, although each linear cohort effect on the intercept was at least marginally significant, the effect of birth cohort was over twice the size of the effect of death cohort (as measured in per-year differences). Furthermore, although persons who began the study farther from birth also had more positive linear slopes at the first occasion, there was no significant effect of death cohort on the linear slope. However, the model fixed effects still only accounted for 4.3% of the total variance in prose recall, suggesting many other factors are likely to relevant than time, years since birth, and years to death at study entry.

5.B. Three-Level Models for Analysis of Separable Dimensions of Within-Person Time

The extent of short-term and long-term changes in physical symptoms and positive affect was examined in 108 older adults using a measurement burst design. Six assessments were collected over a two-week period, and this six-session measurement burst was repeated five times, for a total of 30 possible observations per person.

There were 2,752 total observations for physical symptoms and 2,747 for positive affect. Although there was variability in the actual timing between bursts, it did not significantly predict either outcome beyond just the burst number, and thus all models were specified using session and burst as the metrics of time.

Three-level models were initially estimated for each outcome using maximum likelihood in which the level-1 model predicted differences between sessions, the level-2 model predicted differences between bursts, and the level-3 model predicted differences between persons. Empty means models with random intercepts for level-2 burst mean differences and level-3 person mean differences were first used to partition the variability in each outcome. For symptoms, 30% was across sessions, 20% was across bursts, and 50% was across persons. Thus, the level-2 intraclass correlation of sessions from the same burst and person was $ICC_{L2} = (.20 + .50) / (1.00) = .70$. Of that 70% of the variation captured by the random intercepts at level 2 and 3, 72% was actually at level 3, as given by the level-3 intraclass correlation of bursts from the same person, $ICC_{L3} = (.50) / (.20 + .50) = .72$. For the variability in positive affect, 29% was across sessions, 12% was across bursts, and 59% was across persons, resulting in $ICC_{L2} = .71$ and $ICC_{L3} = .83$.

Saturated means models were then used to examine the pattern of mean differences across sessions and bursts, as shown in Figure 10.5. Linear and quadratic slopes (centered at burst 1) were used to index change across bursts. To capture the differential rates of change shown from sessions 1–2 relative to 2–6, piecewise linear slopes were created. *Slope12* (coded session 1 = −1 and sessions 2–6 = 0) indexed the change from sessions 1–2, and *Slope26* (coded sessions 1–2 = 0 and sessions 3–6 = session − 2) indexed the change from sessions 2–6. The final fixed effects model chosen for symptoms included linear and quadratic slopes for burst, the two piecewise slopes for session, and an interaction of Slope26 with the linear and quadratic burst slopes. The final fixed effects model chosen for positive affect included a linear slope for burst, the two piecewise slopes for session, and an interaction that allowed Slope12 to differ at bursts 1–2 from bursts 3–5. These models did not fit significantly worse than the saturated means model, as indicated by likelihood ratio tests: $-2\Delta LL(23) = 21.1$, $p = .57$ for symptoms, $-2\Delta LL(25) = 21.2$, $p = .68$ for positive affect, indicating that the fixed effects accurately predicted the 30 means.

Random effects were then examined in sequential models, beginning with level-3 random effects for the burst slopes, followed by level-2 and level-3 random effects for the session slopes. All covariances among random effects at the same level were estimated. For symptoms, there was significant variability across level-3 persons in linear change across bursts, $-2\Delta LL(\sim2) = 6.8$, $p = .03$, but not in quadratic change across bursts, $-2\Delta LL(\sim3) = 2.9$, $p = .41$. There was also significant variability in both piecewise slopes across level-2 bursts, $-2\Delta LL(\sim2) = 19.4$, $p < .001$ for Slope12, $-2\Delta LL(\sim3) = 25.0$, $p < .001$ for Slope26, but not across level-3 persons, $-2\Delta LL(\sim3) = 5.5$, $p = .14$ for Slope12, $-2\Delta LL(\sim3) = 1.9$, $p = .60$ for Slope26. For positive affect, there was significant variability across level-3 persons in linear change across bursts, $-2\Delta LL(\sim2) = 23.5$, $p < .001$. There was also significant variability in both piecewise slopes across both level-2 bursts, $-2\Delta LL(\sim2) = 19.1$, $p < .001$ for

Slope12, $-2\Delta LL(\sim 3) = 11.0$, $p = .01$ for Slope26, and level-3 persons, $-2\Delta LL(\sim 3) = 27.2$, $p < .001$ for Slope12, $-2\Delta LL(\sim 4) = 13.3$, $p = .01$ for Slope26.

The final models for symptoms and positive affect are shown in Equations (10.10) and (10.13), respectively, the results of which are given in Table 10.6. Model-predicted means are shown in Figure 10.5. As shown, symptoms initially increased across bursts, the rate of which leveled off in later bursts. Within bursts, symptoms decreased from sessions 1–2 at each burst, but from sessions 2–6 decreased only slightly during bursts 2–4. Positive affect decreased slightly across bursts in a linear fashion. Within bursts, a decrease from sessions 1–2 occurred only in bursts 1–2, but a small increase from sessions 2–6 occurred across bursts as well. Overall, changes across sessions and bursts were minimal, accounting for only 2.5% and 0.6% of the total variance in symptoms and positive affect, respectively (as calculated from the square of the correlation between the actual outcomes and those predicted by the model fixed effects).

A multivariate three-level model was then estimated to examine the possible relationships between symptoms and positive affect; the same univariate models just described were specified for each outcome. Two significant relationships were found, as indicated by Wald tests for their covariances. First was a negative relationship between the level-3 random intercepts ($r = -.403$), indicating that people who reported *more* symptoms on average than other people were likely to report *lower* positive affect on average than other people. In other words, people who reported feeling better also reported being happier. Second was a negative relationship between the level-1 residuals ($r = -.101$), such that in sessions in which symptoms were higher than predicted (i.e., after taking into account all fixed and random effects), positive affect was lower than predicted. In other words, on days when people reported feeling better than usual, they also reported being a little happier than usual, too. A negative relationship was also found between the level-2 burst random intercepts ($r = -.173$), but it was not significant, indicating that within persons, during bursts in which symptoms were higher than usual, positive affect was not lower than usual.

Review Questions

1. When is *time* considered multidimensional rather than unidimensional within persons?
2. How would you interpret a contextual effect of time in an accelerated longitudinal design?
3. When will accelerated time models and within-person time models provide the same results, and when will their results differ?
4. In three-level models, what is the difference between a level-2 and level-3 intraclass correlation?
5. In three-level models, how can a predictor have a random effect at more than one level?

References

Almeida, D. M., Piazza, J. R., & Stawski, R. S. (2009). Interindividual differences and intraindividual variability in the cortisol awakening response: An examination of age and gender. *Psychology and Aging, 24*(4), 819–827.

Bell, R. Q. (1953). Convergence: An accelerated longitudinal approach. *Child Development, 24,* 145–152.

Duncan, S. C., & Duncan, T. E. (2012). Accelerated longitudinal designs. In B. P. Laursen, T. D. Little, & N. A. Card (Eds.), *Handbook of developmental research methods* (pp. 31–45). New York, NY: Guilford Press.

Hoffman, L. (2012). *Considering alternative metrics of time: Does anybody really know what "time" is?* In J. Harring & G. Hancock (Eds.), *Advances in longitudinal methods in the social and behavioral sciences* (pp. 255–287). Charlotte, NC: Information Age Publishing.

Hoffman, L., Hofer, S. M., & Sliwinski, M. J. (2011). On the confounds among retest gains and age-cohort differences in the estimation of within-person change in longitudinal studies: A simulation study. *Psychology and Aging, 26*(4), 778–791.

McArdle, J. J., & Bell, R. Q. (2000). An introduction to latent growth curve models for developmental data analysis. In T. D. Little, K. U. Schnabel, & J. Baumert (Eds.), *Modeling longitudinal and multilevel data* (pp. 69–107). Mahwah, NJ: Erlbaum Associates.

McArdle, J. J., Ferrer-Caja, E., Hamagami, F., & Woodcock, R. W. (2002). Comparative longitudinal structural analyses of the growth and decline of multiple intellectual abilities over the life span. *Developmental Psychology, 38*(1), 115–142.

Mehta, P. D., & West, S. G. (2000). Putting the individual back into individual growth curves. *Psychological Methods, 5,* 23–43.

Miyazaki, Y., & Raudenbush, S. W. (2000). Tests for linkage of multiple cohorts in an accelerated longitudinal design. *Psychological Methods, 5,* 44–63.

Nesselroade, J. R. (1991). The warp and woof of the developmental fabric. In R. Downs, L. Lüben, & D. S. Palermo (Eds.), *Visions of aesthetics, the environment, and development: The legacy of Joachim F. Wohwill* (pp. 213–240). Hillsdale, NJ: Erlbaum.

Raudenbush, S. W., & Bryk, A. S. (2002). *Hierarchical linear models: Applications and data analysis methods* (2nd ed.). Thousand Oaks, CA: Sage.

Sliwinski, M. J. (2008). Measurement-burst designs for social health research. *Social and Personality Psychology Compass, 2,* 245–261.

Sliwinski, M. J., Hoffman, L., & Hofer, S. M. (2010a). Evaluating convergence of within-person change and between-person age differences in age-heterogeneous longitudinal studies. *Research in Human Development, 7*(1), 45–60.

Sliwinski, M. J., Hoffman, L., & Hofer, S. M. (2010b). Modeling retest and aging effects in a measurement burst design. In P. Molenaar & K. M. Newel (Eds.), *Individual pathways of change: Statistical models for analyzing learning and development* (pp. 37–50). Washington DC: American Psychological Association.

CHAPTER 11

ANALYSIS OF INDIVIDUALS WITHIN GROUPS OVER TIME

So far this text has addressed the fundamentals of longitudinal modeling—of quantifying and predicting between- and within-person sources of variation. As introduced back in chapter 1, the statistical purpose of these piles of variance is to represent **dependency**, or sources of residual correlation that arise due to dimensions of sampling. So far, we've seen how random effects represent specific sources of dependency in longitudinal data. For instance, a single dimension of within-person time requires a two-level model of time within persons, which means there is a single origin of dependency—due to persons—to be concerned with. That is, people may differ in their means over time (via a random intercept), in their rates of change over time (via random slopes for effects of time), and in their response to time-varying predictors (via random slopes for those effects as well). Multiple dimensions of within-person time may have additional origins of dependency that require extra levels. For instance, in chapter 10, rates of change across sessions varied randomly across both measurement bursts and persons; because dependency originated from two distinct sources, we used a three-level model to capture both simultaneously.

In chapter 11, we will consider how to model the additional sources of dependency that result from the sampling of persons from different groups. That is, just as *persons* may differ randomly from each other in their means, rates of change, or effects of other predictors, *groups* may differ randomly from each other in these quantities as well. Thus, the goal of this chapter is to expand our longitudinal models to quantify and predict sources of *group* variation in addition to *person* variation. How to model group dependency will depend on how persons are organized within groups, as discussed more generally first. We will then examine two examples of longitudinal data that involve persons in either time-invariant or time-varying groups, each summarized in a sample results section at the end of the chapter as usual. We will also consider other instances of persons nested in groups, such as in family or dyadic longitudinal data, as well as when persons are actually nested within occasions instead of the other way around (i.e., as in panel designs).

1. Concerns in Modeling Individuals Within Groups Over Time

There are many ways in which groups—either pre-existing or purposefully created for a research study—may be integrated into a longitudinal design. Rather than try to describe every possible scenario, let us consider four general organizing questions whose answers will help us determine how to most accurately model the effects of groups within longitudinal data.

1.A. Group Membership: One or Many Groups at Each Occasion?

The first question to answer is whether, *at a given occasion,* persons can belong to only one group or to multiple groups simultaneously. For instance, in educational studies examining student outcomes, including multiple classrooms of students creates one source of group dependency (correlation of students) due to classroom membership. And because classrooms exist within schools, students can also be thought of as members of a school; including multiple schools creates another source of group dependency due to school. Accordingly, a longitudinal model for this type of hierarchical sampling design would need to incorporate dependency due to student, classroom, and school; the model would be organized into levels such that students would be nested in classrooms, and classrooms would be nested in schools.

Membership in multiple groups is not always hierarchical, however. A common example of non-hierarchical multiple group membership is when students are sampled from different neighborhoods *and* from different schools. But not all students who attend the same school will live in the same neighborhood, and not all students who live in the same neighborhood will attend the same school. Accordingly, the groups of schools and neighborhoods are **crossed** rather than nested. Both types of group membership create unique sources of dependency, each of which will then need to be taken into account in building a longitudinal model.

1.B. Persons Within Groups: Exchangeable or Distinct?

The second question in deciding how to model the effects of groups is whether group members can be thought of as *exchangeable* or *distinct*—that is, if their identity should be an organizing variable in building a model for the variance. An example of **exchangeable persons** is students in classes. Although students will differ on measured variables, they are otherwise exchangeable in their identity, which is just "student." Thus, we would model students as *nested* in classes, such that after allowing classes to differ in intercepts and slopes as needed via class-level effects, the residuals of student outcomes from the same class should be independent.

In contrast, an example of **distinct persons** can be found in family research, in which outcomes may be collected from multiple persons in the same family. In this case, the role of the family member (e.g., parent versus child) may be an important defining characteristic beyond other measured variables. Although family members could be modeled as nested in families, this would imply that they are exchangeable. Instead, a more useful approach is to treat the family as the unit of analysis, and then model the outcomes from different family members as multivariate observations of the family. Both approaches—modeling family members as nested in families or as multivariate outcomes of a family—can easily allow intercepts and other fixed effects to differ by a predictor of family role in the model for the means. However, as will be explained in the second section of the chapter, the two approaches differ in their form and interpretation of the model for the variance, such that one modeling strategy may be more useful in some situations than the other. In general, though, exchangeable persons should be modeled as nested within groups, whereas distinct persons are more optimally modeled as separate multivariate outcomes.

It is important to remember that the classification of exchangeable versus distinct persons should always be guided by a study's design and research questions. For instance, gender may be an organizing variable in studying relationship satisfaction in heterosexual couples, in which responses for men and women would be separate outcomes in a multivariate model for couples as the unit of analysis. However, in studying relationship satisfaction in same–sex couples, the members of a pair would then be exchangeable on the basis of gender, in which case persons should be modeled as nested in couples instead. Similarly, in research using twins or siblings to examine heritability, it may be more useful to model persons as nested in families, and use gender as a predictor rather than as the basis of assigning responses into multivariate outcomes. However, in some designs there may be other characteristics more relevant than gender that purposefully distinguish persons in dyads or groups, in which case the multivariate outcomes should be organized by those characteristics instead. For instance, if one member of a dyad was subjected to some type of treatment and the other was not, then it may be more useful to distinguish multivariate outcomes along the dimension of treated versus untreated persons (and then allow gender to predict the outcome of the treated person in different–sex dyads as needed).

1.C. Group Membership: Time-Invariant or Time-Varying?

The examples involving persons nested in groups so far have featured group membership that is constant over time, but group membership could actually change over time. For instance, children may change schools during a study or move to a new class at each grade. Similarly, patients may see different doctors over time. Thus, a third question to consider in deciding how to model the effects of groups in longitudinal data is whether the groups are time-invariant or time-varying. This is not always an easy distinction to make, however. Consider an example of children nested in schools. Although some children may change schools during a study, if most do not, then school membership would be time-varying for only some of the students. Furthermore, even for groups that appear to be time-invariant, because the nature of a group may change as a result of changes in its composition, the *experience* of the group members may change over time. For instance, although persons do not change families over time, families themselves do change over time. A significant life event (e.g., divorce, death of a parent, or introduction of a step-parent) may result in a functionally "different" family in terms of family member outcomes, even when the membership of persons in a family is the same over time. As another example, even if students remain in the same class across time, changes in the classroom environment (e.g., getting a new teacher, or children joining or leaving the class) could create a functionally "different" class. Fortunately, we can extend longitudinal models to include time-invariant or time-varying groups as needed, although the latter will be more complicated to do.

1.D. Sources of Group Dependency: Fixed or Random Effects?

A final question to answer about how to model the effects of groups in longitudinal data is on which side of the model the group differences (i.e., dependency due to group) should be represented. We have two choices: variation across groups can be captured using fixed effects in the model for the means *or* using random effects in the model for the variance. Let us first consider how fixed effects would address dependency arising from time-invariant groups.

In a **fixed effects model for group**, membership in g different groups would be treated as a categorical predictor by including $g - 1$ fixed effects of dummy-coded contrasts for group membership (i.e., for the differences between a reference group as the intercept and each other group). That is, groups are treated as non-exchangeable entities, such that each fixed effect represents only one specific group. If the membership of persons to groups is constant over time for all persons, a model with fixed effects for group is relatively straightforward. The $g - 1$ fixed effects go into the level-2 model for persons (i.e., group would be a time-invariant predictor), thus creating a saturated group means model, in which all mean differences between groups will be perfectly predicted. And as with saturated means models for other categorical predictors (e.g., balanced time, as in this text), a multiple degree-of-freedom χ^2 or F-test can be used to evaluate the significance of omnibus group mean differences (i.e., as in a traditional ANOVA). Similarly, group differences in the effects of predictors could be included by adding $g - 1$ fixed effects for interactions of the predictor by the dummy-coded group contrasts; an omnibus test could be used to test the overall significance of those group-specific interaction terms as well. Other group comparisons of their intercepts or in their effects of predictors can also be requested as needed.

This fixed effects strategy can also be extended to address dependency from multiple time-invariant groups. For instance, if children are nested in schools and in neighborhoods, a set of $s - 1$ contrasts for school membership could predict mean differences across s schools while $n - 1$ contrasts for neighborhood membership predict mean differences across n neighborhoods. Similarly, if children are nested in classes, with c classes in each of s schools, then $s - 1$ contrasts would be needed to describe all school mean differences, and an additional $s*(c - 1)$ school-specific (nested) contrasts would be needed to describe all differences across classes within schools. Critically, because all group variation would then be predicted by fixed effects in the model for the means, we would still only need a two-level model of occasions nested in persons (i.e., differences across groups would not require their own additional piles of variance).

Rather than using fixed effects in the model for the means, the alternative strategy is to use **random effects to model group differences** in the model for the variance. That is, just as per-person random effects allow persons to have their own intercept and slope deviations, per-group random effects can allow each group to have their own intercept and slope deviations. Whether any group random effects are needed is testable via $-2\Delta LL$ tests (as usual), but where these group-based piles of variance belong in the model depends on how persons relate to groups.

If membership of persons to groups is constant over time, then group will become a third level, such that occasions at level 1 would be nested within persons at level 2, and persons would be nested in groups at level 3. The first chapter example will feature a three-level model for such **clustered longitudinal data**. And as we saw in chapter 10, three-level models contains two sets of orthogonal random effects that predict two sources of correlation—in this case, one for persons and one for groups. That is, the level-2 person random effects predict a correlation for the residuals of occasions from the same person, and the level-3 group random effects predict a correlation for the residuals of persons from the same group. Additional memberships of persons in hierarchical groups would similarly be represented as by including these groups as higher levels, such as students at level 2 nested in classrooms at level 3 nested in schools at level 4 (creating three sets of orthogonal random effects that in turn predict three sources of correlation).

Multiple memberships in non-hierarchical groups—for example, students from different schools and different neighborhoods measured over time—can be accommodated by a different type of three-level model, in which schools and neighborhoods are **crossed random effects** at level 3. So, as odd as it sounds, this type of **cross-clustered longitudinal model**, even though it is technically still a three-level model, would have two distinct level-3 models simultaneously: one for variation across schools, and another for variation across neighborhoods. Thus, this type of design would require three sets of random effects for students, schools, and neighborhoods to predict three types of correlation (dependency): The residuals for level-1 occasions from the same student are correlated via the level-2 student random effects, the residuals for level-2 students from the same school are correlated via the level-3 school random effects, and the residuals for level-2 students from the same neighborhood are correlated via the level-3 neighborhood random effects. As a result, the residuals from students who attend the same school *and* live in the same neighborhood are predicted to contain both sources of correlation (and thus to be more related than for students with only one group in common). Models with crossed random effects are new to this chapter; they will also reappear in chapter 12 for use in other repeated measures designs.

Time-varying group membership can also be modeled using fixed or random effects for group, but the models needed to do so will necessarily be more complicated. Let us first consider the case of persons who are mostly nested in time-invariant groups but in which some persons may change groups during the study. A similar problem occurs in cross-sectional designs when persons have previously been members of more than one group. One recommended strategy for such designs is to incorporate the proportion of time spent in each group into the model. We can do so by creating a custom intercept for group. Software usually creates a separate column for each group's intercept (either fixed or random), in which persons who are in the group would have a value of 1 and persons who are not in the group would have a value of 0. Consider as an example a cross-sectional study of high school seniors, in which a student was in school A for grades 9, 10, and 11, but moved to school B for grade 12. To reflect that student's actual group membership accurately, we could assign a value of 0.75 to the intercept column for school A and a value of 0.25 to the intercept column for school B (and 0's otherwise), and do likewise for other students who attended multiple schools. We would then add the custom intercept columns to the model ourselves, rather than relying on the software-created default intercepts that would include only 1 and 0 values. As a result, the expected effect of each school for each student would then be proportional to the time spent in the school.

What if this study were conducted longitudinally throughout high school, such that each student was measured in grades 9 through 12? In this case, we have some choices to make about how the effect of belonging to multiple groups might be included. One perspective is that the effect of group membership operates only at the occasion in which the person is part of the group. Continuing with our previous example, an occasion-specific school effect could be created by giving our example student a value of 1 for the school A intercept when present during grades 9 through 11 and a value of 0 when not present during grade 12, switching to a value of 1 for the school B intercept during grade 12. Thus, the residuals from this student would be predicted to correlate with the residuals of other students from school A only during grades 9 through 11 (and to correlate with the residuals of students from school B during grade 12 instead).

An alternative perspective is a cumulative effect of group membership that stays with its members even after they've left the group. This idea would be operationalized by giving our student a value of 1 for the school A intercept during grades 9 through 11 *and* during grade 12, because the effect of having been to school A should continue even after the student has moved on. The student's school B intercept would also have a value of 1 during grade 12 to reflect the additional effect of being in school B, such that the student's residual is expected to correlate with those of students from school A and school B during grade 12, reflecting both the past and the present.

Finally, an intermediate possibility is that group carryover effects exist but decay over time. For instance, we could assign a value of 0.5 to the student's school

A intercept at grade 12 instead of a value of 1 or 0, which would imply some residual effect of having been at school A, but less of an effect than when the student was actually there. The intercept values may reflect whatever linear or nonlinear decay functions are hypothesized; representing these functions as different fixed or random effects creates non-nested models comparable by AIC and BIC.

In the most extreme case of this type of design, group membership may be completely time-varying, such as when children are in different classes at each occasion. As we'll see later in the second chapter example, the same question regarding the extent of carryover effects of time-varying group membership can be answered by creating custom intercepts as just described and including them as either fixed or random effects. In a fixed effects model, group would be a time-varying predictor, and so the $g - 1$ custom contrasts for membership in g groups would become level-1 predictors instead of level-2 predictors. Fortunately, because group membership would be included for each occasion, we would not need to worry about including between-person differences in group membership in the level-2 model (i.e., the level-1 effects will not be "smushed"). However, in designs in which not everyone changes groups over time, it may be important to distinguish persons who do change groups via a separate level-2 predictor, as the effect of group changes *per se* may be important (above and beyond which groups they belong to). But as in the fixed effects models for time-invariant groups described earlier, because all group differences would be perfectly predicted by the model for the means, we would still only need a two-level model of occasions nested in persons (group would not become a level).

As with time-invariant groups, an alternative to modeling group differences as fixed effects is to include random effects of the custom intercepts for time-varying group membership instead. Consequently, occasions at level 1 would be nested within persons *and* within groups; persons and groups would become crossed random effects at level 2. It's not difficult to imagine how even more complex designs may arise—for instance, students may change classes over time, but classes could be nested within a third level of schools. Crossed and nested effects of groups should be combined however necessary to accurately reflect the sampling of the outcome.

So, now that fixed and random effects models have been described for both time-invariant and time-varying groups, let us consider which strategy we might use for modeling a given set of group differences—should groups be fixed effects or random effects? Either strategy can be an effective and valid way to "control" for group-related dependency (i.e., sources of correlation of the residuals of persons from the same group), but each has its pros and cons. Although a fixed effects model has been recommended when the number of groups is fewer than 10 or so due to the difficulty in estimating random effects variances in small samples (e.g., Snijders & Bosker, 2012), there is a more important issue to consider: *Do you want to know* what *the group differences are, or do you want to know* why *the group differences are?* Although fixed group effects can answer the *what* question, only random effects can answer the *why* question.

Consider, for example, a university study to examine changes in student outcomes over time within its academic colleges. If the purpose of the study is to examine how outcomes differ between specific colleges (e.g., arts and sciences vs. engineering vs. education), a model with $g - 1$ fixed effects for all g group differences will directly answer that question of *what* the group differences are. So, on the plus side, each group's intercept will be perfectly captured and inferences can be drawn about their differences; the same will be true of group-specific predictor slopes after including the additional $g - 1$ fixed effects for the group-specific interaction terms with that predictor. On the minus side, though, because all possible group differences are already explained by the $g - 1$ group fixed effects, group-level predictors cannot also be included. So, if the purpose of the study was to evaluate how academic college characteristics (e.g., number of majors, research funding) *predict* longitudinal student outcomes, then differences across colleges (groups) will need to be modeled using group-specific *random* effects instead of *fixed* effects.

In a random effects model, a group random intercept variance is the analog to the $g - 1$ fixed effects for the dummy-coded group contrasts, whereas a group random slope variance is the analog to the $g - 1$ fixed effects for the group-specific predictor interaction terms. Once group differences are represented by random effects whose variances can be explained by group-level predictors, we will then be able to attempt to find out *why* the group differences are. For instance, we could assess how much college random intercept variance was explained by a main effect of a college-level predictor for number of majors, as well as how much college random time slope variance was explained by an interaction of the number of college majors by time.

The capacity to predict group differences is an important advantage of the random effects model for group differences, but a disadvantage is that random effects variances are not well estimated to the extent that the number of groups is small. Furthermore, the more random effects the model contains, the more likely estimation difficulties are to occur; when that happens, the group differences at higher levels may have to be modeled using fixed effects instead. In addition, although group-specific random intercepts and slopes can be predicted from the model (i.e., using empirical Bayes estimates; see chapter 5), they will be shrunken and potentially biased relative to the actual group estimates that would be obtained from estimating fixed effects per group. Thus, random effects models will be less ideal for making inferences about specific group differences than fixed effects models. This is because random effects models are designed to answer the *why* of group differences, not the *what*—that's what fixed effect models are for.

It's important to note that the same distinction applies to the modeling of variation across persons—that is, persons could also be modeled as fixed effects or random effects. Between-person differences are more commonly represented as random effects given that persons are almost always a sample from some larger population, and because the goal of most studies is the prediction of individual differences. But when the focus of a study is on the differences between specific persons (i.e., the *what* of differences, and not the *why*), modeling persons using fixed effects may be more useful (see Cushing, Walters, & Hoffman, 2014, for an example).

Now that we've considered the important issues in modeling group effects in longitudinal data—the number of group memberships at each occasion, exchangeability of persons in groups, changes in group membership over time, and fixed versus random effects models for group differences—let us continue with some more detailed group examples. In the next section we'll examine three-level longitudinal models of exchangeable persons within a single time-invariant group, and in the following section we'll consider additional types of group-based designs as well.

2. Longitudinal Models for Persons in Time-Invariant Groups

Our first example features data adapted from the Classroom Peer Ecologies Project (as described in chapter 1), in which three observations were collected from third- and fifth-grade students from the same school during a single semester. Because students were nested within a single class throughout the study, a three-level model of level-1 occasions nested within level-2 students nested within level-3 classes will be used to analyze this clustered longitudinal design. Our sample includes a total of 1,731 occasions from 597 students nested within 33 classes who had complete data at a given occasion for all variables to be included, which are described next. Given our sample size of 33 classes, we will use restricted maximum likelihood estimation.

The time-varying outcome is student-perceived student–teacher *closeness*, as measured by the mean of five items rated on a 1 to 7 scale. For demonstration purposes we will examine a predictor at each level of analysis. Descriptive statistics for each variable at each applicable level are provided in Table 11.1; for all quantitative variables, higher values indicate more of the construct. There are two level-1 predictors. First, at each occasion students rated their perceived *victimization* (i.e., bullying by other students), as measured by the mean of four items rated on a 1 to 7 scale. Second, at each occasion separate observers rated the classroom environment on a 1 to 7 scale for its *emotional support* for its students. Finally, we will also examine a level-2 predictor of student gender and level-3 predictors of class grade and class size.

To describe the observed variation at each level, descriptive statistics for lower-level variables at higher levels of analysis are also provided in Table 11.1. That is, for the level-1 predictors of student closeness and victimization, variation across students is indicated by their level-2 student mean variables. Variation in those level-2 student means across classes is indicated by their level-3 class mean variables; similarly, variation in the proportion of girls across classes is indicated by the level-3 class mean for gender. For the level-1 predictor of class emotional support, variation across classes is indicated by the level-3 class mean variable only (there is no level-2 variation across students in class emotional support). Finally, in Table 11.1 the level-1 and level-2 variables were also partitioned into per-level observed variables to convey level-specific variation. That is, the *within-student* level-1 variables represent variation of each occasion relative to the level-2 student's mean, the *within-class* level-1 variable represents variation of each occasion relative to the level-3 class's mean, and the *within-class* level-2 variables represent variation of each level-2 student's mean relative to the level-3 class mean.

Table 11.1 Descriptive statistics per level for all variables in the clustered longitudinal data example.

Level	Variable	# of Observations	Mean	Standard Deviation	Variance	Minimum	Maximum
1	Student Closeness	1731	4.21	0.95	0.91	1.00	6.55
1	Within-Student Closeness	1731	0.00	0.52	0.27	−2.66	2.93
1	Student Victimization	1731	3.13	0.99	0.98	1.29	6.00
1	Within-Student Student Victimization	1731	0.00	0.47	0.23	−2.33	2.19
1	Class Emotional Support	99	4.99	0.74	0.55	2.97	6.25
1	Within-Class Class Emotional Support	99	0.00	0.43	0.18	−1.52	1.20
2	Student Mean Student Closeness	597	4.20	0.80	0.65	1.00	5.65
2	Within-Class Student Mean Student Closeness	597	0.00	0.73	0.53	−2.80	1.80
2	Student Mean Student Victimization	597	3.13	0.87	0.76	1.67	6.00
2	Within-Class Student Mean Student Victimization	597	0.00	0.83	0.69	−1.63	2.66
2	Student Gender (0 = Boy, 1 = Girl)	597	0.50	0.50	0.25	0.00	1.00
3	Class Mean of Student Mean Student Closeness	33	4.22	0.36	0.13	3.35	4.91
3	Class Mean of Student Mean Student Victimization	33	3.13	0.28	0.08	2.50	3.70
3	Class Mean Class Emotional Support	33	4.99	0.61	0.37	3.65	5.88
3	Class Mean Student Gender	33	0.50	0.10	0.01	0.29	0.76
3	Class Mean Size	33	23.09	2.65	7.02	19.00	29.00
3	Class Grade (0 = Grade 3, 1 = Grade 5)	33	0.61	0.50	0.25	0.00	1.00

2.A. Distinguishing Sources of Variation Across Time, Persons, and Groups

So now that we have a descriptive sense of how much variation exists in each variable, we can estimate the proportion of variance at each level by fitting empty means models. First, a three-level empty means model for the level-1 outcome of student–teacher closeness and for the level-1 predictor of student-perceived victimization is shown in Equation (11.1):

Level 1 Occasions : $y_{tsc} = \beta_{0sc} + e_{tsc}$

Level 2 Students : $\beta_{0sc} = \delta_{00c} + U_{0sc}$

Level 3 Classes : $\delta_{00c} = \gamma_{000} + V_{00c}$

Composite : $y_{tsc} = \gamma_{000} + V_{00s} + U_{0sc} + e_{tsc}$

(11.1)

$$ICC_{L2} = \frac{\tau^2_{V_{00}} + \tau^2_{U_{00}}}{\tau^2_{V_{00}} + \tau^2_{U_{00}} + \sigma^2_e} \quad ICC_{L3} = \frac{\tau^2_{V_{00}}}{\tau^2_{V_{00}} + \tau^2_{U_{00}}} \quad ICC_{L3b} = \frac{\tau^2_{V_{00}}}{\tau^2_{V_{00}} + \tau^2_{U_{00}} + \sigma^2_e}$$

in which level 1 is indicated by t for time, level 2 by s for student, and level 3 by c for classes (the subscript i is deliberately not used given that it could refer to students or classes here).

Fitting this three-level model for student–teacher closeness provided a fixed intercept of $\gamma_{000} = 4.215$ (SE = 0.061) for the grand mean (of the class means of the student means). The total variance across levels = 0.918, which was calculated as the sum of the level-3 random intercept variance of $\tau^2_{V_{00}} = 0.090$ (SE = 0.031; 9.81% of the total) for variation across classes, a level-2 random intercept variance of $\tau^2_{U_{00}} = 0.414$ (SE = 0.034; 45.1% of the total) for variation among students in the same class, and a level-1 residual variance of $\sigma^2_e = 0.414$ (SE = 0.017; 45.1% of the total) for variation across occasions from the same student. Using Equation (11.1), $ICC_{L2} = .549$, which was significantly > 0, as indicated by a model comparison of a single-level to a two-level model (ignoring class), $-2\Delta LL(\sim1) = 464.6$, $p < .001$. Again using Equation (11.1), $ICC_{L3} = .179$, which was also significantly > 0, as indicated by a model comparison of a two-level model (ignoring class) to this three-level model, $-2\Delta LL(\sim1) = 40.0$, $p < .001$. Together, these ICCs indicate that, of the total variation in student–teacher closeness over time, 54.9% was across students and classes; of that 54.9%, 17.9% was actually across classes. Expressed in terms of predicted correlations, the correlation of occasions from the same class *and* student was $ICC_{L2} = .549$, whereas the correlation of occasions from the same class only was $ICC_{L3b} = .098$.

Fitting the same three-level model for student-perceived victimization resulted in a fixed intercept of $\gamma_{000} = 3.131$ (SE = 0.047) for the grand mean (of the class means of the student means). The total variance = 0.987, which included a level-3 random intercept variance of $\tau^2_{V_{00}} = 0.033$ (SE = 0.019; 3.3% of the total) for variation across classes, a level-2 random intercept variance of $\tau^2_{U_{00}} = 0.611$ (SE = 0.044; 61.9% of the total) for variation among students from the same class, and a level-1 residual variance of $\sigma^2_e = 0.344$ (SE = 0.014; 34.8% of the total) for the variation across occasions from the same student. Using Equation (11.1), $ICC_{L2} = .652$ and $ICC_{L3} = .051$. So, of the total variation in victimization over time, 65.2% was across students and classes, which was significantly > 0, $-2\Delta LL(\sim1) = 711.8$, $p < .001$; of that 65.2%, only 5.1% was actually across classes, which was still significantly > 0, $-2\Delta LL(\sim1) = 6.0$, $p = .015$. In terms of predicted correlations, the correlation of occasions from the same class *and* student was $ICC_{L2} = .652$, whereas the correlation of occasions from the same class only was $ICC_{L3b} = .033$.

At this point I have to acknowledge a complication regarding the partitioning of variance in three-level models. In examining the level-specific observed variances given in Table 11.1 for closeness and victimization, you will see that they do not match the corresponding level-specific estimated variances from our three-level models. For instance, for closeness, the estimated level-1 residual variance was $\sigma_e^2 = 0.414$, but the observed within-student variance was only 0.272. Similarly, the estimated level-2 random intercept variance was $\tau_{U_{00}}^2 = 0.414$, while the observed within-class variance was 0.532; the estimated level-3 random intercept variance was $\tau_{V_{00}}^2 = 0.090$, while the observed between-class variance was 0.126. So, what's going on? Although the unbalance in these data could be partly responsible (i.e., not all students have three occasions, not all classes have the same number of students), some discrepancy between the observed and estimated level-specific variances would likely still be found even in perfectly balanced data.

The discrepancy between observed versus estimated variance was previously introduced in chapter 5 for two-level models, in which we found that the estimated level-2 random intercept variance $\tau_{U_0}^2$ was smaller than the observed between-person intercept variance. This is because $\tau_{U_0}^2$ has been "corrected" for the between-person variance expected randomly from the level-1 data as indexed by the estimated level-1 residual variance σ_e^2 divided by the level-1 n for number of occasions per person. Consequently, the estimated or "true" level-2 random intercept variance $\tau_{U_0}^2$ = observed between-person intercept variance − (σ_e^2 / n). So, whenever level-1 σ_e^2 is reduced but level-2 $\tau_{U_0}^2$ is not (i.e., by fixed effects of pure level-1 predictors), level-2 $\tau_{U_0}^2$ will increase instead. This same adjustment process occurs twice over in three-level models. As explained in more detail in Figure 11.1, the estimated total variance *above level 1* is corrected for the contribution of level-1 residual variance σ_e^2 per level-1 unit, and the estimated level-3 variance is corrected for the contribution of the level-2 random intercept variance $\tau_{U_{00}}^2$ per level-2 unit.

To help illustrate the influence of sample size at each level on this variance adjustment process, model-estimated variances were predicted using known observed variances at levels 1, 2, and 3 of 60, 30, and 10, respectively. Figure 11.2 shows the percent difference of these model-estimated variances relative to their observed counterparts (which can be thought of as a measure of bias) as a function of sample size. As seen in the top panel, estimated level-1 σ_e^2 will be larger than the observed level-1 variance when level-1 n is small (such as in our current example with only three occasions), which then creates estimated level-2 $\tau_{U_{00}}^2$ that is smaller than the observed level-2 variance. Similarly, as seen in the bottom panel, estimated level-3 $\tau_{V_{00}}^2$ will be smaller than the observed level-3 variance when level-2 n is small (e.g., few students per class).

However, the estimated level-2 $\tau_{U_{00}}^2$ will depend on both level-1 n and level-2 n, as shown in the middle panel. As in two-level models, when level-1 n is small, estimated level-1 σ_e^2 (shown by the gray lines per level-1 n) will be larger than the observed level-1 variance, and so estimated level-2 $\tau_{U_{00}}^2$ (shown by the black lines per level-1 n) will be smaller than the observed level-2 variance. Furthermore, when level-2 n is large, given that estimated level-3 $\tau_{V_{00}}^2$ will then be reduced less, estimated

Total Variance $= \text{Obs3} + \text{Obs2} + \text{Obs1} = \tau^2_{V_{00}} + \tau^2_{U_{00}} + \sigma^2_e$

Obs3 = Observed level-3 variance $\tau^2_{V_{00}}$ = Estimated level-3 variance

Obs2 = Observed level-2 variance $\tau^2_{U_{00}}$ = Estimated level-2 variance

Obs1 = Observed level-1 variance σ^2_e = Estimated level-1 variance

Step 1: Correct all variance above level 1 for the expected contribution of the level-1 variance, as given by level-1 variance σ^2_e over $n1$, the number of level-1 units per level-2 unit:

$$\text{Total Variance} = (\text{Obs3} + \text{Obs2}) \overbrace{-\left(\frac{\sigma^2_e}{n1}\right) + \sigma^2_e}^{\text{Obs1}}$$

Solve for the level-1 variance σ^2_e:

$$\text{Obs1} = \sigma^2_e - \left(\frac{\sigma^2_e}{n1}\right) = \left(\frac{\sigma^2_e n1 - \sigma^2_e}{n1}\right) \rightarrow$$

$$\text{Total Variance above Level 1} =$$

$$\tau^2_{V_{00}} + \tau^2_{U_{00}} + \left(\frac{\sigma^2_e}{n1}\right) = \text{Obs3} + \text{Obs2}$$

$$\text{Obs1} * n1 = \sigma^2_e (n1 - 1) \rightarrow \sigma^2_e = \frac{\text{Obs1} * n1}{n1 - 1}$$

Step 2: Correct the level-3 variance for the expected contribution of the level-2 variance as given by $res2$, a yet unknown level-2 variance, over $n2$, the number of level-2 units per level-3 unit:

$$\tau^2_{V_{00}} + \tau^2_{U_{00}} + \left(\frac{\sigma^2_e}{n1}\right) = \text{Obs3} \overbrace{-\left(\frac{res2}{n2}\right) + res2}^{\text{Obs2}}$$

Solve for $res2$, the expected contribution of level-2 variance to level-3 variance:

$$\text{Obs2} = res2 - \left(\frac{res2}{n2}\right), \quad res2 = \frac{\text{Obs2} * n2}{n2 - 1}$$

Step 3: Solve for the level-2 variance $\tau^2_{U_{00}}$, replacing the level-1, level-3, and obs2 variances already found in the formula for *total variance above level 1* given in step 1:

$$\tau^2_{U_{00}} = \text{Obs3} + \text{Obs2} - \tau^2_{V_{00}} - \left(\frac{\sigma^2_e}{n1}\right) = \overbrace{\text{Obs3} + res2 - \left(\frac{res2}{n2}\right)}^{\text{Obs2}} \overbrace{- \text{Obs3} + \left(\frac{res2}{n2}\right)}^{-\tau^2_{V_{00}}} \overbrace{- \left(\frac{1}{n1} * \frac{\text{Obs1} * n1}{n1 - 1}\right)}^{-\sigma^2_e / n1}$$

$$= res2 - \left(\frac{\text{Obs1}}{n1 - 1}\right) = \left(\frac{\text{Obs2} * n2}{n2 - 1}\right) - \left(\frac{\text{Obs1}}{n1 - 1}\right)$$

Step 4: Express the total estimated variance using observed variances only:

$$\text{Total Variance} = \overbrace{\text{Obs3} - \left(\frac{\text{Obs2}}{n2 - 1}\right)}^{\tau^2_{V_{00}}} + \overbrace{\left(\frac{\text{Obs2} * n2}{n2 - 1}\right) - \left(\frac{\text{Obs1}}{n1 - 1}\right)}^{\tau^2_{U_{00}}} + \overbrace{\left(\frac{\text{Obs1} * n1}{n1 - 1}\right)}^{\sigma^2_e}$$

Figure 11.1 Relationship of observed to estimated variance components in three-level models.

level-2 $\tau^2_{U_{00}}$ will be reduced even more. Finally, level-3 sample size does not factor into these predictions, although level-3 variance will be estimated more precisely when level-3 n is larger (which is also true of the level-2 and level-1 variances by their sample sizes).

This idea of variance correction by level-specific sample size has even more relevance for our other level-1 variable, time-varying class emotional support. Because it is measured for an entire *class* at a given occasion, it will have level-1 and level-3 variance only (i.e., no level-2 variance among students in the same class). This

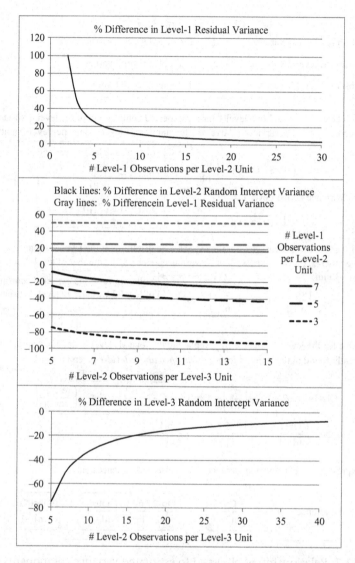

Figure 11.2 Predicted percent difference in estimated variance components relative to observed variance components as a function of sample size per level.

measurement of class emotional support results in a model with only two levels of variance components, as shown in Equation (11.2):

Level 1 Occasions : $y_{tsc} = \beta_{0sc} + e_{tsc}$

Level 2 Students : $\beta_{0sc} = \delta_{00c}$

Level 3 Classes : $\delta_{00c} = \gamma_{000} + V_{00c}$

Composite : $y_{tsc} = \gamma_{000} + V_{00s} + e_{tsc}$ $\qquad$ (11.2)

$$ICC_{L2} = \frac{\tau^2_{v_{00}} + 0}{\tau^2_{v_{00}} + 0 + \sigma^2_e} \quad ICC_{L3} = \frac{\tau^2_{v_{00}}}{\tau^2_{V_{00}} + 0} \quad ICC_{L3b} = \frac{\tau^2_{v_{00}}}{\tau^2_{V_{00}} + 0 + \sigma^2_e}$$

in which U_{0sc} is no longer included, such that level-2 $\tau^2_{U_{00}}$ is assumed to be 0. Even though this is technically now a two-level model, to keep the notation constant throughout the example, we will still refer here to class variance as level 3. This model provided a fixed intercept of γ_{000} = 4.989 (SE = 0.107) for the grand mean (of the class means over time). The total variance across levels = 0.552, which included a level-3 random intercept variance of $\tau^2_{V_{00}}$ = 0.373 (SE = 0.094) for variation across classes and a level-1 residual variance of σ^2_e = 0.179 (SE = 0.006) for the variation across occasions from the same student and class. Using Equation (11.2), $ICC_{L2} = ICC_{L3b}$ = .676, which was significant, $-2\Delta LL(\sim 1)$ = 1,734.4, $p <$ .001 (ICC_{L3} = 1 given level-2 $\tau^2_{U_{00}}$ = 0). Notably, in calculating the number of observations per class, the model combined levels 1 and 2, such that the n used for correcting the estimated level-3 class random intercept variance is actually level-1 n multiplied by level-2 n, or 3*23 using the mean number of students per class. Consequently, the estimated level-3 $\tau^2_{V_{00}}$ is very close to the observed class variance, and estimated level-1 σ^2_e is very close to the observed within-class variance over time.

Given that students from the same class will have the same values of time-varying class emotional support, there is a sense in which the 3*23 sample size used for correcting the level-3 $\tau^2_{V_{00}}$ is greatly exaggerated. In this case, however, we get very different estimates if we average over the students from the same class at each occasion, such that each class then has only its actual three observations (instead of 3*23) with which to correct the estimated class variance. Fitting a two-level model for occasions within classes on the summarized data resulted in a total variance = 0.552, which included a class random intercept variance of 0.280 (SE = 0.094) and a level-1 residual variance of 0.272 (SE = 0.047). Although still significantly > 0, $-2\Delta LL(\sim 1)$ = 23.3, $p <$ .001, the ICC = .507 is smaller than the ICC_{L2} = .676 we found using the original three-level data. Given that there really is no level-2 variation across students within the same class, the latter strategy of using only the actual occasion- and class-specific values would be more appropriate if we were modeling class emotional support as an outcome. But because it will be a predictor of student–teacher closeness (which does have level-2 student variation), its variance will have to be represented at level 1 and level 3 within the three-level models for closeness.

2.B. Evaluating Unconditional Models for Change Over Time Across Persons and Groups

The next step is to evaluate the average pattern of change over time, as well as person- and group-specific variation therein. Given that the three occasions (waves) are balanced across students, we can fit an "answer key" saturated means, unstructured variance model to perfectly reproduce the means, variances, and covariances across waves, as originally presented in chapter 3. For these data, though, we will need to have two distinct levels of unstructured variances and covariances across waves that correspond to students and classes, as shown in Equation (11.3):

$$\textbf{Model for the Means}: \quad y_{tsc} = \gamma_{100}\left(\text{Wave1}_{tsc}\right) + \gamma_{200}\left(\text{Wave2}_{tsc}\right)$$
$$+ \gamma_{300}\left(\text{Wave3}_{tsc}\right)$$

$$\textbf{Model for the Variance}: \quad \mathbf{G} = \begin{pmatrix} \tau_{V_1}^2 & \tau_{V_{1,2}} & \tau_{V_{1,3}} \\ \tau_{V_{2,1}} & \tau_{V_2}^2 & \tau_{V_{2,3}} \\ \tau_{V_{3,1}} & \tau_{V_{3,2}} & \tau_{V_3}^2 \end{pmatrix},$$

$$\mathbf{R} = \begin{pmatrix} \tau_{U_1}^2 & \tau_{U_{1,2}} & \tau_{U_{1,3}} \\ \tau_{U_{2,1}} & \tau_{U_2}^2 & \tau_{U_{2,3}} \\ \tau_{U_{3,1}} & \tau_{U_{3,2}} & \tau_{U_3}^2 \end{pmatrix}$$

(11.3)

in which the notation differs slightly from what we've seen previously so that the subscripts can stay consistent across the models for the means and variance. In the model for the means, rather than specify a fixed intercept and two fixed effects for mean differences from a reference wave, Equation (11.3) more directly shows how the software predicts the mean at each wave in treating wave as a categorical predictor (represented by the three wave-specific dummy codes). In the model for the variance, the $\mathbf{G}$ matrix contains the level-3 class variances and covariances (i.e., of the class means), whereas the $\mathbf{R}$ matrix provides the level-2 student variances and covariances (i.e., of the within-class student deviations). Given the estimation of all possible variances and covariances at the class and student levels, no further level-1 e_{ti} residual variance is possible. This unstructured variance model provides the best-fitting baseline against which to compare more parsimonious models with random intercepts and time slopes for students and classes.

The estimated means for the outcome of student-perceived student–teacher closeness at waves 1, 2, and 3 were $\gamma_{100} = 4.345$, $\gamma_{200} = 4.209$, and $\gamma_{300} = 4.085$, respectively. These three means differed significantly from each other, $F(2, 30.8) = 7.96$, $p = .002$, and appeared to decline linearly. Accordingly, we can specify an alternative but equivalent model for the means of: $y_{tsc} = \gamma_{000} + \gamma_{100}(\text{Wave}_{tsc} - 1) + \gamma_{200}(\text{Wave3}_{tsc})$, in which γ_{000} is the fixed intercept for the predicted mean at wave 1, γ_{100} provides the linear rate of change per wave, and γ_{200} provides the difference in the linear rate of change after wave 2. The advantage of this piecewise slopes model for the means is twofold. First, its three parameters still perfectly predict the three means, but γ_{200} provides a direct test of any deviation from linear change. Second, because these piecewise slopes are equivalent to a saturated means model, REML can still be used to examine whether models with random intercepts and random linear time slopes can approximate the predictions of the unstructured $\mathbf{G}$ and $\mathbf{R}$ matrices from the model in Equation (11.3) that used saturated means instead.

Thus, we continue by starting from a more parsimonious baseline model that includes piecewise mean change, a residual variance at level 1, and random intercept variances at level 2 and level 3 in order to examine variability in linear change across students and classes. As in chapter 10, random effects are allowed to covary only at the same level. Model fit improved significantly by adding a variance of the random linear time slopes across level-2 students (and their covariance with the level-2 random intercept), $-2\Delta LL(\sim2) = 32.0$, $p < .001$, as well as by adding a variance of the random linear time slopes across level-3 classes (and their covariance with the level-3 random intercept), $-2\Delta LL(\sim2) = 37.4$, $p < .001$. This new model did not fit significantly worse than the best-fitting baseline with unstructured $\mathbf{G}$ and $\mathbf{R}$ matrices, $-2\Delta LL(\sim5) = 2.8$, $p = .732$, indicating that the random effects adequately predicted the variance and covariance across waves for students and classes. Furthermore, the wave 3 fixed effect γ_{200} was not significant, indicating that a fixed linear slope adequately predicted the means across waves.

Our new unconditional time model predicting student–teacher closeness is shown in Equation (11.4):

Level 1 Occasions : $y_{tsc} = \beta_{0sc} + \beta_{1sc}\left(\text{Wave}_{tsc} - 1\right) + e_{tsc}$

Level 2 Students :

Intercept: $\beta_{0sc} = \delta_{00c} + U_{0sc}$

Time: $\beta_{1sc} = \delta_{10c} + U_{1sc}$

Level 3 Classes :

Intercept: $\delta_{00c} = \gamma_{000} + V_{00c}$

Time: $\delta_{10c} = \gamma_{100} + V_{10c}$ $\qquad$ (11.4)

Composite : $y_{tsc} = \left(\gamma_{000} + V_{00s} + U_{0sc}\right) + \left(\gamma_{100} + V_{10c} + U_{1sc}\right)\left(\text{Wave}_{tsc} - 1\right) + e_{tsc}$

$$\mathbf{G} = \begin{bmatrix} \text{Level 3} & 0 \\ 0 & \text{Level 2} \end{bmatrix} = \begin{bmatrix} \tau^2_{V_{00}} & \tau_{V_{00,01}} & & \\ \tau_{V_{01,00}} & \tau^2_{V_{01}} & & \\ & & \tau^2_{U_{00}} & \tau_{U_{00,10}} \\ & & \tau_{U_{10,00}} & \tau^2_{U_{10}} \end{bmatrix}, \quad \mathbf{R} = \sigma^2_e \left[\mathbf{I}_{n1 \cdot n2}\right]$$

whose results are given in the first set of columns in Table 11.2. Student–teacher closeness at wave 1 was predicted to be $\gamma_{000} = 4.343$ and to decrease significantly by $\gamma_{100} = -0.130$ per wave, but the fixed linear effect of time only accounted for 1.3% of the overall variance (as given by total R^2). However, there was significant variation across level-3 classes and across level-2 students within classes in both intercepts and linear time slopes. In calculating their ICC_{L3}, 6.2% of the intercept variation and 31.6% of the time slope variation was between classes. The block-diagonal $\mathbf{G}$ matrix for these random effects variances and covariances is also shown in Equation (11.4), in which the level-2 block would be repeated for each person in a group. Finally, the $\mathbf{R}$ matrix per group (the result of multiplying σ^2_e by an $\mathbf{I}$ identity matrix with rows and columns equal to the $n2$ number of persons by $n1$ occasions within that group) would have σ^2_e on the diagonal and 0's elsewhere, as would that group's $\mathbf{V}$ matrix.

Table 11.2 Results from longitudinal models for persons nested in time-invariant groups. Bold values are $p < .05$.

Parameters		Unconditional Time Model (11.4)			Final Conditional Model (11.9)		
		Est	SE	$p <$	Est	SE	$p <$
Model for the Means							
γ_{000}	Intercept	**4.343**	0.045	.001	**4.211**	0.058	.001
γ_{100}	Linear Time Slope (0 = Wave 1)	**−0.130**	0.033	.001	**−0.131**	0.030	.001
γ_{010}	Student Gender (0 = Boy, 1 = Girl)				**0.252**	0.068	.001
γ_{110}	Student Gender by Time				−0.001	0.039	.987
γ_{003}	Class Mean Gender (0 = .50 Girls)				0.545	0.444	.224
γ_{103}	Class Mean Gender by Time				**−1.112**	0.235	.001
γ_{004}	Class Mean Emotional Support (0 = 5)				0.108	0.074	.155
γ_{104}	Class Mean Emotional Support by Time				**0.170**	0.038	.001
γ_{009}	Class Mean Emotional Support by Class Mean Gender				**−2.349**	0.808	.006
γ_{400}	Level-1 Victimization (0 = Student Mean)				−0.075	0.045	.092
γ_{020}	Level-2 Victimization (0 = Class Mean)				−0.053	0.052	.308
γ_{420}	Level-2 Victimization by Level-1 Victimization				**0.109**	0.045	.016
γ_{040}	Level-2 Victimization by Student Gender				**−0.152**	0.073	.038
γ_{021}	Level-2 Victimization by Class Mean Gender				−0.096	0.371	.797
γ_{005}	Level-3 Victimization (0 = 3)				−0.054	0.160	.738
γ_{405}	Level-3 Victimization by Level-1 Victimization				0.157	0.132	.235
$\gamma_{00,11}$	Level-3 Victimization by Class Mean Emotional Support				**−0.778**	0.278	.009
Model for the Variance							
$\tau^2_{V_{00}}$	Class Random Intercept Variance	0.027	0.017	.053	0.019	0.015	.105
$\tau^2_{V_{10}}$	Class Random Linear Time Slope Variance	**0.023**	0.009	.005	0.005	0.005	.153
$\tau_{V_{00,10}}$	Class Intercept-Time Slope Covariance	**0.021**	0.009	.017	**0.020**	0.006	.001
$\tau^2_{U_{00}}$	Student Random Intercept Variance	**0.406**	0.044	.001	**0.395**	0.043	.001
$\tau^2_{U_{10}}$	Student Random Linear Time Slope Variance	**0.049**	0.016	.001	**0.044**	0.016	.003
$\tau^2_{U_{40}}$	Student Random L1 Victimization Slope Variance				**0.095**	0.032	.001
$\tau_{U_{00,10}}$	Student Intercept-Time Slope Covariance	−0.006	0.021	.778	−0.007	0.020	.710
$\tau_{U_{00,40}}$	Student Intercept-L1 Victimization Slope Covariance				0.017	0.027	.525
$\tau_{U_{10,40}}$	Student Time-L1 Victimization Slope Covariance				−0.013	0.013	.339
σ^2_e	Residual Variance	**0.326**	0.019	.001	**0.297**	0.020	.001

Parameters	Unconditional Time Model (11.4)			Final Conditional Model (11.9)		
	Est	SE	p <	Est	SE	p <
<u>REML Model Fit</u>						
Number of Parameters	9			27		
–2LL	4130.1			4069.8		
AIC	4144.1			4089.8		
BIC	4154.6			4104.8		

2.C. Distinguishing Effects of Predictors Across Persons and Groups

Now that we know there are random intercept and random linear time slope differences across classes and across students within classes, we can augment the model in Equation (11.4) to include fixed effects of predictors to explain each source of variation, beginning with level-3 class predictors. Following the convention started earlier, whenever predictor effects are not retained in further models, their subscript numbers will not be re-used (e.g., if a level-3 effect γ_{001} is not retained, the next level-3 predictor will be named γ_{002} rather than using γ_{001} again).

First, we consider to what extent level-3 class random intercept and time slope variance can be explained by class grade (0 = grade 3 and 1 = grade 5) and class size (centered at 23 students). The level-3 intercept equation from Equation (11.4) is now: $\delta_{00c} = \gamma_{000} + \gamma_{001}(\text{Grade35}_c) + \gamma_{002}(\text{Size}_c - 23) + V_{00c}$, and the level-3 time slope equation is now: $\delta_{10c} = \gamma_{100} + \gamma_{101}(\text{Grade35}_c) + \gamma_{102}(\text{Size}_c - 23) + V_{10c}$. The nonsignificant grade effects of $\gamma_{001} = 0.05$ and $\gamma_{101} = 0.03$ indicated no difference between grades 3 and 5 in the intercept or time slope; these grade effects were removed. However, given the small sample size of 33 classes, the marginally significant class size effects of $\gamma_{002} = -0.031$ ($p = .070$) and $\gamma_{102} = -0.021$ ($p = .095$) were retained. These effects indicated that for every additional student in a class, the predicted class mean of student–teacher closeness at wave 1 was lower by 0.031, and the time slope was more negative by 0.021. In computing pseudo-R^2 for the proportion reduction in each pile of variance relative to the unconditional time model in Equation (11.4), the simple main effect of class size explained 18.7% of the original level-3 class random intercept variance, and its interaction with time explained 8.8% of the original level-3 class random time slope variance. The level-2 and level-1 variances were largely unchanged, as to be expected given that class size is a level-3 predictor.

Next we consider to what extent level-2 student random intercept and time slope variance can be explained by gender (0 = boys and 1 = girls). Gender is measured directly at level 2 ($M = 0.497$ and $VAR = 0.250$), but to the extent that classes differ in gender composition, gender may also vary at level 3. As shown in Table 11.1, the proportion of girls in each class ranged from 0.294 to 0.765 ($M = 0.501$, $VAR = 0.011$). Because gender is binary, the ICC for its proportion of between-class variance should be found from an empty model using a logit link and a Bernoulli distribution, rather than from a model than assuming a normal level-1 residual distribution (see chapter 13). In doing so, the class random intercept variance for gender was not estimable. In using observed variances to approximate its ICC instead, 4.11% of the variance in gender was between classes. Although small, because there is some variance across classes, we will include a level-3 class contextual effect for gender in addition to a level-2 student effect. To do so, we include student gender as a predictor in the level-2 model for the student intercept and time slope and as well as class mean proportion of girls (centered at .50) as a predictor in the level-3 model for the class intercept and time slope, as shown in Equation (11.5):

Level 1 Occasions : $y_{tsc} = \beta_{0sc} + \beta_{1sc}(Wave_{tsc} - 1) + e_{tsc}$

Level 2 Students :

Intercept: $\beta_{0sc} = \delta_{00c} + \underline{\delta_{01c}(Girl_{sc})} + U_{0sc}$

Time: $\beta_{1sc} = \delta_{10c} + \underline{\delta_{11c}(Girl_{sc})} + U_{1sc}$

Level 3 Classes :

Intercept: $\delta_{00c} = \gamma_{000} + \gamma_{002}(Size_c - 23) + \underline{\gamma_{003}\left(\overline{Girl}_c - .5\right)} + V_{00c}$

Time: $\delta_{10c} = \gamma_{100} + \gamma_{102}(Size_c - 23) + \underline{\gamma_{103}\left(\overline{Girl}_c - .5\right)} + V_{10c}$

Girl: $\underline{\delta_{01c} = \gamma_{010}}$

Girl*Time: $\underline{\delta_{11c} = \gamma_{110}}$

$$(11.5)$$

Composite :

$$y_{tsc} = \begin{Bmatrix} \gamma_{000} + \gamma_{002}(Size_c - 23) + \underline{\gamma_{003}\left(\overline{Girl}_c - .5\right)} \\ + \underline{\gamma_{010}(Girl_{sc})} + V_{00s} + U_{0sc} \end{Bmatrix} + \\ \begin{Bmatrix} \gamma_{100} + \gamma_{102}(Size_c - 23) + \underline{\gamma_{103}\left(\overline{Girl}_c - .5\right)} \\ + \underline{\gamma_{110}(Girl_{sc})} + V_{10c} + U_{1sc} \end{Bmatrix}(Wave_{tsc} - 1) + e_{tsc}$$

in which the new model effects are underlined for emphasis. The new level-2 placeholders of δ_{01c} and δ_{11c} for the effect of student gender on the intercept and time slope then require their own level-3 equations (which so far just include fixed effects). The level-2 and level-3 effects of student gender can be interpreted similarly as when (correctly) using grand-mean-centering for a level-1 predictor, as was introduced in chapter 8. In the models that follow, pseudo-R^2 values have been calculated using the last reported model as a baseline, such that here the level-3 reductions are relative to the variance remaining after controlling for the effects of class size.

Results from Equation (11.5) were as follows. The simple main effect of gender on the level-2 intercept indicated that, at wave 1, girls felt significantly closer to their teacher by $\gamma_{010} = 0.253$ than do boys in the same classroom (pseudo-R^2 = .039 for the level-2 student random intercept variance). The student gender effect was nonsignificantly weaker by $\gamma_{110} = -0.006$ per wave (pseudo-R^2 = .005 for the level-2 student time slope variance). The nonsignificant level-3 contextual simple main effect of gender indicated that after controlling for student gender, the proportion of girls in a classroom did not predict additional classroom differences in close-ness at wave 1 (i.e., $\gamma_{003} = 0.500 / 10 = 0.050$ greater closeness per 10% additional girls). Furthermore, the level-3 class random intercept variance actually increased (pseudo-$R^2 = -.032$). However, the level-3 gender by time contextual interaction indicated that, after controlling for the difference in the student gender effect over time, the level-3 gender contextual effect was significantly more negative by $\gamma_{103} = -0.924$ per wave (pseudo-$R^2 = .393$ for the level-3 class time slope variance). However, in requesting contextual gender effects per wave, none was actually sig-nificant—this may be due to the lower precision (greater SE) when evaluating con-textual effects conditionally at a single occasion (based on 33 classes) rather than across waves. Regardless, the contextual gender and contextual gender*time effects will be retained given the latter significant interaction.

In addition, in estimating the model in Equation (11.5), the correlation between the level-3 class random intercept and time slope became bounded at 1.0, generat-ing a warning message that the G matrix may not be positive definite. However, because model fit decreased significantly when removing the level-3 random time slope variance, $-2\Delta LL(\sim 2) = 25.3$, $p < .001$, it was retained. Lastly, we can examine a random effect of student gender across classes by adding V_{01c} to the level-3 equa-tion for δ_{01c} to allow variation across classes in the gender difference of student–teacher closeness. The marginally significant improvement in model fit indicated that the gender effect may not be entirely constant across classes, $-2\Delta LL(\sim 3) = 7.7$, $p = .053$. Given the difficulty in estimating level-3 random effects variances in our data, though, the random gender effect across classes was not retained.

2.D. Distinguishing Effects of Predictors Across Time and Groups

We now turn to our time-varying predictor of class emotional support, for which we will first need to examine unconditional models of change to determine how to rep-resent its sources of variance in predicting time-varying student–teacher closeness. However, to do so we will need a two-level data set of occasions within classes given that class emotional support does not vary across students from the same class (and thus only classes could possibly differ in their random intercepts and slopes). A saturated means, unstructured variance model revealed no significant omnibus or pairwise mean differences in emotional support across waves, $F(2, 32) = 0.98$, $p = .388$. Using a saturated means model, a random intercept model did not fit signifi-cantly worse than the unstructured model, $-2\Delta LL(\sim 4) = 3.9$, $p = .419$, and a model with a random linear time slope had a non-positive definite G matrix. Thus, there was no change in class emotional support across waves on average, and there was no random variation in its rate of change across classes.

Consequently, we will only need to represent level-3 variance in mean class emo-tional support (i.e., given its ICC = .507 reported earlier), such as by including class mean emotional support as a level-3 predictor (centered at 5). The level-1 predictor for the within-class effect could be class-mean-centered or grand-mean-centered (i.e., centered at a constant rather than a variable), which would result in a level-3 between-class or contextual class effect, respectively. To maintain symmetry with the within-class and contextual class effects of student gender, we will choose the latter and center time-varying class emotional support at 5. Our new model including level-1 and level-3 effects of class emotional support is shown in Equation (11.6):

Level 1 Occasions:

$$y_{tsc} = \beta_{0sc} + \beta_{1sc}(\text{Wave}_{tsc} - 1) + \beta_{2sc}(\text{EmoSup}_{tsc} - 5)$$
$$+ \beta_{3sc}(\text{Wave}_{tsc} - 1)(\text{EmoSup}_{tsc} - 5) + e_{tsc}$$

Level 2 Students:

$$\text{Intercept: } \beta_{0sc} = \delta_{00c} + \delta_{01c}(\text{Girl}_{sc}) + U_{0sc}$$
$$\text{Time: } \beta_{1sc} = \delta_{10c} + \delta_{11c}(\text{Girl}_{sc}) + U_{1sc}$$
$$\text{EmoSup: } \beta_{2sc} = \delta_{20c}$$
$$\text{EmoSup*Time: } \beta_{3sc} = \delta_{30c}$$

Level 3 Classes:

$$\text{Intercept: } \delta_{00c} = \gamma_{000} + \gamma_{002}(\text{Size}_c - 23) + \gamma_{003}(\overline{\text{Girl}}_c - .5)$$
$$+ \underline{\gamma_{004}(\overline{\text{EmoSup}}_c - 5)} + V_{00c}$$
$$\text{Time: } \delta_{10c} = \gamma_{100} + \gamma_{102}(\text{Size}_c - 23) + \gamma_{103}(\overline{\text{Girl}}_c - .5) \quad\quad (11.6)$$
$$+ \underline{\gamma_{104}(\overline{\text{EmoSup}}_c - 5)} + V_{10c}$$
$$\text{Girl: } \delta_{01c} = \gamma_{010}$$
$$\text{Girl*Time: } \delta_{11c} = \gamma_{110}$$
$$\text{EmoSup: } \delta_{20c} = \gamma_{200}$$
$$\text{EmoSup*Time: } \delta_{30c} = \gamma_{300}$$

Composite:

$$y_{tsc} = \begin{cases} \gamma_{000} + \gamma_{002}(\text{Size}_c - 23) + \gamma_{003}(\overline{\text{Girl}}_c - .5) + \underline{\gamma_{004}(\overline{\text{EmoSup}}_c - 5)} \\ + \gamma_{010}(\text{Girl}_{sc}) + \underline{\gamma_{200}(\text{EmoSup}_{tsc} - 5)} + V_{00s} + U_{0sc} \end{cases} + \\ \begin{cases} \gamma_{100} + \gamma_{102}(\text{Size}_c - 23) + \gamma_{103}(\overline{\text{Girl}}_c - .5) + \underline{\gamma_{104}(\overline{\text{EmoSup}}_c - 5)} \\ + \gamma_{110}(\text{Girl}_{sc}) + \underline{\gamma_{300}(\text{EmoSup}_{tsc} - 5)} + V_{10c} + U_{1sc} \end{cases}(\text{Wave}_{tsc} - 1) + e_{tsc}$$

in which the level-3 model now contains the contextual effects of class emotional support on the class intercept and time slope (γ_{004} and γ_{104}), again underlined for emphasis. The level-1 model has been augmented by the β_{2sc} and β_{3sc} placeholders for the within-class effect of emotional support and its interaction with time, which then requires the δ_{20c} and δ_{30c} level-2 placeholders, which are then defined by the γ_{200} and γ_{300} level-3 fixed effects. Though somewhat cumbersome, this placeholder-based system of equations—and all the empty spaces shown therein—show explicitly just how many more interactions could have been added for the level-1 effects!

The results from Equation (11.6) suggested that our model can be simplified. First, the effect of class size and its interaction with time became decidedly nonsignificant ($\gamma_{002} = -0.025$, $p = .178$; $\gamma_{102} = -0.012$, $p = .204$), indicating no unique effects of class size after controlling for class mean emotional support, and so these class size effects were removed. In addition, neither of our new level-1 effects for within-class emotional support was significant: For every unit greater class emotional support than the class mean, student–teacher closeness at wave 1 was nonsignificantly lower by $\gamma_{200} = -0.024$; this effect was nonsignificantly more positive by $\gamma_{300} = 0.050$ per wave. These effects did not explain any of the level-1 residual variance (it actually increased slightly instead). Furthermore, in trying to estimate a random effect of within-class emotional support across classes by adding V_{20c} to the level-3 equation predicting δ_{20c}, the model would not converge. Thus, given the lack of any fixed or random effects, the level-1 effects of within-class emotional support and its interaction with time were removed.

In our reduced model, we can now interpret the level-3 effects of class emotional support directly as between-class effects (rather than as contextual effects, as they would have been if also including a level-1 effect of within-class emotional support). That is, the simple main effect indicates that for every additional unit of class mean emotional support, class mean student–teacher closeness at wave 1 was nonsignificantly higher by $\gamma_{004} = 0.073$. The interaction of class mean emotional support by time was significant, however, such that the between-class effect became significantly more positive by $\gamma_{104} = 0.169$ per wave, such that at wave 2 it was 0.243 ($p = .018$), and at wave 3 it was 0.412 ($p = .003$). The class mean emotional support by time interaction explained 70.5% of the remaining level-3 class random time slope variance, but the level-3 class random intercept variance increased instead (pseudo-$R^2 = -.084$).

2.E. Distinguishing Effects of Predictors Across Time, Persons, and Groups

Our last predictor to be examined is time-varying student-perceived victimization. But in order to determine how best to specify its higher-level effects in the model, we first need to assess whether it contains level-2 student and level-3 class differences in change over time, in addition to just mean differences at each level (i.e., as indicated by the $ICC_{L2} = .652$ and $ICC_{L3} = .051$ we found earlier). To do so, the models previously estimated for the outcome of student–teacher closeness were also estimated for the predictor of student-perceived victimization. The model from Equation (11.3) with saturated means and unstructured G and R matrices revealed significant mean differences across waves, $F(2, 30.5) = 4.52$, $p = .019$, such that victimization increased slightly across waves ($\gamma_{100} = 3.080$, $\gamma_{200} = 3.125$, and $\gamma_{300} = 3.185$). However, relative to the more parsimonious baseline model with only residual variance at level 1 and random intercept variances at levels 2 and 3, there was no significant variation in the random linear time slopes across level-2 students, $-2\Delta LL(\sim2) = 1.6$, $p = .440$, or across level-3 classes, $-2\Delta LL(\sim2) = 1.0$, $p = .619$. The linear increase of $\gamma_{100} = 0.052$ ($p = .003$) per wave was significant, although the wave 3 contrast γ_{200} was not significant. Consequently, models including predictive effects of victimization will only need to represent mean differences across level-2 students and level-3 classes, as victimization does not show student or class differences in change over time.

There are multiple strategies for including observed variables to represent a time-varying predictor at all three levels of our model, but the primary distinction is whether the predictors are centered around variables (i.e., person-mean-centering and group-mean-centering) or constants (i.e., grand-mean-centering), as shown in the top and bottom panels of Table 11.3, respectively. As was the case for two-level models in chapter 8, so long as a predictor is entered at all three levels and has only fixed effects, these two options will result in equivalent models. While either strategy will result in a purely within-student level-1 effect, the level-2 and level-3 effects will differ depending on which level-1 predictor is included. As shown in the top panel of Table 11.3, centering the level-1 predictor at the level-2 mean will create a pure within-class student effect at level 2; likewise, centering the level-2 predictor at the level-3 mean will create a pure between-class effect at level 3. In contrast, as shown in the bottom panel of Table 11.3, centering the level-1 and level-2 predictors at a constant will create a within-class student *contextual* effect at level 2, and a class *contextual* effect at level 3. To make these interpretations more concrete, let us examine the main effects from both strategies using the model shown in Equation (11.7):

Level 1 Occasions :

$$y_{tsc} = \beta_{0sc} + \beta_{1sc}\left(Wave_{tsc} - 1\right) + \underline{\beta_{4sc}\left(L1vic_{tsc}\right)} + e_{tsc}$$

Level 2 Students :

Intercept: $\beta_{0sc} = \delta_{00c} + \delta_{01c}\left(Girl_{sc}\right) + \underline{\delta_{02c}\left(L2vic_{sc}\right)} + U_{0sc}$

$\quad$ Time: $\beta_{1sc} = \delta_{10c} + \delta_{11c}\left(Girl_{sc}\right) + U_{1sc}$

$\quad\quad$ L1Vic: $\beta_{4sc} = \delta_{40c}$

Level 3 Classes :

Intercept: $\delta_{00c} = \gamma_{000} + \gamma_{003}\left(\overline{Girl}_c - .5\right) + \gamma_{004}\left(\overline{EmoSup}_c - 5\right)$

$$\quad\quad\quad + \underline{\gamma_{005}\left(L3vic_c\right)} + V_{00c}$$

$\quad$ Time: $\delta_{10c} = \gamma_{100} + \gamma_{103}\left(\overline{Girl}_c - .5\right) + \gamma_{104}\left(\overline{EmoSup}_c - 5\right) + V_{10c}$ $\qquad$ (11.7)

$\quad\quad$ Girl: $\delta_{01c} = \gamma_{010}$

Girl*Time: $\delta_{11c} = \gamma_{110}$

$\quad\quad$ L1Vic: $\underline{\delta_{40c} = \gamma_{400}}$

$\quad\quad$ L2Vic: $\underline{\delta_{02c} = \gamma_{020}}$

Composite :

$$y_{tsc} = \begin{cases} \gamma_{000} + \gamma_{003}\left(\overline{Girl}_c - .5\right) + \gamma_{004}\left(\overline{EmoSup}_c - 5\right) + \underline{\gamma_{005}\left(L3vic_c\right)} \\ + \gamma_{010}\left(Girl_{sc}\right) + \underline{\gamma_{020}\left(L2vic_{sc}\right)} + \underline{\gamma_{400}\left(L1vic_{tsc}\right)} + V_{00s} + U_{0sc} \end{cases} + \\ \begin{cases} \gamma_{100} + \gamma_{103}\left(\overline{Girl}_c - .5\right) + \gamma_{104}\left(\overline{EmoSup}_c - 5\right) \\ + \gamma_{110}\left(Girl_{sc}\right) + V_{10c} + U_{1sc} \end{cases}\left(Wave_{tsc} - 1\right) + e_{tsc}$$

Table 11.3 Centering of time-varying student-perceived victimization (vic) predictor in a three-level model for the example of clustered longitudinal data. Coefficients with * are $p < .05$.

Variable-Based Centering	Level 1 ($L1vic_{tsc}$)	Level 2 ($L2vic_{sc}$)	Level 3 ($L3vic_c$)
Name of Predictor and its Levels of Variance	Within-Student (WS) (Level 1 only)	Within-Class (WC) (Level 2 only)	Class Mean (CM) (Level 3 only)
Predictor Equation	$WSvic_{tsc} = Vic_{tsc} - \overline{VIC}_{sc}$	$WCvic_{sc} = \overline{VIC}_{sc} - \overline{VIC}_c$	$CMvic_c = \overline{VIC}_c - 3$
Interpretation (Effect = 0 if omitted)	Within-Student Time Effect ($\gamma_{400} = 0.011$)	Within-Class Student Effect ($\gamma_{020} = -0.129$*)	Between-Class Effect ($\gamma_{005} = -0.025$)

Constant-Based Centering	Level 1 ($L1vic_{tsc}$)	Level 2 ($L2vic_{sc}$)	Level 3 ($L3vic_c$)
Name of Predictor and its Levels of Variance	Time-Varying (TV) Levels 1, 2, and 3	Student Mean (SM) Levels 2 and 3	Class Mean (CM) Level 3
Predictor Equation	$TVvic_{tsc} = Vic_{tsc} - 3$	$SMvic_{sc} = \overline{VIC}_{sc} - 3$	$CMvic_c = \overline{VIC}_c - 3$
Interpretation if Predictors at Level 1, 2, and 3	Within-Student Time Effect ($\gamma_{400} = 0.011$)	Within-Class Student Contextual Effect ($\gamma_{020} = -0.140$*)	Class Contextual Effect ($\gamma_{005} = 0.104$)
Interpretation if Level-1 Effect is Omitted		Within-Class Student Effect ($\gamma_{020} = -0.129$*)	Class Contextual Effect ($\gamma_{005} = 0.104$)
Interpretation if Level-2 Effect is Omitted	Smushed Time and Student Effect ($\gamma_{400} = -0.049$*)		Class Contextual Effect ($\gamma_{005} = 0.021$)
Interpretation if Level-3 Effect is Omitted	Within-Student Time Effect ($\gamma_{400} = 0.011$)	Smushed Student and Class Contextual Effect ($\gamma_{020} = -0.136$*)	
Interpretation if Only Level-1 Effect is Included	Smushed Time, Student, and Class Effect ($\gamma_{400} = -0.048$*)		

in which the definitions of $L1vic_{tsc}$, $L2vic_{sc}$, and $L3vic_c$ and their corresponding estimated fixed effects when using variable-based or constant-based centering are given in Table 11.3. As before, the subscripts are not ordered contiguously within or across levels due to the missing subscripts for the predictors examined previously whose effects have been removed.

Let us begin with the more straightforward results given by variable-based centering, as shown in the top of Table 11.3, in which the level-1 predictor is centered at the level-2 student mean and the level-2 predictor is centered at the level-3 class mean. First, the level-1 within-student effect indicated that student–teacher closeness at the same wave was nonsignificantly greater by $\gamma_{400} = 0.011$ per unit increase in student-perceived victimization relative to the student's mean (pseudo-$R^2 \sim 0$ for the level-1 residual variance). In other words, feeling more victimized *than usual* did not predict how close a student felt to her teacher at that occasion. Second, the level-2 within-class effect indicated that student mean closeness was significantly lower by $\gamma_{020} = -0.129$ for every additional unit of student mean victimization relative to the class's mean (pseudo-R^2 = .022 for the remaining level-2 student random intercept variance). In other words, students who felt more victimized on average across waves *than other students in their class* felt less close to their teachers than other students in their class. Third, the level-3 between-class effect indicated that class mean closeness was nonsignificantly lower by $\gamma_{005} = -0.025$ for every additional unit of class mean victimization (pseudo-R^2 = −.089 for the level-3 class random intercept variance). In other words, classes in which students felt more victimized than in other classes did not feel less close on average to their teacher. To summarize, only the level-2 student within-class effect was significantly negative. Comfortingly, each of these effects would be interpreted in the same way regardless of whether the effects at the other levels are included, because any omitted level-specific effects are assumed to be 0. For completeness of interpretation, though, we will retain the main effects of the victimization predictor at each level.

Now let us consider the results from the model using constant-based centering for time-varying victimization instead (in which each predictor is centered at 3, as shown in the bottom of Table 11.3). The level-1 effect was the same within-student effect just described given that the level-2 and level-3 predictors were also included. However, the level-2 and level-3 effects differ: Whereas variable-based centering created level-specific effects, constant-based centering creates *differences* in effects across levels instead (i.e., contextual effects for incremental contributions after controlling for the lower-level predictors). More specifically, the level-2 within-class student contextual effect indicated that, after controlling for victimization at that wave, for every unit more victimized a student felt than other students in her class, her student mean closeness was significantly lower by $\gamma_{020} = -0.140$. The level-2 contextual effect also indicated that the level-2 effect (given as: $\gamma_{400} + \gamma_{020} = 0.011 - 0.140 = -0.129$) differed significantly from the level-1 effect ($\gamma_{400} = 0.011$) by $\gamma_{020} = -0.140$. The level-3 class contextual effect indicated that, after controlling for both victimization at that wave and student mean victimization, for every unit more victimized a class felt than other classes, class mean closeness was nonsignificantly higher by $\gamma_{005} = 0.104$. The level-3 contextual effect also indicated that the level-3 effect (given as: $\gamma_{400} + \gamma_{020} + \gamma_{005} = 0.011 - 0.140 + 0.104 = -0.025$) differed nonsignificantly from the level-2 effect (given as: $\gamma_{400} + \gamma_{020} = 0.011 - 0.140 = -0.129$) by $\gamma_{020} = 0.104$.

Unlike variable-based centering, in which the effect at each level is the same, regardless of whether the effects at other levels are included, Table 11.3 reports how each coefficient and its interpretation would change if the other predictor effects are omitted when using constant-based centering. First, if the level-1 effect was omitted, it is assumed to be 0, and so the level-2 effect becomes the within-class student effect, but the level-3 effect remains the class contextual effect. However, if the level-2 effect was omitted, it is assumed to be the *same* as the level-1 effect, such that the level-1 effect becomes the smushed time and student effects. The level-3 effect remains the class contextual effect, albeit after controlling for a smushed effect rather than the distinct level-1 and level-2 effects. Similarly, if the level-3 effect was omitted, it is assumed to be the *same* as the level-2 effect, such that the level-2 effect becomes the smushed student and class effects; the level-1 effect would remain the level-1 effect. Finally, if both the level-2 and level-3 effects were omitted, the remaining level-1 effect is smushed effect across all three levels.

If you had trouble following the last paragraph, I can't say I blame you—I had trouble writing it! Unfortunately, it gets even more complicated, because so far we only have a main effect at each level, but the same logic and conditional interpretations would apply in adding interaction terms as well. That is, any interaction effects omitted from a model using variable-based centering are assumed to be 0, whereas in constant-based centering, the assumptions about the terms omitted from a model and the interpretation of those that are left will depend on which specific effects are included. For instance, what if we added an interaction with time for only the level-2 effect of victimization in a model that had all three main effects of victimization? Using variable-based centering, only the within-class student effect would be predicted to change over time, but in constant-based centering, the within-class and between-class effects would be predicted to change equally over time (i.e., a smushed interaction). It's not hard to imagine how complicated interpreting interactions could become when using constant-based centering!

Let us continue by examining whether the victimization effects do change over time. An interaction with time for the level-1 effect can be added as β_{5sc} predicting y_{tsc}, which would become $\beta_{5sc} = \delta_{50c}$ at level 2 and $\delta_{50c} = \gamma_{500}$ at level 3. An interaction with time for the level-2 effect can be added as δ_{12c} to the level-2 equation for the time slope predicting β_{1sc}, which would become $\delta_{12c} = \gamma_{120}$ at level 3. Finally, an interaction with time for the level-3 effect can be added directly as γ_{105} to the level-3 equation for the time slope predicting δ_{10c}. Fortunately for us (given how complex our model is already), no interactions of victimization with time were significant when using variable-based or constant-based centering, so these interactions were removed.

Given the potential problems in interpreting effects using constant-based centering, we will continue augmenting the model from Equation (11.7) using variable-based centering for time-varying student-perceived victimization in order to examine its potential random effects. First, we can examine whether the level-2 within-class student victimization effect varies randomly over classes by adding V_{02c} to the level-3 equation predicting δ_{02c}. However, adding a variance for the random slope of within-class victimization (and its covariances with the level-3 random intercept and time slope) did not significantly improve model fit, $-2\Delta LL(\sim3) = 4.6$, $p = .206$, indicating that the extent to which feeling more victimized than other students in your class predicted feeling less student–teacher closeness did not vary significantly across classes.

Second, we can examine whether the level-1 within-student victimization effect varies randomly over students by adding U_{4sc} to the level-2 equation predicting β_{4sc}. Adding a variance for the random slope of within-student victimization across students (and its covariances with the level-2 random intercept and time slope) significantly improved model fit, $-2\Delta LL(\sim3) = 18.8$, $p < .001$, indicating that the extent to which feeling more victimized than usual predicted feeling less student–teacher closeness at the same wave did vary across students ($\tau^2_{U4sc} = 0.102$). Finally, we can examine whether the level-1 within-student victimization effect also varies randomly over classes by adding V_{40c} to the level-3 equation for δ_{40c}. However, adding a variance for the random slope of within-student victimization across classes (and its covariances with the level-3 random intercept and time slope) did not significantly improve model fit, $-2\Delta LL(\sim3) = 4.7$, $p = .196$, indicating that the extent to which feeling more victimized than usual predicted feeling less student–teacher closeness at that wave did not vary significantly across classes ($ICC_{L3} \approx 0$).

2.F. Summary

Let us summarize the motivations for and results of the analyses conducted so far before moving on. We first examined to what extent the level-3 predictors of class grade and class size could account for level-3 variation across classes in their mean student–teacher closeness and its change over time—that is, whether their main effects could predict the level-3 random intercept variance, and whether their interactions with time could predict the level-3 random time slope variance. No effects remained significant across models, though. Next, we examined whether a level-2 predictor of student gender could account for level-2 variation across students from the same class in their mean student–teacher closeness and its change over time. Girls from the same class felt closer to their teacher than boys (which reduced the level-2 random intercept variance). This student gender effect did not change over time (although it still reduced the level-2 random time slope variance slightly), nor did it vary across classes (there was no level-3 random gender slope). Because classes varied in their proportion of girls, level-3 contextual effects of gender on the intercept and time slope were included as well. Although the contextual effect of having more girls in a class was not significant at wave 1 (and the level-3 random intercept variance increased), this contextual gender effect was more negative across waves (which reduced the level-3 random time slope variance). All four fixed effects of gender were then retained.

We then examined the level-1 and level-3 effects of time-varying emotional support of the class. At level 1 we found that greater class emotional support than usual did not predict greater student–teacher closeness at that wave (no reduction in the level-1 residual variance). This effect did not change over time and did not vary across classes (no level-3 random slope). After removing the nonsignificant level-1 effects, at level 3 we found that greater emotional support than other classes did not predict greater class mean student–teacher closeness (and the level-3 random intercept variance again increased). However, this between-class effect was more positive across waves (which reduced the level-3 random time slope variance).

Finally, we examined the effects of time-varying student-perceived victimization. At level 1, we found that greater victimization than usual did not predict less student–teacher closeness than usual; this effect and its interaction with time did not reduce the level-1 residual variance. However, the effect of greater victimization than usual varied across students (a level-2 random slope), although not across classes (no level-3 random slope). At level 2, we found that greater victimization than other students in a class predicted less student–teacher closeness than other students, which reduced the level-2 random intercept variance; its nonsignificant interaction with time increased the level-2 random time slope variance. The effect of greater victimization than other students did not vary across classes (no level-3 random slope). Last, at level 3 we found that greater victimization than other classes did not predict less closeness than other classes, which increased the level-3 random intercept variance; this effect did not change over time, which increased the level-3 random time slope variance as well.

One side issue to note before continuing further concerns the measurement of lower-level predictors at upper levels. For instance, in this example we created class mean gender to use as a level-3 predictor. In practice, though, whenever not all persons in a group are part of the sample, it may be more informative to use group predictors for the same construct that are measured directly at level 3 instead. For instance, if the actual proportion of girls in each class could be obtained from a separate source, it would better index a gender contextual effect than class mean gender. However, constant-based centering should then be used instead of variable-based centering for the level-2 predictor given that the level-3 predictor is not the sample group mean.

2.G. More on Interactions in Three-Level Longitudinal Models of Persons in Groups

So is this our final model? What other possible effects should we consider? First, it is always a good idea to examine potential nonlinear terms for our fixed effects, which would explain the same piles of variance as for their linear effects. In doing so for our current level-3 predictors in Equation (11.7), the quadratic effects of class mean gender on the level-3 intercept and time slope (entered as γ_{006} and γ_{106} predicting δ_{00c} and δ_{10c}, respectively) were not significant, suggesting a linear contextual effect of gender is sufficient. The same was true for the between-class effect of class mean emotional support on the level-3 intercept and time slope (γ_{007} and γ_{107} predicting δ_{00c} and δ_{10c}, respectively), as well as for between-class mean student-perceived victimization on the level-3 intercept (γ_{008} predicting δ_{00c}). Likewise, the quadratic effect of within-class victimization on the level-2 intercept (δ_{03c} predicting β_{0sc} at level 2, becoming $\delta_{03c} = \gamma_{030}$ at level 3) was also not significant; the binary gender level-2 predictor cannot have a quadratic effect. Finally, the quadratic level-1 effect of within-student victimization (β_{6sc} predicting y_{tsc} at level 1, $\beta_{6sc} = \delta_{60c}$ at level 2, and $\delta_{60c} = \gamma_{600}$ at level 3) was also not significant.

Next, we can consider interactions among predictors at the same level, beginning with the level-3 class mean predictors for gender, emotional support, and victimization. Their 3 two-way interactions and 1 three-way interaction were added to the level-3 class intercept equation for δ_{00c} as γ_{009}, $\gamma_{00,10}$, $\gamma_{00,11}$, and $\gamma_{00,12}$. Although the three-way interaction $\gamma_{00,12}$ and the interaction of gender by victimization $\gamma_{00,10}$ were not significant, the two-way interactions of emotional support with gender (γ_{009}) and with victimization ($\gamma_{00,11}$) were significant and accounted for 33.9% of the remaining level-3 random intercept variance (and 7.3% of the level-3 random time slope variance, unexpectedly). These interactions, to be retained in subsequent models, indicated that the positive effect of having greater class mean emotional support became less positive in classes with more girls and in classes with greater class mean victimization. However, no level-3 interaction effects changed significantly over time (i.e., the terms γ_{009}, $\gamma_{00,10}$, $\gamma_{00,11}$, and $\gamma_{00,12}$ were not significant when added to the level-3 time slope equation for δ_{10c}).

We can continue with by examining interactions among level-2 predictors. Here this only includes an interaction of student gender by within-class victimization. To accurately interpret this level-2 interaction as a within-class effect, though, we must also include the interaction of level-3 contextual gender by within-class victimization. Our new model, also showing our current **G** matrix of random effects variances and covariances (i.e., now including the random effect of level-1 victimization across level-2 students), is shown in Equation (11.8):

Level 1 Occasions :

$$y_{tsc} = \beta_{0sc} + \beta_{1sc}\left(Wave_{tsc} - 1\right) + \beta_{4sc}\left(L1vic_{tsc}\right) + e_{tsc}$$

Level 2 Students :

Intercept: $\beta_{0sc} = \delta_{00c} + \delta_{01c}\left(Girl_{sc}\right) + \delta_{02c}\left(L2vic_{sc}\right)$
$$+ \underline{\delta_{04c}\left(Girl_{sc}\right)\left(L2vic_{sc}\right)} + U_{0sc}$$

Time: $\beta_{1sc} = \delta_{10c} + \delta_{11c}\left(Girl_{sc}\right) + U_{1sc}$

L1Vic: $\beta_{4sc} = \delta_{40c} \qquad\qquad + U_{4sc}$

Level 3 Classes :

Intercept: $\delta_{00c} = \gamma_{000} + \gamma_{003}\left(\overline{Girl}_c - .5\right) + \gamma_{004}\left(\overline{EmoSup}_c - 5\right)$
$$+ \gamma_{005}\left(L3vic_c\right) + \gamma_{009}\left(\overline{Girl}_c - .5\right)\left(\overline{EmoSup}_c - 5\right)$$
$$+ \gamma_{00,11}\left(\overline{EmoSup}_c - 5\right)\left(L3vic_c\right) + V_{00c}$$

Time: $\delta_{10c} = \gamma_{100} + \gamma_{103}\left(\overline{Girl}_c - .5\right) + \gamma_{104}\left(\overline{EmoSup}_c - 5\right) + V_{10c}$

Girl: $\delta_{01c} = \gamma_{010}$

Girl*Time: $\delta_{11c} = \gamma_{110}$

L1Vic: $\delta_{40c} = \gamma_{400}$

L2Vic: $\delta_{02c} = \gamma_{020} + \gamma_{021}\left(\overline{Girl}_c - .5\right)$ (11.8)

Girl*L2Vic: $\delta_{04c} = \gamma_{040}$

Composite :

$$y_{tsc} = \begin{bmatrix} \gamma_{000} + \gamma_{003}\left(\overline{Girl}_c - .5\right) + \gamma_{004}\left(\overline{EmoSup}_c - 5\right) + \gamma_{005}\left(L3vic_c\right) \\ +\gamma_{009}\left(\overline{Girl}_c - .5\right)\left(\overline{EmoSup}_c - 5\right) + \gamma_{00,11}\left(\overline{EmoSup}_c - 5\right)\left(L3vic_c\right) \\ +\gamma_{010}\left(Girl_{sc}\right) + \gamma_{020}\left(L2vic_{sc}\right) + \underline{\gamma_{040}\left(Girl_{sc}\right)\left(L2vic_{sc}\right)} \\ +\gamma_{021}\left(\overline{Girl}_c - .5\right)\left(L2vic_{sc}\right) + \left(\gamma_{400} + U_{4sc}\right)\left(L1vic_{tsc}\right) + V_{00s} + U_{0sc} \end{bmatrix} +$$

$$\begin{bmatrix} \gamma_{100} + \gamma_{103}\left(\overline{Girl}_c - .5\right) + \gamma_{104}\left(\overline{EmoSup}_c - 5\right) \\ +\gamma_{110}\left(Girl_{sc}\right) + V_{10c} + U_{1sc} \end{bmatrix}\left(Wave_{tsc} - 1\right) + e_{tsc}$$

$$\mathbf{G} = \begin{bmatrix} Level\ 3 & 0 \\ 0 & Level\ 2 \end{bmatrix} = \begin{bmatrix} \tau^2_{V_{00}} & \tau_{V_{00,01}} & & & \\ \tau_{V_{01,00}} & \tau^2_{V_{01}} & & & \\ & & \tau^2_{U_{00}} & \tau_{U_{00,10}} & \tau_{U_{00,40}} \\ & & \tau_{U_{10,00}} & \tau^2_{U_{10}} & \tau_{U_{10,40}} \\ & & \tau_{U_{40,00}} & \tau_{U_{40,10}} & \tau^2_{U_{40}} \end{bmatrix}, \quad \mathbf{R} = \sigma^2_e\left[\mathbf{I}_{n1*n2}\right]$$

in which δ_{04c} for the gender by within-class victimization interaction has been added to the level-2 student intercept equation for β_{0sc}, which becomes $\delta_{04c} = \gamma_{040}$ at level 3. The level-3 contextual gender by within-class victimization is given by γ_{021} in the level-3 equation for the within-class victimization effect predicting δ_{02c}. Although it caused the level-2 random intercept to increase slightly rather than decrease, the level-2 interaction of gender by within-class victimization γ_{040} was significant, and indicated that the extent to which girls felt closer to their teacher than boys from the same class was reduced in students who felt more victimized than other students in their class. Alternatively, we could say that the negative effect of within-class victimization was more negative in girls than in boys. The nonsignificant interactions of within-class victimization with contextual gender (γ_{021}) and with between-class gender ($\gamma_{021} + \gamma_{040}$) indicated that the effect of feeling more victimized than others in a class did not differ by the number of girls in the class. However, the remaining level-3 random intercept and random time slope variances were reduced by 6.4% and 1.4%, respectively, further highlighting the "pseudo" nature of pseudo-R^2.

Given the significant student gender by within-class victimization interaction, both interactions for within-class victimization by student gender and by class mean gender will be retained. Fortunately, these interaction effects did not change significantly over time. This was revealed when adding δ_{12c} for the within-class victimization effect and δ_{14c} for the level-2 gender by within-class victimization effect in the level-2 student time slope equation for β_{1sc}, which became $\delta_{12c} = \gamma_{120}$ and $\delta_{14c} = \gamma_{140}$ at level 3; the level-3 gender by within-class victimization effect on the time slope was also added to the former as γ_{121} (as well as the level-3 victimization by time interaction γ_{105}).

So are we done yet? Unfortunately, no—after examining nonlinear effects and interaction of predictors at the same level, we still have cross-level interactions to consider (besides those involving time that we've already tested). Because there are so many potential cross-level interactions, it can be useful to narrow the possibilities down to those motivated by the existing random slopes. For instance, because there was no random variance across classes in the level-2 within-class effects of gender or victimization, their interactions with level-3 predictors are unlikely to be useful. As expected, the level-3 effects of class mean gender, emotional support, and victimization were indeed nonsignificant when added to the level-3 equation for the student gender effect predicting δ_{01c} (entered as γ_{011}, γ_{012}, and γ_{013}) or when added to the level-3 equation for the within-class victimization effect predicting δ_{02c} (entered as γ_{022} and γ_{023}; γ_{021} remained nonsignificant). Similarly, because there was no level-3 random variance across classes in the level-1 within-student effect of victimization, its interactions with the level-3 predictors were also nonsignificant as expected when added to the level-3 equation for the level-1 effect of within-student victimization predicting δ_{40c} (entered as γ_{401}, γ_{402}, and γ_{403}).

In contrast, because the level-1 effect of within-student victimization did vary randomly over students (as given by U_{4sc} in the level-2 equation predicting β_{4sc}), its interactions with level-2 predictors could explain that level-2 random slope variance τ^2_{U40}. Sure enough, the interaction of level-1 by level-2 victimization was significant, as found when adding δ_{42c} to predict β_{4sc}, which became $\delta_{42c} = \gamma_{420}$ at level 3. This interaction indicated that the negative level-1 effect of feeling more victimized than usual was significantly less negative in students who felt more victimized than other students in their class. Alternatively, we could say that the negative level-2 effect of feeling more victimized than other students in a class was significantly less negative when students felt more victimized than usual. For completeness of interpretation across levels, the interaction of level-1 by level-3 victimization was also added (as γ_{401} predicting δ_{40c}) but was not significant, indicating that the level-1 effect of feeling more victimized than usual did not differ by class mean victimization. These interactions explained 7.4% of the level-2 within-student victimization random slope variance τ^2_{U40}. Finally, the level-1 effect of within-student victimization did not differ by gender or class mean gender, as found when adding δ_{41c} to predict β_{4sc}, which became $\delta_{41c} = \gamma_{410}$ at level 3 (and the level-3 interaction with gender was added as γ_{401} predicting δ_{40c}).

Now are we done? Although we have not tested all possible higher-order and nonlinear interactions, this seems like a reasonable place to stop given everything we've found so far. So, at long last, our final model predicting student–teacher closeness is shown in Equation (11.9):

Level 1 Occasions :

$$y_{tsc} = \beta_{0sc} + \beta_{1sc}(\text{Wave}_{tsc} - 1) + \beta_{4sc}(\text{L1vic}_{tsc}) + e_{tsc}$$

Level 2 Students :

$$\text{Intercept: } \beta_{0sc} = \delta_{00c} + \delta_{01c}(\text{Girl}_{sc}) + \delta_{02c}(\text{L2vic}_{sc}) + \delta_{04c}(\text{Girl}_{sc})(\text{L2vic}_{sc}) + U_{0sc}$$

$$\text{Time: } \beta_{1sc} = \delta_{10c} + \delta_{11c}(\text{Girl}_{sc}) \qquad\qquad + U_{1sc}$$

$$\text{L1Vic: } \beta_{4sc} = \delta_{40c} \qquad\qquad + \underline{\delta_{42c}(\text{L2vic}_{sc})} + U_{4sc}$$

Level 3 Classes :

$$\text{Intercept: } \delta_{00c} = \gamma_{000} + \gamma_{003}(\overline{\text{Girl}}_c - .5) + \gamma_{004}(\overline{\text{EmoSup}}_c - 5) + \gamma_{005}(\text{L3vic}_c)$$

$$+ \gamma_{009}(\overline{\text{Girl}}_c - .5)(\overline{\text{EmoSup}}_c - 5) + \gamma_{00,11}(\overline{\text{EmoSup}}_c - 5)(\text{L3vic}_c) + V_{00c}$$

$$\text{Time: } \delta_{10c} = \gamma_{100} + \gamma_{103}(\overline{\text{Girl}}_c - .5) + \gamma_{104}(\overline{\text{EmoSup}}_c - 5) + V_{10c}$$

$$\text{Girl: } \delta_{01c} = \gamma_{010}$$

$$\text{Girl*Time: } \delta_{11c} = \gamma_{110}$$

$$\text{L1Vic: } \delta_{40c} = \gamma_{400} + \underline{\gamma_{405}(\text{L3vic}_c)}$$

$$\text{L1Vic*L2 Vic: } \delta_{42c} = \gamma_{420} \tag{11.9}$$

$$\text{L2Vic: } \delta_{02c} = \gamma_{020} + \gamma_{021}(\overline{\text{Girl}}_c - .5)$$

$$\text{Girl*L2Vic: } \delta_{04c} = \gamma_{040}$$

Composite :

$$y_{tsc} = \begin{bmatrix} \gamma_{000} + \gamma_{003}(\overline{\text{Girl}}_c - .5) + \gamma_{004}(\overline{\text{EmoSup}}_c - 5) + \gamma_{005}(\text{L3vic}_c) \\ + \gamma_{009}(\overline{\text{Girl}}_c - .5)(\overline{\text{EmoSup}}_c - 5) + \gamma_{00,11}(\overline{\text{EmoSup}}_c - 5)(\text{L3vic}_c) \\ + \gamma_{010}(\text{Girl}_{sc}) + \gamma_{020}(\text{L2vic}_{sc}) + \gamma_{040}(\text{Girl}_{sc})(\text{L2vic}_{sc}) \\ + \gamma_{021}(\overline{\text{Girl}}_c - .5)(\text{L2vic}_{sc}) + (\gamma_{400} + U_{4sc})(\text{L1vic}_{tsc}) \\ + \underline{\gamma_{405}(\text{L1vic}_{tsc})(\text{L3vic}_{sc})} + \underline{\gamma_{420}(\text{L1vic}_{tsc})(\text{L2vic}_{sc})} + V_{00s} + U_{0sc} \end{bmatrix} +$$

$$\begin{bmatrix} \gamma_{100} + \gamma_{103}(\overline{\text{Girl}}_c - .5) + \gamma_{104}(\overline{\text{EmoSup}}_c - 5) \\ + \gamma_{110}(\text{Girl}_{sc}) + V_{10c} + U_{1sc} \end{bmatrix}(\text{Wave}_{tsc} - 1) + e_{tsc}$$

whose results are given in the second set of columns in Table 11.2. The model fixed effects accounted for a 10.4% of the total variance in student–teacher closeness. The specific model parameters will be interpreted in the sample results section at the end of the chapter.

One final question to be answered is whether we would have obtained the same pattern of results if we had estimated a truly multivariate clustered longitudinal model—that is, if we had estimated the variances per level for our victimization predictor rather than using variable-based centering to create observed variables to serve as their proxies. Unfortunately, at the present time we are not able to answer that question reliably using existing software (e.g., *Mplus*) for a few reasons. First, REML estimation is currently not readily available within truly multivariate software, but the level-3 random effects variances and covariances as estimated in ML instead will be downwardly biased given that we have only 33 classes. Upon re-estimating our final model in ML to test this conjecture, the level-3 random intercept and linear time slope variances were indeed too small by 43% and 28%, respectively; the level-2 variances were smaller by only 1% to 4%, as expected given the larger level-2 sample size of 597 students across classes. Second, there are software-based restrictions in estimating interaction terms among latent variables. In this case, estimation of the final model within *Mplus* v. 7.11, in which victimization was an outcome instead (i.e., such that its variances were estimated), failed. Thus, software development and/ or alternative estimation routines are still needed for truly multivariate longitudinal models.

2.H. Comparison of Multivariate and Clustered Approaches for Family or Dyadic Data

Earlier in the first section of the chapter we considered the modeling decision point of whether members of a group could be thought of as exchangeable or distinct. The same type of three-level model for time within persons within groups from the previous clustered longitudinal example of students in classes could also be used when group members are distinct, such as for persons from the same dyad (or family) measured repeatedly. What would such models and their alternative look like? For ease of exposition, we will consider a generic design of two distinct persons from the same group (although more than two distinct persons from a group could also be included simultaneously using the same logic and procedures). In practice, this type of distinct person design could arise from repeating sampling of a husband and wife, a parent and a child, a patient and a caretaker, a target subject (i.e., who receives a treatment of some kind) and his or her significant other, or any other kind of meaningful dyad, given the context of the study.

Accordingly, let us consider an example three-level model for dyadic longitudinal data, as shown in Equation (11.10):

Level 1: $y_{tpg} = \beta_{0pg} + \beta_{1pg}(time_{tpg}) + e_{tpg}$

Level 2:

Intercept: $\beta_{0pg} = \delta_{00g} + \delta_{01g}(x_{pg} - \bar{x}_g) + U_{0pg}$

Time: $\beta_{1pg} = \delta_{10g} + \delta_{11g}(x_{pg} - \bar{x}_g) + U_{1pg}$

Level 3:

Intercept: $\delta_{0pg} = \gamma_{000} + \gamma_{001}(\bar{x}_g - C) + V_{00g}$

Time: $\delta_{10g} = \gamma_{100} + \gamma_{101}(\bar{x}_g - C) + V_{10g}$

Level-2 X: $\delta_{01g} = \gamma_{010}$

Level-2 X*Time: $\delta_{11g} = \gamma_{110}$ $\qquad\qquad\qquad$ (11.10)

Composite:

$$y_{tpg} = \left\{\gamma_{000} + \gamma_{001}(\bar{x}_g - C) + \gamma_{010}(x_{pg} - \bar{x}_g) + V_{00g} + U_{0pg}\right\} +$$
$$\left\{\gamma_{100} + \gamma_{101}(\bar{x}_g - C) + \gamma_{110}(x_{pg} - \bar{x}_g) + V_{10g} + U_{1pg}\right\}(time_{tpg}) + e_{tpg}$$

$$\mathbf{G} = \begin{bmatrix} \text{Level 3} & 0 \\ 0 & \text{Level 2} \end{bmatrix} = \begin{bmatrix} \tau^2_{V_{00}} & \tau_{V_{00,01}} & & \\ \tau_{V_{01,00}} & \tau^2_{V_{01}} & & \\ & & \tau^2_{U_{00}} & \tau_{U_{00,10}} \\ & & \tau_{U_{10,00}} & \tau^2_{U_{10}} \end{bmatrix}, \quad \mathbf{R} = \sigma^2_e[\mathbf{I}_{n1*n2}]$$

in which level 1 is indicated by t for time, level 2 by p for person, and level 3 by g for group (i.e., dyad or family). This random linear time model also includes a person predictor x_{pg} (centered at the predictor's group mean $\bar{x}_g$) of the level-2 random intercept and time slope. The group mean predictor ($\bar{x}_g$ centered at a constant C) then predicts the level-3 random intercept and time slope. Finally, also shown is the block-diagonal **G** matrix of random effects variances and covariances (in which the level-2 block would be repeated for each person in a group). The **R** matrix per group (the result of multiplying σ^2_e by an **I** identity matrix with rows and columns equal to the $n2$ number of persons by $n1$ occasions within that group) would have σ^2_e on the diagonal and 0's elsewhere, as would that group's **V** matrix, the same as in previous models.

Let us consider what the three-level model shown in Equation (11.10) can tell us. The random effects at level 3 are between-group differences in the intercept and linear time slope—in other words, they represent the *commonality* across members of the same group in their outcome level at time 0 and in their rates of change. Here, some of that group commonality may be due to persons in that group having more of the X predictor *than other groups* (at level 3). The random effects at level 2 are then the person-specific deviations from the group intercept and linear time slope—in other words, they represent the *discord* among persons from the same group in their outcome level at time 0 and their rates of change. Here, some of this within-group variation may be due to persons having more of the X predictor than the *mean of their group* (at level 2).

However, this three-level model's partitioning of variance into between- and within-group components and their corresponding fixed effects do not directly represent each person as a meaningfully distinct member of the group. For instance, more often of interest in dyadic data are **actor effects**, which concern how a person's predictor relates to that same person's outcome, as well as **partner effects**, which concern how a person's predictor relates to the *other* person's outcome, instead. These ideas are not clearly represented in a three-level model, in which the level-2 person effect is the within-group effect on the same person's outcome of having more of a predictor *than the rest of their group specifically*. In addition, between-group and within-group effects are not likely to be well distinguished given only two persons per group. This becomes even more problematic when some groups only have one person, and in which that person's data then contributes to group-level variance (rather than person-level, within-group variance).

Finally, an additional shortcoming of the three-level model relates the correlations among random effects for persons from the same group that are likely to be of theoretical interest. For instance, if an actor's random intercept or slope is higher than others, is the partner's random intercept or slope likely to be higher as well? And although these correlations are implied by the level-3 random effects, they are not easily quantified directly. The three-level model also assumes the same amount of variability in the intercepts, slopes, and residuals for each type of person in the dyad or family, which may not be likely (and is of course a testable hypothesis).

Fortunately, these issues can be solved by considering another type of longitudinal model for dyadic or family data. Given that time and persons are actually crossed within groups, the assignment of occasions as nested within persons is not our only option. Accordingly, let us examine an alternative model in which persons are modeled as distinct multivariate outcomes in a two-level model of occasions within group (family or dyad), as shown in Equation (11.11):

Level 1 Occasions:

$$y_{tgd} = dvA\left[\beta_{0gA} + \beta_{1gA}\left(time_{tgA}\right) + e_{tgA}\right] + dvB\left[\beta_{0gB} + \beta_{1gB}\left(time_{tgB}\right) + e_{tgB}\right]$$

Level 2 Groups:

Person A Intercept: $\beta_{0gA} = \gamma_{00A} + \gamma_{01A}\left(xA_g - C\right) + \gamma_{02A}\left(xB_g - C\right) + U_{0gA}$

Person A Time Slope: $\beta_{1gA} = \gamma_{10A} + \gamma_{11A}\left(xA_g - C\right) + \gamma_{12A}\left(xB_g - C\right) + U_{1gA}$

Person B Intercept: $\beta_{0gB} = \gamma_{00B} + \gamma_{01B}\left(xA_g - C\right) + \gamma_{02B}\left(xB_g - C\right) + U_{0gB}$

Person B Time Slope: $\beta_{1gB} = \gamma_{10B} + \gamma_{11B}\left(xA_g - C\right) + \gamma_{12B}\left(xB_g - C\right) + U_{1gB}$

Composite:

$$
\begin{aligned}
y_{tgd} = &\left\{dvA\left(\gamma_{00A} + \gamma_{01A}\left(xA_g - C\right) + \gamma_{02A}\left(xB_g - C\right) + U_{0gA} + e_{tgA}\right)\right\} + \\
&\left\{dvA\left(\gamma_{10A} + \gamma_{11A}\left(xA_g - C\right) + \gamma_{12A}\left(xB_g - C\right) + U_{1gA}\right)\right\}\left(time_{tgA}\right) + \\
&\left\{dvB\left(\gamma_{00B} + \gamma_{01B}\left(xA_g - C\right) + \gamma_{02B}\left(xB_g - C\right) + U_{0gB} + e_{tgB}\right)\right\} + \\
&\left\{dvA\left(\gamma_{10B} + \gamma_{11B}\left(xA_g - C\right) + \gamma_{12B}\left(xB_g - C\right) + U_{1gB}\right)\right\}\left(time_{tgB}\right)
\end{aligned}
$$

(11.11)

$$
\begin{array}{cccc}
 & \text{Int-A} & \text{Int-B} & \text{Time-A} & \text{Time-B}
\end{array}
$$

$$
\mathbf{G} =
\begin{array}{r}
\text{Person A Random Intercept} \\
\text{Person B Random Intercept} \\
\text{Person A Random Time Slope} \\
\text{Person B Random Time Slope}
\end{array}
\begin{bmatrix}
\tau^2_{U_{0A}} & \tau_{U_{0A,0B}} & \tau_{U_{0A,1A}} & \tau_{U_{0A,1B}} \\
\tau_{U_{0B,0A}} & \tau^2_{U_{0B}} & \tau_{U_{0B,1A}} & \tau_{U_{0B,1B}} \\
\tau_{U_{1A,0A}} & \tau_{U_{1A,0B}} & \tau^2_{U_{1A}} & \tau_{U_{1A,1B}} \\
\tau_{U_{1B,0A}} & \tau_{U_{1B,0B}} & \tau_{U_{1B,1A}} & \tau^2_{U_{1B}}
\end{bmatrix}
$$

$$
\begin{array}{cc}
 & \text{Res-A} \quad \text{Res-B}
\end{array}
$$

$$
\mathbf{R} =
\begin{array}{r}
\text{Person A Residual} \\
\text{Person B Residual}
\end{array}
\begin{bmatrix}
\sigma^2_{e_A} & \sigma_{e_A,e_B} \\
\sigma_{e_B,e_A} & \sigma^2_{e_B}
\end{bmatrix}
$$

in which level 1 is indicated by t for time, level 2 by g for group (i.e., dyad or family), and person A versus B by dependent variable d. This multivariate model can be estimated in univariate software using a "double-stacked" data structure as introduced in chapter 9, in which the outcomes from both persons would reside in a single column given an additional indicator variable that distinguishes those for each person. In fact, this is the same data structure used in our previous three-level model of time within person within group. However, this multivariate model differs in important ways from the previous three-level model, as described next.

First, let us consider the model for the variance, which now has only two levels. Rather than estimating between- and within-group variances, this multivariate model directly estimates random effects variances *for each distinct person*. An advantage is that the covariances between random effects across distinct persons are then directly estimated as well, which are often of interest. For example, are mothers with higher initial outcomes (than other mothers) likely to be married to fathers with higher initial outcomes (than other fathers)? Are mothers who change more over time likely to be married to fathers who show greater change over time as well? Similarly, the residual variances are estimated separately for each person, with a covariance for residuals at the same occasion that indicates the extent of time-specific concordance after controlling for the change of each individual. In addition, rather than assuming homogeneity, the extent of differential random effects variability across distinct types of persons may also be of interest—for instance, are mothers more variable than fathers? These types of questions can be answered by comparing models with constrained versus unconstrained variance components.

Second, in the model for the means, the person-specific predictor variables (xA and xB) are now included as level-2 *group* predictors only, such that their values would be repeated across all the rows of data from the same group (not just for the same person). This specification allows us to directly examine both their actor and partner effects. As given in Equation (11.11), the *actor* effects of a person's predictor on the *same* person's intercept and time slope are γ_{01A} and γ_{11A} for person A and γ_{02B} and γ_{12B} for person B. The *partner* effects on the *other* person's intercept and time slope are γ_{02A} and γ_{12A} for person A and γ_{01B} and γ_{11B} for person B.

Although it may have been possible to specify equivalent effects in the three-level model, it would be considerably more cumbersome given the decomposition of between-group versus within-group effects of predictors on those corresponding random effects. The multivariate model is generally more flexible for longitudinal analysis of distinct persons from the same group, not only with respect to its random effects, but also its fixed effects. For instance, it is straightforward to see how this multivariate model could be specified to include fixed effects for one person's outcome but not the other. For example, what if partner effects were of interest only for Person A's predictor on Person B's outcome? If so, Person B's partner effects could be eliminated by removing γ_{02A} and γ_{12A} in predicting Person A's intercept β_{0gA} and time slope β_{1gA}. In addition, although not shown here, interaction terms among the xA and xB predictors could also be included in order to examine the incremental effects of belonging to a group where *both persons* have a greater amount of the predictor than other persons of their same type. Finally, the effect of other group-level variables on each distinct person's outcome can also be added.

The multivariate model in Equation (11.11) directly estimates actor and partner effects for the person predictor, but does not directly assess how these effects differ across distinct persons. However, given that these differences are just linear combinations of estimated fixed effects, additional contrasts can be requested in a similar fashion as we've done for other model-implied effects (e.g., as for simple slopes or predicted means using ESTIMATE in SAS, TEST in SPSS, LINCOM in STATA, or NEW in M*plus*). For instance, the difference in the actor effects on the intercept and time slope would be given by $\gamma_{01A} - \gamma_{02B}$ and $\gamma_{11A} - \gamma_{12B}$. Likewise, the difference in the partner effects on the intercept and time slope would be given by $\gamma_{02A} - \gamma_{01B}$ and $\gamma_{12A} - \gamma_{11B}$. Other linear combinations of estimated fixed effects can also be tested as needed.

Considering potential differences in effect size across persons introduces another type of multivariate hypothesis: What if the outcome of interest *is* the difference between distinct persons over time? For instance, the extent to which the *difference* between partners changes over time may itself be an important outcome to consider. Fortunately, the multivariate model from Equation (11.11) can be respecified to directly estimate the difference in outcomes over time between distinct persons from the same group, as shown in Equation (11.12):

Level 1 Occasions :

$$y_{tgd} = \beta_{0g} + \beta_{1g}\left(\text{time}_{tg}\right) + \beta_{2g}\left(\text{dvB}\right) + \beta_{3g}\left(\text{dvB}\right)\left(\text{time}_{tg}\right)$$
$$+ \text{dvA} * e_{tgA} + \text{dvB} * e_{tgB}$$

Level 2 Groups :

Intercept: $\quad\quad\quad\quad\quad \beta_{0g} = \gamma_{00} + \gamma_{01}\left(\text{xA}_g - C\right) + \gamma_{02}\left(\text{xB}_g - C\right)$
$$+ \text{dvA} * U_{0gA} + \text{dvB} * U_{0gB}$$

Time Slope: $\quad\quad\quad\quad \beta_{1g} = \gamma_{10} + \gamma_{11}\left(\text{xA}_g - C\right) + \gamma_{12}\left(\text{xB}_g - C\right)$
$$+ \text{dvA} * U_{1gA} + \text{dvB} * U_{1gB}$$

Intercept Difference: $\quad \beta_{2g} = \gamma_{20} + \gamma_{21}\left(\text{xA}_g - C\right) + \gamma_{22}\left(\text{xB}_g - C\right)$

Time Slope Difference: $\beta_{3g} = \gamma_{30} + \gamma_{31}\left(\text{xA}_g - C\right) + \gamma_{32}\left(\text{xB}_g - C\right)$ $\quad$ (11.12)

Composite :

$$y_{tgd} = \left\{ \gamma_{00} + \gamma_{01}\left(xA_g - C\right) + \gamma_{02}\left(xB_g - C\right) + dvA\left(U_{0gA} + e_{tgA}\right) \right\} + $$

$$\left\{ \gamma_{10} + \gamma_{11}\left(xA_g - C\right) + \gamma_{12}\left(xB_g - C\right) + dvA\left(U_{1gA}\right) \right\}\left(time_{tgA}\right) + $$

$$\left\{ dvB\left(\gamma_{20} + \gamma_{21}\left(xA_g - C\right) + \gamma_{22}\left(xB_g - C\right) + U_{0gB} + e_{tgB}\right) \right\} + $$

$$\left\{ dvB\left(\gamma_{30} + \gamma_{31}\left(xA_g - C\right) + \gamma_{32}\left(xB_g - C\right) + U_{1gB}\right) \right\}\left(time_{tgB}\right)$$

$$\begin{array}{l} \\ \\ \mathbf{G} = \\ \\ \end{array} \begin{array}{r} \text{Int-A} \quad \text{Int-B} \quad \text{Time-A} \quad \text{Time-B} \\ \begin{array}{l} \text{Person A Random Intercept} \\ \text{Person B Random Intercept} \\ \text{Person A Random Time Slope} \\ \text{Person B Random Time Slope} \end{array} \begin{bmatrix} \tau^2_{U_{0A}} & \tau_{U_{0A,0B}} & \tau_{U_{0A,1A}} & \tau_{U_{0A,1B}} \\ \tau_{U_{0B,0A}} & \tau^2_{U_{0B}} & \tau_{U_{0B,1A}} & \tau_{U_{0B,1B}} \\ \tau_{U_{1A,0A}} & \tau_{U_{1A,0B}} & \tau^2_{U_{1A}} & \tau_{U_{1A,1B}} \\ \tau_{U_{1B,0A}} & \tau_{U_{1B,0B}} & \tau_{U_{1B,1A}} & \tau^2_{U_{1B}} \end{bmatrix} \end{array}$$

$$\begin{array}{l} \\ \mathbf{R} = \\ \end{array} \begin{array}{r} \text{Res-A} \quad \text{Res-B} \\ \begin{array}{l} \text{Person A Residual} \\ \text{Person B Residual} \end{array} \begin{bmatrix} \sigma^2_{e_A} & \sigma_{e_A,e_B} \\ \sigma_{e_B,e_A} & \sigma^2_{e_B} \end{bmatrix} \end{array}$$

in which the model for the variance is the same, such that persons A and B have separate random intercepts, random time slopes, and level-1 residuals (via the dvA and dvB interactions with each term). The fixed effects have been modified in an important way, though. Rather than specifying *separate* fixed effects directly for each person, the fixed effects in Equation (11.12) create a simple effect for a reference person and the difference in each effect for an alternative person.

Here's how this works: Note that dvA is no longer attached to any fixed effect. Instead, each fixed effect now has a "main" effect that is shared across persons, including the intercept (γ_{00}), the time slope (γ_{10}), the effects of xA on the intercept and time slope (γ_{01} and γ_{11}), and the effects of xB on the intercept and time slope (γ_{02} and γ_{12}). However, because each predictor also interacts with dvB, the rules of main effects within interaction terms then apply—the main effects become simple effects specifically when the interacting predictor = 0. Here, this means that these main effects are then interpreted as the *simple effects specifically for person A* (when dvB = 0). So, person A's actor effects on the intercept and slope are given by γ_{01} and γ_{11}, whereas the partner effects of person B on person A's intercept and slope would be given by γ_{02} and γ_{12}.

The interactions with dvB then represent the *difference* between person A and person B in each effect. That is, the simple effect of dvB on the intercept (γ_{20}) is the difference between Person A and B when all predictors = 0, and how this person intercept difference depends on xA and xB is given by γ_{21} and γ_{22}. Likewise, the simple effect of dvB on the time slope (γ_{30}) is the difference between persons in the rate of change when all interacting predictors = 0, and how this person slope difference depends on xA and xB is given by γ_{31} and γ_{32}. Although the random effects and residuals could also have been specified as the effect for person A and the difference in the effect for person

B, this may result in a non-positive definite **G** matrix if there is little variability in the differences across persons A and B in the intercepts and slopes, and thus the original specification with separate random effects variances per person was used instead.

More generally, there are three different effects of interest in this example pertaining to each predictor: the effect for person A, the effect for person B, and the difference in the effect between person A and B. Each multivariate model directly provides two of these three effects, but the third can be found through model-implied contrasts. That is, the first multivariate model in Equation (11.11) directly estimated the effects per person (and could be extended to include more than two distinct persons as needed), but the difference in effects between persons would have to be found through additional model-implied contrasts (as described earlier). The second multivariate model in Equation (11.12) directly estimated the effects for a reference person (whomever's dv contrast is missing from the fixed effects), as well as the difference in the effect for an alternative person (and could be extended to include more than one alternative person). Even though the effects for our non-reference person B were not directly estimated, their simple effect of each predictor (as would have been given directly by the first multivariate model) can still be requested from the difference-based model via separate model-implied estimates. For instance, the simple time slope specifically for person B would be given by $\gamma_{10} + \gamma_{30}$. Person B's actor effects on the intercept and slope would be given by $\gamma_{02} + \gamma_{22}$ and $\gamma_{12} + \gamma_{32}$, whereas the partner effects of person A on person B's intercept and slope would be given by $\gamma_{01} + \gamma_{21}$ and $\gamma_{11} + \gamma_{31}$.

As you may have guessed by now, the flexibility of these multivariate models can be extended further by combining either type of fixed effect specification as needed. For instance, to allow an effect to be the same across persons within the first multivariate model in Equation (11.11), we would include its true main effect only, without the "interactions" with the dvA and dvB contrasts. Conversely, to allow an effect only for the reference person A in the second multivariate model in Equation (11.12), we could include it not as a main effect (which would predict both outcomes), but as an "interaction" with dvA (i.e., a nested effect so that it only predicts person A's outcome). Although such hybrid multivariate models can be tricky to specify, they are exceedingly useful in testing custom hypotheses of fixed effects (or linear combinations thereof).

Finally, although described here in the context of dyadic and family data, a multivariate model that directly estimates the difference between outcomes as model parameters is also a very useful alternative to difference score models more generally. This is for two reasons. First, rather than using a difference score as a single univariate outcome, a multivariate model would allow analyses of not only those difference scores (as implemented via fixed effects for the difference between DVs), but also simultaneous analysis of the original DVs themselves as well, providing a more complete picture of results than when considering only their difference scores. Second, the covariances across time of difference scores can be widely variable, even negative, which can be difficult to impossible to approximate with random effects. As a result, predicting the variance and covariance of the original DVs instead using random effects will likely be much easier to do.

3. Special Cases of Persons Within Groups Over Time

It is now time to change gears—to leave our clustered longitudinal data behind in order to examine models for data in which persons change groups over time, as shown in our next example. Later we'll also consider models for when persons are nested within occasions instead.

3.A. Is Time Nested or Crossed With Persons?

As introduced earlier in the chapter, when persons change groups over time, the resulting longitudinal model will have occasions nested within persons and within time-varying groups, such that persons and their time-varying groups will have crossed random effects at level 2 (thus creating two separate level-2 models). Before continuing with this topic, though, I would like to address the issue of why it is that occasions are modeled as nested within persons and groups.

In my experience teaching, the introduction of models with crossed random effects for persons in time-varying groups almost always results in someone asking the one question I dread most—why aren't persons and time (and time-varying groups) also crossed? That is, throughout this text (and indeed, throughout almost all related texts), time is constantly referred to as *nested* within persons. And in longitudinal designs with unbalanced time, in which each person could potentially have his or her own unique set of measurement occasions, time does seem nested within persons. But what about when time is balanced across persons? Then time and persons are indeed crossed, not nested. Furthermore, if persons share at least some of the same measurement occasions in unbalanced designs, then time is still crossed with persons (albeit incompletely). So, why is time almost always modeled as *nested* within persons instead of *crossed?*

If time was modeled as crossed with persons, then persons and occasions would have their own (uncorrelated) level-2 random intercepts. The model would allow mean differences across persons via the level-2 person random intercept, mean differences across occasions via the level-2 occasion random intercept, and the person by occasion interaction would form the level-1 residual. A large number of occasions (i.e., preferably 30 or more; see Hox, 2010) would be required to have sufficient power to estimate a random intercept variance for occasions. It would also likely require a research design in which occasions had meaningful variation beyond just as a way to observe individual change (i.e., in which *time* provides type of some experience that is common across persons). For instance, consider an example study in which persons were measured daily for 30 days. The extent of systematic outcome differences between weekdays and weekends could be examined via a single fixed effect that could potentially explain the random intercept variance for outcome mean differences across the 30 days.

Most longitudinal designs do not meet these requirements of a large number of occasions and meaningful time-specific variation that is independent of persons, and so modeling time as nested within persons is more common. When time is modeled as nested within persons, mean differences across occasions are predicted by fixed effects, such that the saturated means model takes the place of the occasion random intercept. This is why it is useful—when possible to do so in balanced data—to compare the model-predicted means to the saturated means to determine if the mean differences across occasions have been adequately captured by the fixed effects of time. If so, then the level-1 residual will solely reflects the person by time interaction, the same as in the person by time crossed model (i.e., there are no "main effects" of time left unmodeled). Furthermore, random time slopes that allow individual differences in change become the analog to a more general person by occasion random interaction term in the person by time crossed model (which would be considerably more difficult to estimate and predict). So, to summarize the answer to my least favorite question, time is nested within persons whenever we model mean differences across time using fixed effects of time instead of random effects, although we still use random effects of time to describe how those time-related differences vary across persons.

3.B. Longitudinal Models for Persons in Time-Varying Groups

Now let us continue with a new data example, again derived from the Classroom Peer Ecologies Project (see chapter 1), but this time featuring persons nested in time-varying groups. Our example data were collected from the same school during the spring of three consecutive years (labeled years 0, 1, and 2) from students in grades 3, 4, or 5 at the first occasion. The total sample includes 1,214 observations from 486 students (54% boys) in 58 classes (i.e., distinct combinations of students and their teacher each year with at least 10 students per class). There were 18 year 0 classes (six each in grades 3, 4, and 5), 20 year 1 classes (six in grade 4; seven each in grades 5 and 6), and 20 year 2 classes (seven each in grades 5 and 6; six in grade 7). Given the small number of classes each year, we will again rely on restricted maximum likelihood estimation.

The time-varying outcome is teacher-perceived student academic effort, as measured by the mean of four items on a 1 to 5 scale, in which higher scores indicate greater perceived effort ($M = 3.993$, $SD = 0.986$). Let us begin by considering the student variability across years before considering the effects of time-varying classes. Our first step is to estimate an empty means, random intercept model for years within students to examine how much variation in teacher-perceived academic effort is due to student mean differences. Given estimates of $\tau_{U_0}^2 = 0.580$ and $\sigma_e^2 = 0.406$, the ICC = .589, which was significantly > 0, $-2\Delta LL(\sim1) = 340.4$, $p < .001$.

Given that time was balanced across students, we can also examine a saturated means, unstructured variance model as the "answer key" for predicting the student means, variances, and covariances across years. There were significant mean differences across years, $F(2, 385) = 9.26$, $p < .001$; the estimated means were 4.077, 3.903, and 3.924 at years 0, 1, and 2. But only the year 0 mean differed significantly from the others, a trend that would not be described well by a fixed linear time slope. Instead, we will use a piecewise slopes model that includes fixed effects for

Table 11.4 Data structure with which to fit fixed or random effects of time-varying classes.

Student ID	Class ID	Grade	Year	Year 0 Class	Year 1 Class	Year 2 Class	Year 0 Intercept	Year 1 Intercept	Year 2 Intercept	Year 0 Effect	Year 1 Effect	Year 2 Effect
101	1	3	0	1	−99	43	1	0	0	1	0	0
101	−99	4	1	1	−99	43	0	0	0	0	0	0
101	43	5	2	1	−99	43	0	0	1	1	0	1
102	3	3	0	3	21	42	1	0	0	1	0	0
102	21	4	1	3	21	42	0	1	0	1	1	0
102	42	5	2	3	21	42	0	0	1	1	1	1

the deviations between years 0 and 1 and 1 and 2, and in which year 1 becomes the intercept (thus still creating saturated means). A model with these fixed piecewise slopes and a student random intercept only did not fit significantly worse than the "answer key" unstructured variance model, $-2\Delta LL(\sim4)$, = 4.3, p = .366, indicating that the relatively constant variance and covariance across years that could be adequately predicted by a random intercept variance for students.

Because students were nested within different classes across years, our previous three-level model of level-1 occasions nested in level-2 students nested in level-3 classes will not be appropriate—this is because the effect of being in a class should depend on *which class* a student was in during a particular year. Instead, we will consider two alternative ways to describe the effects of time-varying classes: fixed effects or random effects, as described earlier in the first section of the chapter. To use either strategy, though, we must first create custom intercepts to represent the class effects at each occasion, which will require some data restructuring, as described next. The resulting data structure for two example students is shown in Table 11.4.

The first step is to transpose the column that holds the time-varying class ID variable so that the class ID has its own column at each occasion as well. Missing observations for class ID (such as when a student is missing that occasion) should be replaced with an invalid missing data value (e.g., −99) so that the student's data are not subsequently listwise deleted. For example, in Table 11.4, student 101 is missing year 1 data, as is reflected in the time-varying class ID column, as well as in the year 1 class ID column. The next step is to create custom intercepts (as shown in the next three columns) to reflect the current effect of being in a class at that particular occasion. For the year 0 rows, the year 0 intercept is coded 1 if a student was in a valid class at that occasion or coded 0 if not, so that the students with invalid class IDs do not have an effect of class contributing to their predicted outcome. In addition, the year 0 intercept is coded 0 during years 1 and 2, so that the effect of being in the year 0 class no longer applies afterwards. The year 1 and year 2 intercepts would then be created similarly (i.e., coded 1 if the student was in a valid class at that occasion, and coded 0 for an invalid class or during the other occasions). The last three columns of Table 11.4 will be introduced later as part of an alternative model.

Now we are able to estimate occasion-specific fixed effects for classes using our new custom intercepts. Accordingly, a fixed effects model for class as a categorical time-varying predictor in the model for the means is shown in composite form in Equation (11.13):

$$
\begin{aligned}
\text{Effort}_{tsc} = {} & \gamma_{000} + \gamma_{100}\left(\text{Year01}_{tsc}\right) + \gamma_{200}\left(\text{Year12}_{tsc}\right) + U_{0s0} + e_{tsc} \\
& + \gamma_{001}^{0}\left(\text{Class1}_{c}\right)\left(\text{Int0}_{tsc}\right) + \gamma_{002}^{0}\left(\text{Class2}_{c}\right)\left(\text{Int0}_{tsc}\right)\cdots \\
& + \gamma_{00C}^{0}\left(\text{ClassC}_{c}\right)\left(\text{Int0}_{tsc}\right) + \gamma_{001}^{1}\left(\text{Class1}_{c}\right)\left(\text{Int1}_{tsc}\right) \\
& + \gamma_{002}^{1}\left(\text{Class2}_{c}\right)\left(\text{Int1}_{tsc}\right)\cdots + \gamma_{00C}^{1}\left(\text{ClassC}_{c}\right)\left(\text{Int1}_{tsc}\right) \\
& + \gamma_{001}^{2}\left(\text{Class1}_{c}\right)\left(\text{Int2}_{tsc}\right) + \gamma_{002}^{2}\left(\text{Class2}_{c}\right)\left(\text{Int2}_{tsc}\right)\cdots \\
& + \gamma_{00C}^{2}\left(\text{ClassC}_{c}\right)\left(\text{Int2}_{tsc}\right)
\end{aligned}
\tag{11.13}
$$

in which teacher-perceived student academic effort at time t for student s in class c is predicted in the first line by a fixed intercept γ_{000} for the reference year 1 mean, a fixed difference γ_{100} to year 0 (given that Year01 = –1 for year 0 and Year01 = 0 for year 1), and a fixed difference γ_{200} to year 2 (given that Year12 = 0 for year 1 and Year12 = 1 for year 2). Also included in the first line is a student random intercept U_{0s0} that allows a constant student mean difference over time, as well as a time- and student-specific residual e_{tsc}. The second, third, and fourth lines then introduce the class-specific fixed effects for the differences between classes at years 0, 1, and 2, respectively, as indicated by the superscript on their γ fixed effects. Each year has fixed effects up to $C - 1$ classes (given that one class will serve as the reference class for each year) as specified by the class-specific dummy-coded contrasts. Each is entered as an interaction with our year-specific custom intercepts that turn their effects "on" and "off" across years as needed. As a result of this custom intercept specification, each class difference contributes to the predicted outcome only for valid classes, and only for the year in which the student was in that class.

In estimating this model, the fixed intercept and year contrasts are conditional on the reference classes, so we will delay interpreting those for now. Of greater interest is that class mean differences were significant at year 0, $F(17, 884) = 4.58$, $p < .001$, at year 1, $F(19, 881) = 2.51$, $p < .001$, and at year 2, $F(19, 890) = 3.89$, $p < .001$. These fixed effects of class reduced 18.2% of the level-1 time-specific residual variance (resulting in a 2.4% increase in the level-2 student random intercept variance). These results indicate there are significant differences across classes in how much their teachers perceived their students to show academic effort. However, while this fixed effects model has controlled for the dependency due to time-varying class mean differences, it does not allow us to examine the possible reasons for these differences.

Fortunately, we can overcome this limitation by modeling class differences via year-specific random effects instead of fixed effects. That is, we will estimate a *crossed random effects model,* in which years at level 1 are nested within both level-2 students and level-2 time-varying classes, such that students and time-varying classes are crossed at level 2. As you might imagine, multilevel equations quickly become unwieldy for models with crossed random effects (i.e., given that there will be two different level-2 models), so we will use a composite equation only (i.e., with no level-1 placeholders) to describe each new model. Thus, our new model with level-2 random intercepts for both students and classes is shown in Equation (11.14):

$$
\begin{aligned}
\text{Effort}_{tsc} = {} & \gamma_{000} + \gamma_{100}\left(\text{Year01}_{tsc}\right) + \gamma_{200}\left(\text{Year12}_{tsc}\right) + U_{0s0} + e_{tsc} \\
& + U_{00c}^{0}\left(\text{Int0}_{tsc}\right) + U_{00c}^{1}\left(\text{Int1}_{tsc}\right) + U_{00c}^{2}\left(\text{Int2}_{tsc}\right)
\end{aligned}
\tag{11.14}
$$

in which the class fixed effects in lines 2 to 4 have been replaced by class random effects instead, such that an intercept variance across classes will be estimated for each year. To implement this model in software, the default global random intercept must be removed, and three separate random effects for the custom year-specific intercepts must be specified, in which that year's class ID is the nesting identification variable (see the example syntax online for more details).

Results from the model in Equation (11.14) are shown in the first set of columns in Table 11.5. The expected teacher-perceived academic effort in the reference year 1 was γ_{000} = 3.894, which was marginally lower by γ_{100} = −0.182 than in year 0, and nonsignificantly lower by γ_{200} = 0.021 than in year 2. As expected given the previously significant fixed effects for time-varying classes, the three level-2 random intercept variances for class mean differences at years 0, 1, and 2 significantly improved model fit (relative to the same model with only a level-2 student random intercept variance), $-2\Delta\text{LL}(\sim3) = 83.1$, $p < .001$. Given the lack of covariances among the random effects, we can sum the level-1 residual variance, level-2 student random intercept variance, and the per-year level-2 class random intercept variance to create year-specific total variances with which to compute the proportion of variance due to each source. In doing so, the proportion of variance due to level-1 differences across years was 32.6%, 33.8%, and 32.4% at years 0, 1, and 2, respectively. The proportion of variance due to level-2 student mean differences was 59.3%, 61.3%, and 58.9% at years 0, 1, and 2. Finally, the proportion of variance to due to level-2 class mean differences was 8.1%, 4.9%, and 8.7% at years 0, 1, and 2.

Before continuing, it is important to consider other views of how these class effects may operate. That is, our current model hypotheses *acute* effects, such that the effect of a class is present only when a student is actually in that class. An alternative view is that the impact of a class and its teacher will continue in the future even after a student has left the class. We can test this idea empirically by replacing our year-specific custom intercepts with those shown in the last set of columns in Table 11.4. These intercepts represent *transfer* class effects, in which the effect of having been in a year 0 class remains in full during years 1 and 2, and the year 1 effect remains in full during year 2. Additional intermediate hypotheses of less-than-complete transfer could similarly be tested by creating custom intercepts that reflect the residual effect of a class at subsequent occasions (e.g., forming patterns of linear or nonlinear decay).

Table 11.5 Results from longitudinal models of persons nested in time-varying groups. Bold values are $p < .05$. Y0 = year 0, Y1 = year 1, and Y2 = year 2.

Parameters		Unconditional Time Model (11.14)			Final Conditional Model (11.17)		
		Est	SE	p <	Est	SE	p <
Model for the Means							
γ_{000}	Intercept at Y1	**3.894**	0.067	.001	**3.593**	0.116	.001
γ_{100}	Y1 vs. 0	−0.182	0.093	.061	−0.051	0.131	.697
γ_{200}	Y1 vs. 2	0.021	0.093	.826	−0.244	0.154	.125
γ_{001}^{0}	Y0 Grade 5 vs. 3				0.005	0.115	.966
γ_{002}^{0}	Y0 Grade 5 vs. 4				0.118	0.117	.323
γ_{001}^{1}	Y1 Grade 6 vs. 4				0.042	0.133	.755
γ_{002}^{1}	Y1 Grade 6 vs. 5				−0.089	0.125	.481
γ_{001}^{2}	Y2 Grade 7 vs. 5				0.202	0.148	.187
γ_{002}^{2}	Y2 Grade 7 vs. 6				**0.411**	0.147	.012
γ_{010}	Student Gender (0 = Boy, 1 = Girl)				0.077	0.063	.225
γ_{003}^{0}	Y0 Class Mean Gender (0 = .50)				1.254	0.732	.113
γ_{003}^{1}	Y1 Class Mean Gender (0 = .50)				−0.197	0.886	.827
γ_{003}^{2}	Y2 Class Mean Gender (0 = .50)				0.012	0.659	.986
γ_{300}	Time-Varying Aggression (0 = 2)				**−0.606**	0.044	.001
γ_{020}	Student Mean Aggression (0 = 2)				**−0.198**	0.062	.002
γ_{004}^{0}	Y0 Class Mean Aggression (0 = 2)				0.004	0.109	.968
γ_{004}^{1}	Y1 Class Mean Aggression (0 = 2)				0.126	0.137	.368
γ_{004}^{2}	Y2 Class Mean Aggression (0 = 2)				0.068	0.181	.713
Model for the Variance							
$\tau_{U_0}^{2,0}$	Y0 Class Random Intercept Variance	0.081	0.035	.011	0.013	0.012	.143
$\tau_{U_0}^{2,1}$	Y1 Class Random Intercept Variance	**0.048**	0.025	.029	0.024	0.016	.064
$\tau_{U_0}^{2,2}$	Y2 Class Random Intercept Variance	**0.087**	0.038	.011	**0.037**	0.021	.043
$\tau_{U_0}^{2}$	Student Random Intercept Variance	**0.593**	0.049	.001	**0.344**	0.031	.001
σ_e^{2}	Residual Variance	**0.326**	0.018	.001	**0.266**	0.014	.001
REML Model Fit							
	Number of Parameters	8			23		
	−2LL	2984.6			2596.5		
	AIC	2994.6			2606.5		
	BIC	2984.6			2596.5		

Model fit for this alternative transfer of class effects model was significantly improved relative to a model with only student random intercept variance, $-2\Delta LL(\sim3) = 47.2$, $p < .001$. Given that our acute versus transfer class effect models differ in their variance components and are non-nested with the same number of parameters, we can compare them using AIC and BIC. Both were smaller for the acute model, such that the year-specific class effects were preferred. Accordingly, we can continue by examining the extent to which predictors pertaining to each source of sampling (years, students, and time-varying classes) can explain each pile of variance.

To illustrate how to include predictors for time-varying classes, we will begin with a categorical predictor of class grade at each year. Given the structure of these data, though, only some comparisons between grades are possible for each year, as shown in Equation (11.15):

$$
\begin{aligned}
\text{Effort}_{tsc} = {} & \gamma_{000} + \gamma_{100}\left(\text{Year01}_{tsc}\right) + \gamma_{200}\left(\text{Year12}_{tsc}\right) + U_{0s0} + e_{tsc} \\
& + U_{00c}^0\left(\text{Int0}_{tsc}\right) + U_{00c}^1\left(\text{Int1}_{tsc}\right) + U_{00c}^2\left(\text{Int2}_{tsc}\right) \\
& + \gamma_{001}^0\left(\text{G5v3}_c\right)\left(\text{Int0}_{tsc}\right) + \gamma_{002}^0\left(\text{G5v4}_c\right)\left(\text{Int0}_{tsc}\right) \\
& + \gamma_{001}^1\left(\text{G6v4}_c\right)\left(\text{Int1}_{tsc}\right) + \gamma_{002}^1\left(\text{G6v5}_c\right)\left(\text{Int1}_{tsc}\right) \\
& + \gamma_{001}^2\left(\text{G7v5}_c\right)\left(\text{Int2}_{tsc}\right) + \gamma_{002}^2\left(\text{G7v6}_c\right)\left(\text{Int2}_{tsc}\right)
\end{aligned}
\tag{11.15}
$$

in which the new fixed effects are given in lines 3–5. Between-class grade differences (in which the highest grade is the reference at each year) were specified in the same way as the class random intercepts for each year (i.e., as "interacting" with the year-specific custom intercepts to control when their effects will contribute to a student's predicted outcome). There were no significant differences across grades at year 0, $F(2, 20.2) = 0.72$, $p = .499$; the year 0 class random intercept variance actually increased by 3.0%. Likewise, there were no significant differences across grades at year 1, $F(2, 26.2) = 1.32$, $p = .283$, although the year 1 class random intercept variance was nevertheless reduced by 18.6% (again demonstrating why pseudo-R^2 values are named as such). However, there were significant differences across grades at year 2, $F(2, 23.2) = 3.92$, $p = .034$, such that academic effort was perceived to be lower only in grade 7 than in grade 6, which accounted for 35.7% of the year 2 class random intercept variance. To control for grade differences consistently across years, though, all grade effects will be retained.

Next, to illustrate how to examine time-invariant student predictors, we will test the extent to which teacher-perceived student academic effort varies by student gender (in which 0 = boys and 1 = girls). Because student gender is time-invariant, only a single effect across years needs to be included. However, classes did vary in gender composition, ranging from 29% to 65% girls ($M = 0.459$, $SD = 0.067$). Accordingly, we must also include per-year level-2 gender contextual effects by including fixed effects of class mean gender (centered at 50% girls) in interactions with the year-specific class intercepts, as shown in Equation (11.16):

$$
\begin{aligned}
\text{Effort}_{tsc} = {} & \gamma_{000} + \gamma_{100}\left(\text{Year01}_{tsc}\right) + \gamma_{200}\left(\text{Year12}_{tsc}\right) + U_{0s0} + e_{tsc} \\
& + U_{00c}^{0}\left(\text{Int0}_{tsc}\right) + U_{00c}^{1}\left(\text{Int1}_{tsc}\right) + U_{00c}^{2}\left(\text{Int2}_{tsc}\right) \\
& + \gamma_{001}^{0}\left(\text{G5v3}_{c}\right)\left(\text{Int0}_{tsc}\right) + \gamma_{002}^{0}\left(\text{G5v4}_{c}\right)\left(\text{Int0}_{tsc}\right) \\
& + \gamma_{001}^{1}\left(\text{G6v4}_{c}\right)\left(\text{Int1}_{tsc}\right) + \gamma_{002}^{1}\left(\text{G6v5}_{c}\right)\left(\text{Int1}_{tsc}\right) \\
& + \gamma_{001}^{2}\left(\text{G7v5}_{c}\right)\left(\text{Int2}_{tsc}\right) + \gamma_{002}^{2}\left(\text{G7v6}_{c}\right)\left(\text{Int2}_{tsc}\right) \\
& + \gamma_{010}\left(\text{Girl}_{s}\right) + \gamma_{003}^{0}\left(\overline{\text{Girl}}_{c} - .50\right)\left(\text{Int0}_{tsc}\right) \\
& + \gamma_{003}^{1}\left(\overline{\text{Girl}}_{c} - .50\right)\left(\text{Int1}_{tsc}\right) + \gamma_{003}^{2}\left(\overline{\text{Girl}}_{c} - .50\right)\left(\text{Int2}_{tsc}\right)
\end{aligned}
\tag{11.16}
$$

in which the new fixed effects of student and class mean gender are given in the last two lines. The within-class student gender effect was significant, such that the perceived academic effort of girls was higher by $\gamma_{010} = 0.261$ than for boys in the same class, which accounted for 2.3% of the level-2 student random intercept variance relative to the previous model. No contextual or between-class effects of gender were significant; the level-2 class random intercept variances increased by 3.9%, 10.9%, and 9.6% at years 0, 1 and 2. So, although gender composition was not related to class mean perceived academic effort in any year, in order to interpret the student gender effect as specifically within classes, we will retain the contextual gender effects as well.

Last, to illustrate how to include time-varying predictors, we will examine the extent to which teacher-perceived student academic effort is predicted by teacher-perceived student aggression in the same year, as measured by the mean of five items on a 1 to 5 scale, in which higher scores indicate greater perceived aggression ($M = 1.535$, $SD = 0.754$). As in previous chapters, we first need to examine its sources of variance so that all of its potential effects can be properly specified in the model. Preliminary analyses for teacher-perceived student aggression as an outcome revealed an ICC = .516, $-2\Delta LL(\sim 1) = 228.9$, $p < .001$, for the proportion of total variance due to student mean differences before controlling for any time-varying class mean differences. Mean differences across years were marginally significant, $F(2, 374) = 2.52$, $p = .082$, such that year 0 (1.502) was lower than years 1 (1.584) and 2 (1.574). The variances and covariances across students at each year were again adequately predicted by a student random intercept variance, $-2\Delta LL(\sim 4) = 7.4$, $p = .118$ (relative to an unstructured variance model).

Using the crossed random effects model from Equation (11.14), adding the three level-2 class random intercept variances for year-specific class mean differences significantly improved model fit relative to a model with a level-2 student random intercept variance only, $-2\Delta LL(\sim 3) = 233.6$, $p < .001$. The AIC and BIC again preferred the acute class effects model over the transfer class effects model. The proportion of variance in teacher-perceived student aggression due to level-1 differences across years was 29.3%, 32.5%, and 33.1% at years 0, 1, and 2, respectively. The proportion of variance due to level-2 student mean differences was 47.3%, 52.4%, and 53.4% at years 0, 1, and 2, indicating substantial stability across years in students' teacher-perceived aggression. Finally, the proportion of variance due to level-2 class mean differences was 23.4.1%, 15.1%, and 13.5% at years 0, 1, and 2, indicating a sizable amount of the variance in teacher-perceived student aggression depended on which teacher was providing the rating.

Given these results, we need to allow for potentially different effects of teacher-perceived student aggression predicting teacher-perceived academic effort for each year, student, and class. Given that there is no single class to serve as an overall reference point, though, constant-based centering will be more useful for these predictors than variable-based centering. Accordingly, our new model with all possible main effects of teacher-perceived student aggression (each centered at 2 on a 1–5 scale) is shown in Equation (11.17):

$$
\begin{aligned}
\text{Effort}_{tsc} = {} & \gamma_{000} + \gamma_{100}\left(\text{Year01}_{tsc}\right) + \gamma_{200}\left(\text{Year12}_{tsc}\right) + U_{0s0} + e_{tsc} \\
& + U^0_{00c}\left(\text{Int0}_{tsc}\right) + U^1_{00c}\left(\text{Int1}_{tsc}\right) + U^2_{00c}\left(\text{Int2}_{tsc}\right) \\
& + \gamma^0_{001}\left(\text{G5v3}_c\right)\left(\text{Int0}_{tsc}\right) + \gamma^0_{002}\left(\text{G5v4}_c\right)\left(\text{Int0}_{tsc}\right) \\
& + \gamma^1_{001}\left(\text{G6v4}_c\right)\left(\text{Int1}_{tsc}\right) + \gamma^1_{002}\left(\text{G6v5}_c\right)\left(\text{Int1}_{tsc}\right) \\
& + \gamma^2_{001}\left(\text{G7v5}_c\right)\left(\text{Int2}_{tsc}\right) + \gamma^2_{002}\left(\text{G7v6}_c\right)\left(\text{Int2}_{tsc}\right) \\
& + \gamma_{010}\left(\text{Girl}_s\right) + \gamma^0_{003}\left(\overline{\text{Girl}}_c - .50\right)\left(\text{Int0}_{tsc}\right) \\
& + \gamma^1_{003}\left(\overline{\text{Girl}}_c - .50\right)\left(\text{Int1}_{tsc}\right) + \gamma^2_{003}\left(\overline{\text{Girl}}_c - .50\right)\left(\text{Int2}_{tsc}\right) \\
& + \gamma_{300}\left(\text{Agg}_{sc} - 2\right) + \gamma_{020}\left(\overline{\text{Agg}}_s - 2\right) + \gamma^0_{004}\left(\overline{\text{Agg}}_c - 2\right)\left(\text{Int0}_{tsc}\right) \\
& + \gamma^1_{004}\left(\overline{\text{Agg}}_c - 2\right)\left(\text{Int1}_{tsc}\right) + \gamma^2_{004}\left(\overline{\text{Agg}}_c - 2\right)\left(\text{Int2}_{tsc}\right)
\end{aligned}
\tag{11.17}
$$

in which the new fixed effects of student aggression are given in the last two lines. Results are shown in the second set of columns of Table 11.5. The new effects can be interpreted as follows.

First, because of the effects of student mean and year-specific class mean aggression, the level-1 effect of teacher-perceived student aggression is specifically within students and within classes. So, after controlling for a student's own mean aggression and the current class mean aggression, academic effort was perceived to be significantly lower by $\gamma_{300} = -0.606$ for every unit more aggressive a teacher perceived the student to be that year. This level-1 effect accounted for 18.4% of the level-1 residual variance relative to the previous model. Second, the level-2 student contextual aggression effect was also significant, such that after controlling for year-specific level-1 student aggression and level-2 class mean aggression, academic effort was perceived to be lower by $\gamma_{020} = -0.198$ for every unit more aggressive a student was perceived to be than other students. The level-2 between-student effect (i.e., after combining the level-1 and level-2 student contextual effects) accounted for 40.4% of the level-2 student random intercept variance relative to the previous model. Finally, the level-2 class contextual aggression effects were not significant, such that after controlling for year-specific level-1 student aggression and level-2 student mean aggression, level-2 class mean aggression did not predict academic effort during that year. However, the between-class contextual effects (which were significant after combining the level-1 and level-2 class contextual effects) nevertheless accounted for 85.2%, 43.5%, and 40.4% of the remaining level-2 class random intercept variances at years 0, 1, and 2.

These results pose an interesting question—do they reflect biases in teacher perception, or are more aggressive students really less likely to put forth less academic effort? As one might expect, the answer may be a little bit of both. The significantly negative student contextual effect likely reflects true individual differences, given that, consistently across years and teachers, students perceived as more aggressive were also perceived to show less academic effort. The nonsignificant class contextual effects indicate that teachers who generally perceived more aggression in their students didn't necessarily perceive less academic effort. The negative level-1 effect is ambiguous, though, in that it could result from some degree of bias idiosyncratic to a specific teacher–student pairing, or it may be that aggression and academic effort are negatively related within students as well as between students. A research design in which students are rated by multiple teachers at the same time would be needed to more clearly delineate these effects.

So far in this example we have only considered fixed effects of our predictors, but it's important to remember that random effects may be possible as well. That is, level-1 predictors may have random effects over level-2 students or level-2 classes. And as odd as it may sound, level-2 student predictors could have random effects over level-2 classes, and level-2 class predictors could have random effects over level-2 students. Given how complex our model for the variance is already, though, we will forgo examining additional random effects for now. However, in describing crossed random effects models for non-longitudinal repeated measures data, chapter 12 will feature random slopes for level-2 item predictors across level-2 persons.

3.C. Longitudinal Data in Which Time Is Not Level 1

Before concluding the chapter, let us tackle one last topic for longitudinal data involving persons within groups. Earlier in the first chapter example we analyzed clustered longitudinal data, in which occasions were level 1, persons (students) were level 2, and groups (classes) were level 3. This was the appropriate structure because the same students were measured over time, and because the students were in the same class at every occasion. In the last chapter example we still considered time as level 1, but instead had two separate level-2 models for students crossed with classes given that students changed classes over time. Indeed, because time has been level 1 for the entire text so far, it might seem that this will always be the case. Not so—in some research designs, time will *not* be level 1 as a consequence of their differential nesting structure. Let us now consider a few specific examples of how this might occur.

In certain research areas (e.g., political science, business management and strategy), large groups are frequently the unit of analysis, in which outcomes are measured at the level of states, countries, companies, schools, and so on. If these outcomes are collected from the same groups at multiple occasions, then a two-level model of time within groups would be appropriate. All the same logic and procedures for two-level models of time within persons presented throughout the text would be applicable in that case. But what if a longitudinal study of different countries over time also measured characteristics of its residents, but different residents were sampled at each occasion? In that case, persons would be level 1, because they are nested within occasions, such that time would become level 2. Countries sampled repeatedly would then be level 3.

However, this three-level structure is only applicable if the outcome to be predicted has been measured *per person*. If so, then person variables would be level-1 predictors (that could have random effects across occasions and countries), time-varying country variables would be level-2 predictors (that could have random effects across countries), and country variables would be level-3 predictors (that could not have random effects). To avoid smushing the level-1 effects, though, the potential for differential effects of the level-1 person predictors at levels 2 and 3 would need to be allowed. This can be accomplished by including the level-1 predictor's time-specific mean across persons as a new level-2 predictor, and the country mean of those time-specific means (or supplemental country-level information) as a new level-3 predictor. Likewise, the time-varying country predictors would need to have different effects at levels 2 and 3, which can be accomplished by including the variance across countries via a new level-3 predictor. The lower-level predictors could be variable-centered or constant-centered, thus creating between effects or contextual effects, respectively, at the higher levels. Alternatively, the lower-level predictors could be outcomes whose variances at each level would be estimated within multivariate longitudinal models instead (as was presented in chapter 9).

But what if the outcome to be predicted was not measured per person, and instead was measured for an entire country at each occasion? In that case, we would no longer have a three-level model. Individual person predictors would not be included at level 1 because they have nothing to predict! Consequently, the appropriate model for this scenario is a two-level model of time within countries, in which only the time-specific aggregates of the person data could possibly be included as time-varying model predictors (not the original predictor per person). The usual logic and procedures of two-level longitudinal models would then otherwise apply.

Finally, what if the persons *and* the groups change over time? For instance, consider a recurring survey, in which different respondents are sampled at each occasion, and different interviewers collect those responses at each occasion. If the outcome to be predicted is measured per respondent, then respondents would be level 1, nested within interviewers at level 2. But having different respondents and interviewers across occasions means they would *both* be nested within occasions. Whether to treat time as a fixed effect or a random effect (i.e., to make it level 3) would depend on the number of occasions t and whether time-specific predictors are to be included—the same issues as when considering fixed or random effects for a group.

Treating time as a fixed effect would require a model for level-1 respondents nested in level-2 interviewers, and $t - 1$ per-occasion contrasts would have $t - 1$

level-2 fixed effects in the model for the means. The upside is that the $t - 1$ fixed effects would perfectly account for all mean differences over time; adding $t - 1$ interactions of the contrasts with a predictor would also perfectly account for differences across time in the effect of that predictor. The downside is that there would be no variance remaining across time, such that time-specific predictors could not be included. Thus, a fixed effects model for time is likely to be more useful given fewer occasions and the need to *control for*—rather than *predict*—dependency due to differences across time.

In contrast, treating time as a random effect would require a level-3 random intercept variance for differences across time. All other logic and procedures for three-level models would then apply: level-1 respondent predictors could have random effects across interviewers and occasions, level-2 interviewer predictors could have random effects across occasions, and level-3 time-specific predictors could not have random effects. And as before, to avoid smushing the level-1 respondent effects, we should include their interviewer means across respondents as level-2 predictors, as well as their time-specific means across interviewers as level-3 predictors. Likewise, to avoid smushing the level-2 interviewer effects, we should include their time-specific means as level-3 predictors as well.

In summary, time is not always necessarily going to be level 1—where time is located in your model will always be dictated by the sampling design of your outcome variables. Once you determine that, the structure and the levels of your model will define themselves.

4. Chapter Summary

The purpose of this chapter was to describe longitudinal models for persons who belong to one or more groups over time. To properly specific longitudinal models involving groups, several issues are relevant, as discussed in the first section of the chapter. First, do persons belong to only one group at each occasion, or can they belong to multiple groups at once? For the latter case, if the multiple groups are hierarchically organized (e.g., classes in schools), this nesting can be modeled by adding higher levels to the model, such that the random effects at each level are unrelated to those at different levels. In contrast, non-hierarchical groups (e.g., schools and neighborhoods) are said to be crossed, which instead requires uncorrelated random effects at the same level, rather than at a new level. A second issue is whether group members are exchangeable or distinct. An example of exchangeable persons is students in a class, who are all just "students" in the same group. An example of distinct persons is members of a family, in which roles of mother, father, child, and so forth are clearly differentiated. Outcomes from exchangeable persons are modeled as nested within groups, whereas those from distinct persons may be more meaningfully treated as multivariate outcomes (with different variance components) instead. A third issue is whether group membership changes over time. If not, groups become higher levels of the model, such as in the first chapter example of clustered longitudinal data. If group membership does change over time, then groups are modeled as crossed with persons, such as in the second chapter example in which students changed classes across occasions.

After answering these questions, although the necessary model structure should hopefully be clearer, you will still have to decide whether to represent each set of group differences using fixed effects or using random effects. A fixed effects model treats group as a categorical predictor, thus "explaining" all possible group differences in the model for the means. A random effects model instead includes group differences as part of the model for the variance: a random intercept variance captures mean differences across groups, whereas random slope variances capture group differences in the effect of predictors. In either approach, custom-created intercepts can be used to reflect the proportion of time a person has spent in each group, as well as to allow a group's effect to persist over time even after the person has left a group.

The rest of the chapter provided examples of models for persons in groups. The second section detailed the process of fitting three-level models for clustered longitudinal data, in which time was level 1, students were level 2, and classes were level 3. For each level-1 variable, we first examined its variance across levels using empty means models, and then tested the need for fixed and random effects of time. The outcome of student–teacher closeness needed random intercepts and linear time slopes for both students and classes. Accordingly, we then examined level-3 predictors (class grade and class size) to account for class differences in intercept and change over time, as well as a level-2 predictor of student gender to account for within-class student differences in intercept and change over time. We also considered contextual effects of gender at level 3 as a predictor of class differences in intercept and change over time, as well as a potential random effect of student gender across classes.

We continued by examining two time-varying predictors, one pertaining to classes and one pertaining to students. The level-1 predictor of time-varying *class* emotional support had significant mean differences across classes but no fixed or random effects of time. Consequently, we included the observed predictor of emotional support at level 1 and its class mean at level 3 (both centered at a constant) to serve as proxies for its level-1 residual variance and level-3 class random intercept variance. Likewise, the level-1 predictor of time-varying *student* victimization had significant mean differences across classes and across students within classes, but also no fixed or random effects of time. Thus, we used variable-based centering to create level-specific predictors for victimization within students at level 1, within classes at level 2, and between classes as level 3. That is, our observed predictor variables were proxies for victimization's residual variance at level 1, within-class student random intercept variance at level 2, and class random intercept variance at level 3. It's important to note, though, that if either level-1 predictor had random effects of time, then it should have become another outcome instead. Such a truly multivariate model would have allowed separate effects for between-class and/or between-person differences in both intercept and change over time, as well as for within-person variation at each occasion.

We then examined the relative utility of three-level or multivariate two-level models for longitudinal analysis of distinct persons from the same group (e.g., families or dyads). In general, a multivariate two-level model—in which time is nested within group and persons are distinct multivariate outcomes—is more flexible for specifying actor and partner effects, as well as for examining correlations among random effects and residuals for distinct persons from the same group. Multivariate models can also be useful for longitudinal analysis of differences scores, which can be predicted directly within the model along with the original outcomes.

Section 3 then began with a discussion as to why time is usually modeled as nested within persons rather than crossed with persons, and continued with a new example of students who were nested in different classes at each occasion. After creating custom intercepts to represent the group effect at each occasion, we then examined time-varying group differences using fixed effects in the model for the means, as well as random effects in the model for the variance. Given that only random effects permit quantification and prediction of those group differences, we then examined whether those random effects could be predicted by class grade. We also examined the extent to which student random intercept variance could be predicted by gender (and class random intercept variance by contextual gender effects). In addition, given that it shared the same variance structure as our outcome, we included a time-varying predictor at level 1, its student mean at level 2, and its year-specific class means at level 3.

Finally, the last section briefly considered designs in which time is not level 1, which occurs when different persons are measured at each occasion. Ultimately the sampling of the outcome will dictate which level of the model is which, including time.

5. Sample Results Sections

The example analyses in this chapter can be summarized into results sections as follows (which would then need to be expanded to capture the substantively meaningful story, theoretical framework, or set of research hypotheses to be tested). As usual, the amount of detail provided about the process of arriving at the final reported model(s) will usually be far less than the exposition in the chapter, and it will vary based on the goals of the study and the space available. Accordingly, the results sections that follow refer to only some of the intermediate models as benchmarks before interpreting the results from the final models in greater detail.

5.A. Longitudinal Models for Persons in Time-Invariant Groups

Changes in perceived student–teacher closeness across three occasions during the same semester were examined in 597 students who were nested within 33 classes, for a total of 1,731 occasions of data. Third ($n = 13$) and fifth grade classes were included ($n = 20$), with an average of 23 students per class (SD = 2.65, range = 19 to 29). Given the clustered longitudinal design, three-level general linear mixed models were estimated using restricted maximum likelihood, in which level-1 occasions were nested within level-2 students within level-3 classes. Accordingly, fixed effects were tested by their individual Wald test p-values, whereas random effects were tested by the $-2\Delta LL$ between nested models (i.e., a likelihood ratio test) as evaluated by the difference in the model degrees of freedom. All covariances were estimated among random effects at the same level. In calculating pseudo-R^2 for the proportion reduction in each variance component across models, any increases in variance instead of decreases are reported as ~0.

Empty means (i.e., intercept-only) models were first estimated to partition the variance in student–teacher closeness across levels. The level-2 intraclass correlation for the proportion of total variance due to students and classes was $ICC_{L2} = .549$, which was significantly > 0, as indicated by a comparison of a single-level model to a two-level model (ignoring the nesting of students within classes), $-2\Delta LL(\sim1) = 464.6$, $p < .001$. To then partition that student variance, a level-3 intraclass correlation was calculated for the proportion of student variation actually due to variation across classes. The $ICC_{L3} = .179$, which was also significantly > 0, as indicated by a comparison of a two-level model to a three-level model, $-2\Delta LL(\sim1) = 40.0$, $p < .001$. Together, these ICCs indicate that of the total variation in student–teacher closeness over time, 54.9% was across students and classes; of that 54.9%, 17.9% was actually across classes.

Unconditional growth (i.e., time-only) models were then examined, beginning with a saturated means, unstructured variances model in which all possible variances and covariances across waves were estimated separately for level-2 students and for level-3 classes. Given the significant mean differences across waves, $F(2, 30.8) = 7.96$, $p = .002$, each model allowed all means to differ over time by specifying a linear time slope along with a deviation at the third wave. Relative to a model with only a residual variance at level 1 and random intercepts at levels 2 and 3, model fit improved significantly by adding a random linear time slope variance across level-2 students, $-2\Delta LL(\sim2) = 32.0$, $p < .001$, as well as across level-3 classes, $-2\Delta LL(\sim2) = 37.4$, $p < .001$. The resulting model did not fit significantly worse than the unstructured variance model, $-2\Delta LL(\sim5) = 2.8$, $p = .732$, indicating that random intercepts and linear time slopes adequately predicted the variance and covariance across waves for students and classes. Furthermore, the nonsignificant deviation from linear change at the third wave could be removed, given that a negative linear time slope—by which student–teacher closeness became significantly lower by 0.130 per occasion—adequately described average change. Results from the final unconditional growth model, as shown in Equation (11.4), are given in the first set of columns in Table 11.2.

Conditional growth models including predictors were then examined using the random linear time model as a baseline (in which time was centered at the first wave). First examined were fixed effects of class grade (in which 0 = grade 3 and 1 = grade 5) and class size (centered at 23 students) predicting the level-3 intercept and time slope. No class grade effects were significant initially, and thus these effects were removed. The class size effects were marginally significant and predicted lower closeness at wave 1 and a more negative rate of change in larger classes. These class size effects accounted for 18.7% and 8.8% of the level-3 class random intercept and time slope variances, respectively. Both fixed effects for class size were retained.

Level-2 effects of student gender (in which 0 = boys and 1 = girls) and level-3 contextual effects of gender (in which class mean gender was centered at .50) predicting their intercepts and time slopes were then examined. At level 2, girls felt significantly closer to their teacher than boys in the same class, although this effect did not change over time and did not vary randomly across classes. These student gender fixed effects accounted for 3.9% and 0.5% of the level-2 student random intercept and time slope variances, respectively. At level 3, although no wave-specific effects were significant, the contextual gender effect (i.e., the effect of having more girls in a class after controlling for student gender) was significantly more negative over time. These class mean gender fixed effects accounted for ~0% and 39.3% of the remaining level-3 class random intercept and time slope variances. All four fixed effects of gender were retained.

Next examined were the effects of time-varying class emotional support, in which 50.7% of its total variation was between classes. Given that it contained no fixed or random effects of time, only class mean differences needed to be represented at level 3. Thus, time-varying emotional support (centered at 5) and its interaction with time were included at level 1, whereas class mean emotional support (also centered at 5) was included as a level-3 predictor of the intercept and time slope. The nonsignificant level-1 effects indicated that there was no effect of greater emotional support than usual (which did not change over time and did not vary randomly across classes). The level-1 effects were then removed, along with the now nonsignificant effects of class size. The reduced model revealed that the between-class fixed effect of emotional support was significantly more positive over time (and was significantly positive after wave 1), accounting for ~0% and 70.5% of the remaining level-3 class random intercept and time slope variances. Both fixed effects of level-3 class mean emotional support were retained.

The last predictor examined was time-varying student-perceived victimization. As found through empty means models, of its total variation in victimization over time, 65.2% was across students and classes, which was significantly > 0, $-2\Delta LL(\sim1) = 711.8$, $p < .001$. Of that 65.2%, only 5.1% was actually across classes, which also significantly > 0, $-2\Delta LL(\sim1) = 6.0$, $p = .015$. Although victimization increased significantly across waves, $F(2, 30.5) = 4.52$, $p = .019$, there was no significant variation in linear change across students or classes. Consequently, only mean differences in victimization needed to be represented at levels 2 and 3. A level-1 predictor was created as the wave-specific deviation from the student mean, a level-2 predictor was created as the student-specific deviation from the class mean, and a level-3 predictor was created by centering the class mean at 3. The level-1 and level-3 effects were not significant, such that feeling more victimized than usual at level 1 did not predict less closeness at the same wave, and classes who felt more victimized at level 3 did not feel less closeness than other classes. In contrast, the level-2 effect was significantly negative, indicating that students who felt more victimized than other students in their class were predicted to feel less close to their teachers, which accounted for 2.2% of the remaining level-2 random intercept variance. None of these effects changed significantly over time, and the level-1 and level-2 effects did not vary randomly across classes. The level-1 effect did vary randomly across students and was thus retained, $-2\Delta LL(\sim3) = 18.8$, $p < .001$, and indicated that the extent to which feeling more victimized than usual predicts feeling less student–teacher closeness at the same wave varied across students.

Higher-order effects of all retained predictors were then evaluated in sequential models. No quadratic effects were found for any predictor, indicating that their linear effects were likely sufficient. Two-way and three-way interactions were then tested amongst the level-3 predictors. The two-way interactions of class mean emotional support with class mean gender and with class mean victimization were significant and accounted for 33.9% of the remaining level-3 random intercept variance (and 7.3% of the level-3 random time slope variance, unexpectedly). None of the level-3 interactions differed across time. The level-2 interaction of student gender by within-class victimization was significant but did not account for any remaining level-2 random intercept variance. The contextual gender by within-class victimization cross-level interaction was not significant (nor was the between-class interaction), but the remaining level-3 random intercept and random time slope variances were nevertheless reduced by 6.4% and 1.4%. These interaction effects also did not differ over time. Finally, as expected given their lack of random variation across classes, the level-2 within-class effects of gender and victimization and the level-1 effect of victimization did not vary by any level-3 predictor. The level-1 victimization effect—which did vary randomly across students—did not differ by student gender, but did differ significantly by level-2 student mean victimization, and so for completeness the level-1 by level-3 victimization interaction was also added. These interactions with level-1 victimization accounted for 7.4% of the level-2 victimization random slope variance. Results from the final model, as shown in Equation (11.9), are given in the second set of columns in Table 11.2. The model accounted for 10.4% of the total variation in student–teacher closeness (from the square of the correlation between the original outcome and the outcome predicted by the fixed effects). These model effects (and other requested model-implied effects) can be interpreted as follows.

The fixed intercept of $\gamma_{000} = 4.211$ was the expected closeness at wave 1 for a boy who was at his usual level of victimization and who had student mean victimization = 3, as well as who was in a class that has 50% girls, class mean emotional support = 5, and class mean victimization = 3. Closeness declined significantly by $\gamma_{100} = 0.131$ per wave for boys; this linear rate of change over time was nonsignificantly greater for girls by $\gamma_{110} = -0.001$. In addition, at level 2, girls felt significantly closer to their teacher by $\gamma_{010} = 0.252$ than boys in the same class at wave 1; this gender difference was nonsignificantly smaller by $\gamma_{110} = -0.001$ per wave. However, this level-2 gender effect is conditional on a significant interaction with level-2 within-class victimization, as described shortly. At level 3, the contextual effect of gender (i.e., after controlling for student gender) became significantly more negative by $\gamma_{103} = -1.112$ per wave. After dividing each coefficient by 10, for every 10% more girls in a class, class mean closeness was expected to be nonsignificantly different at wave 1 by $\gamma_{003} = 0.055$ and at wave 2 by $\gamma_{003} + \gamma_{103} = 0.055 - 0.111 = -0.056$, but significantly lower at wave 3 by $\gamma_{003} + 2*\gamma_{103} = 0.055 - 2*0.111 = -0.167$. However, the level-3 contextual gender effect was qualified by significant level-3 interactions with class mean emotional support and with class mean victimization, as well as by a nonsignificant interaction with level-2 within-class victimization, as described next.

The between-class effect of emotional support was significantly more positive by $\gamma_{104} = 0.170$ per wave, such that for every additional unit of class mean emotional support, class mean closeness was expected to be nonsignificantly higher by $\gamma_{004} = 0.108$ at wave 1, but significantly higher at wave 2 by $\gamma_{004} + \gamma_{104} = 0.108 + 0.170 = 0.278$ and at wave 3 by $\gamma_{004} + 2*\gamma_{104} = 0.108 + 2*0.170 = 0.448$. So, although students in classes with greater emotional support were predicted to feel closer to their teacher, this level-3 effect was conditionally estimated for classes with 50% girls and class mean victimization = 3, and it differed significantly by these variables. More specifically, the effect of class mean emotional support became less positive by $\gamma_{009}/10 = -0.235$ for every 10% more girls, and less positive by $\gamma_{00,11} = -0.778$ for every additional unit of class mean victimization. To summarize these level-3 interactions, it appears that the benefits of class emotional support on student–teacher closeness were reduced in classes that had more girls and in classes whose students felt more victimized than other classes.

Turning to the level-1 effects of student-perceived victimization, for every unit a student felt more victimized than usual, student–teacher closeness at that occasion was lower by $\gamma_{400} = -0.075$, which was not significant, which was conditional on students with average victimization relative to their class and with class mean victimization = 3. However, the level-1 effect of feeling more victimized than usual became significantly less negative (turning positive) by $\gamma_{420} = 0.109$ for every unit more victimized a student felt than the rest of his class at level 2, such that in students who felt more victimized than the rest of their class, feeling more victimized than usual actually predicted greater student–teacher closeness at those waves. The level-1 victimization effect did not vary by class mean victimization (i.e., it became nonsignificantly less negative by $\gamma_{405} = 0.157$ for every unit greater class mean victimization at level 3).

Turning to the level-2 effects of student-perceived victimization, for every unit more victimized a student felt than others in his class, student mean closeness was nonsignificantly lower by $\gamma_{020} = -0.053$, as conditionally estimated for boys who were at their usual level of victimization, and whose class had 50% girls. However, the level-2 effect of feeling more victimized than others in a class was significantly more negative by $\gamma_{040} = -0.152$ in girls, whose level-2 effect of $\gamma_{020} + \gamma_{040} = -0.053 - 0.152 = -0.205$ was significant. Finally, this level-2 effect was nonsignificantly more negative by $\gamma_{021}/10 = -0.001$ for every 10% more girls in a class. Thus, feeling more victimized than other students in a class had a detrimental effect on student–teacher closeness, but only in girls (and this did not depend on how many girls are in a class).

Finally, turning to the level-3 effects of student-perceived victimization, for every unit more victimized a class felt than other classes, class mean closeness was nonsignificantly lower by $\gamma_{005} = -0.054$, as conditionally estimated for students at their usual levels of victimization and whose class mean emotional support = 5. However, the level-3 effect of feeling more victimized than other classes became nonsignificantly less negative (turning positive) by $\gamma_{405} = 0.157$ for every unit a student feels more victimized than usual at level 1, but significantly more negative by $\gamma_{00,11} = -0.778$ for every unit greater class mean emotional support at level 3. Thus, class emotional support appeared to strengthen the negative effect of class mean victimization.

5.B. Longitudinal Models for Persons in Time-Varying Groups

Changes in teacher-perceived student academic effort were examined in 486 students in 58 classes in grades 3–7 across three years, for a total of 1,214 occasions. Because students were in a different class each year, two-level models with crossed random effects for students and classes at level 2 (and years at level 1) were estimated with restricted maximum likelihood. Fixed effects were tested by their individual Wald test p-values, and random effects were tested by the $-2\Delta LL$ between nested models (i.e., a likelihood ratio test) as evaluated by the difference in the model degrees of freedom. In calculating pseudo-R^2 for the proportion reduction in each variance component across models, any increases in variance instead of decreases are reported as ~0.

Empty means (i.e., intercept-only) models were first estimated to partition the variance in academic effort between years and students. The level-2 intraclass correlation for the proportion of total variance due to students was ICC = .589, which was significantly > 0, as indicated by a comparison of a single-level model to a two-level model, $-2\Delta LL(\sim1) = 340.4$, $p < .001$. Next estimated was a saturated means, unstructured variance model with separate student variances and covariances across years. Given the significant mean differences across years, $F(2, 385) = 9.26$, $p < .001$, the subsequent model included piecewise slopes between years 0–1 and 1–2, with year 1 as the reference (intercept). A reduced model with these fixed piecewise slopes and only a student random intercept variance did not fit significantly worse than the unstructured variance model, $-2\Delta LL(\sim4)$, = 4.3, $p = .366$, indicating that the relatively constant variance and covariance across years that could be adequately predicted by a random intercept variance for students.

The extent to which classes differed in their mean teacher-perceived student academic effort across years was then examined via custom intercepts that allowed a random class effect only when a student was in that given class. Adding three level-2 variances for these custom random intercepts at years 0, 1, and 2 significantly improved model fit (relative to the same model with only a level-2 student random intercept variance), $-2\Delta LL(\sim3) = 83.1$, $p < .001$. The proportion of variance due to level-1 differences across years was 32.6%, 33.8%, and 32.4% at years 0, 1, and 2, respectively. The proportion of variance due to level-2 student mean differences was 59.3%, 61.3%, and 58.9% at years 0, 1, and 2. Finally, the proportion of variance to due to level-2 class mean differences was 8.1%, 4.9%, and 8.7% at years 0, 1, and 2.

The extent to which class mean differences could be predicted by class grade was then examined via fixed effects for differences across the three grades present at each year. There were no significant differences across grades at year 0, $F(2, 20.2) = 0.72$, $p = .499$; pseudo-$R^2 \sim 0$ for the year 0 class random intercept variance. Likewise, there were no significant differences across grades at year 1, $F(2, 26.2) = 1.32$, $p = .283$, although pseudo-$R^2 = .186$ for the year 1 class random intercept variance. However, there were significant differences across grades at year 2, $F(2, 23.2) = 3.92$, $p = .034$, such that academic effort was perceived to be lower only in grade 7 than in grade 6; pseudo-$R^2 = .357$ for the year 2 class random intercept variance. To control for grade differences consistently across years, though, all grade effects were retained.

The extent to which student mean differences could be predicted by gender (coded 0 = boys, 1 = girls) was then examined. Given class differences in gender composition, contextual effects of gender for classes at each year were also added as fixed effects. The within-class student gender effect was significant, such that the perceived academic effort of girls was higher than boys in the same class; pseudo-$R^2 = .023$ for the student random intercept variance. No contextual or between-class effects of gender were significant; pseudo-$R^2 \sim 0$ for the class random intercept variances at years 0, 1 and 2. Although gender composition was not related to academic effort in any year, in order to interpret the student gender effect as specifically within classes, the contextual gender effects were retained.

Last, the extent to which teacher-perceived student academic effort could be predicted by teacher-perceived student aggression during the same year was then examined. Preliminary analyses for student aggression as an outcome revealed an ICC = .516, $-2\Delta LL(\sim 1) = 228.9$, $p < .001$, for the proportion of total variance due to student mean differences before controlling for any class mean differences. Mean differences across years were marginally significant, $F(2, 374) = 2.52$, $p = .082$, such that year 0 was lower than years 1 and 2. The variances and covariances across students at each year were again adequately predicted by a student random intercept variance, $-2\Delta LL(\sim 4) = 7.4$, $p = .118$ (relative to an unstructured variance model). Turning to the class effects, adding the three level-2 class random intercept variances for year-specific class mean differences significantly improved model fit relative to a model with a level-2 student random intercept variance only, $-2\Delta LL(\sim 3) = 233.6$, $p < .001$. The proportion of variance in teacher-perceived student aggression due to level-1 differences across years was 29.3%, 32.5%, and 33.1% at years 0, 1, and 2, respectively. The proportion of variance due to level-2 student mean differences was 47.3%, 52.4%, and 53.4% at years 0, 1, and 2. The proportion of variance to due to level-2 class mean differences was 23.4.1%, 15.1%, and 13.5% at years 0, 1, and 2.

Given these results, separate effects of student aggression were included for each source of variance, including a time-varying predictor at level 1, a student mean predictor at level 2, and year-specific class mean predictors at level 2. Each aggression predictor was centered at 2. The level-1 effect was significantly negative (pseudo-$R^2 = .184$ for the level-1 residual variance). The level-2 contextual and between-student effects were also significantly negative (pseudo-$R^2 = .404$ for the level-2 student random intercept variance). Finally, although the level-2 contextual class effects were not significant, the between-class effects were significantly negative (pseudo-R^2 = .852, .435, and .404 for the class random intercept variances at years 0, 1 and 2).

The final model, as shown in Equation (11.17), accounted for 36.6% of the total variance in teacher-perceived student academic effort (as calculated from the square of the correlation of the original outcome with the outcome predicted by the model fixed effects). In terms of pseudo-R^2, the fixed effects accounted for 84.1%, 48.9%, and 58.0% of the class random intercept variances for years 0, 1, and 2; 41.9% of the student random intercept variance; and 18.3% of the level-1 residual variance. Results are shown in Table 11.5. The expected mean teacher-perceived student academic effort at year 1 was γ_{000} = 3.593 for girls in a grade 6 class with 50% girls, with time-varying, student mean, and class mean aggression = 2. Relative to year 1, the means at years 0 and 2 differed nonsignificantly by γ_{100} = −0.051 and γ_{200} = −0.244. No differences across grades were significant, except that academic effort in year 2 was higher in grade 6 than 7 (γ_{002}^2 = 0.411). No student or class contextual gender effects were significant after accounting for teacher-perceived student aggression, whose effects are interpreted as follows. At level 1, after controlling for a student's own mean aggression and the current class mean aggression, perceived academic effort was significantly lower by γ_{300} = −0.606 for every unit more aggressive a teacher perceived the student to be that year. The level-2 student contextual aggression effect was also significant, such that after controlling for that year's aggression and level-2 class mean aggression, perceived academic effort was lower by γ_{020} = −0.198 for every unit more aggressive a student was perceived to be than other students. Finally, the level-2 class contextual aggression effects were not significant, such that after controlling for that year's aggression and level-2 student mean aggression, level-2 class mean aggression did not incrementally predict academic effort that year.

Review Questions

1. When are persons nested in groups, and when would persons be crossed with groups instead?
2. What types of random effects could potentially be estimated in three-level models?
3. Describe the alternative models for non-exchangeable (distinct) persons from the same group. What are the advantages and disadvantages of each?
4. Contrast and compare fixed and random effects models for group effects. In which situations would one type of model be more useful than the other?

References

Cushing, C. C., Walters, R. W., & Hoffman, L. (2014). Aggregated N-of-1 randomized controlled trials: Modern data analytics applied to a clinically valid method of intervention effectiveness. *Journal of Pediatric Psychology, 39,* 138–150.

Hox, J. J. (2010). *Multilevel analysis: Techniques and applications* (2nd ed.). New York, NY: Routledge.

Snijders, T. A. B., & Bosker, R. (2012). *Multilevel analysis* (2nd ed.). Thousand Oaks, CA: Sage.

CHAPTER 12

ANALYSIS OF REPEATED MEASURES DESIGNS NOT INVOLVING TIME

So far our models for within-person analysis have been presented for longitudinal designs in which when the same variable is measured repeatedly over time, but these models can be useful for other kinds of repeated measures designs as well. To that end, chapter 12 focuses on modeling data from studies in which the same items, stimuli, or trials are administered to each subject. Such repeated measures designs are traditionally analyzed using analysis of variance (ANOVA), in which the individual item responses are aggregated into condition means for each subject (or less commonly, in which the individual subject responses are aggregated into a mean for each item). Yet what is not often recognized is how the assumptions that underlie the use of ANOVA models on such aggregated data are likely to be untenable, resulting in questionable statistical tests of the effects of interest and unnecessary compromises in how the effects of predictors must be specified. Thus, this chapter will present an alternative strategy of *crossed random effects models* (as introduced in chapter 11 for designs in which persons change groups over time).

Because the contents of this chapter represent a departure from typical practice with repeated measures designs, it may be useful to foreshadow the reasons why someone might use crossed random effect models instead of ANOVA models before diving into the specifics. The primary reason to use crossed random effects models is to be able to model multiple sources of variation simultaneously—in repeated measures designs, this includes variation across subjects, variation across items, and their interaction. Even if a design is not fully crossed (i.e., not all subjects respond to all items), because crossed random effects models utilize likelihood-based estimation, all available responses can still be included. In contrast, ANOVA models that are estimated via least squares use listwise deletion, such that both subject and item random variation can only be modeled simultaneously for fully crossed designs with complete data. But missing data is a common problem in repeated measures designs, such as when certain subjects are unable to complete certain items, or when response times are analyzed only for trials in which a correct response was given. Consequently, the use of ANOVA models usually requires a compromise—*subjects* are often treated as the unit of analysis, in which only subject variation is included by aggregating over *items* to create subject condition means. A less common alternative is to treat *items* as the unit of analysis, such that only item variation is included after aggregating over *subjects* to create item condition means. Either way, analyzing these condition means as if they represented all of the original data can cause several problems, as overviewed below.

First, aggregation of responses into condition means assumes any incomplete responses are missing completely at random—that the sample of observed responses accurately represents the original distribution of responses. But to the extent that responses are missing for systematic reasons, those condition means may become biased. Consider, for instance, a visual search task in which both speed and accuracy of response are measured per trial. If the more difficult trials are more likely to be answered incorrectly (such that their longer response times would then be missing), the resulting mean response times for those conditions may be too short, and the effect of difficulty may be artificially reduced. Condition means may also have differential reliability due to the varying numbers of trials that end up contributing across subjects. In contrast, potential biases due to *missingness* can be mitigated to a much greater extent in crossed random effects models because all available responses are used directly under the assumption of missing at random (i.e., conditionally random after accounting for model predictors and outcomes).

Second, aggregating responses into condition means limits the kinds of predictor effects that can be modeled. Specifically, ANOVA models cannot include continuous predictors (i.e., slopes for quantitative variables) for the sampling dimension whose random variation was eliminated from the model. This is because aggregation of items into condition means presupposes that items are distinguished only by categorical predictors (i.e., grouping variables). So continuous predictors for *item* characteristics cannot be examined in *subject* analyses (because we would have already aggregated over items); likewise, continuous predictors for *subject* characteristics cannot be examined in *item* analyses (because we would have already aggregated over subjects). To get around this problem, continuous predictors are often discretized (e.g., via a median split) in order to be included as distinct "conditions" in an ANOVA, a practice that is unnecessary and can be detrimental. In contrast, crossed random effects models can include any kind of categorical or continuous predictors (as well as any interactions), and therefore offer much flexibility. For instance, consider an item predictor of target salience with values ranging from 1 to 10. Rather than include salience as a grouping variable with 10 different levels to be compared (requiring 9 degrees of freedom and much patience to interpret), the effects of increasing salience could instead be summarized with polynomial, nonlinear, piecewise, or other hypothesized trends (i.e., the same kinds of parameters we had used previously for describing the effects of continuous time).

Third, as we will see shortly, the accuracy of tests for the effects of subject or item predictors depends on the inclusion of all random variation across the relevant dimension. For example, if all observed random item variation is not included in the model, then the tests of predictors that pertain to item characteristics may not be accurate. Likewise, if all observed random subject variation is not included in the model, then the tests of predictors that pertain to subjects may not be accurate. This is because even when only categorical predictors are of interest, analyzing condition means makes an untestable assumption that there is no additional variation among units of the same kind (i.e., exchangeability within conditions). In reality, although items such as words, sentences, and pictures are usually carefully selected to vary in the key features of interest, they may not be perfectly equivalent on all other possible features. Ideally, measures of any confounding variables could also be included as controls, but in practice this can become unwieldy or impossible within an ANOVA framework, leaving researchers to defend their strategy on theoretical grounds only. Fortunately, it is possible within crossed random effect models to not only empirically test item exchangeability (i.e., the adequacy of experimental control across items), but to easily include any potentially confounding variables in the model to assess to what extent their inclusion might change the predictor effects of interest.

Finally, although not directly related to aggregation, ANOVA is limited in its capacity to model individual variability and dependency. ANOVA models require homogeneity of variance; the purpose of adjustments for violations of homogeneity is to protect the tests of group mean differences. In contrast, extensions to model heterogeneity of variance (as introduced in chapter 7) are also available in crossed random effects models. Thus, we can examine individual or group differences in *variability* of response as well as in mean response. Furthermore, ANOVA models typically assume dependency within persons due to mean differences only—they cannot address how much subjects vary in their responses as a function of differences between items or experimental conditions. Fortunately, crossed random effects models allow subjects to vary in their effects of item predictors via random effects (i.e., random slope variances), as well as to examine the extent to which subject characteristics can explain each source of subject variation.

Hopefully you now have some indication as to why crossed random effects models can be a useful and flexible tool for analyzing data from repeated measures designs. But before we can move forward, we first need to understand where we've been. Accordingly, the first section of this chapter uses a hypothetical example to describe the traditional ANOVA approaches used to analyze data from designs in which items are the repeated measures, including subjects analyses of variance, items analyses of variance, F' tests, and min F' tests, as well as their problems. The second section then describes how crossed random effects models can overcome the limitations of these ANOVA approaches while offering the aforementioned advantages. These points are illustrated more concretely in the empirical example in the third section. Finally, as in previous chapters, this chapter concludes with summary and sample results sections.

1. ANOVA Models for Repeated Measures Designs of Subjects Crossed With Items

One of the most important implements in the statistical toolbox of those who work with repeated measures designs is the *analysis of variance* (ANOVA) model. As described in chapter 2, ANOVA is a special case of the general linear model for use with continuous outcomes and categorical predictors (i.e., measured or manipulated grouping variables). The model would be called *analysis of covariance* (ANCOVA) if any continuous covariates are included. However, additional terminology is often used to describe ANOVA or ANCOVA within experimental designs. That is, categorical predictors are often called *factors,* and the specific categories are called *levels.* If subjects each receive only one factor level—if subjects are *nested* within factor levels—the factor is *between groups* (or *between subjects*). In contrast, if each subject receives all possible levels of the factor—if subjects are *crossed* with factor levels—the factor is *within groups* (or *within subjects*). The term *repeated measures* is often used as a synonym for a within-subjects factor. Although some texts differentiate between these terms, we will not, and will use the term *repeated measures* to refer generally to within-subjects factors. A research design that combines between-subjects and within-subjects factors is known as a *mixed design* or a *split-plot* design (a term that originated from agricultural and agronomy experiments). Research designs with multiple factors are known as *factorial* designs. For instance, a research design with two between-subjects factors and one within-subjects factor would be called a *three-way mixed factorial design.* The number of "ways" is defined by the total number of factors. Finally, a unique combination of factor levels across predictors is often called a *condition.*

To help illustrate the concepts in this chapter, let us consider an example experiment in which 50 subjects are each presented with 40 sentences, and the outcome is the speed with which a subsequent question about each sentence is answered (response time, or RT). Within this design, there are likely to be systematic differences between subjects (i.e., some subjects will respond faster than others), differences between items (i.e., some sentences will be responded to faster than others), as well as variation due to the unique pairing of a particular subject with a particular item (i.e., remaining residual variation after considering from which subject and for which item a response was obtained). We will use a single predictor to try and explain response differences between the subjects: *verbal fluency* (a continuous predictor). We will use two predictors to try and explain differences in response between the sentences: *active versus passive voice* (a categorical predictor with two levels) and *syntactic complexity* (a continuous predictor).

The ideal analysis for this data would examine the three predictors of interest using all possible responses per item per subject. However, any subject who does not have a response to every item cannot have *any* of his or her data included given that ANOVA traditionally uses listwise deletion. So because subjects are rarely perfectly compliant, it is often impossible to analyze all individual item responses using ANOVA due to incomplete item data. Two solutions for this problem within an ANOVA framework are presented below, and each involves changing the unit of analysis, such that responses are first aggregated into condition means, and then those condition means are analyzed within an ANOVA. Unfortunately, this aggregation eliminates one source of random variation (either subjects or items), which we will see is problematic for assessing the effects of predictors that pertain to that dimension. In addition, continuous predictors for the aggregated dimension will not be able to be examined without turning them into categorical predictors, as shown next.

1.A. Subjects Analysis of Variance: Treating Subjects as Random and Items as Fixed

As introduced earlier, the primary problem with using ANOVA for repeated measures designs of subjects crossed with items is that all relevant sources of variation cannot be modeled simultaneously if there is any incomplete data. The most common approach for circumventing this problem is to first compute a condition mean *across items for each subject*—the analysis of these item condition means across subjects is called an F_1 **ANOVA**. In doing so, the *subject* is now the unit of analysis, and the repeated measures are the item condition mean response times. In this example, although we can easily aggregate item responses as a function of active versus passive sentences, it is unclear how to translate the continuous differences between sentences in syntactic complexity into distinct repeated measures conditions. To do so, we must make another compromise—we will pretend that sentence complexity was measured as "low" versus "high" by taking a median split to form a new predictor. Note that this distortion is necessary in this example to illustrate how these item effects would typically be included in ANOVA models (and is one of its significant limitations, in fact), but is *not* recommended!

Thus, for this F_1 ANOVA, we would begin by computing four item condition means per subject, one for each combination of sentences with active versus passive voice and "low" versus "high" complexity. We would then analyze those four item condition means using a within-subjects factorial ANCOVA, with a between-subjects continuous predictor (or covariate) of grand-mean-centered verbal fluency and within-subjects sentence factors of voice (active vs. passive) and complexity ("low" vs. "high"). In a typical ANOVA, each categorical predictor is coded by the program to create marginal main effects (e.g., as ±0.5 for each level of the predictor here, such that 0 represents the average across levels). The resulting model F_1 ANOVA model is shown in Equation (12.1):

$$RT_{cs} = \gamma_{00} + \gamma_{10}\left(Voice_c\right) + \gamma_{20}\left(Complex_c\right) + \gamma_{30}\left(Voice_c\right)\left(Complex_c\right)$$
$$+ \gamma_{01}\left(Fluency_s\right) + U_{0s} + e_{cs} \tag{12.1}$$

in which RT_{cs} is the response time outcome in item condition c for subject s. The first subscript c denotes effects that pertain to item conditions (created by averaging RTs over the sentences of the same type), and the second subscript s denotes effects that pertain to subjects. Each subscript is numbered in order of appearance of its predictors. Accordingly, in the model for the means, the fixed intercept γ_{00} is the grand mean RT across all conditions and subjects, the main effect of voice γ_{10} is the mean difference between the active and passive voice item conditions, the main effect of complexity γ_{20} is the mean difference between the "low" and "high" complexity item conditions, and the interaction of voice and complexity γ_{30} is how the mean difference between the "low" and "high" complexity item conditions differs between the active and passive voice item conditions (or how the mean difference between the active and passive voice item conditions differs between the "low" and "high" complexity item conditions). Finally, the main effect of fluency γ_{01} is the effect on RT of a one-unit difference in subject verbal fluency.

The F_1 ANOVA model separates the total variance into two terms: the random intercept for each subject U_{0s}, which represents the remaining subject variance in mean RT after controlling for verbal fluency, and the residual e_{cs}, which represents the remaining deviation between each observed and predicted condition mean RT (i.e., the subject by item condition interaction variance). Recall that rather than estimating each U_{0s} and e_{sc} separately, we instead estimate their variances as model parameters (denoted as $\tau^2_{U_{0sub}}$ and σ^2_{F1e}, respectively). As described in chapter 3, the effects of sentence voice and complexity would be tested against the residual variance (σ^2_{F1e}), whereas the effect of subject verbal fluency would be tested against the total variance (from $\tau^2_{U_{0sub}} + \sigma^2_{F1e}$). Although not typically estimated, interactions of fluency with voice and complexity could also added to examine violations of the ANCOVA assumption of regression homogeneity; these would also be tested against the residual variance (σ^2_{F1e}).

At this point, you might be wondering what happened to the differences between items within the same condition. Because the F_1 ANOVA model only analyzes condition means, the within-condition item variance is not included in the model—it was eliminated ahead of time. Accordingly, we have ignored the fact that these items were sampled from a broader population of possible sentences that could have been used. By analyzing condition means (that artificially eliminate the remaining item variation within conditions from the model) we have treated items as *fixed*. In other words, we have assumed that all item differences in RT were due to our *known* effects of voice and complexity, and that no random item variance of *unknown* origin remains (although we have allowed random variation of unknown origin across subjects via U_{0s}).

The problems in treating items as fixed effects have been known for decades (see Clark, 1973; Coleman, 1964), but until recently, analytic techniques that permit treating both items and subjects as random effects simultaneously have not been widely available. Thus, a remedy for the problem of items as fixed effects that is still in practice is to follow the F_1 ANOVA with an additional model in which items are the unit of analysis instead of subjects, as presented next.

1.B. Items Analysis of Variance: Treating Items as Random and Subjects as Fixed

Aggregating over items so that subjects become the unit of analysis as just described is a common approach, but it is not the only option. Alternatively, we could compute a condition *mean across subjects for each item* instead. The analysis of these subject condition means across items is called an F_2 **ANOVA**. In doing so, the *item* is now the unit of analysis, and the repeated measures are the mean response times across subjects in the same condition. Because random item variation is now included in the model, the continuous effect of sentence complexity can be included directly as a covariate. However, just as we were forced to dichotomize continuous sentence complexity in aggregating over items, in aggregating over subjects we will now be forced to dichotomize the continuous subject predictor into conditions of "low" and "high" verbal fluency. Next, we would then analyze those two condition means using a mixed effects ANCOVA, only this time subject verbal fluency would be the *within-items* factor, sentence voice would be the *between-items* factor, and sentence complexity would be a grand-mean-centered *between-items* covariate (with which interactions are not typically estimated). Each categorical predictor would again be coded as ±0.5 to create marginal main effects (such that 0 represents the average across levels). The resulting F_2 ANOVA model is shown in Equation (12.2):

$$RT_{ci} = \gamma_{00} + \gamma_{10}(Fluency_c) + \gamma_{01}(Voice_i) + \gamma_{11}(Fluency_c)(Voice_i)$$
$$+ \gamma_{02}(Complex_i) + U_{0i} + e_{ci} \tag{12.2}$$

in which RT_{ci} is the response time outcome in subject condition c for item i. The first subscript still denotes effects that pertain to conditions (now created by averaging over subjects with each level of fluency); the second subscript now denotes effects that pertain to items. In the model for the means, the fixed intercept γ_{00} is the grand mean RT across all conditions and items, the main effect of fluency γ_{10} is the mean difference between the "low" and "high" verbal fluency subject conditions, the main effect of voice γ_{01} is the mean difference between the active and passive item conditions, and the interaction of fluency and voice γ_{11} is how the mean difference between the "low" and "high" fluency subject conditions differs between the active and passive voice item conditions (or how the mean difference between the active and passive voice item conditions differs between the "low" and "high" fluency subject conditions). Finally, the main effect of complexity γ_{02} is the effect on RT of a one-unit difference in sentence complexity.

In the F_2 ANOVA model for the variance, the random intercept for items U_{0i} represents remaining item variance in mean RT after controlling for sentence voice and complexity (denoted as $\tau^2_{U_{0item}}$), and the residual e_{ci} represents the remaining deviation between each observed and predicted condition mean RT (denoted as σ^2_{F2e}, the item by subject condition interaction variance). The between-items effects of sentence voice and complexity (and their possible interaction) would be tested against the total variance (from $\tau^2_{U_{0item}} + \sigma^2_{F2e}$), whereas subject fluency is a within-items factor, and so its main effect and interaction with sentence voice (or interaction with sentence complexity) would be tested against the residual variance (σ^2_{F2e}).

Because the F_2 ANOVA model only analyzes condition means, any within-condition subject variation is not included in the model—it was eliminated ahead of time. Accordingly, we have ignored the fact that these subjects were sampled from a broader population of possible subjects—by creating condition means that artificially eliminate the remaining within-condition subject variance from the model we have treated subjects as *fixed*, rather than *random*. That is, we have assumed that all differences between subjects in mean RT was due to our one known effect of verbal fluency, and that no random subject variance of unknown origin remains (although we did allow random variation of unknown origin across items via U_{0i}).

What is hopefully becoming clear is that the F_2 items analysis makes the same kind of assumption that is made in the F_1 subjects analysis, just for the other sampling dimension. The F_1 *subjects* analysis eliminates remaining *item* variation within conditions, and the F_2 *items* analysis eliminates remaining *subject* variation within conditions. Therefore, F_1 subjects analyses assume that items are fixed but subjects are random, and F_2 items analyses assume that subjects are fixed but items are random. Accordingly, the results of an F_1 analysis would be informative as to what would happen if the same (fixed) sentences were given to a new set of (random) subjects. Likewise, the results of an F_2 analysis should be informative as to what would happen if a new set of (random) items were given to the same (fixed) subjects. But neither model predicts what would happen with both new items and new subjects, which is usually the point of the study!

The compromise that appears to have been reached in some areas of inquiry is known as the F_1 **by** F_2 **criterion.** In this approach, both the F_1 and F_2 ANOVA models are used to estimate the predictor effects of interest, and only effects that meet the criteria for significance within *both* models are considered reliable. There are several problems with the F_1 by F_2 criterion, as has been discussed elsewhere (see Raaijmakers, 2003; Raaijmakers, Schrijnemakers, & Gremmen, 1999). One problem concerns an imbalance in sample size across dimensions. In research areas in which subjects are plentiful, researchers will commonly employ many more subjects than items. As a result, the effects from the F_1 subjects analysis will be based on a larger sample size and thus will have more power to test the same effects than will the F_2 items analysis. In contrast, subjects may be hard to find in research with special populations, and thus more items than subjects may be used in these cases, with the opposite effect of giving the F_2 items analysis more power than the F_1 subjects analysis. But even in a balanced design with equal numbers of subjects and items, the major problem with the F_1 by F_2 criterion is that quite simply, two wrongs don't make a right. Eliminating random sources of variation within each of the separate models does not solve the problem—all relevant sources of variation need to be included simultaneously. An additional problem is that we were unable to properly test the effects of continuous predictors for the aggregated dimension without dichotomizing them (and introducing measurement error).

1.C. F′ and min F′ for Testing Fixed Effects Through Analysis of Variance

When subjects and items are fully crossed, ANOVA can be used to model both subjects and items as random effects at once, and this model uses the same underlying logic of the crossed random effects models to follow. Specifically, Clark (1973) described a random effects ANOVA in which the responses to each item for each subject can be analyzed. This approach is illustrated in Table 12.1, in which we have simplified our current example by providing the decomposition of total variation after including only one of our item predictors, active versus passive voice, labeled for generality as the *treatment effect*. Table 12.1 shows the expected mean square for each possible effect, where #T = number of treatment conditions = (here, 2),

Table 12.1 Decomposition of variance within a random effects ANOVA (T = treatment, S = subjects, I = items, E = error).

Source of Variance	Degrees of Freedom	Mean Square (MS)	\[Expected Value of Mean Square\]					
			E	S * I (within T)	T * S	S	I (within T)	T
			σ_E^2 σ_{SxI}^2		$\#I * \sigma_{TxS}^2$	$\#T* \#I* \sigma_S^2$	$\#S* \sigma_I^2$	$\#I* \#S* \sigma_T^2$
Treatment	(#T−1)	MS_T	x x		x		x	x
Items (within Treatment)	(#T)*(#I−1)	MS_I	x x				x	
Subjects	(#S−1)	MS_S	x x			x		
Treatment by Subjects	(#T−1)* (#S−1)	MS_{TxS}	x x		x			
Subjects by Items (within Treatment)	(#T)*(#I−1)* (#S−1)	MS_{SxI}	x x					

#I = number of items (here, 40), and #S = number of subjects (here, 50). The "x" entries represent the variance components that are expected to contribute to the expected mean square for each effect. The subscripts on the variances indicate their source (treatments, items, subjects, and any of their interactions). Note that subjects by items interaction variance (σ_{SxI}^2) is not distinguishable from the residual variance σ_E^2 because there is only one unique observation for each subject and item.

Normally an F-ratio is defined so that only one term differs between the numerator and denominator—the F-test then reveals whether that single source of variation is different from 0. With this in mind, Table 12.1 illustrates the problem with both F_1 and F_2 ANOVAs for testing the effect of treatment. In an F_1 subjects analysis, the F-ratio is given by Equation (12.3):

$$F_1 \left(df_T, df_{TxS} \right) = \frac{MS_T}{MS_{TxS}}$$

$$= \frac{\sigma_E^2 + \sigma_{SxI}^2 + \left(\#I * \sigma_{TxS}^2 \right) + \left(\#T * \#I * \sigma_S^2 \right) + \left(\#S * \sigma_I^2 \right) + \left(\#I * \#S * \sigma_T^2 \right)}{\sigma_E^2 + \sigma_{SxI}^2 + \left(\#I * \sigma_{TxS}^2 \right) + \left(\#T * \#I * \sigma_S^2 \right)} \tag{12.3}$$

in which the numerator differs from the denominator by two terms, not one. Thus, the F_1 value could be significant because of significant treatment variance ($\#I*\#S*\sigma_T^2$), as we might hope, or because of significant item variance ($\#S*\sigma_I^2$), which would create an artificially significant result instead. Similarly, in an F_2 items analysis, the F-ratio is given by Equation (12.4):

$$F_2(df_T, df_I) = \frac{MS_T}{MS_I}$$

$$= \frac{\sigma_E^2 + \sigma_{SxI}^2 + (\#I * \sigma_{TxS}^2) + (\#T * \#I * \sigma_S^2) + (\#S * \sigma_I^2) + (\#I * \#S * \sigma_T^2)}{\sigma_E^2 + \sigma_{SxI}^2 + (\#I * \sigma_{TxS}^2) \qquad\qquad + (\#S * \sigma_I^2)} \qquad (12.4)$$

in which the numerator also differs from the denominator by two terms, not one. Accordingly, the F_2 value could be significant because of a significant treatment variance ($\#I*\#S*\sigma_T^2$) or because of significant subject variance ($\#T*\#I*\sigma_S^2$). Thus, if systematic differences remain across items OR subjects beyond those explicitly accounted for by model predictors, neither the F_1 subjects ANOVA nor the F_2 items ANOVA will accurately evaluate the treatment effect.

To solve this dilemma, Clark (1973) proposed an approximate or quasi-F ratio, F' (pronounced "F prime"), defined as shown in Equation (12.5):

$$F'(df_{num}, df_{den}) = \frac{MS_T + MS_{SxI}}{MS_{TxS} + MS_I}, \text{ where}$$

$$df_{num} = \frac{(MS_T + MS_{SxI})^2}{\dfrac{MS_T}{df_T} + \dfrac{MS_{SxI}}{df_{SxI}}} \text{ and } df_{den} = \frac{(MS_{TxS} + MS_I)^2}{\dfrac{MS_{TxS}}{df_{TxS}} + \dfrac{MS_I}{df_I}}$$

$$F'(df_{num}, df_{den}) = \frac{(2 * \sigma_e^2) + (2 * \sigma_{SxI}^2) + (\#I * \sigma_{TxS}^2) + (\#S * \sigma_I^2) + (\#I * \#S * \sigma_T^2)}{(2 * \sigma_e^2) + (2 * \sigma_{SxI}^2) + (\#I * \sigma_{TxS}^2) + (\#S * \sigma_I^2)} \qquad (12.5)$$

in which, after writing the mean squares in terms of their expected values and combining terms, the numerator of F' differs from the denominator by exactly the treatment variance as desired. Thus, F' can provide a solution to the items (or subjects) as fixed effects problem because the treatment effect is evaluated appropriately by modeling both subjects and items as the random effects they actually are. Unfortunately, however, because F' is created from a least squares solution, it cannot be computed when not all pairings of subjects with items are observed, which limits its utility in practice. To combat this problem, Clark (1973) showed how the minimum bound of F' can be computed from separate F_1 and F_2 ANOVAs, as shown in Equation (12.6):

$$\min F'(df_{num}, df_{den}) = \frac{MS_T}{MS_{TxS} + MS_I} = \frac{F_1 * F_2}{F_1 + F_2} \qquad (12.6)$$

in which the numerator degrees of freedom is $\#T - 1$ for the treatment effect, and the denominator degrees of freedom is as defined in Equation (12.5). Given that F' will always be higher than min F', if min F' is significant, then F' will be significant as well. Although the use of min F′ has been criticized for being too conservative (see Raaijmakers et al., 1999), min F′ has been the only way within least squares estimation (i.e., in the traditional ANOVA family of models) to treat both items and subjects as random effects in the presence of missing (or unbalanced) data. Therefore, a less conservative method is needed that still allows for simultaneous analysis of incomplete (or unbalanced) responses from subjects and items. Fortunately, models that use likelihood-based estimation can now be employed to analyze repeated measures data with incomplete responses, and they do so with greater statistical power and under more reasonable assumptions about the missingness than is possible within ANOVA models, as we'll see in the next sections.

1.D. Summary

To summarize the chapter so far, when subjects each respond to the same items, that is, when items are *crossed* with subjects, the optimal analysis should contain all observed responses for each subject to each item. That way, all sources of random variation pertaining to items, subjects, and their interaction can be modeled simultaneously, allowing for the proper evaluation of predictor effects for each dimension. But when not all pairings of subjects and items are observed (i.e., when missing data create an unbalanced or not fully crossed design), an ANOVA model estimated using least squares treating both subjects and items as random effects cannot be used. As a compromise, repeated measures data of this type are typically analyzed one of two ways: by analyzing condition means for each *subject* created by aggregating across *items* within the same condition (F_1 ANOVA; random subjects but fixed items), or by analyzing condition means for each *item* created by aggregating across *subjects* within the same condition (F_2 ANOVA; random items but fixed subjects). But neither approach properly models both subjects and items as random effects, which is problematic for assessing effects of predictors for both dimensions at once. Fortunately, there is an alternative solution that solves these problems and offers other advantages as well.

2. Advantages of Crossed Random Effects Models for Repeated Measures Designs

Rather than aggregating responses over items or subjects, we can include all possible responses from each subject to each item (even given missing data) using a **crossed random effects model.** In this model, individual trials (responses from each subject to each item) at level 1 are nested within subjects *and* within items. Thus, subjects and items are crossed at level 2—in other words, we now have two orthogonal level-2 models simultaneously. Accordingly, rather than using two-level notation (i.e., as typical for longitudinal models), in models with crossed random effects it is often more convenient to write a single composite model. To demonstrate, a crossed random effects model we could fit for our current example (now also including all possible interactions for the sake of illustration) is shown in Equation (12.7):

$$
\begin{aligned}
RT_{tis} = \ &\gamma_{000} + \gamma_{010}\left(Voice_i\right) + \gamma_{020}\left(Complex_i\right) + \gamma_{030}\left(Voice_i\right)\left(Complex_i\right) \\
&+ \gamma_{001}\left(Fluency_s\right) + \gamma_{011}\left(Voice_i\right)\left(Fluency_s\right) + \gamma_{021}\left(Complex_i\right)\left(Fluency_s\right) \\
&+ \gamma_{031}\left(Voice_i\right)\left(Complex_i\right)\left(Fluency_s\right) + U_{0i0} + U_{00s} + e_{tis}
\end{aligned}
\tag{12.7}
$$

in which RT_{tis} is the response time outcome for trial t to item i for subject s. Although the trial t may be perfectly defined by item i and subject s, the t index is included to allow for effects of predictors that pertain to the subject by item unique combination. For instance, when the order of item presentation is randomized across subjects, a predictor for *trial order* might be included as a trial-specific control variable. Thus, the first subscript t indexes predictors pertaining to the specific trials, the second subscript i indexes predictors pertaining to the items, and the third subscript s indexes the predictors pertaining to the subjects. Furthermore, because we are no longer aggregating over any random variance, we no longer need to discretize any of the continuous predictors for subjects or items to become artificial "low" versus "high" conditions in the model.

Accordingly, the model for the means in Equation (12.7) includes the fixed intercept γ_{000} for the expected RT when all predictors are 0, the main effect of sentence voice γ_{010} (the mean difference between active and passive sentences when sentence complexity and subject verbal fluency are 0), the main effect of sentence complexity γ_{020} (the effect on RT of a one-unit difference in complexity when sentence voice and subject verbal fluency are 0), the interaction of sentence voice by complexity γ_{030} (the difference in the complexity slope between sentences of active and passive voice when fluency is 0), the main effect of subject verbal fluency γ_{001} (the effect on RT of a one-unit difference in fluency when sentence voice and complexity are 0), the interaction of sentence voice by subject fluency γ_{011} (the difference in the fluency slope between active and passive sentences when complexity is 0), the interaction of sentence complexity by subject fluency γ_{021} (the difference in the fluency slope for a one-unit difference in complexity when voice is 0), and finally, the three-way interaction γ_{031} (the difference in the sentence voice by complexity interaction for a one-unit difference in fluency).

The crossed random effects model for the variance has three terms: the random subject intercept U_{00s} to represent the subject variation that remains after controlling for fluency (denoted as $\tau^2_{U_{00Sub}}$), the random item intercept U_{0i0} to represent the item variation that remains after controlling for voice, complexity, and their interaction (denoted as $\tau^2_{U_{00Item}}$), and the residual e_{tis} to represent the deviation of each predicted trial RT from the actual trial RT after controlling for everything else (denoted as σ^2_e). Thus, the crossed random effects model accounts for all sources of variation simultaneously—it allows for mean differences of unknown origin across both subjects and items via random effects. Finally, although not seen here, the item predictors could potentially have random slopes over subjects (and less intuitively, the subject predictors could potentially have random slopes over items). Such random slopes are shown later in the chapter.

2.A. Accuracy for Tests of Predictor Effects

At this point, you might be wondering what the real harm is in treating either subjects or items as fixed effects instead of as random effects. This is a fair question, for there is no use in learning how to use an alternative modeling strategy if there is no practical benefit. The answer is that accounting for all sources of variation within a model allows for the most accurate tests of the effects of subject or item predictors in a way that ANOVA models on aggregated data simply cannot.

To illustrate, consider the following simulation study examining Type I error rates for the significance of effects pertaining to items or subjects when their true population effect is 0. Data were created containing an item predictor and a subject predictor, each with two levels and whose fixed main effects were 0. Four conditions were generated, with either small or large variance in mean response due to items remaining after controlling for the effect of the item predictor ($\tau^2_{U00item}$ = 2 or 10), as well as small or large variance due to subjects remaining after controlling for the effect of the subject predictor (τ^2_{U00sub} = 2 or 10). The residual variance for the subject by item interaction was held constant (σ^2_e = 80); similar results were obtained when the total variation was held constant instead. A dataset of complete responses for 30 subjects to 30 items was generated for each of the four item variance by subject variance conditions. This process was repeated 500 times to obtain empirical estimates of the Type I error rate.

Each of the 500 simulated data sets was analyzed using six different models. In four of the models, all 900 responses (30 subjects by 30 items) were analyzed at once. Model 1 included random intercepts for both subjects and items (i.e., crossed random effects for unpredicted random variation in each), and so the residual variance σ^2_e contained only the subject by item interaction variance as it should. Model 2 included a random intercept only for subjects, such that σ^2_e also contained unpredicted random item variance. Model 3 included a random intercept only for items, such that σ^2_e also contained unpredicted random subject variance. Model 4 included no random intercepts, such that σ^2_e contained all unpredicted random variance due to subjects and items. Finally, two additional models were estimated: an F_1 subjects ANOVA (after aggregating items into condition means; Model 5), and an F_2 items ANOVA (after aggregating subjects into condition means; Model 6). The Satterthwaite method was used to estimate denominator degrees of freedom, as in previous chapters (and as was described in chapter 5).

The true fixed effects for both the item and subject predictors were 0, so Table 12.2 gives the proportion of replications per simulation condition and per model in which each fixed effect from the model was mistakenly reported as $p < .05$ (i.e., the empirical Type I error rate). Let us first consider the results from Models 1 through 4 that analyzed all possible responses. When random intercept variances for both subjects and items were included (i.e., subjects and items were treated as random; Model 1), Type I error rates were close to .05, as expected. Correct results were obtained in the fully specified Model 1 for two reasons: (1) Each effect was tested against the proper error term ($\tau^2_{U00sub} + \sigma^2_e$ for the subject effect, $\tau^2_{U00item} + \sigma^2_e$ for the item effect), and (2) each effect was tested with the correct sample size (based

Table 12.2 Simulation study results: Type I error rates for item and subject effects by simulation condition by model. Bold values indicate error rates above .07.

Simulation Condition		Models					
Item Variance	Subject Variance	1: Both Random Effects	2: Random Subjects Only	3: Random Items Only	4: No Random Effects	5: F1 Subjects ANOVA	6: F2 Items ANOVA
Item Predictor:							
2	2	0.03	**0.09**	0.03	**0.09**	**0.09**	0.03
2	10	0.05	**0.14**	0.05	**0.12**	**0.15**	0.05
10	2	0.04	**0.32**	0.04	**0.31**	**0.32**	0.04
10	10	0.05	**0.31**	0.05	**0.29**	**0.33**	0.05
Subject Predictor:							
2	2	0.04	0.04	**0.12**	**0.11**	0.04	**0.12**
2	10	0.05	0.05	**0.34**	**0.34**	0.05	**0.36**
10	2	0.04	0.03	**0.12**	**0.09**	0.03	**0.12**
10	10	0.06	0.06	**0.34**	**0.31**	0.05	**0.37**

on the number of subjects for the subject effect; based on the number of items for the item effect).

In contrast, in Model 2, in which a random intercept variance was included for subjects but not for items (i.e., subjects were treated as random but items were treated as fixed), Type I error rates to detect *subject* effects were around .05 as expected, but Type I error rates to detect *item* effects were much higher, particularly with larger item variation. This is because although the item effect was tested with the same error term as in the correct Model 1 ($\tau^2_{U00sub} + \sigma^2_e$, which was all within σ^2_e given that subject variance τ^2_{U00sub} was not modeled), it was again tested with an incorrect sample size (i.e., for the total number of trials, now ignoring the fact that 30 trials came from the same subject). The opposite pattern was found for Model 3, in which a random intercept variance was included for items but not for subjects (i.e., subjects were treated as fixed but items were treated as random): Type I error rates to detect *item* effects were close to .05 as expected, but Type 1 error rates to detect *subject* effects were much higher, particularly with larger subject variation. This is again because although the subject effect was tested with the same error term as in the correct Model 1 ($\tau^2_{U00sub} + \sigma^2_e$, which was all within σ^2_e given that subject variance τ^2_{U00sub} was not modeled), it was again tested with an incorrect sample size (i.e., for the total number of trials, now ignoring the fact that 30 trials came from the same subject). In Model 4 in which no random intercept variances were included (subjects and items were both treated as fixed), Type I error rates were too high for detecting both subject effects and item effects, and the size of the error rates varied based on the size of the variation in each respective dimension. This was due to testing with an incorrect error term ($\tau^2_{U00item} + \tau^2_{U00sub} + \sigma^2_e$ for each effect, rather than just $\tau^2_{U00sub} + \sigma^2_e$ for the subject effect and $\tau^2_{U00item} + \sigma^2_e$ for the item effect) as well as an incorrect sample size.

Finally, we consider the ANOVA results in analyzing condition means (Models 5 and 6). Model 5 included a random intercept variance for subjects (the F_1 subjects ANOVA), and so Type I error rates for the subject effect were close to .05 as expected because the subject effect was tested with the proper error term ($\tau^2_{U00sub} + \sigma^2_e$) and sample size (based on the number of subjects). But Type I error rates for the item effect mirror those from Model 2, in which items were also treated as fixed—they are too high, especially with larger item variation. As before, there are two reasons for this. First, the item effect was not tested with the proper error term—the remaining $\tau^2_{U00item}$ item variance was artificially removed from the data prior to the F_1 ANOVA by aggregating over items within the same condition, so the item effect had to be tested against the *subject by item condition* version of the σ^2_e residual variance, or σ^2_{F1e}. Second, the item effect was not tested with the correct sample size—because items were not part of the F_1 model, the degrees of freedom were based on the subject by item condition interaction instead. And last but not least, because Model 6 included a random intercept variance for items instead (the F_2 items ANOVA), we see the reverse of the same problem. Model 6 treated items as random, and so Type I error rates for the item effect were close to .05 as expected. In contrast, Type I error rates were much higher for the subject effects, whose variation was artificially removed prior to estimating the F_2 model (i.e., subjects were treated as fixed).

These simulation results demonstrate that when one source of sampling variation is mistakenly treated as fixed (i.e., no remaining variation after controlling for its predictors), tests of the predictor effects pertaining to that dimension are inaccurate. In other words, the goal in testing a subject effect is to see how much random subject variation is accounted for by the subject predictor. If that random subject variation is not in the data *and* in the model (via τ^2_{U00sub}), then the test of the subject predictor will be incorrect. Likewise, the test of how much item variation is accounted for by the item predictor requires that random item variation be included in the data *and* in the model (via $\tau^2_{U00item}$), otherwise the test of the item predictor will be incorrect. Thus, this concern applies when all responses are analyzed but the relevant random effect is simply not modeled (Models 2, 3, and 4), as well as when the random effect is aggregated into condition means in order to use an F_1 or F_2 ANOVA (Models 5 and 6).

These results also suggest that if only one dimension is relevant for testing predictor effects (i.e., when only subject predictors *or* only item predictors are of interest), then it would be "safe" to treat only that one dimension as a random effect. That is, Models 2 and 5 would yield accurate results if only subject predictors are tested; Models 3 and 6 would yield accurate results if only item predictors are tested. However, because predictors related to both subjects and items are typically of interest in repeated measures designs, the most appropriate analysis would model both the subject and item random variation simultaneously—and for designs that are not fully crossed (i.e., in which there is incomplete data), this is the crossed random effects model.

In addition to these issues, however, the flexibility inherent in crossed random effects models can be advantageous for analyzing repeated measures data for several other reasons, as outlined in the beginning of the chapter. We now discuss how crossed random effects models can overcome limitations of traditional ANOVA models for repeated measures data.

2.B. Amount of and Reasons for Missing Responses

One limitation concerns incomplete data, which can be one of the greatest challenges for any researcher. As explained earlier, an ANOVA model estimated using least squares on all possible responses would require listwise deletion for any subjects who do not have complete responses to all items, which may greatly reduce statistical power. To avoid this problem, condition means across items are often computed and then analyzed via an F_1 subjects ANOVA instead (given that all subjects will have a mean for each condition so long as they have at least one observation per condition). However, this approach assumes that any incomplete responses within conditions are **missing completely at random**, which means exactly what it sounds like—that the probability that each response is missing is unrelated to what those responses would have been.

The assumption of missing completely at random is unlikely to be satisfied in many experimental designs, but could be particularly problematic in modeling response time (RT) in tasks in which accuracy is below ceiling, given that RTs for incorrect responses are usually not analyzed. Figure 12.1 shows a hypothetical RT distribution for a subject with higher ability (for whom RTs across items are generally

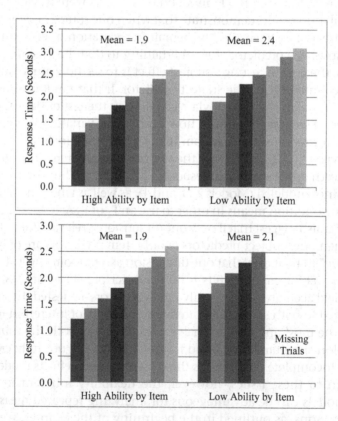

Figure 12.1 Response time distributions by ability: The top panel shows complete data; the bottom panel illustrates bias in mean response time due to incomplete data.

shorter) and for a subject with lower ability (for whom RTs are generally longer). The top panel shows the case where the data are complete (i.e., all items were answered correctly), and in which the RT condition mean would be an appropriate summary of each subject's ability. The bottom panel shows an alternative scenario: If the subject with lower ability provides an incorrect response to the items that would have taken the longest, then the RTs for those missing items (which are definitely *not* missing completely at random here) will not contribute to that subject's condition mean. As a result, the condition mean RT for the lower ability subject may be downwardly biased due to the non-random missing data. This bias in the condition means may unknowingly lead to biased results in analyzing those means.

All may not be lost in the case of non-random missing item responses, however. To continue with our RT example, it might be reasonable to assume that the unobserved values of the missing RTs would be related to the observed data, such as the item predictors (i.e., features that make some items more difficult than others), the subject predictors (i.e., characteristics that might predict how well a subject does in general), and responses from that subject to other items (or responses to that item from other subjects). That is, if a subject tended to have longer RTs to most items, it may be reasonable to assume he or she would have done so on any missing items as well; likewise, it may be reasonable to assume that RT for a missing item would be longer because the other RTs for subjects who did answer the item correctly tended to be longer as well.

To the extent that the probability of missingness can be predicted by predictor variables and other relevant responses, the incomplete data are said to be **missing at random**—this means that after including this predictive information in the model, missing responses are viewed as *conditionally* missing completely at random (such that the missingness is no longer a problem for making correct inferences). This is because the model parameters obtained using likelihood-based estimation are supposed to be optimally reflective of the parameters that would have been estimated had the data been complete (i.e., the missing responses are skipped over in evaluating the multidimensional likelihood for each person, assuming those responses are representative of the overall shape of each dimension). In simulation studies maximum likelihood estimation has been shown to provide unbiased and efficient estimates when the data are in fact missing at random (see Enders, 2010, for a review). Although the assumption of missing at random cannot be formally tested (i.e., because the data we'd need to do so are missing), the inclusion of all relevant item and subject predictors (as well as all available responses from that subject or responses to that item) via crossed random effects models will help in satisfying the assumption of missing at random in order to obtain the least biased model estimates possible.

It is important to note that the predictive information necessary to meet the assumption of missing at random can only be used to the extent that all observed responses actually make it into the model! This is a problem inherent in the F_1 ANOVA model: Any item-level missingness is obscured and assumed missing completely at random because information about which specific responses were missing or why is lost when only condition means are used as outcomes. The same is true for any subject-level missingness in the F_2 ANOVA model. Furthermore, to the extent that item missingness varies across subjects or conditions, condition means will be based on different numbers of responses. Although this unequal reliability is not acknowledged by ANOVA models on condition means, the amount of data contributing to each random effect is taken into account during likelihood estimation of crossed random effects models. Thus, to summarize, rather than reducing power through listwise deletion or analyzing condition means that assume any incomplete responses are missing completely at random, as is required in ANOVA models estimated using least squares, we can utilize crossed random effects models that include all available responses under a more reasonable assumption of missing at random through likelihood-based estimation instead.

2.C. Inclusion of Categorical or Continuous Predictors for Subjects and Items

The second potential limitation of ANOVA models for repeated measures data concerns the specification of predictor effects. ANOVA is used to examine mean differences across levels of a categorical predictor, such as active versus passive sentence voice in our earlier example. Other examples could be the number of items held in memory while completing a second task (e.g., 0, 3, or 6 items) or type of distractors surrounding a visual target (e.g., none, similar, dissimilar). In each of these cases, however, the levels of the predictor are clearly distinct from one another. In contrast, consider one of the other predictor variables from our previous example, verbal fluency. Because verbal fluency was measured continuously *over subjects,* we can include its main and interaction slope effects as a continuous covariate in the F_1 subjects ANOVA (which becomes regression or ANCOVA), given that random subject variation is also included.

But what happens to continuous predictors for item characteristics, such as sentence syntactic complexity in our previous example? Earlier we used an all-too-common solution of dichotomizing syntactic complexity to form categories of "low" and "high" in order to create item conditions for use in an F_1 ANOVA. But then we've introduced measurement error into the predictor, because not all "low" complexity sentences are equally low, and not all "high" complexity sentences are equally high. For instance, given a scale of 1 to 20, a median split at 10 implies that responses to sentences with ratings of 9 and 11 should be just as different as responses to sentences with ratings of 1 and 20, an assumption that is likely to be incorrect. Methodologists uniformly recommend against artificially categorizing a continuous predictor given that it will almost always result in a loss of useful information and can lead to substantially reduced power to detect their effects in some cases, but inflated Type 1 error rates in others (e.g., Cohen, 1983; MacCallum, Zhang, Preacher, & Rucker, 2002; Maxwell & Delaney, 1993). Using only items with extreme levels of the predictor is similarly not recommended for the same reasons (e.g., Preacher, Rucker, MacCallum, & Nicewander, 2005). Clearly an alternative approach is needed that would allow effects of continuous predictors that are measured repeatedly over items to be specified via continuous slopes within the model. Furthermore, the same problem would occur when trying to include a continuous subject predictor into an F_2 items ANOVA (which is why we had dichotomized subject verbal fluency for that model).

There are no straightforward provisions for including continuous predictors pertaining to repeated measures within ANOVA or regression models, although a number of ad-hoc solutions have been developed. One alternative is known as *fixed effects regression* (see Allison, 1994; Lorch & Myers, 1990; Snijders & Bosker, 2012, pp. 45–49; chapter 11 in this text), in which all responses are analyzed, but $N - 1$ dummy indicator variables for N subjects and $N - 1$ subjects by predictor interaction variables are included to control for any within-person residual correlation. Because the dummy indicator variables will account for *all* of the between-subject differences, however, a significant limitation of this approach is that no other subject predictors can then be examined within the model. Likewise, a series of dummy indicator variables included to account for all between-item differences would make it impossible to test effects of any item predictors.

A second alternative is univariate repeated measures ANOVA using modified error terms that properly account for between-subject or between-item variation to assess the significance of fixed effects (Lorch & Myers, 1990). However, given that it is based on least squares estimation, this approach is still limited to random intercepts only (i.e., no random slopes); it also still uses listwise deletion (which assumes any incomplete data are missing completely at random).

Finally, a third alternative is a two-stage approach known as *slopes-as-outcomes* (Lorch & Myers, 1990; Singer & Willett, 2003, pp. 28–44), in which regressions are performed separately for each subject in the first step, and the subject regression estimates are then used as outcomes in a between-subjects analysis (i.e., ANOVA or regression). However, the slopes-as-outcomes method does not account for the differential reliability of the individual regression estimates, which can result in biases in unknown directions. Such two-stage procedures are also statistically inefficient, and have generally been replaced by multilevel models with single-stage estimation.

Crossed random effects models allow main effects of and interactions among categorical or continuous predictors that pertain to subjects, items, or individual trials, thus providing a straightforward solution without the limitations of these ad-hoc approaches. Thus, continuous predictors can be included as such regardless of the sampling dimension they describe and may have linear or nonlinear effects as needed. For instance, the example in the third section of this chapter will illustrate how piecewise slopes can be used to capture both mean differences between groups as well as a linear effect of additional variability within one of the groups.

2.D. Assessing Exchangeability of the Items and Adequacy of Experimental Control

Earlier we saw how the effects of item predictors may be tested incorrectly if not all random item variation is included in the model (and likewise, how effects of subject predictors may be tested incorrectly if not all subject variation is included). In practice, the assessment of item effects is complicated by the extent to which items are *exchangeable* beyond the known item predictors. For example, consider a visual search task in which a subject must find a target X embedded in a field of O distractors. After accounting for the number of distractors (e.g., 5, 10, or 15) and the general location of the target X (e.g., center or periphery of the display), there is little to distinguish one item (i.e., a particular display) from the next within the same condition. When items of the same "type" (as defined by unique combination of the item predictors) do not vary from each other in observed responses, the items can be said to be **exchangeable.** In this example in which the items are created entirely from the two manipulated item features, exchangeability may be a reasonable assumption because the experimenter has purposefully and systematically introduced all of the observed variation across the items. Although manipulated factors usually have clearly distinct factor levels (i.e., grouping variables), they don't have to—the key idea here is that all reasons for item variation are likely to be *known*.

In contrast, in real-world items such as photographs, text passages, or autobiographical memories, the item features of interest (e.g., visual complexity of the photograph, difficulty of the text passage, or strength of the memory) may be measured instead of manipulated, such that it becomes less likely that all items of the same "kind" (i.e., with equal values for their item predictors) can be considered exchangeable. These kinds of items may vary more randomly from each other given that they have been *sampled* from a population of existing items: the domain of all possible photographs, text passages, or memories that could be used in such studies. Furthermore, because the item features may not be under direct experimental control, in addition to the known variation captured by the *measured* item predictors, there is also likely to be variation due to *unknown* factors—additional reasons why the responses to items ostensibly of the type may still differ systematically from each other (e.g., other features of the photographs, text passages, or memories that were not coded for analysis or otherwise controlled for adequately).

Consider from our earlier example the item predictor of active versus passive voice. Can we assume that all active sentences are exactly alike, and that all passive sentences are also exactly alike, and thus that the responses to them would be exactly alike as well? Similarly, would two items with the same level of syntactic complexity (and written in the same voice) necessarily receive the same response? There may be unknown but systematic influences that make some sentences more difficult to read, even after all efforts to equate sentences across conditions.

In repeated measures designs, assuming exchangeability of the items is tantamount to treating items as fixed effects—it assumes that your item predictors can account for *all* of the reasons why responses would differ across items, and thus, that no other random item-specific variation remains within a condition (and that aggregation into condition means does not result in a loss of information). As shown previously, however, all sources of item variation should be in the model (i.e., by including all possible responses and estimating a random effect for systematic item-specific differences). The extent to which that random item variation can be accounted for by the item predictors then becomes a focus of interest. Otherwise, treating items as fixed and exchangeable when they are not can lead to increased Type I error rates for evaluating the significance of item predictors, as was shown by the simulation study earlier.

It's important to note that these concerns about exchangeability of items within conditions apply only when there is more than one item within each condition. If not, all possible item variation is accounted for by including the fixed effects that define the item conditions in the model. For example, if you wished to study children's reactions to toys as a function of toy type (e.g., doll vs. truck) and toy size (e.g., small or large), then at a minimum you would only need a small and large version of one doll and one truck (four toys total). In that case, by including fixed main effects of toy type, toy size, and their interaction, or by including toy type as a four-category predictor (either way, three degrees of for examining the four differences among toys), you would have accounted for all systematic variation across toys (items). In contrast, if multiple exemplars for each condition were used (e.g., five small trucks, five large trucks, five small dolls, five large dolls), then including only the three fixed effects for toy type, toy size, and their interaction presumes that no systematic outcome differences remain among the small trucks, among the large trucks, among the small dolls, and among the large dolls (19 possible degrees of freedom, of which you've spent 3). But what if some of the toys were more novel to the children, more colorful, or otherwise more appealing for systematic reasons besides toy size and type? To the extent that the items differ in their mean responses in unknown ways, this unexplained but systematic variation needs to be specified within the model via a random effect for item (toy).

Finally, a related issue pertains to the adequacy of experimental control of the items. Items such as words are rarely selected arbitrarily—usually great care is taken to ensure that items are balanced across conditions for a plethora of potential confounding variables. Although there is no question that such control procedures can be very useful in limiting the contribution of confounding variables to the obtained item effects, the extent to which these control and counterbalancing procedures were actually successful is rarely examined. This situation can put researchers in a tenuous position—they are left to defend their choices and justify that their method of selection and experimental control was adequate, all the while deflecting criticism about additional factors that could have potentially biased their item effects. ANOVA models conducted on item condition means are rarely used to examine such issues, and thus such arguments are often made on theoretical grounds rather than with empirical evidence.

In contrast, evaluating the adequacy of experimental control is straightforward to do within crossed random effects models. Because all possible responses are modeled, you can include the item predictor variables of interest, as well as any item control variables or additional potentially confounding variables that were measured but that were not controlled for by design. Two issues are then relevant. First, to what extent do the item control variables explain any of the remaining item-to-item variation? The extent to which random item variation remains after including all known item predictors and control variables—that is, the extent to which items can be considered exchangeable—is thus a testable hypothesis within a crossed random effects model. The example in the third section of this chapter illustrates how to do so. Second, to what extent are the effects of the item predictors unaffected by the inclusion of item control variables? If the control procedures were adequate, then those item effects should not change after also including the effects of the item control variables in the model. Further criticism about additional item (or subject) variables that should have been controlled for can be addressed empirically, so long as such those variables were measured for each item (or subject). Regardless of the outcome, however, including potentially confounding variables in the model and assessing the extent of their influence provides an empirical means with which to bolster a theoretical argument about the adequacy of experimental control. Providing such empirical evidence is yet another significant advantage of crossed random effects models over ANOVA models on aggregated data.

2.E. Testing Hypotheses About Variability

A final issue relates to describing variability. Research hypotheses are frequently, if not almost always, centered on the detection of differences in the mean level of an outcome between subjects or between groups. For example, the efficacy of an intervention or experimental manipulation is usually assessed as the extent to which mean differences are found between groups or between experimental conditions. Within-group variation in such cases is usually regarded as a statistical nuisance— as the noise from which the signal of an effect must be separated. But differential within-group variation need not be regarded as merely as a nuisance. The processes under study might exert their effects not only on the mean level of an outcome, but also on the variation of that outcome within groups or within persons, in which case group differences in *subject variability* may also be of direct interest. The assumption that residual variance is the same across groups is called *homogeneity of variance (homoscedasticity)*. Finding differences across groups in the amount of variance is referred to as *heterogeneity of variance (heteroscedasticity)*. Analytic methods for addressing violations of homogeneity of variance within regression and ANOVA have focused primarily on obtaining correct inferences about mean differences in such cases (e.g., Aguinis & Pierce, 1998; DeShon & Alexander, 1996; Grissom, 2000), but generally do not focus on describing or predicting that differential variability. As first demonstrated in chapters 7 and 8, multilevel models can include parameters for heterogeneity of variance in order to test hypotheses about the reasons for the heterogeneity; we will see in this chapter's example how predictors of variability can be incorporated into crossed random effects models as well.

Finally, crossed random effects models provide a means to test hypotheses about *subject variability in predictor effects.* We emphasized earlier how crossed random effects models can simultaneously account for all sources of sampling variation (i.e., treat both subjects and items as random). We now clarify: The crossed random effects models so far have been simplified versions that account only for systematic variation *with respect to the mean response.* That is, the subject random intercept variance captures subject differences in their mean response, and the item random intercept variance captures item differences in their mean response. Any remaining variation pertaining to the subject by item interaction then forms the residual variance. We have limited the model thus far to maintain the analogy to analysis of variance, in which only intercepts can have random effects. Yet systematic sources of variation may still remain because subjects may differ from each other in other ways besides in their mean responses—subjects may differ from each other systematically in their response to the item predictor variables as well.

Using the previous example, for instance, in addition to differences in overall sentence response times across subjects, the difference in response time as a function of active versus passive sentence voice could be larger for some subjects than for others—this is a testable hypothesis via a random slope across subjects for the effect of sentence voice. Random slopes allow subjects to each have their own effect of the predictor, and the model is augmented to include a variance component for these subject-specific slope differences. Furthermore, we can then test whether subject variables can account for these between-subject differences in the effects of item predictors. Continuing our example, it may be that subjects with greater verbal fluency show less of a difference in response time between sentences of active and passive voice. This hypothesis could be specified as a subject fluency by sentence voice interaction, and we could then evaluate the extent to which the subject random slope variance for the effect of sentence voice is reduced after controlling for the interaction. Although such an interaction can be estimated within an F_1 ANOVA model, it could only include an item predictor that is categorical and not continuous (given the need to form item condition means). Furthermore, there would be no formal description of how much of the residual variance was due to between-subject differences in the item effect in the first place. Both of these features are possible to include in crossed random effects models.

3. A Crossed Random Effects Analysis of Subjects and Items

We now examine an extended example to illustrate the concepts presented in this chapter. These data were collected in a study that examined the speed with which changes to digital photographs of 51 driving scenes were detected by 96 younger adults and 57 older adults. Each item was presented for 60 seconds, or until the subject responded, whichever came first, and the outcome for each trial was the natural log of response time in seconds (RT) to detect the change. For further study details, see Hoffman and Rovine (2007). The predictor variables for the items (i.e., the driving scenes) were the *relevance of the change to driving* (i.e., the extent to which the driver in the scene would need to pay attention to the changed object) and the *visual salience of the change* (i.e., how conspicuous the change was within the scene). These item predictors of change relevance and change salience were obtained from a previous study in which separate subjects rated each change on a scale of 0 to 5 for both attributes; ratings were then averaged to create one rating for relevance and one rating for salience for each item. The only predictor variable for subjects was age. The analysis was originally planned as a 2 (age group: young, old) by 2 (change relevance: low, high) by 2 (change salience: low, high) mixed factorial F_1 ANOVA, but several problems related to the previous discussion would need be addressed in doing so.

First, how should the predictor effects be specified in the model? Although there were two distinct age groups sampled (18–32 years and 63–86 years), the older adults are likely to be considerably more heterogeneous in their RTs than the younger adults. As such, treating age as a strictly dichotomous variable would likely misrepresent the mean RT differences among older individuals varying in age (i.e., it would assume a 63-year-old would have the same expected RT as an 86-year-old). Separating the older adults into two groups of "young-old" (i.e., under age 75) and "old-old" (i.e., age 75 or older), as is often done in experimental studies of aging, would also be inappropriate, because this assumes that a "young-old" 74-year-old is more like a 63-year-old than like an "old-old" 75-year-old. We will instead specify the effect of age on RT as a semi-continuous or *piecewise* effect, as was originally introduced for the effect of time in chapter 6. To accomplish this, the continuous age variable is re-coded into two variables, *older group*, in which persons 18 to 32 were coded as 0 and persons 65 and older were coded as 1, and *years over 65*, in which persons 18 to 32 were again coded as 0, but persons 65 and older were coded as their current age minus 65. Then, the main effect of age on RT can be represented with two piecewise effects: The dummy code of *older group* for the mean difference between younger adults and 65-year-olds, and the slope of *years over 65* for the additional increase in RT per year of age over 65. Additionally, because older adults are often more variable from one another than are younger adults (i.e., greater between-subject, level-2 variation), and also show more variability in their own responses across items than do younger adults (i.e., greater within-subject, level-1 variation), differential variability across age groups should be examined in the model as well.

A related problem is how to most accurately capture the effects of the item predictors for change relevance and change salience: Given that they were measured in natural scenes instead of experimentally manipulated, they each range continuously from 0 to 5. An assignment of items into "low" and "high" conditions (as would be needed for an F_1 ANOVA) assumes that all items within each condition would have equivalent RTs. But such distortion of any item (or subject) predictors is unnecessary in a crossed random effects model, which can easily accommodate effects of categorical or continuous predictors that pertain to subjects, items, or their interaction.

Finally, there are two other reasons to analyze all possible item responses rather than aggregate items into condition means. First, because the items were natural scenes that likely varied in a number of unmeasured dimensions besides change relevance and change salience, it would be inappropriate to aggregate these items into condition means that artificially eliminate all this unexplained item variability from the model. So, rather than assuming exchangeability by treating items as fixed effects, we will instead allow for all item variation in the model via an item random intercept. Second, given that the trials in which the change was not detected in 60 seconds were counted as incorrect (because no RT was available), RTs are likely to have been missing for the most difficult items. Analyzing all available RTs in a crossed random effects model takes advantage of predictors of missingness (i.e., change relevance and salience, subject age, and other subject and item responses) to help satisfy the assumption of missing at random. This should result in more accurate results than would be given by an F_1 ANOVA model, as well as potentially greater statistical power given that no listwise deletion of subjects would occur.

3.A. Partitioning Sources of Variation for Subjects and Items

The first step in the analysis should be to examine to what extent there are systematic mean differences across subjects and across items—whether subjects and items both need to have random effects. We can then examine how much of those subject and item differences can be explained by subject and item predictors in conditional models. Given the small item sample size (N_{item} = 51, $N_{subject}$ = 153, N_{total} = 7,646 instead of 7,803 because RT was missing for 157 incorrect trials), we will use restricted maximum likelihood (REML) estimation to prevent any downward bias in the variance estimates that would occur if using ML instead. As usual, the significance of fixed effects will be evaluated via their Wald test p-values, and the significance of random effects will be evaluated using -2ΔLL tests (i.e., likelihood ratio tests using degrees of freedom equal to the difference in the number of estimated parameters) and information criteria (AIC and BIC) between models that include the same fixed effects.

To begin, we estimate an empty means model with no subject or item random effects (i.e., just a single residual error term) as a baseline model, as shown in Equation (12.8):

$$RT_{tis} = \gamma_{000} + e_{tis} \tag{12.8}$$

in which RT_{tis} is the log-transformed response time in seconds for trial t to item i from subject s. As before, the t index is not strictly necessary given that a trial is just the unique combination of subject and item, but is included to illustrate how effects of trial-specific predictors could be accommodated. Thus, the first subscript t indexes predictors pertaining to the specific trials, the second subscript i indexes predictors pertaining to the items, and the third subscript s indexes the predictors pertaining to the subjects. The model for the means has only the fixed intercept, estimated as γ_{00} = 1.61, which is the grand mean RT across all trials. The model for the variance only has e_{tis}, the residual deviation from the sample mean RT for trial t, item i, and subject s, whose variance was estimated as σ_e^2 = 0.69. This empty means, e-only model specifies that the e_{tis} residuals are uncorrelated—that is, it assumes that no systematic differences between subjects or between items are present. Although this model is essentially the worst-fitting model possible, its purpose is to provide a baseline with which to compare more complex models.

A random intercept for subjects is added next, as seen in Equation (12.9):

$$RT_{tis} = \gamma_{000} + U_{00s} + e_{tis} \tag{12.9}$$

in which the model for the variance now also includes U_{00s}, a random intercept for subject s, which is the deviation of that subject's mean RT from the grand mean of the subject RT means of γ_{000} = 1.62. The e_{tis} level-1 residuals now represent the within-subject deviation from the subject RT mean for trial t and item i, and are thus now assumed to be uncorrelated across observations *after* considering from which subject the RT was observed. In other words, Equation (12.9) provides the same empty means, random intercept (for subjects) two-level model that was introduced in chapter 3. However, we are using composite, single-level notation here instead, given that two-level notation gets to be cumbersome once there is more than one level-2 unit to consider.

Because the empty means, e-only model in Equation (12.8) is nested within the empty means, subject random intercept model in Equation (12.9), the improvement in fit from adding the subject random intercept variance can be assessed by comparing their –2 log-likelihood (–2LL) values, or *deviance* values. As introduced in chapter 3, the difference of the –2LL values (–2ΔLL) is distributed as a χ^2 with degrees of freedom equal to the difference in the number of estimated model parameters (so $df = 1$ here). But as described in chapter 5, when adding variances whose possible values are bounded at 0, the –2ΔLL is actually distributed as a mixture of χ^2 distributions with df and $df - 1$, and so using the original df creates a slightly conservative test (which we will acknowledge when relevant by adding a ~ in front of the test df).

For these data, the empty means model with a subject random intercept variance fit significantly better than the empty means model with only a residual variance, –2ΔLL(~1) = 1,746, $p < .001$. The variance of the U_{00s} subject random intercepts was $\tau^2_{U00sub} = 0.17$, and the variance of the e_{tis} residuals was $\sigma^2_e = 0.52$. We can calculate an intraclass correlation for the proportion of total RT variation due to subject mean differences as ICC $= \tau^2_{U00sub} / (\tau^2_{U00sub} + \sigma^2_e) = 0.17 / (0.17 + 0.52) = .25$. Thus, 25% of what was unexplained residual variation is now due to between-subject differences in mean RT—this is significantly different from 0, as indicated by the significant decrease in –2LL from adding the subject random intercept variance.

A random intercept for items is added next, creating an empty means, crossed random effects model, as seen in Equation (12.10):

$$RT_{tis} = \gamma_{000} + U_{00s} + U_{0i0} + e_{tis} \tag{12.10}$$

whose results are shown in the first columns of Table 12.3. The model for the variance now includes U_{0i0}, a random intercept for item i, which is the deviation of that item's mean RT from the predicted mean RT of $\gamma_{000} + U_{00s}$. Likewise, the U_{00s} random intercept for subject s is now the deviation of that subject's mean RT from the predicted mean RT given by $\gamma_{000} + U_{0i0}$. Thus, subjects and items are **crossed random effects** at level 2. The e_{tis} level-1 residuals now represent the within-subject and within-item deviation from the predicted mean for trial t—remaining variation due to a subject by item interaction—and are now assumed to be uncorrelated after considering from which subject *and* from which item the RT was observed.

The addition of the item random intercept variance significantly improved model fit, –2ΔLL(~1) = 1,899, $p < .001$. The level-2 item random intercept variance was $\tau^2_{U00item} = 0.13$, the level-2 subject random intercept variance was $\tau^2_{U00sub} = 0.18$, and the level-1 residual variance was $\sigma^2_e = 0.39$, creating a total RT variance of 0.70 given

Table 12.3 Results for crossed subjects and items example conditional models with random intercepts only. Bold values are $p < .05$.

Model Effects	Equation 12.10			Equation 12.11			Equation 12.12		
	Est	SE	p <	Est	SE	p <	Est	SE	p <
Model for the Means									
γ_{000} Intercept	**1.623**	0.061	.001	**1.613**	0.057	.001	**1.312**	0.048	.001
γ_{010} Item Change Relevance				**−0.050**	0.024	.040	**−0.050**	0.024	.039
γ_{020} Item Change Salience				**−0.138**	0.042	.002	**−0.138**	0.042	.002
γ_{030} Item Relevance by Salience				−0.011	0.020	.569	−0.011	0.020	.568
γ_{001} Subject is Younger vs. Older							**0.590**	0.056	.001
γ_{002} Older Subject Years Over 65							**0.020**	0.004	.001
Model for the Variance									
σ^2_e Residual Variance	**0.390**	0.006	.001	**0.390**	0.006	.001	**0.390**	0.006	.001
$\tau^2_{U00item}$ Item Random Intercept Variance	**0.126**	0.026	.001	**0.094**	0.020	.001	**0.094**	0.020	.001
τ^2_{U00sub} Subject Random Intercept Variance	**0.180**	0.022	.001	**0.180**	0.022	.001	**0.023**	0.004	.001

that these sources of variance are orthogonal (i.e., no covariances are allowed among them). Thus, approximately 26% of the total RT variation is still due to between-subject differences in mean RT (τ^2_{U00sub}), but now approximately 18% is due to between-item variation in mean RT ($\tau^2_{U00item}$), with the remaining 56% as unaccounted-for residual variation representing the subject by item interaction (σ^2_e). Thus, what was unexplained residual variation has now been partly partitioned into systematic variation due to item mean differences, in the same way that the original unexplained residual variation was first partitioned into systematic variation due to subject mean differences.

Finally, to describe the size of the random variation across subjects and items, we can compute 95% random effects confidence intervals as: fixed intercept ±1.96*SQRT(random intercept variance). Using this formula with τ^2_{U00sub} as the random intercept variance, 95% of the individual subject RT means are expected to fall between 0.79 and 2.45. Using $\tau^2_{U00item}$ as the random intercept variance, 95% of the individual item RT means are expected to fall between 0.93 and 2.32. Thus, although there was somewhat greater variation between subjects than between items, both sources of variation are significant—and so random intercepts for both subjects and items should be included in the model along with σ^2_e residual variance.

3.B. Examining Predictors of Item Variation

After examining the need for both subject and item random intercepts, we can now examine the predictors of interest, starting with the item predictors of change relevance and change salience (which each ranged from 0 to 5). Each predictor was centered at 3 to facilitate interpretation of the intercept and their simple main effects, as shown in Equation (12.11):

$$\begin{aligned}
\text{RT}_{tis} = {}&\gamma_{000} + \gamma_{010}\left(\text{Relevance}_i - 3\right) + \gamma_{020}\left(\text{Salience}_i - 3\right) \\
&+ \gamma_{030}\left(\text{Relevance}_i - 3\right)\left(\text{Salience}_i - 3\right) + U_{00s} + U_{0i0} + e_{tis}
\end{aligned} \tag{12.11}$$

for which results are shown in the second columns of Table 12.3. In the model for the means, the fixed intercept $\gamma_{000} = 1.61$ is the expected RT specifically for an item with relevance = 3 and salience = 3. For the other coefficients, the first subscript t indexes predictors pertaining to the specific trials, the second subscript i indexes predictors pertaining to the items, and the third subscript s indexes the predictors pertaining to the subjects. In this model, all predictors are for items only, and thus the first and third subscripts for each fixed effect are 0. Furthermore, given their interaction term, the main effects of change relevance and change salience are each conditional on the 0 value of the other (in which 0 = 3 for each centered predictor). The simple main effect of change relevance indicates that, specifically for an item of salience = 3, RT is expected to be significantly lower by $\gamma_{010} = -0.05$ for every one-unit higher relevance. Likewise, the simple main effect of change salience indicates that, specifically for an item of relevance = 3, RT is expected to be significantly lower by $\gamma_{020} = -0.14$ for every one-unit higher salience. Thus, RTs were significantly faster for items whose changes are more relevant to driving and more visually salient. The nonsignificant relevance by salience interaction indicates that the relevance slope became nonsignificantly more negative by γ_{030} = −0.01 for every one-unit higher salience, or that the salience slope became nonsignificantly more negative by γ_{030} = −0.01 for every one-unit higher relevance. However, we will retain the nonsignificant interaction for now so that we can test higher-order effects involving the relevance by salience interaction in subsequent models.

In the model for the variance, two of the terms carry the same interpretation: The U_{00s} subject random intercept still represents all between-subject variation in mean RT, and the e_{tis} residual still represents all unexplained subject by item interaction variation. After adding item predictors, however, the U_{0i0} item random intercept now represents *leftover* item variance after accounting for the item effects of relevance, salience, and their interaction—the between-item variation that would have been artificially removed from an F_1 ANOVA on item condition means. It is the presence of this remaining between-item variation that allows us to properly test the effects of the item predictors in the first place. The question we are asking is, of the total observed between-item variation in mean RT, how much have we predicted by change relevance and change salience? To provide an answer, we can calculate a *pseudo-R^2* for the proportion reduction in the item random intercept variance relative to the previous model with no item predictors as: pseudo-R^2_{Item} = (0.13 − 0.09) / 0.13 = .25. Thus, of the 18% of the total RT variance originally due to between-item mean differences in the empty model, 25% of it can be predicted by change relevance, change salience, and their interaction.

We can test whether the unexplained item random intercept variance that remains is significantly different from 0 by comparing the current model to a constrained model in which the item random intercept variance has been removed (i.e., no U_{0i0}). The constrained model fit significantly worse, $-2\Delta LL(\sim1)$ = 1,358, $p < .001$, suggesting that substantial item variability remains. In other words, items are *not* exchangeable after controlling for change relevance and change salience— systematic (but unexplained) item-specific mean RT differences still exist, and so the item random intercept variance should remain the model. Finally, as seen in Table 12.3, inclusion of the item predictors had no impact on the amount of subject random intercept variance (τ^2_{U00sub}) or residual variance (σ^2_e), which is expected given that the item predictors by themselves cannot explain between-subject variation or subject by item interaction variation.

3.C. Examining Predictors of Subject Variation

We next examine the subject predictors for age, as shown in Equation (12.12):

$$
\begin{aligned}
RT_{tis} = {} & \gamma_{000} + \gamma_{010}\left(\text{Relevance}_i - 3\right) + \gamma_{020}\left(\text{Salience}_i - 3\right) \\
& + \gamma_{030}\left(\text{Relevance}_i - 3\right)\left(\text{Salience}_i - 3\right) + \gamma_{001}\left(\text{OlderGroup}_s\right) \\
& + \gamma_{002}\left(\text{YearsOver65}_s\right) + U_{00s} + U_{0i0} + e_{tis}
\end{aligned}
\tag{12.12}
$$

in which age has been represented as a piecewise effect as described previously, and for which results are shown in the third columns of Table 12.3. In the model for the means, the fixed intercept of $\gamma_{000} = 1.31$ is now represents the expected RT for an item of relevance = 3 and salience = 3 *specifically for a younger adult.* The effects of relevance, salience, and their interaction (γ_{010}, γ_{020}, and γ_{030}) can be interpreted the same as in the previous model. In Equation (12.12), because the two new predictors are subject variables, their fixed effects have 0's for the first and second subscripts. The main effect of older age group indicates that RT for adults age 65 is expected to be significantly higher by $\gamma_{001} = 0.59$ than RT for younger adults. The main effect of years over 65 in the older adults indicates that RT is expected to be significantly higher by $\gamma_{002} = 0.02$ for every year over age 65. As seen in Table 12.3, relative to the item predictors model in Equation (12.11), these two age effects reduced the subject random intercept variance by: pseudo- $R_{sub}^2 = (0.18 - 0.02) / 0.18 = .87$. Thus, of the 26% of the total RT variance originally due to between-subject differences in the empty model, 87% of it can be predicted by age.

As we did previously for the item variance, we can test whether the subject random intercept variance that remains is significantly different from 0 by comparing the current model to a constrained model without the subject random intercept variance (no U_{00s}). The constrained model fit significantly worse, $-2\Delta LL(\sim 1) = 227$, $p < .001$, suggesting that substantial subject variability remains after controlling for age, and so the subject random intercept variance should remain in the model. Finally, adding the age effects had no impact on the amount of item random intercept variance ($\tau_{U00item}^2$) or residual variance (σ_e^2), as expected given that subject predictors by themselves cannot explain item variation or subject by item interaction variation.

3.D. Examining Subject Differences in the Effects of Item Predictors

Now that fixed effects for both item and subject predictors have been included in the model, we can also examine to what extent the effects of the item predictors show systematic individual differences by adding subject random slopes for the item predictors to the model. Based on the idea that the effect of change salience may differ between younger and older adults, we begin with the random slope for the effect of change salience, as shown in Equation (12.13):

$$
\begin{aligned}
RT_{tis} = {} & \gamma_{000} + \gamma_{010}\left(\text{Relevance}_i - 3\right) + \gamma_{020}\left(\text{Salience}_i - 3\right) \\
& + \gamma_{030}\left(\text{Relevance}_i - 3\right)\left(\text{Salience}_i - 3\right) + \gamma_{001}\left(\text{OlderGroup}_s\right) \qquad (12.13) \\
& + \gamma_{002}\left(\text{YearsOver65}_s\right) + U_{00s} + U_{02s}\left(\text{Salience}_i - 3\right) + U_{0i0} + e_{tis}
\end{aligned}
$$

whose results are shown in the first set of columns in Table 12.4. The model for the variance now includes U_{02s}, a random slope for the effect of salience for subject s, which is the deviation of that subject's slope from the fixed salience slope γ_{020}, and whose variance across subjects is denoted as τ_{U02sub}^2. Although not shown

Table 12.4 Results for crossed subjects and items example conditional models with random slopes. Bold values are $p < .05$.

Model Effects		Equation 12.13			Equation 12.14			Equation 12.15		
		Est	SE	p <	Est	SE	p <	Est	SE	p <
Model for the Means										
γ_{000}	Intercept	**1.312**	0.048	.001	**1.304**	0.048	.001	**1.304**	0.047	.001
γ_{010}	Item Change Relevance	**−0.050**	0.024	.039	**−0.064**	0.024	.010	**−0.064**	0.024	.010
γ_{020}	Item Change Salience	**−0.138**	0.042	.002	**−0.143**	0.043	.002	**−0.143**	0.043	.002
γ_{030}	Relevance by Salience	−0.012	0.020	.567	−0.003	0.020	.893	−0.003	0.020	.894
γ_{001}	Subject is Younger vs. Older	**0.590**	0.056	.001	**0.607**	0.056	.001	**0.618**	0.071	.001
γ_{002}	Older Subject Years Over 65	**0.020**	0.004	.001	**0.021**	0.004	.001	**0.020**	0.006	.001
γ_{011}	Relevance by Age Group				0.014	0.015	.350	**0.038**	0.009	.001
γ_{012}	Relevance by Years Over 65				0.002	0.001	.068			
γ_{021}	Salience by Age Group				−0.015	0.031	.627	0.013	0.017	.460
γ_{022}	Salience by Years Over 65				0.003	0.002	.291			
γ_{031}	Relevance by Salience by Age Group				**−0.025**	0.013	.049	**−0.025**	0.007	.001
γ_{032}	Relevance by Salience by Years Over 65				0.000	0.001	.967			
Model for the Variance										
σ^2_e	Residual Variance: Both	**0.387**	0.006	.001	**0.385**	0.006	.001			
σ^2_e	Residual Variance: Younger							**0.321**	0.007	.001
σ^2_e	Residual Variance: Older							**0.499**	0.014	.001
$\tau^2_{U00item}$	Item Random Intercept Variance	**0.094**	0.020	.001	**0.094**	0.020	.001	**0.095**	0.020	.001
τ^2_{U00sub}	Subject Random Intercept Variance: Both	**0.023**	0.004	.001	**0.023**	0.004	.001			

(Continued)

Table 12.4 (Continued)

Model Effects	Equation 12.13			Equation 12.14			Equation 12.15		
	Est	SE	p <	Est	SE	p <	Est	SE	p <
τ^2_{U00sub} Subject Random Intercept Variance: Younger							**0.011**	0.003	.001
τ^2_{U00sub} Subject Random Intercept Variance: Older							**0.045**	0.011	.001
τ^2_{U00sub} Subject Random Salience Slope Variance: Both	**0.002**	0.001	.009	**0.002**	0.001	.019			
τ^2_{U02sub} Subject Random Salience Slope Variance: Younger							0.002	0.001	.051
τ^2_{U02sub} Subject Random Salience Slope Variance: Older							0.003	0.002	.087
$\tau^2_{U00,02sub}$ Subject Random Intercept-Slope Covariance: Both	−0.000	0.001	.730	−0.000	0.001	.761			
$\tau^2_{U00,02sub}$ Subject Random Intercept-Slope Covariance: Younger							−0.001	0.001	.238
$\tau^2_{U00,02sub}$ Subject Random Intercept-Slope Covariance: Older							0.001	0.003	.713

in Equation (12.13), a covariance between the subject random intercept and random salience slope has also been added (denoted as $\tau_{U00,02sub}$), but no covariance is allowed with the item random intercept variance or with the residual variance.

The new subject random salience slope variance modifies the interpretation of two other variances. First, as explained in chapter 4, the addition of a subject slope variance implies that the amount of subject random intercept variance will vary across levels of the predictor with the random slope. Accordingly, the subject random intercept variance (τ^2_{U00sub}) now represents subject variation in mean RT *specifically when salience is at 3*. Furthermore, the residual variance (σ^2_e) will be smaller because part of what was unexplained subject by item interaction variation is now due to systematic between-subject differences in the effect of item salience, which becomes a separate variance component for another type of subject dependency. As a result, we can no longer compare our variance estimates from this with those from previous models.

To assess whether the U_{02s} subject random salience slope variance (τ^2_{U02sub}) differs significantly from 0, we can compare the −2LL for this random slope model in Equation (12.13) with the −2LL from the previous model in Equation (12.12) without the random slope (but with the same fixed effects in the model for the means in each). Adding a variance for the subject random salience slopes (and their covariance with the subject random intercepts) significantly improved model fit, −2ΔLL(~2) = 8.4, p = .015 (and the smaller AIC and BIC concur), indicating that subjects differ significantly in how much item salience affected their RTs. We can use a 95% random effects confidence interval to describe the size of the random slope variation, calculated as the fixed salience slope ±1.96*SQRT(random salience slope variance). The average salience slope given by the fixed effect was γ_{020} = −0.14 (p = .002) with a random variance of τ^2_{U02sub} = 0.002, such that 95% of the individual subject salience slopes are expected to fall between −0.23 and −0.04. So, although most subjects are expected to respond faster to items of higher salience, the extent of this salience benefit varies significantly by person.

We then examined a subject random slope for item relevance by adding U_{01s}(Relevance$_i$ − 3) to the model shown in Equation (12.13). Adding a variance for the subject random relevance slopes (and their covariances with the subject random intercepts and the subject random salience slopes) did not significantly improve model fit, −2ΔLL(~3) = 2.8, p = .432 (with a smaller BIC but a larger AIC), indicating no significant individual differences in the effect of item relevance on RT. Thus, we retain subject random effects for the intercept and salience slope only.

Given significant subject variation in the effect of salience, the next step is to try and predict that variation with subject predictors—in this example, we will use the piecewise effects of age. In addition, although significant subject variation was not found for the relevance slope, it is still possible that the effect of relevance could vary *systematically* as a function of age, but just not *randomly* across subjects otherwise (see chapter 7 for a discussion of effects that are *fixed, systematically varying,* or *random*). The same can be said for the interaction of relevance by salience— it could vary systematically as a function of age, although not randomly otherwise.

Thus, interactions of older age group and years over 65 with each item effect (relevance, salience, and relevance by salience) were then tested, as shown in Equation (12.14):

$$
\begin{aligned}
RT_{tis} = {} & \gamma_{000} + \gamma_{010}\left(\text{Relevance}_i - 3\right) + \gamma_{020}\left(\text{Salience}_i - 3\right) \\
& + \gamma_{030}\left(\text{Relevance}_i - 3\right)\left(\text{Salience}_i - 3\right) \\
& + \gamma_{001}\left(\text{OlderGroup}_s\right) + \gamma_{002}\left(\text{YearsOver65}_s\right) \\
& \underline{+\left[\gamma_{011}\left(\text{OlderGroup}_s\right) + \gamma_{012}\left(\text{YearsOver65}_s\right)\right]\left(\text{Relevance}_i - 3\right)} \\
& \underline{+\left[\gamma_{021}\left(\text{OlderGroup}_s\right) + \gamma_{022}\left(\text{YearsOver65}_s\right)\right]\left(\text{Salience}_i - 3\right)} \\
& \underline{+\left[\gamma_{031}\left(\text{OlderGroup}_s\right) + \gamma_{032}\left(\text{YearsOver65}_s\right)\right]\left(\text{Relevance}_i - 3\right)\left(\text{Salience}_i - 3\right)} \\
& + U_{00s} + U_{02s}\left(\text{Salience}_i - 3\right) + U_{0i0} + e_{tis}
\end{aligned}
\tag{12.14}
$$

in which the new interactions with age are underlined. Results for this model are shown in the second set of columns in Table 12.4. In the model for the means, the fixed intercept γ_{000} is still the expected mean RT for an item of relevance = 3 and salience = 3 for a younger adult, but now the effects of item relevance, salience, and their interaction (γ_{010}, γ_{020}, and γ_{030}) are also their simple effects for the younger age group. Likewise, the effects for subject older age group and years over 65 (γ_{001} and γ_{002}) are now their simple effects when relevance = 3 and salience = 3.

The interpretation of the new interaction terms can be inferred through their subscripts. Terms with a 1 in the second subscript are for interactions with relevance, such that γ_{011} is the interaction of older age group by relevance and γ_{012} is the interaction of years over 65 by relevance, which can be interpreted as the difference in the relevance slope for the older age group and per year over 65, respectively. Likewise, terms with a 2 in the second subscript are for interactions with salience, such that γ_{021} is the interaction of older age group by salience and γ_{022} is the interaction of years over 65 by salience, which can be interpreted as the difference in the salience slope for the older age group and per year over 65, respectively. Finally, terms with a 3 in the second subscript are for interactions with relevance and salience, such that γ_{031} is the interaction of older age group by relevance by salience and γ_{032} is the interaction of years over 65 by relevance by salience, which can be interpreted as the difference in the relevance by salience two-way interaction for the older age group and per year over 65, respectively.

The model for the variance with respect to subjects includes the U_{00s} subject random intercept, which represents between-subject differences in mean RT after controlling for age, and the U_{02s} subject random salience slope, which represents between-subject differences in the effect of salience, now also after controlling for the age (via the γ_{021} and γ_{022} interactions). The model also includes the U_{0i0} item random intercept, which represents between-item differences in mean RT after controlling for relevance, salience, and their interaction, and the e_{tis} residual, which represents the subject by item interaction variation after controlling for all of the above.

In terms of explaining each source of variance, as seen in Table 12.4, we would expect no real reductions in the subject or item random intercept variances (τ^2_{U02sub} and $\tau^2_{U00item}$) after adding the age-related interaction terms because they represent *constant* mean differences in RT (between persons or between items). Instead, we expect the other two variance components to be reduced by the age by item predictor interactions. First, the subject random salience slope variance (τ^2_{U02sub}) captures between-subject differences in the effect of salience, 15% of which was explainable by age, as determined by the reduction in salience slope variance: pseudo-R^2_{sal} = (0.00241 – 0.00205) / 0.00241 = .15. But because no subject random slope variances were included for the effect of relevance or for the relevance by salience interaction in the model, any systematic variance with respect to those effects is still contained in the residual variance (σ^2_e). In this case, the interactions of age with relevance and with relevance by salience reduced the residual variance by 0.4%, also as determined via pseudo-R^2_e = (0.387 – 0.385) / 0.387 = .004.

The results in Table 12.4 suggest that we can simplify the model in Equation (12.14). The three-way interaction of years over 65 by relevance by salience was not significant, so it was removed first. The three-way interaction of older group by relevance by salience was significant, however, and as such it was retained, along with its three lower-order, two-way interactions (older group by relevance, older group by salience, and relevance by salience). The two-way interactions of relevance by years over 65 and salience by years over 65 were not significant, and they were removed sequentially as well. Finally, we can test whether the subject random salience slope variation that remains is significantly different from 0 (and thus needs to remain in the model) by comparing the current reduced model to a constrained model in which the variance of the subject random salience slopes and their covariance with the subject random intercepts have been removed. The constrained model fit significantly worse, $-2\Delta LL(\sim2) = 6.7$, $p = .035$, suggesting that substantial subject salience slope variability remains. So, because there are additional reasons why the effect of salience differs between subjects besides age, we will retain the subject random salience slope representing this additional subject dependency in the model.

The resulting conditional model is shown in Equation (12.15):

$$
\begin{aligned}
RT_{tis} = {} & \gamma_{000} + \gamma_{010}(\text{Relevance}_i - 3) + \gamma_{020}(\text{Salience}_i - 3) \\
& + \gamma_{030}(\text{Relevance}_i - 3)(\text{Salience}_i - 3) \\
& + \gamma_{001}(\text{OlderGroup}_s) + \gamma_{002}(\text{YearsOver65}_s) \\
& + \gamma_{011}(\text{OlderGroup}_s)(\text{Relevance}_i - 3) \\
& + \gamma_{021}(\text{OlderGroup}_s)(\text{Salience}_i - 3) \\
& + \gamma_{031}(\text{OlderGroup}_s)(\text{Relevance}_i - 3)(\text{Salience}_i - 3) \\
& + U_{00s} + U_{02s}(\text{Salience}_i - 3) + U_{0i0} + e_{tis}
\end{aligned}
\tag{12.15}
$$

although we aren't quite done yet! Our last step is to consider age differences in variability.

3.E. Examining Subject Differences in Variability

Finally, the inclusion of the effects of fixed effects of age in the model for the means allows the intercept for the level of RT and the effects of other predictors on RT to vary as a function of age. In this case, however, we also expect age to have an impact on the *variance* as well as the means. Specifically, because older adults were expected show more between-subject variation and more within-subject variation in their RTs than were younger adults, we tested whether allowing separate variance components by age group would improve model fit (as was first presented in chapter 7). However, because we already have a crossed random effects model with a fairly complex variance structure, we forgo attempting to estimate another subject-level variance component for the scale factor representing individual differences in residual variance.

In this case, because our predictor of variance heterogeneity is a grouping variable, we can specify separate variances per age group directly in the program syntax. First, expanding the model for the variance to include separate residual variances (i.e., a separate **R** matrix) by age group resulted in a significant improvement in fit, $-2\Delta LL(1) = 170$, $p < .001$, such that the older adults had greater trial-level variability than the younger adults. In a second step, subject random intercept variances, subject random salience slope variances, and intercept–slope covariances (i.e., a separate **G** matrix) were then estimated separately for each age group. The difference in the model deviances from adding the three extra variance components was significant, $-2\Delta LL(3) = 21$, $p < .001$, such that the older adults also showed greater between-subject variability in their intercepts and in their effects of salience than the younger adults. These findings provide support for our hypothesis about age

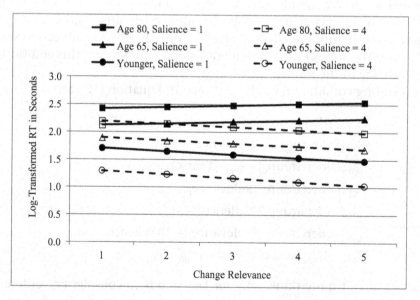

Figure 12.2 Three-way interaction of age group, change relevance, and change salience.

group differences in variability in RT as well as in mean RT. Results for this final model including different **G** and **R** matrices per age group are shown in the third columns of Table 12.4 and depicted in Figure 12.2; the specific model parameters are interpreted in the sample results section that follows.

4. Chapter Summary

Although variants of analysis of variance (ANOVA) are often used to analyze aggregated data from repeated measures designs, this chapter described why alternative approaches should be considered as well. Crossed random effects models offer many significant advantages for analyzing data in which items, stimuli, or trials are measured repeatedly over subjects, as illustrated by the chapter example. Specifically, we were able to model both subjects and items as random effects simultaneously, ensuring appropriate tests of predictors pertaining to each. We were also able to assess to what extent our predictor variables accounted for each source of random variation. Furthermore, we were able to examine slopes for the continuous effects of item predictors measured repeatedly over subjects (change relevance and change salience), as well as piecewise slopes for the effect of a subject predictor of age (representing the difference between the age groups and the slope for age within the older age group). Because crossed random effects models do not require listwise deletion for missing responses and instead use maximum likelihood to estimate model parameters using all available data, this approach is likely to be more powerful and result in less bias than would repeated measures ANOVA using random subjects or random items. Finally, we were also able to examine hypotheses about variability, including predicting subject differences in the effects of salience as a function of age, as well as testing age group differences in between-subject and within-subject variability. In summary, crossed random effects models provide much flexibility for addressing many types of hypotheses within repeated measures designs, and can do so while treating both subjects and items as the random factors that they are, even in the presence of incomplete or unbalanced data.

5. Sample Results Section

A crossed random effects model was used to predict variability across subjects and items in log-transformed response time for 153 observers to detect changes to 51 driving scenes (7,644 total trials; RT was missing for 157 incorrect trials). Restricted maximum likelihood was used to estimate the models; accordingly, the significance of fixed effects were evaluated via their Wald test p-values, and the significance of random effects were evaluated using $-2\Delta LL$ tests (i.e., likelihood ratio tests using degrees of freedom equal to the difference in the number of estimated parameters) and information criteria (AIC and BIC) between models with the same fixed effects.

To begin, three models without predictors (i.e., empty means models) were estimated to partition the total RT variation. Relative to a model specifying a single residual variance, there was significant variability in mean RT across subjects, $-2\Delta LL(\sim1) = 1{,}746$, $p < .001$, and across items, $-2\Delta LL(\sim1) = 1{,}899$, $p < .001$, such that 26% of the RT variation was due to mean differences across subjects, 18% was due to mean differences across items, and the remaining 56% was due to the subject by item interaction (i.e., residual variance). To describe the size of this random intercept variation across subjects and items, 95% random effects confidence intervals were computed as: fixed intercept $\pm$ 1.96*SQRT(random intercept variance). Using this formula, 95% of the individual subject RT means were expected to fall between 0.79 and 2.45, and 95% of the individual item RT means were expected to fall between 0.93 and 2.32. Thus, although there was somewhat greater variation between subjects than between items, both sources of variation were significant, and thus their random effects were retained in the model.

Sequential models were then tested to examine the effects of item predictors (change relevance and change salience) and subject predictors (age, represented as a piecewise effect by two parameters—a mean difference between younger and older adults and a linear slope for age within the older age group). There were significant main effects of change relevance and change salience, such that greater change relevance and greater change salience were each related to shorter RTs, although their interaction was not significant. These three item effects accounted for 25% of the item variation, although significant item intercept variation remained, $-2\Delta LL(\sim1) = 1{,}358$, $p < .001$. There were also significant main effects of age, such that older adults responded more slowly than younger adults, and within the older group, RT increased linearly with age. These two subject effects accounted for 87% of the subject variation, although significant subject intercept variation also remained, $-2\Delta LL(\sim1) = 227$, $p < .001$.

Subject differences in the effects of change relevance and change salience were then examined. Although the effect of change salience varied significantly over subjects, $-2\Delta LL(\sim2) = 8.4$, $p = .015$, the effect of change relevance did not, $-2\Delta LL(\sim3) = 2.8$, $p = .432$. Interaction terms to assess moderation of the effects of change relevance and change salience by age were then added to the model. Although all higher-order interactions with years over 65 were nonsignificant, there was a significant three-way interaction of older age group by change relevance by change salience, as described below. The interactions of (older age group by change relevance) and (older age group by change relevance by change salience) reduced the residual variance by .04%. The interaction of older age group by change salience reduced the subject random salience slope variance by 12%, although significant subject random salience slope variation remained, $-2\Delta LL(\sim2) = 6.69$, $p = .035$. Finally, differential variability across age groups was examined by allowing heterogeneous residual variance and subject random variance by group. Older adults had significantly greater within-subject residual RT variation than did younger adults, $-2\Delta LL(1) = 170$, $p < .001$, as well as significantly greater between-subject variation in mean RT as well as in the effect of salience on RT, $-2\Delta LL(3) = 21$, $p < .001$. Given the multitude of separate variance components, an overall model R^2 was calculated as the square of the correlation between the RT predicted by the fixed effects and the actual RT for each trial, yielding a total $R^2 = .276$ for the final model, as described below.

The third columns of Table 12.4 provide the estimates obtained from the final model; the significance of other model-implied fixed effects reported below was evaluated with additional syntax statements for those estimates. The fixed intercept of $\gamma_{000} = 1.304$ is the expected mean log RT in seconds specifically for a younger adult to an item with change relevance = 3 and change salience = 3. Turning to the subject effects, the simple main effect of older adult group indicates that RT is significantly higher by $\gamma_{001} = 0.618$ in adults age 65 relative to younger adults as evaluated for an item of change relevance = 3 and change salience = 3. The simple main effect of years over 65 indicates that RT is expected to be significantly higher by $\gamma_{002} = 0.020$ for every year over age 65 (which is not conditional on change relevance or change salience given that they did not interact with years over 65).

Turning to the item effects, the simple main effect of change relevance indicates that, for an item with change salience = 3, RT in younger adults is expected to be significantly lower by $\gamma_{010} = -0.064$ for every one-unit higher change relevance. This effect of change relevance is significantly less negative by $\gamma_{011} = 0.038$ in the older age group (in which the effect of change relevance was not significant, as given by $\gamma_{010} + \gamma_{011} = -0.064 + 0.038 = 0.026$, SE = 0.025, $p = .295$). The simple main effect of change salience indicates that, for an item with change relevance = 3, RT in younger adults is expected to be significantly lower by $\gamma_{020} = -0.143$ for every one-unit higher change salience. This effect of change salience is nonsignificantly less negative by $\gamma_{021} = 0.013$ in the older age group (in which the effect of change salience was still significant, as given by $\gamma_{020} + \gamma_{021} = -0.143 + 0.013 = -0.130$, SE = 0.044, $p = .005$).

Finally, the change relevance by change salience interaction indicates that in younger adults, the negative effect of change relevance is expected to become nonsignificantly more negative by $\gamma_{030} = -0.003$ for every one-unit higher change salience. This interaction of change relevance by change salience is significantly more negative by $\gamma_{031} = -0.025$ in the older adults (in which the interaction of change relevance by change salience was not significant, as given by $\gamma_{030} + \gamma_{031} = -0.003 + -0.025 = -0.028$, SE = 0.021, $p = .189$). Thus, although the interaction of change relevance by change salience was not significant within either age group, the difference in this effect across age groups was significant (given that it is tested with a smaller SE than the interaction effect within either group). The pattern of the three-way interaction is shown in Figure 12.2, in which the reduction in RT for items of higher change relevance in the younger adults is essentially the same for items of low or high change salience (solid versus dashed circles), whereas the effect of change relevance is stronger for items of high change salience in the older adults (equally so for adults age 80 in squares or age 65 in triangles, given the lack of interaction with of change relevance with years over 65).

Review Questions

1. Describe the F_1 and F_2 analyses of variance that are often conducted for repeated measures data involving multiple subjects and multiple items. Which sampling dimensions are treated as *fixed* or *random* in each?

2. What problems do missing item responses cause for the F_1 and F_2 analyses of variance?
3. Describe how a crossed random effects model for subjects and items would differ from F_1 and F_2 analyses of variance. What additional benefits can crossed random effects models provide for analysis of repeated measures data?
4. Describe how crossed random effects models can be used to test hypotheses about item exchangeability and adequacy of experimental control.
5. Describe the role of item predictors, subject predictors, and trial-level predictors in a crossed random effects models. Which sources of variation would each account for?

References

Aguinis, H., & Pierce, C. A. (1998). Heterogeneity of error variance and the assessment of moderating effects of categorical variables: A conceptual review. *Organizational Research Methods, 1*(3), 296–314.

Allison, P. D. (1994). Using panel data to estimate the effects of events. *Sociological Methods and Research, 23*(2), 174–199.

Clark. H. H. (1973). The language-as-fixed-effect fallacy: A critique of language statistics in psychological research. *Journal of Verbal Learning and Verbal Behavior, 12,* 335–359.

Cohen, J. (1983). The cost of dichotomization. *Applied Psychological Measurement, 7*(3), 249–253.

Coleman, E. B. (1964). Generalizing to a language population. *Psychological Reports, 14,* 219–226.

DeShon, R. P., & Alexander, R. A. (1996). Alternative procedures for testing regression slope homogeneity when group error variances are unequal. *Psychological Methods, 1*(3), 261–277.

Enders, C. K. (2010). *Applied missing data analysis.* New York, NY: Guilford.

Grissom, R. J. (2000). Heterogeneity of variance in clinical data. *Journal of Consulting & Clinical Psychology, 68*(1), 155–165.

Hoffman, L., & Rovine, M. J. (2007). Multilevel models for experimental psychologists: Foundations and illustrative examples. *Behavior Research Methods, 39*(1), 101–117.

Lorch, R. F., & Myers, J. L. (1990). Regression analyses of repeated measures data in cognitive research. *Journal of Experimental Psychology: Learning, Memory, & Cognition, 16*(1), 149–157.

MacCallum, R. C., Zhang, S., Preacher, K. J., & Rucker, D. D. (2002). On the practice of dichotomization of quantitative variables. *Psychological Methods, 7*(1), 19–40.

Maxwell, S. E., & Delaney, H. D. (1993). Bivariate median splits and spurious statistical significance. *Psychological Bulletin, 113*(1), 181–190.

Preacher, K. J., Rucker, D. D., MacCallum, R. C., & Nicewander, W. A. (2005). Use of the extreme groups approach: A critical reexamination and new recommendations. *Psychological Methods, 10*(2), 178–192.

Raaijmakers, J. G. W. (2003). A further look at the "Language-as-Fixed-Effect Fallacy". *Canadian Journal of Experimental Psychology, 57,* 141–151.

Raaijmakers, J. G. W., Schrijnemakers, J. M. C., & Gremmen, F. (1999). How to deal with the "Language-As-Fixed-Effect Fallacy": Common misconceptions and alternative solutions. *Journal of Memory and Language, 41,* 416–426.

Singer, J. D., & Willett, J. B. (2003). *Applied longitudinal data analysis: Modeling change and event occurrence.* New York, NY: Oxford University Press.

Snijders, T.A.B., & Bosker, R. (2012). *Multilevel analysis* (2nd ed.). Thousand Oaks, CA: Sage.

CHAPTER 13

ADDITIONAL CONSIDERATIONS AND RELATED MODELS

At long last, we've reached the end of our journey together. And despite the length of this journey so far, there is still much left to be covered. The goal of this last chapter is to foreshadow some of the topics we didn't get to, including sample size and power analysis, generalized linear mixed models for non-normal outcomes, and additional related approaches for longitudinal data. I hope this brief introduction may help facilitate continued learning in these areas on your own.

1. Sample Size and Power Analysis in Longitudinal Studies

An important consideration in any research endeavor is the power of the study's design in testing the significance of the hypothesized effects. In longitudinal data, or more generally, in any design in which the outcome has multiple dimensions of sampling, considerations of power will be relevant for *each* of those dimensions. This section briefly reviews concepts of statistical power and how it can be estimated in the context of longitudinal and multilevel studies.

In the tradition of null hypothesis significance testing—as we've used throughout this text—each estimated fixed effect or random effect variance is tested against a null hypothesis of 0. Each test is evaluated using a pre-determined level of significance, or alpha (α). For instance, an $\alpha = .05$ means that in 1 out of 20 tests, a parameter is expected to be declared "significantly different than 0" by chance in our sample ($p < .05$) when it shouldn't have been (i.e., it does not really differ from 0 in the population). More formally, α is the probability of making this type of false positive in declaring significance, known as **Type I error rate**. However, we could also make a wrong decision from the alternative perspective—we could declare a parameter to be *not* significantly different than 0 in our sample when it really does differ from 0 in the population. The probability of making this type of false negative in declaring nonsignificance is known as **Type II error rate**, or beta (β). **Statistical power** (as given by $1 - \beta$) is the probability of actually finding a parameter to be significantly different from 0 in the sample when it should be (i.e., it really does differ from 0 in the population, a correct decision). Traditionally, even though Type I error rate is held to .05, Type II error rate will be targeted at .20, for a targeted power rate of .80.

Statistical power is a nonlinear combination of two things: sample size and effect size for the estimated parameter. Thus, statistical power analysis is the process of solving for one given the other. That is, for a targeted power rate (e.g., .80), what sample size is needed to detect the desired effect size with sufficient power? Alternatively, what effect size can be detected with sufficient power using a specific sample size? Power can be estimated while planning a research study, known as **a priori power analysis**, or it can be estimated after-the-fact given the study's known results, known as **post-hoc** or **a posteriori power analysis**. Let us now consider how to estimate power in planning a study or in describing its results—although we'll see that the latter is generally much easier to do, given that all of the quantities needed are then known!

1.A. Evaluation of Power Across Levels of Analysis

A multitude of resources are available to estimate power for detecting effects in single-level statistical models, ranging from classic textbooks (e.g., Cohen, 1988) to software-based calculators (e.g., SAS P POWER, G*Power). Nevertheless, the process of *a priori* power analysis can still be considerably more challenging in multilevel designs, such as in longitudinal data, given the need to consider the variances that result from dimensions of sampling. As we've seen throughout the text, dependency arising from the repeated sampling of occasions from the same person (or sampling of persons from the same group) can take many forms. These will include not only random intercepts for mean differences, but also random slopes for differences in the effects of predictors. Let us begin with the simpler case of evaluating power to detect fixed main effects of predictors in two-level or three-level models with random intercepts only. We will then consider more complex designs for hypotheses about random slopes and cross-level interactions. The most important thing to remember in planning longitudinal studies, though, is that *power and sample size must take into account dependency across levels of analysis.*

Let us consider a three-level model of time within persons within groups, given that if the number of groups = 1, it will simplify to become a two-level model. At the highest level of the model, the power to detect effects of level-3 group predictors will be based only on the number of groups. That is, because groups are independent, power can be reasonably well approximated using traditional approaches for estimating power in single-level models. For instance, as given by Cohen (1988, p. 102; see also the electronic materials for this text), an effect size in correlation units of $r = .5$ has power = .80 given 28 groups; detecting $r = .3$ or $r = .1$ with power = .80 will require 85 or 783 groups, respectively. Similarly, an effect size in standard deviation units for a between-condition mean difference of $d = .5$ has power = .80 given 64 groups per condition; detecting $d = .3$ or $d = .1$ with power = .80 will require 175 or 1,571 groups per condition, respectively. These examples illustrate the nonlinearity of the relationships among power, sample size, and effect size—it takes a whole lot more sample size to reliably detect small effects! When the number of groups = 1 such that *persons* are independent, the power to detect effects of level-2 person predictors is based only on the number of persons, and it can then be approximated with these traditional approaches for estimating power in single-level models.

In estimating power for the effects of time-varying (level-1) predictors or person (level-2) predictors given multiple level-3 groups, we must then take into account dependency at each level in the predictors. This is because the total level-1 sample size, as calculated from occasions*persons*groups, will not be valid for estimating power for level-1 effects unless there is absolutely no dependency of occasions from the same person *or* dependency of persons from the same group whatsoever. Likewise, the total level-2 sample size given by persons*groups will not be valid for estimating power for level-2 effects unless there is absolutely no dependency of persons from the same group. As we saw in chapter 11, the amount of dependency from constant mean differences across persons and groups can be quantified by level-2 and level-3 intraclass correlations (ICCs) for the variable. We can use these ICCs to estimate **effective sample size**, which is the sample size we *really* have in terms of providing pieces of independent information about a variable at that level of analysis, as shown for levels 1 and 2 in Equation (13.1):

$$
\begin{aligned}
N2_{Eff} &= \frac{n3 * n2}{1 + \left[(n2 - 1) * ICC_{L3}\right]} \\
N1_{Eff} &= \frac{N2_{Eff} * n1}{1 + \left[(n1 - 1) * ICC_{L2}\right]} = \frac{n3 * n2}{1 + \left[(n2 - 1) * ICC_{L3}\right]} * \frac{n1}{1 + \left[(n1 - 1) * ICC_{L2}\right]}
\end{aligned}
\tag{13.1}
$$

in which *n1* is the number of level-1 occasions per person, *n2* is the number of level-2 persons per group, and *n3* is the number of level-3 groups. ICC_{L2} is the proportion of *total* variance that was originally due to between-person (and between-group) mean differences; ICC_{L3} is then the proportion of *between-person* variance that is due to between-group mean differences. $N1_{Eff}$ and $N2_{Eff}$ are the level-1 and level-2 effective sample sizes. The denominator for $N2_{Eff}$ in Equation (13.1) is known as a level-3 design effect, whereas for $N1_{Eff}$ the first denominator is known as the level-2 design effect. A **design effect** is defined as the ratio of sampling variance for a fixed effect to be expected using the current design relative to what would have been obtained from the same number of independent observations instead (Snijders & Bosker, 2012). The design effect is a *multiplier* that describes the sample size needed to obtain the same amount of power as from an independent sample. As shown in Equation (13.1), larger design effects occur with greater numbers of observations per unit and with greater dependency (larger ICCs) of observations.

So how do all of these ideas relate in estimating power? Table 13.1 provides some more concrete examples. The first set of columns lists the effective *n2* per group as a function of actual *n2* and ICC_{L3}. As shown in the second set of columns, only when $ICC_{L3} = 0$ will the total and effective level-2 samples sizes be equal—when persons

Table 13.1 Examples of effective sample sizes in longitudinal data of persons clustered in $n3 = 10$ groups, given predictor intraclass correlations for level-2 n per group ($n2$), ICC for persons in groups (ICC_{L3}), level-1 n per person ($n1$), and the ICC for occasions in persons (ICC_{L2}).

	Level-2 Persons		Level-2 N for 10 Groups		Level-1 Occasions			Level-1 N for 10 Groups	
$n2$	ICC_{L3}	Effective $n2$	Total $n3*n2$	Effective $N2_{Eff}$	$n1$	ICC_{L2}	Effective $n1$	Total $n3*n2*n1$	Effective $N1_{Eff}$
10	.00	10	100	100	4	.00	4	400	400
10	.00	10	100	100	4	.30	2.11	400	210.53
10	.00	10	100	100	4	.60	1.43	400	142.86
10	.00	10	100	100	7	.00	7.00	700	700
10	.00	10	100	100	7	.30	2.50	700	250.00
10	.00	10	100	100	7	.60	1.52	700	152.17
10	.05	6.90	100	69	4	.00	4	400	275.86
10	.05	6.90	100	69	4	.30	2.11	400	145.19
10	.05	6.90	100	69	4	.60	1.43	400	98.52
10	.05	6.90	100	69	7	.00	7.00	700	482.76
10	.05	6.90	100	69	7	.30	2.50	700	172.41
10	.05	6.90	100	69	7	.60	1.52	700	104.95
20	.00	20	200	200	4	.00	4	800	800
20	.00	20	200	200	4	.30	2.11	800	421.05
20	.00	20	200	200	4	.60	1.43	800	285.71
20	.00	20	200	200	7	.00	7.00	1400	1400
20	.00	20	200	200	7	.30	2.50	1400	500.00
20	.00	20	200	200	7	.60	1.52	1400	304.35
20	.05	10.26	200	103	4	.00	4	800	410.26
20	.05	10.26	200	103	4	.30	2.11	800	215.92
20	.05	10.26	200	103	4	.60	1.43	800	146.52
20	.05	10.26	200	103	7	.00	7.00	1400	717.95
20	.05	10.26	200	103	7	.30	2.50	1400	256.41
20	.05	10.26	200	103	7	.60	1.52	1400	156.08

from the same group are independent. Even a small amount of between-group variance is enough to cause a large level-3 design effect. For example, given $n2 = 20$ and $ICC_{L3} = .05$, the design effect = 1.95, creating an effective $n2 = 20 / 1.95 = 10.26$ instead of $n2 = 20$. Thus, for this case you would need to include almost *twice* as many persons when sampling from groups as when sampling independent persons instead.

The deleterious effect of dependency is observed twice over in estimating power for level-1 effects. The third set of columns in Table 13.1 lists the effective $n1$ per person as a function of actual $n1$ and ICC_{L2}. As shown in the last set of columns, the only scenario in which the total and effective level-1 sample sizes will be the same is when both $ICC_{L3} = 0$ and $ICC_{L2} = 0$, or when persons within groups are independent and occasions from the same person are also independent. Otherwise, $N1_{Eff}$ will be reduced given larger level-3 and level-2 design effects. However, when trying to improve power for level-1 effects, the benefit of increasing the number of occasions relative to increasing the number of persons will depend on the dependency of the occasions within persons, which tends to be much greater than the dependency of persons in groups. For instance, an $ICC_{L2} = .60$ for $n1 = 4$ occasions creates a design effect = 2.40, such that for 20 independent persons, you'd have the level-1 power of effective $n1 = 29$, not 80. But if you decided to increase the level-1 total sample size to 140 by adding four more occasions per person so $n1 = 8$, this would create a design effect = 5.20, and an effective $n1$ sample size of still only 31. In contrast, doubling the number of level-2 persons instead (from $n2 = 20$ to 40) would result in a design effect = 2.80, with 160 total level-1 observations and effective $n1 = 57$.

1.B. Suggested Resources for Power Analysis in Longitudinal and Multilevel Data

So far we've considered power for fixed effects in random intercept models. What about power for detecting random slope variances or the cross-level interactions to explain them? For instance, in a two-level longitudinal model, how could we estimate power to detect individual differences in change and level-2 predictors thereof? As reviewed by Hox (2010), in general, research has suggested that the number of level-2 units (e.g., persons) will be more important than the number of level-1 units (e.g., occasions), although the number of level-1 units will help to create a more precise slope estimate for each level-2 unit. This is where power estimation gets tricky, because it is often quite challenging to make reasonable guesses for the effect sizes of unknown variance components *a priori*. Fortunately there are a number of resources that have been developed for these and other complex multilevel designs. Here is a current but non-exhaustive list; corrections and additions will be added to the electronic materials for this text.

Online software *Optimal Design* (Raudenbush et al., 2011) provides options for designing two- and three-level studies, with special emphasis on cluster-randomized trials. Notably, it also helps determine the most cost-effective sampling strategy given known costs of recruiting additional persons or clusters. Online software *PinT* (Power analysis IN Two-level designs) calculates approximate standard errors for fixed effects in two-level models. Examples using these software packages and more details can be found in Hox (2010) and Snijders and Bosker (2012). Finally, online software *GLIMMPSE* (Kreidler et al., 2013) provides power estimation for repeated measures studies and also allows users to address other types of clustered sampling as well.

1.C. Monte Carlo Simulation for Post-Hoc and A Priori Power Analysis

The challenge of *a priori* power analysis lies primarily in selecting appropriate values of all the model parameters necessary to estimate effect size. Fortunately, this process is much easier in post-hoc power analyses, which are conducted on existing data, and thus for which all needed quantities are known. The purpose of a post-hoc power analysis is usually to estimate power for a nonsignificant effect, or relatedly, the sample size necessary to have achieved an acceptable level of power. Such post-hoc power analyses can be conducted using Monte Carlo simulation, such as directly implemented in M*plus*, or by user-created simulation programs in many other software programs. Post-hoc power analysis then proceeds in three steps.

First, the user inputs the obtained values of all parameters, including fixed effects and random effects variances, for the estimated model into the program. Values for the means and variances of model predictor variables and sample sizes per level will also be entered. Second, the program generates hypothetical outcome data consistent with the model, and this simulation process is repeated many times (e.g., 1,000 replications). Third, the same generating model is then estimated on each of the simulated datasets, and the results are tallied across replications. A direct estimate of power is then given by the proportion of replications for which each parameter was significant at the chosen alpha level, given the sample sizes specified. The user can then increase the sample sizes and repeat the second and third steps (simulate new data; analyze the new results) to assess the predicted impact of additional data at each level on estimated power.

Monte Carlo simulation can also be very useful for *a priori* power analysis. Given how difficult it can be to make educated guesses for all the estimated model parameters, repeated simulations using different values provide a direct way to assess the sensitivity of results to such sometimes arbitrary decisions. It also provides a means to examine the relative tradeoffs between increasing sample sizes at each level under a variety of scenarios.

In addition to making assumptions about model parameters in estimating power, we must also believe that the assumptions that underlie our model are correct. As was presented in Appendix 7.A in chapter 7, for the longitudinal models we've examined so far, these assumptions pertain to the conditional independence, normality, and constant variance of all model residuals. Although violations of independence can potentially be addressed by adding additional random effects, assumptions of normality and constant variance may not be reasonable for some types of outcome variables. Accordingly, the next section briefly introduces generalized models for non-normal longitudinal outcomes, as well as the difficulties of estimation in these models.

2. Generalized Longitudinal Models for Non-Normal Outcomes

The term **generalized linear model** is used to refer to a family of models that differ from general linear models in two primary ways: (1) Their model-predicted outcomes follow some other kind of distribution besides normal, and (2) they use link functions to create an unbounded outcome to be predicted by a linear model. Further, just as general linear *mixed* models have both fixed and *random* effects (i.e., they contain multiple piles of variance to capture the dependency created by multiple dimensions of sampling), so do **generalized linear mixed models**. Although there are three main parts of a generalized linear mixed model, only two of these are really new.

First, a novel part of a generalized linear mixed model is its **non-normal conditional outcome distribution**. To review, the general linear mixed models we have seen thus far have used a *normal* conditional distribution to describe the variance remaining in a y outcome after controlling for the model's fixed and random effects, which we have referred to level-1 residual variance. In other words, our overall y outcome has had a normal distribution whose **conditional mean** (i.e., the model-predicted original outcome) was created by the fixed and random effects, and whose residual variance was estimated separately from the mean and assumed to be constant across observations (unless modeled otherwise). Notably, to compute the model likelihood value for each person, we needed the fixed-effect-predicted outcomes ($\hat{y}$), the random effects variances and covariances, *and* the residual variances and covariances. However, for some outcomes (particularly those that are bounded at one or both ends), other conditional distributions besides normal will be more plausible, and thus result in more valid standard errors for the estimated parameters. For instance, binary (0/1) outcomes follow a *Bernoulli* distribution, in which the only parameter is p, the probability of a 1. The model predicts each observation's conditional mean = p, which then determines the conditional variance = $p*(1-p)$. Consequently, models for binary outcomes do not have a separately *estimated* level-1 residual variance (i.e., it is not needed to calculate each person's likelihood). The same will be true in some other generalized linear mixed models as well, such as for counts of events that follow a *Poisson* distribution, whose conditional variance is also determined by the conditional mean.

The second novel part of a generalized linear mixed model is the **link function**, which is how the original bounded outcome becomes a continuous, unbounded outcome to be predicted by the model instead. Although a link function is essentially a transformation, it is not used to transform the original data—instead, the outcome's *conditional mean* is transformed. For instance, the conditional mean to be predicted for a binary (0/1) outcome is the *probability* of having a 1 instead of a 0. Although we could use a linear model to predict the probability of a 1 directly, this could result in predicted probabilities below 0 or above 1 (because a linear slope keeps going). Instead, the linear model will predict a link-transformed outcome that ranges from $\pm\infty$. Critically, though, these predicted outcomes, when converted back into probability (through an **inverse link**), will stay between 0 and 1 where they belong. Similarly, in count outcomes in which negative values are not possible, the conditional mean to be predicted is the expected count of events, and the link function is the natural log. A linear model then predicts the *log* of the expected count instead of the original count so that the expected count will stay positive. Log link functions are also used in heterogeneous variance models (as in chapters 7 and 8) to ensure that predicted variances stay positive (i.e., link functions can be used to transform conditional variances as well as conditional means). Finally, general linear mixed models use an **identity link function**, in which the predicted outcome is just $y*1$ (given that y should already be unbounded).

The last part of a generalized linear mixed model is already familiar—**the linear predictor**, or what we think as a linear combination of fixed and random effects. That is, despite being created for non-normal outcomes, generalized linear mixed models are still *linear* models because their fixed and random effects multiply predictors in a *linear* combination (e.g., intercept + slope*variable + slope*variable . . .) to create model-predicted outcomes. The only difference is that the linear predictor of fixed and random effects directly predicts the conditional mean in the link-transformed, unbounded metric, rather than in the original bounded metric of the outcome.

Notably, random effects in generalized linear mixed models are still assumed to have a multivariate normal distribution and to otherwise function the same as in the models used in this text, with two caveats. One caveat is that, because of the link functions, the fixed effects are no longer the "average" effect for the sample. Instead, they are interpreted as also conditional on the random effects (e.g., γ_{00} will be the expected intercept when all predictors = 0 *and* when $U_{0i} = 0$), such that these models are known as *subject-specific* or *unit-specific* models. The other caveat is that the estimation of generalized linear mixed models proceeds differently than the estimation of general linear mixed models with respect to the random effects, as discussed shortly.

So, to summarize, generalized linear models use *link functions* that create continuous, unbounded outcomes to be predicted by a linear model of fixed and random effects (the *linear predictor*). In transforming back into their original metric (through an *inverse link*), the outcome conditional means will stay within their possible range (e.g., between 0 and 1 for binary data). A non-normal conditional distribution is also selected to best match the outcome's possible values, which may not have a separately estimated level-1 variance. So with these general principles in mind, let us briefly visit some commonly used models. More detailed treatment of generalized models can be found (among other places) in Hedeker and Gibbons (2006) and Stroup (2013).

2.A. Models for Binary, Percent, and Categorical Outcomes

The most common example of generalized linear mixed models is for bounded outcomes, for which general linear mixed models can be problematic. Let us begin with binary outcomes, given that the same principles will apply in predicting percent and categorical outcomes as well. For generality, though, we will forgo the usual subscripts that keep track of levels of analysis.

Most commonly used for binary outcomes is the **logit link**, which is the natural log of the odds ratio for p = the probability of a 1 as follows: logit = $\log[p \, / \, (1 - p)]$. The mapping from probability to the logit (log-odds) scale is symmetric about 0; a logit = 0 corresponds to an odds ratio = $[p \, / \, (1 - p)] = 1$, and a probability of $p = .50$. For example, $p = .90$ becomes logit = 2.2, whereas $p = .10$ becomes logit = −2.2. The logit metric ranges from ±∞, which makes it well suited to be an outcome of the linear predictor of fixed and random effects. Predicted logits can then be converted back to probability p through an inverse link of $p = \exp(\text{logit}) \, / \, [1 + \exp(\text{logit})]$. In Figure 13.1, the solid line illustrates how predicted logits (y-axis) correspond to predicted probabilities (x-axis). As shown, equal distances in logits will correspond to smaller distances in probability as probability approaches 0 or 1. For instance, a one-unit change from logit = 0 to 1 corresponds to $p = .50$ to .73, a difference of .23. Another one-unit change from logit = 1 to 2 corresponds to $p = .73$ to .88, a difference of .15. An additional one-unit change from logit = 2 to 3 corresponds to $p = .88$ to .95, a difference of .07. Thus, the slope relating changes in logits to changes in probability "shuts off" as it heads towards its asymptotes of $p = 0$ or 1, ensuring that the predicted probabilities stay within these bounds. However, it is important to check what your software considers to be "$y = 1$" in these models, as some packages by default predict y = 0 instead of $y = 1$ (e.g., SAS GLIMMIX).

As introduced earlier, binary outcomes follow a discrete Bernoulli distribution, whose conditional mean = p, and whose conditional (residual) variance = $p^{*}(1 - p)$.

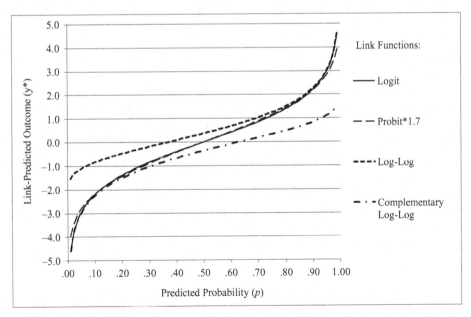

Figure 13.1 Correspondence between predicted probability and model-predicted outcomes when using the logit, probit, log-log, or complementary log-log links in models for binary outcomes.

Thus, the level-1 residual variance is not estimated because it is determined by the conditional mean (and is not assumed constant across all values of the conditional mean, unlike in models with normally distributed level-1 residuals). Further, in calculating the likelihood per person, no level-1 residual variance is included. The height of an observation y in a Bernoulli distribution is given by $[p^y(1-p)^{1-y}]$, such that when y = 1 the height is p, and when y = 0 the height is $1-p$. The lack of an estimated level-1 residual variance means that pseudo-R^2 for the effects of level-1 predictors cannot be computed in the usual way. However, what may happen instead (i.e., the constants used in place of level-1 residual variance) will seem very arbitrary without a little background.

In conceptualizing the model-predicted outcomes in the logit metric, the same model is sometimes written in another way: $y^* =$ (linear predictor) + (e). In this version, y^* is still the predicted logit but is referred to as a *latent* or *underlying* variable, and (e) is used to represent the idea of variance leftover of the *logit* outcome (even though the conditional variance of the *binary* outcome is still determined by the conditional mean). In using the logit link, y^* is assumed to follow a logistic distribution (which looks similar to a normal distribution but will be relatively flatter in this context), whose variance = $s^2(\pi^2/3)$, in which s is a scale factor that modifies the variance when the logistic distribution is used with non-binary outcomes. Thus, the variance for the (e) residual in the logit metric simplifies to $\pi^2/3 = 3.29$, which is then used as a substitute for the un-estimated level-1 residual variance. For instance, in a two-level random intercept model with a logit link, the intraclass correlation can be calculated as ICC = $(\tau_{U_0}^2) / (\tau_{U_0}^2 + 3.29)$. The 3.29 also substitutes for level-1 residual variance in formulas to compute explained variance.

Although Bernoulli is the only distribution used for binary outcomes, other link functions may be used instead. Another option is the **probit link** (also known as *ogive*), written as probit = $\Phi^{-1}(p)$, in which the predicted outcome is the z-score for the area to the left of that probability in a cumulative standard normal distribution. Probits can be converted back into probabilities with an inverse link of $p = \Phi^{-1}(z)$. When y^* is a predicted probit, its level-1 residual distribution is assumed to be standard normal with variance = 1 (instead of a logistic distribution with variance = $\pi^2/3$ as when y^* is a predicted logit). As a result, the scale of the fixed effects in these models will differ by a factor of SQRT($\pi^2/3$). A probit outcome can be translated into a logit outcome as logit $\approx 1.7*$probit to create nearly identical predicted probabilities, as shown in Figure 13.1.

However, the logit and probit link functions each assume that the relationship between the link-predicted outcome and the probability it represents is symmetric before and after $p = .50$. There are two other *asymmetric* link functions better-suited for binary outcomes that are skewed towards 0 or 1. The **log-log link** = $-\log[-\log(p)]$ and is used when 1 is more frequent than 0; its predicted probability can be found with an inverse link of $p = \exp[\exp(-\log-\log)]$. As shown in Figure 13.1, the relationship between the predicted log-log and probability is similar to that of logit or probit*1.7 from $p = .50$ to 1, but it decays more rapidly from $p = .50$ to 0. Alternatively, the **complementary log-log link** (clog-log) = $-\log[-\log(p)]$ is used when 0 is more frequent than 1; its predicted probability can be found with an inverse link of

$p = 1 - \exp[\exp(-\text{clog}-\log)]$. The complementary log-log link predicts the opposite pattern as the log-log (i.e., a more rapid decay from $p = .50$ to 1 instead). Given the same Bernoulli distribution, models with different link functions can be compared via AIC and BIC, as well as by the fit of the predicted probabilities.

These same link functions can be used in predicting other outcomes bounded between 0 and 1, such as percent correct. When percent correct is expressed as the number of successes out of the number of trials, the Bernoulli distribution (for one trial) can be extended to become the discrete *binomial* distribution for multiple trials. The binomial probability of c successes out of n trials is $p(y = c) = [n! \,/\, c! \,(n - c!)]^* p^c (1 - p)^{n - c}$, in which p is the probability of success for each trial, such that the binomial mean $= np$ and variance $= np(1 - p)$. Because the number of n trials is known (and can vary across observations), the model predicts the link-transformed p for the probability of $y = 1$, the same as in models for binary outcomes. The binomial distribution is well suited for percent correct outcomes with floor *or* ceiling effects, but it does predict only one maximum point. A more flexible (but far less intuitive) distribution that can be used with percent correct directly is the continuous *beta* distribution, whose parameters can predict almost any shape for continuous outcomes between 0 and 1. However, the beta distribution does not include values of 0 or 1, although zero-one-inflated beta models also exist for those cases (in which the model can then predict three separate probabilities for outcomes of $y = 0$, $y = 1$, or $0 < y < 1$).

In predicting ordinal and nominal (un-ordered) outcomes, the binary Bernoulli distribution is replaced by a *multinomial* distribution, which works similarly but allows for more than two possible outcomes of a single trial (i.e., it predicts the probability of the outcome that occurred). Models for categorical data represent their C outcome categories using $C - 1$ binary "submodels" estimated simultaneously; models for different outcome types differ by how they create these submodels. To illustrate how each type of submodel is formed, let us consider an example outcome in which $C = 4$, with possible outcomes of 0, 1, 2, or 3. Although the same four link functions can be used as for binary data, logit links tend to be used most frequently.

If the categories are ordered, most common is the **cumulative logit link**, also known as a *proportional odds* or *graded response* model. Its binary submodels distinguish each category transition using all C categories cumulatively. In our example, these submodels would predict the probability of $y \geq 1$, $y \geq 2$, and $y \geq 3$. Each submodel has its own fixed intercept for the expected probability when all predictors = 0, but the predictor fixed effects and random effects variances are assumed to be equal across submodels. Although these assumptions can be tested, in most software for mixed models it is currently hard to do so (or to estimate alternative models with fewer constraints). A less popular (but perhaps more intuitive) link function for ordered categories is the **adjacent category logit link**, also known as a *partial credit* model. Its binary submodels predict each transition separately, such that in our example, they would predict the probability of $y = 1$ instead of 0, of $y = 2$ instead of 1, and of $y = 3$ instead of 2. As with the cumulative logit link, each submodel has its own fixed intercept but is assumed to have the same predictor fixed effects and random effects variances. Models using an adjacent category link can be harder to estimate when some categories have few responses (unlike with the cumulative link, whose submodels each include all responses). Finally, a link function for unordered categories is the **generalized logit link,** also known as a *nominal* model. Its submodels essentially dummy-code each outcome category relative to a reference category. In our example given a reference outcome of $y = 0$, these submodels would predict the probability of $y = 1$ instead of 0, of $y = 2$ instead of 0, and of $y = 3$ instead of 0. Critically, all model parameters are estimated separately for each submodel by default, such that no ordering of categories is assumed whatsoever.

2.B. Models for Skewed Outcomes

Generalized models are often categorized as for *discrete* versus *continuous* outcomes, but it can also be useful to consider how the distributions that allow different shapes may work for an outcome of either type. This section will describe models for outcomes that appear to have skewed distributions, which may occur in either discrete or continuous outcomes.

One type of outcome that often has a skewed distribution is a count of events, such as the number of hospital visits or the number of cigarettes smoked in a day. The expected count of events, called μ, can be predicted using the **natural log link,** such that $\log(\mu)$ is the outcome of the linear predictor, which can be converted back into a predicted count through an inverse link of $y = \exp(\mu)$. $\log(\mu)$ ranges from 0 to ∞, and thus ensures the predicted counts stay positive. There are several related options for the conditional distribution of a count variable. The simplest is the Poisson, a discrete distribution ranging from 0 to $+\infty$ that has a single parameter (called λ) that predicts the probability $p = [\lambda^y * \exp(-\lambda)/y!]$ for each observed count y. Most critically, the Poisson distribution makes the strict assumption that mean = variance = λ, which is not often the case. *Under-dispersion* occurs when the variance is less than predicted by λ; more commonly, *over-dispersion* occurs when the variance is greater than predicted by λ. An alternative for over-dispersed data is the *negative binomial* distribution, whose probability function is quite complex. Most relevant for us here is that it includes an extra k dispersion parameter, such that its mean = λ but its variance = $\lambda + k\lambda^2$. When $k = 0$, the predicted variance = λ as in the Poisson distribution, and so these two models can be compared using a likelihood ratio test to determine if $k > 0$. However, as explained in Stroup (2013), the maximum likelihood function is actually undefined at $k = 0$. He recommends the *generalized Poisson* distribution instead, whose mean = $\lambda/(1 - k)$ and variance = $\lambda/(1 - k)^2$, and for which the maximum likelihood function is defined at $k = 0$.

Each of these distributions for count outcomes predicts at least some 0 values to occur, even though it may be impossible to observe 0 in some types of count outcomes. For instance, hospital records for a patient's number of visits will only include patients with at least one visit (otherwise they wouldn't have a record at all). Simply subtracting 1 from each count won't work, but fortunately, these types of outcomes can be modeled using Poisson and negative binomial distributions that are **zero-truncated** (or *zero-altered*), and which then range from 1 to +∞.

In addition to discrete distributions, there are continuous distributions that could also be used for count outcomes, as well as for outcomes that are truly continuous but skewed (e.g., response time). For example, one option is to predict the log of the outcome by using a log-normal distribution, which ranges continuously from 0 to +∞. As an aside, in this case the same results can be obtained when analyzing a log-transformed outcome using a general linear mixed model as when modeling the original outcome with an identity link and log-normal distribution (i.e., as in SAS GLIMMIX). In the latter model, the log-normal distribution has two parameters: an intercept μ and a scale parameter s, such that the conditional mean = $\exp(\mu)*\text{SQRT}[\exp(s)]$ and the level-1 residual variance = $\exp(2\mu)*\exp(s)*[\exp(s) - 1]$. Another option is a log link with the gamma distribution, which also ranges from 0 to +∞, and whose *shape* and *scale* parameters predict a conditional mean = *shape**scale and a level-1 residual variance = *shape**scale^2. Programs may differ in how they parameterize the log-normal and gamma models, though.

2.C. If and How Much Semi-Continuous Models for Zero-Inflated Outcomes

This last section will consider generalized linear models for outcomes that are not only skewed, but that also have a pile of observations at a lower bound. For instance, in analyzing the number of cigarettes smoked in a day, if the sample includes both smokers and non-smokers, the count outcome y may be **zero-inflated**, meaning that it has more 0 values than predicted. For instance, consider an outcome in which $y = 0$ for 20% of the sample. If a Poisson distribution $\lambda = 3$ (in which λ = mean = variance), then y = 0 is predicted for only 5% of the sample. Similarly, if a negative binomial distribution $\lambda = 3$ and $k = .25$ (in which mean = λ and variance = $\lambda + k\lambda^2$), then y = 0 is predicted for about 10% of the sample. Thus, our sample would have 15% more 0 values than a Poisson distribution or 10% more 0 values than a negative binomial distribution. Fortunately, just there are as zero-*altered* models for count outcomes with no 0 values, there are zero-*inflated* models for count outcomes with too many 0 values (i.e., more 0 values than would be expected given the rest of the distribution). However, these families of models differ in how they conceptualize what a 0 value means and how it should be predicted.

First, the zero-inflated Poisson and zero-inflated negative binomial models focus specifically on how many *extra* 0 values are observed than predicted. In these models, each y outcome is predicted simultaneously by two submodels. One submodel predicts the expected count as usual (ranging from 0 to +∞) using a log link and either a Poisson or negative binomial distribution (as needed). The other binary submodel then uses a logit link and a Bernoulli distribution to predict the probability of y = *extra* 0 for each observation. Thus, these zero-inflated models can be thought of as mixture models, in which the observed zero-inflated outcome is created by an unknown mixture of two distributions (count and Bernoulli).

However, although common in current software, these types of zero-inflated models can be difficult to interpret conceptually, given that the probability of y = "*extra* 0" (as opposed to just y = 0) is arbitrary. In cross-sectional data, the extra 0 values are sometimes described as *structural zeros*. For example, people who reported 0 cigarettes smoked in a day could be non-smokers—meaning they are *structural zeros*—or they could have just not smoked that day (meaning they are *expected* zeros instead). But this explanation falls apart in longitudinal data, in which the probability of being a *structural* zero by definition should not vary over time.

An alternative and simpler approach is used in **hurdle** models, which include the Poisson hurdle and the negative binomial hurdle. These models do not distinguish expected from extra 0 values. In the first submodel (known as the hurdle part), the probability that $y = 0$ versus $y > 0$ is predicted for each outcome using a logit link and a Bernoulli distribution. Second, the expected count for outcomes in which $y > 0$ is predicted using a log link and a zero-*truncated* distribution (either Poisson or negative binomial ranging from 1 to $+\infty$). Conceptually, these two submodels correspond to the idea of "if" and "how much" in predicting the overall zero-inflated outcome. Thus, hurdle models can be easier to interpret than their zero-inflated counterparts (which instead predict the less intuitive quantities of "if extra 0 value" and "how much including expected 0 values"). Hurdle models with multiple "if" parts (e.g., for 0 and 1 vs. $y \geq 2$) are also available.

Although there is no specific number of expected 0 values in continuous outcomes, they can also be zero-inflated relative to the rest of their distribution. The analog to a hurdle model for continuous zero-inflated outcomes is known as a **two-part model**. Although its specification may differ across software, its name is derived from its two submodels. First, the probability that $y > 0$ versus $y = 0$ is predicted for each outcome—note that this direction is backwards relative to the hurdle models, which predict $y = 0$ instead of $y > 0$. Next, outcomes of $y > 0$ are predicted using a continuous distribution, such as normal or log-normal. Thus, the two-part model also corresponds to the idea of "if" and "how much" in predicting a zero-inflated outcome, just using a continuous distribution for the "how much" part instead. In addition, the "if" part could be specified for values other than 0. For instance, in analyzing response times, usually response times are included only for correct answers. Rather than treating accuracy and response time as separate outcomes, they could be examined jointly as outcomes in a two-part model, whose submodels would predict correct or not, and then correct response times. Two-part models could also be used for censored outcomes (e.g., to predict piles at their lower and/or upper bounds).

2.D. Estimation of Generalized Longitudinal Models

The use of non-normal conditional distributions means that generalized linear mixed models will require a different type of maximum likelihood estimation for its random effects than was shown in chapter 5. To review, the previous likelihood function (and its restricted version) for general linear mixed models computed the likelihood for each person's data (or per whatever unit is the highest level of the model) using a multivariate normal distribution for their predicted **V** matrix. However, this was only possible to do by assuming normality for the higher-level random effects *and* for the level-1 residuals. Otherwise, the combination of normally distributed level-2 random effects and a *non*-normal conditional outcome distribution (e.g., Bernoulli, Poisson) does not have a known distribution. Consequently, a different maximum likelihood estimator is needed for such cases. The details of these procedures are technically quite complex, but their general principles can be summarized as follows.

The gold standard of estimation for generalized linear models with random effects is known by several different names, including maximum likelihood via **numeric integration**, via (**adaptive or non-adaptive) Gaussian quadrature**, or just **marginal maximum likelihood**. The key idea is that we cannot simply estimate the variance and covariance of the random effects by trying out different possible estimates across iterations like we did before. Instead, we also have to use those values to **integrate** the random effects out of the likelihood, which is conceptually like summing the area under a curve of the random effect distribution. We can then work with the marginal distribution of the outcomes without the unknown individual random effects getting in the way. To describe this process, let's consider a simplified example in which our only random effect is a random intercept, and that we have a two-level model of four binary outcomes per person. Maximum likelihood estimation would thus proceed in three steps.

The first step is to obtain starting values for all fixed effects and for the random intercept variance. At the first iteration, a model with no random effects can provide starting values for the fixed effects; at later iterations, the current values for all estimated parameters will be updated based on previous iterations. The next step should be to calculate the link-transformed expected outcome from the linear predictor for every observation, but we are missing part of the model equation. That is, although we have current values for the fixed effects, we do not have a value for *each person's* random intercept. However, given that we assume a normal distribution for the random intercepts (always with mean = 0), our current estimate of the random intercept variance tells us what the distribution should look like. We can now make plausible guesses for each person's random intercept values, plug them into the linear predictor, and see how well they work, a process known as **Gaussian quadrature** (in which *Gaussian* refers to the use of a normal distribution). Thus, the second step is for the program to divide the currently proposed random intercept distribution into rectangles, such that the tallest rectangles will be in the center of the distribution. Each rectangle is known as a **quadrature point**; the number of points used will vary by program defaults, by informed selection within the estimator, or by user-inputted values.

Let's say that our current random intercept variance value is 1 (i.e., a standard normal distribution), and that we decide to use only three quadrature points. Thus, at each iteration, each person will "try on" three possible random intercept values: −2, 0, and 2, which represent 10%, 40%, and 10% of the random intercept distribution, respectively. The probability p that $y = 1$ for each outcome can then be calculated as predicted by the fixed effects and the random intercept. But because outcomes from the same person are conditionally independent, what goes into the likelihood is the *joint* probability for the binary outcomes that actually occurred. For example, if $y = 1$ for all four outcomes, then $p*p*p*p$ goes into the likelihood. If $y = 0$ for the fourth outcome instead, then $p*p*p*(1 - p)$ goes into the likelihood instead, and so forth.

Given that each person had to try on three different random intercept values, the three joint probabilities per person have to be combined so that each person contributes only once to the likelihood. To do so, however, we have to take into account how plausible each random intercept value really is by weighting them with the proportion of the distribution they represent. Thus, a random intercept = 0 gets a higher weight than –2 or 2 (which are much less likely in a standard normal distribution). The weighted joint probabilities are then summed into one final likelihood value for each person to indicate the height of that person's data given the current values for all model parameters. However, once the program has a better sense of which random intercept value is most plausible for each person, it goes back and re-rectangles that particular section of the distribution to get a more fine-grained prediction for that person and combines those predictions instead, which is known as **adaptive Gaussian quadrature**. The log likelihood can then be summed across persons as usual under the assumption of independent persons. New values for the fixed effects and random intercept variance are then chosen at each new iteration. The iterations will continue until the model reaches *convergence*, which occurs when the total log-likelihood for the sample does not change more than a pre-specified very small amount.

Although computers nowadays are incredibly fast, this trying-on process for integrating random effects out of the likelihood is still relatively time consuming because it must occur for each person, and it is repeated at every iteration. Further, the process becomes exponentially more complicated as a function of the number of random effects. For instance, let us consider a model that uses 15 quadrature points (i.e., 15 rectangles are tried on by each person at each iteration) to describe change across four binary outcomes. If the model also has a random linear time slope, then each step now requires $15^2 = 225$ rectangle combinations; a random quadratic time slope would then require $15^3 = 3,375$ rectangle combinations. Thus, models with many random effects are especially likely to encounter estimation problems when using numeric integration.

Another critical difference between maximum likelihood when using a multivariate normal distribution (with normal conditional outcomes) and maximum likelihood when using numeric integration (for non-normal conditional outcomes as just described) is how they estimate the model's fixed effects. As was shown in chapter 5 for normally distributed conditional outcomes, the fixed effects can be calculated from the predictor values and the estimated $\mathbf{V}$ matrix. But in generalized linear mixed models the fixed effects are explicitly searched for iteratively as part of the likelihood, in addition to all variance components. Thus, having too many fixed effects can also cause estimation problems in generalized linear mixed models.

Because of the difficulties associated with Gaussian quadrature, simpler approaches to estimation previously developed are still sometimes used. These are called **quasi-likelihood** or **pseudo-likelihood** estimators, and as these names suggest, they have significant limitations. They are not true likelihoods, and so their model −2LL values cannot be used in likelihood ratio tests or other model comparisons. In addition, because research has shown their variance components to be severely underestimated, these methods are no longer favored. Instead, for more complex models the process of Gaussian quadrature can be approximated with Monte Carlo integration, in which random samples of the random effects distributions are "tried on" for a set number of iterations (e.g., 500). In addition, fully Bayesian models can use Markov Chain Monte Carlo to estimate all parameters, which also would not require complete numeric integration.

Finally, one additional complication of generalized linear models arises when the level-1 residuals do not have an estimated variance (e.g., as in the Bernoulli and Poisson distributions in which the variance is determined by the conditional mean). Because residual variance will always remain the same fixed amount, even after level-1 predictors have theoretically explained some of it, the model must change scale as a result. Fortunately, level-2 predictors can reduce the random effects variances without this problem—it is solely a problem with level-1 predictors.

The technical reasons for this change in model scale were described by Bauer (2009), a useful analogy for which is department store "sales" that aren't really sales. For instance, let's say you are the manager of a store, and to break even for a particular shirt, it must sell for $25. If you have lots of these shirts left after a while, you might decide to put it on sale to entice buyers. However, given that it's already priced as low as it can go, you decide to change the tag to make it appear that the original price of the shirt was $50, but now it's 50% off (for an actual price of still $25). If that doesn't work, you might change the price to $100, which is then an amazing 75% off! In the context of generalized linear mixed models, in order for the residual variance to remain the same fixed amount (e.g., 3.29 when using a logit link for binary outcomes) even after including level-1 predictors, the scale of the other model effects (i.e., the original prices for the fixed effects and random effects variances) must increase to reflect the larger level-1 residual variance that theoretically was originally there. Similarly, whenever new random effects are added, the model will change scale such that it then has more overall variance. Thus, this text's analogy—in which all piles of variance are partitioned from the same total—will no longer fit.

3. Alternative Models for Longitudinal Data

Now that we've considered how the models in this text can be extended for use with non-normal outcomes (and all the complications thereof), this final section briefly reviews alternative models for other types of longitudinal data and how they also relate to the models in this text.

3.A. Event History Models

Although *time* has been a central focus of this text, all models have presented the same unidirectional view of time as a predictor. But what if time is conceptually more of an outcome, such that your research question concerns how long it takes for an event to occur? In that case, **event history modeling** (also known as *survival analysis*) will be more useful. As described most succinctly by Singer and Willett (2003), event history models focus on the *whether* and the *when* of event occurrence, although specific model variants will differ in whether the possible event times are discrete occasions or if events can occur in continuously unfolding time instead.

Event history models are often presented using different notation and terminology, but those that use discrete time occasions per person can also be viewed as longitudinal models for dichotomous event outcomes, as described by Hox (2010). The event data would be analyzed in a *stacked* or *long* format (as used throughout this text), in which each row contains a discrete time observation for each person. In the event column, occasions in which the event has not yet occurred are coded 0. When the event occurs, that occasion's outcome is coded 1. After that occasion, however, the outcome is then set to missing to reflect the idea of *hazard*, or that that person is no longer at risk for the event (because it already happened). Given the binary event outcome, the logit or complementary log-log link functions (as presented earlier in this chapter) are used to create an unbounded outcome to be predicted (rather than predicting the conditional probability of event occurrence directly). *Time* can be treated as a categorical predictor (i.e., a saturated means model) or modeled using whatever linear or nonlinear functions are needed. Time-invariant or time-varying predictors of event occurrence can also be included, although it is still important to specify differential between- and within-person types of effects of the latter.

Event history models for continuous time in which only one event can happen per person are more like cross-sectional models. Because time cannot be negative, a log link is used to keep the predicted time to event outcomes positive. In addition, in continuous time the probability of an event happening at any exact time is essentially 0 (as is the probability of any particular value within all continuous distributions). Instead, these models predict the *rate* of event occurrence per unit time (conditionally for those who are still at risk). Event history models for continuous time are known as *semi-parametric* (Singer & Willett, 2003) because although the intercept-like parameter of the model expressing the log of the rate at the beginning of time is arbitrary, these models generally assume that the rate differs proportionally as a function of the model predictors (i.e., proportional odds). Further, these models use only relative, rank ordering of time instead of actual event timing or the distances between events in predicting differences between persons.

3.B. Models for Intensive Longitudinal Data

Longitudinal designs in which *many* occasions are collected within persons (e.g., dozens or hundreds) are sometimes called **intensive longitudinal data** (e.g., Walls & Schafer, 2006). Although the models featured in this text for within-person fluctuation (e.g., chapters 4 and 8) could be used for such data, they are likely to be insufficient to capture all the sources of time-specific within-person dependency. Fortunately, these models can be extended to include other features; specific exemplars of such useful model extensions in this context are described below.

Ecological momentary assessment designs focus on measurement of events and within-person variation as they unfold in real time (e.g., Stone, Shiffman, Atienza, & Nebeling, 2007). Such longitudinal data are not easily defined (or collapsed) into discrete occasions, and thus require models in which time can reflect a truly continuous process, and that take into account varying intervals of report across persons. For instance, **point process models** focus on the rate of occurrence for repeated events, such as cigarette smoking (e.g., Rathbun, Shiffman, & Gwaltney, 2006). These models predict the number of events during each interval (in which the mean is proportional to the length of the interval) using a log link and a Poisson-type distribution. The extent of periodic cycling (e.g., seasonal or diurnal effects) and dependence among events can be examined as a function of time-invariant or time-varying predictors (with the usual concerns about differentiating the effects of between- and within-person sources of variance in the latter).

A more traditional approach to intensive longitudinal data can be found in **time series models**, which estimate parameters that describe auto-regressive patterns and other kinds of time-specific dependency across many occasions collected from a single observational unit. However, conducting a separate analysis for each observational unit does not provide a direct means by which to see how time series parameters differ across units or what factors may predict those differences. Fortunately, time series analyses can be conducted in a multilevel modeling framework, such that fixed and random effects of time series parameters can then be evaluated across units. For example, Rovine and Walls (2006) demonstrated how individual differences in a first-order autoregressive (AR1) effect could be examined by including lagged outcomes as time-varying predictors of a current outcome. Thus, rather than fitting an alternative covariance structure model (e.g., as in chapter 4) that assumes the same AR1 pattern for the residuals of all persons, in their approach, the mean AR1 effect can be estimated as the fixed effect of the previous occasion predicting the current occasion. Individual differences in the AR1 effect can be examined by adding a random slope variance (which can then be explained by other types of person-level predictors through cross-level interactions). Higher-order autoregressive processes (e.g., AR2 or AR3 effects) could also be predicted in a similar fashion.

Time-specific dependency in intensive longitudinal data may also include more dynamic processes, such as a person's oscillation, self-regulation, and return to equilibrium, as well as dyadic influences on each of these. In **dynamic systems modeling** (e.g., Boker & Bisconti, 2006; Boker & Laurenceau, 2006), how rates of change may be predicted by a person's current state is examined by treating the first and second derivatives of each person's time-varying outcome as additional variables. More specifically, in a nonlinear function, the first derivative is the rate of change as evaluated at a particular occasion, whereas the second derivative is the acceleration or deceleration of the rate of change at that occasion (these are equivalent to the instantaneous linear rate of change and *twice* the quadratic rate of change, respectively, as described in chapter 6). These derivatives can be found using observed variable approximations or by estimating them as latent variables in a structural equation model. The analysis then focuses on estimating slopes that describe how the highest-order derivative is predicted by the outcome and the lower-order derivatives, which can create a multitude of different patterns of nonlinear change over time.

For instance, if the slope predicting the *first* derivative by the outcome at that occasion is negative, this will create the same type of negative exponential curve that heads smoothly back toward an asymptote (i.e., an equilibrium achieved over time) from chapter 6. In contrast, if the slope predicting the *second* derivative by the outcome at that occasion is negative, but there is no effect of the first derivative, this will create a continually oscillating pattern of change. However, in predicting the second derivative, negative effects of the first derivative and the outcome at that occasion will create a pattern of oscillation that gradually diminishes over time and eventually rests at equilibrium. In addition, dynamic trajectories that change equilibrium over time can be predicted by adding fixed and random effects of time, while then also including these types of derivative-based relationships to predict nonlinear dynamics among the level-1 residuals. Thus, these models can flexibly but parsimoniously predict many kinds of complex nonlinear trends.

4. Chapter Summary

The purpose of this chapter was to briefly address other topics relevant to the models in this text. First, we considered estimation of statistical power in multilevel models, in which the dependency across levels will strongly influence how much actual power will be found in your sample. In general, greater numbers of observations per upper-level unit and stronger intraclass correlations will create stronger design effects (that will then multiply the sample size needed to achieve the same level of power as in an independent sample). Once design effects are taken into account, traditional approaches for predicting power can be used with random intercept models, although power estimation will be more involved for models with random slopes. Fortunately the number of freely available resources to help with this process continues to grow.

The chapter then headed in a different direction to describe how the longitudinal models in this text can be extended to non-normal outcomes. These generalized linear mixed models have three parts: a link function that creates an unbounded outcome, a linear predictor that combines fixed and random effects to predict that unbounded outcome, and a conditional distribution that better matches the possible outcome values. Specific model variants for types of outcome data were then introduced, including models for binary outcomes, percent correct, ordered and un-ordered categories, counts and other skewed outcomes, as well as "if" and "how much" models for semi-continuous (e.g., zero-inflated) outcomes. We then considered how these models can be estimated using adaptive Gaussian quadrature (i.e., marginal maximum likelihood with numeric integration over the random effects), as well as how the scale of the model must change after including level-1 effects when level-1 residual variance is not estimated. Despite these complications, many of the other general concepts of longitudinal modeling will still apply.

Finally, we briefly visited some related models for longitudinal data not covered in the text, such as event history models that predict the timing of an event. Also related are point process, time series, and dynamic systems models that quantify other aspects of within-person variation, including periodic cycling, auto-regressive process, and regulation processes. Such models are likely to be very useful in exploring the nuances of more intensive longitudinal data.

5. Conclusion

That's all, folks! I sincerely thank you for coming on this journey with me and for making it this far. I hope this introduction has made you now feel more comfortable in the wonderful world of longitudinal analysis, and I hope you plan to stay for a very long time!

References

Bauer, D. J. (2009). A note on comparing the estimates of models for cluster-correlated or longitudinal data with binary or ordinal outcomes. *Psychometrika, 74*, 97–105.

Boker, S. M., & Bisconti, T. L. (2006). Dynamical systems modeling in aging research. In C. S. Bergman & S. M. Boker (Eds.), *Methodological issues in aging research* (pp. 185–229). Mahwah, NJ: Erlbaum.

Boker, S. M., & Laurenceau, J.-P. (2006). Dynamical systems modeling: An application to the regulation of intimacy and disclosure in marriage. In T. A. Walls & J. L. Schafer (Eds.), *Models for intensive longitudinal data* (pp. 195–218). New York, NY: Oxford University Press.

Cohen, J. (1988). *Statistical power analysis for the behavioral sciences.* Mahwah, NJ: Erlbaum.

Hedeker, D., & Gibbons, D. (2006). *Longitudinal data analysis.* Wiley series in probability and statistics. Hoboken, NJ: Wiley.

Hox, J. J. (2010). *Multilevel analysis: Techniques and applications* (2nd ed.). New York, NY: Routledge.

Kreidler, S. M., et al. (2013). GLIMMPSE: Online power computation for linear models with and without a baseline covariate. *Journal of Statistical Software, 45*(10). Available at: www.jstatsoft.org/

Rathbun, S. L., Shiffman, S., & Gwaltney, C. J. (2006). Point process models for event history data: Applications in behavioral science. In T. A. Walls & J. L. Schafer (Eds.), *Models for intensive longitudinal data* (pp. 219–253). New York, NY: Oxford University Press.

Raudenbush, S. W., et al. (2011). *Optimal design software for multi-level and longitudinal research (Version 3.01)* [Software]. Available from www.wtgrantfoundation.org

Rovine, M. J., & Walls, T. A. (2006). Multilevel autoregressive modeling of interindividual differences in the stability of a process. In T. A. Walls & J. L. Schafer (Eds.), *Models for intensive longitudinal data* (pp. 124–147). New York, NY: Oxford University Press.

Singer, J. D., & Willett, J. B. (2003). *Applied longitudinal data analysis: Modeling change and event occurrence.* New York, NY: Oxford University Press.

Snijders, T. A. B., & Bosker, R. (2012). *Multilevel analysis* (2nd ed.). Thousand Oaks, CA: Sage.

Stone, A. A., Shiffman, S., Atienza, A. A., & Nebeling, L. (2007). *The science of real-time data capture: Self-reports in health research.* New York, NY: Oxford University Press.

Stroup, W. W. (2013). *Generalized linear mixed models: Modern concepts, methods, and applications.* Boca Raton, FL: Chapman & Hall.

Walls, T. A., & Schafer, J. L. (2006). *Models for intensive longitudinal data.* New York, NY: Oxford University Press.

AUTHOR INDEX

SUBJECT INDEX